Neighborhood, City, and Metropolis

An Integrated Reader in Urban Sociology

Edited, with Introductions, by
Robert Gutman and David Popenoe
Rutgers University

 Random House New York

Published in the United States by
Random House, Inc., New York, and
simultaneously in Canada by Random
House of Canada Limited, Toronto.

Library of Congress Catalog Card
Number 77-115420

Manufactured in the United States of
America

Printed and bound by
Kingsport Press, Kingsport, Tenn.

Typography by Mel Haber

987654

Neighborhood, City, and Metropolis

Consulting Editor: Marvin Bressler
Princeton University

Preface

Urban sociology is a field with considerable popular appeal. Courses in the subject are widely available on the undergraduate level, and each year there seem to be more and more students in graduate departments who desire to concentrate in the field of urban sociology. The demand for people who are knowledgeable about urban sociology to teach, to fill positions as advisers to government and industry, and to conduct research and evaluate programs dealing with urban problems far exceeds the supply of qualified people.

Along with this popular interest in urban sociology, however, we find a strange situation within the discipline and profession of sociology. Many sociologists, although not unmindful of the manifold difficulties which beset cities, suburbs, and metropolitan regions in the United States today, nevertheless question whether urban sociology constitutes a legitimate field of inquiry. Is the study of social life in urban communities, these critics ask, much different from the study of social life in the society as a whole? Are not the issues which confront urban communities the same issues basically which confront American society at large? Would it not be more appropriate to examine the problems and phenomena of cities in the context of other sociological specializations, such as the study of race and minority relations, local communities, or bureaucracy? Thus, the field of urban sociology has reached a kind of intellectual crisis at the same time that the cities are going through an "urban crisis."

The present reader represents, in effect, an attempt to confront the curious dilemma which now besets the field of urban sociology. It is an effort to define and focus the area of urban sociological specialization in such a way that primary concern is given to the investigation of urban phenomena as related to the continued conceptual development and integrity of sociology as a discipline of scientific inquiry, while at the same time enabling sociologists to remain responsive to the genuine problems and policy issues of urban communities.

We confess that the organization of a reader in these terms has not been an easy undertaking, and many students and critics may well conclude that the effort has been unjustifiably costly. It has not been easy for the reason, among others, that those sociologists who have been most concerned about giving shape and order to the discipline in recent decades have also tended to be less responsive and concerned about the emerging social problems of American society and have been generally uninterested in the field of urban sociology. At the same time, we have found a dearth of theoretical writings or empirical research studies that describe the nature and organization of urban communities while at the same time showing a concern for relating this organization to the leading conceptual advances in the discipline, such as structure-functional theory or new forms of ecological thought. Thus, there is a large gap to be closed. As a consequence, we have sometimes had to force articles and essays written in one mold into our own framework, an objective for which their authors obviously did not intend them. This is one sense in which the organization of our reader may be costly: The author sometimes does not say enough about the issue which interests us in terms of our organization of the field of urban sociology, and putting his article or essay in our context may seem to diminish the significance of his own achievement. If this has happened, we apologize to the authors, but trust they will recognize

and appreciate the objectives we have tried to achieve.

Another sense in which the organization of this reader has been costly is that in our ambition to lend some kind of conceptual order to the field of urban sociology we have been led, we know, to exclude many interesting and important articles and essays that deal with critical social problems of urban communities today. For example, there is very little in this book about the problems of the black community, about poverty, and about drug addiction, crime, and other forms of deviant behavior that are the subject of much public policy discussion at present. We were bothered by these omissions more when we began to compose this book than we are at the present time, in large part because in the last few years a variety of readers and anthologies have been published which deal with these issues in great detail, and some of them with single issues at considerable length.

Though we have omitted materials dealing with important urban problems, this decision should not be interpreted to mean that in our concern for the organization of the field of urban sociology we deny the obligation of sociology to relate to the policy-making process. On the contrary, it is our conviction that there is a large realm in which urban sociology can be made applicable to social planning, and the last section of this reader is given over to an examination of the relation of urban sociology to the work of the practicing professions that operate in urban communities. We would go further and argue that the kinds of concerns which are displayed by the body of this book are a prerequisite to effective planning, that only to the degree that the organization of cities and their relationship to the total society is understood by means of the discipline of sociology can the proposals of the planning professions become effective.

One additional comment about omissions in this book seems essential. We have not striven fully to achieve a completely comparative approach, though we are in total agreement that such an approach to any field of sociology is the best one. We have few materials on preindustrial urban forms, no extensive treatment of urbanization and urbanism in modernizing countries, and so on. The grand scope of urban sociology almost requires that any given book in the field be somewhat selective, and we have chosen to concentrate primarily on urban communities and urbanism in advanced, Western societies. Fortunately, this omission too is compensated for by a host of excellent books which have recently come on the market.

In the period of time during which the development of this reader took place, we were helped in our discussion of its organization and in the selection of readings by numerous colleagues and by our graduate students in urban sociology courses. We are especially grateful for the advice given to us by John E. Bebout, Harry C. Bredemeier, Nathan Glazer, and Virginia Whitney; and by the patience and support shown us by our wives, Sonya R. Gutman and Katharine S. Popenoe, and our editors, Marvin Bressler, Theodore Caris, Charles Lieber, Charles Page, and Arthur Strimling. The preparation of the manuscript was the joint responsibility of our secretaries, Laura Ford and Katharine Lesniak. The development of this reader has been helped immeasurably by the decision Rutgers made several years ago to establish one of the first Urban Studies Centers in an American university.

R. G.
D. P.

Contents

Contemporary Urbanization and Urbanism in the United States: Process and Impact

III

Urban Differentiation 251

Urban Social and Areal Differentiation

Urban Stratification and Cultural Heterogeneity

IV

Urban Ecology 391

Metropolitan Ecological Structure and Growth

Selected Sociocultural Aspects of Urban Ecology

V

Urban Locality Groups   537

Urban Neighborhoods and Social Interaction

Urban Community Power and Decision-Making

VI

Urban Environment and Social Behavior   707

VII

Urban Policy and Planning   789

Projected Trends and Policy Alternatives

Neighborhood, City, and Metropolis

The Field of INTRODUCTION
Urban Sociology:
A Review and
Assessment

The term "urban sociology" . . . is often misunderstood. It does not
mean a special division of sociology dealing with a definite category
of social systems, like, for instance, sociology of the family, which
specializes primarily (though not exclusively) in studies of families as
groups composed of parents and children, or sociology of religion,
whose main task is a comparative study of various kinds of religious
associations, or industrial sociology, which investigates mainly the
social organization of the workers and managers engaged in industrial
production. For the city is not and never was a united social system.—
FLORIAN ZNANIECKI, *Social Relations and Social Roles*

Urban sociology, or the study of cities from the perspective of the discipline of sociology,
has a venerable and distinguished tradition. Thirty to forty years ago it was one of the
largest and primary specialties within sociology, both as an area for research and an area
for teaching. Courses in urban sociology still remain pervasive and popular at the undergraduate level. As a graduate and research endeavor, however, the study of cities was
overshadowed until very recently by the rising popularity of such interests as formal
organizations and bureaucracy, social stratification and social mobility, occupations and
the professions, and modernization and social change. In the last several years urban
sociology has been having something of a renaissance, stimulated primarily by the national
concern for the decline of older American cities, the expansion of metropolitan regions,
and the poor living conditions of urban Negroes. The proliferation of urban studies centers
in universities throughout the country offers tangible evidence of this (even though they
are often dominated by the interests of political science, economics, and city planning).
While this recent activity has given renewed vitality to the field (examples of which are
some of the readings included in this book), it is still too early to tell whether or not urban
sociology can ever again regain its former prominence in the discipline. Many would argue,
in fact, that it has become an untenable academic enterprise and that the field should
be split up into a variety of subspecializations.

Thus, two outstanding characteristics of urban sociology in this country at the present
time seem to be its renaissance and its ambiguity. At the same time that increasing numbers
of students are turning to urban sociology for an understanding of the nature and problems
of cities, many scholars are asking, "What is urban sociology?"; or more pointedly they

3

are saying, "There is no such thing as urban sociology." There are two excellent reasons why urban sociology has ceased to be a neat and tidy focus for sociological research and investigation. First, the study of something so broad and heterogeneous as a city approaches in difficulty and scope the study of the entire society. In this era of specialization it seems simply too complex to study as a specialization in itself. Second, insofar as the study of cities was conducted originally with reference to their differences from rural communities, the predominant and almost total urbanization of American life makes such comparative analysis in this society certainly difficult and in some cases even meaningless.

This seems a most appropriate time and place, therefore, for an assessment of the nature of urban sociology, its position within the discipline of sociology, and its trends and future prospects. How is it that a specialty which is so commonly regarded as a non-specialty could have a renaissance? Is this renaissance well founded and should it be encouraged? Do the variety of things that urban sociologists study all relate meaningfully to one another? If not, how might urban sociology be reorganized in order to make it a more vigorous academic specialization? These kinds of questions are the source for many of the thoughts contained in the discussion which follows and have guided the organization of this book.

The thesis of this introductory article can be previewed quite simply. We agree that problems are inherent in a special field that many leading scholars decry as being confused and ambiguous, that lacks a solid theoretical foundation, that has great difficulty in defining the term urban, that cannot easily decide what belongs in and out of urban courses and texts, and that has been somewhat cut off from the main stream of general sociology. Indeed, these many difficulties have been pointedly brought home to us in the preparation of this book! We regard the current tendency to conceive of urban sociology as the sociology of urban problems as one which in no way helps to clarify the nature of the field; in fact it makes it more of a "nonfield." Finally, we feel that urban sociology must be reorganized and further differentiated along several distinct avenues of development if it is to keep step with current trends and developments in the larger discipline. The nature of this reorganization, together with its implications for this book of readings in urban sociology, will be taken up in the conclusions.

It should be understood that in adopting this view of urban sociology we are talking about it as a specialized research field within the discipline of sociology, rather than as the broad, interdisciplinary problem and policy-oriented field of urban studies or urban affairs. (For the latter approach see Gutman and Popenoe, 1963, and Popenoe, 1965). Our emphasis on urban sociology as a research field, and our discussion of it principally with a view toward enhancing its manageability as an academic pursuit, should not be interpreted as a bias on our part against social science application and a concern with policy and problems. In this essay, however, the structure and function of academic pursuits are considered exclusively from the point of view of *scientific* goals, values, and motivations. Also, it should be said that our thoughts about urban sociology rely very heavily on our views of general sociology and on the distinction between general and special sociology. There is no unanimity of opinion about the precise nature and focus of sociology as a discipline; but we believe that our view of the nature of the discipline, briefly summarized here, is the dominant viewpoint at the present time.

THE RENAISSANCE IN URBAN SOCIOLOGY

Urban sociology probably reached its peak of prestige and prominence in sociology in the late 1920s and early 1930s under the influence of the graduate program at the University of Chicago led by Park, Burgess, and Wirth (Burgess and Bogue, 1964; Faris, 1967). The contrasts between city and country in the United States were still very evident during this period, and it was relatively easy to regard urban settlements as constituting a unique and different form of social organization. Cities, particularly Chicago itself, provided ideal laboratories in which to experiment with the use of the new research techniques of the social survey, participant observation, and life history analysis. The discussion of urban phenomena offered an opportunity also for the many sociologists who wanted to develop sociology into a discipline that was capable of adding insight and understanding to the control of pressing social problems. At this time, urban sociology subsumed a number of important special sociologies which later acquired independent status, including industrial sociology, social stratification, intergroup relations, and mass communications. In addition, urban sociology commanded a broad sphere of general sociological theory directed toward the understanding of large social systems. The main reason for this was that its dominant intellectual orientation was rooted in the theory of human ecology (Park, Burgess, and Mackenzie, 1967). During the twenties and thirties, before the advent of structure-functional analysis and social systems theories in American sociology, the ecologists were almost alone in offering the discipline a reasonably comprehensive and coherent conceptual model for explaining a wide variety of social phenomena at the urban and societal levels.

In the years after World War II, the influence of urban sociology diminished (Introduction, Hatt and Reiss, 1957). Theoretical investigations dealing with cities and urbanization ceased to appear in significant volume, graduate students were attracted by the newer fields that had emerged, and there was considerably less interest in conducting empirical research dealing with urban phenomena. Some of the decline can be attributed to the natural changes in fashion that mark the history of a discipline. Urban sociology was one of the first specialties to be developed in this country, and a new generation of scholars found untried, unplumbed topics more intriguing. Related to this shift in subject matter was the fact that the study of cities during the heyday of the Chicago school was the work of professors and scholars, many of whom had been born in small towns and farming communities and who espoused a distinctly antiurban ideology. The generation which came to populate the discipline after World War II grew up in cities and did not look upon their social organization and way of life as particularly unusual. Many of them preferred to study organizations and systems that were less familiar than the urban neighborhoods and cultures of their youth.

The character of sociology, not only the composition of the sociological fraternity, was changing, too. In its later phases, the work of the Chicago school had tended toward radical empiricism. Its research output emphasized the problems involved in collecting and analyzing demographic data and gave little attention to how these data could be used to modify or reformulate urban theory. This put human ecology and urban sociology, both still heavily influenced by the tradition of Social Darwinism in American thought (Hofstadter, 1955), in a weak position to respond to the attack on their intellectual assumptions coming from scholars influenced by German idealism and other forms of European thought (Alihan, 1938). These newer strains in American sociology, which laid the groundwork for the later invasion of structure-functional analysis and social systems theory into the discipline, believed that social values and cultural norms were the primary determinants of social behavior, stressed the voluntaristic and psychological components in action, and were generally more sophisticated in their understanding of the relations between theory and research (Timasheff, 1966; Hinkle and Hinkle, 1954). Urban sociology also was undermined in the immediate post-World War II period by the growing self-consciousness of sociologists in this country about the scientific status of their discipline, which produced an aversion to a specialty like urban sociology, traditionally oriented to the study of social problems.

As we said earlier, the situation has changed dramatically now, and urban sociology is a very popular subject again. The revival of interest in the field has been helped along to some degree by the willingness of sociologists in general to look upon their work less as a purely scientific and academic enterprise and more as one among a group of policy-oriented disciplines. But undoubtedly the major source of the renaissance in urban sociology is the virtual explosion of public concern about urban problems.

An urban problem can be defined as a problem which is found in, or is associated with, large cities. Traffic congestion, slums, crime and delinquency, racial discrimination, poverty, political corruption—all these are often given as examples of urban problems. Social problems such as divorce and mental illness are not usually associated only with cities, although their incidence probably is higher among urbanized populations. There are other features of urbanized societies which often constitute social problems, including anomie, alienation, commercialism, and conformity; but oddly enough, these are not generally regarded as urban problems by the public.

The outpouring of public interest and political concern for urban problems cannot be attributed to the deterioration of the life situation of urban dwellers. On the contrary, the most common historical and scholarly view is that for the last one hundred years at least, the general quality of life for urban populations has *improved* rather than *deteriorated*. Housing is generally more spacious and the environment more salubrious; there is actually less discrimination and prejudice against Negroes in this country today than a century ago; the economic situation of urban dwellers is generally more favorable, and so on.

The primary reason for the public and political interest in urban problems is that many of the nonurban problems which governed the political discussion of the first half of this century in our country have been "solved" at the same time that our standards of evaluation have become greatly elevated. These "ameliorated" problems include the bread and butter economic issues of jobs and wages, unionization, child labor, and depressions and business stability, as well as the provision of adequate food and clothing. The problems of economic life have been replaced by the problems of the social environment such as race and education, hard-core poverty, crime and delinquency, and the quality of the physical environment. Many of these problems are now found predominantly in the larger cities rather than across the nation as a whole, and this fact, too, focuses attention on "urban" problems. Furthermore, it is necessary to realize that standards of desirable income and housing levels and standards of moral and legal justice have risen in the more affluent sectors of the society. As a result, the recently discovered "invisible" minorities of the large city ghettos stand out in marked contrast both to these standards and to the affluent way of life which has helped to generate the standards. The interest in urban problems also has increased with the rising sense of our capability and capacity to solve them—for example, the prospect that government can "fight a war" against them through processes of democratic planning, and win it. To all these explanations, of course, we must add the recent urban "crisis" phenomena, such as the race riots, which have made the cities an inescapable arena of public and political concern.

Current events have produced powerful pressures on sociologists to define urban sociology as that field within the discipline which focuses on these problems. It is widely reported that students who enroll in courses in urban sociology expect the syllabus to be devoted primarily to materials dealing with race and poverty. Degree candidates in graduate programs have similar expectations. Many of them expect or hope that advanced work in urban sociology will prepare them to fight in the war against poverty or help run the urban school system. Not all students, of course, are concerned with the problems of the inner city. Many are worried about suburbanization and its impact, but even in this context they see urban sociology as a field defined in terms of a set of social problems.

Despite our sensitivity to the urgent need to deal with the dilemmas of cities and suburbs, we nevertheless believe that it is misleading to assume that urban sociology can be defined as the sociological specialty which contains the knowledge about and the solutions to these dilemmas. For one thing, any urban problem of significance is so complex that it can be understood and dealt with only by drawing upon the information and perspective of many fields of sociology, as well as other social science disciplines, and often of disciplines in the natural sciences. For another, to take such a view is to misunderstand the nature of special fields within disciplines. Some fields may have their initial source in the delineation of a set of urgent problems by the norms of a society, but the development of a field is subject to the norms not of society, but of those bodies of systematic knowledge which we call scientific disciplines. These norms demand that the subject matter or phenomena, the models or theories, and the range of facts relating to them or data, be organized into manageable cognitive units that are ordered according to logical rules. The question of the focus and scope of urban sociology, therefore, can be answered only by clarifying the nature of cities and by understanding the characteristics of cities in relation to the broader set of phenomena which are the concern of sociology.

URBAN SOCIOLOGY AS A SPECIAL SOCIOLOGY

We shall now turn to the nature of urban sociology as a particular academic specialty within the discipline of sociology. It first will be necessary, however, to sketch out the defining elements of the discipline of sociology and the properties of a special field of sociology as distinct from the discipline in general.

There is general agreement that sociology, along with each of the other social sciences, is concerned primarily with superorganic or sociocultural phenomena. This distinguishes sociology from the biological and physical sciences, which focus on organic and inorganic phenomena, though the great areas of overlap between these aspects of reality should not be overlooked. Sociocultural phenomena are found primarily in the realm of interacting human beings and the products of their interaction (with the "sociocultural status" of higher forms of animal life remaining somewhat in doubt).

Sociology, and to some degree the sister "behavioral sciences" of anthropology and psychology, has come to analyze and study sociocultural phenomena from the point of view of three distinct frames of reference. These reference points are personality, culture, and society or social systems (Parsons, *et al.*, 1961; Sorokin, 1962; Timasheff, 1966). It must be emphasized that these are mental constructs or analytical and abstracted concepts, not three different kinds of concrete, tangible reality. Nonetheless, they have come to be the major concepts which give principal definition to the three behavioral science disciplines just noted—with sociology concentrating on the social system. This does not mean that each discipline focuses *exclusively* on only one of the major analytical concepts. They are each concerned with all three, that is to say, with sociocultural reality in general; but each looks at this reality from a special vantage point. Thus, psychology studies social and cultural factors from the point of view of the human personality; sociology studies psychological and cultural factors from the reference point of social systems, and so forth.

A fourth major analytical dimension should also be singled out—the relationship between each of these three aspects of sociocultural reality and the biological and physical environments in which they are imbedded. This is also a concern of each of the behavioral sciences, again from one or another of the special vantage points (but it is the *primary* frame of reference for the discipline of geography and the subdisciplines of ethology, biological psychology, and so on).

Sorokin's definition of sociology appeals to us and is generally accepted in the discipline: "Sociology is a generalizing science of sociocultural phenomena viewed in their generic forms, types and manifold interconnections" (Sorokin, 1962). As mentioned earlier, of the four main "branches" of sociocultural phenomena—the cultural, social, personal, and environmental—sociology's *primary* concern is the social (but always in relationship with the others).

There are two forms of sociology within the discipline: general sociology and special sociologies. *General* sociology concentrates on the properties of the sociocultural order (with special reference to the social) which are repeated in time and space, i.e., are common to *all* varieties and classes of sociocultural phenomena. Thus, its concern is the *fundamental* aspects of sociocultural reality, such as basic social processes like cooperation, conflict, differentiation and stratification, and socialization, basic structural qualities of all social systems, and so on. The *special* sociologies (or specialized fields of sociology), however, concern only single classes of sociocultural phenomena—wars, corporations, nation-states, religions. The general-special distinction can be seen quite clearly in the natural sciences. For example, we can consider general biology as distinct from the "specialized biologies" of zoology and botany. It is important to recognize the difference between the rather concrete and "specialized" social and cultural forms and types on the one hand, and, on the other, the four major analytical dimensions of sociocultural reality noted above. Among other things, the various classes and varieties of social phenomena are defined more in terms of the common experience of social reality; the analytical dimensions represent ways of abstracting this empirical reality for purposes of scientific investigation.

The special sociologies are focused on specific major cultural systems (science, religion, language, the fine arts, technology, sociology of knowledge, etc.); on specific basic social systems (or "institutional categories") such as business and industry, the family, education, medicine, government; on various kinds of social change (social movements, wars and revolutions, modernization and economic development, etc.); on various social problems (poverty, race and ethnic relations, health and illness, etc.—sometimes these are included in one of the above areas); on the several stages of the socio-organismic life-cycle (childhood, youth, and aging); on groups distinguished by various formal properties (small groups, formal organizations, locality groups-communities, etc.); and on various aspects of social structure which have emerged as important in modern complex society (mass communications, collective behavior, social planning). Two of the other major social science disciplines, economics and political science, deal with perhaps the most important of the sociocultural institutions—the economy and the polity.

One basic difficulty with urban sociology as we see it, which largely accounts for its ambiguity within the discipline, is that as now practiced it is not a single special sociology comparable to those just listed. Instead, it traditionally has represented a combination of several major analytical dimensions emphasized by general sociology with a number of special sociologies which may not necessarily belong together. This characteristic of urban sociology becomes apparent when we consider the sociocultural phenomenon, the city. It is the city, as we said, which is the essential phenomenon of urban sociology, the study of which conceivably could enable it to have the status of a clearly delineated special sociology.

The city has been approached in three major ways by sociologists. One approach is to regard the city as a small society, distinguished from certain other types of small societies by a set of characteristics which mark it as urban. A second approach looks upon the city as an aggregate of people or a locale with an uncertain or ambiguous status as a group or social organization, whose urban qualities or other phenomena of interest are defined in terms of one or more of the four basic analytical dimensions of sociocultural reality. The third approach is to see the city as a particular type of social group, namely an urbanized local community or territorial group. Let us examine each of these approaches and definitions in turn.

The City as a Small Society

The conception of a city as a small society is a persistent one in sociology. It is the underlying idea of the city in the writings of numerous social historians, such as Pirenne (Pirenne, 1956), and of historical sociologists, including Weber (Weber, 1958). It also is the operating assumption in the literature of the community studies tradition, which attempts to apply schema developed by anthropologists in the study of primitive and rural societies to the investigation of modern communities. There are many examples of this approach, including such classic studies of towns and cities as Middletown (Lynd, 1929) and Yankee City (Warner, 1963).

The common feature of the literature which regards the city in terms of a societal model is the belief that cities and related urban communities such as suburbs and towns (Seeley,

1956; Vidich and Bensman, 1960) encompass a broad range of social institutions and are capable of satisfying all or most of the basic functional needs of these institutions as well as the individual needs of the city's residents—that is, they can be regarded at least for analytical purposes as relatively autonomous and self-sufficient. An intrinsic aspect of this model of cities is that the "explanation" of social life within the city is to be found among factors which are internal to the city as a broad-ranging social system. This model for urban study harks back to earlier periods of Western and Oriental civilizations in which cities were also states, and thus were not only relatively self-sufficient enclaves of civilization but also were capable of exerting their political and religious influence on the hinterland through armed force. The model has proved relevant for the study of cities as late as the preindustrial period (Sjoberg, 1960), but its usefulness is extremely limited for modern cities. Unlike their historical precursors, modern urban communities do not have the responsibility for defense, for example, which is the task of the nation-state. This fact is an outstanding symbol of the increasing interdependence between the contemporary city and the larger society in which it is embedded.

Community studies sociologists, of course, are aware of the new functional relations which obtain between the city and the nation-state and they also are sensitive to the problems this development poses for their view of the city as a relatively autonomous social group. However, they continue to employ the model because of certain practical advantages which it seems to offer in conducting research. It is claimed, for example, that it is difficult to study the larger society directly, just because it is so large and complex, while the fundamental structures and functions of the nation-state are accessible to empirical research at the level of the city or the suburb (Arensberg and Kimball, 1965). This model also provides a useful way of pulling together the many strands of urban life into a coherent unity—a kind of macrosociology of a subsociety. This is especially of pedagogical importance.

Although we recognize the purposes of the attempt to conceive of the city in terms of a societal framework, it is questionable whether such efforts now constitute the basis for a special sociology. It may have provided a viable context in the past, when city-states were more common, and perhaps it continues to make sense for historical and certain kinds of general interpretive studies of cities. But all too often when the contemporary city is looked upon as a small society the product which emerges in the form of sociological analysis is indistinguishable from general sociology dealing with modern society as a whole. The sociology of "life in towns, cities, and suburbs in the United States" is little different from life in the United States.

This weakness is revealed by many textbooks that claim to focus on urban sociology. They usually include chapters on the urban family, the urban church, the urban school system, etc. When one examines their contents it turns out that the things that are described and analyzed are substantially the same phenomena which are discussed in a modern textbook dealing with sociology in general or contemporary society as a whole.

The City as a Population Aggregate

The disappearance of autonomous macrosocieties and the growing interdependence of all structures and localized areas in society present a difficult theoretical problem to the urban sociologist. On the one hand, cities are discernible and visible social entities, if only for the reason already mentioned that the public as well as the formal administrative structure of our society continues to regard them as identifiable groups. On the other hand, as we have just indicated, the heritage of modern sociology rightly points out that these groups are increasingly less coherent and powerful in their own right and have been more and more subject to forces emanating from the larger society and the nation-state.

Confronted with a situation in which there is this kind of confused relation between the organization of sociocultural reality, the available theoretical tradition of the field, and continued public demand for knowledge and understanding of cities, many urban sociologists do not grapple with the problem of defining what kind of group a city is. They have, by default as it were, simply taken the position that cities are agglomerations of people or merely social locales, and have turned their attention instead to understanding certain gross forms of sociocultural reality which have emerged in these agglomerations.

The model of the city as a population aggregate or locale or generalized "community" or environment again leads urban sociology in the direction of general sociology. Its concern tends to view the city in terms of one or more of the four analytical dimensions of sociocultural reality. Sometimes its focus is on urbanism, or the characteristics of the culture of cities that set it apart from the culture of peasant and rural populations (Sorokin and Zimmerman, 1929). Many sociologists have tried to grapple with the problem of defining the city by emphasizing the "unique" forms of social interaction which are found there, including secondary relations and voluntary associations (Park, Burgess, and McKenzie, 1967). Still others, of whom Simmel is a leading example (Simmel, 1950; Plant, 1937), have been interested in clarifying the nature of the urban personality. And it might be argued that the demographic and ecological approaches to the city are nothing more or less than a sustained effort to consider the environmental basis for the city, and thus of most of modern society as a whole, with particular attention to the impact of density and spatial interaction (Gibbs and Hawley, 1961). Wirth's famous article, which we have reprinted, is in many respects the most seminal representative of these approaches to urban sociology; it not only summarizes this interest in the four dimensions of sociocultural reality in cities, but it also goes on to describe the interconnections among them (Wirth, 1938).

The City as an Urbanized Local Community

Many urban sociologists have confronted the task of defining the city as a unique type of group. The group is the urbanized local community or territorial group. It has been pointed out that at least ninety different definitions of the term community are available in sociological literature (Hillery, 1968). Nevertheless, there are a few common features to these definitions which are apposite in relation to our previous discussion. The first is that a community is not a mere agglomeration or locale, it is not an all-purpose society, but it is a kind of group organized along special lines. The behavior of its members is subject to structured patterns of interaction regulated by norms and values which give the group continuity and order and are intrinsic to groups of this type, and this type only. The second is that the community today is recognized as one of many organized groups within a nation-state society and heavily dependent on all other groups and on society as a whole (Popenoe, 1968).

Although most of the major approaches to the local community share these identifying elements, they differ in their views of those structures and functions that are intrinsic to the community or that are best studied at the community level of analysis. One familiar viewpoint (Warren, 1963) is that the community is the organized group responsible for integrating the social functions that have locality relevance. Another approach is to distinguish between work-oriented and residence-oriented activities and functions and then to claim that the community is the organized group centered around residential activities (Reiss, 1959). Finally, some sociologists have argued that the local community consists of that "residual" system which is left over after the major local institutions have been analytically factored out (Hiller, 1941).

The definition of the city as an urbanized local community comes closest to justifying urban sociology as a special sociology. It is this approach which focuses attention on an identifiable and unique type of group phenomenon which is not the subject matter of another specialized field within the discipline. However, to rest on this fact alone the claim that urban sociology is, indeed, a special sociology presents the difficulty that the city so conceived is an increasingly less influential determinant and explicator of the behavior that takes place within the city. For example, in the case of behavior in American cities, the local community group itself is a less significant factor than, say, the American nation-state or many of the large organizations and bureaucracies which set the level of employment, determine the rate of migration, or influence the probability of social mobility. Furthermore, to confine the attention of urban sociologists to the local community level of social analysis almost forces the field to exclude from consideration those very urban problems which are responsible for the renaissance of urban sociology we discussed earlier, on the grounds that many of these problems such as race, poverty, and transportation are determined by events taking place at the societal or intercommunity level of analysis.

URBAN SOCIOLOGY IN PRACTICE

In the last section we considered the problem of urban sociology as a field within the discipline by examining the logical status of various approaches to the definition of the city. However, disciplines and fields, too, have a complicated history, and the subjects they deal with are often determined by factors which are extraneous to the ambition of the social scientist for logical coherence. As we noted earlier, this is certainly the case with urban sociology. The topics which the field is expected to cover often seem to be a grab bag of issues and problems which are considered important by American society but which do not fit neatly in terms of any formal definition of the city. In the present section we wish to review the major classes of topics urban sociology has dealt with in the recent past, to assess their relation to various definitions of the city, and to evaluate their significance in the urban society of this nation today. The method we have used in developing a list of issues is a rough "content analysis" of the leading textbooks in urban sociology that have been published in the last two decades (Anderson, 1959; Bergel, 1955; Boskoff, 1962; Erickson, 1954; Gist and Fava, 1964; Hatt and Reiss, 1957; Sirjanaki, 1964), along with a look at some of the major research monographs that usually are classified as part of the field.

Urban-Rural Comparisons

Many sociologists have suggested that the focus which gives inherent meaning to the field of urban sociology is the investigation of urban-rural differences. Without a rural order, of course, there would be no meaning to the concept of an urban order. Urban-rural contrasts have been constant since the Neolithic period (Childe, 1951) and represent a basic way in which social life has been categorized in the history of social thought.

Studies of urban-rural contrasts (Duncan and Reiss, 1962; Mann, 1965; Sorokin and Zimmerman, 1929) involve essentially the examination of small societies, that is, the comparison of almost every sociocultural aspect of local aggregations of people, including the personality, social system, and cultural and environmental aspects. Sometimes the terms ruralism-urbanism are used to signify this wholesale comparison of large social systems; at other times the term urbanism refers only to the cultural dimension of socio-cultural reality.

It is questionable to what degree urban sociology in a modern nation like the United States can be justified in terms of the distinction between urban and rural culture. Urban-rural contrasts are relatively unimportant in the advanced societies of the contemporary world (Dewey, 1960). In this country they virtually have been obliterated to the point where many city residents, such as recent Negro migrants to ghetto communities in the North, are more "rural" than many middle-class farmers and small businessmen who live in small towns and market centers (Vidich and Bensman, 1960). The agricultural occupation group on which ruralism is based has declined to less than 6 percent of the labor force. At the same time, the concept of urbanism has come to signify a heterogeneous set of subcultures and life styles ranging from slum dwellers in the central cities to gentleman farmers in exurbia (Gans, 1968). Urbanism is, therefore, not a useful term for dealing with community phenomena in our society, although it apparently is still relevant for understanding problems of economic development and basic social processes in parts of Asia, the Middle East, and Latin America (Breese, 1966).

Numerous scholars have pointed to the inadequacies of the urban-rural distinction and have noted the similarity between this concept and the typological classifications for describing social organization in the works of classic social theorists such as Weber, Durkheim, and Töennies (McKinney, 1966). The resemblance suggests that the recognition of the urban-rural distinction really does not belong to a special field of sociology but should rather be considered in the context of general sociological analysis concerned with understanding the underlying social structure of all large-scale societies.

Urbanization

The process through which cities emerge in society, namely "urbanization," is a phenomenon which for long has been of interest to sociology (Hauser and Schnore, 1965). The concept of urbanization can be defined narrowly to refer to the demographic trend of increasing density or population movement to cities (Gibbs, 1961), or it can denote a number of processes which, in combination, have the effect of endowing communities or societies with more complex forms of social organization and culture. In terms of the latter definition, it perhaps would be more accurate to speak of "urbanizing processes" to include industrialization, bureaucratization, and the development of literacy (Popenoe, 1965).

Although "urbanization" has served as a core concept in the formulation of sociological theory for a century or more and is still relevant to understanding modernization in underdeveloped nations, one can question the significance of the process in a society such as ours where almost everyone lives in urban areas and is subject to an urban culture. Even students of the developing countries take the position that the sources and structural implications of increasing density and internal migration are better understood if looked at in conjunction with industrialization and bureaucratization (Reissman, 1964).

Comparative City Studies

A good deal of work has been going on which implies that urban sociology is fundamentally an investigation of the differences in the social structure and culture of cities. The increasing irrelevance of a simple urban-rural continuum is accepted and, instead, research and theoretical activity is directed at classifying types of cities in this country (Hadden and Borgatta, 1965), tracing the connection between major forms of economic and political organization and urban social structure in Western history (Sjoberg, 1960; Mumford, 1961), and examining the ways in which cities adapt to changing technological conditions here and on other continents (Jones, 1966). This literature usually deals with very large and historically significant urban complexes, looking at them as small societies or reflections of large societies, and describing them in terms of the totality of sociocultural reality. One of the key features of this work is its concern with cross-national comparisons.

Comparative city studies illuminate the broad changes which have occurred in urban social organization since the beginnings of human civilization, but to the degree that this work is the product of sociology, it is once more virtually indistinguishable in theoretical orientation from general sociology or social history. The recent studies by ecologists dealing with systems of cities (Duncan, *et al.*, 1960) constitute a possible exception to this generalization. This literature examines the functions of cities from the specialized perspective of their differing roles in the national economy of the United States.

Community Studies

The study of communities as small societies is an enterprise which obviously does not have to be confined to urban communities, but many of the classic community studies by American sociologists have been focused on towns which are distinctly not rural and agricultural in character. We already have mentioned two famous examples: the Lynd's *Middletown* and Warner's *Yankee City* (Stein, 1960). Such studies have not attempted to single out the community as a special kind of group; rather, they have viewed the community as a representative sample of the culture and social structure of American society (Arensberg and Kimball, 1965). Indeed, there is no other way to study American society concretely and empirically except with reference to the behavior which takes place in some community within that society, even when the typicality of the community under scrutiny may not be demonstrable.

The problem of restricting urban sociology to such community studies is that this research usually does not investigate a specific class of phenomena but deals with a wide range of structures and functions. It therefore constitutes the example *par excellence* of the form of sociology which under the guise of a special sociology is really logically indistinguishable from general sociology dealing with society at large. The community studies tradition probably remains an important aspect of American sociology, however, because of its unique contribution to the corpus of research methodology and sociological interpretation.

Urban (Local) Community Studies

A variant of the community studies tradition which continues to generate significant research focuses on distinctive local aggregations of people within metropolitan areas, particularly in slums and suburbs (Gans, 1962 and 1967; Seeley, 1956 and 1959). Just as in the case of the older community studies tradition, this work deals with many facets of social structure and culture simultaneously, even though each researcher tries to concentrate attention on a single aspect of the local community such as the social stratification system (Dobriner, 1963) or the structure of the local decision-making process (Gans, 1967).

This work on subcultures and subsocieties within metropolitan agglomerations is a legacy of the community studies tradition. There are, after all, important contrasts in the social structure and population characteristics of slums and suburbs, stable inner city areas and exurbs, and satellite towns. When applied to these subcultures, the communities studies approach provides a valuable description and appraisal of pluralistic American society. These urban subcommunities, rather than cities as a whole, seem also to be the relevant units with which to compare rural subcultures and small towns.

Locality (Territorial) Groups

A further variation of the interest in smaller communities deals with those normative and functional aspects of communities which arise through the physical proximity of members and residents. It is assumed that such proximity generates a number of competing interests that must be resolved if the common space, or territory, of the residents is to be managed effectively (Hiller, 1941). The functional aspects usually considered relate to such things as the satisfaction of family needs (Barker and Wright, 1954) or leisure demands and the allocation of land (Wilhelm, 1962). The interest in locality groups differs from the other two versions of the community studies tradition by being concerned usually with small locality units such as neighborhoods or natural areas (Keller, 1968), and only with those features of social structure and culture which can be attributed to the experience of sharing a space or geographical area in common.

The relevance of the concept of group needs, processes, and structures based on shared territory is demonstrated in the research dealing with community power structure (Polsby, 1963), problems of local democracy and administration (Greer, 1962), the source and resolution of community conflict (Coleman, 1957), and the social role of neighborhoods (Keller, 1968). Although locality groups are as real as other social groupings, the usefulness of the concept as a basis for defining the boundaries of urban sociology obviously is limited. As we said in our discussion of the urban community concept, compared to social institutions or functional groupings, territorial groups possess relatively little "sociocultural power" (the influence of a particular type of group on other groups, on individuals, and on sociocultural trends). Furthermore, only rarely do they possess in reality the ideal-typical, self-sufficient, and cohesive community structures attributed to them in the literature (Sanders, 1966; Warren, 1963).

Territoriality

The concept of territoriality expresses an interest in the way in which social, cultural, and personality systems are concretely anchored and related in the space of a hypothetically bounded geographical area, such as an urban region (Hawley, 1950). When territoriality is defined in these terms, to refer not to the small area of the neighborhood but to the scale of a metropolis, the concept directs attention to the issues which have traditionally been of importance in human ecology. The ecologists are interested in the impact of the "friction of space" on economic activity, the relation of social organization to the natural resources and available technology in a region, and the distribution of people and activities in space (Quinn, 1950; Schnore, 1965). In the work of some Chicago school sociologists who also thought of urban phenomena as activities conducted within a bounded space, the interest in territoriality has taken the form of the concern for the way in which macrospatial variables, such as the size of a community's population or its density of settlement, influence variables in the sociocultural order (Wirth, 1964; Suttles, 1968).

Since almost 95 percent of social interaction in American society takes place in cities and urban regions, it can be said that most social structures and processes in this country are also influenced by, or have consequences for, the space of urban areas. However, this fact is not license for assuming that territorial ecology and urban sociology are synonymous. We noted earlier that man-environment relationships are a fundamental analytical dimension of all sociocultural systems and, therefore, of general sociology, rather than a defining characteristic of a special sociology. Furthermore, as we saw in the last section, at least two of the three traditional approaches to the nature of cities consider other variables than those which are the principal concern of an ecological framework.

Sociocultural-Material Environment Relationships

The study of the general relations between nonmaterial and material cultures is a rapidly growing branch of urban sociology. The problems studied within this area cover phenomena of different scales, from the environmental basis of the social organization of primitive bands (Steward, 1955) to the social impact of a building or site design (Gans, 1968). The specifically urban aspect deals with the ecological basis of city culture in undeveloped countries (Geertz, 1963), the interrelations between values and social structure and the physical form of an American city (Lynch, 1960), or the response to urban renewal schemes (Fried and Gleicher, 1961; Michaelson, 1968). In contrast to the ecological tradition which was interested primarily in establishing the connection between spatial patterns and economic-demographic phenomena, environmental sociology concentrates on the interaction between environment, social organization, personality and culture (Gutman, 1966).

The direction in which environmental sociology is moving may prove to be a useful subject of sociological investigation. However, it is clear that if it is to succeed in understanding the full complement of relations between space and society, it should be recognized that it is concerned with one of the four analytical dimensions of sociocultural reality. Defined in this way, it is, like human ecology, clearly a subfield within *general* sociology.

Urban Problems

Urban problems are the publicly recognized conflicts between values and situations which are present in cities. Traffic congestion, slums, delinquency, crime, poverty, and racial discrimination are among the greatest of these problems. We have already suggested that social problems of any kind have never been a useful point of reference from which to differentiate special fields within disciplines. Because of their very generalized causal nexus, social problems can only be explained and understood from the point of view of many different special sociologies, several branches of general sociology, and a number of the social science disciplines. This judgment holds even when the primary scholarly interest is in finding solutions to them. The unmanageability of a problem focus is compounded in dealing with urban problems because they include such diverse and relatively unrelated phenomena as air pollution, civic ugliness, and poverty. Indeed, urban problems are almost synonymous with the social problems of contemporary American society, in which case they are the responsibility of the entire discipline of sociology.

TOWARD A REORGANIZATION OF URBAN SOCIOLOGY

Let us consider the implications of what we have said up to now for proposing an organization of the field of urban sociology.

Two broad conclusions emerge from our discussion. One is that many, if not most, of the phenomena and issues which have concerned urban sociologists do not fall within the boundaries of a single special sociology. This is true whether we approach the nature of urban sociology in terms of a definition of the city or whether we assess the variety of topics and problems which have interested scholars who work in the field. From the perspective of a definition of the city, we find that the conception of the city as a small society, which may have been adequate when cities were similar to city-states, or which is still applicable to historical studies of urbanism and contemporary "interpretive" sociology, is no longer sufficient for understanding the organization and functions of cities in large modern societies which are themselves almost wholly urbanized. Our summary of the discussion of the city as a population aggregate or locale reveals that this approach has avoided the problem of identifying the class of group phenomenon which is the subject of a special sociology and instead has devoted its effort primarily to considering the nature of urbanism in its various manifestations. Urbanism, however, is a very ambiguous quality of sociocultural reality. In the sense that it consists of structures and processes underlying *all* groups and institutions in modern society, it seems appropriate to consider it within the context of general sociology, rather than as a specialized field.

A similar conclusion emerged from our examination of the empirical concerns of urban sociologists. The urban-rural distinction, the concept of urbanization, the ecological orientation, the interest in sociology-environment relations, the concern for social problems in cities—all these interests are either equally relevant to a sociology concerned with the total society and the nation-state or they involve a number of special sociologies other than the sociology concerned with cities.

The second broad conclusion revealed by our discussion is that the one class of group phenomena which *is* sufficiently identifiable and analytically distinctive to constitute the basis for a special sociology is not important enough as a determinant of action and behavior in modern American cities to command the exclusive attention of all the many scholars and students who now work as urban sociologists. This class of phenomena is the local community, whether in the form of a city, a suburb, a metropolitan region, or a neighborhood. Indeed, a strong case can be made for the view that the community as a social phenomenon must be closely related to other organized groups operating in mass society if its role and structure in the contemporary social order is to be fully understood (Litwak, 1960). Thus, community sociology might be more allied with other special sociologies, such as the study of primary groups, and less with some of the traditional concerns of urban sociology, such as urbanization or density.

In view of these conclusions, it seems purposeless to regard urban sociology as a single, special sociology which is manageable, theoretically significant, logically integrated, and comparable to most of the other specialized fields within the discipline. On the contrary, the ambition of urban sociologists, in our view, should be to maintain a foothold in the realm of their traditional concerns and, simultaneously, to make an effort to launch urban sociology on the path of increasing differentiation. This is the principal justification both for the publication of this book of readings and for the particular organization we have given to it. To the degree that the available literature makes possible, we have tried to orient the conventional subject matter and classification of urban sociological subjects to the major theoretical and empirical concerns and accomplishments of the discipline as a whole.

Part I presents readings which illustrate various approaches to the nature of urban sociology, including the three principal definitions of the city discussed in this essay. Several of these readings attempt to connect the concerns of urban sociology and the perspective of the field with the discipline as a whole, with the concerns of general sociology, and with other special sociologies.

The readings in Part II deal with urbanism and urbanization from a societal perspective. Although we have pointed out the difficulties in attempting to look upon cities as if they were societies and to regard urbanization as a demographic process, these orientations have been useful in helping us to understand the historical background of contemporary urban communities. Furthermore, the societal perspective helps the student who has been interested only in cities to enlarge his intellectual grasp to include an understanding of the social organization of modern society.

The readings in Part III are directed to amplifying the conception of urbanism as a multifaceted phenomenon defined by increasing organizational complexity, thus tying together a traditional concern of urban sociology with recent developments in the theory of society and social organization. Among the examples of complexity discussed are social stratification, cultural heterogeneity, and spatial differentiation.

Parts IV, V, and VI all deal with subjects which, even though they are not logically exclusive to urban sociology, nevertheless have in practice usually been studied by representatives of this field. The readings in Part IV are about human ecology, some of them written in terms of the conventional ecological interest in the role of the spatial environment in the development of metropolitan economic and social organization; others focus on the social and psychological processes that lead to the redistribution in space of people and their activities. Among our aims in the selection of readings is an attempt to connect the ecological view of cities with developments in the social theory of communication and decision-making.

Part V is given over entirely to studies of the structure and function of local communities. One section of the part deals with the organization of neighborhoods, and several readings relate the function of the neighborhood to alternative forms of primary group organization. The other section presents articles and essays devoted to politics at the local level, most of them emphasizing the rapidly growing theoretical and empirical interest in local power and governmental structures in modern society.

The articles in Part VI discuss theoretical and empirical questions in the emerging field of environmental sociology.

The readings in Part VII deal with the normative and applied aspects of urban sociology. Although the book has been organized around the problem of relating urban sociology to the academic discipline of sociology, our initial discussion of the renaissance in urban sociology today emphasized its source in the accelerating public concern in this country for the problems of cities, suburbs, and metropolitan regions. This concern has, as we repeatedly emphasized, posed a number of issues for the nature of the field defined according to the norms of a scientific enterprise. However, it also has given rise to a considerable literature which, regardless of its intellectual order and neat fit with a disciplinary orientation, has managed to yield a variety of ideas which are important in policy-making and which have also helped to improve the quality of performance in such practicing professions as city planning, architecture, social work, and public administration.

THE FUTURE OF URBAN SOCIOLOGY

We have shown that urban sociology in practice is highly eclectic and have suggested it is largely a matter of history and tradition that the concerns illustrated by our readings continue to be thought of as related and are regarded as appropriate for a single undergraduate or graduate course. Can we expect this tradition to continue?

Naturally, answers to this question must be speculative, but our guess is that the differentiation of the field we have advocated will indeed occur and that the concerns represented by the field of urban sociology today will be redistributed within the sociological enterprise in the future. To the degree that our society becomes more modernized, and as the vestiges of a rural small-town tradition further disappear, there will be decreasing justification for viewing urbanization and urbanism as distinctive social processes and structures even when they are a bridge to further understanding of the total society. From this point of view, in a society which is truly urban—not only in the sense that urban conditions of density, bureaucratization, and industrialization prevail but also in the sense that the ideology of the nation admits and accepts it (White, 1962)—the urbanization and urbanism concerns of urban sociology will be spread more or less throughout the discipline of sociology and all its special fields.

The two other interests which have dominated the organization of this book probably will have somewhat different future developments. As we said, a large modern urbanized society will always require primary groups and local organizations to keep it functioning. An interest in the nature of locality groups, the factors which influence their rise, integrity, or decay, and the function of locality groups in the organization of the total society undoubtedly will persist and perhaps even grow as this functioning becomes more problematic. For this reason we believe that some version of community sociology will survive as a special sociology within the discipline, although the modifying label "urban" is likely to disappear as the urban-rural distinction becomes increasingly less relevant.

We believe that the future will witness, too, an enormous growth in the concern for the interrelations between an environmental dimension of social reality and social and cultural organization. There is already evidence that this is taking place, and here and there throughout the country we have noticed a beginning interest in the field of environmental sociology—building in part on the earlier tradition of ecological sociology. To the degree that this field does in fact develop, it probably will force the sociologist to expand his interest from a concern only with the interrelations between the spatial environment and social organization to include as well a concern for the interrelations between the biological aspects of the environment and social organization. But again it must be pointed out that such a development implies that this aspect of sociological investigation can and will develop independent from urban sociology.

Finally, we feel compelled to end this introduction with a note about the development of an applied and policy-oriented sociology, though this is not the major focus of our book. The main motivation of sociology in the past half century has been the attempt to divest itself of normative concerns in order to develop a sounder and more objective tradition of scientific scholarship. We do not feel that this motivation was wrong—or that the pursuit of sociology as a "pure" social science should in any way be curtailed. But we do believe that the time has come to open the doors of sociology somewhat wider, to give greater legitimation to those whose major concern is to bring a fuller measure of rationality to public decisions and public life in general. The scientific accomplishments of sociology in the last half century represent a vast and underutilized resource in this regard. In many ways policy-oriented sociology could become the finest legacy of the urban sociology tradition.

BIBLIOGRAPHY

Alihan, M. A. *Social Ecology*. New York: Columbia University Press, 1938.

Anderson, N. *The Urban Community*. New York: Holt, Rinehart and Winston, 1959.

Arensberg, C. M., and S. T. Kimball. *Culture and Community*. New York: Harcourt, Brace & World, 1965.

Barker, Roger, and Herbert F. Wright. *The Midwest and Its Children*. Evanston, Ill.: Row, Peterson, 1954.

Bergel, E. E. *Urban Sociology*. New York: McGraw-Hill, 1955.

Boskoff, A. *The Sociology of Urban Regions*. New York: Appleton-Century-Crofts, 1962.

Breese, G. E. *Urbanization in Newly Developing Countries*. Englewood Cliffs, N.J.: Prentice-Hall, 1966.

Burgess, E. W., and D. J. Bogue (eds.). *Contributions to Urban Sociology*. Chicago: University of Chicago Press, 1964.

Childe, V. Gordon. *Man Makes Himself*. New York: New American Library, 1951.

Coleman, J. *Community Conflict*. Glencoe, Ill.: Free Press, 1957.

Dewey, R. "The Rural-Urban Continuum: Real But Relatively Unimportant," *American Journal of Sociology*, 71, 1 (July 1960).

Dobriner, W. M. *Class in Suburbia*. Englewood Cliffs, N.J.: Prentice-Hall, 1963.

Duncan, O. D., *et al. Metropolis and Region*. Baltimore: Johns Hopkins University Press, 1960.

———— and A. J. Reiss. *Social Characteristics of Urban and Rural Communities*. New York: Wiley, 1962.

Erickson, E. G. *Urban Behavior*. New York: Macmillan, 1954.

Faris, R. E. L. *Chicago Sociology*, 1920–1932. San Francisco: Chandler, 1967.

Firey, W. *Land Use in Central Boston*. Cambridge: Harvard University Press, 1947.

Fried, M., and P. Gleicher. "Some Sources of Residential Satisfaction in an Urban Slum," *Journal of the American Institute of Planners*, 27, 4 (November 1961).

Gans, H. J. *The Levittowners; Ways of Life and Politics in a New Suburban Community*. New York: Pantheon, 1967.

————. *People and Plans*. New York: Basic Books, 1968.

————. *The Urban Villagers*. New York: Free Press, 1962.

————. "Urbanism and Suburbanism as Ways of Life" in *Human Behavior and Social Processes*, A. M. Rose, ed. Boston: Houghton-Mifflin, 1962.

Geertz, C. *Agricultural Revolution: The Process of Ecological Change in Indonesia*. Berkeley: University of California Press, 1963.

Gibbs, J. P. (ed.). *Urban Research Methods*. Princeton, New Jersey: D. Van Nostrand, 1961.

Gist, N. P., and S. Fava. *Urban Society*, 5th ed. New York: Crowell, 1964.

Greer, S. *Governing the Metropolis*. New York: Wiley, 1962.

Gutman, R. "Site Planning and Social Behavior," *Journal of Social Issues*, R. Kates and J. Wohlwill, eds., 22, 4 (October 1966).

———— and D. Popenoe (eds.). "Urban Studies: Present Trends and Future Prospects in an Emerging Academic Field," special issue of *American Behavioral Scientist*, 6, 6 (February 1963).

Hadden, J. K., and E. Borgatta. *American Cities*. Chicago: Rand McNally, 1965.

Hatt, P. K., and A. J. Reiss, Jr. (eds.). *Cities and Society*. Glencoe, Ill.: Free Press, 1957.

Hauser, P. M., and L. F. Schnore (eds.). *The Study of Urbanization*. New York: Wiley, 1965.

Hawley, A. *Human Ecology*. New York: Ronald Press, 1950.

Hiller, E. T. "The Community as a Social Group," *American Sociological Review*, 6 (1941).

Hillery, G. A., Jr. *Communal Organizations: A Study of Local Societies*. Chicago: University of Chicago Press, 1968.

Hinkle, R. C., Jr., and G. J. Hinkle. *The Development of Modern Sociology*. Garden City, N.Y.: Doubleday, 1954.

Hofstadter, R. *Social Darwinism in American Thought*, rev. ed. Boston: Beacon Press, 1955.

Jones, E. *Towns and Cities*. New York: Oxford University Press, 1966.

Keller, S. *The Urban Neighborhood.* New York: Random House, 1968.

Litwak, E. "Geographic Mobility and Extended Family Cohesion," *American Sociological Review*, 25 (June 1960).

————. "Reference Group Theory, Bureaucratic Career and Neighborhood Primary Group Cohesion," *Sociometry*, 23 (March 1960).

————. "Voluntary Associations and Neighborhood Cohesion," *American Sociological Review*, 26 (April 1961).

Lynch, K. *The Image of the City.* Cambridge: M.I.T. Press, 1960.

Lynd, R. S., and H. M. Lynd. *Middletown.* New York: Harcourt, Brace & World, 1929.

Mann, P. H. *An Approach to Urban Sociology.* London: Routledge and Kegan Paul, 1965.

McKinney, J. C. *Constructive Typology and Social Theory.* New York: Appleton-Century-Crofts, 1966.

Michelson, W. *Man and his Urban Environment: A Sociological Perspective.* New York: Addison-Wesley, forthcoming.

Mumford, L. *The City in History.* New York: Harcourt, Brace & World, 1961.

Park, R. E., E. W. Burgess, and R. D. McKenzie. *The City.* Chicago: University of Chicago Press, 1967.

Parsons, T. "The Principal Structures of Community," in T. Parsons (ed.), *Structure and Process in Modern Societies.* New York: Free Press, 1959.

————, E. A. Shils, K. D. Naegele, and J. R. Pitts (eds.). *Theories of Society.* New York: Free Press, 1961.

Pirenne, H. *Medieval Cities: Their Origins and the Revival of Trade.* Garden City, N.Y.: Anchor, 1956.

Plant, J. *Personality and the Cultural Pattern.* New York: The Commonwealth Fund, 1937.

Polsby, N. *Community Power and Political Theory.* New Haven: Yale University Press, 1963.

Popenoe, D. "On the Meaning of Urban in Urban Studies," *Urban Affairs Quarterly*, 1, 1 (September 1965).

————. "The Sociocultural Context of People, Groups and Organizations" in *People, Groups and Organizations*, B. P. Indik, and F. K. Berrien, eds. New York: Teachers College, Columbia University Press, 1968.

Quinn, J. A. *Human Ecology.* Englewood Cliffs, N.J.: Prentice-Hall, 1950.

Reiss, A. J. "The Sociological Study of Communities," *Rural Sociology*, 24 (June 1959).

Reissman, L. *The Urban Process.* New York: Free Press, 1964.

Sanders, I. T. *The Community: An Introduction to a Social System.* New York: Ronald Press, 1966.

Schnore, L. *The Urban Scene.* New York: Free Press, 1965.

Seeley, J. "The Slum: Its Nature, Use and Users," *Journal of the American Institute of Planners*, 25, 1 (February 1959).

———— et al. *Crestwood Heights.* New York: Basic Books, 1956.

Simmel, G. *The Sociology of Georg Simmel*, K. Wolff, ed. Glencoe, Ill.: Free Press, 1950.

Sirjamaki, J. *The Sociology of Cities.* New York: Random House, 1964.

Sjoberg, G. *The Preindustrial City.* Glencoe, Ill.: Free Press, 1960.

Sorokin, P. A. *Society, Culture and Personality.* New York: Cooper Square, 1962.

———— and C. C. Zimmerman. *Principles of Rural-Urban Sociology.* New York: Holt, Rinehart and Winston, 1929.

Stein, M. R. *The Eclipse of Community*. Princeton: Princeton University Press, 1960.

Steward, J. H. *Theory of Culture Change*. Urbana: University of Illinois Press, 1955.

Strauss, A. *Images of the American City*. New York: Free Press, 1961.

Suttles, G. *The Social Order of the Slums*. Chicago: University of Chicago Press, 1968.

Theodorson, G. A. *Studies in Human Ecology*. Evanston, Ill.: Row, Peterson, 1961.

Timasheff, N. *Sociological Theory: Its Nature and Growth*, 2nd ed. Garden City: Doubleday, 1966.

Vidich, A. J., and J. Bensman. *Small Town in Mass Society; Class, Power and Religion in a Rural Community*. Garden City: Doubleday, 1960.

Warner, W. L. *Yankee City*. New Haven: Yale University Press, 1963.

Warren, R. L. *The Community in America*. Chicago: Rand McNally, 1963.

Weber, M. *The City*. Glencoe, Ill.: Free Press, 1958.

White, M., and L. White. *The Intellectual Versus the City*. Cambridge: Harvard University Press, 1962.

Wilhelm, S. *Urban Zoning and Land—Use Theory*. New York: Free Press, 1962.

Wirth, L. *Louis Wirth on Cities and Social Life: Selected Papers*, Albert J. Reiss, Jr., ed. Chicago: University of Chicago Press, 1964.

———. "Urbanism as a Way of Life," in *Cities and Society*, Hatt and Reiss, eds. Glencoe, Ill.: Free Press, 1957.

Znaniecki, F. *Social Relations and Social Roles*. San Francisco: Chandler, 1965.

PART I

Theory and Approaches in Urban Sociology

The specific phenomena which concern urban sociology as a field of study can be classified into five categories: (1) urbanization, or the processes through which societies and communities expand in population and become densely settled; (2) urbanism, or the personal, cultural, and social organizational characteristics which are associated with highly urbanized settlements and which are generated, in part, by urbanization; (3) urban environment and ecology, or the reciprocal relationships that prevail between cultural and social features of urban settlements and the natural, physical, and spatial environments; (4) urban locality groups, or the local communities and neighborhoods in an urban setting; and (5) urban policy and planning, or the programs, policies, and plans designed to solve the problems of cities and other urban communities and to guide urban change.

Although these five phenomena have their own distinctive intellectual and methodological problems, three issues of a theoretical sort arise in studying each of them. The first part of the book presents papers and articles dealing with these issues.

One issue of general concern is the nature of a community. The concept of community is undoubtedly one of the most ambiguous in sociology and, indeed, in all of the social sciences. George Hillery ("Definitions of Community," *Rural Sociology*, June 1955) examined the relevant literature and discovered that there were ninety-four different definitions of the term in use. The concept is important because the community is the primary object of *urban* sociological investigation. This is true whether, like Albert Reiss, one is trying to isolate those characteristics of social structure which are the product of unique local conditions or whether, like Herbert Gans, a sociologist is disposed to argue that the significant determinants of local culture primarily stem from the community's ties to the larger society.

A second important issue is the precise meaning of the term "urban." The term itself has an ancient history, the concept on which it is based having been familiar even to Greek society. It seems to be defined in one way by those who are interested in understanding the characteristics of the urban community in broad historical perspective, as is Louis Wirth, in a different manner by a sociologist intent upon distinguishing the variety of settlement types within a metropolitan region, and in still another fashion by someone like Peter Mann who chooses to examine its significance against the background of existing rural and primitive societies. How the concept urban is defined obviously determines in large part the range of communities and issues which are considered an appropriate focus for the student of urban life.

The final issue reflected in the readings of this section is perhaps the most fundamental of the three: Is the concept of the local community, be it urban or otherwise, still relevant to understanding the basic processes, structures, and problems of American cities when the society as a whole possesses so many of those features ordinarily labeled urban, or is the concept of a community an intellectual anachronism? This is only in part a quibble over definitions; it raises the question of how important is the modern community, *per se*, in shaping the lives of its residents.

1. The Sociological Study of Communities   Albert J. Reiss, Jr.

Albert Reiss defines a community as a collective response to the economic and demographic conditions of life that prevail in a particular territorial setting. In his view, this collective response exhibits a particular spatial pattern represented by the distribution of residences and other community activities; it also gives rise to a particular organizational structure, including the class system, the politics, and the associational life of different rural hamlets, towns, and cities. Reiss argues that community differences probably still persist in spite of the increasingly homogeneous culture of American mass society. However, at the same time he adopts this approach, Reiss admits that most sociologists who study communities fail to make explicit the variations in, and causes of, spatial and organizational structure. He reviews at considerable length the evidence of this failure and he examines its intellectual sources. A principal significance of Reiss' paper is that he then goes on to suggest a host of methodological procedures and specific research designs that should help sociologists to delineate the nature and role of community differences in contemporary society.

Albert J. Reiss, Jr., is Professor of Sociology and Director of the Center for Research in Social Organizations at the University of Michigan. He is author of *Crime and Law Enforcement in Major Metropolitan Areas* (1967) and coauthor of *Social Characteristics of Urban and Rural Communities* (1950). He is also editor of *Louis Wirth on Cities and Social Life* (1964) and (with the late Paul K. Hatt) of *Cities and Society: Revised Reader in Urban Sociology* (1957).

Sociologists who study communities do not share a precise definition of community, nor do they agree how observations about community phenomena are to be incorporated into sociological theory. This lack of agreement, in fact, is the *raison d'être* for this paper, since it explores both theoretical and research questions which these writings raise. The discussion that follows will be facilitated, however, if we can make reasonably clear the sense in which this paper deals with the sociological study of community.

Community is viewed in this paper as a territorial system. The more comprehensive territorial definitions of community view it as a form of social or ecological organization arising from the fact that people share a common area for their daily activities. Community thus is viewed as a collective response to conditions of life in a particular territory. We shall say that *a community arises through sharing a limited territorial space for residence and for sustenance and functions to meet common needs generated in sharing this space by establishing characteristic forms of social action.* It is assumed, for the purposes of this paper, that this definition is broad enough to include an interest in both the ecological and the social organization approaches to the study of community.[1] The definition is intended solely to sensitize the reader at the outset to the general perspective followed in this paper. It

This paper was read at a symposium at the University of Wisconsin, May, 1958, in honor of Professor John H. Kolb.

From *Rural Sociology*, Vol. 24 (June 1959), pp. 118–130. Reprinted by permission.

should not be interpreted to mean that a large number of characteristics are used to define a community in either a theoretical or an operational sense. At this juncture in our sociological study of communities, perhaps much is to be said in favor of defining a community in terms of a very small number of variables so that empirical observation may establish what phenomena are associated with them.

Generalizations about Communities

A review of the literature with a view to codifying research on communities shows the multiform nature of the concept of community. A majority of all published research studies purporting to be community studies simply use a territorial area as a sampling context and examine some problematic aspect of human beings within that context. The question naturally arises, why should these studies select a community as the context for the study of a problematic aspect of human behavior? From a scientific point of view there seem to be only two reasons for selecting a community as a context for such studies: one wishes to show either (a) that the generalizations sought are causally independent of the influence of communities or (b) that the generalizations systematically vary with certain stated properties of communities. In either case, there must be a demonstration of *how* variation in properties of communities affects the problematic aspect of human behavior under investigation; this requires testing the null form of hypotheses about the causal consequence of community attributes or variables.[2] Most so-called community context studies do not meet these criteria for the simple reason that either they select only a single community for

investigation, and hence cannot show that their relationships are independent of the context, or they fail to identify properties of communities with which their relationships may vary.

The second largest number of studies of community in the research literature purport to select attributes of communities as the object of investigation. From a scientific point of view such studies should follow a design of comparative community research which bears a close relationship to experimental method. There are studies which approximate such a model, notably in human ecology and demography and to some extent in rural community research. All too often, however, only a single community is selected for study, thereby precluding any investigation of variation in attributes of communities, or some property of the population within a community rather than a community attribute is selected for study. For example, the migrant status of persons within a single community is inferred as a community property.

These comments now lead us to some general observations about the kind of approach to the study of communities which scientific generalization dictates.

1. Community studies should be designed to show systematic variation in the properties of communities and to establish relationships among communities which arise within a larger system or network of communities. This requirement generally means that we must obtain some sample of communities whose parameters in a universe of communities can be inferred or specified (or we must know the parameters). We therefore are not interested in the unique attributes of communities, which often may be all that we are investigating in studies of a single community. The important fact to be recognized here is that

we must first establish that we have some community properties and show how they systematically vary among communities before we can generalize about communities

2. When we wish to examine how community affects any problematic aspect of human behavior under investigation, we must first select some property which systematically varies by community and then, controlling on this test factor, test the null form of the hypothesis about its effect on our observed relationship. For example, suppose we have observed a relationship between the migrant status of persons and the degree of social participation in voluntary organizations, and then we wish to see how "community" affects this relationship. Let us hypothesize that the size of a community will have some effect on this relationship. By the simple technique of partial association we can then examine the effect of size of community on this relationship, assuming we have an adequate sample of the size continuum of communities. Thus, our dummy table might look something like the one given here.

3. Community properties can be viewed as independent, dependent, or intervening variables.

If community properties are viewed as dependent variables, then generally we will need to look to external system variables to produce the variation among communities. Too often, when a property of a community is viewed as a dependent variable, some other property of a community rather than a system condition is taken as the independent variable. Thus, if we seek to explain functional differences in specialization of communities, we shall need to look to an "external" set of conditions which produce the functional variation, rather than to some property of the community which itself may be a source of functional variation. Or, if we wish to show that there is some variation in the status structure of communities, we should not look to internal but to external system conditions primarily.

If community properties are viewed as independent variables, then generally either we should be interested in the relationship among communities, as for example in their exchange relationships or modes of interaction, or we should investigate their effect on the behavior of persons. Many human ecologists treat such properties of communities as their size, spatial organization, degree of urbanization, rate of growth, and functional specialization as the independent variables affecting "relations" among communities and the behavior of residents within them. Characteristic properties of the social organization of communities can similarly be treated as independent variables.

Usually we do not consider community as an intervening variable, yet there seems logical justification for considering it as such in certain research problems. One such instance where a community property

Migrant status	Size of community					
	Small		Medium		Large	
	Social participation score					
	High	Low	High	Low	High	Low
Migrant						
Nonmigrant						

might be considered an intervening attribute is where "community of origin" is attributed to an individual datum, and the intervening effect of this variable on a relationship is investigated. For example, we may wish to investigate the effect of the size of the community of first job on an occupational inheritance relationship.

4. One of the more difficult problems in community research is the delineation of variables or attributes which characterize a community. The substantive nature of these variables depends upon our theory, of course. Still, in a formal sense, there are at least three major types of variables or attributes which merit our consideration.

There are, first, those attributes which are defined by an aggregation of some characteristic of the individuals who are residents in the community (or by an index). This property may be expressed in terms of some measure of descriptive statistics or stochastic analysis. Examples of this kind of characteristic are the size of the population, the relative homogeneity of the population in terms of some demographic or social characteristic, or the attitudes of members toward some "community problem." The property we attribute to a community in this sense must arise from data gathered from individual residents through census or survey techniques or by techniques of social observation.

The second major way we may characterize communities is in terms of some measure of relationship of the individual members to the community. Here we refer to extra-individual properties which are derived from the interaction of individuals. We therefore seek variables which characterize the interaction of inhabitants in terms of community, e.g., their neighboring, their patterns of movement in time and space, or their patterns of community

conflict or consensus. These variables must be measured by techniques which describe and analyze interindividual relationships.

There is, third, a set of characteristics which refer to the community system apart from any *direct* reference to the individual. We may characterize communities in terms of their social institutions or some state of the system, for example. Thus, we may wish to speak of their industrial composition or their moral integration. Our techniques of measurement for these variables are generally inadequate, as are our concepts. Generally we revert to some "less satisfactory" operational measures of the state of a community system which aggregate individual units of observation, e.g., the number of social agencies per 10,000 population or the ratio of productive to maintenance workers in an area.[3]

Our major reason for delineating these three types of community properties is to point up two facts. Most of our research on communities is on the first level, that of characterizing communities in terms of the characteristics of individual inhabitants. The second point is that we have failed to develop satisfactory operational constructs or measures for describing communities in terms of extra-individual properties of the system. This is less true in the field of human ecology than it is in social organization studies of communities, but it remains true for both major fields of investigation.

Theoretical Approaches to the Study of Community Phenomena

All individuals, their interrelationships and institutions, and their social systems can be allocated to territorial space. The geographic distribution of any phenomenon therefore is no satisfactory criterion for designating it as a community property, even if it occurs within a territorial space designated a community. The question naturally arises then: What major criteria shall we apply to designate phenomena as community variables in theory? We have answered this in part with our earlier statement that a community arises through sharing a limited territorial space for residence and sustenance and functions to meet common needs generated by such sharing of space in establishing characteristic modes of action. There appear to be two major frames of reference which attempt to study the community within this framework. Let us examine each of them briefly.

The Community as an Ecological System

Ecologists assume that community structure manifests itself in a spatial and temporal pattern. Hawley observes that in making this assumption we may start with the "wrong end" as we begin with little awareness of community structure itself. We therefore find it difficult to study a space and time which corresponds with community structure.[4] Hawley defines a "community as . . . comprising that area, the resident population of which is interrelated and integrated with reference to its daily requirements, whether contact is direct or indirect,"[5] or "the community includes the area the population of which, however, widely distributed, regularly turns to a common center for the satisfaction of all or a major part of its needs."[6] The ecologist therefore deals only with the symbiotic and commensalistic aspects of communities. Generalizations are sought about the structural features of communities and how these features change in response to external conditions. This "restricted" approach to community study leads to a fairly closed theoretical system,

but this very advantage appears in another sense to be a major limitation of the approach in that it ignores other kinds of community phenomena, namely, the role relationships and institutional forms of action which arise from the fact that individuals are motivated toward particular ends in sharing a territory for residence and sustenance relationships.

The research of the ecologist has in large part been focused on the internal structure of communities and only to a small degree on the external relations of communities. To be sure ecologists in their studies of dominance and of regional networks have focused to some extent on the relations among communities.[7] Yet we have not derived a satisfactory model for the study either of ecological relationships among communities or of the major ecological variables in the intercommunity relationships which occur within a larger matrix or system of communities. This appears to be a major research frontier in human ecology.

Much of the research of the human ecologist deals with relations of production within a community and between communities. This is true of ecological theory as well. Location theory, for example, concentrates to a great extent on productive means and only to a lesser degree on the production-consumption relationship. To be sure the conception of a market implies both, but the ecologist has concentrated less on the consumption than on the production side. This seems true of one of its parent disciplines, economics, as well. Consumption economics appears to be less highly developed than the economics of production. A community, however, is to a large extent a consumption unit. In point of fact, probably most communities "consume" more of what is produced locally than they export unless it is a highly specialized community. Some ecologists have tried to classify communities in terms of a production-consumption or a production-maintenance ratio in recognition of the importance of the consumption organization of a community, and others have described the patterns of retail trade. Despite these pioneer studies, a second major frontier in human ecology appears to be that of concerted research on the consumption organization of a community.

A third major frontier in ecological research lies in the detailed analysis of the residential structure of communities. Ecologists are concerned with the residence as well as the sustenance relationship. Too often in ecology, residence is simply a convenient means for defining a community area or for studying the relation of residents to a sustenance context, as for example in the study of patterns of movement to work or to a central business district. A community, however, consists of a host of residential relationships as well. For example, let us take the problem of temporal patterns of residential movement. Little is known about the daily, weekly, seasonal, and other cyclical patterns of movement in the residential community. What is the nature of the movement among residentially oriented institutions such as the home, church, school, park, residential center, and so on. One might hypothesize that the volume of residential kinds of movement exceeds the volume of movement to and from work, that patterns of residential movement may go counter to patterns of sustenance movement, that the volume of residentially related contacts exceeds the volume of sustenance related contacts, and so on. The human ecologist has essentially ignored all but the "productive" units of a community. The family unit, the child, and other "consuming" units have gained no place as units of

observation in the studies of ecology, but research on residential relationships necessitates observation of these units as well.

Some forty years ago C. J. Galpin wrote his now classic bulletin on agricultural centers, emphasizing the interrelations among parts of a community.[8] In a recent monograph John H. Kolb develops this perspective considerably further, showing the historical development of the town-country community and emphasizing the intercommunity patterns which they form.[9] Kolb's monograph brings together research on these intercommunity patterns and points the way to some of the problems in intercommunity relationships which both the ecologist and the student of social organization need to continue to investigate. The kinds of problems which give rise to intercommunity relations, which he discusses, include such instances as the consolidation of institutions undergoing intercommunity conflict, the functional interdependence of communities for institutional services of various types, and changes in the territorial space of communities as a consequence of competition among them. The study of intercommunity conflict and its resolution and of the increasing functional interdependence of communities is one of the major frontiers for community research. An excellent example of the kind of research which can be done at this frontier and which meets our previously stated criteria of scientific comparative community research is a study completed here at the University of Wisconsin by Burton Kreitlow and James A. Duncan.[10] Comparing heterogeneous and homogeneous communities they show, for example, that residents of the heterogeneous communities were more accepting of programs favorable to school consolidation and improved farming practices.

The Community as a Social System   The conventional treatment of communities, particularly omnibus community studies, presents the community as a microcosm of the larger social macrocosm—as the smallest territorial system which encompasses the major features of society, that is, a society in miniature. A community is usually seen then as possessing a system of stratification, a power structure, characteristic institutions such as educational, religious, and economic ones, and so on, depending upon the "complexity" of its organization. All the major attributes of society therefore are looked for in each community, described, and analyzed.

This is not the place to discuss this approach in detail. Here we wish simply to point out that the characteristic mode of analysis employed in these studies is no different from that used in describing and analyzing the macrocosmic social system. Specific community properties therefore are not identified. Take the case of social stratification as an example. A typical study of "community stratification" fails to show that there is variation in stratification which can be shown to be a property of communities. No systematic study of community variation in stratification can be developed so long as this microcosmic social system approach is followed. There appear to be two major ways out of this dilemma so that we may identify organizational properties of communities which vary systematically. We shall designate these as the *interaction-space approach* and the *social-group approach*. In a real sense the two approaches converge and represent only differences in emphasis. Let us briefly examine each of them.

The interaction-space approach takes as its major focus that the *community involves collective action toward the realization of common goals arising in a residence-sustenance locality*. In brief, a community exists only when there is (a) common recognition of "local" goals, (b) collective motivation with respect to these goals (co-operation, conflict, and so on), and (c) local allocation of resources with respect to these goals.

It perhaps is not unfair to say that this area of research has pretty much been left to persons with a social-problems or action-oriented approach. As a consequence of this fact no systematic approach to the diverse problems which confront communities has been developed. Studies in fluoridation, race relations, taxation, school consolidation, and a host of similar "local" problems generally lead to descriptive studies of the problem in a single community rather than to an investigation of community attributes of these problems and their community variation. This whole approach to community study appears as a research frontier. Perhaps we might point out a few ways in which a systematic approach may be made to some of the problems in this area, however.

A central problem of all communities is the resolution of community conflict. This research frontier is treated in a most seminal way in a recent monograph by James Coleman.[11] Coleman codifies some of the findings from a large number of individual studies on the genesis and resolution of community conflict. While his codification does not always distinguish between community attributes of conflict and more general system properties of conflict, it shows that a problem such as community conflict serves as a means of focusing attention on specific attributes of communities and not on the specific conflict situation, as so often is the case. The kind of questions we then can ask and attempt to answer are such as these: Under what specific conditions in a community does conflict arise, and correlatively under which does conflict over "problems" fail to appear, given similar expectations of conflict. For example, when will there be conflict over school consolidation, school racial desegregation, increased taxation, fluoridation, and so on? Under what conditions are various "equilibriums" reached as "solutions" to any problem of community conflict? The most general question around which research in this area might be designed is that of determining the nature of the processes of decision making in a community. A design for studies of this type might include the following features: (1) select all communities which have recently had a similar decision (e.g., fluoridation, school bond issue, or school desegregation); (2) obtain matched pairs of communities in which the decision was for and against (matching on criteria it is felt desirable to control as sources of variation); (3) examine the pairs for community attributes producing the decision.

A second major type of problem which merits our attention is that of discovering how communities affect patterns of interaction among persons. Much has been written about how size, density of settlement, heterogeneity of the population, and similar characteristics affect social relations among inhabitants. Yet there virtually is no research which compares communities in this respect. Some of my own research has been devised to see how kinds of primary contacts vary among urban, rural nonfarm, and rural farm communities. The results are only suggestive of what we may learn, but they show, for example, that community is more important than social status in determining the amount and types of primary and secondary contacts of inhabitants. Closely related to this is the problem of learning how residence conditions interpersonal relations. While we have a large number of studies of the neighboring relation, it still is far from clear how differences in community structure affect the neighboring relation.

The social-group approach to community study rests on the postulate that *a community system differs from other systems in that locality is a datum in the integration of the system.*[12] Not all interaction which occurs within a territorial area derives from a community. Only those forms of interaction are community which arise within locally defined and implemented value orientations. Several forms of interaction which occur within a territorial community are excluded if we follow this principle. First, all interaction within defined institutions such as the school, the factory, the church, is noncommunity unless the interaction occurs within the context of locally defined values, with agents occupying local roles, and the like. For example, while the school is primarily not of the community in this sense, the controversy over school consolidation, location, or desegregation may have certain community aspects. School consolidation or desegregation in a community may be largely a consequence of extralocal policy; yet at some point there is community policy and decision making on these questions. Second, certain institutions in a community are specialized ones, where residents have little direct relation to the community in which they are located, e.g., state mental hospitals or penitentiaries. To be sure, institutional personnel may be involved in locality relationships or problems, but the residents usually are not.

On the other hand, certain types of institutions are primarily distinguished by their community properties. These include the following: (a) institutions which derive from the residence context, e.g., rooming and lodging houses, patterns of residential spacing, or the local community newspaper;[13] (b) institutions which derive primarily from the consensus process in the community, e.g., the local improvement association, civic associations, and so on; (c) an extralocal institution which utilizes local action to implement both local and extralocal goals, as in the case of local chapters of NAACP, the AMA, or Chambers of Commerce.

An example chosen from the theory of stratification may serve to clarify this approach to community study. There is much controversy in the literature of social stratification over the question whether stratification is a mass society or a local phenomenon. Our problem here is simply to show that a conceptual approach to stratification is possible in local community terms apart from the mass stratification aspects.

We shall begin by noting that the fact that communities vary in some attribute such as the dimensions of the status structure or the amount of in-and-out mobility does not mean that these are community attributes in the sense in which we now are speaking. For one can easily show that these dimensions can arise *outside* a community system as well as *within* a system. We deal in this approach only with those properties which arise within the system. The fact that one community has a predominantly white-collar structure while another has a predominantly working-class structure is primarily a direct consequence of the functional organization of the community, but it also is an indirect consequence of the fact that this functional organization is itself a consequence of the economic interrelations of the community in the larger society. In a very real sense almost any

characteristic of a community is an indirect consequence of the larger social matrix within which a community arises and persists. The size of a community probably is a consequence of where a community fits into some larger system of communities. Despite the fact that a phenomenon such as the stratification structure of a community in a complex society is primarily determined by extralocal factors rather than local ones, it appears there are several senses in which we can view locality attributes. The following, at least, are suggested:

1. A community is an arena for the exercise of status. Persons who occupy similar positions from a mass stratification perspective may have highly different positions in a local community depending upon the composition of the population, the basis for status attribution, or the roles which a person occupies in the community. This local status is nontransferable in contrast with the mass status which is transferable from community to community. Some occupational roles may be so intimately tied to a community status that it may be extremely difficult to move to another community without a great risk or "loss" to the person. This is generally true of the professional with a local "private practice." By way of contrast the person with a "public clientele" may more readily move. Thus, social workers should have a higher rate of community mobility than physicians.

2. Communities may vary in the way in which they facilitate social mobility, apart from the mass avenues to mobility. They may facilitate and retard social mobility (even in the restricted occupational sense) in a number of ways. Local groups may become avenues to mobility, since they involve local chains of acceptance or rejection. A lawyer is generally

disbarred by the *local* bar association for *local* as well as extralocal definitions of malpractice. Or, for example, admission to the medical staff of a hospital often is a function of local rather than medical criteria of acceptance, proving of great consequence for the *career* of the doctor.

3. The position a person has in relation to community ends or values affects *"general position" in the community*. One may be a waitress in an occupational sense, but a prostitute in the community where she works. And, one community may be more tolerant of the prostitute than another, since the value structure may be more tolerant or the local police controls less effective.

4. The choice of the community in which a person will pursue his occupation, particularly if it is a career occupation, and the kind of mobility he experiences probably are a function of his general status in his community of orientation. In general, a person who aspires to upward mobility will move out of his community of orientation if it is a small one where his previous status is communicated. Out mobility from a community, particularly small ones, may therefore be as much a function of general status in the community as it is of "opportunities" apart from status. For, the opportunities will be filled by persons whose known status is consonant with aspired or achieved status, or by immigrants whose previous status is not generally known and communicated. The large community will differ substantially from the small one in this respect, for it is in the large one that status anonymity is more readily preserved.

5. The selection of an occupational status is to some degree a function of the person's willingness to move from his community of orientation. The occupational structure of a community may limit the choice of a career by restricting opportunities to enter or inherit a given occupation.

6. Communities may vary not only in their status-conferring properties but in the degree to which they condition propensities to upward and outward mobility. These differences among communities are a combined function of the value structure and the organizational system. Some school systems, for example, will strongly emphasize achievement and so organize the curriculum and related activities that upward and out mobility is facilitated while others will retard it.

It of course is unclear from the controversy in the literature about the characteristics of "community" or "mass" stratification what behavior is to be explained by either approach. It seems reasonable to postulate that local status determines locally oriented behavior while "mass" status determines mass behavior. To use either status position to predict behavior in the other system relations may be to reduce the predictive power of our variables. The point to be recognized here is that community system variables have theoretical value in stratification theory primarily to explain behavior in the local arena where status is exercised. For example, one might characterize communities in terms of their stratification system and/or some other attributes of their organization (the independent variables) and then show through comparative analysis how these affect the process of decision making in the community (e.g., the power structure and how it functions) and the consequences of the process for the community.

Summary

This paper makes the suggestion that much research on communities fails to meet two important criteria which will permit the development of generalizations about communities. The first failure is that the scientific comparative approach and the techniques of multivariate analysis are not generally applied to the design of community studies. The second failure is that a distinction seldom is maintained between the theoretical properties of communities and properties which are properly classified in other systems. The real frontier of community research is to correct these failures in our theory and design of community research. Like all criticisms, this one suffers from the fact that some research studies do conform to the models briefly discussed in this paper. What merit this discussion has then, if any, may lie in calling attention to these models rather than to our failures.

NOTES

1. Specifically, we wish it to include the type of considerations set forth in Amos Hawley's formulation of human ecology as a theory of community structure, *Human Ecology: A Theory of Community Structure* (New York: Ronald Press, 1950) and at the same time embrace the social organization approach followed in diverse ways by a large number of sociologists, as in the structure-function approach of Talcott Parsons' *The Social System* (Glencoe, Ill.: Free Press, 1951), pp. 91 ff; the teleological-organizational approach of Kingsley Davis' *Human Society* (New York: Macmillan, 1949), pp. 310–313; or the institutional process approach of Robert E. Park and E. W. Burgess *The City* (Chicago: University of Chicago Press, 1925).

2. A critique of community context studies is to be found in the writer's "Some Logical and Methodological Problems In Community Research," *Social Forces*, XXXIII (Oct., 1954), 52–54.

3. We do not wish to pose any artificial opposition of the "dead" controversy of the individual and the group in this three-fold characterization of community attributes. The distinctions are purely heuristic.

4. Amos Hawley, "Discussion," *American Sociological Review*, XIII (1948), 153–156.

5. Amos Hawley, *Human Ecology*, pp. 257–58. Hawley's definition is chosen as representative of the more recent theoretical approaches in human ecology.

6. *Ibid.*, p. 246.

7. See in particular Donald J. Bogue, *The Structure of The Metropolitan Community: A Study of Dominance and Subdominance* (Ann Arbor: University of Michigan Press, 1949), and Walter Isard, Robert A. Kavesh, and Robert E. Kuenne, "The Economic Base and Structure of the Urban Metropolitan Region," *American Sociological Review*, XVIII (1953), 317–21. A paper by Otis Dudley Duncan makes a substantial contribution toward outlining theoretical problems and generalizations in this area, "Human Ecology and Population Studies" in Philip M. Hauser and Otis Dudley Duncan, eds., *The Study of Population* (Chicago: University of Chicago Press, 1959).

8. *The Social Anatomy of an Agricultural Community* (Univ. of Wisconsin Agr. Expt. Sta. Res. Bull. 34, Madison, 1915).

9. *Emerging Rural Communities* (Madison: University of Wisconsin Press, 1959), pp. 8–9 ff.

10. *The Acceptance of Educational Programs in Rural Wisconsin* (Wisconsin Agr. Expt. Sta. Bull. 525; Madison, 1956).

11. *Community Conflict* (Glencoe, Ill.: Free Press, 1957). See also Florian Znaniecki, "Group Crises Produced by Voluntary Undertakings," in Kimbal Young, ed., *Social Attitudes* (New York: Henry Holt, 1931), ch. xi.

12. This approach was suggested to the writer by E. T. Hiller's essay "The Community As A Social Group," *American Sociological Review*, VI (1941), 189–202, and an earlier essay by Florian Znaniecki *op. cit.*

13. See Morris Janowitz, *The Community Press In An Urban Setting* (Glencoe, Ill.: Free Press, 1952) for an analysis of the newspaper as a locality institution in a metropolis.

2. Descriptive Comparison of Rural and Urban Communities

Peter H. Mann

In spite of the present advanced state of urbanization in the United States, urban and rural contrasts still do exist, and they remain obvious and important in less advanced societies. Furthermore, the distinction between urban and rural types continues to provide the student with a sharp and powerful intellectual concept for penetrating the phenomena of urban sociology. Peter Mann analyzes the fundamental differences between urban and rural milieus in terms of eight characteristics: Occupation, Environment, Size of Community, Density of Population, Heterogeneity and Homogeneity of Population, Social Differentiation and Stratification, Population and Social Mobility, and Systems of Social Interaction. His examples are drawn largely from English society, but Mann makes an effort to mention parallel developments in America. The student should recognize that the extremes of the rural-urban continuum are discussed here, on the grounds that this kind of "ideal-type" analysis offers the best way of highlighting the distinctive characteristics of urban communities.

Peter H. Mann is Senior Lecturer in Sociology at the University of Sheffield, in England. He is the author of *Methods of Sociological Enquiry* (1968) and *An Approach to Urban Sociology* (1965).

The highly urbanised form of so much of Western civilisation is a phenomenon of fairly recent development and it is not surprising that the method of contrasting rural and urban groups has been used for a better understanding of changes that have taken place and which are still continuing today.[1] So long as we are clear in our minds as to just *what* we are comparing, the method can be extremely valuable. However, there are two pitfalls which must be carefully avoided if true justice is to be done to the method.

The first pitfall comes with working with the four factors, rural, urban, past and present. The danger lies in comparing rural and urban without taking care to remember (or specify) whether the comparison is at a given time or over a period of time. For example, one can compare the present village with the past village (defining, of course, with what period in the

past one is concerned). One can also compare the past village with the present city. Any comparison using these four variables is a valid one, so long as the time aspect is made clear. But it is not uncommon to find that a comparison of rural and urban is made in which the reader (and perhaps the writer too) has little idea of *when* the comparison is being made. As one example, we find Thomas Sharp saying, "Now the point about the agricultural village, for my present argument, is that it is, or at least was a comparatively simple social organism."[2] Such an argument, ignoring the time factor, must be suspect, since the writer is admitting by implication that a change has taken place in the village and we

From *An Approach to Urban Sociology* (London: Routledge & Kegan Paul; New York: Humanities Press, 1965), Chap. 2, pp. 4–27. Reprinted by permission.

cannot be sure just where in time he is basing his statements.

The second pitfall, closely linked with the first, is that of dealing in stereotypes rather than generalisations. By this we mean to refer to two allied problems. Firstly there is the problem of knowing just what a person is meaning when he refers to a rural community: it may well cover anything from a primitive village in Africa to a village inhabited wholly by wealthy commuters not far from New York. In general this problem is covered to some degree by the implication normally made that the reference is to a village in Western society based mainly upon agriculture as a way of life. This vague definition in itself covers a wide range of differences, but for most general purposes it suffices. The second point concerns the attitudes towards rural communities that are held by many writers. Here we find a wealth of value judgments that are not always made explicit, and it becomes evident that many writers, consciously or unconsciously, are "anti-urban" and "pro-rural." By this we mean that in comparing village and city there is a glorification of rural life which at times is based purely on sentiment, and at times pretty sickly sentiment at that. The thatched cottage, with roses round the door and honeysuckle in the garden is a favourite picture used in greeting cards, calendars and so on. This writer has yet to see a birthday card where a large block of flats is the central pictorial theme. In song and story, and film, the "country life" is the one for me, and "my home town" is always a *small* place, never sounding larger than an overgrown village. The "local yokel" is a figure of fun, but the laughter he arouses is essentially friendly in its spirit: he may be simple, but he is good hearted. His counterpart the city wage-slave never ever raises a joke, he is far too drab and uninteresting, and even if he should show signs of life he is likely to be portrayed as a fat, self-indulgent moron or a slick spivlike character.[3] It would be an interesting topic for research to make a detailed analysis of the various stereotypes such as are mentioned above in the rural-urban contrast. But perhaps the most dangerous aspect of it all lies in the constant emphasis upon urbanism and urban life as a *problem*. Perhaps in the U.S.A. where rural sociology is more advanced, and where rural problems have been very great in fairly recent years, the attitude is more realistic and a better balance is kept. Upton Sinclair's *The Jungle* may be balanced by John Steinbeck's *Grapes of Wrath*. But certainly the position in Great Britain seems to be heavily weighted in favour of the "truly-rural." It will be our contention in future pages that the attitudes of "for rural" and "against urban" do much to obscure the true understanding of both rural and urban life, and place a wholly undue emphasis upon the *problems* of city life. This is not to say that, allowing everyone his own value judgments, there should not be preferences for rural or urban life. The present writer has lived in city and village, and finds much that is attractive in both, with, if anything, a preference for village life. Where the danger lies, surely, is in the idea that city life is very busy and complicated, whereas the village is simple and cosy. It then follows that it would be ideal for us all to live in villages, and, if we cannot do this, then we should try to make our cities as much like villages as possible. Such an argument, we contend, is positively dangerous and can lead to a complete lack of any sensible orientation towards studying the form and structure of urban society. The viewpoint is distorted, and the city stands condemned before it is even put on trial.

The glorification of the rural community is further linked with a harking back to "those good old days" so beloved of song-writers whose memories, or knowledge of facts, appear to be highly selective. Here the two pitfalls join together to make one large hole, and we find a blind groping after a form of life that probably never existed in the past, and certainly could never exist in present life.

If we can avoid the two major errors referred to above it should be possible to make an objective and impartial comparison between rural and urban forms of community. In doing this we shall use the method of the polar contrasts, linked by a continuum. As T. L. Smith points out,

> Rural and urban do not exist of themselves in a vacuum, as it were, but the principal characteristics of each may be found shading into, blending or mixing with the essential characteristics of the other . . . Rather than consisting of mutually exclusive categories, rural and urban, the general society seems to resemble a spectrum in which the most remote backwoods sub-rural [sic] settlements blend imperceptibly into the rural and then gradually through all degrees of rural and suburban into the most urban and hyper-urban [sic] way of living. If such be the case, a scale, rather than a dichotomy, would provide the most satisfactory device for classifying the population or the group according to rural or urban characteristics.[4]

(It is interesting in passing to note that in the above passage Smith gives the prefix "sub" to the most extreme rural pattern, and the prefix "hyper" to the most extreme urban. Perhaps this is meant to imply the development of urban from rural, but it is worth noting as just one example of the way in which attitudes to rural and urban influence the selection of terminology.)

Using the method of analysis put forward by Sorokin and Zimmerman we can see how, "through the classification of a complex and uninterrupted series of phenomena into a few types or classes, they (scientists) overcome the complexity of the concrete reality and give its important traits in the form of a few classes or types of phenomena."[5] Sorokin and Zimmerman consider the principal criterion of difference between rural and urban society to be *occupational*. From this basic difference a further series of differences can be developed, most of which are related in some way to the basic one. Eight characteristics in all are given as a means for comparing what are called the rural urban "words", they are (1) Occupation, (2) Environment, (3) Size of Community, (4) Density of Population, (5) Heterogeneity and Homogeneity of Population, (6) Social Differentiation and Stratification, (7) Mobility, (8) System of Interaction. In this article we shall give each characteristic, with the comparative illustrations made by Sorokin and Zimmerman, and, with each, develop the contrast for our own purposes.

Since agriculture is concerned primarily with the cultivation of crops and the breeding and rearing of animals, the typical rural work is out-of-doors and requires comparatively large areas of land. There is, from this, a further requirement that at least some of the labour force shall live close at hand to the land or, particularly, animals, and it becomes apparent that large communities of agricultural workers are highly unlikely. Rural work also tends to call for a high degree of adaptability; the general farm worker is a man with a variety of skills who can fulfil a number of functions. (It is always a wonder to me, after spending two summers as a student working on farms,

RURAL-URBAN DIFFERENCES SUGGESTED BY
SOROKIN AND ZIMMERMAN

(1) Occupation

Rural	Urban
Totality of Cultivators and their families. In the community are usually few representatives of several nonagricultural pursuits.	Totality of people engaged principally in manufacturing, mechanical pursuits, trade, commerce, professions, governing and other nonagricultural occupations.

that agricultural workers are considered to be unskilled: the man with five years' experience of farm work is surely at least as skilled as the fitter or turner in an engineering works). Conditions vary according to place, but, in general, the agricultural worker is employed in a relatively small labour unit. The "family farm" often has as its only labour force the farmer, his wife, his sons and, possibly, his daughters. Even where outside hands are employed the numbers are still generally small and a comprehensive personal relationship between the farmer and his men is possible. The continuous and relatively unchanging needs of farming make for a tradition which often results in the land being worked by succeeding generations of families. This, in turn, leads to training for farm work beginning at an early age and work and home are closely linked. An example may be cited of a farm known to me, where the farmer, an oldish man, was helped by his three sons, one of whom was married and had twin sons. At the age of four, both the boys could handle a farmtractor and were capable of carrying out many routine farm jobs. It is not suggested that all farms have such a tradition, and the growth (as it appears) of managed farms owned by absentee city businesssmen may cut across this pattern. Nevertheless, in contrast to the industrial type of occupation, the above picture may be used.

With urban occupations a very different system operates. The home and the family group rarely have any direct connection with the occupation of the wage-earner or earners. Few industrial workers have a traditional occupation into which it might be said that they "grew." It is often suggested that coal-mining, dock-work and a few professions such as the church and the armed forces, do have a father-to-son tradition. But even if this is so, the home is not the occupational centre, and in the case of the professions particularly, the following-on of the son in his father's profession may well necessitate his leaving home altogether. Work unit and home unit no longer have the same tie as in agriculture. In the urban setting the choice of occupation open to the young school-leaver is much wider than in the rural area, and the human-industrial structure is correspondingly more complex, depending as it does upon the integration of a huge network of interrelated occupations and processes. Such an organisation makes it extremely difficult for the ordinary worker to understand anything but a small part of the whole, and the possibility of primary relationships on an occupational basis for the *whole* urban group becomes manifestly impossible. Added to this, the breadth of initial choice often leads to rapid specialisation, so that the young man who trains for a particular skill may, in effect, be commiting himself, at an early age, to a particular occupation for life. It is often said that the craftsman has the advantage that, in a slump, he always has his craft, whereas the unskilled man has nothing in particular to offer, but the fact remains that once a skill has been gained the craftsman can rarely change his job (*not* employer) without having to take a less-skilled occupation. The electrician cannot change to plumber, nor the fitter to blacksmith, and in this restriction of occupational movement (which would appear to be increasing as restrictive practices on the part of trades unions grow) may be seen a trend towards immobility. It is worth noting that in the "recession" in the British motor-car industry in 1956 it had to be impressed upon men being laid off that "full employment" did not mean that a man could expect the same job with the same employer for ever and ever, and this was a hard fact which did not appear to be easily digested by some. It would therefore appear that full employment, coupled with an urban industrial structure, has varying results on particular types of workers. Some may move around regularly in search of better conditions or wages whilst the demand for their services is great. Others, particularly the less-skilled, may prefer to remain in the one place, enjoying the fruits of security coupled with good pay. But given the setback of a fall in demand for labour, the necessary mobility between *types* of job of an unskilled sort may be difficult to get. The pattern is, indeed, much more complex than is found in the rural area.

Because it is based upon a *physical* difference, the contrast between rural and urban environment is perhaps the simplest one to understand. Urban problems resulting from the unplanned and relatively uncontrolled development of large cities, with their resulting overcrowding, dirt, noise, and so on, are known to every thinking person, whilst the absence in some rural settings of many of the amenities expected of a modern society is not overlooked by most people. The advantages and disadvantages of the two environments as places for living are not new problems, and perhaps Ebenezer Howard's diagram of the town and country magnets is the most well-known representation of the forces of attraction and repulsion. His solution, the "garden city" is, of course, world famed.

If we accept that the contrast between rural and urban environment brings forward the problems of what is the "best" physical environment, we are likely to become bogged down in a host of value judgments and conditional clauses. Obviously, occupations that are linked completely with a rural environment cannot be carried out in the town: the farmer needs open land for his work, the hunter would get a poor bag stalking along the concrete pavements. Similarly the driver of a London underground train would be hard pressed to find a similar job in the heart of Cornwall. But leaving aside the obvious limitations of environment, we come to the problem of what is, to put it bluntly, the most desirable environment, in general, for the bulk of the population of this country. We know that we are a highly urbanised country, and we know that only a minority of us have occupations that could be called

(2) Environment

Rural	Urban
Predominance of nature over anthropo-social environment. Direct relationship to nature.	Greater isolation from nature. Predominance of man-made environment over natural. Poorer air. Stone and iron.

rural ones. Yet we know also that the countryside has a great attraction for us; witness the streams of cars that swarm out of the town on any sunny weekend, at times so thick that the countryside becomes more congested than the town itself. We have seen how the desire for space and gardens has led to widespread developments of suburbs with a very low building density: such areas are common on the outskirts of the town. These residential areas are not rural in any way (although they may be very near to the open country) yet they have vestiges of rurality in an attempt to make them less urban. The grass verges along the roadside so as to add greenery, the trees planted along the pavement edge, the "cottage-style" modern houses, at times with thatched roofs, all testify to the desire for a layout and a house-design which imitates the rural environment.

We have already mentioned the suggestion that the general population of this country is anti-urban, and when we consider the problem of environment there is ample evidence to support this hypothesis. Howard's idea of the garden city was a brave attempt to gain the best from both worlds, urban and rural together. Yet can it really be said that the idea succeeded? Critics of the garden city concept regard it merely as a delaying action fought against the many factors driving our society towards a more urban mode of life. Whilst not by any means denying the need for plans to control the development of the size of cities, these critics regard Howard's plans as having given rise to the unhappy compromise of the "garden suburb," wasteful of land and creating distances from city centres which appear to be needless. Thomas Sharp says we have created "Neither Town-Nor-Country."[6] To Sharp, town is

town and country is country, and never the two should be confused.

It is interesting to note how urban imitation of rural life is generally an imitation of the past. It is common in city suburbs to find houses built in the 1930's in the "Stockbroker's Tudor" style, and interiors fitted with panelling (wood or plastic) and hung with horse brasses. In the villages themselves the new fits oddly with the old in many cases. An old village, with a higgledy-piggledy layout, may have added to it a new council estate that is no different from one in the centre of any large city. In the villages that have been taken over by city-dwellers and converted into dormitory villages or weekend retreats the houses may be given a new lease of life, with careful restoration and good maintenance. Yet, the "improvements" that are made (windows enlarged, with the addition of steel frames and bottle-glass panes, concrete-block garages added to the brick houses) result in a blurring of the distinction between urban and rural. Perhaps the most notable of all coalescing of rural and urban is to be seen in our seaside resorts, in particular in places where a small village has become a popular holiday resort. Here we find the sweep of sands with its ice-cream vans, its iron piers and its border of concrete promenade, the old fishing village with its host of curio shops and street upon street of boarding houses and hotels. Such places are extremely popular since there is always something to do, even when it rains. One can sit on the sands for hours on end, if one so wishes, but when one tires of sands and sea there are many other attractions of the man-made variety.

In such ways this country is moving towards a position where rural and urban differences are becoming more and more blurred. But the movement is predominantly one of urban superimposed on rural. In this country the rural "predominance of nature over anthropo-social environment" is a waning predominance, and the "direct relationship to nature" is becoming more and more indirect.

If this picture seems harshly drawn, let it be remembered that we are dealing here with what we began by describing as "perhaps the simplest" difference to understand, being based upon a physical criterion.

The problem of "size of community," as a distinguishing factor between rural and urban, is primarily a problem of deciding to what factor the word "size" is to be applied, since "community" can be employed to refer to an area of land as well as a group of people. We shall be led into confusion unless the distinction is made clear. Obviously it would be simplest to lay down an arbitrary boundary line on the map, and say that within this boundary lies our community, urban or rural. But we are then faced with the problem of deciding whether the physical boundary line has any real social meaning, and particularly does this problem arise when we have to deal with village, town or city boundaries where there is an "over-spill" of population. Thus, for a village we might take the boundaries of the parish council, for a town the boundaries of the municipal or county borough. But this method, useful though it may be for the employment of statistical data collected for official purposes, may lead to incorrect readings of the true social composition of the community. We may find that the village boundary, so drawn, excludes the family at the "Big House," or the distant farmer who is an integral part of the village life. In the city there may be excluded the large council estates built outside the city boundary because of shortage of land in the city: it may well also exclude leaders of the community who live in the country villages and commute daily to the city. The problem has been recognised too with regard to the use of census data for cities and towns which form large conurbations; for example, the areas loosely referred to as "Liverpool" or "Manchester" are, in fact, conglomerations of large cities and towns, with no open country or visible marks of division between them. Even on a smaller scale it is difficult to know if any real social distinction can be made in many cases of cities which have a "halo" of urban districts around their boundaries.

Thus the arbitrary choice of limits to the physical community is a choice that is often forced upon one if certain data are required, but in the broadest social meaning these boundaries may be quite misleading.

If, then, the difficult problem of laying down the community boundaries can be satisfactorily solved, the factor of size of community may be considered. Wirth[7] noted the obvious point that "to say that large numbers are necessary to constitute a city means, of course, large numbers in relation to a restricted area or high density of settlement." Thus Wirth's definition of the city as a "relatively large, dense and permanent settlement of socially

(3) Size of Community

Rural	Urban
Open farms or small communities: "agriculturalism" and size of community are negatively correlated.	As a rule in the same country and at the same period, the size of urban community is much larger than the rural community. In other words urbanity and size of community are positively correlated.

heterogeneous individuals," covers three of Sorokin and Zimmerman's criteria of rural-urban differences, but as Wirth adds, there are good reasons for treating the criteria separately. However, when Wirth considers details of population size most of his discussion falls under Sorokin and Zimmerman's later heading of system of interaction. We will also leave such aspects until later, and note only in this present section that communities of 500 and 500,000 people are both composed of individual persons: yet, by the very nature of the community size the lives of the individual persons will differ. The reciprocal conditioning effects which operate between community size and, for example, industrial-occupational structure, leisure activities, housing lay-out and so on, require little elaboration for us to grasp the fundamental ideas. But it is sometimes overlooked that sheer population size alone makes some things possible and others impossible. Many of the benefits and drawbacks of urban and rural life derive basically from population size. A small village could rarely hope to support its own concert orchestra or repertory theatre: a large city must be divided up into small units (e.g. parishes, wards, school districts) with the inevitable differences in social relations from a unit where all things relate to all the people.

Thus, whilst realising that population size in itself is nothing more than heads counted, we must beware being so concerned with the consequences that we forget the basic structure.

One of the problems arising from a discussion on density is to be sure of what we are describing in terms of density. If we accept the dictionary basis of density as a mass: volume ratio, we must consider with what units we are dealing. Density of population may be expressed as so many persons to the acre or square mile, whilst density of dwellings may deal with so many dwelling units (suitably defined) to the acre or other base. With increasing ability to build living accommodation upwards, a ratio of persons to land may be quite misleading unless some further details are given of *how* people are accommodated. One may take a number of examples which could mislead. In many a country village the houses or cottages tend to be small and often crowded together. In a village in which I lived gardens, on the whole, were small and many people had allotments in a field just outside the village. The point now arises in describing density of population and dwellings, what area do we use to compile the ratio? The political-administrative area of a village may well cover several square miles, since farm land will be included, and no land, no matter how useless, will belong to no one. It may well be, then, that a village of a few hundred people which, in living accommodation, is packed tightly round a church or cross-roads, will appear to be very thin on the ground if the denominator for a ratio calculation is the whole area within the political boundary. In urban areas things become very complicated when one tries to compare "high-density" flats

(4) Density of Population

Rural	Urban
In the same country and at the same period the density is lower than in urban community. Generally density and rurality are negatively correlated.	Greater than in rural communities. Urbanity and density are positively correlated.

with "low-density" houses. To try to overcome this difficulty a "net residential density" figure may be used which is "the average number of persons per acre of housing area; which comprises the curtilages[8] of the dwellings, access or internal roads and half the boundary main roads up to a maximum of 20 feet, where these are contiguous to residential property."[9] Distinct from this is "gross density" which is "the average number of persons per acre of the whole neighbourhood." Accepting the value of the distinction here made between net and gross, one is still left with a need for a filling-out of the description of density when an urban residential area is described. We need to know, for any given area, (a) the types of dwellings in which the people live, (b) the use made of land not occupied by the actual buildings themselves, and (c) the division of land between private and public ownership. The principal distinction made between net and gross densities is the restriction of accountable land in the calculation of net density to that which can, in general, be called "residential." But it would be possible to take people from semi-detached houses with reasonable gardens, and re-house them in a single block of flats with a large communal garden round it, and still maintain the same net density. Obviously the environment and mode of life will be changed enormously. For another example, one may consider 200 people living in a city slum, with very small gardens or perhaps only yards. Their net density may be the same as that of 200 people living in a huddle of small terraced cottages in a beautiful village. Yet the one group is surrounded by more slums, factories and shops, whilst the other is surrounded by fields, meadows and woods.

Thus one sees that although the factor of density can be of value in differentiating between rural and urban, one must take care that the basis for whatever statistic is used is clearly understood. There could easily be cases which would qualify for inclusion as awful examples in Darrel Huff's delightful book *How to Lie with Statistics*.

Sorokin and Zimmerman refer to "acquired socio-physical characteristics, such as language, beliefs, opinions, mores, patterns of behaviour and so on."[10] In so far as racial traits are concerned, this is a matter which is more to the fore in the U.S.A. than in Great Britain, though it is noteworthy that the centres of Negro, Chinese, Indian and other Asiatic settlements in this country are all in ports and/or larger cities. Very rarely does one come across a person from another race settled in a country village; even more rare is an ethnic group within the village.

Viewing the rural-urban difference from a somewhat historical point of view, Angell suggests that,

In earlier, simpler societies the local community was equally important as the family and religious institutions in supplying the individual with a sense of basic common values. And it was much more important than the larger society itself which, because communication was poor, could foster such

(5) Heterogeneity and Homogeneity of the Population

Rural	Urban
Compared with urban populations the populations of the rural communities are more homogeneous in racial and psycho-social traits (negative correlation with heterogeneity).	More heterogeneous than rural communities (in the same country and at the same time). Urbanity and heterogeneity are positively correlated.

values only in the most general and abstract way. But the local community had worked out a way of actual common living. It was a world whose culture was in part unique. Over a period of time this culture had come to embody the values that were implicit in the mode of life. People accepted these values as they grew up, just as they did the kind of food they ate or the methods of agriculture they used. Each member of the community was accorded his place in the whole through the operation of accepted principles. He felt himself a member of a moral community.[11]

Angell considers this type of community to be almost extinct today. "The improvements in communication and transportation, the growth of large-scale capitalism and increasing social differentiation have produced a type of life antithetical to this old-fashioned community."[12]

Although it is true that many trends have combined to break down the isolation of the village and thus to reduce its homogeneity of thought and action, nevertheless the straightforward factor of population size can produce homogeneity. In the ordinary agricultural village there is a narrow variety of occupations. Kinship groups may be based largely upon a few well-established families. Religious affiliation locally is limited to "church and chapel." Participant leisure activities may be limited to football and cricket, church youth club and Women's Institute. In political affairs, the parish meeting, or the annual meeting of the parish council makes for the possibility of verbal exchanges between all interested parties;

there is no need for "spokesmen" since all can be present to speak for themselves.[13]

The development of transport and mass-media such as radio, television, popular press and so on, has resulted in a broadening of village life which is antithetical to the suggested homogeneity. With mass culture the villager becomes progressively more a man of the world and less one of the village. The eight a.m. bus to the nearest town, with its load of clerks, craftsmen and typists resounds with discussions of the previous evening's television panel game, or the latest offer of the women's magazine (readership 1.5 millions).

The rural village today, then, is a composite entity. It retains some of its older characteristics, as the stranger or "comerin" may all too quickly find. It is still necessary in many a village to live there for twenty years before one is accepted, and a careless word spoken about Mrs. A. to Mrs. B. may well be received with the news that "Mrs. A.'s husband is the brother-in-law of my mother's cousin, and don't you speak about my family that way." Yet it would be stretching things too far to say that beliefs, opinions, mores and patterns of behaviour derive from the village itself. Even the village school is being replaced by larger, more efficient schools at selected points, fed by the school bus. In so many ways the functions of the village are being taken from it, that it is sometimes difficult to talk of the "village" as a unity at all.[14]

It is perhaps misleading to talk of there being "less" differentiation and stratification in the rural setting than in the urban.

(6) Social Differentiation and Stratification

Rural	Urban
Rural differentiation and stratification less than urban.	Differentiation and stratification show positive correlation with urbanity.

Quite obviously the social differentiation is not of the same type in both areas. The class system of the urban environment, based greatly upon secondary social contacts does not operate in the same way in the village. The village does not have its different types of residential areas to anything like the degree found in the city. There are not large aggregates of professional men, business men, clerks, industrial workers and so on. Whatever there is of an associational character in the village, there is likely to be only *one*, so that membership of the "X" tennis club cannot carry more social status than membership of the "Y" tennis club, since there is only the "Z" tennis club for everyone. Perhaps church and chapel may be regarded as sources of differentiation, socially as well as religiously and if there should be local branches of the political parties here too there may be consideration of status. (In the village in which I lived Conservatives and respectability were regarded as practically synonymous: Socialism was only for the untouchables in the new council houses.)

In the village, however, differentiation and stratification are much more personal matters. One does not see a large Bentley or Jaguar purr past and wonder who the prosperous well-dressed man at the wheel may be. One knows that he is the new owner of the old rectory who bought the farm on the hill (which he now has run by a manager) and that he is really a director of a hire-purchase finance company at the near-by city. This gentleman's status in the village would probably be a rather peculiar one, since he would be "in" the village, but hardly "of" it. But for the people who do function in the village—the parson, the teacher, the doctor, the postman, the grocer, and the butcher, and so on, all these people are known as people, and not merely as representatives of a particular socio-occupational class. If we accept, then, that in the small village everyone will, literally, know everyone else's business, then the *need* for differentiation on a class basis (i.e. by categories) will be much less.

Given the recognition of a hierarchy of occupations, even though there may be only one representative from a particular category, the social relations will still differ between rural and urban, since in the rural setting knowledge of other people in the village will be much greater.

A further development of the greater personal knowledge in the village setting is the handing down of status from one generation to the next. The village system has certain elements of a caste system within it. As T. L. Smith suggests, "the caste principle is not so rigid in urban as in rural societies. . . . Movement from one class to another is easier than in rural society where intimate social contacts make a person's antecedents well known to all members of the community and cause one's position to be largely determined by the status of his immediate ancestors than is the case in the city."[15] Although the concept of a caste system is rather too strong for this case, the idea of a person being born to a certain status is more recognisable in rural than urban life. In the urban setting, with its greater anonymity and social differentiation based more on material goods than antecedents, the individual is judged and classified greatly by what he has attained for himself. Probably his father's occupation would be unknown to 99 percent of his acquaintances. In the village, however, the web of kinship and the general knowledge of family standing marks a person for life. So the bright boy who goes to grammar school, university and on to a professional position in the large city is admired by the rest of the village, but he remains, for them, his father's son. In the city, both where he works and lives, he will be accepted much more by virtue of what he has attained and his village background will be an insignificant factor in the general sum.

With the greater division of labour in the urban setting and the wider field of occupational opportunity open to the individual it can readily be appreciated how the occupational role becomes so much more important in the ascription of social status. In the urban environment, with its great contrasts in occupations, incomes, standards of living, homes and neighbourhoods, primary contacts with all members of the community are obviously impossible. So, with the permanent need for adjustment between individuals, which is facilitated by the ascription of what we call social status, the shorthand symbols of occupation, income, education, place of abode, dress and accent become important reference points.

Sorokin and Zimmerman in their comments on mobility deal with several aspects of it; migratory movements, movement from occupation to occupation, or job to job, and social movement as characterised by rising or falling social status.

It is customary to think of rural-urban mobility in the migratory sense as being from country to town, although the opening up of the American frontier was a movement in the opposite direction. In general, however, there is a steady con-tinuing movement from country to town, or at least from rural to urban. It must be remembered, though, that any movement can be obscured by arbitrary definitions. If a city overflows its boundaries and builds housing estates in its surrounding country area then the houses may well be located in the X Rural District, but the result is not a movement from urban to rural, rather it is an urbanisation of what was previously a rural area. In the case of professional and business people who choose to live outside the city in country villages, it is a further aspect of urbanisation of the rural. The business man, with his car, or daily train, continues with his urban occupation, whilst the family leisure may be split between town and country. It is by no means uncommon today to find villages and small towns where considerable numbers of inhabitants are really more attached to the nearby city than to the village or small town. The increased mobility brought about by car, bus and train has made distances merely relative. Positioned on the right side of the city for easy access to his work, the commuter may find the journey from village to office an easier one than from a suburban district on the other side of the city from his office. A further class of people affected in the mobility problem are those who depend upon local authorities for their housing. The tenants of "council" houses can only have tenancies in accordance with the planning of the local authority. Thus, the applicant for a council

(7) Mobility

Rural	Urban
Territorial, occupational, and other forms of social mobility of the population are comparatively less intense. Normally the migration current carried more individuals from the country to the city.	More intensive. Urbanity and mobility are positively correlated. Only in the periods of social catastrophe is the migration from the city to the country greater than from the country to the city.

house cannot choose for himself where he wants to live—he is limited to the estate built for him and his like. The result may be that a person living in a country town may be offered a council house on a new estate built to expand a particular village. The man may then decide to accept the house, since it offers good cheap accommodation, but to retain his present work in the town, perhaps by choice, or perhaps because the village may not have any vacancies in his particular calling. Council development of this sort can bring about a physical mobility from urban to rural, but socially the migrants become rather divided in their loyalties. I have met people, particularly the housewives, who find this enforced village life tedious and dull, and would give anything to get back to the larger town.

In general, then, it can be seen that there are a number of cases of "false" mobility which should not be accepted without careful scrutiny. It might be said that mobility only really occurs when the individual moves his home *and* occupation from one environment to the other, thus becoming wholly dependent upon the new locality for livelihood and principal social contacts. Living in the one place, be it rural or urban, and travelling daily to the other is not true mobility, though it may result in constant movement.

The "drift from the countryside" to the major towns and cites is likely to attract two particular types of rural person—the best and the worst. As has been mentioned, the "bright boy" who gets a good education is unlikely to find the job he wants in the small village. To "get on" in the world he must move out to work for the large industry or government department. The country-bred bright boys are a considerable gain for the city. At the other end of the scale are the village ne'er-do-wells and

misfits. For them the village is too small because their doings are always noted, whereas the city offers the blessing (for them) of anonymity and "mind your own business." The city, then, gets two particular types for whom the problem of adjustment raises quite different questions.

The conventional considerations of mobility sometimes tend to ignore, or at least, underplay the importance of inter-urban and intra-urban mobility. It is a well-known problem to town planners that work-people cannot be made to move to carefully sited industries. Attempts to "redistribute" the urban population have not met with resounding success. For some reason the worked-out, depressed and depressing colliery town remains more attractive to its sons than the carefully planned and hygienic new town. Yet, given the problems of moving work-people en masse, there remains the constant movement as individuals of people in the higher social classes. Bank employees, insurance men, managers of "chain" stores, teachers of all kinds, and every type of local government officer, may have to move either at the instruction of the employer or to attain personal promotion. Perhaps the most publicised directive towards mobility in recent years has been the memorandum from the Home Secretary to Watch Committees making the explicit recommendation that Chief Constables should be appointed from *outside* the local force. Whilst most Chief Constables are fortunate enough to have houses provided for them, many other less well assisted people may have the worry and financial strain of selling and buying houses each time they move. Some industrial firms, commercial companies and even local government bodies have recognised these problems but for many unfortunates a sum of well over £100 must be put aside for legal and removal costs. A "moving increment" of £50 (taxed) is little inducement in such circumstances.

Mobility within the city is a further point which should not be ignored. In the village a move from one house to another (perhaps from a condemned cottage to a new council house) cannot be an enormous move by the very limitations of the size of the community. In the city, however, a move may be over several miles, with consequent breaking of old neighbourhood relations and a building up of completely new ones. Intra-city mobility may affect several types of people; the occupant of the slum house resettled on the suburban council estate; the couple living in rooms who move to a new block of flats; the flat-dwellers who move to a house because they are starting a family; the expanding family who move to a larger house in search of more space; the declining family, whose children have left home, who seek the small bungalow for retirement. In all, it would be quite reasonable to expect a person who lives his whole life in one city to live in upwards of four dwellings[16] during his lifetime merely for accommodating himself and his family in a dwelling of appropriate size. If mobility brought about by a desire to live in a higher status residential area is considered, then there may well be more moves. As Park comments on the American scene,

Change of occupation, personal success or failure—changes of economic and social status, in short—tend to be registered in changes in location. The physical or ecological organization of the community, in the long run, responds to and reflects the occupational and cultural. Social selection and segregation, which create the natural groups, determine at the same time the natural areas of the city . . . In great cities the divergences in manners, in standards of living, and in general outlook on life in different urban areas is often astonishing . . . this emphasises the importance of location, position and mobility as indices for measuring, describing and eventually explaining, social phenomena.[17]

In all, the picture that the modern city brings to mind is one of a restless, ever-moving population, constantly on the go for one reason or another. Indeed, it is one way of expressing success to describe a person as "getting on." Mobility at all levels and in a host of ways is a part of city life. This is best seen perhaps in the unique situation in London, where it may be said that many daily travellers make a rural-to-urban move each morning, though perhaps it would be truer to call it suburban-to-urban, or even urban-to-urban. We have in the Greater London area the peculiar phenomenon of thousands of people daily moving great distances from home to work; distance which in the provinces would probably be regarded as quite beyond contemplation.[18] Yet with the transport system geared to this principle hardly a thought is given to the daily invasion and retreat, so dulled have our senses become to it.

Mobility, then, is of the very nature of the urban environment. Ranging as it does, however, from migration from one country to another down to a bus-trip to the cinema, we have here a concept which is so great as to require further, more detailed consideration. We shall return to this question later.

In this concluding category the basic argument is quite simple, indeed obvious. If you live in a small isolated community you will know fewer people than you *could* know in a large city. But the people you *do* know in the small community you are likely to know more fully, more intimately

(8) System of Interaction

Rural	Urban
Less numerous contacts per man. Narrower area of the interaction system of its members and the whole aggregate. More prominent part is occupied by primary contacts. Predominance of personal and relatively durable relations. Comparative simplicity and sincerity of relations. "Man is interacted as a human person."	More numerous contacts. Wider area of interaction system per man and per aggregate. Predominance of impersonal, casual and short-lived relations. Greater complexity, manifoldness, superficiality and standardised formality of relations. Man is interacted as a "number" and an "address".

and (if the idea of stability is accepted) for a longer period of time. In the city you "know" a vast number of people, but most of these people are likely to be known superficially or in a segmentary, single-role way. Thus, in the city, the postman is the anonymous man who delivers the letters and to whom we give a tip each Christmas. If the delivery is early in the day we may rarely see him. We are unlikely to know any details of the postman's life. His name, address, marital status, leisure interests and so on will all be a closed book to us. In the small community with one postman we are likely to know the postman as "George Brown," father of two boys and a girl, brother of the garage mechanic, captain of the church bell-ringers, ardent follower of the hunt, etc. etc. In fact, we shall know the postman as a "whole" person.

In the city, one's friends and acquaintances do not form the closed circle of the ideal-type village. Your city friends will have other friends who are little known, or even unknown to you. The circle of friends is a highly personal rather than social affair; each one of us has his or her own circle of friends and acquaintances, and these may differ quite strongly, even between such close people as husband and wife. Given this situation, the individual has no group to which he may be said to "belong" since the form of group interaction tends towards superficiality of

contact rather than depth. The modern cocktail party is a perfect example of the institutionalisation of shallow acquaintance; indeed the essence of this social interaction is summed up in the terms used to describe the conversation—"small-talk" and "cocktail-chatter." Gist and Halbert suggest that, "One has neither the time nor the energy to know intimately all those he meets in the city; therefore he is forced, as a matter of self-protection, to formulate stereotyped conceptions of the multitudes whose faces he perceives; they account for much of the reputed coolness and hard-heartedness of the city."[19] In *Middletown in Transition*, the Lynds postulated that,

> One insensibly becomes a citizen of a wider world as a larger city tends to develop a more metropolitan emphasis . . . Residential areas tend to become more segregated and homogeneous. Such externals as where one lives become more important as placing one in the larger and less familiar population . . . and, personal means of placing one in the group, involving considerations of the kind of person one is, yield to more quickly determinable, shorthand symbols, notably what one owns.

And so on; with any writing on rural-urban contrasts the similarity of views on the form of interaction is apparent. But if reference to Toennies, and Parson's comments on Toennies, is made, it will be noted that Toennies stresses the importance of the "wills" or attitudes which underline the actions. And since social interaction is based on an interaction of ideas then the manifest actions which differ from rural to urban setting must be traceable to different "wills." In this matter R. C. Angell's concept of the "moral" community would seem to be pertinent. He says that "the principle of *moral* community is best exemplified in modern city life by small integrated groups which have worked out an integrated way of life. On the larger scale of territorial aggregates it is seldom that one finds a true moral community, because people who are striving to realise common values in one field have divergent orientations in others."[20] In other words, social interaction is segmentary and not whole.

While pressing this interpretation of the difference in forms of interaction between rural and urban, the temptation to moralise is at times extremely strong. The superficiality of the cocktail party is an easy target for satire (see Dorothy Parker and a host of other American writers). Yet it must be remembered that the rector's tea party or "sherry at the manor house," could be just as boring or tedious. We do not wish to make moralizing comparisons of the one or the other. The real point at issue is the *depth* of social interaction which is likely to take place in the rural and urban setting. What has been suggested is that, within the smaller rural community interaction is more all-encompassing, whether the individual likes it or not. In the city interaction is more segmentary in many ways, but this does not preclude deep friendships arising in this environment. The essential point is that in the rural area the community is there and all are a part of it: in the city each person has his own group of acquaintances, colleagues, companions and friends, and these groups are personal to the individual, but they are not social entities in any larger sense.

NOTES

1. It is recognised that there are criticisms of the rural-urban contrast method.
2. Thomas Sharp in "Design in Town and Village," London, H.M.S.O., 1953, p. 1.
3. Although it must be recognised that the Northern industrial towns are having a current vogue with novels such as *Saturday Night and Sunday Morning* and *A Kind of Loving*, and plays such as *A Taste of Honey*. The latter, however, being a play about a Salford schoolgirl who is made pregnant by a negro sailor and who then goes to live with a young homosexual is not an attempt to depict the ordinary, everyday life of urban dwellers.
4. T. L. Smith, "The Urban and Rural Worlds," in T. L. Smith and C. A. McMahan, *The Sociology of Urban Life*, New York, 1951, p. 43.
5. P. A. Sorokin and C. C. Zimmerman, *Principles of Rural-Urban Sociology*, New York, 1929, p. 15.
6. T. Sharp, *Town Planning*, Chap. 2, Pelican Books, 1940.
7. L. Wirth, "Urbanism as a Way of Life," *American Journal of Sociology*, Vol. 44, July, 1938.
8. "Area attached to a dwelling-house."
9. Ministry of Health, "Design of Dwellings," London, H.M.S.O., 1944.
10. Op. cit., p. 16.
11. R. C. Angell, *The Integration of American Society*, New York, 1941, p. 190–191.
12. Ibid., p. 191.
13. In the village in which I lived it was customary for everyone who turned up at the Annual Meeting of the local church to be elected onto the Parochial Church Council.
14. See G. D. Mitchell, "Social Disintegration in a Rural Community," *Human Relations*, Vol. 3, No. 2, 1950.
15. T. L. Smith and C. A. McMahan, op. cit., p. 51.
16. D. J. Wheeler suggests five household categories for survey purposes in market research in "A New Classification of Households," British Market Research Bureau Ltd., London, 1955.
17. R. E. Park, "The Urban Community as a Spatial Pattern and a Moral Order," in E. W. Burgess: *The Urban Community*, Chicago, 1925, pp. 35–36.
18. Note the areas of greatest population growth between the 1931 and 1951 and 1961 Censuses.
19. N. P. Gist and L. A. Halbert, *Urban Society*, New York, 1948, p. 264.
20. R. C. Angell, op. cit., pp. 20–21.

3. Urbanism as a Way of Life | Louis Wirth

"Urbanism" is one of the most familiar words in the lexicon of urban sociology. It generally refers to certain features of the social structure and culture of cities, including spatial segregation, secondary association, and social heterogeneity, which are reflected in the attitudes, personalities, and ways of life of people who reside in them. Among the major concerns of urban sociology have been the development of meaningful empirical generalizations that could validate the existence of a specific quality called urbanism and the formulation of theories to explain it. Much ferment was generated by this article by Louis Wirth, probably the most widely read essay in the entire literature of urban sociology. It first was published in 1938, as a summary statement of the theoretical conclusions that emerged from the empirical studies conducted by graduate students and faculty at the University of Chicago during the twenty years previous. Wirth regards urbanism as the product of territorial and population size, population density, and demographic heterogeneity. The paper has generated a continuing debate whether the features of urbanism are the result more of these demographic and spatial factors or of cultural and organizational characteristics of American society, such as industrialism, class and ethnic factors, and bureaucracy.

Louis Wirth (1897–1952) was for many years Professor of Sociology at the University of Chicago. His collected papers were published under the title *Community Life anf Social Policy* (1956). He is the author of *The Ghetto* (1928) and many other books.

I The City and Contemporary Civilization

Just as the beginning of Western civilization is marked by the permanent settlement of formerly nomadic peoples in the Mediterranean basin, so the beginning of what is distinctively modern in our civilization is best signalized by the growth of great cities. Nowhere has mankind been farther removed from organic nature than under the conditions of life characteristic of great cities. The contemporary world no longer presents a picture of small isolated groups of human beings scattered over a vast territory, as Sumner described primitive society.[1] The distinctive feature of the mode of living of man in the modern age is his concentration into gigantic aggregations around which cluster lesser centers and from which radiate the ideas and practices that we call civilization.

The degree to which the contemporary world may be said to be "urban" is not fully or accurately measured by the proportion of the total population living in cities. The influences which cities exert upon the social life of man are greater than the ratio of the urban population would indicate, for the city is not only in ever larger degrees the dwelling-place and the workshop of modern man, but it is the initiating and controlling center of economic, political, and cultural life that has

Reprinted by permission from *The American Journal of Sociology*, Vol. 44 (July 1938). Published by The University of Chicago Press. Copyright 1938 by *The American Journal of Sociology*.

drawn the most remote parts of the world into its orbit and woven diverse areas, peoples, and activities into a cosmos.

The growth of cities and the urbanization of the world is one of the most impressive facts of modern times. Although it is impossible to state precisely what proportion of the estimated total world-population of approximately 1,800,000,000 is urban, 69.2 percent of the total population of those countries that do distinguish between urban and rural areas is urban.[2] Considering the fact, moreover, that the world's population is very unevenly distributed and that the growth of cities is not very far advanced in some of the countries that have only recently been touched by industrialism, this average understates the extent to which urban concentration has proceeded in those countries where the impact of the industrial revolution has been more forceful and of less recent date. This shift from a rural to a predominantly urban society, which has taken place within the span of a single generation in such industrialized areas as the United States and Japan, has been accompanied by profound changes in virtually every phase of social life. It is these changes and their ramifications that invite the attention of the sociologist to the study of the differences between the rural and the urban mode of living. The pursuit of this interest is an indispensable prerequisite for the comprehension and possible mastery of some of the most crucial contemporary problems of social life since it is likely to furnish one of the most revealing perspectives for the understanding of the ongoing changes in human nature and the social order.[3]

Since the city is the product of growth rather than of instantaneous creation, it is to be expected that the influences which it exerts upon the modes of life should not be able to wipe out completely the previously dominant modes of human association. To a greater or lesser degree, therefore, our social life bears the imprint of an earlier folk society, the characteristic modes of settlement of which were the farm, the manor, and the village. This historic influence is reinforced by the circumstances that the population of the city itself is in large measure recruited from the countryside, where a mode of life reminiscent of this earlier form of existence persists. Hence we should not expect to find abrupt and discontinuous variation between urban and rural types of personality. The city and the country may be regarded as two poles in reference to one or the other of which all human settlements tend to arrange themselves. In viewing urban-industrial and rural-folk society as ideal types of communities, we may obtain a perspective for the analysis of the basic models of human association as they appear in contemporary civilization.

II A Sociological Definition of the City

Despite the preponderant significance of the city in our civilization, however, our knowledge of the nature of urbanism and the process of urbanization is meager. Many attempts have indeed been made to isolate the distinguishing characteristics of urban life. Geographers, historians, economists, and political scientists have incorporated the points of view of their respective disciplines into diverse definitions of the city. While in no sense intended to supersede these, the formulation of a sociological approach to the city may incidentally serve to call attention to the interrelations between them by emphasizing the peculiar characteristics of the city as a particular form of human association. A sociologically significant definition of the city seeks to select those elements of urbanism which mark it as a distinctive mode of human group life.

The characterization of a community as urban on the basis of size alone is obviously arbitrary. It is difficult to defend the present census definition which designates a community of 2,500 and above as urban and all others as rural. The situation would be the same if the criterion were 4,000, 8,000, 10,000, 25,000, or 100,000 population, for although in the latter case we might feel that we were more nearly dealing with an urban aggregate than would be the case in communities of lesser size, no definition of urbanism can hope to be completely satisfying as long as numbers are regarded as the sole criterion. Moreover, it is not difficult to demonstrate that communities of less than the arbitrarily set number of inhabitants lying with the range of influence of metropolitan centers have greater claim to recognition as urban communities than do larger ones leading a more isolated existence in a predominantly rural area. Finally, it should be recognized that census definitions are unduly influenced by the fact that the city, statistically speaking, is always an administrative concept in that the corporate limits play a decisive role in delineating the urban area. Nowhere is this more clearly apparent than in the concentrations of population on the peripheries of great metropolitan centers which cross arbitrary administrative boundaries of city, county, state, and nation.

As long as we identify urbanism with the physical entity of the city, viewing it merely as rigidly delimited in space, and proceed as if urban attributes abruptly ceased to be manifested beyond an arbitrary boundary line, we are not likely to arrive at any adequate conception of urbanism as a mode of life. The technological developments in transportation and communication which virtually mark a new epoch in human history have accentuated the role of cities as dominant elements in our civilization and have enormously extended the urban mode of living beyond the confines of the city itself. The dominance of the city, especially of the great city, may be regarded as a consequence of the concentration in cities of industrial and commercial, financial and administrative facilities and activities, transportation and communication lines, and cultural and recreational equipment such as the press, radio stations, theaters, libraries, museums, concert halls, operas, hospitals, higher educational institutions, research and publishing centers, professional organizations, and religious and welfare institutions. Were it not for the attraction and suggestions that the city exerts through these instrumentalities upon the rural population, the differences between the rural and the urban modes of life would be even greater than they are. Urbanization no longer denotes merely the process by which persons are attracted to a place called the city and incorporated into its system of life. It refers also to that cumulative accentuation of the characteristics distinctive of the mode of life which is associated with the growth of cities, and finally to the changes in the direction of modes of life recognized as urban which are apparent among people, wherever they may be, who have come under the spell of the influences which the city exerts by virtue of the power of its institutions and personalities operating through the means of communication and transportation.

The shortcomings which attach to number of inhabitants as a criterion of urbanism apply for the most part to density of population as well. Whether we accept the density of 10,000 persons per square mile as Mark Jefferson[4] proposed, or 1,000, which Wilcox[5] preferred to regard as the criterion of urban settlements, it is clear that unless density is correlated with significant social characteristics it can furnish only an arbitrary basis for differentiating urban from rural communities. Since our census enumerates the night rather than the day population of an area, the locale of the most intensive urban life—the city center—generally has low population density, and the industrial and commercial areas of the city, which contain the most characteristic economic activities underlying urban society, would scarcely anywhere be truly urban if density were literally interpreted as a mark of urbanism. Nevertheless, the fact that the urban community is distinguished by a large aggregation and relatively dense concentration of population can scarcely be left out of account in a definition of the city. But these criteria must be seen as relative to the general cultural context in which cities arise and exist and are sociologically relevant only in so far as they operate as conditioning factors in social life.

The same criticisms apply to such criteria as the occupation of the inhabitants, the existence of certain physical facilities, institutions, and forms of political organization. The question is not whether cities in our civilization or in others do exhibit these distinctive traits, but how potent they are in molding the character of social life into its specifically urban form. Nor in formulating a fertile definition can we afford to overlook the great variations between cities. By means of a typology of cities based upon size, location, age, and function, such as we have undertaken to establish in our recent report to the National Resources Committee,[6] we have found it feasible to array and classify urban communities ranging from struggling small towns to thriving world-metropolitan centers; from isolated trading centers in the midst of agricultural regions to thriving world ports and commercial and industrial conurbations. Such differences as these appear crucial because the social characteristics and influences of these different "cities" vary widely.

A serviceable definition of urbanism should not only denote the essential characteristics which all cities—at least those in our culture—have in common, but should lend itself to the discovery of their variations. An industrial city will differ significantly in social respects from a commercial, mining, fishing, resort, university, and capital city. A one-industry city will present different sets of social characteristics from a multi-industry city, as will an industrially balanced from an imbalanced city, a suburb from a satellite, a residential suburb from an industrial suburb, a city within a metropolitan region from one lying outside, an old city from a new one, a southern city from a New England, a middle-western from a Pacific Coast city, a growing from a stable and from a dying city.

A sociological definition must obviously be inclusive enough to comprise whatever essential characteristics these different types of cities have in common as social entities, but it obviously cannot be so detailed as to take account of all the variations implicit in the manifold classes sketched above. Presumably some of the characteristics of cities are more significant in conditioning the nature of urban life than others, and we may expect the outstanding features of the urban-social scene to vary in accordance with size, density, and differences in the functional type of cities. Moreover, we may infer that rural life will bear the imprint of urbanism in the measure that through contact and communication it comes under the influence of cities. It may contribute to the clarity of the statements that follow to repeat that while the locus of urbanism as a mode of life is of course, to be found characteristically in places which fulfil the requirements we shall set up as a definition of the city, urbanism is not confined to such localities but is manifest in varying degrees wherever the influences of the city reach.

While urbanism, or that complex of traits which makes up the characteristic mode of life in cities, and urbanization, which denotes the development and extensions of these factors, are thus not exclusively found in settlements which are cities in the physical and demographic sense, they do, nevertheless, find their most pronounced expression in such areas, especially in metropolitan cities. In formulating a definition of the city it is necessary to exercise caution in order to avoid identifying urbanism as a way of life with any specific locally or historically conditioned cultural influences which, while they may significantly affect the specific character of the community, are not the essential determinants of its character as a city.

It is particularly important to call attention to the danger of confusing urbanism with industrialism and modern capitalism. The rise of cities in the modern world is undoubtedly not independent of the emergence of modern power-driven machine technology, mass production, and capitalistic enterprise. But different as the cities of earlier epochs may have been by virtue of their development in a preindustrial and precapitalistic order from the great cities of today, they were, nevertheless, cities.

For sociological purposes a city may be defined as a relatively large, dense, and permanent settlement of socially hetero-geneous individuals. On the basis of the postulates which this minimal definition suggests, a theory of urbanism may be formulated in the light of existing knowledge concerning social groups.

III A Theory of Urbanism

In the rich literature on the city we look in vain for a theory of urbanism presenting in a systematic fashion the available knowledge concerning the city as a social entity. We do indeed have excellent formulations of theories on such special problems as the growth of the city viewed as a historical trend and as a recurrent process,[7] and we have a wealth of literature presenting insights of sociological relevance and empirical studies offering detailed information on a variety of particular aspects of urban life. But despite the multiplication of research and textbooks on the city, we do not as yet have a comprehensive body of compendent hypotheses which may be derived from a set of postulates implicitly contained in a sociological definition of the city, and from our general sociological knowledge which may be substantiated through empirical research. The closest approximations to a systematic theory of urbanism that we have are to be found in a penetrating essay, "Die Stadt," by Max Weber,[8] and a memorable paper by Robert E. Park on "The City: Suggestions for the Investigations of Human Behavior in the Urban Environment."[9] But even these excellent contributions are far from constituting an ordered and coherent framework of theory upon which research might profitably proceed.

In the pages that follow we shall seek to set forth a limited number of identifying characteristics of the city. Given these characteristics we shall then indicate what consequences or further characteristics follow from them in the light of general sociological theory and empirical research. We hope in this manner to arrive at the essential propositions comprising a theory of urbanism. Some of these propositions can be supported by a considerable body of already available research materials; others may be accepted as hypotheses for which a certain amount of presumptive evidence exists, but for which more ample and exact verification would be required. At least such a procedure will, it is hoped, show what in the way of systematic knowledge of the city we now have and what are the crucial and fruitful hypotheses for future research.

The central problem of the sociologist of the city is to discover the forms of social action and organization that typically emerge in relatively permanent, compact settlements of large numbers of heterogeneous individuals. We must also infer that urbanism will assume its most characteristic and extreme form in the measure in which the conditions with which it is congruent are present. Thus the larger, the more densely populated, and the more heterogeneous a community, the more accentuated the characteristics associated with urbanism will be. It should be recognized, however, that in the social world institutions and practices may be accepted and continued for reasons other than those that originally brought them into existence, and that accordingly the urban mode of life may be perpetuated under conditions quite foreign to those necessary for its origin.

Some justification may be in order for the choice of the principal terms comprising our definition of the city. The attempt has been made to make it as inclusive and at the same time as denotative as possible without loading it with unnecessary assumptions.

To say that large numbers are necessary to constitute a city means, of course, large numbers in relation to a restricted area or high density of settlement. There are, nevertheless, good reasons for treating large numbers and density as separate factors, since each may be connected with significantly different social consequences. Similarly the need for adding heterogeneity to numbers of population as a necessary and distinct criterion of urbanism might be questioned, since we should expect the range of differences to increase with numbers. In defense, it may be said that the city shows a kind and degree of heterogeneity of population which cannot be wholly accounted for by the law of large numbers or adequately represented by means of a normal distribution curve. Since the population of the city does not reproduce itself, it must recruit its migrants from other cities, the countryside, and—in this country until recently—from other countries. The city has thus historically been the melting-pot of races, peoples, and cultures, and a most favorable breeding-ground of new biological and cultural hybrids. It has not only tolerated but rewarded individual differences. It has brought together people from the ends of the earth *because* they are different and thus useful to one another, rather than because they are homogeneous and like-minded.[10]

There are a number of sociological propositions concerning the relationship between (a) numbers of population, (b) density of settlement, (c) heterogeneity of inhabitants and group life, which can be formulated on the basis of observation and research.

Size of the Population Aggregate Ever since Aristotle's *Politics*,[11] it has been recognized that increasing the number of inhabitants in a settlement beyond a certain limit will affect the relationships between them and the character of the city. Large numbers involve, as has been pointed out, a greater range of individual variation. Furthermore, the greater the number of individuals participating in a process of interaction, the greater is the *potential* differentiation between them. The personal traits, the occupations, the cultural life, and the ideas of the members of an urban community may, therefore, be expected to range between more widely separated poles than those of rural inhabitants.

That such variations should give rise to the spatial segregation of individuals according to color, ethnic heritage, economic and social status, tastes and preferences, may readily be inferred. The bonds of kinship, of neighborliness, and the sentiments arising out of living together for generations under a common folk tradition are likely to be absent or, at best, relatively weak in an aggregate the members of which have such diverse origins and backgrounds. Under such circumstances competition and formal control mechanisms furnish the substitutes for the bonds of solidarity that are relied upon to hold a folk society together.

Increase in the number of inhabitants of a community beyond a few hundred is bound to limit the possibility of each member of the community knowing all the others personally. Max Weber, in recognizing the social significance of this fact, pointed out that from a sociological point of view large numbers of inhabitants and density of settlement mean that the personal mutual acquaintanceship between the inhabitants which ordinarily inheres in a neighborhood is lacking.[12] The increase in numbers thus involves a changed character of the social relationships. As Simmel points out:

[If] the unceasing external contact of numbers of persons in the city should be met by the same number of inner reactions as in the small town, in which one knows almost every person he meets and to each of whom he has a positive relationship, one would be completely atomized internally and would fall into an unthinkable mental condition.[13]

The multiplication of persons in a state of interaction under conditions which make their contact as full personalities impossible produces that segmentalization of human relationships which has sometimes been seized upon by students of the mental life of the cities as an explanation for the "schizoid" character of urban personality. This is not to say that the urban inhabitants have fewer acquaintances than rural inhabitants, for the reverse may actually be true; it means rather that in relation to the number of people whom they see and with whom they rub elbows in the course of daily life, they know a smaller proportion, and of these they have less intensive knowledge.

Characteristically, urbanites meet one another in highly segmental roles. They are, to be sure, dependent upon more people for the satisfactions of their life-needs than are rural people and thus are associated with a greater number of organized groups, but they are less dependent upon particular persons, and their dependence upon others is confined to a highly fractionalized aspect of the other's round of activity. This is essentially what is meant by saying that the city is characterized by secondary rather than primary contacts. The contacts of the city may indeed be face to face, but they are nevertheless impersonal, superficial, transitory, and segmental. The reserve, the indifference, and the blasé outlook which urbanites manifest in their relationships may thus be regarded as devices for immunizing themselves against the personal claims and expectations of others.

The superficiality, the anonymity, and the transitory character of urban-social relations make intelligible, also, the sophistication and the rationality generally ascribed to city-dwellers. Our acquaintances tend to stand in a relationship of utility to us in the sense that the role which each one plays in our life is overwhelmingly regarded as a means for the achievement of our own ends. Whereas, therefore, the individual gains, on the one hand, a certain degree of emancipation or freedom from the personal and emotional controls of intimate groups, he loses, on the other hand, the spontaneous self-expression, the morale, and the sense of participation that comes with living in an integrated society. This constitutes essentially the state of *anomie* or the social void to which Durkheim alludes in attempting to account for the various forms of social disorganization in technological society.

The segmental character and utilitarian accent of interpersonal relations in the city find their institutional expression in the proliferation of specialized tasks which we see in their most developed form in the professions. The operations of the pecuniary nexus lead to predatory relationships, which tend to obstruct the efficient functioning of the social order unless checked by professional codes and occupational etiquette. The premium put upon utility and efficiency suggests the adaptability of the corporate device for the organization of enterprises in which individuals can engage only in groups. The advantage that the corporation has over the individual entrepreneur and the partnership in the urban-industrial world derives not only from the possibility it affords of centralizing the resources of thousands of individuals or

from the legal privilege of limited liability and perpetual succession, but from the fact that the corporation has no soul.

The specialization of individuals, particularly in their occupations, can proceed only, as Adam Smith pointed out, upon the basis of an enlarged market, which in turn accentuates the division of labor. This enlarged market is only in part supplied by the city's hinterland; in large measure it is found among the large numbers that the city itself contains. The dominance of the city over the surrounding hinterland becomes explicable in terms of the division of labor which urban life occasions and promotes. The extreme degree of interdependence and the unstable equilibrium of urban life are closely associated with the division of labor and the specialization of occupations. This interdependence and instability is increased by the tendency of each city to specialize in those functions in which it has the greatest advantage.

In a community composed of a larger number of individuals than can know one another intimately and can be assembled in one spot, it becomes necessary to communicate through indirect media and to articulate individual interests by a process of delegation. Typically in the city, interests are made effective through representation. The individual counts for little, but the voice of the representative is heard with a deference roughly proportional to the numbers for whom he speaks.

While this characterization of urbanism, in so far as it derives from large numbers, does not by any means exhaust the sociological inferences that might be drawn from our knowledge of the relationship of the size of a group to the characteristic behavior of the members, for the sake of brevity the assertions made may serve to exemplify the sort of propositions that might be developed.

Density As in the case of numbers, so in the case of concentration in limited space, certain consequences of relevance in sociological analysis of the city emerge. Of these only a few can be indicated.

As Darwin pointed out for flora and fauna and as Durkheim[14] noted in the case of human societies, an increase in numbers when area is held constant (i.e., an increase in density) tends to produce differentiation and specialization, since only in this way can the area support increased numbers. Density thus reinforces the effect of numbers in diversifying men and their activities and in increasing the complexity of the social structure.

On the subjective side, as Simmel has suggested, the close physical contact of numerous individuals necessarily produces a shift in the mediums through which we orient ourselves to the urban milieu, especially to our fellow-men. Typically, our physical contacts are close but our social contacts are distant. The urban world puts a premium on visual recognition. We see the uniform which denotes the role of the functionaries and are oblivious to the personal eccentricities that are hidden behind the uniform. We tend to acquire and develop a sensitivity to a world of artifacts and become progressively farther removed from the world of nature.

We are exposed to glaring contrasts between splendor and squalor, between riches and poverty, intelligence and ignorance, order and chaos. The competition for space is great, so that each area generally tends to be put to the use which yields the greatest economic return. Place of work tends to become dissociated from place of residence, for the proximity of industrial and commercial establishments makes an area both economically and socially undesirable for residential purposes.

Density, land values, rentals, accessibility, healthfulness, prestige, aesthetic consideration, absence of nuisances such as smoke, and dirt determine the desirability of various areas of the city as places of settlement for different sections of the population. Place and nature of work, income, racial and ethnic characteristics, social status, custom, habit, taste, preference, and prejudice are among the significant factors in accordance with which the urban population is selected and distributed into more or less distinct settlements. Diverse population elements inhabiting a compact settlement thus tend to become segregated from one another in the degree in which their requirements and modes of life are incompatible with one another and in the measure in which they are antagonistic to one another. Similarly, persons of homogeneous status and needs unwittingly drift into, consciously select, or are forced by circumstances into, the same area. The different parts of the city thus acquire specialized functions. The city consequently tends to resemble a mosaic of social worlds in which the transition from one to the other is abrupt. The juxtaposition of divergent personalities and modes of life tends to produce a relativistic perspective and a sense of toleration of difference which may be regarded as prerequisites for rationality and which lead toward the secularization of life.[15]

The close living together and working together of individuals who have no sentimental and emotional ties foster a spirit of competition, aggrandizement, and mutual exploitation. To counteract irresponsibility and potential disorder, formal controls tend to be resorted to. Without rigid adherence to predictable routines a large compact society would scarcely be able to maintain itself. The clock and the traffic signal are symbolic of the basis of our social order in the urban world. Frequent close physical contact, coupled with great social distance, accentuates the reserve of unattached individuals toward one another and, unless compensated for by other opportunities for response, gives rise to loneliness. The necessary frequent movement of great numbers of individuals in a congested habitat gives occasion to friction and irritation. Nervous tensions which derive from such personal frustrations are accentuated by the rapid tempo and the complicated technology under which life in dense areas must be lived.

Heterogeneity The social interaction among such a variety of personality types in the urban milieu tends to break down the rigidity of caste lines and to complicate the class structure, and thus induces a more ramified and differentiated framework of social stratification than is found in more integrated societies. The heightened mobility of the individual, which brings him within the range of stimulation by a great number of diverse individuals and subjects him to fluctuating status in the differentiated social groups that compose the social structure of the city, tends toward the acceptance of instability and insecurity in the world at large as a norm. This fact helps to account, too, for the sophistication and cosmopolitanism of the urbanite. No single group has the undivided allegiance of the individual. The groups with which he is affiliated do not lend themselves readily to a simple hierarchical arrangement. By virtue of his different interests arising out of different aspects of social life, the individual acquires membership in widely divergent groups, each of which functions only with reference to a single segment of his personality. Nor do these groups easily permit of a concentric arrangement so that the narrower

ones fall within the circumference of the more inclusive ones, as is more likely to be the case in the rural community or in primitive societies. Rather the groups with which the person typically is affiliated are tangential to each other or intersect in highly variable fashion.

Partly as a result of the physical foot-looseness of the population and partly as a result of their social mobility, the turnover in group membership generally is rapid. Place of residence, place and character of employment, income and interests fluctuate, and the task of holding organizations together and maintaining and promoting intimate and lasting acquaintanceship between the members is difficult. This applies strikingly to the local areas within the city into which persons become segregated more by virtue of differences in race, language, income, and social status, than through choice or positive attraction to people like themselves. Overwhelmingly the city-dweller is not a home-owner, and since a transitory habitat does not generate binding traditions and sentiments, only rarely is he truly a neighbor. There is little opportunity for the individual to obtain a conception of the city as a whole or to survey his place in the total scheme. Consequently he finds it difficult to determine what is to his own "best interests" and to decide between the issues and leaders presented to him by the agencies of mass suggestion. Individuals who are thus detached from the organized bodies which integrate society comprise the fluid masses that make collective behavior in the urban community so unpredictable and hence so problematical.

Although the city, through the recruitment of variant types to perform its diverse tasks and the accentuation of their uniqueness through competition and the premium upon eccentricity, novelty, efficient performance, and inventiveness, produces a highly differentiated population, it also exercises a leveling influence. Wherever large numbers of differently constituted individuals congregate, the process of depersonalization also enters. This leveling tendency inheres in part in the economic basis of the city. The development of large cities, at least in the modern age, was largely dependent upon the concentrative force of steam. The rise of the factory made possible mass production for an impersonal market. The fullest exploitation of the possibilities of the division of labor and mass production, however, is possible only with standardization of processes and products. A money economy goes hand in hand with such a system of production. Progressively as cities have developed upon a background of this system of production, the pecuniary nexus which implies the purchasability of services and things has displaced personal relations as the basis of association. Individuality under these circumstances must be replaced by categories. When large numbers have to make common use of facilities and institutions, an arrangement must be made to adjust the facilities and institutions to the needs of the average person rather than to those of particular individuals. The services of the public utilities, of the recreational, educational, and cultural institutions must be adjusted to mass requirements. Similarly, cultural institutions, such as the schools, the movies, the radio, and the newspapers, by virtue of their mass clientele, must necessarily operate as leveling influences. The political process as it appears in urban life could not be understood without taking account of the mass appeals made through modern propaganda techniques. If the individual would participate at all

in the social, political, and economic life of the city, he must subordinate some of his individuality to the demands of the larger community and in that measure immerse himself in mass movements.

IV The Relation between a Theory of Urbanism and Sociological Research

By means of a body of theory such as that illustratively sketched above, the complicated and many-sided phenomena of urbanism may be analyzed in terms of a limited number of basic categories. The sociological approach to the city thus acquires an essential unity and coherence enabling the empirical investigator not merely to focus more distinctly upon the problems and processes that properly fall in his province but also to treat his subject matter in a more integrated and systematic fashion. A few typical findings of empirical research in the field of urbanism, with special reference to the United States, may be indicated to substantiate the theoretical propositions set forth in the preceding pages, and some of the crucial problems for further study may be outlined.

On the basis of the three variables, number, density of settlement, and degree of heterogeneity, of the urban population, it appears possible to explain the characteristics of urban life and to account for the differences between cities of various sizes and types.

Urbanism as a characteristic mode of life may be approached empirically from three interrelated perspectives: (1) as a physical structure comprising a population base, a technology, and an ecological order; (2) as a system of social organization involving a characteristic social structure, a series of social institutions, and a typical pattern of social relationships; and (3) as a set of attitudes and ideas, and a constellation of personalities engaging in typical forms of collective behavior and subject to characteristic mechanisms of social control.

Urbanism in Ecological Perspective Since in the case of physical structure and ecological processes we are able to operate with fairly objective indices, it becomes possible to arrive at quite precise and generally quantitative results. The dominance of the city over its hinterland becomes explicable through the functional characteristics of the city which derive in large measure from the effect of numbers and density. Many of the technical facilities and the skills and organizations to which urban life gives rise can grow and prosper only in cities where the demand is sufficiently great. The nature and scope of the services rendered by these organizations and institutions and the advantage which they enjoy over the less developed facilities of smaller towns enhances the dominance of the city and the dependence of ever wider regions upon the central metropolis.

The urban-population composition shows the operation of selective and differentiating factors. Cities contain a larger proportion of persons in the prime of life than rural areas which contain more old and very young people. In this, as in so many other respects, the larger the city the more this specific characteristic of urbanism is apparent. With the exception of the largest cities, which have attracted the bulk of the foreign-born males, and a few other special types of cities, women predominate numerically over men. The heterogeneity of the urban population is further indicated along racial and ethnic lines. The foreign born and their children constitute nearly two-thirds of all the inhabitants of cities of one million and over. Their proportion in the urban population declines as the size of the city decreases, until in the rural areas they comprise only about one-sixth of the total population. The larger cities similarly have attracted more Negroes and other racial groups than have the smaller communities. Considering that age, sex, race, and ethnic origin are associated with other factors such as occupation and interest, it becomes clear that one major characteristic of the urban-dweller is his dissimilarity from his fellows. Never before have such large masses of people of diverse traits as we find in our cities been thrown together into such close physical contact as in the great cities of America. Cities generally, and American cities in particular, comprise a motley of peoples and cultures, of highly differentiated modes of life between which there often is only the faintest communication, the greatest indifference and the broadest tolerance, occasionally bitter strife, but always the sharpest contrast.

The failure of the urban population to reproduce itself appears to be a biological consequence of a combination of factors in the complex of urban life, and the decline in the birth-rate generally may be regarded as one of the most significant signs of the urbanization of the Western world. While the proportion of deaths in cities is slightly greater than in the country, the outstanding difference between the failure of present-day cities to maintain their population and that of cities of the past is that in former times it was due to the exceedingly high death-rates in cities, whereas today, since cities have become more livable from a health standpoint, it is due to low birth-rates. These biological characteristics of the urban population are significant sociologically, not merely because they reflect the urban mode of existence but also because they condition the growth and future dominance of cities and their basic social organization. Since cities are the consumers rather than the producers of men, the value of human life and the social estimation of the personality will not be unaffected by the balance between births and deaths. The pattern of land use, of land values, rentals, and ownership, the nature and functioning of the physical structures, of housing, of transportation and communication facilities, of public utilities—these and many other phases of the physical mechanism of the city are not isolated phenomena unrelated to the city as a social entity, but are affected by and affect the urban mode of life.

Urbanism as a Form of Social Organization The distinctive features of the urban mode of life have often been described sociologically as consisting of the substitution of secondary for primary contacts, the weakening of bonds of kinship, and the declining social significance of the family, the disappearance of the neighborhood, and the undermining of the traditional basis of social solidarity. All these phenomena can be substantially verified through objective indices. Thus, for instance, the low and declining urban-reproduction rates suggest that the city is not conducive to the traditional type of family life, including the rearing of children and the maintenance of the home as the locus of a whole round of vital activities. The transfer of industrial, educational, and recreational activities to specialized institutions outside the home has deprived the family of some of its most characteristic historical functions. In cities mothers are more likely to be employed, lodgers are more frequently part of the household, marriage tends to be postponed, and the proportion of single and unattached people is greater. Families

are smaller and more frequently without children than in the country. The family as a unit of social life is emancipated from the larger kinship group characteristic of the country, and the individual members pursue their own diverging interests in their vocational, educational, religious, recreational, and political life.

Such functions as the maintenance of health, the methods of alleviating the hardships associated with personal and social insecurity, the provisions for education, recreation, and cultural advancement have given rise to highly specialized institutions on a community-wide, state-wide, or even national basis. The same factors which have brought about greater personal insecurity also underlie the wider contrasts between individuals to be found in the urban world. While the city has broken down the rigid caste lines of pre-industrial society, it has sharpened and differentiated income and status groups. Generally, a larger proportion of the adult-urban population is gainfully employed than is the case with the adult-rural population. The white-collar class comprising those employed in trade, in clerical, and in professional work, are proportionately more numerous in large cities and in metropolitan centers and in smaller towns than in the country.

On the whole, the city discourages an economic life in which the individual in time of crisis has a basis of subsistence to fall back upon, and it discourages self-employment. While incomes of city people are on the average higher than those of country people, the cost of living seems to be higher in the larger cities. Home ownership involves greater burdens and is rarer. Rents are higher and absorb a larger proportion of the income. Although the urban-dweller has the benefit of many communal services, he spends a large proportion of his income for such items as recreation and advancement and a smaller proportion for food. What the communal services do not furnish the urbanite must purchase, and there is virtually no human need which has remained unexploited by commercialism. Catering to thrills and furnishing means of escape from drudgery, monotony, and routine thus become one of the major functions of urban recreation, which at its best furnishes means for creative self-expression and spontaneous group association, but which more typically in the urban world results in passive spectatorism on the one hand, or sensational record-smashing feats on the other.

Being reduced to a stage of virtual impotence as an individual, the urbanite is bound to exert himself by joining with others of similar interest into organized groups to obtain his ends. This results in the enormous multiplication of voluntary organizations directed toward as great a variety of objectives as there are human needs and interests. While on the one hand the traditional ties of human association are weakened, urban existence involves a much greater degree of interdependence between man and man and a more complicated, fragile, and volatile form of mutual interrelations over many phases of which the individual as such can exert scarcely any control. Frequently there is only the most tenuous relationship between the economic position of other basic factors that determine the individual's existence in the urban world and the voluntary groups with which he is affiliated. While in a primitive and in a rural society it is generally possible to predict on the basis of a few known factors who will belong to what and who will associate with whom in almost every relationship of life, in the city we can only project the general pattern of group formation and affiliation,

and this pattern will display many incongruities and contradictions.

Urban Personality and Collective Behavior It is largely through the activities of the voluntary groups, be their objectives economic, political, educational, religious, recreational, or cultural, that the urbanite expresses and develops his personality, acquires status, and is able to carry on the round of activities that constitute his life-career. It may easily be inferred, however, that the organizational framework which these highly differentiated functions call into being does not of itself insure the consistency and integrity of the personalities whose interests it enlists. Personal disorganization, mental breakdown, suicide, delinquency, crime, corruption, and disorder might be expected under these circumstances to be more prevalent in the urban than in the rural community. This has been confirmed in so far as comparable indices are available; but the mechanisms underlying these phenomena require further analysis.

Since for most group purposes it is impossible in the city to appeal individually to the large number of discrete and differentiated individuals, and since it is only through the organizations to which men belong that their interests and resources can be enlisted for a collective cause, it may be inferred that social control in the city should typically proceed through formally organized groups. It follows, too, that the masses of men in the city are subject to manipulation by symbols and stereotypes managed by individuals working from afar or operating invisibly behind the scenes through their control of the instruments of communication. Self-government either in the economic, the political, or the cultural realm is under these circumstances reduced to a mere figure of speech, or, at best, is subject to the unstable equilibrium of pressure groups. In view of the ineffectiveness of actual kinship ties we create fictional kinship groups. In the face of the disappearance of the territorial unit as a basis of social solidarity we create interest units. Meanwhile the city as a community resolves itself into a series of tenuous segmental relationships superimposed upon a territorial base with a definite center but without a definite periphery and upon a division of labor which far transcends the immediate locality and is worldwide in scope. The larger the number of persons in a state of interaction with one another the lower is the level of communication and the greater is the tendency for communication to proceed on an elementary level, i.e., on the basis of those things which are assumed to be common or to be of interest to all.

It is obviously, therefore, to the emerging trends in the communication system and to the production and distribution technology that has come into existence with modern civilization that we must look for the symptoms which will indicate the probable future development of urbanism as a mode of social life. The direction of the ongoing changes in urbanism will for good or ill transform not only the city but the world. Some of the more basic of these factors and processes and the possibilities of their direction and control invite further detailed study.

It is only in so far as the sociologist has a clear conception of the city as a social entity and a workable theory of urbanism that he can hope to develop a unified body of reliable knowledge, which what passes as "urban sociology" is certainly not at the present time. By taking this point of departure from a theory of urbanism such as that sketched in the foregoing pages to be elaborated, tested, and revised in the light of further analysis and empirical research, it is to be hoped that the criteria of relevance and validity of factual data can be determined. The miscellaneous assortment of disconnected information which has hitherto found its way into sociological treatises on the city may thus be sifted and incorporated into a coherent body of knowledge. Incidentally, only by means of some such theory will the sociologist escape the futile practice of voicing in the name of sociological science a variety of often unsupportable judgments concerning such problems as poverty, housing, city-planning, sanitation, municipal administration, policing, marketing, transportation, and other technical issues. While the sociologist cannot solve any of these practical problems—at least not by himself—he may, if he discovers his proper function, have an important contribution to make to their comprehension and solution. The prospects for doing this are brightest through a general, theoretical, rather than through an ad hoc approach.

NOTES

1. William Graham Sumner, *Folkways* (Boston, 1906), p. 12.
2. S. V. Pearson, *The Growth and Distribution of Population* (New York, 1935), p. 211.
3. Whereas rural life in the United States has for a long time been a subject of considerable interest on the part of governmental bureaus, the most notable case of a comprehensive report being that submitted by the Country Life Commission to President Theodore Roosevelt in 1909, it is worthy of note that no equally comprehensive official inquiry into urban life was undertaken until the establishment of a Research Committee on Urbanism of the National Resources Committee. (Cf. *Our Cities: Their Role in the National Economy* [Washington: Government Printing Office, 1937].)
4. "The Anthropogeography of Some Great Cities," *Bull. American Geographical Society*, XLI (1909), 537–66.
5. Walter F. Willcox, "A Definition of 'City' in Terms of Density," in E. W. Burgess, *The Urban Community* (Chicago, 1926), p. 119.
6. *Op. cit.*, p. 8.
7. See Robert E. Park, Ernest W. Burgess, *et al.*, *The City* (Chicago, 1925), esp. chaps. ii and iii; Werner Sombart, "Städtische Siedlung, Stadt," *Handwörterbuch der Soziologie*, ed. Alfred Vierkandt (Stuttgart, 1931); see also bibliography.
8. *Wirtschaft und Gesellschaft* (Tübingen, 1925), Part I, chap. viii, pp. 514–601.
9. Park, Burgess, *et al.*, *op. cit.*, chap. i.
10. The justification for including the term "permanent" in the definition may appear necessary. Our failure to give an extensive justification for this qualifying mark of the urban rests on the obvious fact that unless human settlements take a fairly permanent root in a locality the characteristics of urban life cannot arise, and conversely the living together of large numbers of heterogeneous individuals under dense conditions is not possible without the development of a more or less technological structure.
11. See esp. vii. 4. 4–14. Translated by B. Jowett, from which the following may be quoted:
    "To the size of states there is a limit, as there is to other things, plants, animals, implements; for none of these retain their natural power when they are too large or too small, but they either wholly lose their nature, or are spoiled. . . . [A] state when composed of too few is not as a state ought to be, self-sufficing; when of too many, though self-sufficing in all mere necessaries, it is a nation and not a state, being almost incapable of constitutional government. For who can be the general of such a vast multitude, or who the herald, unless he have the voice of a Stentor?
    "A state then only begins to exist when it has attained a population sufficient for a good life in the political community; it may indeed somewhat exceed this number. But, as I was saying, there must be a limit. What should be the limit will be easily ascertained by experience. For both governors and governed have duties to perform; the special functions of a governor are to command and to judge. But if the citizens of a state are to judge and to distribute offices according to merit, then they must know each other's characters; where they do not possess this knowledge, both the election to offices and the decision of law suits will go wrong. When the population is very large they are manifestly settled at haphazard, which clearly ought not to be. Besides, in an overpopulous state foreigners and metics will readily acquire the rights of citizens, for who will find them out? Clearly, then, the best limit of the population of a state is the largest number which suffices for the purposes of life, and can be taken in at a single view. Enough concerning the size of a city."
12. *Op. cit.*, p. 514.
13. Georg Simmel, "Die Grosstädte und das Geistesleben," *Die Grosstadt*, ed. Theodor Petermann (Dresden, 1903), pp. 187–206.
14. E. Durkheim, *De la division du travail social* (Paris, 1932), p. 248.
15. The extent to which the segregation of the population into distinct ecological and cultural areas and the resulting social attitude of tolerance, rationality, and secular mentality are functions of density as distinguished from heterogeneity is difficult to determine. Most likely we are dealing here with phenomena which are consequences of the simultaneous operation of both factors.

4. Urbanism and Suburbanism as Ways of Life: A Re-evaluation of Definitions

Herbert J. Gans

Herbert Gans is a leading critic of the interpretation of urbanism set forth by Wirth. Gans argues that of the two gross aspects of urban communities—the spatial-demographic and the social-cultural—the latter is by far more relevant for understanding what goes on in cities and other communities. He makes the argument more specific in the present paper by discussing the role of social class, life-cycle stage and ethnicity as prime determinants of community organization and behavior. His view is that the suburban way of life is the consequence of the social characteristics of the people who live in these communities rather than of the location of the suburbs and their low-density settlement pattern. In the course of elaborating his "anti-environmentalist" position, Gans touches on a number of other issues of contemporary urban theory. He discusses the difficulty of making generalizations about urbanism in the face of the wide diversity of life styles which are exhibited in contemporary communities. Gans also exposes the lack of supporting evidence for the common tendency of journalists, and even sociologists, to attribute social problems, such as personal breakdowns and middle-class divorce, to the quality of suburban life. Finally, he cites examples to point up the dilemma of trying to understand urban communities in modern society without at the same time attending to social factors and institutional changes in the nation as a whole.

Herbert J. Gans, both a sociologist and a city planner, is Professor of City Planning at Massachusetts Institute of Technology. He is the author of *People and Plans: Essays on Urban Problems and Solutions* (1968), *The Levittowners* (1967), and *The Urban Villagers* (1962).

The contemporary sociological conception of cities and of urban life is based largely on the work of the Chicago School, and its summary statement in Louis Wirth's essay, "Urbanism as a Way of Life" (40). In that paper, Wirth developed a "minimum sociological definition of the city" as "a relatively large, dense and permanent settlement of socially heterogeneous individuals" (40, p. 50). From these prerequisites, he then deduced the major outlines of the urban way of life. As he saw it, number, density and heterogeneity created a social structure in which primary group relationships were inevitably replaced by secondary contacts that were impersonal, segmental, superficial, transi-

tory, and often predatory in nature. As a result, the city dweller became anonymous, isolated, secular, relativistic, rational, and sophisticated. In order to function in the urban society, he was forced to combine with others to organize corporations, voluntary associations, representative forms of government, and the impersonal mass media of communications (40, pp. 54–60). These replaced the primary groups and the integrated way of life found in rural and other pre-industrial settlements.

Wirth's paper has become a classic in urban sociology, and most texts have followed his definition and description faithfully (5). In recent years, however, a considerable number of studies and essays have questioned his formulations (1, 5, 13, 15, 17, 19, 20, 23, 24, 27, 28, 30, 35, 38, 41).[1] In addition, a number of changes have taken place in cities since the article was published in 1938, notably the exodus of white residents to low- and medium-priced houses in the suburbs, and the decentralization of industry. The evidence from these studies and the changes in American cities suggest that Wirth's statement must be revised.

There is yet another, and more important reason for such a revision. Despite its title and intent, Wirth's paper deals with urban-industrial society, rather than with the city. This is evident from his approach. Like other urban sociologists, Wirth based his analysis on a comparison of settlement types, but unlike his colleagues, who pursued urban-rural comparisons, Wirth contrasted the city to the folk society. Thus, he compared settlement types of pre-industrial and industrial society. This allowed him to include in his theory of urbanism the entire range of modern institutions which are not found in the folk society, even though many such groups (e.g., voluntary associations) are by no means exclusively urban. Moreover, Wirth's conception of the city dweller as depersonalized, atomized, and susceptible to mass movements suggests that his paper is based on, and contributes to, the theory of the mass society.

Many of Wirth's conclusions may be relevant to the understanding of ways of life in modern society. However, since the theory argues that all of society is now urban, *his analysis does not distinguish ways of life in the city from those in other settlements within modern society*. In Wirth's time, the comparison of urban and pre-urban settlement types was still fruitful, but today, the primary task for urban (or community) sociology seems to me to be the analysis of the similarities and differences between contemporary settlement types.

This paper is an attempt at such an analysis; it limits itself to distinguishing ways of life in the modern city and the modern suburb. A re-analysis of Wirth's conclusions from this perspective suggests that his characterization of the urban way of life applies only—and not too accurately —to the residents of the inner city. The remaining city dwellers, as well as most suburbanites, pursue a different way of life, which I shall call "quasi-primary." This proposition raises some doubt about the mutual exclusiveness of the concepts of city and suburb and leads to a yet broader question: whether settlement concepts and other ecological concepts are useful for explaining ways of life.

The Inner City

Wirth argued that number, density, and heterogeneity had two social consequences which explain the major features of urban life. On the one hand, the crowding of diverse types of people into a small area led to the segregation of homogeneous types of people into separate neighborhoods (40, p. 56). On the other hand, the lack of physical distance between city dwellers resulted in social contact between them, which broke down existing social and cultural patterns and encouraged assimilation as well as acculturation—the melting pot effect (40, p. 52). Wirth implied that the melting pot effect was far more powerful than the tendency toward segregation and concluded that, sooner or later, the pressures engendered by the dominant social, economic, and political institutions of the city would destroy the remaining pockets of primary-group relationships (40, pp. 60–62). Eventually, the social system of the city would resemble Tönnies' *Gesellschaft*—a way of life which Wirth considered undesirable.

Because Wirth had come to see the city as the prototype of mass society, and because he examined the city from the distant vantage point of the folk society— from the wrong end of the telescope, so to speak—his view of urban life is not surprising. In addition, Wirth found support for his theory in the empirical work of his Chicago colleagues. As Greer and Kube (19, p. 112) and Wilensky (38, p. 121) have pointed out, the Chicago sociologists conducted their most intensive studies in the inner city.[2] At that time, these were slums recently invaded by new waves of European immigrants and rooming house and skid row districts, as well as the habitat of Bohemians and well-to-do Gold Coast apartment dwellers. Wirth himself studied the Maxwell Street Ghetto, an inner-city Jewish neighborhood then being dispersed by the acculturation and mobility of its inhabitants (39). Some of the characteristics of urbanism which Wirth stressed in his essay abounded in these areas.

Wirth's diagnosis of the city as *Gesellschaft* must be questioned on three counts. First, the conclusions derived from a study of the inner city cannot be generalized to the entire urban area. Second, there is as yet not enough evidence to prove—nor, admittedly, to deny—that number, density, and heterogeneity result in the social consequences which Wirth proposed. Finally, even if the causal relationship could be verified, it can be shown that a significant proportion of the city's inhabitants were, and are, isolated from these consequences by social structures and cultural patterns which they either brought to the city, or developed by living in it. Wirth conceived the urban population as consisting of heterogeneous individuals, torn from past social systems, unable to develop new ones, and therefore prey to social anarchy in the city. While it is true that a not insignificant proportion of the inner city population was, and still is, made up of unattached individuals (26), Wirth's formulation ignores the fact that this population consists mainly of relatively homogeneous groups, with social and cultural moorings that shield it fairly effectively from the suggested consequences of number, density, and heterogeneity. This applies even more to the residents of the outer city, who constitute a majority of the total city population.

The social and cultural moorings of the inner city population are best described by a brief analysis of the five types of inner city residents. These are:

1. the "cosmopolites";
2. the unmarried or childless;
3. the "ethnic villagers";
4. the "deprived"; and
5. the "trapped" and downward mobile.

The "cosmopolites" include students, artists, writers, musicians, and entertainers, as well as other intellectuals and professionals. They live in the city in order to be near the special "cultural" facilities that can only be located near the center of the city. Many cosmopolites are unmarried or childless. Others rear children in the city, especially if they have the income to afford the aid of servants and governesses. The less affluent ones may move to the suburbs to raise their children, continuing to live as cosmopolites under considerable handicaps, especially in the lower-middle-class suburbs. Many of the very rich and powerful are also cosmopolites, although they are likely to have at least two residences, one of which is suburban or exurban.

The unmarried or childless must be divided into two subtypes, depending on the permanence or transience of their status. The temporarily unmarried or childless live in the inner city for only a limited time. Young adults may team up to rent an apartment away from their parents and close to job or entertainment opportunities. When they marry, they may move first to an apartment in a transient neighborhood, but if they can afford to do so, they leave for the outer city or the suburbs with the arrival of the first or second child. The permanently unmarried may stay in the inner city for the remainder of their lives, their housing depending on their income.

The "ethnic villagers" are ethnic groups which are found in such inner city neighborhoods as New York's Lower East Side, living in some ways as they did when they were peasants in European or Puerto Rican villages (15). Although they reside in the city, they isolate themselves from significant contact with most city facilities, aside from workplaces. Their way of life differs sharply from Wirth's urbanism in its emphasis on kinship and the primary group, the lack of anonymity and secondary-group contacts, the weakness of formal organizations, and the suspicion of anything and anyone outside their neighborhood.

The first two types live in the inner city by choice; the third is there partly because of necessity, partly because of tradition. The final two types are in the inner city because they have no other choice. One is

the "deprived" population: the very poor; the emotionally disturbed or otherwise handicapped; broken families; and, most important, the non-white population. These urban dwellers must take the dilapidated housing and blighted neighborhoods to which the housing market relegates them, although among them are some for whom the slum is a hiding place, or a temporary stop-over to save money for a house in the outer city or the suburbs (27).

The "trapped" are the people who stay behind when a neighborhood is invaded by non-residential land uses or lower-status immigrants, because they cannot afford to move, or are otherwise bound to their present location (27).[3] The "downward mobiles" are a related type; they may have started life in a higher class position, but have been forced down in the socio-economic hierarchy and in the quality of their accommodations. Many of them are old people, living out their existence on small pensions.

These five types all live in dense and heterogeneous surroundings, yet they have such diverse ways of life that it is hard to see how density and heterogeneity could exert a common influence. Moreover, all but the last two types are isolated or detached from their neighborhood and thus from the social consequences which Wirth described.

When people who live together have social ties based on criteria other than mere common occupancy, they can set up social barriers regardless of the physical closeness or the heterogeneity of their neighbors. The ethnic villagers are the best illustration. While a number of ethnic groups are usually found living together in the same neighborhood, they are able to isolate themselves from each other through a variety of social devices. Wirth himself recognized this when he wrote that "two groups can occupy a given area without losing their separate identity because each side is permitted to live its own inner life and each somehow fears or idealizes the other" (39, p. 283). Although it is true that the children in these areas were often oblivious to the social barriers set up by their parents, at least until adolescence, it is doubtful whether their acculturation can be traced to the melting pot effect as much as to the pervasive influence of the American culture that flowed into these areas from the outside.[4]

The cosmopolites, the unmarried, and the childless are *detached* from neighborhood life. The cosmopolites possess a distinct subculture which causes them to be disinterested in all but the most superficial contacts with their neighbors, somewhat like the ethnic villagers. The unmarried and childless are detached from neighborhood because of their life-cycle stage, which frees them from the routine family responsibilities that entail some relationship to the local area. In their choice of residence, the two types are therefore not concerned about their neighbors, or the availability and quality of local community facilities. Even the well-to-do can choose expensive apartments in or near poor neighborhoods, because if they have children, these are sent to special schools and summer camps which effectively isolate them from neighbors. In addition, both types, but especially the childless and unmarried, are transient. Therefore, they tend to live in areas marked by high population turnover, where their own mobility and that of their neighbors creates a universal detachment from the neighborhood.[5]

The deprived and the trapped do seem to be affected by some of the consequences of number, density, and heterogeneity. The deprived population suffers considerably from overcrowding, but this is a consequence of low income, racial discrimination, and other handicaps, and cannot be considered an inevitable result of the ecological make-up of the city.[6] Because the deprived have no residential choice, they are also forced to live amid neighbors not of their own choosing, with ways of life different and even contradictory to their own. If familial defenses against the neighborhood climate are weak, as is the case among broken families and downward mobile people, parents may lose their children to the culture of "the street." The trapped are the unhappy people who remain behind when their more advantaged neighbors move on; they must endure the heterogeneity which results from neighborhood change.

Wirth's description of the urban way of life fits best the transient areas of the inner city. Such areas are typically heterogeneous in population, partly because they are inhabited by transient types who do not require homogeneous neighbors or by deprived people who have no choice, or may themselves be quite mobile. Under conditions of transience and heterogeneity, people interact only in terms of the segmental roles necessary for obtaining local services. Their social relationships thus display anonymity, impersonality, and superficiality.[7]

The social features of Wirth's concept of urbanism seem therefore to be a result of residential instability, rather than of number, density, or heterogeneity. In fact, heterogeneity is itself an effect of residential instability, resulting when the influx of transients causes landlords and realtors to stop acting as gatekeepers—that is, wardens of neighborhood homogeneity.[8] Residential instability is found in all types of settlements, and, presumably, its social consequences are everywhere similar. These consequences cannot therefore be identified with the ways of life of the city.

The Outer City and the Suburbs

The second effect which Wirth ascribed to number, density, and heterogeneity was the segregation of homogeneous people into distinct neighborhoods,[9] on the basis of "place and nature of work, income, racial and ethnic characteristics, social status, custom, habit, taste, preference and prejudice" (40, p. 56). This description fits the residential districts of the *outer city*.[10] Although these districts contain the majority of the city's inhabitants, Wirth went into little detail about them. He made it clear, however, that the socio-psychological aspects of urbanism were prevalent there as well (40, p. 56).

Because existing neighborhood studies deal primarily with the exotic sections of the inner city, very little is known about the more typical residential neighborhoods of the outer city. However, it is evident that the way of life in these areas bears little resemblance to Wirth's urbanism. Both the studies which question Wirth's formulation and my own observations suggest that the common element in the ways of life of these neighborhoods is best described as *quasi-primary*. I use this term to characterize relationships between neighbors. Whatever the intensity or frequency of these relationships, the interaction is more intimate than a secondary contact, but more guarded than a primary one.[11]

There are actually few secondary relationships, because of the isolation of residential neighborhoods from economic institutions and workplaces. Even shopkeepers, store managers, and other local functionaries who live in the area are treated as acquaintances or friends, unless they are of a vastly different social status or are forced by their corporate employers to treat their customers as economic units (30). Voluntary associations attract only a minority of the population. Moreover, much of the organizational activity is of a sociable nature, and it is often difficult to accomplish the association's "business" because of the members' preference for sociability. Thus, it would appear that interactions in organizations, or between neighbors generally, do not fit the secondary-relationship model of urban life. As anyone who has lived in these neighborhoods knows, there is little anonymity, impersonality or privacy.[12] In fact, American cities have sometimes been described as collections of small towns.[13] There is some truth to this description, especially if the city is compared to the actual small town, rather than to the romantic construct of anti-urban critics (33).

Postwar suburbia represents the most contemporary version of the quasi-primary way of life. Owing to increases in real income and the encouragement of home ownership provided by the FHA, families in the lower-middle class and upper working class can now live in modern single-family homes in low-density subdivisions, an opportunity previously available only to the upper and upper-middle classes (34).

The popular literature describes the new suburbs as communities in which conformity, homogeneity, and other-direction are unusually rampant (4, 32). The implication is that the move from city to suburb initiates a new way of life which causes considerable behavior and personality change in previous urbanites. A preliminary analysis of data which I am now collecting in Levittown, New Jersey, suggests, however, that the move from the city to this predominantly lower-middle-class suburb does not result in any major behavioral changes for most people. Moreover, the changes which do occur reflect the move from the social isolation of a transient city or suburban apartment building to the quasi-primary life of a neighborhood of single-family homes. Also, many of the people whose life has changed reported that the changes were intended. They existed as aspirations before the move, or as reasons for it. In other words, the suburb itself creates few changes in ways of life. Similar conclusions have been reported by Berger in his excellent study of a working-class population newly moved to a suburban sub-division (4).

A Comparison of City and Suburb

If urban and suburban areas are similar in that the way of life in both is quasi-primary, and if urban residents who move out to the suburbs do not undergo any significant changes in behavior, it would be fair to argue that the differences in ways of life between the two types of settlements have been overestimated. Yet the fact remains that a variety of physical and demographic differences exist between the city and the suburb. However, upon closer examination, many of these differences turn out to be either spurious or of little significance for the way of life of the inhabitants (34).[14]

The differences between the residential areas of cities and suburbs which have been cited most frequently are:

1. Suburbs are more likely to be dormitories.
2. They are further away from the work and play facilities of the central business districts.
3. They are newer and more modern than city residential areas and are designed for the automobile rather than for pedestrian and mass-transit forms of movement.

4. They are built up with single-family rather than multi-family structures and are therefore less dense.
5. Their populations are more homogeneous.
6. Their populations differ demographically: they are younger; more of them are married; they have higher incomes; and they hold proportionately more white collar jobs (8, p. 131).

Most urban neighborhoods are as much dormitories as the suburbs. Only in a few older inner city areas are factories and offices still located in the middle of residential blocks, and even here many of the employees do not live in the neighborhood.

The fact that the suburbs are farther from the central business district is often true only in terms of distance, not travel time. Moreover, most people make relatively little use of downtown facilities, other than workplaces (12, 21). The downtown stores seem to hold their greatest attraction for the upper-middle class (21, pp. 91–92); the same is probably true of typically urban entertainment facilities. Teen-agers and young adults may take their dates to first-run movie theaters, but the museums, concert halls, and lecture rooms attract mainly upper-middle-class ticket-buyers, many of them suburban.[15]

The suburban reliance on the train and the automobile has given rise to an imaginative folklore about the consequences of commuting on alcohol consumption, sex life, and parental duties. Many of these conclusions are, however, drawn from selected high-income suburbs and exurbs, and reflect job tensions in such hectic occupations as advertising and show business more than the effects of residence (29). It is true that the upper-middle-class housewife must become a chauffeur in order to expose her children to the proper educational facilities, but such differences as walking to the corner drug store and driving to its suburban equivalent seem to me of little emotional, social, or cultural import.[16] In addition, the continuing shrinkage in the number of mass-transit users suggests that even in the city many younger people are now living a wholly auto-based way of life.

The fact that suburbs are smaller is primarily a function of political boundaries drawn long before the communities were suburban. This affects the kinds of political issues which develop and provides somewhat greater opportunity for citizen participation. Even so, in the suburbs as in the city, the minority who participate are the professional politicians, the economically concerned businessmen, lawyers and salesmen, and the ideologicaly motivated middle- and upper-middle-class people with better than average education.

The social consequences of differences in density and house type also seem overrated. Single-family houses on quiet streets facilitate the supervision of children; this is one reason why middle-class women who want to keep an eye on their children move to the suburbs. House type also has some effects on relationships between neighbors, insofar as there are more opportunities for visual contact between adjacent homeowners than between people on different floors of an apartment house. However, if occupants' characteristics are also held constant, the differences in actual social contact are less marked. Homogeneity of residents turns out to be more important as a determinant of sociability than proximity. If the population is heterogeneous, there is little social contact between neighbors, either on apartment-house floors or in single-family-house blocks; if people are homogeneous, there is likely to be considerable social contact in both house types. One need only contrast

the apartment house located in a transient, heterogeneous neighborhood and exactly the same structure in a neighborhood occupied by a single ethnic group. The former is a lonely, anonymous building; the latter, a bustling micro-society. I have observed similar patterns in suburban areas: on blocks where people are homogeneous, they socialize; where they are heterogeneous, they do little more than exchange polite greetings (16).

Suburbs are usually described as being more homogeneous in house type than the city, but if they are compared to the outer city, the differences are small. Most inhabitants of the outer city, other than well-to-do homeowners, live on blocks of uniform structures as well—for example, the endless streets of rowhouses in Philadelphia and Baltimore or of two-story duplexes and six-flat apartment houses in Chicago. They differ from the new suburbs only in that they were erected through more primitive methods of mass production. Suburbs are of course more predominantly areas of owner-occupied single homes, though in the outer districts of most American cities homeownership is also extremely high.

Demographically, suburbs as a whole are clearly more homogeneous than cities as a whole, though probably not more so than outer cities. However, people do not live in cities or suburbs as a whole, but in specific neighborhoods. An analysis of ways of life would require a determination of the degree of population homogeneity within the boundaries of areas defined as neighborhoods by residents' social contacts. Such an analysis would no doubt indicate that many neighborhoods in the city as well as the suburbs are homogeneous. Neighborhood homogeneity is actually a result of factors having little or nothing to do with the house type, density, or location of the area relative to the city limits. Brand new neighborhoods are more homogeneous than older ones, because they have not yet experienced resident turnover, which frequently results in population heterogeneity. Neighborhoods of low- and medium-priced housing are usually less homogeneous than those with expensive dwellings because they attract families who have reached the peak of occupational and residential mobility, as well as young families who are just starting their climb and will eventually move to neighborhoods of higher status. The latter, being accessible only to high-income people, are therefore more homogeneous with respect to other resident characteristics as well. Moreover, such areas have the economic and political power to slow down or prevent invasion. Finally, neighborhoods located in the path of ethnic or religious group movement are likely to be extremely homogeneous.

The demographic differences between cities and suburbs cannot be questioned, especially since the suburbs have attracted a large number of middle-class childrearing families. The differences are, however, much reduced if suburbs are compared only to the outer city. In addition, a detailed comparison of suburban and outer city residential areas would show that neighborhoods with the same kinds of people can be found in the city as well as the suburbs. Once again, the age of the area and the cost of housing are more important determinants of demographic characteristics than the location of the area with respect to the city limits.

Characteristics, Social Organization, and Ecology

The preceding sections of the paper may be summarized in three propositions:

1. As concerns ways of life, the inner city must be distinguished from the outer city and the suburbs; and the latter two exhibit a way of life bearing little resemblance to Wirth's urbanism.
2. Even in the inner city, ways of life resemble Wirth's description only to a limited extent. Moreover, economic condition, cultural characteristics, life-cycle stage, and residential instability explain ways of life more satisfactorily than number, density, or heterogeneity.
3. Physical and other differences between city and suburb are often spurious or without much meaning for ways of life.

These propositions suggest that the concepts urban and suburban are neither mutually exclusive, nor especially relevant for understanding ways of life. They—and number, density, and heterogeneity as well—are ecological concepts which describe human adaptation to the environment. However, they are not sufficient to explain social phenomena, because these phenomena cannot be understood solely as the consequences of ecological processes. Therefore, other explanations must be considered.

Ecological explanations of social life are most applicable if the subjects under study lack the ability to *make choices*, be they plants, animals, or human beings. Thus, if there is a housing shortage, people will live almost anywhere, and under extreme conditions of no choice, as in a disaster, married and single, old and young, middle and working class, stable and transient will be found side by side in whatever accommodations are available. At that time, their ways of life represent an almost direct adaptation to the environment. If the supply of housing and of neighborhoods is such that alternatives are available, however, people will make choices, as if the housing market is responsive, they can even make and satisfy explicit *demands*.

Choices and demands do not develop independently or at random; they are functions of the roles people play in the social system. These can best be understood in terms of the *characteristics* of the people involved; that is, characteristics can be used as indices to choices and demands made in the roles that constitute ways of life. Although many characteristics affect the choices and demands people make with respect to housing and neighborhoods, the most important ones seem to be *class*—in all its economic, social and cultural ramifications—and *life-cycle stage*.[17] If people have an opportunity to choose, these two characteristics will go far in explaining the kinds of housing and neighborhoods they will occupy and the ways of life they will try to establish within them.

Many of the previous assertions about ways of life in cities and suburbs can be analyzed in terms of class and life-cycle characteristics. Thus, in the inner city, the unmarried and childless live as they do, detached from neighborhood, because of their life-cycle stage; the cosmopolites, because of a combination of life-cycle stage and a distinctive but class-based subculture. The way of life of the deprived and trapped can be explained by low socio-economic level and related handicaps. The quasi-primary way of life is associated with the family stage of the life-cycle, and the norms of child-rearing and parental role found in the upper working class, the lower-middle class, and the non-cosmopolite portions of the upper-middle and upper classes.

The attributes of the so-called suburban way of life can also be understood largely in terms of these characteristics. The new suburbia is nothing more than a highly visible showcase for the ways of life of young, upper-working-class and lower-middle-class people. Ktsanes and Reissman have aptly described it as "new homes for old values" (22). Much of the descriptive and critical writing about suburbia assumes that as long as the new suburbanites lived in the city, they behaved like upper-middle-class cosmopolites and that suburban living has mysteriously transformed them (7; 14, pp. 154–162; 25; 36). The critics fail to see that the behavior and personality patterns ascribed to suburbia are in reality those of class and age (6). These patterns could have been found among the new suburbanites when they still lived in the city and could now be observed among their peers who still reside there—if the latter were as visible to critics and researchers as are the suburbanites.

Needless to say, the concept of "characteristics" cannot explain all aspects of ways of life, either among urban or suburban residents. Some aspects must be explained by concepts of social organization that are independent of characteristics. For example, some features of the quasi-primary way of life are independent of class and age, because they evolve from the roles and situations created by joint and adjacent occupancy of land and dwellings. Likewise, residential instability is a universal process which has a number of invariate consequences. In each case, however, the way in which people react varies with their characteristics. So it is with ecological processes. Thus, there are undoubtedly differences between ways of life in urban and suburban settlements which remain after behavior patterns based on residents' characteristics have been analyzed, and which must therefore be attributed to features of the settlement (11).

Characteristics do not explain the causes of behavior; rather, they are clues to socially created and culturally defined roles, choices, and demands. A causal analysis must trace them back to the larger social, economic, and political systems which determine the situations in which roles are played and the cultural content of choices and demands, as well as the opportunities for their achievement.[18] These systems determine income distributions, educational and occupational opportunities, and in turn, fertility patterns, child-rearing methods, as well as the entire range of consumer behavior. Thus, a complete analysis of the way of life of the deprived residents of the inner city cannot stop by indicating the influence of low income, lack of education, or family instability. These must be related to such conditions as the urban economy's "need" for low-wage workers, and the housing market practices which restrict residential choice. The urban economy is in turn shaped by national economic and social systems, as well as by local and regional ecological processes. Some phenomena can be explained exclusively by reference to these ecological processes. However, it must also be recognized that as man gains greater control over the natural environment, he has been able to free himself from many of the determining and limiting effects of that environment. Thus, changes in local transportation technology, the ability of industries to be footloose, and the relative affluence of American society have given ever larger numbers of people increasing amounts of residential choice. The greater the amount of choice available, the more important does the concept of characteristics become in understanding behavior.

Consequently, the study of ways of life in communities must begin with an analysis of characteristics. If characteristics are dealt with first and held constant, we may be able to discover which behavior patterns can be attributed to features of the settlement and its natural environment.[19] Only then will it be possible to discover to what extent city and suburb are independent—rather than dependent or intervening—variables in the explanation of ways of life.

This kind of analysis might help to reconcile the ecological point of view with the behavioral and cultural one, and possibly put an end to the conflict between conceptual positions which insist on one explanation or the other (9). Both explanations have some relevance, and future research and theory must clarify the role of each in the analysis of ways of life in various types of settlement (6, p. xxii). Another important rationale for this approach is its usefulness for applied sociology—for example, city planning. The planner can recommend changes in the spatial and physical arrangements of the city. Frequently, he seeks to achieve social goals or to change social conditions through physical solutions. He has been attracted to ecological explanations because these relate behavior to phenomena which he can affect. For example, most planners tend to agree with Wirth's formulations, because they stress number and density, over which the planner has some control. If the undesirable social conditions of the inner city could be traced to these two factors, the planner could propose large-scale clearance projects which would reduce the size of the urban population, and lower residential densities. Experience with public housing projects has, however, made it apparent that low densities, new buildings, or modern site plans do not eliminate anti-social or self-destructive behavior. The analysis of characteristics will call attention to the fact that this behavior is lodged in the deprivations of low socio-economic status and racial discrimination, and that it can be changed only through the removal of these deprivations. Conversely, if such an analysis suggests residues of behavior that can be attributed to ecological processes or physical aspects of housing and neighborhoods, the planner can recommend physical changes that can really affect behavior.

A Re-evaluation of Definitions

The argument presented here has implications for the sociological definition of the city. Such a definition relates ways of life to environmental features of the city qua settlement type. But if ways of life do not coincide with settlement types, and if these ways are functions of class and life-cycle stage rather than of the ecological attributes of the settlement, a sociological definition of the city cannot be formulated.[20] Concepts such as city and suburb allow us to distinguish settlement types from each other physically and demographically, but the ecological processes and conditions which they synthesize have no direct or invariate consequences for ways of life. The sociologist cannot, therefore, speak of an urban or suburban way of life.

Conclusion

Many of the descriptive statements made here are as time-bound as Wirth's.[21] Twenty years ago, Wirth concluded that some form of urbanism would eventually predominate in all settlement types. He was, however, writing during a time of immigrant acculturation and at the end of a serious depression, an era of minimal choice. Today, it is apparent that high-density, heterogeneous surroundings are for most people a temporary place of residence; other than for the Park Avenue or Greenwich Village cosmopolites, they are a result of necessity rather than choice. As soon as they can afford to do so, most Americans head for the single-family house and the quasi-primary way of life of the low-density neighborhood, in the outer city or the suburbs.[22]

Changes in the national economy and in government housing policy can affect many of the variables that make up housing supply and demand. For example, urban sprawl may eventually outdistance the ability of present and proposed transportation systems to move workers into the city; further industrial decentralization can forestall it and alter the entire relationship between work and residence. The expansion of present urban renewal activities can perhaps lure a significant number of cosmopolites back from the suburbs, while a drastic change in renewal policy might begin to ameliorate the housing conditions of the deprived population. A serious depression could once again make America a nation of doubled-up tenants.

These events will affect housing supply and residential choice; they will frustrate but not suppress demands for the quasi-primary way of life. However, changes in the national economy, society, and culture can affect people's characteristics—family size, educational level, and various other concomitants of life-cycle stage and class. These in turn will stimulate changes in demands and choices. The rising number of college graduates, for example, is likely to increase the cosmopolite ranks. This might in turn create a new set of city dwellers, although it will probably do no more than encourage the development of cosmopolite facilities in some suburban areas.

The current revival of interest in urban sociology and in community studies, as well as the sociologist's increasing curiosity about city planning, suggest that data may soon be available to formulate a more adequate theory of the relationship between settlements and the ways of life within them. The speculations presented in this paper are intended to raise questions; they can only be answered by more systematic data collection and theorizing.

ACKNOWLEDGMENT

I am indebted to Richard Dewey, John Dyckman, David Riesman, Melvin Webber, and Harold Wilensky for helpful comments on earlier drafts of this essay.

NOTES

1. I shall not attempt to summarize these studies, for this task has already been performed by Dewey (5), Reiss (23), Wilensky (38), and others.
2. By the *inner city*, I mean the transient residential areas, the Gold Coasts and the slums that generally surround the central business district, although in some communities they may continue for miles beyond that district. The *outer city* includes the stable residential areas that house the working-and middle-class tenant and owner. The *suburbs* I conceive as the latest and most modern ring of the outer city, distinguished from it only by yet lower densities, and by the often irrelevant fact of the ring's location outside the city limits.
3. The trapped are not very visible, but I suspect that they are a significant element in what Raymond Vernon has described as the "gray areas" of the city (32).
4. If the melting pot has resulted from propinquity and high density, one would have expected second-generation Italians, Irish, Jews, Greeks, Slavs, etc. to have developed a single "pan-ethnic culture," consisting of a synthesis of the cultural patterns of the propinquitous national groups.
5. The corporation transients (36, 38), who provide a new source of residential instability to the suburb, differ from city transients. Since they are raising families, they want to integrate themselves into neighborhood life, and are usually able to do so, mainly because they tend to move into similar types of communities wherever they go.
6. The negative social consequences of overcrowding are a result of high room and floor density, not of the land coverage of population density which Wirth discussed. Park Avenue residents live under conditions of high land density, but do not seem to suffer visibly from overcrowding.
7. Whether or not these social phenomena have the psychological consequences Wirth suggested depends on the people who live in the area. Those who are detached from the neighborhood by choice are probably immune, but those who depend on the neighborhood for their social relationships—the unattached individuals, for example—may suffer greatly from loneliness.
8. Needless to say, residential instability must ultimately be traced back to the fact that, as Wirth pointed out, the city and its economy attract transient—and, depending on the sources of outmigration, heterogeneous—people. However, this is a characteristic of urban-industrial society, not of the city specifically.
9. By neighborhoods or residential districts I mean areas demarcated from others by distinctive physical boundaries or by social characteristics, some of which may be perceived only by the residents. However, these areas are not necessarily socially self-sufficient or culturally distinctive.
10. For the definition of *outer city*, see Note 2.
11. Because neighborly relations are not quite primary and not quite secondary, they can also become *pseudo-primary*; that is, secondary ones disguised with false affect to make them appear primary. Critics have often described suburban life in this fashion, although the actual prevalence of pseudo-primary relationships has not been studied systematically in cities or suburbs.
12. These neighborhoods cannot, however, be considered as urban folk societies. People go out or the area for many of their friendships, and their allegiance to the neighborhood is neither intense nor all-encompassing. Janowitz has aptly described the relationship between resident and neighborhood as one of "limited liability." (20, Chapter 7).
13. Were I not arguing that ecological concepts cannot double as sociological ones, this way of life might best be described as small-townish.
14. They may, of course, be significant for the welfare of the total metropolitan area.
15. A 1958 study of New York theater goers showed a median income of close to $10,000 and 35 per cent were reported as living in the suburbs (10).
16. I am thinking here of adults; teen-agers do suffer from the lack of informal meeting places within walking or bicycling distance.
17. These must be defined in dynamic terms. Thus, class includes also the process of social mobility, stage in the life-cycle, and the processes of socialization and aging.

18. This formulation may answer some of Duncan and Schnore's objections to socio-psychological and cultural explanations of community ways of life (9).
19. The ecologically oriented researchers who developed the Shevsky-Bell social area analysis scale have worked on the assumption that "social differences between the populations of urban neighborhoods can conveniently be summarized into differences of economic level, family characteristics and ethnicity" (3, p. 26). However, they have equated "urbanization" with a concept of life-cycle stage by using family characteristics to define suburbanism with familism (2).
20. Because of the distinctiveness of the ways of life found in the inner city, some writers propose definitions that refer only to these ways, ignoring those found in the outer city. For example, popular writers sometimes identify "urban" with "urbanity," i.e., "cosmopolitanism." However, such a definition ignores the other ways of life found in the inner city. Moreover, I have tried to show that these ways have few common elements, and that the ecological features of the inner city have little or no influence in shaping them.
21. Even more than Wirth's they are based on data and impressions gathered in the large Eastern and Midwestern cities of the United States.
22. Personal discussions with European planners and sociologists suggest that many European apartment dwellers have similar preferences, although economic conditions, high building costs, and the scarcity of land make it impossible for them to achieve their desires.

REFERENCES

1. Axelrod, Morris. "Urban Structure and Social Participation," *American Sociological Review*, Vol. 21 (February 1956), pp. 13–18.

2. Bell, Wendell. "Social Choice, Life Styles and Suburban Residence," in William M. Dobriner (ed.), *The Suburban Community*. New York: G. P. Putnam's Sons, 1958, pp. 225–247.

3. Bell, Wendell, and Maryanne T. Force. "Urban Neighborhood Types and Participation in Formal Associations," *American Sociological Review*, Vol. 21 (February 1956), pp. 25–34.

4. Berger, Bennett. *Working Class Suburb: A Study of Auto Workers in Suburbia*. Berkeley, Calif.: University of California Press, 1960.

5. Dewey, Richard. "The Rural—Urban Continuum: Real but Relatively Unimportant," *American Journal of Sociology*, Vol. 66 (July 1960), pp. 60–66.

6. Dobriner, William M. "Introduction: Theory and Research in the Sociology of the Suburbs," in William M. Dobriner (ed.), *The Suburban Community*. New York: G. P. Putnam's Sons, 1958, pp. xiii–xxviii.

7. Duhl, Leonard J. "Mental Health and Community Planning," in *Planning 1955*. Chicago: American Society of Planning Officials, 1956, pp. 31–39.

8. Duncan, Otis Dudley, and Albert J. Reiss, Jr. *Social Characteristics of Rural and Urban Communities, 1950*. New York: John Wiley & Sons, 1956.

9. Duncan, Otis Dudley, and Leo F. Schnore. "Cultural, Behavioral and Ecological Perspectives in the Study of Social Organization," *American Journal of Sociology*, Vol. 65 (September 1959), pp. 132–155.

10. Enders, John. *Profile of the Theater Market*. New York: Playbill, undated and unpaged.

11. Fava, Sylvia Fleis. "Contrasts in Neighboring: New York City and a Suburban Community," in William M. Dobriner (ed.), *The Suburban Community*. New York: G. P. Putnam's Sons, 1958, pp. 122–131.

12. Foley, Donald L. "The Use of Local Facilities in a Metropolis," in Paul Hatt and Albert J. Reiss, Jr. (ed.), *Cities and Society*. Glencoe, Ill.: The Free Press, 1957, pp. 237–247.

13. Form, William H., *et al.* "The Compatibility of Alternative Approaches to the Delimitation of Urban Sub-areas," *American Sociological Review*, Vol. 19 (August 1954), pp. 434–440.

14. Fromm, Erich. *The Sane Society*. New York: Rinehart & Co., Inc., 1955.

15. Gans, Herbert J. *The Urban Villagers: A Study of the Second Generation Italians in the West End of Boston*. Boston: Center for Community Studies, December 1959 (mimeographed).

16. Gans, Herbert J. "Planning and Social Life: An Evaluation of Friendship and Neighbor Relations in Suburban Communities," *Journal of the American Institute of Planners*, Vol. 27 (May 1961), pp. 134–140.

17. Greer, Scott. "Urbanism Reconsidered: A Comparative Study of Local Areas in a Metropolis," *American Sociological Review*, Vol. 21 (February 1956), pp. 19–25.

18. Greer, Scott. "The Social Structure and Political Process of Suburbia," *American Sociological Review*, Vol. 25 (August 1960), pp. 514–526.
19. Greer, Scott, and Ella Kube. "Urbanism and Social Structure: A Los Angeles Study," in Marvin B. Sussman (ed.), *Community Structure and Analysis*. New York: Thomas Y. Crowell Company, 1959, pp. 93–112.
20. Janowitz, Morris. *The Community Press in an Urban Setting*. Glencoe, Ill.: The Free Press, 1952.
21. Jonassen, Christen T. *The Shopping Center Versus Downtown*. Columbus, Ohio: Bureau of Business Research, Ohio State University, 1955.
22. Ktsanes, Thomas, and Leonard Reissman. "Suburbia: New Homes for Old Values," *Social Problems*, Vol. 7 (Winter 1959–60), pp. 187–194.
23. Reiss, Albert J., Jr. "An Analysis of Urban Phenomena," in Robert M. Fisher (ed.), *The Metropolis in Modern Life*. Garden City, N.Y.: Doubleday & Company, Inc., 1955, pp. 41–49.
24. Reiss, Albert J., Jr. "Rural—Urban and Status Differences in Interpersonal Contacts," *American Journal of Sociology*, Vol. 65 (September 1959), pp. 182–195.
25. Riesman, David, "The Suburban Sadness," in William M. Dobriner (ed.), *The Suburban Community*. New York: G. P. Putnam's Sons, 1958, pp. 375–408.
26. Rose, Arnold M. "Living Arrangements of Unattached Persons," *American Sociological Review*, Vol. 12 (August 1947), pp. 429–435.
27. Seeley, John R. "The Slum: Its Nature, Use and Users," *Journal of the American Institute of Planners*, Vol. 25 (February 1959), pp. 7–14.
28. Smith, Joel, William Form, and Gregory Stone. "Local Intimacy in a Middle-Sized City," *American Journal of Sociology*, Vol. 60 (November 1954), pp. 276–284.
29. Spectorsky, A. C. *The Exurbanites*. Philadelphia: J. B. Lippincott Co., 1955.
30. Stone, Gregory P. "City Shoppers and Urban Identification: Observations on the Social Psychology of City Life," *American Journal of Sociology*, Vol. 60 (July 1954), pp. 36–45.
31. Strauss, Anselm. "The Changing Imagery of American City and Suburb," *Sociological Quarterly*, Vol. 1 (January 1960), pp. 15–24.
32. Vernon, Raymond. *The Changing Economic Function of the Central City*. New York: Committee on Economic Development, Supplementary Paper No. 1, January 1959.
33. Vidich, Arthur J., and Joseph Bensman. *Small Town in Mass Society: Class, Power and Religion in a Rural Community*. Princeton, N.J.: Princeton University Press, 1958.
34. Wattell, Harold. "Levittown: A Suburban Community," in William M. Dobriner (ed.), *The Suburban Community*. New York: G. P. Putnam's Sons, 1958, pp. 287–313.
35. Whyte, William F., Jr. *Street Corner Society*. Chicago: The University of Chicago Press, 1955.
36. Whyte, William F., Jr. *The Organization Man*. New York: Simon & Schuster, 1956.
37. Wilensky, Harold L. "Life Cycle, Work, Situation and Participation in Formal Associations," in Robert W. Kleemeier, *et al.* (eds.), *Aging and Leisure: Research Perspectives on the Meaningful Use of Time*. New York: Oxford University Press, 1961, Chapter 8.
38. Wilensky, Harold L., and Charles Lebeaux. *Industrial Society and Social Welfare*. New York: Russell Sage Foundation, 1958.
39. Wirth, Louis. *The Ghetto*. Chicago: The University of Chicago Press, 1928.
40. Wirth, Louis. "Urbanism as a Way of Life," *American Journal of Sociology*, Vol. 44 (July 1938), pp. 1–24. Reprinted in Paul Hatt and Albert J. Reiss, Jr. (eds.), *Cities and Society*. Glencoe, Ill.: The Free Press, 1957, pp. 46–64. [All page references are to this reprinting of the article.]
41. Young, Michael, and Peter Willmott. *Family and Kinship in East London*. London: Routledge & Kegan Paul, Ltd., 1957.

5. Theory and Research in Urban Sociology

Gideon Sjoberg

Gideon Sjoberg identifies eight "schools" of urban sociology, each of which is defined in terms of the one factor which it regards as primarily responsible for urban growth, the social organization of urban communities, the culture of cities, or urban spatial structure. The eight "schools" are the urbanization, the subsocial, the sustenance, the economic, the environmental (in the spatial or demographic sense of the word), the technological, the value-orientation, and the social power schools. Sjoberg points up the inadequacy of each school's approach and advocates the application of greater effort in the direction of developing a general overall conceptual scheme for interrelating the various factors. His essay is particularly useful for its discussion of ways to resolve the dispute between the environmentalists who regard population growth, density, and spatial dispersion as the sources of urbanism and those urban sociologists who put principal emphasis on the role of changing social values. The paper ends by describing the comparative, cross-national approach to the study of cities as a method for developing urban theory.

Gideon Sjoberg, Professor of Sociology, is currently teaching at the City University of New York. He is author of *The Preindustrial City* (1960), editor of *Ethics, Politics, and Social Research* (1967), and coauthor (with Roger Nett) of *A Methodology for Social Research* (1968).

The Need for More Adequate Theories

The data on cities over the world, though uneven in quality and inadequate on many counts, are nonetheless increasing by leaps and bounds. New materials are constantly being amassed by social scientists of many hues. Unfortunately, these data tend to be ignored by American urban sociologists.[1] Still more likely to be overlooked is the information collected by non-social scientists ranging from newspaper reporters to bureaucratic officials. Persons who occupy governmental posts must draw upon a profusion of materials if they are to engage in rational planning in the industrial-urban or industrializing society. In the Soviet Union, for example, the managerial and political elite increasingly require reliable data on the operation of the industrial-urban complex. Consequently, considerable data are accumulating on the familial, economic, educational, governmental, and other structures, although these materials are frequently published outside the mainstream of social science literature. As new societies enter the industrial-urban orbit, the data on urban centers can be expected to multiply still more rapidly.

Admittedly, use of material gathered by non-social scientists poses special problems for the sociologist; yet for many societies, such as the U.S.S.R. and China, recourse to such information is mandatory. The reports of government officials are

From *The Study of Urbanization*, P. M. Hauser and L. F. Schnore, eds. (New York: John Wiley & Sons, Inc., 1965), Chap. 5, pp. 157–189. Reprinted by permission.

prime sources of data on life in urban centers in these countries.

This is not to deny the need for sociologically oriented descriptive materials on cities, particularly for research projects that are designed to test specific hypotheses. In a real sense, "the more we know, the more we need to know." But to order the ever-accumulating mountains of data and make sense out of seemingly contradictory findings, we must formulate more adequate theories. Indeed this should be our chief goal. Besides facilitating the analysis of existing materials, better theories expose the significant gaps in our knowledge and pave the way for more strategic research.

As Reiss has observed,[2] sociologists have been more interested in studying and theorizing about segments of urban social and ecological structure than in dealing with the totality; and they have tended to use the city as a laboratory for testing theories and hypotheses not specifically related to urban sociology. With increased specialization these trends are likely to persist. Nevertheless, a gestalt perspective —one that views the urbanization process or the urban community in its totality— has much to offer.

Anyone who theorizes about worldwide urban forms faces the task of clarifying and refining some basic concepts, including the community, urbanism, the city, urban society, and ecology. These often are loosely employed in the literature, and many fruitless debates result from the failure of the antagonists to understand each other's definitions of these concepts. Some of the tensions that result from this confusion over definitions will be treated within the context of our discussion.

Types of Theoretical Orientation and Their Respective Schools of Thought

No classification of urban theory can be fully satisfactory. Adherence to any particular system inevitably excludes from consideration certain salient issues. This, however, is not peculiar to urban sociology; it occurs in all theorizing.

The very nature of urban sociology poses certain problems for our analysis. First, most urban sociologists in the United States apparently subscribe to the view that their field must evince a distinctive theoretical or methodological orientation in order to justify its existence. The opposing position, toward which I lean, takes the urban community as the substantive area of study; thus the prime purpose of urban sociology is to understand and predict, by whatever theoretical or methodological tools are available, the social and ecological structure of cities or the actions of their inhabitants.

Another difficulty stems from an "historical accident"—from the fact that in the United States the early students of the city were heavily committed to ecology. Consequently, some writers equate urban sociology with ecology. As the field of ecology has expanded and proliferated in several directions, the boundaries of urban theory have extended accordingly. Nowadays certain of the theoretical orientations associated with urban sociology have been designed to explain the ecological dimension of cities; others are intended to cope specifically with the social sphere. Still other theories seek to account for both the ecology and the social organization of the city.

Some theoretical dilemmas afford the urban sociologist with a unique opportunity to contribute to social theory more generally. For one thing, the urban field is a major battleground for those who stress the impact on urban life of "objective conditions"—the external environment, population structure, and the like—and those who emphasize, for instance, the role of social or cultural values as a key determinant of the so-called objective conditions and of human action in general. Urban sociologists could make a major contribution if they would clarify, perhaps even resolve, some of the issues that separate the antagonists: the "materialists" and "nonmaterialists."[3] At the very least one should seek to be more explicit concerning the assumptions that underlie the selection of one's problems, the collection of data, and the analysis thereof.

Our classification of the major schools of thought in urban sociology is based on the particular variable or variables to which each gives priority. As we shall observe, some schools stress the "external conditions" as determinants of a city's development and social organization, whereas others give priority to values or social power. At the same time, some of these schools of thought include subgroupings that diverge perceptibly from one another because of their differing theoretical or methodological assumptions. We shall at least suggest the range of these disagreements.

The Urbanization School A number of sociologists have examined the impact of the city upon human ecology and social structure. Park and Burgess and their colleagues and students, most notably Wirth and Redfield, have been instrumental in developing and popularizing this theoretical perspective.[4] They drew heavily upon the writings of such European sociologists as Simmel, Maine, Tönnies, Durkheim, and Max Weber.[5] The "urbanization school" has addressed itself, in its own fashion, to an issue of central concern to most leading sociologists—namely, "What are the patterns and processes involved in the transition from a preindustrial, or agrarian, or feudal way of life to an industrial, or urban, or capitalistic order?"

Within modern urban sociology, Wirth's "Urbanism as a Way of Life"[6] is perhaps the most widely cited theoretical orientation. Wirth takes the city—characterized by size, density, and heterogeneity—as the key determinant of many kinds of social action. Redfield, too, in his *Folk Culture of Yucatán*, utilizes the city as a key variable; however, he considers heterogeneity and lack of isolation to be the city's chief characteristics.[7]

To Wirth, and to a degree Redfield, urbanism as a way of life is typified by secularization, secondary-group relationships, voluntary associations, increased segmentation of roles, and poorly defined social norms. The city is, then, a focal point of fluidity and of tenuous social relationships. Implicitly or explicitly the urban center is contrasted with the rural community or, more frequently, with the folk society. The aforementioned characteristics of the urban milieu are regarded as inevitable concomitants of the rise of cities. Significantly, Wirth viewed the effects of urban development as distinctive and independent of those stemming from cultural values or from industrialization; these latter are "held constant." According to this reasoning, all cities, historical and contemporary, share certain key characteristics.

The Wirth-Redfield perspective, though sharply scored in recent years, continues to claim some staunch adherents among students of the city. Recent research, such as that by Smith on preindustrial Tokyo, lends support to Wirth's position.[8] Furthermore, the theorizing of Wirth and Redfield is being perpetuated in introductory textbooks in sociology. But what is more important, many of the ideas of Wirth and Redfield are today being analyzed and researched not by urban sociologists but by those sociologists who speak in terms of "loss of identity," "alienation," or "anomie," in mass societies.[9]

On the other hand, the researches of Babchuk and Gordon, Whyte, Gans,[10] and others on the American scene pinpoint some serious weaknesses of the Wirth perspective. Even for the United States, Wirth exaggerated the amount of secularization and "disorganization" that supposedly typifies the urban setting. We know now that the city is more highly organized than the early Chicago group presumed. Overlooked or deemphasized by writers such as Zorbaugh[11] are certain complex networks of interaction. Slum areas display intricate patterns that often go unobserved by social scientists who come from "the right side of the tracks."[12] And not to be minimized are the bureaucratic organizations that play an increasingly significant role in the lives of American city-dwellers. A mounting body of literature, including the recent studies of Miller and Swanson, documents this trend.[13]

In retrospect it is easy to recognize that Wirth's writings reflect the ethos of the 1920's and 1930's, a period when many American "intellectuals," sociologists among them, were seeking to account for and cope with the stresses and strains of urban life arising from forces such as the First World War, the ingress of large numbers of immigrants from diverse cultures, and the Great Depression. During this era the metropolis was a veritable "seething cauldron."

The limitations of a preoccupation with "disorganization" loom even larger when the Wirth frame of reference is applied to other societies. Oscar Lewis's data support the proposition that in Mexico City urbanization is not necessarily accompanied by a destruction of the social and moral order.[14] And studies of African cities today demonstrate that although the urban milieu is experiencing greatly accelerated change, certain traditional patterns persist alongside the new organizational forms that have emerged.[15] Furthermore, traditional preindustrial cities—including Le Tourneau's Fez and Miner's Timbuctoo[16]—are living testimonials to the fact that cities may evince a quite rigid normative order.

Another shortcoming of the Wirth approach, one that is dramatized particularly in Redfield's early writings, concerns the logical structure of the folk-urban comparison. Redfield saw the folk, or preliterate, society as a closed system. Yet the urban community with which the folk order is contrasted is but a partial system; it survives only because of a hinterland that supplies it with food and raw materials. In effect, Redfield and his followers have been comparing a whole with a part, which is certainly a questionable procedure. Logically, and empirically, the social units to be contrasted are folk versus urban societies and rural versus urban communities. Redfield subsequently modified his position, recognizing that a major distinction obtains between peasants, who form part of a broader society, and preliterates, or folk, who constitute a self-sufficient system that functions apart from any "great tradition."[17]

As for rural-urban differences per se, a number of the generalizations that have emerged from research within the Wirth-Redfield tradition, and are reflected still in sociology textbooks, are badly in need of revision. Numerous patterns that typify the American industrial-urban society are erroneously thought to hold for other social orders as well. By way of illustration, the rural-urban differences that prevail in industrial orders are quite distinct from those that typify preindustrial civilized (or feudal) societies. In the latter, the family organization in its most highly developed form—the large extended family functioning under a single roof—is characteristic of the urban elite rather than of the inhabitants of small villages (where in fact the elite rarely reside). Census materials, though admittedly inadequate in many respects, point to the persistence of these patterns in India today.[18] Then, too, new kinds of rural-urban relationships, depending on the society's level of industrialization, seem to be emerging. In mature industrial orders such as the United States, rural-urban differences are not nearly as marked as those in, say, Southeast Asia. We need to determine just what rural-urban differences hold for all societies and where this is not possible, we need to define the precise limits of the generalizations concerning these differences by identifying the conditions under which specific patterns obtain.

Implicit in the foregoing discussion is another criticism of Wirth and sociologists of like mind: they fail to recognize that the city is shaped along certain lines by the broader, embracing society. Thus, for some problems, the sociologist must consider the city a dependent rather than an independent variable, for much of its ecological and social structure is determined by social forces external to it. Sociologists have perhaps been overly influenced by writers such as Pirenne,[19] who sought to dramatize the social and political independence of the medieval European city. But this thesis is unrealistic for that period even in Western Europe. True, some cities of the past achieved political autonomy, but, in general, cities —certainly contemporary ones—have been mere subsystems subject to societal controls. (We elaborate upon this argument later, especially in our analysis of social power as an independent variable.)

We have been rather critical of the formulations that take the city as an independent variable. At the same time such an orientation is not without some value for the comparative study of cities. In their eagerness to establish the specific "correlates" of urban life, sociologists have generalized all too freely from the American scene, but their emphasis upon the city as a variable cannot be ignored. Urban and rural communities have always diverged and will continue to do so for some time to come.[20]

The city, as the focal point of communication, has always facilitated significant kinds of social change, not the least of which are those stemming from creative intellectual endeavor. Intellectuals have functioned most effectively where the interaction of ideas has been intensive. The city, too, is the repository of the libraries that perpetuate knowledge. Not only does the city provide the necessary conditions for many kinds of social change, including acculturation,[21] but it seems to foster certain varieties of collective behavior, mob action included. Wirth and Redfield rightly gave prominence to the city as a positive force in social change, although often it is more of a "necessary" than a "sufficient" condition. The urban community's precise role in this process, however, awaits clearer theoretical and empirical documentation.

To counterbalance the overemphasis on disorganization, urban sociologists must pay greater heed to social organization, especially to the "differential organization" found among subgroupings within an urban setting, or among different types of cities. Then, too, in societies over the world the city, not the rural area, is the fulcrum of the political, educational, religious, and other organizations (or bureaucracies) that control and support urban life. We must strive to isolate the structural correlates, or functional prerequisites, or imperatives, that hold not only for cities in general but also for specific types of cities. To achieve this a drastic overhaul of the Wirth-Redfield formulation seems mandatory.

Emerging out of the Wirth-Redfield[22] tradition is a group of sociologists[23] who have defined "urbanization" solely in demographic terms.[24] In many instances these writers developed their orientations within the context of other, more elaborate theoretical perspectives (discussed later), and they differ among themselves in some of their methodological and theoretical premises. Thus some approach the study of cities with an eye to discovering patterns or formulating hypotheses, whereas others begin with existing hypotheses and use these as a basis for constructing deductive (axiomatic) theories of a sort.[25]

The primary advantage of the demographic approach to the study of urbanization is that it so readily lends itself to measurement. Now that the metropolitan areas of the world have been roughly delineated, one can more easily formulate and test hypotheses about cities in divergent cultural settings. Certainly, descriptive data on the distribution of urbanites over the world cannot be ignored. Moreover, in contrast to Wirth and Redfield, those sociologists who have adopted the demographic orientation have studied urbanization from the viewpoint of the broader society, which gives them a definite advantage for understanding urban social organization.

Yet special difficulties plague those who define urbanization in demographic terms. In some instances it is unclear whether urbanization is defined in terms of size or whether size is taken as the index of what is urban. Both approaches are legitimate, but the failure to make one's analytical scheme explicit can hardly be defended. In practice it is difficult, if not impossible, in cross-cultural research to take size as the sole criterion of what is urban. It is evident, for instance, that communities of, say, 5000 differ considerably in India, Mexico, and the United States, and any analysis predicated on size alone is a poor one. Even communities in the 100,000 category differ so strikingly in preindustrial and industrial orders that the researcher, to make his analysis meaningful, is likely to introduce criteria other than size into his definition of what is urban. In other words, it is often essential to specify the social conditions under which size is taken as the criterion for urban centers. Actually, Hope Tisdale's article,[26] which gave such impetus to the study of urbanization in demographic terms, has an implicit, and often overlooked, assumption built into her theorizing: she recognized that urbanization is a dependent variable, for it is technology that makes urbanization possible.

The Subsocial School This school, developed by Park and Burgess and often identified as "the Chicago School," has been intent upon studying man in his temporal and spatial dimensions and explaining the resulting patterns in terms of subsocial variables. For upholders of this view the fundamental subsocial variable has been impersonal competition.

In large part, the theorizing of the

Chicago ecologists can be said to represent the confluence of two streams of thought—Social Darwinism and Classical Economics—that swept into prominence during the nineteenth century. Both explain human action in terms of impersonal competition, though the Classical Economists, by casting their theories in terms of a laissez-faire doctrine and focusing primarily on the operation of the marketplace, have functioned within narrower boundaries than the Social Darwinists.

The members of the Chicago School of ecology differ in a number of respects. Burgess, for example, gave more attention to the economic dimension than did Park, who seems to have relied more heavily upon Social Darwinist thinking, though he did not always make this explicit.[27] Consequently, interpretations of the thinking of the Chicago group diverge from one another considerably. Firey,[28] for instance, gives far more attention to the economic facets of the subsocial theory than do certain other critics who play up the Darwinian features.

As to the theorizing and research emanating from this school of thought, Firey,[29] among others, has shown that the resulting generalizations are not fully applicable to American cities. Certain urban patterns cannot be explained in terms of the city's economic organization alone; for example, the factor of sentiment must be recognized. On the basis of research in Austin, Texas, Willhelm and Sjoberg suggest that certain subgroups in American cities, notably businessmen, have incorporated so-called impersonal or subsocial forces into their value system.[30] Thus impersonal forces, as values, are used to justify certain actions in zoning the community.

Although the Chicago School has been sharply criticized, it continues to exert influence. Many of the early studies are still widely cited. Also, certain sociologists (discussed later) have sought to reformulate the Chicago School's theory of ecology, in the process divesting it of many of its Social Darwinistic features.

The Ecological Complex (or Sustenance) School A bridge between the older Chicago School and a highly active group of younger ecologists, prominent among whom are Duncan and Schnore and Gibbs and Martin, was provided first by McKenzie and later by Hawley.[31] These present-day writers have been influenced not only by the earlier Chicago ecologists but also by Durkheim (especially his *Division of Labor*). Classical Economists (including location economists like von Thünen and Lösch), and to some extent the materialist orientation of Marx and his followers. However, among the leaders of this school, Duncan and Schnore diverge perceptibly from Gibbs and Martin, not just in some of their theoretical premises but in their methodology as well. The first two employ the concept of the "ecological complex" and are committed to "induction" or, more accurately, "discovery," whereas the latter stress the notion of "sustenance" and tend to employ a "neo-deductive" approach.[32]

The "ecological complex" of Duncan and Schnore had four basic components: environment, population, social organization, and technology.[33] These variables are seen as functionally interrelated: a change in one leads to modifications in the others. Duncan and Schnore argue that their approach differs significantly from the perspectives of the two other major schools in sociology—the cultural and the social-psychological.

The ecological complex obviously encompasses more than just the urban field, but its chief proponents have focused their attention mainly on the study of cities and urbanization. The major advantage of this framework is its utility for organizing large masses of numerical data, most notably those collected via censuses. Certainly this orientation facilitates the use of measurement.

Metropolis and Region,[34] the major work of Duncan and his associates, enhances our knowledge of the urban hierarchy, or the dominance pattern of cities in American society; in the process it presents an "industrial profile" of some fifty of the largest Standard Metropolitan Areas. Schnore's work also has contributed substantially to the study of metropolitan communities, particularly in the United States.[35]

The shortcomings of the Duncan-Schnore orientation are several. First, the authors have failed to explicate the assumptions underlying their theory—assumptions that affect their interpretation of the empirical data. A clear account of the materialist view they espouse is definitely in order;[36] more crucial still is the need to enumerate those premises apparently adapted from Classical Economics. In addition, the four dimensions of environment, population, social organization, and technology require further refinements. The concept of "social organization," which Duncan and Schnore tend to equate with "the division of labor," is particularly spongy. And in my judgment these four dimensions are not of the same order, that is, on the same level of analysis. For example, the nature of man's "environment" continues to be redefined as a result of changing technology and social organization; the opposite direction of influence is not likely to be encountered, though the environment presents barriers as well as resources, and it contains other

human populations as well as "physical" elements.

Another point of contention in Duncan and Schnore's theorizing is their apparent belief that a value-orientation approach is by nature individualistic (or reductionist). This is doubtful. Values, to be meaningful, must be shared; value systems of necessity are more than individualistic. To study values one must deal with "aggregates." As to the application of the "ecological complex" in actual research, Willhelm contends that both Duncan and Schnore seem to introduce values and other cultural criteria without formally acknowledging this deviation from their theoretical model.[37]

Further comments on the Duncan-Schnore perspective can be introduced in the context of our discussion of the Gibbs-Martin orientation—one that emphasizes sustenance activities rather than the ecological complex. Illustrative of the work of Gibbs and Martin is their study, "Urbanization, Technology, and the Division of Labor." In this they set forth the following propositions:

IA The degree of urbanization in a society varies directly with the division of labor;

IB The division of labor in a society varies directly with the dispersion of objects of consumption. . . .

IIA The degree of urbanization in a society varies directly with technological development;

IIB Technological development in a society varies directly with the dispersion of objects of consumption.[38]

Another proposition tested in an earlier study—namely, "the degree of urbanization in a society varies directly with the dispersion of objects of consumption"—can then be considered as a theorem "derived" from the preceding postulates. Gibbs and Martin advance one other corollary proposition. They then proceed to test the first four propositions rather than any theorems.

Gibbs and Martin, like Duncan and Schnore, have used their so-called ecological approach to organize an impressive amount of empirical data into some meaningful whole. But they falter when they attempt to theorize concerning their framework, especially in the matter of values. Gibbs and Martin write:

> . . . It may be true that, *within* certain limits, socio-cultural values and ideologies influence urbanization. But we do reject these phenomena as possible explanations of the particular relationships observed in this study. This would be the case even if a spatial association between urbanization and certain types of values could be demonstrated. It is entirely possible that as urbanization occurs certain values will come to prevail. Unfortunately, this opens the door to future confusion by making it possible at some later date for observers to conclude that the presence of these values explains urbanization.[39]

But the relationship of values to the division of labor (explored by Gibbs and Martin as well as by Duncan and Schnore) merits far more analytical attention than it has received. The argument that values do not enter into the division of labor prompts the question: how can goods and services be exchanged among elements of a labor force unless certain values are shared by the groups involved? In general, people must agree on a "fair price" if an exchange is to be effected; such an agreement often precedes rather than follows the exchange. The assumption that the division of labor can be entirely dissociated from values has not been demonstrated either theoretically or empirically.

Then, too, the theory of Gibbs and Martin, perhaps more than that of Duncan and Schnore, includes a number of implicit assumptions about "economic man" taken over from Classical Economics—for example, the notion that men strive to maximize "profits" or "economic gain" seems to underlie much of the analysis of the division of labor. The relationship between economic theory and the sustenance organization (or the ecological complex) must be elaborated if this theory is to be extended beyond its present quite descriptive state.

In the end, these modern ecologists have confused the study of a substantive problem (for example, the spatial aspect of human action or of social systems) with a particular theoretical perspective.[40] This is likely to stifle interest in alternative approaches to explanation of the spatial dimension of urban activities.

The Economic School Although the economic orientation is frequently confused with the technological one, and does in fact overlap with it in the works of various social scientists, we treat the proponents of this approach as a separate group.

An important segment of this school, and one to which American sociologists pay little heed, are the Marxists. Social historians in the U.S.S.R. classify cities in terms of Marxian categories: they speak of the slave-owning city, the feudal city, the capitalist city, and the socialist city.[41] Some extensive historical studies of cities have been carried out within this evolutionary framework.[42] It should be informative to observe how neo-Marxist sociologists of the future will modify this orientation to make it more realistic and useful for the analysis of city life.

Another subgroup within the Economic School includes sociologists such as Shevky and Bell and Lacoste who take Colin Clark as their *point d'appui*.[43] Although Shevky and Bell are known almost solely for their methodology, they have adopted Clark's classification of economies into primary, secondary, and tertiary types under the assumption that these are associated with different kinds of urban ecological and social structures. Shevky and Bell avow that:

> . . . *it is not the city which is an underlying "prime mover" in the recent transformation of Western society, but the necessities of economic expansion itself.* Size, density, and heterogeneity, important in describing the urban ambit, are not the significant *structural* aspects of urbanization—for urbanization is a state of a total society, as well as of its cities.[44]

They speak of an increase in the "scale of society," in the scope of social interaction and dependency, as one moves from primary to tertiary forms of production. The structural indicators of this "increasing scale" are (1) changes in the distribution of skills, (2) changes in the structure of productive activity, and (3) changes in the composition of population. Applying Colin Clark's formulation to the study of urban phenomena helps us to see the city in relation to its broader society. And the distinction between secondary and tertiary kinds of economic activity seems useful for distinguishing between two types of "industrial" cities. But the "social area analysis" of Shevky and Bell has to be employed with caution. We must not assume, for instance, that services (tertiary industries) are unique to advanced industrial cities. There may be proportionately more service occupations in preindustrial than in industrial centers,

but the *kinds* of services offered differ markedly in these cities. At the moment, "social area analysis" is little more than a method for manipulating census tract data.

Unfortunately, the proponents of this framework have failed to explicate their theory, and some of their research is only indirectly related to their frame of reference.[45] Greer, who makes much of the increase in the scale of society, neglects to study the impact of the broader societal structure (especially the national political structure) upon the local urban community.[46] Until we possess more satisfactory applications of this theoretical perspective, we must reserve judgment as to its potential utility.

The Environmental School This school of thought has had little impact in urban sociology; yet its leading exponent is avidly read by social scientists, including some sociologists. We are referring to Lewis Mumford, a product of the Patrick Geddes tradition.

Although Mumford is more a moralizer than a scientist, his primary theme is of interest here. He seems to believe that men must somehow come to terms with "nature." To be sure, Mumford discusses technology from time to time, but his chief preoccupation is with the "natural environment." In his view the city (and its inhabitants), to function effectively, must adjust to or even blend into the world of nature. As such, the natural environment is a determinant, with man necessarily accommodating his technology and social organization to it. For Mumford the crucial problems facing society today are products of an imbalance between nature and human culture, including the city as an artifact. In his recent book, *The City in History*, Mumford looks back on Athens as the ideal community that modern cities should emulate.[47]

Our reservations concerning this thesis are many. Mumford seems to suggest that modern man cannot hope to shape his own destiny and must therefore adjust to the environment rather than strive to control the forces of nature. We disagree with this thesis. And we contend that the major problems facing modern urbanites—above all the possibility of an atomic holocaust—are essentially struggles not of man against nature but of man against man.

The Technological School Among those sociologists who give primacy to the technological variable, a line can be drawn between those like Hawley and Ogburn who define technology strictly in terms of terms of tools or energy (the "material conditions") and those who incorporate the concept of "knowhow."[48] We espouse the latter view: that the knowledge of how to make and utilize tools is as much a part of technology as the tools themselves. From this perspective science can be considered as part of technology.

The empirical research of Ogburn, Hawley, and scholars of like mind has advanced our knowledge of the effect of technology upon the spatial ordering of elements within cities and of cities themselves. Yet some of these writers' generalizations concerning the impact of technology upon the spatial and organizational patterning of cities are not as universal as is often assumed. We would certainly not go as far as Ogburn in stating that ". . . the placement of city populations, residences, and places is singularly a function of local transportation as cities themselves are the creation of long-distance transportation. . . ."[49] So too, Hawley's assertion that "the scatter of population about urban centers is a *direct* response to the increased ease of movement"[50] demands careful qualification.

Considerable data have accumulated suggesting that cultural values and power factors, for example, may induce major distortions in the ideal or actual patterns that supposedly result from technological change. The Dotsons' study of Mexican cities, various works on European cities, and Gists' survey of Bangalore suggest that in these industrializing communities, sociocultural factors have slowed the suburbanization process.[51] The patterns found in American cities certainly are not duplicated in all respects. And observe how the Wall in Berlin, a creation of the political structure, has overridden technological factors in determining migration and residence patterns.

These remarks are not intended to minimize the role of technology, least of all industrial technology, in urban ecology and social organization. Certainly its salience is apparent in any comparison of preindustrial and industrial cities.

The implications of technology for urban life can be studied from several vantage points. Besides contrasting cities in preindustrial civilized (or feudal) societies with those in industrial orders, we might compare the differential impact of industrial urbanization on folk and on preindustrial civilized societies. Primitive orders—whether in Africa or New Guinea or parts of Latin America—lack a written tradition and a well-defined literate elite, traits that characterize feudal societies; consequently they appear to have relatively little potential for resisting the impact of industrial urbanization upon their social structure. A literate elite could be a potent force in conserving the traditional way of life.[52]

Another tack might be to examine the impact of various kinds of technology upon the social patterning of cities. We have already indicated that preindustrial and industrial cities, functioning as they do upon distinctive technological bases, diverge perceptibly in many areas of social organization. We must also seek to determine the differential effects of various stages of industrialization upon urban social structure. A pressing need is to compare the present patterns in developing countries of Asia, Africa, and Latin America with earlier forms in Europe. An examination of the variations in the industrial-urban process over the course of European history would also be a profitable venture.[53] The impact of the industrial-urban complex itself upon the rural hinterland is a research area that must not be ignored. The indications are that advanced industrialization obliterates most of the traditional distinctions between city and country. But which, if any, differences will persist?

A necessary goal, but one that is difficult to achieve, is further clarification of certain pertinent theoretical constructs. Technology should be defined in such a manner as to make it operationally researchable, yet theoretically meaningful. The danger lies in defining technology either too narrowly or so broadly as to make analysis meaningless.

The Value-Orientation School A perspective that is at odds with most of the aforementioned schools stresses values, social or cultural, as the key determinant in the study of urban land use and urban social structure. The writings of Max Weber fall within this tradition.[54] In essence, Weber took the values of sociocultural systems as his explanatory variable and the social structure of the city as his dependent variable. This view was perhaps first elaborated, at least with respect to

ecology, in a hitherto obscure and unappreciated article by Znaniecki.[55] More recently Kolb,[56] applying Parsons' pattern-variable approach, has argued that values are the most significant variable for explaining urban ecological and social organization.

More than any other sociologist, Firey has constructed a sound empirical base for those who would take values as a key determinant of a city's ecology.[57] Drawing upon empirical data from Boston, he contrasted the influence of sentiments (that is, values) with that arising from economic factors. Recently, Willhelm extended and revised Firey's position, arguing that economic factors in themselves are values, and that cultural values alone determine man's adaptation to space. Willhelm clearly details the impact of man's concept of time upon his spatial arrangements.[58]

Although the value-orientation approach has been much criticized, social scientists have amassed impressive if rather unsystematic amounts of data demonstrating that values cannot be ignored. Dickinson's *The West European City*, Jones's *A Social Geography of Belfast*, and von Grunebaum's impressionistic essay on Muslim cities all reinforce elements of Firey's theory.[59]

Indeed, it is when we compare cities in highly divergent cultures that we perceive most clearly how values affect urban ecology. Thus in traditional Muslim cities religious values order temporal activities to a high degree. In each part of the city the muezzin's call to prayer at given times of the day sets the pace for numerous activities. And during the month-long festival of Ramadan, people adjust most of their activities to the religious strictures that impose fasting from dawn to sunset. Many daily pursuits take place at night, whereas other activities, especially in the commerical and manufacturing spheres, necessarily undergo some curtailment. Any approach that ignores values cannot explain ecological patterns of this sort.

Values also influence a city's size, density, and heterogeneity—the very characteristics Wirth used to define the city. In the matter of urban expansion some societies' value systems are more permissive than others. In southern Europe, for instance, certain groups have attempted to slow the advance of industrialization. Weber's observations on the function of religious values in the development of economic enterprise have relevance also for the study of urbanization.[60]

Values affect the development not just of cities in general but of specific kinds of cities. Those like Mecca, Benares, Jerusalem, or Rome largely owe their prominence and persistence over many centuries to the positive religious values assigned to them.[61] And today some nations are building capital cities (for example, Brasilia) as showplaces intended to symbolize the country's progress and independence.

The nexus, however, between values and the internal ecology of cities demands more careful exploration even in the United States, to say nothing of the rest of the world. A study by Whyte,[62] though moralistic, is provocative for its discussion of the relationships between values and the influx of a small but significant number of Americans from the suburbs to the central city. A definite association exists between suburban *versus* central-city living and the values people hold. More important still, Whyte and especially Meadows[63] have explored the interconnection between the ideology of city planners and their proposals for remaking the central city. Certainly the early planning programs such as the Garden City movement in England were motivated by strong

negative values toward the industrial city. Purposive city planning (whether locally or nationally inspired) is increasingly shaping urban life in the United States and in Europe, including the Communist bloc. As a result we need many more studies like Orlans' on a planned city in England,[64] and that by Marris on Lagos, Nigeria,[65] detailing how values (along with social power) influence the planning process. Conversely, situations exist where certain values seem to have relatively little effect upon urban land-use patterns.[66]

Many sociologists have proceeded on the assumption that values shape many facets of social structure and social action within the urban context.[67] The notion that the value system is responsible for many of the differences among cities in distinctive cultural settings is explicit in Weber's writings on the city, and in recent decades it has come to dominate the thinking of researchers studying social organization in cross-cultural perspective. But certain drawbacks of this approach call for comment.

First, the precise relationships between values and social structure (or values and ecology) in complex urban communities are difficult to assess. In industrial-urban orders the number of shared values may be few. Drawing upon his own research, Shils observes only tenuous connections between the action patterns of many individuals and subgroups and the more abstract value systems.[68] Certainly it is questionable procedure to assume any one-to-one correspondence between values and the social and ecological organization of urban centers in the United States or any other society.

Second, members of the Value-Orientation School often fail to distinguish among values, ideas, knowledge, beliefs, and the like. To refer to all these varied components of culture as "values," as some writers do, undermines the utility of this frame of reference. Actually, values are those concepts, distinctive of an individual or characteristic of a group, that specify the desirability or undesirability of social phenomena.

Third, an excessive concern with values can lead one to emphasize the differences among cities in various cultures rather than the similarities. Some social scientists assert that special value systems make for unique urban patterns. But my own research on preindustrial cities indicates that for many societies, so-called "unique" cultural patterns in the realms of the family, social class, education, and the like actually have their counterparts in other social orders. This is not to say that the unique should not be sought, but, ultimately, it can be correctly identified only in light of the general.

Sociologists need more satisfactory invariant points of reference by which to assess the impact of values. Parsons'[69] pattern-variable schema—an elaborate effort to isolate a limited number of universal reference points that will hold for all societies—has considerable relevance for the comparative study of urban social structures despite its many evident limitations. Ideally, this approach should enable one to demonstrate that different value systems result in distinctive combinations of pattern variables.

But sociologists can, and must, pursue still other tacks when seeking to isolate universal categories, that is, those that hold for all cities or, more narrowly, for special types such as industrial cities. They can then determine how differing value systems induce deviations from the ideal patterns. This procedure has been followed, at least implicitly, in some ecological studies that have sought to demonstrate

that certain "ideal" arrangements wherein complete dominance of the technological or economic variable has been presumed have in fact been distorted by cultural values. The point is that the perspective which gives prominence to cultural values is not necessarily at odds with the Wirth-Redfield schema or with the technological orientation, to cite only two examples; ideally, these latter perspectives should provide us with reference points by which we can measure, in given types of societies, the effects of values upon urban ecology and social organization.

The Social Power School This group's theoretical schema is the "special interest" approach wherein power becomes the critical independent variable. This was explicitly introduced into urban sociology by Form[70] as a means of explaining urban land-use patterns. Although Form refers to this orientation as a "structural" one, the main variable employed is "social power" as wielded by various groups in the community or nation.

Unfortunately, Form fails to pursue many of the implications of his theory. He focuses upon local community patterns, overlooking the utility of his schema for analyzing the effects of national and international power struggles upon the development of the city, not just in its internal land-use patterns but in its growth and its social organization as well. In fact, a good case can be made for interpreting the entire realm of social planning within the "special interest" frame of reference. With this orientation, and drawing upon existing theories pertaining to competitive group life—for example, the theory of games—one might develop certain general principles about urban life. And though we focus here upon political power, this approach can be extended to cover the effects of social power as wielded by religious or economic or other organizations.

We shall now sketch some of the implications for urban ecology and social organization of political power factors operating on three levels—the local, the national, and the international. Concerning the first of these, Form has discussed the impact of local power decisions upon a city's ecology. This matter has been treated more fully by Meyerson and Banfield, and by Banfield alone.[71] These authors describe how certain land-use patterns are the products of compromise among competing interest groups. Such patterns are prevalent in American cities and undoubtedly find their counterparts in urban centers in other societies. The task that confronts us is that of working out some principles in this sphere that will hold cross-culturally, not just with respect to urban land use but in the area of social organization as well.

A city's ecological structure can be strongly influenced by power decisions on the national level. Recent patterns in the Union of South Africa provide an especially dramatic instance.[72] Here the impact of national power struggles upon the internal spatial and temporal patterns of cities is clearly evident. The national "pass" laws sharply curtail the movement of Natives into, and within, urban centers. Moreover, in recent years large numbers of Natives have been forcibly removed from tracts in and near the centers of cities such as Johannesburg and relocated in newly created communities on the outskirts. In Johannesburg these new sites are miles from the central city, forcing many Natives to travel long distances to their places of employment. Purposive land use changes such as these, seeking as they do to implement the policy of apartheid, demon-strate the futility of interpreting *all* land-use change within frames of reference solely devoted to value orientations or technology. Still less appropriate would be a materialistic or biotic framework. By global standards the cities of South Africa are highly industrialized, but a sizable portion of the urban labor force has been transplanted to residential areas well removed from their occupational situses. This is not a "rational" deployment of workers from the standpoint of furthering industrialization. Nor can values fully account for this large-scale population movement. Although the Afrikaners highly value spatial, and social, apartheid, the Natives have not always relinquished their urban residence voluntarily. Already leading a marginal existence, they have suffered further hardships as a result of their removal to outlying areas. Unquestionably the decisive "intervening variable" permitting these new arrangements has been the social power of the Afrikaners, who wield control of the society's governmental (including military) organization and economic structure. As a result, they are able to put some of their values into practice despite the protests of the Natives, some Britishers, and the governments of other countries.

Power factors on the national level influence not only the city's internal ecology but its growth as well. Historical evidence indicates that the rise and fall of cities has been closely associated and even determined by the rise and fall of empires.[73] More narrowly, many cities today owe their existence to purposive social planning by the national government. In the U.S.S.R. the Communist leadership has sought to promote industrial urbanization in part by obliterating via the exercise of police powers, the traditional peasant way of life.[74] Although the peasantry resisted for a time, ultimately they had to capitulate. For one thing, the collectivization of farms, by implementing the industrialization of agriculture, made many agriculturists redundant and thus drove them into the urban labor force. In the process the central government gained further control over the agricultural surplus and was thereby enabled to sustain the expanding urban population.

Another facet of this problem is observable in modernizing societies. In India, for example, disagreement exists between certain elements who desire heavy industry and large cities and those who advocate light industries and smaller cities. The course of urban development in India will rest in high degree upon which faction emerges the victor in this struggle.

Power decisions on the national level also affect the urban community's social organization. In the United States the Supreme Court's rulings on desegregation, reinforced by the power of the federal government, have left their clear impress upon the social structure of cities from Little Rock to New Orleans, to Birmingham and beyond. So too, the world over, most notably in countries undergoing purposive social change, the impact of national governmental decisions on the activities of the local urban community's inhabitants can be dramatic. Russia since the Revolution has experienced a vast upheaval in its urban social structure, and the reports filtering out of Communist China indicate that its central government has effected radical transformations in almost every sphere of urban life, but particularly in the intellectual, the political, and the economic realms. The sheer weight of the social power wielded by the Communist oligarchy is obliterating patterns that were fixed over millennia. No analysis of urban social organization can

be deemed adequate unless it considers the impact of the changes initiated and/or reinforced by the vast powers of modern national governments. Nor can we overlook the conflicts between local and national power groups that this process engenders.

The implications for cities of international power struggles have been almost totally ignored by sociologists. But the struggle for dominance among nations has given strong impetus to industrialization and urbanization in many parts of the world. Thus in many developing countries external considerations are forcing modifications in the traditional social organization. In many cases the elite itself is encouraging this process, for if this group is to maintain social status and power on the international level, and if it is to escape subjugation to some new kind of colonialism, it must advance its country's industrial urbanization, even though in the end this elite will undoubtedly suffer some diminution in its power and status within the society. Japan's industrial urbanization, for instance, was stimulated, in part at least, by the ruling group's concern with external status and power considerations.

But what about those power struggles on the international scene that culminate in war? These leave a still firmer impress upon urban centers, as has been amply demonstrated in preindustrial and industrial communities throughout history. The Second World War was certainly no exception. The German occupation of Polish cities, for example, had profound repercussions for their spatial and temporal patterns and their social organization and above all for the ghettos and the very existence of the Jewish population.[75] The procedures and techniques devised by the Nazis to obliterate the Jews (a largely urban population) point to the complexities of the organizational apparatuses that can arise in industrial-urban centers in time of crisis, as well as to the almost insuperable difficulties an urban subgroup may experience. (As a brief aside, we observe that few urban sociologists concerned with social organization in rapidly changing urban communities, particularly organization of the informal sort, have examined the functioning of the underground movements in European cities occupied by the Germans.)

International conflicts have other kinds of repercussions for cities. Berlin, after its division into the Western and Eastern sectors, has developed two quite different ecological and social organizations. Or consider the impact of bombing on cities in Europe and Japan. The possible effects of nuclear weapons upon urban life over the world staggers the imagination. Overall, the implications of social power for urban centers may be implicit in sociological writings, but their fuller theoretical significance awaits exploration.

Interrelationships among the Schools: Special Problems

We have surveyed the dominant theoretical orientations in the field of urban sociology. What can we conclude from this discussion? First, each of these perspectives has certain strengths and weaknesses. None of them, in their present form, can be viewed as adequate. Even researchers who strive toward formal deductive models have failed to explicate some of their key assumptions.

Second, these theoretical orientations can be refined only if urban sociologists pay greater heed to certain problems that inhere in sociological theory. American urban sociology is still primarily intent

upon data gathering, not upon building theoretical systems. This preoccupation with particulars, though for many purposes a desideratum, is partly responsible for the reluctance of many sociologists to examine some of the more general issues implied in comparative research. Cross-cultural research demands more abstract categories and analytical techniques than does the study of cities within a single cultural setting. Only at higher levels of abstraction do many of the significant similarities among cities emerge, and, as indicated later, comparative study forces one into the kind of abstract conceptualization that the empiricist might hesitate to undertake.

Third, the interrelationships among the variables employed by the different schools demand careful attention.[76] We have already suggested some of these. Thus the expansion of technology, notably industrialization, not only gives impetus to urbanization but is itself spurred by the growth of cities. Also, definite ties exist between technological advance and the dominant ideology and power structure. A society's value orientation, or ideology, determines to a marked degree the manner in which social power is applied.

Moreover, although certain structural arrangements, with their particular supporting values, appear in all cities at a given level of technology, these configurations may readily be distorted by special constellations of power or values in given societies. But only an awareness of the universal patterns among cities enables us to discern the impact of these "unique" value systems or power arrangements. The unique, after all, is demonstrable only in terms of some general standard. An urgent need is for more careful attention to the social conditions under which particular generalizations seem to hold.

We should also seek to resolve the disagreements between those who stress values and those who emphasize "external conditions" as factors in the spatial and social structure of cities.[77] A necessary step in this direction is the recognition by sociologists that their theoretical assumptions shape their choices of project, their methods, and their analyses; but they must do more. We would like to suggest one possible approach.

A vast amount of evidence has accumulated demonstrating that material objects or artifacts are interpreted differently in divergent cultural settings. Indeed, as Sorokin argues, material objects form part of culture only when they become "vehicles," that is, when they become meaningful to the actor. Yet Sorokin also contends that one's "conceptual system" —for example, his ideas, values, and beliefs—must be objectified in terms of certain vehicles. Although he believes that meanings affect these vehicles and play havoc with their "natural" properties, such vehicles as artifacts and tools simultaneously impose limitations and modifications upon meanings.[78] Indirectly at least, Sorokin suggests that the "external world" sets limits to the kinds of concepts, including values, that can raise and persist.

In line with this reasoning, we offer the following neo-evolutionary hypothesis: *as industrial urbanization proceeds and as the technological environment becomes increasingly complex, the possibility of evaluating one's external environment in a variety of ways is concomitantly lessened.* Thus preliterate societies display a very wide variety of values in, for example, the familial, political, and religious spheres. In contrast to this, values, ideas and beliefs in industrial-urban systems are more circumscribed. After all, the "vehicles"

in this setting are highly complex. If a society is to sustain atomic research facilities, mass transportation and communication, and a host of other advanced technologies, certain cultural values seem mandatory. One must positively value not only the complex tools but the scientific knowledge which is an integral part of this technology. Consequently, it is in the scientific-technological-economic sphere that specific values are most frequently shared across sociocultural systems. As one enters the realm of religion and the cultural arts, one can expect to find a greater variety of values among industrial-urban systems.[79]

Formulating and Testing Hypotheses in a Comparative Setting

The logical query is: what next? Because sociologists still have so much to learn about comparative analysis, it is likely that their energies in the years to come will be devoted primarily to formulating more adequate propositions, to engaging in discovery rather than in the formal testing of well-defined hypotheses. But this last must not be neglected; especially do we need to test those hypotheses that form part of some logico-deductive model.

As we observed earlier, however, the impediments to effective comparative research are such that a rigorous testing of many hypotheses will probably not be accomplished to the satisfaction of the more rigorous empiricists. A harsh fact is that a number of research techniques currently in favor among urban sociologists are not readily exportable to other cultural settings; they have been formulated to fit a constellation of traits that are rather unique to American cities. Warner's Index of Status Characteristics is a case in point.[80]

Here the occupational category can be applied cross-culturally to evaluate social status or class position, but those relating to house type and dwelling area and, by implication, housing seem to be poor indices of social status in, say, contemporary Russian cities.[81] A realistic portrayal of the status or class configuration of cities in other societies (assuming that comparable data are available in the first instance) would require drastic revision of Warner's method. Similarly, the various segregation indices, the Shevky-Williams-Bell technique, perhaps even the Queen and Carpenter urbanism index[82]—all of which have gained acceptance among sociologists in many quarters—must be substantially altered before they can be utilized in certain social orders, and in some societies they appear not to be applicable at all. For one thing, these devices presuppose methods of data collection that are realized in relatively few societies. The Shevky-Williams-Bell technique, for example, has been criticized by sociologists on several counts, but its most glaring defect is its culture-boundedness.[83] Its effectiveness rests upon the availability of certain types of data assembled in a specified manner, particularly in terms of census tracts or similar areal units. To reiterate, these techniques have proved their general usefulness for certain research purposes in societies like the United States, but their utility in cross-cultural study appears to be sharply limited at the present time.

Urban sociologists also face problems when they must rely upon data gathered by non-social scientists, notably government functionaries. As we stressed earlier, industrial-urban societies must amass prodigious bodies of information in order to plan rationally and function efficiently. Even in the United States, where untold

numbers of questionnaires are distributed by public and private agencies, the demand for data still seems to exceed the supply. Because of their limited numbers and scanty resources, social scientists must rely upon these materials when studying certain problems.

Government bureaucrats, however, are rarely interested in collecting information specifically directed to scientific generalization on a worldwide basis. They are more often concerned with data bearing on the industrialization and urbanization of their own societies. Even in the United States and other advanced industrial countries, a great deal of social-scientific research is geared to the requirements of governmental and other bureaucracies as these seek to resolve specific problems. Pertinent in this regard is Shryock's discussion of the pressures exerted on the United States Bureau of the Census as it has devised classificatory schemes such as the Standard Metropolitan Area (SMA). For reasons of prestige, Chambers of Commerce all over the country vie to have their particular communities included in the classification, and many exert pressures for greater elasticity in the classification scheme— pressures that threaten to undermine the "scientific validity" of the SMA concept.[84]

The problems of gaining adequate standardized data are greatly magnified, of course, in comparative study. The cross-cultural consistency that does exist in such matters as census categories is mainly attributable to the efforts of United Nations agencies. Perhaps more significant is the fact that industrial-urban communities and societies around the world must deal with similar social problems.

Another quite formidable barrier to research in many societies is the resistance of the leaders to the activities of social scientists. The use of rigorous research procedures within and among societies thereby becomes circumscribed. For our knowledge of Chinese cities today, to cite an instance, we must often resort to indirect sources such as the comments of foreign visitors to China, interviews with refugees, the observations of newspapermen, and the writings of Chinese laymen. All nations restrict, in varying degrees, the dissemination of official governmental data, including census materials. Even in the United States sociologists can hardly probe with impunity into any and all facets of urban life. In certain instances indirect evidence is the best that can be obtained. But a source of optimism lies in the fact that the range of freedom for social research in industrial-urban orders seems to be expanding rather than contracting. One reason for this is that a great deal of data on the operation of the industrial order must be diffused if modern cities are to function effectively.

What is mandatory is a realistic appraisal of the methodology of scientific inquiry as it relates to cross-cultural research. Through ingenious use of census materials obtained from numerous societies, Jack Gibbs[85] has been able to examine certain aspects of world urbanization, and by piecing together scattered materials, Inkeles and Rossi[86] have advanced our knowledge of the comparative ranking of occupations in industrial-urban societies. Cross-cultural studies of this kind, however, treat only a relatively narrow range of problems, and the empirical categories employed generally permit only gross comparisons.

The methodology of comparative inquiry needs rethinking, and urban sociologists must prepare to assist in this task. Although Max Weber's ideal type and Howard Becker's constructed type[87] have been much criticized, we must not minimize the utility of typologies in comparative study. Plainly, we need some conceptual tools to bridge the gaps between data that are not strictly comparable on an empirical plane. Moreover, sociologists should make greater use of the "negative case" method. We agree with Karl Popper that one can disprove a scientific hypothesis but can never prove one with finality.[88] In light of this, we need more research aimed at refuting or setting limits to existing propositions. Moreover, we can use the negative case approach to set up careful research designs that can be duplicated by social scientists in other societies. In essence we must use some modification of Florian Znaniecki's "method of analytical induction."[89] Possessing only limited time and resources and facing the special difficulties of comparative research, sociologists should seek out strategic negative cases with an eye to refuting existing notions and replacing them with more tenable generalizations. At the very least, this procedure should reduce considerably our area of ignorance.

NOTES

1. We have only to read Scott Greer's theoretical effort, *The Emerging City* (New York: Free Press of Glencoe, 1962), to observe how little attention some writers give to cities in other societies.
2. Albert J. Reiss, Jr., "The Sociology of Urban Life 1946–1956" in Paul K. Hatt and Albert J. Reiss, Jr. (Eds.), *Cities and Society: The Revised Reader in Urban Sociology* (New York: Free Press of Glencoe, 1957), pp. 10–11.

3. The cleavage between the "materialists" and the "nonmaterialists" in sociology is generally ignored in survey studies dealing with social theory see, for example, Don Martindale, *The Nature and Types of Sociological Theory* (Boston: Houghton Mifflin, 1960). But this neglect is not an index of its importance, for the differing assumptions about reality influence one's choice of research problem and explanatory variables. The "materialists,"

who differ to some degree among themselves, reject the study of values, attitudes, ideas, or beliefs or else seek to predict these by studying objective conditions. Moreover, they tend to examine the social order in highly mechanistic terms. A comparison of "materialists" and "nonmaterialists" is complicated by the heterogeneity of the latter. Included within this category are those who study values and ideas within a mechanistic framework and those who employ a more voluntaristic orientation. Although a detailed examination of these issues lies beyond the scope of this essay, our comparison of the Subsocial or the Ecological Complex (or Sustenance) School with the Value-Orientation School suggests some of the divergencies between the "materialists" and "nonmaterialists" in urban sociology.

4. See Robert E. Park, *Human Communities* (New York: Free Press of Glencoe, 1952).
5. Georg Simmel, "The Metropolis and Mental Life," in Hatt and Reiss, *op cit.*, pp. 635–646; Henry Sumner Maine, *Ancient Law* (London: J. Murray, 1930); Emile Durkheim, *The Division of Labor in Society*, trans, and ed. by George Simpson (Glencoe, Ill.: Free Press, 1947); Max Weber, *The City*, trans. and ed. by Don Martindale and Gertrud Neuwirth (New York: Free Press of Glencoe, 1958); Ferdinand Tönnies, *Fundamental Concepts of Sociology*, trans. and supplemented by Charles P. Loomis (New York: American Book Co., 1940).
6. Louis Wirth, "Urbanism as a Way of Life," in Hatt and Reiss, *op. cit.*, pp. 46–63.
7. Robert Redfield, *The Folk Culture of Yucatán* (Chicago: University of Chicago Press, 1941). In some respects Redfield's definition of the "city" makes him less "materialistic" than Wirth.
8. Robert J. Smith, "Pre-Industrial Urbanism in Japan: A Consideration of Multiple Traditions in a Feudal Society," in Thomas C. Smith (Ed.), *City and Village in Japan*, Part II of *Economic Development and Cultural Change*, 9 (October 1960), pp. 241–257. It should be stressed that Smith does qualify the Wirth position in terms of recent research findings. Some scholars continue to adhere quite closely to the traditional Wirth framework; see, for example, Marshall B. Clinard, "A Cross-Cultural Replication of the Relation of Urbanism to Criminal Behavior," *American Sociological Review*, 25 (1960), pp. 253–257.
9. Joseph Bensman and Bernard Rosenberg, *Mass, Class, and Bureaucracy* (Englewood Cliffs, N. J.: Prentice-Hall, 1963); Maurice R. Stein, *The Eclipse of Community* (Princeton: Princeton University Press, 1960).
10. Nicholas Babchuk and C. Wayne Gordon, *The Voluntary Association in the Slum*, University of Nebraska Studies, No. 27 (Lincoln: University of Nebraska, 1962); William F. Whyte, *Street Corner Society* (Chicago: University of Chicago Press, 1943); Herbert J. Gans, *The Urban Villagers* (New York: Free Press of Glencoe, 1962).
11. Harvey W. Zorbaugh, *The Gold Coast and the Slum* (Chicago: University of Chicago Press, 1929).
12. In fairness to the early Chicago sociologists, we must recognize that certain researchers did perceive recurrent social patterns within the urban slum; see, for example, Nels Anderson, *The Hobo* (Chicago: University of Chicago Press, (1923).
13. Daniel R. Miller and Guy E. Swanson, *The Changing American Parent* (New York: Wiley, 1958).
14. Oscar Lewis, "Urbanization Without Breakdown: A Case Study," *Scientific Monthly*, 75 (1952), pp. 31–41. At the same time, life in the urban slum in Mexico City may exhibit considerable instability; see Oscar Lewis, *The Children of Sanchez* (New York: Random House, 1961).
15. A. L. Epstein, *Politics in an Urban African Community* (Manchester: Manchester University Press, 1958); Aidan Southall (Ed.), *Social Change in Modern Africa* (London: Oxford University Press, 1961); Peter Marris, *Family and Social Change in an African City* (Evanston: Northwestern University Press, 1962).
16. Roger Le Tourneau, *Fès: Avant le Protectorat* (Casablanca: Société Marocaine de Librairie et d'Edition, 1949); Horace Miner, *The Primitive City of Timbuctoo* (Princeton: Princeton University Press, 1963).
17. See Robert Redfield, *Peasant Society and Culture* (Chicago: University of Chicago Press, 1956). Actually, in one of his articles, written with Milton Singer, "The Cultural Role of Cities," *Economic Development and Cultural Change*, 3 (1954), pp. 53–73, Redfield implicitly abandons the notion that the city is the key independent variable.
18. K. M. Kapadia, "Rural Family Patterns: A Study of Urban-Rural Relations," *Sociological Bulletin*, 5 (1956), p. 119; S. C. Dube, *Indian Village* (Ithaca: Cornell University Press, 1955), p. 133. Other deviations from American urban-rural differences occur in family patterns in India. There appear to be rather insignificant urban-rural differentials in the total number of children born to women who were married during 1930–1939; see Philip M. Hauser (Ed.), *Urbanization in Asia and the Far East* (Calcutta: UNESCO, 1957), pp. 117–118.
19. Henri Pirenne, *Medieval Cities* (Princeton: Princeton University Press, 1925).
20. The study of rural-urban differences has generated a vast literature, and much research will no doubt be carried out along these lines in modernizing societies. See Michael Kenny, *A Spanish Tapestry* (Bloomington: Indiana University Press, 1962), and R. D. Lambert, "The Impact of Urban Society Upon Village Life," in Roy Turner (Ed.), *India's Urban Future* (Berkeley: University of California Press, 1962), pp. 117–140. In fact, such studies still have significance: consider the rural-urban differences in industrial societies, as exemplified in Otis Dudley Duncan and Albert J. Reiss, Jr., *Social Characteristics of Urban and Rural Communities, 1950* (New York: Wiley, 1956).
21. Ralph Beals, "Urbanism, Urbanization and Acculturation," *American Anthropologist*, 53 (1951), pp. 1–10.
22. Wirth, *op. cit.*, Redfield, *op. cit.*

23. See Hope Tisdale, "The Process of Urbanization," *Social Forces*, 20 (1942), pp. 311–316; Harley L. Browning, "Urbanization in Mexico," unpublished Ph.D. dissertation, University of California (Berkeley), 1962; Duncan and Reiss, *op. cit.*

24. "Urbanization is a process of population concentration. It proceeds in two ways: the multiplication of points of concentration and the increase in size of individual concentrations." This is the definition set forth by Tisdale, *op. cit.*, p. 311.

25. Kent P. Schwirian and John W. Prehn, "An Axiomatic Theory of Urbanization," *American Sociological Review*, 27 (1962), pp. 812–825.

26. Tisdale, *op. cit.*

27. Robert Ezra Park, "Human Ecology," and Ernest W. Burgess, "The Growth of the City: An Introduction to a Research Project," in George A. Theodorson (Ed.), *Studies in Human Ecology* (Evanston: Row Peterson, 1961), pp. 22–29 and 37–44.

28. Walter Firey, *Land Use in Central Boston* (Cambridge: Harvard University Press, 1947).

29. *Ibid.*

30. Sidney M. Willhelm and Gideon Sjoberg, "Economic vs. Protective Values in Urban Land Use Change," *American Journal of Economics and Sociology*, 19 (1960), pp. 151–160.

31. For example, Amos H. Hawley, *Human Ecology* (New York: Ronald Press, 1950).

32. In oversimplified terms, the researcher who stresses "discovery" analyzes data with an eye to formulating or generating hypotheses. The patterns emerge out of the analysis. See Norwood Hanson, *Patterns of Discovery* (Cambridge: Cambridge University Press, 1958). In "deduction," ideally we have a set of logically interrelated postulates from which hypotheses are derived. We proceed to test the hypotheses, and this automatically involves a test of the postulates. See Karl Popper, *The Logic of Scientific Discovery* (New York: Science Editions, 1961). I refer to Gibbs and Martin's approach as "neo-deductive" because they seem to test their "postulates" directly.

33. Otis Dudley Duncan and Leo F. Schnore, "Cultural, Behavioral, and Ecological Perspectives in the Study of Social Organization," *American Journal of Sociology*, 65 (1959), pp. 132–146; Otis Dudley Duncan, "Human Ecology and Population Studies," in Philip M. Houser and Otis Dudley Duncan (Eds.), *The Study of Population* (Chicago: University of Chicago Press, 1959), pp. 678–716; Leo F. Schnore, "Social Morphology and Human Ecology," *American Journal of Sociology*, 63 (1958), pp. 620–634. The most explicit criticism of the Duncan-Schnore position is Sidney M. Willhelm, "The Concept of the 'Ecological Complex': A Critique," *American Journal of Economics and Sociology*, 23 (1964), pp. 241–248.

34. Otis Dudley Duncan et al., *Metropolis and Region* (Baltimore: Johns Hopkins University Press, 1960).

35. Leo F. Schnore, "Urban Form: The Case of the Metropolitan Community," in Werner Z. Hirsch (Ed.), *Urban Life and Form* (New York: Holt, Rinehart and Winston, 1963), pp. 167–197; Leo F. Schnore, "Social Problems in the Under-

developed Areas," *Social Problems*, 8 (1961), pp. 182–201; Leo F. Schnore, "The Statistical Measurement of Urbanization and Economic Development," *Land Economics*, 37 (1961), pp. 229–245.

36. Some of the assumptions underlying the materialist view of society can be found in A. K. Saran, "The Marxian Theory of Social Change," *Inquiry*, 6 (1963), pp. 70–128.

37. Sidney M. Willhelm, *Urban Zoning and Land-Use Theory* (New York: Free Press of Glencoe, 1962), pp. 25–26.

38. Jack P. Gibbs and Walter T. Martin, "Urbanization, Technology, and the Division of Labor: International Patterns," *American Sociological Review*, 27 (1962), pp. 667–677. Also, Jack P. Gibbs and Walter T. Martin, "Toward a Theoretical System of Human Ecology," *Pacific Sociological Review*, 2 (1959), pp. 29–36.

39. Gibbs and Martin, "Urbanization, Technology, and the Division of Labor," *op. cit.*, p. 677. In light of this general comment, it is interesting that Gibbs and Martin include certain knowledge and *beliefs* in their definition of technology (p. 672). Would not a belief system regarding technology be an ideology?

40. Materialism as a theory should be openly represented in sociology, but to equate it with ecology is likely only to confuse the issues involved.

41. "Gorod," *Bol'shaya Sovetskaya Entsiklopediya*, XII, 2nd ed. (Moskva: Gosudarstvennoe nauchnoe izdatel'stvo, 1952), pp. 172ff.

42. SH.A. Meskhia, *Goroda i Gorodskoĭ Stroĭ Feodal'noĭ Gruzii*: XVII–XVIII vv. (Tbilisi, U.S.S.R.: Izdatel'stov Tbilisskogo Gosudarstvennogo Universiteta Imeni Stalina, 1959).

43. Eshref Shevky and Wendell Bell, *Social Area Analysis: Theory, Illustrative Application, and Computational Procedures* (Stanford: Stanford University Press, 1955); Norbert Lacoste, *Les Caractéristiques Sociales de la Population du Grand Montréal* (Montréal: Université de Montréal, 1958); Surinder K. Mehta, "A Comparative Analysis of the Industrial Structure of the Urban Labor Force of Burma and the United States," *Economic Development and Cultural Change*, 9 (1961), pp. 164–179.

44. Shevky and Bell, *op. cit.*, p. 8.

45. See Amos H. Hawley and Otis Dudley Duncan, "Social Area Analysis: A Critical Appraisal," *Land Economics* 33 (1957), pp. 337–344, and the *Pacific Sociological Review*, 5 (1962), with the debate among Bell and Greer, Van Arsdol et al. and Schnore.

46. Greer, *op. cit.*

47. Lewis Mumford, *The City in History* (New York: Harcourt, Brace & World, 1961).

48. Hawley, *op. cit.*, William F. Ogburn, "Inventions of Local Transportation and the Patterns of Cities," in Hatt and Reiss, *op. cit.*, pp. 274–282. Fred Cottrell, *Energy and Society* (New York: McGraw-Hill, 1955).

49. Ogburn, *op. cit.*, p. 281.

50. Hawley, *op. cit.*, p. 421, italics added.

51. For example, Noel P. Gist, "The Ecology of Bangalore, India: An East-West Comparison," *Social Forces*, 35 (1957), pp. 356–365; Floyd

Dotson and Lillian Ota Dotson, "Urban Central-ization and Decentralization in Mexico," *Rural Sociology*, 21 (1956), pp. 41–49; Emrys Jones, *A Social Geography of Belfast* (London: Oxford University Press, 1960).

52. The difficulties that nonliterate groups face in coping with modern changes can be inferred from the data in Melville J. Herskovits, *The Human Factor in Changing Africa* (New York: Knopf, 1962).

53. Some of these variations can be inferred from David S. Landes, "The Structure of Enterprise in the Nineteenth Century: The Cases of Britain and Germany," Reprint No. 152, Institute of Industrial Relations, Berkeley, University of California, 1960.

54. Weber, *op. cit.*

55. Florian Znaniecki, "The Sociological Approach to Rural and Urban Ecology," *Arbeiten des XIV. Internationalen Soziologen Kongresses*. Bucuresti, Mitteilungen, Abeilung D.—Stadt und Land, I (1939?), pp. 147–166.

56. William L. Kolb, "The Social Structure and Function of Cities," *Economic Development and Cultural Change*, 3 (1954), pp. 3–46.

57. Firey, *op. cit.*

58. Willhelm, *Urban Zoning and Land-Use Theory*, *op. cit.*, *passim*.

59. Robert E. Dickinson, *The West European City* (London: Routledge and Kegan Paul, 1951); G. E. von Grunebaum, *Islam* (Menasha: American Anthropological Association, Memoir No. 81, 1955). Chap. 8; Jones, *op. cit.* Also, Jack C. Fisher, "The Continuity of Urban Patterns Under Socialism," Ann Arbor: University Microfilms, 1962. Fisher clearly demonstrates the importance of tradition in determining land-use patterns in Yugoslavian cities.

60. Max Weber, *The Protestant Ethic and the Spirit of Capitalism* (London: George Allen and Unwin, 1930). Cf. Robert N. Bellah, *Tokugawa Religion* (New York: Free Press of Glencoe, 1957).

61. See C. Snouck Hurgronje, *Mekka in the Latter Part of the Nineteenth Century*, trans. by J. H. Monahan (London: Luzac, 1931).

62. Editors of Fortune, *The Exploding Metropolis* (Garden City: Doubleday, 1958).

• 63. Paul Meadows, "The Urbanists: Profiles of Professional Ideologies," *1963 Yearbook, School of Architecture* (Syracuse: Syracuse University, forthcoming). Also see Jane Jacobs, *The Death and Life of Great American Cities* (New York: Random House, 1961), and the controversies surrounding this work.

➤ 64. Harold Orlans, *Stevenage* (London: Routledge & Kegan Paul, 1952).

65. Marris, *op. cit.* For example, Marris observes that one argument for slum clearance was that "Central Lagos was the heart of the Federal capital, and its development was urgent for the sake of national pride" (p. 90).

66. See Fisher's discussion, *op. cit.*, of the impact of the Communist ideology and value system upon the older cities of Yugoslavia.

67. Values have constituted the key independent variable in the works of Weber, Parsons, Soro-kin, and many others.

68. Edward Shils, "Primordial, Personal, Sacred and Civil Ties," *British Journal of Sociology*, 8 (1957), pp. 130–145.

69. Talcott Parsons, *The Social System* (New York: Free Press of Glencoe, 1951).

70. William H. Form, "The Place of Social Structure in the Determination of Land Use: Some Implica-tions for a Theory of Urban Ecology," *Social Forces*, 32 (1954), pp. 317–323.

71. Martin Meyerson and Edward C. Banfield, *Politics, Planning and the Public Interest* (New York: Free Press of Glencoe, 1955); Edward C. Banfield, *Political Influence* (New York: Free Press of Glencoe, 1961). In general, the idea of a monolithic power structure, as propounded by Floyd Hunter and others, is of little value for interpreting or analyzing the social structure and ecology of most industrial cities. See Floyd Hunter, *Community Power Structure* (Chapel Hill: University of North Carolina Press, 1953).

72. For example, Leo Kuper et al., *Durban: Study in Racial Ecology* (New York: Columbia University Press, 1958); "Johannesburg Pushes Apartheid Evacuations," *Christian Science Monitor*, August 29, 1956, p. 6; Colin Legum, "South Africa: The West at Bay," *The Nation*, 197 (August 10, 1963), pp. 70–73.

73. Gideon Sjoberg, "The Rise and Fall of Cities: A Theoretical Perspective," *International Journal of Comparative Sociology*, 4 (1963), pp. 107–120.

74. Barrington Moore, Jr., *Terror and Progress: USSR* (Cambridge: Harvard University Press, 1954), Chaps. 2 and 3.

75. Emmanuel Ringelblum, *Notes from the Warsaw Ghetto*, trans. and ed. by Jacob Sloan (New York: McGraw-Hill, 1958); Raul Hilberg, *The Destruc-tion of the European Jews* (Chicago: Quadrangle Books, 1961).

76. For a somewhat different perspective on these matters, see Leonard Reissman, "Class, the City, and Social Cohesion," *International Review of Community Development*, No. 7 (1961), pp. 39–51. Also, William M. Dobriner, *Class in Suburbia* (Englewood Cliffs, N. J.: Prentice-Hall, 1963).

77. More generally, the "phenomenological" orienta-tion of Alfred Schutz may well offer one avenue of escape from the "idealist" vs. "materialist" dilemma. See Alfred Schutz, *Collected Papers, I, The Problem of Social Reality* (The Hague: Martinus Nijhoff, 1962). To Schutz, the "funda-mental reality" resides neither in material objects nor in ideas or concepts (including values) but in the interrelationships between the two.

78. Pitirim Sorokin, *Social and Cultural Dynamics*, Vol. IV (New York: American Book Co., 1941), pp. 165–167.

79. The fact that science and technology are highly cumulative would seem to account in part for some of these patterns. It is interesting that Sorokin, who has attacked the "material-non-material" dichotomy, is forced to admit, in the face of criticism, this special feature of the scientific technological sphere. P. J. Allen (Ed.), *Pitirim A. Sorokin in Review* (Durham: Duke University Press, 1963), p. 427.

80. W. Lloyd Warner et al., *Social Class in America: A Manual of Procedure for the Measurement of*

Social Status (Chicago: Science Research Associates, 1949).

81. Robert A. Feldmesser, "Social Status and Access to Higher Education: A Comparison of the United States and the Soviet Union," *Harvard Educational Review*, 27 (1957), p. 98 Cf. Ellen Hellmann, *Racial Laws versus Economic and Social Forces* (Johannesburg: South African Institute of Race Relations, 1955), p. 20.

82. Shevky and Bell, *op. cit.;* Stuart A. Queen and David B. Carpenter, *The American City* (New York: McGraw-Hill, 1953).

83. The Shevky-Bell procedure can be used in studying cities with appropriate data in other societies. See Dennis C. McElrath, "The Social Areas of Rome: A Comparative Analysis," *American Sociological Review*, 27 (1962), pp. 376–391.

84. Henry S. Shryock, Jr., "The Natural History of Standard Metropolitan Areas," *American Journal of Sociology*, 63 (1957), pp. 163–170.

85. Jack P. Gibbs (Ed.), *Urban Research Methods* (Princeton: Van Nostrand, 1961).

86. Alex Inkeles and Peter H. Rossi, "National Comparisons of Occupational Prestige," *American Journal of Sociology*, 61 (1956), pp. 329–339.

87. For a discussion of typologies, see John C. McKinney, "Constructive Typology and Social Research," in John T. Doby (Ed.), *An Introduction to Social Research* (Harrisburg: Stackpole, 1954), Chap. 7.

88. Popper, *op. cit.*

89. Florian Znaniecki, *The Method of Sociology* (New York: Farrar and Rinehart, 1934).

Urbanism and Urbanization

PART II

This section presents readings which discuss the historical development of urban societies and urban communities, the factors responsible for the emergence of urbanism, and the general characteristics of urbanization and the urban social order in the United States today.

The first group of readings describe the development of urbanization on the world scale. The first cities emerged in the Middle East six or seven thousand years ago, a very short time span given the total history of human societies. They were not much larger than the small villages that one can still find in primitive societies today. By the beginning of the Christian era occasional population agglomerations of 100,000 people had been developed in Greece, in the Roman Empire, and among some of the Indian societies of Latin America. Almost all of these urban communities were independent city-states possessing their own defense, religious, and political systems. Although they were pre-industrial and based on an agricultural economy, none of them could have developed or survived without an economic surplus made possible by the invention of metal and wooden tools and through new systems for administering land and farms.

The modern metropolis familiar to us in Western nations, made up of millions of people and extending its social and economic network over hundreds of miles, is a very recent phenomenon of urbanization, having emerged in Europe and the United States only in the last century. It is heavily dependent on intensive and complex systems of manufacturing, production technology, and advanced systems for distribution and exchange. The absence of this kind of firm industrial base presents serious difficulties for the equally populous but poverty-ridden and poorly organized cities which now are emerging in the underdeveloped nations.

The readings in the second group concern the development of urbanism in the United

States. American urbanization shares numerous characteristics with urbanism in all Western nations, including extensive suburbanization, rapid population growth, the decline of central cities, and tremendous population mobility. All these characteristics are accentuated in this country. The specifically American characteristics include a unique degree of political autonomy for local governments, a system of meeting social demands primarily through the free market mechanism, and a philosophical tradition which looks upon the city as a source of social evil. This combination of rapid growth with "home rule" capitalist economics and an antiurban attitude have given rise to many of the difficulties which American urban communities experience in their relation to the larger society.

Origins and Evolution of Urban Communities and Urbanization

6. The Urban Revolution | V. Gordon Childe

Towns and cities developed six to seven thousand years ago in the Middle East in the rich alluvial valleys of the Nile, Tigris, and Indus rivers. Our knowledge of their social organization, as well as of the similar settlements which developed a few milennia later in Central America, is inferred from remains of buildings and other artifacts dug up by archeologists. V. Gordon Childe, an archeologist himself, discusses ten distinguishing features of this first urban revolution and the technological and agricultural events responsible for its emergence. The features he lists are almost identical with those mentioned by Wirth, except that they exist in more rudimentary form. For example, Childe points out that the formation of cities coincided with the shift from a system of community cohesion based on ties of kinship to cohesion achieved through the functional complementarity of differentiated social roles. However, occupational differentiation in these early settlements was still simple and elementary. As a consequence, cities could flourish only because solidarity based on functional interdependence was buttressed by barbarian ideology and moral beliefs founded in religion and temple worship.

V. Gordon Childe (1892–1957) was Professor Emeritus of Prehistoric European Archeology at the University of Edinburgh and Director of the Institute of Archeology in London, England, at the time of his death. Among the many books for which he is famous are *Social Evolution* (1951), *What Happened in History* (1942), and *Man Makes Himself* (1936).

The concept of "city" is notoriously hard to define. The aim of the present essay is to present the city historically—or rather prehistorically—as the resultant and symbol of a "revolution" that initiated a new economic stage in the evolution of society. The word "revolution" must not of course be taken as denoting a sudden violent catastrophe; it is here used for

From *The Town Planning Review*, XXI, 1 (April 1950), pp. 3–17.

the culmination of a progressive change in the economic structure and social organization of communities that caused, or was accompanied by, a dramatic increase in the population affected—an increase that would appear as an obvious bend in the population graph were vital statistics available. Just such a bend is observable at the time of the Industrial Revolution in England. Though not demonstrable statistically, comparable changes of direction must have occurred at two earlier points in the demographic history of Britain and other regions. Though perhaps less sharp and less durable, these too should indicate equally revolutionary changes in economy. They may then be regarded likewise as marking transitions between stages in economic and social development.

Sociologists and ethnographers last century classified existing pre-industrial societies in a hierarchy of three evolutionary stages, denominated respectively "savagery," "barbarism" and "civilisation." If they be defined by suitably selected criteria, the logical hierarchy of stages can be transformed into a temporal sequence of ages, proved archaeologically to follow one another in the same order wherever they occur. Savagery and barbarism are conveniently recognized and appropriately defined by the methods adopted for procuring food. Savages live exclusively on wild food obtained by collecting, hunting or fishing. Barbarians on the contrary at least supplement these natural resources by cultivating edible plants and—in the Old World north of the Tropics—also by breeding animals for food.

Throughout the Pleistocene Period—the Palaeolithic Age of archaeologists—all known human societies were savage in the foregoing sense, and a few savage tribes have survived in out of the way parts to the present day. In the archaeological record barbarism began less than ten thousand years ago with the Neolithic Age of archeologists. It thus represents a later, as well as a higher stage, than savagery. Civilization cannot be defined in quite such simple terms. Etymologically the word is connected with "city," and sure enough life in cities begins with this stage. But "city" is itself ambiguous so archaeologists like to use "writing" as a criterion of civilization; it should be easily recognizable and proves to be a reliable index to more profound characters. Note, however, that, because a people is said to be civilized or literate, it does not follow that all its members can read and write, nor that they all lived in cities. Now there is no recorded instance of a community of savages civilizing themselves, adopting urban life or inventing a script. Wherever cities have been built, villages of preliterate farmers existed previously (save perhaps where an already civilized people have colonized uninhabited tracts). So civilization, wherever and whenever it arose, succeeded barbarism.

We have seen that a revolution as here defined should be reflected in the population statistics. In the case of the Urban Revolution the increase was mainly accounted for by the multiplication of the numbers of persons living together, i.e., in a single built-up area. The first cities represented settlement units of hitherto unprecedented size. Of course it was not just their size that constituted their distinctive character. We shall find that by modern standards they appeared ridiculously small and we might meet agglomerations of population today to which the name city would have to be refused. Yet a certain size of settlement and density of population is an essential feature of civilization.

Now the density of population is determined by the food supply which in turn is limited by natural resources, the techniques for their exploitation and the means of transport and food-preservation available. The last factors have proved to be variables in the course of human history, and the technique of obtaining food has already been used to distinguish the consecutive stages termed savagery and barbarism. Under the gathering economy of savagery population was always exceedingly sparse. In aboriginal America the carrying capacity of normal unimproved land seems to have been from .05 to .10 per square mile. Only under exceptionally favourable conditions did the fishing tribes of the Northwest Pacific coast attain densities of over one human to the square mile. As far as we can guess from the extant remains, population densities in palaeolithic and pre-neolithic Europe were less than the normal American. Moreover such hunters and collectors usually live in small roving bands. At best several bands may come together for quite brief periods on ceremonial occasions such as the Australian corroborrees. Only in exceptionally favoured regions can fishing tribes establish anything like villages. Some settlements on the Pacific coasts comprised thirty or so substantial and durable houses, accommodating groups of several hundred persons. But even these villages were only occupied during the winter; for the rest of the year their inhabitants dispersed in smaller groups. Nothing comparable has been found in pre-neolithic times in the Old World.

The Neolithic Revolution certainly allowed an expansion of population and enormously increased the carrying capacity of suitable land. On the Pacific Islands neolithic societies today attain a density of 30 or more persons to the square mile.

In pre-Columbian North America, however, where the land is not obviously restricted by surrounding seas, the maximum density recorded is just under 2 to the square mile.

Neolithic farmers could of course, and certainly did, live together in permanent villages, though, owing to the extravagant rural economy generally practised, unless the crops were watered by irrigation, the villages had to be shifted at least every twenty years. But on the whole the growth of population was not reflected so much in the enlargement of the settlement unit as in a multiplication of settlements. In ethnography neolithic villages can boast only a few hundred inhabitants (a couple of "pueblos" in New Mexico house over a thousand, but perhaps they cannot be regarded as neolithic). In prehistoric Europe the largest neolithic village yet known, Barkaer in Jutland, comprised 52 small, one-roomed dwellings, but 16 to 30 houses was a more normal figure; so the average local group in neolithic times would average 200 to 400 members.

These low figures are of course the result of technical limitations. In the absence of wheeled vehicles and roads for the transport of bulky crops men had to live within easy walking distance of their cultivations. At the same time the normal rural economy of the Neolithic Age, what is now termed slash-and-burnt or jhumming, condemns much more than half the arable land to lie fallow so that large areas were required. As soon as the population of a settlement rose above the numbers that could be supported from the accessible land, the excess had to hive off and found a new settlement.

The Neolithic Revolution had other consequences beside increasing the population, and their exploitation might in the end help to provide for the surplus increase.

The new economy allowed, and indeed required, the farmer to produce every year more food than was needed to keep him and his family alive. In other words it made possible the regular production of a social surplus. Owing to the low efficiency of neolithic technique, the surplus produced was insignificant at first, but it could be increased till it demanded a reorganization of society.

Now in any Stone Age society, palaeolithic or neolithic, savage or barbarian, everybody can at least in theory make at home the few indispensable tools, the modest cloths and the simple ornaments everyone requires. But every member of the local community, not disqualified by age, must contribute actively to the communal food supply by personally collecting, hunting, fishing, gardening or herding. As long as this holds good, there can be no full-time specialists, no persons nor class of persons who depend for their livelihood on food produced by others and secured in exchange for material or immaterial goods or services.

We find indeed to day among Stone Age barbarians and even savages expert craftsmen (for instance flint-knappers among the Ona of Tierra del Fuego), men who claim to be experts in magic, and even chiefs. In palaeolithic Europe too there is some evidence for magicians and indications of chieftainship in pre-neolithic times. But on closer observation we discover that today these experts are not full-time specialists. The Ona flintworker must spend most of his time hunting; he only adds to his diet and his prestige by making arrowheads for clients who reward him with presents. Similarly a pre-Columbian chief, though entitled to customary gifts and services from his followers, must still personally lead hunting and fishing expeditions and indeed could only maintain his

authority by his industry and prowess in these pursuits. The same holds good of barbarian societies that are still in the neolithic stage, like the Polynesians where industry in gardening takes the place of prowess in hunting. The reason is that there simply would not be enough food to go round unless every member of the group contributes to the supply. The social surplus is not big enough to feed idle mouths.

Social division of labour, save those rudiments imposed by age and sex, is thus impossible. On the contrary community of employment, the common absorbtion in obtaining food by similar devices guarantees a certain solidarity to the group. For cooperation is essential to secure food and shelter and for defence against foes, human and subhuman. This identity of economic interests and pursuits is echoed and magnified by identity of language, custom and belief; rigid conformity is enforced as effectively as industry in the common quest for food. But conformity and industrious cooperation need no State organization to maintain them. The local group usually consists either of a single clan (persons who believe themselves descended from a common ancestor or who have earned a mystical claim to such descent by ceremonial adoption) or a group of clans related by habitual intermarriage. And the sentiment of kinship is reinforced or supplemented by common rites focused on some ancestral shrine or sacred place. Archaeology can provide no evidence for kinship organization, but shrines occupied the central place in preliterate villages in Mesopotamia, and the long barrow, a collective tomb that overlooks the presumed site of most neolithic villages in Britain, may well have been also the ancestral shrine on which converged the emotions and ceremonial activities of the villagers below. However, the solidarity thus idealized and concretely symbolized, is really based on the same principles as that of a pack of wolves or a herd of sheep; Durkheim has called it "mechanical."

Now among some advanced barbarians (for instance tattooers or woodcarvers among the Maori) still technologically neolithic we find expert craftsmen tending towards the status of full-time professionals, but only at the cost of breaking away from the local community. If no single village can produce a surplus large enough to feed a full-time specialist all the year round, each should produce enough to keep him a week or so. By going round from village to village an expert might thus live entirely from his craft. Such itinerants will lose their membership of the sedentary kinship group. They may in the end form an analogous organization of their own—a craft clan, which, if it remain hereditary, may become a caste, or, if it recruit its members mainly by adoption (apprenticeship throughout Antiquity and the Middle Age was just temporary adoption), may turn into a guild. But such specialists, by emancipation from kinship ties, have also forfeited the protection of the kinship organization which alone under barbarism, guaranteed to its members security of person and property. Society must be reorganized to accommodate and protect them.

In pre-history specialization of labour presumably began with similar itinerant experts. Archaeological proof is hardly to be expected, but in ethnography metalworkers are nearly always full time specialists. And in Europe at the beginning of the Bronze Age metal seems to have been worked and purveyed by perambulating smiths who seem to have functioned like tinkers and other itinerants of much more

recent times. Though there is no such positive evidence, the same probably happened in Asia at the beginning of metallurgy. There must of course have been in addition other specialist craftsmen whom, as the Polynesian example warns us, archaeologists could not recognize because they worked in perishable materials. One result of the Urban Revolution will be to rescue such specialists from nomadism and to guarantee them security in a new social organization.

About 5,000 years ago irrigation cultivation (combined with stockbreeding and fishing) in the valleys of the Nile, the Tigris-Euphrates and the Indus had begun to yield a social surplus, large enough to support a number of resident specialists who were themselves released from food-production. Water-transport, supplemented in Mesopotamia and the Indus valley by wheeled vehicles and even in Egypt by pack animals, made it easy to gather food stuffs at a few centres. At the same time dependence on river water for the irrigation of the crops restricted the cultivable areas while the necessity of canalizing the waters and protecting habitations against annual floods encouraged the aggregation of population. Thus arose the first cities—units of settlement ten times as great as any known neolithic village. It can be argued that all cities in the old world are offshoots of those of Egypt, Mesopotamia and the Indus basin. So the latter need not be taken into account if a minimum definition of civilization is to be inferred from a comparison of its independent manifestations.

But some three millennia later cities arose in Central America, and it is impossible to prove that the Mayas owed anything directly to the urban civilizations of the Old World. Their achievements must therefore be taken into account in our comparison, and their inclusion seriously complicates the task of defining the essential preconditions for the Urban Revolution. In the Old World the rural economy which yielded the surplus was based on the cultivation of cereals combined with stockbreeding. But this economy had been made more efficient as a result of the adoption of irrigation (allowing cultivation without prolonged fallow periods) and of important inventions and discoveries—metallurgy, the plough, the sailing boat and the wheel. None of these devices was known to the Mayas; they bred no animals for milk or meat; though they cultivated the cereal maize, they used the same sort of slash-and-burn method as neolithic farmers in prehistoric Europe or in the Pacific Islands today. Hence the minimum definition of a city, the greatest factor common to the Old World and the New will be substantially reduced and impoverished by the inclusion of the Maya. Nevertheless ten rather abstract criteria, all deducible from archaeological data, serve to distinguish even the earliest cities from any older or contemporary village.

(1) In point of size the first cities must have been more extensive and more densely populated than any previous settlements, although considerably smaller than many villages today. It is indeed only in Mesopotamia and India that the first urban populations can be estimated with any confidence or precision. There excavation has been sufficiently extensive and intensive to reveal both the total area and the density of building in sample quarters and in both respects has disclosed significant agreement with the less industrialized Oriental cities today. The population of Sumerian cities, thus calculated, ranged between 7,000 and 20,000; Harappa and Mohenjo-daro in the Indus valley must have approximated to the higher figure. We can only infer that Egyptian and Maya cities were of comparable magnitude from the scale of public works, presumably executed by urban populations.

(2) In composition and function the urban population already differed from that of any village. Very likely indeed most citizens were still also peasants, harvesting the lands and waters adjacent to the city. But all cities must have accommodated in addition classes who did not themselves procure their own food by agriculture, stockbreeding, fishing or collecting—full-time specialist craftsmen, transport workers, merchants, officials and priests. All these were of course supported by the surplus produced by the peasants living in the city and in dependent villages, but they did not secure their share directly by exchanging their products or services for grains or fish with individual peasants.

(3) Each primary producer paid over the tiny surplus he could wring from the soil with his still very limited technical equipment as tithe or tax to an imaginary deity or a divine king who thus concentrated the surplus. Without this concentration, owing to the low productivity of the rural economy, no effective capital would have been available.

(4) Truly monumental public buildings not only distinguish each known city from any village but also symbolize the concentration of the social surplus. Every Sumerian city was from the first dominated by one or more stately temples, centrally situated on a brick platform raised above the surrounding dwellings and usually connected with an artificial mountain, the staged tower or ziggurat. But attached to the temples, were workshops and magazines, and an important appurtenance of each principal temple was a great granary.

Harappa, in the Indus basin, was dominated by an artificial citadel, girt with a massive rampart of kiln-baked bricks, containing presumably a palace and immediately overlooking an enormous granary and the barracks of artizans. No early temples nor palaces have been excavated in Egypt, but the whole Nile valley was dominated by the gigantic tombs of the divine pharaohs while royal granaries are attested from the literary record. Finally the Maya cities are known almost exclusively from the temples and pyramids of sculptured stone round which they grew up.

Hence in Sumer the social surplus was first effectively concentrated in the hands of a god and stored in his granary. That was probably true in Central America while in Egypt the pharaoh (king) was himself a god. But of course the imaginary deities were served by quite real priests who, besides celebrating elaborate and often sanguinary rites in their honour, administered their divine masters' earthly estates. In Sumer indeed the god very soon, if not even before the revolution, shared his wealth and power with a mortal viceregent, the "City-King," who acted as civil ruler and leader in war. The divine pharaoh was naturally assisted by a whole hierarchy of officials.

(5) All those not engaged in food-production were of course supported in the first instance by the surplus accumulated in temple or royal granaries and were thus dependent on temple or court. But naturally priests, civil and military leaders and officials absorbed a major share of the concentrated surplus and thus formed a "ruling class." Unlike a palaeolithic magician or a neolithic chief, they were, as an Egyptian scribe actually put it, "exempt from all manual tasks." On the other hand, the lower classes were not only

guaranteed peace and security, but were relieved from intellectual tasks which many find more irksome than any physical labour. Besides reassuring the masses that the sun was going to rise next day and the river would flood again next year (people who have not five thousand years of recorded experience of natural uniformities behind them are really worried about such matters!), the ruling classes did confer substantial benefits upon their subjects in the way of planning and organization.

(6) They were in fact compelled to invent systems of recording and exact, but practically useful, sciences. The mere administration of the vast revenues of a Sumerian temple or an Egyptian pharaoh by a perpetual corporation of priests or officials obliged its members to devise conventional methods of recording that should be intelligible to all their colleagues and successors, that is, to invent systems of writing and numeral notation. Writing is thus a significant, as well as a convenient, mark of civilization. But while writing is a trait common to Egypt, Mesopotamia, the Indus valley and Central America, the characters themselves were different in each region and so were the normal writing materials—papyrus in Egypt, clay in Mesopotamia. The engraved seals or stelae that provide the sole extant evidence for early Indus and Maya writing, no more represent the normal vehicles for the scripts than do the comparable documents from Egypt and Sumer.

(7) The invention of writing—or shall we say the inventions of scripts—enabled the leisured clerks to proceed to the elaboration of exact and predictive sciences—arithmetic, geometry and astronomy. Obviously beneficial and explicitly attested by the Egyptian and Maya documents was the correct determination of

the tropic year and the creation of a calendar. For it enabled the rulers to regulate successfully the cycle of agricultural operations. But once more the Egyptian, Maya and Babylonian calendars were as different as any systems based on a single natural unit could be. Calendrical and mathematical sciences are common features of the earliest civilizations and they too are corollaries of the archaeologists' criterion, writing.

(8) Other specialists, supported by the concentrated social surplus, gave a new direction to artistic expression. Savages even in palaeolithic times had tried, sometimes with astonishing success, to depict animals and even men as they saw them— concretely and naturalistically. Neolithic peasants never did that; they hardly ever tried to represent natural objects, but preferred to symbolize them by abstract geometrical patterns which at most may suggest by a few traits a fantastical man or beast or plant. But Egyptian, Sumerian, Indus and Maya artist-craftsmen—full-time sculptors, painters, or seal-engravers —began once more to carve, model or draw likenesses of persons or things, but no longer with the naive naturalism of the hunter, but according to conceptualized and sophisticated styles which differ in each of the four urban centres.

(9) A further part of the concentrated social surplus was used to pay for the importation of raw materials, needed for industry or cult and not available locally. Regular "foreign" trade over quite long distances was a feature of all early civilizations and, though common enough among barbarians later, is not certainly attested in the Old World before 3,000 B.C. nor in the New before the Maya "empire." Thereafter regular trade extended from Egypt at least as far as Byblos on the Syrian coast while Meso-potamia was related by commerce with the Indus valley. While the objects of international trade were at first mainly "luxuries," they already included industrial materials, in the Old World notably metal the place of which in the New was perhaps taken by obsidian. To this extent the first cities were dependent for vital materials on long distance trade as no neolithic village ever was.

(10) So in the city, specialist craftsmen were both provided with raw materials needed for the employment of their skill and also guaranteed security in a State organization based now on residence rather than kinship. Itinerancy was no longer obligatory. The city was a community to which a craftsman could belong politically as well as economically.

Yet in return for security they became dependent on temple or court and were relegated to the lower classes. The peasant masses gained even less material advantages; in Egypt for instance metal did not replace the old stone and wood tools for agricultural work. Yet, however imperfectly, even the earliest urban communities must have been held together by a sort of solidarity missing from any neolithic village. Peasants, craftsmen, priests and rulers form a community, not only by reason of identity of language and belief, but also because each performs mutually complementary functions, needed for the well-being (as redefined under civilization) of the whole. In fact the earliest cities illustrate a first approximation to an organic solidarity based upon a functional complementarity and interdependence between all its members such as subsist between the constituent cells of an organism. Of course this was only a very distant approximation. However necessary the concentration of the surplus really were with the existing forces of production, there seemed a glaring conflict on economic interests between the tiny ruling class, who annexed the bulk of the social surplus, and the vast majority who were left with a bare subsistence and effectively excluded from the spiritual benefits of civilization. So solidarity had still to be maintained by the ideological devices appropriate to the mechanical solidarity of barbarism as expressed in the pre-eminence of the temple or the sepulchral shrine, and now supplemented by the force of the new State organization. There could be no room for sceptics or sectaries in the oldest cities.

These ten traits exhaust the factors common to the oldest cities that archaeology, at best helped out with fragmentary and often ambiguous written sources, can detect. No specific elements of town planning for example can be proved characteristic of all such cities; for on the one hand the Egyptian and Maya cities have not yet been excavated; on the other neolithic villages were often walled, an elaborate system of sewers drained the Orcadian hamlet of Skara Brae; two-storeyed houses were built in pre-Columbian *pueblos*, and so on.

The common factors are quite abstract. Concretely Egyptian, Sumerian, Indus and Maya civilizations were as different as the plans of their temples, the signs of their scripts and their artistic conventions. In view of this divergence and because there is so far no evidence for a temporal priority of one Old World centre (for instance, Egypt) over the rest nor yet for contact between Central America and any other urban centre, the four revolutions just considered may be regarded as mutually independent. On the contrary, all later civilizations in the Old World may in a sense be regarded as lineal descendants of those of Egypt, Mesopotamia or the Indus.

But this was not a case of like producing like. The maritime civilizations of Bronze Age Crete or classical Greece for example, to say nothing of our own, differ more from their reputed ancestors than these did among themselves. But the urban revolutions that gave them birth did not start from scratch. They could and probably did draw upon the capital accumulated in the three allegedly primary centres. That is most obvious in the case of cultural capital. Even today we use the Egyptians' calendar and the Sumerians' divisions of the day and the hour. Our European ancestors did not have to invent for themselves these divisions of time nor repeat the observations on which they are based; they took over—and very slightly improved systems elaborated 5,000 years ago! But the same is in a sense true of material capital as well. The Egyptians, the Sumerians and the Indus people had accumulated vast reserves of surplus food. At the same time they had to import from abroad necessary raw materials like metals and building timber as well as "luxuries." Communities controlling these natural resources could in exchange claim a slice of the urban surplus. They could use it as capital to support full-time specialists— craftsmen or rulers—until the latters' achievement in technique and organization had so enriched barbarian economies that they too could produce a substantial surplus in their turn.

7. The Origin and Growth of Urbanization in the World   Kingsley Davis

Kingsley Davis discusses the continuation of the "urban revolution" into our own era. Adopting a cross-national perspective, he describes the gross movements of people to urban centers and the factors that induced these shifts in population. The focus of his paper is the great upturn in world urbanization that accompanied the industrial revolution of the nineteenth century. Between 1800 and 1950, the rate of urbanization accelerated more rapidly than during any previous period of world history. Since the growth of cities during this era was the product of technological developments in manufacturing rather than in agriculture, it took place in those continents where the machine age struck in its more advanced forms first, namely Europe, North America, and Oceania. Davis suggests that the continued progress in world industrialization will probably result universally in growth on the metropolitan scale already common in the large urban regions of the United States, including the pattern of suburbanization. He notes, too, that the gap between the developing and advanced countries is diminishing. Our rate of urbanization and that of European countries has begun to level off or decline, while in Asia and Latin America the rate has only recently begun to take off and move forward rapidly.

Kingsley Davis is Professor of Sociology and Director of the Institute of International Urban Research at the University of California, Berkeley. He is the author of *Population and Welfare in Industrial Societies* (1960), *Human Society* (1949), and many other books.

Urban phenomena attract sociological attention primarily for four reasons. First, such phenomena are relatively recent in human history. Compared to most other aspects of society—e.g., language, religion, stratification, or the family—cities appeared only yesterday, and urbanization, meaning that a sizable proportion of the population lives in cities, has developed only in the last few moments of man's existence. Second, urbanism represents a revolutionary change in the whole pattern of social life. Itself a product of basic economic and technological developments, it tends in turn, once it comes into being, to affect every aspect of existence. It exercises its pervasive influence not only within the urban milieu strictly defined but also in the rural hinterland. The third source of sociological interest in cities is the fact that, once established, they tend to be centers of power and influence throughout the whole society, no matter how agricultural and rural it may be. Finally, the process of urbanization is still occurring; many of the problems associated with it are unsolved; and, consequently, its future direction and potentialities are still a matter of uncertainty. This paper examines the first and last points: the origin, growth, and present rate of progress of urbanization in the world. Since good statistics on urban concentration do not exist even today for substantial parts of the world, and hardly exist for any part during most of the time since cities have been in existence, we are forced to rely on whatever credible evidence can be found and so can reach only broad conclusions concerning early periods and only approximations for recent times. Nevertheless, it can be said that our information, both statistical and nonstatistical, is much better today than when Adna Weber wrote his classic treatise on comparative urbanization at the turn of the present century.[1]

The Rise of Early Urban Centers

Because the archeological evidence is fragmentary, the role of cities in antiquity has often been exaggerated. Archeologists in particular are inclined to call any settlement a "city" which had a few streets and a public building or two. Yet there is surely some point in not mistaking a town for a city. Moreover, what is important is not only the appearance of a few towns or cities but also their place in the total society of which they were a part. Thus, even though in particular regions around the Mediterranean and in southern and western Asia many towns and a few cities arose prior to the Christian Era, there were severe limitations both on the size that such cities could reach and on the proportion of the total population that could live in them.

Speaking generally, one can agree with the dominant view that the diverse technological innovations constituting Neolithic culture were necessary for the existence of settled communities.[2] Yet one should not infer that these innovations, which began some 8,000–10,000 years ago, were sufficient to give rise to towns as distinct from villages. Even though the Neolithic population was more densely settled than the purely hunting or food-gathering peoples, it was nevertheless chiefly engaged in an occupation—agriculture—which requires a large amount of land per person. The Neolithic population density was therefore not a matter of town concentration but rather a matter of tiny villages scattered over the land.

What had to be added to the Neolithic complex to make possible the first towns? Between 6000 and 4000 B.C. certain inventions—such as the ox-drawn plow and wheeled cart, the sailboat, metallurgy, irrigation, and the domestication of new plants—facilitated, when taken together, a more intensive and more productive use of the Neolithic elements themselves. When this enriched technology was utilized in certain unusual regions where climate, soil, water, and topography were most favorable (broad river valleys with alluvial soil not exhausted by successive cropping, with a dry climate that minimized soil leaching, with plenty of sunshine, and with sediment-containing water for irrigation from the river itself), the result was a sufficiently productive economy to make possible the *sine qua non* of urban existence, the concentration in one place of people who do not grow their own food.

But a productive economy, though necessary, was not sufficient: high productivity per acre does not necessarily mean high per capita productivity. Instead of producing a surplus for town dwellers, the cultivators can, theoretically at least, multiply on the land until they end up producing just enough to sustain themselves. The rise of towns and cities therefore required, in addition to highly favorable agricultural conditions, a form of social organization in which certain strata could appropriate for themselves part of the produce grown by the cultivators. Such strata—religious and governing officials, traders, and artisans—could live in towns, because their power over goods did not depend on their presence on the land as such. They could thus realize the advantages of town living, which gave them additional power over the cultivators.

The first cities, doubtless small and hard to distinguish from towns, seem to have appeared in the most favorable places sometime between 6000 and 5000 B.C. From that time on, it can be assumed that some of the inventions which made larger settlements possible were due to towns and cities themselves—viz., writing and accountancy, bronze, the beginnings of science, a solar calendar, bureaucracy. By 3000 B.C., when these innovations were all exercising an influence in Egypt, Mesopotamia, and India, there were in existence what may be called "true" cities. After that there appears to have been, for some 2,000 years, a lull during which the most important innovations, toward the end of the period, were alphabetic writing and the smelting of iron. Curiously, the cities in the regions where city life had originated eventually went into eclipse, and it was not until Greco-Roman times that new principles made possible, in new regions, a marked gain in city existence. The fact that the greatest subsequent cultural developments did not occur primarily in the regions where the first cities arose suggests that cities are not always and everywhere a stimulant of economic and social advance. Childe admits that, if anything, the first cities had a stultifying effect on cultural progress,[3] due perhaps to the unproductive insulation and excessive power of the urban elite. There is no doubt that the religio-magical traditionalism of the early cities was profound.

Why was there so little urbanization in ancient times, and why did it proceed so slowly from that point? The sites of the earliest "cities" themselves show that they were small affairs. The walls of ancient Babylon, for example, embraced an area of very roughly 3.2 square miles,[4] and "Ur, with its canals, harbors, and temples, occupied some 220 acres; the walls of Erech encompass an area of just on two square miles."[5] This suggests that the famous Ur could hardly have boasted more than 5,000 inhabitants and Erech hardly more than 25,000. The mounds of Mohenjo-daro in Sind cover a square mile,[6] and Harappa in the Punjab had a walled area visible in 1853 with a perimeter of $2\frac{1}{2}$ miles.[7] These were evidently "cities" of 5,000–15,000 inhabitants, yet they were the chief centers for the entire Indus region, an area nearly two-thirds the size of Texas. Less is known about the earliest Egyptian cities, for they were built with mud bricks and have long since disappeared beneath the alluvial soil. Tell el 'Amarna, the temporary capital built much later, about 1400 B.C., perhaps held something like 40,000 people. The wall of Hotep-Sanusert, an earlier capital built about 1900 B.C. on the Fayum, measured 350 by 400 meters[8] and inclosed an area of approximately one-twentieth of a square mile. Thebes, at the height of its splendor as the capital of Egypt about 1600, was described by Greek writers as having a circumference of 14 miles. By a liberal estimate it may have contained 225,000 inhabitants.

To the questions why even the largest cities prior to 1000 B.C. were small by modern standards, why even the small ones were relatively few, and why the degree of urbanization even in the most advanced regions was very slight, the answer seems as follows: Agriculture was so cumbersome, static, and labor-intensive that it took many cultivators to support one man in the city. The ox-drawn plow, the wooden plowshare, inundation irrigation, stone hoes, sickles, and axes were instruments of production, to be sure, but clumsy ones. Not until iron came into use in Asia Minor about 1300 B.C. could general improvement in agriculture be achieved. The static character of agriculture and of the economy generally was fostered perhaps by the insulation of the religio-political officials from the practical arts and the reduction of the peasant to virtually the status of a beast of burden. The technology of transport was as labor-intensive as that of agriculture. The only means of conveying bulky goods for mass consumption was by boat, and, though sails had been invented, the sailboat was so inefficient that rowing was still necessary. The oxcart, with its solid wheels and rigidly attached axle, the pack animal, and the human burden-bearer were all short-distance means of transport, the only exception being the camel caravan. Long-distance transport was reserved largely for goods which had high value and small bulk—i.e., goods for the elite—which could not maintain a large urban population. The size of the early cities was therefore limited by the amount of food, fibers, and other bulky materials that could be obtained from the immediate hinterland by labor-intensive methods, a severe limitation which the Greek cities of a later period, small as they remained, nevertheless had to escape before they could attain their full size.

There were political limitations as well. The difficulty of communication and transport and the existence of multifarious local tribal cultures made the formation of large national units virtually impossible. The first urban-centered units were city-states, and when so-called "empires" were formed, as in Egypt, in the Sumerian region,

and later in Assyria, much local autonomy was left to the subordinated areas, and the constant danger of revolt prevented the extension of the hinterlands of the cities very far or very effectively. It is symptomatic of the weakness of the early cities that they were constantly threatened and frequently conquered not only by neighboring towns but also by nonurban barbarians. Each wave of barbarians tended to rebuild the urban centers and to become agricultural and sedentary, only to be eventually overwhelmed in turn by new invaders. Other limiting factors were the lack of scientific medicine (which made urban living deadly), the fixity of the peasant on the land (which minimized rural-urban migration), the absence of large-scale manufacturing (which would have derived more advantage from urban concentration than did handicraft), the bureaucratic control of the peasantry (which stifled free trade in the hinterland), and the traditionalism and religiosity of all classes (which hampered technological and economic advance).

The limitations explain why we find, when the sites furnish adequate evidence, that the earliest cities were small affairs, usually no more than towns. Whether in the new or in the old world, even the biggest places could scarcely have exceeded 200,000 inhabitants, and the proportion of the total population living in them must have been not more than 1 or 2 percent. From 50 to 90 farmers must have been required to support one man in a city.

Subsequent City Development

If urbanization was to escape its early limitations, it had to do so in a new region, a region more open to innovation and new conceptions. As it turned out, the region that saw a later and greater urban development was farther north, the Greco-Roman world of Europe, flourishing approximately during the period from 600 B.C. to 400 A.D. Iron tools and weapons, alphabetic writing, improved sailboats, cheap coinage, more democratic institutions, systematic colonization—all tended to increase production, stimulate trade, and expand the effective political unit. Towns and cities became more numerous, the degree of urbanization greater. A few cities reached a substantial size. Athens, at its peak in the fifth century B.C., achieved a population of between 120,000 and 180,000. Syracuse and Carthage were perhaps larger.

The full potentialities of the ancient world to support a large city were realized only with the Romans. Through their ability to conquer, organize, and govern an empire, to put the immediate Italian hinterland to fruitful cultivation, to use both force and trade to bring slaves, goods, food, and culture to the imperial capital, they were able to create in Rome (with the possible exception of Constantinople some centuries later) the largest city that was to be known in the world until the rise of London in the nineteenth century. Yet, despite the fact that Rome and Constantinople came to hold populations of several hundred thousand, they were not able to resist conquest by far less urbanized outsiders. The eclipse of cities in Europe was striking. Commerce declined to the barest minimum; each locale became isolated and virtually self-sufficient; the social system congealed into a hereditary system.[9] When finally towns and cities began to revive, they were small, as the following estimates suggest: Florence (1338), 90,000; Venice (1422), 190,000; Antwerp (sixteenth century), 200,000; London (1377), 30,000;[10] Nuremberg (1450), 20,165; Frankfort (1440), 8,719.[11]

Yet it was precisely in western Europe, where cities and urbanization had reached a nadir during the Dark Ages, that the limitations that had characterized the ancient world were finally to be overcome. The cities of Mesopotamia, India, and Egypt, of Persia, Greece, and Rome, had all been tied to an economy that was primarily agricultural, where handicraft played at best a secondary role and where the city was still attempting to supplement its economic weakness with military strength, to command its sustenance rather than to buy it honestly. In western Europe, starting at the zero point, the development of cities not only reached the stage that the ancient world had achieved but kept going after that. It kept going on the basis of improvements in agriculture and transport, the opening of new lands and new trade routes, and, above all, the rise in productive activity, first in highly organized handicraft and eventually in a revolutionary new form of production—the factory run by machinery and fossil fuel. The transformation thus achieved in the nineteenth century was the true urban revolution, for it meant not only the rise of a few scattered towns and cities but the appearance of genuine urbanization, in the sense that a substantial portion of the population lived in towns and cities.

The World Trend from 1800 to 1950[12]

Urbanization has, in fact, gone ahead much faster and reached proportions far greater during the last century and a half than at any previous time in world history. The tremendous growth in world trade during this period has enabled the urban population to draw its sustenance from an ever wider area. Indeed, it can truly be said that the hinterland of today's cities is the entire world. Contemporary Britain, Holland, and Japan, for example, could not maintain their urban population solely from their own territory. The number of rural inhabitants required to maintain one urban inhabitant is still great—greater than one would imagine from the rural-urban ratio *within* each of the highly urbanized countries. The reason is that much of agriculture around the world is still technologically and economically backward. Yet there can be no doubt that, whether for particular countries or for the entire globe, the ratio of urban dwellers to those who grow their food has risen remarkably. This is shown by the fact that the proportion of people living in cities in 1950 is higher than that found in any particular country prior to modern times and many times higher than that formerly characterizing the earth as a whole.

The rapidity of urbanization in recent times can be seen by looking at the most urbanized country, England. In 1801, although London had already reached nearly the million mark (865,000), England and Wales had less than 10 percent of their population in cities of 100,000 or more. By 1901 no less than 35 percent of the population of England and Wales was living in cities of 100,000 or more, and 58 percent was living in cities of 20,000 or more. By 1951 these two proportions had risen to 38.4 and 69.3 percent, respectively.

Britain was in the van of urban development. A degree of urbanization equal to that she had attained in 1801 was not achieved by any other country until after 1850. Thereafter the British rate of urbanization began slowly to decline, whereas that of most other countries continued at a high level. By assembling available data and preparing estimates where data were lacking, we have arrived at figures on urbanization in the world as a whole,

beginning with 1800, the earliest date for which anything like a reasonable estimate can be obtained. The percentage of the world's population found living in cities is as shown in Table 1. It can be seen that

TABLE 1. PERCENTAGE OF WORLD'S POPULATION LIVING IN CITIES

	In Cities of 20,000 Plus	In Cities of 100,000 Plus
1800	2.4	1.7
1850	4.3	2.3
1900	9.2	5.5
1950	20.9	13.1

the proportion has tended to do a bit better than double itself each half-century and that by 1950 the world as a whole was considerably more urbanized than Britain was in 1800. As everyone knows, the earth's total population has grown at an extremely rapid rate since 1800 reaching 2.4 billion by 1950. But the urban population has grown much faster. In 1800 there were about 15.6 million people living in cities of 100,000 or more. By 1950 it was 313.7 million, more than twenty times the earlier figure. Much of this increase has obviously come from rural-urban migration, clearly the most massive migration in modern times.

In 1800 there were apparently less than 50 cities with 100,000 or more inhabitants. This was less than the number in the million class today and less than the number of 100,000-plus cities currently found in many single countries. By 1950 there were close to 900 cities of 100,000 or more people, which is more than the number of towns and cities of 5,000 or more in 1800.

As yet there is no indication of a slackening of the rate of urbanization in the world as a whole. If the present rate should continue, more than a fourth of the earth's people will be living in cities of 100,000 or more in the year 2000, and more than half in the year 2050. For places of 20,000 or more, the proportions at the two dates would be something like 45 percent and 90 percent. Whether such figures prove too low or too high, they nevertheless suggest that the human species is moving rapidly in the direction of an almost exclusively urban existence. We have used the proportion of the population in cities of 20,000 and 100,0000 or more as a convenient index of differences and changes in degree of urbanization. Places of less than 20,000 also fit a demographic definition of "urban." When, therefore, more than a third of the population of a country lives in cities of the 100,000 class (38.4 percent in England and Wales in 1951), the country can be described as almost completely urbanized (81 percent being designated as "urban" in the English case in 1951). We thus have today what can be called "urbanized societies," nations in which the great majority of inhabitants live in cities. The prospect is that, as time goes on, a greater and greater proportion of humanity will be members of such societies.

The question may be raised as to how such an extreme degree of world urbanization will prove possible. Who will grow the food and fibers necessary for the enormous urban population? The answer is that agriculture may prove to be an archaic mode of production. Already, one of the great factors giving rise to urbanization is the rather late and as yet very incomplete industrialization of agriculture. As farming becomes increasingly mechanized and rationalized, fewer people are needed on the land. On the average, the more urbanized a country, the lower is its rural density.[13] If, in addition to industrialized agriculture, food and fiber come to be increasingly produced by manufacturing

processes using materials that utilize the sun's energy more efficiently than plants do, there is no technological reason why nearly all of mankind could not live in conurbations of large size.

The Regional Pattern of Urbanization

The highest levels of urbanization are found today in northwestern Europe and in those new regions where northwest Europeans have settled and extended their industrial civilization. The figures are as shown in Table 2.[14] Oceania is the most

TABLE 2. PERCENTAGE OF WORLD'S POPULATION LIVING IN CITIES BY REGIONS

	In Cities of 20,000 Plus	In Cities of 100,000 Plus
World	21	13
Oceania	47	41
North America (Canada and U.S.A.)	42	29
Europe (except U.S.S.R.)	35	21
U.S.S.R	31	18
South America	26	18
Middle America and Caribbean	21	12
Asia (except U.S.S.R.)	13	8
Africa	9	5

urbanized of the world's major regions, because Australia and New Zealand are its principal components. North America is next, if it is defined as including only Canada and the United States. The regions least urbanized are those least affected by northwest European culture, namely, Asia and Africa.

The figures for world regions are less valuable for purposes of analysis than are those for individual countries. The latter show clearly that urbanization has tended to reach its highest point wherever economic productivity has been greatest—that is, where the economy is industrialized and rationalized. This explains why urbanization is so closely associated with northwest Europeans and their culture, since they were mainly responsible for the industrial revolution. Of the fifteen most urbanized countries in the world, all but one, Japan, are European in culture, and all but four derive that culture from the northwest or central part of Europe.

The rate of urbanization in the older industrial countries, however, is slowing down. During the twenty years from 1870 to 1890 Germany's proportion in large cities more than doubled; it nearly doubled again from 1890 to 1910; but from 1910 to 1940 the increase was only 36 percent. In Sweden the gain slowed down noticeably after 1920. In England and Wales the most rapid urbanization occurred between 1811 and 1851. Contrary to popular belief, the fastest rate in the United States occurred between 1861 and 1891. Since, as we noted earlier, there has been no slowing-down of urbanization in the world as a whole, it must be that, as the more established industrial countries have slackened, the less-developed countries have exhibited a faster rate. In fact, such historical evidence as we have for underdeveloped areas seems to show that their rates of urbanization have been rising in recent decades. This has been the case in Egypt, where the rate is higher after 1920 than before; in India, where the fastest urbanization has occurred since 1941; in Mexico, where the speed-up began in 1921; and in Greece, where the fastest period ran from 1900 to 1930. Asia, for example, had only 22 percent of

the world's city population in 1900 but 34 percent of it in 1950, and Africa had 1.5 percent in 1900 but 3.2 percent at the later date.

With respect to urbanization, then, the gap between the industrial and the pre-industrial nations is beginning to diminish. The less-developed parts of the world will eventually, it seems, begin in their turn to move gradually toward a saturation point. As the degree of urbanization rises, it of course becomes impossible for the rate of gain to continue. The growth in the urban proportion is made possible by the movement of people from rural areas to the cities. As the rural population becomes a progressively smaller percentage of the total, the cities no longer can draw on a noncity population of any size. Yet in no country can it be said that the process of urbanization is yet finished. Although there have been short periods in recent times in England, the United States, and Japan when the city population increased at a slightly slower rate than the rural, these were mere interludes in the ongoing but ever slower progress of urban concentration.

The Tendency toward Metropolitan Expansion

The continuance of urbanization in the world does not mean the persistence of something that remains the same in detail. A city of a million inhabitants today is not the sort of place that a city of the same number was in 1900 or in 1850. Moreover, with the emergence of giant cities of five to fifteen million, something new has been added. Such cities are creatures of the twentieth century. Their sheer quantitative difference means a qualitative change as well.

One of the most noticeable developments is the ever stronger tendency of cities to expand outward—a development already observed in the nineteenth century. Since 1861, the first date when the comparison can be made, the Outer Ring of Greater London has been growing more rapidly than London itself. French writers prior to 1900 pointed out the dispersive tendency,[15] as did Adna Weber in 1899.[16] There is no doubt, however, that the process of metropolitan dispersion has increased with time. This fact is shown for the United States by comparing the percentage gains in population made by the central cities with those made by their satellite areas in forty-four metropolitan districts for which Thompson could get comparable data going back to 1900. The gains are as shown in Table 3.[17] The difference in-

TABLE 3. PERCENTAGE INCREASE IN POPULATION IN 44 METROPOLITAN DISTRICTS IN THE UNITED STATES, 1900–1940

	Central Cities	Rest of Districts
1900–1910	33.6	38.2
1910–20	23.4	31.3
1920–30	20.5	48.7
1930–40	4.2	13.0

creases, until in 1930–40 the population outside the central city is growing more than three times as fast as that inside the central city. Furthermore, Thompson has shown that *within the metropolitan area outside the central cities* it was the "rural" parts which gained faster than the urban parts, as the percentage increases per decade shown in Table 4, indicate. Clearly, the metropolitan districts were increasingly dependent on the areas outside the central

TABLE 4. PERCENTAGE POPULATION INCREASE OUTSIDE CENTRAL CITIES IN 44 METROPOLITAN DISTRICTS

	Urban Parts	Rural Parts
1900–1910	35.9	43.2
1910–20	30.2	34.5
1920–30	40.6	68.1
1930–40	7.3	28.1

cities, and especially upon the sparsely settled parts at the periphery of these areas, for their continued growth. Thompson showed that, the greater the distance from the center of the city, the faster the rate of growth.[18]

The same forces which have made extreme urbanization possible have also made metropolitan dispersion possible, and the dispersion itself has contributed to further urbanization by making large conurbations more efficient and more endurable. The outward movement of urban residences, of urban services and commercial establishments, and of light industry—all facilitated by improvements in motor transport and communications— has made it possible for huge agglomerations to keep on growing without the inconveniences of proportionate increases in density. In many ways the metropolis of three million today is an easier place to live and work in than the city of five hundred thousand yesterday. Granted that the economic advantages of urban concentration still continue and still push populations in the direction of urbanization, the effect of metropolitan dispersion is thus to minimize the disadvantages of this continued urban growth.

The new type of metropolitan expansion occurring in the highly industrial countries is not without its repercussions in less-developed lands as well. Most of the rapid urbanization now occurring in Africa and Asia, for example, is affected by direct contact with industrial nations and by a concomitant rise in consumption standards. Although private automobiles may not be available to the urban masses, bicycles and busses generally are. Hence Brazzaville and Abidjan, Takoradi and Nairobi, Jamshedpur and New Delhi, Ankara and Colombo, are not evolving in the same manner as did the cities of the eighteenth and nineteenth centuries. Their ecological pattern, their technological base, their economic activity, all reflect the twentieth century, no matter how primitive or backward their hinterlands may be. Thus the fact that their main growth is occurring in the present century is not without significance for the kind of cities they are turning out to be.

Future Trends in World Urbanization

Speculation concerning the future of urbanization is as hazardous as that concerning any other aspect of human society. Following the direction of modern trends, however, one may conclude that, with the industrial revolution, for the first time in history urbanization began to reach a stage from which there was no return. The cities of antiquity were vulnerable, and the degree of urbanization reached was so thin in many societies as to be transitory. Today virtually every part of the world is more urbanized than any region was in antiquity. Urbanization is so widespread, so much a part of industrial civilization, and gaining so rapidly, that any return to rurality, even with major catastrophes, appears unlikely. On the contrary, since every city is obsolescent to some degree—more obsolescent

the older it is—the massive destruction of many would probably add eventually to the impetus of urban growth.

The fact that the rate of world urbanization has shown no slackening since 1800 suggests that we are far from the end of this process, perhaps not yet at the peak. Although the industrial countries have shown a decline in their rates, these countries, because they embrace only about a fourth of the world's population, have not dampened the world trend. The three-fourths of humanity who live in underdeveloped countries are still in the early stages of an urbanization that promises to be more rapid than that which occurred earlier in the areas of northwest European culture.

How urbanized the world will eventually become is an unanswerable question. As stated earlier, there is no apparent reason why it should not become as urbanized as the most urban countries today—with perhaps 85–90 percent of the population living in cities and towns of 5,000 or more and practicing urban occupations. Our present degree of urbanization in advanced countries is still so new that we have no clear idea of how such complete world urbanization would affect human society; but the chances are that the effects would be profound.

In visualizing the nature and effects of complete urbanization in the future, however, one must guard against assuming that cities will retain their present form. The tendency to form huge metropolitan aggregates which are increasingly decentralized will undoubtedly continue but probably will not go so far as to eliminate the central business district altogether, though it may greatly weaken it. At the periphery, it may well be that the metropolis and the countryside, as the one expands and the other shrinks, will merge together, until the boundaries of one sprawling conurbation will touch those of another, with no intervening pure countryside at all. The world's population doubles itself twice in a century, becoming at the same time highly urbanized, and as new sources of energy are tapped, the possibility of centrifugal metropolitan growth is enormously enhanced. If commuting to work could be done with the speed of sound and cheaply, one would not mind living two hundred miles from work. Almost any technological advance from

now on is likely to contribute more to the centrifugal than to the centripetal tendency. It may turn out that urbanization in the sense of emptying the countryside and concentrating huge numbers in little space will reverse itself—not, however, in the direction of returning people to the farm but rather in that of spreading them more evenly over the land for purposes of residence and industrial work. "Rurality" would have disappeared, leaving only a new kind of urban existence.

NOTES

1. Adna F. Weber, *The Growth of Cities in the Nineteenth Century* (New York: Columbia University Press, 1899).
2. V. Gordon Childe, *Man Makes Himself* (rev. ed.; London: Watts, 1941), chaps. v–vi; *What Happened in History* (London and New York: Penguin Books, 1946 [first printed in 1942]), chaps. iii–iv.
3. *Man Makes Himself*, p. 227.
4. Deduced from data given in Marguerite Rutten, *Babylone* (Paris: Presses Universitaires de France, 1948), p. 34.
5. Childe, *What Happened in History*, p. 87.
6. Stuart Piggott, *Prehistoric India* (Harmondsworth: Penguin Books, 1950), p. 165.
7. Childe, *What Happened in History*, p. 118.
8. Pierre Montet, *La Vie quotidienne en Égypte* (Paris: Hachette, 1946), p. 16.
9. Henri Pirenne, *Medieval Cities* (Princeton: Princeton University Press, 1939), pp. 84–85.
10. Pierre Clerget, "Urbanism: A Historic Geographic and Economic Study," *Annual Report of the Smithsonian Institution for 1912* (Washington, D.C.: Government Printing Office, 1913), p. 656.
11. Henri Pirenne, *Economic and Social History of Medieval Europe* (London: Routledge & Kegan Paul, 1936), p. 172.
12. The writer acknowledges with pleasure the collaboration of Mrs. Hilda Hertz Golden in the statistical work on which this and succeeding sections are based. Such work has been done as part of a continuing program of comparative urban research in the population division of the Bureau of Applied Social Research, Columbia University.
13. See Kingsley Davis and Hilda Hertz, "Urbanization and the Development of Pre-industrial Areas," *Economic Development and Cultural Change*, III (October, 1954), 6–26. See also the writer's paper, "Population and the Further Spread of Industrial Society," *Proceedings of the American Philosophical Society*, XCV (February, 1951), 10–13.
14. From Kingsley Davis and Hilda Hertz, "The World Distribution of Urbanization," *Bulletin of the International Statistical Institute*, XXXIII, Part IV, 230.
15. Paul Meuriot, *Des agglomérations urbaines dans l'Europe contemporaine* (Paris: Bélin Frères, 1898), pp. 249–78. Literature on the movement of industry and people to the periphery of cities is cited, and a theoretical discussion of the subject given, in René Maunier, *L'Origine et la fonction économique des villes* (Paris: Giard & Brière, 1910), pp. 231–314.
16. *Op. cit.*, pp. 458–75.
17. Warren S. Thompson, *The Growth of Metropolitan Districts in the United States, 1900–1940* (Washington, D.C.: Government Printing Office, 1948), p. 5. The picture is much the same for the rest of the metropolitan districts for decades in which comparability could be established.
18. *Ibid.*, p.9.

8. The Role of Urbanization in Economic Development: Some International Comparisons

Bert F. Hoselitz

A continuing concern of students of urban phenomena is the relative significance of urbanization and industrialization as social processes responsible for the growth of cities and the development of modernized societies. Does increasing population density and migration of farmers and peasants to cities precede the emergence of the factory system and modern production methods, or can urbanization occur in volume only after a nation has experienced considerable industrial progress? Bert Hoselitz investigates this issue by examining the sources of urban growth and economic progress in India and other developing nations today in comparison to similar trends in America and Europe during the nineteenth century. He concludes, first of all, that on the strictly demographic level, India now and our country in the past exhibit comparable rates of urbanization. Second, Hoselitz shows that the migration to cities and the emergence of large urban settlements in developing nations are trends which continue even when the industrial base to support them is lacking. Third, and as a consequence of the independence of industrialization and urbanization, cities in India and other parts of Asia and in Latin America are inhabited by more peasant groups and more often exhibit rural patterns of life than was true in American and European towns and cities a century ago.

Bert F. Hoselitz is Professor of Economics and Social Science at the University of Chicago. He is the author of many books and articles in the area of economic growth, including *Theories of Economic Growth* (1960) and *Sociological Aspects of Economic Growth* (1960). He has also written *A Reader's Guide to the Social Sciences* (1965).

Rapid urban growth is a relatively new phenomenon in India. Up to the end of the First World War some urban growth took place, but neither the proportion of the total population in urban places nor the rate of increase of the urban population itself was startling. With the decade 1921 to 1931, urbanization became a noticeable phenomenon in India, and the rate of urban growth has accelerated with each decade since then. Moreover, the cities and larger towns (i.e., urban places with more than 20,000 inhabitants) have grown more rapidly than those with only quasi-urban features. These trends of urban growth in India during the last few decades are presented in Table 1.

Two facts, above all, should be noted: (1) The percentage variation of the total population living in urban places has been increasing each decade since 1901, and (2) the rate of increase during the five decades 1901 to 1951 in towns with 20,000 or more inhabitants has been almost twice as fast as the rate of growth of all urban places together (i.e., 112 percent as against 59 percent). These data apparently understate the rate of urban growth somewhat, since the Indian census, on which these data are based, does not list population of metropolitan areas, but only of towns and

From *India's Urban Future*, Roy Turner, ed. (Berkeley: University of California Press, 1962), Chap. 8, pp. 157–181. Reprinted by permission.

TABLE 1. URBAN GROWTH IN INDIA SINCE 1881

Year	British India	India (boundaries of 1948)			
	Percentage of urban population	Percentage of urban population	Per cent variation per decade	Percentage of urban population in towns 20,000+	Percentage variation per decade in towns 20,000+
	(1)	(2)	(3)	(4)	(5)
1881	9.3	—	—	—	—
1891	9.4	—	—	—	—
1901	10.0	10.91	—	5.61	—
1911	9.4	10.57	−3.12	5.48	−2.32
1921	10.2	11.38	7.66	6.08	10.95
1931	11.1	12.13	6.59	6.97	14.64
1941	12.8	13.91	14.67	8.88	27.40
1951	—	17.34	24.66	11.89	33.90
1901–51	—	—	58.94	—	111.94

Column 1, Kingsley Davis, *The Population of India and Pakistan* (Princeton, N.J., 1951), p. 127; columns 2–5, Ashish Bose, "The Process of Urbanization in India" (Doctoral dissertation, University of Delhi, 1959), p.167.

town groups, and we may assume that data for metropolitan areas would show a more rapid rate of growth, especially of the larger cities and towns.

A datum which is often selected from these figures is the fact that in 1901 (or 1891) the proportion of the urban population of India was around 10 percent, and that this proportion was roughly similar to the share of the urban population in the United States in 1840. But, whereas in the five decades between 1840 and 1890 the share of the urban population in the United States rose from 10.8 percent to 35.1 percent, in India it rose only from 10.9 percent in 1901 to 17.3 percent in 1951. Hence the rate of urbanization in India was much slower than in the United States, though the parallel is somewhat vitiated by the fact that in India the rate of urbanization accelerated from 1901 onwards, whereas in the United States from 1840 to 1890 it tended to slow down gradually.[1]

The purpose of these comparisons is either to determine the comparative speed of urban growth in India, as against the United States, or to extrapolate from American past experience the future trends of Indian urban growth. But there are a number of reasons why comparisons between the United States and India have serious shortcomings. Culturally the United States and India are very different and it would be difficult to select two countries more different in social structure. The growth of the United States falls entirely in the period of modern capitalism; there are no survivals in American culture of previous feudal or tribal systems of social organization; moreover, though an overwhelming proportion of the American population did live in rural areas in the 18th and early 19th centuries, rural America was at that time culturally an outlying province of Britain and Europe. Even in the early stages of American history, the urban centers played an overwhelming role culturally, and, as Lampard has pointed out, from the very early times the United States had an essentially urban civilization.[2] Finally, and most importantly the growth of American society in the 19th century took place through the settlement of new land. Urban growth was not merely a process of already existing urban centers growing larger; new cities were founded, and this was possible and necessary because of the spatial expansion of the population over previously uninhabited country. The experience of urban growth in countries like the United States, Canada, or Australia is relevant if comparisons are made with Siberia or Brazil, or perhaps even the western portions of China, but not if our concern is with India, a country which in its main outlines has maintained a fairly stable settlement pattern for hundreds and even thousands of years. Moreover, unlike American society, which fundamentally is a modern society, Indian society has roots which go back deep into its past. Though Harappa and Mohenjo Daro are irrevocably gone, we should not forget that Banaras was a principal urban center in the time of the Buddha; that Patna, a state capital in modern India, is located on the site of Pataliputra, the capital of the Magadha empire; and that Delhi, the national capital of India, was once Indraprastha, one of the legendary capitals of the Mahabharata.

Comparisons between India and the United States, whether they deal with historical or contemporary trends, must, therefore, be highly imperfect, because of the profound differences in culture and traditions of the two societies. Similar though somewhat less profound differences exist if India is contrasted with Europe. Europe had a feudal social structure not so long ago, and its society was organized along tribal lines at a time when India had seen the rise and fall of empires which embraced a large portion of the subcontinent. Moreover, in many European countries we will encounter manifold traditions which date back to a time in

which most of the population lived in more or less self-contained village communities and in which the few scattered urban centers, rather than specializing in the production of finished goods and exchange with the countryside, performed mainly administrative functions for surrounding territories. As we shall see later, a wide distance separates the European and the Indian city culturally and administratively. But, in terms of social structure and even in terms of demographic developments, the countries of Europe in the 19th century are less distant from 20th-century India, and hence patterns or urbanization in 19th-century Europe are more appropriate as a yardstick of developments in modern India than corresponding data from the United States.

In Tables 2 and 3 are presented some data on the rate of urban growth in various countries during the 19th and 20th centuries. In Table 2 urban places with more than 20,000 inhabitants are considered, since smaller towns frequently do not exhibit genuine urban characteristics in terms of social structure or even economic specialization. Though in many countries the census authorities have designated much smaller central places as "urban," it was decided to confine our comparisons to places with 20,000 inhabitants or more, in order to avoid differences arising from different definitions of "urban" and "rural," and in order to enhance the probability that only places with genuine urban features would be included.

Table 2 shows that the share of population in these effectively urban places increased in India during the sixty-year period 1891 to 1951 from 4.8 percent to 11.9 percent, or in round figures from almost 5 percent to almost 12 percent. In most European countries the rate of growth was somewhat faster. If we omit from con-

TABLE 2. POPULATION IN CITIES WITH OVER 20,000 INHABITANTS IN SELECTED COUNTRIES (IN PERCENT OF TOTAL POPULATION)

Country	c. 1800	c. 1850	c. 1890	c. 1920	c. 1950
England and Wales	16.9	34.9	53.7	—	—
Scotland	13.9	27.7	42.4	—	—
Ireland	5.9	8.7	15.3	—	—
France	6.8	10.7	21.1	—	—
Belgium	8.7	16.6	26.0	—	—
Netherlands	24.5	21.6	29.4	—	—
Germany	4.6	13.0	21.9	—	—
Prussia	6.0	7.8	23.0	—	—
Bavaria	3.7	6.1	15.8	—	—
Switzerland	1.5	5.4	13.2	—	—
Sweden	3.0	3.4	10.8	—	—
Denmark	10.9	9.6	20.2	—	—
Norway	0.0	4.2	13.8	—	—
Scandinavia	4.1	4.9	13.8	—	—
Spain	9.8	9.6	18.0	—	—
Portugal	10.4	10.6	8.0	—	—
Iberian peninsula	9.9	9.8	15.5	—	—
Austria	4.4	4.2	12.0	—	—
Hungary	2.3	4.6	10.6	—	—
Austro-Hungarian Empire	3.5	4.4	11.5	—	—
Russia	2.4	3.6	7.2	—	—
United States	3.8	9.8	23.8	—	—
India	—	—	4.8	6.1	11.9

For countries other than India, Adna F. Weber, *The Growth of Cities in the Nineteenth Century* (New York, 1899), *passim*; for India, Bose, *op. cit.,* p. 170.

sideration those countries which already had more than 10 percent of their population in urban places of more than 20,000 inhabitants at the beginning of the 19th century, we find that in Germany the rate of population increase in these effectively urban centers during the fifty years from 1800 to 1850 was faster than in India, and that in Austria-Hungary the rate of population growth was about the same as in India, but took only forty years, from 1850 to 1890. Proportions of the effective urban population similar to those in India in 1890 were found in Scandinavia in 1850, and in Switzerland in 1850. In both regions the rate of urban growth was faster than in India during the last sixty years, since in Scandinavia the effectively urbanized share of the population grew to 13.8 percent in forty years, and in Switzerland to 13.2 percent in the same forty years. On

the other hand, the rate of urban growth in Russia was approximately equal to that of India.

Considering the entire experience of European urban growth during the nineteenth century we may conclude, however, that with the exception of a few cases (e.g., Britain, Germany, Belgium and the Netherlands, and, to a lesser extent, France) India's rate of effective urbanization during the last fifty to sixty years follows, on the whole, the same pattern as that established in Europe during the period of incipient industrialization in each country. Thus, although India's urban population in the first half of this century grew at a somewhat slower rate than the urban population of Europe during most of the 19th century, the rate of urbanization in India is not abnormally slow, and is commensurate in general magnitude with

TABLE 3. INCREASE OF POPULATION IN CITIES WITH MORE THAN 100,000 INHABITANTS (SELECTED COUNTRIES, SELECTED PERIODS)

Country	Factor by which population multiplied in cities of 100,000 in 1925			Factor by which city population is multiplied in period cited	
	c. 1815 (1)	c. 1870 (2)	c. 1925 (3)	Period (4)	Multi-plicand (5)
England and Wales	1.0	5.4	12.5	1800–1850	5.3
Scotland	1.0	3.7	6.7	—	—
Ireland	1.0	1.8	3.0	—	—
France	1.0	2.3	4.2	1850–1890	2.8
Belgium	1.0	2.9	7.4	1850–1890	2.3
Netherlands	1.0	1.7	4.8	1850–1890	3.4
Germany (frontiers of 1914)	1.0	3.0	11.8	1850–1890	6.0
Prussia	—	—	—	1850–1890	8.6
Bavaria	—	—	—	1850–1890	4.5
Switzerland	1.0	3.3	10.6	—	—
Scandinavia	1.0	2.3	8.4	—	—
Austria (frontiers of 1914)	1.0	2.7	8.1	1850–1890	3.4
Hungary (frontiers of 1914)	1.0	1.6	4.3	1850–1890	3.2
Russia	—	—	—	1850–1890	3.2
Poland	1.0	2.7	14.1	—	—
United States	—	—	—	1850–1890	7.0
		1901	1951		
British India	—	—	—	1890–1955	6.1
India	—	1.0	2.84	1901–1951	4.9

Columns 1–3 (for all countries except India), Helmut Haufe, *Die Bevölkerung Europas* (Berlin, 1936), pp. 225–226; columns 4–5 (for all countries except India), Weber, *op. cit., passim*; columns 1–5 (for India), *Census of India, 1951*, I, Part II-A, and International Urban Research, *The World's Metropolitan Areas* (Berkeley and Los Angeles: University of California Press, 1959), pp. 47–49, 52.

European growth rates. Moreover, the speed of urban growth in India (as can be seen from column 5 of Table 1) has increased considerably in successive decades, and this pattern again repeats the experience of most European countries. Hence from the purely democraphic standpoint India's progress of effective urbanization shows approximately the same characteristics as the corresponding trends in the various European countries.

In Table 3 are presented some data on urbanization in still larger urban centers, i.e., in places with populations of more than 100,000 inhabitants, which in conformance with Indian practice we will designate as "cities." Table 3 is composed of two parts; the first three columns show

the rate of multiplication of population which at the end point was residing in cities of more than 100,000 inhabitants, and the last two columns show the multiplication of population resident in urban centers with more than 100,000 population at the starting and the final points of the period indicated. In other words, in the first three columns are described the growth rates of cities which ended up with populations of more than 100,000, though at earlier dates some might not have contained 100,000 inhabitants. In the last column we take the population resident at the beginning of the period in all places with more than 100,000 inhabitants and compare it with the population resident at the end of the period in all places having more than 100,000 inhabitants. (The beginning and end dates of the period are given in column 4). On the whole, the two parts of Table 3 show a fairly high concordance; the periods selected for the last two columns of Table 3 are those which showed in each country the fastest rate of city growth as compared with other periods.

Table 3, like Table 2, shows that the demographic trend in India's large cities in the last half-century resembles rather closely that of the large cities in European countries. In the first fifty years of this century the population living in Indian cities which now have more than one lakh population almost tripled. This record compares roughly with that of Belgium, Austria, and Germany in the first half of the 19th century, and exceeds the rate of growth of population of large cities in Hungary, Ireland, and Scandinavia in the same period.

Similarly, the rate of growth of the city population in India during the 20th century does not fall behind comparable growth rates in European countries during the period of their most rapid urbanization. From the sociological standpoint this section of Table 3 is more significant than the first three columns. It shows by what factor the population resident in large cities was multiplied over a period of forty to fifty years. In other words, it shows that in the first fifty years of this century the population of India in cities of one lakh or more population increased almost fivefold, and that in the sixty-five years from 1890 to 1955 this population in the territory of the former British India increased more than six-fold. Not many European countries show such high rates of growth, though in the United States the population in cities of more than 100,000 inhabitants increased sevenfold in the

forty years from 1850 to 1890 and in Prussia the rate of increase in the same period was even more than eight-and-a-half-fold.

These rates of growth are of great significance. Students of urbanization are agreed that, to the extent to which the process of modernization is mediated through urban centers, the larger cities play a more crucial role, and that, in general, the larger a city, the more important is its general mediating function in the process of social change and acculturation. To some extent, therefore, the rapidity with which a country modernizes, or at least with which psychological attitudes favorable to modernization are created, is dependent upon the growth of its cities and especially the large cities. And here the performance of India in the most recent past does not seem to lag behind analogous periods in many European countries; if we add to this, moreover, that urbanization has been increasingly rapid in the last two or three decades (a fact which emerges from Table 1) and may be expected to continue at even higher speed than in the recent past, the gradual development of a larger urban sector in Indian society will constitute one of the important "environmental" preconditions for rapid modernization.

II

We may conclude that on the strictly demographic level the over-all trends of Indian urbanization in the first half of the 20th century show substantial similarities with analogous periods in the urbanization process in Europe. We now shall turn to the consideration of whether the social and economic conditions of the process of urbanization also show analogies, and what similarities and differences in the two processes may appear.

An important difference between European countries in earlier phases of economic development and India at the present is revealed by Table 4. There the approximate distribution of the labor force in eight European countries is presented at a time when the proportion of their population in urban centers with more than 20,000 inhabitants was roughly the same as that of India in 1951. Some of these countries were substantially industrialized, but other countries were chiefly producers and exporters of primary products, as shown in Table 4.

What is important to note is that at a time when the degree of urbanization was roughly the same in these countries as in India now, the share of the labor force in manufacturing was substantially larger than in India in 1951 and the share of the labor force in agriculture was substantially smaller. In more explicit terms, whereas at a roughly equivalent degree of urbanization in the European countries only a little

more than half of the population derived its livelihood from agriculture, more than two thirds of the population derived their livelihood from agriculture in India in 1951; and whereas more than a quarter of the European population derived its livelihood from manufacturing, only a tenth of India's population depended upon manufacturing for its livelihood.

It is, of course, true that precise comparisons of this kind are imperfect, that the classification of the labor force is somewhat arbitrary, and that the differences may be somewhat smaller than shown in the table. But the difference in the relative weight of industry and agriculture is so striking between late-19th-century Europe and mid-20th-century India that even the correction of inaccuracies in classification would not lead to a very substantial change in the picture.

Given the degree of urbanization, the countries of Europe were more industrialized than India is now. The lag in industrial development, as compared with late-19th-century Europe, is not only exhibited

TABLE 4. DISTRIBUTION OF LABOR FORCE AND SHARE OF URBANIZATION (SELECTED COUNTRIES)

| Country | Year | Percentage of working force | | | Percent of population in towns with over 20,000 inhabitants |
		Agriculture	Manufacturing	Services	
Austria	1890	43	30	27	12.0
Ireland	1851	47	34	19	8.7
France	1856	53	29	19	c. 10.7
Norway	1890	55	22	23	13.8
Sweden	1890	62	22	16	10.8
Switzerland	1888	33	45	22	13.2
Portugal	1890	65	19	16	8.0
Hungary	1900	59	17	24	c. 10.6
Average (unweighted)		52.1	27.3	20.6	11.0
India	1951	70.6	10.7	18.7	11.9

Columns 1–3, Simon Kuznets, "Quantitative Aspects of the Economic Growth of Nations, II: Industrial Distribution of National Product and Labor Force," *Economic Development and Cultural Change*, V, No. 4 (July, 1957), Supplement, pp. 77, 82–90; column 4, Table 2 of this paper.

by the lesser degree of industrialization in India's countryside, but also in her cities. A rough composition of the urban occupational structure can be gained from the distribution of livelihood classes among which the urban population is distributed. The Indian census presents eight livelihood classes, the first four of which are designated as "agricultural classes" and include farmers, tenants, agricultural laborers, and landowners. The fifth class is composed of persons depending upon manufacturing, the sixth on commerce, the seventh on transport, and the eighth on miscellaneous services. Only 40 percent of India's total population in livelihood class V resides in cities, and the corresponding figures for livelihood classes VI, VII, and VIII are 60.2 percent, 66.3 percent, and 50.2 percent, respectively. In other words, the majority of persons depending upon manufacturing live in rural areas, as do one half of those depending upon services, two fifths of those depending upon commerce, and one third of those depending upon transport.

If we look at these data from a different standpoint, i.e., from that of the occupational composition of the urban population we find that 25 percent of this population depends upon manufacturing, 20 percent upon commerce, 6 percent upon transport, 35 percent upon miscellaneous services, and the remaining 14 percent upon agriculture and landownership. To be sure, the proportion of population dependent upon manufacturing increases as the size of the city increases, but even in cities of the largest size (i.e., cities with more than 100,000 inhabitants) only 29 percent of the population derives its livelihood from manufacturing, and the proportion of this class declines to 24.9 percent in towns with population of 50,000 to 100,000 inhabitants and to 22.9 percent in towns with 20,000

to 50,000 inhabitants. Similar decreases of a few percentage points with declining city size can be noted in other typically urban occupational groups, i.e., transport, commerce, and other services. In towns with populations below 10,000 inhabitants less than one fifth of the population depends upon manufacturing for a livelihood and more than one third on various forms of agricultural occupations.[3]

In contrast to this, the proportion of persons deriving their livelihood from manufacturing and mining in Germany in 1882 showed the following numerical characteristics; in cities of more than 100,000 inhabitants 47.3 percent derived its livelihood from what the Indian census would call class V livelihood (manufacturing and mining), in towns between 20,000 and 100,000 inhabitants this proportion was 52.8 percent, and in towns between 5,000 and 20,000 inhabitants it was 53.6 percent. In other words, roughly half the urban populations (rather than a quarter as in India) depended upon manufacturing and mining.[4]

In brief, one of the characteristics of India's economy, as compared to that of late-19th-century Europe, is its lower level of industrialization, not only in the rural areas, but also in the cities. This means that urban growth has proceeded with a smaller relative accumulation of industrial capital in urban centers, and this in turn has the consequence that relatively fewer employment opportunities in manufacturing and related occupations become available in urban areas for immigrants to the cities. To this should be added that the external aspects of manufacturing in India and in late-19th-century Europe are also different. We have no comprehensive data on the distribution of persons occupied in manufacturing in India as between plants of different size. But it is well known that a large portion of the Indian labor force in manufacturing is employed in the so-called "unorganized" sector, i.e., in small cottage or handicraft-type shops, employing usually few, if any, employees who are not members of the owner's family. Though this is true of almost all enterprises located in rural areas and small towns, it is also true of a large proportion of enterprises engaged in manufacturing in cities and large towns. Important reasons for the preponderance of so many small-scale enterprises are the very inefficient capital market, the absence or malfunctioning of effective institutions for combining many small capitals into one of larger size, and the over-all low level of saving in the community. These factors tend, moreover, to inhabit the development of many external economies in urban areas which are generally acknowledged to have been important factors in the economic development of Western countries. Moreover, the small size of many industrial firms also prevents the exploitation of internal economies, i.e., economies of scale of production. Thus, the comparatively low level of urban industrialization, combined with the preponderance of many small enterprises in industry, places impediments in the path of economic development in India which were either absent or much less significant in comparable periods in the Western more highly developed countries.

The scarcity of capital and the small size of many industrial enterprises is the result of yet another difference between India and the countries of Europe during their early phase of industrialization. Both in 19th-century Europe and in present-day India a sizable portion of the urban population is composed of migrants. We have noted earlier the very rapid rates of growth of large towns and cities, and it is

quite clear that a multiplication of the urban population by several times in a few decades can take place only because constant sizable migration to the cities occurs. In Europe, capital formation in urban areas occurred with sufficient rapidity so that the new arrivals sooner or later could find employment in industry or associated occupations. To be sure, there were often violent fluctuations in industrial employment due to the business cycle, and, quite apart from this, there was never a smooth correlation between additions to the urban labor force and additions to the urban capital stock providing employment for the newcomers. This means that during the 19th century, when European cities grew so rapidly, there were sometimes prolonged periods of excess labor supply in urban areas; but in the long run the period of European industrialization and urbanization must be regarded as one characterized by a shortage of labor—especially if it is compared with present-day India. In other words, in spite of temporary hardships and misery which new arrivals to the urban labor force may have encountered in 19th-century Europe, in the long run profitable employment opportunities opened up for them.

This, in turn, had the result of creating an open and well-functioning labor market in European cities, and also made possible a substantial degree of upward social mobility through economic achievement. In present-day India these conditions are absent in most cities, or at best present only to a very limited degree in a few. The simultaneous presence of small, cottage-type enterprises and large factories producing similar or identical commodities, but with a much lower net productivity of labor in the former, leads to great variations in earnings between the large, modern plants and the small, more primitive ones.

This disrupts the labor market, and strong tendencies favoring the development of noncompeting groups make themselves felt. This development, in turn, impedes social mobility and at the same time tends to contribute to misallocation of resources and, often, to prolonged unemployment. A fractionalized, internally disrupted labor market exists in many Indian cities not only for unskilled or semiskilled labor, but even for more highly skilled (especially white-collar) occupations; and a portion (though by no means all) of the so-called "educated unemployment" of Indian cities is attributable to the imperfections in the mechanism of allocating human resources.

Compared with European cities during a corresponding period of economic development, the cities of India, therefore, show the following economic features; urban industry is less developed and is characterized by a larger number of small-scale and cottage-type enterprises; the urban labor force, therefore, is made up of a smaller portion of industrial workers, and a larger portion of persons in miscellaneous, usually menial, unskilled services; the urban labor market is fractionalized and composed of mutually noncompeting groups, thus impeding optimum allocation of resources and preventing upward social mobility and relief in the amount of unemployment. All these features make economic development more difficult in India today than was the case in Europe in the 19th century. They also are a cause for the lower level of earnings and productivity in Indian urban occupations.

Why, in view of these relative disadvantages, do urban centers, and especially the larger urban centers, grow at approximately the same pace as did the cities of Europe in the 19th century? Though part of the growth is due to the natural increase of population, we have seen that sizable migration to the cities does take place. Moreover, the bulk of cityward migrants are young males in the early ages of their active working life.[5] There is considerable discussion of whether "push" factors or "pull" factors prevail in inducing persons to move to the cities of India, and this discussion is somewhat repetitive of arguments raised in Europe in the 19th century. I believe that in both cases the proponents of the preponderance of push factors are more accurate, but the actual conditions and developments in rural areas, which tended to push the population out, are different.

The main reason for Indians leaving the villages is the high population density in agricultural regions and the smallness of the amount of land available to cultivators —in brief, the sheer excess of human resources on the land. In Europe there also developed an imbalance between human and nonhuman resources in agriculture, not because of excessive agricultural population density, but because of the rationalization of agriculture and the creation of larger-sized farms. By the end of the third quarter of the 19th century, 74 percent of all farmland in England and Wales was in farms of 100 acres and more. At around 1890, 44.9 percent of all agricultural land of France was in farms of that size, and in eastern Germany between 55 and 60 percent of all agricultural land was in farms of more than 100 hectares (about 250 acres).[6] In other words, in Europe large-scale agriculture was on the rise. The small- and middle-sized grain farmers became increasingly squeezed and turned to the production of specialized crops (wine, vegetables, or fruits) or high-grade foods (meat, dairy products, eggs). This had the result of improving greatly the efficiency of agriculture, and, though the total income of small farmers and agricultural laborers did not catch up with that of urban workers and employees, the rural population did, on the whole, participate in the rising living standards resulting from economic growth. The rationalization of agriculture also caused them to participate in technical progress and the associated rise in the productivity of labor. Thus, the agricultural sector participated fully in the fruits of the industrial revolution, although in many parts of Europe there appeared various lags and leakages in relative farm incomes. Protection was resorted to in order to overcome, at least partially, these frictions. The important point, however, is that not only was more capital applied to agriculture as economic growth progressed, but education spread to the countryside rapidly, communications were swiftly improved, the rural population became increasingly familiar with machines and their operation, and the cultural gap which divided city and country became narrowed.

In India the pressures which are operative on the cityward migrants are of a very different kind from those predominant in 19th-century Europe. Here it is not the modernization of agriculture which leads to a geographical and functional redistribution of the labor force of the country but the sheer pressure of population—the low (and declining) man-land ratio.[7] Some idea of the contrasting pressure of human resources on land, as between European countries in the 19th century and present-day India is presented in a paper which appeared elsewhere and which shows that the countries of northern and western Europe had available roughly from 3 to 5 times as much cultivable land per farm household in the mid-19th century as is available today for each Indian farm household.[8] This means not only that the short-run effects of population growth exerted less pressure on existing agricultural resources in Europe than in India, but also that it was easier to produce and mobilize a food surplus on European farms which could be made available for the urban population. This, in turn, meant that the entire outlook of the European farmer, from the outset of rapid industrialization, could be more directly oriented toward marketing all or part of his crop, rather than producing primarily for his subsistence. Here, again, the most important aspect is not the purely economic one, but the sociocultural one. The greater degree of commercialization of agriculture produced attitudes among the farm population which made them more responsive to fluctuations in relative prices and more receptive to innovations in techniques of agricultural production. Hence European agriculture showed a much greater degree of flexibility in its resource-allocation patterns, and could therefore take part more effectively in the all-pervasive process of economic growth than can Indian agriculture, which today is so largely oriented toward subsistence production.

These conditions determine differences in the reasons for rural-urban migration in Europe and India, as well as differences in the quality of migrants. Though some European writers in the 19th century made much of the socio-cultural rural-urban differences which were presumed to prevail then, these were different from those prevailing in India today, since in over-all attitudes and values the newcomers to European cities and towns were little different from those of the urban population. In India, on the other hand, the cultural impact exerted by the city on the countryside is small, and the attitudes of a large part of Indian urbanites towards educational standards, innovations, capital formation, and entrepreneurship are little different from those of the rural population. In brief, in Europe urban cultural values tended to overwhelm and gradually eliminate those of the countryside. In India we find a small, highly urban sector with very new and modern values, and close beside it a mass of urbanites whose distance from rural culture and social structure is almost nil. It is often said that India lives in her villages. This is true not only of her rural population, but also of a large sector of her urban people.

III

These observations bring us to the third aspect of the role of the cities, their cultural and social impact. It has been shown in the preceding sections of this paper that, although the demographic patterns of urban growth in 20th-century India and in 19th-century Europe were rather similar, the underlying economic conditions accompanying this process of urbanization differed considerably. Social and cultural conditions are associated more closely with economic than with demographic changes, and for this reason it would not be surprising to find that differences between European and Indian urbanization in the sociocultural sphere also are greater than in the demographic field. One of the factors which contributes to this difference is that many of the largest and most important cities of India were foreign creations, imposed upon Indian society from the outside, rather than natural growths within the native social structure. This is not to say that Bombay, Madras, and Calcutta—and other large

cities of India—are not thoroughly Indian today. But the outlook of the urban elite in these and other large centers differs from that of the rural elite and the elite in small towns. And in a country like India, where educated persons are still in a minority, the attitudes and opinions of the elite play a very important role in setting the general cultural framework for a society. The urban elite in the large centers is Westernized, has a European or at least European-style education, often uses English as a language of communication, and is far removed in attitudes and style of life from the peasants and the mass of poorer urban workers. The elite in the rural areas and in smaller towns is less removed from the common people, it speaks one of the vernacular languages, and in its religious practices, its social views, and even its ordinary daily behavior patterns is closer to the masses. To be sure, there are differences in wealth and power between the elite and the common people even in the countryside or the small towns, but the cultural and behavioral gap is narrower and in many instances completely absent. This means that the distance between the dominant ideology in Indian cities and the Indian countryside is great, and that the overcoming of this gap for the newly arrived migrants is difficult, often requiring more than a generation to be accomplished.

This has the consequence that the urban population in India is made up of several layers of differentially "urbanized" persons. In particular, there exist within the confines of large cities considerable sectors of persons who culturally—i.e., in attitudes values, and behavior—are villagers. Some of them have come recently from a village, others may have resided in a city for some time, and still others may have been born there. Since these persons have still a village outlook, they often have not severed their ties with the village. Many of them return more or less regularly to their villages. Even though they were born in the city, some keep alive their interest in property in the village their parents came from and maintain close ties with the extended family, parts of which continue to live in the ancestral home. These groups also have not overcome the general economic outlook of villagers. They are employed as unskilled workers, and they form usually the most poorly paid sector of the population. They have unsteady and irregular employment, a large proportion of them is illiterate, and, in spite of the impact of the demonstration effect upon them, they have patterns of consumption which are little removed from those of villagers.

In Indian cities there are several intermediate groups between these completely village-like "urbanites" and the sophisticated, Westernized members of the metropolitan elites who resemble in many aspects persons in similar social positions in the great cities of the West. These intermediate groups tend to narrow the gap somewhat between the extremes. Moreover, there existed a cultural gap even in the cities of 19th-century Europe. But it was never so wide and so persistent as in India.

Next in importance to the wide gap between urban elite and rural culture in India is the great variety of particularistic groups. Indian society is notably dissected into groups whose behavior patterns, customs, occupations, and even food practices vary. Some of the lines separating these groups are the result of linguistic and tribal differences, but within the linguistic or tribal grouping there are sharp differences of caste, or jati. It is irrelevant for our purposes how this

variety of small caste groups, each with its own rules and norms, has originated— i.e., whether it is the result of fission and segmentation of earlier larger groups or, as Iravati Karve argues, is the result of a process of constant addition and agglomeration of new groups. It is equally irrelevant whether this great variety of small subgroups is the result of some religious or ritual theory or is the outcome of the political heterogeneity and absence of effective political control over large areas in India's history. It is a fact that caste is important in many parts of India, especially in the rural parts; that caste is hierarchically organized; that it tends to establish barriers to free movement and free interaction; and that— in spite of official condemnation of "communalism"—caste still manifests its strength in many fields of social action.

In urban centers, largely through the impact of Western values, but partly also under the influence of economic necessity, the divisive features of caste have become greatly mitigated in many public contacts, but have been largely maintained in private, more intimate relations. Persons of different castes will work together and visit the cinema or theater together, but they will not (or only rarely and in unusual circumstances) visit each other's homes, intermarry, or form close friendships. The migrants who come to the city, and who usually leave behind a strongly caste-ridden society, come into a situation in which their caste relations are ambiguous. They soon learn, however, that in private relationships the ordinary divisions set up by caste are, on the whole, valid also in the city. In more concrete terms, neighbors, friends among whom one may visit, and persons from whom one can receive aid or counsel in adversity or difficulty are normally only persons belonging to the same caste or, at most, a related caste. Hence arrangements for living are made in which the rural settlement patterns are, in part, transferred to the city. In Europe, in contrast, caste never existed. Discrimination in the choice of living space took place there also, but a person could and did move out of certain neighborhoods if and when his economic and social position permitted. Though there is a tendency for this to happen also in India, it is usually possible only for persons in the highest social positions or with relatively great wealth, and many Indian cities, especially many of the smaller cities and medium-sized towns, are spatially comparable to agglomerations of larger and smaller villages rather than to organically inter-related population centers.

There is yet a third sociocultural difference between Europe and India, relating primarily to the cultural tradition of towns and cities. In Europe, at least in western and central Europe, towns very early became independent political bodies. In territories where the central power was weak, e.g., Italy and Germany, the degree of political autonomy of urban centers was high, but it was also in evidence in the more highly centralized monarchies of England and France. The city-state is a European invention, and the city-state was never formally stronger than in medieval Europe. Moreover, the medieval city-state, unlike the ancient city-state, did not arise out of a combination of tribes, but through contract. One of the points forcefully stressed by Max Weber, in describing the uniqueness of the European medieval city, is the fact that its origin is an usurpation of rights by burghers who formed a sworn fraternity, thus exempting themselves from the effective overlordship of some territorial ruler. To be sure, city charters often appeared as grants of a lord, who in this way saved face, but, as Weber points out, the effective instrument in the formation of the Occidental city was the *conjuratio*, the sworn contract by the citizens for purposes of joint protection and defense, even—in extreme cases—against the lord.[9] This resulted in the establishment of an independent government of the urban community which could own property and tax the citizens. It meant that some representative body of the citizens was charged with taking measures for the common defense, that this body could impose laws and ordinances, that it provided for special economic privileges of the citizens, and that it was responsible for the construction of walls and moats and streets and squares —in brief, for public works for and on behalf of the citizens.

Thus, in Europe, urban institutions developed which made for the unified rational administration of the city; city governments developed which had as their function the regulation of relations among citizens and between citizens and strangers; and authorities were constituted which were responsible for the provision of structures and other public works in the common interest of all citizens. Though this cannot be called planning in the modern sense, it was the forerunner of modern city planning. One needs only to look at maps showing the successive extensions of city walls in medieval cities to see that these new walls were planned with the ecological pattern of the entire city in mind; that not only the economic and civic-political needs of the community, but also its recreational and aesthetic needs, were considered.[10]

India never had a tradition of urban self-government of this kind. The Indian cities always were appendages to a court or other administrative center, to a temple or other place of worship or pilgrimage, or to a colony of merchants. To be sure, many of the functions which were performed by European cities were also performed by Indian cities. Just as the preindustrial cities of Europe, so the cities of India had principally governmental or religious, educational or cultural functions, but at the same time were economic centers, i.e., nuclei of trade. Especially the cities newly founded by Europeans were markets, and the victory of the British over the Dutch and French in Bengal ultimately decided the rise of Calcutta. But, although Indian cities functionally performed a role similar to that of the preindustrial cities of Europe, they never had the political and administrative autonomy of European cities, never developed governments of their own, and never created institutions representing exclusively the civic interests of their inhabitants. Even where we have instances of city planning in India—as, for example, in Jaipur or Lucknow—the plan embraces not the city as a whole, but merely a small area around the court or a central area in which the royal palace and the main cult buildings had their site. Ecological planning of the city as a whole is a concept which first was introduced into India with the foundation of New Delhi in 1911.

Let me summarize. When we turn to the sociopolitical sphere and contrast the process of urbanization in India with that of 19th-century Europe, again we find several crucial differences. First, the cultural gap between the dominant city elite and the rural masses is even greater in India than was the case in Europe in its early stages of industrialization. This makes the adjustment problems for city-ward migrants in India more difficult, but it also produces in the urban population an intermediate sector of very im-

perfectly committed urbanites. Secondly, Indian society is much more broken up into mutually exclusive groups than was European society. Class barriers in 19th-century Europe were high and often difficult to surmount, but caste barriers are even more nearly impervious. Though in certain urban roles caste tends to lose its vigor, it maintains itself in others and hence continues to play a divisive role, fractionalizing the urban population—especially in housing and community-living aspects.[11] Thirdly, India has no tradition of urban autonomy and urban independence in administration. Such concepts as zoning or the provision of parks, open spaces, and other public amenities for community use have been absent from Indian thinking and are only now being introduced. Urban finances have, in the past, been deplorable, and urban tax receipts continue to be insufficient even for the installation and maintenance of vital services. Major public works in urban areas, to the extent to which they were undertaken at all, were the result of action not by the citizens or their representatives, but by some ruler or other powerful person who had his residence in a city or town. Indian cities, even in the very recent past, thus have not grown in any orderly fashion, but—like Indian society as depicted by Iravati Karve—by addition and agglomeration.

The result is that Indian cities—even some of the largest ones—show sizable quarters which have preserved their rural character and in which life is carried on under general conditions only little different from those of the village. This in turn is reflected in the style of life and attitudes of that part of the urban population which has not broken its ties with village life and is only partially and incompletely "urbanized." Hence the cultural impact of the "city" in the modernization process in India is exerted upon a population which is culturally and psychologically farther removed from accepting change than was the European population in the 19th century and hence under much less favorable environmental conditions than was the case in Europe. Moreover, whereas the cultural elements produced in the European city were elaborations of already indigenous culture complexes, in India many of the new cultural elements come from a foreign culture. These cultural impediments are added to other obstacles in the path to rapid economic growth in India.

IV

In the preceding sections we have attempted a comparison between urbanization in India today and the process of urban growth in the early stages of European industrialization, and have found that these two episodes show significant differences in the economic and social spheres, though the demographic picture is very similar. In order to round out our analysis of Indian urbanization in a world setting it is incumbent upon us now to examine the similarities and differences that exist between Indian urbanization and this process in other developing countries. Unfortunately, a comparison between India and other developing countries must remain brief and perhaps somewhat superficial. In part this is due to limitations of the available data; even demographic data are scarce and of doubtful validity, and economic and sociocultural data are in even more imperfect state. But in part it is also due to the limitations of this writer, who must rely for comparative material primarily on second-hand and third-hand sources.

The demographic picture, as one might expect, does not differ very much in other developing countries from that of India. The African experience is still very recent; though urbanization has been rapid there, it is mostly a postwar phenomenon. In fact, some African cities have grown in the recent past at a more rapid rate than has been recorded almost anywhere else. It seems that a number of factors are responsible, chief among them the growth of political self-determination and the economic development of the region. Whether and to what extent African patterns of urban growth will ultimately resemble those of other countries, it is as yet premature to say, though some field studies have been made which seem to indicate that in the sociocultural sphere many phenomena familiar from the urbanization process of India and other Asian countries also tend to occur in Africa.[12]

In Latin America, also, the demographic trends of urban growth have been similar to those of India. In fact, cities and towns there have grown even more rapidly. In Venezuela, for example, the proportion of the population in places with more than 20,000 inhabitants was 5.3 of the country's total in 1891. By 1951 this proportion had risen to 31.3 percent. Similar trends were observable in Mexico, Chile, Puerto Rico, and Panama.[13] In Latin America it is also the large cities which have grown most rapidly. For example, whereas in 1940 there were four metropolitan areas with more than a million inhabitants in all Latin America, and another five with 500,000 to one million inhabitants, in 1955 there were eight metropolitan areas with more than a million and another ten with 500,000 to one million inhabitants. Moreover, in 1940 there were altogether twenty cities with more than 200,000 inhabitants in all of Latin America, whereas in 1955 this number had increased to forty-six. Their population rose from 13,423,000, or 10.8 percent of the total population, in 1940 to 36,895,000 or 19.2 percent of the total population, in 1955.[14] This is a very rapid increase, no matter with what other region or period we compare it.

All these data show that during World War II and the postwar period urban growth has proceeded rapidly in Latin America, and that, above all, the additions to the larger urban centers have been even greater than in India. It is interesting to consider whether in the socioeconomic field the Latin-American pattern resembles more that of 19th-century Europe or that of present-day India. In many ways the countries of Latin America are intermediate between those of Europe and those of South and East Asia. Capital is relatively scarce, but not as scarce as in Asia. Average incomes in most countries are several times above those of the countries of Asia, but (with the rather spurious exception of Venezuela) well below those of Europe. The elites of Latin-American countries are Westernized, deriving their culture from that of the Iberian peninsula. The masses in many Latin-American countries are Negroes, Indians or mestizos, many of whom are culturally far apart from the urban upper-class elites. In fact, though caste does not exist in Latin America, the cultural differences between urban elites and rural masses are as wide as those in India and the gap, though primarily one of economic and social class, is as difficult to surmount as that in the poorer countries of Asia and Africa. Some upward social mobility does exist, especially in countries like Mexico or Brazil which have shown rapid economic growth in the last few decades, but, on the whole, the cleavages in Latin-American society have remained as severe as they

were upon the attainment of independence.

Evidence on the socioeconomic impact of urban places in Latin America is scanty. Some of the most perceptive work on sociocultural change in Latin-American cities has been done by Oscar Lewis, who has found, on the whole, a remarkable persistence of rural behavior patterns and attitudes among recently urbanized populations.[15] Lewis's studies have been made mostly among the lower-class urban dwellers of Mexico City. He found, among other things, that peasants who had recently arrived in Mexico City maintained and, if anything, strengthened the extended family ties they had before; religious life become more disciplinary and all pervasive, and their religious outlook, contrary to the preconceived ideas of some urban sociologists, did not become more secular; the use of village remedies and beliefs persisted, and the system of *compadrazgo* remained strong; above all, these recent migrants tended to settle in so-called *vecindades* which tended to become small, socially more or less self-contained communities within the city, enhancing cohesive and personalized ties among their members. Lifetime friendships were established within the *vecindad*, and the daily face-to-face relationships resembled those of a village situation. Most marriages occurred within a *colonia* (a group of neighboring and related *vecindades*), and most members of *vecindad* were related by either kinship or *compadrazgo* ties.

This picture, which has been underlined by Joseph A. Kahl (who also found similar sociocultural relations among recent immigrants and, indeed, large portions of the poorer inhabitants of African cities), seems to indicate that culturally the cities of Latin America have close resemblances with those of India, and that Lewis may not be far wrong when he speaks of a "culture of poverty," i.e., a generalized pattern of sociocultural relation typical of peasants and poor urbanites in the developing countries of Asia, Africa, and Latin America.[16]

Finally, we may ask whether the urbanization process in Latin America (and other developing countries) is associated with economic features similar to those of India. We have seen earlier that the main economic problems arising in Indian urbanization are partly a result of the low degree of industrialization in both urban and rural areas, combined with a dense agricultural population and with a scarcity of capital, which moreover becomes available often only in small, fractionalized amounts. The economic environment in which urbanization in Latin America has proceeded has in part been different. Indigenous capital also is not abundant and, as in India, investment in agricultural land or urban real estate, or even in commerce is preferred, as compared with investment in industry. But population pressure on agricultural resources is less severe than in India, and relatively larger amounts of private foreign capital—mostly in the extractive industries, but during the last few years increasingly in manufacturing—have become available. Much of this capital has come from the United States.[17] Thus, the scale of operations of modernized industry is relatively larger in Latin-American cities than in India. Though many handicrafts and small industries continue to exist, their output frequently is not competitive with that of the modern, more highly mechanized factories; even though small and large plants may be found in the same industry, the output of each tends to find a market among different social or local groups. To be sure, we witness also serious imperfec-

tions in the labor markets of Latin-American cities; we find many aspects of labor-management relations there which are also encountered in India—e.g., a sharp division between blue-collar and white-collar occupations, or a high degree of paternalism on the part of the employers; and we find relatively labor-intensive methods of industrial production.[18] But, whereas the relative backwardness of urban industry in Latin America is the result of the imperfect and partial adoption of a modern technology imposed upon a population which still lacks many of the skills and educational endowments required for its efficient operation, the relative backwardness of urban industry in India is primarily an outflow of the general conditions under which Indian industry functions. Some of the causes for the industrial backwardness of India are the same as those in Latin America, but in addition the very different resource endowment and the structure of capital and industrial investment resulting from it are superimposed in India (and also other countries in South Asia) to compound the impediments in the path of rapid economic development.

Summarizing this very sketchy overview of the comparative role of the urban impact in various developing regions of the world, we may conclude that developments in sub-Saharan Africa are as yet unclear and difficult to predict, but are likely to show—in the realm of social adjustments—some of the features now encountered in India. Latin America appears to be in the intermediate position between India (and other South Asian countries) on the one hand and the advanced European countries on the other. Demographic patterns of urbanization showing an early rapid growth which gradually slows down appear to parallel one another in all regions, with the European and other advanced countries being in a decidedly later phase of the urban growth process than Latin America, Africa, or Asia. In social relations the differences between the advanced countries and the underdeveloped countries appear greatest, perhaps because the cultural complex of industrialism is indigenous with western and central Europe and is a foreign importation into the under-developed countries. The economic function and impact of cities in various parts of the world appears to be greatly modified by the general resource endowment of the various nations. In densely populated Asia, where demographic pressures are higher than elsewhere in the world, the relatively low ratio between nonhuman and human resources creates conditions of poverty which prevent the full impact of urban centers from exerting itself sharply. In Latin America, where the ratio

between resources and population is more favorable, urban centers provide more of the amenities and external economies for a well-functioning industry, although the level of skill and education of the human resources in these countries is yet inadequate to make full use of the opportunities created by the urban environment. It appears, therefore, that the model to be followed by urban developments in India is not the pattern established by the United States, Europe, or Latin America. Rather, India must work out her own solutions in the framework of her own sociocultural and economic conditions. Perhaps the history of urban growth in China and Japan may provide some more useful guidelines for India than the experience of Western countries. But it would go far beyond the limitations of this paper and the knowledge of this writer to attempt to substantiate this suggestion in greater detail.

NOTES

1. See Ashish Bose, "The Process of Urbanization in India" (Doctoral dissertation, University of Delhi, 1959), pp. 168–169. A similar comparison between Indian and United States urban growth, although not with the period 1840–1890, but an earlier period (1790 to 1850), is made by Kingsley Davis, *The Popultion of India and Pakistan* (Princeton, N.J., 1951), pp. 127–128.
2. Eric Lampard, "Urban-Rural Conflict in the United States, 1870–1920: An Ecological Perspective on Industrialization," a paper read at the University of Michigan, May, 1959. [Mimeo-graphed.]
3. All data in this and the preceding paragraph are from Bose, *op. cit.*, pp. 217–218.
4. See A. F. Weber, *The Groth of Cities in the Nineteenth Century* (New York, 1899), *passim*.
5. Estimates of recent migration to the large cities of India have been published in S. N. Agarwala, "A Method for Estimating Decade Internal Migration in Cities from Indian Census Data," *Indian Economic Review*, IV, No. 1 (February, 1958), 59–76; a comprehensive study of rural-urban migrations in later-19th-century Europe is found in P. Meuriot, *Les agglomérations urbaines dans l'Europe contemporaine* (Paris, 1897), pp. 309–332.
6. See Meuriot, *op. cit.*, pp. 285–287.

7. The increasing population pressure on agricultural resources in India is the main theme of the Report of Shri R. A. Gopalaswami, I.C.A., the census commissioner of the last census; see *Census of India*, 1951, I, Part I-A, 138–150, and Part I-B, Appendixes I and V. For a more recent analysis see *Report on India's Food Crisis and Steps to Meet It* (Delhi, 1959), pp. 9–20, by the Agricultural Production Team of the Ford Foundation.
8. See Bert F. Hoselitz, "Population Pressure, Industrialization and Social Mobility," *Population Studies*, XI, No. 2 (November, 1957), 126. This paper is also reprinted in Bert F. Hoselitz, *Sociological Aspects of Economic Growth* (Glencoe Ill., 1960).
9. See Max Weber, *The City*, trans. and ed. Don Martindale and Gertrude Neuwirth (Glencoe, Ill., 1958), chap. ii.
10. For a publication which graphically represents some planned urban growth in medieval cities see F. L. Ganshof, *Étude sur le développement des villes entre Loire et Rhin au moyen âge* (Brussels, 1943), especially the Appendix (maps).
11. For some examples of this see the sections on "Neighborhood Relations," and "An Indian 'Ghetto,'" in A. Bopegamage, *Delhi: A Study in Urban Sociology* (Bombay, 1957), pp. 93–109.

12. See the reports in International African Institute, *Social Implications of Industrialization and Urbanization in Africa South of the Sahara* (Paris, 1956).
13. See Kingsley Davis and Ana Casis, "Urbanization in Latin America," *Milbank Memorial Fund Quarterly*, XXIV (April, 1946), 197–198. For Venezuelan data see Ministerio de Fomento, Oficina Central del Censo Nacional, *Octavo Censo de Población* (Caracas, 1954), *passim*.
14. Based on data presented in Davis and Casis, *op. cit.*, pp. 192–194, and International Population and Urban Research, *The World's Metropolitan Areas* (Berkeley and Los Angeles: University of California Press, 1959), pp. 43–45.
15. See his "Urbanization without Breakdown: A Case Study," *Scientific Monthly*, LXXV, No. 1 (July, 1952), 31–41; and "The Culture of the Vecindad in Mexico City: Two Case Studies,"

Actas del III Congreso Internacional de Americanistas (San José, Costa Rica, 1959), I, 387–402.
16. See J. A. Kahl, "Some Social Concomitants of Industrialization and Urbanization: A Research Review," *Human Organisation*, XVIII, No. 2 (Summer, 1959), 53–74; also the works by Oscar Lewis cited in note 15.
17. See Research Center in Economic Development and Cultural Change, *United States Business and Labor in Latin America* (a study prepared at the request of the Committee on Foreign Relations, U.S. Senate, 86th Congress, 2nd Session [Washington, 1960]), pp. 9–35, especially pp. 28–33.
18. See, for example, United Nations, Department of Economic Affairs, *Labour Productivity of the Cotton Textile Industry in Five Latin-American Countries* (New York: 1951), *passim*, but especially pp. 6–10, 13–16.

9. The Nature of the City | Max Weber

In the course of elaborating a definition of the essential city as a closed settlement, Max Weber presents a pithy and informative history of urban development prior to the twentieth century. He points out that cities have served at least one of a combination of functions to meet the needs of the nations, states, or hinterlands of which they were a part. These functions have included centers for trade and commerce, centers for production, consuming or shopping areas, concentrations of decision-making and administrative services, sources for military power and protection, religious centers, and centers for the generation of cultural expression and innovation. Weber concludes his discussion with the important point that the city as an urban community is historically a peculiarity of Western society. Only in Europe (and then later in America) did the residents of towns and cities have political autonomy, and only there did they share common statuses and patterns of association which set them off from the population of the surrounding society. This tradition of the urban community established the framework for many of the issues which still concern urban sociology in the United States. Cities and towns still are governed by "home rule" and are supposed to be capable of caring for their own residents' needs, even though they often lack adequate resources and power to do these jobs.

Max Weber (1864–1920), probably the most influential sociologist of this century, was Professor of Economics at the University of Munich at the time of his death. He is most noted for *The Protestant Ethic and the Spirit of Capitalism* (English translation, 1956) and *The Theory of Social and Economic Organization* (English translation, 1947), as well as for *The City* (English translation, 1958).

Economic Character of the City: Market Settlement

The many definitions of the city have only one element in common: namely that the city consists simply of a collection of one or more separate dwellings but is a relatively closed settlement. Customarily, though not exclusively, in cities the houses are built closely to each other, often, today, wall to wall. This massing of elements interpenetrates the everyday concept of the "city" which is thought of quantitatively as a large locality. In itself this is not imprecise for the city often represents a locality and dense settlement of dwellings forming a colony so extensive that personal reciprocal acquaintance of the inhabitants is lacking. However, if interpreted in this way only very large localities could qualify as cities; moreover it would be ambiguous, for various cultural factors determine the size at which "impersonality" tends to appear. Precisely this impersonality was absent in many historical localities possessing the legal character of cities. Even in contemporary Russia there are villages comprising many thousands of inhabitants which are, thus, larger than many old "cities" (for example, in the Polish colonial area of the German East) which had only a few hundred inhabitants. Both in terms of what it would include and what it would exclude size alone can hardly be sufficient to define the city.

Economically defined, the city is a settlement the inhabitants of which live primarily off trade and commerce rather than agriculture. However, it is not altogether proper to call all localities "cities" which are dominated by trade and commerce. This would include in the concept "city" colonies made up of family members and maintaining a single, practically hereditary trade establishment such as the "trade villages" of Asia and Russia. It is necessary to add a certain "versatility" of practiced trades to the characteristics of the city. However, this in itself does not appear suitable as the single distinguishing characteristic of the city either.

Economic versatility can be established in at least two ways: by the presence of a feudal estate or a market. The economic and political needs of a feudal or princely estate can encourage specialization in trade products in providing a demand for which work is performed and goods are bartered. However, even though the *oikos* of a lord or prince is as large as a city, a colony of artisans and small merchants bound to villein services is not customarily called a "city" even though historically a large proportion of important "cities" originated in such settlements.[1] In cities of such origin the products for a prince's court often remained a highly important, even chief, source of income for the settlers.

The other method of establishing economic versatility is more generally important for the "city"; this is the existence in the place of settlement of a regular rather than an occasional exchange of goods. The market becomes an essential component in the livelihood of the settlers. To be sure, not every "market" converted the locality in which it was found into a city. The periodic fairs and yearly foreign-trade markets at which traveling merchants met at fixed times to sell their goods in wholesale or retail lots to each other or to

First published in *Archiv für Sozialwissenschaft und Sozialpolitik*, Vol. 47, p. 621 ff. (1921). Last edition: *Wirtschaft und Gesellschaft* (Tübingen: J. C. B. Mohr, 1956) Vol. 2, p. 735 ff. [All the notes in this translation are those of the editors.]

consumers often occurred in places which we would call "villages."

Thus, we wish to speak of a "city" only in cases where the local inhabitants satisfy an economically substantial part of their daily wants in the local market, and to an essential extent by products which the local population and that of the immediate hinterland produced for sale in the market or acquired in other ways. In the meaning employed here the "city" is a market place. The local market forms the economic center of the colony in which, due to the specialization in economic products, both the non-urban population and urbanites satisfy their wants for articles of trade and commerce. Wherever it appeared as a configuration different from the country it was normal for the city to be both a lordly or princely residence as well as a market place. It simultaneously possessed centers of both kinds, *oikos* and market and frequently in addition to the regular market it also served as periodic foreign markets of traveling merchants. In the meaning of the word here, the city is a "market settlement."

Often the existence of a market rests upon the concessions and guarantees of protection by a lord or prince. They were often interested in such things as a regular supply of foreign commerical articles and trade products, in tolls, in moneys for escorts and other protection fees, in market tariffs and taxes from law suits. However, the lord or prince might also hope to profit from the local settlement of tradesmen and merchants capable of paying taxes and, as soon as the market settlement arose around the market, from land rents arising therefrom. Such opportunities were of especial importance to the lord or prince since they represented chances for monetary revenues and the increase in his treasure of precious metal.

However, the city could lack any attachment, physical or otherwise, to a lordly or princely residence. This was the case when it originated as a pure market settlement at a suitable intersection point (*Umschlageplatz*)[2] where the means of transportation were changed by virtue of concession to non-resident lords or princes or usurpation by the interested parties themselves. This could assume the form of concessions to entrepreneurs—permitting them to lay out a market and recruit settlers for it. Such capitalistic establishment of cities was especially frequent in medieval frontier areas, particularly in East, North, and Central Europe. Historically, though not as a rule, the practice has appeared throughout the world.

Without any attachment to the court of a prince or without princely concessions, the city could arise through the association of foreign invaders, naval warriors, or commercial settlers or, finally, native parties interested in the carrying trade. This occurred frequently in the early Middle Ages. The resultant city could be a pure market place. However, it is more usual to find large princely or patrimonial households and a market conjoined. In this case the eminent household as one contact point of the city could satisfy its want either primarily by means of a natural economy (that is by villein service or natural service or taxes placed upon the artisans and merchants dependent on it) or it could supply itself more or less secondarily by barter in the local market as that market's most important buyer. The more pronounced the latter relation the more distinct the market foundation of the city looms and the city ceases by degrees to be a mere appendaged market settlement alongside the *oikos*. Despite attachment to the large household it then became a market city. As a rule the quantitative expansion of the original princely city and its economic importance go hand in hand with an increase in the satisfaction of wants in the market by the princely household and other large urban households attached to that of the prince as courts of vassals or major officials.

Types of Consumer and Producer City

Similar to the city of the prince, the inhabitants of which are economically dependent upon the purchasing power of noble households are cities in which the purchasing power of other larger consumers, such as rentiers, determines the economic opportunities of resident tradesmen and merchants. In terms of the kind and source of their incomes such larger consumers may be of quite varied types. They may be officials who spend their legal and illegal income in the city or lords or other political power holders who spend their non-urban land rents or politically determined incomes there. In either of these cases the city closely approximates the princely city for it depends upon patrimonial and political incomes which supply the purchasing power of large consumers. Peking was a city of officials; Moscow, before suspension of serfdom, was a land-rent city.

Different in principle are the superficially similar cities in which urban land-rents are determined by traffic monopolies of landed property. Such cities originate in the trade and commerce consolidated in the hands of an urban aristocracy. This type of development has always been widespread: it appeared in Antiquity; in the Near East until the Byzantine Empire; and in the Middle Ages. The city that emerges is not economically of a rentier type but is, rather, a merchant or trade

city the rents of which represent a tribute of acquisitors to the owners of houses. The conceptual differentiation of this case from the one in which rents are not determined by tributary obligations to monopolists but by non-urban sources, should not obscure the interrelation in the past of both forms. The large consumers can be rentiers spending their business incomes (today mainly interest on bonds, dividends or shares) in the city. Whereupon purchasing power rests on capitalistically conditioned monetary rentier sources as in the city of Arnheim. Or purchasing power can depend upon state pensions or other state rents as appears in a "pensionopolis" like Wiesbaden. In all similar cases one may describe the urban form as a consumer city, for the presence in residence of large consumers of special economic character is of decisive economic importance for the local tradesmen and merchants.

A contrasting form is presented by the producer city. The increase in population and purchasing power in the city may be due, as for example in Essen or Bochum, to the location there of factories, manufactures, or home-work industries supplying outside territories—thus representing the modern type. Or, again, the crafts and trades of the locality may ship their goods away as in cities of Asiatic, Ancient, and Medieval types. In either case the consumers for the local market are made up of large consumers if they are residents and/or entrepreneurs, workers and craftsmen who form the great mass, and merchants and benefactors of land-rent supported indirectly by the workers and craftsmen.

The trade city and merchant city are confronted by the consumer city in which the purchasing power of its larger consumers rests on the retail for profit of foreign products on the local market (for example, the woolen drapers in the Middle Ages), the foreign sale for profit of local products or goods obtained by native producers (for example, the herring of the Hansa) or the purchase of foreign products and their sale with or without storage at the place to the outside (intermediate commercial cities). Very frequently a combination of all these economic activities occurred: the *commenda* and *societas maris* implied that a *tractator* (travelling merchant) journied to Levantine markets with products purchased with capital entrusted to him by the resident capitalists.[3] Often the *tractator* traveled entirely in ballast. He sold these products in the East and with the proceeds he purchased oriental articles brought back for sale in the local market. The profits of the undertaking were then divided between *tractator* and capitalist according to pre-arranged formulas.

The purchasing power and tax ability of the commercial city rested on the local economic establishment as was also the case for the producers' city in contrast to the consumers' city. The economic opportunities of the shipping and transport trade and of numerous secondary wholesale and retail activities were at the disposal of the merchants. However the economic activity of these establishments was not entirely executed for the local retail trade but in substantial measure for external trade. In principle, this state of affairs was similar to that of the modern city, which is the location of national and international financiers or large banks (London, Paris, Berlin) or of joint stock companies or cartels (Duesseldorf). It follows that today more than ever before a predominant part of the earnings of firms flow to localities other than the place of earning. Moreover, a growing part

of business proceeds are not consumed by their rightful receivers at the metropolitan location of the business but in suburban villas, rural resorts or international hotels. Parallel with these developments "city-towns" or city-districts consisting almost exclusively of business establishments are arising.

There is no intention here of advancing the further casuistic distinctions required by a purely economic theory of the city. Moreover, it hardly needs to be mentioned that actual cities nearly always represent mixed types. Thus, if cities are to be economically classified at all, it must be in terms of their prevailing economic component.

Relation of the City to Agriculture

The relation of the city to agriculture has not been clear cut. There were and are "semi-rural cities" (*Ackerburgerstaedte*) localities which while serving as places of market traffic and centers of typically urban trade, are sharply separated from the average city by the presence of a broad stratum of resident burghers satisfying a large part of their food needs through cultivation and even producing food for sale. Normally the larger the city the less the opportunity for urban residents to dispose of acreage in relation to their food needs at the same time without controlling a self-sufficient pasture and wood lot in the manner of the village. Cologne, the largest German city in the Middle Ages, almost completely lacked the *All-mende* (commons) from the beginning though the commons was not absent from any normal village of the time. Other German and foreign medieval cities at least placed considerable pastures and woods at the disposal of their burghers.

The presence of large acreages accessible to the urbanite is found more frequently as one turns attention to the south or back toward antiquity. While today we justly regard the typical "urbanite" as a man who does not supply his own food need on his own land, originally the contrary was the case for the majority of typical ancient cities. In contrast to the medieval situation, the ancient urbanite was quite legitimately characterized by the fact that a *kleros, fundus* (In Israel: *chelek*) which he called his own, was a parcel of land which fed him.[4] The full urbanite of antiquity was a semi-peasant.

In the Medieval period, as in Antiquity, agricultural property was retained in the hands of merchant strata. This was more frequently the case in the south than in the north of Europe. In both medieval and ancient city states agricultural properties, occasionally of quite exorbitant size, were found widely scattered, either being politically dominated by municipal authorities of powerful cities or in the possession of eminent individual citizen landlords. Examples are supplied by the Cheronesic domination of the Miltiades or the political or lordly estates of medieval aristocratic families, such as the Genoese Grimaldi, in the provinces or overseas.

As a general rule inter-local estates and the sovereign rights of individual citizens were not the objects of an urban economic policy. However, mixed conditions at times arose such that according to the circumstances estates were guaranteed to individuals by the city. In the nature of the case this only occurred when the individuals whose estates were guaranteed by the city belonged to the most powerful patricians. In such cases the estate was acquired and maintained through indirect help of civic power which in turn might share in its economic and political usufruct. This was frequently the case in the past.

The relation of the city as agent of trade and commerce to the land as producer of food comprises one aspect of the "urban economy" and forms a special "economic stage" between the "household economy" on the one hand and the "national economy" on the other.[5] When the city is visualized in this manner, however, politico-economic aspects are conceptually fused with pure economic aspects and conceived as forming one whole. The mere fact that merchants and tradesmen live crowded together carrying on a regular satisfaction of daily needs in the market does not exhaust the concept of the "city." Where only the satisfaction of agricultural needs occurs within closed settlements and where—what is not identical with it—agricultural production appears in relation to non-agricultural acquisition, and when the presence or absence of markets constitutes the difference, we speak of trade and commercial localities and of small market-towns, but not of cities. There were, thus, hidden non-economic dimensions in the phenomena brought under review in the previous sections. It is time to expand the concept of the "city" to include extra-economic factors.

The Politico-Administrative Concept of the City

Beside possessing an accumulation of abodes the city also has an economic association with its own landed property and a budget of receipts and expenditure. Such an economic association may also appear in the village no matter how great the quantitative differences. Moreover, it was not peculiar to the city alone, at least in the past, that it was both an economic and a regulatory association. Trespass

restrictions, pasture regulations, the prohibition of the export of wood and straw,
and similar regulations are known to the
village, constituting an economic policy
of the association as such.

The cities of the past were differentiated
only by the kinds of regulations which
appeared. Only the objects of political
economic regulation on behalf of the
association and the range of characteristic
measures embraced by them were peculiar.
It goes without saying that measures of
the "urban economic policy" took substantial account of the fact that under the
transportation conditions of the time the
majority of all inland cities were dependent
upon the agricultural resources of the
immediate hinterland. As shown by the
grain policies of Athens and Rome this was
true for maritime cities. In a majority, not
all, of urban trades areas, opportunity was
provided for the natural "play of the
market." The urban market supplied the
normal, not the sole, place for the exchange of products, especially food.

Account also must be taken of the fact
that production for trade was predominantly in the form of artisan technology
organized in specialized small establishments. Such production operated without
or with little capital and with strictly
limited numbers of journeymen who were
trained in long apprenticeship. Such production was economically in the form of
wage worker as price work for customers.
Sale to the local retailers was largely a
sale to customers.

The market conditions of the time were
the kind that would naturally emerge,
given the above facts. The so-called
"urban economic policy" was basically
characterized by its attempt to stabilize
the conditions of the local urban economy
by means of economic regulations in the
interest of permanently and cheaply feeding the masses and standardizing the
economic opportunities of tradesmen and
merchants. However, as we shall see,
economic regulation was not the sole
object of the urban economic policy nor,
when it historically appears, was it fully
developed. It emerges only under the
political regime of the guild. Finally it can
not be proved to be simply a transitional
stage in the development of all cities. In any
case, the urban economic policy does not
represent a universal stage in economic
evolution.

On the basis of customer relations and
specialized small establishments operating
without capital, the local urban market
with its exchange between agricultural and
non-agricultural producers and resident
merchants, represents a kind of economic
counterpart to barter as against systematically divided performances in terms of
work and taxes of a specialized dependent
economy in connection with the *oikos*,
having its basis in the accumulation and
integration of work in the manner, without
exchange occurring inside. Following out
the parallel: the *regulation* (urban economic
policy) of the exchange and production
conditions in the city represent the counterpart to the *organization* (traditional and
feudal-contractual) of activities united in
the economy of the *oikos*.

The very fact that in drawing these distinctions we are led to use the concepts of
an "urban economic area" and "urban
area," and "urban authority," already
indicates that the concept of the "city"
can and must be examined in terms of a
series of concepts other than the purely
economic categories so far employed.

The additional concepts required for
analysis of the city are political. This
already appears in the fact that the urban
economic policy itself may be the work of
a prince to whom political dominion of the

city with its inhabitants belongs. In this case when there is an urban economic policy it is determined *for* the inhabitants of the city not *by* them. However even when this is the case the city must still be considered to be a partially autonomous association, a "community" with special political and administrative arrangements.

The economic concept previously discussed must be entirely separated from the political-administrative concept of the city. Only in the latter sense may a special *area* belong to the city. A locale can be held to be a city in a political-administrative sense though it would not qualify as a city economically. In the Middle Ages there were areas legally defined as "cities" in which the inhabitants derived ninety percent or more of their livelihood from agriculture, representing a far larger fraction of their income than that of the inhabitants of many localities legally defined as "villages."

Naturally, the transition from such semi-rural cities to consumers', producers' or commercial cities is quite fluid. In those settlements which differ administratively from the village and are thus dealt with as cities only one thing, namely, the kind of regulations of land-owning, is customarily different from rural land-owning forms. Economically such cities are differentiated by a special kind of rent situation presented in urban real estate which consists in house ownership to which land ownership is accessory. The position of urban real estate is connected administratively with special taxation principles. It is bound even more closely to a further element decisive for the political-administrative concept of the city and standing entirely outside the purely economic analysis, namely, the fortress.

Fortress and Garrison

It is very significant that the city in the past, in Antiquity and the Middle Ages, outside as well as within Europe, was also a special fortress or garrison. At present this property of the city has been entirely lost, but it was not universal even in the past. In Japan, for example, it was not the rule. Administratively one may, with Rathgen,[6] doubt the existence of cities at all. In contrast to Japan, in China every city was surrounded with a gigantic ring of walls. However, it is also true that many economically rural localities which were not cities in the administrative sense, possessed walls at all times. In China such places were not the seat of state authorities.

In many Mediterranean areas such as Sicily a man living outside the urban walls as a rural worker and country resident is almost unknown. This is a product of century-long insecurity. By contrast in old Hellas the Spartan polis sparkled by the absence of walls, yet the property of being a "garrison-town" was met. Sparta despised walls for the very reason that it was a permanent open military camp.

Though there is still dispute as to how long Athens was without walls, like all Hellenic cities except Sparta it contained in the Acropolis a castle built on rock in the same manner as Ekbantama and Persepolis which were royal castles with surrounding settlements. The castle or wall belonged normally to Oriental as well as to ancient Mediterranean and ordinary medieval cities.

The city was neither the sole nor oldest fortress. In disputed frontier territory and during chronic states of war, every village fortified itself. Under the constant danger of attack in the area of the Elbe and Oder Rivers Slavic settlements were fortified, the national form of the rural village seems early to have been standardized in the form of the "hedge-enclosed" circular area with a single entrance which could be locked and through which at night cattle were driven to the central protection of the village area. Similarly, walled hill retreats were diffused throughout the world from Israelite East Jordan to Germanic territories. Unarmed persons and cattle took refuge within in times of danger. The so-called "cities" of Henry I in the German East were merely systematically established fortresses of this sort.

In England during the Anglo-Saxon period a "burgh" (borough) belonged to each shire whose name it took. Guard and garrison duty as the oldest specifically "civic" obligations were attached to certain persons or pieces of land. When in normal times such fortresses were occupied guards or vassals were maintained as a permanent garrison and paid in salaries or in land. There were fluid transitions from the permanently garrisoned fortress to the Anglo-Saxon burgh, the "garrison-city," in the sense of Maitland's theory, with a "burgess" as inhabitants. The burgess received its name from its political position which like the legal nature of its civic land and house property was determined by the duty of maintaining and guarding the fortress.

However, historically neither the palisaded village nor the emergency fortification are the primary fore-runners of the city fortress, which was, rather, the manorial castle. The manorial castle was a fortress occupied by the lord and warriors subordinated to him as officials or as a personal following, together with their families and servants.

Military castle construction is very old, doubtlessly older than the chariot and military use of the horse. Like the war chariot the importance of the castle was determined by the development of knightly and royal warfare. In old China of the classic songs, in India of the Vedas, in Egypt and Mesopotamia, in Canaan, in Israel at the time of the Song of Deborah, in Greece during the period of the Homeric epics, and among the Etruscans, Celts, and Irish, the building of castles and the castle-principality were diffused universally. Old Egyptian sources speak of castles and their commanders and it may be assumed that they originally accommodated just as many small princes. From old documents it can be inferred that in Mesopotamia the development of the provincial kingships was preceded by a castle-dwelling princedom such as existed in Western India at the time of the Vedas and such as was probable in Iran at the time of the oldest *Gathas*. The castle was certainly universally dominant in Northern India on the Ganges during the time of political disintegration. In this last instance, the old Kshatriyas whom the sources show to be peculiarly sandwiched between the king and nobility, were obviously princes.

In the period of Christianization, castle construction was pressed in Russia. It appears also during the dynasty of Thutmose in Syria at the time of the Israelite confederation (Abmilech). Old Chinese literature also provides irrefutable evidence of its original occurrence. The Hellenic and Asia Minor sea-castle was as universally diffused as piracy. There must have been an interim period of especially deep pacification to allow the Cretan unfortified palaces to arise in the place of the castle. In this area later castles like the Decelia,[7] so important in the Peloponnesian Wars, were originally fortresses of noble families.

The medieval development of a politically independent gentry opened with the *castelli* in Italy. In Northern Europe the independence of the vassals was also bound up with enormous castle construction as established by Below.[8] Even in modern times individual deputyship in Germany has been dependent upon possession by the family of a castle, even if only the meager ruins of one. Disposal of a castle originally signified military dominion over the country. The only question was: In whose hands? It could be in the hands of the individual lords, or confederations of knights, or of a ruler who could depend on the trustworthiness of his vassals, ministers, or officers.

The City as the Fusion of Fortress and Market

In the first stage of its development into a special political form the fortified city was incorporated in or dependent upon a castle, the fortress of a king, noblemen, or association of knights. Such nobles either resided in the fortress themselves or maintained a garrison of mercenaries, vassals, or servants therein. In Anglo-Saxon England the right to possess a "haw," a fortified house in a "burgh," was bestowed as a privilege on certain land owners of the surrounding countryside. In Antiquity and Medieval Italy the cityhouse of the nobleman was held in addition to his rural castle. The inhabitants or residents adjoining the castle, sometimes all, sometimes special strata, were bound as citizens (burgess) to the performance of certain military duties such as building and repair of the walls, guard duty, defense service and, at times, other military services such as communication and supply for the urban military noble. In this instance the burger is a member of his estate because, and insofar as, he participates in the military association of the city.

Maitland[9] has worked this out with especial clarity for England. The houses of the "burgh" were in the possession of people having the duty of maintaining the fortification. This contrasts with the village. Alongside royal or aristocratically guaranteed market peace appears military jurisdiction. The politically oriented castle and economically oriented market with the market area of the towns at times simultaneously serving both functions, again drill field and assembly area of the army and the place of pacific economic exchange on the other, often stand in plastic dualism beside one another.

The military drill field and economic market are not everywhere spatially separated. The Attic *pnyx* was a much later development than the *agora* which originally served the economic traffic as well as political and religious activities. On the other hand in Rome from ancient times the *comitium* and *campus martius* were separated from the economic *fora* as in the Middle Ages the *piazza del campo* at Siena (a tournament place still used today as a place for holding races between the wards of the city), as the front of the municipal place, is distinct from the *mercato* at the rear. Analogously in Islamic cities the *kasbeh*, the fortified camp of the warriors, was spatially separate from the *bazaar*. In Southern India the political city of notable men appears separately alongside the economic city.

The relation between the garrison of the political fortress and the civil economic population is complicated but always decisively important for the composition of the city. Wherever a castle existed artisans came or were settled for the satisfaction of manorial wants and the needs of the warriors. The consumption power of a prince's military household and the protection it guaranteed attracted the merchants. Moreover the lord was interested in attracting these classes since he was in position to procure money revenues through them either by taxing commerce or trade or participating in it through capital advances. At times the lord engaged in commerce on his own, even monopolizing it. In maritime castles as ship owner or ruler of the port the lord was in a position to procure a share in piratical or peacefully won sea-borne profits. His followers and vassals resident in the place were also in position to profit whether he voluntarily gave them permission or, being dependent on their good will, was forced to do so.

The evidences of the participation of the ancient city lords in commercial activities are many. Vases from old Hellenic cities like Cyrene picture the king weighing goods (*silphion*). In Egypt at the beginning of historical time a commercial fleet of the Lower-Egyptian Pharaoh is reported. Widely diffused over the world, but especially in maritime "cities" where the carrying trade was easily controlled, the economic interest of resident military families flourished beside the monopoly of the castle chieftain, as a result of their own participation in commercial profits. Their capacity to participate in the civic economy often shattered the monopoly (if it existed) of the prince. When this occurred the prince was considered only to be *primus inter pares* in the ruling circle or even simply as equal. The ruling circle comprised the urban sibs domiciled through landed property and deriving capital from some form of peaceful commerce, especially the *commenda* capital in the Middle Ages, or from personal participation in piracy or sea war. Often the prince was elected for short times and in any case he was decisively limited in power. In ancient maritime cities since Homer's time yearly municipal councils

gradually appeared. Quite similar formations often occur in the early Middle Ages. In Venice they formed a counter balance to the doges though with very different leadership positions depending on whether a royal count or vicomte or bishop or someone else was lord of the city. Equivalent developments also appear in other typical commercial cities.

Thus in early Antiquity and in the Middle Ages the urban commercial capitalists, the financiers of commerce, the specific notable persons of the city, have to be separated in principle from the domiciled holders of commercial "establishments," the merchants proper. To be sure the strata often blended into each other. However, with this we already anticipate later explanations.

In the hinterland, shipping points, terminals, crossings of rivers and caravan routes (for example, Babylon) could become locations of similar developments. At times competition arose between the priest of the temple, and priestly lord of the city, for temple districts of famous gods offered sacred protection to inter-ethnic elements. Such areas could provide locations for politically unprotected commerce. Thus a city-like settlement, economically supplied by temple revenues, could attach itself to the temple district in a manner similar to the princely city with its tributes to the prince.

Individual cases varied depending on the extent to which the prince's interest in monetary revenues predominated in the granting of privileges for merchandising and manufacturing independent of the lordly household and taxed by the lord. On the other hand, the lord could be interested in satisfying his own needs hence in acting in ways strengthening his own powers and monopolizing trade in his own hands. When attracting foreigners by offering special privileges the lord also had to take into consideration the interests and "established" ability (which was also important for himself) of those already resident, who were dependent on his political protection or manorial supplies.

To this variety of possible development must be added the effects of the political-militaristic structure of the dominating group within which the founding of the city or its development occurred. We must consider the main antitheses in city development arising therefrom.

Associational and Status Peculiarities of the Occidental City

Neither the "city," in the economic sense, nor the garrison, the inhabitants of which are accoutred with special political-administrative structures, necessarily constitute a "community." An urban "community," in the full meaning of the word, appears as a general phenomenon only in the Occident. Exceptions occasionally were to be found in the Near East (in Syria, Phoenicia, and Mesopotamia) but only occasionally and in rudiments. To constitute a full urban community a settlement must display a relative predominance of trade-commerical relations with the settlement as a whole displaying the following features: (1) a fortification; (2) a market; (3) a court of its own and at least partially autonomous law; (4) a related form of association; and (5) at least partial autonomy and autocephaly, thus also an administration by authorities in the election of whom the burghers participated.

In the past, rights such as those which define the urban community were normally privileges of the estates. The peculiar political properties of the urban community appeared only with the presence of a special stratum, a distinct new estate. Measured by this rule the "cities" of the Occidental Middle Ages only qualify in part as true cities; even the cities of the eighteenth century were genuine urban communities only in minor degree. Finally measured by this rule, with possible isolated exceptions, the cities of Asia were not urban communities at all even though they all had markets and were fortresses.

All large seats of trade and commerce in China and most of the small ones were fortified. This was true also for Egyptian, Near Eastern, and Indian centers of commerce and trade. Not infrequently the large centers of trade and commerce of those countries were also separate jurisdictional districts. In China, Egypt, the Near East, and India the large commercial centers have also been seats of large political associations—a phenomenon not characteristic of Medieval Occidental cities, especially those of the North. Thus, many, but not all of the essential elements of the true urban community were at hand. However, the possession by the urbanites of a special substantive or trial law or of courts autonomously nominated by them were unknown to Asiatic cities. Only to the extent that guilds or castes (in India) were located in cities did they develop courts and a special law. Urban location of these associations was legally incidental. Autonomous administration was unknown or only vestigial.

If anything, even more important than the relative absence of autonomous administration, the appearance in the city of an association of urbanites in contradiction to the countryman was also found only in rudiments. The Chinese urban dweller legally belonged to his family and native village in which the temple of his ancestors stood and to which he conscientiously maintained affiliation. This is similar to the Russian village-comrade, earning his livelihood in the city but legally remaining a peasant. The Indian urban dweller remained a member of the caste. As a rule urban dwellers were also members of local professional associations, such as crafts and guilds of specific urban location. Finally they belonged to administrative districts such as the city wards and street districts into which the city was divided by the magisterial police.

Within the administrative units of the city, wards and street districts, urban dwellers had definite duties and even, at times, rights as well. In the attempt to secure peace, city or street districts could be made liturgically responsible collectively for the security of persons or other police purposes. It was possible thus for them to be formed into communities with elected officials or hereditary elders. This occurred in Japan where one or more civil-administrative body (*Machi-Bugyo*) was established as superior to self-administered street communities. However, a city law similar to that of Antiquity or the Middle Ages was absent. The city as corporate *per se* was unknown. Of course, eventually the city as a whole formed a separate administrative district as in the Merovingian and Carolingian Empires, but as was still the case in the Medieval and Ancient Occident, the autonomy and participation of the inhabitants in local administration were out of the question. As a matter of fact, local individual participation in self-administration was often more strongly developed in the country than in the relatively large commercially organized city.

In the village, for example, in China, in many affairs the confederation of elders was practically all-powerful and the Pao-Chia[10] was dependent on them, even though this was not legally expressed. Also

in India the village community had nearly complete autonomy in most significant circumstances. In Russia the mir enjoyed nearly complete autonomy until bureaucratization under Alexander III. In the whole of the Near Eastern world the "elders" (in Israel, *sekenim*)[11] originally of the family and later chiefs of noble clans were representatives and administrators of localities and the local court. This could not occur in the Asiatic city because it was usually the seat of a high official or prince and thus under the direct supervision of their bodyguards. However, the city was a princely fortress and administered by royal officials (in Israel, *sarim*)[12] who retained judicial power.

In Israel the dualism of officials and elders can be traced in the royal period. Royal officials everywhere triumphed in bureaucratic kingdoms. Such royal bureaucrats were not all-powerful but subject to public opinion often to an astonishing degree. As a rule the Chinese official was quite powerless against local associations such as the clans and professional associations when they united in a particular case. At every serious united opposition of the clans and local associations the Chinese Official lost his position. Obstruction, boycott, closing of shops, and strikes of artisans and merchants in response to oppression were a daily occurrence, setting limits on the power of officials. However, such limits on official power were of a completely indeterminate kind.

In China and India the guilds and other professional associations had competencies with which the officials had to reckon. The chairman of the local associations often exercised extensive coercive powers even against third parties. However all their powers involved only special competencies of particular association in particular questions of concrete group interest.

Moreover, there was ordinarily no joint association representing a community of city burghers *per se*, even the concept of such a possibility is completely lacking. Citizenship as a specific status quality of the urbanite is missing. In China, Japan, and India neither urban community nor citizenry can be found and only traces of them appear in the Near East.

In Japan the organization of estates was purely feudal. The *samurai* (mounted) and *kasi* (unmounted) ministerial officials confronted the peasant (*no*) and the merchants and tradesmen who were partly united in professional associations. However, here too, the concepts of a "citizenry" and an "urban community" are absent. This was also true in China during the feudal period. After the feudal period in China a bureaucratic administration of literati qualified for office in terms of examinations leading to academic degrees confronted the illiterate strata among whom appeared economically privileged guilds of merchants and professional associations. But in this period in China, too, the ideas of an "urban citizenry" and "urban community" are missing. This was true even though in China as well as in Japan the professional associations were self-administered. Moreover while the villages were self-administered the cities were not. In China the city was a fortress and official seat of imperial authorities in a sense completely unknown in Japan.

The cities of India were royal seats or official centers of royal administration as well as fortresses and market places. Guilds of merchants and castes largely coinciding with professional associations were present, enjoying considerable autonomy especially with respect to their own legal competence and justice. Nevertheless, the hereditary caste system of Indian society with its ritualistic segregation of the professions, excluded the emergence of a citizenry and urban community. And though there were numerous castes and sub-castes of traders and artisans they cannot be taken together and equated with the Occidental burgher stata. Nor was it possible for the commercial and artisan castes of India to unite in a form corresponding to the medieval urban corporations for caste estrangement hindered all inter-caste fraternization.

To be sure in India during the period of the great salvation religions, guilds appeared with hereditary elders (*schreschths*) uniting in many cities into an association. As residues from this period there are, at present, some cities (Allahabad) with a mutual urban *schreschth* (elder) corresponding to the occidental mayor. Moreover, in the period before the great bureaucratic kingdoms there were some politically autonomous cities in India ruled by a patriciate recruited from families supplying elephants to the army. Later this phenomenon almost completely disappeared. The triumph of ritualistic caste estrangement shattered the guild associations and royal bureaucracies in alliance with the Brahmans swept away, except for vestiges, such trends toward a citizenry and urban community in Northwestern India.

In Near Eastern Egyptian antiquity the cities were fortresses and official administrative centers with royal market privileges. However, in the period of the dominion of the great kingdom they lacked autonomy, community organizations, and a privileged citizen estate. In Egypt during the Middle Empire office feudalism existed; in the New Empire a bureaucratic administration of clerks appeared. "Civic privileges" were bestowed on feudal or prebendal office holders in localities comparable to the privileges of bishops in old

Germany. However, civic rights were not bestowed on an autonomous citizenry and even the beginnings of a "city patriciate" have not been found.

In contrast to the complete absence of a citizenry in ancient Egypt were the phenomena in Mesopotamia, Syria and especially Phoenicia, where at an early period typical city-kingdoms emerged at intersection points of sea and caravan traffic. Such civic kingdoms were of intensified sacred-secular character. They were also typified by the rising power of patrician families in the "city-house" (*bitu* in the Tel-el-Amarna tablets) in the period of charioteering.[13] In the Canaanite city an association of chariot-fighting knights possessing urban residences appeared. This knighthood kept the peasant farmers in a state of debt servitude and clientship as in the case of the early Hellenic polis. It was obviously similar in Mesopotamia where the "patrician" as a land-owning full burgher economically qualified for war service is separated from the peasant. Immunities and privileges of this stratum were chartered by the king. However, with the mounting military power of the government this also disappeared. Politically autonomous cities and a burgher stratum of Occidental type are as little to be found in Mesopotamia as is a special urban law alongside royal law.

Only in Phoenicia did the landed patriciate engaging in commerce with its capital manage to maintain its dominion over the city state. However, the coins of the time *am Sôr* and *am Karthadast* in Tyre and Carthage hardly indicate the presence of a ruling "demos" and if such was ever the case it was only at a later time. Thus a true citizenry only partly developed. In Israel, Juda became a city-state but the elders (*sekenim*) who in the early period governed the administration as chieftains

of patrician sibs were thrust into the background by the royal administration. The *gibborim* (knights) became royal attendants and soldiers. In contrast to the countryside, the royal *sarim* (officials) ruled in the large cities. Only after the exile did the community (*kahal*) or fellowship (*cheber*) appear as an institution on a confessional basis under the rule of priestly families.[14]

Nevertheless, all these phenomena indicate that here on the coasts of the Mediterranean Sea and on the Euphrates appeared the first real analogies of a civic development equivalent to that of Rome at the time of the reception of the Gens Claudia. The city is ruled by a patriciate resident in the city with powers resting on monetary wealth primarily won in commerce and secondarily invested in landed property, debt slaves and war slaves.[15] The military power of the urban patriciate was a product of its training for knightly warfare, a training often spent in feuds against one another. The patricians were inter-locally diffused and united with the king or *schofeten* or *sekenim* as *primus inter pares*. Such a patriciate like the Roman nobility with consuls was threatened by the tyranny of the charismatic war king relying upon recruited bodyguards (Abimelech, Jepthah, David). Prior to the Hellenic period this stage of urban development was nowhere permanently surpassed.

Obviously such a patriciate also dominated in cities of the Arabian coast during the period of Mohammed, remaining in existence in those Islamic cities where the autonomy of the city and its patriciate was not completely destroyed as in the larger state. Under Islamic rule ancient oriental conditions were often preserved, whereupon a labile ratio of autonomy between urban families and princely officials appears. Resident city families enjoyed a position of power resting on wealth from urban economic opportunities and invested in land and slaves. Without formal legal recognition the princes and their officials had to take account of the power of the patriciate in the same manner that the Chinese Pao Chia had to take account of the obstruction of clan elders of the villages and merchant and professional associations. However, the city was not thereby necessarily formed into an independent association. Often the contrary occurred, as may be exemplified.

Arabian cities like Mecca were settlements of clans such as remained typical in the Middle Ages to the threshold of the present Snouck Hurgronje[16] has proven that the city of Mecca was surrounded by the *bilad* representing lordly property of an individual *dewis* of sibs descending from Ali—such were the *hasnaidic* and other noble sibs. The *bilad* was occupied by peasants, clients, and protected Bedouins. *Bilads* were often intermixed. A *dewis* was any sib one ancestor of which was once a sherif. Since 1200 the sherif himself belonged without exception to the Alidic family *Katadahs*. Legally the sherif should have been installed by the governor of the caliph (who was often unfree and once, under Harun al Rashid, was a Berber slave). However in reality the sherif was chosen from the qualified family by election of the chieftains of the *dewis* who were resident in Mecca. For this reason as well as the fact that residence in Mecca offered opportunities to exploit pilgrims, the heads of the class (*emirs*) lived in the city. Between them at times alliances obtained with agreements for preserving the peace and establishing quotas for dividing chances for gain. Such alliances were terminable at any time, dissolution signaling the start of a feud inside and outside the city. Slave troops were employed in such feuds and the defeated group was exiled from the city.

However, despite defeat the community of interest between hostile families as against outsiders led to observance of the courtesy of sparing the goods and lives of members of the families and clientele of the exiles. Such courtesies were observed under the threat of general mutiny of one's own partisans.

In modern times the city of Mecca recognizes the following official authorities: 1. On paper the collegiate administrative council (*Medschlis*) installed by the Turks appears as the authority; 2. In fact the Turkish governor is the effective authority, occupying the position of protector (in former times usually the ruler of Egypt); 3. Authority is shared by the four *cadis* of the orthodox rights who are always noble men of Mecca, the most eminent (schafitic) for centuries being nominated from one family by the sherif or proposed by the protector; 4. The sherif simultaneously is head of the urban corporation of nobles; 5. The guilds, especially the cicerones, followed by the butchers, corn merchants and others; 6. The city ward with its elders is partly autonomous. These authorities competed with each other in many ways without fixed competences. A party to a legal suit selected the authority appearing most favorable of whose power against the accused seemed to be most strong. The governor was unable to prevent an appeal to the *cadi* who competed with him in all matters of ecclesiastical law. The sherif was held to be the proper authority of the natives especially in all matters concerning the Bedouins and caravans of pilgrims. The governor was dependent on the willingness of the sherif to cooperate. Finally, here as in other Arabic areas, particularly in the cities, the cooperation of the nobility was decisive for the effectiveness of authority.

In the ninth century a development

reminiscent of Occidental circumstances occurred when with the flight of the Tuluniden and Deschafariden, in Mecca the position of the richest guilds, that of the butchers and corn merchants, held the balance of power. However, it was still unconditionally true at the time of Mohammed that only the noble *koreischitic* families were militarily and politically important, thus, a government by guilds never arose. Slave troups sustained by profit-shares of resident urban families continually sustained their power. In a similar manner, in medieval Italian cities power continually tended to glide into the hands of the knightly families as wielders of military power.

The idea of an association which could unite the city into a corporate unit was missing in Mecca. This furnished its characteristic difference from the ancient polis and the early medieval Italian commune. However, when all is said and done, this Arabic condition—of course omitting specific Islamic traits or replacing them by Christian counterparts—may be taken to typify the period before the emergence of the urban community association. It is also typical for Occidental commercial sea cities.

So far as sound information extends, in Asiatic and Oriental settlements of an urban economic character, normally only extended families and professional associations were vehicles of communal actions. Communal action was not the product of an urban burgher stratum as such. Transitions, of course, are fluid but precisely the largest settlements at times embracing hundreds of thousands even millions of inhabitants display this very phenomenon. In medieval Byzantine Constantinople the representatives of urban districts were leaders of party divisions who financed circus races (as is still the case for the horse race of Siena). The Nika revolt under Justinian was a product of such local cleavages of the city. Also in Constantinople, from the time of the Islamic Middle Ages until the sixteenth century, only merchants, corporations, and guilds appear as representatives of the interests of the burghers beside purely military associations such as the *Janitscharen* and *Sipahis* and the religious organizations of the *Ulemas* and *Dervishes*. However, in sixteenth century Constantinople there is still no city representation. Similarly in late Byzantine Alexandria, beside the power of the patricians, relying upon the support of very sturdy monks, and the competitive power of the governor relying on a small garrison there was no militia of particular city districts. Within the districts of the city only the circus parties of rival "greens" and "blues" represented the leading organizations.

NOTES

1. For the place of the household or oikos-economy cf. Max Weber, *General Economic History*, trans. Frank H. Knight (Glencoe: The Free Press, 1950) pp. 48, 58, 124 ff., 131,146, 162 and Johannes Hase Broek, *Griechische Wirtschaftsgeschichte* (Tübingen: J. C. B. Mohr, 1931) pp. 15, 24, 27, 29, 38, 46, 69, 284.
2. Charles H. Cooley's theory of transportation took the break in communication either physical or economic as the most critical of all factors for the formation of the city.

3. Weber, *General Economic History*, pp. 205, 206 and W. Silberschmidt, *Die Commenda in ihrer Frühesten Entwicklung* (1884).
4. Pöhlmann, *Aus Altertum und Gegenwart*, p. 124 ff.; Weber, *General Economic History*, p. 328; Weber, *Ancient Judaism* (Glencoe: The Free Press, 1952), p. 465.
5. Weber has in mind distinctions introduced by Gustave Schmoller.
6. Karl Rathgen, "Gemeindefinanzen" in *Verein für Sozialpolitik* (Leipzig: Duncker & Humblot,

1908–10) and *Allgemeine Verfassungs und Verwaltungsgeschichte* (Leipzig: Huebner, 1911).

7. Hill commanding the pass between Pentelicus and Poenes, occupied by the Spartans in 413.

8. Georg Below, *Der deutsche Staat des Mittelalters* (Leipzig: Zuelle & Meyer, 1914); *Territorium und Stadt* (München: R. Oldenberg, 1900).

9. Frederic William Maitland, *The Charters of the Borough of Cambridge* (Cambridge: University Press, 1901) and *The Court Law* (London: Quaritsch, 1891).

10. Even until recent times every ten families constituted a "pao" formally under a headman. A hundred families constituted a "Chia" under a "Pao Chia" also called "Ti Pao." We read Pao-Chia for Taotai.

11. Weber, *Ancient Judaism*, p. 16.

12. *Ibid.*, p. 18.

13. Weber, *Ancient Judaism*, p. 14 f.

14. *Ibid.*, p. 385 f.

15. In all these areas in the early period enslavement for debt appears and debt slaves are found alongside slaves captured in battles—battles at times being actually slave raids.

16. Snouck Hurgronje, *Mekka in the Latter Part of the 19th Century* (London: Luzac, 1931).

10. The Preindustrial City | Gideon Sjoberg

The considerable variation which exists among the characteristics of urban settlements is brought fully into focus in this discussion of the preindustrial city by Gideon Sjoberg. The author deals with settlements which developed before the industrial revolution of the nineteenth century as well as with the cities of Asia, Africa, and Latin America that only now are beginning to experience the influence of modern technology. Making use of an implied definition of cities as dense concentrations of population, Sjoberg challenges a number of stereotyped notions about the ecological, economic, political and organizational correlates of urbanization. He points out, for example, that in the preindustrial city the business district is rarely located at its geographic center, the family structure is often consanguineal and clan-like rather than nuclear and conjugal, there is little fragmentation of work, social mobility is minimal, and there is often no formal machinery for regulating social life. Perhaps more than any other paper in this section, this article should help the reader to understand the intimate connection between the social organization of contemporary urban communities and the broader social structure of America. It also should enable him to distinguish between the universal features of cities and those characteristics which are the product of historical differences in national cultures and stages of technological development.

Gideon Sjoberg is Professor of Sociology at the City University of New York. Several of his published works are cited on page 85 of this volume.

In the past few decades social scientists have been conducting field studies in a number of relatively non-Westernized cities. Their recently acquired knowledge of North Africa and various parts of Asia, combined with what was already learned, clearly indicates that these cities are not like typical cities of the United States and other highly industrialized areas but are much more like those of medieval Europe. Such communities are termed herein "preindustrial," for they have arisen without stimulus from that form of production which we associate with the European industrial revolution.

Recently Foster, in a most informative article, took cognizance of the preindustrial city.[1] His primary emphasis was upon the peasantry (which he calls "folk"); but he recognized this to be part of a broader social structure which includes the pre-industrial city. He noted certain similarities between the peasantry and the city's lower class. Likewise the present author sought to analyze the total society of which the peasantry and the pre-industrial city are integral parts.[2] For want of a better term this was called "feudal." Like Redfield's folk (or "primitive") society, the feudal order is highly stable and sacred; in contrast, however, it has a complex social organization. It is characterized by highly developed state and educational and/or religious institutions and by a rigid class structure.

Thus far no one has analyzed the pre-industrial city *per se*, especially as it differs from the industrial-urban community, although Weber, Tönnies, and a few others perceived differences between the two. Yet such a survey is needed for the understanding of urban development in so-called underdeveloped countries and, for that matter, in parts of Europe. Such is the goal of this paper. The typological analysis should also serve as a guide to future research.

Ecological Organization

Preindustrial cities depend for their existence upon food and raw materials obtained from without; for this reason they are marketing centers. And they serve as centers for handicraft manufacturing. In addition, they fulfil important political, religious, and educational functions. Some cities have become specialized; for example Benares in India and Karbala in Iraq are best known as religious communities, and Peiping in China as a locus for political and educational activities.

The proportion of urbanites relative to the peasant population is small, in some societies about 10 percent, even though a few preindustrial cities have attained populations of 100,000 or more. Growth has been by slow accretion. These characteristics are due to the nonindustrial nature of the total social order. The amount of surplus food available to support an urban population has been limited by the unmechanized agriculture, transportation facilities utilizing primarily human or animal power, and inefficient methods of food preservation and storage.

The internal arrangement of the pre-industrial city, in the nature of the case, is closely related to the city's economic and social structure.[3] Most streets are mere passageways for people and for animals used in transport. Buildings are low and crowded together. The congested conditions, combined with limited scientific knowledge, have fostered serious sanitation problems.

More significant is the rigid social segregation which typically has led to the formation of "quarters" or "wards." In some cities (e.g., Fez, Morocco, and Aleppo, Syria) these were sealed off from each other by walls, whose gates were locked at night. The quarters reflect the sharp local social divisions. Thus ethnic groups live in special sections. And the occupational groupings, some being at the same time ethnic in character, typically reside apart from one another. Often a special street or sector of the city is occupied almost exclusively by members of a particular trade; cities in such divergent cultures as medieval Europe and modern Afghanistan contain streets with names like "street of the goldsmiths." Lower-class and especially "outcaste" groups live on the city's periphery, at a distance from the primary centers of activity. Social segregation, the limited transportation facilities, the modicum of residential mobility, and the cramped living quarters have encouraged the development of well-defined neighborhoods which are almost primary groups.

Despite rigid segregation the evidence suggests no real specialization of land use such as is functionally necessary in industrial-urban communities. In medieval Europe and in other areas city dwellings often serve as workshops, and religious structures are used as schools or marketing centers.[4]

Finally, the "business district" does not hold the position of dominance that it enjoys in the industrial-urban community. Thus, in the Middle East the principal mosque, or in medieval Europe the cathedral, is usually the focal point of community life. The center of Peiping is the Forbidden City.

Economic Organization

The economy of the preindustrial city diverges sharply from that of the modern industrial center. The prime difference is the absence in the former of industrialism which may be defined as that system of production in which *inanimate* sources of power are used to multiply human effort. Preindustrial cities depend for the production of goods and services upon *animate* (human or animal) sources of energy —applied either directly or indirectly through such mechanical devices as hammers, pulleys, and wheels. The industrial-urban community, on the other hand, employs inanimate generators of power such as electricity and steam which greatly enhance the productive capacity of urbanites. This basically new form of energy production, one which requires for its development and survival a special kind of institutional complex, effects striking changes in the ecological, economic, and social organization of cities in which it has become dominant.

Other facets of the economy of the preindustrial city are associated with its particular system of production. There is little fragmentation or specialization of work. The handicraftsman participates in nearly every phase of the manufacture of an article, often carrying out the work in his own home or in a small shop nearby and, within the limits of certain guild and community regulations, maintaining direct control over conditions of work and methods of production.

In industrial cities, on the other hand, the complex division of labor requires a specialized managerial group, often extra-community in character, whose primary function is to direct and control others. And for the supervision and co-ordination of the activities of workers, a "factory system" has been developed, something typically lacking in preindustrial cities. Occasionally centralized production is found in preindustrial cities—e.g., where the state organized slaves for large-scale construction projects. Most commercial activities, also, are conducted in preindustrial cities by individuals without a highly formalized organization; for example, the craftsman has frequently been responsible for the marketing of his own products. With a few exceptions, the preindustrial community cannot support a large group of middlemen.

The various occupations are organized into what have been termed "guilds."[5] These strive to encompass all, except the elite, who are gainfully employed in some economic activity. Guilds have existed for merchants and handicraft workers (e.g., goldsmiths and weavers) as well as for servants, entertainers and even beggars and thieves. Typically the guilds operate only within the local community, and there are no large-scale economic organizations such as those in industrial cities which link their members to their fellows in other communities.

Guild membership and apprenticeship are prerequisites to the practice of almost any occupation, a circumstance obviously leading to monopolization. To a degree these organizations regulate the work of their members and the price of their products and services. And the guilds recruit workers into specific occupations, typically selecting them according to such particularistic criteria as kinship rather than universalistic standards.

The guilds are integrated with still other elements of the city's social structure. They perform certain religious functions; for example, in medieval European, Chinese, and Middle Eastern cities each guild had its "patron saint" and held periodic

festivals in his honor. And, by assisting members in time of trouble, the guilds serve as social security agencies.

The economic structure of the preindustrial city functions with little rationality, judged by industrial-urban standards. This is shown in the general nonstandardization of manufacturing methods as well as in the products and is even more evident in marketing. In preindustrial cities throughout the world a fixed price is rare; buyer and seller settle their bargain by haggling. (Of course, there are limits above which customers will not buy and below which merchants will not sell.) Often business is conducted in a leisurely manner, money not being the only desired end.

Furthermore, the sorting of goods according to size, weight, and quality is not common. Typical is the adulteration and spoilage of produce. And weights and measures are not standardized: variations exist not only between one city and the next but also within communities, for often different guilds employ their own systems. Within a single city there may be different kinds of currency, which, with the poorly developed accounting and credit systems, signalize a modicum of rationality in the whole of economic action in preindustrial cities.[6]

Social Organization

The economic system of the preindustrial city, based as it has been upon animate sources of power, articulates with a characteristic class structure and family, religious, educational, and governmental systems.

Of the class structure, the most striking component is a literate elite controlling and depending for its existence upon the mass of the populace, even in the traditional cities of India with their caste system. The elite is composed of individuals holding positions in the governmental, religious, and/or educational institutions of the larger society, although at times groups such as large absentee landlords have belonged to it. At the opposite pole are the masses, comprising such groups as handicraft workers whose goods and services are produced primarily for the elite's benefit.[7] Between the elite and the lower class is a rather sharp schism, but in both groups there are gradations in rank. The members of the elite belong to the "correct" families and enjoy power, property, and certain highly valued personal attributes. Their position, moreover, is legitimized by sacred writings.

Social mobility in this city is minimal; the only real threat to the elite comes from the outside—not from the city's lower classes. And a middle class—so typical of industrial-urban communities, where it can be considered the "dominant" class— is not known in the preindustrial city. The system of production in the larger society provides goods, including food, and services in sufficient amounts to support only a small group of leisured individuals; under these conditions an ˙ ꞌan middle class, a semileisured group, ˍ.ꞏꞏot arise. Nor are a middle class and extensive social mobility essential to the maintenance of the economic system.

Significant is the role of the marginal or "outcaste" groups (e.g., the Eta of Japan), which are not an integral part of the dominant social system. Typically they rank lower than the urban lower class, performing tasks considered especially degrading, such as burying the dead. Slaves, beggars, and the like are outcastes in most preindustrial cities. Even such groups as professional entertainers and itinerant merchants are often viewed as outcastes, for their rovings expose them to "foreign" ideas from which the dominant social group seeks to isolate itself. Actually many outcaste groups, including some of those mentioned above, are ethnic groups, a fact which further intensifies their isolation. (A few, like the Jews in the predominantly Muslim cities of North Africa, have their own small literate religious elite which, however, enjoys no significant political power in the city as a whole.)

An assumption of many urban sociologists is that a small, unstable kinship group, notably the conjugal unit, is a necessary correlate of city life. But this premise does not hold for preindustrial cities.[8] At times sociologists and anthropologists, when generalizing about various traditional societies, have imputed to peasants typically urban kinship patterns. Actually, in these societies the ideal forms of kinship and family life are most closely approximated by members of the urban literate elite, who are best able to fulfil the exacting requirements of the sacred writings. Kinship and the ability to perpetuate one's lineage are accorded marked prestige in preindustrial cities. Children, especially sons, are highly valued, and polygamy or concubinage or adoption help to assure the attainment of large families. The preeminence of kinship is apparent even in those preindustrial cities where divorce is permitted. Thus, among the urban Muslims or urban Chinese divorce is not an index of disorganization; here, conjugal ties are loose and distinctly subordinate to the bonds of kinship, and each member of a dissolved conjugal unit typically is absorbed by his kin group. Marriage, a prerequisite to adult status in the preindustrial city, is entered upon at an early age and is arranged between families rather than romantically, by individuals.

The kinship and familial organization displays some rigid patterns of sex and age differentiation whose universality in preindustrial cities has generally been overlooked. A woman, especially of the upper class, ideally performs few significant functions outside the home. She is clearly subordinate to males, especially her father or husband. Recent evidence indicates that this is true even for such a city as Lhasa, Tibet, where women supposedly have had high status.[9] The isolation of women from public life has in some cases been extreme. In nineteenth-century Seoul, Korea, "respectable" women appeared on the streets only during certain hours of the night when men were supposed to stay at home.[10] Those women in preindustrial cities who evade some of the stricter requirements are members of certain marginal groups (e.g., entertainers) or of the lower class. The role of the urban lower-class woman typically resembles that of the peasant rather than the urban upper-class woman. Industrialization, by creating demands and opportunities for their employment outside the home, is causing significant changes in the status of women as well as in the whole of the kinship system in urban areas.

A formalized system of age grading is an effective mechanism of social control in preindustrial cities. Among siblings the eldest son is privileged. And children and youth are subordinate to parents and other adults. This, combined with early marriage, inhibits the development of a "youth culture." On the other hand, older persons hold considerable power and prestige, a fact contributing to the slow pace of change.

As noted above, kinship is functionally integrated with social class. It also reinforces and is reinforced by the economic organization: the occupations, through the guilds, select their members primarily on the basis of kinship, and much of the work is carried on in the home or immediate vicinity. Such conditions are not functional to the requirements of a highly industrialized society.

The kinship system in the preindustrial city also articulates with a special kind of religious system, whose formal organization reaches fullest development among members of the literate elite.[11] The city is the seat of the key religious functionaries whose actions set standards for the rest of society. The urban lower class, like the peasantry, does not possess the education or the means to maintain all the exacting norms prescribed by the sacred writings. Yet the religious system influences the city's entire social structure. (Typically, within the preindustrial city one religion is dominant; however, certain minority groups adhere to their own beliefs.) Unlike the situation in industrial cities, religious activity is not separate from other social action but permeates family, economic, governmental, and other activities. Daily life is pervaded with religious significance. Especially important are periodic public festivals and ceremonies like Ramadan in Muslim cities. Even distinctly ethnic outcaste groups can through their own religious festivals maintain solidarity.

Magic, too, is interwoven with economic, familial, and other social activities. Divination is commonly employed for determining the "correct" action on critical occasions; for example, in traditional Japanese and Chinese cities, the selection of marriage partners. And nonscientific procedures are widely employed to treat illness among all elements of the population of the preindustrial city.

Formal education typically is restricted to the male elite, its purpose being to train individuals for positions in the governmental, educational, or religious hierarchies. The economy of preindustrial cities does not require mass literacy, nor, in fact, does the system of production provide the leisure so necessary for the acquisition of formal education. Considerable time is needed merely to learn the written language, which often is quite different from that spoken. The teacher occupies a position of honor, primarily because of the prestige of all learning and especially of knowledge of the sacred literature, and learning is traditional and characteristically based upon sacred writings.[12] Students are expected to memorize rather than evaluate and initiate, even in institutions of higher learning.

Since preindustrial cities have no agencies of mass communication, they are relatively isolated from one another. Moreover, the masses within a city are isolated from the elite. The former must rely upon verbal communication, which is formalized in special groups such as storytellers or their counterparts. Through verse and song these transmit upper-class tradition to nonliterate individuals.

The formal government of the preindustrial city is the province of the elite and is closely integrated with the educational and religious systems. It performs two principal functions: exacting tribute from the city's masses to support the activities of the elite and maintaining law and order through a "police force" (at times a branch of the army) and a court system. The police force exists primarily for the control of "outsiders," and the courts support custom and the rule of the sacred literature, a code of enacted legislation typically being absent.

In actual practice little reliance is placed upon formal machinery for regulating social life.[13] Much more significant are the informal controls exerted by the kinship, guild, and religious systems, and here, of course, personal standing is decisive. Status distinctions are visibly correlated with personal attributes, chiefly speech, dress, and personal mannerisms which proclaim ethnic group, occupation, age, sex, and social class. In nineteenth-century Seoul, not only did the upper-class mode of dress differ considerably from that of the masses, but speech varied according to social class, the verb forms and pronouns depending upon whether the speaker ranked higher or lower or was the equal of the person being addressed.[14] Obviously, then, escape from one's role is difficult, even in the street crowds. The individual is ever conscious of his specific rights and duties. All these things conserve the social order in the preindustrial city despite its heterogeneity.

Conclusions

Throughout this paper there is the assumption that certain structural elements are universal for all urban centers. This study's hypothesis is that their form in the preindustrial city is fundamentally distinct from that in the industrial-urban community. A considerable body of data not only from medieval Europe, which is somewhat atypical,[15] but from a variety of cultures supports this point of view. Emphasis has been upon the static features of preindustrial city life. But even those preindustrial cities which have undergone considerable change approach the ideal type. For one thing, social change is of such a nature that it is not usually perceived by the general populace.

Most cities of the preindustrial type have been located in Europe or Asia. Even though Athens and Rome and the large commercial centers of Europe prior to the industrial revolution displayed certain unique features, they fit the pre-industrial type quite well.[16] And many traditional Latin-American cities are quite like it, although deviations exist, for, excluding pre-Columbian cities, these were affected to some degree by the industrial revolution soon after their establishment.

It is postulated that industrialization is a key variable accounting for the distinctions between preindustrial and industrial cities. The type of social structure required to develop and maintain a form of production utilizing inanimate sources of power is quite unlike that in the pre-industrial city.[17] At the very least, extensive industrialization requires a rational, centralized, extra-community economic organization in which recruitment is based more upon universalism than on particularism, a class system which stresses achievement rather than ascription, a small and flexible kinship system, a system of mass education which emphasizes universalistic rather than particularistic criteria, and mass communication. Modification in any one of these elements affects the others and induces changes in other systems such as those of religion and social control as well. Industrialization, moreover, not only requires a special kind of social structure within the urban community but provides the means necessary for its establishment.

Anthropologists and sociologists will, in the future, devote increased attention to the study of cities throughout the world. They must therefore recognize that the particular kind of social structure found in cities in the United States is not typical of all societies. Miner's recent study of Timbuctoo,[18] which contains much excellent data, points to the need for recognition of the preindustrial city. His emphasis upon the folk-urban continuum diverted him from an equally significant problem: How does Timbuctoo differ from modern industrial cities in its ecological, economic, and social structure? Society there seems even more sacred and organized than Miner admits.[19] For example, he used divorce as an index of disorganization, but in Muslim society divorce within certain rules is justified by the sacred literature. The studies of Hsu and Fried would have considerably more significance had the authors perceived the generality of their findings. And, once the general structure of the preindustrial city is understood, the specific cultural deviations become more meaningful.

Beals notes the importance of the city as a center of acculturation.[20] But an understanding of this process is impossible without some knowledge of the preindustrial city's social structure. Although industrialization is clearly advancing throughout most of the world, the social structure of preindustrial civilizations is conservative, often resisting the introduction of numerous industrial forms. Certainly many cities of Europe (e.g., in France or Spain) are not so fully industrialized as some presume; a number of preindustrial patterns remain. The persistence of preindustrial elements is also evident in cities of North Africa and many parts of Asia; for example, in India and Japan,[21] even though great social change is currently taking place. And the Latin-American city of Merida, which Redfield studied, had many preindustrial traits.[22] A conscious awareness of the ecological, economic, and social structure of the preindustrial city should do much to further the development of comparative urban community studies.

NOTES

1. George M. Foster, "What Is Folk Culture?" *American Anthropologist*, LV (1953), 159–173.
2. Gideon Sjoberg, "Folk and 'Feudal' Societies," *American Journal of Sociology*, LVIII (1952), 231–239.
3. Sociologists have devoted almost no attention to the ecology of preindustrial centers. However, works of other social scientists do provide some valuable preliminary data. See, e.g., Marcel Clerget, *Le Caire: Étude de géographie urbaine et d'histoire économique* (2 vols.; Cairo: E. & R. Schindler, 1934); Robert E. Dickinson, *The West European City* (London: Routledge & Kegan Paul, 1951); Roger Le Tourneau, *Fés: Avant le protectorat* (Casablanca: Société Marocaine de Librairie et d'Édition, 1949); Edward W. Lane, *Cairo Fifty Years Ago* (London: John Murray, 1896); J. Sauvaget, *Alep* (Paris: Librairie Orientaliste Paul Geuthner, 1941); J. Weulersse, "Antioche: Essai de géographie urbaine," *Bulletin d'études orientales*, IV (1934), 27–79; Jean Kennedy, *Here Is India* (New York: Charles Scribner's Sons, 1945); and relevant articles in American geographical journals.
4. Dickinson, *op. cit.*, p. 27; O. H. K. Spate, *India and Pakistan* (London: Methuen & Co., 1945), p. 183.
5. For a discussion of guilds and other facets of the preindustrial city's economy see, e.g., J. S. Burgess, *The Guilds of Peking* (New York: Columbia University Press, 1928); Edward T. Williams, *China, Yesterday and Today* (5th ed.; New York: Thomas Y. Crowell Co., 1932); T'ai-ch'u Liao, "The Apprentices in Chengtu during and after the War," *Yenching Journal of Social Studies*, IV (1948), 90–106; H. A. R. Gibb and Harold Bowen, *Islamic Society and the West* (London: Oxford University Press, 1950), Vol. I, Part I, chap. vi; Le Tourneau, *op. cit.*; Clerget, *op. cit.*; James W. Thompson and Edgar N. Johnson, *An Introduction to Medieval Europe* (New York: W. W. Norton & Co., 1937), chap. xx; Sylvia L. Thrupp, "Medieval Guilds Reconsidered," *Journal of Economic History*, II (1942), 164–173.
6. For an extreme example of unstandardized currency cf. Robert Coltman, Jr., *The Chinese* (Philadelphia: F. A. Davis, 1891), p. 52. In some traditional societies (e.g., China) the state has sought to standardize economic action in the city by setting up standard systems of currency and/or weights and measures; these efforts, however, generally proved ineffective. Inconsistent policies in taxation, too, hinder the development of a "rational" economy.
7. The status of the true merchant in the preindustrial city, ideally, has been low; in medieval Europe and China many merchants were considered "outcastes." However, in some preindustrial cities a few wealthy merchants have acquired considerable power even though their role has not been highly valued. Even then most of their prestige has come through participation in religious, governmental, or educational activities, which have been highly valued (see, e.g., Ping-ti Ho, "The Salt Merchants of Yang Chou: A Study of Commercial Capitalism in Eighteenth-Century China," *Harvard Journal of Asiatic Studies*, XVII [1954], 130–168).
8. For materials on the kinship system and age and sex differentiation see, e.g., Le Tourneau, *op. cit.*; Edward W. Lane, *The Manners and Customs of the Modern Egyptians* (3d ed.; New York: E. P. Dutton Co., 1923); C. Snouck Hurgronje, *Mekka in the Latter Part of the Nineteenth Century*, trans. J. H. Monahan (London: Luzac, 1931); Horace Miner, *The Primitive City of Timbuctoo* (Princeton: Princeton University Press, 1953); Alice M. Bacon, *Japanese Girls and Women* (rev. ed.; Boston: Houghton Mifflin Co., 1902); J. S. Burgess, "Community Organization in China," *Far Eastern Survey*, XIV (1945), 371–373; Morton H. Fried, *Fabric of Chinese Society* (New York: Frederick A. Praeger, 1953); Francis L. K. Hsu, *Under the Ancestors' Shadow* (New York: Columbia University Press, 1948); Cornelius Osgood, *The Koreans and Their Culture* (New York: Ronald Press, 1951), chap. viii; Jukichi Inouye, *Home Life in Tokyo* (2d ed.; Tokyo: Tokyo Printing Co., 1911).
9. Tsung-Lien Shen and Shen-Chi Liu, *Tibet and the Tibetans* (Stanford: Stanford University Press, 1953), pp. 143–144.
10. Osgood, *op. cit.*, p. 146.
11. For information on various aspects of religious behavior see e.g., Le Tourneau, *op. cit.*; Miner, *op. cit.*; Lane, *Manners and Customs;* Hurgronje, *op. cit.*; André Chouraqui, *Les Juifs d'Afrique du Nord* (Paris: Presses Universitaires de France, 1952); Justus Doolittle, *Social Life of the Chinese* (London: Sampson Low, 1868); John K. Shryock, *The Temples of Anking and Their Cults* (Paris: Privately printed, 1931); Derk Bodde (ed.), *Annual Customs and Festivals in Peking* (Peiping: Henri Vetch, 1936); Edwin Benson, *Life in a Medieval City* (New York: Macmillan Co., 1920); Hsu, *op. cit.*
12. Le Tourneau, *op. cit.*, Part VI: Lane, *Manners and Customs*, chap. ii; Charles Bell, *The People of Tibet* (Oxford: Clarendon Press, 1928), chap. xix; O. Olufsen, *The Emir of Bokhara and His Country* (London: William Heinemann, 1911), chap. ix; Doolittle, *op. cit.*
13. Carleton Coon, *Caravan: The Story of the Middle East* (New York: Henry Holt & Co., 1951), p. 259; George W. Gilmore, *Korea from Its Capital* (Philadelphia: Presbyterian Board of Publication, 1892), pp. 51–52.
14. Osgood, *op. cit.*, chap. viii; Gilmore, *op. cit.*, chap. iv.
15. Henri Pirenne, in *Medieval Cities* (Princeton: Princeton University Press, 1925), and others have noted that European cities grew up in opposition to and were separate from the greater

society. But this thesis has been overstated for medieval Europe. Most preindustrial cities are integral parts of broader social structures.

16. Some of these cities made extensive use of water power, which possibly fostered deviations from the type.

17. For a discussion of the institutional prerequisites of industrialization see, e.g., Bert F. Hoselitz, "Social Structure and Economic Growth," *Economia Internazionale*, VI (1953), 52–77, and Marion J. Levy, "Some Sources of the Vulnerability of the Structures of Relatively Non-industrialized Societies to Those of Highly Industrialized Societies," in Bert F. Hoselitz (ed.), *The Progress of Underdeveloped Areas* (Chicago: University of Chicago Press, 1952), pp. 114 ff.

18. *Op. cit.*

19. This point seems to have been perceived also by Asael T. Hansen in his review of Horace Miner's *The Primitive City of Timbuctoo*, *American Journal of Sociology*, LIX (1954), 501–502.

20. Ralph L. Beals, "Urbanism, Urbanization and Acculturation," *American Anthropologist*, LIII (1951), 1–10.

21. See, e.g., D. R. Gadgil, *Poona: A Socio-economic Survey* (Poona: Gokhale Institute of Politics and Economics, 1952), Part II; N. V. Sovani, *Social Survey of Kolhapur City* (Poona: Gokhale Institute of Politics and Economics, 1951), Vol. II; Noel P. Gist, "Caste Differentials in South India," *American Sociological Review*, XIX (1954), 126–137; John Campbell Pelzel, "Social Stratification in Japanese Urban Economic Life" (unpublished Ph.D. dissertation, Harvard University, Department of Social Relations, 1950).

22. Robert Redfield, *The Folk Culture of Yucatan* (Chicago: University of Chicago Press, 1941).

Contemporary Urbanization and Urbanism in the United States: Process and Impact

11. The City | Lewis Mumford

Lewis Mumford has long been America's most noted urban critic. His theme in the present essay is American history looked at as the history of the rising importance of cities and metropolitan areas. He divides urban development into three stages: the provincial, the commercial, and the industrial. He analyzes American cities of each period in terms of the relation between dominant social institutions and the expression of the prevailing pattern of dominance in buildings, architectural styles, and city plans. Mumford argues that the disorder in metropolitan areas is a sign of the failure of industrial civilization to create a humane society. This view of city life represents a strain of antiurban criticism that goes back to the Founding Fathers. In this case, it is embellished by an attack on New York City and its Region and the influence which this urban complex has exerted on growth throughout the United States. The virulence of Mumford's antimetropolitan feeling is perhaps the one quality which makes the paper, written in the 1920's, seem a little out of date. With the development of other urban centers, such as Los Angeles and Chicago, New York is less a dominant force than it was forty years ago. And the spread of the metropolitan order to all parts of the nation is evidence that it has come to be an accepted, if not completely admired, way of life for a majority of Americans.

Lewis Mumford, social philosopher and historian, was born in New York City and now lives in Amenia, New York. Among his most famous books are *The Myth of the Machine* (1967), *The City in History* (1966), *The Culture of Cities* (1938), and *Technics and Civilization* (1934).

Preface

The City was written for the symposium on Civilization in the United States, edited by Harold Stearns:* published in 1922. It was, I believe, the first historic analysis of its kind to be published in the United States; and both in its perceptions and its omissions it bears witness to the current state of thought. I was twenty-six when I wrote that essay, and still had much to learn, both about that large part of the history of my country which had hardly been touched by any of the historians, and about the development of cities themselves: yet I am not ashamed to publish it along with my maturer work, even though it tempt some unfriendly critic to remark how little I have learned since.

Despite more than a generation of constructive effort toward the improvement of cities, led by Frederick Law Olmsted, the elder, one of the great artists of the nineteenth century, comparatively little work had then been done in the detailed history of American city building or in a sociological analysis of the processes themselves. The advance of the Chicago school of urban sociologists had been somewhat tangential, and such works as Carl Bridenbaugh's Cities in the Wilderness, or John Coolidge's Mill and Mansion, still lay in the future. For more than a generation, we had indeed had among us the most brilliant and penetrating critic of architecture America has yet produced, Montgomery Schuyler, one of the first to make a sound critical appraisal of the Roeblings, Richardson, Adler and Sullivan; but good though Schuyler was, his field was the individual building, not the corporate organization and plan.

There are many points in my essay that would now have to be amplified; and certain uninformed judgments remain, like that on Richardson, which I myself have since corrected in various other places; still I leave it as it stands, because its errors have but little capacity for mischief. In my contribution to the Survey Graphic's Regional Planning Number, May 1925, I made a somewhat different analysis of our urban growth, dividing it into an initial period of settlement, with three subsequent migrations, leading to the possibility of a fourth migration which would be in the nature of a wholesale resettlement of the country.

Even before 1922 I had left behind the notion that metropolitanism was a mark of progress or a conclusive phase in the development of cities: hence my unsparing criticism of the Regional Plan for New York, sponsored by the Russell Sage Foundation, whose naïve premises I criticized at the very beginning of their work and whose final report I analyzed in some detail in the New Republic in 1932. The assumptions about continued population growth and urban concentration which the Russell Sage planners regarded as so eminently sensible and unchallengeable have now been proved worthless, for the very civilization that supported these beliefs is, in many areas, in an advanced stage of disintegration.

Meanwhile these false premises did great harm by distracting attention from the real problems that confronted our cities and by failing to work out any strategy for dealing with these problems. As so often happened during the last quarter century, the self-styled practical men

* Copyright 1922 by Harcourt, Brace and Company, Inc.

turned out to be the weak irresponsible dreamers, afraid to face unpleasant facts, while those of us who were called dreamers have, perhaps, some little right to be accepted—at least belatedly—as practical men. By now history has caught up with our most dire prophecies. That is at once the justification of our thinking and the proof of its tragic failure to influence our contemporaries.

Provincial and Commercial Eras

Around us, in the city, each epoch in America has been concentrated and crystallized. In building our cities we deflowered a wilderness. Today more than one-half the population of the United States lives in an environment which the jerry-builder, the real estate speculator, the paving contractor, and the industrialist have largely created. Have we begotten a civilization? That is a question which a survey of the American city will help us to answer.

If American history is viewed from the standpoint of the student of cities, it divides itself roughly into three parts. The first was a provincial period, which lasted from the foundation of Manhattan down to the opening up of ocean commerce after the War of 1812. This was followed by a commercial period, which began with the cutting of canals and ended with the extension of the railroad system across the continent, and an industrial period, that gathered force on the Atlantic seaboard in the thirties and is still the dominant economic phase of our civilization. These periods must not be looked upon as strictly successive or exclusive: the names merely express in a crude way the main aspect of each era. It is possible to telescope the story of America's colonial expansion and industrial exploitation by following the material growth and

the cultural impoverishment of the American city during its transformations.

The momentum of the provincial city lasted well on to the Civil War. The economic basis of this period was agriculture and petty trade: its civic expression was, typically, the small New England town, with a central common around which were grouped a church—appropriately called a meeting house—a school, and perhaps a town hall. Its main street would be lined with tall suave elms and bordered by reticent white houses of much the same design as those that dotted the countryside. In the growing towns of the seaboard this culture was overthrown, before it had a chance to express itself adequately in either institutions or men, and it bloomed rather tardily, therefore, in the little towns of Concord and Cambridge, between 1820 and the Civil War. We know it today through a largely anonymous architecture, and through a literature created by the shool of writers that bears the name of the chief city. Unfortunately for the further development of what we might call the Concord culture, the agricultural basis of this civilization shifted to the wheat-growing West; and therewith channels of trade were diverted from Boston to ports that tapped a richer, more imperial hinterland. What remained of the provincial town in New England was a mummy-case.

The civilization of the New England town spent itself in the settlement of the Ohio Valley and the great tracts beyond. None of the new centers had, as provincial towns, any fresh contribution to make. It had taken the culture of New England more than three centuries before it had borne its Concord fruit, and the story of the Western movement is somehow summed up in the legend of Johnny Appleseed, who planted dry apple seeds, instead of grafts from the living tree, and hedged the roads he traveled with wild apples, harsh and puny and inedible. Cincinnati and Pittsburgh jumped from a frustrate provincialism into the midst of the machine era; and so for a long time they remained destitute of the institutions that are necessary to carry on the processes of civilization.

West of the Alleghenies, the common, with its church and school, was not destined to dominate the urban landscape: the railroad station and the commercial hotel had come to take their place. This was indeed the universal mark of the new industrialism, as obvious in nineteenth-century Oxford as in Hoboken. The pioneer American city, however, had none of the cultural institutions that had been accumulated in Europe during the great outbursts of the Middle Age and the Renaissance, and as a result its destitution was naked and apparent. It is true that every town which was developed mainly during the nineteenth century—Manchester as well as Milwaukee—suffered from the absence of civic institutes. The peculiarity of the New World was that the facilities for borrowing from the older centers were considerably more limited. London could export Madox Brown to Manchester to do the murals in the Town Hall: New York had still to create its schools of art before it had any Madox Browns that could be exported.

With the beginning of the nineteenth-century, market centers which had at first tapped only their immediate region began to reach further back into the hinterland, and to stretch outward, not merely for freights but for immigrants, across the ocean. The silly game of counting heads became the fashion, and in the literature of the thirties one discovers that every commercial city had its statistical lawyer who was bold enough to predict its leadership in "population and wealth" before the century was out. The chief boast of the American city was its prospective size.

Now the New England town was a genuine community. In so far as the New England community had a common social and political and religious life, the town expressed it. The city which was representative of the second period, on the other hand, was in origin a trading fort, and the supreme occupation of its founders was with the goods life rather than the good life. New York, Pittsburgh, Chicago, and St. Louis have this common basis. They were not composed of corporate organizations on the march, as it were, towards a New Jerusalem: they were simply a rabble of individuals "on the make." With such a tradition to give it momentum it is small wonder that the adventurousness of the commercial period was exhausted on the fortuities and temptations of trade. A state of intellectual anesthesia prevailed. One has only to compare Cist's Cincinnati Miscellany with Emersons' Dial to see at what a low level the towns of the Middle West were carrying on.

Since there was neither fellowship nor social stability nor security in the scramble of the inchoate commercial city, it remained for a particular institution to devote itself to the gospel of the "glad hand." Thus an historian of Pittsburgh records the foundation of a Masonic lodge as early as 1785, shortly after the building of the church, and in every American city, small or big, Odd Fellows, Mystic Shriners, Woodmen, Elks, Knights of Columbus, and other order without number in the course of time found for themselves a prominent place. (Their feminine counterparts were the D.A.R. and the W.C.T.U., their juniors, the college Greek letter fraternities.) Whereas one will search American cities in vain for the labor temples one discovers today in Europe from Belgium to Italy, one finds that the fraternal lodge generally occupies a site of dignity and importance. There were doubtless many excellent reasons for the strange proliferation of professional fraternity in the American city, but perhaps the strongest reason was the absence of any other kind of fraternity. The social center and the community center, which in a singularly hard and consciously beatific way way have sought to organize fellowship and mutual aid on different terms, are products of the last decade.

Perhaps the only other civic institution of importance that the commercial towns fostered was the lyceum: forerunner of the elephantine Chautauqua. The lyceum lecture, however, was taken as a soporific rather than a stimulant, and if it aroused any appetite for art, philosophy, or science there was nothing in the environment of the commerical city that could satisfy it. Just as church going became a substitute for religion, so automatic lyceum attendance became a substitute for thought. These were the prayer wheels of a preoccupied commercialism.

The contrast between the provincial and the commercial city in America was well summed up in their plans. Consider the differences between Cambridge and New York. Up to the beginning of the nineteenth century New York, at the tip of Manhattan Island, had the same diffident, rambling town plan that characterizes Cambridge. In this old type of city layout the streets lead nowhere, except to the buildings that give onto them: outside the main roads the provisions for traffic are so inadequate as to seem almost a provision against traffic. Quiet streets, a pleasant aspect, ample domestic facilities were the desiderata of the provincial town;

traffic, realty speculation, and expansion were those of the newer era. This became evident as soon as the Empire City started to realize its "manifest destiny" by laying down, in 1811, a plan for its future development.

New York's city plan commissioners went about their work with a scarcely concealed purpose to increase traffic and raise realty values. The amenities of city life counted for little in their scheme of things: debating "whether they should confine themselves to rectilinear and rectangular streets, or whether they should adopt some of those supposed improvements, by circles, ovals, and stars," they decided, on grounds of economy, against any departure from the gridiron design. It was under the same stimulus that these admirable philistines had the complacency to plan the city's development up to 155th Street. Here we are concerned, however, with the results of the rectangular plan rather than with the motives that lay behind its adoption throughout the country.

The principal effect of the gridiron plan is that every street becomes a thoroughfare, and that every thoroughfare is potentially a commercial street. The tendency towards movement in such a city vastly outweighs the tendency towards settlement. As a result of progressive shifts in population, due to the changes to which commercial competition subjects the use of land, the main institutions of the city, instead of cohering naturally—as the museums, galleries, theaters, clubs, and public offices group themselves in the heart of Westminster—are dispersed in every direction. Neither Columbia College, New York University, the Astor Library, nor the National Academy of Design—to seize but a few examples—is on its original site. Yet had Columbia remained at Fiftieth Street it might have had some effective working relation with the great store-houses of books that now occupies part of Bryant Park at Forty-second Street; or, alternatively, had the Astor Library remained on its old site it might have had some connection with New York University—had that institution not in turn moved!

What was called the growth of the commercial city was really a manifestation of the absence of design in the gridiron plan. The rectangular parceling of ground promoted speculation in land-units and the ready interchange of real property: it had no relation whatever to the essential purposes for which a city exists. It is not a little significant that Chicago, Cincinnati, and St. Louis, each of which had space set aside for public purposes in their original plans, had given up these civic holdings to the realty gambler before half of the nineteenth century was over. The common was not the center of a well-rounded community life, as in New England, but the center of land-specula-tion—which was at once the business, the recreation, and the religion of the com-mercial city. Under the influence of New York the Scadders, whom Martin Chuzzle-wit encountered, were laying down their New Edens throughout the country.

Broadway as Symbol

It was during the commercial period that the evolution of the Promenade, such as existed in New York at Battery Park, took place. The new promenade was no longer a park but a shop-lined thoroughfare, Broadway. Shopping became for the more domesticated half of the community an exciting, bewildering amusement; and out of a combination of Yankee "notions," Barnumlike advertisement, and magis-terial organization arose that *omnium gatherum* of commerce, the department store. It is scarcely possible to exaggerate the part that Broadway—I use the term generically—has played in the American town. It is not merely the Agora but the Acropolis. When the factory whistle closes the week, and the factory hands of Cam-den, or Pittsburgh, or Bridgeport pour out of the buildings and stockades in which they spend the more exhausting half of their lives, it is through Broadway that the greater part of their repressions seek an outlet. Both the name and the institu-tion extend across the continent from New York to Los Angeles. Up and down these second-hand Broadways, from one in the afternoon until past ten at night, drifts a more or less aimless mass of human beings, bent upon extracting such joy as is possible from the sights in the windows, the con-tacts with other human beings, the occa-sional or systematic flirtations, and the risks and adventures of purchase.

In the early development of Broadway the amusements were adventitious. Even at present, in spite of the ubiquitous movie, the crowded street itself, at least in the smaller communities, is the main source of entertainment. Now, under normal con-ditions, for a great part of the population in a factory town one of the chief instincts to be repressed is that of acquisition (collection). It is not merely that the average factory worker cannot afford the luxuries of life: the worst is that he must think twice before purchasing the necessities. Out of this situation one of Broadway's happiest achievements has arisen: the five and ten cent store. In the five and ten cent store it is possible for the circumscribed factory operative to obtain the illusion of unmoderated expenditure—and even ex-travagance—without actually inflicting any irreparable rent in his purse. Broadway is thus, in more than one sense, the great compensatory device of the American city. The dazzle of white lights, the color of electric signs, the alabaster architecture of the moving-picture palaces, the esthetic appeals of the shop windows—these stand for elements that are left out of the drab perspectives of the industrial city. People who do not know how to spend their time must take what satisfaction they can in spending their money. That is why, although the five and ten cent store itself is perhaps mainly an institution for the proletariat, the habits and dispositions it encourages are universal. The chief amusement of Atlantic City, that opulent hostelry-annex of New York and Philadelphia, lies not in the beach and the ocean but in the shops which line the interminable Broadway known as the Boardwalk.

Broadway, in sum, is the facade of the American city: a false front. The highest achievements of our material civilization—and at their best our hotels, our department stores, and our Woolworth towers are achievements—count as so many symptoms of its spiritual failure. In order to cover up the vacancy of getting and spending in our cities, we have invented a thousand fresh devices for getting and spending. As a consequence our life is externalized. The principal institutions of the American city are merely distractions that take our eyes off the environment, instead of instruments which would help us to mold it creatively a little nearer to humane hopes and desires.

Consequences of Industrialism

The birth of industrialism in America is announced in the opening of the Crystal Palace in Bryant Park, Manhattan, in 1853. Between the Crystal Palace Exhibition and the Chicago World's Fair in 1892 lies a period whose defects were partly accentuated by the exhaustion that followed the Civil War. The debasement of the American city during this period can be read in almost every building that was erected. The influence of colonial architecture had waned to extinction during the first half of the century. There followed a period of eclectic experiment, in which all sorts of Egyptian, Byzantine, Gothic, and Arabesque ineptitudes were committed—a period whose absurdities we have only in recent years begun to escape. The domestic style, as the century progressed, became more limited. Little touches about the doors, moldings, fanlights, and balustrades disappeared, and finally craftsmanship went out of style altogether and a pretentious architectural puffery took its place. The "era of good feeling" was an era of bad taste.

Pittsburgh, St. Louis, and Chicago give perhaps the most naked revelation of the industrial city's characteristics. There were two institutions that set their mark upon the early part of this period. One of them was the Mechanic's Hall. This was usually a building of red brick, structural iron, and glass, whose unique hideousness marks it as a typical product of the age of coal-industrialism, to be put alongside the "smoke-halls" of the railroad termini. The other institution was the German beer-garden—the one bright spot on the edge of an urban landscape that was steadily becoming more dingy, more dull, and more depressing. The cities that came to life in this period had scarcely any other civic apparatus to boast of. Conceive of Pittsburgh without Schenley Park, without the Carnegie Institute, without the Library or the Museum or the Concert Hall, and without the institutions that have grown up during the last generation around its sub-Acropolis—and one has a picture of

Progress and Poverty that Henry George might have drawn on for illustration. The industrial city did not represent the creative values in civilization: it stood for a new form of human barbarism. In the coal towns of Pennsylvania, the steel towns of the Ohio and its tributaries, and the factory towns of Long Island Sound and Narragansett Bay was an environment much more harsh, antagonistic, and brutal than anything the pioneers had encountered. Even the fake exhilaration of the commercial city was lacking.

The reaction against the industrial city was expressed in various ways. The defect of these reactions was that they were formulated in terms of an escape from the environment rather than in a reconstruction of it. Symptomatic of this escape, along one particular alley, was the architecture of Richardson, and of his apprentices, McKim and White. No one who has an eye for the fine incidence of beautiful architecture can avoid a shock at discovering a monumental Romanesque building at the foot of Pittsburgh's dingy "Hump," or the hardly less monstrous beauty of Trinity Church, Boston, as one approaches it from a waste of railroad yards that lie on one side of it. It was no accident, one is inclined to believe, that Richardson should have returned to the Romanesque only a little time before Henry Adams was exploring Mont St. Michel and Chartres. Both men were searching for a specific against the fever of industrialism, and architects like Richardson were taking to archaic beauty as a man who was vaguely ill might have recourse to quinine, in the hope that his disease had sufficient similarity to malaria to be cured by it.

The truth is that the doses of exotic architecture which Richardson and his school sought to inject into the American city were anodynes rather than specifics. The Latin Renaissance models of McKim and White—the Boston Public Library and Madison Square Garden, for example—were perhaps a little better suited to the concrete demands of the new age; but they were still a long way from that perfect congruence with contemporary habits and modes of thought which was recorded in buildings like Independence Hall. Almost down to the last decade the best buildings of the industrial period have been anonymous, and scarcely ever recognized for their beauty. A grain elevator here, a warehouse there, an office building, a garage—there has been the promise of a stripped, athletic, classical style of architecture in these buildings which shall embody all that is good in the Machine Age: its precision, its cleanliness, its hard illuminations, its unflinching logic. Dickens once poked fun at the architecture of Coketown because its infirmary looked like its jail and its jail like its town hall. But the joke had a sting to it only because these buildings were all plaintively destitute of esthetic inspiration. In a place and an age that had achieved a well-rounded and balanced culture, we should expect to find the same spirit expressed in the simplest cottage and the grandest public building. So we find it, for instance, in the humble market towns of the Middle Age: there is not one type of architecture for fifteenth-century Shaftesbury and another for London; neither is there one style for public London and quite another for domestic London. Our architects in America have only just begun to cease regarding the Gothic style as especially fit for churches and schools, whilst they favor Roman mode for courts, and the Byzantine, perhaps, for offices. Even the unique beauty of the Bush Terminal Tower is compromised by an antiquely "stylized" interior.[1]

With the beginning of the second decade of this century there is some evidence of an attempt to make a genuine culture out of industrialism—instead of attempting to escape from industrialism into a culture which, though doubtless genuine enough, has the misfortune to be dead. The schoolhouses in Gary, Indiana, have some of the better qualities of a Gary steel plant. That symptom is all to the good. It points perhaps to a time when the Gary steel plant may have some of the educational virtues of a Gary school. One of the things that has made the industrial age a horror in America is the notion that there is something shameful in its manifestations. The idea that nobody would ever go near an industrial plant except under stress of starvation is in part responsible for the heaps of rubbish and rusty metal, for the general disorder and vileness, that still characterize broad acres of our factory districts. There is nothing short of the Alkali Desert that compares with the desolateness of the common American industrial town. These qualities are indicative of the fact that we have centered attention not upon the process but upon the return; not upon the task but the emoluments; not upon what we can get out of our work but upon what we can achieve when we get away from our work. Our industrialism has been in the grip of business, and our industrial cities, and their institutions, have exhibited a major preoccupation with business. The coercive repression of an impersonal, mechanical technique was compensated by the pervasive will-to-power—or at least will-to-comfort—of commercialism.

We have shirked the problem of trying to live well in a régime that is devoted to the production of T-beams and toothbrushes and T.N.T. As a result, we have failed to react creatively upon the environment with anything like the inspiration that one might have found in a group to medieval peasants building a cathedral. The urban worker escapes the mechanical routine of his daily job only to find an equally mechanical substitute for life and growth and experience in his amusements. The Gay White Way with its stupendous blaze of lights, and Coney Island, with its fear-stimulating roller coasters and chute-the-chutes, are characteristic by-products of an age that has renounced the task of actively humanizing the machine, and of creating an environment in which all the fruitful impulses of the community may be expressed. The movies, the White Ways, and the Coney Islands, which almost every American city boasts in some form or other, are means of giving jaded and throttled people the sensations of living without the direct experience of life—a sort of spiritual masturbation. In short, we have had the alternative of humanizing the industrial city or dehumanizing the population. So far we have de-humanized the population.

Exodus to Suburbia

The external reactions against the industrial city came to a head in the World's Fair in Chicago. In that strange and giddy mixture of Parnassus and Coney Island was born a new conception of the city—a White City, spaciously designed, lighted by electricity, replete with monuments, crowned with public buildings, and dignified by a radiant architecture. The men who planned the exposition knew something about the better side of the spacious perspectives that Haussmann had designed for Napoleon III. Without taking into account the fundamental conditions of industrialism, or the salient facts of economics, they initiated what shortly came to be known as the City Beautiful movement. For a couple of decades Municipal Art societies were rampant. Their program had the defects of the régime it attempted to combat. Its capital effort was to put on a front—to embellish Main Street and make it a more attractive thoroughfare. Here in esthetics, as elsewhere in education, persisted the Brahminical view of culture: the idea that beauty was something that could be acquired by anyone who was willing to put up the cash; that it did not arise naturally out of the good life but was something which could be plastered on impoverished life; in short, that it was a cosmetic.

Until the Pittsburgh Survey of 1908 pricked a pin through superficial attempts at municipal improvement, those who sought to remake the American city overlooked the necessity for rectifying its economic basis. The meanness, the spotty development, and the congestion of the American city were at least in some degree an index of that deep disease of realty speculation which had, as already noted, caused cities like Chicago to forfeit land originally laid aside for public uses. Because facts like these were ignored for the sake of some small, immediate result, the developments that the early reformers were bold enough to outline still lie in the realms of hopeless fantasy—a fine play of the imagination, like Scadder's prospectus of Eden. Here there have been numerous signs of promise during the last decade; but it is doubtful whether they are yet numerous enough or profound enough to alter the general picture.

At best, the improvements that have been effected in the American city have not been central but subsidiary. They have been improvements, as Aristotle would have said, in the material bases of the good life: they have not been improvements in the art of living. The growth of the American city during the past century has meant the extension of paved streets and sewers and gas mains, and progressive heightening of office buildings and tenements. The outlay on pavements, sewers, electric lighting systems, and plumbing has been stupendous; but no matter what the Rotary Clubs and Chambers of Commerce may think of them, these mechanical ingenuities are not the indices of a civilization. There is a curious confusion in American between growth and improvement. We use the phrase "bigger and better" as if the conjunction were inevitable. As a matter of fact, there is little evidence to show that the vast increase of population in every urban area had been accompanied by anything like the necessary increase of schools, universities, theaters, meeting places, parks, and so forth. The fact that in 1920 we had sixty-eight cities with more than 100,000 population, thirty-three with more than 200,000, and twelve with more than 500,000 does not mean that the resources of polity, culture, and art have been correspondingly on the increase. The growth of the American city has resulted less in the establishment of civilized standards of life than in the extension of Suburbia.

"Suburbia" is used here in both the accepted and in a more literal sense. On one hand I refer to the fact that the growth of the metropolis throws vast numbers of people into distant dormitories where, by and large, life is carried on without the discipline of rural occupations and without the cultural resources that the Central District of the city still retains in its art exhibitions, theaters, concerts, and the like. But our metropolises produce Suburbia not merely by reason of the fact that the people who work in the offices, bureaus, and factories live as citizens in a distant territory, perhaps in another state: they likewise foster Suburbia in another sense. I mean that the quality of life for the great mass of people who live within the political boundaries of the metropolis itself is inferior to that which a city with an adequate equipment and a thorough realization of the creative needs of the community is capable of producing. In this sense, the "suburb" called Brookline is a genuine city, while the greater part of the "city of Boston" is a suburb. We have scarcely begun to make an adequate distribution of libraries, meeting places, parks, gymnasia, and similar equipment, without which life in the city tends to be carried on at a low level of routine—physically as well as mentally. (The blatantly confidential advertisements of constipation remedies on all the billboards tell a significant story.) At any reasonable allotment of park space, The Committee on Congestion in New York pointed out in 1911, a greater number of acres was needed for parks on the lower East Side than was occupied by the entire population. This case is extreme but representative.

It is the peculiarity of our metropolitan civilization, then, that in spite of vast resources drawn from the ends of the earth, it has an insufficient civic equipment, and what it does possess it uses only transiently. Those cities that have the beginnings of an adequate equipment, like New York—to choose no more invidious example—offer them chiefly to the traveler. As a traveler's city New York is near perfection. An association of cigar salesmen or an international congress of social scientists, meeting in one of the auditoriums of a big hotel, dining together, mixing in the lounge, and finding recreation in the theaters hard by, discover an environment that is ordered, within its limits, to a nicety.

It is this hotel and theater district that we must charitably think of when we are tempted to speak about the triumphs of the American city. Despite manifold defects that arise from want of planning, this is the real civic center of America's Metropolis. What we must overlook in this characterization are the long miles of slum that stretch in front and behind and on each side of this district—neighborhoods where, in spite of the redoubtable efforts of settlement workers, block organizers, and neighborhood associations, there is no permanent institution, other than the public school or the sectarian church, to remind the inhabitants that they have a common life and a common destiny.

Civic life, in fine, the life of intelligent association and common action, a life whose faded pattern still lingers in the old New England town, is not something that we daily enjoy, as we work in an office or a factory. It is rather a temporary state that we occasionally achieve with a great deal of time, bother, and expense. The city is not around us, in our little town, suburb, or neighborhood: it lies beyond us, at the end of a subway ride or a railway journey. We are citizens occasionally: we are suburbanites (*denizens, idiots*) by regular routine. Small wonder that bathtubs and heating systems and similar apparatus play such a large part in our conception of the good life.

Prospects of Metropolitanism

Metropolitanism in America represents from the cultural angle, a reaction against the uncouth and barren countryside that was skinned, rather than cultivated, by the restless, individualistic, self-assertive American pioneer. The perpetual drag to New York, and the endeavor of less favorably situated cities to imitate the virtues and defects of New York, is explicable as nothing other than the desire to participate in some measure in the benefits of city life. Since we have failed up to the present to develop genuine regional cultures, those who do not wish to remain barbarians must become metropolitans. That means they must come to New York, or ape the ways that are fashionable in New York. Here opens the breach that has begun to widen between the metropolis and the countryside in America. The countryman, who cannot enjoy the advantages of the metropolis, who has no center of his own to which he can point with pride, resents the privileges that the metropolitan enjoys. Hence the periodical crusades of our State Legislatures, largely packed with rural representatives, against the vices, corruptions, and follies which the countryman enviously looks upon as the peculiar property of the big city. Perhaps the envy and resentment of the farming population is due to a genuine economic grievance against the big cities—especially against their banks, insurance companies, and speculative middle-men. Should the concentration of power, glory, and privilege in the metropolis continue, it is possible that the city will find itself subject to an economic siege. If our cities cannot justify their existence by their creative achievements, by their demonstration of the efficacy and grace of corporate life, it is doubtful whether they will be able to persuade the country to support them, once the purely conventional arrangements by means of which the city browbeats the countryside are upset. This, however, brings us to the realm of social speculation; and he who would enter it must abandon everything but hope.

Metropolitanism is of two orders. At its partial best it is exhibited in New York, the literal mother city of America. In its worst aspect it shows itself in the sub-metropolises which have been spawning so prolifically since the eighties. If we are to understand the capacities and limitations of the other great cities in America, we must first weigh the significance of New York.

The forces that have made New York dominant are inherent in our financial and industrial system; elsewhere those same forces, working in slightly different ways, created London, Rome, Paris, Berlin, Vienna, Petrograd, and Moscow. What happened in the industrial towns of America was that the increments derived from land, capital, and association went, not to the enrichment of the local community, but to those who had a legal title to the land and the productive machinery. In other words, the gains that were made in Pittsburgh, Springfield, Dayton, and a score of other towns that became important in the industrial era were realized largely in New York, whose position had been established, before the turn of the century, as the locus of trade and finance. (New York passed the 500,000 mark in the 1850 census.) This is why, perhaps, during the seventies and eighties, decades of miserable depression throughout the industrial centers, there were signs of hope and promise in New York: the Museums of Art and Natural History were built: Life and Puck and a batch of newspapers were founded: the Metropolitan Opera House and Carnegie Hall were established: and a dozen other evidences of a vigorous civic life appeared. In a short time New York became the mold of fashion and the glass of form, and through the standardization, specialization, and centralization which accompanies the machine process the Metropolis became at length the center of advertising, the lender of farm mortgages, the distributor of boiler-plate news, the headquarters of the popular magazine, the publishing center, and finally the chief disseminator of plays and motion pictures in America. The educational foundations which the exploiter of the Kodak has established at Rochester were not characteristic of the early part of the industrial period—otherwise New York's eminence might have been briskly challenged before it had become, after its fashion, unchallengeable. The increment from Mr. Carnegie's steel works built a hall of music for New York long before it created the Carnegie Institute in Pittsburgh. In other words, the widespread effort of the American provincial to leave his industrial city for New York comes to something like an attempt to get back from New York what had been previously filched from the industrial city.

The future of our cities depends upon how permanent are the forces which drain money, energy, and brains from the various regions in America into the twelve great cities that now dominate the countryside, and in turn drain the best that is in these sub-metropolises to New York. Today our cities are at a crossing of the ways. Since the 1910 census a new tendency has begun to manifest itself, and the cities that have grown the fastest are those of a population from 25,000 to 100,000. Quantitatively, that is perhaps a good sign. It may indicate the drift to Suburbia is on the wane. One finds it much harder, however, to gauge to qualitative capacities of the new régime; much more difficult to estimate the likelihood of building up, within the next generation or two, genuine regional cultures to take the place of pseudo-national culture which now mechanically emanates from New York. So far our provincial culture has been self-fertilized and sterile: our provincial cities have substituted boosting for achievement, fanciful speculation for intelligent planning, and a zaniacal optimism for constructive thought. These habits have made them an easy prey to the metropolis, for at its lowest ebb there has always been a certain amount of organized intelligence and cultivated imagination in New York—if only because it is the chief point of contact between Europe and America. Gopher Prairie has yet to take to heart the fabel about the frog that tried to inflate himself to the size of a bull. When Gopher Priairie learns its lessons from Bergen and Augsburg and Montpellier and Grenoble, the question of "metropolitanism versus regionalism" may become as active in America as it is now in Europe.

Those of us who are metropolitans may be tempted to think that the hope for civilization in America is bound up with the continuance of metropolitanism. That is essentially a cockney view of culture and society, however, and our survey of the development of the city in America should have done something to weaken its self-confident complacence. Our metropolitan civilization is not a success. It is a different kind of wilderness from that which we have deflowered—but the feral rather than the humane quality is dominant: it is still a wilderness. The cities of America must learn to remold our mechanical and financial régime, for if metropolitanism continues they are probably destined to fall by its weight.

NOTE

1. This paragraph—like the article on Machinery and the Modern Style I published in The New Republic in 1921—antedated the lucubrations of Le Corbusier on the same subject.

12. The Growth and Structure of Metropolitan Areas

William M. Dobriner

Several papers presented earlier in this volume make the point that metropolitan development is the process which distinguishes contemporary urbanism. William Dobriner explores the meaning of this claim with reference to census materials and demographic and social science studies concerned with the New York Region. He argues that the social and economic differences within the Region are grasped most easily if one thinks in terms of three concentric zones: the Central Core, the Suburban Zone, and the Rural-Urban Fringe. The Central Core is characterized by high density populations with a good deal of land devoted to commercial and industrial use. The second Zone includes not only suburban, bedroom communities but also industrialized satellite cities. In the Rural-Urban Fringe the prevailing use of land has no established pattern as yet: it is the frontier for the expanding metropolis. The paper also includes a review of attempts by other sociologists to define the nature of the metropolis. The convergence of definitions proposed by different scholars suggests that the experience of the New York Region is roughly similar to other metropolitan areas in the United States.

William M. Dobriner is Professor of Sociology at Hofstra University, New York. He is the author of *Social Structures and Systems* (1969) and *Class in Suburbia* (1963); and he edited *The Suburban Community* (1958).

In 1900, metropolitan areas claimed 31 percent of the total population. Today, 2 out of 3 Americans live in urban places, but over 60 percent of the total population lives in metropolitan areas. Census forecasts suggest that by 1975 the population of the United States will exceed 220 million, an increase of roughly 40 million over 1960, 63 percent of whom will live in metropolitan areas.

The growth of metropolitan centers, however, is merely one facet of the urban revolution of the last sixty years. Although metropolitan areas have demonstrated amazing growth, the component parts are by no means growing at the same rate. In 1900, for example, the population of the *central cities* of metropolitan areas constituted 61.9 percent of the total metropolitan unit while the suburban and fringe areas outside of the cities were only 38.1

percent of the total area. By 1960, however, the picture had changed. Central cities claimed barely half of the total population of metropolitan areas.

The 1960 Census for the New York Standard Metropolitan Statistical Area dramatically illustrates the national trend. While New York city lost a total of 109,973 persons between 1950 and 1960, its suburban counties were registering spectacular gains. Nassau County increased 93 percent over the decade. Rockland 53 percent, Suffolk 141 percent, and Westchester 29 percent. In this manner, while New York City lost about one and a half percent of its population during the decade, its suburbs increased by 75 percent.

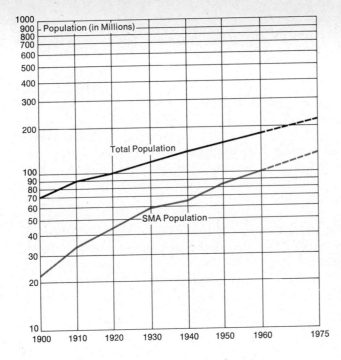

Figure 1. Population growth in the United States and in standard metropolitan areas, 1900–1975. (Source: *Guiding Metropolitan Growth:* A Statement on National Policy by the Research and Policy Committee of the Committee for Economic Development, p. 13.)

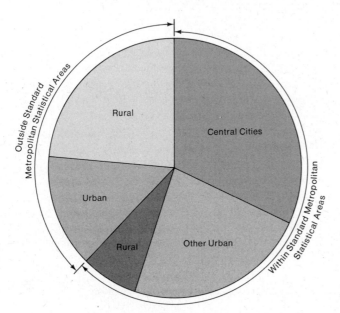

Figure 2. Population by type of residence in metropolitan and non-metropolitan areas: 1960. (Courtesy of the Department of Commerce, Bureau of the Census.)

From 1900 until 1920 central cities were growing faster than their tributary rings.[1] However, in each decade since 1920 the rings have been growing faster than the central cities. Thus, the comparative growth rates between central cities and their rings have now become considerable. In the decade between 1940 and 1950, rings grew almost two and a half times as fast as central cities. The result has been that the suburban population alone is estimated at more than 50 million. The trends in the New York metropolitan area are clearly reflected on the national level. According to the 1960 Census, about 84 percent of the 28 million population increase during the decade 1950–60 occurred in the nation's metropolitan areas.[2] However, the increase in these areas from 89,316,903 in 1950 to 112,885,178 in 1960 (26.4 percent) saw the suburban rings growing at a much faster rate than central cities. The increase of central cities in the decade (5.6 million) to a total of 58 million by 1960 constituted a 10.7 percent increase; in contrast, outlying suburban areas grew from 36.9 million population in 1950 to 54.9 million in 1960 for an increase of 48.6 percent.

The growth rates for central cities are clearly continuing to decline. Indeed, the trend is for the central cities of the largest metropolitan areas to have even slower rates of growth than the central cities of

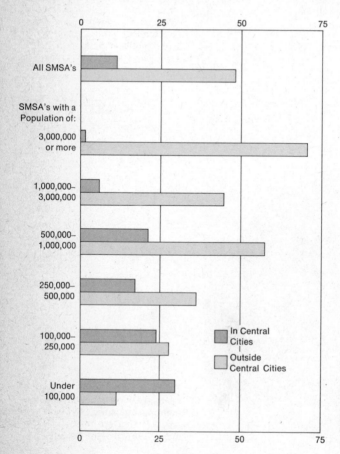

Figure 3. Change in population in and outside central cities by size of standard metropolitan statistical areas: 1950–1960, in percent. (Courtesy of the Department of Commerce, Bureau of the Census.)

smaller metropolitan areas. We have already noted that New York City lost population during the 1950–60 decade. In the five metropolitan areas of 3,000,000 or more the growth in central cities was only 1 percent. In contrast, however, the growth of the suburban rings of these great metropolitan centers was 71 percent. As size declines, the growth rate of central cities increased in relation to the suburban areas. In the case of the smaller metropolitan areas of less than 100,000, the growth rate (29 percent) exceeded the suburban rate (11 percent).

It is clear that population is moving toward the suburbs and the claim of central cities is decreasing. For the country as a whole, the outlying rings of metropolitan centers accounted for about two-thirds of the total U.S. population increase

since 1950 and for more than three-fourths of the total increase within metropolitan areas. Furthermore, the trend of central city loss and suburban gain is expected to continue. By 1975, the Committee for Economic Development (see Fig. Four) estimates the central city population will have dropped to 42 percent of the metropolitan total, while the suburban and fringe areas outside will have grown to 57 percent of the entire metropolitan complex. This almost reverses the central city-suburban population proportions established for metropolitan areas at the turn of the century.

Although cities, as a distinguishable community form, have existed for over five thousand years, the city in its metropolitan guise is scarcely one hundred years old. And while *urbanism* and *the city* are

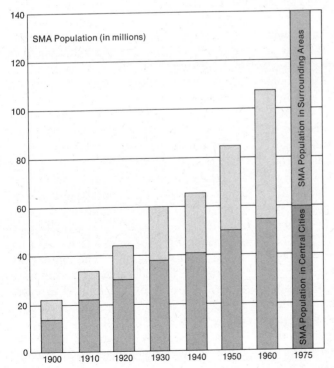

Figure 4. Distribution of metropolitan population between central cities and surrounding areas, 1900–1975. (Source: *Guiding Metropolitan Growth:* A Statement on National Policy by the Research and Policy Committee of the Committee for Economic Development, p. 15.)

subject to varied interpretations, so too, is *metropolis*. Although there are literally hundreds of experts today dealing with the many facets of metropolitan matters, both scientific and practical, no one is quite sure what a metropolis really is. The many faces of metropolitanism seen by the specialists only serve to illustrate the significant ·point that *metropolis* and *metropolitan* are conceptual entities—constructs which categorize certain emergent and dominant properties of modern urban life. Accordingly, definitions of the critical features of metropolitanism will vary as each specialist abstracts out of the total empirical context those patterns that have particular relevance to his investigation. The metropolitan area, therefore, will be viewed by the Bureau of the Census in terms of its needs for clear statistical delimitation between other community forms—rural and urban. Then too, metropolitanism may be conceptualized in terms of an area of economic dominance from the core city outward into its hinterland. The metropolitan area may be thought of as a transportation network without regard for political boundaries. On a more complex level, the metropolitan area may be regarded as a vast spatial structure consisting of functionally interdependent economic, political, and social subsystems. The result may be a super-organized concentration that takes in portions of two or three states in a highly specialized and differentiated functional integration of areas that go well beyond the political limits of the core city.

Indeed, the process of metropolitan growth has proceeded so far that the unit "metropolitan area" in the aforementioned sense may no longer apply to the larger, integrated metropolitan aggregates that are flowing into each other across the nation. The "boundaries" of metropolitan areas are fusing to form super-metropolitan entities that have been called "strip cities" or, as Jean Gottmann has termed the integration of metropolitan areas from southern New Hampshire all the way to the Appalachian foothills in Virginia, "Megalopolis."

According to a study made by *U.S. News and World Report* (Sept. 18, 1961; see Figure Five) the thirteen major "strip cities" in the United States—Boston to Washington, Albany to Erie, Cleveland to Pittsburgh, Toledo to Cincinnati, Detroit to Muskegon, Chicago-Gary to Milwaukee, St. Louis to Peoria, Seattle to Eugene, San Francisco to San Diego, Kansas City to Sioux Falls, Fort Worth-Dallas-San Antonio-Houston, Miami-Tampa-Jacksonville, and Atlanta to Raleigh—contain half the population of the country (89,395,469) and have increased more than 25 percent from 1950. Of the total 212 metropolitan areas in the nation, 119 fall within 13 giant strip city patterns. Not only did half of the population live within these super-metropolitan constellations, but 109 billion dollars in retail trade or 54.7 percent of the total consumer market was expended there.

Yet no matter how one looks at the metropolis he is bound to perceive selectively. No matter how broad and inclusive the view, or how abstract the delineating categories, one is bound to leave out something that someone else regards as crucial. No definition is entirely adequate. No view is universal. However, by leaving something out, the scientific investigator hopes he can logically and empirically control the limited variables he wants to study. It is only by this kind of artificial abstraction out of the phenomenological chaos around us that we can make any sense out of the world in which we live. Since the metropolis is the newest, largest,

Figure 5. The thirteen major strip cities in the United States. (Courtesy of the Department of Commerce, Bureau of the Census.)

and most complex unit in which residential, political, and economic functions fuse into a single massive entity, our sense of its structures and processes is still incomplete. But every year we fill in more of the picture. Our perceptions sharpen, our concepts become more precise, our data more reliable, and thus our knowledge grows.

The Bureau of the Census has struggled constantly to develop statistical referents which subsume the spatial and functional integration of great cities and their tributary hinterlands. The term "metropolitan district" was used in the Census of 1940 and earlier. Essentially this term was applied to an urban area with one or more central cities of 50,000 or more in population, in addition to including adjacent, contiguous, or adjoining units with popula-

tion densities of 150 or more per square mile. In the Census of 1950, the Bureau adopted the term "Standard Metropolitan Area" which included a city of 50,000 or more in population, in addition to the entire county in which the city was located and all contiguous counties which are economically and socially integrated into the metropolitan complex.

Terms such as "metropolitan district" and "standard metropolitan area" are the arithmetic constructs through which the Bureau of the Census gathers data on the metropolitan areas of the nation. They were designed as convenient statistical guides suitable for the purpose of the Census. For other purposes the Census concept of metropolitan area might not usefully apply.

We are primarily concerned with the metropolitan area as a spatial structure which reflects the underlying functional specialization and integration of the area. On this level, the units of analysis go considerably beyond the demographic and political variables utilized by the Census. In the main, metropolitan areas are conceived of in terms of three specialized subareas. These are variously referred to as "rings," "zones," "belts," etc., and they stand in a particular spatial or *ecological* relationship to each other. While the vocabularies differ, and there has been little systematic effort spent on the formal delineation of functional rings

within the metropolitan complex, there is enough consistency (particularly from the empirical studies) to warrant the "three ring" view. For example, R. D. McKenzie, a pioneer in the field of metropolitan studies, discussed "three tapering zones of influence" within the metropolitan district in connection with traffic and shopping patterns.[3] Boskoff distinguishes three bands within the "urban region" or metropolitan context.[4] He suggests the central city, the suburban zone, and urban fringes. Schnore analyzed metropolitan growth rates as broken into central cities, urban rings, and rural ring.[5] Duncan and Reiss, in the analysis of differential growth

Figure 6. A model metropolitan area showing the relationship between the central city, suburban zone, and rural-urban fringe.

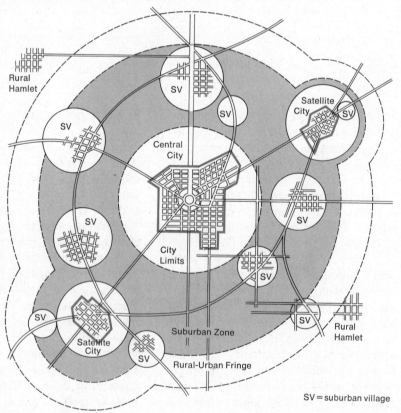

SV = suburban village

rates within the metropolitan area, distinguish three basic metropolitan units: central cities, suburbs, and urban fringe.[6] Lazerwitz, in his study of socioeconomics and demographic change within metropolitan areas focused on three belts: central residential area, suburban residential belt, and adjacent residential belt.[7] Hoover and Vernon, in their study of the New York Metropolitan Region, conceived of the area in terms of three basic zones: The Core, The Inner Ring, and The Outer Ring.[8]

Although their language varies, ecologists, demographers, economists, sociologists and political scientists *think* of the metropolitan area in terms of three differentiated zones. We can, therefore, assume that this view of metropolitan centers is generally useful. Since there is general agreement that the zones *are there*, but not complete accord on the terms used to describe these areas, we shall identify them as (1) the Central Core, (2) the Suburban Zone, and (3) the Rural-Urban Fringe. Having identified these zones, however, the logical task is to inquire into those factors which have led to the three-ring view of metropolitan centers. In the interest of brevity we shall take the central city—the core area—as a given quantity and shall concentrate our discussion on the communities and zones which lie beyond the core city.

The Bureau of the Census does not provide a definition of *suburb* even for its own limited statistical purposes. Neither has the term received much formal attention by sociologists. Adna Weber, in his classic study of city growth written in 1899, commented on suburban expansion and the loss of population from certain areas of London, Berlin, and New York.[9] Certainly, the idea of the suburbs has been around a long time. Unfortunately, only a few writers in recent years have begun to ask if the idea of the suburbs in terms of structure and function within the metropolitan complex has much meaning and usefulness. Within the past decade, the term *suburb* has been heavily reappraised.

Boskoff defines suburbs as ". . . those *urbanized nuclei* located outside (but within accessible range) of central cities that are politically independent but economically and psychologically linked with services and facilities provided by the metropolis."[10] In addition, he stresses the "economic and social . . . bonds of dependence . . ." between suburb and central city. According to Walter Martin "*Suburb* refers to the relatively small but formally structured community adjacent to and dependent upon a larger central city."[11] Fava: "Suburbs . . . refers particularly to the residential or dormitory variety, characterized by dependence on the city occupationally and for various specialized types of shopping and recreation. A working definition would comprise the area outside the legal city limits but within commuting distance."[12] Hallenbeck suggests that in order to understand the "social geography" of cities it is necessary "to go beyond municipal boundary lines" where there are "distinct communities that stand apart."[13]

All of these views of the suburbs, which are representative of the literature, rest heavily on two basic characteristics—characteristics which critically, or as Martin says "definitively," differentiate the suburb from all other forms of community organization. These are: the physical and political separation of the suburb from the central city, and the economic dependence of the suburb on the core city as particularly seen in the suburban commuting pattern. Suburbs may indeed be much more than this, but if a community is to be regarded as suburban in its simplest and most elementary form, it must be physically removed from the central city and it must rely heavily on the urban economy.

A metropolis, at least in part, consists of a densely populated, highly urbanized core surrounded by a belt of politically independent but economically dependent suburban communities. At least, this seems to be the prevailing view. However, the term *suburban* is meaningful when applied to many species of community. The varieties, kinds, and types of suburb go back in the literature at least 40 years when Taylor first discussed the character of "satellite cities."[14] These were centers of production and employment and were not residential. Later, in the 1920's, Harlan Douglas differentiated suburbs as *residential, industrial*, and *mixed* types.[15] For Douglas, the two basic modes of suburban life were the "centers of consumption"—the residential suburbs and "centers of production"—the industrial suburb. Taylor's satellite city and Douglas' suburb of production are essentially one. Still later, and moving into the contemporary tradition, Harris distinguished between housing or dormitory suburbs, and manufacturing and industrial suburbs.[16] Schnore has recently contrasted the characteristics of residential suburbs and "employing satellites."[17] According to Schnore, in *spatial* terms both satellites and suburbs are "indistinguishable from adjacent areas" and must be viewed as "constituent parts of a larger urban complex—the metropolitan area." Continuing his distinction, Schnore maintains that "goods and services tend to flow out of the employing satellites to other areas . . . while persons are attracted into these for employment." Of the residential suburbs Schnore maintains they "tend to receive an influx of

goods and services for the consumption of their inhabitants." In terms of their characteristic functions within the metropolis, the residential suburbs are "suppliers of labor and consumers of commodities," while the employing satellites are "consumers of labor and suppliers of commodities."

Satellites tend to be older than residential suburbs and are found most often in industrialized sections of the northeast and north-central areas of the nation. In addition, suburbs and satellite cities tend to have contrasting types of populations. In general, satellites contain younger populations than do residential suburbs with a trend toward the lower socioeconomic class and status groups. Along similar lines, the population of satellite cities, contrasted with a model residential suburb, have a lower average education, lower average rent levels, high proportions of foreign-born whites, higher fertility rates, higher percentages of tenant-occupied buildings, and a work force in which two out of three workers are in the blue collar occupations.

In contrasting the comparative growth rates of residential suburbs and the employing satellites, Schnore demonstrated that the suburbs were growing almost twice as fast as the satellites. Furthermore, the suburbs were becoming even more residential in character, while the satellite areas, in addition to the central cities, were becoming more industrialized.

In the zonal view of the patterning of metropolitan areas, Zone I consists of the densely populated and highly commercialized and industrialized core, while Zone II consists of a belt of rapidly growing suburban communities and industrialized satellite cities. Of the two, suburbs and satellites, the suburbs seem to predominate slightly on the national average.

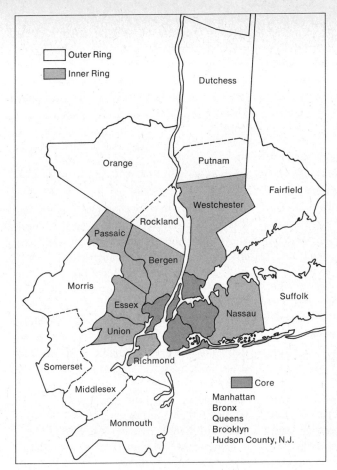

Figure 7. The three main zones of the New York metropolitan region. (Reprinted by permission of the publishers [Harvard University Press] from Edgar M. Hoover and Raymond Vernon, *Anatomy of a Metropolis*, charts by H. I. Forman. Copyright © 1959 by Regional Plan Association, Inc.)

Beyond the suburban belt lies the third zone of the metropolitan area which goes by a variety of names. Some call it "the rural ring," "urban fringe," "the outer ring," "the rural-urban fringe," and the like. We have called it the "rural-urban fringe" and by that we identify it as the last belt or area in which metropolitan or urban patterns are still evident. Essentially this belt consists of a geographic area in which the prevailing use of land is neither clearly urban nor suburban (residential, industrial, commercial) or rural (agricultural). It is that area where the expanding metropolis is currently waging its imperialistic war. This is the belt where the new suburban colonies and satellite cities will emerge in a few years. Thus, from an ecological view, the rural-urban fringe represents that spatial dimension of the entire area in which new urban functions, largely in the form of suburban residential areas and employing satellites, eat into the rural countryside. As such, it is a heterogeneous area of instability and change. On one side of the illusive and fragmentary boundary of the urban fringe lies the ring of suburban villages and satellite cities and on the other, beyond suburbia and the interurban railways, past the commuter railroad, the expressway and parkway systems, the mass-produced subdivisions, the land opens up and the signs of the city fade. Beyond the rural-urban fringe all volatile and instable lie the small villages, the pokey economies, and the sleepy roadways of rural America.

Of "exurbia" much need not be said here. The term was first introduced by A. C. Spectorsky in his book *The Exurbanites* several years ago.[18] Since then the term has enjoyed some popular currency. But *exurbia*, in the sense that Spectrosky employed the term, does not constitute a dimension of the metropolitan area that is unique or new. He used it to refer to the semirural residential sites of the executive elite of the communications industry. situated on certain tightly zoned sections of Long Island's "north shore;" in Fairfield, Connecticut; Rockland, New York; and Bucks County, Pennsylvania, the "exurbs" constitute a rural escape from the high pressure bureaucracies of the communications world. In a technical and sociological sense, they have no ecological relevance apart from the three rings already noted. What "exurbs" may exist will be found in the suburban zone or urban fringe. In terms of social stratification they are upper-middle class and even lower-upper by virtue of the high incomes of those who reside there. What goes on in "exurbia," however, that has any sociological relevance can be adequately met within the conceptual framework of the ecology of metropolitan areas and the stratification system. In short, the "exurbs" are simply expensive upper-middle and upper-class suburbs characterized by a self-conscious and rigorously maintained rurality.

Up to this point we have been discussing the spatial patterning of the metropolitan area in terms of three basic zones and the characteristics of two peculiarly metropolitan forms—the suburb and satellite city. But one might legitimately ask—what are the variables that went into the differentiation of these areas? What are the empirical referents which social scientists employed delineating and separating these zones? Before sketching out some of the differences between these units within the metropolitan complex, and how they were determined, we suggest again the conceptual nature of the zones. At best, the three rings of metropolitan areas are intellectual constructs, abstractions, symbolic instruments, that have been built up from a base of empirical uniformities and regularities observed within the metropolitan framework. For other analytic purposes, and with other bases for the delineation of these areas, five, ten, or even fifteen zones might appear in the structure of the metropolis. For the moment, we will look at a few descriptive studies which analyze metropolitan areas within the three zone framework.

Edgar M. Hoover and Raymond Vernon's volume *Anatomy of a Metropolis* is a study of the social metabolism of the New York metropolitan region. In their approach to the region, which covers 22 counties, three states, 16 million people, and 7 million jobs, Hoover and Vernon employed the three ring approach. Significantly they point out that jobs and people within the three zones vary in critical ways.

The Core The five core counties of Manhattan, Bronx, Queens, Brooklyn, and Hudson County, New Jersey, contain 54 percent of the Region's population and 64 percent of the jobs. By the mid-1950's only 9 percent of the core's land suitable for development was still vacant. According to Hoover and Vernon, income levels, ethnic characteristics, family composition, and general life styles within the core differ critically from the other two zones of the region.

Perhaps the most dramatic difference between the core and inner ring (suburban zone) is the concentration of nonwhites and Puerto Ricans within the core. Census data reveal that nonwhites in New York City increased by 41 percent from 1950 to 1957. Indeed, between 1950 and 1960, 1,293,508 more white persons moved out of the city than moved in. In the same decade, 162,845 more nonwhites (mostly Negroes) and 273,677 Puerto Ricans moved into New York than moved out.

By 1960, 612,574 Puerto Ricans were living in the city. They constituted approximately 8 percent of the city's total population, which represents an increase of 148 percent over 1950. Manhattan, the inner core, contained 36.8 percent of the total Puerto Rican population, while Brooklyn had 29.4 percent and the Bronx, 30.5 percent. In 1960, the city's Negro population was put at 1,087,931 or 14 percent of the total city. Manhattan contained 36 percent of the total Negro population, although this percentage is declining each decade as Negroes move outward.

The concentration of Puerto Ricans and Negroes in the core is clearly reflected in the ethnic and racial composition of the city's public schools. Negro and Puerto Rican children make up 75 percent of the elementary school enrollment in Manhattan, nearly half of the elementary pupils in the Bronx, and 41.7 percent in Brooklyn. The role of economic class and mobility aspirations is sharply indicated by the kinds of training received by the racial and ethnic groups of the core. Negroes and Puerto Ricans, who constitute 22 per-

cent of the city's total population, contributed only 16 percent of the academic high school students while making up 43.5 percent of the vocational high school students. Negroes and Puerto Ricans contributed 44.6 percent of the enrollment in the academic high schools in Manhattan and 51.5 percent of the enrollment in Manhattan's vocational high schools.

The concentration of nonwhites in Manhattan's core is by no means unique. In Philadelphia, for example, Negroes constituted 51 percent of the public school enrollment in the spring of 1962. The increase of Negroes in the public schools of Philadelphia has been rising about 2 percent a year.

While ethnic and racial minorities are highly concentrated in the core and follow the national pattern, there is evidence to suggest that they too are suburban bound. The Puerto Rican Government's Migration Division had estimated New York City's Puerto Rican population to be 720,000 as of December 31, 1960. However, the considerably lower census count of 650,000 has been interpreted to mean that Puerto Ricans are spreading out from the core to find jobs and homes in the outlying zones of the metropolitan area. Where 56 percent of the Puerto Rican population lived in Manhattan in 1950, only 36.8 were living there by 1960.

The same pattern is holding true for Negroes. Suburban Nassau County increased in nonwhites from 2.6 percent in 1950 to 3.2 percent in 1960. In the four New York suburban counties of Westchester, Rockland, Nassau, and Suffolk there were in 1960, 147,000 Negroes or nearly twice as many as there were in 1950. In 1950, the nonwhite population of the New York suburban area was 5.3 percent of the total population; by 1960 it had increased to 6.8 percent. While these are comparatively small gains in terms of total population, the trend is nevertheless significant for the future.

Families in the core (particularly Manhattan), according to Hoover and Vernon, can be differentiated into two contrasting model forms. At one end are the unskilled, low-income service workers consisting largely of Negro and Puerto Rican families. From Harlem all the way to the Bowery they live in the city's worst housing and provide cheap labor for the core's industries. They are, in the main, New York's current incoming migrant population. Like the Germans and Irish, Italians and Jews who preceded them, they start at the bottom and perhaps in three generations may struggle into the middle class. Unlike the former immigrant groups, however, the Negroes, and Puerto Ricans to some extent, face the additional barrier of race in their progress up the class ladder. For "The Newcomers," as Oscar Handlin calls them, Manhattan, the inner core, has been the traditional starting place.

Literally high above the crowded, noisy, squalid, lower-class "barrios" of Manhattan live the "other element" along what remains of residential Park Avenue and the surviving smart neighborhoods of Manhattan. They are the upper-middle and upper-class executives and professionals (many without children) who find all the work and play they can handle conveniently located within a few city blocks. For them, suburbia has no siren call. They are well educated, well paid, and their world, in spite of the physical proximity, is incredibly insulated and apart from the darker-skinned people who toil and struggle around them.

Toward the outer core in Brooklyn and Queens the economic extremes are less visible. Housing is in better repair and the stark five-storey apartment building and

rows of converted two-family frame houses of imitation stone and brick constitute the architectural landmarks of the zone. This is the residential area of the lower-middle income groups—the lower white collar worker and semiskilled wage earner. Then too, there are the small, closed neighborhoods of racial and ethnic minorities. And almost always, within earshot, the periodic rumble of the subways or elevated hauling to and from Manhattan.

The Inner Ring Around the populous core in a semiarc range the counties of the inner ring—Richmond, Union, Essex, Bergen, Passaic, Westchester, and Nassau, containing 30 percent of the region's population and 24 percent of its jobs. Forty-five percent of the inner ring's land suitable for development stood vacant in the mid-1950's. The average number of residents per acre of residential land in the core is 104 contrasted with 14 in the inner ring.

Hoover and Vernon characterize the inner ring as "the locale of the sociologist's Suburbia." Indeed, as the second zone of the metropolitan area, the inner ring corresponds in almost all respects to the suburban zone as suggested earlier. The only exception would be Richmond. Although its population probably resembles the suburban model rather than the urban, Richmond (Staten Island) is still politically a part of New York City: as such it could not logically be considered as a *suburb* of itself.

Toward the inner part of the inner ring, that area closest to the core, the population is predominantly lower-middle in income. The work force consists largely of the lower white collar groups and semiskilled blue collar workers who commute to Manhattan or elsewhere in the core.

Moving out into the inner ring the

quality of the housing improves. The apartment houses all but disappear, and the modern single-family house on the 60 by 100 plot, that universal symbol of suburban America, stands triumphant everywhere. The ratio of skilled workers to semiskilled and unskilled rises in addition to a steady increase in the number of white collar workers. Now interspersed within the respectable middle-class ethos of the area are older, greener, zoning-protected, status-conscious, well-cared-for upper-middle class and upper-class suburbs. Here the work force is professional or executive.

Beyond the old established suburban villages, on the fringes of the suburban zone (inner ring) and blurry edge of the rural-urban fringe (outer ring) there is an area of intense construction. This is the land of the model home standing amid a flurry of brave banners and nostalgic signs—"Five Oaks," "New England Village," and "The Knolls." There are suburbs for all price classes. They range from new "custom built" ten-room contemporaries, split-levels, "authentic Cape Cods" that have been completely "modernized" for "contemporary suburban living," all the way to the basic and unadorned five-room, cellarless ranch. Spread through the area of new construction particularly along the rail lines are older settlements, and satellite cities with established but growing pockets of Negro neighborhoods.

The Outer Ring Beyond the suburban area lie the counties of Monmouth, Middlesex, Somerset, Morris, Orange, Rockland, Putnam, Dutchess, Fairfield, and Suffolk, representing three states and consisting of two and a half million people out of the entire region's sixteen. Eighty percent of the outer ring's land was still undeveloped in the mid-1950's.

According to Hoover and Vernon the differences among the counties and settlements of the outer ring are as important as the similarities in these areas remote from Manhattan and each other. The outer ring includes rapidly industrializing Middlesex, the fox-hunting clubs and genteel country living of Morris and Somerset, the lush and sophisticated exurbias of Orange, Dutchess, and Putnam to the north along with Rockland and Fairfield. Fairfield in particular is characterized by two very distinct personalities—the industrial area of Bridgeport with half of its employed residents working in the manufacturing industries in contrast to the upper-middle class commuting executives and professionals who live along the shore of Long Island Sound or in the thinly settled interior.

Of the outer ring, Hoover and Vernon summarize its character as an "area touched with the attributes of rural living." It is open and spacious and certainly more rural in appearance than urban. Yet, the discerning observer will note the increasing frequency of suburban tract development as signs of things to come. The outer ring is still essentially a belt that has to realize fully its role in the metropolitan structure. As such it is more future than present. Hoover and Vernon suggest that the social and economic importance of the area may be in the significant changes that it undergoes within another generation.

The Hoover and Vernon study of the New York metropolitan area demonstrates some basic differences between the three zones both in terms of their institutional functions within the metropolis and the characteristics of the populations within the rings. The differences they found which separated one zone from the other conforms to the socioeconomic profiles of metropolitan central cities and their rings in other great population centers throughout the nation.

Duncan and Reiss have compared the demographic characteristics of central cities with suburban and fringe areas by utilizing the data from the 1950 census.[19] They found that central cities have somewhat more females than do the suburbs, with sex ratios of 93.5 and 95.1 respectively. Furthermore, the suburban population was slightly younger than the central population with a medial age of 30.9 years in comparison with the central city media of 32.7 years. In addition, the suburban population had a considerable excess of persons aged 13 and under and a slight preponderance of individuals in the age groups 14–19 and 25–44. On the other hand, central cities have a relatively larger number of persons aged 45 and older than do the suburbs.

In the main, suburbs have higher fertility ratios than do central cities. According to Duncan and Reiss, in their sample of central cities there were 452 children under 5 years of age per 1000 women in the age interval 20–44; in comparison, there were 534 children per 1000 women in the suburban population. In terms of marital status, for whites of both sexes, the percentage married is greater in the suburbs than in central cities. In addition, there are fewer persons in the single, widowed, and divorced categories in the suburban zone. Furthermore, the suburban family is somewhat larger than the central city family, 3.6 and 3.4 members respectively.

In terms of racial composition, the pattern Hoover and Vernon found in the New York metropolitan area is also a national metropolitan characteristic. The suburbs are predominantly white. Three times as many Negroes reside in the central cities as in the suburbs. In educational achievement, white suburban residents seem to be a full year ahead of persons residing in central cities, with education levels of 11.3 and 10.3 respectively. On the other hand, for nonwhites, the central city median in education exceeded the suburban by 0.2 a year.

To summarize, when compared with central cities, suburbs have higher fertility ratios, higher percentages of married persons, lower percentages separated, higher percentages in primary families, high socioeconomic status in the labor force, higher median income, lower median age, a higher percentage of mobile families, and a higher level of educational achievement.

Bernard Lazerwitz, utilizing data assembled by the Survey Research Center of the University of Michigan from the period 1950 to 1956 found that the suburban belts around standard metropolitan area central cities had increased with families characterized by higher incomes, skilled and semiskilled occupations, child raising, and living in more expensive houses.[20] In addition, Lazerwitz found that over this six-year period, the areas beyond the suburban belt (the metropolitan ring) had greater increases in families whose heads had business or professional occupations and who lived in moderate cost housing than did central cities. According to Lazerwitz, the data that emerged from his study indicated an increased suburban concentration of skilled and semiskilled family heads. This would suggest a growth in suburban occupational heterogeneity as more families continue to leave the central city area. Finally, this study generally supported the findings of the differences between central city population with suburban and fringe zones.

The three studies just cited all reveal that there are significant empirical differences between the three metropolitan rings that are generally employed by students of the metropolitan area. We have thus sketched out certain features and characteristics of metropolitan areas, particularly in demographic and ecological terms. Our particular concern, however, lies in the second zone of the metropolitan area,

a zone which now includes over fifty million people. The suburbs is an area of the modern metropolis which many authorities now suggest represents the living style, mores, and folkways, the dreams and aspirations—and indeed which typifies the primary values—of American society.

NOTES

1. Donald J. Bogue, *op. cit.* (Dobriner), p. 25.
2. *United States Census of Population* 1960, *United States Summary.* Number of Inhaibtants, PC(1) 1A, U. S. Department of Commerce, Bureau of the Census. pp. XXIV-XXVII, *passim.*
3. R. D. McKenzie, "The Rise of Metropolitan Communities," *Recent Social Trends.* Reprinted in Paul K. Hatt and Albert J. Reiss (eds.) *Reader in Urban Sociology* (Glencoe, Ill.: The Free Press, 1951), pp. 91–103.
4. Alvin Boskoff, *The Sociology of Urban Regions* (New York: Appleton-Century-Crofts, 1962), p. 132.
5. Leo F. Schnore, "Metropolitan Growth and Decentralization," *The American Journal of Sociology*, LXIII (September 1957).
6. Otis Dudley Duncan and Albert J. Reiss, Jr., *Social Characteristics of Urban and Rural Communities*, 1950 (New York: John Wiley & Sons, 1956), *passim.*
7. Bernard Lazerwitz, "Metropolitan Residential Belts," *American Sociological Review*, XXV (April 1960), p. 245.
8. Edgar M. Hoover and Raymond Vernon, *Anatomy of a Metropolis* (Cambridge, Mass.: Harvard University Press, 1959), p. 9.
9. Adna F. Weber, *The Growth of Cities in the Nineteenth Century* (New York: Columbia University Press, 1899).
10. Alvin Boskoff, *op. cit.*, p. 133.
11. Walter T. Martin, "The Structure of Social Relationships Engendered by Surburban Residence," *American Sociological Review*, XII (August 1956).
12. Sylvia Fleis Fava, "Suburbanism as a Way of Life," *American Sociological Review*, Vol. 21 (February 1956), pp. 34–37.
13. Wilbur C. Hallenbeck, *American Urban Communities* (New York: Harper & Row, Publishers, 1951), p. 201.
14. Graham R. Taylor, *Satellite Cities* (New York: Appleton-Century-Crofts Inc., 1915).
15. Harlan Douglas, *The Suburban Trend* (New York: The Century Company, 1925), *passim.*
16. Chauncey D. Harris, "Suburbs," *The American Journal of Sociology*, XLIX (July 1943), pp. 1–13.
17. Leo F. Schnore, "Satellites and Suburbs, " *Social Forces*, Vol. 36 (December 1957), pp. 121–129. Reprinted in William M. Dobriner, *op. cit.*, pp. 109–121.
18. A. C. Spectorsky, *The Exurbanites* (Philadelphia: J. B. Lippincott Co., 1955).
19. Otis Dudley Duncan and Albert J. Reiss Jr., *op. cit.*, *passim.*
20. Bernard Lazerwitz, *op. cit.*, p. 245.

13. City and Suburb: The Economics of Metropolitan Growth

Benjamin Chinitz

In this selection, Benjamin Chinitz introduces the concepts and data of the economic analyst to define a metropolis and to examine the sources of metropolitan growth in the United States. To Chinitz, a metropolis is an economic unit which, for purposes of analyzing its structure and progress, may be compared to a business firm or a nation's economy. When it is looked at in this way, the metropolitan area turns out to be a highly efficient unit. The concentration of people, plants, stores, and services in a closely packed territory helps to lower production costs and make commodities available more cheaply and expeditiously to the consumer. In discussing the reasons why some metropolitan areas are better organized and grow faster than others, Chinitz pays special attention to the experience of New York and Pittsburgh. He argues that the two regions have a similar endowment of natural resources. However, New York offers a cluster of diversified industries, services, and amenities which help to attract new firms and residents, whereas Pittsburgh's growth is constrained by an overspecialized, heavily capitalized industrial economy.

Benjamin Chinitz is Professor of Economics at Brown University. He was formerly Deputy Assistant Secretary of Commerce for Regional Economic Research and Planning. He is the author of *Freight and the Metropolis* (1960) and *Rate Discrimination in Ocean Transportation* (1956); and he is editor of *City and Suburb: The Economics of Metropolitan Growth* (1964).

The Movement into Metropolitan Areas

What lies behind the rapid and accelerating growth of metropolitan areas in the United States? Why is a larger and larger proportion of the nation's growing population choosing to live and work within the confines of the metropolitan complexes which cover a relatively minuscule portion of the nation's total area? The answer lies partly in the changes in patterns of production. Over the past century there have been drastic shifts in the kinds of goods which society wants and in the inputs which are required to produce them efficiently. But there have been shifts in consumption patterns as well, as more and more Americans achieve both the income

with which to afford the good things in life and the leisure in which to enjoy them. And many of the refinements of twentieth-century living are most easily acquired— and often best enjoyed—in proximity to a fairly large number of other people with similar tastes and demands.

Push and Pull One of the most obvious effects of industrialization and economic progress has been a steady drop in the extent to which people live directly off the land. For many decades the proportion of Americans employed in agriculture, mining, fishing, forestry, and the other

From Benjamin Chinitz, *City and Suburb: The Economics of Metropolitan Growth* © 1964. Reprinted by permission of Prentice-Hall, Inc., Englewood Cliffs, New Jersey.

"primary" industries whose products are the fruits of nature more or less in their original state has been declining sharply— from 40 percent of the total work force employed at the turn of the century to only 10 percent in 1960. This is in part because the demand for the products of primary industries has not nearly kept pace with the long-term growth of income and consumption in the United States. When people find themselves twice as rich as they were before, they do not generally —at least in this country—eat twice as much or use twice as much cloth to cover themselves. Rather, they tend to expend their increased wealth on higher-quality goods and even more on different types of consumption which cannot be satisfied by the products of farm or forest, of sea or mine. They tend to spend a larger and larger share of their income on cars and entertainment, on education for their children and medical care for their families —goods which are either the end product of a long and complicated fabrication process or which are not really tangible "goods" at all.

Not only is the demand for the products of the land-bound primary industries steadily decreasing in proportion to the total demand for goods and services in the United States, but the number of man-hours required to produce any given quantity of these primary products has been dropping sharply and persistently. Since 1947, American labor productivity in agriculture and mining has more than doubled—an increase more rapid than that which has characterized most manufacturing industries and much more rapid than that experienced in the growing service sectors. In sum, the direct fruits of the land represent a shrinking portion of the population's total consumption of goods and services, and every year fewer people are required to satisfy each unit of demand that remains.

With the decline of agriculture and the extractive industries, which together have always formed the economic backbone of rural and small-town life, it is not surprising that more and more people should move into the cities and their surrounding areas. Man is a social animal: he desires privacy but he generally desires companionship more. As technological process enables more and more people to earn their living within smaller and smaller areas, their reaction is to move closer to their fellow men and to the goods and services which are available in full variety only to a large, compact market. In general, it is the metropolitan areas which can best provide these while offering, at the same time, a choice of urban, suburban, or rural living within their boundaries.

If the decline in the importance of primary industries has provided the push toward metropolitan areas, the pull has come from the increasing importance of other industries. The fastest-growing segment of the economy in recent years has been that vast complex of functions generally lumped together as the "service" or "tertiary" sector. This area of American economic life includes trade and distribution activities, such business services as finance, advertising, research, and central office administration, and an enormous variety of personal services, of which education, medical care, repair services, and entertainment represent only a small part. The reasons for the rapid growth of employment in these industries (which has averaged 3 percent annually since 1947 as compared with an annual growth rate of 1 percent for employment in the nation as a whole) reflect those already advanced for the decline of agriculture and the extractive industries. More and more of the income of the American people is spent on the services provided by these industries. At the same time, these industries have so far been those least affected by technological progress; labor productivity has increased far less rapidly in the service industries than in either agriculture or manufacturing, so that the share of national employment accounted for by the services sector has risen even more than the share of national output accounted for by its "products."

Production Trends The kinds of labor or skills required for the production of services are very different from those required in farming or mining. The changed requirements have, in general, a strong urban bias. The need for physical strength and manual dexterity has been almost entirely replaced by the need for a high level of literacy, for professional and technical knowledge, for clerical skills, for the kind of sophistication that allows ease and familiarity in the handling of complicated processes and large bodies of information. And people with the kind of background, education, and inclinations to encourage the development of these attributes are generally to be found in cities—and in greatest supply in the large cities which form the core of metropolitan areas. For those service industries which require a large female clerical force (with its characteristically high turnover rate as girls leave their jobs to marry and have babies), only a metropolitan area can provide a large enough pool of potential workers within easy commuting distance. In addition, the metropolitan area, with its close-linked, far-reaching network of utilities and services, offers access to a large supply of technical and office skills while allowing the employer to choose between an urban location in the center or a suburban one nearer the periphery.

For manufacturing, the third major sector of the American economy (and until recently the largest), the situation is more complicated and the relationship to increasing metropolitanization less clear-cut. The trend seems to be toward decentralization of manufacturing activity. During much of this century manifacturing employment has tended to spread out and away from its historical concentration in the large urban centers, and the share of the nation's manufacturing jobs accounted for by large metropolitan areas seems to have declined slightly.

The chief cause of this dispersion of activity has unquestionably been the development of new modes of transportation. In the days when rail and waterways were the most efficient means of moving both people and goods from one place to another, it was not only natural but essential for manufacturing activity to cluster in the large cities which grew up at the nodal points of these transport systems. With the advent of the automobile and the truck and the development of an increasingly widespread network of roads to carry them, this situation changed rapidly. Freed from their dependence on fixed lines of transportation, manufacturers were able to consider other factors in choosing their locations, and in many cases these other considerations led them out of the great urban centers into the nonmetropolitan parts of the country.

By mid-century, however, the decentralizing effect of the truck and the automobile had been largely spent, and a variety of forces operating in favor of a new metropolitan concentration came to the fore. Some of these forces consist of still newer developments in transportation which tend to restore the historical advantage of the metropolitan area. The advent of jet transport is one such development; another is the increasing importance of piggyback transport (the carrying of truck trailers on specially designed railroad flat cars). These new transport modes have acted as brakes on decentralization because the expense of constructing a modern jet airport, or of maintaining the complex and expensive terminal facilities required for efficient piggyback operations, can be supported only by the concentration of people and the large markets found in metropolitan areas.

Other forces are also at work to halt the dispersion of manufacturing activity. One important factor is the steadily decreasing dependence of manufacturing on specific raw material inputs. The importance of raw materials in the manufacturing process has been lessening for a number of reasons —one of which is industrial advancement itself. Manufactured goods are subjected to a constantly increasing amount of processing. The natural fruits of the earth pass through ever more numerous and ever more complex operations before they reach their final form: iron is turned into steel of a hundred different qualities and characteristics before it is made into cars or machines or instruments; wood is converted into paper or cardboard and then turned into hundreds of kinds of boxes and containers. The effect of all this processing is, of course, to reduce the role played by raw material costs in the total cost of the finished product.

The resource inputs required in the manufacturing process are not only becoming less important, relatively, but they are also becoming more and more diversified. The tendency of technological progress during this century seems to have been, on balance, to reduce the dependence of a manufacturing process on any particular raw material. A hundred years ago,

the quality of steel and the cost of its production were both heavily dependent on the quality of the coal and of the pig iron available for making it; today low-grade coal or other fuels can be utilized just about as well, and scrap iron can be used along with pig iron without any sacrifice of quality. The creation of a vast pipeline network has sharply reduced the energy-cost disadvantages suffered by producers far from petroleum and natural gas supplies; the advent of slurry pipelines may do the same for coal-users in the near future. More and more, advances in technology are enabling men to make use of nature's most plentiful and ubiquitous resources—air, water (and soon, perhaps), solar heat—both as energy sources and as the basic ingredients for some of the manmade materials which are in many cases replacing natural raw materials in the manufacturing process.

As technology has reduced the dependence of manufacturing on raw materials, it has increased the dependence of one manufacturing operation on another. As the chain of fabrication and assembly has grown longer and more complex, the outputs of a number of manufacturing industries—of the chemicals and metals industries, for example—have increasingly become the inputs of others. This increased specialization leads to an increased interdependence among various types of manufacturing establishments. Manufacturers of intermediate or producer goods must be close to industrial markets of sufficient size to support their large-scale operations —close, that is, to a large cluster of other manufacturing firms. Producers of final goods must have easy access both to the intermediate goods needed as inputs and to the markets for the final product. In these terms, the solution for both groups is the same: to cluster close to one another within the large metropolitan areas which alone can provide both inputs and markets in sufficient scale and variety to meet their total needs.

All in all, then, the forces pulling manufacturing employment into the metropolitan areas seem to be increasing rather than diminishing in strength. This is not to deny, of course, that there are also forces at work in the opposite direction. One of these centrifugal forces is the difference in labor costs between metropolitan and nonmetropolitan areas. Although certain manufacturing industries depend heavily on the low-wage labor culled from the new immigrant and other disadvantaged minority groups congregated in some of the largest cities—the reliance of the New York garment industry on low-wage Puerto Rican labor is an example—the fact remains that wages are typically higher in the nation's metropolitan centers than in smaller urban or nonurban locations. There are several reasons for this pattern: labor unions tend to be better organized in the big cities and their bargaining strength therefore greater there than elsewhere; living costs are typically lower outside the boundaries of metropolitan areas; and the steady decrease in agricultural and mining jobs feeds an excess labor supply in rural areas and small towns which exerts a continuous downward pressure on wages in such areas. Similarly, there are often differentials in space costs between metropolitan and nonmetropolitan areas. Although a metropolitan complex typically includes suburban and even rural locations, space shortages do arise as the complex grows, and firms with particular space requirements may find that these needs can be satisfied more readily, or at lower cost, beyond metropolitan boundaries.

Consumption Trends So far, there have been a number of shifts in the pattern of production in the United States which may help to explain why a growing proportion of the nation's jobs are to be found in metropolitan areas. But the picture is not complete without some mention of the shifts in tastes and technology which make the metropolitan area an increasingly desirable place in which to *live* as well as to *work*. We have already mentioned some of the reasons why services, which occupy an increasingly large portion of American consumer demand, are best produced in a metropolitan setting. But since services are characteristically difficult to transport from one place to another, they are best consumed in a metropolitan setting as well. Institutions of higher education, highly specialized medical or legal facilities, theaters, symphonies, and nightclubs—it is on such things that more and more of America's growing wealth is being spent, and they are available in greatest abundance within metropolitan areas.

Although the advantage of metropolitan areas is greatest in the provision of highly specialized services, recent advances in technology seem to be creating a tendency for their advantage to increase in the consumption of certain tangible goods as well. This was not always so; the most important innovations made available to the consumer during the first half of this century—electricity, the radio, the automobile, the movies, television—all tended to reduce the disadvantages of living outside of metropolitan areas, to make more and more of the niceties enjoyed by the city-dweller available to his rural neighbor as well. But today, the complexity and vast expense of many of the items demanded by both individuals and business firms may once again be widening the gap between metropolitan and nonmetropolitan living.

For instance, as we have already pointed out, it takes a metropolitan area to support a jet airport, although the same is not true of the smaller facilities required to service propeller aircraft. In the days when almost all the medical equipment available could fit into the doctor's black bag, the sick man in a rural farmhouse was just as likely to be cured as the one in the big city; today much of the lifesaving equipment which scientific advances have made available is so complex and expensive that only the larger hospitals can afford it. Similarly, almost any businessman anywhere can afford a desk calculator, but it is generally in metropolitan areas that one finds the great computer complexes whose services an increasing number of firms desire but only the largest can afford to provide for themselves.

What do all these changes portend for the future growth of metropolitan areas? In the production sector, the forces of attraction and repulsion will doubtless continue to work against each other. By now the effect of the decline in agricultural and mining employment is largely spent, simply because there are few jobs left in these industries; but the expansion of jobs in the service industries, and particularly such business services as data-processing and research, will continue and perhaps accelerate. For the manufacturing sector, some new developments—such as the availability of atomic power for industrial use—are likely to continue the process of emancipation from sources of raw materials and increase the attractions of metropolitan locations. Other changes—such as developments in the manufacture of steel which serve to reduce the scale required for efficient production—are likely to operate in the direction of decentralization. As more and more manufacturing workers exchange their blue collars for white ones,

the attractions of an urban labor force will grow, but these advantages could be nullified if space, labor, and other costs of doing business increase disproportionately as part of the growing pains of metropolitan areas.

In consumption trends, too, the future is far from clear. It is certain that the demand for complex and expensive goods and sophisticated services—items best consumed in a metropolitan setting—will continue to grow faster than the demand for goods and services as a whole. But as people get richer and transportation more rapid, more people will be able to live where they please and spend their money where they can get what they want.

Which set of forces will prove the stronger, the centripetal or the centrifugal? The signs suggest that the trends which have prevailed throughout this century will continue, that a larger and larger share of the nation's population will live and work within metropolitan areas. Whether such areas grow faster or more slowly than the nation as a whole, there is no question that they are going to grow or that this growth will engender new benefits and opportunities, new challenges and difficulties. The manner in which the benefits and opportunities are utilized and the challenges and difficulties met and overcome will play a large role in determining the quality of life in our country.

The Structure of the Metropolitan Economy

So far, we have talked about metropolitan areas as if they were all the same, as alike as bottles of homogenized milk. Actually, they come in an assortment more varied than the wines of France, often with nothing more in common than conformity to the minimum standards of size and density set by the Bureau of the Census. They range in size all the way from greater New York's more than 10 million inhabitants down to the 65,000 people who together form the Standard Metropolitan Statistical Area of San Angelo, Texas. Some of these metropolitan areas were great urban centers even before the nation was born; others earned the title only in 1960. Some, like New York and San Francisco, are great trading, financial, and cultural centers as well as the homes of an enormous variety of manufacturing establishments whose products are marketed throughout the country. Others, like Pittsburgh and Detroit, have grown up as one-industry towns, heavily committed to the production of a single commodity or of closely related groups of commodities and generally with relatively little involvement in the "nonproductive" business and consumer service or distribution activities which have come to be regarded as metropolitan specialties.

The *raison d'être* of any metropolitan area is specialization and trade with the outside world. And because any area's structure and development are very closely tied up with the kinds of specialties it offers in trade, it is both customary and convenient to divide the metropolitan economy into two parts: those industries directed toward other markets and those directed chiefly toward the local market. These two fundamental divisions are often termed the *basic* and *local-market oriented* sectors, respectively.

Basic Industries It is by its pattern of specialization, its export or basic industries, that a metropolitan area is most easily characterized, and it is in this segment of the economy that the different areas exhibit the widest diversity. Some of the areas

developed because their natural resource endowments or their strategic locations gave them a distinct advantage in one or two industries. Some have remained closely associated with these traditional specialties ever since (as, for example, Pittsburgh with steel, Akron with rubber, Omaha with meat-processing, Minneapolis with flour-milling), although those areas which have continued to grow and thrive in the mid-twentieth century have all broadened their original export base to include a variety of new specialties as well. Others acquired their major specialties almost by accident, as Detroit acquired the automobile industry, and then built up a real advantage in those lines of production through what may be loosely termed the economies of agglomeration. Some metropolitan areas specialize in the large-scale heavy manufacturing industries whose customers are mainly other industries, while others concentrate on consumer products. And some, including nearly all of the greatest metropolitan giants, specialize in a great variety of industries, large-scale and small-scale, exporting both producer goods and consumer goods. The New York metropolitan area, for example, accounts for more than 30 percent of the nation's total employment in nearly one hundred of the nation's 446 manufacturing industries. It is beyond the scope of this discussion to list all the goods New York exports to the markets of the nation, but many have certain things in common: they tend to be consumer goods, of high value in relation to their weight or bulk, and highly unstandardized (that is, subject to frequent and drastic changes). The nation's other great metropolises—Chicago, Los Angeles, and Philadelphia, for example—also produce several hundred different types of manufactured goods and, although they do not export all or even most of them to other areas, each one possesses a long and varied list of export specialties.

All metropolitan areas have in common their heavy dependence on trade and specialization, but it is a dependence at a very different level, and in a very different sense, from that of a farm or small town which sells a single product and relies on the outside world to provide it with nearly all the other necessities of life. For another common characteristic of metropolitan areas is their very high degree of economic self-sufficiency. No metropolitan area produces everything it consumes, of course, and trade must involve imports as well as exports, but most metropolitan areas are capable of providing for a large proportion of their own needs. In making this assertion, we must remember the difference between a city and a metropolitan area. Cut off from the outside world, New York City would starve to death in short order, but the New York metropolitan area might survive a little longer, although it would find its diet painfully restricted. For the New York metropolitan area includes not only the city and its bedrooms, but also the truck and potato farms of Suffolk County and the dairy farms of outer Westchester. The same variety of land use is characteristic of nearly all of the nation's metropolitan areas.

Local-Market Industries Metropolitan areas are more alike in the goods they produce for local consumption than in those they produce for export. This is because there are certain types of goods which consumers everywhere demand and which are easily or feasibly transported over long distances—dairy products and most fresh foods are one example, newspapers are another—and it is these goods which nearly every metropolitan area produces for itself. Areas vary tremendously, of course, in the breadth of their production for local consumption—the largest metropolitan areas tend to produce some of almost every type of manufactured good (many of them largely for local consumption), while the smaller ones must rely on a wider variety of imports. And a particular area's exports naturally help to determine the things which it makes for its own use as well. But it is possible to classify certain industries or products as generally local-market oriented, and almost every metropolitan area is engaged to a greater or lesser extent in the production of such goods.

It is above all the production of nontangible services that characterizes the self-sufficiency of metropolitan areas. We have already explained some of the reasons for which many business and consumer services are best produced in a metropolitan setting. Many are, by their nature, difficult to export. Some can, of course, be exported in indirect ways: a metropolitan area can serve as a wholesaling or financial center for the surrounding region or even, as with New York's Wall Street or Hartford's insurance complex, for the entire nation. People come into the metropolitan area to take advantage of almost any of its services and then go home again; sometimes they even stay home and simply send their problem, be it a delicate machine in need of repair or a question on financial reorganization. But the fact remains that it is largely for their own consumption that metropolitan areas generate the vast complex of services which gives all such areas, however diverse their underlying structures, a common look, and distinguishes them from the nonmetropolitan parts of the nation.

Once started, this process tends to feed

upon its own growth. This is partly because metropolitan-dwellers tend to have a greater demand for services and higher incomes with which to satisfy these demands than does the population at large. But it is also partly a function of the difficulties or "diseconomies" inevitably associated with metropolitan living—difficulties which require an increased number and variety of people to be offset. It takes a good many more middlemen, for example, to get a fresh egg to a housewife in midtown Manhattan than to one in a small town or rural area. Similarly, it requires more laundries, policemen, window-washers, and government clerks to maintain the customary American standards of individual cleanliness, comfort, convenience, and safety in a metropolitan setting.

Variations in Growth Rates

Metropolitan areas as a whole are expanding—not only in absolute size, but also in the proportion of the nation's people and jobs encompassed within their borders. As has been noted, despite their great variety of export production patterns, all—or almost all—metropolitan areas have certain things in common: a high degree of self-sufficiency in providing the goods and services required by their own markets and, most particularly, a heavy involvement in a particular set of highly specialized and refined service activities. But despite this vigorous over-all growth and the similarities which stamp metropolitan economies, the growth experiences of individual metropolitan areas have varied enormously. During the most recent decade some, like Phoenix, Arizona, have doubled in size; others, like Pittsburgh and Boston, have remained almost at a standstill; a very few—Jersey City, for example—have actually lost ground.

What has caused some metropolitan areas to grow at an explosive rate and others not to grow at all? There are a few very simple answers—factors which help to explain the diversity of growth experience but which by no means represent the whole story nor even the major part of it. One of these factors is geographical location. Like people, metropolitan areas tend to grow faster when they are young; thus those areas located in the newer, more recently settled and industrialized parts of the country are in general growing faster than those in the long-established parts of the nation. In general, such areas have grown faster in the West than in the East, faster in the South than in the North, fastest of all in the Southwest and slowest of all in the Northeast.

Size is another of the simple factors which seems to play a role in the rate of growth. In general—and with some outstanding exceptions, such as Los Angeles—the nation's largest metropolitan areas have not been growing as fast as some of the smaller ones. An examination of the pressures which arise to impede metropolitan growth will reveal why rapid expansion should come more easily to a small or middle-sized metropolitan area than to a giant one.

Such factors as location and size are actually only a partial explanation of the differences in growth. In every region of the country and in every size category there are metropolitan areas which have been enjoying vigorous growth and others whose growth had been sickly or nonexistent. Other, more subtle factors are involved—some of them related to observable differences in the structure of the metropolitan economy (in the employment "mix" or industry "mix" of one area as opposed to that of another) and others to intangible differences in the ability to adjust to shifts both in consumer demand and in the competitive advantages possessed by a particular area or region to satisfy some part of the total demand.

The Direct Influence of "Mix" To begin with, an area's population and employment are more likely to grow rapidly if the export activities which underlie its economic structure are concentrated in fast-growing rather than slow-growing industries. For an industry to be fast-growing in terms of employment, two things are required: total demand for its output must be expanding vigorously, and labor productivity in that particular line must not be rising so fast as to prevent a growth of output from being translated into employment growth as well. An area specialized in the aircraft industry, for instance, which has been fast-growing on both counts during the postwar era, would be expected to exhibit a higher rate of over-all growth than another heavily committed, say, to coal-mining, an industry in which slackening demand and rapidly rising labor productivity have combined to produce a rapid nationwide drop in employment.

A fast-growing mix of industries will not insure an area's growth, however, if competitive shifts cause a shrink in its share of the industries in which it is specialized. This question of industry share is closely related both to size and to geographical location. The population and income of the United States, once heavily concentrated in the nation's northeastern quadrant, have been steadily spreading out more evenly over the nation as a whole. At the same time, a number of technological changes have combined to make many manufacturing industries more closely market-oriented than ever before. As a result, many of the older and larger industrial centers, particularly in the Northeast, are finding that their traditional industrial specialties, areas in which they once dominated national production, are following the markets across the country, either through the relocation of established plants or the construction of new plants.

But age and location are by no means the only determinants of competitive shift. The nature of an area's labor market, the cost and availability of land within its boundaries, its relation to the nation's ever-changing transportation network, the tax structure and financing possibilities it offers to new enterprises, and the degree to which it is able to offer services and facilities important to new manufacturing establishments—all these factors and many more help to determine a metropolitan area's advantage or disadvantage in holding its share of a particular industry or attracting a larger one.

New York and Pittsburgh: A Contrast Differential rates of growth among metropolitan areas are explained in part by differences in industry mix and in part by competitive shifts in industry shares. But there is still another factor. It may be helpful to compare specifically the growth experiences of two major metropolitan areas: New York and Pittsburgh. Both are among the nation's oldest industrial centers, located in the northeastern quadrant of the country. Both owe their rise to industrial predominance to certain unique natural endowments: New York above all to its great Atlantic port, which long represented the major link between the sources of supply in the Old World and the markets of the United States; Pittsburgh to a combination of its rich endowments of fuel—chiefly coal and, to a lesser extent, natural gas—and its strategic location at the confluence of two major rivers (which won the city the title "Gateway to the West"). Both have seen the original advantage bestowed by their natural endowments eroded by technological change and by developments in the rest of the country. Both have watched their early specialties—New York, its flour-milling, copper- and sugar-refining, and all the manufacturing and commercial activities connected with its ports; Pittsburgh, its coal-mining and steel and glass production—either suffer a decline in national demand or disperse widely to other parts of the country. Yet the New York area has continued to expand at a healthy rate, while Pittsburgh's growth has all but ground to a halt. Why?

A careful study of the statistics reveals that New York's industry-mix is growing faster than the national average; Pittsburgh's, slower. But this is the beginning, not the end of the explanation. Despite the fact that its traditional industrial specialties have not kept pace with the over-all rate of national growth in recent decades and that its own share in them has been steadily shrinking as the process of dispersion continues, Pittsburgh's pattern of industrial specialization today does not differ radically from that of its economic heyday. Its heaviest specialization—now, as then—is in the production of iron, steel, metal, and glass, and in the manufacture of heavy industrial machinery and equipment. New York's production pattern, on the other hand, has changed radically. As its original specialties declined, others developed. By the end of the nineteenth century, New York was the nation's leader in the production of ready-to-wear apparel and in the printing and publishing industries. More recently, these specialties have been supplemented by still newer industrial concentrations: in aircraft, chemicals, electrical equipment, electron-

ics, and scientific instruments. New York's industry mix is not fast-growing today because the area was lucky or far-sighted in its original industrial structure; rather, it possesses some particular attraction for new, rapidly expanding industries as such, which seems to insure that its industry mix, while constantly changing, will always be fast-growing, and that as its share of established specialties is gradually eroded, new ones will spring up to replace them.

The key, then, seems to be that New York has diversified its industrial structure, while Pittsburgh has been left clinging to its declining specialties. But what determines the degree of diversification—the ability to adjust to change and make the most of it? After all, an area does not choose its industries; in a free-enterprise economy, at least, the industries choose the area. The answer seems to lie in the type of atmosphere an area offers, and in the services and facilities it provides for industrial newcomers. New York has long since ceased to attract industries on the basis of specific natural endowments. Rather, it bases its appeal on the advantages of clustering—advantages in the form of a wide variety of specialized services in production, transportation, and marketing. These are the advantages which accrue, in certain types of industries, from being located close to one's competitors and to as many specialized business services as possible—services which a manufacturing firm would otherwise have to provide for itself. New York, with its heavy concentration of wholesale, retail, transportation, finance, communications, government, central office, and business and consumer service functions, offers a rich soil in which new industries can flourish.

Pittsburgh, on the other hand, offers a much thinner selection of such services, not only because it is smaller than New

York, but because it has retained a degree of commitment to historic roots unusual in the mid-twentieth century. Having established its economy on the new, large-scale, heavy manufacturing industries in which it had a distinct natural advantage, Pittsburgh has continued to grow from this rather narrow base rather than branching out into the nonmanufacturing service sectors. While New York has a larger-than-average proportion of its total employment in the sectors described as "soil" for new industries, Pittsburgh's proportion in most of these sectors—with the exception of research and central office administration—is distinctly below average. It appears to be in the process of catching up with other metropolitan areas, but its long-standing handicap in this respect helps to explain why, as its original advantages have declined in importance and the industrial specialties founded on them have declined or dispersed, new industries have not sprung up in their place fast enough to maintain a satisfactory over-all rate of growth.

Pittsburgh is the subject of a three-volume report issued early this year by the Pittsburgh Regional Planning Association. The flavor of the findings is conveyed in the selection, "Pittsburgh Takes Stock of Itself," by Edgar M. Hoover, the man who directed the research summarized in these volumes. More than any other major metropolitan study, this one of Pittsburgh puts the spotlight on the economic structure of the area as a determinant of economic growth.

The attraction of a well-rounded business environment is greater for some industries than for others. Industries which are characteristically small in scale, highly competitive, and with unstandardized products are those which most urgently require outside services and facilities of many types. Only a handful of manufacturing industries require such services once they are solidly established, but most of them do in the beginning. Thus, large metropolitan areas have traditionally acted as incubators for new products and new processes. It is in the early stages of technical development in a given industry that uncertainty about the future is at its greatest. It is then that what the metropolitan area has to offer is most important to the new firm. By permitting the businessman to rely on already existing supplies of space, labor, and transportation, and on established financial facilities and business services, the metropolis permits him to keep his own commitment to a minimum without sacrificing any of the essential nonproductive ingredients which may spell the difference between success and failure. It is this incubator function which the New York metropolitan area performs superlatively well.

Today, as manufacturing industries are increasingly freed from dependence on raw material resources, and as the accelerating rate of technological change increases the degree of uncertainty associated with many lines of production, it is likely that more and more industries will become increasingly dependent on their external environment. This implies that the creation of a climate favorable to diversification, through the provision of a competent labor force and of the wide variety of the skills and facilities categorized as the service sectors, will play a larger and larger role in determining a particular area's growth rate. Insofar as the creation of such a climate involves an increase in the number of jobs in the service industries, it will of course contribute directly to the growth of employment as well, particularly since many of these industries are themselves highly sensitive to the existence of their counterparts (research establishments, for example, clearly prefer to locate where a cluster of such establishments already exists). In two ways then—directly by creating more jobs and more income in response to an ever-increasing demand, and indirectly by enhancing an area's attractiveness to fast-growing manufacturing industries—the expansion of the nonproductive sectors of the metropolitan economy may prove the key to sustained growth.

Shifts within the Metropolis

We have talked about two types of change fundamental to the economics of metropolitan areas: the trend toward increasing metropolitanization in the United States as a whole, and the determinants of shifts among metropolitan areas in the form of widely diverse growth experiences. But equally striking shifts have been taking place within metropolitan areas—changes in internal structure and composition which, particularly in the case of the older and larger areas, pose at least as many problems as do the broader shifts and are closely related to them.

There is nothing homogeneous about a metropolitan area. Each of them divides into at least two distinct parts: the urban core or central city, and the surrounding suburban ring (which often shades off into rural countryside at the outer edges or in pockets far from main transportation lines). In the largest areas, it is possible to make further breakdowns—to distinguish an "inner" and "outer" ring, for example —and in nearly all it is possible to identify the distinctive core of the core: the central city's central business district. Obviously, as a metropolitan area grows it must grow

outward, since there are severe limitations on how far up or down it can go. Thus, in the process of growth, the relative importance of the urban core shrinks and that of the surrounding ring expands. This is in part a trick of statistics, for the boundaries of a metropolitan area are not fixed; they grow as the area grows, so that new acreages and populations are continually being annexed. But there is more to the outward shift than simple annexation. There is no question that particular people and particular jobs tend to move out of the central city into the surrounding ring, and that this flow is almost always greater than the flow in the opposite direction. Nor is it simply that the relative importance of the city shrinks and that of the suburbs grows uniformly in every direction; rather, the particular function and specialization pattern of each of these parts changes drastically, and in the process the whole complexion of the metropolitan area is altered.

In the larger metropolitan areas, at least, the proportion of population living within the central city has been falling since the beginning of the century. During the same period, or at least as far back as can be measured reliably—generally, since 1929— the central cities' share of certain important employment categories (manufacturing, wholesaling, retailing) has been falling with equal regularity. It is not possible to make any simple statement about the two parallel trends since they interact on and influence each other in a variety of complex ways. But, if the movement of population is assumed as given, it is easy to see why certain types of jobs naturally follow. If people move to the suburbs, the grocery stores, hardware stores, laundries, and hairdressers—the retail and personal service industries—inevitably accompany them, as in fact they have.

Shifts in Manufacturing Manufacturing employment, however, provides the most solid evidence of an outward redistribution, gradual but steady, in the great majority of the principal metropolitan areas. No matter the standard of measurement—the proportion of metropolitan area manufacturing jobs accounted for by the central city, the rate of manufacturing employment growth in the city and in the suburbs, or the share of total employment accounted for by manufacturing in the city and in the surrounding areas—there is no question that, over the past fifty years, manufacturing has grown more rapidly in the surrounding rings of the great metropolitan areas than in the central core. These changes cannot be explained directly by movements of population; indeed, manufacturing employment is much more likely to effect intrametropolitan shifts in the distribution of population than to be affected by them. Rather, these changes relate to the kinds of advantages a manufacturing firm is likely to derive from a central location, the way these advantages have changed over time, and the types of manufacturing operation for which they are most important.

The data on manufacturing employment show, with remarkable consistency, that manufacturing firms located in the urban center of a metropolitan area are smaller in average size than those located on the periphery. This is no mere coincidence; it is intimately tied up with the function which a central location performs for a manufacturing establishment. This is, in brief, to provide all the facilities and services which a firm does not want to provide for itself: rental space for the firm which does not want to buy or build; a large labor market to supply appropriate workers to the firm which cannot import or train its own; transportation facilities

to establishments which find it cheaper to make fractional use of existing facilities than to supply their own; specialists who enable the manufacturer to subcontract out almost any portion of its operations which it cannot economically perform itself; proximity to a cluster of competitors, which minimizes the need for marketing facilities. By locating close to such a complex of outside facilities, the small firm can reduce its handicap vis-à-vis its larger competitors, and the firm operating at a high level of uncertainty can keep its commitments to a minimum. And these suppliers who must, in turn, have a large enough market to make their operations pay are inevitably found in greatest abundance at the urban core.

In certain types of manufacturing industries, chiefly those producing unstandardized and continuously changing products—the apparel industry is an obvious example—the level of uncertainty remains forever high and the importance of external suppliers always great. But in many industries this dependence is transitional, to be outgrown as the firm expands. For such industries, the outward movement of firms is an integral part of the growth process itself—for as a firm moves from dependence on external services to reliance on scale economies derived from its own operations, the advantages of a central urban location tend to be increasingly overshadowed by its disadvantages.

The chief difficulty an urban firm is likely to encounter as it grows is lack of space. In most established urban centers, it is very difficult and expensive for a firm to expand efficiently. And as a firm reaches the size where it becomes more economical to provide for its own transportation needs than to rely on outside facilities, the problem of traffic congestion and lack of parking and loading space at its urban location may become acute. Thus the greater availability of open sites is probably the most important single factor underlying the move to the suburbs.

As firms grow up and move away from their urban origins, new ones spring up to take their place. But in recent decades the replacement has not been rapid enough to sustain a rate of manufacturing growth at the center equal to that in the rings; in many large metropolitan areas, in fact, the number of manufacturing jobs in the urban core has declined not only relatively but also absolutely. Technological changes have had something to do with this: first, the increase in transport flexibility which accompanied the development of trucking; and, more recently, the trend toward integrated, continuous production processes—processes which demand single-story, extensive plant layouts for greatest efficiency and thus increase the disadvantages of cramped, multistory structures. But probably even more important are the inevitable results of the growth-and-decay process. As the central city grows older and more congested, the expense of modernizing obsolescent structures increases until it becomes cheaper to build anew on open land than to modify existing structures. And as the shift to the periphery continues, the suburban areas develop industrial complexes of their own and are increasingly able to provide many of the services which were once the exclusive characteristic of the urban center. More and more fledgling firms may be attracted to a suburban location, rather than waiting to move there after they reach a particular stage of expansion.

Many of the forces which tend to push manufacturing operations out of the metropolitan center and into the rings also affect wholesaling operations, al-though the outward shift in this sector has so far been less pronounced. Obsolescent inner-city structures, changed transportation networks, and the horizontal-layout demands of modern goods-handling methods are causing a more rapid growth of wholesaling employment at the periphery than in the urban center.

Population, manufacturing, retailing, household services, and—to a lesser extent —wholesaling are all moving out of the central city. Yet the central cities show no signs of emptying—many, in fact, seem more congested and densely packed than ever. What is filling the vacuum? In part, the answer lies in the discussion of manufacturing. The centers of most of the large metropolitan areas continue to attract "exotic," highly competitive types of manufacturing. But there is another type of function, increasingly important in twentieth-century society, in which both inputs and outputs are even more heterogeneous, and unstandardized rapid communication and face-to-face contacts even more important than for the exotic manufacturing industries. These are the highly specialized areas of finance, business services, and central office administration, whose inputs are skill or knowledge or information, whose outputs are not goods but service or advice or decisions. It is these establishments—banks and law offices, advertising agencies and central administrative offices, consulting firms and government agencies—which are filling more and more of the central cities of most urban areas, and are becoming the primary function of the core of the core, the city's central business district.

This, then, is the general pattern of employment in the modern metropolis: a central urban core which dominates the surrounding rings in the performance of office, financial, and business service functions and which also houses those types of manufacturing, wholesaling, and retailing in which the need for maximum opportunities for face-to-face contacts with suppliers or customers or both provides a strong incentive for clustering. Surrounding it is the suburban ring or rings, attracting an increasing share of the manufacturing and wholesaling activities in the area, as well as those retailing and household service operations designed to satisfy routine, day-to-day demands. At the outer fringes of the metropolitan area there is likely to be a certain amount of activity dependent on the soil—activities which are likely to be dying off rapidly unless they are of the sort essential to the well-being of the metropolitan dwellers themselves, such as dairy farms or truck gardens.

Population Shifts Certain types of jobs have been moving out of the metropolitan areas for many decades; the people, in most cases, began moving out even earlier. The history of any city reveals a continuous outward flight of residents, as inventions and changing tastes make once-satisfactory dwellings obsolescent and as industrial and commercial operations encroach on them, making renovation difficult and expensive and threatening them with crowding and dirt and noise. Generally, it is the well-off who move first and farthest in search of space and fresh air and privacy. By the early years of this century, the development of streetcar and subway lines made it increasingly possible for the middle classes to follow and, in the years since World War II, the ubiquity of automobile ownership has greatly accelerated an exodus emphasized by postwar suburban housing developments ringing nearly every metropolitan area. As one group moves outward, its place in the abandoned and obsolescent residential areas is generally taken by a group one step lower on the economic ladder, so that socioeconomic levels tend to drop steadily toward an area's core. In some of the older metropolitan areas, in fact, the process has gone one step further; not only have the rich and the people of moderate means moved out, abandoning urban residence to those too poor to move, but the slums themselves have begun to creep outward, creating an absolute decline in the city's population.

These generalizations, however, conceal the wide variety of patterns actually found among the metropolitan areas of the United States. Depending on the particular stage of development and pattern of specialization, metropolitan areas differ tremendously in the distribution of their activities and their inhabitants. For some, the outward shift of population and jobs has spelled the absolute decline of the central city; for others, it has signaled the opportunity for a huge boom of renovation and office-building construction at the core, as the city adjusts itself to its new and specialized functions. In some areas, important manufacturing industries have good reason to cling to their location at the core (Manhattan's garment industry is an example); in others, the industrial mix is such that virtually all manufacturing operations are heeding the outward pull. Some central cities still harbor large residential areas in which new middle- and upper-class housing is being built; in others, almost the only residents are the slum-dwellers and the only residences are the crumbling structures they have taken over from the more fortunate, perhaps interspersed with a few apartment-enclaves of those well-to-do whose very special kinds of housing needs can be satisfied by high-rise buildings.

Conflicting Trends When all the infinite variety has been taken into account, metropolitan areas still face a set of common problems—problems which act as barriers to their orderly growth. One is the severe imbalance frequently created by the outward shifts in population and employment. As many types of jobs move into the periphery, the central cities are becoming more and more specialized in functions which require chiefly professional technical, and clerical workers—a skilled and literate work force. But the skilled and literate groups are precisely those segments of the population which are increasingly choosing to live outside the urban center. The slum-dwellers, on the other hand, are poorly suited to fill the city's office and service jobs; the jobs for which they are suited—the less skilled occupations involved in many types of manufacturing, wholesaling, and household service operations—are moving farther and farther away from them.

The increased cross-hauling of people this imbalance implies represents at best an increased expenditure of time and resources, often complicated by the growing traffic congestion in many metropolitan areas. But it may mean more than that. By reducing the availability of an appropriate labor force, it can make both suburbs and city less attractive to new establishments in the relevant sectors. And it can leave the city slum-dwellers, stranded, raising the unemployment rate and the welfare burden which must be borne by the area's center.

In many metropolitan areas, the increasing traffic congestion makes it harder and harder to carry out many functions efficiently within the urban core, and harder and harder to get into the center from the periphery. A related difficulty is the increasing expense of reclaiming obsolescent structures and outmoded sites, an expense which not only works against the return of the middle-class or affluent city-dweller, but also reduces the attractiveness of urban locations for nonresidential uses. These are, of course, primarily problems of the central city. But the problems of the city are inevitably the problems of the metropolitan areas as well, for despite the increasing importance of the suburban sections, the economic well-being of any metropolitan area is still heavily dependent on the city around which it has grown. The movement toward complementary specialization of functions in city and suburb serves, in fact, to increase the interdependence between the two.

Metropolitan Problems

These are some of the major pressures operating to check the growth of metropolitan areas—a growth which is being fed by strong pressures of its own. In some areas these difficulties have already become acute; in others they will not have to be faced for many years to come. But they are problems with which every metropolitan area, sooner or later, will have to deal; the more fortunate or far-sighted ones preventively, others in search of a cure or at least a palliative.

Modern man does not attribute all his dissatisfaction with the world around him to his metropolitan abode. But the metropolis does get tagged for more than its fair share of his gripes. No doubt the new spatial arrangements have created new problems and intensified others which existed before. But the metropolis is also indicted for problems which are revealed rather than fostered by the new spatial patterns.

Crime, delinquency, perversion, poverty,

slums: all these have become more visible and therefore seemingly more acute. It is easier to count noses in the city than in the country. The density dimension—squalor per square mile—adds urgency to a problem which is fundamentally measured by the frequency of its occurrence among people.

The distinction between the emergence of a new problem and the revelation of an old one will help to focus attention on those problems which are uniquely metropolitan in character. The resolution of old problems in the new setting is a challenge worthy of attention.

Some further distinctions are in order. Dissatisfaction with the current state of affairs implies one or more of three essentially different kinds of judgments. The most basic is a value judgment which challenges the wisdom of the current allocation of resources among competing needs. "We will master space travel before we solve the commuting problem, and isn't that idiotic?" is an indictment of the values which seem to prevail in Congress. The argument is that the solution of the metropolitan transportation problem would yield social benefits greater than those conferred upon society by the space program. Galbraith is making a similar value judgment when he argues that an affluent society should devote more of its wealth to the alleviation of pressing social problems.

The popular discontent with the quality of life in the metropolitan areas is basically of this character. More should be spent to improve housing, to relieve traffic congestion, to control air pollution, to provide adequate recreational facilities. More should be allocated to these needs even if it means less can be allocated to other national programs.

One hesitates to debate values because they do not necessarily rest on tidy logical arguments. But one is entitled to ask whether the devotion of more resources to these problems would indeed bring us that much closer to their solution. Could we profitably spend another $5 billion on the alleviation of urban problems? We know how to get to the moon, or—to put it more accurately—we know how to learn how to get to the moon and how to get there if the funds are made available. Can we say the same for progress toward the solution of problems of the metropolitan area? No one will deny that we have made progress in our understanding of the mechanics of metropolitan development and in the design of instruments to guide that development along desirable lines. But how fast can we accelerate this process of discovery and engineering with additional funds?

This brings up the second class of gripes which are implicit in many criticisms of metropolitan form. Are we using our resources efficiently? If we add up the total social effort in the metropolis—federal, state, local, private—couldn't we get better results for the same expenditure if we were more efficient in the management of our resources? A classical argument along these lines: If we spent less on roads and more on rapid transit we could get more transportation capacity for a given expenditure on transportation. Another: If we spent less money on tearing down old buildings and more on their rehabilitation we could get more urban renewal for a given expenditure.

This is a more subtle attack on the way we manage our affairs and is more characteristic of the academic than of the common man. But many private interests have a stake in the argument and they contribute to its vigor.

Finally, there are those who challenge the very goals which are implicit in current programs to improve the metropolitan milieu. The planners who decry suburban "sprawl" will fortify their arguments with complaints if inefficiency but fundamentally they are against the way of life because they feel it does not contribute to the improvement of society and the progress of civilization. Recent tirades against current fashions in urban renewal are also in this vein.

14. Springdale and the Mass Society

Joseph Bensman and Arthur J. Vidich

Many towns and villages in the United States have developed numerous features of the culture of urbanism without having grown in population, become more densely settled, or been swallowed within the expanding boundaries of an urban region. For this reason it can be said that America is now an almost entirely urban society in the face of the fact that a quarter of the people do not live in metropolitan areas. Arthur Vidich and Joseph Bensman, in a selection from their study of an upper New York State community they call Springdale, discuss the means by which distant cities and the larger society shape local culture and social organization. First, they point to the role of the mass media, of formal organizations such as the agricultural extension service, and of continuous in- and out-migration, in imparting to small towns the values, norms, and beliefs that dominate the national society. Secondly, Vidich and Bensman discuss the importance of "institutional connectors" operating through the occupational system. People who work or reside in rural areas are dependent for their livelihood on economic and political organizations which have their roots beyond Springdale. The pattern of social change they describe is one in which strong horizontal ties that once held together the membership of local communities have been replaced by vertical bonds which extend through the centralized structures of large corporations, trade unions, and professional associations. The ambiguous position of local communities in urban society is reflected in what the authors call the "psychological ambivalence" of Springdale residents. They praise rural virtues and disapprove of urban institutions at the same time that the influence of the city forces them to respect and admire the competence of national organizations. The outcome is the surrender of local politics to the decision-making process and power of mass society.

Joseph Bensman is Associate Professor of Sociology at City College of the City University of New York. He is the author of *Dollars and Sense* (1967) and coauthor of *Mass, Class and Bureaucracy* (1963) and of *Small Town in Mass Society* (1958).

Arthur J. Vidich is Professor of Sociology and Anthropology at the New School for Social Research, New York City. He is coauthor of *Small Town in Mass Society* (1958) and coeditor of *Reflections on Community Studies* (1964) and *Sociology on Trial* (1963).

The Ambivalent Attitude to Mass Society

Springdalers have a decided respect for the great institutions that characterize American society. The efficiency, organizational ability and farflung activities of giant government and business enterprise inspire them with awe. The military might of the nation and the productive capacity of industry lend a Springdaler a sense of pride and security, and the continuous development and successful application of science assure him that he is a participant in the most forward-looking and progressive country in the world. Anyone who would attack the great institutions of America would have no audience in Springdale: "Everybody knows this country wouldn't be what it is if it weren't for free enterprise and the democratic form of government." When the Springdaler is on the defensive he will tell the critic, "If you don't like it here you can go back to where you came from."

The Springdaler also sees that the urban and metropolitan society is technically and culturally superior to his own community. He sees this in his everyday life when he confronts the fact that his community cannot provide him with everything he needs: almost everyone goes to the city for shopping or entertainment; large numbers of people are dependent on the radio and television; and everyone realizes that rural life would be drastically altered without cars and refrigerators. Springdalers clearly realize how much of local life is based on the modern techniques, equipment and products which originate in distant places.

The community is constantly dependent on cultural and material imports and welcomes these as a way of "keeping up with the times." However, they believe that the very technical and cultural factors that make for the superiority of the "outside" also account for the problems of living that cities exhibit. The "city masses," while they have easier access to progress, are also the ready-made victims of the negative aspects of progress. In contrast, rural life, because it is geographically distant, can enjoy progress and avoid the worst features of the industrial mass society; Springdalers can believe that they are in a position to choose and utilize only the best of two worlds, that the importations, if properly chosen, need not affect the inner life of the community.

Because it is possible to choose only the best, the Springdaler can believe that, in spite of some disadvantages, his is the better of two worlds. This belief in the autonomy or, at worst, the self-selective dependency of rural life makes it possible for the community member publicly to voice the following conceptions concerning the relationships between his town and mass society:

1. That the basic traditions of American society—"grass-roots democracy," free and open expression, individualism— are most firmly located in rural society. The American heritage is better preserved in the small town because it can resist bad city influences and thereby preserve the best of the past.
2. That the future hope of American society lies in rural life because it has resisted all "isms" and constitutes the only major bulwark against them.
3. That much of the progress of society is the result of rural talent which has migrated to the cities. In this way rural

From *Small Town in Mass Society: Class, Power, and Religion in a Rural Community*, by Arthur Vidich and Joseph Bensman (Princeton University Press, 1958), pp. 80–107. Reprinted by permission of Princeton University Press.

society has a positive influence on urban life; rural migrants account for the virtues of city life. "Everyone knows that most of the outstanding men in the country were raised in small towns" and Springdalers proudly point to several local names that have made good on the outside.

4. That "when you live in a small town you can take or leave the big cities—go there when you want to and always come back without having to live as they do." There is the belief that "if more people lived in small towns, you wouldn't have all those problems."

These summarize the types of beliefs that are frequently stated in public situations. The observer who is willing to go beyond the public statements discovers that Springdale has a great variety of direct and intimate connections with a wide range of institutions of the mass society. Moreover, these institutions affect many phases of the community, have consequences for its internal local functioning and in some ways control the direction of social change within it.

Springdale is connected with the mass society in a variety of different forms. The cumulative effect of these various connections makes possible the continuous transmission of outside policies, programs and trends into the community even though the effects of the transmission and the transmitting agents themselves are not always seen. Outside influences can be transmitted directly by a socially visible agent such as the extension specialist who lives in the community for the purpose of acting upon it. Outside interests and influences can also be expressed indirectly through members of the community: policies and programs of relatively invisible outside interests are transmitted by *heads* of local branches of state and national organizations, by *heads* of local businesses dependent on outside resources and by *heads* of churches attached to larger organizations. In some instances the community is affected by the consequences of decisions made by business and government which are made with specific reference to the community, i.e., the decision to build a state road through the community or the decision to close down a factory. Plans and decisions that refer directly to the community are made from a distance by invisible agents and institutions. Perhaps most important are the mass decisions of business and government which are transmitted to the rural scene by the consequences of changes in prices, costs and communications. These affect the town even though they are not explicitly directed at it, and they comprise the invisible social chain reactions of decisions that are made in centers of power in government, business and industry. The invisible social chain reactions emanating from the outside no doubt alter the life of the community more seriously than the action of visible agents such as the extension specialist.

These types of transmission do not represent mutually exclusive channels, but rather exist in complex interrelationship with each other. They merely suggest the major ways in which the community is influenced by dynamics which occur in the institutions of mass society. How these combined dynamics in their varior combinations affect the fabric of life in Springdale can be seen by examining the way in which cultural importations and economic and political connections shape the character of community life. In their net effect they influence the psychological dimensions of the community.

Cultural Importations from Mass Society

The external agents of cultural diffusion range from specific observable individuals placed in the local community by outside institutions to the impact of mass media of communications and successive waves of migration. The consequence of these modes of diffusion lies in the effect which they have on local styles of living.

Formal Importing Organizations The adult extension program of the land grant college is mediated at the local level by the county agent and the home demonstration agent who respectively are concerned with farming methods and production, and patterns of homemaking and family life. These agents carry out their program through the Farm and Home Bureau organizations. In Springdale township these agencies have a membership of 300–400 adults. The county agent is primarily concerned with introducing modern methods of farm production and operation and with fostering political consciousness among the farmers. As a type of executive secretary to the local Farm Bureau whose officers are local farmers, the agent acts as an advisor in planning the organization's program, which includes such items as production and marketing problems, parity price problems and taxation problems.

The organizational structure of the Home Bureau parallels the Farm Bureau. From skills and techniques and personnel available at the extension center, local programs consist, for example, of furniture refinishing or aluminum working as well as discussions on such topics as child-rearing, nutrition, penal institutions and interior design. The Home Bureau extension specialist trains a local woman in information and techniques which are reported back to the local club. This program, geared as it is to modern homemaking, child-rearing and the feminine role, has the effect of introducing new styles and standards of taste and consumption for the membership.

Other institutional connectors similar to the above in organizational structure account for the introduction of still other social values and social definitions. The 4-H Club, the Future Farmers of America and the Boy and Girl Scouts, as well as the Masons, Odd Fellows, American Legion, Grange and other local branches of national organizations and their auxiliaries, relate the Springdaler to the larger society through the social meanings and styles of activity defined in the programs, procedures and rituals of the national headquarters. State and national conventions, but not office holding, of these as well as church organizations directly link individuals to the outside. In effect these arrangements regularize and institutionalize the communication and organizational nexus between the small town and the point of origin of new ideas and values.

New cultural standards are also imported by agents who are not permanent residents of the town or who have only a transient relationship with it. These include the teachers at the central school, many of whom view their jobs as a temporary interlude in a progression of experience which will lead to a position in a city system. The other agents of contact are a wide variety of salesmen and "experts" who have a regular or irregular contact with business, government and private organizations. From the surrounding urban centers and the regional sales offices of farm implement and automobile manufacturers and nationally branded products, modern methods of merchandizing and business practice are introduced. Experts in civil defense, evangelism, fire-fighting, gardening, charity drives, traffic control and youth recreation introduce new techniques and programs to the local community. This great variety and diversity of semi-permanent and changing contacts in their cumulative effect act as a perpetual blood transfusion to local society. The net effect that these agents have as transmitters of life styles depends in a measure on their position and prestige in the community. The differential effect of these cultural contacts is treated below.

The Ubiquity of Mass Media Social diffusion through the symbols and pictorial images of the mass media of communications has permeated the community, reducing the local paper to reporting of social items and local news already known by everyone. Few individuals read only the local weekly paper; the majority subscribe to dailies published in surrounding cities and in the large metropolitan areas. This press, itself part of larger newspaper combines, presents an image of the passing scene in its news and nationally syndicated features to which the population of an entire region is exposed.

The mass culture and mass advertising of television and radio reach Springdale in all their variety. Television, particularly, is significant in its impact because for the first time the higher art forms such as ballet, opera and plays are visible to a broad rural audience. National events such as party conventions, inaugurations and investigative hearings are visible now to an audience which was previously far removed from the national centers of action and drama. Because of the relative geographic isolation of Springdale, television has made available entirely new areas of entertainment, information and

education. It has created new leisure-time interests, has introduced new modes of leisure-time consumption and has led to the acceptance of standardized entertainment models. Wrestling, Arthur Godfrey and Howdy-Doody are common symbols of entertainment. Equally available and pervasive among the classes and individuals to whom they appeal are pocket books, comic books, and horror and sex stories. Micky Spillane, Willie Mays, Davy Crockett and other nationally prominent personages as well as nationally branded products are as well known and available to the small town as they are to the big city. The intrusion of the mass media is so overwhelming that little scope is left for the expression of local cultural and artistic forms.

However, the diffusion of the printed word is not limited to the mass media; it is present also in the realm of education, both religious and secular. The state department of education syllabus defines minimum standards and content for subject matter instruction. Courses of Sunday School instruction are available for all age levels, and each faith secures its material from its own national religious press. In each of these major institutional areas the standards and *content* of instruction are defined in sources available only in standardized form.

The Immigrant as a Cultural Carrier Specific individuals are carriers of cultural diffusion, and the volume and extent of migration in and out of the community suggests the degree and intimacy of its contact with the mass society. In a community which is regarded as stable and relatively unchanging by its own inhabitants, only 25 percent of its population was born locally. Another 25 percent has moved into the community since 1946 and 55 percent are new to the community since 1920. Moreover, of the 45 percent who have moved to the community since 1932, more than 30 percent have lived for a year or longer in cities with populations in excess of 25,000; 7 percent in cities with populations in excess of one-half million.

Each decade and each generation introduces a new layer of immigrants to the community. The agricultural and business prosperity of the 1940's and early 1950's has brought city dwellers to farms and to businesses on main street, and the housing shortage has led workers to reclaim long-abandoned farm dwellings. The 12 percent of new people who moved into Springdale in the Thirties came in response to the effects of the depression. From 1918 to 1928 the Poles moved onto farms abandoned by descendants of original settlers. Indeed, the ebb and flow of migration extends back to such eras of political and economic upheaval as the depression of the 1890's, the civil war, the depression of the 1830's and the mass movement of people during the Indian Wars and the opening of the territory in the early 1800's. Each new wave of migrants, bringing with it the fashions and thought styles of other places, influences the cultural development of the community.

The cumulative consequences of these channels of diffusion and the quantity and quality of the "material" diffused denies the existence of a culture indigenous to the small town. In almost all aspects of culture, even to speech forms, and including technology, literature, fashions and fads, as well as patterns of consumption, to mention a few, the small town tends to reflect the contemporary mass society.

Basically, an historically indigenous local culture does not seem to exist. The cultural imports of each decade and generation and the successive waves of migration associated with each combine to produce a local culture consisting of layers or segments of the mass culture of successive historical eras. In the small town the remaining elements of the gay-ninety culture are juxtaposed against the modern central school. The newer cultural importations frequently come in conflict with the older importations of other eras. The conflict between "spurious" and "genuine" culture appears to be a conflict between two different ages of "spurious" culture.

The Economic Nexus: Occupational Gatekeepers to the Mass Society

Simply because individuals pursue given occupations, their interconnections with mass society follow given patterns. They may be direct employees of specific organizations of the mass society; they may be the objects and targets of the programs of mass organizations; they may be trained by and in great institutions or their skills may be utilized only in urban areas. Because of these occupational characteristics they are specially qualified, accessible and available as transmitters of specific organizational and cultural contacts and contents.

Because these individuals in their occupational roles as gatekeepers are treated as specialists by both the community and mass society, occupation even more than life style becomes a crucial dimension of community life. The content, quality and amount of cultural importation accounted for by an individual is a function of the specific occupational nexus which he has to both the community and mass society.

The Professionals A number of institutional representatives who are residents of the town receive their position in the community by virtue of their connections with outside agencies. Their position in the community is secured in part by the institution to which they are connected and by the evaluation of the role they are imputed to have in the agency which they locally represent.

The group of individuals who possess a borrowed prestige based on their external affiliations fall largely in the professional category. They are individuals who uniformly possess a college education. Among their ranks are included lawyers, ministers, doctors, teachers, engineers, and a variety of field representatives of state and federal agencies who settle in the community for occupational purposes. All of these individuals, except one or two, have migrated to the community as adults. In addition to the prestige which they are accorded by virtue of being "educated," their overwhelming characteristic as a group lies in the influence which they have in mediating between the town and the larger society. They possess the knowledge and techniques necessary for connecting the small town to the intricate organization of the mass bureaucratic society. They possess "contacts" with outside agencies and their role requires an ability to understand "official" documents and forms, and to write appropriate letters to appropriate bureaus. Thus, for example, the lawyer is counsel to political bodies as well as to free associations and other local organizations, in which capacities he gains an extensive and intimate knowledge of affairs of the town and thereby acquires a position of influence. In like manner the technical knowledge of state educational regulations and policies possessed by the highschool principal is indispensable to the locally constituted school board.

In addition to the prestige and influence which segments of this group possess by virtue of their education and institutional role, they are accorded a respect and, in some cases, awe because of the power which they are imputed to have in manipulating the outside world; they can accomplish things for the community which no one else can.

Moreover, this professional group as a whole, including the relatively transient teaching staff, are felt to have access to styles of taste and consumption which are considered different from those available to the rest of the community. As a result these institutional connectors are considered outside the ordinary realm of prestige assignments and social stratification. That is, their social position in the community is not guaranteed by conforming to standards which are indigenous to the community but, rather, by imputed conformance to "alien" or "exotic" standards of urban life.

As a result of this dual position, individuals in this group, especially those who have come from or have resided for some time outside the community, are able to influence styles of consumption and thought in the community. They do this in three main areas of activity: in organizational activities, community projects and social fashions. They have been prime movers in setting up a formal program of youth recreation and in vigorously participating in and supporting local cultural activities such as plays, recitals and educational talks. In the P.T.A. they constitute the bloc favoring those modern methods and programs which bring the outside world to the small town —talks by foreign university students, race relations discussions and sociodramas in dating and parent-child relationships. Ideas for the development of a community center and adult education programs emanate from and are supported by them. In terms of dress styles and personal adornment as well as home furnishings and styles of party giving, this group is in the forefront of innovation.

This innovating group of middle-class newcomers is supported by a group of college-educated locals who act as a bridge between the new standards and local society. In supporting these new standards, the local group absorbs some of the resentment which is directed at the innovating group by both the farmers and merchants.

It must be noted that the professionals' psychological orientation to accentuate the "elite" cultural values of mass society is more than merely a product of their residence, education or background in the mass society. The limitations on economic success and the limited professional opportunities in the community means that the drive toward success through work and investment is not fully available to them. The possession of alien cultural standards makes it possible for the professionals to reject the success drive by accepting meaningful standards alternative to those available to the rest of the community; they distinguish themselves in the community by their identification with external values.

Businessmen   For storekeepers, filling station operators, appliance dealers, automobile and farm equipment dealers and feed mill operators, the external world is a source of supply for the goods and commodities which they sell on the local market. Their position in relation to their source of supply and the overall condition of the national economy determines the level of their business activity, ceilings on their potential income, and hence indirectly their style of life. To analyze this group we must consider separately the position

of the independent shopkeeper, the businessman who operates on a franchise and the feed mill and farm implement dealer.

The shopkeepers who make up the bulk of the business community have experienced a slow and gradual decline in their class position relative to other groups in the community. This is mainly due to the breakdown of their monopolistic position with respect to the local market, but it is also related to the rise of other groups. The development of the automobile, the appearance of the chain stores in surrounding areas and the expansion of mail order sales have placed them in a competitively disadvantageous position. Moreover, the nationally branded and advertised product, with its fixed profit margin determined by the producer, has tended in a general way to determine his volume/profit ratio in a way increasingly disadvantageous to him. His decrease in profits in relation to volume has driven him to a greater competition with other local shopkeepers—a competition which takes place in the form of despecialization, greater reliance on credit trade and keeping his shop open for long hours. The first two of these responses to his dilemma have further depressed his profit/volume ratio: in the one case by reducing his return on his investment and in the other case by increased losses due to bad debts. He keeps his business open in an effort to improve his investment/profit ratio and this he can do only by staying in the store himself.

The economic position of the small storekeeper prevents him from reinvesting earnings in his own business. He sees little to be gained by modernizing and expanding his store in an effort to increase profits. Hence, the very bases on which the business group could achieve a class ascendancy are not open to it. Moreover, the long hours which he keeps in his store prevent him from holding a secondary occupation and limit his activities in community affairs. As a result he lives in an atmosphere of social and economic scarcity relative to his position thirty years ago and relative to other segments of the community. This accounts for the dominant psychology of scarcity-mindedness which is characteristic of this most numerous segment of the business class.

The position of the businessman who operates on a *franchise* is more obviously linked to the mass society. Usually he not only has a single source of supply, but also his source of supply (a petroleum company, for example) specifies the business practices and standards which must be maintained in order to retain the franchise. If the retail outlet is owned by the supplier (as with some filling stations) rents may be charged on a sliding scale according to volume of business—less volume, less rent—with the consequence that the profit margin of the local operator is not fixed.

More important, however, are the combined effects of the distribution policies of the petroleum products companies and appliance producers. Most of the big producers of these products maintain a local outlet; in some cases a single product may be retailed in two or three small-scale local outlets. In at least one line, household appliances, price cutting has become a standard form of competition. The effect of this proliferation of outlets is to depress the business chances of any single operator retailing a given branded product.

This group responds to its economic situation by increasing business hours, by carrying secondary lines and by intensive competition for "service" trade. Business is conducted at almost any hour of the day or night. Since these are one-man businesses, other members of the family are

soon incorporated in the work process; children are helpers, wives act as secretaries and clerks. In the extreme case, the family life of the filling station operator orients itself almost completely to "keeping the business open"; the husband and wife are on duty together or the husband is absent from home except to sleep. This group is known to the community primarily through its occupational circumstances and its relationships are based upon being entrepreneurs and having a clientele. As individuals they are relatively unimportant to the community since there is a high rate of turnover of franchises.

There are three individuals in the business class who are exceptions. These are the feed mill operators and the farm implement dealers who in Springdale consist of one feed mill operator located on the periphery of the township, one implement dealer located in the village, and one large-scale combined feed mill, housing supply and farm implement partnership. Because they service an agricultural industry which since the early Forties has been prosperous, they are favorably situated in the local economy.

In terms of their customer relationships they are most intimately tied to the farmers, especially to the prosperous farmers who do most of the buying. Because of their market position their economic fate is intimately related to that of the farmers. In the period of farm ascendancy at the time of the study, they too were prosperous and exhibited all of the same aspects of expansion, investment and opportunity-consciousness already described for the farmer. In addition, however, because they are businessmen and the most successful businessmen, they have achieved the respect, admiration and enmity of the business community as well as of the town at large.

They are the most heavily capitalized group of individuals in the community and play an important credit function in the local agricultural economy. Because of the farmer's economic dependence on them and the interlocking character of their mutual fate, the feed mill and implement dealers identify themselves with the farmer's interests. In local politics they are in a position to provide the leadership in organizing the farmer's interests and frequently act as spokesman for the farm community. This is particularly true of the feed mill and implement partnership since it is the community's dominant enterprise; the other feed dealer is less important because his business is small and is located on the periphery of the town, and the other implement dealer is unimportant politically because being an Italian he is ethnically peripheral.

Thus two sub-groups of the business community, shopkeepers and franchise operators, experience a social and economic decline relative to a third, the feed and implement dealers.

These shifts in relative success are linked to accessibility to economic opportunity which is largely defined by external forces.

Industrial Workers Industrial workers represent a curious gap in the relationship of the rural community to mass society. Individuals who live in Springdale but work outside on products which are geared to a national market are not understandable to other members of the community because the rural community lacks the perceptual apparatus necessary to understand industry and the industrial process. The industrial worker lives in the community, but the occupational basis of his existence is not subject to the social pigeon-holing by others necessary to

making judgments and assessments of him.

Industrial workers consist mainly of individuals and their families who have migrated to the community in an effort to escape city life and to seek cheaper housing as well as land for home gardens. Due to the ecological conditions of the rural community (a large number of abandoned farm dwellings and the breakup of large houses into apartments), in-migrating as well as native industrial workers live in a scattered pattern throughout the township. As a consequence of their work routine, which involves, in addition to their work in a factory, one or two hours of commuting plus, in many cases, the operation of an extensive garden, home improvements and the care of livestock or a secondary occupation, this group tends to be relatively socially isolated in its day-to-day contact with the rest of the community. Their work carries them to the city where they can do their shopping and engage in city activities. As individuals some of the industrial workers strive to become involved in community activities and many of them maintain an affiliation with one of the local churches.

This dependence on outside industry affects the internal stratification pattern of local society. There are apparently no fixed standards available to other groups in the community, especially the farmers and businessmen, by which a social class position can be assigned to industrial workers relative to their own class position. Industrial processes tend not to be understood by the non-industrial groups and, therefore, these latter groups are not able to assign evaluations of skill, workmanship and prestige to the various individuals engaged in industrial activity. There is some evaluation of industrial workers based on an evaluation of the shop in which they work since sharp differences in working conditions and security benefits exist from shop to shop, but this is insufficient to assign differential status to individuals who work at different jobs in the same shop.

A rather minimal evaluation rests on the general attitude other groups have to industrial workers as a generic type. Local workers are viewed with a mixture of envy and pity; envied because they have what is regarded as a short work day, good pay and little responsibility to their jobs; pitied because their opportunities for economic advancement are "arbitrarily" limited.

Because of the paucity of data and criteria available to other groups for ranking individual workers, the problem of the social definition of their position is left in large measure to definitions of positions which individuals give to themselves. Thus the industrial worker in the small town, more than individuals in any other group, is in a position to create his own social standing. He can do this partly by church affiliation, but primarily through affiliation with auxiliary church organizations, participation in commnuity organizations, association in social circles and by demonstrating his ability to work hard improving his home and cultivating a respectable garden.

But even given these criteria, the bulk of the industrial group is not socially *visible* to the rest of the community. That is, they are not conceived as a group because there is no single framework available to other groups to give their perception a perspective.

Their major occupational role exists outside the framework of the local society. This would suggest that even in a relatively "simple" rural community there is no single standard for social stratification. That is, social stratification in this type of situation represents a plurality of unrelated dimensions, often in conflict or not even coherent, in the midst of which groups of individuals may exist as congeries. This has been pointed out in the literature of urban stratification, but it has always been assumed that the small-scale rural society could be stratified from top to bottom, an hypothesis which this observation suggests is not the case. A major reason why a single standard of stratification cannot be used is that a single standard presupposes knowledge which makes assessment possible. The Springdaler does not have the knowledge of the complex industrial commercial processes of modern society to be able to locate individuals in these processes.

Farmers As noted earlier, there are two classes of farmers, the rational and the traditional. A major difference between them is the way they organize their production in relation to the mass market and government regulations.

Those who gear themselves to the mass market address themselves to favorably pegged prices, subsidies and quotas. As a consequence when prices and regulations are favorable they accept the favorable environment as a condition for their operations. They invest and expand, work hard and are successful. Their success stimulates confidence and buoyancy and produces an expansionist psychology.

In a peculiar way the traditional farmers who as a group do not gear themselves to the mass market do this specifically because of their relations with the mass market. As older farmers they have learned from the depression that they can be economically vulnerable, and they have learned that they can survive in the community by being immune to the market. The depression experience was so bitter for them that they have learned nothing since. Thus it happens that at the time of the study they were still living in the market of the early Thirties.

To show how the internal status position of the farmer is related to the institutional structure of the larger society, account must be taken of the fluctuations in the agricultural economy over the past thirty years. The agricultural depression beginning after World War I and extending to the beginning of World War II placed the farmer in a depressed (indebted) economic position. The decline of the farmer in Springdale was more extreme than in the nation at large during this period because Springdale is a marginal agricultural area with relatively poor land and a high rate of feed purchases. Farmers were either dispossessed, displaced or they retrenched to a heavily indebted minimum standard of consumption and operation. In this period the farmer verged on being declassed or actually was declassed.

Today the farmer is an important and ascendant segment of the rural middle class. From a position of near bankruptcy in 1933 he had risen (at the time of the field work for this study) to a position of heavy capitalization and social prominence. His rise coincided with the rationalization of marketing procedures (the Federal Milk Price Order in the New York Milk Shed), federal agricultural policies, and the rise in the market value of his products since the early 1940's. Specific agricultural policies which have contributed to his rise include the price support program, farm credit programs, and fertilizer and other land improvement give-aways. A little recognized source of preferential treatment given him by an outside agency lies in the structure of United States income tax laws, which allow for rapid depreciation of plant and equipment, little accountability on cash sales and a broad base of allowable operating expenses.

Although the status of all farmers is equally linked to decisions and policies of these larger institutional structures (the price structure and federal agricultural legislation), all farmers do not equally orient their operations to legislation and regulations oriented to him. At this point the rate of status ascendancy of the individual farmer is probably directly related to the extent to which he accepts the preferential treatment accorded him in these larger policy decisions. Those who have been most swift and efficient in adjusting to the changing conditions of the agricultural economy over the past twenty years constitute the most rapidly ascending segment of farmers.

As a consequence of the character of the institutional connectors which link the farmer to the great society, the status of the farmer relative to other local groups is relatively independent of local community forces. By the same token, his status is directly related to price structures and mass decisions and policies. Alterations in these external forces, such as a tumbling in farm prices, can cause an upheaval in the status structure of the local community.

This analysis does not exhaust the class groups. Other groups are occupationally less directly connected with the mass society and its markets. The aristocrats are oriented to the market only by fixed interest rates established in previous economic periods; their income from annuities, insurance payments, and fixed inheritances declines in an inflationary period. The shack people, with the exception of their consumption function, are separated from the market by their unwillingness to direct their attention to it for any sustained period of time, even though their consumption standards are inflated at those times when they do address themselves to the market. The marginal middle-class groups economically are not in a position to be directly and importantly related to the market except through the general price level. Their relationship to the market is mediated through their imitation of more prestigeful and successful groups which are located in the community.

Occupation, Class and Community

It will be noted that the above analysis of the impact of mass society, as stated in the framework of occupation, stands in contrast to the analysis of class which was stated as differences in style of life. The difference is understandable only in terms of the different economic and psychological functions of these two elements. Style of life is related to preferences in expenditure of time, energy and money. Occupation deals with source of income rather than its expenditure. Obviously there is a connection between the two: that is, it is difficult in the long run to spend in excess of one's income. The possession of income however does not by itself guarantee a style of living. In addition to income, the elements necessary to guarantee a style of living are taste, aspirations, habits and skills. This means that individuals in the same occupational class may be affiliates of different social classes as in the case of segments of the marginal middle class. In recognizing this, one sees that social class has an independent volitional character from occupational categories. However, one cannot forget that through time the means available for consumption are products of income and that those

factors which affect the income of members of a given social class also affect an individual's class eligibility. It is specifically at this point that the relationship of occupational classes to the mass society is important in its effect on the internal social classes of Springdale and, moreover, on the cultural and psychological character of these social classes.

Those groups which are favorably linked to the mass society are in a position to be socially, economically and politically ascendant in the community; in Springdale these are the rational farmers. Those groups which are unfavorably linked— segments of the marginal middle class— find it difficult to achieve the wherewithal to practice the preferred styles of life. Moreover, a favorable position with respect to certain aspects of mass society can and does in the long run produce optimism, buoyancy, aggressiveness and high self-esteem among members of a given class. Thus the psychological foundation of the class of rational farmers has changed over time. On the other hand, a negative position *vis à vis* mass society produces feelings of penury, scarcity, defensiveness and defensive social snobbery. Each of these sets of attitudes becomes a basis for further social and economic orientations for the affected classes.

The Political Surrender to Mass Society

Local political institutions consist of a village board, a town board and local committees of the Republican and Democratic parties. The jurisdiction of the village board includes powers of control and regulation over a variety of community facilities and services—street lighting, water supply, fire protection, village roads, street signs and parks. To carry out the functions empowered to it, it possesses the power of taxation. The town board is concerned chiefly with fire protection, the construction and maintenance of roads; through its participation on the county board of supervisors, it participates in programs connected with welfare, penal and other county services.

However, at almost every point in this seemingly broad base of political domain the village and town boards adjust their action to either the regulations and laws defined by state and federal agencies which claim parallel functions on a statewide or nationwide basis or to the fact that outside agencies have the power to withhold subsidies to local political institutions.

Local assessment scales and tax rates are oriented to state equalization formulas which partially provide the standardized basis on which subsidies are dispersed by the state. State highway construction and development programs largely present local political agencies with the alternative of either accepting or rejecting proposed road plans and programs formulated by the state highway department.

The village board, more than the town board, is dependent on its own taxable resources (taxes account for almost half its revenues) and best illustrates the major dimensions of local political action. The village board in Springdale accepts few of the powers given to it. Instead, it orients its action to the facilities and subsidies controlled and dispensed by other agencies and, by virtue of this, forfeits its own political power. Solutions to the problem of fire protection are found in agreements with regionally organized fire districts. In matters pertaining to road signs and street signs action typically takes the form of petitioning state agencies to fulfill desired goals "without cost to the tax-payer." On

roads built and maintained by the state there is no recourse but to accept the state traffic bureau's standards of safety. A problem such as snow removal is solved be dealing directly with the foreman of the state highway maintenance crew through personal contacts: "If you treat him right, you can get him to come in and clear the village roads." In other areas of power where there are no parallel state agencies, such as for garbage collection or parks, the village board abdicates its responsibility.

As a consequence of this pattern of dependence, many important decisions are made for Springdale by outside agencies. Decisions which are made locally tend to consist of approving the requirements of administrative or state laws. In short the program and policies of local political bodies are determined largely by acceptance of grants-in-aid offered them—i.e., in order to get the subsidy specific types of decisions must be made—and by facilities and services made available to them by outside sources.

Psychologically this dependence leads to an habituation to outside control to the point where the town and village governments find it hard to act even where they have the power. Legal jurisdictions have been supplanted by psychological jurisdictions to such an extent that local political action is almost exclusively oriented to and predicated on seeking favors, subsidies and special treatment from outside agencies. The narrowing of legal jurisdictions by psychologically imposed limits leads to an inability to cope with local problems if outside resources are not available.

Power in local political affairs, then, tends to be based on accessibility to sources of decision in larger institutions. Frequently this accessibility consists merely of the knowledge of the source, or it may mean a personal contact, or an ability to correspond to get necessary information. Under these circumstances, power in the political arena is delegated to those with contacts in and knowledge of the outer world and to those who are experts in formal communication with impersonal bureaucratic offices. These are, on the individual level, the lawyer and, on an institutional level, the political party. The lawyer gains his paramountcy through technical knowledge and personalized non-party contacts up the political hierarchy with other lawyers. He is the mediator between the local party and the party hierarchy, and transforms his personalized contacts into political indispensability in the local community. His access to outside sources of power determines his power and predominance in the local community.

The Social Psychological Consequences of the Rural Surrender

A central fact of rural life then, is its dependence on the institutions and dynamics of urban and mass society. The recognition of this dependence and the powerlessness associated with it give to the agents and institutions of the great society a degree of respect and admiration which, however, does not always connote approval. Rather, there is a high degree of ambivalence with respect to these agents and institutions. They have respect because of their power and wealth, and because their norms have the legitimacy of acceptance in wide areas of the society at large. On the other hand, the very dominance of the mass institutions causes resentments, since, in the light of this dominance, rural life in its immediacy is devalued. Hence, for example, although the standards of the land grant college are accepted, the institution and its agents may be resented for the role they play in innovation.

The phenomenon of psychological ambivalence to the mass society is particularly reinforced by the fact that slight changes in the policies and dynamics of the mass institutions can have profound effects on the rural way of life and on its major social and economic classes—i.e., parity policies, industrial relocations, new state roads and state subsidization formulas. In response to these conditions, the members of the rural community and their political spokesman resent their dependency and powerlessness and channelize it into anti-urban politics and policies. In relation to the outer world, there exist two types of political victory; when rural rather than urban areas get a disproportionately large share of the benefits of the state budget and when the city can be made the object of investigation on ground of corruption or vice by politicians surrounded by a halo of rural images. At the same time a personal identification with important urban political officials lends an individual prestige in the rural community.

But this continuous transvaluation of the attitudes toward urban life and its representatives are never so simple as the dependence-resentment mechanism would suggest. For such political and psychological currents are supported by intricately articulated images of the mass society and rural self images, described in Chapter Two, which for the purposes of this discussion can be termed counterimages.

These images, themselves, are a product of complex institutional developments and reflect the process of urban penetration. For it is uniquely ironical that the self-image of the rural community and its image of urban life are in part the products of the penetration of urban mass media.

Through these media the people of Springdale see urban life dominated by crime, dirt, filth, immorality, vice, corruption and anti-Americanism. The urban center is seen as a jungle of man's inhumanity to man; the large political center as a "dog-eat-dog" world of investigations and counterinvestigations with few clearly defined heroes. It sees the urban middle classes confronted by apparently hopeless personal problems and moving from crisis to crisis without end. It is because of the mechanism of resentment that the Springdaler can see wide class differences in urban society and be unaware of class in his own environment.

Contrariwise, the mass media frequently present rural life in idyllic terms. The *Saturday Evening Post* cover brings forth the image of the cracker barrel, the virtues of life close to soil and stream and of healthy, simple, family living. The weekly press carries syndicated columnists who extol the virtues of ruralism. Political as well as feature speakers who come to town invariably reinforce the town's image of itself: "The false life of cities," "If America were made up of small towns like Springdale, this would be a better country." "The goodness of America lies in the small town where life and nature meet to make for genuine living." The urban man of knowledge and the university scientist verbalize their own image of rural life and in doing so shape the self-image of the rural audience.

Separate urban images exist for the various segments which epitomize the rural community. The farmer is strong, self-reliant and capable. He is warm, affectionate and devoted but these characteristics are frequently hidden under a crusty, gruff exterior. He is a good businessman and a sharp trader capable in the final analysis of outwitting others, especially the city slicker. Outside of a few old gossips, communtiy life is richly warm and filled with a wide variety of social interchange, gatherings and genuinely spontaneous self-expression. The rural dweller is religious, moral and upright, though capable of "cutting-up" in a way which is both amusing and tolerable. The villains, the sharp-dealers, the frauds, when not urban types, exist in order to provide the protagonist and the community with an effective demonstration of its values in action.

The above picture, of course, is only a profile of the images presented to the rural consumer of mass media. Numerous exceptions exist, as, for example, the image of rural corruption often present in the violent type of pocket novel. Another notable exception is the absence in the mass media of an image of the rural, commuting, industrial worker. His place in rural society is difficult to stereotype, particularly since it stands in sharp contrast to the image of the self-reliance and independence of the rural community as personified by the farmer. Thus the lack of definition of the rural industrial worker in the mass media corresponds to the lack of a definition of industrial workers held by the residents of Springdale, including the lack of a self-definition by the industrial workers themselves.[1]

The mass media then provide the raw materials out of which the rural resident can and does form personal images which enable him to approach the psychological demands of his situation. The rural target of the mass media thus can select those elements of the total output which enable him to meet those psychological needs, ignoring both the materials and the implications which are not congruent with the manner in which he wishes to structure his perception and images.

From the standpoint of the producer of mass media, to complete the picture, the image presented of rural life and life in general reflects not only his estimate of his audience (since not all of the mass media are specifically aimed at the rural market) but also the psychological climate of the urban centers where images of rural life are produced. The romanticization of rural life in press and radio reflects the need of the urban dweller to conceive of rural life as simpler and freer from the complexities, tensions, and anxieties which he faces in his own world. Rural life is thus conceived as a counterimage which highlights his own situation. However, when presented to the rural resident, it serves as an image which enables the rural dweller to form symbolic and ideological resistance to urban society. It is thus through the mass media that the negative reactions to mass society of both the rural and urban dweller are linked; and it is as sets of similar responses to the negative aspects of urbanism that both urban and rural dwellers find a common symbolic meeting ground.

In addition to images which may be the peculiar product of the mass media, Springdalers hold negative images of the major urban institutions. Washington is populated by corrupt politicians, influence peddlers and communists. Cities are hotbeds of radicalism and atheism. Industrial workers led by racketeers are lazy, highly paid and incapable of performing the complex managerial practices necessary to success in farm and small business management. Big universities and city churches are seats of secularism and the city influence is held responsible for local immorality and corruption. These images in their complex articulation enable the rural resident to take pride in his situation, to meet the psychological threat of his power-lessness in a mass society and to organize political action which expresses both his economic interest and his psychological needs.

It must be remembered, however, that the central fact of rural life is ambivalence: the negative image of urban life goes hand in hand with respect for the power, the wealth and the legitimacy of acceptance of urban values. The most contrary values are thus held in complex, psychologically balanced constellations. As a result, the response of rural residents to urban institutions is not stable through time. Slight shifts in their situations can cause the most varied responses. Their political loyalties are subject to sudden shifts in phase with shifts in farm income, price levels and the policies of state and federal governments. Anti-urban elements are held in check or can develop relatively easily. Furthermore, the balance of power and influence within the community can and does vary with relatively slight shifts in the external situation affecting these groups.

Hence, those factors which appear to be decisive in determining the action of the rural community are factors which originate in areas outside the rural community. Thus, even when the rural community attacks the urban mass society, the nature of the attack, its intensity and the situations which bring it forth are, in large part, the products of urban mass society. Rural life, then, can be seen as one area in which the dynamics of modern urban mass society are worked out.

There is always the danger of considering all aspects of mass society as responding only to the dynamics of mass society, so that when one completes one's analysis mass society dissolves into a response to itself. It must be remembered that there is a reciprocal relationship between Springdale and mass society in which Springdale, taken as one of thousands of similar communities, exerts itself upon and shapes the mass society. This reciprocal relationship is found primarily in the area of politics. The analysis of this relationship brings into focus an entirely new set of perspectives on the life of the community.

NOTE

1. Industrial workers who live in the country are caught in the cross pressures which exist between their positions as workers and the dominant and hostile definitions which their culture give to their position. They tend to be anti-union, yet desire the benefits which they think unions give to workers. But these desires are not frequently expressed at a verbal level. In the absence of alternatives and in the presence of a dominant cultural stand against unions, the industrial workers affirm the dominant values of the community, including personal pride in the paternalistic concern of their employers. This is done with no apparent psychological cost to the workers.

15. On the Impact of Urbanism on Social Organization, Human Nature and the Political Order

Philip M. Hauser

In this paper, Hauser presents a comprehensive survey of the impact of the emergence of cities on our social order. The decline in family size, the emphasis on rationality, the rise in crime and delinquency rates, and the weakening of the two-party system—all these facets, and many more, of contemporary America are traced to the urbanization process. However, Hauser states that these evidences of social disorganization should not be regarded as intrinsic deficiencies of the urban way of life. They are the temporary expression of inevitable dislocations caused by the emergence of a new stage of the continuing revolution in environmental conditions that began with the Neolithic period. Hauser also is careful to emphasize the liberating influences on personality, behavior, values, and individual opportunity that stem from the growth of the metropolis. Many of the difficulties of the metropolis itself are attributed to the insufficiencies of its governmental organization. These will be overcome when the central cities and suburbs become more alike in social structure and population composition.

Philip M. Hauser is Professor of Sociology and Director of the Population Research Center at the University of Chicago. He is the author or editor of numerous books, including *World Population Problems* (1965), *The Handbook for Social Research in Urban Areas* (1964), and *The Population Dilemma* (1963), and is the coeditor of *The Study of Urbanization* (1964). Professor Hauser is past President of the American Sociological Association (1967–68), of the American Statistical Association (1962), and of the Population Association of America (1950).

Man as the only culture-building animal on the globe not only adapts to environment but creates environment to which to adapt. The urban or metropolitan area is one of man's more complex cultural constructs which, on the one hand, is an impressive symbol of achievement and, on the other, the matrix of serious and pressing problems. Product of the cumulative effects of the various "revolutions," ranging from the "neolithic" to the "industrial," the urban area today faces the prospect of adjustment to still further revolutions. These revolutions are being generated by electronic and atomic technology, which together with developing rocketry may produce new and as yet unvisualized dimensions of change, or even result in the annihilation of the metropolis altogether.

It is generally believed that the neolithic revolution with its invention of domesticated plants produced the first relatively widespread and fixed human settlements. The emergence of an agricultural economy and increasing dependence on its products led gradually to the abandonment of the nomadic existence. Neolithic settlements were relatively small population groupings, villages rather than towns, whose size was limited by technological, economic, social and political factors. The appearance of larger population aggregations, the town and the city, depended on developments which did not appear until the metal ages. The emergence of a metropolitan area of a million or more is probably a modern phenomenon dependent on the technology and the economic, social and political organization identified with the industrial revolution.

Since the first city of one million or more inhabitants was probably nineteenth century London, it may be said, in broad perspective, that it took man, or closely related ancestors, some one hundred thousand to one million years to produce the modern metropolis. But the metropolis not only is the consequent of such developments; it is also a determinant of further development. Urbanism has profoundly affected the social order; it has modified the nature of human nature and has produced vast changes in the political order.

It is to the consideration of aspects of these changes, or aspects of "urbanism as a way of life," that this essay is addressed.

II

The fact that living in the city makes a difference in the way of life has been noted by the writers of antiquity, as well as by more recent observers. Durkheim, in pursuing his interest in "social morphology," succinctly stated, in a relatively little-known note, the relationship of the nature of physical conditions of living and population agglomerations to "social life":

> Social life rests on a substratum whose size as well as its form is determined. This substratum is constituted by the mass of individuals who make up society, the way in which they are distributed on the soil, and the nature and configuration of all sorts of things that affect collective relationships. The social substratum differs according to whether the population is large or small and more or less dense, whether it is concentrated in cities or dispersed over the countryside, how cities and houses are constructed, whether the area occupied by the society is more or less extensive, and according to the kind of boundaries that delimit it.[1]

Increased size and density of population produce the equivalent of a mutation in

From *Confluence* (Spring 1958), pp. 57–69. Reprinted by permission.

social structure and organization. Great variations in physical spacing and accessibility of people to one another lead to quite different social orders. In the most abstract documentation of this observation, it may be indicated that in a density situation of 35 persons per square mile (common in non-urban areas) the individual can, within a 3 mile radius, reach fewer than 1,000 persons. If the population density is 10,000 persons per square mile (a common figure in cities) the person has access within a 3 mile radius to over 280,000 people.

Durkheim differentiated between social orders whose cohesion was derived from "mechanical solidarity" and those whose coehsion was "organic," arising from the division of labor. He envisaged these differentiations as consecutive developments in keeping with his historical and evolutionist approach. Organic solidarity was typical of the more recent and more complex social orders. Tönnies produced a similar distinction between "community" and "society," as existing simultaneously. Redfield and Wirth capstoned this development of "ideal-type" constructs in amplifying the distinction beteeen "folk society" on the one hand and "urbanism as a way of life" on the other.

The urban social order is the opposite of the folk society which Redfield described as small, isolated, homogeneous, with simple technology, with simple division of labor, largely independent economically, characterized by strong organization of conventional understanding with no systematic knowledge in books and with no "market" complex. Wirth, in describing the "urban mode of life," emphasized the way in which the physical mechanism of the city, including the pattern of land use, land values, transport and communication facilities, influenced urban living. He emphasized the dominance of the city over its hinterland. He pointed to the way in which the essential abstract characteristics of the city—"size," "density" and "heterogeneity" resulted in "the substitution of secondary for primary contacts, the weakening in the bonds of kinship and the declining social significance of the family, the disappearance of the neighborhood, and the undermining of the traditional bases of social solidarity."

In connection with the general impact of urbanism on the social order as described above, it must be noted that in the United States "heterogeneity" played a peculiarly important role because this nation has been largely peopled by diverse ethnic groups from Europe and by the Negro from Africa. Our cities during the nineteenth and early part of the twentieth century were made up predominantly of the foreign born and their immediate descendents. During the last four or five decades, and especially since thè onset of World War II, our cities have been subject to relatively large streams of Negro migrants, shifting from the South to the North and to the West. Thus the emergence of the urban mode of life in the United States has, in comparison with most other Western nations, been more vitally affected by the admixture of diverse ethnic and racial groups. This process is by no means complete. In Chicago, in 1950, for example—and this is not an atypical situation—the "foreign white stock" as defined by the United States Census (that is, the foreign born plus native of foreign or mixed parentage) made up about 45 percent of the population; and the non-white made up an additional 15 percent. Thus the third generation or earlier white population of Chicago, and of many of our large metropolitan areas, constitute a minority.

The changes described are of course reflected in changes in social institutions. Because the family has in our society traditionally been recognized as the primary social unit, it is a convenient unit through which to trace many of the influences of urbanism on social institutions. The colonial family in early American history was the keystone of social organization. For example, it was a basic and largely self-sufficient economic unit; it provided for the security and protection of its members; and it was the center for their affectional and recreational life.

Even this most solidly rooted of our social institutions, however, has not been able to withstand the impact of urbanization. Compared with the colonial family, the modern urban family is smaller; it is more often childless and has fewer children, if fertile. The urban family collectively and individually is much more mobile; it possesses comparatively little economic or social unity; is much more frequently broken by separation or divorce; and, as my colleague William F. Ogburn demonstrated some time ago, has long since lost many of its various historic functions, or shared them with new, specialized, urban institutions. The relationship of husband and wife, parents to children, children to each other and of the "small" to the "large" family have been redefined in the urban setting. The relations of family members to one another compete in depth, range, influence and satisfaction with extra-family relationships.

As old institutions, including the family, were modified, new institutions emerged in response to new needs. These have given rise to specialized types of agencies such as the police department, public health services, insurance, workmen's compensation laws, unemployment compensation, labor unions and civilian defense organizations. In brief, the urban environment has forced modification of our inherited institutions and has precipitated the need for the formation and development of new institutions.

One of the most important differences between the urban and "folk" environment as it affects the conduct of the person is to be found in the extent to which he is faced with the necessity of exercising choice, of substituting rational for traditional ways of doing things. In the "folk" setting there is generally a prescribed way of dealing with most situations, certainly the most important recurrent situations in life. In the city there are almost always alternatives—and the person is forced to make a choice.

These basic changes in the nature of human nature in the urban setting are expressed, of course, in changes in modes of thought and action and in personality types. Max Weber recognized this in his construction of "ideal-types" of social behavior—the "traditional," the "purposive-rational," the "valuational" and the "emotional"; types which Riesman has adapted and popularized in his categories of "directedness"—"tradition-direction," "inter-direction" and "other-direction."

Enforced rationalism and urban living, together with rapid social change, provide the matrix for social and personal disorganization, blatant manifestations of the frictions of urbanism as a way of life.

Social disorganization is the intermediate stage between social organization and social reorganization. Contemporary manifestations of social disorganization in the United States are products of cultural friction originating in the differential rates of change among the components of our social heritage and engendered by the great tide of social change set in motion by the impact of industrialization and urbanization.

The juvenile delinquent and the criminal are manifestations of the breakdown of inherited social controls. They are symptoms of the deteriorating influence in the urban environment of such social institutions as the family and the church, of the waning grip of our mores, of the inadequacy, as yet, of the emergent new controls represented by such substitute institutions as the school, the court, the prison and the reformatory. The pauper, early industrial sweated labor, the radical and revolutionist, the unemployed, the aged dependent and the striker are some of the by-products of rapid change and its attendant frictions in our economic organization and in its impact on other aspects of total social organization. The corrupt political boss, the "big fix," the grafter, the "short pencil" operator and the unscrupulous lobbyist mirror the disorganization of political institutions caught in the vortex of rapid social change. Modern war, as a symptom of social disorganization, can be described largely as an outgrowth of the new forms of international contact and international economic, social and political interdependence which precipitate new frictions and problems for the peaceful resolution of which an adequate international social heritage —adequate international institutions, processes and patterns of conduct and thought —have not yet emerged.

Urban existence in breaking down the inherited vestiges of a "folk" order is producing many forms of disorganization. But it has also opened up new vistas for self-expression and new opportunities for shaping both man's environment and his destiny. For the same processes of social change that produce social and personal disorganization free man's mind from the constraints of the past and promote the exercise of ingenuity and creativity. It is not merely a coincidence that the great centers of learning, invention, innovation, art and culture have historically been located in urban areas.

In the new urban matrix of social interaction, a new human nature has been bred which is still in process of social evolution. The "city mentality," characterized by its sophistication, objectivity, utilitarianism and rationalism, is on the one hand a product of the urban environment, and on the other a major force producing and influencing changes in our social heritage, in our economic, social and political institutions and in the urban environment itself.

III

Many of our pressing contemporary problems in government and in politics are symptoms of the strains arising from the anachronism represented by our twentieth century industrial, urban, economic and social order and eighteenth and nineteenth century forms of government and political structure.

The city as the symbol of the twentieth century order is the nub of the many sore political problems of the day. The great metropolitan areas of the country have long since outgrown their inherited governmental structures. Arising as geographic, economic, demographic and social entities, they are nevertheless subjected to layer upon layer of local governmental structure. The 168 Standard Metropolitan Areas delineated by the Federal government in 1950 contained over 16,000 governmental units (including school districts) with powers to tax and to spend. They thus averaged some 100 governmental units per Standard Metropolitan Area; and the larger SMA's had about a thousand governmental units.

The city in the United States is usually the corporate creature of a state, with boundaries rigidly defined by a state charter. In contrast, the economic, population and social phenomena which it symbolizes, but of which the metropolitan area rather than the city is the expression, are not so rigidly defined.

As a result chaos is evident in many of our metropolitan areas in respect to problems with which prevalent forms of governmental structure are ill-equipped to deal. These include such area-wide problems as traffic control, highways, public transport, water and air ports, water supply, sanitation, housing, crime, recreation, health and welfare and the like. The pressures created by the area-wide problems may be expected to mount. It may be anticipated in the coming decades that new governmental mechanisms will emerge to complement or to supplant present forms of local government.

An acute aspect of problems of local government is evident in the conflict of interests between central cities and the metropolitan rings or suburbs. Mayor Zeidler of Milwaukee in a recent paper has predicted increasing political cleavage between central cities and their suburban areas, and has suggested that suburban areas may unite with downstate areas in coalition against central cities.

Certainly there is a basis for drawing such a generalization in recent voting behavior. But such projections overlook at least several factors which may conceivably produce a quite different situation, perhaps even within the next two decades.

For one thing, by 1975, of a total possible population of 228 millions in the United States, about two-thirds—or about 150 million persons—are likely to be resident in Standard Metropolitan Areas, with only a third of the population in the remaining areas of the country. Of the population within the Standard Metropolitan Areas, only half will be resident in central cities and the remainder will live in suburban areas. Certainly it will be true that suburban area populations together with non-standard metropolitan area populations will greatly surpass central city populations, in fact surpass them by a ratio of two to one. But the community of interest between metropolitan suburban populations and non-metropolitan area populations is easily exaggerated. The following are among the considerations that indicate that community of interest between suburban and central city populations will grow closer rather than further apart, and tend to preclude suburban-non-metropolitan area coalition.

Standard Metropolitan Areas are at present absorbing 97 percent of the total population increase of the nation, with disproportionate increases in outlying suburban areas which, between 1950 and 1955, grew 7 times as rapidly as central cities (28 percent as compared with 4 percent). The rapidity of metropolitan area growth, especially suburban growth, together with the fact that a relatively large proportion of suburban growth is derived from the central cities through migration, is likely to mean that suburban areas will more closely resemble central cities in the next two decades than they have in the past decade. That is, the continued process of metropolitan area growth is extending so far beyond central city boundaries that large parts of suburban areas will contain working-class and lower-middle-class populations of the type which was previously located in inner zones of central cities when metropolitan areas as a whole were smaller. Many political analysts tend to assume that migrants from central cities to suburbs become conservative and Republican when they come in association with the higher social-economic strata previously associated with suburban living. But these political analysts fail to recognize that by the time the suburbs contain 50 to 60 percent of the population in Standard Metropolitan Areas, which may be the case by 1975, they will no longer be made up entirely of upper- and upper-middle-class groups.

Another acute aspect of contemporary problems in local government and politics is evident in the widespread concern about the growing Negro population in central cities. Some political analysts assume that the Negro migrant to the central cities will retain his low social-economic characteristics and previous political behavior; and visualize that "a kind of economic caste system will develop." They believe that lower-class Negroes will remain in central cities with the suburbs containing the white upper-income groups.

This assumption completely ignores the past history of migration to cities and the processes by which migrants have been absorbed into "urbanism as a way of life." The Negro migrant to the central city will, without question, follow the same patterns of social mobility blazed by the successive waves of immigrants who settled in our central cities. Just as the immigrant underwent a process of "Americanization," the in-migrant Negro is undergoing a process of "urbanization." The Negro is already rising and will continue to rise on the social-economic scale as measured by education, occupation, income and the amenities of urban existence. Furthermore, the Negro, in time, will diffuse through the metropolitan area and occupy outlying suburban as well as central city areas.

These observations should not be construed to deny the possibility, in the short run, of central cities becoming vast non-white areas of lower economic status than the suburbs. The forces described above, however, are likely, in the longer run, to produce an admixture of low and high economic status and white and non-white populations both in the central cities and in the suburbs.

The influence of the city on the political order is of course by no means confined to the problems of government in the metropolitan area itself. Our founding fathers, who agreed on the Federal-State system of government as provided for in the Constitution, never envisaged the rise of the metropolitan area and the concentration of our population in them. It is small wonder, then, that this rural preindustrial governmental structure shows the great strains manifest in "downstate-upstate," urban-rural and regional and sectional conflicts of interests; or, in the "rotten borough" situations which sometimes obtain in the urban representation in state legislatures. It is small wonder, also, that voices are heard from time to time to mutter about the vestigial character and "fifth wheel" functions of State government.

Quite apart from the problems of governmental structure and levels of government, urbanism has greatly affected the role of government itself, the character of public administration, the nature of representative government, the political party system and the substance of political issues.

There is no doubt that the complex of technological, economic and social changes which constitute "urbanism" is the major factor in the rapidity with which governmental functions have proliferated, often despite the express intent of administrations. The urban way of life, the increasing interdependence of the elements of the social order and the increasing inability of traditional and inherited social institutions to cope with the new problems of urban living have led inexorably to the multiplication of government functions, powers and personnel; and the process is still under way.

The complex and often technical character of the urban problems has changed the requirements of "governing." In the urban setting, public administration requires many technical and professional skills. The "expert" has emerged as a new and powerful element in government, and bureaucracy has become an indispensable tool in the functioning of society.

Urbanization has also brought great changes in the nature of representative government. Representative government as provided for in the United States was an adaptation of the "democracy" of the Greek city state. It is one thing, however, for a representative to speak for a small, homogeneous, rural, agricultural constituency; and quite another thing to "represent" a heterogeneous population of one-quarter to one-half million persons with diverse and sometimes conflicting interests. The emergence of the public opinion poll may be regarded as an invention in the urban scene for the measurement of the "will" of the urban population. It may play an increasingly important role in representative government in the years to come.

Urbanism is also increasing the strains to which our two party system is being subjected. The historic differences which led to the formation of our political parties are more and more obscured by the problems of our complex urban order. As a result there is a wider range of interests, political philosophies and policies within each of our great political parties than between them. The increased choice forced upon the urbanite, discussed above, extends also to the choice of political parties. The urban voter is more apt to choose than to inherit his political preferences; therefore the increasing importance of the "independent" vote. In the state of transition in which we still find ourselves, the citizen, in voting, often has little notion of just what men, principles and policies he is supporting; and the elected official often operates with no better awareness of the policy preferences of the electorate.

Finally, in respect of issues, the problems of urbanism have fashioned the foremost political issues of the century. First, as has been noted above, the very role of government has become a major political issue, underlying in a fundamental way the multitudinous specific issues which flare into prominence in election campaigns. The great disputes about the Federal Reserve System, the income tax, workmen's compensation laws, the enfranchisement of women and the anti-trust laws, to mention but a few, were generated earlier in this century as frictions of the changing urban order. The "New Deal" of Franklin D. Roosevelt aimed at the solution of perhaps the major single complex of problems confronting Western urban civilization—the frictions and swings of the business cycle and especially the problems precipitated by economic depression. "Social" legislation continued in President Truman's "Fair Deal" and into President Eisenhower's Republican administration despite the latter's avowed opposition to "creeping socialism." It is an ironic fact that the "Little Rock affair," although it represents a pathetic effort to cling to eighteenth and nineteenth century political slogans as well as to pre-urban forms of living, will probably hasten the dissipation of what little is left in substance to "state's rights"; this, at a time when there has been a Presidential effort to return a number of governmental functions from the Federal to State governments.

IV

It must be recognized that the experience described here is largely of the West, and, in some respects, especially the experience of the United States. The social, personal and political influences of urbanization in American society, discussed above, may be readily comprehended as products of the transition from a folk to an urban order. The non-material elements of contemporary society may be described as being in various stages of accommodation to changing technology, economic structure, physical spacing and accessibility of population as manifested in the urban setting. The major influence of urbanism on our social and political institutions and ideologies has been, in brief, to make them, in varying degrees, obsolescent.

The problems of urbanization—social, personal and political—are but symptoms of the frictions produced by the differential rates of change in our social heritage. But reorganization can never be achieved without a certain amount of disorganization. We can be comforted by the many obvious advantages and advances which the industrial revolution and the city have brought with them, including an ever-rising standard of living and an unprecedented opportunity for personal expression and creativity.

The adjustments necessary to achieve an integrated and consistent social heritage can conceivably be attained in time through "natural" processes—through the forces which produce the "strain toward consistency" in our culture. This process of social evolution perhaps parallels the biological "struggle for existence" and the "survival of the fittest," but in the area of culture traits and culture complexes.

Unlike the rest of the animal kingdom, however, man has it within his power to speed up the social evolutionary process—to accelerate the adjustment of social and political institutions and ideologies to the new requirements forced by technological and structural change. Indeed, one of the most important influences of urbanization lies in the emancipation of the person from the rigidities and restraints imposed upon him by tradition, in the new opportunity—in large measure forced upon him by the nature of urban existence—to be a rational animal and to intervene in the processes of social change so as to exert some control over its tempo and its direction.

NOTE

1. In *L'Annee Sociologique*, Vol. II, 1897–1898. Called to my attention and translated by my colleague, Otis Dudley Duncan.

PART III

Urban
Differentiation

Although numerous characteristics have been used to distinguish the urban community, the principal one, which sets it apart as a social type from other forms of communities, is a high degree of differentiation. Community differentiation can be defined as the division of the population of a community into separate aggregates or groups different from one another in terms of specifiable aspects that are accessible for purposes of analysis and understanding. These differentiated aggregates or groups are functionally interdependent.

There are four sociologically important kinds of differentiation in a community. These four are: (1) status and role in significant social institutions in the community, particularly the occupational role in the economy; (2) location in a territory; (3) the values, norms, beliefs, attitudes, and life styles exhibited by residents; and (4) ranking in terms of income, prestige, or power assigned to the groups and aggregates formed around the other aspects of differentiation. The specific types of community differentiation corresponding to these four aspects are designated respectively: role differentiation, areal differentiation, cultural differentiation, and rank differentiation.

The readings in the first section deal with role and areal differentiation. We see evidence of the importance of *role differentiation* in the sheer volume of occupations which exist in any metropolis and in the way in which the interrelations among them constitute a system of interdependent economic activities. This form of differentiation overlaps *areal differentiation*. Slums attract residents and workers whose occupations either are at the bottom of the occupational scale of prestige or are entirely outside the realm of legitimate, socially approved activities. Suburbs traditionally have been inhabited by white-collar occupational groups, although recently this particular association between role and areal differentiation has been modified by the development of cheaper housing and transportation in the suburbs. The tie between these two forms of differentiation sometimes is so strong that knowledge of the occupational composition of a city or other area in a metropolis is a convenient index for predicting other characteristics of a community, including the life-style of residents and its location in the region.

The selections in the second section are concerned with cultural and rank differentiation. In the American city the key to *cultural differentiation* usually has been ethnic group membership and race. The Negro-white relationship obviously still is crucial as a source of life-style difference, but with the stoppage of European immigration in the 1920s, nationality differences have become less significant. Religious group membership has tended to take up the role in cultural differentiation once played by ethnic factors. *Rank differentiation* is found even in pre-urban communities, but it is more pronounced in cities and in the metropolis, mainly as a way of introducing some kind of order and efficiency into the pattern of social relationships produced by the proliferation of role, areal, and cultural differentiation. In addition to being more explicit as a form of differentiation in urban than in other types of communities, rank differentiation is perceived in a new way under the anonymous conditions of urban life.

Urban Social and Areal Differentiation

16. The Classification of Cities

Edgar F. Borgatta
and
Jeffrey K. Hadden

The most basic kind of urban differentiation is the difference among cities (the kind of difference which concerned Reiss in his article in Part I). The authors of previous selections, whether they were economists, sociologists, historians, or anthropologists, introduced some set of concepts for describing these differences. The present selection has two special merits: It reviews the available classification schemes systematically, and it calls attention to their virtues and shortcomings. The authors, Jeffrey Hadden and Edgar Borgatta, argue that existing typologies fall into three categories. The first includes schemes which describe cities in terms of an evolutionary or historical progression from simple forms of social and spatial organization to forms that are more complex. In the second category are typologies that focus on the economic activities of an urban community or its functional role in the larger society. The final category is made up of schemes based on the study of city characteristics by means of factor analysis. The selection appeared originally as a chapter in a research monograph proposing a new factor-analytic approach to classifying cities.

Edgar F. Borgatta is Brittingham Research Professor of Sociology at the University of Wisconsin. He is editor of *Sociological Methodology* (1968) and coeditor of the *Handbook of Personality Theory and Research* (1968).

Jeffrey K. Hadden is Associate Professor of Sociology at Case-Western Reserve University. In addition to being coauthor (with Edgar F. Borgatta) of *American Cities: Their Social Characteristics* (1965), he is coeditor of *Metropolis in Crisis* (1967).

To the unaccustomed observer, the city often appears to be a bewildering maze, or a puzzle with an almost infinite number of pieces. But the human mind has a unique capacity for simplifying and reducing great amounts of information into smaller categories, and, in one way or another, most men come to "understand" the city.

This unique mental operation involves "classifying," "typing," "generalizing," "abstracting," or "boiling-down" the information. Whatever the name used, the operation is the same—reducing a large amount of complex information into a small number of concepts. Thus, we may refer to a city with such adjectives as "continental," "big," "old," "gay," "dirty," "conservative," "wide-open," or "cultured." These terms convey a complex image, and the transmitter and recipient of the message generally "understand" the implications of the concept being used. For example, if a city is described as "wide-open," we might expect to find gambling, organized crime, prostitution, etc. If a city is described as "cultured," we might expect to find museums, theaters, support of classical music forms, etc.

There are many ways to classify cities, but they are not all equally useful. Some names convey images that are understood by most people, others have meaning only for a few. In general, however, popular classification concepts do not have exactly the same meaning for the persons who use them.

Scholars, like the journalist and the man on the street, have attempted to classify cities. Sometimes their classifications have been rather sophisticated, but at other times it is doubtful whether their efforts have led us any further than popular conceptions. In this chapter we examine some of the many approaches to the classification of cities. As we stated in the first chapter, the objective of the research reported in this book is to examine the possibility of deriving a small set of variables that will permit the classification and prediction of a wide range of urban phenomena. It is, obviously, not possible to derive such a set of variables from "library research," but examination of the existing literature is an essential step in any inquiry; it provides the "theoretical" basis for including relevant variables in any empirical investigation.

There are many ways of classifying cities, and in the history of writing about cities a great number of classificatory schemes have been employed. Size, historical development, economic activity, geographical location, and occupational structure are only a few of the bases that have been utilized to classify cities. A comprehensive review of the literature would be a monograph in itself. Thus, our review attempts to be representative of a number of kinds of approaches rather than exhaustive. Specifically, we focus on three approaches to urban classification: historical-evolutionary, economic specialization or functional, and factor-analytic. Notably missing from our review are classification schemes that deal with economic base, relationship of cities to their tributary areas, and regional location.[1]

Historical Bases of Classification

Underlying principles for the classification of cities are not independent of each other. For example, a historically oriented classification that has as a basis an evolu-

From *American Cities: Their Social Characteristics* (Chicago: Rand McNally, 1965), Chap. 2, pp. 8–19. Reprinted by permission.

tionary concept must bear some relationship to another system that is concerned with classification at some given period by type of culture.

Historical evolutionary analyses occurring early in geography, economics, and sociology provided one general framework of classification of urban centers or concentrations of populations. The continuum usually posited was one from simplicity of aggregates to high differentiation and technological specialization with urban centers of civilizations. There are many such analyses in social science literature, including the general presentations to be found in the early work of Lewis Henry Morgan and Herbert Spencer. It is obvious that classifications of urban centers involving such notions of developmental or evolutionary differentiation are still current in our common thinking. For example, in speaking of Latin American or Asian areas, it is not uncommon to use the term "a relatively *modern* city." The implication is not only one of technological development but of involvement of many aspects associated with modern western civilization. And, on the other hand, it is not uncommon to encounter designation of cities as belonging to "*underdeveloped* areas."

The longitudinal-developmental type of classification is global and becomes extremely difficult to apply to urban centers high on the scale. The reasons for this, obviously, are that the differentiation among cities implies differences that are not attributable to being higher or lower in the scale of development. High civilization may be signified in some classifications by the development of arts, by the development of industry, and by the modal standard of living, etc.; these may not turn out to be equivalent.

The writings of Lewis Mumford have popularized concern with the historical development of urban life.[2] Mumford's terminology, possibly as much as his historical acumen, has drawn attention to the development of the complex culture of the city.

In his description of stages. Mumford describes pre-urban village communities under the concept *Eopolis. Eopolis* refers to the developing urban community marked by partial division of labor in the economic sphere and differentiation in the crafts and sciences. Older family types and religious organizations persist, and the community is seen as existing within narrow regional confines. The *Metropolis*, which generally corresponds to our common use of the term, has a central location, adequate and secure food supply, and is involved in exchange, economically and culturally, with other communities and regions. Division of labor becomes highly specialized, and familism decreases at the expense of individualism. The *Megalopolis* is represented by bigness. Complex organization, bureaucracy, impersonality, and general dominance of the region by urban centers characterize the *Megalopolis*. The development of economic dominance of the city, with emphasis on what may sometimes be identified as the vices of bigness such as white collar crime, deterioration of areas and development of undesirable living situations, loss of local organization and autonomy, etc., characterize the stage called *Tyrannopolis*. The final stage representing total disorganization and the reassertion of rural community is called *Necropolis.*

Mumford's historical analysis presents not only a romantic stylization of the cycle, but a Rousseauian value premise as well. It represents one among many versions of historical classification by developmental stages and illustrates well how this longitudinal view enters into the notions of classification of cities.

A more recent but equally speculative classification, emphasizing specialization in part, was presented by Riemer in 1952.[3] In the period extending through the fall of Rome, cities were institutional centers. During the Middle Ages, trading centers developed. In the later Middle Ages and into the Renaissance, industrial centers came to the fore. Finally, as the Industrial Revolution emerged, metropolitan and resort centers developed.

Geographers' conceptualizations of the historical development of cities have often dealt with the evolution of land use. A representative set of suggestions is found in the work of Taylor.[4] In analyzing changes in land use, he suggests stages of the *infantile* (distinctions between residential, commercial, and industrial areas are not clear), *juvenile* (mixture of shops, offices, and small industries, but with some segregation of a commercial district in the center), *early mature* (higher status residential areas moving toward periphery of the center), and *mature* (characterized by industrial concentration at railways, growth along railway and road patterns, and separation of industrial segments from the residential segments). In larger cities additional processes are noted including assimilations of local centers, construction of communication and transportation facilities, and development of controls of the allocation and additional construction of the city.

A somewhat different approach to the historical classification of cities is presented by the economic historian, N. S. B. Gras.[5] Gras argues the thesis of the concomitance of technology and development of community structures appropriate for the level of technology. The development of western civilization is seen to have major phases of collectional, cultural nomadic, settled village, town, and metropolitan economies. Historically, the complexity of production and exchange systems and dependence upon the local area vary inversely, and differentiation and specialization are concomitants of this growing complexity.

In describing the last stage of his phases of development, Gras says, "the . . . metropolitan economy is the organization of producers and consumers mutually dependent for goods and services, wherein their wants are supplied by a system of exchange concentrated in a large city which is the focus of local trade and the center through which normal economic relations with the outside are established and maintained."[6] He further points out that the later phase (metropolitan economy) may exist in the presence of earlier phases (e.g., villages), but the latter are subordinate and perform different functions for the larger center. Gras was also one of the earlier writers to recognize acutely the interdependence between the city and its adjacent tributaries. He notes that the city "must possess a hinterland, a tributary adjacent territory, rich in natural resources, occupied by a productive population and accessible by means of transportation."[7]

Functional or Economic Specialization Theories

It has long been recognized that cities differ according to their economic base or productive specialization. For example, this was observed as early as the fourteenth century by the Arab philosopher, ibn-Khaldun, who noted that certain cities specialize in crafts and activities, and that mutual cooperation among cities is "innate in civilization."[8] Many typologies appear in the literature that seem to have been developed in a speculative manner. Some appear to have resulted from the author's acquaintance with a particular city or cities, while others appear to be "intuitively self-evident" about the nature of cities.

One of the earlier attempts in this century to construct a classification of cities according to their economic specialization was that of Tower.[9] He classified cities into four groups: (1) commercial, (2) industrial, (3) political, and (4) social centers and health resorts. Each type of city owed its location to geographical factors. *Commercial centers* grow up under conditions which favor trade and communication, such as natural bodies of water or established trade routes. *Industrial cities* are also frequently commercial cities because of the flow of communication and traffic, but they also tend to emerge near supplies of raw materials. *Political centers* are located near the center of accessibility for the majority of the population. And *social centers* and *health resorts* are found in locations which are attractive for the tourist.

Aurousseau[10] grouped twenty-eight classes of towns and cities under six major headings. The first grouped capital and revenue centers into *administrative cities*. The second group included fortress towns, garrison communities, and naval bases which he called *defense towns*. The third grouped university towns, cathedral towns, art centers, religious and pilgrimage centers into *culture centers*. The fourth grouped manufacturing and craft cities into *production centers*. The fifth group was called *communication links* and included depots, mining, fishing, lumber, market, bridge-head, navigation, export, import, supply, and similar centers. Finally, health, tourist, and holiday centers were grouped into *recreation centers*.

Aurousseau also felt that the geographical location of a city determined its economic specialization. Generally, one type of activity overshadows the rest, but Aurousseau asserted that ". . . many are conveniently situated for the discharge of more than one function."[11] In describing the location of cities according to function, Aurousseau noted that administrative cities *ought* to be located centrally but observed that often they are not. Defense cities, naturally, are located at places of strategic military advantage. Cultural centers have no regular distribution, but tend to occur at the junction of old routes. Two factors, source of power and presence of raw materials, determine the location of centers of production. The location of communication centers depends on whether the function it serves is collection, transfer, or distribution. Finally, recreational centers appear at points that have some strong or novel attraction, such as climate or scenery.

A somewhat more parsimonious classification pivoting on production and distribution of goods was developed by McKenzie.[12] The first type consisted of communities such as agricultural, fishing, mining, and lumbering towns and were called *primary service communities*. A second type was primarily occupied with the task of distribution and is referred to as a *commercial community*. The *industrial community* constituted a third type and was, of course, principally involved in production. A final type lacked an economic base and included cities specializing in such activities as education, recreation, defense, and administration.

A most critical note on the importance of the typology by specialization is found in a National Resources Committee Report of 1937 which stated:

> . . . cities *must be* distinguished according to the principal function they serve. Whatever

uniformities there may be found in the life of urbanities, it will make some difference whether the city in which they live is an industrial, a commercial, or residential city; a capital, an educational center, or a resort; whether it depends upon mines, oil wells, timber, a port, a river, or railroad; and whteher its economic base is unitary or multiple, balanced or unbalanced.[13]

Classification of cities by specialization as mentioned above by no means exhausts the speculative attempts to build classifications of urban communities. They may, however, be considered as early representatives of this particular approach of classifying cities according to their economic specialization. Later examples are easily located. For example, Gist and Halbert in this earlier tradition delineated production, trade and commerce, political, cultural, health or recreational, and diversified centers.[14]

More recently Cahnman differentiates between consumption- and production-oriented cities.[15] The former includes fortresses, court cities, administrative, religious, and educational centers. The latter includes manufacturing cities named by the type of product produced. The author sees the borderline between consumption-oriented and production-oriented cities as blurred, with cities engaged in distribution and finance occupying a position between the two types. This classification scheme may also be viewed as a historical classification since the consumption-oriented city is seen to predate the production-oriented, with the latter not reaching its peak until the Industrial Revolution.

The major criticism of these studies is, of course, that they did not delineate clearly the inclusiveness of the types defined. Their categories often were not mutually exclusive, nor were they able to

weigh or otherwise give meaning to cities that obviously fell into one or more categories. Furthermore, little effort was made to relate these types to other variables.

A significant step towards a systematic empirical classification of cities was made by William F. Ogburn.[16] He began by noting the relationship between technological advancement and division of labor. Specialization in modern times is not only characteristic of men, but cities also tend to concentrate particular types of activity. In a manner similar to classifications mentioned above, Ogburn distinguished seven types of specialization: (1) trading centers, (2) factory towns, (3) transportation centers, (4) mining towns, (5) pleasure resorts, (6) health resorts, and (7) college towns. The criteria used in determining these types is not clear, but it would appear that they were selected because of the availability of census data for these categories.

In much of the work prior to Ogburn, the establishment (naming) of types constituted an end in itself. The identification of cities belonging to a particular type was mainly illustrative. Ogburn proceeded two important steps beyond this point. First, he established criteria for identifying cities belonging to the various types. Second, having identified cities belonging to each type, he compared them with a hypothetical "average city" on a large number of social and economic characterisitcs.

The existence of types was determined by a deviation from an "average city." Thus, for example, the "average city" had 17 percent of its working population engaged in trading activity. Cities with greater than 20 percent of their labor force in buying and selling were classified as "trading centers." A "representative" group of "trading centers" were aggregated and summary scores on a number of demographic, social, and economic characteristics were obtained. These scores were then compared with the "average city." Thus, Ogburn was able to speak of the "average trading center" relative to the "average city." In parallel, he followed this procedure for each of the types.

Although Ogburn's study had some rather serious methodological shortcomings, it stands as a landmark in comparative urban research and constitutes a significant advance in the classification of cities. His work was an early attempt to classify cities through empirically derived rather than *ad hoc* arbitrary criteria. It was the first attempt to systematically identify cities belonging to a class and also the first attempt to apply the classification.

A number of classifications of economic specialization have appeared since Ogburn's classic study. In 1943 Chauncy Harris published a paper entitled "A Functional Classification of Cities in the United States."[17] Harris was apparently unaware of the comprehensive study by Ogburn that had been published six years prior to his own investigation. In his introductory comments, Harris noted that "... the literature on the functions of cities ... is sadly deficient in studies of criteria for distinguishing types and in classifications including more than a few *well known type* examples."[18] While Harris proposed that his study was an attempt to remedy these deficiencies, his work is subject to the very criticisms he made of previous studies.

Using occupational and employment figures, his classification was based on "... the activity of *greatest importance* in each city."[19] He determined the activity of greatest importance by "... an analysis of cities of *well known types*"[20] and then arbitrarily assigned higher percentage cutting points to some activities than others.

Nine types of cities were described as follows: (1) manufacturing, (2) retailing, (3) diversified, (4) wholesaling, (5) transportation, (6) mining, (7) educational, (8) resort or retirement, and (9) others. The classification "others" includes cities of "known types" that Harris was unable to differentiate on a statistical basis. These include regional capitals, political capitals, army bases, naval bases, professional centers, and financial centers.

The number of cities falling into each type of specialization was reported, but identification of cities belonging to each type was not presented beyond examples.[21] With the exception of a few comments on regional location and city size, almost no effort was made to relate classification scheme to anything else.

While the Ogburn classification is, in our judgment, more sophisticated, the Harris classification has received more attention and has subsequently been revised four times.[22] The first and most substantial revision was by Kneedler and appeared just two years after the original Harris article. Kneedler made only minor modifications of the economic specialization categories and the arbitrary procedure for deriving the categories, but a number of new dimensions were added. One such dimension was called "metropolitan status." Cities were classified as (1) *independent cities* if they were not part of a metropolitan district, (2) *central cities* if they were the principal politically defined city of a metropolitan district, and suburbs if they were part of the metropolitan district, but not the central city. Suburbs were in turn classified according to an employment-residence ratio as "employing suburbs," "balanced suburbs," and "dormitory suburbs."

Another dimension of the Kneedler revision was a "manufacturing ratio," which was an expression of the number employed in manufacturing as a proportion of the number engaged in manufacturing, retail and wholesale trade, and service establishments. Still another dimension that applied to suburbs only was an index of rent level. This rent index was an expression of the rent level of the suburb relative to the rent level of the entire metropolitan district.

In addition to expanding the Harris classification, a unique feature of Kneedler's work was the actual publication of the classification data for cities. Thus, for the first time, a source of classification data was published that could be utilized for comparative analyses of cities of various types. Kneedler did some preliminary analyses of her data and found that there were systematic relationships between the type of economic specialization and geographic location and population size.

Subsequent revisions of the Harris-Kneedler classification by Jones and his associates involve only minor changes. In the most recent revision, several social and economic characteristics of each city have been printed in parallel with the classification system. In addition, some cross-tabulation analyses of these data by size, region, and metropolitan status appear. One cannot but wonder, however, why the social and economic characteristics presented were not tabulated by type of economic specialization. One would assume that the reason for developing economic specialization categories would be to demonstrate that cities with particular specializations vary systematically on social, economic, or other characteristics. Yet this has never been empirically demonstrated.

Jones, Forstall, and Collver claim that this information "... will be enlightening and useful to users of other governmental

data in the *Municipal Year Book*, enabling them to compare particular cities with places possessing similar characteristics. Moreover, the classificatory data can be used by social scientists as a basis for grouping cities in order to study the relationship between communal types and political and other social behaviors."[23] It is not possible to assess the extent to which these data have been "enlightening and useful," but a review of literature reveals that social scientists have taken little interest in doing empirical analyses of the raw data as suggested by the authors.

In addition to the Harris-Kneedler classification, a number of other studies have appeared since Ogburn's classic study.[24] Many of these have remained at the intuitive level and thus have added little either by way of refinement or new insight. A study by Nelson, however, is methodologically noteworthy.[25] We observed that in Ogburn's study cities were classified into types according to a deviation from the "average city." The proportional deviation necessary to be included in a type was not consistent from one type to another and neither were the criteria for selecting a particular deviation specified. In Nelson's study, cities that deviated more than one standard deviation from the mean on a particular criterion were included in a type. Another feature of the Nelson classification was that it permitted a city to be included in more than one type of specialization.

The most comprehensive economic specialization classification of American cities to appear since the Ogburn study was that of Duncan and Reiss which appeared in 1956 as one of the "Census Monograph Series."[26] The Duncan and Reiss volume closely parallels the design of the earlier Ogburn study and may be considered as an extension and replication. As in the Ogburn study, Duncan and Reiss explored the variation in demographic, social, and economic characteristics of cities for four "independent variables": size, regional location, population growth or decline, and economic specialization. The major focus of the monograph was on the construction of a classification system of cities and a systematic comparison of the characteristics of cities according to the typology.

The classification developed was essentially built on four dimensions: (1) manufacturing, (2) trade, (3) "minor" types of specialization, and (4) income. Each city had a profile to reflect its position in each of the dimensions, and, as in the Nelson study, each city could have more than one type of specialization. Cities were also grouped according to size and metropolitan status, the latter distinguishing communities as Standard Metropolitan Areas, central cities, suburbs, and independent cities.

On the first dimension they selected the upper and lower quintiles of the proportion of persons engaged in manufacturing in Standard Metropolitan Areas and urban places and classified these as "high" and "low" respectively on manufacturing. The residual group was excluded from analysis.

The second dimension differentiated communities on the basis of per capita wholesale and retail trade. Duncan and Reiss concluded that the major differentiation of social characteristics pivots on whether or not a city specialized in retail trade, but their classification of trading centers was more elaborate than this basic dichotomy. They first determined quartiles for wholesale sales per capita and retail sales per capita and combined them in a two-dimensional paradigm yielding sixteen categories. These classes were then combined to yield a ninefold

classification of wholesale-retail trade. Later they further collapsed the categories into five groups with the following classification: (1) wholesale trade centers, (2) retail trade centers, (3) trade centers, (4) maintenance trade centers, and (5) nontrade centers.

The third dimension consisted of five "minor" types of specialization: (1) higher education, (2) public administration, (3) transportation, (4) military, and (5) entertainment and recreation. Cities were classified as "educational" centers if they fell in the upper quintile of the percentage of persons twenty to twenty-four years of age enrolled in school. The upper decile on the percentage of persons employed in a particular activity determined the classification of "public administration," "transport," and "entertainment and recreation" centers. Military centers were classified by a ratio of the size of the community and the number of persons in the armed forces. The authors noted that these types were selected from a larger number of theoretical types and suggested that the possibility of identifying additional types be examined.

The final dimension was based on the median income of families in 1949. As in the first dimension, income was divided into quintiles, with the upper and the lower quintiles retained for analysis.

We will not discuss the findings of the Duncan and Reiss volume here since intrinsically the relationships involved are merely a part of the raw correlation matrix that serves as the basis of one of our analyses. Rather, let us turn briefly to a summary and evaluation of the functional or economic specialization classifications. First of all, the reader can see from the studies presented here that there has been a relatively long history of differentiating cities on bases involving economic specialization. There have been a wide variety of methodological approaches used, ranging from speculation to precise statistical specifications, although on *ad hoc* arbitrary bases. However, the larger proportion of classifications fall into the former rather than the latter category. And even when statistical procedures have been employed, the lack of parallelism in the results is rather discouraging. Thus, for example, one major United States city received a different classification in each of four studies.[27]

Another major problem with the classification systems is that classification tends to be an end in itself rather than a means to some other end. Little is gained, for example, if a city is identified as a "retailing center," unless this information allows us to predict something else about the city. But very little has been done to relate the functional categories to other characteristics of cities. Until there has been substantially more effort to relate the functional classifications to something else, we find ourselves quite in agreement with Duncan and his collaborators who concluded ". . . there is little need for just another functional classification of cities, however ingenious its methodology."[28]

. . .

Factor Analytic Classifications

Our own approach to the classification of cities begins with a different emphasis than the classifications discussed thus far. Rather than imposing *ad hoc* conceptualizations on the data, we wanted to explore the possibility of deriving some independent underlying dimensions on which cities could be characterized and differentiated. In short, we wanted to develop a

system of classification that would minimize the importance of any preconceived order that classifiers might have while maximizing whatever underlying order there might be in the data. We would argue that classification systems are not appropriately evaluated as being either "right" or "wrong," but rather as "useful" or "not useful." In this case, our own notion of usefulness involves the ability to inclusively and parsimoniously describe the characteristics on which human communities vary.

Factor analysis is a useful procedure for ordering the relationships among a large set of variables.... The technique can appropriately be applied to the problem of classifying cities.

The application of factor analytic procedures to the study of urban units is relatively recent, yet considering the time span since the first study, the number of studies involved is not large. The first application of factor analysis to the classification of urban units was by Daniel O. Price in 1942, and we shall review briefly the objectives and the data he presented.[29]

In his factor analysis of metropolitan centers, Price stated his objectives as follows: "The purpose of factor analysis is to locate the smallest number of fundamental variables which will explain all the correlations observed."[30] He accepted the utility of the procedure as described in an SSRC Bulletin at that period of ". . . simplification of the system and in suggesting what are the fundamental variables."[31] In interpreting his results, Price stated the following: "If the sociologist is attempting to get some orderly picture of society, he must, as far as possible, locate the fundamental factors in society from which the other characteristics can be predicted, and factor analysis seems to be a method for moving in that direction."[32]

It must be emphasized that there is nothing magical proposed by Price in this first application, and subsequently people who have utilized the technique have been equally modest in suggesting what is involved. The procedure is one of matrix transformation by a technique well known to mathematics long before psychologists stumbled upon it. Extravagant claims for the technique seem to occur more often in informal comments of critics than in the formal presentations in Price and the subsequent applications of the technique in this area. In short, the suggestion involved in Price's justification for his study is that if one is studying the relationship among indices, the objective generally is to "explain" relationships among variables, usually by explicit or implicit partialling procedures. If this is the case, parsimony requires location of a reference set of variables that will make such explanations systematic and inclusive, as well as simple by use of a minimum of variables. For this purpose factor analysis is seen as eminently suitable as an approach.

NOTES

1. The following sources are not intended to be comprehensive, but they should lead the interested reader to the relevant literature for the latter three types of classification. Brian J. L. Berry and Allen Pred, *Central Place Studies: A Bibliography of Theory and Application* (Philadelphia: Regional Science Research Institute, 1961); Otis Dudley Duncan, W. Richard Scott, Stanley Lieberson, Beverly Duncan, and Hal H. Winsborough, *Metropolis and Region* (Baltimore: The Johns Hopkins Press, 1960); Richard B. Andrews, "Mechanics of the Urban Economic Base," *Land Economics* (1953–1956), XXIX–XXXII (series of articles); Donald J. Bogue, *The Structure of the Metropolitan Community: A Study of Dominance and Subdominance* (Ann Arbor: Univ. of Michigan, Horace H. Rackham School of Graduate Studies, 1950); Donnell M. Pappenfort, "The Ecological Field and the Metropolitan Community: Manufacturing and Management," *American Journal of Sociology*, LXIV (January, 1959), 380–385.

2. Lewis Mumford, *The Culture of Cities* (New York: Harcourt, 1938).

3. Svend Riemer, *The Modern City* (New York: Prentice-Hall, Inc., 1952).

4. Griffith Taylor, *Urban Geography* (New York: Dutton, 1946).

5. N. S. B. Gras, *An Introduction to Economic History* (New York: Harper, 1922).

6. *Ibid.*, p. 185.

7. *Ibid.*, p. 187.

8. ibn-Khaldun, *The Muqaddimah*, trans. Franz Rosenthal (London: Routledge and Kegan Paul, 1958), Vol. II, p. 302.

9. W. D. Tower, "The Geography of American Cities," *Bulletin of the American Geographical Society*, XXXVII (1905), 577–588.

10. Marcel Aurousseau, "The Distribution of Population: A Constructive Problem," *Geographical Review*, XI (October, 1921), 569–572.

11. *Ibid.*, p. 569.

12. R. D. McKenzie, *The Metropolitan Community* (New York: McGraw-Hill, 1933).

13. National Resources Committee, *Our Cities: Their Role in the National Economy* (Washington, D.C.: U.S. Government Printing Office, 1937), p. 8.

14. Noel P. Gist and L. A. Halbert, *Urban Society* (New York: Crowell, 1956).

15. Jean Comhaire and Werner J. Cahnman, *How Cities Grew* (Madison, N.J.: Florham Park Press, 1959).

16. W. F. Ogburn, *Social Characteristics of Cities* (Chicago: International City Managers' Ass., 1937).

17. Chauncy D. Harris, "A Functional Classification of Cities in the United States," *Geographical Review*, XXXIII (January, 1943), 86–99.

18. *Ibid.*, p. 86. (emphasis added)

19. *Ibid.* (emphasis added)

20. *Ibid.*, p. 85. (emphasis added)

21. Harris does indicate in a footnote, however, that a list of the functional classifications of cities may be obtained on request. Thus, it is possible that the omission of the classification table from the publication may have been an editor's decision.

22. Grace Kneedler, "Economic Classification of Cities," *Municipal Year Book*, 1945 (Chicago: The International City Managers' Ass., 1945); pp. 30–38; Table ,IV; Victor Jones, "Economic Classification of Cities and Metropolitan Areas," *Municipal Year Book*, 1953 (Chicago: The International City Managers' Ass., 1953), pp. 49–57; Tables II, IV; Victor Jones and Andrew Collver, "Economic Classification of Cities and Metropolitan Areas," *Municipal Year Book*, 1960 (Chicago: The International City Managers' Ass., 1960), pp. 66–77, 87–88; Tables IV, VI; Victor Jones, Richard L. Forstall, and Andrew Collver, "Economic and Social Characteristics of Urban Places," *Municipal Year Book*, 1963

(Chicago: International City Managers' Ass., 1963), pp. 85–157.

Other studies have incorporated the essence of the Harris-Kneedler classification. For example, John F. Hart applied the classification with only minor modifications to the Southern United States in "Functions and Occupational Structure of Cities of the American South," *Annals of the Association of American Geographers*, XLV (September, 1955), 269–286.

Similar classifications have been used in the Netherlands and Australia: H. J. Keoning, "Een Typologie van Nederlandse Steden," *Tijdschrift voor Economische en Sociale Geographie*, XLI ste Jaargang (August-September, 1950), 187–206; Murray G. A. Wilson, "Some Population Characteristics of Australian Mining Settlements," *Tijdschrift voor Economische en Sociale Geographie*, LIII ste Jaargang (May, 1962), 125–132.

23. Jones, Forstall, and Collver, *op. cit.*, p. 86.

24. A partial list includes: Murray H. Leiffer, *City and Church in Transition* (Chicago: Willett, Clark and Company, 1938); Arthur M. Weimer and Homer Hoyt, *Principles of Urban Real Estate* (New York: Roland Press, 1939); John W. Alexander, "United States Cities: Employment Category by Size of Settlement," *Annals of the Association of American Geographers*, XLII (June, 1956), 237–238; T. Lynn

Smith, "The Functions of American Cities," in T. Lynn Smith and C. A. McMahan (eds.), *The Sociology of Urban Life: Text and Readings* (New York: Dryden Press, 1951), pp. 97–103; Egon E. Bergel, *Urban Sociology* (New York: McGraw-Hill, 1955); Thomas O. Wilkinson, "A Functional Classification of Japanese Cities: 1920–55," *Demography*, I (1964), 177–185; Gunnar Alexandersson, *The Industrial Structure of American Cities* (Lincoln: Univ. of Nebraska Press, 1956).

25. Howard J. Nelson, "A Service Classification of American Cities," *Economic Geography*, XXXI (July, 1955), 189–210.

26. Otis Dudley Duncan and Albert J. Reiss, Jr., *Social Characteristics of Urban and Rural Communities*, 1950 (New York: Wiley, 1956).

27. Duncan, *et al.*, *op. cit.*, p. 34.

28. *Ibid.*, p. 36.

29. Daniel O. Price, "Factor Analysis in the Study of Metropolitan Centers," *Social Forces*, XX (May, 1942), 449–455.

30. *Ibid.*, p. 451.

31. Paul Horst, Paul Wallin, Louis Guttman, *et al.*, *The Prediction of Personal Adjustment* (New York: Social Science Research Council, Bulletin 48, 1941) p. 65.

32. Price, *op. cit.*, p. 455.

17. Occupational Composition and Metropolitan Hierarchy: The Inter- and Intra-metropolitan Division of Labor

Omer R. Galle

In a large, urban-industrial nation, cities do not exist in isolation, but are highly interdependent, bound together by the integrative forces of the economy, transportation and communication technology, and population mobility. As a result, the characteristics that differentiate cities do not occur at random, but rather exhibit an overall pattern that makes it possible for us to speak of a system or hierarchy of cities. One such pattern in the United States, along with its implications for understanding urban differentiation, is discussed in this paper by Omer Galle. He points out that the fifty-six largest metropolitan areas can be classified into eight groups. Each of these groups has a somewhat special role to play in the industrial structure of the national society. The cities making up these groups can be arranged into a hierarchial order defined in terms of the capacity of a group of cities located high in the order to determine the industrial characteristics of the cities in a lower position. Galle shows that this hierarchy is reflected in the occupational composition of American cities. On the basis of this finding, the author goes on to speculate about the possibility of using the concept of a system of cities to explain variations in the social and political characteristics of urban communities.

Omer R. Galle, who received his doctorate from the University of Chicago, is Assistant Professor of Sociology at Vanderbilt University.

Introduction

That small communities vary in occupational compositions is evident in the contrasts between a one-company mining town and a college town. Large communities also display marked variations in occupational structure. For example, in 1950 the Washington, D.C., Standard Metropolitan Area (SMA) employed 27.5 per cent of its labor force as clerical and kindred workers, whereas 11.8 per cent of the Charleston, West Virginia, SMA labor force were similarly employed.[1] Wilkes-Barre–Hazleton had 43 percent of its labor force employed as operatives and kindred workers; in the Miami SMA 11 per cent were so employed.

The occupational structure of a community is perhaps the most important single aspect of its social structure, and has implications for a wide range of community processes.[2] Some speculations about these implications will be presented later. The major task of this paper, however, will be to demonstrate the sizable variations in occupational structure that exist among the large metropolitan areas of the United States and to examine the relationship between the occupational structure of a community and its position in a national system of cities.

Occupational composition has been found to vary with city size,[3] and with functional specialization.[4] Size, however, is but one index of a city's interrelations with other cities, as is functional specialization. A more complex classification will be useful, particularly in assessing differences between metropolitan areas, all of which are at one end of the size scale.

The Concept of a System of Cities In preindustrial times, the city was considered the core of an independent community, and together with its immediate hinterland constituted an integrated and self-sufficient entity.[5] The rise of modern technology, with its rapid means of transportation and communication, has changed this situation. An industrial nation such as the United States can be viewed as an integrated system of urban centers and interrelated regions, with each segment of the total system contributing its unique component to the total division of labor.

In this paper, attention will be focused on a set of fifty-six large metropolitan areas, comprising all SMA's of 300,000 or more population in 1950. These SMA's contained 43.6 per cent of the total population of the United States in that year. Any classification of metropolitan areas according to their positions in a national system of cities must utilize a combination of criteria, including size and function. Such a classification has been developed by Duncan and his collaborators, taking account of population size; per capita measures of value added by manufacture, wholesale sales, business service receipts, non-local loans, and demand deposits; and a detailed study of the industrial structure and trade areas of each SMA.[6] The classification scheme is shown in Table 1.

The "metropolitan hierarchy" depicted in Table 1 is multidimensional and identifies eight classes of metropolitan areas. Among the manufacturing SMA's (the left side of the table), the "Diversified Manufacturing with Metropolitan Functions" is

Paper No. 14 in the series, "Comparative Urban Research," issuing from the Population Research and Training Center, University of Chicago, under a grant from the Ford Foundation. A preliminary version of this paper was read at the 1962 annual meetings of the American Sociological Association.

TABLE 1. THE METROPOLITAN HIERARCHY*

National Metropolis (N)

New York
Chicago
Los Angeles (D)
Philadelphia (D)
Detroit (M)

Diversified Manufacturing with Metropolitan Functions (D)

Boston (N)
Pittsburgh (N)
Saint Louis
Cleveland
Buffalo
Cincinnati

Regional Metropolis (R)

San Francisco (N)
Minneapolis–St. Paul
Kansas City
Seattle
Portland
Atlanta
Dallas
Denver

Diversified Manufacturing with Few Metropolitan Functions (D)

Baltimore
Milwaukee
Albany–Schenectady–Troy
Toledo
Hartford
Syracuse

Dually Classified Regional Capitals (CD & CM)

Louisville (CD)
Birmingham (CM)
Indianapolis (CD)
Columbus (CD)
Richmond (CD)

Specialized Manufacturing (M)

Providence
Youngstown
Rochester
Dayton
Allentown–Bethlehem–Easton
Akron
Springfield–Holyoke
Wheeling–Steubenville
Charleson, West Virginia

Regional Capital (C)

Houston
New Orleans
Memphis
Omaha
Forth Worth
Nashville
Oklahoma City
Jacksonville

Special Cases (S)

Washington, D.C.
SanDiego
San Antonio
Miami
Tampa–St. Petersburg
Norfolk–Portsmouth
Wilkes-Barre–Hazleton
Knoxville
Phoenix

* Adapted from Otis Dudley Duncan, William Richard Scott, Stanley Lieberson, Beverly Davis Duncan, and Hal H. Winsborough, *Metropolis and Region* (Baltimore: Johns Hopkins Press, 1960), p. 271.

the only one of the three groups to show strong relationships with moderately large contiguous hinterlands. Each, however, encounters strong competition for these surrounding areas from other centers close by. The "Diversified Manufacturing with Few Metropolitan Functions" are SMA's of somewhat smaller size and have less developed trading and financial activities than manufacturing centers with metropolitan functions. The "Specialized Manufacturing" SMA's have the lowest average per capita wholesale sales and the highest average per capita value added by manufacture of the eight groups of SMA's. Because of their special functions, all three groups of manufacturing SMA's have relationships with many parts of the country, so that much of what would be considered their "hinterlands" are of a diffuse and non-contiguous nature.

Each of the "Regional Metropolises" has a fairly large contiguous hinterland over which it exerts relatively uncontested dominance. These SMA's have the highest average per capita wholesale sales for any of the groups of SMA's in the table and show some strength in manufacturing, although not as much as the manufacturing types of SMA's. The "Regional Capitals" are in many ways similar to the regional metropolises, and many of the differences between these two type of SMA's can be attributed to size. The regional capitals exert their dominance over smaller contiguous hinterlands; they have a slightly lower average per capita wholesale sales, and an average per capita value added by manufacture lower than all groups of SMA's, except the special cases. The "Dually Classified Regional Capitals," while not separated into a distinct group in *Metropolis and Region*, are so treated here. These SMA's combine some of the characteristics of both major types of

SMA's (the regional centers and the manufacturing centers), with moderate evidence of both manufacturing activity and regional relationships.

Whereas the six types of SMA's described above are relatively homogeneous groups, the remaining two are not. The "National Metropolises," the five largest SMA's are "not products of regional forces, but are created by larger factors in the total national economy."[7] New York and Chicago clearly stand apart from the other three in such measures as per capita wholesale sales, business service receipts, nonlocal loans, and demand deposits. The other three SMA's are transitional between national metropolises and other types of SMA's (as noted by their secondary classification symbols in parentheses in the table). The "Special Cases," listed at the bottom of the table, are also a heterogeneous group. They form a residual category containing SMA's that vary widely in function, from the nation's capital (Washington, D.C.), to tourist centers (e.g., Miami), to concentration in coal mining (Wilkes-Barre–Hazleton), to military centers (e.g., San Diego). In the following analysis, the national metropolises and the special cases, because of their internal heterogeneity, will not be studied; attention will be focused on the six groups of relatively homogeneous SMA's.

Occupational Differentiation

In the following analysis we will investigate more systematically the variations in occupational composition of large metropolitan communities. Table 2 shows the mean percentage employed in each of the eight broad Census occupational categories for each of the six homogeneous groups of

SMA's. The manufacturing SMA's tend to have a greater proportion of their labor force classified as craftsmen, foremen, and kindred workers, and as operatives and kindred workers, while the regional centers have relatively more workers in the categories of managers, clerical, sales, and service workers. The dually classified regional capitals tend to be in between the two extremes of the regional metropolises and specialized manufacturing centers.

It is clear from the results shown in Table 2 that the classification scheme presented in *Metropolis and Region* is helpful in tracing some of the regularities of occupational differentiation. This classification system states that, among the large metropolitan communities of the United States, there exist fairly distinct groupings of cities that differ in accordance with the dissimilar tasks they perform within the national economy. Table 2 indicates that not only do these different types of communities perform dissimilar tasks, but

TABLE 2. MEAN PER CENT DISTRIBUTION OF EMPLOYED CIVILIAN LABOR FORCE, EIGHT BROAD OCCUPATIONAL CATEGORIES, BY TYPE OF SMA*

Type of SMA

Occupational Category	Regional Metropolis	Regional Capital	Dually Classified Regional Capital	Diversified Manufacturing, with Metropolitan Functions	Diversified Manufacturing with Few Metropolitan Functions	Manufacturing
Total	100.00	100.00	100.00	100.00	100.00	100.00
Professional, technical, and kindred workers	10.70	9.25	9.46	9.88	10.41	8.74
Managers, officials, and proprietors, including farm	12.45	11.76	9.99	9.63	10.11	9.32
Clerical and kindred workers	17.79	15.88	15.89	15.81	16.64	12.83
Sales workers	9.08	8.45	8.44	7.90	7.81	7.08
Craftsmen, foremen, and kindred workers	14.70	14.98	15.09	16.44	16.42	16.90
Operatives and kindred workers	15.44	16.41	20.40	21.47	21.53	28.33
Service workers, including private household	11.85	13.87	12.45	10.51	10.02	8.71
Laborers, including farm and mine	6.80	8.15	7.08	7.26	5.90	7.01
Occupation not reported	1.19	1.25	1.20	1.10	1.16	1.08

* Compiled from Bureau of the Census, *Census of Population, 1950* (Washington, D.C.: Government Printing Office, 1953), II, Part 1, Table 90, 150–51.

they also vary in their occupational composition. In order to draw the causal inference that the cities have dissimilar occupational structures, *because* they perform different tasks in the national economy more information is needed.

The Industrial Profile The industrial profile of a community consists of all those industrial categories in which the given community employs a substantially greater proportion of its labor force than does the labor force of the United States as a whole.[8] It is the group of industries in which a community specializes and that tie that community to the national system of cities. It follows from this that the non-profile industries of the various communities will be quite similar, since these industries consist mainly of those activities that any city of this size needs to maintain itself. The concept of industrial profile is in many respects similar to the economists' idea of economic base, or Alexandersson's notion of "city-forming" industries.[9]

Occupation and industry are two quite different concepts, and the classification of the labor force by one does not necessarily imply a set distribution with respect to the other. However, insofar as the division of labor along functional lines seems to be logically pre-eminent in the determination of a community's role in the national economy, industrial structure is here viewed as a basic determinant of occupational structure. Thus, the unique differences between types of cities in their occupational composition should be a function of the different modes of industrial specialization. The occupational structure of the non-profile industries may be expected to be quite similar in all types of cities.

Using the cross-tabulation of occupation by industry for each SMA that is available from the 1950 Census,[10] the occupational distributions of profile and non-profile industries have been compiled.[11] For each of the six homogeneous groups of SMA's, Table 3 shows the mean occupational distribution for profile and non-profile industries and for the total experienced civilian labor force. For convenience, all the blue-collar occupations have been considered together. With this exception, the occupational distributions for the total labor force, shown in Panel A of Table 3, are identical with the mean occupational distributions exhibited in Table 2. That much of the variation in occupational composition is accounted for by the industrial profiles of the respective cities can be seen from Table 4. In this table, the variances for each of the five occupational groups over the forty-two SMA's for workers in profile industries, in non-profile industries, and in the total labor force are shown. All five of the variances for the profile industries are significantly larger than their non-profile counterparts.[12] The question now arises as to whether the variations in occupational composition are systematic with respect to the groups of cities delimited by the authors of *Metropolis and Region*. The results of an analysis of variance are indicated in Table 3.

With only minor exceptions, the results in Table 3 are consistent and quite striking. Within the profile industries, the differences between types of SMA's in the mean percentages in each occupational category are much larger than the differences between the occupational distributions for the total labor force. The regional centers, led by the regional metropolises, have relatively more workers in white-collar occupations, while the manufacturing SMA's have much greater proportions of their labor forces (in the profile industries) in blue-

TABLE 3. MEAN PER CENT DISTRIBUTION, BY TYPE OF SMA, OF TOTAL EMPLOYED CIVILIAN LABOR FORCE OF PROFILE INDUSTRIES AND OF NON-PROFILE INDUSTRIES

Occupational Category	Type of SMA					
	Regional Metropolis	Regional Capital	Dually Classified Regional Capital	Diversified Manufacturing, with Metropolitan Functions	Diversified Manufacturing, with Few Metropolitan Functions	Specialized Manufacturing
A. The Total Employed Civilian Labor Force						
Total	100.00	100.00	100.00	100.00	100.00	100.00
Professional, technical, and kindred workers	10.70	9.25	9.46	9.88	10.41	8.74
Managers, officials, and proprietors, including farm*	12.45	11.76	9.99	9.63	10.11	9.32
Clerical and kindred workers	17.79	15.88	15.89	15.81	16.64	12.83
Sales workers*	9.08	8.45	8.44	7.90	7.81	7.08
All blue-collar workers, including occupations not reported*	49.98	54.66	56.22	56.78	55.03	62.03
B. The Profile Industries						
Total	100.00	100.00	100.00	100.00	100.00	100.00
Professional, technical, and kindred workers	8.96	9.28	6.99	8.29	9.61	5.69
Managers, officials, and proprietors, including farm*	11.88	9.35	5.65	4.82	4.47	2.76
Clerical and kindred workers*	27.00	21.51	17.56	15.90	19.33	11.70
Sales workers*	10.21	6.52	4.27	2.38	1.86	1.04
All blue-collar workers, including occupations not reported*	41.95	53.34	65.53	68.61	64.73	78.81

TABLE 3 (*Continued*)

C. The Non-profile Industries

Total	100.00	100.00	100.00	100.00	100.00	100.00
Professional, technical, and kindred workers	10.98	9.44	10.32	10.58	10.64	10.52
Managers, officials, and proprietors, including farm	12.72	12.56	11.61	12.11	12.65	13.29
Clerical and kindred workers	14.77	13.79	15.13	15.82	15.18	13.43
Sales workers*	8.85	9.08	9.97	10.73	10.50	10.73
All blue-collar workers, including occupations not reported	52.68	55.13	52.97	50.76	51.03	52.03

* The Kruskal-Wallis *H*-test indicates that this extreme clustering of rankings within groups would occur with a probability of less than 0.001 if all groups had the same mean rank, and the rankings were in fact random over all groups (see William H. Kruskal and W. Allen Wallis, "Use of Ranks in One-Criterion Variance Analysis," *Journal of the American Statistical Association*, XLVII, No. 260 [December, 1952], 583–621).
Source: Bureau of the Census, *Census of Population, 1950* (Washington, D.C.: Government Printing Office, 1953), Vol. II, Parts 2–49, Table 84.

collar occupations. The differences between the means in the profile industries are significant well past the 0.0001 level of probability for all occupational categories except the professional, technical, and kindred workers. The mean proportion of blue-collar workers in specialized manufacturing centers (78.81 per cent) is almost twice as large as the corresponding figure for the regional metropolises (41.95 per cent). Similarly, the regional metropolises have a mean of 11.88 per cent of their profile-industry labor force in the managers, officials, and proprietors category, as compared with only 2.76 per cent for the specialized manufacturing centers.

Among non-profile industries the systematic differences evident for the total labor force and for the labor force in profile industries are, with the exception of the sales workers category, not present. Even the blue-collar category, which is probably the most heterogeneous occupational group, does not show a significant *H*-value in the analysis of variance.

With regard to the profile industries, the regional metropolises have the highest mean percentage employed in the sales workers category, and the specialized manufacturing centers the lowest. In the non-profile industries, on the other hand, the regional metropolises have the lowest mean percentage employed as sales workers, and the specialized manufacturing centers the highest (along with the diversified manufacturing centers with metropolitan functions). That is, there is almost a complete reversal in the direction of the differences between the means in the non-profile sales workers. It is possible that in the central-place metropolises, such as the regional centers, some of the activities that are generally thought to be non-profile (maintenance activities) are pre-empted by the profile industries that are already specialized in this area, and serving more than the local community, while in the non-central-place oriented cities (the manufacturing SMA's) this is not the case.[13]

TABLE 4. ESTIMATED VARIANCES AND STANDARD DEVIATIONS OF OCCUPATIONAL PER CENT DISTRIBUTIONS OF TOTAL EXPERIENCED CIVILIAN LABOR FORCE, PROFILE INDUSTRIES, AND NON-PROFILE INDUSTRIES OVER ALL 42 SMA'S

	Variances		
Occupational Category	Total Labor Force	Profile Industries	Non-profile Industries
Professional, technical, and kindred workers	1.93	20.18	1.76
Managers, officials, and proprietors, including farm	2.24	13.83	1.40
Clerical and kindred workers	5.47	47.45	1.82
Sales workers	0.72	14.63	1.17
Blue-collar workers, including farm and mine	24.54	240.32	7.39

Of the five occupational categories shown in Table 3, only the category of professional, technical, and kindred workers group fails to show any significant systematic differences between the six types of SMA's, either for the profile industries, the non-profile industries, or the total labor force. It should be noted here that all these occupational groupings are quite broad and consequently quite heterogeneous. This is especially true for the professionals; within this broad category there are physicians, judges, dentists, and other "service" professionals whose work is generally ubiquitous in all communities of sufficient size. There are also engineers, chemists, natural scientists, and other technical workers whose work is not primarily dependent upon the general public, but upon the industrial structure of the city. We thus have two trends working at cross-currents with each other. Those communities with a high level of industrial activity would have a large proportion of the technical component of the professional category, while those cities that serve as distributive and integrative central places for a large hinterland would tend to have more of the service type of professional.[14]

Discussion

The basic purpose of this study has been to specify the relevance of a community's place in the general system of cities for its occupational structure. In light of this relationship, the importance of the industrial-profile concept should be emphasized. In fact, the industrial profile comprises a different set of industries for each city. Since occupational structure is determined to a great extent by industrial structure, much of the observed variation in the occupational composition of profile industries for the different types of SMA's may be accounted for by the varying composition of the industrial profiles. It is also possible that some of the variation is due to different occupational compositions of the same industries in two or more different types of communities. Although this would be the next step in further work, no attempt has been made here to differentiate between these two effects. The avowed purpose of the study, however, has already been accomplished. If the reasoning with respect to the industrial profile is accepted, then we have shown that the differing occupational structures of large metropolitan communities are accounted for in large part by the specialized tasks these communities perform in the national economy.

It must be emphasized that this is not a circular statement. Industry and occupation are not the same. When classified by industry, the labor force is grouped into categories of productive functions for the community. When classified by occupation, the labor force is sorted into groups that denote the specific tasks performed by individuals, regardless of what they are producing as a final product. The original classification of SMA's was delimited by a careful study of the productive and distributive functions of each area. That the occupational distributions of the different types of communities exhibit systematic variation because of this is an empirical finding and supports the basic hypothesis of this paper.

Implications According to Rossi, "We know a great deal from the geographers and ecologists about the location of human settlements, how to classify cities by their important functions, but we do not have much knowledge about how these factors affect the social lives of the communities."[15] In this paper, a systematic variation in occupational composition has been shown, and the reasons for these variations have been identified. Although the implications for the "social lives" of the communities involved are more difficult to specify, some speculations concerning the consequences of the observed differences in occupational composition may be advanced.

Duncan and Schnore have suggested that the perspective of the human ecologist has a primary contribution to make to the study of power in the local community.[16] Hawley has suggested that "dominance" in the local community is attached to those functional units that control the flow of sustenance into it.[17] In a "company town," for example, where one firm employs the majority of the labor force, that company occupies a unique power position in the community. Whereas dominance is more diffuse and the situation therefore more complicated in the large metropolis, the profile industries play comparable dominant roles in these areas. The dominance may be less centralized, but the functional niche is similar. Although the industries that are in this dominant position may or may not exercise their "functional" power, they have the potential to do so. Other groups may organize for the prime purpose of combating this corporate power and gaining some control over community decisions.[18] Rossi has suggested that in large cities voluntary organizations, such as civic groups and the Community Chest, may play an important role in the power complex of the community.[19] The dominance of the profile industries may also be manifested in relationships with the political machinery of the community.

In his paper on "Community Power and Urban Renewal Success," Hawley examined the effect of the size of the managerial component of the labor force on the success of a city in urban renewal programs.[20] His data show an inverse relationship between the relative numbers of managers, officials, and proprietors in a city's labor force and the amount of progress achieved on the city's urban renewal program. He concludes that a smaller managerial component indicates a centralization of the control of "power" in the community, which in turn facilitates the control over decisions such as whether to undertake or continue programs of urban renewal.

Pinard has examined a number of demographic variables and their relation to the decision of a community to accept or reject fluoridation of their water supply.[21] He found that the communities that had a low proportion of managerial and professional workers had greater success in passing fluoridation measures. He also confirms Hawley's suggestion that power can be used to block collective action by pointing out that the intensity of approval *or* disapproval is greater in the communities with a smaller "social elite."

Neither Hawley nor Pinard examined the causes of variation in the relative size of the upper white-collar occupations between cities. Similarly, we have not examined the SMA's studied here with respect to success in urban renewal planning or fluoridation projects. Combining our results with the results of their two papers, however, it can be predicted that the power structure varies systematically with the functional position of the community in the system of cities.

It could be argued that since the major portion of the variation in percentage of managers is accounted for by the profile industries, and since the profile industries do not employ the major proportion of the labor force in any of the SMA's, the power accruing to these industries will manifest itself only in their internal structure. This is significant in and of itself, but the unique position that the profile industries hold suggests community-wide repercussions in the power structure. The industrial profile of a city consists of those industries that relate the local community to the national system. Hawley has suggested that these industries are important in the community-wide power structure. "The relative numbers in the key industry should prove decisive.... What constitutes a key industry, of course, is contingent upon the function the city performs for the regional and national society."[22] In any case, the papers of Hawley and Pinard, and the results presented here, along with the preceding speculative re-marks suggest that the ecological study of community power is well worth more detailed investigation, both with respect to the internal dynamics of power within the city, and with respect to generalizations about differences in power structures between cities.

As these brief remarks indicate, we feel that a more careful study of the interrelations between the position of a city in the national system of cities, its occupational structure, and other internal characteristics of the city may be a useful means of getting at aspects of power structure, and other community social processes, especially in the large metropolitan areas where the "community study method"[23] has yet to be proven economically feasible. In the course of this type of study, it may be well to re-examine the utility of a typological classification of cities, such as the one from *Metropolis and Region*. Cities actually vary in a more or less continuous manner, and categorizing them into distinct groups is a rather crude technique. It may be more appropriate to try to construct a multiple-variable approach to community structure, utilizing many if not all of the variables used in the *Metropolis and Region* scheme, and perhaps other variables, in an attempt to study a more specific aspect of community structure or community social life. The use of a multiple-variable approach would also allow analysis of a wider range of cities and a more detailed examination of the relevant aspects of a city's position in the national system of cities.

Conclusion

It has been suggested that it is fruitful to view the local community as an integral part of the total system of urban places and related regions in the national economy.

Local cities perform different tasks in the maintenance and growth of the system as a whole that cause them to become differentiated with respect to each other in their internal aspects as well.

In applying our hypothesis to actual data, we have considered only the largest metropolitan areas of the United States as of 1950, and have examined the internal division of labor for these areas as reflected in their occupational composition. We have demonstrated that the occupational structure of a city exhibits systematic variation with respect to the community's place in the system of cities. These differences can, in large part, be attributed to the industrial profile of the city—that part of the city's economic activity that relates the local community to the system of cities. This, we feel, is the major contribution of this paper.

The position a city holds in the national system of cities is a factor determining its social structure. We would suggest that community researchers who try to argue that their particular community is "typical" of all American communities are doomed to failure.[24] It might be more meaningful to try instead to specify where their community stands with respect to the national system of cities, and to consider whether this fact makes any difference in their powers of generalization. It is our firm belief that in many cases it will.

ACKNOWLEDGMENTS

The author would like to thank Otis Dudley Duncan, Karl E. Taeuber, Alma F. Taeuber, and Robert W. Hodge for helpful comments and criticisms. Most of the computational work was ably performed by Mark Warden.

NOTES

1. The following data are gathered from U.S. Bureau of the Census, *Census of Population, 1950* (Washington, D.C.: Government Printing Office, 1953), II, Part I, Table 90, 150–51.
2. See, e.g., Otis Dudley Duncan and Beverly Duncan, "Residential Distribution and Occupational Stratification," *American Journal of Sociology*, LX (March 1955), 493–503 [reprinted in this volume]; Frank W. Notestein, "Class Differences in Fertility," *Annals of the American Academy of Political and Social Science*, November, 1936, pp. 1–11; and Liston Pope, "Religion and the Class Structure," *Annals of the American Academy of Political and Social Science*, March, 1948, pp. 84–91.
3. Otis Dudley Duncan and Albert J. Reiss, Jr., *Social Characteristics of Urban and Rural Communities, 1950* (New York: John Wiley & Sons, 1956), pp. 95–102.
4. *Ibid.*, Part IV, esp. Tables 124, 137, 138, and 139.
5. Amos H. Hawley, *Human Ecology* (New York: Ronald Press Co., 1950), pp. 239–45. For a more detailed exposition of the ideas outlined in this discussion of the "system of cities" concept, see also Chauncy D. Harris, "The Market as a Factor in the Localization of Industry in the United States," *Annals of the Association of American Geographers*, XLIV, No. 4 (December 1954), 315–48; Brian J.L. Berry and W. L. Garrison, "Recent Developments in Central Place Theory," *Papers and Proceedings*

of the Regional Science Association, 1958; Edgar M. Hoover, "The Concept of a System of Cities," *Economic Development and Cultural Change,* Vol. III (1955); Donnell M. Pappenfort, "The Ecological Field and the Metropolitan Community: Manufacturing and Management," *American Journal of Sociology,* LXIV, No. 4 (January 1959), 380–85.
6. For a detailed description of classification procedures see Otis Dudley Duncan, William Richard Scott, Stanley Lieberson, Beverly Davis Duncan, and Hal H. Winsborough, *Metropolis and Region* (Baltimore: Johns Hopkins Press, 1960), chap. xi, and esp. pp. 259–75.
7. *Ibid.*, p. 266.
8. For a detailed discussion of the construction and use of industrial profiles, see *ibid.*, pp. 200–230.
9. Gunnar Alexandersson, "City-forming and City-serving Production," in Harold M. Mayer and Clyde F. Kohn (eds.), *Readings in Urban Geography* (Chicago: University of Chicago Press, 1959), p. 111.
10. Bureau of the Census, *Census of Population, 1950,* Vol. II, Parts 2–49 (the state volumes), Table 84.
11. Modifications were made in the industrial profiles of the SMA's to facilitate their use with the intermediate industrial classification used in the occupation by industry table for SMA's of the Census volumes. The original profiles were constructed from the detailed classification. For a

more detailed explanation of the procedure followed in the modification of the industrial profiles, see the complete report (Omer R. Galle, "Community Structure and the Metropolitan Hierarchy" [unpublished research report, Population Research and Training Center, University of Chicago, 1962]).

12. K. A. Brownlee, *Statistical Theory and Methodology in Science and Engineering* (New York: John Wiley & Sons, 1960), p. 220.

13. The significant differences in the sales category in non-profile industries may also be due to an imprecise method of "operationalizing" the industrial profile concept for use in studying occupational differentiation. In modifying the industrial profiles to the occupation by industry table of the Census volumes, only those industries which were listed separately in the "industrial profile" tables in *Metropolis and Region* were included in the "operational" industrial profile. This meant that some non-local services, such as wholesale trade and others, were almost always included in the regional centers, and almost always excluded in the manufacturing centers, though in fact they should have been included in all SMA's.

14. In the original analysis, this was in fact found to be the case (see Galle, *op. cit.*).

15. Peter H. Rossi, "Theory, Research, and Practice in Community Organization," *Social Science and Community Action*, ed. Charles R. Adrian (East Lansing: Board of Trustees, Michigan State University, 1960), p. 22.

16. Otis Dudley Duncan and Leo F. Schnore, "Cul-

tural, Behavial and Ecologicoral Perspectives in the Study of Social Organisation," *American Journal of Sociology*, LXV, No. 2 (September, 1959), 139.

17. Hawley, *op cit.*, pp. 229–30.

18. *Ibid.*, pp. 210–11.

19. Peter H. Rossi, "Theory and Method in the Study of Power in the Local Community" (a paper presented at the 1960 annual meetings of the American Sociological Association), pp. 38–39. It is, of course, possible that the executives of the profile industries utilize these voluntary organizations as one channel through which their power is exercised.

20. Amos H. Hawley, "Community Power and Urban Renewal Success," *American Journal of Sociology*, LXVIII, No. 4 (January, 1963), 422–31.

21. Maurice Pinard, "Structural Attachments and Political Support in Urban Politics: The Case of Fluoridation Referendums," *American Journal of Sociology*, LXVIII, No. 5 (March, 1963), 513–26.

22. Hawley, "Community Power and Urban Renewal Success," *op. cit.*, p. 431.

23. Conrad M. Arensberg, "The Community-Study Method," *American Journal of Sociology*, LX, No. 2 (September, 1954), 109–24.

24. Almost all community studies make some attempt to generalize to some larger universe of communities. For one of the more lyrical examples see W. Lloyd Warner, *Democracy in Jonesville* (New York: Harper & Bros., 1949), p. xv. For a more recent example see Robert A. Dahl, *Who Governs?* (New Haven, Conn.: Yale University Press, 1961), pp. 1–8.

18. Urbanism Reconsidered: Scott Greer
A Comparative Study of
Local Areas in a Metropolis

Another important aspect of urban differentiation is social differentiation within the city. In most American cities this kind of differentiation has the interesting characteristic of being associated with spatial or ecological differentiation: People with similar occupations, values, interests, and styles of life are clustered together in the same part of the city. The truth of the claim that such social areas, as they have come to be called, do exist is revealed in the paper by Scott Greer. For his study of social participation in Los Angeles, Greer was able to select two census tracts in which the residents were alike in terms of economic and racial characteristics but differed in terms of family structure. Greer assumed that family structure (as measured by fertility, percent of working women, and percent of single-family detached dwellings in an area) was a particularly sensitive indicator of the degree of urbanization of a population. He also believed that this measure of "urbanization" was the major variable associated with differences in the residents' involvement with local community affairs. Greer's investigation confirmed his thesis. He found that large families with nonworking mothers and living in single family homes (low-urbanization) were much more likely to be interested and involved in neighborhood and local community life than the smaller, apartment-dwelling families with working mothers (high-urbanization). Apart from its usefulness in elaborating the concept of social area, the paper is important in helping to modify the notion that there is a single urban way of life in American communities.

Scott Greer is Professor of Sociology and Political Science and Director of the Center for Metropolitan Studies at Northwestern University. His many publications include *Urban Renewal and American Cities* (1965), *Metropolitics* (1963), *Social Organization* (1962), *Governing the Metropolis* (1962), and *The Emerging City: Myth and Reality* (1962).

The investigation of the internal differentiation of urban population has been concerned chiefly with economic rank and ethnic diversity, and with the differences which accompany variations in these factors. Such studies throw little light upon the broad, non-ethnic, cultural differences generated in the metropolitan environment, i.e., upon "urbanism as a way of life." While there has been much concern, theoretically, with the effects of the metropolitan ambit upon all social relationships, most of the empirical basis of urban theory has been the study of small "natural areas" or the study of gross regularities in census data, arranged spatially for analysis.

Perhaps the best evidence bearing upon this larger question of "urbanism" has been the study of urban neighborhoods. The work of Donald Foley, for example, indicates that in a sample of Rochester residents (1) the neighborhood pattern still exists to some degree, but, (2) many individuals do not neighbor and do not consider their local area to be a social community.[1] Such studies approach the propositions that urban society is functionally rather than spatially organized and that urbanites are mobile, anonymous, and lacking in identification with their local area.

To gauge the generality of Foley's conclusions, however, one needs to know where the neighborhoods he studied fit in an array of neighborhoods. Because wide variation exists, the relation between the area studied and others is crucial for the hypothesis tested; most of Rochester may be much more neighborhood oriented, or much less so, than the area studied.

The Shevky-Bell typology of urban subareas is useful in this connection, for it allows any census tract to be located in three different arrays by means of three indices constructed from census data.[2] It is hypothesized that these represent three dimensions within urban social space, each statistically unidimensional and independent of the others. The dimensions are social rank, segregation, and urbanization.[3] The last largely measures differences in family structure, and, it is assumed,

Revised version of paper read at the annual meeting of the American Sociological Society, September, 1954. The study was carried out by the Laboratory in Urban Culture, a research facility of Occidental College, with the support of the John Randolph Haynes and Dora Haynes Foundation. I wish to express gratitude to Ella Kube, Research Associate, for assistance in the computation and analysis upon which the report is based.

From *American Sociological Review,* Vol. XXI (February 1956), pp. 19–25. Reprinted by permission.

indicates corollary differences in behavior. Thus, when social rank and segregation are controlled, differences in the index of urbanization for specific tract populations should indicate consistent variations in social behavior. One purpose of the present research was to determine the nature of such corollary differences, and particularly differences in social participation.

This report is based upon a pilot study of differences in social participation between sample populations in two Los Angeles areas (census tracts 35 and 63).[4] The two tract populations are nearly identical with respect to two of the indices (social rank and segregation) and differ on the third, urbanization. For simplicity in presentation the tract with the higher urbanization index score (tract 63) will hereafter 'be called the high-urban tract, the other (tract 35) the low-urban tract.

The two sample tracts compare as follows. *History:* the low-urban tract is in an area that thirty years ago was separately incorporated for a brief time; the high-urban tract has always been a part of Los Angeles proper. *Location:* the low-urban tract is approximately fifteen minutes from the city center by auto; the high-urban tract is about half as far. (The low-urban tract is adjacent to the competing centers of Glendale and Pasadena.) *Social rank:* both tracts fall within the large middle range, being slightly above the median for the County. The social rank index for the low-urban tract is 68, for the high-urban tract, 66, as of the 1950 census of population, based upon the standard scores developed by Shevky with 1940 census data. *Ethnicity:* in neither tract does the foreign-born and non-white population amount to more than 5 per cent. *Urbanization:* the two tracts represent the extremes of the middle range of the urbanization index, within which a majority of the Los

Angeles County census tracts lie. The low-urban tract had an urbanization index of 41, the high-urban tract, 57. There are much more highly urban tracts at middle rank, and much lower ones, in the County. The sample is weighted against the instrument, so that if striking and consistent variations appear in this middle range, they probably indicate more extreme variations at the poles.

The Field Procedure and the Sample

The field study included scheduled interviews on the participation of adult members of households in formal organizations, neighboring, cultural events, visiting, domestic activities, the mass media, the kin group, and other social structures.

Visiting was measured by questions concerning friends or relatives who were visited regularly at least once a month. The respondent was asked to give the address of the residence visited, both as a control over the accuracy of the information, and as a clue to social space position in the Shevky-Bell typology. Neighboring was measured by Wallin's "Neighborliness Scale," which was developed for a similar population in Palo Alto, California.[5] The scale assumes that neighborliness is unidimensional and can be measured by a small battery of questions referring to the degree of interaction with neighbors. The reproducibility for the present sample has not yet been determined. Cultural events were recorded and categorized in the manner devised by Queen, in his studies of social participation in St. Louis.[6] Individuals were asked about their attendance in the past month at movies, classes and study groups, athletic contests, lectures and speeches, museums and exhibits, musical events, and stage shows. They were also asked the location of the event and who accompanied them. Special schedules of questions were developed for the purpose of describing participation in formal organizations of various sorts, definitions of the local area, domestic participation, neighborhood play of children, and other aspects of participation which will not be reported here.

An area random sample was interviewed in each tract, with 161 respondents in the low-urban tract, 150 in the high-urban tract. These households represented approximately 7 per cent of the populations of the two census tracts chosen. The housewife was the respondent, and the response rate was over 85 per cent, being higher in the low-urban area. Interviewers were advanced and graduate students at Occidental College, and the average interview time was approximately one hour.

The two samples of households compare as follows:

Income: 20 percent of the households in each area had less than $3,000 annually; 37 percent in the low-urban area and 31 percent in the high-urban area had annual incomes between $3,000 and $5,000; 35 percent in the low-urban area and 38 percent in the high-urban area had over $5,000 annually. Those who did not know or declined to state were 8 percent in the low-urban area, 11 percent in the high-urban area. The chief difference was a preponderance of middle income households in the low-urban area, with somewhat more heterogeneity in the high-urban area. *Occupation*: using the blue collar-white collar break, the samples were identical. In both areas, 72 percent of the employed respondents were white-collar. Seventy-two percent of the husbands in each area were in clerical jobs or higher.

Education: if education is divided into three classes, elementary or less, some high school or completed high school, and some college

or more, the low-urban sample is slightly more homogeneous. Both respondents and husbands are 60 percent high-school educated, with approximately 15 percent below and 25 percent above this class. In the high-urban sample the middle category accounted for only 50 percent, with approximately 25 percent below and 25 percent above this class.

Such differences are not great but seem to indicate a consistent tendency towards somewhat more heterogeneity in the high-urban sample. It includes a slightly higher proportion of low-income, low-education persons, and also a slightly higher proportion of high-income, high-education persons. The high-urban sample is also more heterogeneous with respect to ethnicity. Although the percentage of non-white and foreign-born is similar in the two samples (9 for the low-urban sample, 11 for the high-urban) differences in religious affiliation indicate more ethnic diversity in the high-urban sample.

The low-urban area sample is much more homogeneous and Protestant in affiliation and preference. The high-urban sample however, includes sizeable representations of the minority American religious beliefs: Jews and Roman Catholics are, together, only 20 percent of the low-urban sample; they are 37 percent of the high-urban sample. This heterogeneous and non-Protestant population in the high-urban sample is probably, to a large degree, made up of second and later generation ethnic individuals. Since the census tracts with high indexes of segregation in middle economic ranks are usually found in the more highly urbanized areas of the Shevky-Bell grid, it is likely that "later generation ethnics" (not identified in census data) are also concentrated in the more highly urbanized tracts of the middle social rank.

Such a correlation between second and later generation ethnic populations and urbanization, however, does not allow the reduction of the urbanization dimension to the ethnic component. In truth, many of these individuals are in process of leaving their ethnic status behind. Instead, it may be said that one of the attributes indicated by the urbanization index is apt to be the presence of second and later generation ethnics in the midst of acculturation. Such heterogeneity between faiths and within faiths is one of the conditions that give highly urbanized populations their particular characteristics.

Empirical Findings

Table 1 gives differences in participation between two areas with respect to the localization of community. The low-urban sample differed sharply and consistently in the direction of more participation in the local community. Their neighboring score was higher, they were more apt to have friends in the local area, and these constituted a larger proportion of all close friends, i.e., those visited at least once a month. They were more apt to go to cultural events such as movies, athletic contents, stage shows, and study groups, in the local area, and they were more apt to use local commercial facilities of certain types.

The low-urban sample had a higher rate of membership and participation in formal organizations other than church, and, more important, a larger proportion of their organizations were local in nature. A large majority of the respondents' organizations held meetings in the local area, and although the husbands' organizations usually met outside the area, still a much larger proportion met locally than did in the

TABLE 1. LOCAL COMMUNITY PARTICIPATION IN TWO URBAN AREAS

Type of Social Participation	Low Urban*	High Urban*
Per cent of respondents with high neighboring scores (Scale types 2 through 5)	67†	56†
N of respondents	(162)	(150)
Per cent of respondents with friends in the local area	50	29
N of respondents	(162)	(150)
Per cent of all respondents' friends who live in local area	41	25
N of all friends	(441)	(316)
Per cent of respondents attending cultural events in local area, of those attending any cultural events	45	18
N attending any events	(101)	(92)
Per cent of respondents' formal organizations which meet in:		
Local area	62	26
Other areas	35	71
No response	3	3
N of organizations	(126)	(67)
Per cent of respondent's formal organizations with the majority of members residing in:		
Local area	57	33
Other area	18	18
Scattered over the city	23	45
No response	2	4
N of organizations	(126)	(67)
Per cent of husbands' formal organizations (as reported by respondent) which meet in:		
Local area	21‡	5‡
Other areas	73	86
No response	6	9
N of husbands' organizations	(104)	(57)
Per cent of husbands' formal organizations (as reported by respondent) with the majority of members residing in:		
Local area	25	10
Other area	23	12
Scattered over the city	45	77
No response	7	1
N of husbands' organizations	(104)	(57)

* P (χ^2) <.01, with exceptions noted below.
† P (χ^2) slightly above .05 level: $\chi^2 = 3.77$.
‡ P (χ^2) between .01 and .02 levels.

high-urban sample. Furthermore, the members of formal organizations to which the low-urban sample belonged were more apt to live in the immediate local community. In the high-urban sample other members were most apt to be scattered over the metropolis as a whole.

Further indication of the differential importance the local based organization had for these two samples is the greater familiarity of the low-urban sample with local community leaders. (See Table 2.)

TABLE 2. RESPONDENTS' ABILITY TO NAME LEADERS OF THE LOCAL AREA AND OF LOS ANGELES

	Low Urban	High Urban
Per cent of respondents who could name at least one local leader	32*	21*
N of respondents	(162)	(150)
Per cent of respondents who could name at least one Los Angeles leader	38†	37†
N of respondents	(162)	(150)

* P (χ^2) between .02 and .05 levels.
† Difference not significant.

While the samples were equally able (and unable) to name Los Angeles leaders, there was a significantly higher proportion who could name local leaders in the low-urban area sample. This probably indicates a uniform engagement of the middle-rank populations in the affairs of the metropolis as a whole, but definite variations in their interest and involvement with respect to local affairs.

It is sometimes stated, almost as an axiom, that the urban milieu results in the extreme attrition of kin relations. The present study indicates this to be questionable. The most important single kind of social relationship for both samples is kinship visiting. A large majority of both

samples visit their kin at least once a month, and *half of each sample visit their kin at least once a week*. These data, reported in Table 3, are consistent with the findings of

TABLE 3. KIN VISITING IN TWO URBAN AREAS

Per Cent Visiting Kin	Low Urban*	High Urban*
Once a week or more often	49	55
At least once a month, but less than once a week	24	21
A few times a year, but less than once a month	11	8
Never	5	9
No kin in Los Angeles	11	7
No of respondents	(162)	(150)

* No significant difference between low and high urban area samples.

Bell in his comparable study of social areas in the San Francisco Bay Region.[7]

Both samples indicated complacency with their neighborhood and said they were satisfied with it as a home, but in giving their reasons for liking it, they tended to differ. The low-urban sample described their area as a "little community," like a "small town," where "people are friendly and neighborly." The high-urban sample, on the other hand, most frequently mentioned the "convenience to downtown and everything," and spoke often of the "nice people" who "leave you alone and mind their own business." The high-urban sample seemed less committed to remaining in their present area—a higher proportion stating that there were other neighborhoods in the city in which they would rather live.

A tendency toward differential association with populations at a similar level of urbanization is indicated in the visiting patterns of the two samples outside their local areas. The residences of close friends and the meeting places of social circles are almost mutually exclusive for the two samples. Furthermore, when the census tracts in which are located the homes of the friends they visit are categorized by urbanization scores, clear differences appear. The low-urban sample is more apt to have friends in other low-urban areas, while the high-urban sample is apt to visit in other high-urban areas. (See Table 4.)

TABLE 4. RESIDENCE OF FRIENDS VISITED, OUTSIDE OF THE LOCAL AREA, BY URBANIZATION INDEX SCORE[*]

	Low Urban[†]	High Urban[†]
Per cent of friends living in tracts with urbanization index score of		
1–20	13	12
21–40	35	25
41–60	41	33
61–80	8	19
81–100	3	11
N of friends visited	(180)	(162)

[*] Friends' addresses which could not be coded (80 in the Low Urban area, 65 in the High Urban) are excluded.
[†] $P (\chi^2) < .001$.

When it is recalled that these two samples are almost identical with respect to social rank and segregation, the importance of the urbanization dimension is underlined. These visiting patterns refer to well structured friendship relations of probable importance. Such differential association may result from proximity, as well as selective visiting by levels of urbanization. The relative importance of proximity will be measured through the use of the intervening opportunities model. However, even if such differential association is to a large degree a function of spatial proximity, its significance in certain respects would remain. For, if populations at given levels of urbanization interact more intensely within those levels than with other popula-

tions, such interactions should result in fairly stable networks of informal communication and influence. The content of such communications should vary with urbanization.

Summary and Interpretation

In order to investigate empirically the complex of notions surrounding the nature of urban social behavior, the Shevky-Bell typology, applied to sub-areas in Los Angeles County, was used to select two neighborhoods which differed clearly on the index of urbanization. Social rank was not used as the chief factor accounting for differential social participation, as was the case in the studies of Komarovsky, Goldhamer, and others.[8] Instead, rank was controlled, and the urbanization dimension was tested for broad differences in social participation.

It should be noted that this study investigates the effects of urbanization at a *particular* level of rank and segregation; at other levels, the effects of urbanization remain problematical. It is hoped that future studies will clarify, for example, the effects of differential urbanization at higher and lower social ranks, as well as in segregated populations. The Shevky-Bell typology, based upon a three dimensional attribute-space model of urban society, calls attention not only to three separate factors, but also to the possibility that the particular effects of one may be transformed as either or both of the others vary.

However, the urbanization dimension was the focus of the present study. It was not identified with the older notion of urbanism which implies that all city populations are changing in the direction of atomistic, mass society.[9] Instead, it was assumed that there is a continuum of alternative life-styles at the same economic level and that these are concentrated in different urban sub-areas. In this framework, the low-urban areas are just as characteristic of modern urban society as are the high-urban areas. Both types continue to be alternatives in the urban complex. In this view, the Shevky-Bell index of urbanization is a putative means of identifying such variations in "ways of life." Instead of concentrating on urbanism as *a way* of life, the present study was focused upon the variations possible.

Two social aggregates, inhabiting tracts with similar economic rank and ethnicity but varying with respect to the urbanization index, were sampled. The sample populations were then studied by means of reported social participation.

The findings are consistent with the hypothesis that, where rank and ethnicity are equal, differences in the urbanization index will indicate differences in social behavior. Had the index identified populations not significantly different, doubt would have been cast upon its utility at the level of individual social behavior, for the urbanization dimension of modern society, as conceived by Shevky in his theoretical structure, implies such differences in social behavior.[10] However, the present study indicates that the index, constructed primarily with items related to family structure, does identify differences in social participation which are associated with variations in family structure but not derived solely from them. The general validity of the hypothesis must rest upon further studies in Los Angeles and other urban complexes. Although this study and that of Bell indicate the urbanization dimension does affect social participation to an impressive degree, the regularity with which these differences form a continuum at this intersection of social rank and segregation, and the nature of the hypothesized continuum, remain to be spelled out. Still, in the interpretation of the findings here reported, the following implications come to mind:

1. The local area in the contemporary American metropolis may be viewed as attracting population, not only by the economic rank and ethnic composition of the population already in the area, but also by the degree of urbanization characteristic of the area—the way of life common to the older inhabitants.

2. Such areas may attract populations on at least two different functional bases: (1) the demographic and the cultural characteristics of the older settlers, who give the area its "tone," may attract people, as seems true in the low-urban sample, or, (2) the area as a socially neutral, but convenient base of operations for various segmental interests, may attract people as in the high-urban sample. Such different principles of attraction would tend to produce greater homogeneity of background and interest in low-urban areas, and from this similarity a higher degree of community-type behavior and of conformity would be expected.

3. A continuum is hypothesized for nonsegregated, middle-rank areas. At one pole lie the local areas which select a predominantly "old American" population with similar jobs, aspirations, incomes, who wish to raise children, neighbor, participate in local community groups, and, in brief, carry on a life in many ways similar to that of the small towns described by Warner and his associates.[11] At the other pole lie those areas of the city which are more heterogeneous, with fewer children and little interest in the local area as a social arena. Such areas may approach, in many ways, the ideal type of urban environment hypothesized by Wirth.[12]

4. In this perspective, the local area is important as a framework for interaction, as a "social fact," just where it is least repre-

sentative of the total urban society. The small community, as studied by Warner and others, is a very poor example of the urban complex, since it will include the fewest elements of urban society as a whole. At the same time, the high-urban tract as a sample of urban society is only slightly less biased, for in it the local area as a social fact disappears altogether. Thus it is not possible to use either the model of a small, spatially enclosed community or the stereotype of the continually more atomistic mass society in describing social participation in the contemporary metropolis.

There are, however, certain common structural threads running through the fabric of modern society. As Paul Hatt noted, the indices developed by Warner and others to measure social status may be generalized to the total society, since the various methods correlate highly with one universal attribute—occupation.[13] The present approach is, then, to ask: How does this attribute become defined and organized, how does it influence participation, in different sub-areas of the metropolis?

A tentative answer is that the individual's social position is defined differently and his social participation is patterned differently as the focus shifts from the low-urban populations to the high-urban populations. One may envisage the low-urban areas as somewhere between the small town and the conventional picture of metropolitan living. Where the local area is a social fact, where common interests and associations obtain, generalizations derived from small community studies may have validity. For here the individual's status will result, in part, from participation in a known and used local organizational structure and from family ties that are publicly understood.

When, however, high-urban populations are considered, social participations is organized around position in other organizational contexts, as for example, the corporation, politics, the labor union, or perhaps, as Riesman has suggested, categories derived from the popular culture of the mass media.[14] Here also are many individuals whose life, aside from work, is ordered by participation in small informal groups, and informal groups only, floating within the vast culture world of the market and the mass media. In such populations the locally defined community is largely irrelevant to status and participation. Associations are spread geographically, but ordered and concentrated in terms of selected interests. Family, in this context, is still important. It is slightly more important in the high-urban sample described. But it is probably much more private in its reference. In fact, kin relations may be seen as growing in importance just because of the diminished reliance placed upon neighborhood and local community.

What has been sketched above is a tentative model which will allow the use of contributions from earlier research, (studies of small cities, natural areas, the apartment house family, the surburban fringe) within a framework which integrates and orders them in relation to one another. Such a frame of reference also relates, eventually, to the increasing importance of large-scale organizations in a society which allows many alternative life patterns for individuals at the same functional and economic level.

NOTES

1. Donald L. Foley, "Neighbors or Urbanites? The Study of a Rochester District," *The University of Rochester's Studies of Metropolitan Rochester*, Rochester, New York, 1952.
2. Eshref Shevky and Wendell Bell, *Social Area Analysis*, Stanford, California: Stanford University Press, 1955. See also, Eshref Shevky and Marilyn Williams, *The Social Areas of Los Angeles*, Berkeley and Los Angeles: The University of California Press, 1948.
3. For a description of the statistical analysis and testing of the typology, see Wendell Bell, "Economic, Family, and Ethnic Status," *American Sociological Review*, 20 (February, 1955), pp. 45–52.
4. The extension of the study to include two additional sample tracts will be reported later; results are generally consistent with the findings reported here. Rank and segregation are the same in the added tract samples, but the new tracts extend to the extremes of the urbanization index within middle economic rank.
5. Paul Wallin, "A Guttman Scale for Measuring Women's Neighborliness," *American Journal of Sociology*, 49 (November, 1953), pp. 243–246.
6. Stuart A. Queen, "Social Participation in Relation to Social Disorganization," *American Sociological Review*, 14 (April, 1949), pp. 251–256.
7. Wendell Bell (with the assistance of Maryanne Force and Marion Boat), "People of the City," (processed) Stanford University Survey Research Facility, Stanford, California, 1954.
8. Mirra Komarovsky, "The Voluntary Associations of Urban Dwellers," *American Sociological Review*, 11 (December, 1946), pp. 868–896; Herbert Goldhamer, "Voluntary Associations in the United States," unpublished Ph.D. thesis, University of Chicago, 1942.
9. See Louis Wirth, "Urbanism as a Way of Life," *The American Journal of Sociology*, 44 (July, 1938), pp. 1–24 [reprinted in this volume].
10. Shevky and Bell, *op. cit.*, especially Chapter II.
11. See, for example, W. Lloyd Warner and associates, *Democracy in Jonesville*, New York: Harper and Brothers, 1949.
12. Wirth, *op. cit.*
13. Paul K. Hatt, "Stratification in the Mass Society," *American Sociological Review*, 15 (April, 1950), pp. 216–222.
14. David Riesman, in collaboration with Reuel Denny and Nathan Glazer, *The Lonely Crowd, A Study of the Changing American Character*, New Haven: Yale University Press, 1950, especially Chs. X, XI, XII.

19. The Slum: Its Nature, Use, and Users   John R. Seeley

The sociocultural sub-areas of urban communities that command the great bulk of scholarly and public attention are slums and suburbs. John R. Seeley's paper on the nature of slums is divided into two parts. In the first part, he discusses the social definition of a "slum" and whether slums are eradicable. Seeley concludes that sub-areas called slums will probably always be with us. The definition of a slum area, he argues, is relative to the standards of a society; when general standards are raised those areas and persons at the bottom of the social ladder will continue to be thought of as slum communities and slum-dwellers. Furthermore, the slum satisfies the social and psychological needs not only of those who dwell in them, but also of individuals at the top of the income scale who profit from the availability of a disadvantaged population. In the second part of the paper Seeley examines the variety of groups and types of individuals who inhabit slums and the reasons why they live in them. Some persons live there more or less permanently because the other communities of the city do not provide a suitable environment for them. Other slum-dwellers are there by necessity too, but move in and out in response to the capacity of the larger community to satisfy their need for housing, jobs, and a way of life. According to Seeley, a considerable proportion of the persons living in slums are there because they choose the area deliberately. The slum is a community from which they can launch their drive for social and economic advancement, or else it contains a population that offers a ready market for the goods and services the entrepreneurial slum-dweller can provide.

In view of the fundamental ineradicability of the slum phenomenon in human society, Seeley is led throughout his paper to consider the probable impact of urban renewal and redevelopment programs. He concludes that what these programs usually accomplish is the redistribution of the slum population and slum areas to other parts of the urban community.

John R. Seeley has served as Dean of the Center for the Study of Democratic Institutions in Santa Barbara, California, and was formerly Professor of Sociology and Chairman of the Department at Brandeis University. He is the author of *The Americanization of the Unconscious* (1967), *Crestwood Heights* (1956), and several other books.

To cling to a dream or a vision may be heroic—or merely pathetic. Slum-clearance, slum renewal, or, more grandiosely, the extirpation of the slum, is for many planners just such a dream: brightly imagined, cherished, fought for, often seeming—but for stupidity here or cupidity or malice there—at very fingertip's reach. To ask how realistic this orientation is, what is possible at what costs and to whose benefit, is almost as idle-seeming an enterprise to many as it would be to raise doubts about the sanctity of American motherhood or the soundness of the American home. If a direct challenge to the orthodox view seems too bold, let us tease at the fabric of the dream only a little, to see how it appears—and perhaps still shimmers—in the cooler light of moderately disinterested curiosity as against the warm glow of programmatic commitment.

I

The very notion of a "slum" depends on a number of more primitive notions. We must invoke at least—(and I believe only) —the notions of

Space
Population
A value-position defining "goods" and "ills"
Dispersion in the distribution of any good (or ill) among the population so that, in that respect, all men are not equal
Correlation[1] among goods (or ills) so that one good tends to be attended by another, rather than offset by an ill
Concentration (in space) of those who have the most (and also those who have the least) of what there is to get

Any alteration in any of the realities that lie behind these six terms changes what "the slum problem" is; the elimination of any corresponding reality eliminates slums; and anything short of that guarantees the slum's survival. It cannot be over-emphasized that no change in the plane of living—as for example, the doubling of all real incomes—would remove the problem. It is not a matter of absolutes. In a society where nearly everyone walks, the man with a horse is a rich man, and the man without is a poor man; in a society

Reprinted by the permission of the *Journal of the American Institute of Planners* (Volume XXV, No. 1, February, 1959).

where nearly everyone has (or could have) a car, the man who can only afford a bicycle is *by that much* disadvantaged, and, potentially, a slum dweller. The criteria for what is a slum—as a social *fact*—are subjective and relative: for one brand of mystic this world is a slum (relative to the next) and for another there *is* no slum, because the proper objects of desire are as available in one area as another.

Since, for the planner, space is an eternal datum and population is also given, at least in the moderately long run, any attempt to "deal with" the slum must turn on affecting in some way one of the other factors. Since, commonly, the value-position from which goods or ills are to be defined is uncritically received from the culture or projected by the individual planner, this too appears as something given—although this unexamined accept-ance undoubtedly leads to much of the defeat and frustration which the planner encounters and manufacturers. We shall have to return to this question of values later, but for the moment we may ask, what is possible if indeed a single value-scheme—the value-scheme of middle-class materialism—is applicable? The answer, if the analysis is correct so far, is obvious: we can attempt an attack on any one or on all of the remaining factors: dispersion, correlation, and concentration. These are discussed in decreasing order of difficulty.

To attempt to diminish the dispersion in the distribution of any one good—say, money—is actually a matter of high politics rather than "planning" in the customary sense. Two courses are classically open politically: the periodic redistribution of goods gained; and the blocking of oppor-tunities to gain them. An example of the first is the combination of income taxation or succession-duties with "equalizing" distribution of the proceeds—as, for

instance, by differential "social security benefits." An example of the second—insofar as it is effective at all—lies in anti-trust or antimonopoly proceedings, more particularly in the form which they have taken in recent years, that is, the prevention of particularly blatant potential concentra-tions before they actually occur. Not only is this whole route attended by vexing ethical and political problems, but also limits are set for it by the culture and, in the ultimate analysis, by economics itself. We may or may not be anywhere near those limits in North America, but it is obvious that dispersion-reduction beyond a certain point may, in fact, reduce the total of what there is to distribute—may, in fact, reduce it to the point where the least advantaged are in absolute, though not relative, terms more disadvantaged than before. We may discover limits and optimum points by trial-and-error or experiment in the course of history, but this clearly falls outside the planning procedure. This leaves us with correlation and concentration to examine.

An attack upon the correlation of goods with goods and ills with ills, in the life of any person or group, is notoriously difficult. Nothing multiplies like misfor-tune or succeeds like success. As the work of Bradley Buell[2] so unequivocally demon-strated for the whole range of problems with which social work deals, disaster is so wedded to further disaster in the lives of families that the combined case-load of innumerable separate agencies in a city is very largely represented by only a small core of "multi-problem families," families in which economic dependency may be the child of poor nutrition and poor physical health and the father of overcrowding and desperate family relations and poor mental health—and so, in a new and horrible incest, in turn the father of its own father, more economic dependency

. . . and so on. And what Buell finds for social work problems is not restricted to that field. Within single problem-fields themselves, diseases tend to follow diseases in the field of medicine, just as one bungled social relation generally follows another, as students of society observe, and one psychological catastrophe is the ancestor of the next in the case history of almost any psychiatric patient. Every social agency, every "caretaker institution,"[3] is concerned to break up or diminish these correlations or to palliate their effects; but the whole apparatus can deal with only the few, worst cases; and nothing short of a society quite different from any yet seriously contemplated is likely to make sensible inroads upon the fact of correlation itself. In any case, this too falls outside the domain of local, or even regional, planning. So we are left with geographic concentration as our last point, seemingly, of promising attack. And it is this point, if I am not mistaken, that the weight of the planners' planning has so far largely fallen.

The problem of "deconcentration" may be seen as the problem of moving from the present state of a heterogeneity of neighborhoods each homogeneous within itself to a homogeneity of neighborhoods each heterogeneous within itself. Upon succeeding, we should no longer be able to write of *The Gold Coast and the Slum*[4] but only, perhaps, of the gold coast within the slum and the slum within the gold coast. It is hard to doubt that—if we are willing to pay the price—here we *can* be successful. And it is equally hard to doubt that some increases in positive goods and some diminutions in positive evils would follow upon such a geographic transfer of the "variance" in fortune from the "between communities" label to the "within communities" one.

No one, perhaps, has put the case for the positive benefits so well as Catherine Bauer who brings knowledge, experience, vision, and passion to her task.[5] She argues, in reality, from the full depth of her feelings, but, in form at least, from primitive democratic principles against the one-class, one-occupation, one-economic-level community and for the broad-spectrum neighborhood where a child may at least encounter the aged, the ethnically strange, the poorer, the richer, the better, the worse, the different, and, therefore, the educative and exciting. The essence of her argument, I think, is that since the efficacy of our type of democracy depends on the achievement of consensus even in a highly differentiated society, whatever militates against "understanding" diminishes the national welfare. This is a telling point, especially if lack of direct exposure does militate against "understanding," and if increased exposure promotes it.

Another argument for "deconcentration" can be made, I believe, on negative grounds; and for some it may have considerable force. The argument is that the very concentration of evils or ills is itself an additional ill or evil—quite separate from the mere sum of the evils concentrated. I think this is a valid point. Anyone who has watched a child checking quite equally his separate bruises and scratches before bedtime, only to be suddenly overborne emotionally, as their totality dawns upon him, will know what is meant at an individual level.[6] The pervasive air of squalor of a Tobacco Road or any of its innumerable counterparts is, I think, differentiable from the separately existent miseries that otherwise go to make it up.

However, even at this level of analysis, things are not so simple as they seem. If it is true that the concentration of the defeated and despairing casts a pall, a psychological smog, of defeatism and despair, it is also true that "misery loves company" and that support to bear the hurt comes chiefly from the hurt. Beyond this, awareness of one's disabilities and disasters is heightened if they must be borne in the presence of the able and successful; and this awareness—unless it can lead to a remedy—is itself an additional, and perhaps disabling, disaster. It is also to be noted that to the extent that compresent misery adds to misery at one end of the scale, the "slum," compresent abundance adds to the sense of abundance and security at the other end, the elite community or "gold coast." Thus, at the very least, "deconcentration" is not likely to be an unmixed good to anyone or even a mixed good to everyone.

Things are much less simple again if we are willing to be realistic and to recall for re-examination one of the premises accepted for the sake of argument earlier: that the question may properly be examined at all in the light of the planner's value-system, or the one he assumes to represent the society at large. The first possibility we shall not even examine; few would argue seriously that an urban plan should rest ultimately purely on the private preferences of the urban planner who plans to please himself. The second is worth some study.

It is a persistent illusion characterizing, I believe, only the middle-class meliorist, and only the middle-class meliorist in America—where it is least true!—that there is some particular case-applicable value-system that may be ascribed to the society at large. I do not doubt that *at a very high level of abstraction* consensus around value-statements can be obtained: America believes in justice; it simply divides on segregation. America believes in due process; it divides, however, on the propriety of what happens at many a Congressional investigation. What is at issue regarding the slum is a case and not an abstraction, and around it Americans divide, not simply in terms of slum-dwellers versus non-slum-dwellers, but within as well as between both groups.

It must be recognized at the outset, I believe, that the slum is almost as much a "social necessity" for some sizable segment of the elite as is, say, an adequate, centralized, and appropriately located medical center. I do not mean this only in the relatively trivial sense, referred to earlier, in which those who enjoy the greater proportion of social goods also desire protection against the debris entailed in their production. I mean it in the quite literal sense that, like the supermarket in its locus, or the central business district in its locus, the slum provides on an appropriate site a set of services called out by, produced for, delivered to, and paid for by the self-same elite whose wives are likely to adorn with their names the letterheads of committees to wipe out or "clean up" the slum. Many of the services provided by the slum are not within the monetary reach of slum people: the bulk of the bootlegging, the call-girl services, a great part of what some feel able to call "vice," the greater part of the gambling, and the whole set of connections that connect the underworld with the overworld serve the latter rather than the former, and are as much a response to effective (that is, money-backed) demand as is the price of a share of A. T. & T. or General Motors.

Given this "effective demand," taking it for granted that such demand will indeed call out "supply" somewhere, the question for the planner—at least in the moderately long run—must not be *whether*? but *where*? To the degree that the services are highly specialized, as many of them are,[7] there seems no economically appropriate locus for them too far from the core of the central city proper. To the degree that the services are not so specialized, they will generally have already found their way— by a combination of economic logic with police pressure—to the ring of satellite municipalities immediately outside the city itself.

If these services, and a whole chain of other "opportunities" that the slum presents, were solely of interest and profit to an elite group who already had most of what there was to get, a case might be made out for the abolition of the slum (if possible) as being in the public interest. (There is a sense in which this is true just as, no doubt, sinlessness or prohibition are in the public interest.) But this view of a one-sided exploitative interest in the maintenance of the slum by *outside* landlords or "service" users simply will not fit the facts. The facts are that the slum-dwellers also have sizable investments, of interest, of sentiment, and of opportunity, both in the site of these services and its appurtnenances and in the way of life that goes on there.

Slums differ, of course, and I have lived intensively only in one, Back-of-the-Yards, Chicago, in the early 'forties, and, together with others,[8] have studied another, "Relocation Area A" in Indianapolis. I do not intend to give in detail any account of the former, especially as the main features of a somewhat similar area were sketched in William Foote Whyte's *Street Corner Society*.[9] Something of the intensity, excitement, rewardingness, and color of the slum that I experienced is missing from his account of his slum, either because his *was* different or because sociological reporting militates against vibrancy of description (or, perhaps, because we cut into the material of our participant-observer experience in different ways). In any case, I would have to say, for what it is worth, that no society I have lived in

before or since, seemed to me to present to so many of its members so many possibilities and actualities of fulfillment of a number at least of basic human demands: for an outlet for aggressiveness, for adventure, for a sense of effectiveness, for deep feelings of belonging without undue sacrifice of uniqueness or identity, for sex satisfaction, for strong if not fierce loyalties, for a sense of independence from the pervasive, omnicompetent, omniscient authority-in-general, which at that time still overwhelmed the middle-class child to a greater degree than it now does. These things had their prices, of course—not all values can be simultaneously maximized. But few of the inhabitants whom I reciprocally took "slumming" into middle-class life understood it, or, where they did, were at all envious of it. And, be it asserted, this was not a matter of "ignorance" or incapacity to "appreciate finer things." It was merely an inability to see one moderately coherent and sense-making satisfaction-system which they didn't know, as preferable to the quite coherent and sense-making satisfaction-system they did know. This is not analogous to Beethoven versus boogie-woogie, but more nearly to the choice between English and French as a vehicle of expression. (I will not even say which is which.)

Possibly I can give a clearer impression of the variety of dwellers in one slum and the variety of uses they make of it by quoting at length from the published report of the Indianapolis area that we studied. Section II of this paper is accordingly taken from that report.[10]

II Types of Slum-Dwellers

There are always, of course, innumerable ways of classifying a population so immensely various as that of the slum, or, perhaps, of any urban area. We were struck again and again (both when we examined the way in which these people thought about themselves and when we examined behavior objectively) by two major differences: the difference between necessity and opportunity, and the difference between permanence and change.

Quite obviously, for many the slum constitutes a set of opportunities for behavior which they want (at least at the conscious level) to indulge in or to be permitted. For others, equally obviously, the slum constitutes a set of necessities to which, despite their wants, they have been reduced.

Similarly—though changes are *possible* —some are in the slum and feel they are in the slum on a temporary basis only, and others are there and feel they are there to stay. These distinctions establish four major types:

1. The "permanent necessitarians"
2. The "temporary necessitarians"
3. The "permanent opportunists"
4. The "temporary opportunists"

The meaning of these terms[11] will become clear as we proceed. Schematically, these might be represented as follows:

TABLE 1. PRINCIPAL SLUM TYPES: AREA "A"

	Relation	
Time	Necessity	Opportunity
Permanent	1	3
Temporary	2	4

Within each of these primary types, the data cast up a dozen or more fairly obvious subtypes whose characteristics are worth recording. The chart below (Table 2), which locates some twelve of these, fills in some details for the chart above (Table 1) and gives an orderly way of arranging

TABLE 2. TYPES AND SUBTYPES OF SLUM-DWELLERS: AREA "A"

Primary reason for slum involvement

Likeliest term of involvement	Necessity	Opportunity
Permanent	1. a. The indolent b. The "adjusted" poor c. Social outcasts	3. a. Fugitives b. Unfindables c. "Models" d. "Sporting Crowd"
Temporary	2. a. The respectable poor b. The "trapped"	4. a. Beginners b. "Climbers" c. "Entrepreneurs"

what is to follow in this section.

1. The Permanent Necessitarians Those in the slum permanently and by necessity evidently include at least three subtypes: the "indolent," the "adjusted poor," and the "social outcasts." In Area "A," these three subtypes seem to constitute the greater part of that "hard and unmovable core," which in turn constitutes about half of the population still living in Redevelopment Commission property. These are the people who feel they "cannot" leave the area, and who will or can do nothing to find alternative housing.

The "indolent" are those whose most striking characteristic[12] is a general apathy or immobility. Whether from inherited characteristics, disease, maleducation, malnutrition, the experience of perennial defeat, religiously founded "resignation," or mere valuation of other things—these are the do-nothings, those who "have no get up and go," those whose immobility is grounded now in their very physique or character.

Whatever the cause for the "indolence," and no matter what miracles feeding, better care, or therapy (physical or psychological) could accomplish for such people in the very long run, at least in the short run no plan looking to them for even moderate effort or initiative is a feasible one. "Care" and "custody" are the only public-policy alternatives to neglect;[13] rehabilitation, if possible at all, would be a long, hard, slow process of uncertain outcome or economy.

The "*adjusted poor*" represent similarly, though likely less immovably, a population living in the slum by necessity but adapted by deep-seated habit (and now almost by preference) to its ways. This group represents the concentration in the area of the destitute, or nearly destitute, whose adaptation consists in "acceptance" of the nearly unfit-for-human-habitation shacks and shanties, holes and cellars of the area —provided only they be available at "that low rent." Among them are many of those who value independence fiercely enough that they would rather cling to this most marginal physical existence in independence than accept relative comfort in dependency—even supposing they could have the latter. (At least this is their first and habitual reaction. Some few who were persuaded later to move into Lockefield Gardens are now glad they made the exchange of relative independence for relative comfort.) In this group are many of the very old, the "single" women with many dependents, and other persons prevented in one way or another from working continuously enough or at pay high enough to qualify for a more respectable poverty. Many, if not most of these, are still in the area in Redevelopment Commission property, "unable to move" and unlikely, in the absence of harder necessity than they yet know, to do so.

The last subgroup among the "permanent necessitarians" are the "*social outcasts*."[14] Police evidence, tradition, and common gossip have it that these people were relatively prominent in Area "A" at one time, but left when redevelopment became imminent or even earlier. These people included the "winoes," the drug addicts, peddlers and pushers, the "hustlers," prostitutes and pimps, and others whose marginal, counter-legal, or "shady" activities both excluded them from better-organized neighborhoods and made the slum a more receptive or less rejecting habitat.

In any case, by 1955 these had largely disappeared from the area. By that date, all that was left of this group seemed to be those living in common-law relationships, a handful of "winoes," and a few others living habitually in unconventional ways, for whom the slum provided escape, refuge, sympathy, tolerance, and even some stimulation by the very fact of their being together.

2. The Temporary Necessitarians The "*respectable poor*," who are in the slum by necessity but whose residence there is or may be more temporary, usually spend a good part of their lives in it—now in and now out, although mostly in. Though slum-dwellers, and often as poor financially as the "adjusted poor," these people are unadjusted or unreconciled to the slum in the sense that all their values and identifications and most of their associations are outside it. They pay their bills, mind their own business, remain well inside the law, hold the aspirations and, within their means, practice the lifeways of a socially higher class, most of whose members far outrank them economically.

Some of these wind up in public housing, but more often than not they resist such a solution, hoping that "things will take a turn for the better," a turn that will permit them to live more nearly where they feel they belong and how they feel they should. For many of these, redevelopment provided either the money (if they owned their homes) or the incentive or both that made that "turn for the better" reality rather than wish.

The "*trapped*" are people who, having bought a home (or had one left to them by a parent or relative) at a time when the area was not so run down, one day find themselves living right in the middle of a slum. Blight filters insensibly in and around them, destroying the value of their property. Though many remain, through a program such as redevelopment many more are induced finally to get out.

3. The Permanent Opportunists Those who are in the slum to stay, primarily because of the opportunities it affords, are the fugitives, the unfindables, the "models" and the "sporting crowd."

The *fugitives* are really of two types: those whose encounters with the law or the credit agency have led them into a life of subterfuge and flight, more or less permanent; and those whose nature or experience has decided them to flee the exigencies of rigorous competition in a better area in their own business or profession.

The former, probably not numerous, are really using the possibility of anonymity which the slum offers. To them it offers literal sanctuary or asylum, a cover or protection from the too-pressing inquiries of the more respectable world. These people, poorly circumstanced for the most part, had also left Area "A" in large numbers before our study began.

The latter, seeking escape from the status struggles of the world outside, or looking for a more easily maintained economic niche, occupied some of the best property within the area, and when catapulted out by redevelopment, found successful ways to maintain themselves and even to enhance their position outside the area. Many of them were merchants, doctors, lawyers, or other professionals who had served that part of the population that was later to migrate to the "better neighborhoods" with them. (They resembled the "climbers" discussed below, except that they did not want or expect to escape from their refuge in the slums.)

Somewhat like the first group of fugitives are the "*unfindables.*" By definition, we had no contact with them, although we did have contact with those who had had contact. From their descriptions, there is suggested the presence in the population (before the advent of redevelopment) of a sizable "floating population," who could not readily be located, rarely got counted in any census, and lived a shadowy kind of existence both in terms of location and social identity. These were not so much people in flight as people whose individualism of outlook and whose detachment from urban ways led them to seek no clear social identity (or to operate under many). Some could be found by laboriously following a chain of vague touch-and-go relationships, some only by sorting out and tracing down a variety of "names" and nicknames under which each had serially or simultaneously lived. Most could not be found at all—with our resources or the census-taker's. These, too, had mostly disappeared from the area by the time we came, although some were left, and the memory of others was still green.

The "*models*" constitute a rare but interesting type. These are people who have somehow become, or conceived of themselves as, social or religious missionaries. They are people who stay in the slum (actually, or as they interpret their own behavior) primarily in order to "furnish an example" or "bring a message" to "the others," the "less cultured," or the "unsaved." Some of them are people who were first among "the trapped," but who have adapted further by finding a satisfying permanent life in the slum; the satisfaction consists in bringing culture or religious light to "those still less fortunate." Some of them patently find some martyr-like satisfaction in such "service," but others more soberly find genuine relatedness and utility in this adaptation.

Some of these remained in Area "A"; some went early. Those who went seemed shortly to find themselves cast in the same role in their new neighborhoods.

Finally among the (relatively) permanent opportunists are the members of the "*sporting crowd*." This term, in local use, evidently connotes a range of characters noted primarily for their jollity and informality—perhaps a certain breezy off-handedness is their distinguishing characteristic—rather than for any necessary preference for illegal or marginal activities as such. They live in the slum for a complex of reasons. First, living in the slum leaves them more money to spend on "other things"; second, having spent a large share of their incomes on those "other things," what is left is only enough for slum rents; third, the slum is the place to meet others similarly situated; fourth, the slum itself provides (or, rather, in the case of Area "A," did provide once) facilities for their pursuits, such as taverns, book-making and other betting facilities, and so on. Marginal to this type are those who have been described to us as ranging from "the roughnecks who make it unsafe for others to be in the area" to the less violent

types who just create nuisances, which, as one woman explains, ". . . cause you to be afraid to have a friend visit, because you never know whether someone is going to walk in on you without any clothes on." The informality, rather than roughness or nudity as such, is the hallmark of this group.

These, too, by now have mostly fled the area.

4. The Temporary Opportunists It remains to describe the temporary opportunists, a most important group both because of their numbers and because the slum of these people is a way—perhaps the only way—to the pursuit of those things that American culture has taught them are worth pursuing: "self-improvement," independence, property, a savings account, and so on. It may be only for this group that the general reader will feel fully sympathetic, and it may be only here that he will ask himself, "How are these people to get where we want them to get, if we systematically destroy the slums which are the traditional, if unspoken-of, way of getting there?" The question is a good one, and the study leaves its answering to the wisdom of the agencies, public and private, charged or self-charged with such responsibility.

We find that in this group there are three subtypes: the "beginners," the "climbers," and the "entrepreneurs."

The "*beginners*" are mostly the unattached immigrants to the city who have neither helpful kin nor access to powerful agencies of assimilation, such as churches and ethnic associations. The slum is simply their "area of first settlement" where they rest on arrival in the city not for "the pause that refreshes" so much as for the pause that instructs, the pause that permits them a precarious period in which to "get oriented," find a first job, and learn the elements of urban living. Many of these are young married couples, some with first children, trying to learn simultaneously to be citizens, husbands and wives, and parents in the urban manner. Their slim resources, financial, educational, and psychological, necessitate a place to stay that will not strain these resources much further; the slum furnishes an opportunity to rest, to gather fresh forces, and to prepare for moving on as soon as may be— if disease, misfortune, or the fortune of more children does not exert more "drag" than can be overcome. From this source the city replenishes its labor force at the lower economic levels, and its "respectable poor" and other types at the lower social rungs.

The "*climbers*" are somewhat similar to the beginners except that they may have been in the city for some time and that their plans are somewhat more long-term and ambitious. These are the ones who live in the slum in what amounts to a period of apprenticeship, self-denial and self-sacrifice with a view to accumulating enough goods, money, and know-how to leap later into a much "better" area, a considerably higher standard of living, and a much more "respectable" way of life. They are "saving"—out of the very stuff of their own lives—the material and non-material means of achieving better housing, greater status, "success," and home-ownership.

For many of these, the period of stay becomes protracted because the dream tends to become embellished even as savings accumulate, and the time to move seems always "a little later, when we have a little more." Redevelopment, for many of these, helped toward a settlement with

reality by putting period to an unduly prolonged stay in the slums or overextended plans; for a few, it cut off the possibility of any great "improvement" at all, insofar as it caught them in the initial phases of their plans. Some of those thus "caught" simply moved into neighboring slums to begin again. Some abandoned plans for ownership and became renters outside the area.

Last are the "*entrepreneurs*," a special class of climbers, oriented similarly to the climbers, mostly more ambitious, but saving out of businesslike enterprises—rather than their own miseries—the wherewithal to escape misery in due time. Beginning usually as people of small financial means, they establish a small business or, more frequently, make the slum itself their business. They somehow (frequently by a kind of financial skin-of-your-teeth operation) get hold of a duplex or house that can be "subdivided." That part of it in which they do not themselves reside must, if possible, pay the costs of the whole, and moreover, yield "a little something" so that more property can be bought as time goes by. Often they purchase property, first, in the slum and, later, in better neighborhoods. In the case of at least one person in the area, a drug store was eventually purchased out of the money thus saved by living in the slums.

This kind of person lives a large part of his life in the slum, but usually leaves about the time he reaches fifty. He may by then own enough slum property to live very comfortably in a better neighborhood; or he may out of his small-scale slum business operation develop a larger business in a different area, becoming thus an undifferentiable element of the respectable business community.

III

If the earlier part of this paper made— or even labored—the point that in no way within reach of local planning could the slum be "wiped out," and if the second part drew attention via a particular case to the general situation of a vast variety of people coexisting in the slum's complex fastnesses, what, it may be asked, happens when planned steps are nevertheless taken to "do something" about an area, in this case to "redevelop" it. No general answer can be given—it depends on the steps and the people—except that the greater part of what happens is a redistribution of phenomena in space. We say "the greater part of what happens" because, as is evident from the original report,[15] this is not all that happens: in the very act of relocation *some* "positive" potentialities

that were formerly only latent are released or actualized. As far as the redistribution in space is concerned, it is hard to say whether it should be viewed as "deconcentration": it is rather like a resifting and resorting, a speeding up of the city's "natural" ecological processes, with results both "good" and "bad," certainly unintended as well as intended. In this process, opportunities are created for some and destroyed for others, or very often for the same person; certainly, lifelong adjustments or habituations, comfortable and uncomfortable, productive and non-productive, are overset, disturbed, interrupted, or destroyed. Moreover, in most cases one population is advantaged and another further disadvantaged, and it is not at all clear that the balance is tipped in favor of those who initially had least —perhaps, rather, the contrary.

NOTES

1. "Positive correlation," of course.
2. See Bradley Buell, *Community Planning for Human Services* (New York: Columbia University Press, (1952).
3. To use the phrase of Erich Lindemann.
4. See Harvey Zorbaugh, *The Gold Coast and the Slum* (Chicago: University of Chicago Press, 1937).
5. See, e.g., Catherine Bauer, "Good Neighborhoods," *The Annals of the American Academy of Political and Social Science*, Vol. 242 (1945), pp. 104–115.
6. Cf. Bruno Bettelheim, *Love is Not Enough* (Glencoe: Free Press, 1950).
7. Compare, for instance, the (twelve at least) institutionalized sets of provisions for sex satisfaction demanded and supplied in a large mid-Western metropolis simply out of the changes to be rung on gender, race, and activity as against passivity. Omitting further variations and refinements, and using an obvious code, we have: (*MNA–MNP*), (*MNA–MWP*), (*MNP–MWA*), (*MWA–MWP*), (*FNA–FNP*), (*FNA–FWP*), (*FNP–FWA*), (*FWA–FWP*), (*MN–FN*), (*MN–FW*), (*MW–FN*) and (*MW–FW*).
8. Mr. Donald A. Saltzman and Dr. B. H. Junker.
9. Second edition (Chicago: University of Chicago Press, 1958).
10. *Redevelopment: Some Human Gains and Losses* (Indianapolis: Community Surveys, 1956), pp. 48–59. Field work by Mr. Donald A. Saltzman

and others; report by Mr. Saltzman, Dr. B. H. Junker, and the author in collaboration.
11. The distinction—like other human distinctions—must not be "overworked." The difference betweeen necessity and opportunity is largely subjective—a necessity welcomed with joy is often regarded as an opportunity; an opportunity accepted only with regret may be construed as a necessity. Even "permanent" and "temporary" refer largely subjectively to expectations and intentions, though they also partly (on that account) refer objectively to probabilities of later behavior.
12. It should not be overlooked that we have classified only by the most obvious characteristic. Many people have several characteristics, e.g., one could find examples of the "indolent-adjusted poor" or the "adjusted poor and trapped."
13. "Neglect," as used here, means "leaving them alone" or "not interfering" with the "natural" process by which these people are able to get along and to subsist.
14. They are so classified although some of them belong no doubt among the permanent opportunists (those who feel they *chose* the slum as a place of operation rather than that they were excluded from better areas) and some (those few who find their way to "respectable" roles) among the "temporary necessitarians." The peculiar arrow in Chart 2 symbolizes this difficulty of classification.
15. *Ibid*, pp. 67–143.

20. The Suburban Community   Herbert J. Gans
and Its Way of Life

The development of the contemporary American suburb has led to a vast outpouring of commentary in the popular press, most of it satirical about the habits of the suburbanite or critical of the impoverished moral quality of suburban life. Gans challenges the view that whatever may be at fault with middle-class American life is the result of the suburban settlement pattern. He admits that many suburbs around large central cities have distinctive social forms, that their spatial organization is less dense, more haphazard than cities, and that they offer amenities and facilities which are sometimes more luxurious and in other places less commodious than big cities. However, Gans attributes the unique characteristics of suburban culture not to these spatial and environmental factors but rather to the family, social class, and ethnic characteristics which the residents of the suburbs bring with them when they settle there. He defends his viewpoint by describing the neighboring habits, the values and interests, and the political process in different suburban communities, to show that they differ markedly depending upon whether their inhabitants are working class, lower-middle class or upper-middle class.

Herbert J. Gans is Professor of City Planning at Massachusetts Institute of Technology. Several of his published works are cited on page 70 of this volume.

This paper attempts a brief description and an even briefer evaluation of the surburban community and the surburban way of life. The purpose of the analysis is to consider the major variables that affect both of these, and more specifically, to propose two hypotheses: First, that there is no one suburban community or way of life, but that the phenomena which we see in suburbia can be explained by and large by the behavior patterns and norms associated with the age-group and the classes who have moved there. And second, that the difference between the suburbs and the city have been wildly exaggerated, and that once we take age and class into account, the remaining differences are relatively minor. These two hypotheses then lead to a logical evaluative conclusion: that the major problems to be found in suburbia are those associated with the life-cycle and the class position of the people involved.

I shall not attempt to define what I mean by suburb now: the definition that I have in mind will emerge as I develop my analysis. Let me say only that I shall discuss primarily—although not exclusively—the low density, single family housing areas that have sprung up outside the city limits of most Canadian and American metropoli in the last fifteen years to house the young white middle class. Some of these areas are what S. D. Clark calls packaged suburbs—and since I have been studying one of the Levittowns, these are what I know best. Others

Paper read at the Eastern Canadian Sociological Association Conference, Toronto, February 15, 1963. The full study of Levittown reported herein has been written up in *The Levittowners* (New York: Pantheon Books, 1967); also published in Laura Balbo and Guido Martinotti, *Metropoli e Sottocomunitá* (Italy: Marsilio Editori, 1966). Reprinted by permission.

are small subdivisions which are scattered all over the once rural landscape. Although there are some significant differences between these two types of suburban subdivision, they do not loom large in the kind of analysis I shall attempt, and I shall treat them as one.

From a historical perspective, the packaged suburbs are perhaps the most novel element of the suburban growth, for while there have been company towns and large subdivisions before, the pre-planned community which is not a company town is a new combination of old elements. But beyond that, the post-war suburbia is really not novel at all. It is only the latest phase of the urban growth process, the expansion of the city—albeit outside the city limits—in a normal pattern. As always this expansion follows the major transportation routes, and as always the move is made by young people, who find that raising a family in the city has become difficult or undesirable. In times past, the people who moved to the outer edges of the urban area were either very rich, or of an income level that could not afford rowhouses or two-family dwellings. Today, the availability of the automobile, and the improvements in mass production and mass financing of housing has made it possible for these latter to move into single family houses.

Why they do so is, I think, fairly obvious. It is easier to raise children in a house than in an apartment building. Not only is there more space inside and outside, but the supervision of small children is much facilitated. A mother can put her children in the backyard, or even on the street, and can do other things without worrying about the safety or the quality of the playmates of her children. If she is a middle-class person—and she usually is—she believes supervision to be important, and

rejects the working class norm that older siblings can take care of younger ones, and that by the time the child, or the male child, is six, it can be allowed to run loose.

In addition to the fact that people get much more space for relatively little more money, they seem to feel that renting is a waste of money; owning a house gives them an equity or promise of one. But perhaps even more important than the financial equity is the emotional one: the desire to be the owner of four walls, within which one is in control of one's destiny. Privacy from the rest of the world, and the freedom to do what one wishes within these walls is perhaps especially important to people whose privacy and freedom is a limited in their worklives, and in many other spheres as well. And finally, there is a desire for land, a garden to work in as well as a wish to own some land, which can be traced back to the rural tradition of those of Anglo-Saxon background and of the children of European peasants as well. In short, I would agree with S. D. Clark in that most people come to suburbia because of the house, and would add only the home and the land to this formulation. In the rest of the paper, I want to discuss the community and the way of life that is associated with house, home and land.

II

Sociology has always paid a great deal of attention to the concept of community: the idea of an aggregate of people who occupy a common and bounded territory in which they establish and participate in shared institutions. This emphasis perhaps reflects the fact that the pioneers of American sociology stemmed from and favored rural and small town America. When and where the economy was based on land, the communities that grew up around the production of marketing of agricultural goods played a significant role in people's lives. Moreover, the technology of that era required that people be relatively close to their work, both in the rural areas and in the cities, so that economy, community, and for that matter, way of life were interrelated and affected by the costs and frictions of space. But today, most of our economic institutions are little concerned with spatial factors: they need to be accessible to the large markets, but even then have considerable freedom of location. The same is true of those parts of the labor force who have a relatively high amount of job security. Once the fear of job loss is gone people can reside in what are called bedroom communities, although it would be more correct to call them child-rearing ones.

But what kinds of communities are these? I have already noted that most people buy a house, with only a sidelong glance at the people who are to be their neighbors to make sure that these appear to be compatible. Upper middle class people are likely to consider the quality of the schools; Catholic, the presence of a church; and Jews, the availability of coreligionists, but for the most part, non-house concerns are minor in the purchase decision.

Once people have moved into the house, their horizon broadens the spaces beyond. Women, restricted in their mobility by children, and in many cases by a little noticed difficulty in using the automobile, become involved with the block or the street-front, both for social contact with neighbors so as to escape at least temporarily the long hours of childish conversation and for mutual aid in everyday life. And homeowners, who are concerned with maintaining the value and status image of their house, must make sure that their

neighbors share their concern, and thus there develops on every block a social system devoted to exerting the social control necessary to maintain the houses and front-lawns on the street to a common standard of upkeep.

Now some people, especially in the working class, find many of their friends on the block as well, so that for them, it is a vital part of their social universe. But most people realize that too much social intimacy with the people close by can have undesirable results as easily as desirable ones, and look elsewhere for new friends. They go to churches, social and activity clubs, as well as civic organizations to find friends—and this explains much of the hyperactivity that is found in many new suburbs. Voluntary associations, be they secular or sacred, classify people not only by subtler divisions of age and class than house price does initially, but they also classify by norms affecting leisure time. Thus, a Methodist has somewhat different recreational standards than a Presbyterian, and so does a person who joins an organization set up to benefit children as compared with one who joins a lodge or a veterans organization—especially since the latter is in some ways the suburban equivalent of the neighborhood tavern.

In any case, regardless of where friends are found, the suburban resident eventually establishes a set of friendships that may be scattered all over the subdivision, or even over adjacent ones, thus involving him in life beyond the house and the block.

Most people do not remain active in the organizations to which they have flocked in the search for friends, but the organizations remain, and they are an important part of life in the suburbs, at least for an active minority. Some are people who participate for occupational reasons: lawers and insurance salesmen, for example, who can establish new contacts as well as a reputation for community service. Others are people who enjoy organizational activity in itself, because it permits them to have the feeling of usefulness or power they do not get on the job or in the kitchen. And for yet others, notably in the upper middle class, community activity is an accepted part of a way of life that stresses activity and service as ends in themselves. But beyond what these organizations do for people active in them, they exist because there are public services which either cannot be carried out by the local government, or which are carried out by non-governmental agencies because people enjoy doing them, or are unwilling to pay for them—and because it satisfies a desire for service to others based on Judaic-Christian concepts of charity to help those who need it. Moreover, there are national organizations, like the Kiwanis, Lions, or the Boy Scouts who function largely through local branches. Most of these organizations want to grow, and thus make considerable effort to establish branches in the new suburbs. In this process, they hasten—as well as rationalize —the formation of organizations. This is also true of the churches, whose planning is more total and effective than that of most secular organizations in America. In Levittown, for example, the major Protestant denominations had the churches financed and all but built before people had moved in.

The final level of social organization I want to discuss is the government and the political party system. This also involves a minority of the people—usually those who are professional politicians if not by vocation then by temperament. As long as the parties provide the municipal services that are required by law or consensus, the average resident pays little attention to them or to the government. If he is middle class, he will vote even when there are no issues that touch him, but when there are such issues, and controversies develop, he may become active, putting pressure on the government and his party to bend the final solution his way. This kind of protest is perhaps more common in the suburb than in the city, but even so it is rare, partly because politicians run the government so as to minimize controversy, and partly because even in a small suburb, the average person will find that although he can protest to the politician in person, he will not get much personal satisfaction if his constituency is at all heterogeneous.

In most cases, the constituency is heterogeneous. If the subdivision is as large as a Levittown—which may mean 17,000 families—it is heterogeneous because it is so big. If the subdivision is small, it is usually one of many within a politician's constituency. And if there is heterogeneity, there is likely to be difference of opinion, reflecting the values and the incomes of the different resident blocs. Thus, upper middle class people are very much concerned that the public school prepare their children for a good college, and ideally they want it to be a prep school. Working class people, on the other hand, do not have the money for such schools, and in most cases, their concept of education is to prepare their children for the kind of white collar work that requires only a high school education. They want the public school to be more vocational. Lower middle class parents are in the middle; they expect their children to go to college, but to a state or community college rather than to a Harvard, and are unwilling—if not unable—to pay for more than this.

But even more fundamental values come into play here. Upper middle class people, who start teaching their children at home long before they are of school age, want nursery schools, kindergartens, and small classes to give their children individual attention. Working class people, especially if they are Catholic, think of the school as helping them to discipline their children so that they will stay out of trouble, and see no disadvantages in the large, sternly run classroom. Lower middle class people, who live much more through their children than others, want to keep them at home as long as possible, and reject the upper middle class notion that children are ready to learn at age 3 or 4. Thus, when these groups form a single constituency for a school system—or on other matters for a political party—there is apt to be disagreement about how to allocate public funds, and in many cases, political conflict as well. Since the school is the most costly, and in some ways the most important public agency in the suburbs, it is the major source of governmental conflict. But one must not exaggerate this: I, for one, was amazed by how little attention lower middle class parents in Levittown paid to the school and what their children were or were not learning—but then the school system and its personnel were by and large lower middle class themselves.

Let me now put these observations together into three conclusions about the extent and significance of the suburban community, the variations in it, and the differences between it and the urban one. The first point is that the community as a spatially defined unit of social organization is really not very important in the life of the suburbanite. I have tried to show that the vital center of suburban life is the home, and to a lesser extent, the block and the network of friends. Only a minority of people are involved in organizations, and in the day-to-day activities of the govern-

ment. Moreover, the relations which people develop with neighbors and other residents are for the most part voluntary—there is no other necessary tie between homeowners beyond the maintenance of house and lawn upkeep. Also, many of the services provided by government could be—and sometimes are—provided by private enterprise.

In short, the community is really little more than a system of administrative and political organizations for the provision of public services—and for gaining agreement as to what these should be—as well as a set of voluntary associations which carry out other services that cannot be provided either by private enterprise or the individual homeowner. I do not mean to denigrate these functions, but only to suggest that the concept of community and the reality contained in the concept are much less significant than they have been been thought to be by sociologists and, for that matter, by planners and other public officials. Perhaps the clearest indication of this is the fact that the boundaries of suburban communities are on the whole arbitrary; they were set in the days when rural needs and horse-and-buggy transportation set definite limits, but they remain intact today. There are of course good reasons for this. Not only have political systems developed around them that are hard to alter, but because homeowners are taxpayers, they find it to their interest to maintain the smallness of suburban municipalities.

The minor role of the community does not mean that the suburbs lack what is commonly called a sense of community. This term is used in two ways, to refer to primary or quasi-primary relations between people, and to the feelings of loyalty for the institutions within the political boundaries. Community exists in the suburb in both senses. People do relate to neighbors, and there is a considerable amount of mutual trust and mutual aid among people who did not know each other before they became neighbors. Moreover, suburbanites get to know many people other than immediate neighbors: they say hello to a large number of them, and in this, and in the informal chit-chat that goes on between them, storekeepers and other local functionaries, the suburb is much like the small town. People do not know each other's ancestors of course, but that is the major difference. The second sense of community is also present. It is expressed usually through a feeling of loyalty for the place when it is spoken ill of—but some of that is personal self-defense. There is also some identification with the high school athletic team, the one community institution about which consensus is most easily obtained, and of course when hostile elements—be these Acts of God or the influx of low status people—threaten the community, people do band together to save the reality and the image in which they invested their savings.

The second point is that there is no one suburban community; but there are suburban communities which differ widely from each other, because of the age and class backgrounds of the people who live within their boundaries. Now there are many ways of classifying suburban communities, but it seems to me that once we have identified the predominant age and class groups, and in some cases, ethnic and religious allegiances, and beyond this, the distribution of these, that is, the homogeneity or heterogeneity of the population, and the nature of the dominant groups, if any, we can understand most of the events that take place in these communities. Not all, to be sure, but most. It is these characteristics which affect the nature, quality and importance of the school system, of the array of municipal services other than a few basic and universal ones, and of the range of voluntary associations and their activities. The description I gave of class differences in the conception of education and of the role of the school can thus be extended to other community institutions, and the identification of the dominant age-group and class blocs will go far to tell us which institutions are most powerful. Similarly, the amount of population heterogeneity should indicate the amount of political and social conflict in the community over the make up of these institutions and the allocation of resources to them.

Finally, it is useful to know what is suburban about these communities. The types of institutions and organizations that make up the suburban community are on the whole the same that are found in small towns and in cities, and when the populations are similar in age and class, the specific institutions and organizations may be very much the same. For example, veterans' groups are powerful in working class residential areas, be these small towns, cities or suburbs. The essential differences are perhaps three. First, cities, and to a lesser extent, small towns contain economic institutions other than stores, and because of their function and the size of their investment—I am of course thinking mostly of industrial firms—these play a leading role in the activities of the community institutions. Second, suburban communities are demographically less heterogeneous than cities and most small towns. The city is the home of the very rich and the poor; as well as of middle class people too old or too tied down to move to the suburbs, and in the United States, of a non-white population which is almost entirely poor as well. It is also the home of the single-person or childless household, and of the highly urbane. The demographic differences have two important consequences for the community. These populations support a variety of institutions and organizations that are not to be found in most suburban areas. Also, the greater amount of heterogeneity in the city—abetted by size—also affects the centralization of functions, and the amount of feedback between functionaries and members, government officials and citizens, politicians and voters.

A final difference lies in the newness of the modern suburb: it is the first settlement built for the automobile age. This is not very important: all it does is to make life a little more convenient for most of its inhabitants, and less convenient for others, that is, those who depend on mass transit: women who do not drive or have no cars, and teenagers.

There are of course, many other differences of varying import, but I want to stress an opposite point: the many similarities of city and suburb as communities. Indeed, once demographic differences are noted, the similarities are quite striking. This is especially true if we forget for the moment the existence of the city center. When we go into residential neighborhoods in the city, much of what I have said about the suburb as community applies as well. Here too, life centers about the house and the block, and for the minority of actives there are voluntary associations, some city-wide, but most functioning within smaller areas such as neighborhoods or districts. In fact, if one compared suburban and city residential areas with populations of roughly similar age and class, one would find remarkably few differences, other than those I have mentioned previously. This is most true in the outer parts of the city, where the housing is largely of the detached or rowhouse type, but it is even

true of apartment areas. For example, from what I have seen of some new high rise apartment projects in New York City, the coffee klatsches of people on the same floor, the development of project organizations, and the protest campaigns against the builder for his failure to carry out promises suggest that in some things, the resemblance to suburbia looms large.

It is true that the city has a clearly identifiable and dominant center, but this is also true of packaged suburbs, and it is even coming to be true of complexes of subdivisions adjacent to huge shopping centers. The city center has a bigger city hall, and it has a complex of cultural institutions that cannot be found in the suburbs, but in the shopping centers of upper middle-class suburbs, art galleries, art theaters, and good libraries are springing up, and their high school auditoria are increasingly hosts to the big-name performers in various of the arts. At the same time, most city centers have ceased to be places of cultural innovation and creativity. What has happened is that culture, like every other major consumer product, is now produced in a handful of major cities. In the United States, these are New York, and a quartet of subcenters, Boston, Chicago, San Francsico and Los Angeles. The smaller cities have become less important in this respect, and the young people with innovative talent desert them increasingly. And since in our day even artists and cultural innovators marry young and have families, it may happen that a generation from now, there will be suburban areas which can be called locations of cultural creativity, either because creative people live in them, or because suburban artist colonies will develop along the line of the rural and small town or resort art colonies that can be found all over Canada and the United States.

III

Before I go on to the evaluation, I would like to consider—in a much briefer but parallel fashion—the suburban way of life. My points will be the same as those which I tried to make for the suburban community: there is no single suburban way of life, but ways are best differentiated by the age and class of the people who pursue them, and that the ways of life to be found in the suburbs do not differ significantly from those found elsewhere.

The notion of a suburban way of life has been emphasized in the mass media, and in the social criticism of the literary intellectuals, but most of what has been said is myth rather than reality. I won't bore you with the content of the myth: of homogeneity, conformity, hyperorganization and hypersociability, compensated by excessive amounts of alcohol, fornication, and mental illness. The myth has been well debunked by such sociologists as Ktsanes and Reissman, Berger, Dobriner, Clark, and Greer. The myth exists largely because the upper middle class people who write mass media entertainment and social criticism either live in the city—or would if their wives and children would let them—and confuse the suburb with the ways of life of the upper middle class and lower middle class. In attacking the homogeneity, conformity and pettiness of the suburbs, they are really attacking the lower middle class; in depicting alcoholism, adultery and intense social competition in suburbia, they are commenting on a highly exaggerated version of the life of the upper middle class people in such competitive occupations as show business, advertising, architecture, and academia. Their confusion of settlement with way of life is no different than that of Anglo-Saxon critics 100 years ago, who blamed the city for the existence of crime, vice, degradation, alcoholism, and the like that are found among lower class populations wherever they live. When the small town society of the Anglo-Saxon elite was endangered by immigration, the critics attacked the city; now that the city is losing its power to the suburbs, the critics take after the suburb.

Since the large majority of the people who have settled in post-war suburbia are lower middle class, their way of life has generally been identified as *the* suburban one. But whether they live in the city or in the suburb, the child-rearing lower middle class is strongly home-oriented: its major recreation is the care of home and children. Its social life is focussed on friends and neighbors, rather than on relatives, and it swells the membership rolls of churches and voluntary social organizations. It has always been anti-urban even when it lived in the city, and it made little use of city culture even when it was close. Indeed, in some ways, lower middle class culture is ideally suited to suburbia, because the nuclear family is so important, the tie to the extended family weak, and the lack of need for the city so marked.

But the other classes move to suburbia too. Berger's study of California factory workers has shown that working class groups can maintain their way of life in the suburbs, and working class suburbs are therefore quite different from middle class ones. In them, house upkeep is usually poorer, but the gardens are more densely planted though more with vegetables perhaps than lawn. Organizations and churches are fewer, and less sparsely attended, friendships are closer to home, and wherever possible, social life is taken up largely with relatives. The schools are usually poorer in quality, and the football teams are better; and taverns or roadhouses usually spring up in the environs of working class suburbs. It is perhaps true that working class culture is less congruent with suburbia than middle class culture. This is especially true of the women, and if my findings in Levittown are generally applicable, some of them miss the daily contact with their mothers, the closeness to childhood friends, as well as the hustle-and-bustle of working class neighborhood street life, and the entertainment facilities of the downtown area.

The upper middle classes lived in the suburbs before anyone else could afford to do so, and their way of life there differs from both of the previous ones. This way of life is marked by the more extensive and intensive participation in community activities, be they social, cultural or civic: by less emphasis on the home as the center of life, by even fewer ties to relatives than in the lower middle class, and more shared activities as well as partying with friends, by greater demands on the children to do well in school and outside of it, and by more interest in culture and civic virtue. This way of life has been so well described by John Seeley and his associates in *Crestwood Heights* that I need to say no more about it.

These ways of life are not visible from looking at suburban subdivisions, but they become quite evident on closer inspection, and they stand out especially clearly when they are found side by side in uneasy harmony, as is the case in a heterogeneous suburb. And at close view, one can see also what has been found in several studies of people who moved from city to suburb: that these ways are on the whole independent of suburbia, that they exist in the city as well as in the suburb, even though they are less easily seen in the bigger community. Thus, it is

evident that there is no one suburban way of life, or for that matter an urban one. Rather, there are ways of life that are best distinguished by class, and to a lesser extent by age, and these are found in all settlement types.

Indeed, the differences between these ways of life in city and suburb are perhaps even smaller than the differences between city and suburb as community. The ownership of a single family house and a yard make for more outdoor family living, although the barbecue pit can be found in city neighborhoods as well. People in the suburbs perhaps do more gardening, but I suspect that they spend less time at parks or on Sunday drives. Women who socialize with their neighbors do so more than in most city neighborhoods, because neighbors are more compatible, but working class people who come from ethnic enclaves in the city say there is less neighboring in the suburbs. For men there is more peace and quiet in the suburbs, partly because the house is more spacious, and the yard a pleasant diversion. Alternatively, some women say there is too much peace and quiet; they feel isolated from the downtown stores. Certainly the ties to old friends and to relatives are stretched in the move to the suburbs, sometimes to the breaking point, saddening those who depended on them, and gladdening those for whom confrontations with parents or in-laws meant conflict. Life is perhaps somewhat slower in the suburbs, but those who are in a hurry are so everywhere.

Most of the differences boil down to those of scale: one's private housing space is bigger, while the public social organizations and areas are smaller: it is easier to move around in social and physical space. And associated with this is a lesser degree of population heterogeneity. There is thus less involuntary contact with people who are highly different—one can evade the signs and areas of utter poverty by living in the suburbs. Some argue that this blinds people—and especially children—to the bitter realities of this world, but one can also argue that absence from them reduces hostility toward them, and allows for more understanding. And suburban children do not lack contact with other problems: mental illness, alcoholism, marital conflict and the like. At the same time, there is closer contact with people who are somewhat different: in the suburbs I have studied, people of different religions and ethnic groups socialize more than they do in most city neighborhoods. Thus, on the suburban street on which I lived, second-generation Italians lived next to and with Poles, Irish, Jews, and with small town Southerners. It may be that suburbia is more of a melting pot than the city ever was.

Yet all of these differences are in the last analysis minor. What really matters, the nature and quality of family life, the extent to which the individual can live as he wishes, the things he aspires to for himself and his children, and the activities he pursues outside the home are by and large little affected by where he lives. They are functions of the amount of education he has had, the kind of job he holds, the income he makes, and the life cycle stage he is in.

I am of course oversimplifying somewhat for the purpose of emphasis, for one cannot reduce ways of life entirely to functions of age and class. For example, religion and ethnicity must be considered too. This comes out clearly in my Levittown data, for Jews, Irish Catholics, and Italian Catholics report that life has changed more since they left the city, or that the move has brought some discomfort, where-as Protestants report this less often. The former have clearly been socialized to live in urban ethnic-religious enclaves, although most of them soon become enthusiastic suburbanites. Yet this does not alter my basic point: that the things which matter most in peoples' lives are not influenced so much by place of residence as by national and regional changes in the economy, society, and culture, of which both city and suburb are an intrinsic part.

IV

In conclusion, I want to pull some of those observations together and make explicit some of the evaluative comments that have been implicit in what I have said before. It should be clear that I conceive the suburban community and its way of life as nothing especially unusual, but rather as a more visible expression of behavior patterns and attitudes that are found in all settlement types.

Beyond that, my observations lead to the conclusion that because people have been able to move voluntarily, and to choose where they would live, social relationships between them are superior to those in the city. Not only is family life somewhat freer and less tense—largely because people have gotten more space—but child-rearing is considerably less strained than it is in apartments, and children are more of a joy and less of a burden. The somewhat greater homogeneity of age and class makes it easier for people to find friends, to get along with neighbors, and generally, to trust and help each other more, to be kind to each other and tolerant of differences more, and to work with each other for common aims. Suburbia is not the Garden of Eden, of course, and conflicts between neighbors, organizations, and political opponents are as frequent as in any other social group.

And like other people, suburbanites have problems. I am most familiar with the problems of people in low and medium priced communities, and restrict myself to them in this discussion. Uppermost perhaps are financial problems, for home-ownership is ultimately more expensive than renting, even if one gets more space for one's money. (I gather that in Canada, where down payment requirements are much higher than in the United States, a move to the suburbs can impoverish families, but this is not the case in the United States.) Rather, the costs of the homeownership, coming as they do at the time as the family is growing, force people to tighten their budgetary belts. Sometimes this is accompanied by marital disputes over how to spend what money there is; more often, people take out the problem on public services, by voting against increased taxes and depriving themselves of services which they should have—as well as those which someone else thinks they should have—and which really do not cost very much. But in our society it is easier for people to vote against taxes than to cut down on personal expenditures. In part, the problem results from dependence on local property taxes, and I hope that when the next wave of suburban building begins at the end of this decade, wage and income taxes will be used to pay for municipal services, and federal aid will be available to help the suburban areas through their birth pains.

Teenagers seem to suffer in suburbia, because they are cut off from meeting places and entertainment facilities, and from access to those available in the city. And some working class women find it difficult to cope with separation from mothers and other relatives with whom they were close in the city, although some of these women find partial substitutes among neighbors. In a predominantly lower middle class community, upper middle class people suffer somewhat from lack of compatible people, and from access to cultural facilities, but then they work all the harder in the community to obtain these for themselves and others. But this isolation does not seem to be a problem in upper middle class suburbs.

Some women suffer from what they call being stuck at home: from having to spend all day with children, either because they cannot relate to the neighbors, or because household duties make it impossible for them to get out. This problem is not by any means limited to the suburbs, although women who lived near relatives in the city could visit with them, or leave their children with them while they escaped for a few hours to the downtown department store. Their problems could be solved by more apartment building in the suburbs, so that parents—affluent ones at least—who wanted to, could move out there with them, and by more adequate mass transit so that such women can get back to the city more easily. What is harder to solve is the problem of career and job opportunities for women who want to work while raising a family. These opportunities are few in the city, but even fewer in the suburbs. Some women find substitute rewards by working in voluntary organizations or in political ones, but it is not quite the same.

Almost all of these problems are those of specific class and lifecycle groups, and it is really quite difficult to find problems that affect all people in suburbia—other than the war against crabgrass. This does not explain away the problems, but only suggests that these two variables are more important than place of residence, and that even in considering problems unique to either city or suburb, we must study them in terms of their consequences for old and young, middle class and working class.

While suburbanites have their share of problems, their general level of contentment with suburbia is so high that it is safe to say that they will remain in suburbia, and more important, that the next generation of young people will want to live there as well. Since their numbers will be large, and the time when they will start looking for housing will soon be upon us, it is not too early to begin thinking about the next suburban building boom. Two problems are particularly relevant: the shortage of land for low-density housing, and the increasing distance of it from the city. The land shortage will probably force builders to develop new housing types that provide the advantages of single family housing at a somewhat higher density: possibly a rowhouse that offers more privacy than those that have been built in the past. The increasing decentralization of industry will mean that many of the next generation's breadwinners will not have to travel to the city every day, but even so, I think the time has come for the development of high speed mass transit systems between city and suburb. The technology has long been available, but the tougher problem of persuading politicians and voters that the government must make the initial—and high—capital investment necessary to develop a system good enough to persuade people to leave their cars at home has not yet been solved.

More suburban housing will also mean more urban sprawl, but this does not strike me as a real problem. The arguments against it have been based on the need to save agricultural land, even though we have more farmland and farmers than we can possibly use even today, and on esthetic grounds. While urban sprawl is not very pretty, I think it is less desirable or feasible to force people to raise their children in high rise apartment houses. Moreover, I do not think that we have a right to even think seriously about the esthetics of urban sprawl until we do away with the urban slums, which are not only infinitely more ugly, but which, unlike urban sprawl, produce so much human misery and degradation.

Urban Stratification and Cultural Heterogeneity

21. Peninsula People: Social Stratification in a Metropolitan Complex

Harold M. Hodges, Jr.

Several urban sociologists have suggested that social class is the most important variable defining the culture and organization of social areas, including both the areas called suburban communities and the denser neighborhoods of cities. Harold Hodges' paper utilizes data about the population of the San Francisco region to describe the social class system which is roughly typical of most American metroplitan areas. He locates six social classes, ranging from the upper class which comprises only two-tenths of one percent of the Bay Area population, to the lower-lower class, whose members constitute between fifteen and twenty percent of the residents of this metropolis. In other communities, of course, the proportions in a particular class may be different, but because our society is now highly and rather uniformly urbanized, the styles of life and the attitudes he describes for each class are generally applicable throughout the United States. Although there are many studies of the class composition of urban communities and its connection with ecological patterns, Hodges is one of few to discuss the subject with reference to the total range of settlements that exist within a typical metropolitan region.

Harold M. Hodges, Jr., is Professor of Sociology at San Jose State College in California. He is the author of *Social Stratification: Class in America* (1964) and *Penninsula People* (1964) and coauthor of *Education and Society* (1963).

"We are a classless people": of all the venerable American myths, few, it would appear, have demonstrated more remarkable staying power than this.

That it has endured as so cherished an element in the American dream is not altogether illogical. For our democratic heritage and its accompanying ideology are premised on the compelling assumption that our worth is determined not by our ancestry, but by what we, as individuals, accomplish in our own lifetimes by dint of our own efforts.

But to deny that we are a classless people, to assert that in fact social classes are salient ingredients in the American social frabic, is not to deny the worth of the doctrine of equality; it is rather, in an important sense, to affirm it.[1] Nor is such an assertion fraught with ugly Marxian overtones of class consciousness and class conflict. It is a neutral statement of fact, devoid of connotations of inferiority and superiority. It is a valid statement of fact, and not the mere fanciful creation of theorists, because copious evidence increasingly corroborates both the conclusive reality and the substantial everyday consequence of social-class divisions in American society.[2]

For many Americans—educators, for example—or social workers, psychiatrists, clergymen, probation officers, personnel and advertising men, social classes[3] are not simply forces, such as death and taxation, that one must live with; they are decisive elements which help shape and color virtually every facet of our lives. As such, they must be comprehended with clarity and insight. Helpful as it is for the person who would know the behavior, motives, and values of others to understand the "typical" American, it is infinitely more critical that he understand, say, the "middle-class," and, better, the "lower-middle-class" American. We shall shortly see why.

Yet what knowledge of social classes is available is, on the whole, piecemeal and fragmentary. To date, for example, there has been no comprehensive investigation of the American class structure on a national scale. Numerous accounts, among them August Hollingshead's" Elmtown's Youth" and Lloyd Warner's "Yankee City,"[4] have treated the question of social stratification on the level of the local community.[5] But "Main Street, U.S.A." —small-town America—typifies our country more in fiction and memory than in fact. Contemporary America, and even more certainly tomorrow's America, may be better visualized in terms of sprawling metropolitan complexes: of central cities, their suburban peripheries, and neighboring satellite communities. Accordingly, the descriptive portrait of social-class differences which follows is postulated on the conviction that urban-suburban America is sociologically more meaningful than the Elmtowns, Yankee Cities and similar small and stable communities described 15 and 20 years ago.

The report is based on the findings of a still-continuing investigation[6] into the relationships between social-class membership and a diverse array of attitudinal, behavioral, and life-style factors.[7] In the course of the undertaking, now in its sixth year, a random sample of more than 3,000 "heads of household" in the populous (1960 population: approximately 2,000,000) three-county San Francisco "Peninsula area" completed comprehensive questionnaires (forced-choice and

Reprinted by permission from *Education and Society*, W. Warren Kallenback and Harold M. Hodges, Jr., eds. (Columbus, Ohio: Charles E. Merrill Books, Inc.), pp. 389–420. Copyright © 1962 by Harold M. Hodges, Jr.

open-ended) and a variety of clinical and depth-type tests.[8]

Despite a deliberately minimal use of such standard sociological cautionary terms as "typically" and "generally," it must be remembered that the class-linked differences described are, without exception, differences not of kind, but of degree. Although the verbal sketches are, for illustrative purposes, broad-stroked, the actual qualities which differentiate class from class are—with some notable exceptions—commonly less striking and vivid.

Just as the boundaries which separate one class level from the next are not hard-and-fast, but insensibly blurred, overlapping, and imprecise, so is the complex of values and behavior which characterizes an "upper" or "lower-middle" individual energized by other than purely class-related considerations: it is compounded, too, of hereditary and constitutional elements, of such diverse subcultural forces as age, sex, family, ethnic, and regional influences, and, above all, of those uniquely idiosyncratic factors which make all of us mavericks as much as conformists.[9] As with social class, so too with comparisons between Dane and Greek, Ozark hillbilly and Bronx-dweller: each such affiliation is of undeniably critical import, yet other cultural impresses are similarly at work in qualifying and modifying these national and regional biases.[10]

The "class portraits" which follow must, finally, be recognized for what they are: mere partial vignettes, tapping what appear to be certain class-related characteristics among given people (residents of the San Francisco Peninsula) at a given time (the late 1950s and early 1960s). They cannot be safely generalized to the whole of the American population. Some distinctions will seem ruthlessly pat and

others makeshift and tentative. The vast majority of the conclusions are based on statistical examination of empirical evidence; others are more impressionistic, deriving from analyses of tape-recorded interviews, responses to open-ended questions, and Rorschach protocols. The reader, lastly, must constantly remind himself that tags of identity, no matter what their technical "validity," are forever in danger of glossing over a central truth: however else we might define or categorize him, every last person on earth is an individual, unlike any other human who has ever existed.[11]

Lower-lower Class: Despair, Anger, Apathy

Of every six Peninsula families, at least one inhabits this lowermost position in the class hierarchy.[12] In the broad occupational sense the occupant of this level is an unskilled "lower-blue-collarite"; but his employment is characteristically sporadic and marginal, his marketable talents are few, and he is the last to be hired and the first to be fired. He entered the labor arena in his middle teens after dropping out of school just short of the eighth grade,[13] he was still a teenager when he married (a legal formality bypassed by at least one "husband" in ten at is class level), and he fathered the first of his four or five children before he was old enough to vote. He had achieved social and legal adulthood at an age when his upper-middle-class contemporaries faced another five years of schooling and celibacy. If his marriage has endured—and the odds are just short of even that it has not or will not—he is likely to find that it is strife-ridden; he rarely admits an abiding love for his wife and children, and he is plagued by in-law troubles.

The lower-lower-class Peninsula dweller lives in cramped quarters: typically in a dilapidated tenement, a jerry-built "suburban" slum, or in a fast-deteriorating postwar government housing development— a dwelling littered with debris and enjoying at best a minimal level of sanitation. Although the monthly family income of the "LL"—some $250—is the most he has ever realized (more than two wives in three at this level are gainfully employed outside the home), it is consumed more rapidly than it is earned. Only occasional items in his household have not been purchased on an installment plan, and he is perennially in debt. This, then is the objective plight of the LL. His subjective predicament—his private world of dreams, goals, cravings, and frustrations—is no less severe because it is less visible to the untutored eye.[14]

Virtually every one of the lower-blue-collarite's major life goals—geared, apparently, to a middle-class frame of reference vividly portrayed for him by the mass media, the advertising industry, and even the schools—has somehow been stifled or thwarted. Reluctantly and for the most part subconciously, he realizes that he has fallen short of the American dream occupationally, educationally, residentially, and in the realm of material possessions. Although his childhood aspirations in each of these spheres were markedly less pretentious than those entertained by his middle-class counterparts, his actual achievements have, in relative terms, lagged even more markedly.

To ask precisely why the LL has failed to achieve upward occupational-economic mobility is to pose a question which, given our present state of knowledge, is inherently unanswerable; it will nonetheless be worth while to consider a few of the partial clues afforded by the research. In the first place, the LL's lowly position in the class[15] hierarchy is due infinitely less to intellectual deficiency or slothfulness than to what, for want of a more precise term, may be called "cultural deficiency." Unassimilated and marginal, the LL is encumbered by deeply ingrained values and life-styles which are inevitably at odds with the middle-class values and life-styles which facilitate upward mobility. Unskilled, ill-educated—often tethered by the additional incubus of skin color—he is frequently trapped in a vicious circle which effectively suppresses his haphazard and infrequent efforts to break through the class barrier.

It may be hypothesized that the "cultural deficiency" which inhibits so many LLs (some, remember, will achieve a measure of upward mobility) is due in the main to (1) a set of values and traditions "inherited" from his three in four grandparents who came from rural or village areas and/or (2) a simple adaptation on the part of a vulnerable and insecure person to what must certainly seem an omnipotent and brutal environment. And of all the rural survivals (or adaptations) which most persistently impede movement into higher reaches of the class system, none would appear more an incumbrance than the LL's pervasive sense of closeness to kin. Despite the frequency of bitter husband-wife conflicts, the LL seems especially fearful of venturing beyond the familiar confines of his family group; although he "neighbors" more frequently and intimately than those in other levels, he derives the greater part of his psychic support from intimate interaction with relatives: from visits to taverns, front-porch gossip, and watching the fights on television with brothers, brothers-in-law, or same-sex cousins. In consequence, he is more unwilling than any to leave "home" for better employment opportunities,[16] he possesses an abiding sense of loyalty toward kinfolk (an unwritten code of mutual aid prescribes that near-relatives come to one another's unstinting assistance in times of trouble), and, perhaps most importantly, his network of lower-class convictions, habits, and life styles is consistently reinforced and insulated by his like-minded relatives. The latter, predictably, live near: almost half of all LLs—in comparison to one in ten middle-class Peninsulans—claim close relatives living within a four-block radius of their own dwellings.

If he is less removed from a rural heritage, we might expect that the LL would subscribe to such "patriarchal" values as husband-father dominance and wife-child subservience. And it is he, indeed, who most readily concurs that "the wife's place is in the home" (with LL wives in hearty accord!),[17] that the husband should "run the show," and that the child is ideally obedient, quiet, and even servile to parental dictates. The LL parent appears to abide by this dogma in practice as much as in theory. Consistent with the pithy yet representative comment of one respondent that "my pa did it that way and, by God, what's good enough for him is good enough for me," the lower-blue-collar mother knows nothing of Dr. Spock or "new-fangled" ways of infant-training. Instead, she does as her mother did: the errant baby or child is punished with dispatch and often with harshness for "being bad"—for toilet accidents, messiness, crying, fighting, and, above all, sassing or talking back.[18]

But it is the deeper-seated, less manifest recesses of the LL's personality configuration that most tellingly distinguish him from his white-collar counterparts. The LL is at the very nadir of the American class, status, and power hierarchy; yet he is, we will recall, at the threshold of this system because he has incorporated many of its central values. His status is thus as marginal as it is "lowly": he is on the outside looking in. He subscribes to certain middle-class ideals (in particular such goals as material well-being, progress, and upward mobility), yet he is simultaneously attached to antagonistic and even contradictory convictions taught him by his agrarian forebears. The consequence can only be a cruel impasse: he is at once seduced by the success ethic, and balked in his efforts to realize its rewards. The resultant frustration, conscious or not, is very real. In congruence with much of contemporary theory and research, it would seem to go far in helping account for the psychodynamics of LL status. Space limitations will not allow a full exposition of the matter, but certain central components in the "LL personality" can be profitably analyzed in this light.

Chief among the hypothetical responses to the frustrations experienced by the study's lower-lower-class subjects are three generalized reactions which proved in fact to be characteristic: (1) a fusion of cynicism, distrust, despair, and pessimism; (2) hostility and anger focused on "others"; and/or (3) apathy and withdrawal from the larger social arena. The first constitute basic ingredients in what has come to be known as "misanthropy"; the misanthrope, by dictionary definition, is one who hates or distrusts people in general. Other people (except for intimates and relatives), the LLs concurred, are simply not to be trusted: they are selfish and are out to cheat or take advantage of one's weaknesses. "People," they seemed to assert, "are no good." Success of any sort is best accomplished by connections, pull, or underhanded dealing, and no one—television repairman, doctor, butcher, union official, businessman—is truly honorable and worthy of trust. The dog-eat-dog specter of the jungle, it seems, is very real in the lowermost echelons of the Peninsula blue-collar world. Coupled with this outlook was an ill-defined sense of pessimism, aloneness, and despair, of what the sociologist defines as "anomie." "Human nature being what it is," the LL characteristically agreed, "there will always be war and conflict"; the future is bleak and hopeless, and there is nothing we little men can do to avert it.

For many LLs the reaction was less muted but almost as indirect; to them, something was not only vaguely "wrong," but some one or some thing—scapegoats—must be blamed. Theirs, in a word, is what students of personality call an "extrapunitive" reaction (the "intrapunitive" person, in contrast, fixes the blame on himself when things go wrong).[19] Although misanthropy is considered by many to be one form of extrapunitiveness, what has come to be popularly known as *authoritarianism* is an even more personalized, hate-infused way of fixing the guilt on others.

Much has been written about the causes and dynamics of authoritarianism since the concept came into prominence shortly after World War II. Suffice it at this point to remark that the distorted attitudes which warp the authoritarian's vision are in large part deeply imbedded products of early childhood experiences.[20] The authoritarian tends, among other things, to be one who thinks, perceives, and structures most of his life in a categorical, black-and-white sort of way. His world is peopled by weak and strong, pure and impure, good and bad. He wants his heroes (typically strong and tough-minded men who are leaders of the good—or majority—cause)

to be unequivocally heroic, and his villains (weak, pussyfooting members of minority causes: "un-Americans," intellectuals, artists, homosexuals, long-hairs) to be clearly villainous. The investigation's LL was patently the most authoritarian subject in the entire sample.[21] The world for him is not simply divisible into two hard-and-fast categories, but those in the wrong category, transgressors of the mores—delinquents, alcoholics, beatniks, opiate addicts, perverts—are deserving of harsh punishment, for they are what "ails this world."

For many LLs, particularly the elderly, the most effective way of coping with life appears to be a reaction blended of apathy and resignation. They belong to few or no formal organizations except for the Roman Catholic or Baptist churches (for a growing minority, especially those Negroes who have recently migrated from the Deep South, fundamentalist or emotion-laden sects afford a religious outlet). Some of the younger LLs are disinterested members of trade unions and a sparse handful of the older still claim memberships in fraternal orders, but for most social life is limited to relatives and occasional neighbors. Nor is the lower-blue-collar Peninsulan ego-involved in his community. "Girlie" and movie magazines, the television and comic sections of the newspaper: these are among his rare links with the larger world of affairs. Even the 1960 presidential election, which evoked more interest in his ranks (because of the religious overtones for Catholics and fundamentalists[22]) than any contest since the F.D.R. era witnessed a scant 25 per cent turnout at the polls. His, it seems evident, is a fatalistic what-can-I-do-about-it, why-bother? universe; he has retreated into the comfortable womb-like sanctuary of the cocoon.

Upper-lower Class: Marlboro Man . . . or Milquetoast?

There is a sharper hiatus between the lower-lower class and the upper-lower than between the world of the latter and the world of the lower-middle. Yet in many telling and predictable ways the upper-blue-collarite (approximate statistical markings: he comprises one-third of the Peninsula's residents, completed 10 to 11 years of schooling, reaps a $5,500-$6,500 annual family income, and occupies a semi-skilled or skilled occupational status) is less like the white collarites just above him than he is like his LL peers.[23] Thus in comparison to subjects in the middle and upper class levels, the UL is like the LL—only "less so"—in his proclivity for authoritarian, anomic, misanthropic, and patriarchal values; he is almost as intolerant of Mexican-Americans, Oriental-Americans, and Negroes, and is even more anti-Semitic (the most prejudiced of all toward Jews is the lower middle).

But undue stress on the similarities between those in the two blue-collar levels might belie the even more numerous dissimilarities which amply warrant the conclusion that the UL inhabits a class level distinctly his own. To illustrate the point more vividly, we shall first remark on the "uniquely" UL attributes—those which are not merely intermediate between LL and LM characteristics but are more or less singular.

In sharp contrast to the LL, the upper-blue-collarite seems infinitely more confident and ebullient; he is less concerned with his self image among strangers and, unlike the LL, rates himself as aggressive and friendly rather than shy and "uncomfortable among people I don't know." Whether such "self-ascriptions" are valid —are truly the way the typical UL honestly sees himself—is in good part academic; the important issue is that he seems confident to the point of brashness and "inner-directed" in terms of David Riesman's typology.[24] It is as though he walks boldly rather than timidly, that he is vigorously self-assertive, almost pugnacious. By way of amplification, the UL is the apparent personification of the "Marlboro Man": he describes himself as "strong and silent," "tough-minded," and "manly"; he is less forgiving than any of "sissiness" in men and boys; his favorite movies and television shows are horse operas; John Wayne and Clark Gable are his professed ideals. He is far and away the most avid outdoorsman, hunter, and fisherman, the heaviest of smokers. He more than any likes beer, and poker is his card game.

Yet in a puzzling reversal of form, and in particular contradiction to his independent, devil-may-care stance, the upper-blue-collarite is apparently plagued by "status concern." One of life's most important goals, he declares, is "raising one's social position"; and most vital of all in choosing a career (even more vital than income and job satisfaction) is the prestige which attaches to it. Neighborgood "status competition" is also of disproportionate concern to the UL, and he more than any would admit to "extreme disappointment" were his similarly circumstanced neighbors to acquire newer and bigger cars,[25] extensively remodel their homes, or buy their wives "expensive furs." Somewhat perversely, too, this self-styled "he-man" is likelier than the male at any other level to help his wife with such "womanly" domestic chores as grocery shopping, dishwashing, and table setting.[26]

The upper-blue-collarite's leisure-time pace is less restricted than the LL's; not so given to such passive entertainment as movies and television (the LL watches the latter more than four hours a night and, alone among the others, appears to be enjoying television more and more),[27] he is an ardent baseball, boxing, and wrestling fan, bowler, and "do-it-yourself" addict. He has, in comparison to his neighbors in the white-collar ranks, little or no truck for gardening, and he is only reluctantly being converted to back-yard barbecuing. Likelier than the LL to entertain friends he met at work, more than four in five of his and his wife's most intimate acquaintances are themselves classifiable as upper-lower class.[28] And when he and his wife do act as hosts, they eschew bridge, rarely serve hard liquor, and tend to break up into all-male or all-female gossip groups. The UL is more active in clubs than the LL; he tends to prefer such veterans' organizations as the American Legion or V.F.W. and occasional fraternal orders (in particular the Elks); she is especially active in the P.T.A.[29] and in auxiliaries to her husband's clubs.

His new-found affluence—no level in the entire sample has obtained such marked yearly income increases as his (between 1950 and 1960 his average annual wages increased more than 50 per cent) —has witnessed what may prove to be far-reaching changes in the upper-blue-collar way of life. For one thing many in his ranks have moved into the same suburban tracts occupied by lower-middle-class families, and an increasing proportion boast the basic amenities traditionally associated with the American middle-class style of life. The physical move to suburbia rarely, at the time of the study, connoted an actual move into middle-class ranks (absolute social-class mobility requires more than the mere material symbols of middle-class status; it involves what amounts to a social-psychological absorption of the most

subtle middle-class values, life-styles, and behavior patterns—a conquest which few can essay in less than a generation). But because many UL children grow up with middle-class children,[30] it may be safely predicted that many will themselves bridge the gap. In the meanwhile their parents frequently become "marginal" cases: "lower-middle class" to the outward eye, yet still, in the main, actually "upper-lower class" in the important realms of friendships and deep-seated values. The leap from blue-collar to white-collar status (and the move amounts to a leap in social and psychological terms) warrants brief analysis less because of the strains which attend it than because of its apparently increasing frequency: no Peninsula class level has "lost" more members to the next highest class than the upper-lower— and no level has gained more from the next lowest than the lower-middle.[31]

Lower-middle Class: Puritanism, Frugality, and the Bible

If his upper-lower next-door neighbor stands out as a distinct sort, so does this salesman, clerical worker, foreman, lathing contractor, and proprietor of the corner drug store. In a real sense his social-class level is the most unique and variant of all; yet in another, concrete context, he represents that most illusive of all animals: the "typical" American.

His is what has been called the "level of the common man." And though barely one in three Peninsula-dwellers are members of his class, his common-ness is not a qualitative matter, but a quantitative one. For he is the mythical average man in many ways. His traits include an annual income of between $8,000 and $9,000, a high-school diploma,[32] and a tract home in the suburbs. In fact "suburbia"—an illusive and hard-to-pinpoint geographic entity[33]—"is," in a statistical sense, the lower-middle class; for more than three-fourths of the Peninsula's "non-urban" single-family dwelling units are evaluated at $15,000 to $20,000, and an estimated two-thirds of these are occupied by families designated as "lower middle." But the LM is average in other respects than income, education, and residence. He, many market analysts have come to realize, is virtually the "common de-nominator" that purveyors of the mass media speak of so fondly. Take, for ex-ample, his consumption preferences in four of the media. More than those in other class levels, "his" magazines—*Life, Reader's Digest, Saturday Evening Post*, and *Ladies' Home Journal* . . . his television menu—Perry Mason, The Un-touchables, Gunsmoke, Jack Benny, and Groucho Marx . . . his pet comic strips—Gasoline Alley, Dixie Dugan, Mary Worth, Dick Tracy, and Joe Palooka . . . his cinema preferences—for five successive years, his favorite movie stars were rated first in "box-office appeal" by *Variety*—have time and again been recognized as *national* favorites.[34]

Undue emphasis upon the lower middle's typicality might, however, obscure his uncommon aspects. And these are many. For one thing, perhaps most importantly of all, the investigation's LM appears to be a "reincarnation" of the nineteenth-century American; if the LL's essential bent was old world and agrarian, the LM's may be said to be middle western and small town.[35] It is almost as though he had stepped into the mid-twentieth century through the pages of Booth Tarkington or Sinclair Lewis. His orientation appears, in short, to be rear-guard (where the upper-middle's, we shall see, is more avant-garde).

A person who is puritanical is, according to one dictionary definition, one who is "extremely or excessively strict in matters of morals and religion";[36] this would seem an apt description, too, of the modal lower-middle-class Peninsulan. At no other level, certainly, was there such rigid insistence upon toeing the ethical and sexual line: upon righteous conduct and conformance with accepted standards of goodness and honesty. And for many LMs, the feeling ran deeper; for them such rectitude meant an unforgiving demand that others be incorrupt and virtuous. Thus, in the words of one questionnaire item, the LM was least willing of all to "remain on friendly, first-name terms with a person who . . . drinks heavily . . . has poor table manners . . . swears . . . has secret extra-marital affairs . . . expresses disbelief in God and the Bible." Atheism and pro-fanity, in particular, are cardinal sins to LM eyes. "Sex" is a naughty word to many a LM, and he is less at home than most with an off-color joke. In a somewhat related sense, he expresses the greatest degree of fear that his own son or daughter might depart from his or her appropriate sex role—that his son might be thought a sissy or his daughter a tomboy and unladylike.

If puritanism is a central lower-middle trait, so is the "Protestant Ethic." The characteristic LM belief that hard work, frugality, saving for a rainy day, and proving oneself in the market place are virtues: these are central to the aggregate of values made famous by Max Weber and R. H. Tawney and epitomized earlier by Ben Franklin in *Poor Richard's Alman-ack*. That the LM should hold such quali-ties to be worthy makes sense, for his ranks are heavily peopled by the entrepre-neurs and small businessmen for whom the Protestant Ethic is a historical article of faith. Yet there is a minority within the Peninsula lower-middle class—a growing minority—who are less willing to abide by these tenets: these consist, by and large, of the many younger LMs who are salaried employees of large enterprises—the occupational grouping which C. Wright Mills included in his designation "new middle class."[37] Incongruously, however, the majority of LMs—whatever their occupations, salaried or self-employed—*behaved* as though thrift and frugality were mere lip-service ideals. For comparisons of mean annual incomes at each level with estimated values of dwelling units and cars and amounts spent on furnishings and clothes point to an inescapable conclusion: it is above all the lower-middle who spends above his means. Particular manifestations of what Veblen labeled "conspicuous consumption" vary with each class level; but at no other level did respondents spend so high a proportion of their incomes on such commodities as did the LMs. The contradiction between ideal and practice was glaring.[38]

A third major component of the lower-middle value system is religiosity. For religion, at least as the LM conceives it, is a dominant motif in his life. He claims the most frequent church attendance (half his numbers attend weekly), active memberships in church-related clubs, Bible reading, and beliefs that Biblical precepts are of paramount importance for children and adults alike. Like the blue collarites, his ranks include more Roman Catholics than adherents of any other single faith; yet in a relative sense the most characteristic LM denominational preference is Methodist.[39]

At no level is political-economic conservatism so deeply entrenched as at the lower middle. That barely less than one-half of the LM voters cast their lot with the Nixon-Lodge ticket in 1960 (the LM figure was identical to that of the actual Peninsula-wide vote[40]) belies the proportion at this class level who favor Goldwater (one-third of registered LM Republicans) or Byrd (one-fourth of LM Democrats) as presidential nominees in 1964. On other measures of conservatism, too, the LM more than any opposed increased social security legislation, the growing power of trade unions, the employment of "intellectuals" at cabinet level, and the general encroachment of the federal government on states' rights.[41]

Less "organization prone" than the UMs, but more so than the blue-collarites, the lower-middle belongs to many clubs; but his favorites, at least in numerical terms, are the fraternal order (especially the Elks, Shriners, Masons, and Oddfellows), the chamber of commerce, and assorted religious auxiliaries. He, more than any, is a baseball aficionado, and it is his sons who provide the bulk of local Pony and Little League rosters. But whatever his propensity for extracurricular activities, no one is more of a homebody than the LM; he spends more time than any at the family dinner table, on family vacations and week-end auto trips, and barbecuing and gardening in the "back yard." His, in fact, is the sole level where husbands claim greener thumbs than wives.

In conclusion, one final and rather sober inference is adducible about the status of the lower-middle in the Peninsular socioeconomic hierarchy: his position is more precarious and ill-defined than ever before. That he clings so tenaciously to the images of the "white collar" and small-town America—and their attendant symbols of respectability—may be symptomatic of the fact that he is at least subliminally aware of his plight.

In a stark economic context he is this

era's "forgotten man." Most consequentially, his is the only level where the value of the "real" dollar has actually shrunk; to purchase basic staples he, unlike the majorities in other class levels, must work longer hours in the 1960s than he did in the 1950s. In the critical dimension of power, too, his lot appears to be worsening; in the battle of giant vested interests his chamber of commerce is certainly no match for the N.A.M. on the one side and the A.F.L.-C.I.O. on the other.

Finally, the composition—and thus the traditional value orientation—of the lower-middle class is also in a process of profound permutation. As the well-defined dikes which once separated skilled blue collar from white collar callings become ever hazier, and as the "new" middle class eclipses the "old," the qualities which have historically differentiated the lower-middle class as a class apart are certain to undergo radical changes.

Upper-middle Class: Tomorrow's American

If the Peninsula's lower-middle class citizen approximates the "average" American, his peer in the next-highest status niche may—at the calculated risk of too glib an analogy—be said to depict the American of "tomorrow." The comparison is dictated less by foresight than hindsight. For it is well documented that yesterday's UM Peninsulan was the first to adopt what have now become nation-wide fancies: the split-level ranch home, the Ivy-League style in men's clothes, the sports car, the barbecue addiction, and the hi-fi craze, to mention the more obvious.

But this is merely part of the UM's many-faceted makeup. Scarcely one subject in seven, characteristically the professional, semi-professional, independent businessman, or corporate employee who has gone a year or two beyond his A.B. degree, belongs to the upper-middle level.[42] Yet his numerical insignificance is abundantly offset by his disproportionate influence in the market place, political arena, and the amorphous world of life-styles.[43]

What, in thumbnail style, are the more distinctive qualities which prevail in the Peninsula's upper-middle level? Variegated as they are, at least one intrinsic theme seems to consistently thread its way through the whole of the UM ethos. It relates essentially to interpersonal relations and a basic way of perceiving others. No one word describes it. But the words flexible, trusting, democratic, tolerant, and non-dogmatic come most quickly to mind. Its antithesis is most relevantly represented by the lower-blue-collarite's character: rigid, defensive, authoritarian, parochial, and suspicious, to re-phrase some of the major traits reviewed earlier. Because this is the rule, there are, of course, exceptions: the outlook of *some* UMs is indistinguishable from *the* "lower-class" outlook. But the mood we have described is the prevailing upper-middle-class temper, and it helps explain much of what we shall take to be the upper-middle character.

Thus, though by several measures the most "child-centered" of all subjects, the UM parents appeared to be less anxious and more easy-going in the sphere of child-rearing and disciplining. They are, for example, more tolerant and understanding of children's tantrums, messing, fighting, and sassing. This general aura of permissiveness (the often caricatured dominant-child-submissive-parent was rarely encountered) was observable, moreover, through the entire span of parent-child relationships. Less apprehensive and hurried than lower-class mothers in the realms of weaning and toilet-training

infants, UM parents were more democratic in later phases of their children's
lives. The "children-should-be-seen-but-
not-heard" dictum was as rare among
UMs as it was common among LLs, and
even in adolescence upper-middle
youngsters were youngest of all when
allowed to go out on their first unchap-
eroned dates.[44]

Deviates, too—delinquents, homosexuals, and drug addicts as well as such
lesser norm-flaunters as people who swore,
drank excessively, professed atheism, or
engaged in extra-marital affairs—incurred
less wrath from UMs than from those at
other levels. If, in fact, the LMs were the
most puritanical and Victorian of all, the
UMs were the least so. In related vein, the
upper-middles displayed the greatest degree
of faith in their fellow-humans' motives,
were the least pessimistic and despondent
in outlook, and were by far the most
forgiving of others' frailties and discerning
of their own: they were the least "anomic,"
"misanthropic," and "authoritarian" of
all. And where the LLs had preponderantly
described themselves as shy and retiring,
the average UM respondent depicted
himself as one who is "at ease" among
others: as gregarious and sociable. If, on
the other hand, the LL purports to be
inner-directed in inclination (and we must
recall the conflicting evidence), the logical
inference that the prevailing UM tenor is
more other-directed is not warranted by
the data. For in consequence of efforts to
tap at least some dimensions of Riesman's
three character constructs, "other-directed-
ness"—a compelling need to "do as those
around us do"—appeared to be more of
an upper-lower and even lower-middle
than an upper-middle propensity. The
member of the latter level seemed, in
contrast, less impressionable and more
certain of himself. Nor was the UM so
self-conscious as those in other levels; he
was at least willing to agree, for instance,
that ". . . It is difficult, when in a crowd
of strangers, not to be concerned with how
I look to them—about the sort of impression I am making." Neither (professedly)
was he as concerned as the others with
what neighbors or strangers thought of his
garden, home, car, and clothes.[45] Lest the
UM be mistakenly taken as a flawless
paragon of virtue, it is only fair to remind
ourselves that the "tests" designed to
measure various components of personality
are at best imperfect stabs at reality.[46]
What is more, the description of such
findings, if not quite caricatures, are
written in consciously bold relief in order
to highlight the more relevant and contrasting class-linked qualities. There exists
the possibility, finally, that like so many
"character" and "intelligence" tests, such
measures (together with their criteria of
"goodness") are not altogether culture-
free: free of a bias which might best be
characterized in terms of "seeing—and
judging—the world through middle-class
glasses."[47]

Almost three-fifths of the Peninsula
upper-middles were, in terms of their
parents' class levels, "upward mobile."
And the key to their mobility, especially if
they were 45 years of age or younger, was
the college diploma. As much an instrument of status validation to the UM as
the white collar is to the LM, the bachelor's
degree predictably dominated much of the
upper-middle-class vision. "Education"
and "career"—and the two are indissolubly linked—may be said, in fact, to
be the most focal UM concerns. At the
family dinner table, at parties, in terms
of values they would instill in their children,
"career" crops up again and again as a
central UM value. And when he is not
talking "shop," it appears, the man at this

level is talking education—especially to his children. Even as early as the kindergarten-primary years, he apprehensively scans his children's school performances less—as with the UL and LM—for signs of social adjustment than for indications of academic competence. Especially if he himself is a graduate of a state college or university, he wants his offspring to go to some such "prestige" school as Stanford, Harvard, Yale, or Princeton,[48] yet admittance to such institutions is increasingly limited to only the ablest students.[49] He knows this and his consequent concern amounts at times, to a virtual panic; it would appear meaningful, then, that it was he, especially, who led the many local fights for a curtailment of "progressive education" practices; his characteristic answer to the question "what is wrong with our public schools?" was the "life adjustment ideal"! Where, at lower levels, the lower-class parent might stress toughness and obedience and the lower-middle parent morality, frugality, and religiosity, the representative upper-middle parent urged his children to attain top academic marks and win out in classroom competition.[50]

Count Alexis de Tocqueville, Lord James Bryce, and countless observers ever since have observed that Americans are passionate "joiners"—that the man without some sort of formal affiliation is a virtual pariah. Had they observed with greater caution, they might have more precisely qualified this characteristic with the hedge, "certain" Americans: the Americans we would classify today as "upper-middle." For it is unquestionably at this level that (to borrow from sociological gobbledy-gook) "organization proneness" most emphatically prevails. It is not, however, the lodge or fraternal order which claims upper-middle allegiance,

but the service club: Rotary, especially, and the likes of Kiwanis, Lions, professional societies, and the big-city chambers of commerce. Upper-middle wives, too, are the most avid clubwomen. If not all Helen Hokinson sorts, they certainly prove likeliest of all to pack the seats at neighborhood improvement meetings, to belong to garden, alumnae, and bridge clubs, and to campaign vigorously for charitable enterprises. What is more she, like her husband, is frequently elected "president" of some such group.[51] And her children, too, are elected to school offices more frequently than others and belong to more such organizations as Boy Scouts and Girl Scouts. Predictably, the UM's civic consciousness and involvement is mirrored in the voting booth; in seven cases in ten a Republican,[52] more than 85 in every 100 at his class level turned out to vote at the 1960 presidential election.

The UM is not very "religious"; not, that is, in the manner of the LM; he attends church (and his children Sunday school) almost as frequently as those in other levels. But there is abundant evidence—including his own testimony—that he takes his religion more socially than literally, more ceremoniously than moralistically; liturgy, ritual, and tradition: these appear to be the most telling religious pulls for the UM. Even among his numbers baptized and raised in the Catholic church, there are far more "faith shifters" than at any other social-class level. And it is *into* three denominations in particular that upper-middle respondents have elected to move: Presbyterian, Episcopal, and Congregational.[53] And that childhood religious background is less and less compelling as one ascends the class ladder is hinted by the respective proportions of respondents at each level who were baptized, confirmed, and reared as Roman

Catholics yet who married non-Catholics (LL: 18%; UL: 22%; LM: 47%; UM: 84%). While the matter of marriage is relevant, it should be noted that the broken-marriage rate is lowest of all at the upper-middle-class level: less than one marriage in ten had been dissolved by divorce, separation, desertion, or annulment. The important question, "why?" is too complex to allow the analysis it merits; yet certain circumstances which research has linked with marital success especially predominate at the UM level and warrant mention: upper-middle subjects are presumably more "mature" because they marry later (he averaged 25 and she nearly 23); prior to marriage each had dated for a longer time and had dated a larger number of partners; the parents of each had, according to their children, experienced "happier" marriages, and, perhaps most importantly of all, both more readily subscribed to the "democratic-companionship"—in contrast to the autocratic-patriarchal—ideal-type marital union.

If the Peninsula's upper-middles differed from subjects at other class levels in the realms of attitudes, deep-seated value complexes, organizational activity, and political and religious bents, they differed, too, in their leisure-time proclivities.

And it is here that what behavioral scientists shun as "value judgments" almost necessarily impinge on any attempt at description and analysis.[54] Reservations notwithstanding, the undertaking's UMs were plainly more sophisticated and more discriminating than any but the "uppers" in the arena of leisure. The "fine arts," for example—ballet, opera, symphonic music, the theater, poetry, literature, and graphic art—drew their most enthused devotees from people at this level. They read more books—an average of at least one a month and, more consequentially, they read what arbiters of literature would certainly define as "superior" books. They rarely attended motion pictures, but when they did (from four to six times a year) they typically preferred foreign and "art" fare or sophisticated domestic comedy; representative of their favorite actors and actresses were Greta Garbo, Marlene Dietrich, Barbara Bel Geddes, Grace Kelly, Audrey Hepburn, Cary Grant, Jack Lemmon, Alec Guinness, Jimmy Stewart, and Peter Sellers.[55] Their television tastes were similar to their cinematic: they rarely watched television and the one half who did watch on other than special occasions averaged less than 20 minutes a night in front of their sets. What is more, the viewers at the UM level were becoming weary of television (during recent years television watching has dramatically decreased at the "top" of the class ladder and increased at the bottom); commercials as well as the fare had alienated a significant number of them to the point of vocal disgust.[56] Aside from "Channel 9"—an educational-cultural outlet in San Francisco area—their favorite fare, even after its demise, was Playhouse 90; other representative upper-middle preferences were discussion panels (their first choice in 1962 was Open End), news analyses (none devoted as much allegiance to Huntley and Brinkley as they), and sportscasts (notably college and professional football).[57]

Magazine likes were just as sharply class-linked. Thus where those in the lower classes were inclined to indulge in the "pulps" and the LMs were fondest of the giant mass-circulation periodicals, the characteristic UM preferences were *Time, Sunset,*[58] *U.S. News and World Report, Sports Illustrated, New Yorker, Harper's, Atlantic,* and *Saturday Review.* Newspaper choices were more variegated, although blue-collarites tended to prefer evening papers and white-collarites morning papers (except for the group, largely those who commuted to San Francisco, who read both morning and evening newspapers); the former expressed a greater interest in local and community news, whereas those in the middle classes, especially the UMs, were more partial to national and international doings.[59] In a word, the LLs and ULs were generally more "localistic" and the UMs more "cosmopolitan" in outlook.[60]

The generic cultural-esthetic bent among the upper middles roughly corresponds to what Russell Lynes has identified in tongue-in-cheek manner as "upper-middle-brow"; it is from this social-class level, too, that the vast majority of "high-brows" are drawn.[61] But the latter, who by definition are virtually classless (for their often self-conscious intellectual-esthetic tastes tend to transcend class as well as national boundaries), are a distinct minority even in UM circles in San Francisco. Yet it has been they (more recently identified by Lynes as "upper bohemians") who in many instances have first supported what have eventually become major UM interests: high-fidelity music, for example, and modern ballet and opera, the "little theatre," poetry recitals, contemporary jazz, the *haute cuisine*, and "serious" paperback books.[62]

Before inquiring into the qualities of the last of the Peninsula class levels—the "upper"—it will be relevant to examine certain contentions advanced by William H. Whyte, Jr. in his much-quoted *The Organization Man*. Perhaps middlewestern and Atlantic-seaboard "suburbia" differs radically from its Pacific-slope counterpart. But even in neighborhoods predominantly peopled by middle-management employees of such giant concerns as I.B.M., Ford, and Lockheed, there was little or no evidence of the hyper-conforming "organization man." There was only infrequent "neighboring" in such areas; intimate acquaintances with next-door neighbors were uncommon, and individuality—not cautious conventionality—overwhelmingly prevailed. Concordant with Whyte's hypotheses, the upper-middles were the most "geographically mobile" of all: less than one in 25 had lived in their current dwellings for as long as a decade, and the average span of local residence was less than five years. Yet a sense of "rootlessness" appeared to be rare and only occasional friendships stemmed from first encounters at work or in the neighborhood. In like vein, we have already noted that "the" Peninsula suburbanite is—whatever his income or class level—a mythical being. He lives in suburbia more out of circumstances than choice; he identifies far more with "the city" than with his immediate environs, and if he is indeed similar to those who live nearby, it is not because he mirrors his neighbor: it is because both share a common social-class heritage. Somewhat similarly, some students of American society believe social-class "cultures" to be little more than "occupational cultures." The allegation, if the undertaking's findings have been read aright, is in part quite valid. For if there is one central determinant of social-class membership it is (except, perhaps, at the uppermost levels) occupational role. Yet it is possible to interpret such a diagnosis too neatly. The basic LL and UL callings might be definable, respectively, as "unskilled" and "skilled." But the LM and, especially, the UM occupational duties are certainly far too motley in every important context to "explain" what we have described as class-related values and behavior. Occupation in the general and abstract sense certainly accounts for social-class membership; but the consequences of such membership—especially for the entire family—surely transcend mere occupational values. There is, finally, nothing sacroscant about such labels as "upper" and "upper middle"; although traditional usage suggests such names, other designations—perhaps alphabetical or numerical—are no less worthy. Nor is the term "social class" necessarily the best; "culture unit," "socio-economic division," and "subcultural level" are among many which might prove equally as suitable.

Upper-class: Eccentricity, Ancestor Worship, and Insouciance

Of all the social-class designations, none has been simultaneously so apparent yet so misunderstood and misused. For "upper class" connotes many things for many people: privilege, power, and wealth justly or unjustly gained; ostentation, snobbery, immorality, gentility, lavish leisure, and inconspicuous consumption: in fact, the entire catalog of the commendable and uncommendable, the esteemed and the begrudged. The image, like so many popular impressions of the renowned and envied, is concocted of part truth and good part fiction. Yet what the "truth" is must remain unanswerable until "upper class" has been faithfully defined; and opinions are sharply divided even among the more diligent students of the matter. Thus for some, membership "at the top" is conceived in terms of power: massive, selfish, conniving power in the eyes of orthodox Marxians; interlocking, mutually buttressing powers—a complementary meshing of interests among such power

elites as the military, industrial, and governmental—to the late C. Wright Mills, or conflicting yet "countervailing" power blocks (i.e., big labor, big government, big business) according to John K. Galbraith.[63] For others, upper-class rank is more a corollary of high esteem or status; to them the elite is made up families which have enjoyed sufficient generations of prestige (blended, of course, with wealth and power) to merit the designation "aristocratic." A similar but variant opinion holds that a "new" society is taking the place of the "old." The old consists of stable, conservative, old-guard families, and is as inevitably represented in the sacrosanct pages of the *Social Register* as it is in the membership lists of the ultra-exclusive clubs: San Francisco's Pacific Union, Boston's Somerset, or Philadelphia's The Philadelphia clubs, for example; they are the "Proper Bostonians" and Philadelphia's "Main Liners." The new society is younger and less inhibited; blended of European blue bloods, international celebrities, café society, the very rich, and the very powerful, its membership is more fluid and its stance less snobbish and far less staid.[64]

The *Social Register*, "old society" criterion was elected as this study's measure of upper-class membership, but only after considerable pre-testing and preliminary analysis. For the Peninsula's "power elite," though tacitly admitted to exist, was found to be too ill-defined and amorphous to measure. And the "rich"—those with annual incomes of $50,000 or more—were found to be little more than wealthy UMs: people whose basic values differed so slightly from those of the upper middles that they simply did not warrant a separate class designation.[65]

Numerically insignificant—less than one

in every 500 Peninsula families is listed in the pages of the *Social Register*—the upper class is nonetheless highly influential as a "reference group": a membership to which many aspire and which infinitely more consciously or unconsciously imitate. Its characteristics may be delineated briefly.

The ranks of the upper class—of the "Us" are only rarely characterized by conspicuous and showy consumption: costly debuts, mansions, hosts of servants, gala parties, glittering limousines and furs; this is the rare but publicized side of the coin. Not opulence and certainly not ostentatious display, but more nearly "inconspicuous" consumption—"tweeds," flat shoes, battered stationwagons, quiet parties: these are Peninsula upper-class earmarks. There is, of course, a minority "jet set" which boats a faster, more public life, and there are many in the U ranks who are ultra-fashionable in the realms of clothes, homes, and cars, and others still who boast chauffeurs and $100,000 homes. But the upper class, if it is to be judged accurately, cannot be legitimately assessed in such terms.

However conservative or however flamboyant, the U is heavily addicted to a seemingly unending chain of parties big and small, dances, charity balls, first nights at the theater and opera, and frequent sorties to the Sierra ski slopes, resort homes at Lake Tahoe or the beach, and his box seats at the San Fransico Giants' Candlestick Park. He drinks more frequently—and more heavily—than those at other levels, but he is less given to smoking. When he entertains, he is likelier to host bigger parties than the UMs—or smaller, for most typically he and his wife will entertain another couple with dinner followed by bridge ("the" UM game, incidentally) or dominoes. He likes form-

ality: white-tie affairs and, at work, dark or banker's grey suits with vests; his wife often prefers simple and "basic" black.[66]

The modal upper-class Peninsulan is likeliest of all to live in "the city": notably in San Francisco's exclusive Pacific Heights area or, if not, in more spacious and grandiose Hillsborough (less than half an hour's freeway time south of the city) or "exurban" (and quite "horsey") Woodside. Half his numbers are California born and half have lived in their present homes for eight or more years: longer, in both instances, than any, even those at the lowermost class level. He attended school at either Stanford, California, Yale, or Harvard (his mean educational attainment is equal to that of the UM, and like the UM, he has done at least some postgraduate work); she was likelier than he to have gone to a private school (Burke's, for example) and thence to Stanford, California, Vassar, or a two-year "finishing" school in the East. Fewer Us attend church than those at any other level. More than half are nominally Episcopalian, but fewer find themselves at church on Sunday than for weddings.

The U, finally, is in many ways more akin to the UL and LL than to his middle-class peers. Like the LL, for example, he is more tradition-oriented (although more given to ancestor worship, heirlooms, and insignia—or intimations—of high status in earlier generations); and like the Ls in general he claims to be tougher-minded,[67] more introvertive, and in accord with the ideals that husbands and parents should be dominant. He is less permissive than the UM parent toward infants and children, and like the L favors obedience and quietness. Nor is he so wedded to his career; likelier to follow in his father's occupational footsteps, even when he has not "inherited" the job, he, more than

TABLE 1. SOCIAL STRATIFICATION IN CALIFORNIA SUBURBS*

Level	Markings	Personality	Habitat	Diversions
Upper .2%	Listing in the Social Register	Conservative; indulges in "inconspicuous consumption"	Doings in "the city"	Partying, gin-rummy, watching baseball; foreign films
Upper-middle 10–15%	Professional or executive position, college diploma; $11,000 per year	The "joiner"—gregarious, hyperactive, socially at ease; concerned with "career" and "school"; child-centered and easy-going with children; takes his religion more socially than literally.	Service clubs like Kiwanis and Lions	Do-it-yourself projects. *Time*, *Harper's* Playhouse 90 on TV; bridge, golf
Lower-middle 35%	Whitecollar clerk, neighborhood businessman, or foreman; 7,600 per year; a tract home in the suburbs	Togetherness—active church-going; the "typical" American. *Says* he saves for a rainy day, but more likely than anybody else to own a Cadillac Lincoln or Buick.	Church lodge, PTA	Bible-reading; gardening (Mr. says he has a greener thumb than Mrs.); the "national favorites"—*Life, Reader's Digest, Saturday Evening Post;* Perry Mason, Ed Sullivan, 77 Sunset Strip; canasta, watching football

Upper-lower 35–40%	A union man: skilled or semi-skilled blue-collar worker; 11 years schooling; $5,500 per year	Closest to the cigarette-ad ideal of the two-fisted, tatooed he-man; ill-at-ease among strangers; wants to improve social position. Likes masculine men and feminine women, but helps with dishes and diapers; has migraine headaches, insomnia.	1) The great out-of-doors 2) Sears, Ward's Penney's (buying everything on time)	On TV, westerns like Cheyenne and Gunsmoke; poker
Lower-lower 15–20%	Usually unskilled laborer; 8 years schooling or less; $3,000 per year;	A misanthrope— pessimistic about the future, wary of strangers. Apathetic towards politics. Loyal to family and kinfolk. Wants to be liked; fearful of being an odd-ball or unpopular. "Children should be seen, not heard."	In front of the TV (and waits up for the late-late show)	Bowling; pool; on TV, westerns such as Wagon Train, wrestling and boxing. For wife: romantic magazines.

*Based on sample of about 2,000 heads of households in the "peninsula area," from San Francisco to San Jose. Originally appeared in Robert J. Havighurst and Bernice L. Neugarten, *Society and Education* (Boston: Allyn and Bacon, Inc., 1962), pp. 32–33. Reprinted by permission. (This chart was constructed by Havighurst and Neugarten on the basis of an earlier report on the "Peninsula People" data.)

the UM with a similar educational background, is found in such callings as banking, stockbroking, medicine, or architecture. Yet even more than the upper middle, the U appears to be "at home" among others, more insouciant and at ease no matter what his current social surroundings. Not quite so flexible and democratic, certainly not as gregarious and emphatic, he seems in many ways the most nonconforming and individualistic of all Peninsulans. Much of his social life and public decorum is rigidly straitjacketed by custom, yet he is frequently given to eccentricities which are rare at all levels except the "upper bohemian" segment of the middle class: to a curious blend of formality and casualness, diffidence and outspoken candor, of reverence and irreverence toward tradition. Like the upper middle, he is "at home abroad," yet he feels less compulsion to smile at strangers.

This, in brief, is the class system which prevails on the "Peninsula." It is still ill-defined, its boundaries imperceptibly merge, and the whole of its substance is in a constant state of dynamic flux. At no level are its members rigidly governed by its unwritten norms, yet at all levels deeply embedded values as well as everyday behavior are class-typed beyond our faintest comprehension.

What of the future? None but seers can vividly foretell. But to an educated guess will allow a terse if rough-hewn prophecy of things to come.

Most saliently of all, America's social-class affiliations should simultaneously become less—and yet more—consequential in shaping their destinies, perceptions, and behaviors. Less consequential because the American people, like all who belong to industrialized "mass" societies, are fast becoming an ever more homogeneous people with a mass, common-denominator culture. And yet more consequential because the very forces which are making them "more alike" are at the same time making social class a relatively (if not absolutely) more potent instrument.[68]

A word of amplification is in order. Toward the end of the nineteenth century and the beginning of the twentieth, no society on earth seemed more heterogeneous—composed of more diverse racial and ethnic elements—than the United States. But even before immigration had dwindled to a trickle, the massive pressures which were to cast Americans into more and more of a look-alike mold were at work.[69]

The pressures are too numerous to detail, but among them were increasingly effective means of mass production (and its correlative mass-marketing operations), transportation, and communication. Simultaneously, the once-potent differences on the American cultural landscape were being flattened by the world's first truly democratic system of mass education. This movement was in turn indissolubly linked with mass literacy, the mass production and marketing of books and periodicals, and an ever more vigorous and pervasive advertising industry.[70] In the meanwhile unionization and federally legislated social security and taxation measures were, together with an economy which benefitted the "have nots" more than any element in the population,[71] shaping an economic structure which bulged the more in the middle as it became narrower at its peak and its base.

These were the more tangible, "real-life" elements making for homogenization. They were hastened and buttressed in turn by certain "American" experiences and ideological commitments which have blunted and distorted our vision of social stratification. Each merits brief analysis.

(1) Lack of a feudal, aristocratic heritage: because our nation was started, in at least one sense, from "scratch," we have not faced the trenchant fuedal survivals—both legal and psychological—which have impeded the growth of social democracy in so much of Europe and Latin America; nor have we ever known a native hereditary aristocracy; we have, in fact, been consciously anti-aristocratic. (2) Democratic idealism: the doctrine of demoracy is, of course, the very pith of our official philosophy and the heart of the libertarian concept that all citizens are legal equals. (3) Frontier psychology: If the frontier closed with the advent of this century, the "psychology" which accompanied it— the "go-west-young-man" faith in individual initiative, survival of the fittest, and ever-available abundance—did not die. (4) The Protestant Ethic philosophy: akin to the other ideological commitments was the Protestant Ethic belief which vitalized the commercial and industrial revolutions; for it sanctioned salvation via individual effort rather than hereditary privilege or redemption in the next world. (5) The Horatio Alger myth: the Alger legend, finally, was of a piece with the "log-cabin-to-White-House" and "rags-to-riches" themes; for each ordained that "Every-man" could, like Jackson, Lincoln, Ford, and Carnegie, struggle from humble beginnings to the very pinnacle by dint of grit, determination, and hard work.

Because each of these beliefs has so much in common with the others, they have effectively blended into the national article of faith which we know as the American creed. They have not only obscured the cold realities of social class and class differences, but they have served as the very incentives which have helped so significant a proportion of Americans to actually bridge the gaps in our socio-economic structure.

NOTES

1. Because social as much as economic rank is determined, in the long run, by talent and marketable skills rather than hereditary privilege, it can be argued that the American stratification system has functioned more as an elevator than a barrier—that despite obvious flaws and short-term exceptions, it has made for *de facto* equality.
2. Historical experience virtually ordains that social stratification connotes one thing for Americans and another for the peoples of the Old World. Particularly in such agrarian, semi-feudal states as Spain or tradition-permeated societies as England, survivals of the three-estate system of stratification—hereditary nobility and "gentlemanly" occupations and schools are prime examples— make class divisions more tangible and class consciousness more pervasive; the nearest American equivalent is our own "deep south." Correlatively, what Talcott Parsons has called the "particularistic" style of social outlook—the popular division of men into categories based on *inherited* differences—is generally more prevalent in Europe than in the United States.
3. The concept of "social class," it must be warned, is neither (1) universally accepted in the social sciences, (2) conceived in precisely the same way by all students of social stratification, nor (3) commonly designated by the same label.
4. Captivating as such sociological accounts may be, the subtle texture of social class is often more readily amenable to the stylistic graces of the novelist. For richness of insight and deftness of contrast, few have better described upper-class Americans than Henry James, Edith Wharton, F. Scott Fitzgerald, and J. P. Marquand; Sinclair Lewis remains the unparalleled chronicler of the middle classes, while the varying nuances of lower-class behavior have been variously conveyed by William Faulkner, John Dos Passos, Erskine Caldwell, Nelson Algren, John Steinbeck, James T. Farrell, and John O'Hara.
5. In addition, hundreds of studies appear annually which are devoted to such class-related facets of life as infant-training and child-rearing procedures, recreational habits, political orientation, consumer behavior, formal affiliations, freindship patterns, and a multitude of attitudinal and psychological variables.
6. The study will be reported in detail in two books: *Social Stratification: Class in America*, and *Peninsula People: Social Stratification in Suburbia* (forthcoming).
7. Although the variables derived in the main from the findings and theories of earlier students, many were suggested by the initial, "free-exploration" phases of the present study.

8. A more detailed and technical description of the investigation's research design, sampling techniques, and statistical procedures is available upon request from the author; space considerations preclude their inclusion here. Footnoted technical references have been pared to the barest minimum for the same reason.

9. Nor, of course, can every last individual be precisely class typed; conscious rebels and zealous individualists aside, many are simply "marginal": en route between one class level and the next, or indeterminantly on the fringe of two levels. Similarly, there are many who are Europeans more than Germans, or cosmopolites more than Texans.

10. Like "nation" and "region," the concept "social class" comprises considerably more than some such statistical *category* as 20–24-year-old, female, or Democrat; each class level is more nearly a subculture, and the members of a given class, although unknown to one another, are linked because they share similar life experiences, occupational roles, styles of life, educational backgrounds, formal affiliations, consumption behavior, leisure-time preferences, and choices of mass media. They tend to think and act alike because they share common "universes of discourse."

11. The humanist might object to sociological efforts to "pigeonhole" what are after all individuals with private souls; yet pigeonholing is an honorable occupation, at least as ancient as Herodotus and Plato, and it has been utilized, often magnificently, by philosophers, playwrights, poets, and novelists: by Kant and Sartre, Moliere and Strindberg, Keats and Eliot, Dickens and Faulkner. The "I.B.M." or questionnaire sociologist, armed with calculating machine, infertile imagination, and a mystical language of inelegant gobbledygook, is in part a genuine spectre, in part a straw man. For in sociology as in history, belles-lettres, philosophy, and the arts, there are not only sharply conflicting schools of thought, but scholars whose talents, inclinations, and modes of discourse vary radically.

12. The term "lowermost" is not so subjective a designation as it appears; for at least one thoroughgoing national opinion survey corroborates what common sense dictates: unskilled occupations enjoy materially lesser prestige than do occupations in other categories.

13. That his younger brothers will remain in school two years longer than he points up a matter of consequence to the educator: the burgeoning floodtide of lower-class youngsters who pose problems altogether unique, for their subculture is drastically different from that of the heretofore typical middle-class child's.

14. For a more thoroughgoing analysis of the subjective lower-class world, see the recent article by Albert K. Cohen and Harold M. Hodges, Jr., "*Characteristics of the Lower-Blue-Collar Class,*" *Social Problems, X* (Spring, 1963), 303–304.

15. Throughout this paper the concept "class" will be used loosely; in truth it has many components, among them, as Max Weber suggested, economic wherewithal (class), social esteem (status), and the ability to influence the destinies and decisions of others (power).

16. The "ethic of workmanship"—pride and ego-involvement in the work sphere— is even rarer in the lower-lower than in the upper-lower ranks; work for the LL is merely an unpleasant means to an end and it is rarely "brought home" and discussed at the dinner table.

17. For a more extensive discussion of this point—and the apparent contradiction between practice and ideal— see Cohen and Hodges, *Ibid.*

18. Perhaps in partial consequence of such authoritarian relationships, there proved to be more overt conflict between parents and their adolescent offspring at the lower-lower level than at any other; and at no other level did teenage and pre-teen boys so readily turn to all-male "gangs" (not necessarily "delinquent" gangs) for leisure and as guidelines to values and conduct. It is possible too, that the basic LL distrust of authority figures—policemen, teachers, and "bosses," for example—is also due in part to such parent-child interaction.

19. It was as though the LL was plagued by a diffused but constant "chip-on-the-shoulder" sense of repressed hostility.

20. That harsh, punitive infant-training and child-rearing is a corollary of authoritarianism poses a provocative question about the relationship between authoritarianism and social class; see Harold M. Hodges, Jr., *Social Stratification: Class in America*, pp. 210–217.

21. To affirm that the LL is "more" authoritarian is not to declare that those at the other extreme of the class scale—the uppers and upper-middles— are altogether lacking in this quality; it is simply to assert that a significantly higher proportion of lower-blue-collarites proved to be authoritarian according to the measures used to assess this characteristic in this study.

22. At no other class level did the election evoke such strong and vocal religiously hued sentiments; more than four in five LLs who had voted against Eisenhower-Nixon in 1956 voted for the Nixon-Lodge ticket in 1960. Perhaps more significantly, the LL vote was rarely a "proletariat" vote; he did not find the *system* wanting, merely other people.

23. Although the time-honored blue collar-white collar distinction is fast losing meaning in an increasingly automated work world which may soon see the bulk of all employees classifiable as "dial-watching," button-pushing technicians; the two lower classes share numerous similarities which legitimately mark then as a sphere apart; in like manner, we may refer to "the" middle class. Yet much is lost in such sweeping distinctions, just as the concept of the "average" American must gloss over Vermonter, Hoosier, Brooklynite, Texan, and Southern Californian.

24. For comments on the relationships between the Peninsula findings and Riesman's character types, see David Riesman, *The Lonely Crowd* (Yale paperback edition, 1961, p. XXI) and Seymour M. Lipset and Leo Lowenthal, *Culture and Social Character* (Glencoe, Illinois: The Free Press, 1961, p. 435); an attempt at "measuring" Riesman's "other," "tradition" and "inner"-directed types was essayed during the investigation.

25. His car is apparently a prepotent "status symbol" for the UL; and among second-hand buyers, a

greater proportion in his ranks than in any own Cadillacs, Lincolns, and Chryslers.

26. The UL's is the only class level where husbands tend to adopt their wives' religious preferences.

27. Aside from western (especially "Gunsmoke" among the men and "Maverick" among the women), the ULs more than any prefer comedies (Red Skelton, Bob Hope, Lucille Ball) and variety shows (Lawrence Welk, Ed Sullivan).

28. The percentages of "four closest friends" occupying the same social-class positions as the subjects: LL: 81; UL: 72; LM: 63; UM: 75, and U: 80.

29. P.T.A. groups in the Peninsula appear to derive their principal numerical support from UL and LM parents; many upper and upper-middle parents explain that other obligations preclude such activities.

30. Yet even in neighborhoods where LM and UL children live in approximately equal numbers, more than two-thirds of pre-teenagers' "best friends" are drawn from their own class levels.

31. Census data indicate, however, that the relative proportions of America's male work force in blue-collar and white-collar occupational categories have remained fairly constant during the past half century; this is largely because the skilled occupational level—the upper-lower—has drawn heavily from the diminishing ranks of farmers, semi-skilled, and unskilled. The most frequent UL-to-LM jump in the Peninsula study consisted of a move from skilled laborer (e.g., electrician) to small businessman (e.g., electrical contractor); yet the mortality rate among such starts was high: of every ten who had attempted such a move, five had been unsuccessful and had returned to blue-collar work.

32. The traditional emblem of white-collar status has been the high-school diploma; yet more than two in five Peninsula UL youngsters are now completing the twelfth grade, while the LM boy and girl are steadily expanding their educational horizons: approximately one in every two of the latter are now completing two years of "college" (typically, junior college) and, within 10 to 15 years, will apparently be earning a bachelor's degree. But in a proportional sense, the true floodgates on the school scene are opening toward the bottom of the class ladder.

33. Despite the numerous caricatures of the "kaffee-klatsching robots" who presumably people suburbia (see, for example, *Time* magazine, June 20, 1960, or *The Atlantic Monthly*, April, 1960), the suburbs in the Peninsula area proved to be far more heterogeneous than homogeneous according to dozens of measurable characteristics; "the suburbanite," in short, was nonexistent.

34. Respondents at other levels occasionally named the above as their favorites, too; but the LMs made the same choices with greater frequency.

35. In fact the LM was likelier than any other to have grown up in (a) the middle west and (b) a small or middle-sized town.

36. *Webster's New World Dictionary of the American Language, College Edition* (Cleveland and New York: The World Publishing Company, 1959), p. 1182.

37. There is evidence, albeit fragmentary, that mem-

bers of the Peninsula's "new" middle class—such "organization men" as corporation employees, military personnel, salaried salesmen, and teachers —adhere more readily to that constellation of values which William H. Whyte, Jr. has termed the "Social Ethic."

38. An interesting, but as yet unanswerable question arises: is the LM's professed puritanism and sexual morality practiced as well as it is preached?

39. Two-thirds of LMs change to their spouses' faiths when they marry; the same pattern prevails at all levels except for the LL, where the two in five who shift faiths are largely non-Catholics.

40. The lower-middle vote was, in fact, the only vote which almost exactly paralleled the local vote during the past five presidential elections; he appears to be the ephemeral "pivotal voter."

41. Both the John Birch Society and the Christian Anti-Communist Crusade derived their heaviest Peninsula-area support from the LM class, notably from its entrepreneurial elements; but intensive analysis reveals that the appeal of ultra-conservatism is as much "psychological" as it is class or group-linked.

42. This representative UM subject is, like those in the other levels, between 40 and 41 years old; many of the older men in this level, especially those in their 60s and 70s, have completed as few as 11 or 12 years of formal schooling. That some of the study's younger lower-middle subjects had completed college calls our attention to the fact that social-class membership is determined by far more than formal education.

43. Before examining the UM, we must once again remind ourselves of two cardinal points which, if overlooked, would grossly distort our perception of social stratification: (1) "the" American cannot be fully comprehended until his many component memberships (among them, regional, ethnic, and age as well as class) are understood, and (2) the concept social class, like the concepts "girl," "teenager," or "Jew," embraces a multitude of sub-types and variations— not to mention wholly unique individuals. In truth, then, there is no such thing as "a" Negro, "a" Texan, or "a" lower-middle-class American.

44. As in the whole of the United States so among the Peninsula people, adolescence appears to be increasingly prolonged; this was notably so among the upper-middles where—according to parental admission—adolescence is more and more intruding into the "pre-teen" years in the form of dating, drinking, smoking, high heels, mascara. and lipstick; it is protracted, too, at the other end owing to the tendency of UM boys to undertake graduate work and delay their entry into the labor market and marriage. Less volitional and of far more critical consequence is the impasse encountered by the LL adolescent when he is unable to find full-time employment.

45. Illustrative of UM opinions are two statements which respondents at this level emphatically disagreed with: "it would be embarrassing to arrive at a party and find that I had worn entirely the wrong sort of clothes," and "it would be embarrassing to discover that my neighbors considered me "different' or an 'odd-ball'." Riesman, it must be recalled, did not intend his

typologies to be confused with individual personality propensities; rather, they represent character
types which are common to particular societies
(and subcultures) at particular times.

46. Although major conclusions are based on a variety
of measurements—on depth and clinical tests as
well as open-ended personal interviews—their
validity has yet to be confirmed.

47. The "bad" boy, in the eyes of far too many
teachers, is simply the lower-class boy: bored,
restless, noisy, unkempt, dirty, trouble-making,
rude; this is but one of many instances in which
teachers must ideally combine psychological with
sociological "know-how" if they are to effectively
deal with their charges.

48. The two in five UMs who "inherited" their
status were, in fact, preponderantly graduates of
such schools as these (far more, too, had majored
in liberal arts and had belonged to "name"
fraternities or sororities). Sons and daughters of
upper-middle professionals and business executives, the whole style of life of these "core" UMs
differed so radically from that of the "parvenu"
(upward-mobile) UMs that their "level" almost
constituted a class within a class. In essence, they
were simply "more upper middle" than their
parvenu counterparts; yet they were less innovative, future-oriented, gregarious in inclination, and
geographically mobile. For a more detailed analysis
of this core-parvenu distinction, see Ruth Shonle
Cavan, *The American Family* (3rd ed.; New York:
Thomas Y. Crowell Co., 1963), pp. 86, 132–34.

49. Whether the UM concern that children attend
"Ivy-tinged" preparatory schools and colleges is
actuated more by status than educational motives
is a matter of conjecture; but the further we ascend
the class ladder the likelihood that
parents will send their sons to "St. Grottlesex"-
type prep schools: if not to St. Paul's, St Mark's,
Grotton, or Middlesex, then to such California
equivalents as Thacher or Cate. And unlike other
parts of the country Peninsula girls, especially,
are sent to private schools.

50. Almost one-half of the upper-middle spouses,
significantly, first met "at school."

51. Here again, it seems, we uncover another clue into
the characteristic UM personality syndrome:
gregarious, hyperactive, socially at ease, he is a
diametric counterpart of lower-class torpor, non-
involvement, and lack of assurance.

52. If the LM tended to be conservative in political
stance, the UM is more "liberal" in inclination;
thus (to cite one of several measures) the Republicans in his midst were likeliest of all to favor Rockefeller and Lodge to Goldwater, and the Democrats
to prefer Stevenson and Humphrey to Byrd. It is at
the UM level, nonetheless, that the most vocal
opposition to President Kennedy has been
expressed.

53. Even more "upper-middle" in membership, but
smaller numerically, are the Christ Scientist and
Unitarian churches; the percentages of all respondents who claim to have "inherited" their
religious faiths—to have followed parental faiths
varies denominationally: Roman Catholic: 99%;
Methodist: 80%; Baptist: 76%; Episcopalian:
60%; Presbyterian: 35%; Congregational: 11%.
Whatever her current religious faith, the lower the

class level of the wife, the likelier she is to follow
the faith of her parents.

54. For in the purest terms of "relativism" and
"ethical neutrality" nothing—no work of art or
literature, cuisine or nature—is inherently superior
or inferior; truth and beauty, these concepts would
dictate, are not eternal verities but are humanly
defined by given people at given times.

55. A sizable minority of UM men preferred the
"sexy-sultry" type: Sylvano Mangano, Sophia
Loren, Marilyn Monroe, Kim Novak.

56. Although the center of gravity among local
video viewers has been visibly shifting toward the
blue-collar pole of the class hierarchy, open-ended
interviews and unsolicited comments from LMs
as well as UMs indicate that a "hungry" market
exists for upper-middle-class-type fare; the
television market, like those in the other media, is
thus not one but many.

57. These represented relative (and unique) UM
choices; in the purely numerical sense the
favorite UM options included Gunsmoke,
Maverick, and Perry Mason (with the latter two
eliciting their most enthusiastic support from
wives).

58. A west-coast magazine devoted to gourmet-type
food, travel, and gardening.

59. Even so mundane a matter as liking for comic
strips proved to be class-tinged; characteristic
preferences at each level: UM: Gordo, King Aroo,
Peanuts, Dondi; LM: Skeezix, Joe Palooka,
Judge Parker, Dick Tracy, Mary Worth, Dixie
Dugan, Our Boarding House, and Out Our Way;
UL: Will-Yum, Smokey, Dilly, Mark Trail; LL:
Skymaster, Alley Oop.

60. In newspaper as with magazine and book preferences, the UMs' interests were also quantitatively different; they read a greater number and
variety of sources and they spent more time at
reading.

61. For Lynes' amusing yet informative account of
"brow-level" differences, see his "Highbrow,
Lowbrow, Middlebrow" in *Harper's* (September,
1949); a more serious and discursive analysis in
the same vein: Dwight Macdonald, *Masscult,
Midcult* (New York: Partisan Review, 1961), 78 pp.

62. Yet, though a numerically sparse element, the
"highbrows" appear to exert a disproportionate
influence on UM tastes in literature, poetry,
music, and the stage. There is evidence, too, that
their influence is increasing.

63. Akin to Galbraith's definition is the political
"balance of powers" concept.

64. Characteristic of the heterogeneous "new society"
membership: shipping magnate Aristotle Onassis,
Princess Margaret and Lord Snowdon, the Duke
and Duchess of Windsor, Elsa Maxwell, Jack and
Jackie Kennedy, Noel Coward, Henry Ford II;
the "old," although the boundaries often overlap,
would include such names as Lodge, Saltonstall,
Harriman, Belmont, Rockefeller, Biddle, Carnegie,
DuPont, Vanderbilt, and Stettinius.

65. In fact the UM core-parvenu dichotomy proved
far more discriminating than the "middle"-"high"
income measure; this would appear to be one more
convincing demonstration that not income, but
basic, deeply incorporated values and life-styles
are the essential, cataclysmic ingredient in what

we call social-class membership. See Harold M. Hodges, Jr., *Social Stratification: Class in America* Chapters VII and VIII.

66. "Tweeds and flats" are more her wear for neighborhood walks or the country.

67. Yet he, and in particular his wife, devote more time and energy than any to charitable endeavors; her Junior League (the one national upper-class organization) is a prime example, See Hodges, *op. cit.*, pp. 106–107.

68. As the forces making for sameness and homogenization shatter the once-formidable dikes—regional, racial, ethnic, religious, social-class, and even age and sex—which historically cast Americans into so many distinct types, the role enacted by social class has, in relative terms, become increasingly transcendent.

69. This is not to forecast a grim Orwellian world of other-directed automatons, but merely to point out the direction in which we have moved and, apparently, will continue to move.

70. A nearly identical trend is visible wherever industrialization and a psychology of abundance is an increasingly puissant force; thus the so-called "westernization" of Japan and "Americanization" of so much of western Europe.

71. During the past half century the discrepancies between the wealthiest and most impoverished tenths of the American population have been drastically reduced: what is more, the "deprived" elements—Negroes, Mexican-Americans sharecroppers, itinerant and unskilled laborers— have realized the most dramatic gains of all in "real income."

22. Urbanism, Anonymity, and Status Symbolism

William H. Form and Gregory P. Stone

A major characteristic of urban stratification is that city dwellers use symbols of status to define class membership because social contacts do not provide sufficient time to acquire personal knowledge about all the people one sees or meets. Taking this assumption as their starting point, William H. Form and Gregory Stone investigate which social classes are most easily recognizable through symbolic means and what the content is of the symbols which urban residents employ in judging each other. The authors report that "down-and-outers" and "high class" people are identified readily, and the lower status group especially so. They classify the content of status symbols into six categories. Of the six, they claim that behaviors which are indicative of what they call "style symbolism" predominate in the appraisal of all social categories. The paper concludes with an especially interesting discussion of how the lay public regards the criteria which sociologists use in determining social status.

William H. Form is Professor of Sociology at Michigan State University. He is coeditor of *Industrial Relations and Social Change in Latin America* (1965) and coauthor of *Influentials in Two Border Cities* (1965) and *Industrial Sociology* (1964). He has contributed many other works in industrial and community sociology.

Gregory P. Stone is Professor of Sociology at the University of Minnesota, the author of many articles in books and journals, and coeditor of *Social Psychology Through Symbolic Interaction* (1970).

Problems and Method

In small towns of the United States, where every man may know almost every other, participation in the daily life of the community is widely evaluated. On the basis of such community-wide evaluations, the participating person and his family may be assigned to a social class.[1] Such assignments may encompass the lifetime of a person, for changes in assignments are not easily accomplished locally. In contrast to the intimate and enduring appraisals of the small town may be placed the anonymous and often fleeting appraisals of the city.[2] In the mass society of the city many social contacts are segmental and the participants often strangers. Consequently, the urbanite may frequently rely upon appearance rather than reputation:[3] status may be temporarily appropriated[4] by the "correct" display and manipulation of symbols, while in the small town it is more permanently manifested by the direct enactment of rights and duties. The bestowal of status in the city is often an inference from symbolism to social position; in the small town the bestowal of status proceeds from the evaluation of rights and duties appropriate to social position, and the relevant symbolism is basically symptomatic.

The conspicuous contrast in modes of appropriation and assignment of status suggests that the techniques for the study of differentiation in small towns are not directly applicable to the city, where considerable attention must be directed to variations in the display and manipulation of relevant symbols.

The present study seeks to answer the following questions:

1. What symbolism is relevant for the appropriation and assignment of status in the city?
2. Is there consensus on status symbolism?
3. How are inferences made from appraisals of such symbolism validated?
4. Are the symbols employed by sociologists to assess the status of his informants the symbols employed by the informants themselves?

To answer these questions, an interview schedule was administered to an "analytic sample"[5] of one hundred and twenty-five adults representing numerically equivalent groupings residing in three widely differing socioeconomic areas of Lansing, Michigan, a middle-sized city of approximately 100,000 population.[6] The construction of the schedule was built around the theoretical contributions of Erving Goffman, Max Weber, and Hans Speier.

Goffman contrasts collective symbols which represent commonalities among social categories with status symbols which represent differences among social categories.

> Persons in the same social position tend to possess a similar pattern of behavior. Any item of a person's behavior is, therefore, a sign of his social position. A sign of position can be a status symbol only if it is used with some regularity as a means of "placing" socially the person who makes it. Any sign which provides reliable evidence of its maker's position—whether or not laymen or sociologists use it for evidence about position—may be called a *test of status*. ... By definition, then, a status symbol carries *categorical* significance, that is, it serves to identify the social status of the person who makes it. But it may also carry expressive significance, that is, it may express the point of view, the style of life, and the cultural values of the person who makes it.

... Status symbols are used because they are better suited to the requirements of communication than are the rights and duties which they signify.[7]

Interview questions, therefore, were designed to elicit from respondents the signs and symbols they employ to appraise the social positions and life-styles of anonymous others in status terms.

The adoption of Weber's formulation of three dimensions as a way out of the existing confusion characterizing current stratification studies is now part of an institutionalized pattern of behavior in the social sciences.[8] Concern with coexisting dimensions of stratification dictated the use of open-ended questions in the interview schedule. Although the instrument was designed to cast the informant in a status-relevant role, it provided him some opportunity to adopt other economic or politically appraising roles in accord with his orientation to the various stratification orders. Weber further observes that status groups are characteristically distinguished by their intrinsic tendency toward social closure particularly as manifested in connubial and commensal exclusiveness.[9] Accordingly, questions were focused upon those criteria employed by informants in deciding whether or not to invite anonymous others into commensal and connubial association.

Finally, the design of the interview schedule took into account Speier's contention that "for honor to arise it is essential that there be bearers, bestowers and observers of honor."[10] This important research distinction made over twenty years ago has scarcely been utilized in studies since that time. The great bulk of stratification research has been oriented to the general question: "Who bears what status and what behavioral and attitudinal consequences ensue?" Status bestowal and status observance have seldom been subjected to intensive scrutiny, except instrumentally to examine variations on the general theme.[11] This study devotes much attention to the bestowal and observation of status.

Observations of Status: Appraisals of Four Status Categories

Many investigators have explored the perceptual cues or symbolism used by people to identify their own status and the status of others in community settings. One of the most searching investigations of the symbolism which people use in their appraisals of others is the Duncan and Artis study of stratification in a Pennsylvania rural community.[12] More recently, the problems of whether people see social classes as discrete entities and whether there is a consensus upon subjective class identification have been explored. Thus, Lenski concluded that "social class" is popularly conceived as a series of continuous positions instead of discrete groups.[13] A study by Rose reveals that college students and their parents disagree sharply not only on their own social class but on the distinctions between upper- and lower-middle-class categories.[14] In Goffman's terms the tests of status for them are inadequate for the placement and appraisal of others and themselves.

The inadequacy of symbolism to observe status bearers seems to stem in large part from the nature of stratification in the city. As Kaufman says: "The question here is whether urbanites have sufficient consistency of behavior or 'status equilibrium' as they participate in highly segmentalized worlds, so that patterns may be delineated at any level."[15]

Confusion is due also to the symbolism in the mind of the researcher as well as that in the mind of the informant.[16] However, there is a third possibility—that informants may be differentially oriented in their appraisals of others. Thus, at times, they may appraise others in class (economic) terms; at other times, in terms of the power others command; and, at still other times, the assessment may be in status terms, that is, in terms of the prestige attached to others' behavior, appearance, or position in life.[17] It is this third possibility with which the research is concerned.

Respondents in the sample were asked how they would recognize members of four social categories ("high society," "middle class," "working class," and "down-and-outers")[18] in the anonymity of the central business district either on the street or in a department store. Their responses were analyzed first to ascertain the stratification dimensions (class, status, or political power) of their observations.[19] Inspection of Table 1 shows that roughly 15 per cent of the observations of "high society," "working class," and "down-and-outers" took into account at least two of the three stratification dimensions for which responses were coded.[20] In contrast, more than 25 per cent of the "multiple observations" were directed toward the "middle class." If, as Weber suggests, members of classes are

fundamentally in conflict with each other, while members of status groups emulate and exclude each other, then the relationships generated by the two orders are fundamentally incompatible. It would follow that observations and appraisals proceeding in terms of multiple stratification dimensions would be ambiguous and anomalous.

Confirmation of the ambiguous character of the symbolism employed was obtained from an analysis of the degree of certainty with which the different social categories were recognized by the informants. "Down-and-outers" were most readily identified, followed by the "working class" and "high society." Greatest uncertainty characterized the observations and appraisals of the "middle class."

Upper-, middle-, and lower-stratum respondents placed different emphases upon the stratification dimensions used to identify the four social categories. Specifically, lower-stratum respondents frequently employed a class symbolism to identify "high society" and the "middle class" and predominantly status symbolism to identify the "down-and-outers." The symbolism used to distinguish the "working class" (the category nearest their own) was the most ambiguous. On the other hand, informants from the middle socioeconomic

TABLE 1. STRATIFICATION DIMENSIONS OBSERVED IN AN ANONYMOUS SITUATION

Stratification Dimensions	Social Categories							
	High Society		Middle Class		Working Class		Down-and-Outers	
	No.	Per Cent	No.	Per Cent	No.	Per Cent	No.	Per Cent
Status	89	71.2	86	68.8	78	62.4	82	65.6
Class	34	27.2	34	27.2	42	33.6	26	20.8
Power	6	4.8	1	0.8	—	—	3	2.4
Indeterminate	18	14.4	39	31.2	26	20.8	33	26.4
Total*	147	117.6	160	128.0	146	116.8	144	115.2

* Percentages computed from an N of 125.

stratum of Lansing were much more consistently oriented toward status, for they primarily used status symbols to identify "high society," the "working class," and the "middle class." Only the "down-and-outers" were frequently observed in class terms. However, as was the case with lower-stratum respondents, the middle stratum employed a vague symbolism in observing the "middle class" (the social category nearest their own). Informants drawn from the highest socioeconomic levels had least difficulty in observing status as evidenced by their consistently precise appraisals. "High society," the "middle class," and the "down-and-outers" were all appraised in predominantly status terms, while class symbolism was most frequently employed in the observation of the "working class."

In sum, all groups identified "down-and-outers" readily and with least equivocation. Lower-stratum informants were able to identify "high society" with greatest facility; middle-stratum informants, the "working class"; and upper-stratum respondents, the "middle class."

Symbolic Content of the Appraisals Having established that there were frequent

ambiguities and inconsistencies in stratification observations, the data were again examined to determine whether the symbolism employed in these observations varied from one social category to another. To accomplish this, the content of the symbolism was classified under six headings: (1) style symbolism, emphasizing the "strategy" rather than the content of appearance; (2) displays of possessions; (3) social identities emphasizing occupation, education, and other social attributes and group affiliations; (4) imagery or the appearance of the members of the social categories; (5) physical appearance or organic references; and (6) attitudinal references.

Table 2 summarizes variations in the symbolism used toward the different social categories. Three inferences in the form of hypotheses for future testing may be drawn from these data. First, style symbolism predominated in the observation and appraisal of all social categories. This finding supports Weber's contention that "'status groups' are stratified according to the principles of consumption as represented by special 'styles of life.'"[21] The finding also supports Riesman's hypothesis that the prototype of the

TABLE 2. SYMBOLIC CONTENT OF THE OBSERVATIONS AND APPRAISALS OF FOUR SOCIAL CATEGORIES

| | Social Categories | | | | | | | |
| | High Society | | Middle Class | | Working Class | | Down-and-Outers | |
Symbolic Content	No.	Per Cent	No.	Per Cent	No.	Per Cent	No.	Per Cent
Style	102	81.6	90	72.0	95	76.0	102	81.6
Possessions	79	63.2	43	34.4	89	71.2	59	47.2
Social identities	42	33.6	45	36.0	44	35.2	33	26.4
Images of appearance	13	10.4	—	—	22	17.6	86	68.8
Organic references	—	—	—	—	35	28.0	25	20.0
Attitudinal references	—	—	50	40.0	—	—	81	64.8
Total*	236	188.8	228	182.4	285	228.0	386	308.8

* Percentages computed from an *N* of 125.

changing American "character" is reflected in changing styles of consumption —from a preoccupation with the "hardness of the materials" (the display of possessions per se) to a preoccupation with the implementation of the materials in the strategies of human relations.[22] In general, matters of taste and style may be crucial in setting the temporary status arrangements formed in the anonymous situations of city life.[23]

The second inference from Table 2 points to a relative lack of emphasis given to any particular mode of symbolism other than style in the observation and appraisal of the "middle class." Coupled with earlier evidence concerning the ambiguity and uncertainty that attends appraisals of the "middle class," it would appear that the "middle class" is not a status symbol at all; rather, in Goffman's terms, it may best be understood as a collective symbol. Third, the data reveal that images of appearance increase as the general status of the social category decreases. Apparently people have least difficulty portraying the "down-and-outers" and the "working class" and greatest difficulty portraying the "middle class" and "high society." Perhaps status disqualification tends to become symbolically stylized in American society to a greater extent than status qualification.

With respect to differences among the categories, several clear trends appear. The "down-and-outers" seem to be the most visible group to which tests of status may be easily and clearly applied. Their style of life is distinguished by excessive drinking, shabby dress, obscene language, and slovenliness. In the imagery of the observer a shuffling gait, stooped posture, and the expression of indifferent attitudes (such as laziness and indolence) are characteristic of the category.

Members of the "working class" were identified not only by characteristic styles but also by object symbolism which singled out typical hats, shoes, occupational uniforms, or lunch pails. Categorical symbols betraying social identities based on occupation, education, or consumption (as evidenced by the stores they are seen patronizing) were also often employed, as were organic cues such as the condition of hands, teeth, and hair.

Observations of anonymous members of "high society" focused upon visible and audible evidence of life-style (manners, conversation, and dress) and the public display of possessions (jewelry, expensive clothing, and imposing limousines). More attention was directed to symbols of income, occupation, education, and family status which defined the social identities of the "middle class" than to other modes of symbolism, with the exception of style.

Interstrata Consensus on Status Symbolism Determination of consensus among different strata with respect to the kind of symbolism employed in observations and appraisals of different social categories poses a twofold problem. On the one hand, a consensus on symbolism implies that a substantial majority of respondents within each stratum applies the symbolism in question. On the other hand, such a consensus also implies a substantial agreement among respondents, irrespective of their stratum membership. Arbitrarily defining a substantial majority as 60 per cent or more of the respondents from each of the three strata interviewed, it may be seen from Table 3 that the symbolism employed in the observations of the "middle class" did not command a majority of the respondents. Substantial majorities did employ symbolism emphasizing varieties of style in their observations of "high

TABLE 3. SYMBOLIC CONTENT OF OBSERVATIONS AND APPRAISALS OF FOUR SOCIAL CATEGORIES

Symbolism Applied to Four Social Categories	Socioeconomic Strata of Respondents					
	Upper		Middle		Lower	
	No. (N = 32)	Per Cent	No. (N = 51)	Per Cent	No. (N = 42)	Per Cent
"High Society":						
Style	24	75.0	44	86.2	34	80.9
Manners	11	34.4	15	29.4	5	11.9
Mode of dress	19	59.4	28	54.9	29	69.0
Conversational style	14	43.8	18	35.3	10	23.8
Possessions	19	59.4	29	56.8	31	73.8
Clothing	18	56.2	25	49.0	22	52.4
Car*	2	6.3	4	7.8	11	26.2
Wealth*	1	3.1	2	3.9	9	21.4
"Middle Class":						
Style*	21	65.6	44	86.2	23	54.7
Mode of dress*	16	50.0	33	64.7	15	35.7
Grooming	8	25.0	13	25.5	4	9.5
Conversational style	4	12.5	15	29.4	1	2.4
Manners*	4	12.5	21	41.2	2	4.8
Social identitites	10	31.2	19	37.2	16	38.1
Occupation	5	15.6	1	2.0	6	14.3
Economic position	3	9.4	7	13.7	9	21.4
Attitudinal references	11	34.4	17	33.3	13	30.9
"Working Class":						
Style	26	81.2	42	82.3	27	64.3
Manners	7	21.9	13	25.5	3	7.1
Mode of dress	23	71.9	37	72.5	25	59.5
Conversational style*	10	31.2	25	49.0	2	4.8
Possessions	23	71.9	34	66.6	32	76.2
Clothing	22	68.8	29	56.8	30	71.4
Social identities*	17	53.1	17	33.3	10	23.8
Occupation	5	15.6	9	17.6	3	7.1
Social participation	9	28.1	7	13.7	7	16.7
Organic references*	7	21.9	24	47.0	4	9.5
Hands*	7	21.9	18	35.3	3	7.1
"Down-and-Outers":						
Style	28	87.5	43	84.3	31	73.8
Excessive drinking*	1	3.1	14	27.4	6	14.3
Mode of dress*	18	56.2	32	62.7	14	33.3
Grooming	18	56.2	24	47.0	15	35.7
Conversational style*	6	18.8	22	43.1	10	23.8
Possessions	18	56.2	27	52.9	14	33.3
Clothing*	15	46.9	24	47.0	10	23.8
Images of appearance*	24	75.0	31	60.8	11	26.2
Haggard	6	18.8	8	15.7	1	2.4
Gait and posture	6	18.8	8	15.7	2	4.8
Attitudinal references*	18	56.2	13	25.5	13	30.9
Shiftless	11	34.4	7	13.7	10	23.8

* Indicates significant associations between mentions and non-mentions of the category concerned by socioeconomic strata below the .05 level as measured by the chi-square test.

society," the "working class," and "down-and-outers." Moreover, clear majorities reported that the display of possessions facilitated their placements of anonymous members of the "working class."

Yet, whether there is substantial agreement among the different strata upon these symbolic modes remains problematical. On the positive side it might be argued that the absence of significant association between mentions and non-mentions of the symbolism in question by socioeconomic strata requires that the null hypothesis of no difference be accepted—that agreement does, in fact, exist. However, if a rigorous criterion of agreement is applied, for example, that the association of mentions versus non-mentions of a symbolic mode by socioeconomic strata be at a probability level of .95 or greater, as indicated by the chi-square test, then instances of agreement are not found with reference to the symbolism employed to identify the four social categories. Application of this criterion elicited only one instance of substantial agreement: the application of attitudinal symbols to the "middle class" was a consistent feature of the observations of that category on the part of a third of all three strata.

When the data in Table 3 are examined for instances of major disagreement among the strata with reference to the symbolism used in observations of others, the application of style symbolism is most characteristic of respondents representing the middle socioeconomic stratum of Lansing. Only in the case of observations directed toward "down-and-outers" does another stratum, the highest grouping, apply the symbolism of style relatively more frequently than the middle stratum. As opposed to the latter, lowest-stratum informants apply symbols of style least frequently. The single exception to this is the highest stratum, whose observations of "high society" emphasized style somewhat less frequently than did the lowest stratum. The display of possessions was apparently not crucial for placements and appraisals of the "middle class." Yet, for two of the three remaining categories, observations on the display of possessions such as clothing and cars were most often employed by respondents from the lowest socioeconomic stratum and least often employed by middle-stratum respondents. The crucial areas of disagreement among strata seem generally to be that middle-stratum informants tend to emphasize the stylization of appearance by anonymous others and that lower-stratum informants tend to emphasize the substance of appearance and the objects displayed. Specific instances as well as exceptions to the generalizations are provided in Table 3.

Bestowals of Status: Admission of Strangers to Commensal and Connubial Association

The encouragement of commensal and connubial relations is a basic process solidifying and equilibrating the status claims of a group.[24] Consequently, the acceptance of a stranger into commensal or connubial association is generally a bestowal of equal status by those who tender the invitation or sanction the acceptance. Presumably, decisions to accept the stranger are based upon inferences drawn from the symbolism he proffers in the anonymous situation. Undoubtedly, such inferences must be validated subsequently. However, we are concerned here only with the kind of symbolism the informants said was relevant for their decision to bestow status upon strangers. The process whereby informants validate inferences underlying such decisions shall be considered in a later section.

Acceptance of the Stranger into Connubial Association[25] Acceptance of a stranger as a potential member of a family is a crucial decision, because status commitments to him are necessarily intensive, extensive, and enduring, involving as they do other family members. The following situation was presented to the respondents:

If your daughter came home one night and told you she was in love with a young man you didn't know, what would be the first questions you would ask her about him?

Only the broadest categories of status symbolism applied in this situation can be summarized here. Responses were classified according to queries concerning the family of orientation of the stranger, his other social identities, style symbolism, and "personality" attributes. Of these categories, only that of social identities, other than family of orientation, was employed by itself as a basis for deciding whether to accept the prospective son-in-law. In this case, as may be seen from Table 4, there was a slight tendency for respondents from the lower socioeconomic stratum to use

only this kind of information as a basis for their decision. In the analysis of the specific requirements of social identities, the lower-stratum informants were most concerned with whether the stranger had a job and whether he was a good provider. Middle-stratum informants were more concerned with his specific occupation, religion, and mobility prospects on the job. Respondents from the upper stratum focused their inquiries upon the education, religion, and financial position of the "candidate." In addition, middle-stratum respondents evidenced the greater tendency to include the "style" of the stranger in their appraisals. Reluctant to arrive at any final decision in the matter, they most often expressed the desire to get more information about the stranger and to "test" the love relationship. Their inquiries about his family of orientation centered around questions of "background" and morality. Respondents from the upper stratum asked many vague but seemingly important (to them at least) questions about the young man's family.

In general, the impressions from these findings support existing theory, especially

TABLE 4. SYMBOLIC CONTENT OF DECISIONS TO ACCEPT A STRANGER INTO POTENTIAL CONNUBIAL ASSOCIATION

| | Socioeconomic Strata of Respondents | | | | | |
| | Upper | | Middle | | Lower | |
Symbolic Content of Decisions	No.	Per Cent	No.	Per Cent	No.	Per Cent
Family of orientation and other social identities	12	37.5	12	23.5	11	26.2
Family of orientation, other social identities, and style	6	18.8	17	33.3	10	23.8
Family of orientation, other social identities, and personality attributes	1	3.1	2	3.9	2	4.8
Other social identities and style	4	12.5	6	11.8	4	9.5
Other social identities and personality attributes	1	3.1	—	—	1	2.4
Other social identities only	3	9.4	4	7.8	7	16.7
Inapplicable	5	15.6	10	19.6	7	16.7
Total	32	100.0	51	99.9	42	100.1

as developed by Warner and Lynd. When the bestowal of status is enduring and permanent, the substance and strategy of the *appearance* of the status-bearer becomes insignificant in the appraisal; the *repute* of his position and participation in the larger social organization is crucial.

Acceptance of the Stranger into Commensal Association The decision to invite a stranger to one's home is considerably less crucial, status-wise, than accepting him as a potential family member. Consequently, a less searching scrutiny would be expected prior to the decision to invite him home. To elicit the kind of symbolism respondents would employ in making such a decision, they were asked to react to this situation:

If you met a stranger downtown and took a strong personal liking to him (her), what kinds of things would you want to know about him before you would invite him to your home?

Again, it appears that the stranger's social identities are crucial in the resultant appraisals, but little attention is paid specifically to his family of orientation. In this case, however, as may be seen from Table 5, appraisals of the stranger's social identity were most often made, in conjunction with his "style," by all informants regardless of socioeconomic circumstance. Upper-stratum respondents, however, were somewhat more concerned with style than were others. They paid special attention to the stranger's manners, breeding, mode of conversation, leisure activities, and similar attributes. Middle-stratum informants were somewhat more preoccupied with his occupation, family, education, religion, ethnicity, and place of residence. More frequently than any other stratum, lower-stratum respondents took into account the personality attributes of the stranger, his friendliness or responsiveness to themselves. One gains an impression from the data that lower-stratum respondents regard the stranger's acceptance of their invitation as a bestowal of status upon themselves.

This brief investigation of the bestowal of status upon strangers seems to suggest the following hypotheses. Bestowal of status commits the person as his observations of status do not. The more enduring the commitment, the less relevant is the

TABLE 5. SYMBOLIC CONTENT OF DECISIONS TO ACCEPT A STRANGER INTO POTENTIAL COMMENSAL ASSOCIATION

| | Socioeconomic Strata of Respondents | | | | | |
| | Upper | | Middle | | Lower | |
Symbolic Content of Decisions	No.	Per Cent	No.	Per Cent	No.	Per Cent
Social identities only	2	6.3	5	9.8	2	4.8
Social identities and style	13	40.6	23	45.1	20	47.6
Social identities and personality attributes	—	—	1	2.0	—	—
Social identities, style, and personality attributes	6	18.8	9	17.6	5	11.9
Style only	5	15.6	4	7.8	2	4.8
Style and personality attributes	1	3.1	3	5.9	6	14.3
Personality attributes only	—	—	2	3.9	2	4.8
Inapplicable	5	15.6	4	7.8	5	11.9
Total	32	100.0	51	99.9	42	100.1

TABLE 6. MODES OF VALIDATING STATUS INFERENCES

Modes of Validating Status	Socioeconomic Strata of Respondents							
	Upper		Middle		Lower		Total	
	No.	Per Cent	No.	Per Cent	No.	Per Cent	No.	Per Cent
Observation	7	21.9	6	11.8	16	38.1	29	23.2
Indirect interrogation	20	62.4	31	60.8	10	23.8	61	48.8
Direct interrogation	6	18.8	19	37.2	17	40.5	42	33.6
Total*	33	103.1	56	109.8	43	102.4	132	105.6

$$\chi^2 = 17.8981 \,; p < .01$$

* Some informants employed more than one mode of validation. Percentage are computed from a total N of 125, consisting of 32 upper-stratum, 51 middle-stratum, and 42 lower-stratum respondents.

style of the other and the more relevant is the repute of his position and participation in the larger social organization. The more transient the commitment, the more relevant the style of the other and the less relevant his position and participation. Finally, the absence of any significant associations between symbolic content of the bestowals and socioeconomic stratum of the respondent may indicate a greater interstrata consensus in the status symbolism employed in bestowals than in observations of status.

Validations of Status Inferences

Because the bestowal of status upon the stranger commits the person to a relationship, the decision to bestow status must be validated. The person somehow must assure himself that the stranger is, in fact, deserving of the status bestowed. To ascertain how such validations are accomplished, informants were asked how they would go about finding out the answers to questions they would ask about a stranger before inviting him to their homes. Validations were undertaken in three general ways. Relying completely upon the appearance of the stranger, some informants merely used observation for the validation

of their status inferences. Others asked the stranger direct questions to secure the information they needed. Most informants were indirect in their interrogations. Raising seemingly irrelevant points of discussion, they expected the stranger to reveal himself in the course of conversation, or they would search for mutual friends and acquaintances, delay their decision to invite him, and check with mutual friends and acquaintances prior to committing themselves.

Table 6 shows that the socioeconomic stratum of the respondent was associated with the mode of validation employed. Upper-stratum informants employed indirect modes of validation more frequently than we would expect by chance. However, the cells contributing most to the chi square indicate that the most significant tendencies are represented by lower-stratum informants employing observation as a mode of validation and avoiding indirect interrogation, while middle-stratum informants tend generally to avoid observation as a mode of validation.[26]

Status Symbolism of the Sociologist

One of the routine tasks of the sociologist is precisely the placement of persons, and, to accomplish these placements, he takes into account the symbols that people present. An attempt is made in this final section to inquire into the relative importance which laymen place upon the symbolism which the sociologists use, insofar as the laymen use such symbols in their placements and appraisals of others. To this end informants were asked to rate the indexes sociologists have used in their stratification studies as "important," "irrelevant," or "unimportant." The test of "importance" was whether they used the index in question in their own judgments and appraisals of others. Table 7 presents the list of indexes they judged to be unimportant or irrelevant.

Seven of the twelve indexes presented—household furnishings, income, occupation, organizations and clubs, types of house, clothing, and type of neighborhood—were judged by a majority of the respondents to be unimportant or irrelevant in appraising others. This is somewhat sur-

prising in view of the fact that such indexes as income and occupation are so often used by sociologists in their placements of respondents. It may be that respondents may have taken advantage of this question to "play down" status differences in their community. Furthermore, the same index is certainly construed differently by respondents from different strata. Thus, over 90 per cent of all respondents judged "family" to be important for the appraisal of others, but the different connotations of the term for upper- and lower-stratum respondents has frequently been noted in the literature. Despite such stringent qualifications of the data, there appears to be a general absence of significant differences in the appraisals of status indexes among the socioeconomic strata. Such an absence may indicate that the sociologist is, in fact, employing indexes which are relevant for the community at large and not characteristic of particular segments or strata of the community. In this respect two indexes

TABLE 7. STATUS INDEXES JUDGED UNIMPORTANT OR IRRELEVANT FOR THE APPRAISAL OF STATUS

Status Indexes	Upper No. (N = 32)	Per Cent	Middle No. (N = 51)	Per Cent	Lower No. (N = 42)	Per Cent	Total No. (N = 125)	Per Cent
Clothing	15	46.9	23	45.1	25	59.5	63	50.4
Credit rating	15	46.9	23	45.1	22	52.4	60	48.0
Education*	2	6.3	5	9.8	16	38.1	23	18.4
Family	4	12.5	4	7.8	4	9.5	12	9.6
Household furnishings	20	62.4	31	60.8	33	78.6	84	67.2
Income	17	53.1	32	62.7	28	65.7	77	61.2
Occupation*	12	37.5	27	52.9	33	78.6	72	57.6
Organizations & clubs	17	53.1	37	72.5	31	73.8	85	68.0
Race	12	37.5	20	39.2	25	59.5	57	45.6
Religion	15	46.9	23	45.1	21	50.0	59	47.2
Type of house	26	81.2	38	74.5	33	78.6	97	77.6
Type of neighborhood	17	53.1	22	43.1	24	57.1	63	50.4

Column group header: Socioeconomic Strata of Respondents

* Significant below the .01 level as indicated by the chi-square test for mentions versus non-mentions of the index by socioeconomic stratum of respondent.

were differentially evaluated by the respondents.

Judgments of the unimportance and irrelevance of education and occupation were significantly associated with the socioeconomic stratum of the respondent. In both instances fewer upper-stratum and more lower-stratum respondents than would be expected by chance judged these indexes to be unimportant or irrelevant for their appraisals of others. Since education and occupation are very frequently used by sociologists in stratifying communities, it may be argued that they are really viewing the community through the eyes of higher status groupings—that their stratifications may be ideologically biased. The other, and perhaps more pertinent, interpretation would acknowledge that the members of the higher strata of the community are in fact the bestowers of community status; but, until more searching investigations of precisely the mechanisms of status bestowal are undertaken, the problem will remain unresolved.

ACKNOWLEDGMENT

The authors are indebted to Arnold Rose for a critical reading of the manuscript.

NOTES

1. Essentially the technique of "evaluative participation" discussed extensively in W. Lloyd Warner, Marchia Meeker, and Kenneth Eels, *Social Class in America* (Chicago: Science Research Associates, 1949).
2. The opportunity for anonymity is enhanced in the urban environment, but in time anonymous contacts become personal (see Gregory P. Stone, "City Shoppers and Urban Identification: Observations on the Social Psychology of City Life," *American Journal of Sociology*, LX [July, 1954], 36–45; Joel Smith, William H. Form, and Gregory P. Stone, "Local Intimacy in a Middle-sized City," *American Journal of Sociology*, LX [November, 1954], 276–84).
3. For a competent summary of the issues involved see Ruth Rosner Kornhauser, "The Warner Approach to Social Stratification," in *Class, Status and Power*, ed. Reinhard Bendix and Seymour M. Lipset (Glencoe, Ill.: Free Press, 1953), pp. 243–55.
4. Weber observes: "The development of status is essentially a question of stratification resting upon usurpation. Such usurpation is the normal origin of almost all status honor" (Hans Gerth and C. Wright Mills [trans. and eds.], *From Max Weber: Essays in Sociology* [New York: Oxford University Press, 1946], p. 188).
5. A term employed by Eysenck in his critique of the sampling method employed by Richard Centers' study of the psychology of social classes (see H. J. Eyednck, "Social Attitude and Social Class," *British Journal of Sociology*, I [March, 1950], 57–58).
6. The use of a similar sampling device in a Minneapolis study is reported in Neal Gross, "Social Class Identification in the Urban Community," *American Sociological Review*, XVIII (August, 1953), 398–404. Gross's point that such samples are not "representative" of the community

populations from which they are drawn is to be underscored. Since Lansing, Michigan, is not a large metropolitan center, the present study is being replicated in the metropolitan area of Minneapolis–St. Paul.
7. Erving Goffman, "Symbols of Class Status," *British Journal of Sociology*, II (December, 1951), 295. The relevance of the last assertion applies a fortiori to the urban circumstance. Although the meaning attached here to "status" differs from that employed by Goffman, his observation that statuses may be ranked in prestige terms essentially captures our conception of status as used by Weber. Moreover, we substitute the term "appraise" for Goffman's "rank" to avoid the assumption of a hierachical status arrangement.
8. Neal Gross, "A Critique of 'Social Class Structure and American Education,'" *Harvard Educational Review*, XXIII (Fall, 1953), 300.
9. Gerth and Mills (trans. and eds.), *op cit.*, pp. 187–88.
10. Hans Speier, "Honor and Social Structure," *Social Research*, February, 1935, p. 76.
11. In this view one of the greatest shortcomings of current stratification research derives from the assumption that the entire community observes (confirms) the status of its members. Clearly observers of status may be proliferated and set apart in the social arrangements of the community; indeed, they may not be located in the community at all!
12. Otis Dudley Duncan and Jay W. Artis, *Social Stratification in a Pennsylvania Rural Community* (Pennsylvania State College Agricultural Experiment Station Bull. 543 [State College, Pa., October, 1951]).
13. A conclusion derived from the conception of the community as an undifferentiated status audience (see Gerhard E. Lenski, "American Social Classes: Statistical Strata or Social Groups?" *American*

Journal of Sociology, LVIII [September, 1952], 139–44).

14. Arnold M. Rose, "The Popular Meaning of Class Designation," *Sociology and Social Research*, XXXVIII (September–October, 1953), 14–21.
15. Harold F. Kaufman, "An Approach to the Study of Urban Stratification," *American Sociological Review*, XVII (August, 1952), 434.
16. Gross, "Social Class Identification in the Urban Community," *op. cit.*
17. The perspective of the observer is also a function of the larger social-historical context. The stratification imagery of working-class members of an urban community with a history of industrial conflict, for example, revealed a more predominantly (but not at all exclusive) class orientation than did our own interviews (cf. the suggestive study by Jerome G. Manis and Bernard N. Meltzer, "Attitudes of Textile Workers to Class Structure," *American Journal of Sociology*, LX [July, 1954], 31–35).
18. In line with the research aim to study status symbols, the designations "high society," "middle class," etc., were used because the investigators felt that these designations tended to evoke status imagery on the part of the respondents rather than class or power imagery.
19. A by-product of this analysis demonstrated the greater empirical applicability of the concepts "class" and "power" as compared to the concept "status". In the present state of our theoretical knowledge there is no gainsaying the fact that class and political power admit of more rigorous and precise "operational" definition than does status.
20. Since each "indeterminate" response was a discrete categorization of a single informant's response to the question, "multiple observations and appraisals" may be computed by subtracting the percentage of "indeterminate" responses from 100 and subtracting that result from the total percentage of "determinate" responses.
21. Gerth and Mills (trans. and eds.), *op. cit.*, p. 193.
22. The hypothesis has been presented many times by Riesman, but for its initial statement see David Riesman, Nathan Glazer, and Reuel Denny, *The Lonely Crowd* (New York: Doubleday Anchor Books, 1953), pp. 133–88. Elaborations directly relating to the area of stratification research may be found in Lincoln Clark (ed.), *Consumer Behavior, II: The Life-Cycle and Consumer Behavior* (New York: New York University Press, 1955), pp. 1–18. Concerning strategies of human relations see Erving Goffman, "On Face-Work," *Psychiatry*, XVIII (August, 1955), 213–31.
23. Some evidence confirming this assertion was afforded by Bevode C. McCall, currently conducting a study of stratification in Chicago. He reports the importance of matters of taste in the appraisals that Chicagoans make of one another.
24. On this point see, *inter alia*, Herbert Spencer's analysis of "visits" in his *Principles of Sociology* (New York: D. Appleton & Co., 1895), Vol. II, Part IV, chap. v, pp. 105–12. The status relevance of connubial relations is, of course, widely documented in the stratification literature.
25. In the interview respondents were queried about status tests in a commensal situation *prior to* inquiries concerning the connubial situation. With this procedure, application of the unusually severe tests of marriage was not suggested for the commensal situation.
26. These data may be compared with findings reported in Leonard Schatzman and Anselm Strauss, "Social Class and Modes of Communication," *American Journal of Sociology*, LX (January, 1955), 329–38.

23. Class and Mobility in a Nineteenth-Century City   Stephan Thernstrom

Mobility between social classes is usually thought to be one of the inevitable consequences of urbanization and the emergence of cities. Indeed, the opportunity for dramatic personal success which urban life is supposed to offer is generally regarded as one of its great benefits. Stephan Thernstrom examines the mobility experiences of working class families in "Yankee City" during the middle and late nineteenth century. Yankee City is a pseudonym for Newburyport, Massachusetts. He points out that it was common for laborers to leave the smaller cities of New England for Boston and New York, or to go West. However, Thernstrom doubts that many of them improved their social position by doing so. Among those who stayed in Newburyport, a few rose into the middle class, most remained members of a floating, itinerant laboring class, and a substantial proportion acquired homes and real estate and thus became members of what he calls the property-owning working class. Thernstrom concludes that the positive impact of urbanization on social mobility has been exaggerated. The reader will be impressed by the ingenious manner in which the author makes use of sketchy historical data to treat a very significant theoretical issue in the study of cities.

Stephan Thernstrom is Associate Professor of History at Brandeis University and a member of the Joint Center for Urban Studies at Harvard-MIT. He is the author of *Poverty, Planning, and Politics in the New Boston* (1969) and *Poverty and Progress: Social Mobility in a Nineteenth-Century City* (1964).

American legend has it that the United States has long been "the land of opportunity" for the common man. No other society has so often celebrated social mobility, none has made a folk hero of the self-made man to quite the same degree. The idea of the distinctive fluidity of our social order has been a national obsession for more than a century.

This has been the myth. How has it squared with social reality? The literature on social mobility in contemporary America is abundant, but social scientists have made few efforts to examine the problem in historical depth. One of the most glaring gaps in our knowledge of nineteenth-century America is the absence of reliable information about the social mobility of its population, particularly at the lower and middle levels of society. And ignorance of the past, in this instance, clouds our understanding of the present as well. Recent scholarly disputes over the charge that the American class structure is becoming increasingly rigid have been heated but inconclusive.[1] The question of whether it is actually more difficult to rise from the bottom social ladder in the United States today than it was in the America of Horatio Alger can hardly be settled when so little is known about the actual extent of social mobility in our society prior to 1900.

The only systematic mobility research in America which extends back into the nineteenth century has examined the social origins of members of the American business elite. Valuable as this research has been, it must be said that very little can be learned about the range of mobility opportunities at the base of the social pyramid from a survey of the class origins of those who climbed to its very pinnacle. "Room at the top" is perhaps less important than room at the middle, and about room at the middle a century ago the business elite studies are silent.

This essay summarizes some of the findings of a small-scale enquiry which ventures into this important but virtually unexplored territory. For some years now I have been analyzing the career patterns of hundreds of obscure workmen living in a small New England city in the latter half of the nineteenth century, using evidence drawn from original manuscript schedules of the U.S. Census, local tax and school records, and a variety of other sources. Rates of intra-generational and inter-generational occupational mobility, property mobility, and geographical mobility were determined for the sample population, and these discoveries were used to reinterpret the social history of the community and to explain the successful integration of its industrial working class. A few of the chief conclusions of the study will be reviewed here, with particular attention to those of special interest to the sociologist.[2]

The site of the research was Newburyport, Massachusetts, a city which already enjoys a certain notoriety as the scene of W. Lloyd Warner's "Yankee City" inquiry. Since Vol. IV of the Yankee City study, *The Social System of the Modern Factory*, is one of the most important sources of the influential "blocked mobility" hypothesis, it seemed particularly appropriate to conduct my own study of social mobility in Newburyport. A full critical discussion of what Warner and his associates failed to understand about the community as a result of their ahistorical, functionalist methodological preconceptions cannot be included in this article, but it is important to point out here that nineteenth-century Newburyport was not the dormant, self-contained "predominantly old American" *Gemeinschaft* village portrayed in the Yankee City volumes. Both Warner's image of the community in the 1930's when his study was carried out, and his assumptions about the city's history were badly distorted. In the latter half of the nineteenth century Newburyport underwent a drastic economic and social transformation and became a booming industrial city with its full quota of factories and immigrants. The point is important, for it means that the data on social mobility reported below pertain not to a deviant community representing a "substitute cultural profile," but to a city exposed to the same massive social forces which were altering the face of hundreds of other American communities in those years.[3] To observe nineteenth-century Newburyport is not to view New York or Chicago in microcosm, of course, but this small New England city can legitimately serve as a case study of the social effects of processes which affected New York and every other American city to a greater or lesser degree. For this reason, these findings concerning social mobility in one nineteenth-century city, though hardly a satisfactory index of the openness of the national class structure of the era, seem to me to provide a useful new starting point for gauging long-term mobility trends in our society.

Sample and Procedures

The population studied consisted of all male residents of Newburyport who reported "laborer" as their occupation on a U.S. Census schedule for 1850, 1860, or 1870, and all the sons of these men listed in the Newburyport schedules.[4] These obscure unskilled workmen and their children stood at the very bottom of the community social ladder, suffering from the classic disabilities of a depressed social group: unemployment, illiteracy, bad housing, poor diets. Roughly two-thirds of them were recent immigrants to the United States, uprooted Irish peasants driven to the New World by the terrible famine of the late 1840's. And the native-born Americans in the group were largely newcomers to urban life as well, migrants from the declining marginal farms of rural New England, men lacking capital or useful skills. The limited resources available for the study made it necessary to focus on a relatively small group. The unskilled laborers of the city were chosen as the least favorable case with which to test popular American mythology about mobility opportunities. This choice imparted certain biases to the findings, of course; downward mobility, for instance, could not be explored, for these were men who could fall no lower on the social scale. But this seemed the most interesting starting point for a mobility inquiry. If many of these impoverished common laborers and their sons actually made significant social gains, it would seem particularly impressive testimony to the fluidity of the social structure.

The career patterns of laborers in the sample were traced through 1880. The selection of the 1850–1880 period was fortuitous (manuscript census schedules were unavailable before 1850 and after 1880) but not unfortunate, for these three decades were of decisive importance in the social and economic history of the community. It was in just these years that Newburyport, still a sleepy pre-industrial town of 7,000 in 1840, experienced the sudden shock of rapid population growth, mass immigration, and economic transformation. By 1880 a modicum of industrial peace and social stability had been restored in Newburyport, a development which cannot be properly understood without some grasp of the mobility patterns disclosed in the sample study.

Men on the Move: The Problem of Geographical Mobility

The most common form of mobility experienced by the ordinary laborers of nineteenth-century Newburyport was mobility out of the city. Slightly less than 40 percent of all the unskilled laborers and their children living in the community at mid-century were still listed there in the Census of 1860; of the 454 men in this class in 1860, but 35 percent were to be

found in the city a decade later; the comparable figure for 1870–1880 was 47 percent. The first generalization to make about the "typical" Newburyport laborer of this period, it appears, is that he did not live in Newburyport very long! For a majority of these permanent transients, Newburyport provided no soil in which to sink roots. It was only one more place in which to carry on the struggle for existence for a few years, until driven onward again.[5]

Did these men on the move make their fortunes elsewhere in the Great West or the Great City, as American folklore would have it? It was impossible, regrettably, to trace these individuals and thereby to provide a certain answer as to how many of them were successful in other communities. In the absence of a magical electronic device capable of sifting through tens of millions of names and locating a few hundred there was no way of picking out former residents of Newburyport on later national censuses. It is important to note, however, that in only a handful of these cases was the laborer migrating from Newburyport in a particularly strategic position to take advantage of new opportunities in another community. If, for instance, the son of a laborer, unencumbered as yet with family responsiblities, was fortunate enough to possess a substantial savings account and perhaps a high school education or some experience in a skilled or nonmanual occupation, his employment prospects after migration were obviously excellent. Such cases, however, were rare. The great majority of laborers who left Newburyport departed under less auspicious circumstances. Without financial resources, occupational skill, or education, frequently with heavy family responsibilities, the range of alternatives open to these men in their new destination was slender. Laborers like these were not lured to leave the city by the prospect of investing their savings and skills more profitably elsewhere; they left when the depressed state of the local labor market made it impossible for them to subsist where they were. As a result of the collapse of 1857, for example, Newburyport suffered a population decline estimated by the local newspaper as "more than one thousand." Most of these departures, it was thought, were cases of workers moving to "locations where work is more abundant."

That the geographical mobility of men in these circumstances dramatically improved their prospects of upward social mobility seems unlikely. The telling objection which has been advanced against the famous "safety valve" theory of the frontier applies here.[6] Migrant laborers from the city rarely had the capital or knowledge necessary to reap the benefits of the supply of "free land" at the frontier. Most often these workmen probably remained within the unskilled labor market centered in Boston and extending out to Lowell, Lawrence, Lynn, and smaller cities like Newburyport and Chicopee. And it is doubtful that a laborer without capital or skills found it notably easier to advance himself in Boston than in Newburyport. The great metropolis offered alluring opportunities at the top to those with the proper requisites, but to the common laborer who drifted there from Newburyport it probably meant more of the same.

The present study necessarily focused on the settled minority of workmen who remained within the community for a decade or more and whose careers could therefore be traced. It is highly improbable, however, that our lack of precise knowledge of the later careers of migrants from Newburyport has led to an underestima-tion of the upward mobility achieved by local laborers. An inquiry of this kind, indeed, is biased to some degree in the opposite direction. To analyze the social adjustment of workmen who settled in a particular city long enough to be recorded on two or more censuses is to concentrate on laborers who were most resistant to pressures to migrate, and these tended to be men who had already attained a modicum of economic security in the community. Thus four-fifths of the local unskilled laborers who owned real property in 1850 were still living in Newburyport in 1860, a persistence rate of 80 percent; the comparable figure for propertyless laborers in this decade was 31 percent. Migration was, in this sense, a selective process. Masses of unskilled newcomers—from rural areas and from abroad—streamed into the nineteenth-century city. Large numbers of these men were unable to establish a secure place for themselves in the community. Unemployment was always a possibility, and all too often a grim reality. When jobs were too few to go around, the rumor of work in Lawrence, or Lynn or Holyoke was enough to draw these men on. Workmen who remained in a particular city for any length of time were therefore a somewhat select group, because to find sufficiently stable employment to maintain a settled residence in a community was itself success of a kind to the laborer. In tracing the changing social position of groups of Newburyport workmen we must keep this relationship between geographical mobility and social mobility clearly in mind. The process of internal migration within the unskilled labor market removed many of the least successful laborers from the community; the following analysis of occupational and property mobility in Newburyport applies only to a settled minority from the total unskilled laboring population which passed through the community between 1850 and 1880.

Patterns of Intra-generational Occupational Mobility

In mid-nineteenth-century America there were few dissenters from the proposition that a uniquely open, perfectly competitive social order had emerged in the New World, a social order in which any man, however lowly his origins, could rise to a station befitting his true worth. A note of skepticism about the ideology of mobility, however, occasionally crept into the immigrant press. Thus the *Pilot*, organ of the Boston Irish, observing that "if the school of adversity is the best place to learn, few will be disposed to question the great opportunities enjoyed by us to acquire a knowledge of mankind," mounted a sharp attack on the myth of America as "the paradise of the poor man." Just how was the lot of "the poor man in America

superior to the poor man in Austria or Italy?" The trinity of poverty, misery, and vice had been exported to the United States with eminent success. The braggart's "boastful tongue is silenced in hard times like these." And even in times of great prosperity, estimated the editors, 95 out of 100 ordinary workmen were fated to "live and die in the condition in which they were born." These opposed claims may be put to empirical test; this report on the social mobility experiences of laborers in a New England community is one such test.

An overview of the intra-generational occupational mobility of hundreds of unskilled laborers employed in Newburyport between 1850 and 1880 is provided in Table 1.[7] Occupational mobility was defined simply as a job shift from one to another of four broad categories: unskilled manual occupations, semiskilled manual occupations, skilled manual occupations, and nonmanual occupations. In the original study more refined categories were employed at a later stage of the analysis,

TABLE 1. OCCUPATIONAL AND GEOGRAPHICAL MOBILITY OF THREE GROUPS OF LABORERS, 1850–1880

Occupational Status Attained

Year	Unskilled	Semiskilled	Skilled	Nonmanual	Rate of persistence*	Number in sample
			1850 census group			
1860	64%	16%	15%	5%	32%	55
1870	36	39	9	15	64	35
1880	57	21	7	14	40	14
			1860 census group			
1870	74	12	8	5	33	74
1880	69	19	6	6	65	48
			1870 census group			
1880	79	6	10	5	41	102

* This column provides a measure of the geographical mobility of workmen in the sample. The rate of persistence of a group for a particular decade is defined as that proportion of the group recorded on the census at the start of the decade that is still present in the community at the end of the decade. Thus 32 percent of the unskilled laborers of 1850 still lived in Newburyport in 1860; 64 percent of the men in this group as of 1860 still lived in Newburyport in 1870, and so forth.

but these crude ones are well suited for this brief report on the chief findings.

The simplest generalization which suggests itself is that less than half of the unskilled workmen in Newburyport at the time of the Census of 1850, 1860 or 1870 remained there for as much as a decade, and that only a minority of those who did climbed up the occupational ladder at all.[8] On the whole the likelihood of moving into a higher status occupation varied inversely with the status of the occupation. By far the most widespread form of vertical occupational mobility was into positions of only slightly higher status than unskilled labor—such semiskilled jobs as factory operative, fisherman or watchman. The common workman who resided in Newburyport in this period had only a slight chance of rising into a middle-class occupation, even when "middle class" is generously defined to include a petty clerkship or the proprietorship of a tiny grocery or a subsistence farm. Nor was his prospect of entering a skilled craft very great. From 75 to 85 percent of these men remained near the bottom of the job ladder in the low-skill, low-pay occupational universe. The great majority continued to work as day laborers; most of those who did change occupations became semiskilled workmen, performing simple manual tasks at slightly higher wages and with somewhat more regular employment than they had previously enjoyed.

Comparison of the fortunes of the three groups of laborers studied suggests that the mobility prospects of those who arrived in Newburyport after 1850 were somewhat less favorable. Table 1 shows that workmen in the 1860 and 1870 groups tended to cluster more heavily towards the bottom of the occupational scale than laborers already working in the city in 1850. There was in fact a modest tightening of the local

opportunity structure after 1850, a point to which we shall return later.[9] But much of this seeming change was an ethnic phenomenon. When the occupational distribution of foreign-born and native-born workmen in these years is tabulated separately it becomes evident that the immigrant was distinctly slower to rise occupationally than his Yankee counterpart, and that the apparent trend registered in Table 1 may be largely attributed to the higher proportion of foreign-born laborers in the two later groups.

Fathers and Sons: Patterns of Inter-generational Occupational Mobility

If nineteenth-century Americans professed great optimism about the laborer's chances of "pulling himself up by his own bootstraps," they were more optimistic still about his children's prospects of rising in the world. A distinction between the situation of the first-generation immigrant and the second-generation American was frequently drawn in mobility folklore. A promotional book on *The Irish in America*, for example, was careful to say that in the New World "the rudest implements of labor may be the means of advancement to wealth, honour, and distinction, *if not for those who use them*, at least for those who spring from their loins."

Table 2 summarizes the career patterns of youths who sprang from the loins of the common laborers of Newburyport. The data are arranged by age groups, so that the adult occupations of laborers' sons as well as their initial jobs as teenagers are displayed. Not all of the fathers of these youths actually remained unskilled laborers throughout this entire period, of course, but for the present this variable can be ignored. A majority of them did in fact remain laborers, and, as we shall see shortly, those who did climb a notch or two upwards had little success in passing on their advantage to their off-spring.

In one important respect the sons of these laborers fared better than their fathers. Unskilled manual laborers in Newburyport during these years character-istically remained common laborers; the odds that one of these men would hold the same lowly position ten years later were at least two to one. But the sons of these unskilled workmen, Table 2 reveals, did not typically gravitate to unskilled jobs. In none of the age cohorts at any of the four censuses between 1850 and 1880 had a majority of these sons inherited their

fathers' occupations; no more than one in four, on the average, were employed as common laborers.

If most of these youths moved upwards on the occupational ladder, however, few moved very far. The great majority of mobile sons found semiskilled manual employment, and most of the rest entered a skilled trade. The contrast between generations was not at all sharp in the upper ranges of the occupational scale. It is striking that entry into an occupation which carried middle class status was almost as difficult for the son of a common laborer as for his father.

The children of foreign-born workmen suffered from special disabilities in the occupational competition, as did their fathers. As Table 3 clearly shows, the

TABLE 2. OCCUPATIONAL AND GEOGRAPHICAL MOBILITY OF SONS OF LABORERS, 1850–1880 *

Occupational Status Attained

Year	Unskilled	Semiskilled	Skilled	Nonmanual	Rate of of persistence	Number
			Youths born 1830–1839			
1850	39%	56%	6%	0%	—	18
1860	10	76	7	7	29%	41
1870	11	48	30	11	56	27
1880	11	42	37	11	63	19
			Youths born 1840–1849			
1860	11	84	2	4	54	57
1870	28	45	17	10	32	58
1880	21	46	17	17	33	24
			Youths born 1850–1859			
1870	23	59	11	7	54	95
1880	33	40	20	8	44	76
			Youths born 1860–1869			
1880	25	60	7	8	56	73

* The reader may be surprised to see the number of youths in a group increasing from decade to decade in some instances, at the same time that the persistence rate figure indicates that half to two thirds of the group members left Newburyport each decade. The explanation is that large numbers of youths were coming *into* the city during these years as well, and that these have been included in the analysis.

proportion of native youths in skilled and nonmanual positions was consistently higher than the proportion of sons of immigrant stock; the latter clustered heavily near the bottom of the occupational scale. But these ethnic differences in mobility opportunities narrowed somewhat in the post-Civil War years. The popular belief that second generation Americans labored under no special handicaps in the race for occupational status was excessively optimistic, but Table 3 hints at the beginning of a trend towards some equalization of opportunities. It is noteworthy, however, that by 1880 none of these youths had advanced through the mobility channels so often stressed in impressionistic accounts of immigrant life —politics and religion. To become a priest required education; to become a ward boss required some education too, and a well-organized, politically conscious constituency. The Irish of Newburyport, and later groups as well, eventually attained these requisites, but only after long years of struggle.

Since these mobility data display the career patterns of two generations of men over a period of some decades, it is possible to explore a question which has rarely been examined by students of social mobility. Was occupational mobility a cumulative process, in the sense that a father's upward mobility positively influenced his son's prospects for occupational advance? A rather surprising, though tentative, answer is suggested by Table 4 which classifies the sons of Newburyport laborers according to the highest occupation held by their father in the 1850–1880 period. No consistent positive relationship between the occupational mobility of fathers and sons appears. The children of laborers mobile into a semiskilled occupation were more successful than the sons of static laborers in both the semiskilled and skilled callings, as we would expect. But workmen who climbed into a skilled trade were unable to transfer higher status to their children; their sons found skilled jobs less often than the sons of semiskilled men, and were the least successful of all the groups at penetrating the nonmanual occupations. And the sons of the small elite of laborers whose rose into a nonmanual occupation during this period, paradoxically, clustered in unskilled laboring jobs more heavily than the sons of men still at the bottom of the occupational scale. The children of these highly mobile fathers, it is true, showed up much better than the other groups in the nonmanual category. But even so, only a third of them attained middle class occupational status, and this, for technical reasons, is an inflated estimate.[10] The table, however, is only

TABLE 3. OCCUPATIONAL DISTRIBUTION OF SONS OF NATIVE AND FOREIGN-BORN LABORERS, 1850–1880

	1850		1860		1870		1880	
Occupational category	Native	Foreign	Native	Foreign	Native	Foreign	Native	Foreign
Number in sample	19	14	34	76	37	148	37	158
Unskilled	26%	71%	12%	8%	8%	27%	19%	27%
Semiskilled	53	21	53	88	38	55	38	50
Skilled	21	7	18	3	27	14	24	15
Nonmanual	0	0	18	1	27	5	19	8

TABLE 4. OCCUPATIONAL STATUS ATTAINED BY LABORERS' SONS ACCORDING TO THE HIGHEST OCCUPATION OF THEIR FATHERS

Son's occupation at the last census on which he was listed in the 1850–1880 period	Unskilled	Semiskilled	Skilled	Nonmanual
Number in sample	234	38	23	24
Unskilled	26%	3%	9%	29%
Semiskilled	54	63	70	29
Skilled	13	24	17	8
Nonmanual	8	10	4	33

suggestive. Differences in the age distribution of sons in the four categories, impossible to control when the sample is so small, or some other variable may have been responsible for the pattern disclosed in Table 4. But it remains impressive that the cross-tabulation provides no positive support for the belief that exceptionally mobile workmen imparted exceptionally high mobility aspirations to their children, nor for the hypothesis that a mobile father was able to ease his son's entry into a higher status occupation.

Property, Savings and Status

Occupation, of course, is not the sole determinant of social status; men make certain social advances without changing their occupations at all. Class is not unidimensional; as Weber notes, "only persons who are completely unskilled, without property and dependent on employment without regular occupation, are in a strictly identical class status."[11]

The social group examined here consisted of men who did at one time hold a "strictly identical class status" in a nineteenth-century New England city. By any criterion the unskilled manual laborers of Newburyport at mid-century stood at the bottom of the social ladder. But how permanent was their lowly status? An assessment of the extent of occupational mobility out of the unskilled laboring class has been presented. The other major determinant of class status suggested by Weber—possession of property—should now be considered.

The facile optimism of nineteenth-century celebrants of the American way of life has been viewed with suspicion by twentieth-century historians. Few students of American labor history have expressed much optimism about the economic situation of the urban working class during the 1850–1880 period. Wages for unskilled and semiskilled labor were never very high in the best of times, and unemployment was endemic to the economic system. These three decades were punctuated by a national financial panic in 1857, a postwar slump, and a prolonged depression in the 1870's. A fairly characteristic judgment of working class opportunities for property mobility is Shlakman's verdict for Chicopee, Massachusetts: "Savings accumulated during the good years were eaten up in the frequent and severe depression periods." Another scholar reports that wages in Holyoke in this period were "little more than enough to live on."[12]

An equally pessimistic diagnosis of the economic prospects of the laboring class might easily have been returned by an observer of the Newburyport scene in 1850. And in many respects the lot of the laborer in 1880 seemed little better. Real earnings of unskilled workmen seem to have increased only slightly, if at all, in this period, and efforts to improve wages by collective action were still doomed to failure.

A careful tracing of the economic position of individual working class families through a variety of local records, however, yielded some surprising findings. Table 5, for example, which indicates the extent of real property ownership in the three groups, shows that real estate was strikingly available to working-class men who remained in Newburyport for any length of time. From a third to a half of these workmen were able to report some property holdings on the census schedules after a decade of residence in the city;

after twenty years the proportion of owners had risen to 63 percent in one group and 78 percent in another. The typical size of these accumulations, by men who had once lived on the margin of subsistence, was similarly impressive. The range of reported holdings was fairly wide, but the median figure was $600 or more for each group at each census. Only an insignificant fraction of these propertied workmen held less than $300, while a large and rising proportion reported accumulations valued at $1,000 or more.[13] Furthermore, a majority of the laboring families who settled in Newburyport in these years had accounts in local savings banks, and accumulations of several hundred dollars were not uncommon. That an ordinary workman in Newburyport might in time accumulate a sizeable property stake was not a mere possibility: it was a strong probability.

TABLE 5. PROPERTY HOLDINGS OF LABORING FAMILIES *

		Property Owners		Percentage Distribution by Value			
Year	Number of families	Number	Percent	Under $300	$300–999	$1000 or more	Median holding
			1850 census group				
1850	175	18	11%	0%	72%	28%	$600
1860	71	23	32	0	70	30	800
1870	49	38	78	8	47	45	800
1880	34	18	53	0	56	44	950
			1860 census group				
1860	256	28	11	4	86	11	700
1870	105	50	48	8	46	46	800
1880	70	44	63	5	52	43	800
			1870 census group				
1870	256	74	29	5	53	42	700
1880	121	49	41	6	61	33	700

* It may be noticed that the group numbers here are somewhat larger than those in the occupational mobility tables preceding. This is because the unit of study has shifted from the individual to the family. If the father in the 1850 group died in 1868, obviously no occupation would be listed for him in the Census of 1870. But if one of his employed sons continued to live with the family in 1870, the family would still be included in these property calculations.

Inferences about the economic position of workingmen based on raw wage data and dubious guesses as to "minimum" family budgets, it appears, can be extremely misleading. And confident estimates of the disastrous impact of seasonal and cyclical economic fluctuations on ordinary working-class families may be equally unreliable. In actuality, the depression of the middle and late 1870's, the second most severe and prolonged economic collapse in American history, did little to disturb the patterns of property mobility described here. A random check of 50 of the property-owning laboring families recorded in the Newburyport Assessor's Valuation Lists for 1870, 1873, 1876 and 1880 revealed that one-third of them actually increased their property holdings between 1873 and 1876, during the depths of the slump. In 1880 only 3 of the 50 were substantially poorer than they had been in 1870; 26 had increased their accumulation of taxable property. The depression may well have slowed the pace at which local workmen discharged the mortgages on their homes, but rarely did it reverse the gains already made. The very low rate of foreclosures on mortgages held by local workmen in this period is further testimony of the remarkable ability of settled working-class families to weather hard times.

Three reasons help to explain the striking ability of these families to accumulate property on pittance wages and to preserve it through prolonged depressions. First, it must be remembered that the most impoverished laborers, the working-class families hardest hit in a depression, were forced to go on the road; a study of laborers settled in a particular community deals with a selected minority who tended to be the last to be fired in hard times and the first to be rehired when the economy picked up.

A second point of great importance is that these settled laboring families were rarely dependent on the income of the chief wage earner alone. One member of family might often be out of work, but it was highly unusual for all able-bodied family members to be out of work simultaneously. The local newspaper gave an illuminating instance. Tim Harrington sent his wife and children to work; when they were employed he bought only the family flour out of his weekly wages and deposited the surplus in the savings bank. Unemployment rarely cut off the entire income of such families and ate up their savings; it commonly blocked only a portion of their income, and temporarily prevented further accumulation.

This is not to suggest, however, that these multiple income families could live comfortably and still put money in the bank. It cannot be emphasized too strongly that the real estate holdings and savings accounts of Newburyport laborers depended on ruthless *underconsumption*. Few of these families earned much above the "minimum" subsistence figure estimated by the Massachusetts Bureau of the Statistics of Labor, but they very often managed to consume much less than this "minimum" and to save the difference. A luxury like drinking, for example, was out of the question. The workman who wished to accumulate and maintain a property stake in the community had compelling reasons for sobriety; it was no coincidence that a Roman Catholic Temperance Society was formed in Newburyport at just the time that the Irish immigrants began their climb upward into the propertied sector of the working class.

Money in the bank and a place to live without paying rent did provide security against extreme want, and did give a man a certain respectability. Entry into the propertied sector of the working class was thus an important form of social mobility. But it was mobility within narrow limits, mobility which tended to close off future opportunities rather than open them, as Table 6 reveals. Common sense suggests

TABLE 6. OCCUPATIONAL STATUS ATTAINED BY LABORERS' SONS ACCORDING TO THE PROPERTY HOLDINGS OF THEIR FATHERS

| | *Father's Maximum Property Holding in the 1850–1880 Period* | | |
Son's occupation at the last census on which he was listed in the 1850–1880 period	Less than $300	$300-899	$900 or more
Number in sample *	121	65	48
Unskilled	24%	22%	35%
Semiskilled	59	57	38
Skilled	7	18	21
Nonmanual	11	3	6

* The numbers here are smaller than in Table 4, because property data were analyzed only for families resident in Newburyport for a decade or more during the period.

that youths from the thrifty, respectable, home-owning segment of the working class would develop higher ambitions than the children of laborers living at the bare subsistence level, and that they would possess superior resources in the contest for better jobs. Table 6, however, suggests that this was not the case in Newburyport. Property mobility and inter-generational occupational mobility were not necessarily complementary forms of social mobility; indeed, in some instances they were mutually exclusive. The sons of property-owning workmen entered skilled manual callings more often than sons of property-less laborers, but they remained disproportionately concentrated in unskilled

positions and, most surprising, somewhat underrepresented in nonmanual positions.

This striking discovery recalls an aspect of working-class property mobility about which the prophets of the nineteenth-century success creed were understandably silent. The ordinary workman of Newburyport could rarely build up a savings account or purchase a home without making severe sacrifices. To cut family consumption expenditures to the bone was one such sacrifice. To withdraw the children from school and to put them to work at the age of ten or twelve was another. As Table 6 shows, the sons of exceptionally prosperous laborers did *not* enjoy generally superior career opportunities; the sacrifice of their education and the constriction of their occupational opportunities, in fact, was often a prime cause of the family's property mobility.

This pattern was particularly characteristic of the Irish working-class families of Newburyport. Immigrants and their children, we saw, moved upwards on the occupational scale with greater difficulty than their Yankee counterparts. When we consider property mobility, however, the roles of the two groups are reversed. More than 60 percent of the foreign-born laborers of the community accumulated significant property holdings within a decade; the comparable figure for native workmen was little more than 40 percent. That Irish working-class families were especially successful in accumulating property but especially unsuccessful in climbing out of the low-status manual occupations was hardly a coincidence. The immigrant laborer received wages no higher than those of the Yankee workman, but he had a greater determination to save and to own. Perhaps the land hunger displayed by the Irish laborers of Newburyport was a manifestation of older peasant values. In any case, it was a hunger which could be satisfied to a remarkable extent by even the lowliest laborer—but only at a price. The price was not only ruthless economy; equally necessary was the employment of every able-bodied member of the family at the earliest possible age. The cotton mill or the shoe factory was not to provide the teen-agers of the second generation with the education a rapidly industrializing economy was making increasingly necessary, as the exceptionally low mobility of Irish youths into non-manual occupations so plain reveals.[14]

Mobility, Class Conflict and Social Control

These findings about working-class social mobility reveal something of importance about the social consequences of urbanization and industrialization in nineteenth-century America. To set them in their proper historical context, and to relate them fully to the problems of disorder and social control which emerged as the forces of change reached into quiet villages and towns across the land cannot be attempted in the limited space available here. A few brief comments, however, may suffice to suggest how these findings can deepen our understanding of social change in the American city.

Until the 1840's, Newburyport had been a compact, stable, tightly-integrated community, dominated, in Henry Adams' phrase, by "a social hierarchy in which respectability, education, property and religion united to defeat and crush the unwise and vicious."[15] The Federalist social system of old Newburyport collapsed when the industrialization and rapid urban growth of the 1840's drastically altered the composition of the Newburyport population and the relationship between the community's social classes. A host of anxieties about "the poor and the working classes of the city" developed then, anxieties reflecting changes both in the character of the local working class and in the institutional setting which had formerly promoted deference and subordination of lower-class elements. The old constraining network of religious, economic, political and personal controls had been drastically weakened; the charitable, educational, and legal institutions on which the burden of social control now fell seemed hopelessly inadequate substitutes.

Community fears focused particularly on the newly-arrived Irish, but in fact the separation of the Irish from Newburyport life was part of a larger social process which severed the entire lower class, foreign and native, from its traditional bonds to the community. The immigrant was naturally the most vulnerable target of the stereotypes. "When the paupers, criminals, and intriguing Jesuits are poured in upon us, then let every true-blue American show all such the way they should be received." The facile coupling suggested the ease with which a further equation could be made. Perhaps the impoverished and the immoral, the immigrants and the drifters, the coal-porters and the gravel-diggers were all part of the same class. If in fact only the foreign-born members of this class were, strictly speaking, "alien," in a deeper sense all were coming to be seen as alien to the traditional values of the community. The deep undercurrents of anxiety beneath the optimistic rhetoric of local politicians, ministers, and newspaper writers at mid-century, sometimes came to the surface, as in the editorial complaining that the imminent exhaustion of America's free land would mean that "the great safety valve of our prosperity will be forever closed." Then, as land became concentrated in the hands of "the strongest class," "the most indolent class" would be driven off the land and forced into the cities. In the sprawling cities, "the strife of competition" would become "a hundred fold more severe," and the gulf between "exaltation" and "degradation" would grow ever wider. In a similar vein, the Fourth of July oration delivered at City Hall in 1850 evoked an apocalyptic vision of a bloody struggle between "the *have-alls* and the *lack-alls*" which would end in either anarchy or tyranny.

These lurid fears rested on the premise that the alienated "lack-alls" of America were a permanent class, with a consciousness of their separate identity and a determination to fight for their interests. That this premise was false soon became clear to Newburyport residents, as the processes of mobility analyzed in this essay began to operate. Before long, the undifferentiated mass of poverty-stricken laboring families, the "lack-alls" who seemed at mid-century to be forming a permanent class, separated into three layers. On top was a small but significant elite of laboring families who had gained a foothold in the lower fringes of the middle-class occupational world. Below them was the large body of families who had attained property mobility while remaining in manual occupations, most often of the unskilled or semiskilled variety; these families constituted the stable, respectable, home-owning stratum of the Newburyport working class. At the very bottom of the social ladder was the impoverished, floating lower class, large in numbers but so transient as to be formless and powerless.

That movement into middle-class occupations inspired commitment to middle-class norms and promoted the integration of mobile working-class families into the community is obvious. But what was the significance of the much more common form of social advance achieved by the laboring families of Newburyport—mobility from the floating group of destitute unskilled families into the respectable, propertied sector of the working class? Nineteenth-century propagandists took a simple view. The property-owning laborer was "a capitalist." If there was a working class in America, as soon as "a man has saved something he ceases to belong to this class"; "the laborers have become the capitalists in this new world." Accumulated funds, however small, were capital, and the possession of capital determined the psychological orientation of the workman. It was the nature of capital to multiply itself; he who possessed capital necessarily hungered for further expansion of his holdings. To save and to invest was the first step in the process of mobility; it inspired a risk-taking, speculative mentality conducive to further mobility. The distinction between the "petty capitalist" workman and the rich merchant was one of degree. To move from the former status to the latter was natural; it happened "every day." Similar assumptions lie behind the still-popular view that "the typical American worker" has been "an expectant entrepreneur."[16]

This was sheer fantasy. A mere handful of the property-owning laborers of Newburyport ventured into business for themselves. More surprising, the property mobility of a laboring man did not even heighten his children's prospects for mobility into a business or professional calling. Indeed, the working-class family which abided by the injunction "spend less than you earn" could usually do so only by sacrificing the children's education for an extra paycheck, and thereby restricting their opportunities for inter-generational occupational mobility.

Furthermore, the use these laborers made of their savings testifies to their search for maximum *security* rather than for *mobility* out of the working class. An economically rational investor in nineteenth-century Newburyport would not have let his precious stock of capital languish in a savings bank for long, and he certainly would not have tied it up in the kind of real estate purchased by these laborers. The social environment of the middle-class American encouraged such investment for rising profits, but the working-class social milieu did not. The earning capacity of the merchant, professional. or entrepreneur rose steadily as his career unfolded—the very term "career" connotes this. The middle-class family head was ordinarily its sole source of support, and the family was able both to accumulate wealth and to improve its standard of living out of normal increments in the salary (or net profits) accruing to him over the years.

Ordinary workmen did not have "careers" in this sense. Their earning capacity did not increase with age; in unskilled and semiskilled occupations a forty-three-old man was paid no more than a boy of seventeen. Substantial saving by a working-class family thus tended to be confined to the years when the children were old enough to bring in a supplementary income but too young to have married and established households of their own.

The tiny lots, the humble homes, the painfully accumulated savings accounts were the fruits of those years. They gave a man dignity, and a slender margin of security against unpredictable, uncontrollable economic forces which could deprive him of his job at any time. Once the mortgage was finally discharged, home ownership reduced the family's necessary expenses by $60 to $100 a year, and a few hundred dollars in the savings bank meant some protection against illness, old age, or a sluggish labor market. While a cynical observer would have noted the possibility that home ownership served also to confine the workman to the local labor market and to strengthen the hand of local employers, who were thus assured of a docile permanent work force, few laborers of nineteenth-century Newburyport were disposed to think in these terms.

If, however, families belonging to the propertied stratum of the working class had not set their feet upon an escalator which was to draw them up into the class of merchants, professionals and entrepreneurs, they had established themselves as decent, hard-working, church-going members of the community. In this sense, the ordinary workmen of Newburyport could view America as a land of opportunity despite the fact that the class realities which governed their life chances confined most of them to the working class. The gospel of success, it may be suggested, had symbolic truth to these obscure men. Not one rose from rags to riches, but all of them could see that *self-improvement was possible*. This sense of satisfaction, and the conformity to community norms which it inspired, cannot be further documented here,[17] but it provides an essential clue to the social history of Newburyport as the community peacefully adjusted to the challenges of an industrial civilization.

A Note on Mobility Trends in the United States

The U.S. Census of 1850 counted 62 cities of more than 10,000; by the end of the century the number stood at 440. Can a study of social mobility patterns in one of these communities tell us anything about the others? Is it possible, on the basis of the Newburyport example, to draw any broader conclusions about the social structure of nineteenth-century America? I believe that it is, to some degree. There are good theoretical grounds for believing in certain uniformities in the impact of urbanization and industrialization within a given society, and a few suggestive fragments of evidence gathered by other investigators tend to support the view that the patterns of working-class mobility found in Newburyport in the latter half of the nineteenth century were the result of forces which were operating in much the same way in cities throughout the entire society. The point can only be asserted here; the skeptical reader will find a full discussion of it in the book from which this essay is drawn.

If this be granted, the present study, coupled with scattered evidence concerning social mobility in several American cities in the twentieth century, allows us to reappraise the blocked mobility hypothesis. If the level of mobility opportunities open to unskilled workmen and their children in nineteenth-century Newburyport was at all representative of other American cities of the period, the contrast between the boundless opportunities of the past and the constricted horizons of the present drawn by writers like Warner is a romantic illusion. To rise from "the bottom of the social heap" has not become increasingly difficult in modern America; if anything, Tables 7 and 8 suggest, it has become somewhat less difficult.

Studies of the intra-generational occupational mobility rates of unskilled laborers are regrettably scarce; the available evidence, however, is relatively unambiguous. Table 7 compares the Newburyport findings with the results of mobility inquiries

TABLE 7. OCCUPATIONAL STATUS ATTAINED BY UNSKILLED LABORERS OVER TEN-YEAR PERIODS, SELECTED CITIES, 1850–1950*

	Unskilled	Semiskilled	Skilled	Nonmanual	Number in sample
Newburyport					
1850–1860	64%	16%	15%	5%	55
1860–1870	74	12	8	5	74
1870–1880	79	6	10	5	102
Norristown					
1910–1920	70	14	8	10	825
1920–1930	70	12	10	8	925
1930–1940	52	30	10	8	1180
1940–1950	51	26	12	12	1065
Chicago, Los Angeles, New Haven, Philadelphia, St. Paul, San Francisco					
1940–1950	65	26	26	9	—

* The Norristown data were drawn from local city directories by Sidney Goldstein; see *Patterns of Mobility, 1910–1950: The Norristown Study* (Philadelphia, 1958), pp. 169, 175, 178, 185. The figures for the six major cities are from Gladys L. Palmer, *Labor Mobility in Six Cities: A Report on the Survey of Patterns and Factors in Labor Mobility, 1940–1950* (New York, 1954), p. 115. Semiskilled, skilled, and service workers are combined in one category in the Palmer report, unfortunately, but the unskilled and nonmanual estimates are acceptable for comparative analysis. The number of unskilled laborers in the sample is not reported, but the survey as a whole is based on some 13,000 work history schedules collected in the six cities.

TABLE 8. OCCUPATIONAL STATUS ATTAINED BY SONS OF UNSKILLED LABORERS, SELECTED SAMPLES, 1860–1956 *

Sample	Unskilled	Semiskilled	Total of unskilled and semiskilled	Skilled	Nonmanual	Number in sample
Newburyport 1860–1830	22%	49%	71%	19%	10%	245
San Jose, Calif. ca. 1900	60	4	64	16	20	70
Indianapolis 1910	36	20	56	28	16	1195
New Haven 1931	—	—	72	13	15	153
San Jose 1933–34	42	17	59	14	28	242
Indianapolis 1940	30	32	62	16	21	675
U.S. National Sample 1945	38	20	58	17	25	41
Chicago, Los Angeles, San Francisco, Philadelphia 1950	20	34	54	27	20	—
Norristown 1952	14	34	48	24	28	86
U.S. National Sample 1956	25	28	53	28	20	87

* The Newburyport figures represent the distribution of occupations held by laborers' sons aged twenty or over in 1860, 1870, or 1880. The age limitation was essential to avoid an overrepresentation of boys holding their first jobs. Most of the other studies reported made some attempt to eliminate very young males, but the varying age limits of the samples remain an inescapable source of variation between the studies. The San Jose figures were calculated from Percy E. Davidson and H. Dewey Anderson, *Occupational Mobility in an American Community* (Stanford, 1937), pp. 20, 29. The ca. 1900 estimate for San Jose is not very reliable since it depends on a retrospective estimate (in 1933–34) by respondents of the regular occupation of their fathers and grandfathers. Unskilled and semiskilled occupations, unfortunately, were not distinguished in the New Haven survey; John W. McConnell, *The Evolution of Social Classes* (Washington, 1942), p. 216. The Indianapolis figures are for all of Marion County, Indiana, which includes some suburban and rural fringes around Indianapolis as well as the city itself. They were calculated from the detailed mobility tables included in Rogoff's *Recent Trends in Occupational Mobility*. The 1945 sample of the adult white population of the U.S. is reported in Richard Centers, "Occupational Mobility of Urban Occupational Strata," *American Sociological Review*, XIII (1948), pp. 197–203. The 1950 data for Chicago, Los Angeles, San Francisco, and Philadelphia were gathered in the Occupational Mobility Survey carried out under the auspices of the Committee on Labor Market Research of the Social Science Research Council, seven university research centers, and the U.S. Bureau of the Census and were published in Stanley Lieberson, *Ethnic Patterns in American Cities* (Glencoe, Ill., 1963), pp. 186–187; the number in the sample was not reported. The Norristown figures, based on data from the Norristown Household Survey, are for adult whites; see Sidney Goldstein, ed., *The Norristown Study* p. 109. The 1956 national sample was selected by the Survey Research Center of the University of Michigan; reported in S. M. Miller, "Comparative Social Mobility: A Trend Report and Bibliography," *Current Sociology*, IX (1960), p. 78.

dealing with Norristown, Pennsylvania between 1910 and 1950, and with six major metropolitan centers in the decade 1940–1950. The career patterns of common workmen in these cities displayed a striking resemblance, it is clear, and the small differences which can be detected indicate slightly superior opportunities in the twentieth-century community. Only one laborer in twenty from the Newburyport sample rose into a nonmanual position, while the figure for Norristown, Chicago, Los Angeles and the others was approximately one in ten. The tremendous expansion of menial white-collar and sales positions which has produced these new opportunities in the nonmanual occupations has also tended to blur income and status differentials between manual and nonmanual callings, of course, so that upward mobility into a routine white-collar job means less of a status advance than it did a century ago. While this is an important qualification, it remains the case that the rise from an unskilled laboring position to virtually any nonmanual occupation represents significant upward mobility. Mobility of this kind is not being blocked; it appears to be on the increase in the modern American city.

Much more is known about the occupational attainments of the sons of unskilled laborers in the United States, and it is possible to conclude with some confidence that in the past century there has been a mild trend towards greater upward mobility. The available evidence is summarized in Table 8. The occupational categories used in the various studies reported there varied slightly, and there were differences in sampling techniques which could produce artificial variations. The consistency of the findings, given these facts, is impressive.

Of the sons of unskilled laborers employed in nineteenth-century Newburyport, seven out of ten held unskilled or semiskilled jobs themselves and one was in a nonmanual position of some kind; of the sons of unskilled laborers working in Norristown in 1952, five out of ten held unskilled or semiskilled positions, while three were in nonmanual callings. The data from San Jose, Indianapolis, New Haven and the other communities listed on Table 8 covering the years 1900–1956, indicate that this contrast reflects a genuine trend. It may be objected that the first column of the table, which shows the extent of direct inheritance of unskilled manual positions in these several cities, does not reveal any such clear trend. Neither does the second column, which measures movement in semiskilled occupations. But this should come as no surprise, for the Newburyport evidence showed that the unskilled and semiskilled occupations constituted a common occupational universe; while there were status differences between these two job cagetories, they were small and movement between the two was very easy. The same held true in other American communities, Table 8 shows clearly; the concentration of laborers' sons in unskilled jobs and in semiskilled jobs fluctuated widely from city to city, but the concentration of sons in the *low-skill occupational universe* (column three) varied relatively little. The unskilled and semiskilled total is a better indicator of mobility trends than either separately, and it shows a modest but definite improvement in the prospects of youths of lowly birth. More than two-thirds of them remained in low-status callings in Newburyport; a figure this high was reported in only one of the nine twentieth-century studies, and the lowest concentration of sons in unskilled and semiskilled work was found in the three post-World War II inquiries.[18]

The converse of this decline in the tendency of youths from unskilled working-class families to remain in the low-skill occupational universe, of course, was their growing representation in the skilled and nonmanual occupations. The skilled column of Table 8 actually presents a rather confused picture; the variation in skilled opportunities from community to community was sizeable, and it is difficult to see any clear trend, though the fact that three of the four highest figures were from the post-war studies should be a valuable reminder that the disappearance of the glassblower and the shoemaker of old must not be confused with a disappearance of the skilled crafts themselves.

The evidence of a modest trend towards increased mobility from the bottom of the occupational scale into business, professional, and white-collar callings is fairly persuasive. A few of the figures seem surprising, but it is surely significant that the six studies covering the 1933–1956 period show two to three times as many laborers' sons in nonmanual positions as the figures for Newburyport in the latter half of the nineteenth century and for Indianapolis in 1910.[19] In recent decades white-collar and professional occupations have made up an ever-increasing segment of the American occupational structure, and during the same period the American educational system has become markedly more democratic. The fruits of these two developments are graphically displayed here, in the rising proportion of laborers' sons who no longer face the necessity of making a living with their hands. Whatever the effects of mechanization, the closing of the frontier, the narrowing of class differences in fertility, and a host of other factors which have inspired gloomy prophecies of an increasingly rigid class structure in the United States, their combined effect has evidently been insufficient to offset these forces making for improved mobility opportunities for men at the bottom of the occupational ladder.[20]

Nor does it seem likely that a serious case could be made that opportunities for property mobility are declining. If it is not at all clear that the distribution of income in the United States has become markedly more equal in recent decades, it is incontestable that in every occupational class absolute levels of real income have risen dramatically. The extraordinary devotion to home ownership displayed by the Irish working-class families of Newburyport has not been uniformly displayed by American workmen in subsequent decades, but other forms of investment —the automobile, for example, have become increasingly important. The two Middletown volumes are rich with data concerning these changes in the working-class style of life, and a few later studies supply evidence on property mobility in the post-World War II period. Chinoy's suggestive report, *Automobile Workers and the American Dream*, shows in convincing detail how, for factory workers lacking any reasonable prospects of upward occupational mobility, "the constant accumulation of personal possessions" has provided substitute gratifications which allow them to retain a belief that they are "getting ahead."[21]

Whether our index of the openness of the class structure be the extent of intra-generational occupational mobility, of inter-generational occupational mobility, or property mobility, therefore, it is difficult to resist the conclusion that chances to rise from the very bottom of the social ladder in the United States have not declined visibly since the nineteenth century; they seem, in fact, to have increased moderately in recent decades.

To say this is not to say that opportunities are boundless in present-day America, that ours is a society in which every "deserving" man holds a status in accord with his "true merit." Opportunities are neither boundless nor are they equal in the United States today, as an abundance of sociological research into class differences testifies. The mere fact of being born into a middle-class or a working-class home still profoundly influences the life chances of every American —his prospects of obtaining a college education, finding a good job, living in decent housing, even his prospects of enjoying mental and physical health and living to an advanced age.

All this is true, but we can obtain some true perspective on the present only when we shed the rose-tinted spectacles through which the American past has characteristically been viewed. In the States today the climb upward from the bottom rungs of the social ladder is not often rapid or easy, but *it never was*, if the experiences of the working-class families of nineteenth-century Newburyport are at all representative. Few of these men and few of their children rose very far on the social scale; most of the upward occupational shifts they made left them manual workmen still, and their property mobility, though strikingly wide-spread, rarely involved the accumulation of anything approaching real wealth. This was not the ladder to the stars that Horatio Alger portrayed and that later writers wistfully assumed to have been a reality in the days of Abraham Lincoln and Andrew Carnegie. It was, however, social advancement of a kind immensely meaningful to men whose horizons of expectations were not those of an Alger hero. Low-level social mobility of this sort does not seem more difficult for the American working-class family today; quite the contrary.

ACKNOWLEDGMENT

I am indebted to the Joint Center for Urban Studies of the Massachusetts Institute of Technology and Harvard University for generously supporting the research on which this article is based.

NOTES

1. Important statements of the blocked mobility hypothesis include: W. Lloyd Warner and J. O. Low, *The Social System of the Modern Factory* (New Haven, 1947), pp. 182–185, 87–89; Robert S. and Helen Merrell Lynd, *Middletown: A Study in American Culture* (New York, 1929), pp. 51, 65–66; *Middletown in Transition: A Study in Cultural Conflicts* (New York, 1937), pp. 67–72, 471; J. O. Hertzler, "Some Tendencies Towards a Closed Class System in the United States," *Social Forces*, XXX (1952), pp' 313–323.

   For the opposite view, see Gideon Sjoberg, "Are Social Classes in America Becoming More Rigid?" *American Sociological Review*, XVI (1951), pp. 775–783; Ely Chinoy, "Social Mobility Trends in the United States," *American Sociological Review*, XX (1955), pp. 180–186; William Petersen, "Is America Still the Land of Opportunity? What Recent Studies Show about Social Mobility," *Commentary*, XVI (1953), pp. 477–486; Natalie Rogoff, *Recent Trends in Oc-*

   cupational Mobility (Glencoe, 1953); Elton F. Jackson and Harry J. Crockett, Jr., "Occupational Mobility in the United States: A Point Estimate and Trend Comparison," *American Sociological Review*, XXIX (1964), pp. 5–15.

2. It was not possible, in this brief essay, to describe in detail the procedures followed and the sources used. The skeptical reader will find a fully documented account in my book. The notes included here are intended only to clarify and to suggest some connections between by findings and those of other researchers.

3. For the argument that Newburyport embodies a "substitute cultural profile," see Florence Kluckhohn, "Dominant and Substitute Profiles of Cultural Orientations: Their Significance for the Analysis of Social Stratification," *Social Forces*, XVIII (1949–50), pp. 376–393. A host of critics have attacked the assumption that small and seemingly static communities like Newburyport and Morris, Illinois ("Jonesville") are adequate

laboratories for observing American social life. The critics are surely right to insist that the city Warner calls "Yankee City" must be considered a deviant case in many respects. My point, however, is that Newburyport was far less deviant than Warner made it out to be. See ch. viii and the appendix to my book for a full discussion of this.

4. Errors were undoubtedly made in tracing the careers of these hundreds of individuals. For a variety of reasons such errors are most likely to have led to some overestimation of the extent of migration out of the community, and perhaps some underestimation of the frequency of upward occupational mobility. However, a cross check against the Newburyport Assessor's lists revealed few mistakes and suggests that the margin of error in gathering data was relatively small.

5. This remarkable volatility of the local population, it should be noted, was not a working class phenomenon. During the three decades studied, Newburyport experienced something very close to a complete turnover of population. Of the 2,025 families recorded in the city directory of 1849, only 360 were listed in the directory of 1879. The social consequences of this are considered at length in ch. vii of my book. Nor is it likely that Newburyport was an exceptionally unstable community. Merle Curti found that less than 50 percent of each of several occupational groups in Trempealeau County, Wisconsin, remained there for as long as a decade in the 1850–1880 period; *The Making of an American Community: A Case Study of Democracy in a Frontier County* (Stanford, 1959), pp. 65–77. The population of Rochester, New York, appears to have been even less stable at this time. Only 47 percent of a sample of 500 names drawn from the 1849 city directory could be located in the 1855 edition, and the figure fell to 20 percent in 1859. See Blake McKelvery, *Rochester, the Flower City, 1855–1890* (Cambridge, 1949), p. 3. The whole question requires systematic study by American social and economic historians. For some valuable methodological suggestions, see Eric E. Lampard, "Urbanization and Social Change: On Broadening the Scope and Relevance of Urban History," in Oscar Handlin and John Burchard, ed., *The Historian and the City* (Cambridge, 1963), pp. 225–247.

6. Carter Goodrich and Sol Davison, "The Wage Earner in the Westward Movement," *Political Science Quarterly*, L (1935), pp. 161–185, and LI (1936), pp. 61–110; Fred A. Shannon, "A Post Mortem on the Labor Safety Valve Theory," *Agricultural History*, XIX (1945), pp. 31–37; Clarence H. Danhof, "Farm-Making Costs and the 'Safety Valve;' 1850–1860," *Journal of Political Economy*, IL (1941), pp. 317–359. It is impressive that sample surveys conducted in Saskatchewan and Alberta in 1930–1931 revealed that a significant number of the farm operators of the prairie provinces had some previous experience in unskilled or semiskilled employment; see C. A. Dawson and Eva R. Younge, *Pioneering in the Prairie Provinces: The Social Side of the Settlement Process* (Toronto, 1940), pp. 120–123, 318. But many of these men had been born and raised on farms; and it is probable that relatively few of them had ever worked as laborers in cities hundreds of miles from the frontier. For other negative evidence on this point, see Oscar Handlin, *Boston's Immigrants: A Study in Acculturation* (Rev. ed., Cambridge, 1959), p. 159 and the literature cited there.

7. A word of warning is in order here. The discussion which follows is based on a series of tables which display in percentages the changing occupational distribution of several groups of men and boys. Scrutiny of the absolute numbers from which these percentages were calculated will reveal that, in some instances, occupational shifts by relatively few men appear as a rather dramatic percentage change. These changes in the occupational adjustment of even a small group of individuals are suggestive, but the reader must recall that this is an interpretative essay based on fragmentary data, not a large-scale, definitive statistical study.

It must also be remembered that these conclusions refer not to the entire working class population of the community but to *unskilled* laborers and their sons. Recent mobility research suggests the likelihood that an investigation of the career patterns of *skilled* families would have revealed substantially greater movement into nonmanual occupations. Presumably it would also have disclosed evidence of downward occupational mobility, since skilled workmen (unlike common laborers) have status to lose.

8. The career patterns of three distinct groups of laborers are analyzed here. The first of these groups consists of all Newburyport residents listed as unskilled laborers on the manuscript schedules of the U.S. Census of 1850. The second consists of men first listed as laborers in Newburyport on the Census of 1860, and the third of unskilled workmen new to the community in 1870.

9. It should be pointed out that the overall *shape* of the Newburyport occupational structure changed very little during this thirty-year period. The proportion of the labor force employed in skilled manual trades declined slightly between 1850 and 1880, and the semiskilled and nonmanual categories expanded slightly. It seemed pointless, therefore, to employ special techniques in an effort to control for the effects of changes in the occupational structure and to isolate "pure mobility."

10. For want of a better place to put them, youths working on farms owned by the fathers were ranked as nonmanual employees. Many of them, it is reasonable to assume, later entered ordinary manual laboring positions. There was no evidence of this, however, during the period studied.

11. Max Weber, *The Theory of Social and Economic Organization* (New York, 1947), p. 425.

12. Vera Shlakman, *Economic History of a Factory Town: A Study of Chicopee, Massachusetts* (Northampton, 1936), pp. 193–194; Constance M. Green, *Holyoke, Massachusetts* (New Haven, 1939), pp. 44, 105. Edgar W. Martin's *The Standard of Living in 1860: American Consumption Levels on the Eve of the Civil War* (Chicago, 1942) concludes that the typical urban working-class

family of the period had negligible prospects of saving anything but a tiny fraction of its income.

13. The 1880 figures on Table 5 suggest a slowing of the trend towards more widespread property ownership and larger holdings, but this is a statistical artifact. The estimates for 1850, 1860 and 1870 come from manuscript schedules of the U.S. Census. No question about the ownership of real or personal property was included in the Census of 1880, unhappily, so local tax figures had to be used for that year, and those are notoriously conservative. A comparison of responses to census property questions in 1850, 1860 and 1870 with assessor's lists for the same years indicates that the 1880 figures on Table 5 are some 10 percent lower than they would have been had census data been available.

14. Cf. Oscar Handlin's discussion of the differences between the adjustment of the Irish and the Jews in nineteenth-century New York: *The Newcomers: Negroes and Puerto Ricans in a Changing Metropolis* (Cambridge, 1959), opp. 26–27. For other suggestive evidence, see Curti, *The Making of an American Community*, pp. 183–187; Otis Dudley Duncan and Stanley Lieberson, "Ethnic Segregation and Assimilation," *American Journal of Sociology*, LXIV (1959), pp. 364–374.

15. Cf. the excellent discussion of the Federalist elite of the day in Norman Jacobson, "Class and Ideology in the American Revolution," in the first edition of Stephan Thernstrom, *Poverty and Progress: Social Mobility in a Nineteenth-Century City*.

16. For a recent elaboration of the familiar view that the psychology of the American working class has been "entrepreneurial" see Gerald N. Grob, *Workers and Utopia: A Study of Ideological Conflict in the American Labor Movement, 1865–1900* (Evanston, 1961), pp. 165–166, 189. The classic expressions of this approach are to be found in the writings of "the Wisconsin school" of labor history; see John R. Commons *et al.*, *History of Labor in the United States*, 4 vols. (New York, 1918–1935) and Sleig Perlman, *A Theory of the Labor Movement* (New York, 1928). For a perspective on working-class life closer to that taken here, see Richard Hoggart, *The Uses of Literacy: Aspects of Working Class Life, With Special Reference to Publications and Entertainments* (London, 1957); Ely Chinoy, *Automobile Workers and The American Dream* (Garden City, N.Y., 1955); S. M. Miller and Frank Riessman, "Are Workers Middle Class?" *Dissent*, VIII (1961), pp. 507–513 and the works cited there; Miller and Riessman, "The Working Class Subculture: A New View," *Social Problems*, IX (1961), 86–97; Herbert J. Gans, *The Urban Villagers: Group and Class in the Life of Italo-Americans* (Glencoe, 1962).

17. See ch. vii of my book for a full discussion.

18. The high concentration of sons in the low-skill occupational universe in New Haven was probably due largely to the fact that the sample included many more very young men than any of the others: the minimum age for inclusion in the New Haven Sample Family Survey was only sixteen, and all respondents were unmarried and living at home.

19. Both of the San Jose estimates seem high, but the ca. 1900 figure warrants little confidence for reasons advanced in the note to Table 8. It is quite possible, of course, that California attracts a disproportionately ambitious and talented migrant population, and this may be reflected in both San Jose figures.

20. It can be objected, of course, that the trend towards somewhat greater access to nonmanual jobs for men of working-class origins has been accompanied by a decline in the relative status of nonmanual as against manual occupations; see C. Wright Mills, *White Collar: The American Middle Classes* (New York, 1951) for a discussion of the dramatic expansion of menial white-collar occupations in recent decades and the consequent blurring of income and other status differentials between blue-collar and white-collar work. This is indeed an important point, but it may be doubted that many white-collar workers evaluate their status as negatively as Mills does. Certainly in present-day America most shifts from manual to nonmanual positions would still be considered upward mobility by most observers.

21. Chinoy, *Automobile Workers*, 124.

24. Patterns of Adjustment of Negroes and Puerto Ricans in a Changing Metropolis

Oscar Handlin

From the nineteenth century until recently, the Irish, Italian, and Jewish immigrants who congregated in the cities of the Eastern seaboard occupied the lower rungs of the class system. The same is now true of the Negro and Puerto Rican population. The connection between class and race is confirmed in this selection by Oscar Handlin, who here traces the changing social role of these various groups in the history of New York City. He shows that their fate is not predetermined or unalterable. The status of the Negroes, for example, and the tensions which frequently have arisen between them and the white majority, have oscillated over the last century, in response to forces at work in the city and in the nation. Among these forces have been the rate of migration of Negroes into New York, the degree of economic prosperity or depression, and the changing spatial distribution of the black population. Handlin concludes the selection by considering whether it will be possible for the Negro and Puerto Rican groups to repeat the history of assimilation and integration which has characterized earlier waves of newcomers to New York.

Oscar Handlin is Winthrop Professor of History at Harvard University. He has written numerous books, including *The American People: The History of a Society* (1966), *Fire-Bell in the Night: The Crisis in Civil Rights* (1964), and *The Newcomers* (1962), and is coeditor of *The Historian and the City* (1963).

Too often a sense of panic at the presence of strangers has obscured the understanding of the process by which they become parts of the community to which they migrate. This is as true of the Negroes and Puerto Ricans as it was of their predecessors. That panic leads to exaggerated estimates of the numbers involved, as when responsible newspapers guessed that there were 600,000 Puerto Ricans in the city at a time when it held a little more than one-fourth that number.[1]

The same kind of fear also created an exaggerated impression of the novelty of contemporary urban problems. Too often it was assumed that there was precedent neither for the diffusion of New York's population into its suburbs, nor for the reception in the city of groups like the Negroes and the Puerto Ricans.[2]

The data for historical comparison indicates that, in adjusting to metropolitan life, the Negroes and the Puerto Ricans faced problems similar to those already encountered by earlier immigrants. The transition from rural to urban surroundings was difficult in itself, and it was complicated by serious cultural discrepancies between the old life and the new. Like their predecessors also, the Negroes and Puerto Ricans filled the lowest occupations and suffered in consequence from poverty, inferior housing, and their concomitant social disorders.

There were, however, two significant

Reprinted by permission of the publishers from Oscar Handlin, *The Newcomers*, Cambridge, Mass.: Harvard University Press. Copyright, 1959, by Regional Plan Association, Inc.

differences between these and earlier immigrants. The Negroes and Puerto Ricans found their adjustment complicated by their dark skins in a period when a great deal of social tension focused on the issue of color difference. Furthermore, there had been significant changes in the character of the metropolitan community to which they came. In 1820, the scale of settlement was small enough so that neighborhood, city, and region were identical. In 1850 region and city were still the same, but the districts of residence had been differentiated in a variety of neighborhoods. Twenty years later the urban region had spread beyond the city's political boundaries. In 1900 the municipality had expanded to take in that part of the region within New York State. Since then still more rapid diffusion of the population has broadened the region, reduced the relative size of the city, and altered the character of the neighborhood. Those changes in the context of metropolitan life are certainly factors in establishing the pattern of adjustment by Negroes and Puerto Ricans.

It will be well to begin the analysis of that pattern with an examination of the total social context within which it developed. A consideration of certain broad changes in the whole New York community and of the experience of the older ethnic groups in the region since 1928 will supply a background against which the problems of the Negroes and the Puerto Ricans can be more meaningfully evaluated.

New York in the 1920's seemed to be entering upon a period of stability. With the end of large-scale immigration from Europe and the slackening of the rate of population growth, there was often talk in that decade that the city had reached an era of maturity. It seemed to be approaching a turning point beyond which it would cease to expand and be compelled to plan within limited resources. The very concern with regional planning in these years reflected that conviction. This sentiment was fortified by the onset of the depression, a time for retrenchment and for a careful hoarding of resources. This atmosphere suffused the years down to the outbreak of the war in 1941.

There followed a period, which has lasted until the present, of renewed expansion and of prosperity. The new conditions were significantly reflected in changes in both social and economic trends. The revival of business activity and of relatively full employment, the reappearance of labor shortages, and the rise in family incomes transformed the basic material terms of life in the city. These conditions were associated with the growing stability of family life, the rise in the birth rate, and the resumption of population growth.

The result of both trends was a renewal of the process of rapid expansion to the suburbs which had slackened noticeably in the 1930's. The move out of the central city was associated, as it had been in the past, with the difficulties of accommodating middle-class ideals to the practical problems of urban life. The renewed emphasis on the togetherness of a sound family relationship and the desirability of rearing children in good neighborhoods led directly back to the one-family house on its own plot. The virtues of home ownership and of the high status that it brought now, however, could only be attained outside the city limits; population growth and rising land values made that certain, and inexorably stimulated the shift to the suburbs.

The postwar dispersal of residences bore striking similarities to earlier movements of population from the city. But the patterns of commuting that developed with it were distinctive in several important respects. The fact that a good deal of industry was now located on the outskirts meant that a good deal of passenger traffic moved to work around the periphery and from the city outward as well as toward the center. More important, this movement, unlike those of the past, was not accompanied by an extension of public transportation. The automobile made it possible for many individuals and groups to move about freely and to select their residences almost without reference to their place of work. But it also led to significant contractions of the services available through public transportation; and high costs made additions to those facilities impossible.

This factor magnified the differential among income groups. In the absence of public transportation it became more difficult for the less well-to-do to follow the more prosperous to the suburbs. The man without an automobile of his own had access only to a contracting area of settlement. That in turn intensified the association between suburban residence and status.

The alternation of depression and prosperity, of contraction and expansion, helped to explain the development of the older ethnic groups in the city. In the decade or so after 1928, a general sense of tightness led to widespread fear of the loss of position. Those who were already well established were on the defensive, while groups which were seeking to become established felt greater pressure than ever before. The situation heightened the consciousness of group identity; it placed a high premium on belonging to the proper groups and attached a strong handicap to belonging to the improper ones. An uneasy suspicion that the opportunities of the future might be more restricted than those of the past made discrimination in employment and in education more intense than ever before. At every level there was a marked desire to hold on—the Anglo-Saxons to their professional and managerial positions, the Irish and Germans to their places as clerks or skilled craftsmen.

There remained some measure of social mobility. The sons of unskilled workers were still becoming lawyers or teachers or being trained for those positions, particularly among the newer groups like the Italians and the Jews. This was due in part to the continued vitality of the conception of equality of opportunity in most sectors of the educational system; in part it was due to a change in the character of the labor force, within which many fewer unskilled hands were needed. But for the moment this occupational upgrading had unfortunate consequences. It meant that more people were prepared for the better places in the economy than could be absorbed under current economic conditions. The result was a high degree of tension between the groups moving up and those already established, with the latter using various devices of discrimination to their own advantage.

The tension of the struggle for status was reflected most acutely in the competition for desirable housing. The Jews and the Italians pressed on into better neighborhoods, moving steadily out of Manhattan into Brooklyn and the Bronx as the spread of apartment houses made facilities available to them. As earlier, the process displaced the older residents. But now such shifts evoked bitterness and resentment often exacerbated through the influence of real estate brokers who feared that patterns of open occupancy would have an unsettling effect upon values. Falling prices for housing entailed substantial costs for people who had to sell. As the "tip-point" approached in a neighborhood and it became clear that its character would change, fear of financial losses added to the general sense of insecurity among established groups. Informal methods of restriction through restrictive covenants or gentlemen's agreements became the last desperate line of defence against social as well as pecuniary loss.[3]

Such threats to the external symbols of status were at the root of the group conflicts of the late 1930's. The activities of the Christian Front, of the *Brooklyn Tablet*, and of similar movements had a particular attraction to the threatened Irish and Germans for they stood in greatest danger from the adverse effects of the depression. But the strain was felt also by the Jews and Italians who considered themselves under attack and blocked off from the opportunities for advancement. For people who were established, ethnic identification was a badge of their status, while for those who were seeking to become established it was a token of that which held them back.

The change since 1939 and particularly since 1945 has been striking. Every index shows a noteworthy decline in discrimination in employment. Slight pockets of prejudice against Jews and Italians persist only in a limited number of jobs, such as those of hotel desk clerks, in which a stereotyped appearance remains important; and these are rarely worth competing for. More generally, favorable economic conditions, the disrepute into which discrimination fell during the war, and the fair employment practices act have gone a long way toward resolving this problem.

With the renewal of prosperity and the disappearance of unemployment, the competition for jobs gave way to a competition for men. The transformation of the labor force through which the number of professional, managerial, and clerical places grew while the number of unskilled jobs declined, now made itself felt more positively.[4] Shortages were particularly prominent in those areas which had seemed most restricted before 1939—in the professions and the ranks of skilled labor. In ironic contrast with the situation before the war, some medical schools were undersubscribed and the heavy demands for doctors, teachers, and engineers could not be filled. These shortages, combined with a more intense transformation of the labor force, eased the problem of social mobility. Wide areas toward the top of the occupational ladder were now thrown open for the advance of the children of the laborers. Middle-class status was therefore within the reach of many second and third generation new immigrant families. As discrimination declined and opportunities widened, ethnic identification ceased to be a serious impediment.

This change coincided with a rise in the birth rate and a strengthening of family life, both of which were now also associated with middle-class status. The result was a renewed trend toward movement out of apartments and into single-family houses, away from the center of the city and into the suburbs. The trend was stimulated by government policy which eased the process of acquiring small homes and also by the great emphasis on education which was connected with the future advancement of children.

The result was a concerted shift toward the periphery by all those who aspired to a rise in status. Between 1950 and 1957 an outburst of new construction, wherever in the region empty land was available, put numerous new dwelling units at the disposal of those who sought improved housing and contributed to the massive movement of population outside the central city. Only those too fixed in their ways to break familiar neighborhood ties or too old to hope for a change in career remained in the earlier centers of settlement; and such people required relatively little space. Clusters of Italians thus stayed in Greenwich Village and of Jews in the East Side. A few young married couples moved into new apartment projects, drawn before their babies arrived by the attractiveness of urban life. But they hardly compensated for those who left. The East Side and Manhattan in general lost steadily in number of residents; and there was a general decline in the density of settlement of the most heavily populated areas of the city.[5]

The automobile and new highway systems had thrown open an immense region of suburban residences into which the growing population moved. The areas of desirable homes were more sharply detached from the areas of production and, to a significant degree, remoteness from the center of the city became a measure of income.

The movement was still one by groups, for the values of the suburb could best be realized within an ethnic mold. It would be fruitless to attempt to map the specific migration of each of the many groups that participated in the process; but the general characteristics of the migration are clear. The new suburbs recreated in a modified form the patterns of life of the old neighborhoods. Yet the rapid widening of the total area of settlement removed the sharpness of competition among ethnic groups; so much space became available that one did not have to interfere with another. While a few very select neighborhoods are still closed by gentlemen's agreements and restrictive covenants, even these devices are surreptitious and on the way toward disappearance.[6]

Two factors in particular eased competition. Since the value of real estate was rising, people who left a neighborhood generally profited when they sold their homes. Furthermore, the very motives that induced the move to the suburbs heightened the consciousness of ethnic identity. Family feeling, the desire to preserve connections with children, the need for communal ways of expending leisure time, and the search for social identity emphasized the value of belonging to churches, societies, and similar ethnic organizations.

These associations showed a striking vitality. Although their ranks were no longer being replenished by immigration, they gained strength through the acquisition of an indigenous quality that relieved them of the taint of foreignness. After 1945, the religious element was more often stressed in these affiliations than earlier; but within the broadly recognized categories of Protestant, Catholic, and Jew, narrower groups retained their individuality as did some outside those categories, like the Greeks and Russians. Even when these associations lost their original function, as when the government after 1933 assumed many of the burdens formerly carried by private philanthropic or benefit societies, they shifted to some other basis. What was critical was the sense of identification they gave their members, not the specific task they performed. And which identification was much less important than the desire for some identification. Belonging to some group was more and more often what mattered, not belonging to any particular one. Often an individual now found it difficult to attain the kind of anonymity that the city provided in the 1920's; but he was no longer penalized for the affiliations toward which ethnic ties drew him.

Since being an Italian or a Jew no longer

bore the odium of distinctive inferiority, ethnic preferences entered prominently into the choice of residence, often out-weighing such other considerations as access to the place of employment. The result was a decline in the competition for common space and, therefore, a reduction of tension. The last twenty years have thus presented a marked contrast to the ten that preceded them.

Movement to the suburbs was thus an indication of the establishment of a new relation among place of residence, occupa-tional status, family stability, and the ethnic community, a relation established in the context of postwar economic expansion. That relation, not the simple facts of the spread of settlement or the character of the Negroes and Puerto Ricans, is at the heart of the problems of adjustment of the present and of the immediate future.

The changes in the character of the wider community have shaped the course of Negro and Puerto Rican adjustment in the past three decades. From 1929 to the end of the 1930's both groups suffered from the precarious effects of the depres-sion. From 1939 onwards, the shortage of unskilled labor relieved them of the economic burdens of marginal employment but compelled them to confront the new problems of group life.

Both groups entered the labor market, as earlier immigrants did, at the bottom of the occupational hierarchy. Neither in the South nor in Puerto Rico had these immigrants been able to accumulate education or capital. Furthermore, the Negroes were hampered by color and the Puerto Ricans by ignorance of English. But more important was the fact that, as newcomers, they had to accept whatever jobs were available. Even those who arrived

with skills or had had training in white collar occupations had to take whatever places were offered to them.

As a result they became mostly unskilled marginal laborers. The earliest forms of employment they found were in the con-struction and garment industries which had formerly depended on Europeans. The earlier gains of New York's Negroes were now wiped out by the inundation from the South. The black men, like the Puerto Ricans, were frequently unemployed; their wages were low; and their conditions of labor were poor. They had therefore to supplement their incomes through the labor of women, in homework, shops, or domestic service. Both groups had come to accept such additional earnings at home.[7]

The depression struck the Negroes with particular severity. Since they were in an exposed position by virtue of their mar-ginal status in the labor force, they were the first to be fired and the last to be rehired. And since they had few resources they were vulnerable to every setback. The decade of the 1930's therefore was one of unremitting hardship. The gap between the median family incomes of the Negroes and Puerto Ricans on the one hand and of non-Puerto Rican whites on the other widened; and a careful student at the end of the decade could see little prospect of improvement.[8]

The renewed demand for manpower after 1939 eased the employment problem; and prosperity enabled the growing number of Negroes and Puerto Ricans to find re-munerative places, despite those aspects of the occupational pattern that tended to diminish the dependence of the economy on unskilled labor and despite the shrink-age in number of jobs relative to industrial output. Although the continued inflow of newcomers who were unskilled or who faced a period of adjustment to the new situation added to the number of low-paid laborers in the city, these were not as helpless as their predecessors. They came with superior information on job prospects and could return if disappointed. They did not therefore constitute the massive pool of hands with no alternative at all that had been available to the region's low-wage industries in the 1850's or 1890's or even the 1930's.

Family incomes rose steadily after 1940 and the differential between Negroes and Puerto Ricans on the one hand and non-Puerto Rican whites on the other narrowed perceptibly. The disparity in earnings in the 1950's was less likely to spring from differences in the rate of pay for a given job than from the fact that the Negroes and Puerto Ricans were clustered in the least rewarding occupations. The improvement in the economic situation of these groups was the product of prosperity, of trade union activity, and of conscious government policy embodied in the state fair employment practices act.[9]

The effective reduction of unemployment and the elimination of discriminatory wage scales only clarified another and more fundamental problem—that of how the members of these groups were to be enabled to repeat the climb out of the ranks of unskilled labor to which ever more of them aspired. The general insecurity of these people and their recency in the city emphasized the importance of internal distinctions and put a substantial premium on the ability to rise in occupational status. The inclination of their press to identify every individual in terms of his salary illustrated the weight ascribed by Negroes and Puerto Ricans to the level of earnings.

Thus far they have had only limited and qualified success in escaping from unskilled labor. At the start two traditional avenues of upward mobility were open to the Negroes and Puerto Ricans as they had been earlier immigrants—the first in areas in which they dealt with members of their own groups, the second in areas in which talent had the opportunity to assert itself without suffering from the limitations of their ethnic backgrounds.

The first Negro opportunities came through enterprises which catered to colored people and which depended upon the patronage of their neighbors. Madame C. J. Walker, who early in the century had earned a fortune through the sale of a hair straightener, was a classic example. Barber and beauty shops, funeral parlors, restaurants, bars, liquor stores, night clubs, and other small businesses are sprinkled through the Negro districts—about 5,000 of them in Harlem, 2,000 elsewhere in the city. The expansion of the total size of the group has gradually increased the potential support for establishments of this sort. The Puerto Ricans similarly moved out of the ranks of labor by opening groceries, meat markets, *bodegas*, and other little shops that catered to the distinctive tastes of their fellows.[10]

The patronage of both groups also maintained a certain number of professional men, lawyers, insurance and real estate brokers, and doctors, who added to the middle-class element in the population. Somewhat incongruously, entry to that status was also possible for a limited number who earned their wealth through policy and other forms of gambling and through rackets associated with narcotics, vice, unions, and business. These callings, which existed on, and over, the margin of legality, had always offered opportunities to outsiders not as inhibited as established respectable Americans in their attitudes toward alcohol, sex, lotteries, or violence.

They now afforded some Negroes and Puerto Ricans a means of rising.[11]

The second channel of mobility was much narrower and opened an escape from labor to a still smaller group. But it had a high symbolic value, since through it were available both wealth and recognition by the whites. In the theater, art, music, and athletic worlds, talent was more or less absolute; and discrimination was much less effective than in other realms. This accounted for the high incentive among Negroes and Puerto Ricans to seek these pursuits as a way up; and it accounted also for the popularity and high status among them of prize fighters, musicians, and the like, a popularity of which the incidence of reference in magazines and newspapers is a striking index.[12]

All these means of rising are, however, self-contained and limited. They are more available to some elements of the Negro and Puerto Rican population than to others; the West Indian colored people, for instance, are better prepared for urban life and more aggressive than the natives, and have profited as a result. But, in sum total, such economic opportunities affect only very small numbers. Furthermore, they depend upon the maintenance of group solidarity; and, to the extent that these immigrants become adjusted to the New York environment, such means of rising may actually become less effective and still more limited. Paradoxically, the decline in discrimination has already had that effect. In recent years the Negroes have been relatively well treated in mid-town and Bronx stores; they have been accorded charge facilities and improved services. Chain and department stores also earn good will by advertising in the ethnic media. As a result a substantial part of expenditures has been diverted away from local shops. Buying downtown, in fact,

is sometimes a sign of superior status. Such trends certainly have weakened the position of the retailer or professional who depends upon an ethnic clientele.[13]

Some sectors of both the Negro and Puerto Rican population accept the situation and grow bitter or apathetic in consequence—with deleterious social effects. But a substantial and growing percentage, particularly in the second generation, are determined to find wider and better ways out. Only a few succeed as well as the Negro doctor in Sheepshead Bay, four-fifths of whose patients are white. But the number who seek the widest scope for their abilities is constantly expanding; and the second generation shows a perceptible rise in occupational level over the first.[14]

To some extent some such people have managed to escape from unskilled labor by moving into the service trades, occupations that are better paid than jobs in industry and yet in which they do not compete at a disadvantage against better established elements of the labor force. Here too there are significant limits however; and the fact that the Puerto Ricans have done better than the Negroes in these fields reflects the continuing importance of color prejudice as a selective factor.

Beyond this level, moreover, the hardships of achieving a rise in status are magnified. It is difficult to measure the extent to which such a rise has already taken place. But it is possible to analyze the factors that condition the capacity of these groups to move upward.

Their predecessors climbed either as entrepreneurs or as fee- or salary-receiving skilled employees. In both respects the Negroes and Puerto Ricans, for the moment, stand at a disadvantage as compared with earlier immigrants.

The failure is not due primarily to ethnic attributes. There has been some disposition to blame the lag in Negro development on their lack of capacity for business; the failure of the caterers to expand early in the century, for instance, has often been ascribed to their inability, as a group, to adopt modern methods or to adjust to new conditions. Or, alternatively, their slowness as compared with the Puerto Ricans or Chinese has been ascribed to cultural traits, ethnically determined.[15]

There is some validity to these explanations. But it is essential, in advancing them, to treat them in the context both of the conditions created by color prejudice and of the economic terms within which business now operates.

The cultural traits which handicap the Negro entrepreneur are closely related to the prejudice from which he has suffered. Thus, it seems true that the Negroes find it particularly difficult to develop the practices of saving, or to hold on to a surplus that can be used as capital, or to transmit to their children the nest egg that will permit them to make an advantageous start in life. This difficulty is, in part, a result of the peculiar patterns of consumer expenditure within the group. Like other people whose income has been uncertain and sporadic they have wasteful spending habits. The recollection of long periods of deprivation encourages "mad spending sprees" when funds become available. There is a kind of pride in reading that a housekeeper who inherits $100,000 buys a big car; that a stewardess has a $1,000 perfume collection; that a windfall is splurged on a wardrobe; or that a picnic at the Kerhonson Country Club consumes 1,000 chickens and 200 fifths of whiskey. In addition, the heavy cost of funerals, the temptation of debt with its heavy concealed charges, and inexperience in the techniques of economical urban shopping needlessly eat up family resources.[16] Yet, beyond these particular manifestations of inadequate management lies a more general sense of insecurity and uncertainty about the future that weakens incentives for saving. In the absence of clearly defined, attainable objects, in the absence sometimes even of the hope for improvement, it seems futile to economize and no loss to seek the pleasures of the moment in immediate consumption. Significantly, the Negroes who most frequently have capital available for investment are ministers and other salaried and professional men whose incomes run above the levels of expenditure accepted as appropriate for them. In that respect the Negroes seem closer to the Irish of the past than to the Jews or Italians.

The difference in the experience of the Puerto Ricans is enlightening. To some, but to a lesser, extent, the Puerto Rican immigrants bring with them habits that also discourage capital accumulation. They come from the class least likely to save at home; and even those who did hold on to surpluses were accustomed to investing it only in real estate. They too were likely to contract a high volume of debt and to show few liquid assets. Yet, from among these newcomers, as from among the West Indian Negroes, a substantially larger percentage of entrepreneurs have emerged. In part that was due to the fact that on the island the shopkeeper was a familiar figure and even the jíbaro was acquainted with the idea that through trade one could achieve a rise in status. But it was also due to the fact that color has not been for the Puerto Ricans as determining a barrier as for the Negro; and they have in the very act of migration often defined their own goals of improvement.[17]

However, the advantage is relative only. For all these groups, external factors, derived from the changing context within which business operates, are even more of an impediment than ethnic traits. The Puerto Ricans do not suffer from the same handicaps as the Negroes and yet face almost as much difficulty in establishing themselves. The path of the independent small businessman who aims to break out from within the limited patronage of the ethnic circle is more difficult now than earlier. There are still vestiges of the tradition by which the peddler became a shopkeeper and then a department store owner; or by which the grocer became a wholesaler or distributor; or by which the subcontractor became a manufacturer. But it is not as easy now as formerly to move along these lines. For everyone, the growing advantages of bigness put the small and new competitor at a disdvantage. Suburban shopping centers remote from the center of town make expansion difficult for entrepreneurs who begin with the limited patronage of a neighborhood ethnic group. As a result it seems unlikely that independent small business will provide an important access to a future rise in status for either group.

The fact that the capital required is larger and more difficult to come by is particularly burdensome to these groups. On the one hand, their own members are not given to corporate investment, especially since the Negroes at least still have bitter recollections of the disastrous outcome of Marcus Garvey's enterprises in the 1920's. The only financial institution run by colored people is the Carver Savings and Loan Association. On the other hand, both groups find it difficult to negotiate business loans, not only because of overt prejudice but even more because of persistent stereotypes among bankers of what constitutes a good risk.[18]

The alternative to entrepreneurship as a means of rising is to break into the developing complex of positions as professional, managerial, or clerical employees and fee receivers. This channel of advancement is likely in the future to be much more important than in the past. Economic and social trends, which have magnified the importance of large enterprise and of government, have also expanded the clerical, managerial, and professional ranks in the American economy, so that these now seem the most accessible means of rising. Yet, although access to these situations depends less upon inherited wealth or connections than upon skill, prejudice and certain stereotypes of suitability have heretofore restricted the number of eligible Negroes and Puerto Ricans in them. Resentment at exclusion from such positions led to organized protests by the Citizens League for Fair Play, as far back as 1933. But the general restriction of opportunities in that decade kept such protests ineffective.

The importance of discrimination in this area has become clear since the end of the depression. The difficulty of Negroes and Puerto Ricans in penetrating it, despite the vast expansion of opportunities, stands in contrast to the experience of other prewar minorities like the Jews and Italians, who have had the advantage of a longer residence in the city and who also have not been burdened by the handicap of color.[19]

There are signs of improvement although the pace is slow. Substantial numbers of Puerto Ricans and Negroes show an avid desire for advancement that is reflected in a widespread interest in commercial education. As in the case of the Irish earlier, the first breakthrough has been in government employment. Apart from the greater sensitivity of the state as an employer to the issue of public policy involved in discrimination, the growing weight of the Negro and Puerto Rican groups as a political factor has produced openings in the civil service. There has been a steady penetration of the police and fire departments, the public schools, and the offices of municipal, state, and federal agencies.[20]

Politics also became the means for wider social action. The state fair employment practices act forbade discrimination on the grounds of race or ethnic origin. It had an effect upon certain labor unions and large-scale employers and set a standard of practices that was important, whatever the degree of enforcement. The machinery of administration in the State Commission Against Discrimination is relatively weak but the effects of the standard it sets are significant. The rise in importance of the Negroes and Puerto Ricans as consumers has similarly influenced employers anxious to have their patronage. Finally, the growing concern of the trade unions in the metropolitan area with the problem has operated in the same direction.[21]

The effects of the more general drop in bias are not readily measurable. A recent study by the State Commission on Discrimination of the hotel industry in New York City showed a striking penetration into some of these jobs within significantly restricted limits. In the first place the Puerto Ricans have made more progress than the Negroes; and the advance for either group has been slightest in the case of white-collared administrative positions in which the employee comes in contact with the public, that is, in which appearance is important. Both restrictions indicate that color remains a barrier to such employment.[22]

While prejudice and discrimination are real and important factors they do not in themselves complete the picture. For, while they operate to depress the condition of the Negroes and Puerto Ricans, they are reinforced by deficiencies in the education and preparation of many individuals in those groups. Ironically, for instance, after the airlines had been persuaded in 1958 to hire colored hostesses, it proved difficult to find an appropriate applicant. Altogether apart from the factor of prejudice, the number of qualified applicants is not as large as it was in the case of earlier groups at a comparable stage of development. Discrimination has thus depressed the underprivileged while the conditions produced by deprivation become the grounds —or at least the pretext—for continued discrimination.[23]

The connection between the schools and social mobility makes the educational system of special concern to the Negroes and Puerto Ricans. For, through the schools the lower elements of the labor force, or at least their children, have in the past and may in the future acquire the means of pulling themselves upward economically. In both groups conscientious parents continue to believe in that possibility.[24]

Hence the great concern of both groups with the school system, even beyond its vocational and trade aspects. There are efforts to encourage participation in the P.T.A.'s; and the press regularly notes evidence of scholastic honors or achievements and publicizes the availability of scholarships. But the Negroes and Puerto Ricans nevertheless feel that they are deprived of genuine equality of educational opportunity. The problem arises in part from the fact that so many of these people are immigrants and in part from the conditions they encounter on arrival.[25]

In 1910, before the migration northward became serious, the level of literacy of the Blacks was only slightly below that of the whites in the city.[26] But in the next four decades the relation changed as the newcomers paid the price for retardation in the areas from which they came. There has been more recent improvement both in the South and in Puerto Rico. But some gap remains and is reflected in the fact that the median number of school years for both groups is lower than that for whites. There is also evidence of an unusually high level of absenteeism among children within the legal school age.[27]

To some extent the deficiency in preparation is reinforced by the conditions children from these groups find upon arrival. A variety of factors prevent many of them from concentrating upon their studies—the inability to use correct English, their own poverty and sometimes the necessity for part-time work, the lack of privacy at home, and the remoteness of the goals toward which education leads. The result is often a high rate of truancy. All too often, also, even those students who attend docilely merely sit out their lessons, without the incentive to pay attention to what transpires in the classroom.[28]

The parents are sometimes inclined to ascribe all these difficulties to discrimination against them by the educational system. There is some, but not total, validity to these complaints. Public schools in New York City and in the other communities of the metropolitan area are not segregated by law; assignments are made primarily on the basis of residence. But in homogeneous neighborhoods in which most children have a common ethnic background, the schools are in effect segregated without legal formality and reflect the character of the population in their district. The process is cumulative. Members of other groups caught within the boundaries of a Negro or Puerto Rican district flee to the suburbs or to the private schools. That offers the individual a refuge, but often only compounds the general difficulty, for the result has been a perceptible change in the character of the public schools. The report of the Superintendent of Schools for 1957 showed a drop of 20,000 in the number of white pupils, 12,740 of them having left for Long Island, 4,781 for New Jersey, and 2,606 for Westchester and Rockland counties. Negroes then formed 20.1 per cent and Puerto Ricans 15.4 per cent of the school population. But they were highly concentrated. Fully 455 of the 704 schools in the city were homogeneous to the extent that 90 per cent or more of their students were either Negro or white or Puerto Rican.[29]

Given the nature of the neighborhoods in which they live, it is not surprising that the education of Negro and Puerto Rican children should proceed generally under inferior conditions. The schools they attend are, by their very character, housed in the oldest buildings, have the least desirable reputations, and are shunned by the best teachers.

There has been some conscious effort to meet the special needs of these groups, and particularly the language problems of the Puerto Ricans. But the difficulties created by residential segregation are not readily surmountable. Many Negro parents, alive to the importance of the problem, are sensitive or suspicious of any arrangement that hints at discrimination; and there has been some pressure on the Board of Education to effect a change by altering the lines of the school districts and the procedures for teacher assignment. This is unlikely to give more than minor relief, however. To prove really effective such changes would call for a total readjustment of the city's educational pattern; and the losses entailed in doing so might well nullify any social gains.[30]

The experience of earlier groups shows the importance of three other modes of coping with the problem of providing equal educational opportunities throughout the society. There ought, of course, to be a general improvement of all schools. More important, a decline in discrimination that would ease the prospects of upward mobility and put the rewards of education within reach of the minorities would give such pupils the incentive that would itself raise the level of their schooling. It would also give more scope for the recognition of individual differences among students. The lack of such incentives has been as great an educational deterrent for children of these groups in New York as it was in the South or in Puerto Rico. Finally, greater freedom of movement would extend to the Negroes and Puerto Ricans, or to selective groups among them, the opportunity to escape to better neighborhoods and better schools.[31]

Education is thus linked not only with the problems of occupational mobility but also with those of housing, which is likely to prove the most critical area of social conflict in the next two decades.

NOTES

1. *New York Times,* October 14, 1947.
2. See, in general, for example, Amos H. Hawley, *Changing Shape of Metropolitan America* (Glencoe, 1956), 12ff.; Morton Grodzins, "The New Shame of the Cities," *Confluence,* VII (1958), 29ff.
3. See, for example, Rhetta M. Arter, *Exploring Montclair* (New York, 1956), 9, 10.
4. A. J. Jaffe and R. O. Carleton, *Occupational Mobility in the United States 1930–1960* (New York, 1954), 11.
5. E. M. Hoover and Raymond Vernon, *Anatomy of a Metropolis* (Cambridge, 1959), 183ff.; Rhetta M. Arter, *Between Two Bridges: A Study of Human Relations in the Lower East Side* (New York, 1956), 9, 11, 18; [Dan W. Dodson], *Public Education in Greenwich Village* (New York, 1954), 7, 8; Charles Abrams, *Forbidden Neighbors* (New York, 1955), 140ff.
6. See Alan Wood, "I Sell My House," *Commentary,* XXVI (1958), 383ff.; Harry Gersh, "Gentlemen's Agreement in Bronxville," *ibid.,* XXVII (1959), 109ff.; Arter, *Exploring Montclair,* 6, 9; Abrams, *Forbidden Neighbors,* 218.... See George E. Haynes, *Negro at Work in New York City* (New York, 1912), 69ff.; Lawrence R.
7. Chenault, *Puerto Rican Migrant in New York City* (New York, 1938), 44, 74; *Negro Population,* 519, 522; *A Summary in Facts and Figures,* April, 1957, p. 19; Paul K. Hatt, *Background of Human Fertility in Puerto Rico* (Princeton, 1952), 85; C. Wright Mills, Clarence Senior, and Rose K. Goldsen, *The Puerto Rican Journey* (New York 1950), 69.
8. Gunnar Myrdal, *An American Dilemma* (New York, 1944), 380. For the Negroes, see *ibid.,* 365; Charles L. Franklin, *Negro Labor Unionist of New York* (New York, 1936), 81ff., 271ff.; Morton Zeman, "A Comparative Analysis of White-Nonwhite Income Differences in the United States" (University of Chicago Ph.D. thesis, 1955), 4ff. For the Puerto Ricans, see Chenault, *Puerto Rican Migrant,* 73, 74.

9. Zeman, "Comparative Analysis," 23, 194ff. For the Negroes, see *Ebony, The Negro Market* (Chicago, 1955), 9; New York City Commission on Intergroup Relations, *Fact Sheet on the Sharkey-Brown-Isaacs Bill* (June 7, 1957) and *Non-White Family Income in New York City 1953–54.* For the Puerto Ricans, see A. J. Jaffe, *Puerto Rican Population of New York City* (New York, 1954), 20, 23ff.; Mills, *Puerto Rican Journey,* 23, 37, 60ff., 75; Dan Wakefield, *Island in the City* (Boston, 1959), 196ff. For the fair employment practices act, see New York State Commission Against Discrimination, *Reports of Progress* (annual); "The Operation of State Fair Employment Practices Commissions," *Harvard Law Review,* LXVIII (1955), 685ff.
10. James W. Johnson, *Black Manhattan* (New York, 1930), 283; Stan Opotowsky, "Harlem," a series in *New York Post,* March 1958; Jesus de Galindez, *Puerto Rico en Nueva York* (New York, c. 1951), 25; John H. Burma, *Spanish-Speaking Groups in the United States* (Durham, 1954), 164ff.
11. J. L. Roman, "Raquets de Nueva York," *El Diario de Nueva York,* March 26, 1957 ff.; *New York Amsterdam News,* August 23, 1958; p. 1; below, p. 102; above, p. 37. Myrdal is in error in the statement that Negroes started policy in New York (*American Dilemma,* 330. 331). Its history in the city reaches back to the first half of the nineteenth century.
12. This statement is based upon an examination of the publications listed below, p. 106, through 1957 1958. See also Johnson, *Black Manhattan,* 74ff., 175ff.
13. See *La Prensa,* February 4, 1958, pp. 2, 3; also George E. Haynes, *Negro at Work in New York City* (New York, 1912), 101ff.
14. *New York Amsterdam News,* March 15, 1958; Jaffe, *Puerto Rican Population,* 57, 59–61.
15. Myrdal, *American Dilemma,* 307ff.; Haynes, *Negro at Work in New York City,* 99; Christopher Rand, *The Puerto Ricans* (New York, 1958), 37ff.

16. These examples are from *Jet*, April 11, 1957, p. 6. July 4, 1957, p. 47, January 29, 1958, pp. 42, 50ff., August 7, 1958, p. 44; *Ebony*, August, 1957, p. 35. See also Myrdal, *American Dilemma*, 367ff.

17. See MacCoby and Fulder, "Savings among Upper-Income Families in Puerto Rico," Fernández Méndez, *Portrait of a Society*, 81ff.; Elena Padilla, *Up from Puerto Rico* (New York, 1958), 153ff.; Julian H. Steward, *et al.*, *People of Puerto Rico* (Urbana, 1956), 241.

18. Edmund D. Cronon, *Black Moses, The Story of Marcus Garvey* (Madison, 1955), 50ff.

19. See, for example, Gary S. Becker, *Economics of Discrimination* (Chicago, 1957), 77.

20. For attitudes in Puerto Rico, see Paul K. Hatt, *Backgrounds of Human Fertility in Puerto Rico* (Princeton, 1952), 76–78; for New York, see special supplement, *La Prensa*, January 29, 1958; *Westchester County Press*, June 29, 1957.

21. See above, note 9; . . . .

22. New York State Commission Against Discrimination, *Employment in the Hotel Industry* (report of March 1958); and *Puerto Rican Employment in New York City Hotels* (report of October 1958); *New York Amsterdam News*, April 19, 1958; SCAD *Newsletter*, II, No. 2 (March 1959), 2.

23. See, in general, Zeman, "Comparative Analysis," 108, 112ff.

24. See Padilla, *Up from Puerto Rico*, 198ff.; Mills, *Puerto Rican Journey*, 161ff.; Steward, *People of Puerto Rico*, 481ff.

25. See, for example, *Jet*, April 11, 1957, p. 24, August 7, 1958, p. 42; *Ebony*, April, 1957, pp. 83ff.; Wakefield, *Island in the City*, 149ff.

26. See statistics in *Negro Population*, 388.

27. See statistics in *Negro Population*, 415; also J. Cayce Morrison, *The Puerto Rican Study 1953–1957* (New York, 1958), 110; *A Summary in Facts and Figures*, April 1957, p. 6; Joseph Monserrat, *Background and General Information on Puerto Rico* (New York, 1952), 2; Trumbull White, *Puerto Rico and Its People* (New York, 1937), 209ff; V. S. Clark, *et al.*, *Porto Rico and Its Problems* (Washington, 1930), 73ff.; Jaffe, *Puerto Rican Population*, 17; Dan W. Dodson, *Between Hell's Kitchen and San Juan Hill* (New York, 1952), 25. .

28. Padilla, *Up from Puerto Rico*, 210; Morrison, *Puerto Rican Study*, 117, 129, 142.

29. Reported in *New York Times*, January 6, 1958. See also Tables 24–26; Morrison, *Puerto Rican Study*, 152ff., 172ff.; Jaffe, *Puerto Rican Population* 50, 51.

30. On the problems of the Puerto Ricans, see Morrison, *Puerto Rican Study*, 13ff.; Clarence Senior, *Strangers and Neighbors* (New York, 1952), 38, 39; Padilla, *Up from Puerto Rico*, 201ff. On the Negro reaction, see, for example, *New York Amsterdam News*, March 15, 1958, p. 1, for the problems in P.S. 2 and P.S. 70 in the Bronx. See also, William Jansen, Superintendent of Schools, *Report #1 on Integration* (New York, 1957); *New York Times*, September 30, 1957, pp. 1, 25, October 6, 1957, sec. IV, p. 5.

31. See M. M. Tumin and A. S. Feldman, "Status, Perspective and Achievement: Education and Class Structure in Puerto Rico," *American Sociological Review*, XXI (1956), 464ff.; Morrison, *Puerto Rican Study*, 129, 142.

25. Urban Differentiation: Problems and Prospects   Dennis C. McElrath

The selections presented so far point to three bases of differentiation within urban communities: class, ethnicity, and family status or life-cycle stage. Dennis McElrath's paper adds a fourth dimension: migration status, or the rate of movement of individuals across social boundaries. He implies that the four criteria exhaust the range of significant variables not only for understanding what is happening within any particular city but also for comprehending the differences which prevail among urban communities. McElrath also believes that by concentrating attention on these dimensions, and the ways in which they are being transformed, the sociologist can hope to predict the future development of cities.

Dennis C. McElrath is a Fellow of Adlai E. Stevenson College and Associate Professor of Sociology at the University of California, Santa Cruz. He is coeditor of *The New Urbanization* (1968).

Cities are focal points for a great variety of America's ills. City people daily clog highways, befoul air, pollute water, challenge sewer systems, make streets hazardous and public spaces lethal. Their sick, indigent, deviants, and aged make demands; their slums spread; their race relations sicken our conscience; their children run amuck; and their girls go bad.

Most of these problems, however, though identified with urban America, are not unique to this growing sector of society. It is patently impractical, undesirable, and almost meaningless in a complex society undergoing rapid and widespread change to separate the city, with its problems and prospects, from the larger society. Cities today are part-societies where everyday activities are linked to greater polities, economics, and extended networks of kin and friend. Much current discussion of urban affairs nevertheless treats this portion of society without reference to the whole. It is a curious abstraction to view both social order and its concomitant problems within the community as static or discrete, since all activities in an urban society are interwoven to form a large fabric whose pattern, like an "op" painting, constantly vibrates, restructures, moves unceasingly, and never settles down. The fascination of urban sociology lies in defining and understanding this constantly changing organization of thousands of disparate yet widely interdependent acts performed daily by all the people of the city and all those linked to it by interdependence or interaction. A profoundly important perspective may be thus gained for evaluating, formulating, and implementing enlightened public policy.

Such a perspective is not easy to acquire. No neat theory of urban social organization exists today even though the current renascence in urban studies and its attendant affluence has greatly increased research, writing, and systematic thinking in this area. What is being formed, instead, are sets of related ideas which are grounded in careful observations and which hang together well enough to be termed theoretical frames of reference. Basically, the framework for analysis of urban problems and prospects which is used here relates broad changes occurring in the larger society to the activities and opportunities of people settled in local areas of the city. This patterned sifting and sorting of people into local areas is part of the present transformation of urban communities, and a source of many current difficulties.

Of the several recent and significant influences, industrialization and urbanization are the two major changes most instrumental in transforming society through healing or eliminating old divisions within it and yielding new ones. Industrialization has destroyed the traditional skill hierarchy, supplanting a set of distinctions based on an equation of age and seniority with skill, and substituting for it a new hierarchical division topped, for the moment, by those who possess highly specific technical skills. This current division apparently operates in all advanced industrial countries.[1]

An additional and serendipitous result of the new industrialization is the greatly diminished relevance of sex as a basis for limiting access to resources and rewards in the community. Recent expansion of the tertiary sector of industries and the dramatic enlargement in size and scale of many enterprises has widened the opportunity for gainful employment of women outside the household. It has yielded thereby a viable alternative to a style of life which centered on household, children, family, and kin. This new division, moreover, stemming from changes in the mode and scale of production, does not rest on the possession of certain types of skills but rather on opting one style of life over another. The distinction here, therefore, is between "urbanism" as characterized by small families and women working; and "familism," a life style associated with larger families and women at home.[2]

As Durkheim, among others, points out, the process of industrialization thus erases older distinctions based on an age-graded, sex-selective division of labor.[3] These older, ascriptive molds for the allocation of tasks and resources fall into disrepute only to be replaced by other sets of constraints, based on achieved skills and the exercise of a choice of life style. The newer constraints are buttressed by and defended in terms of the prevailing morality of "a career open to talents" and "the maximization of personal choice."

Viewed simply as the process of concentrating a large proportion of the population in a relatively few locations, urbanization inevitably produces new divisions within the community. The spatial consolidation of peoples destroys the internal homogeneity of the community because, in effect, it can be accomplished only by a major spatial redistribution of the population. This redistributive process yields two analytically distinct divisions within the urban community.

The first may be termed "migration status" and is based upon the extent to which movement from a place of origin to an urban center represents a movement across important *social boundaries.* Thus the experience of Whyte's organization

man in going from one suburb to another across the country is not a movement over social boundaries. Whyte's organization man is not a stranger to the suburb: he is merely an urban man on the move. On the other hand, a strip miner's migration from Appalachia to Chicago traverses fewer miles, yet it crosses a much wider social gap. The miner is a newcomer to the city, and his choices are constrained not merely by his redundant skills or an option to a particular style of life but also by *the novelty and alienness of a complex urban world.*

Ethnic heterogeneity within the urban community is another consequence of the redistribution of people associated with urbanization. To the extent that cities draw upon populations with different physical or cultural backgrounds their composition is altered; and the urban community is divided by social visibilities.[4]

Both migration status and ethnic status are byproducts of the current pattern of urbanization in America. In its present form, this pattern results in the accumulation of substantial urban populations, each with distinct migration experiences and a variety of social visibilities. Like the divisions engendered by industrialization, these divisions also operate so as to limit access of individuals to the resources and rewards of the community. Unlike the constraints based on acquired skills and choice of life style, however, limitations arising from these sources are not directly legitimized by the prevailing public morality. But their indirect support is revealed by a close scrutiny of the "melting pot" ideology which indicates a widespread acceptance of the view that inequity is just and legitimate as long as cultural pluralism and inappropriate ruralism persists. In addition, the continuing American dilemma in race relations exposes the persistence of an indirect buttressing of inequity based on physical visibility.

Urbanization and industrialization, then, yield four basic dimensions of social differentiation along which the rewards and resources of urban communities are distributed. In the city the range of opportunities available to an individual or family is subject to the multiple constraints of economic status (based on skills); family status (based on life style option); migration status (based on migration experience); and ethnic status (based on social visibility).

Allocation of resources in terms of each of these status dimensions is, to some extent, legitimized by prevailing norms. In addition, all four statuses act in concert to delimit the range of opportunities open to urbanites. This is especially applicable in the case of housing opportunities. A long list of studies conducted in cities and metropolitan areas throughout the United States attests to the fact that all of these dimensions operate both separately and in combination to structure the pattern of residential settlement in American cities.[5] This accumulated evidence indicates that local areas contain distinctive types of populations occupying different constellations of statuses and, as a consequence, have markedly different needs, demands, information, facilities, and modes of action.

Sets of relatively discrete problems are associated with the operation of each of these dimensions. Economic status distinguishes local area populations in terms of the prevalent level of skills and other resources. Thus when localities are arrayed along this dimension they vary in concomitant needs and demands associated with occupational and educational achievements. At the lower levels of economic status, where localities contain substantial proportions of unskilled and uneducated workers, most of these problems resolve into the absolute constriction of life chances arising from poverty and ignorance. At somewhat higher statuses, lack of specific skills, skill redundancy, precarious employment, and highly unstable and insecure career trajectories are major issues. Above this lie the worries of the middle class: a scattering of problems concerned with extended educational training prior to employment, early plateauing of career trajectories, all the insecurities of while collar employment, and prolonged retirement and widowhood.

Important differences in concerns are observed as well between local areas arranged by family status. In urban localities where most people dwell in apartments, where wives work, families are small, and where there are many single people either just beginning their careers or retired from them, there exists some concern for the maintenance and improvement of the urban ambient. Occasionally worry is expressed about maintaining safe public spaces or preserving lively neighborhoods. For the most part, the world of the urban man is a world of career and consumption not oriented to the locality, where personal problems have more to do with economic status, ethnicity, and migrancy than with life style.[6] The public problems of these areas, however, are great. For the most part they revolve around decay and sterile renewal, a shrinking tax base, and the creation of a residential scene which perhaps only few people want and within which even the committed urbanite finds it difficult to persist.[7]

A quite different picture is observed, however, in familistic areas characterized by high fertility and women at home. Here, among the mortgaged single family dwellings of suburbia and in the familistic areas of the central city there exists a much greater concern for and involvement in the local area. Children blaze paths of interaction, bind local knots of interdependence, and magnify the importance of schools, neighborhood, and local community. In these areas current problems derive from the rearing of children and, often, the rapid, recent creation of vast horizontal neighborhoods.[8]

Ethnic status designates localities in terms of the presence of culturally and physically visible minorities. These areas are focal points associated with problems of shedding social visibilities and assimilation into the larger community. In the case of the culturally visible this process is generally a matter of three or four generations in America.[9] With the physically visible, the rate of assimilation is appreciably slower, for their stigmata may be erased only through amalgamation or by *defining the differences as socially meaningless* in the acquisition of benefits of the community. This process, requiring dramatic normative and attitudinial changes is, to be sure, lengthy and its results often volatile.[10]

Finally, migration status identifies a set of local problems arising from the absence of urban skills and magnified by local reactions to newcomers.[11] Historically, the difficulties which beset migrants were empirically and socially confused with ethnic status. It is now clear that the necessary skills, resources, and even motives for action in a large scale urban society are qualitatively distinct from the requirements of the little communities of the hinterland and foreland. The problems of the migrants arise from inappropriate responses to an urban world. Even when the experience of migration is less dramatic, constraints arise from the alienness of the new environment and the severing of old ties, modes of action, connections, and amenities. For migrants, then, basic problems involve the acquisition of urban skills and the establishment of new and meaningful relations with the alien community.

Each of these dimensions identifies sets of personal and social concerns which are problematic in our time. Only a few of these are isolated above; but even this listing indicates how the significance and relevance of urban problems systematically varies from one locality in the city to another, in accordance with the relative standing of the population of each along four basic dimensions of social differentiation.

These are not isolated findings gleaned from occasional samples of a few scattered studies: the evidence is garnered from a large number of separate investigations which span the nation and several decades, and it is consistent evidence. From Providence to San Diego, all four dimensions differentiate between populations and define the problems of each.[12] Within any community a greater understanding of the assets and activities of local area residents is gained by taking into account their standing along each of these dimensions and, more importantly, by considering the configuration of their standings. Their resources are limited not only by the prevalence of migrants, ethnics, an urban life style, or semi-skilled workers, but also by the combined influence of all of these limits.

This is critical to the present discussion because many of the enduring problems which presently plague cities arise from compounding inequity and constraint in localities within the community. Residents of an urban ghetto are disproportionately disadvantaged by the accumulation of limits stemming from low economic status, high levels of ethnicity, migrancy, and an urban life style. It is, however, not only a compounding of effects among the spatially isolated disadvantaged which is problem generating; difficulties also arise because these status dimensions are frequently crystallized among the advantaged as well.

The combined assets of localities which contain a high proportion of skilled, white, Protestant, long-term urbanites when conjoined with an option to familism usually involves an alignment with the amenities of suburbia. Not only does this result in the oft decried drainage of tax support from the central city but also in the removal of a significant sector of the population from a daily confrontation with the problems of the urban core. The highly disadvantaged who are entrapped in localities suffering from compounded deprivations thus become invisible to their opposites in suburbia.[13] The compounding of extremes of deprivation on the one hand, and of advantage on the other, thus presents problems in addition to those which are directly associated with each dimension of differentiation.

Status crystallization at the extremes of each dimension, conjoined with residential segregation, is not, however, the usual condition in cities. Most localities beyond a minimum level of economic status vary widely in life style. Ethnicity and migrancy are often compounded in the extreme as, for example, in urban areas settled by Negroes from the rural South who are generally of low economic status. But this does not always obtain: "hillbillies" are unskilled, rural-to-urban migrants. However, they are not physically visible, while most Negroes in Chicago are visible; but these latter are often urban men—not migrants—and occasionally highly skilled. In fact, in almost every city studied, it is not possible to predict accurately where a locality stands along any one continuum

from a knowledge of its standing along another. Each of the four dimensions is, except possibly at the extremes, quite independent of all of the others.[14] This independence of the different ways of distributing resources within the community means that each local area is characterized by a fairly distinct status profile and, in turn, by a particular constellation of relevant problems and concerns. This metropolitan mosaic contains few concerns which are shared by all segments of the community. What is highly problematic in one locality is viewed with passive disinterest in another across the tracks or out among the trees of suburbia. But now, by careful analysis of mass data, we can begin to isolate these different types of localities and mixtures of interests and perhaps even begin to mobilize personal and community resources in terms of their needs.

The community, however, is not static and the divisions which now separate localities are being altered by advancing industrialization and urbanization. If present trends continue, it is likely that several of these dimensions will cease to affect large segments of the community and, more importantly, that the range of variation of localities along each will shift radically. First, the general rise in economic status of most localities in metropolitan areas, as observed in the last two censuses, is considered likely to continue. This change has resulted in a general upward shift for most localities and a marked increase in the proportion of highly advantaged localities. But the proportion of highly disadvantaged localities at the lowest levels of economic status has not altered greatly.

It is difficult to tell at this time if this upward increase in the average economic status will continue to be accompanied by a widening of the range of inequity.

Perhaps present efforts to raise the skills and education of the most disadvantaged will result in the upward progression of the *average* economic status, accompanied by a shrinking range of inequity or, at the least, a fairly constant range.

The proportion of familistic localities has increased in nearly all metropolitan areas each decade since 1940. In addition, it has been observed that this life style is by far the most prevalent in (1) those areas of the nation which have experienced the greatest growth (the Southwest and Far West); (2) those sections of all metropolitan areas which have experienced greatest growth (the suburbs and fringe areas); and (3) among those economic groupings which have most increased in status (upper and middle class).[15] It is likely that, given this strong thrust, this style of life will continue to be chosen by an increasingly large proportion of the total society. Further, with increasing economic status, it is probable that urban life style, at least in its present form, will be increasingly limited to those entrapped in the central city and unable to move.

The extreme form of migration status —the result of a radical shift from peasant to urban life—is likely to disappear in the next few decades. This will be due to both a diminution in the rate of rural to urban migration (we are running out of farmers) and the continued extension of urban forms throughout America and the continued increase in the intensity of involvement of all people in urban life. This long-term trend in the urbanization of American society is not likely to cease. Less extreme forms of migration status associated with movement that does not cross steep social boundaries will, however, probably persist since there is no evidence that the rate of long distance or short distance residential movement is likely to diminish. Changes in communications technology may, however, alter the social significance of this movement.

Proximate changes in ethnic status are difficult to assess in the light of recent changes in immigration policies which will affect the volume of immigration and the distribution of physical and cultural visibilities, as well as the distribution of skills among immigrants. Recent fluctuations in the migration patterns of Puerto Ricans also make projections with respect to this large minority difficult. Finally, current changes in norms and attitudes surrounding race relations will have a profound effect on the relevance of physical visibility to the distribution of resources within the community and concomitant problems. It is likely, however, that Negroes will continue to migrate to the urban North and West; that they will suffer inequities based on race alone; and that in many instances these will be compounded with disadvantages which stem from migrancy and low economic status.

In sum, the twin processes of urbanization and industrialization have yielded a fourfold division within the urban community. Each of these separately and in concert produce many current problems. The future course of these processes may heal some divisions and, possibly, bring about new ones.

NOTES

1. See Seymore Martin Lipset & Reinhard Bendix, Social Mobility in Industrial Society (1959); Neil J. Smelser, The Sociology of Economic Life (1963); and Wilbert E. Moore & Bert F. Hoselitz (Eds.), Industrialization and Society (in collaboration with UNESCO) (1963), for general discussions of this process and significant consequences.
2. See Eshref Shevky & Marilyn Williams, The Social Areas of Los Angeles (1949); and Eshref Shevky & Wendell Bell, Social Area Analysis: Theory, Illustrative Application and Computational Procedures (1955), for an insightful synopsis of this transformation.
3. Emile Durkheim, The Division of Labor in Society cc. 3–8 (1949).
4. W. L. Warner & Leo Srole, The Social Systems of American Ethnic Groups (1945); Nathan Glazer and Daniel Patrick Moynihan, Beyond the Melting Pot: The Negroes, Puerto Ricans, Jews, Italians, and Irish in New York City (1963); Oscar Handlin, The Newcomers (1963).
5. Cf. Warner & Srole, op. cit. supra note 4, and other volumes of the Yankee City series for careful observations on the role of migrancy, ethnicity and class on patterns of settlement completed some twenty years ago. Recent materials include: Beverly Duncan & Philip Hauser, Housing a Metropolis—Chicago (1960); Stanley Lieberson, Ethnic Patterns in American Cities: A Comparative Study Using Data from Ten Urban Centers (1963); Anderson & Bean, The Shevky-Bell Social Areas: Confirmation of Results and a Reinterpretation, 40 Social Forces 119 (1961); Anderson & Egeland, Spatial Aspects of Social Area Analysis, 26 Am. Socio. Rev. 392 (1961); Bell, The Social Areas of the San Francisco Bay Region, 18 Am. Socio. Rev. 39 (1953); Bell, Economic, Family, and Ethnic Status: An Empirical Test, 20 Am. Socio. Rev. 45 (1955); Bell, The Utility of the Shevky Typology for the Design of Urban Subarea Field Studies, 47 J. Soc. Psy. 71–83 (1958); Bell, Social Areas: Typology of Urban Neighborhoods, in Marvin Sussman (ed.), Community Structure and Analysis (1959); John C. Bollens, Explaining the Metropolitan Community (1961); Goldstein & Mayer, Population Decline and the Social and Demographic Structure of an American City, 29 Am. Socio. Rev. 48 (1964), Greer, Urbanism Reconsidered, 21 Am. Socio. Rev. 19 (1956); Kahl, A Comparison of Indexes of Socio-Economic Status, 20 Am. Socio. Rev. 317 (1955); Walter C. Kaufman, A Factor-Analytic Test of Revisions in the Shevky-Bell Typology for Chicago and San Francisco, 1950 (unpublished Ph.D. thesis in Northwestern University Library, 1961); McElrath The Social Areas of Rome: A Comparative Analysis 27 Am. Socio. Rev. 376 (1962); Mack & McElrath, Urban Social Differentiation and the Allocation of Resources, 352 Annals 25–32 (1964); Schmid, MacCannell & Van Arsdol, Jr., The Ecology of the American City: Further Comparison and Validation of Generalizations, 23 Am. Socio. Rev. 392 (1958); Robert C. Tryon, Identification of Social Areas by Cluster Analysis (1955); Van Arsdol, Jr., Schmid & Camilleri, A Deviant Case of Shevky's Dimensions of Urban Sturcture, Research Studies of the State College of Washington (June 1957); Van Arsdol, Jr., Schmid & Camilleri, The Generality of Urban Social Area Indexes, 23 Am. Socio. Rev. 277 (1958); Van Arsdol, Jr., Schmid & Camilleri, An Application of the Shevky Social Area Indexes to a Model of Urban Society, 37 Social Forces 26 (1958).
6. Cf. Bell, Social Choice, Life Styles and Suburban Residence, in William M. Dobriner (Ed.), The Suburban Community 225–47 (1958).
7. For a lively presentation of this polemic, see Jane Jacobs, The Death and Life of Great American Cities (1961); as well as The Editors of Fortune, The Exploding Metropolis (1961).
8. See especially Mowrer, The Family in Suburbia, in Dobriner, op. cit. supra note 6, at 147–64, as well as several other chapters in this volume.
9. Warner & Srole, op. cit. supra note 4, and Lieberson, op. cit. supra note 5, are especially pertinent.
10. See works cited supra note 4.
11. Ibid.
12. Shevky & Williams, op. cit. supra note 2; Shevky & Bell, op. cit. supra note 2; and the last eighteen items of note 5 supra, are pertinent, along with several pieces in George A. Theodorson (Ed.), Studies in Human Ecology, esp. Part II (1961); Marvin B. Sussman (Ed.), Community Structure and Analysis (1959); as well as the excellent discussion in Scott Greer, The Emerging City: Myth and Reality (1962).
13. Cf. Michael Harrington, The Other America: Poverty in the United States (1962).
14. Cf. the several articles by Van Arsdol and others, supra note 5; and also Ralph Ellison, The Invisible Man (1952).
15. Dennis McElrath, The New Urbanization and Trip Generation [forthcoming].

Urban Ecology PART IV

Neighborhood, city, and metropolis are concepts which imply not only a way of life and a particular system of social and cultural differentiation, but also a specific territory in which urban people live and work. Indeed, the fact that human activities have a location in geographical space is sufficiently important as a generator of community characteristics and problems to have given rise to a specialty within sociology, human ecology. The concern of the ecologists with the way in which sociocultural phenomena are patterned in space is now duplicated by the interest of several other disciplines in "territoriality," including regional science, geography, and city planning. The readings in this part draw on all these fields.

A prime intention of these readings is to point up the ways in which space is relevant to understanding the large-scale urban territorial unit, namely the metropolitan region. The selections presented in the first section describe the physical structure of the metropolitan community, discuss the reasons for its dispersed spatial organization, and consider some problems this pattern generates. The fundamental concept here is "the friction of space," the costs and hazards which the rootedness of activities and populations to land imposes on the efficient and economical exchange of commodities and workers in an urban area. In recent decades the development of the automobile and the jet plane have liberated interrelated activities from their dependence on spatial proximity resulting in an increasing tendency for urban activities to spread out through a region. This tendency has been further facilitated by rapid developments in communication technology including closed circuit television and improved telephone service. The willingness of Americans to learn to use these new technologies and to adapt to their demands constitutes one of the remarkable social changes of the present century. However, it is possible that consumer styles

391

and preferences will change again, and the implications of this for the spread city pattern and metropolitan growth are difficult to estimate.

The second section includes readings which try to dig underneath the macroecological level and to understand the impact of social organization, cultural standards, and psychological responses on people's decision about land use and the location of activities in metropolitan regions. How are the major economic and technological forces leading toward suburbanization experienced by the individual family faced with the need for more housing space or a safer neighborhood? What impact have these forces had on the residents of ghetto areas who, because of poverty and discrimination, are unable to flee the central city? In what way do the processes of metropolitan expansion interrelate with the goals and preferences of different occupational groups? To what degree is the demand of business and real estate developers for downtown land constrained by sentimental attachments to existing land uses or by the role of local politicians? The articles that provide answers to these questions reflect the point of view of a modern school of ecological thought, a school which emphasizes the social and cultural factors determining spatial location, as distinct from the traditional focus on economic and biological processes.

Metropolitan Ecological Structure and Growth

26. Urban Form: The Case of the Metropolitan Community   Leo F. Schnore

The study of the spatial structure of urban communities is the province of that specialty within sociology known as human ecology. Leo Schnore reviews the contribution of the field to understanding the metropolis. He points out that research dealing with spatial structure has progressed from an interest in the evolution of the metropolitan community to a concern for its internal organization and, more recently, to the investigation of systems of metropolitan regions (see the selection by Galle in Part III). Schnore argues that ecology has contributed fundamental knowledge of the structure and dynamics of the metropolis and thereby also has developed a scientific basis for the formulation of urban policies. However, he emphasizes that ecological studies suffer from two important deficiencies. Because of the kind of data available, existing research offers a "snapshot" rather than an historical portrait of metropolitan growth, and previous studies depend too heavily on a conception of the metropolis as a closed social system. The author takes off from this criticism to discuss three frontiers for future research into spatial structure.

Leo F. Schnore is Professor of Sociology at the University of Wisconsin. He is the author of *The Urban Scene* (1965) and coeditor of *Urban Research and Policy Planning* (1967) and *The Study of Urbanization* (1965) ; and he has contributed a number of other works in the field of ecology and demography.

Does urban sociology offer any distinctive contributions to the study of urban life and form? It was one of a number of specialized approaches to the city and its problems that appeared almost simultaneously in the twenties as new subfields within the traditional academic disciplines. Urban life and form soon became the focus of the whole Chicago School of sociologists led by Robert E. Park. As Albert J. Reiss, Jr., has observed, these men "saw three principal areas of sociological inquiry into urban life: the study of the ecology of the city, of its social organization, and of the psychology of its inhabitants."[1]

These three areas have not received equal attention over the years. In his "The Growth of the City" of 1923, Ernest W. Burgess, Park's colleague, sketched the outlines of "the ecology of the city," asserting that land uses, population, and urban institutions were distributed in a series of concentric zones focusing upon the urban core, the central business district. Fifteen years later, Louis Wirth, in "Urbanism as a Way of Life," provided a virtual catalog of hypotheses concerning the distinctive features of urban social organization and psychology. In the years that have followed, the themes set out in these two expositions have been restated a number of times, and some of them have come under sharp attack, but far more attention has been given to the topics treated by Wirth.[2] Students of the urban scene, whether sociologists or not, have been less interested in the morphology of the city than in interpersonal relations in the city milieu and the role of the larger urban environment in shaping personality development. The result is that we have a substantial literature devoted to sociological treatments of *urban life*. The subject of *urban form* poses another problem altogether.

What is urban form? One can quickly become lost in a semantic bog if he is unwilling to accept arbitrary limitations on the uses of such a term, but the subject of urban form has not been a popular sociological specialty, no matter what meaning may be read into the phrase. *For present purposes, we shall simply take "form" as the rough equivalent of "spatial structure," and hold that one of the largest contributions to general urban studies on the part of sociology lies in the work that has been done on the spatial structure of the metropolitan community.* This subject subject represents a logical extension of the earlier interests of Chicago sociologists in the ecology of the city, and constitutes a continuing interest on the part of some sociologists in the morphology of urbanism. Economists and geographers share these concerns, but we will limit ourselves to the efforts of sociologists working in the ecological tradition.

Theory and Research on the Metropolitan Community

The seminal theoretical work on "metropolitanism," *An Introduction to Economic History*, published in 1922 by N. S. B. Gras, was actually an interpretive historical inquiry, not a sociological treatise. Rejecting earlier theories that posited a series of evolutionary stages of economic organization culminating in the national economy, Gras argued for recognition of the "metropolitan economy" as the successor to the "town economy," with London after the mid-sixteenth century regarded as the prototype.[3] His views exerted a profound influence upon the thinking of many sociologists—most notably, R. D. McKenzie, a student of Park and Burgess, who subsequently taught at the University of Michigan. McKenzie published a full-scale monograph on *The Metropolitan Community* in 1933, the first statistical treatment of the subject. He turned away from Gras's historical concerns and identified "the metropolitan community" as the product of revolutionary changes in local transportation and communication occurring in the twentieth century:

> By reducing the scale of local distance, the motor vehicle extended the horizon of the community and introduced a territorial division of labor among local institutions and neighboring centers which is unique in the history of settlement. The large center has been able to extend the radius of its influence; its population and many of its institutions, freed from the dominance of rail transportation, have become widely dispersed throughout surrounding territory. Moreover, formerly independent towns and villages and also rural territory have become part of this enlarged city complex . . . The metropolitan community, therefore, comprises a cluster or constellation of centers. Smaller cities and towns tend to group themselves around larger ones somewhat as planets group themselves around a sun.[4]

The study of "the city" as a continuous area of dense settlement was thus supplemented by the recognition of clusters of cities forming a "supercommunity." This larger entity gained its unity through a territorial division of labor between more or less specialized parts, including the metropolis itself and the nearby hinterland, urban and rural, and McKenzie brought together a variety of materials—mainly from census sources—in order to document "the rise of the metropolitan community."

Research on this broader area of interdependent relations was greatly facilitated by the recognition of "metropolitan" units on the part of data-collecting agencies of the federal government. Beginning in 1910, population statistics were made available for "metropolitan districts" consisting of large cities and the immediately adjacent territory beyond their borders. With minor revisions in criteria, these units continued to be delineated by the Bureau of the Census up through the census of 1940, and they were used exclusively for the reporting of population data. In advance of the 1950 census, responsibility for this activity shifted to an interdepartmental committee consisting of representatives of a large number of federal agencies, and many additional series of social and economic data have been regularly reported for Standard Metropolitan Areas (1950) and Standard Metropolitan Statistical Areas (1960). It is only recently, then, that "metropolitan" data have come to be available on matters other than those covered in the decennial census of population. These matters deserve mention here because the character of the available data seems to have had a large part in shaping the research that has been carried out. Norman B. Ryder's observation concerning fertility research bears repeating here:

> It does not seem unfair to assert that the existence of vast stores of official data . . . has made the development of the subject excessively dependent on these stores, so that the forms in which data are presented in these sources have become the frames of reference for analysis. To put the point in the form of a question: Have demographers chosen their methods and concepts because they are theoretically relevant or because the data already exist in these forms?[5]

TABLE 1. POPULATION OF CENTRAL CITY AS A PERCENTAGE OF TOTAL METROPOLITAN AREA POPULATION, SELECTED CITIES, 1850–1960*

Census Year	New York	Cincinnati	Boston	St. Louis	Buffalo	Cleveland	Detroit	Syracuse	Phoenix	Austin
1850	*50*	—	26	50	30	27	24	26	—	—
1860	48	67	26	58	42	46	33	31	—	—
1870	43	70	30	67†	51	63	42	41	—	—
1880	43	67	35	68	57	75	49	42	—	—
1890	41	66	26	72	66	79	62	61	—	—
1900	68†	63	43	71	69	85	68	64	27	47
1910	67	54	42	68	68	*86*	76	69	32	53
1920	66	50	41	68	67	83	77	71	32	61
1930	64	47	36	60	63	73	72	72	32	68
1940	64	43	35	57	60	69	68	70	35	79
1950	61	35	34	51	53	62	61	65	32	82
1960	53	47†	28	38	41	49	44	51	66†	88†

* Standard Metropolitan Areas as defined in 1950, with definitions retrojected to earlier census years. The italicized entries designate the census dates at which the central cities contained maximum proportions. In four cases (New York, Boston, Phoenix, and Austin) this maximum is not the largest percentage shown in the column because city areas were considerably extended by annexation of territory after decentralization was under on the older areal basis.

† A major annexation to the central city occurred in the preceding decade.

Whatever the answer to this question, it does appear that empirical research on "metropolitan" topics has been rather one-sided. McKenzie described the rise of the metropolitan community as an emerging system characterized by two principal trends:

(1) The increase in the aggregate population of the community and the expansion of the area within which local activities are carried on in common; (2) the increased mobility of products and people, resulting in a wider range of individual choice, more specialization of local services and a more closely-knit community structure.[6]

Studies of these latter processes—increased mobility, specialization—are rather hard to find. Granted, migration, residential mobility, and commuting have been studied in a metropolitan context from time to time, but the mobility of products—commodities and services—has received less attention than the mobility of people. Intrametropolitan "specialization of local services" has been largely ignored, at least as it may represent an unfolding process observable over time, and no one has seriously tried to grapple with the question of whether or not the metropolitan area is tending toward "a more closely knit community structure." These are not trends that can be easily inferred from inspecting a series of census reports.

At the same time, it must be said that the other processes identified by McKenzie —population growth and territorial expansion—have been thoroughly documented by subsequent research. In particular, we have three excellent historical-demographic analyses of twentieth-century developments by Warren S. Thompson, Donald J. Bogue, and Amos H. Hawley.[7] Not only do we have data for metropolitan areas in the aggregate, but we can also trace the experience of individual areas in some detail. If one is interested in the decentralization of residential population, for example, it is possible to assemble historical statistics in a simple way that permits the approximate dating of relative outward shifts in particular places. (See Table 1.) Our study has suggested that at least one city, New York, was decentralizing as early as the 1850's, and that it was joined by nine others before the turn of the century. At the same time, this inquiry has demonstrated that it was not until the 1920's, when automobile ownership became widespread, that a majority of large American cities began to exhibit growth rates lower than those of their surrounding rings.[8]

Census materials, then, have been employed to establish the main trends of metropolitan growth and expansion over the years. But what of the evolving spatial structure of the metropolitan community? McKenzie spoke of it as a "new type of supercommunity organized around a dominant focal point and comprising a multiple of differentiated centers of activity."[9] What do we know of the evolution of this urban form? Unfortunately, we must depend upon cross-sectional "snapshots" if we wish to learn anything more than the gross facts of population redistribution.

Prewar Metropolitan Patterns: Three Studies

As we shall see, ecological studies of the spatial structure of the metropolitan community also tend to be based on census materials. Five investigations deserve close attention, particularly from the standpoint of research design. The first three portray the ecology of the metropolitan community as it existed on the eve of World War II.

The Structure of the Metropolitan Community The first of these studies was the extremely ambitious doctoral dissertation written at the University of Michigan by Donald J. Bogue. Using materials from the 1939 "economic censuses" (business and manufacturing) in combination with 1940 population census data, Bogue assigned every square foot of the continental United States to one or another of 67 preselected "metropolitan communities," and examined patterns of population density, wholesale and retail trade, services and manufacturing according to broad distance zones and directional sectors.[10] Presented as "a study in dominance and subdominance," it demonstrated the existence of a complex but orderly geographic division of labor between spatial units spread over a wide landscape extending far beyond the city itself. Understandably enough, this study has not been replicated for other years. Confined as it is to 1939–1940 materials, it yields a richly detailed cross-sectional view of the level of territorial differentiation achieved in a highly industrialized society favored by an advanced system of transportation and communication, and it fully deserves recognition as a classic contribution to metropolitan research.

Other studies, much smaller in scope, have adopted major elements of Bogue's design, assigning outlying areas to one or another metropolis and proceeding to search for spatial patterns in demographic, social, or economic characteristics.[11] In actual fact, however, there are reasons for doubting the utility of a full-scale replication of the Bogue study, given one of its major characteristics—the assumption of a set of "closed" metropolitan communities, wherein the experience of a particular area is implicitly regarded as independent of the experience of other areas occupying positions in the total spatial structure of the national economy. Nevertheless, this research must be regarded as a major accomplishment—a breakthrough both substantively and methodologically—for it pointed the way to a structural interpretation of census materials.

Differentiation in Metropolitan Areas Still another study—also a doctoral dissertation from the University of Michigan —has taken up the question of the territorial division of labor, but in a more restricted area.[12] This study, by Leslie Kish, demonstrated the existence of an orderly pattern of differentiation among subcommunities found within the immediate orbit of the metropolis, that is, within the metropolitan community itself rather than in the broader metropolitan region studied by Bogue. Some nine demographic, economic, and political characteristics of incorporated places as of 1940 were examined in a probability sample of twenty-four areas. Again, distance was of central concern, and it was found that subcenters near the central city were much more variegated than those at greater distances; within an "inner metropolitan belt," in fact, high levels of differentiation were clearly observable, while substantially lower levels were found in areas beyond the immediate sphere of metropolitan influence.

With the use of an ingenious measure of intraclass correlation, Kish was able to show bands of "metropolitan influence" varying in width according to the size of the metropolis. Other than the size factor, however, this study stressed variation *within* metropolitan areas, ignoring area-to-area variation, and it implicitly took the metropolitan community as a "closed" system. Again, one must be struck by the cross-sectional nature of the inquiry, and a whole series of questions is likely to occur to the reader concerning trends over time in levels of differentiation. For example, when did the patterns observed in 1940 emerge? Have the bands of influence been expanding at a measurable rate? Are suburbs becoming more differentiated or more like each other? Despite his inability to answer such questions, Kish produced important bench mark data, and provided significant details on another facet of metropolitan spatial structure.

Metropolitan Site Selection A third study of prewar patterns was more directly concerned with the economic aspect of metropolitan spatial structure. In addition, it involved an attempt to derive longitudinally oriented propositions from cross-sectional data. We refer to "Metropolitan Site Selection," by Walter Isard (an economist) and Vincent H. Whitney (a sociologist), a study of the territorial differentiation of retail trade in subcenters of 10,000 or more inhabitants, found in a series of seven distance zones ranging up to seventy miles from the metropolitan center.[13] The spatial structuring of retail activities was clearly manifested in the data. As of 1939 (the data of the Census of Business used in the study), total per capita sales were substantially higher in the central city than in the nearby suburban zones; beyond about twenty miles, however, per capita sales rose in a roughly regular gradient with distance. This pattern was interpreted by the authors as a reflection of the drawing power of the metropolis, which tends to attract shoppers from the immediately contiguous zones. At a greater distance, the "friction of

space" presumably operated to discourage longer trips to the metropolitan center, and functioned as a protective barrier against the competition of the metropolis, guranteeing higher sales for smaller outlying cities that served as trade centers for their own immediate hinterlands. More important, Isard and Whitney were able to show orderly variations by distance in specific trade categories: the center was heavily specialized in general merchandising and exhibited "dominance" over the nearby suburbs in such lines as apparel and jewelry, but not in food sales and in the automotive group, where sales were more evenly distributed.

Despite the clarity of the major findings, certain characteristics of the Isard-Whitney research design make for difficulties in interpretation. Like the studies by Bogue and Kish, it took the metropolitan area as a kind of "closed system," though this seems justifiable in a study of retail trade patterns. In addition, however, the study was highly aggregative, combining data for ten metropolitan centers and their surrounding cities; the results were thus presented in the form of weighted averages —averages that are heavily influenced by the patterns exhibited in the largest places, and that may conceal a great amount of variation from area to area. Moreover, the authors excluded a number of outlying places near cities of intermediate size, and they further eliminated all cities that had fewer than 5000 inhabitants in 1890, "in order to diminish as far as possible the special effect of suburban cities whose growth has been primarily associated with the centrifugal flow of population from the central cities."[14]

These limitations were imposed in an effort to develop an historical argument; Isard and Whitney assumed that the outlying cities had been very similar to each other in terms of retail structure in 1890, and they then interpreted the "site selection" patterns observable in 1939 as the product of trends over time in the direction of greater trade specialization that followed upon major improvements in local transportation and communication. Yet their data are intrinsically cross-sectional in form, and a longitudinal argument is necessarily strained. Technically speaking, the effects of aggregating the data over ten metropolitan regions and the consequences of arbitrarily eliminating outlying cities are also extremely difficult to assess. Replications of this study would be improved if they were confined to individual areas and if they allowed the full range of city types to be represented. Moreover, historical inferences would be more soundly based if a series of observations at different points in time were employed.

Metropolitan Patterns: Two Recent Studies

The studies by Bogue, Kish, and Isard and Whitney provide a wealth of cross-sectional evidence on the internal spatial structure of the metropolitan community just prior to World War II. Two more recent investigations that have focused on postwar patterns were carried out at the University of Chicago by Donnell Pappenfort and by Otis Dudley Duncan and his colleagues.

The Ecological Field and the Metropolitan Community The Pappenfort study demonstrated the utility of postulating a more inclusive "field" within which individual metropolitan communities are found.[15] Using data for production units (factories) located in Illinois, and their spatially separate administrative centers (home offices) located throughout the United States, Pappenfort was able to show that production units in Illinois are dissimilarly distributed according to the location of their administrative centers. Illinois factories with Illinois home offices are distributed with primary reference to Chicago, the dominant metropolis in the state. At the same time, Illinois factories with administrative offices outside the Chicago Standard Metropolitan Area are located with reference to the influence of adjacent and even more distant metropolitan areas. According to Pappenfort, "the consistency of the relationships suggests that they may reflect general principles of ecological organization on the national level that the contemporary interpretation of the metropolitan community [as a closed system] does not include."[16]

Metropolis and Region Further confirmation for this more inclusive structural conception is found in *Metropolis and Region*, by Otis Dudley Duncan and his colleagues. Like the other works discussed above, this study was cross-sectional in orientation, designed to yield "a mid-century bench mark." Frankly ecological in outlook, it assumed that "to understand metropolitan communities we must examine them in the context of a more inclusive system."[17] The "more inclusive system" turns out to be more than the "region" as it is ordinarily conceived in the literature of metropolitanism, for it often embraces the whole of the national economy and society. In the case of manufacturing, for example, it was shown that the "urban hierarchy" is a national system, while broad regions appear to have relatively self-contained hierarchies for the provision of certain services. As the authors showed, each kind of metropolitan function may entail a distinctive type of regional relationship.

The notable advance achieved by this study was the incorporation of an "open system" conception of the metropolis in the very design of the research. Much of the novelty of the study stems from this fact, together with the related use of actual data on interarea exchanges—tabulations of the flow of commercial and financial payments and receipts between each of thirty-six zones making up the Federal Reserve System. These interregional data were complemented by materials on the spatial patterning of bank loans. Similarly, new light was cast on the concept of "metropolitan dominance." Unlike Bogue's classic study (and others influenced by it), the approach taken by Duncan and his colleagues "does not rest on a prior classification of nonmetropolitan parts of the country into metropolitan regions [and] metropolitan influence or 'dominance' is not conceived as flowing to each hinterland areal unit from a single metropolitan center."[18] Instead , the nonmetropolitan territory of the United States was examined in terms of Pappenfort's concept of a generalized "ecological field."

Two Issues in Research Design

Cross-sectional versus Longitudinal Studies One could easily make a case for a research program essentially based on straightforward replications of the five ecological studies reviewed above. Certainly our understanding of metropolitan structure would be considerably enhanced by the asemblage of many more "snapshots" for additional dates, so that gross trends could be detected. These studies capture certain static aspects of an evolving structure at certain points in time, but they tell us very little indeed about the nature of that evolution. Drawing longitudinal inferences from cross-sectional data involves hazards that are too familiar to require discussion here. But the difficulties involved in actually conducting longitudinal studies when one is working with data assembled on an areal basis are less widely recognized. To take only one example, consider the implications of the simple fact that most census data are reported for political units—cities, counties, states—as of a particular point in time.

Political boundaries change, and even if one is content to confine himself to research on demographic matters, ignoring questions of spatial structure, there is a serious practical difficulty that faces anyone conducting research on population growth or other changes within metropolitan areas, namely, the possibility of *changes in the territorial units under study*. Thus, only one serious effort has been devoted to a careful assessment of annexation as a "component" of population growth in metropolitan centers and rings; Bogue examined this factor, along with the contributions of natural increase and net migration, for the 1940–1950 decade. This problem turns out to be much more severe for the 1950–1960 intercensal period, when three out of four metropolitan centers extended their legal limits.[19] Thus, the best intentions in the world may be frustrated by the form in which mass data are made available. Anyone who has had experience in working with these materials quickly comes to appreciate why cross-sectional research designs are so frequently used in the investigation of problems that seem to cry out for longitudinal study.

Open versus Closed Systems We have also observed that most of the work that has been done on this subject exhibits a kind of "intrametropolitan" bias, for it takes the metropolitan community as a relatively self-contained or quasi-independent system. We have seen that efforts to identify the place of the metropolitan community in some larger field are recent and rare. Like everyone else, sociologists acknowledge the fact of interdependence when they observe that metropolitan agglomerations inevitably depend upon other areas for food and fiber, but they seem to ignore the implications of this fact in carrying out their studies. Again, however, there are practical reasons that influence the design of metropolitan research. The "simple" problem of determining the spatial limits of the metropolitan community makes it clear that there are many difficulties in attempting to bound what is literally an "open system."

This matter can be best understood if one contrasts the problems facing an investigator who prefers to undertake a comparative analysis of a number of places rather than an intensive study of a particular area. As an example, consider Gottmann's monumental work on *Megalopolis*, the densely settled northeastern seaboard of the United States.[20] This remarkable study provides a noteworthy example of an open-system conception, analyzing a sprawling series of "super-communities" that could hardly be understood without reference to its place in the nation and the world. The extent to which this unique cluster of contiguous metropolitan areas exhibits internal unity is still an open question, but it is quite clear that the study of any particular area is more likely to sensitize the investigator to the relations between it and the outside world than a study that attempts simultaneously to deal with a number of areas, all of which are interrelated in some

degree. Just as we found pressing practical reasons for cross-sectional rather than longitudinal designs, we come to appreciate the difficulties involved in working with an open-system conception in comparative analyses of the metropolitan community. To say that something is difficult, however, is not to say that it is impossible, and we shall see that there are at least a few points at which the metropolitan system can be "opened" in a way that permits its study as part of a still larger system.

Two Subjects for Future Research

Let us consider the future directions that ecological analysis might take, building upon the work that has already been accomplished, and taking account of the issues discussed above. Two broad topics seem particularly amenable to an approach that takes the spatial structure of the metropolitan community as a point of departure: "population shifts" on the one hand, and "movement systems" on the other. In both cases, questions of research design are crucial, but work is somewhat farther advanced in the first instance.

Population Shifts   As we have noted, the growth and territorial expansion of the metropolitan aggregate over time has been charted in detail, but these population movements have yet to be linked to historical shifts in social and economic organization. Thus, Reiss has asked "what is the relationship between *types* of economic organization, or functional specialization, and metropolitan growth? Historical research is particularly needed on the relationship between urban aggregation and changes in economic organization."[21] Changes in industrial and occupational composition of individual metropolitan areas provide one means of accounting for differentials in population growth. Certain sectors of the national economy are growing rapidly, while others are lagging. Are these changes reflected in the growth of individual metropolitan areas? The larger ecological field should be kept in the forefront of such an analysis, and an open-system conception appears to be necessary, for the growth of any particular metropolitan area is achieved only at the expense of other parts of the nation.

Within the metropolitan community itself, however, the redistribution of residential population may be regarded as incidental to the internal reorganization of spatial relations. As a consequence, a closed-system approach still has some utility. Nevertheless, the unresolved problems are many and vexing. To take only one example, consider the sheer description of the phenomenon variously labelled decentralization, deconcentration, or suburbanization. Despite the considerable attention devoted to this subject, much remains to be learned. As Duncan has observed:

> Extensive attempts to measure the [suburban] trend and efforts to isolate its determinants are prominent in the literature . . . This is a field of research with more than ordinary difficulties of conceptualization and measurement. All too often researchers . . . have somewhat naively accepted findings of differential growth rates between central and peripheral portions of urban communities as evidence of a specific process of "suburbanization" or "decentralization," without attempting an operational distinction between these alleged processes and the normal tendency for expansion to occur on the periphery of the community area . . . One may hazard a guess as to the approach needed to clarify this problem. *Comparative studies in considerable longitudinal depth* should match a city of a given size at a recent date with one of the same size at a remote date and note whether the recent pattern of growth is a more dispersed or "suburban" one than that occurring at the earlier period. An adequate comparison would require detailed examination of patterns and changes of population density.[22]

Assuming that the existing problems of terminology and measurement can be solved, shifts in residential population must still be linked to *other* processes occurring within the metropolitan community. One of the logical next steps consists of treating the growth of subareas as responsive to changes in the local housing inventory. The recent attention to the changing spatial structure of "housing opportunities" in two case studies by Beverly Duncan and her colleagues points the way toward resolving many of the difficulties that attend research focusing exclusively upon the movements of residential population.[23] Thus, longitudinal studies of closed metropolitan systems continue to offer considerable promise, especially as questions of timing are brought to the fore.

In this connection, a whole family of research questions is related to the problem of "history." Efforts at urban renewal and the troubles facing central business districts have made us all conscious of the obsolescence of the metropolitan core. But we are even more conscious of the differences between metropolitan areas than we are of the similarities among them. One factor that produces differences is the constant turnover visible in the metropolitan community —families being formed and dissolving, firms entering business and failing, etc. Each of these units begins its life and is obliged to take its place in an existing structure. Moreover, each cohort—or set of units "born" in a given year—emerges in an era marked by a somewhat different technological repertoire, and its activities are likely to be affected by the character of the tools and techniques of the age. But elements of technology are readily diffused, and may make for similarities that outweigh the differences.

One can conceive a model of "incremental growth and residues," wherein *the timing of major periods of growth* may be the crucial factor in accounting for the differences and similarities among metropolitan communities and their areal parts. The growth rings observable in a tree's trunk tell us not only its age, but also something of its year-to-year experience, whether favorable or unfavorable. It is commonplace to remark on the differences between pre- and post-auto cities, at least with respect to general form and physical structure. If one adds some attention to the

TABLE 2. GROWTH RATES, 1940–1950, IN METROPOLITAN SUBURBS AND SATELLITES OF 10,000 OR MORE INHABITANTS, BY FUNCTIONAL TYPE AND OTHER CHARACTERISTICS

Selected Characteristics of Metropolitan Suburbs	Percent Increase in Population, 1940–50			Number of Suburbs		
	Residential	Employing	All	Residential	Employing	All
A. *Regional location*						
Northeast	13.3	6.1	8.1	65	110	175
North Central	30.0	17.1	22.8	65	57	122
West	63.6	47.1	53.1	37	43	80
South	77.4	47.4	60.4	20	19	39
B. *Central city size*						
500,000 or more	27.8	12.4	18.2	136	142	278
100,000–500,000	36.1	13.8	21.6	32	40	72
less than 100,000	79.5	36.9	42.9	19	47	66
C. *Suburban size, 1940*						
50,000 or more	15.1	10.0	11.5	17	31	48
25,000–50,000	18.8	14.9	15.8	18	55	73
10,000–25,000	30.9	19.1	24.4	90	102	192
less than 10,000	104.1	92.6	99.3	62	41	103
D. *Distance from central city*						
0–10 miles	27.2	16.4	20.8	112	92	204
10–20 miles	40.8	18.2	25.3	61	84	145
over 20 miles	29.4	15.9	18.1	14	53	67
E. *Metropolitan area economic base*						
Manufacturing	23.6	12.2	16.1	79	105	184
Diversified	33.0	19.3	23.9	89	98	187
Retail	68.9	23.4	29.2	17	23	40
Other	412.7	64.8	103.4	2	3	5
F. *Suburban rent level*						
Low	31.7	12.8	15.9	7	26	33
Average	29.0	15.1	18.8	91	173	264
High	36.3	44.1	38.4	89	30	119
G. *Age of suburb*						
more than 50 years	21.8	12.2	15.0	102	178	280
40–50 years	33.1	36.2	34.6	35	31	66
30–40 years	51.8	66.2	57.5	25	12	37
less than 30 years	116.6	168.5	126.6	25	8	33
All suburbs	31.9	17.0	22.1	187	229	316

Leo F. Schnore, "The Growth of Metropolitan Suburbs," *American Sociological Review*, 22 (April 1957), pp. 165–173.

historical variations in the style and architectural design of homes, shops, and factories, much of the physical appearance of contemporary metropolitan communities can be understood by reference to their periods of florescence. Internally, one can detect cross-sectional differences between whole residential neighborhoods, shopping areas, and industrial districts that are the products of history.[24]

Still another line of analysis involves the study of short-term growth differentials within metropolitan areas in terms of the roles played by various subareas—whether "neighborhoods" within the great city or "suburbs" in the ring. Here again, cross-sectional research designs appear to be appropriate. The results of one such study are shown in Table 2. These data represent an effort to portray recent growth differentials between two types of metropolitan subcenter: (1) "residential suburbs," having more employed residents than jobs, and (2) "employing satellites," having more jobs than employed residents. The guiding assumption is that variations in growth are associated with these typological differences.

In this kind of demographic-ecological research, it is desirable to distinguish the components of population change—natural increase versus net migration. As Table 3

TABLE 3. COMPONENTS OF POPULATION CHANGE IN THE CONSTITUENT PARTS OF THE DETROIT STANDARD METROPOLITAN AREA, 1940–1950

Area	Percent Change, 1940–1950, Due to:		
	Natural Increase	Net Migration	Total Change
Total Standard Metropolitan Area	15.9	10.9	26 8
A. Central city	14.1	−0.2	13.9
B. Total ring	19.8	34.3	54.1
1. Small subcenters and fringe	20.0	67.3	87.3
2. Large subcenters (10,000 or more)	19.6	5.6	25.2
a. Employing satellites	17.8	−3.8	14.0
b. Residential suburbs	23.6	25.7	49.3
Employing satellites			
Pontiac	16.4	−5.5	10.3
Dearborn	26.6	22.8	49.4
Ecorse	24.5	11.4	35.9
Hamtramck	12.9	−25.9	−13.0
Highland Park	7.5	−16.2	−8.7
Wyandotte	24.7	−4.3	20.3
Residential suburbs			
Mount Clemens	23.8	−5.5	18.3
Saint Clair Shores	26.7	63.8	90.5
Birmingham	23.6	14.5	38.1
Ferndale	24.4	7.4	31.8
Royal Oak	30.5	56.4	86.9
Grosse Pointe Park	2.3	1.1	3.4
River Rouge	20.1	0.7	20.8
Lincoln Park	30.3	62.1	92.4

Source: Original computations derived from vital statistics and census reports, 1940–1950. Satellites and suburbs are operationally defined in Leo F. Schnore, "The Functions of Metropolitan Suburbs," *American Journal of Sociology*, 61 (March 1956), pp. 453–458.

demonstrates, satellites and suburbs within a single metropolitan area may experience highly dissimilar forms of growth and decline, ranging from the rapid growth of such residential suburbs as Lincoln Park, Royal Oak, and St. Clair Shores—growth stemming from both natural increase and net in-migration—to the actual losses registered in the employing areas of Hamtramck and Highland Park, both of which are politically independent enclaves within the city of Detroit that are losing large numbers of people as land uses change and as population groups replace each other.

With respect to the areal sources of in-migration—the more variable of the two components of population change—some further effort should be devoted to distinguishing "streams" of migration (for example, city to ring, intracity, ring to city), and to considering distance as well as direction of movements; survey-based studies have elucidated different "reasons" for moves of varying distance and direction, and migrant selectivity also appears to vary according to type of stream. For example, the city-to-ring stream appears to select families in the expanding phase of the family cycle, while the countercurrent is often said to be made up of older persons whose children have moved out of their parental homes to establish their own households.[25]

Still another phase of metropolitan population redistribution that is deserving of further analysis is the changing color composition of the larger urban agglomeration and its various parts. A recent study has thrown some light upon the relative decentralization of white and nonwhites in the twelve largest metropolitan areas between 1930 and 1960. Table 4 shows the expected patterns—mounting proportions in the rings—for the total populations and for the whites in each area. In six areas, however, the 1960 proportion of nonwhites found in the ring is actually *lower* than that found there in 1930. In another five areas, there is practically no change in this proportion, and the San Francisco-Oakland SMSA provides the only real exception to the common pattern.[26] While this study makes use of the gross distinction between the central city and the ring, the use of finer areal units (for example, census tracts) permits a more detailed examination of changes in the color composition of metropolitan communities. No matter how fine the observational grain, however, descriptions of trends in the redistribution of such subgroups should be linked to changes in land use, and particularly to shifts in the spatial structure of the housing market.

In summary, more imaginative uses of the very rich materials from the Census of Population and Housing and other similar sources of mass data will certainly yield greater returns than have been heretofore realized. We know the main trends. What seems to be required is the *systematic interpretation of major population shifts as responses to other changes in the spatial structure of the metropolitan community*. Despite the fact that much basic descriptive work has been accomplished, much remains to be learned about the causes of population growth and territorial expansion of the metropolitan system. The needed work includes conceptual clarification, the development of appropriate research designs, and the resolution of some basic problems of measurement. We need more demographic "facts," and we need them assembled in more useful ways, for the data should also serve for testing hypotheses concerning changes in ecological structure and their role in bringing about major population shifts.

TABLE 4. PERCENTAGE OF POPULATION IN THE RINGS OF THE TWELVE LARGEST STANDARD METROPOLITAN STATISTICAL AREAS (1960), BY RACE: 1930-1960

Percentage of Population in Rings, by Race: 1930–1960

Standard Metropolitan Statistical Areas (1960)	Total Population				White				Nonwhite			
	1960	1950	1940	1930	1960	1950	1940	1930	1960	1950	1940	1930
Twelve largest SMSA's: all	50.0	38.5	33.0	31.2	54.9	40.9	34.2	32.1	17.0	16.7	17.8	19.3
New York	27.2	17.4	14.4	13.1	29.5	18.3	14.6	13.2	10.9	8.8	10.8	10.5
Los Angeles–Long Beach	58.1	49.1	42.8	40.7	61.1	51.0	43.7	41.3	27.3	21.0	22.3	27.1
Chicago	42.9	30.1	25.7	24.1	48.8	32.7	26.9	25.1	9.0	8.1	8.2	8.2
Philadelphia	53.9	43.6	39.6	37.8	59.9	46.9	41.4	39.0	21.6	21.7	25.0	26.4
Detroit	55.6	38.7	31.7	28.0	63.0	41.8	33.2	29.0	14.1	16.1	12.7	12.8
San Francisco–Oakland	60.2	48.2	35.9	31.9	64.1	49.6	36.2	32.0	33.0	34.8	28.8	28.4
Boston	73.1	66.8	65.1	64.0	74.9	67.8	65.7	64.4	22.4	24.2	33.3	37.5
Pittsburgh	74.9	69.4	67.7	66.9	77.6	71.4	69.1	67.9	37.9	39.5	47.7	48.4
St. Louis	63.6	50.2	44.3	40.7	69.7	53.2	46.1	42.2	27.7	28.9	28.3	26.6
Washington	61.8	45.2	31.7	30.0	77.0	53.8	35.9	30.0	16.0	16.9	18.3	21.1
Cleveland	51.2	37.6	30.7	27.6	59.5	41.6	32.7	29.1	2.8	3.0	3.8	4.8
Baltimore	45.6	32.4	24.6	22.4	54.6	36.1	26.3	23.2	14.3	17.1	16.7	18.3

Source: Harry Sharp and Leo F. Schnore, "The Changing Color Composition of Metropolitan Areas," *Land Economics*, 38 (May 1962). Table III, p. 179.

Movement Systems McKenzie referred to the increased mobility of products and people as a typically metropolitan trait, and some attention has been devoted to the recurrent circulation of various elements within the metropolitan community. Traffic studies, in particular, have yielded a wealth of information on commuting and other types of trip, and they tell us a great deal about the spatiotemporal structure of the urban complex. The relevance of these flows and exchanges has been ably identified by Donald L. Foley in a statement concerning the internal functioning of the city:

> In the contemporary large American city a mosaic of functional areas has evolved seemingly as an inevitable counterpart of the broader fact of economic specialization. Ecologists term this process segregation. So long as a city is characterized by specialization and, specifically, by segregation, we can expect that communication and movement among these divergent functional areas will be necessary if that city is to function as an integrated community . . . The development of efficient communication devices, particularly the telephone and postal service, has made it possible for much daily activity to be handled without movement of persons. Nevertheless . . . a vast amount of daily travel is necessary . . . Movement of persons in the course of carrying out day-to-day activities provides a dynamic mechanism by which the city's various functional areas are linked.[27]

But more than the city per se is involved in the circulation process. The entire metropolitan complex manifests patterned movements in space. After all, one of the key features distinguishing the modern metropolis from large cities of the past is the ease and rapidity of exchange or movement, whether of persons, commodities, or information. Moreover, smaller cities, which also enjoy the advanced transportation and communication facilities of the metropolis, share this relative ease of movement. The unique features distinguishing internal movement in the metropolitan community appear merely to reflect the enhanced complexity associated with a far-flung system of interdependent nuclei.

Compared to small cities, where the regular ebb and flow of traffic is so readily visible, it appears that physical movement in the metropolitan community is much less simple with respect to direction and over-all orientation. In contrast with the simple in-and-out movement between center and periphery of the small city, the metropolitan community appears to have a very high proportion of *lateral movements*, in complicated crosscurrents and eddies. Commuting, in particular, is not merely a matter of centripetal and centrifugal flows morning and evening, but a confusing and asymmetrical compound of variously oriented threads of traffic, overlaying the older (and perhaps rudimentary) center-oriented pattern.

This greater complexity of movement, of course, is related to the feature that we have identified as typologically essential to metropolitanism—functional interdependence reflected in an extreme territorial division of labor. This interdependence between the constituent segments of the whole metropolitan community is only achieved via specialization of land use, and areal specialization requires complex movement systems. Certainly the existence of 1960 census data on workplace, together with comparative use of more than 150 "origin–and–destination" traffic studies in American cities, should yield a more realistic cross-sectional image of this aspect of metropolitan circulation.[28] (In fact, the *recurrent intracommunity* movement of people manifested in "commuting flows" might soon be more adequately understood than the *nonrecurrent intercommunity* movement known as migration.)

The internal circulation of commodities and services, and the flows of waste, fuel, and power, remain virtually unexplored in the ecological literature, despite their presumed importance. These are truly "functional prerequisites" for the maintenance of modern metropolitan communities. Moreover, the internal flow of information has not been charted in detail. The rapid circulation of intelligence may be regarded as one of the crucial permissive factors allowing a sprawling metropolitan population to act in concert. Widely dispersed activities are only integrated, coordinated and synchronized by easy means of communication. The frequently noted separation of production phases of manufacturing from central office functions is a case in point. Physical processes requiring large amounts of land have shifted toward the periphery, while managerial and clerical functions have remained in the metropolitan center, where they enjoy the advantages of numerous "external economies." Such a separation would be unthinkable without the assurance of a rapid and continuous flow of information between the spatially discrete parts making up the metropolitan system.

But more than *internal* circulation is at issue. We possess only a limited understanding of the *external* flows and linkages that give coherence to the whole national system of cities. Granted, intercity traffic in people (via common carriers and automobile) and in certain commodities can be measured with some precision, and the exchange of messages between communities can be similarly assessed, but we have an imperfect understanding of the routes and volumes of such flows as streams of capital.

The work of Duncan and his colleagues in *Metropolis and Region* points the way to studies of intercity and interregional flows, conducted from a spatial-structural point of view. Another question that should be answered in the near future has to do with the "megalopolis" or "strip city." The new 1960 census data on workplace (coded in terms of counties and large cities) should permit an assessment of the extent to which neighboring metropolitan areas are actually linked into some larger unity via exchanges of commuters. All in all, the place of "movement systems" in the functional integration of the metropolitan community would seem sufficiently important to warrant more concerted research effort, whether conducted from the standpoint of an open or closed system.

The Exportability of the Metropolitan Concept

It might appear from the foregoing discussion that metropolitan theory and research is characterized by an ethnocentric preoccupation with the United States, and some writers have asserted that this is the case for urban sociology in general and metropolitan studies in particular.[29] This is not the place in which to debate questions concerning urban sociology's "proper" objectives, for example, whether or not truly "global" propositions should be the goal. Actually, it is rather remarkable to find that the drumfire of criticism directed against the ethnocentrism of urban sociology has reached a crescendo at the very time that advances are being made in a comparative direction. Although the criticisms would have had some real point and force in earlier years, when "comparative urban research" consisted largely of scattered case studies of individual cities in other cultures, recent work on metropolitan topics has been conducted on a scale that promises at least the possibility of discovering cross-cultural regularities. Let us consider some concrete examples.

Perhaps the most impressive undertaking of all is the literally global research being conducted by a group of scholars at International Urban Research, University of California (Berkeley). This center, under the direction of Kingsley Davis, is the successor to the office established at Columbia University in 1951 as the World Urban Resources Index. Its major product to date is a volume delineating metropolitan areas on a worldwide scale. Though it has some technical limitations, this compilation of basic data provides enormously useful information on some 720 agglomerations in every part of the

world.[30] These demographic materials have been employed in a number of recent comparative studies, and others are under way.

Some of these investigations have been worldwide in scope, examining the correlates of metropolitanization around the world as of the early fifties, and studying the recent growth of large metropolitan agglomerations in some eighty countries and territories in the various major world regions.[31] Table 5 provides a regional summary, and illustrates one of the uses of these new materials, based on metropolitan units possessing a high degree of comparability. The table shows clearly that higher rates of metropolitan growth are found in the under-developed areas, while lower rates are exhibited in the industrialized regions of the world. At the same time, metropolitan areas are capturing a

TABLE 5. METROPOLITAN GROWTH IN WORLD REGIONS, ca. 1940–ca. 1952 BY 1937 LEVEL OF PER CAPITA ENERGY CONSUMPTION

			*Indices of Metropolitan Growth**			
Regions	Per Capita Energy Consumption (Kilowatt Hours), 1937†	Degree of Metropolitanization, ca. 1940	Average Annual Percentage Growth of Metropolitan Population	Ratio of Metropolitan Growth to Total Growth	Percentage of Total Growth Claimed by Metropolitan Areas	Excess Growth of the Metropolitan Population
North America	10,074	51.6	2.1	1.40	77.2	1.50
Oceania	3,543	53.3	2.4	1.00	55.0	1.03
Europe	3,117	33.7	1.1	1.57	55.1	1.64
U.S.S.R.	1,873	17.7	1.9	3.80	84.7	4.79
South America	758	17.7	3.7	1.68	37.7	2.13
Middle America	702	16.0	4.3	1.79	32.1	2.01
Africa	686	9.0	3.9	2.44	23.2	2.58
Asia	286	10.5	3.8	2.53	24.2	2.30
All regions	1,676	21.4	2.0	1.67	39.1	1.83

* Source: International Urban Research, University of California (Berkeley).
† Source: Nathaniel B. Guyol, *Energy Resources of the World* (Washington, D.C.: U.S. Department of State, 1949), Table 43.
Source: Jack P. Gibbs, and Leo F. Schnore, "Metropolitan Growth: An International Study," *American Journal of Sociology,* 66 (September 1960), p. 164.

very high proportion of the total increase accruing to the industrialized nations. These facts are surely not surprising, but they do document the existence of patterns that had been discussed only impressionistically prior to this study. These same materials have also been employed in case studies of particular countries. Wilkinson, for example, has used them to launch an investigation of metropolitanization in Japan, and other recent inquiries have focused upon metropolitan development in Italy and the United Kingdom, where explicit contrasts with U.S. patterns can be drawn.[32]

All of the foregoing studies deal primarily with population aggregation, with special emphasis upon *levels* of metropolitanization and *rates* of metropolitan growth. As in the literature on American metropolitan communities, it must be said that there are fewer examples of frontal assaults upon problems of spatial structure. For many years, "comparative" ecological work consisted of case studies of the spatial structure of individual towns and cities in other parts of the world. The cumulative impression yielded by these scattered accounts led many students in the field to believe that cross-cultural regularities were not be found. Reviewing these works, Noel P. Gist concluded that they

> . . . present ample evidence that ecological theory based on the study of American cities is not necessarily applicable to cities in other parts of the world. The few Latin American studies, for example, clearly indicate that the prevailing ecological configurations in American cities of the United States are not characteristic of cities below the Rio Grande, although technological and other factors are tending to produce ecological patterns more nearly like those of the North.[33]

In actual fact, however, there is some evidence suggesting that large urban agglomerations throughout the world *do* manifest patterned regularities in spatial structure, at least if one confines attention to a specific feature for which data are available from many times and places. Whereas other aspects of urban life and form may very well exhibit profound variations from culture to culture, one formal feature displays a striking similarity in many cultures. More specifically, the residential redistribution of urban dwellers according to social class exhibits a fairly high degree of predictability with reference to the center of the urban complex. Given growth and expansion of the entire aggregate, and given appropriate improvements in transportation and communication technology—in short, given metropolitan development—the upper strata tend to shift from central to peripheral residence, while the lower classes increasingly take over the central area abandoned by the elite.[34]

Although this generalization is necessarily modest in scope, a reading of the available evidence suggests that other and more significant cross-cultural regularities might be found if they were made the objects of diligent search. (These regularities, of course, need not be in the form of universals.) In any event, a serious effort to extend the geographic scope of metropolitan research is well under way.

Conclusions

We have here assumed that the sheer growth of *metropolitanism* might cause us to focus on this particular mode of "urban form." With Duncan and his colleagues, we are persuaded that the continuing study of the metropolitan community is no mere intellectual exercise. In their words:

> At a time when journalists are making the "exploding metropolis" virtually a household word there is no need to plead the timeliness of an essay on metropolitanism. But though our topic is timely we are not primarily concerned to diagnose a social problem or to suggest remedies for the manifold ills of metropolitan areas. The maladies on this familiar roster—traffic congestion, housing obsolescence, frictions among shifting population groups, financial quandaries, governmental fragmentation, and the like—are most likely not fundamental problems in themselves. Rather, they symptomatically reflect an accumulation of lags in the mutual adjustment of units and functions of the metropolitan community— lags which are perhaps inevitable in a period of sporadic and unco-ordinated, though not related, changes in community structure.[35]

Whether we have been successful in persuading others of the importance of the matters discussed here must be left to the judgment of the reader. We have said that urban form has received scant attention by sociologists, except for those who employ an ecological approach and focus on spatial structure. The virtues of the body of work reviewed here seem to lie in its treatment of the metropolitan community as a functioning whole—an interaction system —and in the data it provides on some of the more gross morphological features of the metropolitan community as they are reflected in space and time. Some progress has been made in developing an understanding of the constituent areal parts of this supercommunity, and in identifying the internal linkages between them. More recent ecological research has provided an account of the place of the metropolitan community in a larger field or system external to it, and to which it is inevitably responsive. Finally, metropolitan research is becoming less confined to the United States.

Nevertheless, all of the existing problems would not be solved by simple appreciation of the facts of internal and external interdependence provided by an ecological perspective. Whether longitudinal or cross-sectional in orientation, a full-fledged theory of urban form requires much more attention to the units or building blocks with which we intend to work, and far more effort must be directed toward the development of empirically oriented taxonomies. Despite the efforts of sociologists, economists, political scientists, and geographers, we are still obliged to work with rather crude typologies—central cities, rings, classifications of the economic base, community specialization. Similarly, we make do with such oversimplified polarities as "residential suburbs" versus "employing satellites." Finally, we have not even started to develop the full implications of the concept of "megalopolis," an elusive but challenging concept which has yet to be subjected to searching critical scrutiny. Studies of morphology require attention to taxonomic questions, and these are the tasks for the future.

NOTES

1. Albert J. Reiss, Jr., "Urban Sociology, 1945–55," in Hans L. Zetterberg, ed., *Sociology in the United States of America: A Trend Report* (Paris: United Nations Educational, Scientific, and Cultural Organization, 1956), p. 108. In addition to urban sociology and urban geography, the University of Chicago also served as the birthplace of the scientific study of city politics.

2. Ernest W. Burgess, "The Growth of the City: An Introduction to a Research Project," *Publications of the American Sociological Society*, 18 (1924). pp. 85–97; Louis Wirth, "Urbanism as a Way of Life," *American Journal of Sociology*, 44 (1938), pp. 1–26 [reprinted in this volume]. Two recent treatments of Wirth's central themes may be found in William L. Kolb, "The Social Structure and Functions of Cities," *Economic Development and Cultural Change*, 3 (1954), pp. 30–46; Philip M. Hauser, "On the Impact of Urbanism on Social Organization, Human Nature and the Political Order," *Confluence*, 7 (1958), pp. 57–69 [reprinted in this volume]. The available textbooks in urban sociology all depend heavily upon Wirth's formulation. The ecology of the city is treated in James A. Quinn, *Human Ecology* (Englewood Cliffs, N.J.: Prentice-Hall, Inc., 1950), and in Amos H. Hawley, *Human Ecology: A Theory of Community Structure* (New York: The Ronald Press Company, 1950).

3. N. S. B. Gras, *An Introduction to Economic History* (New York: Harper & Row, Publishers, 1922). See also N. S. B. Gras; "The Rise of the Metropolitan Community," in E. W. Burgess ed., *The Urban Community* (Chicago: University of Chicago Press, 1926), pp. 183–191.

4. R. D. McKenzie, *The Metropolitan Community* (New York: McGraw-Hill Book Company, Inc., 1933), pp. 6 and 71.

5. Norman B. Ryder, "Fertility," in Philip M. Hauser and Otis Dudley Duncan, eds., *The Study of Population: An Inventory and Appraisal* (Chicago: University of Chicago Press, 1959), p. 413. For background on the emergence of official metropolitan units, see Henry Shryock, Jr., "The Natural History of Standard Metropolitan Areas," *American Journal of Sociology*, 63 (1957), pp. 163–170.

6. R. D. McKenzie, "The Rise of Metropolitan Communities," in Research Committee on Social Trends, *Recent Social Trends* (New York: McGraw-Hill Book Company, Inc., 1933), reprinted in Paul K. Hatt and Albert J. Reiss, Jr., eds., *Cities and Society* (New York: The Free Press of Glencoe, 1957), p. 202.

7. Warren S. Thompson, *The Growth of Metropolitan Districts in the United States, 1900–1940* (Washington, D.C.: Government Printing Office, 1947); Donald J. Bogue, *Population Growth in Standard Metropolitan Areas, 1900–1950* (Washington, D.C.: Housing and Home Finance Agency, 1953); Amos H. Hawley, *The Changing Shape of Metropolitan America: Deconcentration Since 1920* (New York: The Free Press of Glencoe, 1956). The main trends are summarized in Leo F. Schnore, "Metropolitan Growth and Decentralization," *American Journal of Sociology*, 63 (1957), pp. 171–180.

8. See Leo F. Schnore, "The Timing of Metropolitan Decentralization: A Contribution to the Debate," *Journal of the American Institute of Planners*, 25 (1959), pp. 200–206.The subtitle refers to a previously published exchange: Robert Schmitt, "Suburbanization: Statistical Fallacy?" *Land Economics*, 32 (1956), pp. 85–87, and Amos H. Hawley, "A Further Note on Suburbanization," *ibid.*, pp. 87–89.

9. *Op. cit.*, pp. 6–7.

10. Donald J. Bogue, *The Structure of the Metropolitan Community: A Study in Dominance and Subdominance* (Ann Arbor: University of Michigan Press, 1950). The large size of the units under study suggests that they might better be regarded as extensive "metropolitan regions" rather than "metropolitan communities," for the latter term has come to be used to designate the localized area whose population is integrated with reference to daily activities; as such, it is roughly coterminous with the commuting area or the local labor market. Bogue's units are mapped in F. Stuart Chapin, Jr., *Urban Land Use Planning* (New York: Harper & Row, Publishers, 1957), p. 98.

11. For example, see Theodore R. Anderson and Jane Collier, "Metropolitan Dominance and the Rural Hinterland," *Rural Sociology*, 21 (1956), pp. 152–157. This is a study of the hinterlands of four metropolitan centers in Missouri.

12. Leslie Kish, "Differentiation in Metropolitan Areas," *American Sociological Review*, 19 (1954), pp. 388–398.

13. Walter Isard and Vincent H. Whitney, "Metropolitan Site Selection," *Social Forces*, 27 (1949), pp. 263–269.

14. *Ibid.*, p. 264.

15. Donnell M. Pappenfort, "The Ecological Field and the Metropolitan Community: Manufacturing and Management," *American Journal of Sociology* 64 (1959), p. 380.

16. *Ibid.*, p. 385.

17. Otis Dudley Duncan *et al.*, *Metropolis and Region* (Baltimore: The Johns Hopkins Press, 1960), p. 4.

18. *Ibid.*, p. 8.

19. Donald J. Bogue, *Components of Population Change 1940–1950: Estimates of Net Migration and Natural Increase for Each Standard Metropolitan Area and State Economic Area* (Oxford, Ohio, and Chicago: Scripps Foundation for Research in Population Problems, Miami University, and Population Research and Training Center, University of Chicago, 1957); Leo F. Schnore, "Municipal Annexations and the Growth of Metropolitan Suburbs, 1950–1960," *American Journal of Sociology*, 67 (1962), pp. 406–417.

20. Jean Gottmann, *Megalopolis: The Urbanized Northeastern Seaboard of the United States* (New York: The Twentieth Century Fund, Inc., 1961).

21. Albert J. Reiss, Jr., "Research Problems in Metropolitan Population Redistribution," *American Sociological Review*, 21 (1956), p. 572.

22. Otis Dudley Duncan, "Human Ecology and Population Studies," in Hauser and Duncan, eds., *The Study of Population*. p. 697. Italics added.

23. Beverly Duncan and Philip M. Hauser, *Housing a Metropolis—Chicago* (New York: The Free Press of Glencoe, 1960); and Beverly Duncan, Georges Sabagh, and Maurice D. Van Arsdol, Jr., "Patterns of City Growth," *American Journal of Sociology*, 67 (1962), pp. 418–429.

24. An enlightening informal discussion of the evolution of housing areas is contained in a work by Hoover and Vernon, who observe that "each successive residential development can be thought of as responding to the conditions of its period and depositing a record of the past." Edgar M. Hoover and Raymond Vernon, *Anatomy of a Metropolis* (Cambridge: Harvard University Press, 1959). p 208.

25. Philip M. Hauser, *Population Perspective* (New Brunswick, N.J.: Rutgers University Press, 1960), pp. 115–117.

26. Harry Sharp and Leo F. Schnore, "The Changing Color Composition of Metropolitan Areas," *Land Economics*, 38 (1962), Table III, p. 179.

27. Donald L. Foley, "Urban Daytime Population: A Field for Demographic-Ecological Analysis," *Social Forces*, 32 (1954), pp. 323–324.

28. See Leo F. Schnore, "Three Sources of Data on Commuting: Problems and Possibilities," *Journal of the American Statistical Association*, 55 (1960), pp. 8–22.

29. The most vigorous expression of this view is to be found in Gideon Sjoberg, "Comparative Urban Sociology," in Robert K. Merton, Leonard Broom, and Leonard S. Cottrell, Jr., eds., *Sociology Today: Problems and Prospects* (New York: Basic Books, Inc., 1959). An explicit criticism of the ethnocentrism of "metropolitan" research and theory is contained in Thomas O. Wilkinson, "Urban Structure and Industrialization," *American Sociological Review*, 25 (1960), pp. 356–363.

30. Suzanne R. Angelucci *et al.*, *The World's Metropolitan Areas* (Berkeley: University of California Press, 1959). See also, Jack P. Gibbs and Kingsley Davis, "Conventional versus Metropolitan Data in the International Study of Urbanization," *American Sociological Review*, 23 (1958), pp. 504–514. Because "Standard Metropolitan Areas" in the U.S. were accepted at face value, 147 of the 720 metropolitan areas were delineated by the use of criteria other than those described in the publication, and there is no evidence that the IUR criteria were tested for metropolitan areas in this country. Boundary changes for cities around the world are not reported, so that the population data (shown for two dates) must be used with caution in attempting to assess the significance of any changes in city versus ring population, but total metropolitan growth can be studied.

31. Leo F. Schnore, "The Statistical Measurement of Urbanization and Economic Development," *Land Economics*, 37 (1961), pp. 229–245; Jack P. Gibbs and Leo F. Schnore, "Metropolitan Growth: An International Study," *American Journal of Sociology*, 66 (1960), pp. 160–170; Jack P. Gibbs, "The Growth of Individual Metropolitan Areas: A Global View," *Annals of the Association of American Geographers*, 51 (1961), pp. 380–391.

32. See Thomas O. Wilkinson, *op. cit.*, and his "Agricultural Activities in the City of Tokyo," *Rural Sociology*, 26 (1961), pp. 49–56. See also Leo F. Schnore, "Le aree metropolitane in Italia," *Mercurio*, 3 (1960), pp. 19–24; and, *idem*, "Metropolitan Development in the United Kingdom," *Economic Geography* 38 (1962), pp. 215–233.

33. Noel P. Gist, "The Urban Community," in Joseph B. Gittler ed., *Review of Sociology: Analysis of a Decade* (New York: John Wiley & Sons, 1957), p. 170.

34. See Gideon Sjoberg, *The Preindustrial City: Past and Present* (New York: The Free Press of Glencoe, 1960), pp. 97–99. A detailed review of the available evidence for the United States and Latin America may be found in Leo F. Schnore, "On the Spatial Structure of Cities in the Two Americas: Some Problems in Comparative Urban Research," mimeographed paper prepared for the Committee on Urbanization, Social Science Research Council, n.d.

35. Duncan *et al.*, *op. cit.*, p. 1.

27. The Historic and the Structural Theories of Urban Form: Their Implications for Urban Renewal

William Alonso

Almost all discussions of spatial structure emphasize that the different social areas of the urban community are distributed within concentric zones of settlement. The poor tend to live in the center of the metropolis, adjacent to factories and commercial establishments, while the more affluent families are located at the region's outer edge. William Alonso examines two complementary theories for explaining this phenomenon. One is the traditional ecological theory associated with the Chicago school of sociology, which argues that the pattern is the result of the historical conditions under which American cities have grown. The other theory is structural. It asserts that a combination of tastes, costs, and income conditions operating on the urban population in the present is responsible for the distribution of peoples, cultures, and land uses. Alonso discusses the fact that current governmental policy for renewing the central areas of large cities is based on the ecological-historical theory. If this theory is inadequate, as Alonso suggests it may be, serious doubts may be raised about the probable effectiveness of urban renewal programs.

William Alonso is Professor of Regional Planning at the University of California, Berkeley. He is the author of *Location and Land Use* (1964) and coeditor of *Regional Development and Planning* (1964).

An explanatory theory of urban form has been developing in recent years that provides an alternative to the classic theory developed by R. Haig (1926)[1] and by Park and Burgess (1925).[2] The new theory has emerged so gradually and it differs from the older theory in apparently so slight a degree that it has gone unrecognized as being in conflict with the older theory. Yet the difference is a most important one not only from a scientific point of view but also for the vast urban renewal program that is so vigorously being pursued by our cities. This program is implicitly based on the older theory, and depends on its validity for its success. Should the new theory prove more nearly correct, there is grave danger that much of the current renewal effort will fail.

Both theories are interested in a broad range of urban phenomena but it will be useful to focus on a paradox that has intrigued students of American cities since the turn of the century. This is that land values tend to drop with distance from the center of the city, while family income tends to rise with distance. The paradox is, then, that the well-to-do live on cheap land while the poor live on expensive land.

The older theory explains this phenomenon in terms of the passage of time, and may be called an *historical theory*. In brief, it holds that as a city grows the houses near the center of the city become old and therefore unsatisfactory to high-income families. The rich then build new houses where open land is available which, of course, is on the periphery of the city. Those of lower income then move into the vacated houses.

From *Land Economics*, XL, 2 (May 1964), pp. 227–231. Reprinted by permission.

415

The moving parts of this theory are the aging of structures, sequential occupance by income levels, and population growth, for the number of low-income families must increase to provide a demand for the houses vacated by the well-to-do. The urban area grows much like a tree in cross-section, by means of a growth ring which leaves behind old, rigid tissue. Land values do not play an essential part in the argument and seem to receive slight mention in recent statements of the theory although earlier writers placed emphasis on speculation to explain high central land values. Homer Hoyt, whose sector theory is an important variant of this type of theory, explains: "The wealthy seldom reverse their steps and move backwards into the obsolete houses which they are giving up . . . As they represent the highest income group, there are no new houses above them abandoned by another group. Hence the natural trend of the high rent [high rent for dwellings: it should not be confused with high land values] area is outward, toward the periphery of the city."[3]

In spatial terms the clearest statement of the historical theory remains the "concentric zones hypothesis" of Burgess. The Burgess theory is the spatial equivalent of the filtering process or trickle-down theory of the housing market according to which new houses are built only for the well-to-do but in time pass on to those of lower income. Thus, society provides housing for the poor not by building directly for them but by letting the wealthier absorb most of the depreciation costs before the house is handed on.

By the historic theory, then, the location of the rich depends on the availability of land. Residential urban renewal, whatever its original statement of intentions, has taken on a typical form. It clears decayed housing in the center of urban areas and replaces it with more expensive housing, confident that the newness of the buildings will attract those of high income. The previous low-income residents are thus displaced and move elsewhere, typically away from the center. In effect, it makes land available in the center for high-income housing, while still endorsing the trickle-down view of the housing market. If correct, this means that Americans will no longer follow each other like lemmings from the center to the surburbs and then to the exurbs as population grows and buildings age. Rather, this centrifugal expansion will now be turned inward and the growth ring will be near the center. The suburbs, as time goes by and buildings age, will become available to those of lower income. But of course the new central housing built by urban renewal will in time age also and the wealthy will once again be on the move. If they are not to go to the suburbs again urban renewal will have to provide them with buildable land near the center. Logically this should be the land ringing the areas now being renewed, which will by then be occupied by the oldest structures. Following this reasoning, urban renewal in the long run will be a ring expanding outward *through* the urban mass, leaving behind a gradient of housing that ages toward the center and pushing against the oldest housing of the urban area until the center is once again the oldest and the process starts again. Thus, the simple movement outward of high income to the suburbs will be replaced by a convection flow like that of boiling water in a pot.

This is a very simplified view of the distant future of urban renewal. It is clear that the moving ring of renewal cannot always be of the type used today. Institutional devices may be modified to permit renewal by the free market and less direct governmental intervention. Depending on a host of factors, such as the quantity and condition of the housing stock and the structure of the demand forces, rehabilitation may become more important. For the process to work there must be a balance of the rates of population growth, new construction, aging of buildings, and the structure of demand, according to income, age, and type of families. If there is, for instance, a very rapid increase of low-income demand, the filtering process may not deliver enough dwellings to the lower sector of the market and overcrowding, invasion, and accelerated social obsolescence will result. In the extreme case, as in the developing countries, there would result a complicated alternation of high- and low-income rings. If, on the other hand, population growth slows down or the structure of income rises rapidly at the bottom, there would be a softening of the demand for old, central accommodations so that the centrifugal growth may leave a hole in the center, manifested in high vacancies, lower densities, reconversions, and the other phenomena of "gray areas." This appears to be the case in metropolitan areas and of course is the ideal situation for urban renewal according to the historical theory.

But the practice of urban renewal is based on the assumption that if high-cost housing is offered in the center, it will attract high-income people. Recent investigators have suggested that the peripheral position of the rich may be the result of the structure of market forces rather than the consequence of historical development. That is to say, that the rich may be in the suburbs because they prefer to be there rather than because they have nowhere else to go. In the words of Vernon and Hoover, "higher-income people use their superior purchasing power to buy lower density housing, but at the cost of a longer journey-to-work."[4] Note that in this explanation it is lower density rather than newness that makes the suburbs attractive to the wealthy.

The reason for the preference for ample space over shorter journey-to-work becomes clear by the simultaneous consideration of the value of land, the cost of commuting, and travel and space preferences. Most Americans prefer to have ample land, as shown by the popularity of the single-family home and as anyone can learn merely by talking to people. As with all desirable things that can be bought, the wealthy tend to buy more land than the poor, all other things being equal. Coupling this greater purchasing power with lower land prices away from the center, it is clear that the savings in land costs are far greater for the rich than for the poor. For instance, if one would buy 10,000 square feet and the other 2,500, a drop in price of 50 cents per square foot would mean a savings of $5,000 for one and only $1,250 for the other.[5] Consider now that such a move would cost $500 per year in added commuting costs: this would represent 20 cents per square foot for the poor man but only 5 cents per square foot for the wealthy one.[6]

If typical American tastes are a liking for ample land and a relative willingness to commute, it is clear that more distant but cheaper per-square-foot sites are more attractive to the wealthy than to the poor. Accessibility, which diminishes with increasing distance, behaves as an "inferior good;" that is to say that, although accessibility is desirable, people as they become wealthier will buy less of it because they prefer to substitute for it something else (land). Such inferior goods are not rare: for instance, the per capita consumption of wheat and its products has declined steadily in this country as people in their affluence prefer to substitute meat and other foods for bread.

This explanation of the more-land-but-less-accessibility phenomenon may be called *structural* to distinguish it from the Burgess-Hoyt historical explanation in that it represents the working out of tastes, costs, and income in the structure of the market. It does not rely on the historical process although this process is undeniable and has been a strong influence reinforcing the structural forces. To put it another way, the structural theory says that a city which developed so quickly that the structures had no time to age would still show the same basic urban form: low income near the center and high income further out. The structural theory is not an alternative to the historical theory; rather, they are complementary. Thus far, both have acted in the same direction. But now urban renewal, relying entirely on the logic of the historical theory, has set them at odds for, while it provides central land, it cannot afford sufficiently low prices to permit low densities[7] so that the structural forces will continue to pull high-income people (and therefore new construction) to the suburbs.

Under these conflicting circumstances the net result of urban renewal will be unclear, particularly because the structural forces depend on tastes and these are very difficult to evaluate. For instance, the fragmentary evidence I have seen of societies where apparently no great value is placed on ample land for the home (*i.e.*, societies in which the rich do not occupy very much more land than the poor) suggests that there the rich tend to live near the center. This is in agreement with the structural theory because, as there is no attraction in the substitution of space for accessibility, greater purchasing power is used to buy accessibility. Indeed, there is in the United States a substantial minority of the well-to-do that does prefer accessibility to space and this minority lives in luxury apartments or town houses in the central areas. Much of the demand for the new construction of urban renewal is undoubtedly attributable to previous neglect of this sector. It is also instructive to follow the location of middle-class families through their life cycle: the young couple lives in a central apartment, moves to the suburbs as the family grows, and returns to the center after the children leave home, thus reflecting their changing space-preferences with changing family size.

Taste or preference for space are possibly words too weak to denote what is really meant by this key variable of the structural theory. Rather, the nature of the demand for space in this country seems to be a deeply ingrained cultural value, associated not only with such functional needs as play space for children, but also with basic attitudes toward nature, privacy, and the meaning of the family. A preference so deeply rooted in a culture is not likely to change suddenly. But in the last three years there has been a startling increase in the proportion of new dwellings in multiple structures and it has been suggested that this reflects such a change of taste. Whereas from 1954 to 1956, 89 per cent of new dwellings were single-family homes and only some 11 per cent of new dwellings were in multiple structures, the current rate is well over 30 per cent. Have the well-to-do, who are the consumers of most new housing, begun to prefer accessibility to space? In a sense this may be the case: as metropolitan areas have grown bigger and roads more congested it may be that some have come to feel that the commuting trip is too long and have returned to central locations. However, the prospective vast road building and mass transit improvement programs may again reduce time-distances (much as the popularization of the automobile did in the 1920's) and re-restablish the almost complete preponderance of the single-family house.

But there is another explanation, more powerful than that of distance, for the increase in apartment construction. We have mentioned the convection-flow life cycle of the American middle-class family. The young and the old need apartments while it is those in their thirties that power the demand for single-family homes. Those reaching the age of thirty these days are those who were born in the Great Depression when the birth rate fell dramatically. Thus, in the 1960 to 1970 decade there is less demand for single-family homes because there are 9 per cent fewer people coming into their thirties than in the 1950 to 1960 decade. But this situation will change sharply in 1970: there will be an increase of almost 40 per cent among those reaching their thirties in the 1970–1980 decade over the 1960–1970 decade. Thus, we may attribute much of the shift from single to multiple dwellings to temporary changes in the age composition of the population rather than to fundamental changes in taste and we may expect that these changes will be short-lived.

Urban renewal is a magnificent opportunity to reshape our cities. Today there is money, public support, legal power, and human energy of a scale that could not have been imagined a few years ago. The urgency of urban problems and the many years of frustration of those concerned with them have naturally led to a rush of activity now that the means are available. In spite of the conviction of the planning profession as a whole that comprehensive planning is necessary, too often urban renewal has consisted of one project and then another, with no overall plan. It is precisely this lack of a comprehensive urban (*i.e.*, metropolitan) plan that has obscured the implicit theoretical structure of renewal, for a comprehensive plan is the marriage of the goals of a community with an understanding of the structure of the community. The implicit exclusive reliance on the historical theory (which is incomplete without the structural theory) raises the danger of large-scale failure through a lack of understanding of the workings of the urban system and a misinterpretation of the structure of demand. It is a false empiricism to scoff at theory as too abstract. Empiricism requires an evaluation of results and it will be many years before the long-range effects of current experiments in urban renewal become clear. At a time when we are so vigorously rebuilding our cities it is important that we be as intelligent as possible about it. We must make explicit the theories of urban structure under which we are proceeding. If the historical theory by itself is correct, current renewal procedures stand a good chance of success. But if it needs the complement of the structural theory, current renewal projects are skimming a narrow and specialized sector of demand which will soon dry up. In many cities stand acres of cleared land awaiting development and investors face time lags of years from the inception to the completion of development. The reaction-time of the urban renewal process is too slow to permit a purely pragmatic approach. Vacant land and vacant buildings are frightening possibilities.

NOTES

1. Robert M. Haig, "Toward an Understanding of the Metropolis," *Quarterly Journal of Economics*, May 1926.

2. Ernest W. Burgess, "The Growth of the City" in *The City*, editors, R. E. Park and E. Burgess (Chicago, Illinois: University of Chicago Press, 1925).

3. Homer Hoyt, *The Structure and Growth of Residential Neighborhoods in American Cities* (Washington, D.C.: Federal Housing Administration, 1937), p. 116.

4. Edgar M. Hoover and Raymond Vernon, *The Anatomy of a Metropolis* (Cambridge, Massachusetts: Harvard University Press, 1959), p. 169.

5 Of course, greater quantities will be bought at the more distant location because of price elasticity, but the essence of the argument is unchanged and it is simpler to view the quantity of land bought by each individual as unchanging with location.

6. The analysis of the effect of income on location is developed more fully in my *Location and Land Use* (Cambridge, Massachusetts: Harvard University Press, 1964).

7. Even in cases in which extraordinary subsidies (in excess of 90 percent) afford the redeveloper central land at a price comparable to that of suburban land in order to permit low densities, the resulting pattern has been more urban (ten or more families per gross acre) than suburban (four or less familes per gross acre). The subsidy per family of providing 100-by-100-foot lots at suburban land prices in a renewal area would be in the order of twenty to forty thousand dollars.

28. The Functions of Transportation | Scott Greer

Transportation is the process that leads to the exchange of people, goods, and services. Greer discusses how it integrates activities distributed at different points in the metropolitan region. Not only does transportation link preestablished sites but the development of new means of transportation is an important determinant in the location of urban settlements and land uses. A dramatic example of this impact is the proliferation of urban growth around freeway interchanges and air terminals, the contemporary equivalent of the burgeoning settlements near railway stops in the last century. Much of Greer's analysis relies on the concept of the space-time ratio, the amount of time it takes to traverse a given spatial distance. He emphasizes that this ratio is constantly shrinking because of advances in transportation technology. As a result, an urban network can extend over an ever wider area with no loss of efficiency and coordination. Meanwhile, the resident of a metropolis gains increasing locational freedom in deciding where to live and work.

Scott Greer is Professor of Sociology and Political Science and Director of the Center for Metropolitan Studies at Northwestern University. Several of his published works are cited on page 277 of this volume.

One way in which sociologists approach the meaning of a social pattern such as transportation is to ask: What is its *function*? By this they mean, What are its consequences for other aspects of human life? What is the task of a transportation system, within the complicated mass of human activities, which leads men to perpetuate it through time? How does the transportation segment of the economy stay in business? In answering these questions, we shall *define* transportation in terms of its consequences for other human activity.[1]

Transportation is the circulation of men, energy, and goods, controlled by social actors for social ends. Such circulation is as old as human life, for no society can interrelate the activities of its members save through movement, given the physiological nature of man. Human activities are always spatially separated and conjoined. But if we look for the reasons behind the large-scale, specialized, mechanical transport systems, our attention is drawn to what has been termed the geographical division of labor.

Human activities on different sites tend to vary, one from another, and yet these various activities are frequently complementary—mutually useful or necessary. At the simplest level we find product differentiation due to differences in environment. One tribe lives on the sea coast and has access to salt and fish, while another lives in the interior and has access to fruit, honey, and game. At the most complex level we have product differentiation due to a rational division of labor. The research chemist's product is basic to that of the farmer in the Iowa fields.

The latter type of differentiation interests us particularly; it is due to the economic advantages of rationally dividing labor and allocating it to different groups of people.

It is a process which can greatly increase efficiency and productivity. Such differentiation of activity can come about, however, only when there are methods for integrating the activity of the different groups. The product of the soil chemist, a recipe, must get to the factory: the factory's product must get to Iowa. The products of all the subcontractors must be assembled so that a finished automobile results, then the automobile must be exchanged for all the economic necessities of life for the constituent groups.

We have spoken as if the chief kinds of differentiation were in material products, for this is easier to conceive. However, it is equally important to note that these products are the results of *human activities* differentiated over space. Sometimes there are no tangible products, only processes of social action (as in a football game, where activity over space is highly integrated— and disintegrated—through time). Social actions are the basic subject matter of sociology, and the ways in which they are integrated are of supreme interest to the sociologist.

The means of integration are *communication*, or the flow of messages which allows men to order behavior over time and space, and *transportation*, or the circulation of men, energy, and goods, which permits cooperation over space. The transportation system allows a continual flow of energy (from food to nuclear fuels) into the human collective, its machines and toys, and back into the nonhuman environment from which further energy is procured. It allows people widely separated in space to depend upon one another, as the resident of the central city depends upon those who run dairy farms in the hinterland, and creameries in the suburbs, for his morning milk. But when they do so, they become mutually dependent upon the larger system, the flow of goods and human energy which provides cash for the farmer, food for the urbanite: they are interdependent.

Thus the function of transportation is the integration of human activity over space through the exchange of products and activities, the collection and distribution of men, energy, and goods.

Two Transportation Revolutions

Since transportation is a principal mechanism for integrating the results of the geographical division of labor, the transport system is one of the limits upon such development. If transportation is costly and painful, complementary products will be exchanged only when they are *very* valuable. We have authenticated cases of trade-routes in the Neolithic era, when flint mines of northern Europe exported tools to the Mediterranean littoral. Though transportation was by human back and foot, it was worth doing, for flint was the basic industrial material of the Stone Age. For the most part, however, societies that move on foot do not trade widely or extensively.

If trade is difficult or impossible, this has further consequences. Since there is no need for a surplus, over and above the needs of the local community for a given product, each village produces for itself and limits its production to local needs. Societies made up of such local producers and consumers are called subsistence economies. For most of the million years or so of man's residence on earth he has lived in such societies. When, however, more effective transportation media are

devised, the small and isolated village communities begin to be connected by the trader. He collects their surpluses, deposits them in warehouses and moves them to a market where they can be exchanged for complementary products which may find their way back to the original villages as payment. Such a trader is binding together the activities and products of men scattered over space.

As this occurs, other uses are made of improved transport. It is now possible for men in one place to rob those far away, hauling the products of their labor home for consumption. Very similar to such plundering is the levying of taxes by the stronger centers upon the total population It was out of plunder, taxation, and trade that cities were born. First in the Middle East, then around the Mediterranean basin and along the coasts of Asia, cities developed as men made use of water transportation and drayage.

The improved transportation of the classical ages made possible a widespread network of interdependence, an extension of society wider than mankind had ever known before. This extension of social structure we call "increase in scale";[2] based upon geographical division of labor and integration through trade and empire, it makes possible large urban concentrations of population which, unable to support themselves directly, must depend upon supplies from the hinterland. The widespread network of interdependence, with cities at the intersections of the bonds, produces "civilization"—a world of wide horizons, wealth, and a differentiation of human behavior such as the village world never knew. Priests, soldiers, traders, artisans, civil servants, politicians, walk the streets of the city.

Still, the cities of the classical empires, though they seem contemporary in many respects, were severely limited in their size because their society was limited in the scale it could attain. Lacking the technology which has made nonhuman energy sources available to later civilizations, the empires were heavily dependent upon human and animal labor. Their basic sources of energy were, then, food and feed produced by the peasant villages—and these were very limited sources of supply. At the same time, the transportation system was slow, inefficient, and rigid. The best method of transport was by water, but primitive equipment and lack of navigational tools and knowledge limited ships in size and in route (for the most part they hugged the coast, navigating by landmarks). Land transport was even more inefficient: the horse-collar was not invented before the medieval era, and the poor animals drew burdens by means of nooses around their necks, which severely limited their load.

Not until the age of steam was a society of radically different scale than the Roman Empire possible. With steam power, in railroad and ship, it became possible to transport great masses of material over great distances in a relatively short period of time. Equally important, as Gilmore points out, the steamboat or railroad can move well in either direction, upstream, against the tide, or uphill against the force of gravity. This makes possible *equal interchange* between cities (located on the coast to take advantage of water transport) and the inland valleys and plateaus. It makes possible a continental economy, with an astonishingly complex division of labor.[3]

The application of steam to transport coincided with its application to work in general. For the first time societies had access to a vast source of energy which was not derived, directly or indirectly, from the agricultural products of the villages.

However, steam power was most economical when large plants were built around the energy converters. This caused the rapid development of the factory in the nineteenth century as a basis for the urban economy, and a change from the city as governmental and market center, to the city as workshop for the entire society or, as in the case of England, the entire world. Cities increased in size and a larger proportion of the population became urban dwellers, while the countryside became more dependent upon the city. The goods returned to the countryside in exchange for farm products became staples of the rural way of life; eventually the farmer was as specialized as the urban dweller, and quite unable to subsist on the product of his land and his hands.

Steam power depends upon inflexible structures, however; the weight of the engine forced the development of iron rails, and these limited the train to a single transportation line. One comes to the railroad—the railroad cannot oblige by reciprocating.[4] In the same way, power generated by steam cannot be transported easily for any distance: it must be used under one roof. Thus the use of steam transport and power produced the highly concentrated urban settlements which Lewis Mumford has called the "cities of the eotechnic age"—the primitive age of urban civilization.[5]

These are the cities which form the core of most contemporary metropolitan areas. However, the conditions that produced them no longer hold. The transportation of men and energy is now possible through media which are infinitely more flexible than the steam engine and its applications. The internal combustion engine has made possible transport of passengers and goods wherever roads are passable. The developments in the use of electrical energy make possible an electrical power grid which can spread over hundreds of miles, supplying energy at equal cost to any point on the grid. The consequences have been profound; many of them are recognizable as aspects of the metropolitan transportation problem.

These technological innovations have made possible a society which is not only of very large scale, with an infinitely complex division of labor and a vast integrative network, but one which is infinitely *fluid*. Commitment to given spatial locations, a consequence of poverty in transport, is less and less important as a limit upon human action. Because of this fluidity, the work force moves ever further from its place of work (commuting by automobile or helicopter); factories leave the center of the city (where the railroads cross and coal could be hauled cheaply) for the distant suburbs. Factories move also across the nation, from Jersey City to Phoenix. The human population, more mobile with each increase in scale, changes residence frequently within and between cities.[6]

Improvements in transport are important, then, because they are improvements in the mechanism of integration. This may be summarized in one statement: the space-time ratio is steadily decreasing. The cost in time for traveling a given distance is dwindling, and, as some have said, space is translated into time in the metropolitan society. This shift in the space-time ratio is apparent in the transportation of people, goods, and energy (such as electricity); it is also occurring in the transmission of messages. The implications of these changes are that space, for all practical purposes, is never unalterably fixed. It is a barrier to the extension of human activities, but as the mechanism of extension improves, space shrinks. Thus the Chicago

of the horse-drawn street railway was miniature compared with the metropolis of today, but when we remember the limited speed of movement, it seems likely that it looked just as vast then to its human population, and, for human purposes, it *was* just as vast.

The consequence of the shrinking space-time ratio is that more space can be used for activities which remain just as closely coordinated as before. A greater horizontal area can be included in one network of control, at the same cost in time and human energy.

Another way of putting it is that men have much greater locational freedom; they are no longer forced to place houses within walking distance of the factory, and the factory on a spur line of the railroad. As this occurs, those explanations of human behavior which assume that the costs and constraints of circulation are determining must take account of such change or become misleading. One form of such explanation might be called "map determination"; the spatially near at hand is assumed to be more important than the distant—whether this is a market, a job, a friend, or neighbor. It assumes that people will follow the principle of least effort, and neighbor more with those next door—trade at the nearest grocery store— and even marry the nearest marriageable female.

This approach rests upon the notion that interaction is necessary for integration, and that interaction is easier with those near at hand. However, these notions, while useful, make sense only when *we turn geographical space into social space*. As we do this, the effects of geographical nearness or distance are translated through the space-time ratio. Thus, a map of a nation in terms of social space would be laid out, not in miles of the earth's surface, but in units which express the ease and speed of movement from one part to another. Monument Valley, in the wild desert country of northeastern Arizona, is much further from Phoenix in time, in cost, and in sheer human effort, than is San Francisco.

The social size of America has been progressively shrinking, not steadily, but in fits and starts, with the introduction of the steamboat, the railroad, the electric train and streetcar, the automobile, the airplane, and now the jet airplane. Some of these innovations affect the space-time ratio between different parts of the country very differently—the railroads relate east and west much more closely than north and south, for example. Others tend to equalize the space-time ratio between all parts of the country (as the automobile has done and, lately, the airplane and helicopter).

Such changes have had profound effects upon the regional variations and the community structure of the society. The declining space-time ratio, together with the increase in scale and integration of the continental economy has increased the dependence of all segments upon the larger system. It has also increased the flow of cultural messages from one end of the nation to the other, thus decreasing regional and local isolation. One result has been an increasingly urban-derived and urban-centered mode of life for Americans at large. Another has been a change in the functions of the small, local community.

Observation indicates that people usually have used the same transportation means and have been willing to travel about the same distance to participate in their folk institutions as to purchase staple commodities . . . (but) . . . that distance is greater than in pre-automobile days. As a result,

in areas relatively well supplied with cars, there has been a notable transfer of functions from smaller to larger centers. In many areas the cross-roads store and the country church have vanished and the functions performed by these have been transferred to a village. In other cases, part or all of the functions of the village have been transferred to the farm market center. . . . Thus, there has been a considerable transfer of functions from open country to villages and from villages to market towns.[7]

This has combined with a continued increase in the proportion of the population living in metropolitan areas and a decline in the farming population. As farming becomes a business supplying a national market, the economies of scale lead to larger farms, and mechanization reduces the need for farm population. Each decade finds a greater proportion of the population living on a smaller proportion of the territory of the United States.[8] At the same time that the society becomes metropolitan, however, the very nature of the metropolitan community is changing; this is also a result of changes in the space-time ratio.

The Space-time Ratio and the Shape of the City

The great cities of America are largely the products of the age of steam; the expanding scale and shrinking space-time ratio resulting from steam power made them possible and necessary. However, they were also shaped and constrained by the inflexibility of the steam engine, for railroads were basically impractical for short-haul transportation of passengers. Thus the railroad changed the space-time ratio between cities but not within them; great numbers of people concentrated in urban areas, but, within them, moved about by foot or horse and carriage. Some results are evident in this description of the older portion of St. Louis:

> The central city of the area thus is far more densely settled than are the centers of most newer metropolitan areas. Growing up in the age of coal and steam, the older portions of St. Louis City reflect the high premium placed on land near transportation facilities —the river and the railroads. Location of industry in such sections of the city brought the construction nearby of extensive, crowded residential districts to house the labor force. On the outer edges of settlement, newer properties were developed for the higher income groups, which had the time and facilities to travel longer distances to work and shop.[9]

The need to minimize the space-time ratio for circulation within the central city, when foot and carriage were the principal media, led to the construction of multi-storied factories and warehouses, row-houses without yards, and many-storied tenements and apartment houses. Railroad commutation, practical when stops are few and far between, made possible the commuter suburbs of the upper classes.

The appearance of the electric streetcar permitted greater dispersion of the city, along the routes which the streetcar followed, for the streetcar could transport passengers cheaply and make stops at each block. As Cottrell puts it, residential development produced a distribution "like a number of strings of beads radiating from a central point, the rails serving as the thread and the communities centered around the suburban railway station being the beads."[10]

In the earlier city of foot traffic and the horse carriage, a great many facilities had been decentralized, so that they might be within easy walking distance of their clients. (In this respect they served the purposes of the villages which Gilmore discusses.) With the development of streetcar transport, however, movement to the central business distrct became easy and the downtown section flourished.[11] The electric transportation system, radiating from the center of the city, focused activity in the downtown district. At first the automobile accentuated the trend, for it allowed even easier access to the central business district; soon, however, it became apparent that the automobile's effect was, at best, a mixed blessing for the downtown businesses.

> . . . the energy costs of the congestion that arises from using automobiles and trucks in the cities built around streams, railroads, and trolley cars mount much more rapidly than any energy gains that might come from so using automotive units there. . . . It is now much cheaper to bring power and materials to residence areas, or to empty spaces in which such residence areas and their associated services can be built up, than to redesign and rebuild the central city in order to make it an efficient means to use modern (energy) converters. The story of the movement from the central city is well documented.[12]

In short, the densely built-up neighborhoods on narrow streets, which served the city in the Age of Steam, cannot become wheel borne by automobile and truck without producing extreme congestion. Such congestion quickly detracts from the value of the automobile as a means of transport. It also, and what is perhaps more important, detracts from the central city as a place of residence or plant location.

Most location within the central city took place when there was no choice. Factories were built where transportation was cheapest. Houses were crowded near them, taking advantage of proximity in a world that moved on foot. The broadcast distribution of the automobile throughout the urban population placed, within easy driving distance, not only the areas between the spokes of the public transportation system, but areas far beyond the end of the streetcar lines. Access to distant areas allowed the urban population to purchase private space around their houses, which were chiefly horizontal single-family houses instead of multiple-unit apartments. We do not know if the inhabitants of the city in the Age of Steam would have all chosen to live in such houses had they been practical (though the residences of the wealthy would indicate that to be likely); certainly, when the choice became available, American urban populations voted overwhelmingly for the larger lots and the single-story, single family dwelling of the suburbs.

The development of extensive, diffused, residential neighborhoods to house the new growth of the city also encouraged the building of factories in the outlying areas. Taking advantage of the same changes in the space-time ratio which allowed the population to move its residence, suburban areas developed industrial parks which compete successfully with the central city for new industry. And, as the city expands, circumferential highways around the city become as important as those which lead inward to the city center. Where arteries inward cross the circumferential, we see the development of giant supermarket shopping centers, competing effectively with the central city, for they are at the crossroads of the new transportation media based upon the internal combustion engine.[13]

Thus the center of the city, the eotechnic city, is losing much of the population which once inhabited it; the skilled worker and white-collar worker, the prosperous and the wealthy, move outward. The core of the city retains, chiefly, the poor who can afford no better. Of these, new migrants into the city are an important proportion, and ethnic groups, Negroes and Puerto Ricans in Manhattan, Mexicans and Negroes in the old center of Los Angeles, are very important. Around the center of the city, however, the great neighborhoods built up during the age of the streetcar retain much of the working-class population in the metropolitan area. This must be kept in mind when such extreme statements are made, as "The central city is rapidly becoming an ethnic ghetto." For the population of the central city as a whole probably differs less radically from that in the suburbs than it did 40 years ago, when suburbanites were wealthy residents of the commuter towns, on the North Shore out of Chicago, or the Main Line out of Philadelphia. Today's suburbs include a great many tract-developments housing the middle class of clerical and factory workers, as well as those for the wealthy. Suburban neighborhoods appear to be the best selling items in the residential housing market for all who can afford them. As Robert Wood puts it:

Thus suburbia, residential, commerical, and industrial, became a permanent characteristic of urban life in the United States, and urban life itself was transformed from compact, congested cities into "metropolitan areas." By 1957, 174 of these metropolitan complexes contained 108 million people and 15,658 separate governments. Over 47 million of those people lived outside the central city, producing 36 per cent of the national value added by manufacturing and accounting for over 20 per cent of national retail sales.[14]

But we must remember that 61 million persons continue to live in the central cities. The central city still contains a majority of the population in most major metropolitan areas, though a shrinking majority with every decade of suburban expansion and central city population stability. Few central cities are declining in absolute numbers; it is simply that the over-all urban population increase is going to the suburbs. If we consider the proportion of space already built-up in most central cities, it is clear that new housing in the city requires the demolition of existing structures. Furthermore, if it demands extensive space, it must be located outside the central city, for land prices in the city are very high and demolition is costly.

As a result of changes in the space-time ratio, vast areas on the peripheries of the older cities were thrown open for settlement. The central city, which once contained all or most of the population as well as the functions of the metropolitan area, now contains only certain portions. In the division of labor, the central city is still the locus of most commerical activity, governmental agencies, industries, entertainment, and public facilities. In the geographical division of rewards (residences and neighborhoods), the central city houses the very poor in its tenements, the segregated ethnic minorities in its ghettos, the factory workers and lower middle-class in its decent but aging middle and outer neighborhoods, and the prosperous folk who prefer an urban milieu in its giant apartment houses.[15]

The Shape of the City and the Circulation System

The fanning out of the residential areas of the metropolis, while much of the work still remains concentrated in locations at the center, requires a tremendous diurnal movement of population toward small areas of the central city. The standardization of the work-day means that almost all of the labor force is en route simultaneously. The consequences are that during the peak rush hours in morning and afternoon, a large proportion of the automobiles of the metropolitan area are obstructing each other's paths. This results in slow speeds, difficult driving, increased accidents, and concentrated exhaust fumes, some of the attributes of the metropolitan transportation problem.

However, from one point of view, the very congestion indicates that the streets are being *well used*; the public investment is not wasted. One reason is that the automobile is still a faster means of movement than the public transportation lines.[16] In addition it is much more flexible; many neighborhoods are so diffuse that public transportation could serve them only at a loss. They do not generate enough business for the cost of operating buses. Thus the automobile represents a gain in the fluidity of the metropolitan population and a net social gain, for it makes land valuable for human residence and work which was once used only for pasture. However, this increased fluidity not only allows the location of residences in the outskirts, but also *decreases the comparative value* of the older structures in the center of the city. Row houses cannot compete as residences with the ranch houses of the suburbs; loft buildings cannot compete as warehouses with the horizontal plants of industrial parks.

At the same time, the differential space-time ratio in travel between various parts of the metropolis changes. Congestion on the arteries and lack of parking space in the downtown districts handicap the central business district in comparison with the suburban shopping centers.[17] This weakens the relative business position of the downtown stores and banks; it also has an effect upon the large-scale civic shows and resources. David Riesman puts it this way: "The city today, for many, spells crime, dirt, and race tensions, more than it does culture and opportunity. While some people still escape from the small town to the city, even more people are escaping from the city to the suburbs."[18] The net consequence of the decreased space-time ratio, and the differential ratio within the metropolitan area, is an increased blurring in the focus of urban life

upon the old, traditional center of the city. For many, this is a problem, if not an incipient disaster.

There are, thus, two basic types of metropolitan transportation problem. First, there is concern with improving the rate, ease, and cost of circulation within the metropolitan area as a whole. Second, there is concern for the effects of the automobile revolution upon the shape of the city; specifically, men are worried about the declining importance of the central city as symbol and hub of the metropolitan area.

NOTES

1. It is interesting to note that as early as 1894 Charles Horton Cooley published, as his doctoral dissertation, a study of transportation and society. See his "The Theory of Transportation" in R. C. Angell, ed., *Sociological Theory and Social Research* (New York: Holt, 1930).
2. For a discussion of increase in scale and a bibliography, see Scott Greer, *Social Organization* (New York: Random House, 1955).
3. Cf. Harlan W. Gilmore, *Transportation and the Growth of Cities* (Chicago: Free Press, 1953).
4. For a discussion of those characteristics of steam such as energy source which affects its social use, see Fred Cottrell, *Energy and Society* (New York: McGraw-Hill, 1955), Ch. 5.
5. Lewis Mumford, *Technics and Civilization* (New York: Harcourt, Brace, 1934).
6. Twenty-four percent of the people in Los Angeles in 1950 had lived in another residence in 1949. "Residential Mobility, 1949–50, in the Ten Largest Standard Metropolitan Areas of the United States," Detroit Area Study, Survey Research Center, University of Michigan, Project 843, #1211: May, 1957.
7. H. W. Gilmore, *Transportation and the Growth of Cities*, pp. 97 and 107.
8. R. D. McKenzie, "The Rise of Metropolitan Communities," in *Recent Social Trends in the United States*, pp. 445 ff.

9. *Path of Progress for Metropolitan St. Louis*, p. 8.
10. F. Cottrell, *Energy and Society*, p. 101.
11. H. W. Gilmore, *Transportation and the Growth of Cities*, p. 115.
12. F. Cottrell, *Energy and Society*, p. 108.
13. For clear documentation of the advantages held by shopping centers in the suburbs, see C. T. Jonassen, *The Shopping Center Versus Downtown*, Bureau of Business Research, College of Commerce and Administration, Ohio State University, 1955.
14. Robert C. Wood, *Suburbia, Its People and Their Politics* (Boston: Houghton Mifflin, 1959), p. 64.
15. For analysis of one metropolitan area in these terms, see *Background for Action*, First Public Report, The Metropolitan St. Louis Survey, Pt. 1, "The People" (University City, Mo., 1957).
16. See the data summarized by Francis Bello in "The City and the Car," in The Editors of *Fortune*, *The Exploding Metropolis* (New York: Doubleday, 1958).
17. Cf. C. T. Jonassen, *The Shopping Center Versus Downtown*, pp. 89–94.
18. David Riesman, "The Suburban Dislocation," in *Annals of the American Academy of Political and Social Science*, Vol. 314 (November, 1957), p. 131.

29. On Social Communication and the Metropolis

Karl W. Deutsch

Social communication is the process of exchanging information within human groups. In many circumstances, social communication can be substituted for transportation as a force leading to coordination and integration in the metropolitan community. If an individual can send a message to a site, he may not have to go there in person. According to Karl Deutsch, one of the great achievements of the metropolis is that it provides opportunities for these substitutions. He looks upon the modern urban community as a "huge engine of communication, a device to enlarge the range and reduce the cost of individual and social choices." Deutsch is equally aware, however, that an individual can suffer from an excess of information, stimuli, and opportunity—or what he calls "communication overload." He observes in this context that the flight to the suburbs is an available means for escaping a surfeit of stimuli. Deutsch concludes his paper by posing a number of issues that social research should examine in order to arrive at reasonable standards for metropolitan communication.

Karl W. Deutsch is Professor of Government at Harvard. He is the author of *The Analysis of International Relations* (1968), *Nationalism and Social Communication* (Revised Edition, 1966), *The Nerves of Government* (1963), and many other books in the fields of national government and international relations.

Any metropolis can be thought of as a huge engine of communication, a device to enlarge the range and reduce the cost of individual and social choices. In the familiar telephone switchboard, the choices consist of many different lines. Plugging in the wires to connect any two lines is an act of commitment, since it implies foregoing the making of other connections. The concentration of available outlets on the switchboard permits a wider range of alternative choices than would prevail under any more dispersed arrangement. It also imposes less stringent conditions of compatibility. The limits for the potentially useful size of a switchboard are fixed by the capacity of the type of switching and control equipment available.

The facilities of the metropolis for transport and communication are the equivalent of the switchboard. The units of commitment are not necessarily telephone calls but more often face-to-face meetings and transactions. For any participant to enter into any one transaction usually will exclude other transactions. Every transaction thus implies a commitment. The facilities available for making choices and commitments will then limit the useful size of a metropolis.

Contact Choices: The Product of Cities

From this perspective, the performance of a metropolis could be measured in terms of the average number of contact

George Braziller, Inc.—from "On Social Communication and the Metropolis" by Karl W. Deutsch from *The Future Metropolis*, edited by Lloyd Rodwin; reprinted with the permission of the publisher. Copyright © 1960 by the American Academy of Arts and Sciences. Reprinted by permission also of Constable, London.

choices which it offers to its inhabitants within, say, one hour of round-trip commuting time, at the prevailing levels of effort and equipment.[1] Efficiency in cities, as in other organizations, differs from effectiveness. Effectiveness is the probability of carrying out a given type of performance, regardless of cost, while efficiency consists in low cost for a given performance. The more persons or services available to a city dweller within a round trip of one hour, the more effective would be his city or metropolitan area, and the cheaper the cost of maintaining a metropolis area; and the cheaper the cost of maintaining a metropolis that places, say 1,000,000 people and 50,000 public and private institutions, firms or service points within a given commuting radius, the more efficient the metropolis could be said to be. The effectiveness of a metropolis could be measured in contact choices within one hour of travel time, while the efficiency of the same city would be measured by the ratio of such choices to some unit of cost. How many choices will $100 per capita buy for the residents of city X? As in many problems of design, one criterion cannot entirely override another. Some increases in effectiveness may have to be sought even at the price of rising costs, and some gains in efficiency may be worth some concessions in performance.

According to this view, the essential performance of the metropolis is in the enhancement of the range and number of such choices, and the basic cost is the maintenance of a system of facilities that makes a wide range of choices possible. One might ask: how many choices can an individual buy at a cost he can afford— and how many such choices on the average can the community buy for different groups of people, at prices it can afford? For each type of city and for each type of communication and transport system, it might then be possible to sketch demand and cost curves based either on the best available knowledge, or on prevailing practice.

Large cities, of course, serve many other functions. They offer playgrounds for children, lanes for lovers, shelter for residents and transients. But houses, playgrounds, and lovers' lanes are found in villages as well, and so sometimes are factories, power stations, mills, inns, manor houses and castles. Almost any one kind of installation found in a metropolis can also be found in the countryside. It is the multiplicity of different facilities and of persons, and the wide choice of potential quick contacts among them, that makes the metropolis what it is. And this essential character applies to large cities in underdeveloped as well as in advanced countries.

This general function of the metropolis is facilitated by its geographic location at some nodal point in a larger transportation network. The more the arteries that intersect at the site of the city, the greater the opportunities the city has to facilitate a wide range of choice. Again, the larger the city, the more diversified its industries, repair shops, and service installations— hospitals, research institutes, libraries, and labor exchanges—the wider the range of possible choices among them. The larger, the more diversified, the more highly skilled and educated the population, the greater the range of available personal choice either with respect to organizations or to opportunities in the world of culture, recreation and the arts.

In terms of economics, particularly in regard to the location of industrial enterprises, many of these considerations appear as external economies, actual or expected. Roads, port and rail connections, municipal services, the supply of skilled and unskilled labor, and the availability of high-level professional and scientific talent —all appear as so many potential factors of production, and some of them may even appear as free goods, against which no additional items of cost need to be budgeted. As will be evident later, the expectation may not be an altogether realistic one: the effective attractions of the area for new industries may lead after a time lag of some years or decades to substantial problems of congestion and overload. Yet locating in or near a great city is not only an exercise in economic rationality. Often the decision is made in intuitive and human terms; and most often perhaps the economic reasoning and the human preferences for location may seem to reinforce one another. Both tend to seek a widening range of choice at low, or at least tolerable, costs of choosing; and just this is the special advantage of the city. The rising proportions of industrial staff whose jobs are oriented to communication, service or professional functions may reinforce this attraction.

The power of the metropolis as an engine of communication is thus attested indirectly by its power of attraction over people. Though this power has an economic component, in the aggregate it is far more than economic. "How ya gonna keep 'em down on the farm, after they've seen Paree?" asked an old song; and the sociologists and anthropologists of the 1940's and 1950's have been reporting the vast attraction of urban areas in Asia and Africa to former villagers, far beyond any immediate economic or social push. They are held even in the squalor of the shanty towns and *bidonvilles*. If freedom is the opportunity to choose, then the metropolis, in so far as it is an engine for facilitating choice, is also one of liberation. This liberation may be physical, in terms of the

visits, the meetings, the sights now possible, or psychological and vicarious, in terms of the choices and experiences which can now be made in the imagination. In either case, it is a liberation whose reality and whose social, political, and psychological relevance cannot be doubted.

Communication Overload: The Disease of Cities

People come to large cities because there, among other reasons, they find a wider range of choice within their individual limitations than they are likely to find anywhere else. Inevitably this means that every metropolis must offer each of its residents enough freedom for a wide range of choices to be significant to them; and this also means enough freedom so that serious problems of peak loads and of recurrent, possibly growing, overloads are imposed on the city's many but limited facilities. Recurrent overloads are thus not an alien disturbance intruding into the even functioning of the metropolis. They are, on the contrary, an ever possible result of the essential nature of the metropolis as a device for facilitating a wider range of free choices.

To put it differently, the likelihood of such overloads is a result of the probability of coincidences in human choices and behavior under conditions of freedom. These overloads are not only the occasional loads, for which reserve capacities must be provided, but also the regular rush-hour loads, the result of relatively synchronized hours for work and recreation which in turn permit a larger range of choices than staggered hours would.

Despite their origin, however, recurrent overloads will tend to paralyze many functions, and eventually to blight the very structure of a metropolis. It is for good reason that waiting-line theory has become a fast growing field in operations research and social science. Taken together, increasing overloads of this kind reduce or destroy many attractions of the metropolis as well as the economic value of many of the capital investments in it.

Even in the absence of such overloads, the very effectiveness of a metropolis may produce subtle changes in its culture and in the cast of mind of its residents. A wider range of relevant choices implies ordinarily an additional burden on those who are choosing. Some years ago, Clifton Fadiman wrote a thoughtful article "The Decline of Attention" in modern, and especially American culture.[2] Since then Richard Meier has written of "attention overload" and of the "communication-saturated" society as characteristic problems of modern—and thus particularly of urban and metropolitan—culture.[3] These, too, are overloads in communication, but they occur not in streets and telephone lines but within the minds and nervous systems of people.

To increase the range of visible and relevant choices that confront a person usually means to increase the opportunity cost of whatever course he may eventually choose. Whatever he does will necessarily imply foregoing something else that also has appeared relevant and in a sense attractive. The wider the range of relevant choices we put before a person of limited physical and psychic resources and capabilities, the more acute and pressing we make his problem of economy in allocating his own time, attention and resources; and if he has been raised in a "conscientious" culture, such as the American or Northwest European, we are quite likely also to have increased his vague but nagging sense of self-doubt and misgiving as to whether he has made the best choice, and thus the best use, of his opportunities.

Cities therefore may produce a pervasive condition of communications overload. Whereas villagers thirst for gossip, city dwellers with more ample choices may crave privacy. But the internal communications overload of other people makes them less receptive to our needs. Their limited attention or their real need for privacy may tend to exclude us, and in the midst of crowds of neighbors we may experience persistent loneliness. Such loneliness, inflicted on us by others, is the obverse of our own need for privacy; and our own limited capabilities for concentration, attention, and responsiveness will make both their and our loneliness less likely to be overcome.

What people cannot overcome, they may try to gloss over. The poets and the social scientists—both critics of our culture—have catalogued the many rituals of self-deception that men practice: the reading of mass media that purvey illusions of "inside information" to the millions commonly excluded from it; the fancy dress of conformity which they don, from ivy league dress to the black leather jackets of youth gangs, or beatnik beards and sandals. Even these foibles that convey a sense of belonging, of identity, should be seen in perspective. People indulge in them, not necessarily because they are more shallow or stupid than their forebears in a village or small town, but because the commitments the metropolis imposes—of greater freedom, wider choices, greater burdens on their attentions and their powers of response—have temporarily become too much for them.

This temporary overburdening may be particularly acute for newcomers from some radically different cultural background. Then the effects of psychological uprooting through contact with the wider opportunities of metropolitan life are superimposed on the effects of the shock of a new culture and the weakening of the traditional bonds of family and familiar authority.

Communication overloads may be reduced through effective cues for orientation. Consider, for example, the practice of the old city builders, who placed the most important structures of visual attraction, such as cathedrals, palaces, or monuments, at the nodal points in the street network of the city. The nodal points, as the term is used here, were those located at the main intersections of the city's traffic flow, and hence most often observed as the city's landmarks, and they were also those points most useful for orientation. The experience of visual beauty in a place of visual usefulness was thus often an inevitable part of a city dweller's daily coming and going. It is perhaps not too fanciful to surmise that this combined experience of perception and clarity of orientation in such cities as London, Paries, Bern, Cologne or Prague contributed, and still contributes to the charm of those cities and to the feeling of their inhabitants that they were members of a deep and rich culture. Bridges can fulfil a similar orienting function: the San Francisco Bay Bridge and the Golden Gate Bridge come readily to mind, together with the Embarcadero Tower of the old ferry building, visible for a long distance along the major artery of Market Street.

In many modern metropolitan areas, however, these conditions are no longer fulfilled. Major intersections in many American cities are often adorned with gasoline stations or car lots, with flimsy, low, shop buildings with large neon signs. At the same time, many of the largest, most expensive, and sometimes most impressive constructions are put on side lots, well away from the main intersections, as for example Rockefeller Center, the Lever and Seagram buildings, the United Nations building or the Museum of Modern Art in New York City. In Boston, the John Hancock building, tallest and most monumental in the city, is tucked away on a side street.[4] Many of our visible landmarks are only of very limited help in orientation, and are best seen from afar or by special visit. At the same time, many of the major intersections passed daily by most of us are either nondescript or appallingly ugly and give subtle but depressing impressions of disorientation, tiredness, or tension.

Such crucial traffic points cannot be easily abandoned. When elegant entertainment and shopping shifted from the central intersection of Times Square to the area of Rockefeller Center, the old subway system became less convenient to users of the Center, who have to make their way there and back by foot, bus, or taxi and who thus have increased congestion. This contrast between the changing fashions in regard to neighborhoods and the unchanging nature of fixed intersections in a major traffic network helps to make the market mechanism such an unsatisfactory instrument for the development of these crucial sites.[5]

Overloads on some of the public and private services available in an urban area may sometimes be reinforced in their effects by a shrinking, or even an atrophy, of these services. Services vulnerable to this kind of process include service and repair shops, stockrooms, and parts depots, hospitals and clinics, libraries and museums. Many of the services of these institutions might be needed on Saturdays, in some cases, as is true of the cultural institutions, or on Sundays, or often for many hours on each work day. Institutions such as supermarkets and suburban shopping centers provide such longer hours of service, but many others do not, and some now curtail the amount of service previously offered. Much of this situation seems caused by rising labor costs, by fixed budgets, by the rising cost of able managers for small or middle-sized undertakings, or by the difficulty of dividing units of managerial effort so as to obtain management for some extra hours daily or weekly, and perhaps by some subtle development in American metropolitan areas that makes the personnel in service industries prefer shorter hours to more pay. This may be a rational choice, but it may become less so if too much of the new leisure is frittered away in waiting for delayed services. An increase in staff, with additional compensation for staggered hours (already practiced in suburban supermarkets), might be one approach an affluent society could well explore. In any case, freemarket forces alone seem unlikely to overcome the persistent gap between the rising need for services in metropolitan areas and the actual volume of services rendered.

Suburbs: An Escape from Overloads

In the congested metropolis, a major effect of the cumulative overloads on communications, transport, and other urban amentities is frustration. Withdrawal to a suburb offers partial surcease. Taxes play a role in these frustrations. The late Justice Holmes once said he did not mind paying taxes, for this was the way he bought civilization; but exasperated city dwellers may flee to the suburbs from a metropolis where so much tax money buys so little in civilized living. The remedy is not to lower the urban tax cost as such but to improve the quality of metropolitan government and metropolitan living by attacking the whole range of overloads. Several lines for such an attack have been proposed, but most are proposals for escape. When put into practice they have not been markedly successful. For example, the shift in population to dormitory suburbs around the old cities has produced mounting burdens on commuting. A farther shift to some twenty-five or fifty miles from the city would make commuting prohibitive for many; whereas some men have been able to afford the financial and physical costs, their wives have found themselves marooned in a more or less rural environment, deprived of most of the choices and opportunities that make city life attractive.

The schemes for satellite towns are more far-reaching: each would be near the city, with separate though limited facilities for employment, shopping, services, and entertainment. Some towns of this kind have been built, but in Britain, at least, they have proved less popular than expected.[6] Still more far-reaching schemes for decentralization would break up the large cities altogether in favor of a wide scattering of major factories and administrative offices over much greater regions. Such a proposal would require a heavy reliance on medium- and long-distance transport and on telecommunications, as well as the acceptance of rural (or nearly rural) isolation.

All these schemes are unsatisfactory in the same fundamental respect. For escape from the frustrations of the metropolis, they would sacrifice the primary purpose of the large city—a wider range of choice with a low cost. The search for more effective ways of dealing with urban problems cannot ignore this basic function of a metropolis, it must rather be the starting point.

A Strategy of Search for Solutions

The concept of a metropolis as a device for facilitating choice in communications can contribute first of all to answering some general questions, from which one may proceed to more specific surmises and to ways in which both the tentative general answers and the specific surmises can be tested. The first questions might be these: what is the usual ratio of the cost of transport and communication facilities to the cost of shelter? how does this ratio change for different types of cities? how is it influenced by an increase in the scale of a city, as measured by its total population?

There are several ways of exploring this inquiry; they should give us interchangeable indices of the same underlying fact.[7] The proportion of communication costs to shelter costs could be measured in terms of the ratio of total capital investment in communication and transport facilities to the total capital investment in shelter. Or it could be measured in terms of the ratio of current expenditure of communication and transport to current expenditure on shelter; or in terms of the ratio of total manpower employed in communication and transport to the manpower employed in the construction and maintenance of shelter. Doubtless, a range of further indicators of this kind for related ratios might be developed, but those already given should serve amply to illustrate the point.

One could also study the ratios of some appropriate nonmonetary indicators, such as the physical proportions of certain relevant facilities. The known ratio of the area of land that is devoted to streets in a city to the land area devoted to dwellings and gardens could perhaps be used more effectively within the context of the other ratios noted above.

Other types of large-scale organization could be studied. As taller skyscrapers are built, what is the change in the ratio of space devoted to elevator shafts to the total volume of the building? As corporations grow bigger, what is the ratio of telephone calls and written messages to some measure of the total volume of company activities? Such questions are aimed not merely at promoting speculation but also at suggesting a surmise to be tested: as the size and functions of a city grow, the proportion of resources devoted to transport and communications may have to grow faster, or at least as fast, if increasing overloads are to be avoided. It may be that some lag may produce no ill effects. Then the crucial question would be: what lag in the growth of such facilities is acceptable? Research may disclose a range of acceptable or desirable proportions for investment in such facilities and thus offer a potentially useful tool to planners.

What would life be like in an otherwise normal metropolis if its transport and communication facilities had been deliberately somewhat overdeveloped by present-day standards? Suppose its streets and intersections were hardly ever jammed, its parking spaces rarely unavailable, its public transport frequent, rapid, clean and uncrowded, its telephone lines usually free, with quickly available connections? If this sounds too much like utopia, it might still be asked: how much improvement in well-being in a city could be purchased by how large an investment in drastically improved transport and communication?

Some years ago, Sigfried Giedion drew attention to the late nineteenth-century shift to the pavilion system in large exhibitions, away from the earlier practice of centralizing all major exhibits in one giant building of the Crystal Palace type.[8] Giedion suggested that, as the exhibitions and the crowds of visitors grew larger, they gave rise to intolerable demands for more corridors to keep the crowds moving. The solution devised was to break up the exhibition into scattered pavilions, and to let the visitors make their way from one to another across the network of footpaths or across the open ground. People preferred to walk hundreds of yards in the open to the next pavilion rather than push their way for dozens of yards along some crowded corridor or hall. The principle may be relevant perhaps to the metropolis and the problems of urban decentralization.

Again, the question of cost arises. The shift to the pavilion system made the visitors themselves responsible for keeping dry and warm, a cost previously borne by the management of the single central hall. When a shift occurs from a compact city to a spreading network of suburbs, costs are also shifted from the city government to suburban families, who must now maintain one or two cars and pay toll rates for most of their telephone calls. In addition, there is now the financial, physical, and nervous cost of commuting. The decisive factor is the increase in delay in arriving and in the danger and tension. The ten or twelve miles between Wellesley and Boston may require twenty-five to thirty minutes with light traffic and good weather, in bad weather or dense traffic, forty-five minutes or more; and there are perhaps a hundred intersections. Over an adequate expressway the same trip might take fifteen to twenty minutes, with less tension and fatigue. A radial and peripheral system of improved expressways, permitting safe traveling speeds of seventy miles an hour—assuming corresponding improvements in the safety features of cars—would permit a city to double its effective radius and quadruple its potential area of integration. Our road experts have told us that "speed kills" if

resorted to at the wrong time and place. But our city planners might well remind us that delays, too, can kill when their cumulative burden is added over a long period to an intensive working day.

Safe speed is not cheap. It cannot be achieved except by planned investment under public guidance. But it could do much to humanize life in our cities. The day may come when a profession of specialized expediters may watch over the smooth and quick flow of traffic and communication in our metropolitan areas, to identify and remove bottlenecks and overloads before their effects become cumulative and choking.

The same considerations apply even more strongly to public transportation. Improved and publicly subsidized rail transport—on the ground and underground—offers perhaps some of the most promising opportunities to combine high speed in mass transportation with safety at tolerable cost. The old-style commuting trains that take forty minutes for twenty miles not only exhaust their passengers but also drive more and more people to the somewhat faster highways. A drastic improvement in the speed and caliber of public transportation might relieve the pressure on the road system. Similarly, an extension of local telephone call rates to the entire suburban area—on the analogy of the successful principle of uniform postal rates—might reduce some of the need to travel back and forth and thus further reduce the pressure on the transport system. Still another step might be the partial staggering of service hours, so that more stores and service facilities would be available for more hours daily, thus reducing the peak loads when all stores open or close. Rotating assignments and staggered hours might require more employees, but it might pay off in higher profits for the stores and in greater freedom for the community.[9]

None of these improvements would be cheap, and none easy to achieve. Such improvements, however, might be a key factor in rehabilitating our metropolitan areas. What is needed is a realistic analysis of the problem of peak loads and of the rising capital requirements for transport and communication. Only a substantial investment in transportation and communications can make metropolitan decentralization practicable, and only a substantial strengthening of public control over strategic land sites can restore beauty to our cities. Ways will have to be found to let planners use the powers of the community to guide urban growth toward a clear and pleasing pattern of new and old landmarks where people can once again feel well-oriented, exhilarated, and at home.

The various lines of research suggested in these pages have a common origin and a common goal. Our inquiry has centered on the function of a metropolis in aiding its residents in their choices and in their search for responses. The ranges and costs of such choices and responses are basic to our analysis. Proportionately accelerated investment in communications, together with an improved knowledge of the general order of magnitude of these proportions, suggests a possible approach to urban decentralization. It also points up the need for greater clarity and beauty in our cities, and perhaps also for more responsive government, capable of integrating a wider range of metropolitan and suburban services, if the expanded metropolis is to become a genuine home for its people.

NOTES

1. This would be analogous to measuring the performance of a switchboard or of a central telephone exchange in terms of the number of potential calls among which an average subscriber might be able to choose, say, for ten cents, or within thirty seconds time for dialing automatic switching, signaling, and the first response of the called party.
2. Clifton Fadiman, "The Decline of Attention," in *The Saturday Review Reader* (New York: Bantam Books, 1951), pp. 25–36.
3. I am indebted for the term to Richard L. Meier; see his "Characteristics of the New Urbanization" (multigraphed, University of Chicago, 1953), especially pp. 3–5.
4. There are exceptions in many cities, to be sure. The Prudential Building in Chicago, the Coliseum Exhibition Hall at Columbus Circle in New York, and the Liberty Mutual Building in Boston are all at major intersections. These seem to have been exceptions, however, so far as major post-1930 construction is concerned.

5. Many users of the new facilities have employed a new transport system—the taxicab—but the cost to the community includes not only the cab fare but also the surface traffic jams and perhaps the exclusion of a marginal class of customers for the new facilities.
6. Lloyd Rodwin, *The British New Towns Policy*, Cambridge, Harvard University Press, 1941.
7. See Paul F. Lazarsfeld's discussion on the interchangeability of indices in his article, "Evidence and Inference in Social Research," *Dædalus*, 1958, no. 4, pp. 99–130 (*On Evidence and Inference*).
8. Sigfried Giedion, *Space, Time and Architecture* (Cambridge, Harvard University Press, 1941), pp. 262, n–11, 725–727, 736–742, 757.
9. For a discussion of some limiting factors and of the forces tending to pull the working hours of the whole community into a single rhythm, see Vilhelm Aubert and Harrison White, "Sleep: A Sociological Interpretation," *Acta Sociologica*, 1960, *4*: no. 3, 1–16.

30. Socioeconomic and Technological Forces in Urban Expansion

John W. Dyckman

Urban growth in the ecological sense is the expansion of urban social networks over ever larger spatial areas. John Dyckman describes recent patterns of population redistribution within metropolitan regions and between regions in the United States. He examines the major forces responsible for these changes, including the shift from an agricultural to an industrial and service-oriented economy, increasing population growth, accelerating labor force demand, and the development of the automobile and the jet airplane. Using this analysis he proceeds to examine the implications of these forces for urban growth during the next few decades. Dyckman believes that the population will continue to be concentrated along the Atlantic and Pacific coasts and that the dispersion to suburban settlements within regions will also persist. He makes this assumption on the grounds that these patterns reflect not only the underlying economic and demographic pressures but also the dominant consumer preferences of urban residents. He is careful to point out, however, that tastes and styles of life have changed several times in the course of American history and that future changes could well upset the accuracy of his predictions.

John W. Dyckman is Professor of City and Regional Planning and Chairman of the Department of City and Regional Planning of the University of California, Berkeley. He is coauthor of *Capital Requirements for Urban Development and Renewal* (1961).

One of the best ways to gain insight into the forces which are at work changing our society is to attempt an assessment of future states. When confronted with the need for decision about futures, the forecaster looks hard at the present forces and scrutinizes the past for evidence of their persistence. In this spirit, much of this essay is about the future.

For the most part, however, the future considered is nearby. The commitments of city planners predispose them to a long-range view; improvements such as dams, irrigation systems, highways, streets, and other public works last upwards of fifty years and continue to have consequences throughout their lifetime. Urban renewal has made city planners acutely conscious of the usefulness of many buildings over fifty years old. It is to be expected, then, that the Corps of Engineers prepares forecasts in its major river basin studies for the year 2010, the National Capital Planning Commission has undertaken a plan for the year 2000, and other forty- and fifty-year plans find favor. This paper, however, is directed to another purpose, that of setting the stage for *policy* planning.

Policy-making is not a "technical" art. It proceeds more tentatively and incrementally than the planning of works. Policies are at once statements of desired goals and guides to action. Implementation may be by direct or indirect controls. To the extent that the path of indirection is

From *Urban Expansion, Problems and Needs*, papers presented at the Administrator's Spring Conference. Washington, D. C.: Government Printing Office, April 1963, pp. 1–27.

439

favored, the policy must take account of a complex interplay between opportunities and motives. In such a brief overview as this, the emphasis is heavily on the opportunities. But in the actual working out of policies, many opportunities will be discarded and new ones elected. The choices of millions of decision makers cannot be adequately simplified for an exercise of this kind.

Elsewhere I have called attention to the fact that technological developments were making possible both centralization and decentralization of the functions of the city.[1] In this sense, the technological change was "nondiscriminating." The decisive factors in the actual pattern that would develop were these changes in taste and life style elected by a population that was relatively wealthy. A similar luxury of choice might be denied to a country like India, where per capita wealth and income were substantially lower than in the United States. The relation between average level of income and the form of development of urban places is very intimate. Thus in the United States it might be possible in the year 2000 to enjoy an even greater degree of functional specialization of places than we now have, both within and between metropolitan areas. At the same time a country like India may be able to afford, and to realize gains from, a much less specialized urban function.

It is not unlikely that the United States will see high-density (as measured by activity per unit of area) center cities, utilizing modern communication technology for information storage and exchange, but with virtually no residence in center city except a mass variant of the nineteenth-century men's club. Residential areas may be a great deal more scattered than at present, and recreation may be place-specialized on a grander scale. This latter trend is well marked today, when in the wintertime Southern California, Florida, and Arizona are virtually suburbs of New York and Chicago. As average income per capita increases (and it shows signs of continuing to do so in the United States at least), and as real costs of transportation become cheaper, the potential for extending this kind of functional specialization is sizably enhanced.

To a substantial extent, too, we are entering a world phase in which the functional specialization and division of labor is truly global. The summer in Europe is already competitive with the erstwhile fashionable vacation spots in this country. (A travel agent on Martha's Vineyard told me in 1960 or 1961 that his bookings to Europe for old customers even then had exceeded his bookings on the Vineyard.) In a more subtle way, this breakdown of distance will have great influence on our domestic land policies. Much has been made of the potential loss of agricultural land to urban subdivisions in metropolitan areas, for example, especially where that land has special suitability for a relatively unique type of cultivation. But instead of examining its uniqueness in a United States context, we will soon be obliged to consider it in world terms, for the tendency to common markets and the break-up of tariff barriers is now strong.

As power sources and technological innovations permit, we will also see an increasing alteration of geography and micro-climate. One of the most promising applications of atomic power is in earth moving, in the creation of harbors and canals and reversing rivers. The changes wrought by such works will create new specializations, new absolute and comparative advantages in traditional kinds of production. And these works will drain land, create new areas, and alter the urban land supply. With change in the micro-climate, they will create amenity on an appreciable scale. As for conventional types of production—for example, agri-culture—new developments (such as hydro-ponics) will drastically modify land require-ments.

Changes of this order are not explored in this paper. While their pursuit is both fascinating and profitable, they cannot be effectively incorporated in next year's urban policy. By choice, this paper follows a conservative policy of looking only at the United States and at well-underway present trends. It focuses on the decisions of the present consumers and producers, without indulging in what might be allowable flights of fancy about the fickle tastes of these actors. If in consequence it is somewhat pedestrian, it is at least in the justifiable American tradition of not looking further than one Administration ahead.

Forces Producing Urban Expansion

With our population moving rapidly to pass 200 million, with the rural and agri-cultural labor force necessary to supply foodstuffs and raw materials for that population declining and the "surplus" rural population moving to metropolitan areas, with metropolitan population spill-ing over the old city boundaries and covering the countryside, in the process replacing land formerly in agricultural use with suburban settlement, and with government-military sponsorship of new research and technology centers in the hitherto non-industrial South and West, it is obvious to social observers that the pattern of urban settlement in America is entering a period of qualitative change.

To understand this change, it is, of course, necessary to be aware of the main social, economic, and technological forces at work in the society. But the most important of these forces are well-known. I sum-marized some of them in an article in *Daedalus* (see note 1), and Kenneth Boulding has made a succinct statement of them.[2] It may be more useful at this point to go somewhat further and reach into the dynamics that seem to be at work within these broad parameters of change.

To attempt to assay these dynamics is frankly a speculative exercise. My strategy of speculation is very crude. First, it tries to infer motives and incentives from the actions of the broad classes of decision-makers effecting some of these changes and, second, it tries to sketch the environ-ment of action limiting these decisions. There is a teleological bias in this method. It tends to see action as adaptive and motives as roughly "economizing" in the sense of seeking a solution efficient for the values of the actor, so that the values are often inferred from the action. Thus the approach is "rationalistic," with all the weaknesses of this method.

Barring catastrophic occurrences, like atomic war, and startling reversals of policy, such as opening of immigration on an unrestricted basis, the population of the United States in the near and middle future has been determined, within rough limits at least, by decisions already made. Both the future levels of population and the demographic composition of the totals will be considered, therefore, as powerful environmental factors limiting the scope of future choices. The implications of the growth and aging of our present demo-graphic base deserve an extended treat-ment, which is reserved for the next section of this paper.

Let us begin, then, by considering three

well-observed types of decisions: (1) the decisions to move from rural areas to the cities; (2) the decisions to make inter-regional shifts from North and East to South and West; and (3) the decisions to locate on the periphery, in suburban and exurban portions of the metropolitan areas. These decisions will be of interest not only because of their consequences for the pattern of urban settlement in America but also because of their implications for the preferences of Americans for styles of urban living. This latter set of findings will perhaps be of the greater interest in possible policy formation, though it is necessarily the more speculative endeavor.

Some of the decisions, however, are so well documented that they are scarcely the subject of speculation today. The first great class of moves in the process of urban expansion, for example, has been going on for so long and has been so well observed that it no longer seems to need an explicit rationale. The move off the farm into the city has been in process for more than a hundred years in America and has furnished the stuff for one of the great themes in traditional American literature. The decisions to move from rural to urban settings were largely founded on economic bases; for opportunities, in the sense of potentially greater income and economic and social mobility, have long been greater in cities than in the country for a large part of the rural population. In addition, strong motives of escape from a culturally poor and restricted environment to one richer in communication and exchange of information have been a force in urban migration.

In an important sense, the motive underlying this migration has been a desire to improve efficiency in consumption on the part of the migrants—though the richer consumption is made possible by the economies of agglomeration in the productive centers. Lately, this pattern has undergone substantial change. Moves from rural areas to cities, or from less urbanized to more highly urbanized regions, still may result in economic advantage. But for many, the economic and even cultural differentials have been increasingly reduced. Agriculture itself has become industrialized, in the sense of high capitalization of the process. Costs of communication, in relative terms at least, have been greatly reduced. The popular culture of rural areas today differs very little from that of urban areas. The well-capitalized farmer is, as Boulding says, little distinguishable from the exurbanite.[3] In fact, the gentlemen farmers of exurbia may adopt more of the traditionally rural cultural patterns than the modern factory-farmer. Where the agricultural working force has not been reduced by mechanization, as in some fruit and vegetable growing, it has been reduced by the suburbanization of the land.

Since we may expect that the flow of capital into agriculture has effectively substituted for labor inputs and tended to equalize factor proportions in urban and rural areas, the displacement of agricultural workers by machinery cannot be expected to produce very large migrations into the cities in the future. But one powerful noneconomic complex of forces operates to continue to swell urban population: The migration of Negroes from the South to the northern cities has social and political as well as economic roots. At the present rates of change of southern white attitudes and of movement of Negroes out of the South, it seems likely that the decline in Negro population of the southern small towns and rural areas will continue until the source is virtually depleted. For despite actions of the Supreme Court, the fundamental social changes necessary to give southern Negroes hope of equality or to extend hopes or change expectations have not been forthcoming.

Meanwhile, to a lesser extent than the small towns are contributing to the central cities, they are being absorbed into the metropolitan areas. Those small towns outside metropolitan regions which do not themselves provide a probable nucleus for such a region are declining in population and economic importance. The country is being metropolitanized at a very fast rate; within a decade or two, three-quarters of the population of the country will live in metropolitan centers. At or near that point, the ratio may be approaching an asymptote.

Locational Decisions: Regional Trends

The regional shift to south and west is in part a similar "evening-out" process. California has just become the most populous state in the Union, and the South and Far West may be expected to grow at a more rapid rate than the older centers of the North and East through several decades. To some extent, this growth reflects predictable decisions by entrepreneurs seeking outlets for capital— old centers, such as Boston, have exported capital for generations. But in recent years, the growth of the Far West, in particular, has been more rapid than the rate which would be produced by any drive for equalization of returns on investment. The movement has, rather, been spearheaded by the conscious decisions of an affluent people to seek the amenity in life-style provided by these areas.

The most striking case is found in the growth of research industries in California. The rapid growth of research, particularly government contract research in elec-

tronics, weapons, and space technology, has been a prominent feature of the American economy in the last decade. With the aid of government-financed contracts, a huge research complex has emerged in Southern California and lesser complexes in Northern California, Arizona, and other parts of the West and the South. The locational pulls moving these activities to the new regions have included some consideration of defensive dispersion, but they are found even more significantly in the individual decisions of a large number of the technicians themselves. Many of these space-engineers and scientists found roots in the West in wartime service at Western air bases or in the aviation industry that flourished on the West Coast in World War II. But many others are simply seeking the fringe benefits afforded by Western climate, natural attractions, and life-style.

These engineers are able to exert a strong influence on locational decision for two reasons: (1) the ease of access of new or young firms into the defense industries and (2) the continued shortage of skilled scientific personnel relative to the government-induced demand. A new research firm may be set up on the strength of a single government contract, and that firm typically is footloose and free to make virtually any locational choice. Larger companies competing for skilled personnel find salary rates relatively fixed by the nature of their contracts and use fringe benefits as a powerful recruiting device.

The decisions of these engineers are of interest in our speculation about urban expansion not only for their impact on the growth of research industries in the Far West and Southwest, but especially for the example they provide of locational and urban life-style decisions in a situation of relatively free choice. Moreover, these engineers are the prototypes of the functional operatives of the cybernated society. It would be a mistake to think of these technicians as "unusual"; they are typically not the most creative scientists in our society, but the organization men of the new scientific Establishment. It is a mistake to think of their choices as the eccentricities of "genius"; genius, so far as we are able to identify it, seems to be randomly distributed. And if the most original work is not produced in this climate, these are at least conditions under which quantities of research can be produced effectively on order. In some areas, notably Southern California, these researchers are virtually interchangeable parts in a large research machine, for they form a labor pool which is most economical for rapid assembly of task-force teams.

What do their choices tell us about the preferences of the technicians' skill-band, which is expected to play such an important role in a more nearly automated and cybernated society? Richard L. Meier has calculated a list of the converging influences that serve as attraction for new research complexes.[4] This list is strongly weighted by the preferences of the new technicians. It includes the following items:

1. Access to cultural and natural amenity (including outdoor recreation and wooded building sites)
2. Adjacency to major research-oriented universities, hospitals, and similar institutions
3. Proximity to large capital-intensive installations
4. Existence of a professional-class suburban environment
5. Exit on a metropolitan expressway

In addition, Meier lists another item: availability of cheap, general-purpose structures. But though much has been made of this potential (incubator) function of existing structures, I fail to find the evidence on this score either conclusive or instructive. Whatever the locational pattern of future research installations, the experience of recent years offers informing insights into the preferences of the rising "meritocracy" in a relatively unrestrained choice situation (characterized by cost-plus contracts, a seller's market for professional skills, geographic mobility, new industry with absence of seniority ties, and so on). Given this freedom of choice, the life-style chosen by the new professionals seems to have the following aspects:

1. Desire for a suburban setting, preferably in relatively homogeneous circumstances of high educational level, good schools, "highbrow" middle-class taste
2. Preference for outdoor recreation, usually in the form of highly individual activities and romantic rural contracts
3. Favoring of informality and diversity in entertaining, rather than the relatively formal entertaining of the older-era well-to-do
4. Surprisingly high tolerance for automobile commuting
5. Strong bias in favor of free-standing houses

The romantic individualism in rural recreational taste of the new engineers may stem from a predominantly "protestant" upbringing, but it also may be the leisure-differentiating response of men who are most aware of the imminent disappearance of both rural life and individuality. In a similar vein, many high-income urbanites seem to be increasingly drawn to center city residence as the face-to-face contact, which once was so functional in the city, has increasingly become a luxury in an era when communications functions of a less sensitive and rich kind are handled exceedingly well by telephone, television, and other media.

One of these points, the preference for suburban environment, takes us to a third context of decision: the intra-metropolitan "game." Metropolitan growth has always been peripheral. The qualitatively new aspect of present growth is the realization that in virtually every major metropolitan area of the country, development "outside" the city will soon overbalance the core. This circumferential weighting is effected less by hollowing out the core than by extending the domain of the outskirts. If we consider the whole metropolitan area as the "city," we see that this extension has had the effect of reducing average density.

Again, let us look at the calculations of the decision-makers. Here, too, the forces in this movement are the actions of the individual's "optimizing" or "efficiency-seeking" behavior. Each potential land user seeks the best trade-off of locational efficiency in consumption and production, or his "optimum" position at given cost. The trade-off of gains and costs is usually one of amenity and amount of space, on the one hand, and travel time and cost to work, on the other. We are all aware that one impact of the extension of the expressway systems in metropolitan areas has been the reduction of travel time from outlying points to employment centers, with an added bonus in cases where employment has been able to move, in its turn, outward to the new labor pool. Only slightly less obvious is the realization that the amount of space which can be purchased for a given residential dollar increases more rapidly with distance in many metropolitan areas than does the corresponding cost (in time and money) of travel to the desired destinations.

Depending on the price elasticity of demand for space by the residential locators, this relative cost situation can be a powerful decentralizing factor.

The trend is strengthened by the use of public resources to open up opportunities for the private actors. By pushing highways, water, utilities, and so forth, the government opens land before existing demand has been fully absorbed by the market in older places, thus opening the opportunity for individual decision-makers to find lower-cost positions for a given consumption goal. While the resulting pattern may not be the most efficient in terms of government cost, the argument might be made that the resulting lower-density pattern of development increases community welfare by permitting the realization of strong space preferences.

The "scatteration" which is most conspicuously wasteful of public utility development is a product of the entrepreneurial organization of land development. Given the existence of a market for fees in land, the legal conditions of holding such fees, and the liabilities imposed by present patterns of taxation, along with the practices of finance and extension of credit, it can be demonstrated that the pattern of scatteration is a rational response to market opportunities on the part of land developers. In particular, the incentive of the land developer to seek to open new land at certain points in the balance between acquisition and holding prices and market demand may allow us to predict the developing scatteration with some reliability. Jack Lessinger has attempted to develop such a model, which he has tested in the Santa Clara Valley, California.[5]

Given this organization and the existence of a band of widely different positions in space preference and ability to pay for space, the development is not likely to be compact or orderly in most metropolitan areas. Remember that the gains from compact organizations are social, not individual—at least in the short-run reckoning.

The Environment of Urban Change

The Future Impact of Present Demographic Composition—The Negro in the City As indicated earlier, Negro migration to northern cities will be high through the 1960s, but thereafter will slow down perceptibly as Negroes in the North and West outnumber those in the Old South and the source of inmigration begins to dry up. But Negro natural increase— which is presently higher than that of whites in urban areas for reasons of age distribution and persistence of rural cultural modes—will continue to support the rapid growth in the Negro share of city populations in the face of declining inmigration. Philip Hauser has pointed out that the birth rate of the Negro population of Chicago more than doubled—from a rate of 18 per thousand to 37 per thousand —in the period from 1940 to 1957, while its death rate decreased from 15 per thousand per year to 10 per thousand per year. At the Chicago rate, the impact of natural increase alone would double the urban Negro population in 27 years. The concentration of the Negro population in the central cities—and often in ghettoes within those cities—along with their concentration in lower-income occupations, restricted work skills, and generally unfavorable social status, continues to be the most important fact in the internal life of the cities.

As a specialized consumer in a relatively compartmentalized segment of the market,

the Negro has been singled out for the special treatment of the "race" market, has been confined to certain neighborhoods of the city, and has been served by public welfare programs in the very areas in which he has been denied equal treatment in the market. Witness the fulsome supply of public housing for Negro areas and the formidable difficulties presented to Negroes seeking to obtain loans for home ownership.

But as Negroes come to be a majority in the old cities and gain in political power, they may be able to end this era of patronizing treatment. Perhaps the most foreboding aspect of the struggle for this equality is the fact that the Negro is making his move for first-class citizenship at a time when the terms of trade in the market for productive resources are turning against unskilled labor. Many of the young people face a shrinking job market in which even the modest skills of previous industrial societies are in short demand. Only the services bid to be avid employers, and as the standard of living in the material sector of the economy goes up, the ability to earn the money for the high-level consumption it symbolizes by work in services falls short. The main route out of this morass which our society offers is through education.

We may expect that school facilities and learning climate will be prizes in the struggle for enhanced opportunity, just as they even now are marginally decisive attractions in many residential locational choices. The issue of inferior schooling resulting from *de facto* residential segregation and the neighborhood organization of schools is being hotly debated in New York and Chicago and will inevitably be raised in other urban centers. If the neighborhood school principle gives way first, it will mark the end of the most important single distinguishing mark of neighborhood identity and could end the special status of communities within cities. If, on the other hand, neither residential segregation nor the neighborhood school arrangement yields, the odds will be against securing first-class public schooling for the minority (or future majority) children.

For the most serious obstacle to achievement in the ghetto schools is the defeatist and defensive "culture of poverty," as Oscar Lewis has defined this term. Middle-class and aspirant, socially mobile lower-class families shun this culture, which they find pervading the slum school. They seek the highly regarded schools in certain middle-class neighborhoods chiefly to escape the ghetto schools, rather than from any clear expectations of the performance of the others. Unless the defensive armor is broken up, by one means or another, the large concentration of unemployed, out-of-school youth found by James Conant[6] in a number of northern city areas will grow by steady accretion.

In short, though the Negro is contributing greatly to the growth of the American city (adding over 2 million a decade in migration alone, and constituting about a quarter of the population in a number of northern industrial centers), he is responsible for little of the suburban expansion and has scarcely participated in the new technology that is changing labor force requirements and industrial location and creating a new group of "style leaders." At present this Negro urban population represents an enormous potential which, if released, could add considerably to the tide of suburbanization, home ownership, and other trends in urban life. If dammed up, this energy, located at the heart of the great historical urban centers of the country, could become a corrosive force speeding the social and economic decomposition of the old cities.

Age Composition of the Population

Throughout the 1950s the cities felt the burden of the postwar baby boom, for the number of school-age children increased more rapidly than total population, assessables, or income. The steady rise in urban spending was ascribable in large measure to increased school costs. In the period ahead, the influx of elementary school children is expected to taper off. But despite a more "normal" flow of new arrivals in school, there may be little respite from the mounting burden of school costs. For the elementary school budget of the fifties is moving up into high school, where per pupil costs are higher by a factor of 20 to 25 percent. (High school enrollments are expected to increase 48 percent in the 1960s, compared with a mere 6 percent increase in elementary school enrollments.) Any drive to improve the quality of our secondary schools, particularly through recruitment of accomplished personnel, would mean salary increases, smaller classes, and other expensive inducements. The much needed programs for the underprivileged areas of the cities could cost even more.

But the implications of inferior schooling are not the most serious while the student is in school, but at the point of drop-out from high school, when vocational or other occupational training may be needed, or on graduation, when competition for admission to college results in many graduates being turned away. In states like California, where the state attempts to provide higher education at various levels of academic proficiency, the investment of the state in higher education facilities is one of the most potent forces in urbanization. The development of a new campus is the signal for the growth of a new town or the expansion of a sleepy or stagnant community into a booming city.

Finally, whatever the career courses taken by the eighteen-and-over age group, within five or ten years after high school they will marry and form households in large numbers. The housing industry and the hundreds of products associated with it depend on a vigorous rate of family formation. The babies born between 1946 and 1952 will be in the marrying age group during the latter half of the sixties and the early seventies. We may expect a new wave of demand for inexpensive housing, similar to the V.A. push following World War II, and again we may expect to see that search lead to the outskirts of cities where land is cheapest (unless this group is willing and able to occupy older sections which have somehow been forced down in price).

Labor Force Consequences of Demographic Composition

Considered in conjunction with estimates of economic growth and technological developments—particularly automation and "cybernation"—the present labor force potential poses a serious urban-planning problem. We have met the problem tangentially in the consideration of the Negro and the adolescent in the city. The portion of the population able to enter the labor force depends on demographic factors, and the portion actually making itself available for work depends on cultural as well as economic considerations. The portion actually at work depends, of course, on the state of the economy and on the character of productive technique used in a given level of output; it is also dependent on the social organization of the work force and this has an effect on the spatial organization of the city, and is affected by it.

The main demographic factor to be considered is the size of the work force potential in the years ahead, for that size is large compared with the probable demand for labor, given continuation of the other conditions mentioned. The "productive" age groups will be swollen with many new arrivals from adolescent ranks—some 26 million will be entering the job market in the sixties. (Despite the attrition of death, age, illness, and voluntary withdrawal, this bulge will push net annual addition to the labor force to at least 3 million a year by 1970.) In addition, a higher percentage of women will be in the labor force and since there will be a higher portion of women in the population, this, too, will represent an incremental factor.

If there are jobs for these labor force participants—and that is by no means assured—they are likely to be forming families. As gainfully employed young marrieds, where will they choose to live? With what will they want to equip households?

But even more important, what will happen to social organization of the labor force in the struggle to find reasonably "full employment," and how will the reorganization affect the city?

Consider the possibility that the time-input of the individual worker is cut to spread the work. If this cut takes the form of reducing the work week, holding the work day constant (some production experts feel that the work day is now at minimum length for efficiency of operation), the obvious outcome will be still longer weekends. This could signal a whole range of urban rearrangements:

more two-house living, with a semiweekly rhythm of oscillation between "exurb" and town apartment; the possibility of spreading some of the weekend shore and mountain traffic crush to other days of the week; revision of the shopping patterns—perhaps an end to the sharp differentiation of weekend from weekdays in stores, clubs, and so on. For any breakthrough in the present pattern will expose the archaic and obsolete roots of the prevailing diurnal and seasonal pattern. If the "spreading" seeks to take the form of shorter hours per day—as foreshadowed in the New York electricians' agreement—it could mean real realignment of the morning and evening traffic jam stoked by the journey to work. With much of the city on a two-shift basis—and the five-hour day scarcely lends itself to any other arrangement if a serious effort is made to utilize capital intensively—a markedly different physical pattern of the city could develop. With the time at work absolutely less, the individual worker—depending on the possibilities and inclinations for moonlighting, and other job opportunities—might be willing to accept an even longer journey to work than is presently the case. This could lead to more dispersed settlement. The shift arrangements could be a "one-step stagger"—with two peaks —or further staggered, to provide several lower peaks in commuter load. If workers maintained roughly the present average journey-to-work and home-residence pattern, the result could take the form either of a great expansion of the cultural and recreational opportunities near or connected with the workplace or of a similar expansion at or near the residence.

With the shorter work day and spreading of the labor input, the possibility of economically decentralizing productive plants might actually be reduced. With two shifts doing the work of the former one, the plant must assemble twice as many workers (measured by individuals with separate residence). But this means access to a labor pool of twice the size, and in some locations this may not be feasible. Thus the external economies of access to the labor pool may actually be more important with the "spread the work" schemes.

Another answer to the changing balance between population and labor force requirements is a gradual change in the labor force participation age at the upper end of the distribution. Earlier retirement has the social appeal of "reward" for those who have worked rather than "denial" of the opportunity to work, whatever the appeal of the experienced worker to his employer or the former's attachment to his job. With the aid of Social Security, pension funds, and assorted employee participation plans, many workers now retire at sixty or sixty-five. An advancement of the age of eligibility or earlier compulsory retirement could open positions for youthful job seekers.

Putting aside the merits of this proposal and considering only its impact on urban settlement, early retirement might be expected to be a force accelerating the movement of population to such amenity centers as Florida and California. The number of persons in the population who will be over sixty-five in 1975 is estimated by Census sources as 21 million. By advancing retirement to age fifty-five, for even one-third of the group in the labor force, we would add about 6 million to the retirement rolls. The retired cadre would be about 30 percent of the size of the labor force.

Retirement breaks the residential tie to workplace and frees the former worker for shift of location with the seasons or at his pleasure. Whereas the normal life-cycle aging may lead to exchange of dwelling unit for another better suited to the size needs of the expanding or contracting family, retirement may signal a dramatic break with place. In addition to the migration to Florida, Arizona, and California, there has been a substantial contribution by elder persons to the mobile homes market. Both these trends will continue, and they would be substantially speeded up by an extensive policy of early retirement. About one-third of the people in the United States are tied to a regular place of work, and many of these are undoubtedly retired persons who have acquired jobs outside the fields of their regular long-time employment. Such jobs may be necessary to supplement social security or retirement benefits. The supply of these jobs in areas of high amenity is one of the limitations on further shifts of older people to the areas. Various service industries now provide the bulk of this employment, and the automation of services could further reduce opportunity in the over–sixty-five job market.

Because, unlike natural resources, people incorporate feedback information into their decisions and adapt their behavior accordingly, population is not a passive boundary condition in urban development. The fertility cycles are evidence of this. Fertility accompanies early marriage. In our country early marriage may mean earlier entry into the labor force (and for some, postponement of or withdrawal from higher education). We experienced a "baby boom" in the early postwar period of the late forties and early fifties. This kind of boom may, however, soon be self-correcting.

If the high labor force influx generated by above-average postwar fertility is not matched by a corresponding growth of jobs, and if lack of job opportunity postpones marriage and child bearing and encourages delay in entry into the labor force, there will be a decline in the fertility rate, if not in numbers born, at the full maturing of the postwar babies. For the cities, however, demand that does not show up in one form will appear in another, usually with Federal stimulation. The "drop" in the labor force of 314,000 persons observed in the year 1961–1962 may be a symptom of the response of women and youth to the decline in job opportunities in 1961. Many of the young people who do not find the job picture attractive will show up in public educational programs, some at the higher levels. Married women who do not return to school for more training may displace domestic workers, tightening that market. In the main, however, the most important effect will be the postponement of marriage and childbearing, for this will appear in the future years as an easing of potential pressure on housing and school demand.

Regional differences in job opportunity are difficult to estimate, but it is clear that the bulk of the jobs in the seventies will be found in the metropolitan areas. There is little likelihood that any "back to the country" movement will ease the population pressure on the urban areas. The extractive industries have not only become more highly mechanized with each year, but they are becoming increasingly transformed into chemical industries that benefit from the external economies of urban areas, including the research facilities. For some time at least, the most abundant source of jobs will be in the urban service industries. Ultimately, however, the relatively high cost of services will lead to some mechanization and eventual automation, with substitution of machines for people. An early sign of this can be seen in the new self-service dry-cleaning machines, which are invading one of the traditional strongholds of the services. The teaching machines, though now confined to classroom use, are another example. What will happen to the traditional neighborhood when the school can be carried about, the corner cleaner is obsolete, and the grocery store is entirely automated? Perhaps the barber shop will continue to be a gathering place, but even this is not secure.

Technical Changes Affecting the Physical City

As an artifact of our culture, the city is bound to be affected by changes in the productive techniques of that culture, which we label "technology." A long procession of economic historians has paraded the evidence for the impact of mode of production on city size and form. Students of industrial location have filled in this historical march with a rationale for the decisions of the decisive enterprises. In recent years we have noted a marked change in the terms on which these decisions have been made. Where once location was largely dictated by considerations of "weightlosing," movement toward the point where resource assembly costs and marketing costs were an optimum trade-off, we have been witnessing a steady decline of the influence of these factors.

This development was predicted by Patrick Geddes, who saw, well before our time, the general movement of the technology from mechanical technique to chemical and electronic transformations. In the latter the traditional transport cost considerations have shrunk with the declining importance of "weight," and chemical advances have made possible the utilization of relatively ubiquitous, less

"special" resources. This long-range perspective tends to vindicate Mumford's agitation in the thirties for the application of a "neotechnic" technology to American cities.

The shift from the locational economics of a coal-powered steel-fabricated economy to those of plastics, silicates, and synthetics should not be allowed to obscure an even more significant development: the rise of a communications technology that threatens to burst the bounds of place for many traditional functions. The very term "communication" is more general and pervasive than "production" or "distribution." It stands simply for interaction, though the transmittal of information is usually also implied. Ways of achieving this interaction—which is ultimately the reason for the assembly of people in urban places—have been undergoing the most rapid development.

If transportation technology is considered along with communication technology, the alteration of place ties is made more apparent. But the larger changes to come will be the result of the modification not only of ways of reaching places, but of the very reasons for going to them. Transportation technology, particularly with the jet airplane, reached a stage of development in the fifties when long-time quantitative changes introduced real qualitative differences. The fact that the country is only "five hours wide and two hours deep" for those with the money to fly has made possible appearances by businessmen or politicians on both coasts in the same working day (provided they travel west). Under the impact of jet travel, a new hierarchy of urban places has been developing which adds to the "clumping" of cities in "megalopolitan" centers. A study of the geography of air travel by Edward J. Taaffe shows the emergence of four dominant centers in the nation: New York, Chicago, Los Angeles–San Francisco (which in the jet age is, however it may horrify natives of the latter, one port), and Dallas-Houston. Each of these has a distinct hinterland for "collecting" traffic and a well-defined pattern of exchange with the others.

This agglomeration of activity around the larger center is enormously facilitated by the rapid development of an expressway-highway network, which greatly reduces travel time to the metropolis from surrounding cities and towns. (The extent to which time is reduced is understated by simply comparing road time with existing rail or common carrier schedules. A great part of the saving comes from the ability to leave at will, without regard to the waiting time required by fixed schedules.) As a result of these developments, the functional boundaries of the metropolis have been greatly expanded, whatever the permanence of its political boundaries. Substantial areas of land are thereby "opened" to settlement, in the sense that they are possible locations for actors in the affairs of our society and afford potential bases for discharging given functions.

Development of communication technology has tended to make the smaller cities and open spaces within the metropolitan area convenient as well as physically assessible sites for carrying on business. The telephone—which Americans utilize more intensively and extensively than any people in the world—establishes the minimum contact, though it has a relatively narrow band of communication possibilities. Television has greatly extended the potential for place-to-place communication, though it has been largely one-way thus far. The telephone is reasonably close to the limits of its exploitation in business

use. Americans own phones at the rate of 38 per hundred persons, compared with a world average of 4.3 phones per hundred. We could reach a situation in which virtually no adult was ever out of reach of a phone before doubling this rate. At present, the desire to escape from the contact by phone and to secure some privacy from its signals has reached significant proportions with many people, and this flight from overly insistent modes of communication may grow.

The business uses of television have scarcely been tapped. Thus far they have been confined to the occasional closed-circuit sales talk and spying on shoplifters. As two-way communication becomes more convenient, we may expect a substantial replacement of trips to consummate business dealings of all kinds (in the course of which many legal problems of the validity of certain contracts and other agreements are bound to be raised). Further advances in transistors will make possible a highly economic sending and receiving apparatus for future television equipment. Wide use of microfilm, magnetic tapes, and other data-storing devices has already had a potential space-economizing impact on the business district, though expansion of space-use per person by executives has masked this development.

By successive reduction of weight/output and information/transmission cost ratios, the technology has made possible greater concentration of activity at a given point. At the same time, these developments permit any chosen point to be reached more easily from a wider range of locations. The resulting pattern has been one of polarization of activities on a national scale, with dispersion within metropolitan regions.

Technology alone does not determine this pattern. It is the outcome of the indirect effects of technological change—especially as manifest through income effects—in combination with our mode of social and economic organization. The rise in real income—and improvement in transportation techniques must be reckoned an important contribution to this rise—has permitted more people to indulge a preference for more space per person, particularly land space. The decentralization of land-use decisions and private ownership of land, business, and other resources, have, in turn, permitted the expression of these individual preferences, both basic characteristics of our mode of social and economic organization.

Thus, while New York City has become ever more ascendant in the national decision scene and has gained as a seat of power and clearing house for an ever-greater volume of actions and decisions, its gross population density has fallen to one-fourth its level of a century ago. Since World War II, New York City has constructed more new office space than all the other large cities of the nation combined, but the population density of Manhattan, where this building is concentrated, has declined. According to Henry Cohen, the present density of Manhattan is only 25 percent higher than the gross density for all New York City in 1860. The New York example shows dramatically the combined centralizing and decentralizing forces of our technology at work. The nation-shrinking technology of jet airplanes, telephones and television, and other devices has made it possible to administer nationwide enterprises effectively from a single location in New York. At the same time New Yorkers themselves have been enabled to purchase four times as much space per person as their nineteenth-century predecessors by growth in income,

relative cheapness of automobiles, public support of highway building, extension of utilities, favorable home financing, and so forth.

Throughout our four jet-based metropolitan complexes similar effects can be noted. Within the older cities, moreover, an effect analogous to that taking place on the national scale is observable. Population activities are simultaneously moving farther out toward the periphery and building up the inner core, leaving the intermediate "grey" areas to wither. This is at once the effect of greater functional specialization of areas and changing allocation of time by consumers. The grey areas, moreover, have just the wrong density for the present-day tastes—they are too dense for the automobile-based style of life and neither concentrated nor central enough for the high-value transactions of the core city. Left behind by changing family and ethnic composition, by changing income and tastes, they are not valuable enough locationally to justify writing off the substantial "sunk" investments in streets, utilities, buildings, and institutions in private—or even public—redevelopment. In consequence of this functional obsolescence, they receive little new investment and serve chiefly as entrepots for the new inmigrants to the city.

At the national level a corresponding polarization of activity may be observed. Though California and the Pacific Coast generally have been experiencing rapid population growth, and the former is now the largest state in numbers, the center of gravity of the nation's population has not shifted markedly westward. Rather, the population has shifted more dramatically from the interstices between the boundaries of the metropolitan regions toward the metro centers, with some tendency to move toward all the coasts—Atlantic, Gulf, Pacific, and Lakes—and an inevitable evening-out toward the less densely occupied South and West. True, California has special attractions which permit it both to be more selective in its attractiveness and get more than its share: but this is just the case of the prettiest girl at the Cotillion at which all will dance.

For the national as well as the metropolitan distribution has its grey areas. Over half the living Americans born in Arkansas no longer live there, and half the rural population of Oklahoma left the state in the decade 1940–1950. The Great Interior of the nation is hollowing out, with the population being drawn toward the periphery, despite the presumed greater vulnerability of the coasts to wartime attacks. In the world of jet air travel there is no need for passengers to stop at the intervening interior towns, and there is a strong incentive for population to be within at least the outer ring of the metro-area, where the expressways will provide convenient links with the metropolitan transport center. Since industry is less resource-based and more market-oriented, and since the people are moving into the coastal metropolitan areas, the whole process is self-reinforcing.

Some Economic Restraints on Urban Expansion

Can our economy afford to write off the capital invested in the grey areas of the nation and the cities? Clearly, the public costs of allowing individuals to realize the full potential of the rising standards of living and corporations to compete in following the markets have to be considered in national economic policy. National policies—from subsidy of the airlines to cost-plus contracts for defense research organizations—have strengthened the tendencies toward national metropolitanization. Within metropolitan areas, the generous no-down-payment V.A. financing and the policies of the FHA. have undoubtedly contributed to the *drangnach*-suburbs of the post World War II era. Is this permissive policy beginning to run up against the friction of fiscal woes?

Collapse of the land quest of urban dwellers has been widely predicted for at least a decade, with rising suburban public costs and taxes most frequently given as the reason. Per capita spending by local government increased at a rate of 7 percent a year toward the end of the 1950s, chiefly as a result of rising costs for public education and the arriving bulge of school-age children. The less-dense pattern of land occupancy adds costs, and the opening of new areas of settlement has the effect of greatly concentrating this burden —at least socially—in the write-off period of the underutilized facilities left behind. The cost of the community facilities required by a new dwelling unit in the typical suburban subdivision is equal to, or exceeds, the $15,000 average cost of the house. If Luther Gulick's figure of $1100 average urban investment per capita is applied to the expected increase of 30 million in urban population in the 1960s, an increment of $33 billion in urban investment will be required over the decade. In our ACTION study, Reginald Isaacs and I calculated that almost four times that amount would be required by a twelve-year program which would aim at completely renewing all urban areas in the country, at the same time providing for new urban growth.[7] Our total would have been greatly reduced by the simple policy expedient of forsaking investment in the national grey areas and by "rationalizing" the internal structure of metropolitan areas. But even under the unreal and ambitious presumption that local goals would be accorded equal priority and all local plans would be realized up to some minimum level, the somewhat surprising fact emerges that the entire bill of goods for urban spending is less than the accumulated ten-year difference in the present rate of growth in our economy and the 5 percent a year "forced draft" rate advocated by the influential Rockefeller Brothers Fund Report of 1958.

Taking our economy as a unit, and looking only at its absolute level of affluence, it is apparent that we can afford the cost of our present pattern. It is also apparent that a more efficient pattern could be achieved from the standpoint of conserving the national supply of capital. But the political decisions to save and reallocate these funds are not made by a national planning board, and in the absence of such central direction, allocations are made by the various markets. There is little doubt that the present pattern is responsive to market demand and reflects some measure of consumer sovereignty. If "amenity" is considered a legitimate consumer good, we may say that the community welfare is enhanced by the successful pursuit of space-amenities and climate-amenities by so many Americans. The claims of planners that these amenities, or comparable ones, can be more efficiently produced by other patterns of development will be heard only to the extent that we are willing to relax our goals of freedom of enterprise decisions and consumer self-determination. In the meantime, the distribution of these amenities—natural or man made—becomes the most significant resource base in the locational pattern of the economy.

The Problem of Governmental Organization

Those limits to the realization of the "free enterprise" pattern of land occupation that are presently most serious arise out of the organization of government itself. The overspill of old political boundaries in the growth of the metropolis and the imbalances in legislatures occasioned by the shifts of population between states and regions have vexed our whole present generation of political scientists. The functional metropolis of the present day is an envelope of hundreds of governments and quasi-governments. Unfortunately for some, the taxables are poorly distributed, as are the service loads. And unfortunately for all, local government in general, having relinquished the most important taxes to the Federal and state governments, has been handicapped by limited tax powers.

The political scientist and public administration expert see the functional city split into scores of taxing units without regard to functions, hamstrung on tax leeway, and burdened with new, higher service demands stimulated by the rising expectations of a more affluent population. Since the new technology is so effective in overcoming space frictions, and since the metropolitan area is so well tied together by the spreading highway transportation network, it seems only too obvious that the solution is to consolidate the various governments and form a new level, metropolitan government. Even in metropolitan areas which do not span state lines—thereby complicating this issue—the response to the idea of metropolitan government by citizens has not been enthusiastic.

One explanation for the lack of enthusiasm for the METRO idea has been the class and ethnic ecology of the various constituent communities and their competitive stakes in independence. Another could be the tremendous stake in existing arrangements enjoyed by the multitudinous officials administering the present pattern. Whatever the forces militating against metropolitanization of the administration of cities, and however lukewarm citizen response, it appears likely that the very recognition of these regions by the Federal government in its programs will strengthen *de facto* metro bodies. In fact, the Federal government, since it operates largely through the state apparatus in its grants and assistance programs, will create a vested interest for state planning in recognizing these metro regions.

In an era in which many more citizens literally have two or more homes, what is going to happen to traditional political organization around the place of residence? First, note that political representation accorded *place* is already breaking down. The recent Supreme Court rulings in the cases of organization of the electorate in Tennessee and Michigan have dealt a severe blow to the representation of geographic areas and have leant weight to the doctrine of the equal representation of individuals. In part this is a reflection of the wider understanding of the functional unity and interdependence of states and the nation. It is a relatively short step from this appreciation to the acceptance of the functional unity of metropolitan areas, though there will undoubtedly continue to be a lag in elevating this understanding to a principle of organization, for the reasons that Edward Banfield and others have stressed—that is, we could have more Teterboros and Emeryvilles, as well as Winnetkas and New Canaans.[8] But politically, this simply transfers the problem of representation and control to a higher level. In the case of the vital issue of taxation and finance, this power and control, has largely drifted to the Federal Government, where it has been substantially augmented by the great power of allocation of defense contracts, currently such an important part of the national business. If we cannot get metropolitan government, and I am willing to concede that voluntary consolidation is highly improbable, it is likely that we will see states, where they correspond to or contain whole metropolitan regions, organize services on a regional basis. This is all the more likely if the power of rural legislators over state government is broken in the urban-rural states. Then the way will be clear for the urban areas to demand such service.

One advantage of the state involvement with metropolitan affairs will be the potential for exercising state controls over problems—such as air pollution and water pollution—which cannot be confined to the single community, or worse, which often lead to competition between communities. The case of the Los Angeles smog is a good example. Since automobiles are licensed by the state and are free to travel anywhere in its domain, the state of California has undertaken to combat the smog-generating exhaust of automobiles—which is felt chiefly in Los Angeles, with its concentration of autos and particular climatic conditions—by requiring suppressors on all autos registered in the state. At least area-wide jurisdiction is required for the effective handling of air or water pollution by industry, since the ratables provided by plants are highly desired, while the effects of the pollution are shared by communities which do not reap the tax benefits.

The response of the consumer to controls—whether economic or political—is one of the crucial unanswered questions of the future of the cities. In the past, the American consumer has responded to rationing by black markets and to zoning by subversion (though we may take some comfort in the fact that more law-abiding nations, Germany, for example, have been capable of activities, which, while never antisocial, were sometimes antihuman). From the earliest days of the American cities, the citizens have demonstrated the keenest interest in individual achievements and the most profound indifference to the publicly managed environment. Accounts of the early development of the queenly cities of the Ohio Valley, like Louisville and Cincinnati, stress the beauty of the homes and the churches and refer only in passing to the fact that the sewage ran in a stream down the center of the unpaved streets and pigs roamed the sidewalks long after the cities were well built-up.

As the total population of a metropolitan area becomes of an order of tens of millions, nonetheless, certain problems reach the critical stage, however dispersed the residential settlement. Air pollution, water pollution, and the obdurate transportation issue are not alleviated by lower density residential development so long as the central city remains a focus of the activity. If these byproducts of high volumes of activity in the city cannot be controlled, the limits of city size will soon be reached. Signs of the feedback influence of these nuisances can be observed in the decisions of enterprises to escape from city traffic to suburban locations, and in a few cases to small towns, and in moves from Los Angeles to Phoenix to escape the smog. In the grand frontier tradition, many Americans still seem to feel that the most effective vote is cast with one's feet.

The time is not far away, however, when the supply of unspoiled places will be virtually used up. At that time the citizen will need to face the choice of the pattern and density of settlement and the survival of the city more squarely. This responsibility will sometimes be difficult to locate. Pollution of streams, for example, is exacerbated by the huge quantities of discharged detergents emptied into the water by urban sewage systems. In the United States, these detergents are made from alkylaryl sulfatonate, a product of the petroleum industry, which does not break up in the bacterial action of treatment plants but floats downstream on top of the water, creating a harmful film on the surface. Germany has recently passed a law requiring the use of biodegradable detergents, which will break down in treatment. Any move in that direction in the United States, if it could get past the obstacles that would be thrown up by the oil companies and soap companies, would also have to survive the clamor of consumers, who might have to pay higher prices for detergents if existing arrangements were disturbed.

The optimism of the American consumer, who seems to feel that every ill generated by quirks of taste can be met by the development of a remedial product, is not disposed to put the brakes on present trends in the urban culture. Campaigns which have been remarkably successful elsewhere, like the British smoking–lung cancer publicity, do not seem to dim the enthusiasm of the American consumer for following where his taste leads. On this evidence, there is no justification for the sanguine expectation that the American city dweller will give up the automobile as a means of commuting to work and will take to mass transit in large numbers. For a time, the best for which we can hope is that transit can hold its own in those few cities where it is still very important. Ultimately, if this base is preserved, we may be able to build upon it in the future, when a major break-through in urban transit can be realized and the attractive flexibility and convenience of the automobile can be combined with the compactness, speed, and efficiency of the mass transit carrier.

Control of Land Development

If we seem committed, for a time to come, to the automobile city, are we equally fastened to the present pattern of land development? Unless we are willing to pursue a policy requiring an incredible amount of political courage—the effective expropriation of speculative values established in the inner rings of metropolitan areas—it seems likely that we are. The sprawling character of the major metropolitan areas is largely dictated by the action of the real estate (particularly, land) market. As development proceeds on the periphery of the city, with the extension of streets, utilities, and services, land prices rise rapidly. When those prices are too high for speculative builders and other buyers, there is pressure to extend the urbanized area farther out, leaving behind the hard core of "over-priced" vacant land. In rapidly growing areas, and with the aid of the popular expressways, this process has been greatly speeded up in recent years. The cheap houses which official governmental policies favor can be built most easily on the cheapest land— which typically is farthest out from the center city.

The most direct way to achieve a less "scattered" pattern—short of governmental invasion of the private building business—is by "squeezing out" the value of the unbuilt-upon land in the inner rings, thereby accelerating a ripeness for development which normally would come about only when the whole region was so large that the high-value center would overspill the sites. But squeezing out is a painful process. It is equivalent to expropriation of developmental value—even though that value may be realizable within the time period hoped for by the holder. Many schemes, from the Henry George single-tax to various compensation devices, have been proposed to "compact" development. All involve some limitation on the freedom of action of the entrepreneur dealing in land, and all would require mobilization of political force.

It should be clear that the prevailing clamor for urban "open space" must be dovetailed with land development policy. Scatteration leaves many open spaces; indeed, this is the source of much of the criticism of it. The spaces left "open" in scattered or dispersed development are themselves spread about, usually are not in large contiguous lumps, and tend to be in private hands which hold out prospects for future development. In contrast, open spaces sought by the land planners are of the nature of greenbelts. To achieve the latter it would be necessary not only to compact development, but also to secure large tracts of adjoining land against future development. Again, the most direct way to achieve this is by public acquisition. There is no easy way.

If the present pattern of land development prevails, we have been told, the open space around cities will disappear. The Regional Plan Association of New York, for example, has pointed out that if prevailing zoning restrictions on sizes of residential lots in suburban areas were to be maintained, the future population of the New York region would occupy all the land now open. Of course, the simple application of this arithmetic disguises the very operation of the land market which concerns us. Aside from the question of whether four-acre zoning would be maintained in the face of sufficient economic demand (an unlikely prospect in view of past experience), there is the obvious action of demand on prices of land. Demand would in this case push the prices so high in a short time that consumers who would be able to buy such lavish amounts of space could not be found in large numbers. Thus it is most unlikely that all the open space around any metropolitan center will be fully occupied into the relatively distant future. The real issues are the relative desirability of scattered open space compared with solid blocks of open space and the relative desirability of large-scale intervention in the land market compared with freedom to pursue profit in this market.

In all this discussion, we have not allowed the consumer scope to be perverse. More from lack of space than for lack of interest we have avoided the speculative exploration of taste, leadership, and style effects. Conceivably, by some miracle of devious status seeking, the subway train could be elevated to high fashion or the streetcar made fashionable for party going as well as for journeying to work. Conceivably, too, consumers might react with distaste to lawns, trees, shrubs, and ground around the house. It is not improbable that once two-way closed-circuit television is common, great importance will be attached to face-to-face contacts, the telephone will decline as a primary business instrument, and meeting places in the center city will have even greater importance than at present.

For the only thing certain about consumer behavior is that it is restless and ever seeking. It is our cross that the urban pattern for which we must plan and set policy is still shaped in large measure by such behavior. But most of us would not really want it otherwise.

NOTES

1. "The Changing Uses of the City," *Daedalus* (Winter 1961).
2. Kenneth Boulding, "The Death of the City," Harvard Conference on the City in History, Summer 1961.
3. *Ibid.*
4. Richard L. Meier, Address to the American Institute of Planners' Annual Meeting, Detroit, Michigan, November 1961.
5. Jack Lessinger, "The Rural-Urban Fringe—Study of Santa Clara Valley," unpublished manuscript.
6. James Conant, *Slums and Suburbs*, (New York: McGraw-Hill, 1961).
7. J. W. Dyckman, R. R. Isaacs, and P. R. Senn *Capital Requirements for Urban Development and Renewal* (New York: McGaw-Hill, 1961).
8. E. C. Banfield and M. Meyerson *Politics, Planning and the Public Interest* (Glencoe, Illinois: Free Press, 1955).

ted Sociocultural Aspects of Urban Ecology

31. The Consumer Votes by Moving

Janet Abu-Lughod
and
Mary Mix Foley

Residential mobility is a basic ecological process, and the question of why people move has long interested urban scholars. This form of mobility is associated with neighborhood invasion, population succession, and the other large-scale processes identified with the concept of urban growth. Janet Abu-Lughod and Mary Mix Foley review the research literature dealing with the subject. They cite the evidence to show that approximately one-fifth of the American population change their dwelling units each year. Most of this migration consists of movement within the region of residence. It is especially marked among families with young children, people who rent rather than own their dwellings, and those who are in the lower income groups. The propensity to move reflects dissatisfaction with the space available in the house, rather than with shortcomings in the design of the dwelling or with the problems of the neighborhood. Residential mobility motivated by a concern about the adequacy of the space within the house apparently has been increasing since 1900. The authors conclude their paper by examining the implications of these research findings for predicting the future course of metropolitan expansion.

Janet Abu-Lughod is Associate Professor of Sociology at Northwestern University. Mary Mix Foley coauthored *Modern Church Architecture* (1962).

Mobility occurs when the occupant of a dwelling vacates it to establish residence in another one. By moving, the consumer adapts his housing to his changing needs and also expresses his preferences and values on the housing market. The degree of residential turnover can therefore be a sensitive index to the rapidity with which consumer needs and preferences are changing, and—less sensitively—to the efficiency with which the housing stock is satisfying these demands. In attempting to make such inferences, however, it is important to differentiate between mobility which is the result of actual housing dissatisfaction and that which has other causes.

About 20 percent of the United States civilian population changes its address annually.[1] Of this group of movers, nearly two-thirds (or about 13 percent of the total population) travel only short distances, remaining within the same community or county. These movers are trying primarily to adjust housing to household needs and preferences. The remaining one-third (or about 7 percent of the population as a whole) go longer distances, migrating to another county or even to a new state or region. Although a change in housing is a by-product of these latter moves, it is seldom the motivating factor. Most long-distance migrants are moving in hope of better working opportunities, as a result of actual job transfers or offers, or (especially if retired or in ill health) in search of a pleasanter climate.

The rates of both types of mobility are important in estimating housing demand and in describing the pattern of growth experienced by metropolitan areas. Statistics on long-distance mobility are of particular value in relation to migratory movements. High mobility into a specific region requires a larger housing stock than does regional stability. Thus the

regions of in-migration (traditionally the West Coast) may experience housing shortages out of proportion to the situation in other parts of the country. Since this long-distance mobility is related primarily to job of climate considerations, it has little to do with satisfactions or dissatisfactions of a housing nature and reveals little about housing preferences.

Short-range mobility, on the other hand, and the stated reasons for the change in residence, do reflect consumer attitudes toward housing. But even within this group there are exceptions. Of the approximately 13 percent of the population which makes short-distance moves each year, some 2 to 3 percent can be classified as involuntary movers. Their dwellings have been taken away from them through fire, demolition, forced sale, or eviction. Another 1 percent or more move because a new family desiring an independent household has been formed out of members of previous households. Perhaps only 8 percent of all families are actually moving voluntarily this year because of dissatisfaction with their current dwelling. Thus, it is clear that, although 20 per cent of the population moves each year, only about two-fifths of this number can be considered as an index to changing consumer needs and preferences which are strong enough to produce mobility. Without any inherent dissatisfaction with the dwelling occupied, a certain amount of mobility is both logical and necessary.

Abnormal conditions also diminish the direct logical consequence of dissatisfaction. A housing shortage lowers mobility rates even when dissatisfaction is high.

From *Housing Choices and Housing Constraints* by Foote, Abu-Lughod, Foley & Winnick. Copyright © 1960 by McGraw-Hill, Inc. Used by permission.

This situation was typical of the war and early postwar period. Rises in cost of better dwellings can also reduce mobility. This is quite obvious in the case of the low-income consumer who cannot afford to improve his housing. But cost inequities can occur even when the desired housing is of objectively lower value, as under rent control. There have been many instances of small "uncontrolled" apartments costing must more than larger "controlled" ones, thus distorting the normal tendency of families to adjust their space requirements. Another example is that of the aging homeowner who, having paid off his mortgage debt, is restrained from seeking smaller quarters by their higher out-of-pocket costs.

Even when opportunities offered by the housing market are quite adequate, a time lag may occur between dissatisfaction and an actual move. In periods of normal vacancy, there is ample evidence that less than half the consumers who are dissatisfied with their housing actually translate their desire to move into action.[2] Although these restraints on mobility may obscure the housing discontent which exists, extreme mobility clearly indicates consumer dissatisfaction. High rates of mobility may arise from rapidly changing consumer needs and standards which outstrip the ability of the housing market to provide appropriate dwellings. Or they may be the penalty for a previous era of insensitivity to the desires of consumers. Mobility in its most exaggerated form—for instance, the rapid turnover of dwellings in a declining neighborhood—is in itself destructive, wasting resources, speeding deterioration, and disorganizing the community.

From the above examples it can be seen that some forms of mobility play a positive role in the appropriate allocation of housing, whereas other forms of mobility (or barriers to it) may have a negative effect. In a rational operation of the housing market, logical change of dwelling to meet changing family circumstances should probably be facilitated. Ideally, also, some attempt should be made to lessen change of dwelling due to shortcomings of the housing stock or its environment.

Since this study is limited to existing surveys and since these deal primarily with mobile consumers, the chapter will concentrate on defining those groups within the population who do move and on isolating the most important causes of their mobility. However, some studies have been undertaken which measure "mobility potential," the number of families who wish to move or are contemplating a move. In this way, at least some of the latent housing dissatisfaction can be gauged. The various mobility patterns—both long- and short-distance—will also be considered as they affect the different parts of the metropolis, specifically the city proper as against the suburbs.

The Mobile Housing Consumer

As has been stated previously, approximately 20 percent of the civilian population moves each year. If a different 20 percent of the population moved each year, a full 100 percent of the population would have changed residences by the end of five years. Instead, over a five-year period, 50 to 60 percent of the population change their address. After ten years, approximately 75 percent have moved; by the end of twenty years, 90 percent of the population are no longer living in the homes they occupied at the beginning of that period (see Figure 1).[3]

For the purposes of this study, the five-year interval has been selected. Individuals

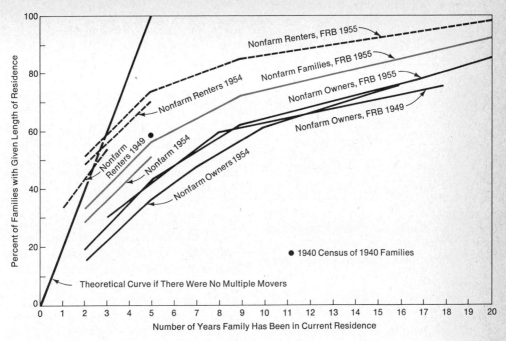

Figure 1. The multiple mover. Actual duration-of-occupancy curves compared with theoretical curve. Note: Percent above line are stable; percent below line are mobile.

and families who have moved once or more during that period are classified as "mobile," the remainder as relatively stable. However, a further refinement can be made by isolating the multiple mover. Only one study of a national urban sample contains the information needed to estimate his role.[4] This poll found that 53 percent (1,320 persons) of the 2,490 interviewed had moved once or more during the preceding five years, to produce a total of 3,290 moves for the survey group. A small minority, 15 percent of the total interviewed, made three or more moves during the time period and accounted for over half of the total moves made by the entire group. This restless minority can be termed extremely mobile.

Translated into number of population rather than percentages (and transferred from a sample group to a national level

and from a 1940 population to a 1956 one of 170 million),[5] this means that some 90 million people in the United States move one or more times within five years and that of these, 25½ million move three or more times. On the other hand, nearly 80 million persons do not move at all.

The characteristics of the mobile 90 million, accentuated by the very mobile 25½ million, are roughly sketched below.

The Characteristics of Movers

Renters Are More Likely to Move Than Owners Mobility rates for renters are, on the average, twice to three times as high as those for owners. This difference is evident no matter what data sources are consulted. Figure 2 combines all national mobility rates which distinguish between owners and renters. Rates for renters are in every case substantially above those for owners. In no case do the rates come within 20 points of each other.

KEY TO SOURCES

Year	Numbers	Data collector
1934–36	2, 3, 4, 12, 16, 21	WPA
1940	8, 20	U.S. Census
1949	7, 11, 13, 17	Federal
1954	1, 6, 9, 14, 18	Reserve
1955	5, 10, 15, 19	Board

Several reasons for this differential are obvious. Renters are, on the average, younger than homeowners and are therefore less likely to have achieved what they consider to be a permanent housing solution. In Branch's study, nearly four-fifths of respondents under thiry years of

Figure 2. Percentage of U.S. nonfarm owner and renter households or families which had moved to present dwelling less than one, two, three, four, or five years before survey date.

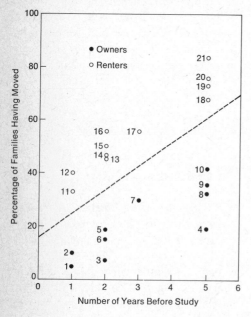

age expressed a preference for owning, but only a little more than one-fourth of this group had translated desire into mortgage payments, as compared with two-thirds of those over fifty. Since their rental quarters are often considered little more than a temporary expedient, these are quite likely to be exchanged for more suitable accommodations if such become available, whether the new dwelling be another rental unit or owned housing.

In general, also, the consumer believes that the rental dwelling is less suited to family needs than is the owned home. The reason for this belief is at least partly founded in fact. Owned housing is predominantly the single-family detached house with a yard, but two-thirds of all rental units are in multifamily structures. Figure 3, which gives yearly mobility rates for housing of various types under different tenure forms, shows that families who own homes are least likely to have moved to them within the year. On the other hand, families renting apartments in multifamily structures are most likely to have moved to them recently (one-third of such families have occupied their dwellings for under a year). The higher mobility rates for renters can therefore be partly explained in terms of the type of housing which renting implies.

However, if this were the only reason, those renters who do not live in apartments, but rent single-family houses, should be no more likely to move than homeowners. Instead, they show a mobility rate exactly midway between that for apartment renters and single-family homeowners. Therefore, there must be other differences between the rental and owner groups beyond the type of housing which they occupy.

Of first importance among these residual differences is doubtless the predilection of

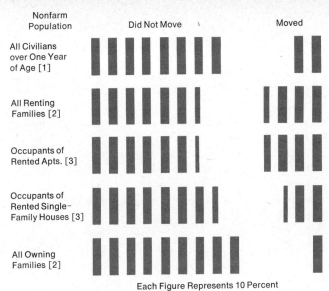

Nonfarm Population	Did Not Move	Moved

All Civilians over One Year of Age [1]

All Renting Families [2]

Occupants of Rented Apts. [3]

Occupants of Rented Single-Family Houses [3]

All Owning Families [2]

Each Figure Represents 10 Percent

Figure 3. Percentage moving each year by tenure class. (Source: [1] U.S. Bureau of the Census, computed average 1948–1955, from annual figures appearing in selected issues of *Current Population Reports*. [2] "Survey of Consumer Finances," *Federal Reserve Bulletin*, reprinted from selected issues. [3] Theoretical estimate derived by applying a mobility rate 50 percent higher for apartment renters than for single-family-house renters. The values were selected to average the known mobility of nonfarm renters in 1949 [Source 2]. Justification for this assumption is found in the only study distinguishing between these two rental types. See T. Earl Sullenger, "Social Significance of Mobility," *American Journal of Sociology*, vol. 55, May, 1950, pp. 559–564.)

Americans for homeownership. Ninety percent of the nonfarm population considers owning the preferable form of tenure, and fully 70 percent actively desire it for themselves. Thus, when homeownership is achieved, a goal has been reached and one impetus to move is dispelled. Conversely, the renter who wants to own (and this is approximately 25 percent of the total population) tends to be restless and dissatisfied regardless of the objective quality of his rental housing.

Although of less basic importance than the ideological preference for homeownership, the mere fact that it is easier to move from rented quarters undoubtedly influences mobility. When a renter decides to move, he finds a new place, gives his notice, packs his belongings, and usually spends less than $100 on the move. Little time, money or effort is expended. When an owner decides to move, he often is unable to negotiate for new housing until he has sold his present home. This may take months in time and heavy costs

in legal fees. In addition his cost of moving runs substantially higher, about $1,000. The expense, time, and trouble associated with a move made by a homeowner often may be enough to inhibit mobility even though the motivation to move exists. That is, homeownership in itself may be an obstacle to mobility and, indeed, is so recognized by some homeowners.[6]

Although over-all mobility rates have not altered substantially during the past twenty-five years, and although renter mobility consistently remains higher than owner mobility, Figure 2 does reveal one interesting and significant change: the discrepancy between mobility rates of renters and owners has decreased steadily. That is, over the years, renters have become more "stable" in their market behavior, and owners have become more "mobile."

It is not difficult to find an explanation for this phenomenon. The period of greatest discrepancy was the Depression. During that period, home building all but ceased and few families shifted from rental to owner tenure; in fact, the movement was in the opposite direction. There were few "recent buyers" among homeowners to raise the mobility rate. Those who did own, and who managed to avoid foreclosure, tended to remain in the same house, rather than buy a second one. Among renters, however, there were both previous renters adjusting their housing expenditures to curtailed incomes and families who had lost their homes by foreclosure. The one-year mobility rate for renters in the mid-thirties was ten times the one-year rate for owners. By 1940, this gap had narrowed slightly, coinciding with the slow recovery of the late thirties.

Then during the war and afterwards the situations first of the renter and later of the owner were reversed. The gap between owner and renter mobility was narrowest during the period between 1940 and 1947, partly because rent control inhibited renter mobility. The postwar period, especially in the fifties, is characterized by relatively higher owner mobility rates (about 40 percent of the owner families residing less than five years in their current homes) and by relatively lower renter mobility rates (about 70 percent to 75 percent of the renter families occupying their current quarters for less than five years). The high mobility rate for owners can be explained only by the fact that homeownership and home buying have been sustained on a very high level. About 10 percent of all owner families bought houses in 1956. Over a five-year period, some families purchased two houses, thus yielding a five-year net mobility rate of 40 percent.

It seems safe to predict that if economic prosperity continues and homeownership continues to rise, the discrepancy between the mobility rates of renters and owners will continue to diminish. It will never disappear, however. As previously outlined, rental housing is less suited to what the consumer perceives his needs to be; also, renters are in a stage of family growth which requires more rapid change of housing accommodations.

Movers Are Younger than Nonmovers
Age is directly related to mobility. Individuals aged between twenty and twenty-four are more likely than any others to move during a given year. Between 1954 and 1955, 42 percent of all persons within that age group did move. Mobility gradually decreases with each year of age until, after sixty-five years, less than 10 percent of the age group move within a year's time.[7] (See Figure 4A.)

The same relationship is evident in family mobility. The younger the head of the family, the less likely it is to be living in the same residence it occupied five years earlier. Families with heads aged below forty-five have higher than average mobility rates; those with heads over forty-five have rates lower than the average.[8] (See Figure 4B.)

This relationship between youth and mobility accounts for part of the association between stability and homeownership, since owners, on the average, are older than renters.

The 1955 *Survey of Consumer Finances* shows that, in the age group between 18 and 24 years, only 16 per cent are homeowners. This rises to 45 per cent in the group aged 25 to 34; to 61 percent in the group aged 35 to 44; and to 69 percent for the group aged 55 to 64.

The relationship between age and mobility operates not only among those who have moved, but among those who plan to move. The *Survey of Consumer Finances* found this to be true in measuring mobility potential among families with heads of

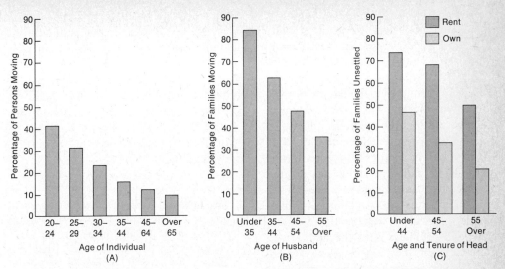

Figure 4. Age and mobility: (A) percentage of civilians moving between 1954 and 1955 by age of individual; (B) percentage of husband-and-wife families moving between 1935 and 1940 by age of husband; (C) percentage of families potentially mobile in 1954 by age and tenure of family head.

varying age and tenure. Renters were far more likely than owners to be anticipating a move, but younger renters had a higher mobility potential than older renters. Among owners, 47 percent of families in which the head was under forty-five years were planning to move, as compared with only 33 percent of owner families headed by men aged between forty-five and fifty-four, and 21 percent of owner families in which the head was fifty-five years old or over (Figure 4C).[9]

Lack of mobility in the oldest age group—that over sixty-five years old—is due partly to their high rate of home-ownership but partly also to the fact that they are no longer subject to the various pressures (job changes, family expansion, rises in social status with increased income) which motivate younger families to move. The one motive which they do have— reduction in family size—is not a pressing one and often is overbalanced by a fear of losing their independence. Hence the

tendency on the part of the elderly to cling to their owned homes even after maintenance has become a taxing and too costly chore for curtailed energies and incomes.

At the opposite end of the scale is the high mobility of young men and women aged between twenty and twenty-four. This is partly explained by the fact that these are the ages when marriage and the establishment of independent households are most usual and when migration from farms to cities or from one region or city to another is most likely. At these ages, mobility is primarily individual rather than family mobility. It is expressed in the housing market as a demand for small rental units, often furnished, and often of relatively low cost.

On the other hand, mobility between twenty-five and forty-five years is predominantly family mobility and is explained primarily by growth in family size. The presence of young children in a family, which changes the nature of its housing requirements, is perhaps the single most important cause of mobility during the middle years. In fact, families with young children make up the most mobile group within any age level, and it is among this group that the largest proportion of renters who want to own are found.

Figure 5 shows the relationship between family composition and mobility. Full families, consisting of both parents and their young children, show the greatest tendency to change their residences. When only one child is present, a larger proportion of their moves are to other communities and counties. With the addition of more children, the tendency is to concentrate moves within the same community or county. Single individuals and, to a lesser extent, childless couples are far less mobile, when age is controlled.

Not only is mobility highest for young families with children, but the desire for

mobility is also greatest for this group. Measures of mobility potential[10] show that the consumers most anxious to alter their housing are young families still growing or just reaching maximum size. Indeed, during the first decade of marriage, the average family makes some two-thirds of all the moves it will make during its entire history. Rossi cogently summarizes why this should be so:

The housing needs of a *young* household are most likely to be "out of balance," as it were, with its actual housing. This is the period in the family's life cycle where the greatest amount of change in household size and composition takes place. It is also the period in which the household, because of the financial demands made upon it by these rapid changes in size and composition is least likely to be able to bring housing into line with its needs.[11]

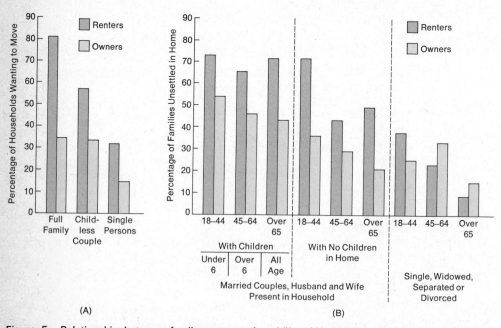

Figure 5. Relationship between family status and mobility. (A) Mobility potential by family and tenure, Philadelphia sample, 1950; (B) mobility potential by family status, age of head, and tenure, U.S. nonfarm families, 1955.

Obviously, then, the demand for housing expressed by the mobile family groups, whose heads are under forty years of age, is for larger quarters, owned homes, and usually suburban locations. In addition there is a latent demand for such housing which is not expressed on the market because of lack of resources. To look only at the demand expressed by persons actively seeking a different dwelling gives a somewhat distorted image of the total distribution of housing demand and the total distribution of housing consumers.

Movers Have Lower Incomes than Nonmovers Between 1949 and 1950, the median income for nonmovers was $42 more than the median for the entire male civilian labor force over fourteen years of age ($2,578 as opposed to $2,536). The median income for those who moved within the same county was $2,356, or $80 less than the over-all median. The median income for those who migrated to other counties or states was a full $465 less than the over-all median—a low of $2,071.

However, this relationship between low income and mobility can be partly explained by youth, since the young are more mobile (particularly to different counties or states), and income is then at its lowest. Confirming this interpretation is the fact that expectation of higher income (again typical of youth) predisposes the consumer to move more than does the prospect of stable or diminishing income.

A survey undertaken in the early 1950s showed that some 45 per cent of nonfarm, owner families who expected their income to be higher in the immediate future also expected to be moving; only 25 percent of the owner families who expected no substantial change in their incomes planned to move. Among renters the same relationship exists, but in more extreme terms. Of renter families, 80 per cent of those optimistic about future income increases were planning to move, as contrasted with only 52 percent who expected no substantial change in their economic circumstances.[12]

Although undoubtedly much of the apparent relationship between low income and mobility can be explained by youth, some part of it cannot be so explained, since, for every age group—except the unusual interval between fourteen and twenty-four years—mobile workers have lower incomes than nonmobile workers. This residual mobility difference between income groups is probably partly due to the migration to the cities of unskilled rural labor and to the rapid turnover of rented dwellings in slum or declining neighborhoods.

Another factor may be the differential mobility rates for specific occupations. In 1955, for example, census figures showed that workers in the primary industries of agriculture, fishing, and mining, and the secondary industries of construction and manufacturing had higher than average mobility rates. On the other hand, male workers employed in transportation, communication, and other public utilities, professional men and those in related services, and the self-employed in nonagricultural industries had mobility rates substantially below the average (19.1, 18.8, and 12.0 percent, respectively, having moved between 1954 and 1955).[13] It would seem self-evident that the latter group of occupations would pay more than the former. Statistics for the year 1954 show this to be true, in general. In that year the low-mobility group of occupations uniformly showed substantially higher incomes than the high-mobility group ($8,854 for professional and technical people as compared to $1,867 in agriculture, for example), with the one exception of transportation-communication, in which earnings were, however, roughly comparable to those in manufacturing, the highest-paid of the high-mobility group ($4,932 in manufacturing as compared to $4,676 in transportation-communication).[14]

A case has also been made for the correlation of mobility with high income. William H. Whyte, Jr., in *The Organization Man* writes:

> . . . the experience of direct mail people indicates that address changes are more frequent in the $5,000 and over bracket. There are also indications that address changes are becoming more frequent in this group. In 1953, 14.8 percent of *Fortune's* subscribers changed addresses during the year. In 1954, 16.6 percent, and in 1955, 17.4 percent.[15]

Although these figures would certainly indicate that mobility is increasing in the middle- and upper-income groups, it is quite possible that young adults and transient workers, with low incomes but with the very highest mobility rates, seldom order by mail. Moreover, these highly mobile consumers do not subscribe to an expensive business magazine.

Movers Have More Education than Non-movers It has been found that mobile persons have more formal education than do those who display stable behavior in the housing market. In general, however, this education-mobility relationship is probably another facet of the youth-mobility tie. It is well known that the average years of schooling completed by young persons is higher than the average for older persons—a testimony to the dramatic gains in mass education over the past generation.

In some measure, however, it may be true that education per se induces mobility. Advanced training increases the job potential and therefore those with higher education may be expected to range farther afield in seach of employment. In particular, those who have gone away to college, especially from small towns, tend to take jobs in other cities after they graduate, rather than returning home again. According to recent census figures and the *Time* study, *They Went to College*,[16] only 27.3 percent of high school graduates aged between twenty-five and thirty-four were interstate migrants. Of those who had had at least one year of college, 45.5 percent crossed state lines. Of those who had completed college in another state, and who had worked their way through, 69 per cent did not return to their original home town.

Furthermore, these college-educated young people, even after the start of their careers, may be more likely to receive offers which take them to another city from that in which they first obtained employment. Recruiting for the higher-status jobs in large national corporations, for teaching positions, for government service, for publishing, and similar fields which require a high educational level, is not limited to the local community. A possible confirmation of this lies in the fact that professionals and those in related services, in marked contrast to every other occupational group, are most likely to make an *intercommunity* move when they change residences. Although their overall mobility is not high (18.8 percent having moved between 1954 and 1955), 55 percent of these moves were to other communities or counties.[17]

Professional employment, like college training, is still far from typical of the population as a whole. Indeed, education-linked mobility might be more than counteracted by the mobility of rural migrants with comparatively little formal schooling. The education-mobility association must therefore, in the over-all picture, be counted as another function of youth.

The Mobility Profile From the preceding discussion of mobility factors, a fairly accurate picture of the mobile consumer can be drawn. The typical mover is a young person (or family) with a comparatively low income, who is currently renting an apartment. If this renter expects a rise in salary, or if he wants to own his own home, or if young children are part of the household—or all three—the mobility potential is increased. As possibly portentous deviants from this general mobility profile, it appears that the incidence of moves (at least long-distance moves) is quite high, and may even be increasing, among consumers of middle to high income, with a high educational level, particularly those in corporate or professional employment.

Why People Move

Intercommunity as Opposed to Intra-Community Mobility As was pointed out at the beginning of the chapter, there are two distinct types of mobility: the long-range or intercommunity move and the short-range or intracommunity move (Figure 6). Whereas the former is primarily job-motivated, the latter is chiefly housing-motivated. Furthermore, long-range moves are dominated by the attractiveness or positive "pulls" of the new location; short-range moves are dominated by dissatisfaction with the previous residence.

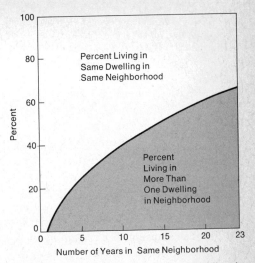

Figure 6. Percentage of individuals residing in more than one dwelling unit in the same neighborhood by length of residence in that same neighborhood. (Source: Special tabulations prepared for ACTION from data collected in Gallup poll, Ballot 453k, Feb. 24, 1950, questions 26a and b. [*Data were made available through the courtesy of the American Institute of Public Opinion.*])

Intercommunity Moves Among a randomly selected sample of in-migrants to Kalamazoo, Michigan,[18] for example, 57 percent of the reasons given for moving were related to economic or job considerations. Almost two-thirds were related to the attractive influences of the new environment, which included, in addition to economic opportunity, the desire to lead a better life, to escape from undesirable large city conditions, or to live in a healthier climate. Only 4 percent of the reasons given were directly related to housing. Furthermore, the higher the level of education and socio-economic status, the more likely were attractive "pulls" to dominate the motives for moving.

Confirmation of the overwhelming importance of economic considerations in intercommunity mobility is found in comparable data for the town of Norris-town, Pennsylvania.[19] A study of migrants into this community revealed that 63 percent of the men who moved there from outside the general area had been motivated by job reasons. Of the women, almost half had moved because their husbands had changed jobs; another 22 percent had migrated as brides of husbands already residing in Norristown.

Intracommunity Moves Conversely, perhaps three-fifths of those who move within the same community are seeking primarily to better their housing. The remaining two-fifths have either been forced to move or have done so as a by-product of some other decision. In a 1940 study which analyzed the reasons given for mobility within the preceding five-year period, 59 per cent concerned voluntary attempts to obtain more suitable housing.[20] Similar distributions of stated motives appear in studies of Flint, Michigan, and Philadelphia.[21]

Housing Dissatisfaction: a "Cause" of Mobility Not all dissatisfied housing consumers move (even locally) and not all movers are dissatisfied with their previous dwellings. Low-level discontent coupled with inertia may keep some householders in unsatisfying quarters. At least twice as many households are not satisfied with their housing as move in any year. Still others may have their moving plans frustrated by conditions in the housing market or by economic incapacities to achieve a different standard of housing. In addition, moving does occur in the absence of conscious dissatisfaction and planning, as when some change in circumstances forces a move (sudden loss of income or of the dwelling itself by fire or flood) or when an appealing opportunity presents itself almost accidentally.

Nevertheless dissatisfaction with current housing does underlie the majority of decisions to move within the same community. As shown in various studies, slightly over 60 percent of intracommunity movers are so motivated. The major sources of discontent which lead them to move can be summarized in descending order of importance:[22]

1. Space within the dwelling (usually too little, occasionally too much)
2. The neighborhood surrounding the dwelling (particularly the social composition of the neighborhood; secondarily its physical characteristics)
3. Cost of housing (invariably too high, or too high for value received)
4. Secondary sources of dissatisfaction, such as poor design or layout of the dwelling; difficulties with the landlord; tensions within the household not necessarily related to the quality of the dwelling; and other more vague and amorphous causes of discontent

Such dissatisfactions may be accepted temporarily during a period of housing shortage or until slim family earnings increase. They may also be more permanent irritants, as in the case of the low-income consumer who has little hope of bettering either earnings or housing. On the other hand, actual deterioration of the dwelling and its surroundings may render previously satisfactory housing unsuitable.

It is interesting to note that cases in which discontent develops later are far more common than those in which it is present from the beginning of occupancy. Note further that dissatisfaction with housing is as much or more the result of changing family needs as it is of changes in the quality of the dwelling itself or of its environment.

This is particularly true of space complaints. Enlargement of family size is the most frequent cause of space dissatisfaction, almost independently of objective density of occupancy. Families seem to adjust to a particular level of density (whether it be high or low), but the addition of a new person tends to create feelings of overcrowding even when objectively there is enough space for all. Rossi found it to be true that more families living at densities exceeding one person per room registered space complaints as a primary cause of moving than did less crowded families. But fully twice as many families who had expanded in size cited space complaints as did those families whose size had remained constant.

Dissatisfactions with neighborhood are also often the result of changes in family status. A neighborhood environment which is suited to the needs of the young couple becomes inadequate when children reach school, or even toddling, age. A working wife finds her previously satisfactory neighborhood location undesirable when she ceases to work. Obviously, a major shift in job location can render a previously convenient dwelling quite unsuitable.

Of those movers who complained about their previous neighborhood, half were disturbed by its social composition. Less than one-quarter cited the physical structure of the previous area and an even smaller percentage the inadequacy of community or municipal services. In almost three-fifths of these cases there had been no discernible change either in the neighborhood or in the family's objective needs. Where changes had occurred, changes in needs were equally as important as actual deterioration of the area.

Cost complaints, although widespread, tend to be incidental, or somewhat ineffective in precipitating a move, unless they are felt in conjunction with other dissatisfaction. For instance, a young couple paying a moderate rental for a small city apartment may not feel the price too high for the small space until after children arrive. Then they would tend to seek larger quarters elsewhere, in a section of the city with lower housing costs.

As a general rule, renters register more cost complaints than do owners, not necessarily because their financial burden is heavier, but because it is somewhat less flexible than that of owners. On the other hand, owners are more sensitive to neighborhood inadequacies, which, it might be presumed, could indicate a concern with cost as "property value."

Obviously, then, dissatisfaction with housing contains a subjective element. There is some uniformity between level of satisfaction and objective characteristics of the dwelling, its cost and its surrounding environment and location. But correlation is not complete, since satisfaction is always partly a subjective phenomenon, varying from family to family, and depending upon the different standards by which they judge, as well as the different goals which they look forward to achieving.

Nevertheless, the major reasons for housing dissatisfaction do point to a general area of agreement and to one particular housing consumer. Space, neighborhood, and cost motives for moving all corroborate the finding that young families in the expanding stage of the family cycle are the most mobile type of household within the population.

The Changing Patterns of Mobility

The preceding pages have charted the mobility of housing consumers according to age, tenure, income, and education. Also defined were the major housing dissatisfactions which tend to precipitate a move. Still to be answered is the question of where the various consumers are going, and how their moves (or non-moves) affect the pattern of the metropolitan area. With this question, job-oriented mobility, as well as those moves made in order to obtain better housing, assume civic importance. Long-range trends in mobility become strategically relevant. And the movements of special groups within the population are of particular interest.

Intercommunity Movement Trends In 1850, 25 per cent of the native-born white population were living in states other than those in which they were born. By 1890, this interstate mobility had dropped to 20 percent of the native white population, and it continued to fall until 1920. But from 1920 onward a countertrend set in, and long-distance mobility began to rise once more. Today, interstate migration of the native white population is roughly comparable to 1850, with somewhat more than 25 percent of the population living in states other than where they were born. Interregional migration rates have followed the same pattern, dipping between 1900 and 1920 and then rising again to an earlier level of over 10 percent.[23]

Although these figures can mean that interstate and interregional mobility rates have not increased substantially over the past one hundred years, they reveal the extraordinary phenomenon of a completely settled country in which interstate and interregional moves are even more frequent than they were while settlement was still taking place. Furthermore, 25 percent of an 1850 population of 23 million meant a movement of 5¾ million people. Twenty-five percent of today's 170 million population means a movement of 42½ million people, or 7½ times as many as were living in other states in 1850.

This is a different kind of mobility from that which was dominant during the settlement of America. It reflects partly the general rural-urban shift which, over the years, has brought farm and small-town residents to the larger cities; partly, increased job mobility which takes workers from one city to another across the country.

Of particular interest within this general trend is the recent Southern shift, including the agricultural movement away from cotton, which has been displacing low-income rural workers, white and Negro, sending them to the city and often to the North. Nor should one overlook the moves made in search of a pleasanter climate, notably to the West Coast, certain Southwestern states, and Florida, which have given these regions such dramatic population rises, preponderantly of older people. However, since World War II an unprecedented industrial boom has drawn also a great many younger families with children, particularly to California, somewhat less dramatically to Florida. Migratory farm workers, such as the "Okies" moving into California during the Depression, have also contributed to the western shift.

In contrast to the ebb and flow of white migration is the interstate migration rate of the nonwhite population (mainly Negro), which follows a quite different pattern. Since 1850, it has increased almost steadily, until today it exceeds that of the white population. These moves are, and always have been, mainly a migration from rural areas into the larger cities and, in the case of the Negro, from the South to the North.

Intracommunity Movement Trends But the intercounty, interstate, and interregional moves, whether white or Negro, represent only about one-third of all the moves which occur in any given year. The other two-thirds are local moves, the majority of which are housing-motivated. Of this type of mobility in the nineteenth century almost nothing is known. However, it is unlikely that many moves in 1850, and even somewhat later, were primarily concerned with a change in housing. In 1850, 85 percent of the population lived in rural areas, and farm families are seldom motivated to change residences in order to obtain more suitable housing. Their houses are a part of the farm and may be neglected, improved, enlarged, or even replaced without any mobility being recorded for the farm family. When urban population was an insignificant part of the total, housing-motivated mobility must have been much less important than it is today, when more than 4 out of 5 Americans live in nonfarm communities. In earlier days, there could not possibly have been the dominant pattern of housing mobility seen in the foregoing analysis of the median housing consumer: from small rented apartment to larger rented apartment, to owned small home, to owned larger home.

Today, this pattern has been further emphasized by the change in the American family from a three- or even four-genera-tion household to a one- or two-generation household. When children remain in the parental home during their adult years, early marriage years, and even beyond the time when they have children of their own, mobility rates are low. This was the typical family pattern of earlier decades. Today, many unmarried children establish independent households, newly married couples move to their own dwellings at once, and the three-generation household has become an infrequent and undesired occurrence. Higher mobility rates undoubtedly result from this family pattern.

That housing-oriented mobility has increased in the past half century, we have no doubt. However, the only available direct evidence of this increase comes from the sample study of Philadelphia families in 1950 (Figure 7).[24] The findings of this study indicate that families founded before 1910 moved less frequently during their first decade of existence than did families of more recent origin. Seventy-one percent of the families formed before 1910 had low mobility records, making only one or two moves during the first ten years of existence. Of families formed in 1940, only 40 percent made as few as one or two moves between then and 1950. Three times as many of the latter families made five or

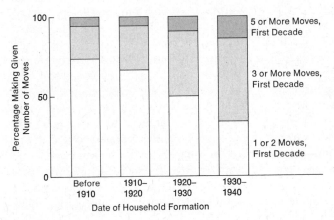

Figure 7. Distribution of households making a given number of moves during the first decade of duration. (Source: Unpublished draft of a study on mobility by Peter Rossi. The published version of the study [*Why Families Move*, Free Press, Glencoe, Ill., 1955] unfortunately omits these exploratory data. Figures are derived from a subsample of 632 families residing in four small areas of Philadelphia in 1950.)

more moves during their first decade as did families founded before 1920. Figure 7 also shows the relation between the date of family formation and the number of moves made during the first decade.[25]

Population Shifts Both these new types of mobility, job-motivated and housing-motivated, are important, but for different reasons. These become apparent when the population movement each year is broken down in its component parts, roughly as follows:

Interstate, Intercounty, or Interregional Of the approximately 7 percent of the population making long-distance moves each year, the white majority are moving predominantly:

1. From rural area or small town to city or suburb
2. From city to city
3. From the suburbs of one city to the suburbs of another
4. From the city to the suburbs of another city
5. From central city to suburbs, where these are in a different state or county
6. To the North, South, and West

The nonwhite (mainly Negro) minority is moving predominantly (1) from rural area to city, (2) from South to North.

Intracommunity or Intracounty Of the approximately 13 percent of the population making short-distance, housing-motivated moves each year, the white majority are moving predominantly (1) within the city proper; (2) within the suburbs; (3) from city to suburb, where these are in the same county or state. The nonwhite minority is moving predominantly within the city proper.

The nonwhite shift, although smaller in percentage of total population, is concentrated mainly in one direction, into the city. The white shifts are made in a great many different directions. But the net result is a shift away from the central city. Thus, the significant job-motivated mobility is that which brings the Negro and other nonwhites into the city. The significant housing-motivated shift is that which takes the white to the suburbs. What these moves mean in relation to each other can best be seen in specific examples of both large and medium-sized cities.

In 1957, New York City (population: 7,812,509) gained 311,000 Negroes and 304,000 Puerto Ricans. It lost 720,000 whites. By that time 20 percent of New York City residents were either Negro or Puerto Rican. Although the city showed a net loss since 1950 of 79,448 persons, its New York and New Jersey suburban areas gained 1,278,078, the Connecticut suburban gain being uncounted.[26]

From 1950 to 1956, the Negro population of Syracuse, New York (population 214,000), rose by nearly 100 percent. In that period, the city gained 4,767 Negroes and lost 10,767 whites. Although the city showed a net loss of 6,000 people, the suburbs gained 60,000, all except 400 of them white. Of the Syracuse city population, 4.3 percent is now nonwhite; of the nonwhite group, almost all are Negro (there are a few Indians and a negligible number of Orientals).[27]

From 1950 to 1957, Chicago gained 197,000 nonwhites, mostly Negro. It showed a net loss of 93,000 whites. The loss would have been much greater were it not for the very large (although uncounted) gain in rural Southern whites, congregating, like the Negroes, in the central city.[28]

Since 1940, Indianapolis, Indiana (today's population 450,000), has experienced an industrial and birth rate boom which has increased the population by over 63,000 people, most of them in the suburbs. The Metropolitan Planning Commission expects that within the next eighteen years, the eight suburban counties surrounding Indianapolis will be entirely filled up, tripling the size of the metropolitan area. Unlike the other cities cited, the Negro population has increased by only 3 percent. The majority of newcomers are workers drawn from the Indiana farm and small-town population, white workers from the rural South, and executives from all over America. In 1940, Indiana had a 60:40 farming to industry population ratio; it is now 65 percent industrial to 35 percent agricultural.[29]

Although the increase of nonwhites may be much slower in some cities than in others, and indeed may be outweighed by white gains in some sections of the country, it is nevertheless evident in most of the larger cities.

There is no reason to expect that the migration of nonwhites and rural whites to the city and to the North will stop, although it may be temporarily slowed or halted by unforseen factors. Indeed, in the long run it can be expected to increase as agriculture in general becomes more mechanized and larger in its scale of operation. Coupled with the net shift of whites away from the city and of Northern whites toward the South and West, this means, over the years, a redistribution of population which must have profound effects upon metropolitan areas in all sections of the country. Within this pattern of mobility cities today must plan for the future.

NOTES

1. Since 1947, the Bureau of the Census has published annual statistics showing the number of civilians who, at the end of the year, lived in a different dwelling from that occupied when the year began. These statistics have shown such remarkable uniformity over a ten-year period that it seems plausible to accept close to 20 percent as a normal rate of postwar mobility. However, the census figures underestimate the number of *moves* as opposed to the number of persons moving, since they fail to record more than one move per year per mover.
2. George Katona and Eva Mueller, *Consumer Expectations 1953–56*, University of Michigan, 1956. About 70 per cent of the renters and 34 per cent of the owners in 1954 expressed a desire to move, although actually only 33 per cent of the renters and probably 10–12 percent of the owners did move.
3. Works Progress Administration, Division of Social Research (prepared by Peyton Stapp), *Urban Housing: A Summary of Real Property Inventories Conducted as Work Projects 1934 to 1956*, 1938; see especially p. 21, U.S. Summary (yearly and five-year net mobility rates for the mid-1930s—24 percent and over 55 percent respectively).
   U.S. Bureau of the Census, *Population and Housing—Families—General Characteristics, United States, Cities of 100,000 and Metropolitan Districts of 200,000 or More*, a separate volume, but issued as part of the *Sixteenth Census of the United States*, table 18, pp. 50–51. (Five-year net mobility rate for 1935–1940, 61 per cent.)
   Melville C. Branch, Jr., *Urban Planning and Public Opinion*, Bureau of Urban Research, Princeton, N.J., 1942. (Five-year net mobility rate between 1935 and 1940, 53 percent.)
   U.S. Bureau of the Census, "Internal Migration in the United States: April, 1940 to April, 1947," *Current Population Report, Population Characteristics*, ser. P–20, no. 14, Apr. 15, 1948; see table 4, p. 16 for nonfarm migration. (Seven-year mobility rate of 58.8 percent; from this estimate, a five-year mobility rate of 50 per cent.) Decline partly due to change in unit of mobility: from a household count in earlier studies to an individual count in this study. Also most young men—the most mobile group within the population—were serving in the Armed Forces.)
   Federal Reserve Board, *Survey of Consumer Finances*, selected issues from 1948 to 1958. (Family mobility information is available for selected years and varying time intervals in the *Federal Reserve Bulletin*. These data indicate that by 1955, the five-year net mobility rate had reached 57 per cent.)
   Projections for ten- and twenty-year mobility rates are based on the preceding statistics.
4. Branch, *op. cit.*
5. Because of this shifting of the base of estimation, the figures are only the roughest kind of estimate.
6. A study of a Buffalo sample of 788 homeowners reported in the *President's Conference on Home*

Building and Home Ownership, vol. IV, 1924, revealed that 12 percent of those owners interviewed reported that home-ownership had interfered with moving to another community to take a better job; 7 percent felt that ownership kept them from adjusting their housing to changed family needs; 5 per cent said that it had interfered with moving closer to work or to the children's school, etc. Cited by R. Dewey and W. Slayton, "Urban Redevelopment and the Urbanite," in Coleman Woodbury (ed.), *The Future Cities and Urban Redevelopment*, University of Chicago Press, Chicago, 1952, p. 326.

7. U.S. Bureau of the Census, *Current Population Reports*, April, 1954– April, 1955.

8. 1940 Census on Family Mobility as cited in Glick, "The Family Cycle," *American Sociological Review*, vol. XII, April, 1947, pp. 164–174.

9. Katona and Mueller, *op. cit.*

10. Figure 5A defines mobility potential as that percentage expressing a desire to move within a year. Peter Rossi, *Why Families Move*, Free Press, Glencoe, Ill., p. 72. Figure 5B defines mobility potential as the percentage stating that they feel that they are not settled in a satisfactory home. Federal Reserve Board, *op. cit.*, 1955.

11. Rossi, *op. cit.*, p. 72.

12. Katona and Mueller, *op. cit.*, table 39, p. 87. Data are for June, 1954.

13. U.S. Bureau of the Census, "Mobility of the Population of the United States: April, 1954 to April, 1955," *Current Population Reports, Population Characteristics*, ser. P–20, no. 61, Oct. 28, 1955. Based on computations from data appearing in table 5, p. 12.

14. Glenn Beyer, *Housing: A Factual Analysis*, The Macmillan Company, New York, 1958, pp. 6, 8; citing U.S. Bureau of the Census, "Family Income in the United States: 1954 and 1953," *Current Population Reports*, ser. P–60, no. 20, December 1955, p. 17.

15. William H. Whyte, Jr., *The Organization Man*, Doubleday, New York, 1957, p. 298.

16. E. Haveman and P. S. West, *They Went to College*, Harcourt, Brace, New York, 1952. (Survey by *Time*, analysis by Columbia University Bureau of Applied Social Research.)

17. U.S. Bureau of the Census, *op. cit.*

18. Ralph Turner, "Migration to a Medium-sized American City: Attitudes, Motives, and Personal Characteristics Revealed by Open-end Interview Methodology," *The Journal of Social Psychology*, vol. 30, 1949, pp. 229–249. Turner studied 200 family heads over twenty-one years of age who had moved to Kalamazoo from a distance of over 25 miles during the period four to ten months before survey date. Of these respondents, randomly selected from a master list of all in-migrants to the community, there were 161 men with families; 9 unmarried men; 16 unmarried women; 5 widows and 1 widower; 5 divorced women and 1 divorced man.

19. Sidney Goldstein, *Patterns of Internal Migration: Norristown, Pennsylvania, 1910–1950*, preliminary report issued by University of Pennsylvania Behavioral Research Council, July, 1953, vol. II, p. 60. (Hectographed.) In comparing these figures with those of Turner, it should be borne in mind that Turner interviewed only heads of households, whereas Goldstein interviewed all movers.

20. Branch, *op. cit.*, p. 21. The answers have been regrouped somewhat for this analysis. Total adds to more than 100 percent because multiple reasons were given by many respondents. The reasons, in order of descending importance, were to secure better quarters or a better location, 18 percent; to build or buy a home, 16 percent; to obtain more space in the dwelling, 13 percent; and to reduce costs or space, 12 percent. The remaining reasons were forced to move because of a change in, or destruction of, previously occupied dwelling, 13 per cent; to be closer to job, 10 percent; miscellaneous, 30 percent.

21. Betty Tableman, *Intracommunity Migration in the Flint Metropolitan District*, University of Michigan Institute for Human Adjustment, 1948; and Peter Rossi, *Why Families Move*, Free Press, Glencoe, Ill., 1955, table 8–1, p. 135.

22. In this and the following discussion, the authors are indebted to the material collected and analyzed by Rossi, *op. cit.*, on 273 Philadelphians who moved voluntarily between 1945 and 1950 in an attempt to better their housing conditions.

23. U.S. Bureau of the Census, *Statistical Abstract of the United States*, 1956, tables 27, 28, 33, 34, pp. 33–39; see also *Historical Statistics*, 1945, and Supplement, ser. B 205–230, p. 31.

24. Data were collected by Rossi in connection with his research on *Why Families Move*. These figures appear in a hectographed prepublication draft but have not been incorporated into the published version.

25. Nevertheless, since the new mobility pattern was established, countertrends have appeared which decrease mobility, thus preventing a continual, over-all rise: for example, an increasing percentage of persons in the older age brackets; an increase in homeownership; the widespread ownership of cars, and the improvement of the highway system, which allows workers to change jobs without changing residences. Over the past twenty-five years there has been little net change in over-all mobility. During the 1930s, when housing was easily obtained and jobs were not, mobility remained at a fairly constant level of 55 to 60 percent over a five-year period. The early 1940s saw a dip to about 50 percent, due to housing shortage and the absence of young men —traditionally the most mobile group—who were serving in the Armed Forces. By 1955, the five-year mobility rate had risen once more to 57 per cent, a point roughly equivalent to the early thirties.

26. U.S. Bureau of the Census, *Special Census: New York City, 1957*.

27. Eunice Grier and George Grier, *Race Relations in Syracuse*, New York State Commission Against Discrimination, January, 1958, Summary, iii; "The People: Numbers and Distribution," pp. 1, 2.

28. *Population Growth in the Chicago Standard Metropolitan Area*, Chicago Community Inventory, University of Chicago, 1958.

29. Indianapolis City Planning Commission.

32. The Metropolitan Area as a Racial Problem   Morton Grodzins

The late Morton Grodzins demonstrates the usefulness of thinking about the problems of black-white relations in American society in terms of the spatial structure of metropolitan regions. He discusses such matters as the growing concentration of blacks in central cities, their declining proportion in suburban areas, the sources of the present black population distribution, and the processes through which the racial compositions of metropolitan areas are changed. Grodzins argues that a wide variety of difficulties from which the nonwhite population suffers can be attributed ultimately to the prevailing pattern of residential segregation, including high rates of unemployment, poor education, disease and delinquency, and the relative lack of political power for blacks. Perhaps the most original and interesting sections of the paper are the final ones, in which the author describes four kinds of population and locational policies for upsetting prevailing patterns and bringing about a more even distribution of blacks within metropolitan areas. These policies touch on the following issues: the control of black migration to northern population centers, the recruitment of whites back into the central cities, controlled suburbanization of blacks, and redistribution of blacks to small metropolitan areas and away from the ten large cities in which they are now concentrated.

Morton Grodzins (1917–1964) was Professor of Political Science at the University of Chicago. He was the author of numerous books, including *The American System* (1966) and *A Nation of States* (1963), and coauthor of *Government and Housing in Metropolitan Areas* (1958).

Almost nothing is being done today to meet what is likely to be the nation's most pressing social problem tomorrow. The problem can be simply stated in all its bleakness: many central cities of the great metropolitan areas of the United States are fast becoming lower class, largely Negro slums.

The Great Schism of Population

Some 95 million people, more than half the population of the United States, now live in what the Bureau of the Census defines as a standard metropolitan area: a central city of at least 50 thousand population with its ring of satellite communities "essentially metropolitan in character and socially and economically integrated with the central city." Fewer than one-third of the nation's population lived within these areas in 1900; slightly more than half resided there in 1950; and it is estimated that 70 percent of the nation's total population will be metropolitan area dwellers by 1975.

The fourteen largest metropolitan areas, those with populations of over one million, contain more than half of the total metropolitan population and almost one-third of the nation's. These areas attract the largest number of Negro in-migrants from the South, and in them, generally, Negroes constitute a larger proportion of the total

From *The Metropolitan Area as a Racial Problem*, University of Pittsburgh Press, 1958, pp. 1–28. Reprinted by permission of the publisher.

population.[1] The consequences of the urban-suburban racial and class bifurcation, therefore, are most acute in these largest metropolitan areas. Some smaller metropolitan areas face the same problems in less acute form while others, because of their small number of Negroes, do not face them at all.

For several decades the Negro population of the great cities has been increasing more rapidly than the white population. The great changes come in time of full employment, and the explosive growth, as measured by the decennial censuses, took place between 1940 and 1950. In that decade, the total population of the fourteen largest metropolitan areas increased by 19

percent, the total Negro percentage gain (65.1 percent) being more than four times greater than the white increase (15.6 percent). Negroes increased proportionately more rapidly in both central cities and suburbs, but the significant growth differential was inside the great cities. Whites increased by 3.7 percent, Negroes 67.8 percent. (For individual cities, see Figure 1.) The Negro population at least doubled in four central cities while whites in five cities decreased in number.

As late as 1950 nonwhites constituted only a minor fraction of the total population in most of the central cities of the fourteen largest metropolitan areas. Washington, D.C., with nonwhites totalling

Figure 1. Center cities: largest metropolitan areas; population growth, by race, 1940–1950.

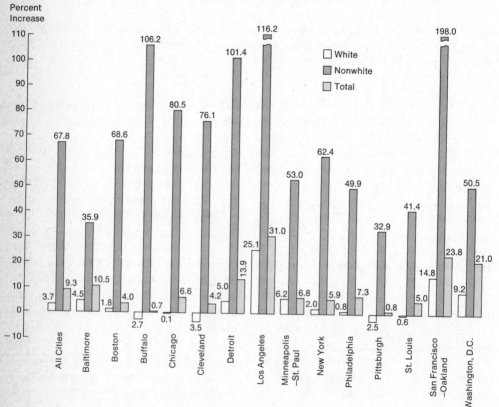

35.4 percent of total population, and Baltimore (23.8 percent) had the largest group of nonwhites in proportion to total population. In addition to these, only three other cities had 1950 Negro populations in excess of 15 percent; three had less than 10 percent.

Continued Negro migration, the comparatively greater rate of natural increase among nonwhites, and the exodus of whites to the suburbs will dramatically raise the proportion of nonwhites in central cities. The few special censuses that have been made since 1950 indicate this trend. In Los Angeles nonwhites moved up from 6.5 percent of the population in 1940, to 11 percent in 1950, to 14 percent in 1956. In Chicago, according to a careful unofficial estimate by Otis Dudley Duncan and Beverly Duncan of the University of Chicago, Negroes now comprise 19 percent of the total, compared with 8 percent in 1940.[2] The city is expected to be one-third Negro by 1970. An official census in New York City showed that nonwhites in the nation's largest city increased by 41 percent from 1950 to 1957, while the white population decreased by 6 percent. Nonwhites made up 13 percent of New York's population in 1957, as compared with 6 percent in 1940 and 10 percent in 1950. (Only a tiny fraction of New York's Puerto Rican population is enumerated as being "nonwhite.") New York City officials have forecast that in 1970 Negroes and Puerto Ricans together will constitute 45 percent of the population of Manhattan and nearly one-third of the entire city. Washington, D.C. may already have an actual Negro majority.

Estimates of future population trends must take into account some reurbanization of white suburbanites as the proportion of older people increases and the suburbs become less attractive to those whose children have grown up and left home. Even making allowances for shifts of this sort, all evidence makes it highly probable that within 30 years Negroes will constitute from 25 to 50 percent of the total population in at least 10 of the 14 largest central cities.

The suburbs of the metropolitan areas exhibit very different population trends. Negroes made up only 4 percent of their population in 1940 and less than 5 percent in 1950. (Central city nonwhites were 9 percent of total population in 1940, 13.2 percent in 1950.)

Some suburban areas experienced nonwhite percentage gains between 1940 and 1950, and even the fourteen-area totals show Negro increases greater than white ones. But the actual number of Negroes was small. A suburban nonwhite gain of 130 percent in Minneapolis-St. Paul, for example, represented an actual increase of exactly 337 persons. Moreover, even the nonwhite "suburban" increases noted are rarely to the suburbs themselves. Rather they largely represent Negro migration to the smaller industrial towns within the metropolitan rings of the central cities. Special censuses made of suburban places since 1950 strengthen the impression of Negro exclusion. There is evidence of absolute decreases in the numbers of Negroes in some suburban areas; in other areas there has been a movement of one or two nonwhite families into all-white communities. The only statistically significant suburban growth of Negro population, however, has taken place in industrial fringe cities—Gary, Indiana, for example —or in segregated Negro dormitory communities—Robbins, Illinois, for example.

The growing racial schism of population between central cities and suburbs is revealed sharply in the megaphone-like

Percent

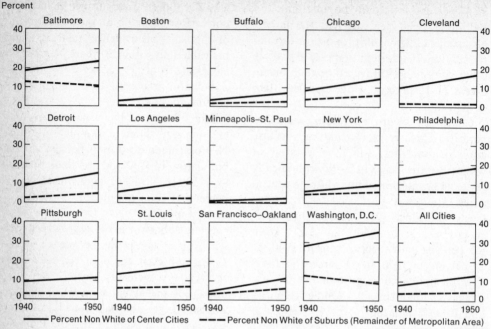

Figure 2.   Largest metropolitan areas; percent nonwhites, center cities and suburbs, 1940 and 1950.

lines of Figure 2. There is no exception in the 14 cities to the pattern of a widening gap between Negro city percentages and Negro suburban percentages. Where Negroes in 1940 were proportionally most numerous in both central cities and suburbs (as in Baltimore and Washington, D.C.), the subsequent decade saw nonwhites decrease markedly as a percentage of suburban populations and increase markedly as a percentage of central city populations. This record very likely traces the future for other cities whose urban-suburban population distribution by race in 1950 approximated the 1940 distribution of Baltimore and Washington.

The general picture of the future is clear enough: large nonwhite concentrates (in a few cases, majorities) in the principal central cities; large white majorities, with segregated Negro enclaves, in the areas outside.

Growth Patterns within Cities

The pattern of Negro population growth within the central cities follows established and well-understood patterns. It is based upon in-migration from the South, and it is accelerated by a larger rate of natural increase of the nonwhite in-migrants in comparison with the older white residents. Migration has been the source of the largest increase in most non-southern cities, and continued industrial expansion may actually increase this movement in the years immediately ahead. The "push" from the South may grow stronger as the consequence of growing white antagonisms following attempts to enforce the Supreme Court's nonsegregation decisions. And the "pull" of the northern cities may become more forceful as the Negro communities there become larger and more firmly established and as information concerning job and other opportunities correspondingly flows back to relatives and friends. On the other hand, the relatively more rapid natural increase of Negroes, in comparison with white residents, will almost certainly become less striking with the passage of years.

The spatial expansion of Negro population in the larger cities follows roughly similar patterns. One universal rule is that residential concentrations are segregated. In every major city with a considerable number of Negroes there exists a "black belt" or a series of "black areas." In Chicago, 79 percent of all Negroes in 1950 lived in census tracts in which at least 75 percent of the residents were Negroes. At the opposite extreme, 84 percent of the non-Negroes resided in census tracts in which less than 1 percent of the residents were Negro,[3] and the disparity would be even higher if Negro servants "living in" were not counted. Chicago's segregation pattern is somewhat extreme, but all cities follow this pattern. Negroes live preponderantly or exclusively with Negroes, whites with whites.

A second rule is equally general: once an urban area begins to swing from predominant white to predominant Negro occupancy, the change is rarely reversed. Between 1920 and 1950 in Chicago there are no cases in which areas of predominantly Negro residents reverted to areas of white occupancy. More than this, a neighborhood with a substantial proportion of Negroes (say 25 percent) rarely retains its mixed character for a considerable period of time. The Duncans, in their intensive study of neighborhood changes in Chicago, found not a single instance between 1940 and 1950 of a census tract "with mixed population (25–75 percent nonwhite) in which succession from white to Negro occupancy

was arrested"[4] though, as they remark, the succession was more rapid in some tracts than in others. Postwar programs of public housing and urban renewal have somewhat altered this rule, in some cases establishing new Negro concentrates where they had not previously existed and in others demonstrating that relatively stable interracial patterns of living can be achieved.[5] But new housing programs in predominantly Negro areas have for the most part meant the simple exchange of one Negro population group for another; and urban renewal programs, by displacing Negro families in one area, have frequently had the effect of hastening the succession of adjacent areas to all-Negro occupancy.

A third generalization is that the pattern of Negro residential expansion is from the core of the city outward. The original concentration is almost everywhere near the center of the city. It subsequently expands radially or in concentric circles. A map by zones for virtually every city with a sizeable Negro population shows higher percentages of Negro residence in areas closest to the city center with decreasing proportions as the distance from the city center increases.

A fourth generalization is also possible. The Negro population moves generally into areas already characterized by high residential mobility. Furthermore, there is a rough comparability between the social characteristics of the in-migrant Negro population and the out-migrant white population with respect to such factors as educational attainment, rate of unemployment, room crowding, home ownership, and white collar employment.[6] Lower-class Negroes, in other words, tend to move into lower-class neighborhoods; middle-class Negroes into middle-class neighborhoods. The "piling up" process—the gross overcrowding of dwellings and areas—occurs only after the transition from white to Negro dominance has taken place.

The "Tipping" Mechanism

The process by which whites of the central cities leave areas of Negro in-migration can be understood as one in the social-psychology of "tipping a neighborhood." The variations are numerous, but the theme is universal. Some white residents will not accept Negroes as neighbors under any conditions. But others, sometimes willingly as a badge of liberality, sometimes with trepidation, will not move if a relatively small number of Negroes move into the same neighborhood, the same block, or the same apartment building. Once the proportion of non-whites exceeds the limits of the neighborhood's tolerance for interracial living (this is the "tip point"), the whites move out. The proportion of Negroes who will be accepted before the tip point is reached varies from city to city and from neighborhood to neighborhood.

The process is not the simple one of "flight" that is a part of the real estate mythology of changing neighborhoods. It may take a number of years before the "invaded" neighborhood becomes an all-Negro one. Nor is the phenomenon uniformly one in which Negroes "push" whites out. As already noted, areas of heavy Negro in-migration are most often areas already characterized by high mobility; and the process of Negroes taking up vacancies as they occur cannot be conceived as one in which the old residents have been "pushed." This is to say that tipping may come slowly and does not necessarily indicate any immediate downgrading of the given neighborhood. What it signifies is the unwillingness of white

groups to live in proximity to large numbers of Negroes.

Many people in many ways for many purposes have explored how the tip point operates. Real estate operators, seeking the higher revenues that come with Negro overcrowding, talk freely among themselves about "tipping a building" or "tipping a neighborhood." (Sometimes this can be done by selling a single house to a "block busting" family.) Quakers in the Philadelphia suburbs of Concord Park and Greenbelt Knoll have utilized the tip point for the opposite purpose: to build interracial communities. They have concluded that this goal can be achieved only if the proportion of Negroes is rigidly controlled and does not exceed the point at which whites (even Quakers) will refuse to participate. An official of these developments has written: "Early in our sales program we found that white buyers would not buy without assurance that Negroes would be in a minority."

Public housing officials have faced the tip-point phenomenon from another angle. In some Eastern cities it is possible to maintain low cost housing projects on an interracial basis as long as nonwhites do not exceed roughly 20 percent of the total residents. Once this point is reached, whites will not remain in, or move into, the project. One method used to combat the process of tipping public housing has been to raise rents. This has the effect of decreasing the number of Negroes who can afford to live in the projects. So the tip point leads to a shifting of public housing goals, subordinating the first principle of low rentals to that of maintaining interracial occupancy.

In a few areas around the country Negroes and whites live side by side without fuss or fanfare. This is true even in Chicago, where segregation patterns are extreme, and examples of "open occupancy" can be found from New York to San Francisco.[7] Furthermore, in recent years, there has been a tendency for a single Negro family—usually of considerable income and of the professions—to find a dwelling in an all-white neighborhood. In every such case of "interracial living," however, some factor—economic or other—limits the ingress of Negro residents.

Education and community organization can extend tolerance and thus increase the proportion of Negroes in a given area before the tip point is reached. But the limits have not proved to be infinitely elastic. Even where goodwill, community effort, and financing have been maximized, the psychology of tipping has operated. The only interracial communities in the United States, with the exception of some abject slums, are those where limits exist upon the influx of nonwhites.

Patterns of Suburban Exclusion

The sheer cost of suburban housing excludes Negroes from many suburban areas. Furthermore, the social satisfactions of slum or near-slum existence for a homogeneous population have been insufficiently studied, and it is undoubtedly true that many Negro urban dwellers would not easily exchange life in all-Negro big-city neighborhoods for interracial suburban homes, even if moderately priced. The crucial fact, however, is that Negroes do not have any free choice in the matter. They are excluded from suburbia by a wide variety of devices.

Social antagonisms of suburban communities are themselves effective. Where it is plainly understood that Negroes are not wanted, Negro suburbanization is for all practical purposes impossible. In addition, suburban communities use their control of zoning, subdivision, and building regulations to achieve exclusion. Minimum lot sizes are increased to two or more acres; requirements for expensive street improvements are made—and then waived only in favor of "desirable" developments; large-scale building operations are defined as "business" for zoning purposes, thus excluding the possibility of low or moderate income suburban building; the suburb itself purchases all vacant land parcels that are large enough for subdivision and resells only to favored purchasers; builders are required to obtain certificates from the school board that educational accommodation will be adequate for the new residences; ordinances regulating "look alike" features or requiring certain building materials make home building expensive.

Where legal barriers of this sort are not sufficient to maintain a "white only" policy, land use controls are used informally—and of course illegally—to exclude Negroes. A Philadelphia builder recently told an interviewer that he would very much like to sell suburban houses to Negroes, but that it was impossible because it would ruin him economically. "If I sold just one suburban home to a Negro, the local building inspectors would have me moving pipes three-eighths of an inch every afternoon in every one of the places I was building; and moving a pipe three-eighths of an inch is mighty expensive if you have to do it in concrete."[8]

These practices are combined with social and economic pressures upon white owners of older homes and upon real estate brokers. Mortgage bankers habitually discriminate against the Negro buyer in the white neighborhood, and not always for purely economic reasons. Where all else fails, suburban residents have often turned to violence to prevent Negro occupancy. The total suburban facade is relatively impenetrable.

Suburban restrictions are everywhere aimed at Negroes as a racial group and not simply against people of low or moderate income. When such restrictions are applied uniformly, they of course also affect whites. But even this has an indirect effect upon the Negro concentrates within the cities. If middle- and lower-class whites who live next door to the slums were able to move to the suburbs, their places would quickly be taken by the slum-dwellers, especially those Negroes whose presence in the slums is due less to income than to the prejudice which excludes them from more desirable places. By raising the price of housing in the suburbs, land use regulations reduce the movement of the white middle and lower classes out of the city. And this in turn holds the slum-dweller in the slums and, accordingly, the Negro in the ghetto.

Consequences of Population Distribution

Some of the consequences of the urban-suburban racial and class schism are already apparent, and others can be reasonably predicted.

Social Consequences Within the cities the first result is a spreading of slums. There is no free market for Negro housing. The Negro population always increases faster than the living space available to it. New areas that open up to Negro residence become grossly overcrowded by conversion of one-family houses to multiple dwellings and by squeezing two or more Negro families into apartments previously occupied by a single white one. Though complete statistical evidence is lacking, it is likely that Negroes pay substantially more rent for such accommodations than do whites, and the higher rent itself produces higher densities. Housing occupied by Negroes is more crowded, more dilapidated, and more lacking in amenities such as private baths than housing occupied by whites with equivalent incomes.

Income factors account in part for the condition of life of the Negro community. Negroes are heavily over-represented in low income jobs: in the menial services, in unskilled and semi-skilled factory labor, and in "dirty work" generally. In this respect they are not unlike some earlier immigrants to the city; the Irish and the Poles, for example, also settled mainly in the slums.

Like previous newcomers to the city tasting the freedom of urban life for the first time, a significant portion of the Negro group does not possess the stable patterns of thought and action that characterize the "better" older inhabitants. And, as with all immigrant groups, old community patterns of control do not operate well in the new environment. Family disorganization among urban Negroes is high as measured by such indices as broken marriages, families headed by females, and unrelated individuals living in the same household. The development of social stabilization pivoted on family and community ties takes place against great odds. How does a mother keep her teen-age son off the streets if an entire family must eat, sleep, and live in a single room? What utility can be found in sobriety among a society of drinkers and in a block of taverns? What opportunity for quiet amidst the din of a tightly packed, restless neighborhood?

The conditions of urban life, rather than

socializing new Negro residents to "desirable" life patterns, frequently have the opposite effect. They encourage rowdiness, casual and competitive sexuality, and a readiness for combat. The result is that the neighborhoods acquired by Negro residents eventually spiral downward. Disease and crime rates are high. Family stability is further prejudiced. Filth accumulates. The slum spreads outward.

These very conditions of life in the predominantly Negro neighborhoods lead the larger population to resist the expansion of Negro residential areas. The racial attribute—skin color—is added to the social attributes of lower class behavior. And while Negroes, like other urban immigrants, can readily lose undesirable social attributes, they cannot lose their color. They therefore do not have the mobility of other immigrant groups. They are racially blocked, whatever their social *bona fides*.

The Negro "black belts" of the great American cities as a consequence are by no means homogeneous. The very concentration of population within them plus the visible badge of color give them a spurious air of likeness. They contain, in fact, wide ranges of every social attribute: from illiteracy to high learning, from filth to hospital-like hygienic standards, from poverty to riches, from political backwardness to sophistication. Though the casual observer of the "black belt" neighborhoods sees only slums, the fact is that in every such area there are sub-areas, frequently on the periphery of the high-density mass, that are anything but slums. These are usually neighborhoods of newest acquisition, inhabited by the well-to-do of the Negro community. Density is low, lawns and gardens are well-tended, church attendance is high, neatness and cleanliness are apparent, parental standards of pro-priety for children higher than for comparable white groups.

Negro neighborhoods in the shadows of white luxury apartments are not unknown; but the more usual pattern is for low-income non-Negroes to occupy a buffer zone between all-Negro and the better white neighborhoods. Some of these are themselves new migrants to the city: Southerners and Japanese-Americans in Chicago, Puerto Ricans in New York, for example. Others are old residents on the lower ends of the income scale, people who, like the Negroes themselves, do not find success in life, or life itself, easy.

With the exodus of middle and upper classes to the suburbs, lower-income groups constitute a larger and larger fraction of the population of the central cities. Members of these groups generally exhibit a greater degree of intolerance and racial prejudice than do other whites. And the increasing juxtaposing of the Negro and the low-income non-Negro populations produces increased interracial tensions. Shirley Star of the National Opinion Research Center has shown that the greatest white animosity towards Negroes is found on the edge of the expanding Negro residential areas where whites fear their block or neighborhood will soon be "invaded."[9] In these lower class and lower-middle class transitional areas, violence is incipient. Individual differences within the minority group are ignored. A young white resident of such an area in Chicago recently beat a Negro to death with a hammer. "I just wanted to get one of them," he explained, "which one didn't matter."

The total situation produces Negro communities in which people live their whole lives without, or with minimum, contact with the other race. With a Negro population numbering in the hundreds of thousands, and with this population densely concentrated, one can live, eat, shop, work, play, and die in a completely Negro community. The social isolation of the northern urban Negro is, for very large numbers, more complete than it ever was for the Negro rural resident in the South.

Even in education, the urban residential segregation of the non-southern cities has produced consequences that are not dissimilar to what the South is trying to maintain by the use of violence and unconstitutional law. If segregation is defined not in legal terms but in the numbers of students who attend all-Negro schools, then it is undoubtedly true that more Negro students are segregated in the schools of New York and Chicago than in any other cities or some states.

This general picture of segregation needs some qualification. A small number of church groups have succeeded in building interracial congregations. Qualified Negro workers are finding employment in places previously barred to them, not only in manufacturing, but also in the professions and in retail establishments. On a few blocks in urban America, Negroes and whites have demonstrated that they can live together as neighbors. Labor unions, though traditionally anti-Negro, have in some places accepted Negroes as full partners in leadership as well as membership.

These are evidences of advances toward social integration. Other advances have been made within the Negro community itself. As this community in a given city grows larger, satisfactory career lines, economic security, and the home and community life that accompany such developments become possible. Here, however, Negroes and whites meet each other across separate societies rather than within a single group. The Negro shares with whites the better things of life, but he does

so in isolation with other Negroes. The disadvantaged segregated community even produces advantages for some individuals within it, providing protected markets for Negro professionals and businessmen and protected constituencies for Negro political and church leaders. Yet even those who profit from segregation suffer from it. They feel the pin-pricks as well as the sledges of discrimination, and they must suppress their dissatisfaction in accordance with standards of conduct expected of all "better" people, whatever their race.

The larger evidence is neither that of social integration nor of intracommunity social gains. Rather it is evidence pointing to the expansion of Negro slums within the largest cities and the separation of whites and Negroes by intracity neighborhoods and especially on central city-suburban lines.

Economic Consequences Population shifts bring with them major economic consequences. Of first importance is the further decline of a large segment of business activity and associated property values, in the central cities. For reasons only remotely related—or unrelated—to the Negro-white population distribution, the economic feasibility of decentralized retail shopping has already been demonstrated. Suburban shopping centers have captured a large segment of the market in clothing, furniture, and other consumption goods; almost everywhere the "downtown" shops of the central cities have lost ground, absolutely and proportionally, to the peripheral developments. Retail sales in the central business district of Chicago decreased by 5 percent between 1948 and 1954, while sales in the metropolitan area outside the city increased by 53 percent. The relative sales loss of downtown areas has been even greater in other central cities.

Further developments can be foreseen. The downtown stores, with nonwhite and low-income customers more and more predominant in their clientele, will tend to concentrate on cheaper merchandise. "'Borax' for downtown, Herman Miller for the suburb," is already a slogan of the furniture business. The decline of the central-city department store will be accompanied by a general deterioration of the downtown area. There are some striking exceptions, most notably in mid-town Manhattan. But in most cities—Chicago, Boston, Los Angeles are good examples— the main streets are becoming infested with sucker joints for tourists: all night jewelry auctions, bargain linens and cheap neckties, hamburger stands and jazz dives. The slums, in other words, are spreading to the central business districts.

A further, though more problematic, development is that the offices of the large corporations will join the flight from the city, taking along with them their servicing businesses: banks, law offices, advertising agencies, and others. The rapid development of closed circuit television, facsimile reproduction, and other technical aids relieves these businesses of the necessity of clustering at a central point. Their exodus from the city is already underway. New highways will make it easier in many places to get from one suburb to another than from suburb to downtown; and the losses of giving up central headquarters can be amortized over a number of years, frequently at considerable tax savings. Even the downtown hotel is likely to give way to the suburban motel except for convention purposes, an incidental further boost to the honkey-tonk development within the downtown business areas.

The rule seems to be a simple one: retail trade, the white collar shops, and the service industries will follow popula-

tion. (Once their exodus is well underway, they also lead population.) The same general rule at least partially applies for manufacturing: the greatest suburbanization of manufacturing has taken place in those metropolitan areas where there has also been the most marked suburbanization of population, and some evidence indicates that manufacturing precedes population, rather than vice versa. Though the central cities have lost some manufacturing to both suburban and non-metropolitan areas, they have nevertheless maintained the preponderant share of the nation's total manufacturing enterprise. As Kitagawa and Bogue have shown, "the over-all spatial distribution (of manufacturing) in the United States has changed comparatively little in the past 50 years."[10] The relative immobility of heavy industry has the result of fixing the laboring and semi-skilled groups, including large numbers of Negroes, within the central cities.

Even a conservative view must anticipate the exodus of a large segment of retail and other nonmanufacturing businesses from downtown centers. Abandonment of these centers will lead to a host of municipal problems, not least of which is the loss of a substantial tax base. These economic developments are at once a step towards, and a consequence of, the city-suburban bifurcation of races that promises to transform many central cities into lower class ethnic islands. Successful attempts by central cities to encourage the establishment of new manufacturing plants as a means of rebuilding their tax base will of course hasten this process.

Political Consequences Whatever the melancholy resemblance between older segregation patterns of the rural South and newer ones of the urban North, one important fact is different: the Negroes of the North possess the suffrage. How will they use it if they become the majority group—or at least the largest single group —in some of the great cities of the nation?

The most likely political development is the organization of Negroes for ends conceived narrowly to the advantage of the Negro community. Such a political effort might aim to destroy zoning and building restrictions for the immediate purpose of enlarging opportunities for desperately needed Negro housing against stubborn social pressures. If successful, the outcome might merely extend the Negro ghetto and cause a further departure of white populations to the suburbs. Yet the short-run political appeal of this action cannot be denied.

What the Negroes seek for themselves in Chicago in 1975 or 1985 might not be any more selfishly conceived than what Irish-dominated city councils in Boston and New York have sought in the past. In one essential field, Negro leadership may be more advantageous to the whole population: lacking devotion to the parochial schools, it would not be mean in the support of public schools. The rub lies in the very visibility of Negro domination. Even on the assumption of Negro leaders and followers demonstrating wisdom and forbearance, what would be the consequence in one or more major cities of the city councils becoming predominantly Negro? What will be the situation in a state legislature when the largest group of big-city representatives are Negroes?

At the very least, cities politically dominated by Negroes will find it more difficult to bring about the urban-suburban cooperation so badly needed in so many fields. They will find greatly exacerbated what is already keenly felt in a majority of states: the conflict between the great urban center and the rural "downstate" or

"upstate" areas. Similar unfortunate effects will follow in the national Congress, once a number of large cities are largely represented by Negro congressmen. The pitting of whites against Negroes, and of white policies against Negro policies, does not await actual Negro urban domination. The cry has already been raised in state legislatures. The conflict can only grow more acute as race and class become increasingly coterminous with local government boundaries.

In the long run, it is highly unlikely that the white population will allow Negroes to become dominant in the cities without resistance. The cultural and economic stakes are too high. One countermeasure will surely present itself to the suburbanites: to annex the suburbs, with their predominantly white populations, to the cities. This will be a historic reversal of the traditional suburban antipathy to annexation. But in the perception of suburbanites it will be justified: they will be annexing the city to the suburbs.

The use of annexation to curb Negro political powers is already underway. It was an explicit argument used by political leaders favoring an annexation to Nashville in 1952. And other recent annexations, largely confined to the South, have taken place at least partially to deny Negroes political powers they would otherwise achieve.

Other actions to the same end can be expected, especially the gerrymandering of Negro populations so as to deny them equitable representation in legislative bodies of city, state, and nation. Tuskegee, Alabama, was gerrymandered in 1957 to exclude all but a handful of Negro voters from city elections, and steps are currently under way to divide Macon County among five neighboring counties. Negroes have long lived within the city, and the county has for many years been preponderantly Negro, but only recently have the Negroes exercised their franchise in any numbers. In the border city of Cincinnati, fear of growing Negro political power was an important reason for the 1957 action that repealed proportional representation and subsequently defeated the reform City Charter Committee. During the campaign over proportional representation, whispering campaigns urged defeat of the system in order to prevent Theodore M. Berry, Negro vice-mayor, from becoming mayor, as well as to prevent Negroes from moving into white neighborhoods. The total political picture of continued racial bifurcation forecasts a new round of political repression aimed at Negroes. For this one, they will be better armed—effective numbers, economic strength, political sophistication, and allies in the white population.

Toward Solutions

If racial separation and segregation lead to evil consequences, the cure is obvious; the separation should be ended. For no problem is a solution more easily stated: white populations should be brought back into the central cities, and Negroes should be allowed to choose freely where they want to live in all areas of central cities and suburbs alike. No solution is more difficult to implement.

Racial exclusiveness may be conceived as an "American dilemma" in moral terms, or a Marxian problem of class antagonisms, or a Freudian expression of instinctual attractions and cultural taboos. From these perspectives the "race problem" may be solved, if at all, only through the slow marches of gradual social change. Neither laws, nor adult education,

nor *ad hoc* institutional programs can be decisive.

It can certainly be assumed that for a long time for some people in some places no program of residential integration will be palatable or acceptable. Yet it is also true that people are not frozen in antagonistic attitudes, that change is possible, and that the change can best be achieved by actual successful experiences in interracial living. Most importantly, plans can be built upon the great diversity of outlook and attitude among the urban populations of midcentury America.

Creating a Free Real Estate Market The most important general step to be taken is to remove the restrictions on where Negroes may live. This is, in the first place, an act of simple justice. Of greater relevance here, if nonwhites possessed genuine residential mobility, it would go a long way toward eliminating the great social costs of the present population distribution. From free movement, it follows that (1) there would be less overcrowding in Negro areas; (2) there would be fewer and smaller all-Negro neighborhoods; and (3) individual Negroes would self-selectively distribute themselves, as white populations do, among neighborhoods whose social characteristics are roughly homogeneous and roughly similar to their own.

It should not be supposed that the removal of restrictions would end Negro residential concentrations. Income factors alone will confine many Negroes to the least desirable residential areas for a long time to come. Considerations of sociability are also an important concentrating factor. Investments in businesses and living quarters will keep even many of those who can afford to move as residents of all-Negro areas. Yet many Negroes now live in Negro neighborhoods simply because they have no other place to go. With the occupational upgrading and increased income that Negroes are achieving in ever-growing numbers, there is no doubt that freedom to choose residences would result in a scattering of Negro families throughout the entire urban area.

That many Negroes would continue to reside in areas of all-Negro concentration, even under circumstances that permit dispersion, would, in fact, make easier the dispersion process. Only a limited number of non-whites can afford, and wish, to move to white neighborhoods. This means that there could be a relatively complete dispersion of those so inclined, without their number becoming large in any single neighborhood.

The case of nondiscrimination housing laws can best be argued in these terms. Such laws would allow the widespread dispersion of nonwhites. Given the limited number of nonwhites who would choose in the foreseeable future to take advantage of such laws, their main impact would be in preventing the kinds of concentration that frequently turn present "open occupancy" communities into crowded all-Negro slums.

Nondiscriminatory laws, however, can do more harm than good unless they are enacted in large jurisdictions. The smallest effective area is probably a very large city. In smaller areas their effect might be to create the flight of white residents to "lily-white" jurisdictions. The full effect of nondiscriminatory laws can be felt only if, in a given region, there are no such areas to which to flee. Even under this circumstance, laws against discrimination may produce a scattering of all-Negro residential pockets rather than genuine dispersions unless attempts are made to prevent the concentration of Negroes in any given neighborhood.

Panic flights of old-resident whites at the appearance of one or a few new-resident Negro families will be discouraged if the old residents know that, no matter where they move, a similar development might take place. The new residents in most cases will seek to avoid another all-Negro neighborhood. The interests of old and new residents become congruent on the points of maintaining neighborhood standards and mixed, rather than all-Negro, occupancy. Other less happy outcomes are of course possible. But nondiscrimination laws, where combined with a sensitivity to the importance of not crowding Negroes into any single area, provide opportunities for giving Negroes the free residential choice they should have while simultaneously producing minimum disturbance in existing communities.[11]

Controlled Migration The case for nondiscriminating laws thus rests largely on the point that they would filter nonwhites in relatively small numbers to white communities. Laws of this sort are difficult to enforce. (How does one prove discrimination if a seller decides not to sell?)

Population groups are infinitely facile in frustrating unpopular laws. Public acceptance is necessary if interracial living is to be made possible.

The tipping phenomenon has meant that interracial communities in the United States (outside some slum areas) exist only where there also exist limits on the influx of nonwhites. In the usual case, these limits have been economic in nature. Thus the Kenwood region of Chicago is a truly interracial one. Homes in this neighborhood are large and expensive to maintain, and municipal housing codes are rigidly enforced. Pure economic pressures, combined with community acceptance of those Negroes who can afford to live there, have produced an upper-middle class interracial neighborhood.

In other cases, control of in-migration has been consciously contrived. The developers of the Philadelphia suburbs of Concord Park and Greenbelt Knoll have announced their intention of maintaining a white-Negro ratio of 55—45. Prospective purchasers place their names on a waiting list, and a purchase is made possible only if it maintains the desired racial distribution.

It is doubtful that many population groups, other than confirmed, egalitarian Quakers, would accept a ratio of Negroes at this high a point. On the other hand, Negro political leads in the large cities could probably not remain political leaders if they were willing to accept controlled interracialism, set at a ratio that most whites would accept.

Nevertheless, experimentation with various systems of controlled migration is highly desirable. The tip-point phenomenon is so universal that it constitutes strong evidence in favor of control. Without control there has been a total failure to achieve interracial communities involving substantial numbers of Negroes anywhere in the great urban areas of America. Where controlled migration has been achieved, so has interracial living.

Many methods can be found to implement a controlled migration. A free real estate market, accompanied by enforced, adequate housing codes, is the preferred mechanism. The direct rationing of sales, as in the Philadelphia suburbs, is possible in a number of different forms. Community organizations of all types, including church groups, can be mobilized. Informal pressures upon real estate operators and mortgagers can be effective. The private, if not public, support of Negro leaders for controlled migration can be achieved. At Concord Park and Greenbelt Knoll, the builders found no opposition from Negroes to a balanced community pattern, once it was explained that the larger goal was to break down racial segregation. Many Negroes will support policies aimed at avoiding all-Negro communities if alternative housing opportunities are available.

The moral problem is not an easy one. It is the problem of placing limits upon Negro in-migration to particular urban and suburban areas. It means fostering a smaller discrimination in favor of scotching a larger one. Whatever the difficulties of such a position, it seems to be, for a large number of Negroes and whites alike, a preferable alternative to the present pattern of segregated population groups.

Returning White Population to Central Cities Values of urbanism, other things being equal, compete easily with the suburban way of life. The other things now *not* equal include: modern, moderate priced housing; cleanliness and green space; good schools; safety against hoodlum attack; a sense of neighborhood solidarity. If such amenities were available, the attractions of urban life would almost certainly be sufficient to bring large numbers of white residents back into the cities. The cities offer a diversity of living conditions, a choice of companionship, and a range of leisure time activities that cannot be matched by the suburbs with their relatively closed and static conditions of life. The isolation of the dormitory suburbs, the large fraction of life demanded for commuting, and the social restriction of village living have already produced a swelling protest. Some segment of the metropolitan population is certainly composed of confirmed suburbanites, and no changes in the central city would attract them. But urban life would beckon large numbers if it could compete with suburbia in terms of the economics of housing, the safety and comfort of families, and the social solidarity of neighborhoods.

No precise data exist concerning the extent to which the suburban sadness has already started a return flow to the cities. Certainly that flow has been considerable, especially among older couples, the more wealthy, and the childless. (The Chicago Gold Coast and the Manhattan luxury apartment would make important foci of research for measuring this flow.) What needs to be done is to bring into this stream the larger numbers of young and middle-aged couples who have families and who are not wealthy. Developments within the suburbs—the overcrowding of schools, the blighting of badly planned residential areas, and the full flowering of the un-inhibited automobile culture—will provide an additional push toward the cities.

Whatever may be accomplished by individual home owners and real estate specialists will not be sufficient to reverse the massive population trends described earlier. The effort must be aided by governmental action. The important point is that governmental programs must be on a far larger scale than any action thus far undertaken.

The basic unit of operation must be a large site: a complete neighborhood or even a complete area of the city. The scale of urban renewal must be conceived not in square blocks, but in square miles. Destruction or rehabilitation of old urban dwellings and the building of new neighborhoods must be planned not in tens of acres but in hundreds. Whole sections of cities will have to be made over in order to attract an influx of stable white population groups.

Rebuilding on this scale is important for many reasons. And it would provide one opportunity to achieve interracial communities. Many white families affirm that they move to the suburbs not because they have Negroes for neighbors but because of the neighborhood deterioration that accompanies the high densities and rowdy behavior of the in-migrants. Large rebuilt areas, strictly controlled against over-crowding, would have the effect of removing such objections. Very large sums of public money will be required for this sort of program, but the obstacles are political rather than economic.[12] Intricate collaborative devices among the local, state, and federal governments will be necessary. The history of urban redevelopment thus far, with few exceptions, is a history of too little, too late. Anything less than a massive program may have admirable local effects for particular population fractions, as when adequate housing is substituted for slum housing over several blocks for a few residents in New York's Harlem. These ameliorative programs are not to be criticized. But they do not attack the basic problem of the bifurcation of races on urban-suburban lines. To meet this problem, the rebuilding of entire sections of major cities is necessary.

The Suburbanization of Negroes Any extensive rebuilding of central cities will displace Negro populations who inhabit the very urban areas not in need of re-building. No progress is possible unless a redistribution of the Negro population simultaneously occurs. One objective must be a migration of Negroes to suburban areas.

It is widely assumed that opening suburbs to Negroes would be readily achieved if there existed a single local government whose jurisdiction covered the entire metropolitan area. This is certainly too optimistic a view of the matter. Even under a metropolitan government, the people in outlying areas would not be without ability to resist, politically and socially, the incursion of what they consider "undesirable elements" into their communities. In Chicago and in many other places, residents of "better" neighborhoods *within* the central city have successfully opposed housing measures which threatened to bring Negro residents into their areas. If the free distribution of nonwhite groups is not politically feasible on an interneighborhood basis, the creation of a metropolitan government will certainly not make it so on an intercity one. A single government for a whole area might conceivably provide a more satisfactory political arena for the eventual solution of distributing nonwhite groups throughout an entire metropolitan area, but will not *ipso facto* guarantee that distribution.

Nor is it true that restrictions on the migration of Negro and other nonwhite groups to the suburbs is solely a class or economic matter. Any examination of the variety of suburban conditions leads to the conclusion that urban blight and the dilapidated housing and social conditions that accompany it are not uniquely characteristic of the central cities. Rather, blight exists in varying degrees of intensity in all parts of the metropolitan area, central city and suburbs alike. In all but the very newest of planned suburban developments, many dwelling units exist which, in the terms of the Bureau of the Census, "should be torn down, extensively repaired, or rebuilt." Only a fraction of these units are Negro dwellings. In many metropolitan areas a larger proportion of dwelling units outside than inside the central city are dilapidated or lack running water.[13]

Despite these facts, in many suburban areas the extravagances of legal restrictions covering suburban building should be examined for their effect upon maintaining Negro urban concentrations. Provisions covering lot sizes, sidewalks, streets, building setbacks, and building materials often have very little to do with the maintenance of standards of health and decency. They are, rather, frankly established to stabilize or to upgrade community levels, including the maintenance of their racial character. The effect is to make suburban housing too expensive for even the Negroes who otherwise could afford, and would prefer, suburban living. Less extravagant building and housing codes would certainly lead to some greater degree of Negro suburbanization. This can be accomplished without producing additional suburban slums. The antidote to over-stringent building restrictions is not their complete abolition.

Nondiscriminatory housing laws would, as we have seen, go a long way in encouraging some suburbanization of Negroes. Other discriminating practices—many of them extra-legal—should be ended. If local building inspectors cannot be trained to administer laws impartially, they should be replaced by officials who can, under state or federal supervision. If local police forces will not protect the property and lives of Negro purchasers of suburban homes, then procedures for training, replacing, or penalizing such officials must be adopted. If established realtors will not sell to Negroes, others should be encouraged, and perhaps paid, to do so.

Social attitudes change more slowly than laws, and only a moderate incursion of Negroes into established suburbs can be expected in the near future. The best chance for even this modest development is under community auspices on the basis of controlled migrations. The need for Negro suburban housing will greatly exceed the receptivity of the established suburbs, especially if central city rebuilding is undertaken on the scale that it is needed. This sharply raises the question of the desirability of encouraging all-Negro suburbs.

The negative consideration is obvious: all-Negro suburbs would simply substitute one sort of segregated life for another. On the other hand, there is much to be said on the positive side. Such suburbs would be a large factor in redressing the present imbalance in the urban-suburban population distribution. As we have seen, this in itself is a highly desirable step. Secondly, such communities, adequately planned and constructed, would provide a great improvement in living conditions, superior to both the urban and suburban slums in which so large a proportion of Negroes now reside. Thirdly, and perhaps most importantly, the all-Negro middle-class suburb could very well constitute a significant step in the direction of large-scale interracial communities. Present conditions of life of the largest fraction of the Negro population discourage, rather than encourage, the habits of thought and conduct deemed desirable by the large white community. The middle-class Negro suburb would foster such attributes. If class, in addition to skin color, is a principal cause of segregation, then the class differential may be overcome by the middle-class suburban life.

As in so many planned social changes, schemes for all-Negro suburban communities may produce unexpected ill consequences. One deserves mention. Grant the truth of what has been said: that good suburban housing in a good suburban neighborhood will aid in producing a Negro population of model, middle-class, social attributes, and that nothing distinguishes this group from middle-class whites except skin color. It is then easily assumed that interracial living is the next step. But the opposite assumption must also be entertained: that whites will continue to resist interracial living. In this event Negroes will all the more resent their segregation and whites will have no line except the color line on which to take a stand. If Negro-white tensions pivot exclusively on color, they may be exacerbated to a new point of bitterness.

Despite such dangers, the more persuasive evidence is that Negro-white tensions will decrease, not increase, as the populations become socially more alike. For this reason, as well as the need to meet short-run housing requirements, experiments with all-Negro suburban communities should be encouraged.

Negroes to Smaller Cities Discussion of the possible distribution of some Negroes to points outside the larger metropolitan areas does not fall strictly within the purposes of this paper. Yet is it worth noting that Negroes are greatly underrepresented in virtually all places outside the South and the larger urban areas of the rest of the country. Without considering non-southern rural areas (where Negroes constitute a smaller fraction of the population than anywhere else), the cities under 250 thousand in the Northeast are, in all size classes, less than 2.9 percent Negro; in the North Central states, less than 4.2 percent; and in the West, less than 2.7 percent.[14] A program of encouraging migration to these smaller cities would somewhat mitigate the large city, urban-suburban racial bifurcation and, at the same time, establish important new opportunities for integrated living. The effects of such an effort should not be overestimated. For example, if one un-realistically assumes it were possible for non-southern cities of from 10 thousand to 250 thousand population to be increased 5 percent in total population by an in-migration of Negroes, the total number so placed would be fewer than 900 thousand. This is only some 150 thousand more than the number of Negroes in New York City at the 1950 census.

Nevertheless, attempts to locate Negroes in cities of this size—as well as in smaller urban areas—would be worthwhile. Since employment opportunities in industry constitute the most important attraction for Negro in-migrants, success of such at-tempts would pivot upon the availability of such jobs for Negroes (therefore a shortage of white workers) and upon in-formation concerning such opportunities being disseminated among potential mi-grants. The former factor will to a large extent depend upon further industrial growth in small- and medium-size urban areas. The factor of publicity is more immediately controllable. The information flow now directed at potential migrants from the South (by such organizations as the Urban League) could very well be focused more sharply on the existing and emerging opportunities outside the larger metropolitan areas.

No single measure will solve the problem in any single area, and the same combina-tion of measures will not be appropriate as leverage points in any two areas. What strikes the observer is the paucity of imagination that has been brought to bear on the issue. The Quaker communities in the Philadelphia area provide a model for one kind of controlled migration that is only slowly being taken up in other places. The investment in almost any city of, say, a million dollars in a revolving fund for the

purchase of homes to foster interracial neighborhoods, with careful planning and public relations, could make a dent in the pattern of segregation. A well-staffed, resourceful office with the objective of publicizing successes of interracial resi-dential contacts would be a valuable positive aid to enlarging those contacts and no less valuable a means of dissipating images of disagreeableness and violence that widely prevail.

Action programs of this sort are obvious needs. Beyond them there exists a wide range of more experimental possibilities for both private and public agencies. For example, there are a number of newly built areas in the central cities whose attractiveness and proximity to work and recreational facilities make them highly desirable living places. Lake Meadows, in Chicago, is a good example of this sort of development. Nevertheless, these areas tend to become all-Negro communities because of their relatively small size, or their situation close to older Negro slums, or other factors. It might be possible to make such newly built areas model inter-racial neighborhoods. How can white residents be attracted to them? A private foundation might bring the attractions of such developments to the attention of whites by maintaining a good small museum at such a site or by arranging concerts there (but at no other nearby place) of outstanding musical groups, or by providing superior park and swimming facilities, or indeed by partially subsidizing rental costs for limited periods. The marginal attractions needed to bring whites into such intrinsically attractive areas may in many cases be quite small; and once a pattern of interracial living is successfully achieved it may be expected to continue as subsidies are diminished. Private organ-izations could in a similar way reward suburban communities that make it easy for Negroes to take up residence.

The national government may not be barred from an analogous type of activity. A good case can be made for a federal program to provide suburbs with aid for community facilities they already need and will need even more in years to come: schools, parks, libraries, swimming pools, and similar amenities. It is commonplace for federal legislation to establish conditions that must be met by local governments before they qualify for financial aid. The question arises: is it possible to write a federal law that would supply aid for community facilities on a priority basis to those suburbs containing a given minimum of Negro residents? Constitutional and political questions immediately arise. Clearly no requirement based directly upon a racial classification would meet constitutional standards. Yet it is not beyond the realm of legal creativity to find another scheme of definition that would foster the end of racial distribution and yet remain within constitutional limits. The more difficult objection is political, but it is by no means insurmountable. Even southern congressmen might support such a measure if for no other reason than glee over the embarrassment of their northern colleagues. The larger point is not to argue for the desirability or feasibility of this particular measure, but rather to suggest the need for inventive action. The growing consequences of the population schism, plus the plight that many suburbs will soon find themselves in, combine to bring within the realm of probability even schemes that at first blush seem impossible of achievement.

The whole discussion of "solutions" now rests too largely upon moral terms. The wealth of the United States has historically been used to remove issues from the idealistic to a cash basis, and in this issue, too, cash may be a great salve for moral wounds. This is not meant to be a cynical statement. It is, rather, counsel for the strategy of induced social change. Payment in the form of needed community facilities should accompany other types of action.

Church, social work, and educational institutions must prepare the ground for interracial living and must be ready to act when tensions occur. Indeed, mobilization of resources must take place over a very wide range: from training police officers in problems of race relations to the establishment of special community programs for the improvement of interracial contacts; from the provision of social services for Negro in-migrants to education programs for prospective employers of Negroes; from block activity preparing the way for Negro neighbors to nation-wide programs that implement basic Negro civil rights. Every community facility—churches, schools, labor unions, recreational groups, economic organizations, and government —can be enlisted. Here, as with almost all programs of civic change, working through established institutions and existing voluntary groups is the best avenue to success.

Conclusion

It is frequently argued that problems created by the present distribution of Negroes in the large metropolitan areas are only transitory problems. They will solve themselves through the normal processes of acculturation. This view holds that every immigrant wave to the great cities has at least initially produced disadvantaged ethnic islands. With the passage of time, however, these islands have given way as the second and third generations have acquired cultural characteristics of the larger society and broken away from the habits of conduct of their immigrant fathers and grandfathers. This is the pattern of the Jews in New York, the Poles in Chicago, the Italians in San Francisco. There is some evidence that the Negro group is going through the same process as its members surmount social, vocational, professional, and residential barriers. All the problem needs is time. The American melting pot will work for Negroes as it has for others.

This is a hopeful view. Despite many examples of successful interracial adjustment, it is a view not substantiated by either history or available data. The example of earlier European immigrants all concern white populations. No statistically significant evidence exists indicating the inevitable dissolution of the Negro concentrations. As with Japanese-Americans before World War II, acceptance by the larger community for a relatively few Negroes is being accompanied by life within closed communities for the relatively many. (The Japanese community in Los Angeles grew continuously between 1900 and 1942.) The factor of skin color, alone, is one cause for the different course of development. The very size of the Negro concentration in the larger cities, resulting in the establishment of an entire Negro economic and social life, can also be expected to obstruct the decline of the communities in which that life flourishes. To this must be added the disinclination of many white groups to accept Negroes as neighbors and social companions. The total picture for the future, if present trends are unaltered, is the further breaking down of some boundaries of the closed community affecting proportionately small

numbers of Negroes. For the largest numbers, segregation will continue and probably increase, rather than decline.

This is almost certainly the correct prognosis for the immediate 30 years ahead. To the extent that the natural acculturation argument is one covering the distant future—say 80 or 100 years—it may have greater accuracy. But to that extent it is largely irrelevant. The central cities of the metropolitan areas dominate the nation not only in population but also in retail and wholesale sales, manufacturing, and the provision of services to individuals and businesses. They set the tone and pattern for the entire complex of community interdependence in politics, economics, and cultural life. If the analysis presented here is accurate, the whole nation is faced with a wide range of deleterious consequences. And these consequences will take their toll long before the "natural desuetude" of segregation is accomplished. This is the justification for taking all positive steps possible to end the present patterns of segregation.

Another reason for not disturbing the current population distribution might lie in the danger that dispersion would deprive Negroes of the political power they have acquired as the consequence of concentration. This is not a valid argument for two reasons.

On the one hand, it does not take into account the genuine gains that accrue to the Negro population as the consequence of dispersion. Increasing strain in race relations seems always to accompany concentrated numbers. Where a minority group is dispersed, it is less visible, less likely to be considered a unit, less feared, less subject to discrimination. Where it is concentrated and segregated, it is more likely to be relegated to a subordinate position, and its members have fewer opportunities for assimilation into the larger social structure.

On the other hand, dispersion of residential areas would not necessarily lead to a decline in Negro political power. The 100 percent Negro voting districts can be viewed as a type of gerrymandering in which political power is lost by the very concentration of voters. Negroes constituting 50 percent of the voters in two election districts (or 25 percent in four districts) will wield more political power than if they composed 100 percent of a single district. What is to be avoided is the halfway house: not enough dispersion to prevent clear subordination, with not enough concentration to make numbers politically effective. Within the larger metropolitan areas this is an unlikely possibility. The gains to be made by Negroes from political action built upon concentration can never equal those that can be achieved by dispersion throughout the metropolitan areas.

The programs suggested for overcoming Negro concentrations face great obstacles. They arouse the ire of the ignorant and the prejudiced. They are disquieting to even the fair-minded and the sophisticated who live good lives and who perform their civic duties conscientiously. And they will be bitterly opposed by a wide range of people: owners, mortgagers, and others who profit from the present patterns of land use; political leaders in the central cities, including Negro leaders, who fear the dissipation of established constituencies, as well as political leaders of other areas whose tenure will be disturbed by the incursion of new voters into their districts; old residents of suburbs and the better central-city neighborhoods who hold strongly to their comfortable social situations and established shopping, social, and educational patterns. Even those with humanitarian motives will voice opposition to some plans on the grounds that they constitute an unwarranted interference in the life patterns of the poor. And Negro groups and leaders will not easily be won over to some aspects of the proposed program. They will, for example, see large-scale urban renewal as a displacement and an imposition, before its advantages will be apparent. Negroes have already in many cities distinguished themselves for their opposition to smaller-scale programs of urban renewal.[15] Some of this opposition may be blunted: as when Negro opposition to urban renewal is placated by well-planned programs of relocation housing. But every such move, in turn, is likely to increase opposition from other sources: in the example given from areas in which the relocation housing is to be placed.

Despite difficulties and despite the uncertainty of success, all efforts are justified. The stakes are high: the preservation and further development of many facets of urban American life, for whites and Negroes alike. By building a non-discriminatory housing market in both city and suburbs, income and social attributes, not race, can be maximized as the criteria for residential location. By rebuilding large areas of central cities, white populations can be induced to return to those cities. By combating restrictions against Negro occupancy of suburbs, a flow of nonwhites can be started in that direction. By attracting Negroes to jobs in the smaller cities outside the South, where they are now underrepresented, some of the present and potential city-suburban population imbalance may be corrected. By encouraging through community resources the controlled migration of Negroes into all areas of city and suburbs, a significant redistribution of Negroes and whites can take place.

All these measures minimize the dangerous operation of the tip-point psychology. Here, as elsewhere, nothing succeeds like success, and a demonstration that such a program can produce results in one metropolitan area of the nation will be important for all areas. The only way to avoid the consequences of racial schism is to bridge it.[16]

NOTES

1. Otis D. Duncan and Albert J. Reiss, Jr., *Social Characteristics of Urban and Rural Communities, 1950* (New York: John Wiley & Sons, 1956), p. 60.
2. The Duncans' figure for 1956 supersedes an estimate made in 1955 by Donald Bogue and illustrates the difficulties of making projections. Bogue estimated that Chicago's Negro population would reach between 19 and 24 per cent of the total by 1965 (*An Estimate of Metropolitan Chicago's Future Population: 1955 to 1965*, a report published jointly by the Chicago Community Inventory, University of Chicago, and Scripps Foundation, Miami University); the Duncans' closer look revealed that the 19 percent figure had been reached by 1956 (*Chicago's Negro Population*, a report by the Chicago Community Inventory, University of Chicago, 1956). I am indebted to Otis and Beverly Duncan for answering many questions concerning the problems of this paper and for their criticism of an early draft.
3. Otis D. Duncan and Beverly Duncan, *The Negro Population of Chicago* (Chicago: University of Chicago Press, 1957), p. 96.
4. *Ibid.*, p. 120.
5. With respect to the latter point see Robert C. Weaver, "Integration in Public and Private Housing," *Annals of the American Academy of Political and Social Science*, March, 1956, p. 87.
6. Otis D. Duncan and Beverly Duncan, *op. cit.*, pp. 14–16, chaps. vii, viii.
7. See, for example, Davis McEntire, "A Study of Racial Attitudes in Neighborhoods Infiltrated by Non-Whites" (mimeographed) (Berkeley: University of California, 1955); Arnold M. Rose, Frank J. Atelsek, and Lawrence R. McDonald, "Neighborhood Reactions to Isolated Negro Residents: An Alternative to Invasion and Succession," *American Sociological Review*, October, 1953, pp. 497–507; Robert C. Weaver, "Integration in Public and Private Housing," *loc. cit.*; also the mimeographed reports of the Committee on Civil Rights in Manhattan, "Open Occupancy Living in the Bronx" (May, 1957); "Summary of Survey on Country-Wide Instances of Open Occupancy Housing" (May, 1957).
8. Quoted from Edward C. Banfield and Morton Grodzins, *Government and Housing in Metropolitan Areas* (New York: McGraw-Hill Book Co., 1958).
9. See Shirley A. Star, "Interracial Tension in Two Areas of Chicago: An Exploratory Approach to the Measurement of Interracial Tension," unpublished doctoral dissertation, Department of Sociology, University of Chicago, December, 1950.
10. Evelyn M. Kitagawa and Donald J. Bogue, *Suburbanization of Manufacturing Activity Within Standard Metropolitan Areas* (Published jointly by Scripps Foundation for Research in Population Problems, Miami University, and Population Research and Training Center, University of Chicago), 1955, p. 15.
11. See Robert C. Weaver, "The Effect of Anti-Discrimination Legislation Upon the FHA- and VA-Insured Housing Market in New York State," *Land Economics*, Vol. XXXI, No. 4, November, 1955, pp. 303–13.
12. See Edward C. Banfield and Morton Grodzins, *op. cit.*
13. Victor Jones, "Local Government Organization in Metropolitan Areas," *The Future of Cities and Urban Redevelopment*, ed., Coleman Woodbury (Chicago: University of Chicago Press, 1953).
14. Otis D. Duncan and Albert J. Reiss, Jr., *op. cit.*, p. 60.
15. For good reasons, it should be added. Renewal programs are largely slum clearance programs and, therefore, largely affect Negro populations. Since alternative housing is frequently unavailable, the effect of slum clearance is often one of packing Negroes even tighter into existing Negro areas, usually in the periphery of the cleared zone. A study by the Urban League of Chicago showed that between 1948 and 1956, 86,000 people in Chicago were displaced by urban renewal, highway, and other programs. Almost 57,000 of these were Negroes. Constituting fewer than 20 percent of the city's population, Negroes made up more than 65 percent of the displaced population. See *Chicago Urban League Newsletter*, Vol. 2, No. 4, September-October, 1957, pp. 3–4.
16. Earlier versions of portions of these materials have been published as "Metropolitan Segregation," *Scientific American*, October, 1957, pp. 33–41; and "The New Shame of the Cities," *Confluence*, Vol. 7, No. 1 (Spring, 1958), pp. 29–46.

33. Residential Distribution and Occupational Stratification

Beverly Duncan
and
Otis D. Duncan

One of the major contributions of sociology to our understanding of spatial structure has come through its investigations of the way in which residential patterns are affected by considerations of social status. Otis and Beverly Duncan explore the major dimension of social status—occupation—in its relationship to the urban form of Chicago. To measure the relevant aspects of spatial structure, the Duncans develop a battery of four indices, designed to express the degree of residential segregation of occupations, the isolation of occupational groups from each other, the concentration of occupations in low-rent areas, and the degree of centralization of the occupations. Their analysis provides strong support for the proposition that spatial distance between occupation groups is closely related to their social distance. Their most important finding is that residential segregation follows a \|-pattern: The occupations at the extremes of the occupational scale are more highly segregated than the low white-collar and top blue-collar jobs located in the middle of the scale. The authors discuss a number of factors that could account for this pattern, including the possibility that locational and neighborhood preferences formed during childhood persist into the adult years.

Beverly Duncan is Research Associate at the Population Studies Center, University of Michigan. She is the author of many research monographs and articles, including *Family Factors and School Dropout: 1920–1960* (1965), and is coauthor of *Housing a Metropolis: Chicago* (1960).

Otis Dudley Duncan is Professor of Sociology and Associate Director of the Population Studies Center at the University of Michigan. He is coauthor of *Statistical Geography* (1961), *Metropolis and Region* (1960), *Social Characteristics of Urban and Rural Communities* (1956), and a number of other books.

The idea behind this paper was forcibly stated—in fact, somewhat overstated—by Robert E. Park: "It is because social relations and so frequently and so inevitably correlated with spatial relations; because physical distances so frequently are, or seem to be, the indexes of social distances, that statistics have any significance whatever for sociology. And this is true, finally, because it is only as social and psychical facts can be reduced to, or correlated with, spatial facts that they can be measured at all."[1]

This study finds a close relationship between spatial and social distances in a metropolitan community. It suggests that a systematic consideration of the spatial

aspect of stratification phenomena, though relatively neglected by students of the subject,[2] should be a primary focus of urban stratification studies. Aside from demonstrating the relevance of human ecology to the theory of social organization, the study offers further evidence for the suitability of a particular set of methodological techniques for research in comparative urban ecology.[3] These techniques are adaptable to a wide variety of problems

Reprinted by permission from *The American Journal of Sociology*, Vol. LX (March 1955), pp. 493–503. Published by The University of Chicago Press. Copyright 1955 by The University of Chicago.

in urban ecological structure, permit economical and objective comparisons among communities, and thus overcome some of the indeterminacy of a strictly cartographic approach. The techniques are here applied to only one metropolitan community, Chicago; however, comparative studies, conducted on an exploratory basis, indicate their ability to produce significant results.

Data and Method

The sources of data for this study, except as noted otherwise, were the published volume of 1950 census tract statistics for Chicago and adjacent areas[4] (coextensive with the Chicago Metropolitan District, as delineated in 1940), and the census-tract summary punch cards for this area obtained from the Bureau of the Census. The ecological analysis pertains to employed males fourteen years old and over, classified into the eight major occupation groups listed in the tables below. The occupation groups disregarded in this analysis (farmers and farm managers, farm laborers, private household workers, and occupation not reported) include only twenty-one thousand of the one and a half million employed males in the Metropolitan District.

A portion of the analysis is carried through with the census tract as the area unit. There are 1,178 census tracts in the Metropolitan District, of which 935 are in the city of Chicago and 243 in the adjacent area. The remainder of the analysis rests on a scheme of zones and sectors, delineated rather arbitrarily. Tracts were assigned to circular zones, concentric to the center of the city at State and Madison streets, with one-mile intervals up to fourteen miles, two-mile intervals up to twenty-eight miles, and with residual categories of tracts

more than twenty-eight miles from the city center and tracts in the adjacent area too large to be classified by zones. The latter category contains only 1.4 percent of the employed males. Five sectors were established, with boundaries approximating radial lines drawn from the city center. The North Shore sector runs along Lake Michigan through such suburbs as Skokie, Evanston, Lake Forest, and Waukegan; the Northwest sector extends through Park Ridge and Des Plaines to Arlington Heights; the West sector includes the suburbs of Cicero, Oak Park, and Berwyn, running out as far as Wheaton and Naperville; the Southwest sector is approximately bisected by a line running through Blue Island, Harvey, and Chicago Heights to Park Forest; and the South Shore sector runs along Lake Michigan through the Indiana suburbs of East Chicago, Hammond, Gary, and East Gary. Combining the zone and sector schemes yielded a set of 104 zone-sector segments; that is, area units averaging about ten times the size of a census tract, though with considerable variation in area and population.

The spatial "distance" between occupation groups, or more precisely the difference between their areal distributions, is measured by the *index of dissimilarity*.[5] To compute this index, one calculates for each occupation group the percentage of all workers in that group residing in each area unit (tract or zone-sector segment). The index of dissimilarity between two occupation groups is then one-half the sum of the absolute values of the differences between the respective distributions, taken area by area. In the accompanying hypothetical example the index of dissimilarity between occupations A and B is 20 percent (i.e., 40/2). This may be interpreted as a measure of displacement: 20 percent of the workers in occupation A would have to move to a different area in order to make their distribution identical with that of occupation *B*.

Area	A	B	Diff.
1	10%	15%	5%
2	20	15	5
3	40	25	15
4	30	45	15
Total	100%	100%	40%

When the index of dissimilarity is computed between one occupation group and all other occupations combined (i.e., total employed males except those in the given occupation group), it is referred to as an *index of segregation*.[6] An equivalent and more convenient means of computing the segregation index is to compute the index of dissimilarity between the given occupation group and total employed males (i.e., all occupations), "adjusting" the result by dividing by one minus the proportion of the total male employed labor force included in that occupation group.

The indexes of segregation and dissimilarity were computed on both a tract basis and a zone-sector segment basis to determine the effect of the size of the area unit on the results. While the indexes for tracts are uniformly higher than for zone-sector segments, this effect can be disregarded for purposes of determining the relative positions of the occupation groups. The product-moment correlation between the two sets of segregation indexes in Table 2 is .96. The correlation between the two sets of dissimilarity indexes in Table 3 is .98, with the segment-based index (*s*) related to the tract-based index (*t*) by the regression equation, $s = .8t - 1.3$. These results indicate that for the kind of problem dealt with here the larger, and hence less homogeneous, unit is as serviceable as the smaller

one. This suggests that some of the recent concern about census-tract homogeneity may be misplaced.[7]

The *index of low-rent concentration* is obtained by (1) classifying tracts into intervals according to the median monthly rental of tenant-occupied dwelling units; (2) computing the percentage distribution by rent intervals for each occupation group and for all occupations combined; (3) cumulating the distributions, from low to high rent; (4) calculating the quantity $\Sigma X_{i-1} Y_i - \Sigma X_i Y_{i-1}$, where X_i is the cumulated percentage of the given occupation through the *i*th rent interval, Y_i is the cumulated percentage of all occupations combined, and the summation is over all rent intervals; and, finally, (5) "adjusting" the result (as for the segregation index) to obtain an index equivalent to the one obtained by comparing the given occupation group with all other occupations combined. This index varies between 100 and −100, with positive values indicating a tendency for residences of the given occupation group to be in areas of relatively low rent and with negative values indicating relative concentration in high-rent areas.

The *index of centralization* is computed in the same fashion, except that tracts are ordered by distance from the center of the city, that is, are classified according to the zonal scheme. A negative index of centralization signifies that the given occupation group tends to be "decentralized," or on the average located farther away from the city center than all other occupations, while a positive index is obtained for a relatively "centralized" occupation.[8]

Occupation and Socioeconomic Status

Selected nonecological indicators of the relative socioeconomic status of the major

TABLE 1. SELECTED INDICATORS OF SOCIOECONOMIC STATUS OF THE MAJOR OCCUPATION GROUPS

Major Occupation Group*	Median Income in 1949†	Median School Years Completed‡	Edwards' Socio-economic Group§	Per Cent Nonwhite‖
Professional, technical, and kindred workers	$4,387	16+	1	2.7
Managers, officials, and proprietors, except farm	4,831	12.2	2	2.2
Sales workers	3,698	12.4⎰		⎧2.8
Clerical and kindred workers	3,132	12.2⎱	3	⎩7.4
Craftsmen, foremen and kindred workers	3,648	9.5	4	4.9
Operatives and kindred workers	3,115	8.9	5	12.4
Service workers, except private household	2,635	8.8	5–6	23.0
Laborers, except farm and mine	2,580	8.4	6	27.4

* Does not include farmers and farm managers, private household workers, farm laborers, and occupation not reported.
† For males in the experienced labor force of the Chicago Standard Metropolitan Area, 1950. Source: *1950 U.S. Census of Population*, Bulletin P-C13, Table 78.
‡ For employed males twenty-five years old and over, in the North and West, 1950. Source: *1950 U.S. Census of Population*, Special Report P-E No. 5B, Table 11.
§ Approximate equivalents. Source: Alba M. Edwards, *Comparative Occupation Statistics for the United States, 1870 to 1940* (Washington, D.C.: Government Printing Office, 1943).
‖ For employed males in the Chicago Metropolitan District, 1950. Based on nonwhites residing in census tracts containing 250 or more nonwhite population in 1950. These tracts include 95.8 percent of all nonwhite males in the Metropolitan District.

occupation groups are shown in Table 1. The professional and managerial groups clearly have the highest socioeconomic rank, while operatives, service workers, and laborers are clearly lowest in socioeconomic status. The ranking by socioeconomic level would probably be agreed on by most social scientists. The major occupation groups correspond roughly with the Alba Edwards scheme of "social-economic groups." Edwards does not separate sales workers and clerical workers by "social-economic group," and the group of service workers, except private household, contains individual occupations various classified by Edwards as skilled, semiskilled, and unskilled, predominantly the latter two.

A ranking in terms of median income results in two reversals in rank. The 1949 median income of male managerial workers in the Chicago Standard Metropolitan Area was about $500 greater than that of

professional workers, although both were substantially above that for sales workers. The median income for the craftsmen-foremen group was about $500 higher than that for clerical workers. In fact, the median income for the craftsmen-foremen group was only slightly below that for sales workers, whereas the median income for clerical workers was only slightly above that for operatives.

However, in median school years completed, professional workers clearly rank first, while there is little difference in the medians for the managerial, sales, and clerical groups. The median drops sharply, over 2.5 years, for the craftsmen-foremen group and declines further for each group in the order of the initial listing.

In the Chicago Metropolitan District the proportion of nonwhites in an occupation group appears to be closely related to its socioeconomic status. The proportion is very low in the professional, managerial, and sales groups, but it is somewhat higher for clerical workers than for the craftsmen-foremen group. Increasing proportions are observed for operatives, service workers, and laborers, in order.

The suggested ranking is in general conformity with the National Opinion Research Center's data on popular attitudes toward occupations, except that sales occupations appear to rank below clerical and craft occupations in the NORC results.[9] An inadequate sampling of occupational titles within the sales group may account in part for the low prestige rating of sales workers obtained by the NORC. Furthermore, their data do not differentiate prestige ratings by sex. Particularly in a metropolitan area, the male sales worker group is more heavily weighted with such occupations as advertising, insurance, and real estate agents and sales representatives of wholesale and manufacturing concerns than is the case for female sales workers, among whom retail sales clerks are the large majority.

The failure of different bases of ranking to give identical results has been discussed by writers on stratification in terms of "disaffinity of strata" and "status disequilibrium."[10] The reversals in rank between the professional and managerial groups and the clerical and crafts workers are most frequent. The upshot seems to be that no one ranking can be accepted as sufficient for all purposes. The examination of residential patterns discloses other instances of disequilibrium, which are of interest both in themselves and as clues to the interpretation of those already noted.

Residential Patterns

Four aspects of the residential patterning of occupation groups are considered. The first is the degree of residential segregation of each major occupation group with respect to all others, that is, the extent to which an occupation group is separated residentially from the remainder of the employed labor force. The second is the degree of dissimilarity in residential distribution among major occupation groups, that is, the extent to which pairs of occupation groups isolate themselves from one another. The third aspect is the degree of residential concentration of each occupation group in areas characterized by relatively low rents. Finally, the degree of centralization of each major occupation group (i.e., the extent to which an occupation group is concentrated toward the center of the metropolitan community)

TABLE 2. INDEX OF RESIDENTIAL SEGREGATION OF EACH MAJOR OCCUPATION GROUP, FOR EMPLOYED MALES IN THE CHICAGO METROPOLITAN DISTRICT, 1950

Major Occupation Group *	By Census Tracts	By Zone-Sector Segments
Professional, technical, and kindred workers	30	31
Managers, officials, and proprietors, except farm	29	20
Sales workers	29	20
Clerical and kindred workers	13	9
Craftsmen, foremen, and kindred workers	19	14
Operatives and kindred workers	22	16
Service workers, except private household	24	20
Laborers, except farm and mine	35	29

* Does not include farmers and farm managers, private household workers, farm laborers, and occupation not reported.

is examined. In each case the spatial patterning of the residences is considered in relation to socioeconomic level.

A clear relationship of the ranking of major occupation groups by socioeconomic status and by degree of residential segregation is shown in Table 2. Listed in the order given there, the indexes of residential segregation from a ∪-shaped pattern. The highest values are observed for the professionals and the laborers and the lowest value for the clerical workers. The degree of residential segregation varies only slightly among the professional, managerial, and sales groups; however, it declines markedly for the clerical workers and then increases regularly for each successive group.

This finding suggests that residential segregation is greater for those occupation groups with clearly defined status than for those groups whose status is ambiguous. The latter groups are necessarily subject to cross-pressures from the determinants of residential selection; for example, the clerical group has an income equivalent to that of operatives but the educational level of managerial workers.

To check the hypothesis that spatial distances among occupation groups parallel their social distances, the indexes of dissimilarity in residential distribution among major occupation groups are shown in Table 3. As previously indicated, a listing of major occupation groups by socioeconomic level can at best only roughly

TABLE 3. INDEXES OF DISSIMILARITY IN RESIDENTIAL DISTRIBUTION AMONG MAJOR OCCUPATION GROUPS, FOR EMPLOYED MALES IN THE CHICAGO METROPOLITAN DISTRICT, 1950
(Above diagonal, by census tracts; below diagonal, by zone-sector segments)

Major Occupation Group*	Prof., Tech., Kindred	Mgrs., Offs., Props.	Sales Wkrs.	Clerical Kindred	Crafts-men, Fore-men	Oper-atives, Kin-dred	Service, Exc. Priv. Hshld.	Labor-ers, Exc. Farm and Mine
Professional, technical, kindred workers	—	13	15	28	35	44	41	54
Managers, officials, and proprietors, except farm	8	—	13	28	33	41	40	52
Sales workers	11	7	—	27	35	42	38	54
Clerical and kindred workers	20	18	17	—	16	21	24	38
Craftsmen, foremen, kindred workers	26	23	25	12	—	17	35	35
Operatives, kindred workers	31	29	30	16	14	—	26	25
Service workers, except private household	31	31	30	19	25	19	—	28
Laborers, except farm and mine	42	41	42	32	30	21	24	—

Column group heading: *Major Occupation Group*

* Does not include farmers and farm managers, private household workers, farm laborers, and occupation not reported.

approximate a social distance scale. Similarly, a measure of dissimilarity in residential distribution can only approximate the spatial distance between groups—the index measures only the dissimilarity of the residential distributions with respect to a particular set of areas and is insensitive to other important aspects of the spatial pattern such as proximity of areas of concentration.

Nonetheless, the data in Table 3 indicate the essential correspondence of social and spatial distance among occupation groups. If it is assumed that the ordering of major occupation groups corresponds with increasing social distance (e.g., the social distance between professional and sales workers is greater than that between professional and managerial workers), and if it is assumed that the index of residential dissimilarity approximates the spatial distance between the two groups, the expected pattern would be the following: Starting at any point on the diagonal, the indexes would increase reading up or to the right (down or to the left, in the case of the indexes below the diagonal, based on zone-sector segments). It is clear that the expected pattern, though not perfectly reproduced, essentially describes the observed pattern. The exceptions are few and for the most part can be explained hypothetically; such hypotheses provide clues for additional research.

The least dissimilarity is observed between professional and managerial workers, managerial and sales workers and professional and sales workers. Furthermore, the dissimilarity of each of these groups with each other occupation group is of approximately the same degree. In fact, three of the inversions of the expected pattern concern the comparison between the managerial group and sales workers; that is, the residential dissimilarity

of sales workers with craftsmen-foremen, operatives, and laborers is slightly greater than that of the managerial group, although their difference in terms of socioeconomic level is presumably less.

The residential distribution of clerical workers is more dissimilar to the distribution of sales workers, professional, and managerial workers than to that of the craftsmen or the operatives. Hence, although clerical workers are often grouped with professional, managerial, and sales workers as "white-collar," in terms of residential distribution they are more similar to the craftsmen and operatives than to the other white-collar groups.

The remaining inversions of the expected pattern involve service workers, except private household. One-fifth of these are "janitors and sextons." Presumably a substantial proportion of the janitors live at their place of work in apartment buildings housing workers in the higher status occupation groups.[11] It is hypothesized that this special circumstance accounts for the tendency of service workers to be less dissimilar to the higher status groups than expected on the basis of socioeconomic status.[12] At the same time the color composition of the service group presumably acts in the opposite direction. In so far as residential segregation on basis of color, cutting across occupational lines, exists within the metropolitan community, occupational status is rendered at least partially ineffective as a determinant of residential location. These factors, however, probably do not wholly explain the largest single deviation from the expected pattern, the much larger index of dissimilarity between craftsmen-foremen and service workers than between clerical and service workers.

The first column of Table 4 shows the indexes of low-rent concentration of the

TABLE 4. INDEXES OF LOW-RENT CONCENTRATION AND OF CENTRALIZATION FOR MAJOR OCCUPATION GROUPS, CHICAGO METROPOLITAN DISTRICT, 1950

Major Occupation Group *	Index of Low-Rent Concentration (Total Employed Persons)	Index of Centralization (Employed Males)					
				Sector			
		Metro-politan District	North Shore	North-west	West	South-west	South Shore
Professional, technical, and kindred workers	− 32	− 14	− 15	− 20	− 29	− 20	5
Managers, officials, and proprietors, except farm	− 30	− 12	− 20	− 16	− 19	− 15	1
Sales workers	− 25	− 5	− 15	− 12	− 12	− 9	8
Clerical and kindred workers	− 9	5	7	2	1	5	9
Craftsmen, foremen, and kindred workers	11	− 8	6	− 6	− 7	− 5	− 26
Operatives, kindred workers	29	10	21	16	18	8	− 4
Service workers, except private household	7	21	16	18	20	16	36
Laborers, except farm and mine	32	7	9	21	30	16	− 1

* Does not include farmers and farm managers, private household workers, farm laborers, and occupation not reported.

occupation groups. Some caution must be exercised in interpreting them, since the tabulation on which they are based did not distinguish between male and female workers, and the indexes had to be computed for total employed persons rather than males. It is clear, nonetheless, that the degree of low-rent concentration is inversely related to the socioeconomic status of the occupation groups. All four of the white-collar occupation groups have negative indexes, signifying relative concentration in high-rent areas, whereas all four of the blue-collar groups have positive indexes. Again, there is a relatively sharp break between the clerical and the other three white-collar groups. The managerial group has a slightly greater index of low-rent concentration than the professional group, despite the higher income level of

the former. It is even more striking that the low-rent concentration of craftsmen-foremen is substantially higher than for clerical workers, again the reverse of the relative positions on income. It can be shown that in 1940 the combined clerical and sales group tended to spend a larger proportion of its income for rent than did the group of craftsmen, foremen, and kindred workers. For example, for tenant families with wage and salary incomes between $2,000 and $3,000 in 1939, and without other income, 63 percent of the families headed by a clerical or sales workers paid $40 per month or more rent, as compared with only 38 percent of families whose heads were craftsmen, foremen, or kindred workers.[13]

The index of low-rent concentration for service workers, although positive, is low compared to the other blue-collar groups. This exception to the expected pattern no doubt has the same explanation as advanced above; that is, that a substantial proportion of service workers live in comparatively high status areas in connection with their place of employment.

The indexes of centralization of the occupation groups are given in Table 4, both for the Metropolitan District as a whole and within each of the five sectors. According to the Burgess zonal hypothesis, there is an upward gradient in the socioeconomic status of the population as one proceeds from the center to the periphery of the city. Hence one would expect the degree of residential centralization of an occupation group to be inversely related to socioeconomic status. The data provide general support for this hypothesis, although there are some significant exceptions. Thus, for the Metropolitan District as a whole, three of the four white-collar indexes are negative (indicating relative decentralization), and three of the four blue-collar indexes are positive (indicating relative centralization). The exceptional cases are again the clerical and craftsmen-foremen groups.

In three of the five sectors (Northwest, West, and Southwest), the hypothesized pattern of centralization indexes is perfectly reproduced, except for the inversion between clerical workers and the craftsmen-foremen group, which appears in all sectors. For the North Shore sector the principal deviation from the pattern is the comparatively low degree of centralization of service workers and laborers. In this sector the managerial group is somewhat more decentralized than the professional group, as is also true in the South Shore sector. The latter sector exhibits a quite marked departure from the expected pattern, in that the only decentralized occupations are those in the blue-collar category. There is a small measure of confirmation for the hypothesized pattern, in that within the white-collar category the least centralized groups are the professional and managerial, and within the blue-collar category the most decentralized is the craftsmen-foremen group. The high index for service workers is doubtless due to the relatively high proportion of nonwhites in this occupation, and the relatively central location of the South Side "Black Belt," a large portion of which falls in the South Shore sector. The decentralization of the other blue-collar groups is attributable to the presence of the Indiana industrial suburbs on the periphery of the South Shore sector. A similar effect of some industrial suburbs at the northern end of the North Shore sector is observable in the low centralization index for laborers in that sector. It is apparent that expectations based on the zonal hypothesis must be qualified by recognizing distortions of the zonal pattern produced by peripheral industrial concentrations. Such concentrations appear only in certain sectors, and, where they are absent, the zonal hypothesis leads to a realistic expectation concerning the pattern of residential centralization by socioeconomic status.

Residential Separation and Dissimilarity of Occupational Origins

There are good reasons for supposing that residential patterns are related to occupational mobility. For example, ecologists have noted a tendency for advances in socioeconomic status to be accompanied by migration toward the city's periphery. Residential segregation is doubtless one of the barriers to upward mobility, in so far as such mobility is affected by the opportunity to observe and imitate the way of life of higher social strata. Among the findings reported above, at least one may have an explanation that involves mobility. It is surprising that the residential patterns of sales workers do not differ more than they do from those of professional and managerial workers; since the income of sales workers is well below that of either, they rank lower in prestige, and their educational attainment is substantially less than that of professional workers. But there are data which suggest that a sizable proportion of sales workers are moving to a higher occupational level, or aspire to such a move, anticipating it by following the residential pattern of the higher group. The Occupational Mobility Survey found that for males employed in both 1940 and 1950 there was a movement of 23 percent of the men employed as sales workers in 1940 into the group of managers, proprietors, and officials by 1950. This is the largest single interoccupational movement in the mobility table, except that 23 percent of laborers moved into the group of operatives and kindred workers.[14] Another aspect of occupational mobility is illuminated by the data in Table 5, which shows indexes of dissimilarity among the major occupation groups with respect to the distribution of each group by major occupation group of the employed male's father.[15] These indexes, therefore, pertain to differences among the major occupation groups in background, origin, or recruitment. The hypothesis to be tested is that, the greater the dissimilarity between a pair of occupation groups in occupational origins, the greater is their dissimilarity in residential distribution.

TABLE 5*. INDEXES OF DISSIMILARITY IN DISTRIBUTION BY FATHER'S OCCUPATION AMONG MAJOR OCCUPATION GROUPS, FOR EMPLOYED MALES IN SIX CITIES IN THE UNITED STATES, 1950

Major Occupation Group

Major Occupation Group†	Mgrs., Offs., Props.	Sales Wkrs.	Clerical, Kindred	Craftsmen, Foremen	Operatives, Kindred	Service, Incl. Priv. Hshld.	Laborers, Exc. Mine
Professional, technical and kindred workers	20	16	27	38	39	34	46
Managers, officials, and proprietors, except farm	—	11	28	31	34	30	42
Sales workers	—	—	26	35	37	35	47
Clerical and kindred workers	—	—	—	18	20	28	39
Craftsmen, foremen, kindred workers	—	—	—	—	14	25	31
Operatives, kindred workers	—	—	—	—	—	22	23
Service workers, including private household	—	—	—	—	—	—	20

* Source: Unpublished data from Occupational Mobility Survey, Table W-9. For description of sampling and enumeration procedures see Gladys L. Palmer, *Labor Mobility in Six Cities* (New York: Social Science Research Council, 1954).
† Does not include farmers and farm managers and occupation not reported. A small number of private household workers are included with service workers, and a small number of farm laborers with laborers, except mine.

The pattern of Table 5 is clearly like that of Table 3. The indexes of dissimilarity with respect to residence, computed on the zone-sector segment basis, correlate .91 with the indexes for occupational origin. The correlation is .94 for the residential indexes based on census tracts, with the regression of the tract-based index (t) on the index of dissimilarity in occupational origin (u) being $t = 1.2u - 1.8$. The hypothesis is thereby definitely substantiated.

In Table 5 all but one of the inversions of the pattern expected on the assumption of an unequivocal ranking of the occupation groups involve the sales and service workers. Sales workers are closer to professional workers with respect to occupational background than are the managerial workers and farther from each of the blue-collar groups. Actually, a more consistent pattern would be produced by ranking sales workers second in place of the managerial group. In this respect the data on occupational origins are more consistent with the ecological data than are the data on socioeconomic status in Table 1. In terms of the indexes of dissimilarity in occupational origins, service workers are closer to the first three white-collar groups than are any of the other blue-collar groups. However, in comparisons among the clerical and blue-collar groups, service workers clearly rank next to last, or between operatives and laborers. Again, the factor of occupational origins is more closely related to residential separation than are the indicators of socioeconomic status.

The last point deserves emphasis. Not only do the indexes of dissimilarity on an area basis have the same general pattern as those on an occupational origin basis but also the deviations from that pattern occur at the same points and in the same direction. This cannot be said regarding the

several indicators of socioeconomic status. If income determined residential separation, managers would outrank professionals, and clerical workers would be virtually identical with operatives in their separation from other groups. If education determined residential separation, there would be substantial differences between the indexes for professional workers and managerial workers. Neither of these hypotheses is borne out by the data, whereas differences in occupational background lead to accurate, specific predictions of the pattern of differences in residential distribution.

The ecological analysis has provided strong support for the proposition that spatial distances between occupation groups are closely related to their social distances, measured either in terms of conventional indicators of socioeconomic status or in terms of differences in occupational origins; that the most segregated occupation groups are those at the extremes of the socioeconomic scale; that concentration of residence in low-rent areas is inversely related to socioeconomic status; and that centralization of residence is likewise inversely related to socioeconomic status. These results are in accord with accepted ecological theory, provide support for it, and demonstrate the relevance of ecological research to the theory of social stratification.

These generalizations, however, are perhaps no more significant to the advancement of knowledge than are the instances in which they do not hold and the additional hypotheses advanced to account for the exceptions. Conventional measures of socioeconomic status do not agree perfectly as to the rank order of the major occupation groups, nor do the several ecological indexes. The prime case in point occurs at the middle of the socioeconomic scale, at the conventional juncture of white-collar and blue-collar occupations. Clerical and kindred workers have substantially more education than craftsmen, foremen, and kindred workers, and the clerical occupations are usually considered of greater prestige than the craft and related occupations. However, craftsmen-foremen have considerably higher incomes on the average, and, among males, their nonwhite proportion is smaller. The pattern of the indexes of dissimilarity in residential distribution clearly places the clerical group closer to the other white-collar groups than the craftsmen-foremen are, and the clerical workers' index of low-rent concentration is less than that of the craftsmen and foremen. But in terms of residential centralization the clerical group tends to fall with the lower blue-collar groups, and the craftsmen-foremen group with the other white-collar groups. In general, it would appear that "social status" or prestige is more important in determining the residential association of clerical with other white-collar groups than is income, although the latter sets up a powerful cross-pressure, as evidenced by the comparatively high rent-income ratio of clerical families. To account fully for the failure of clerical workers to be residentially decentralized like the other white-collar groups, one would have to consider work-residence relationships. Data on work-residence separation for a 1951 Chicago sample show that clerical workers resemble craftsmen, foremen, and kindred workers in the degree of separation much more than they do sales, managerial, or professional workers.[16]

Perhaps the most suggestive finding of the study is that dissimilarity in occupational origins is more closely associated with dissimilarity in residential distribution than is any of the usual indicators of socio-economic status. This result can only be interpreted speculatively. But one may suppose that preferences and aspirations concerning housing and residential patterns are largely formed by childhood and adolescent experiences in a milieu of which the father's occupation is an important aspect.

The discovery that "status disequilibria" are reflected in inconsistencies in the ordering of occupation groups according to their residential patterns provides a further reason for distinguishing "class" from "social status" elements[17] within the complex conventionally designated as "socioeconomic status." Apparently, attempts to compound these two can at best produce a partially ordered scale; at worst, they may obscure significant differences in life-style, consumption patterns, and social mobility.

There is one imporant qualification of the results reported. Like census tracts, broad occupation groups are not perfectly homogeneous. The managerial group includes proprietors of peanut stands as well as corporation executives, and night-club singers are classified as professional workers along with surgeons. One would therefore expect to find a much sharper differentiation of residential patterns if more detailed occupational classifications were available. In particular, the points at which cross-pressures on residential location develop should be more clearly identified.

Further research should seek other forces producing residential segregation. Ethnic categorizations other than race are doubtless relevant though difficult to study directly for lack of data. In general, the patterns described here would be expected to hold for females, but significant deviations might also occur, in part because the residence of married females is probably determined more by their husbands' occupation than by their own, and in part because the occupations that compose each of the major occupation groups are different for females from those for males (as mentioned above in regard to sales workers). Both race and sex would bear upon residential patterns of private household workers, who are predominantly female and nonwhite. A final class of especially important factors is the effect of the location of workplaces on residence. There is evidence that residences are not distributed randomly with respect to places of work. If location of work is controlled, an even sharper differentiation of residential patterns than that described here may be revealed.

ACKNOWLEDGMENTS

Reprinted by permission from *The American Journal of Sociology*, Vol. LX (March 1955,) pp. 493–503. Published by the University of Chicago Press. Copyright 1955 by TheUniversity of Chicago.

NOTES

1. The Urban Community as a Spatial Pattern and a Moral Order," in *The Urban Community*, ed. Ernest W. Burgess (Chicago: University of Chicago Press, 1926), p. 18.
2. See, however, the discussion of "dwelling area" by W. Lloyd Warner *et al.*, *Social Class in America* (Chicago: Science Research Associates, 1949), pp. 151–54.
3. Otis Dudley Duncan and Beverly Duncan, "A Methodological Analysis of Segregation Indexes," forthcoming in *American Sociological Review;* Donald J. Bogue, *The Structure of the Metropolitan Community* (Ann Arbor: University of Michigan, 1949), p. 72; Richard W. Redick, "A Study of Differential Rates of Population Growth and Patterns of Population Distribution in Central Cities in the United States: 1940–1950" (paper presented at the 1954 annual meeting of the American Sociological Society, Urbana, Illinois).
4. *1950 United States Census of Population*, Bulletin P–D10.
5. For the use of the index of dissimilarity as a "coefficient of geographic association" see National Resources Planning Board, *Industrial Location and National Resources* (Washington, D.C.: Government Printing Office, 1943), p. 118.
6. For discussion of the index of dissimilarity as a segregation index see Duncan and Duncan, *op. cit.*, and the literature there cited.
7. Jerome K. Myers, "Note on the Homogeneity of Census Tracts: A Methodological Problem in Urban Ecological Research," *Social Forces*, XXXII (May, 1954), 364–66; Joel Smith, "A Method for the Classification of Areas on the Basis of Demographical Homogeneous Populations," *American Sociological Review*, XIX (April, 1954), 201–7.
8. The indexes of low-rent concentration and of centralization are formally identical with the index of urbanization proposed in Otis Dudley Duncan,"Urbanization and Retail Specialization, *Social Forces*, XXX (March, 1952), 267–71. The formula given here is a simplification of the one presented there; and the area units and principle of ordering are, of course, different.
9. National Opinion Research Center, "Jobs and Occupations: A Popular Evaluation," *Opinion News*, IX (September 1, 1947), 3–13.
10. Cf. Pitirim A. Sorokin, *Society, Culture, and Personality* (New York: Harper & Bros., 1947), pp. 289–94, on disaffinity of strata. On status disequilibrium cf. Émile Benoit-Smullyan, "Status, Status Types, and Status Interrelations," *American Sociological Review*, IX (April, 1944), 154–61; Harold F. Kaufman, *Defining Prestige in a Rural Community* ("Sociometry Monograph," No. 10 [New York: Beacon House, 1946]).
11. Cf. Ray Gold, "Janitors versus Tenants: A Status-Income Dilemma," *American Journal of Sociology*, LVII (March, 1952), 486–93.
12. This effect has been definitely noted in data, not shown here, for female private household workers, about one-fourth of whom "live in."
13. Data for the Chicago Metropolitan District, 1940, from Table 11, *Families: Income and Rent, Population and Housing, 16th Census of the United States: 1940*.
14. Based on unpublished Table W-56 of the Occupational Mobility Survey, taken in six cities in 1951. For description of the sampling and enumeration procedures see Gladys L. Palmer, *Labor Mobility in Six Cities* (New York: Social Science Research Council, 1954), chap. i and Appendix B.

15. These indexes are based on the aggregated results of sample surveys in six cities in 1951. Although separate data are available for Chicago, these were not used here, because the sample was too small to produce reliable frequencies in most of the cells of the 8×9 table from which the dissimilarity indexes were computed. (In the intergeneration mobility table the classification of father's occupations included the group "farmers and farm managers" as well as the eight major occupation groups listed in Table 5. This was desirable, since a significant proportion of fathers —though very few of the sons in this urban sample—were farmers.)

16. Beverly Duncan, "Factors in Work-Residence Separation: Wage and Salary Workers, Chicago, 1951" (paper presented at the annual institute of the Society for Social Research, Chicago, June 5, 1953).

17. See "Class, Status, Party," in *From Max Weber: Essays in Sociology*, ed. H. H. Gerth and C. W. Mills (New York: Oxford University Press, 1946).

34. Sentiment and Symbolism as Ecological Variables   Walter Firey

Explanatory models of metropolitan growth usually emphasize the hegemony of market forces in shaping the pattern of urban activities. Walter Firey's paper is one of the earlier writings within the ecological literature to point out that land speculators, real estate developers, zoning boards, and other powerful interests influencing the growth of cities operate in a context of social values and norms. Usually these values support the market mechanism, but sometimes, as in this case taken from the history of Boston's urban core, the prevailing values place a higher priority on the preservation of amenities. Firey examines the dispute over density levels and open space on Beacon Hill, the North End, and the Commons. He shows that from the mid-nineteenth century onward space in some areas was treated in terms of its symbolic importance. Because of the sentimental feelings of the residents, the low-rise housing and the gardens were maintained in the Hill and the Commons, even though these areas were extremely valuable potentially for more intensive development and use.

Walter Firey is Professor of Sociology, University of Texas. He is the author of *Law and Economy in Planning* (1965), *Mind, Man and Land: A Theory of Resource Use* (1960), and *Land Use in Central Boston* (1947).

Systematization of ecological theory has thus far proceeded on two main premises regarding the character of space and the nature of locational activities. The first premise postulates that the sole relation of space to locational activities is an impeditive and cost-imposing one. The second premise assumes that locational activities are primarily economizing, "fiscal" agents.[1] On the basis of these two premises the only possible relationship that locational activities may bear to space is an economic one. In such a relationship each

From *American Sociological Review*, Vol. 10 (April 1945), pp. 140–148. Reprinted by permission.

activity will seek to so locate as to minimize the obstruction put upon its functions by spatial distance. Since the supply of the desired locations is limited it follows that not all activities can be favored with choice sites. Consequently a competitive process ensues in which the scarce desirable locations are preempted by those locational activities which can so exploit advantageous location as to produce the greatest surplus of income over expenditure. Less desirable locations devolve to corresponingly less economizing land uses. The result is a pattern of land use that is presumed to be most efficient for both the individual locational activity and for the community.[2]

Given the contractualistic milieu within which the modern city has arisen and acquires its functions, such an "economic ecology" has had a certain explanatory adequacy in describing urban spatial structure and dynamics. However, as any theory matures and approaches a logical closure of its generalizations it inevitably encounters facts which remain unassimilable to the theoretical scheme. In this paper it will be our purpose to describe certain ecological processes which apparently cannot be embraced in a strictly economic analysis. Our hypothesis is that the data to be presented, while in no way startling or unfamiliar to the research ecologist, do suggest an alteration of the basic premises of ecology. This alteration would consist, first, of ascribing to space not only an impeditive quality but also an additional property, viz., that of being at times a symbol for certain cultural values that have become associated with a certain spatial area. Second, it would involve a recognition that locational activities are not only economizing agents but may also bear sentiments which can significantly influence the locational process.[3]

A test case for this twofold hypothesis is afforded by certain features of land use in central Boston. In common with many of the older American cities Boston has inherited from the past certain spatial patterns and landmarks which have had a remarkable persistence and even recuperative power despite challenges from other more economic land uses. The persistence of these spatial patterns can only be understood in terms of the group values that they have come to symbolize. We shall describe three types of such patterns: first, an in-town upper class residential neighborhood known as Beacon Hill; second, certain "sacred sites," notably the Boston Common and the colonial burying-grounds; and third, a lower class Italian neighborhood known as the North End. In each of these land uses we shall find certain locational processes which seem to defy a strictly economic analysis.

The first of the areas, Beacon Hill, is located some five minutes' walking distance from the retail center of Boston. This neighborhood has for fully a century and a half maintained its character as a preferred upper class residential district, despite its contiguity to a low rent tenement area, the West End. During its long history Beacon Hill has become the symbol for a number of sentimental associations which constitute a genuine attractive force to certain old families of Boston. Some idea of the nature of these sentiments may be had from statements in the innumerable pamphlets and articles written by residents of the Hill. References to "this sacred eminence,"[4] "stately old-time appearance,"[5] and "age-old quaintness and charm,"[6] give an insight into the attitudes attaching to the area. One resident reveals rather clearly the spatial referability of these sentiments when she writes of the Hill:

It has a tradition all its own, that begins in the hospitality of a book-lover, and has never lost that flavor. Yes, our streets are inconvenient, steep, and slippery. The corners are abrupt, the contours perverse. . . . It may well be that the gibes of our envious neighbors have a foundation and that these dear crooked lanes of ours were traced in ancestral mud by absent-minded kine.[7]

Behind such expressions of sentiment are a number of historical associations connected with the area. Literary traditions are among the strongest of these; indeed, the whole literary legend of Boston has its focus at Beacon Hill. Many of America's most distinguished literati have occupied homes on the Hill. Present day occupants of these houses derive a genuine satisfaction from the individual histories of their dwellings.[8] One lady whose home had had a distinguished pedigree remarked:

I like living here for I like to think that a great deal of historic interest has happened here in this room.

Not a few families are able to trace a continuity of residence on the Hill for several generations, some as far back as 1800 when the Hill was first developed as an upper class neighborhood. It is a point of pride to a Beacon Hill resident if he can say that he was born on the Hill or was at least raised there; a second best boast is to point out that his forebears once lived on the Hill.

Thus a wide range of sentiments— aesthetic, historical, and familial—have acquired a spatial articulation in Beacon Hill. The bearing of these sentiments upon locational processes is a tangible one and assumes three forms: retentive, attractive, and resistive. Let us consider each of these in order. To measure the retentive influence

that spatially-referred sentiments may exert upon locational activities we have tabulated by place of residence all the families listed in the Boston *Social Register* for the years 1894, 1905, 1914, 1929, and 1943. This should afford a reasonably accurate picture of the distribution of upper class families by neighborhoods within Boston and in suburban towns. In Table 1 we have presented the tabulations for the three in-town concentrations of upper class families (Beacon Hill, Back Bay, and Jamaica Plain) and for the five main suburban concentrations (Brookline, Newton, Cambridge, Milton, and Dedham). Figure 1 portrays these trends in graphic form. The most apparent feature of these data is, of course, the consistent increase of upper class families in the suburban towns and the marked decrease (since 1905) in two of the in-town upper class areas, Back Bay and Jamaica Plain. Although both of these neighborhoods remain fashionable residential districts their prestige is waning rapidly. Back Bay in particular, though still surpassing in numbers any other single neighborhood, has undergone a steady invasion of apartment buildings, rooming houses, and business establishments which are destroying its prestige value. The trend of Beacon Hill has been different. Today it has a larger number of upper class families than it had in 1894. Where it ranked second among fashionable neighborhoods in 1894 it ranks third today, being but slightly outranked in numbers by the suburban city of Brookline and by the Back Bay. Beacon Hill is the only in-town district that has consistently retained its preferred character and has held to itself a considerable proportion of Boston's old families.

There is, however, another aspect to the spatial dynamics of Beacon Hill, one that pertains to the "attractive" locational

TABLE 1. NUMBER OF UPPER CLASS FAMILIES IN BOSTON, BY DISTRICTS OF CONCENTRATION, AND IN MAIN SUBURBAN TOWNS, FOR CERTAIN YEARS

	1894	1905	1914	1929	1943
Within Boston					
Beacon Hill	280	242	279	362	335
Back Bay	867	1166	1102	880	556
Jamaica Plain	56	66	64	36	30
Other districts	316	161	114	86	41
Suburban Towns					
Brookline	137	300	348	355	372
Newton	38	89	90	164	247
Cambridge	77	142	147	223	257
Milton	37	71	106	131	202
Dedham	8	29	48	69	99
Other towns	106	176	310	403	816
Total in Boston	1519	1635	1559	1364	962
Total in Suburbs	403	807	1049	1345	1993
Totals	1922	2442	2608	2709	2955

Tabulated from: *Social Register, Boston.*

role of spatially referred sentiments. From 1894 to 1905 the district underwent a slight drop, subsequently experiencing a steady rise for 24 years, and most recently undergoing another slight decline. These variations are significant, and they bring out rather clearly the dynamic ecological role of spatial symbolism. The initial drop is attributable to the development of the then new Back Bay. Hundreds of acres there had been reclaimed from marshland and had been built up with palatial dwellings. Fashion now pointed to this as the select area of the city and in response to its dictates a number of families abandoned Beacon Hill to take up more pretentious Back Bay quarters. Property values on the Hill began to depreciate, old dwellings became rooming houses, and businesses began to invade some of the streets. But many of the old families remained on the Hill and a few of them made efforts to halt the gradual deterioration of the district. Under the

aegis of a realtor, an architect, and a few close friends there was launched a program of purchasing old houses, modernizing the interiors and leaving the colonial exteriors intact, and then selling the dwellings to individual families for occupancy. Frequently adjoining neighbors would collaborate in planning their improvements so as to achieve an architectural consonance. The results of this program may be seen in the drift of upper class families back to the Hill. From 1905 to 1929 the number of *Social Register* families in the district increased by 120. Assessed valuations showed a corresponding increase: from 1919 to 1924 there was a rise of 24 percent; from 1924 to 1929 the rise was 25 percent.[9] The nature of the Hill's appeal, and the kind of persons attracted, may be gathered from the following popular write-up:

To salvage the quaint charm of Colonial Architecture on Beacon Hill, Boston, is the object of a well-defined movement among

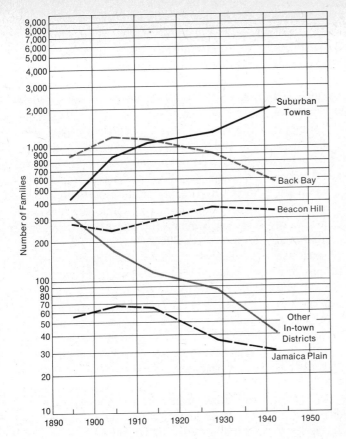

Figure 1. Number of upper-class families in Boston by districts of concentration, and in suburbs, for certain years.

writers and professional folk that promises the most delightful opportunities for the home seeker of moderate means and conservative tastes. Because men of discernment were able to visualize the possibilities presented by these architectural landmarks, and have undertaken the gracious task of restoring them to their former glory, this historic quarter of old Boston, once the centre of literary culture, is coming into its own.[10]

The independent variable in this "attractive" locational process seems to have been the symbolic quality of the Hill, by which it constituted a referent for certain strong sentiments of upper class Bostonians.

While this revival was progressing there remained a constant menace to the character of Beacon Hill, in the form of business encroachments and apartment-hotel developments. Recurrent threats from this source finally prompted residents of the Hill to organize themselves into the Beacon Hill Association. Formed in 1922, the declared object of this organization was "to keep undesirable business and living conditions from affecting the hill district."[11] At the time the city was engaged in preparing a comprehensive zoning program and the occasion was propitious to secure for Beacon Hill suitable protective measures. A systematic set of recommendations was drawn up by the Association regarding a uniform

65-foot height limit for the entire Hill, the exclusion of business from all but two streets, and the restriction of apartment house bulk.[12] It succeeded in gaining only a partial recognition of this program in the 1924 zoning ordinance. But the Association continued its fight against inimical land uses year after year. In 1927 it successfully fought a petition brought before the Board of Zoning Adjustment to alter the height limits in one area so as to permit the construction of a four million dollar apartment-hotel 155 feet high. Residents of the Hill went to the hearing en masse. In spite of the prospect of an additional twenty million dollars worth of exclusive apartment hotels that were promised if the zoning restrictions were withheld the petition was rejected, having been opposed by 214 of the 220 persons present at the hearing.[13] In 1930 the Association gained an actual reduction in height limits on most of Beacon street and certain adjoining streets, though its leader was denounced by opponents as "a rank sentimentalist who desired to keep Boston a village."[14] One year later the Association defeated a petition to rezone Beacon street for business purposes.[15] In other campaigns the Association successfully pressed for the rezoning of a business street back to purely residential purposes, for the lowering of height limits on the remainder of Beacon street, and for several lesser matters of local interest. Since 1929, owing partly to excess assessed valuations of Boston real estate and partly to the effects of the depression upon families living on securities, Beacon Hill has lost some of its older families, though its decline is nowhere near so precipitous as that of the Back Bay.

Thus for a span of one and a half centuries there have existed on Beacon Hill certain locational processes that largely escape economic analysis. It is the symbolic quality of the Hill, not its impeditive or cost-imposing character, that most tangibly correlates with the retentive, attractive, and resistive trends that we have observed. And it is the dynamic force of spatially referred sentiments, rather than considerations of rent, which explains why certain families have chosen to live on Beacon Hill in preference to other in-town districts having equally accessible location and even superior housing conditions. There is thus a noneconomic aspect to land use on Beacon Hill, one which is in some respects actually diseconomic in its consequences. Certainly the large apartment-hotels and specialty shops that have sought in vain to locate on the Hill would have represented a fuller capitalization on potential property values than do residences. In all likelihood the attending increase in real estate prices would not only have benefited individual property holders but would have so enhanced the value of adjoining properties as to compensate for whatever depreciation other portions of the Hill might have experienced.

If we turn to another type of land use pattern in Boston, that comprised by the Boston Common and the old burying grounds, we encounter another instance of spatial symbolism which has exerted a marked influence upon the ecological organization of the rest of the city. The Boston Common is a survival from colonial days when every New England town allotted a portion of its land to common use as a cow pasture and militia field. Over the course of three centuries Boston has grown entirely around the Common so that today we find a 48-acre tract of land wedged directly into the heart of the business district. On three of its five sides are women's apparel shops, department stores, theaters and other high-rent locational activities. On the fourth side is Beacon street, extending alongside Beacon Hill. Only the activities of Hill residents have prevented business from invading this side. The fifth side is occupied by the Public Garden. A land value map portrays a strip of highest values pressing upon two sides of the Common, on Tremont and Boylston streets, taking the form of a long, narrow band.

Before considering the ecological consequences of this configuration let us see what attitudes have come to be associated with the Common. There is an extensive local literature about the Common and in it we find interesting sentiments expressed. One citizen speaks of:

> . . . the great principle exemplified in the preservation of the Common. Thank Heaven, the tide of money making must break and go around that.[16]

Elsewhere we read:

> Here, in short, are all our accumulated memories, intimate, public, private.[17]
> Boston Common was, is, and ever will be a source of tradition and inspiration from which the New Englanders may renew their faith, recover their moral force, and strengthen their ability to grow and achieve.[18]

The Common has thus become a "sacred" object, articulating and symbolizing genuine historical sentiments of a certain portion of the community. Like all such objects its sacredness derives, not from any intrinsic spatial attributes, but rather from its representation in peoples' minds as a symbol for collective sentiments.[19]

Such has been the force of these sentiments that the Common has become buttressed up by a number of legal guarantees. The city charter forbids Boston

in perpetuity to dispose of the Common or any portion of it. The city is further prohibited by state legislation from building upon the Common, except within rigid limits, or from laying out roads or tracks across it.[20] By accepting the bequest of one George F. Parkman, in 1908, amounting to over five million dollars, the city is further bound to maintain the Common, and certain other parks, "for the benefit and enjoyment of its citizens."[21]

What all this has meant for the spatial development of Boston's retail center is clear from the present character of that district. Few cities of comparable size have so small a retail district in point of area. Unlike the spacious department stores of most cities, those in Boston are frequently compressed within narrow confines and have had to extend in devious patterns through rear and adjoining buildings. Traffic in downtown Boston has literally reached the saturation point, owing partly to the narrow one-way streets but mainly to the lack of adequate arterials leading into and out of the Hub. The American Road Builders Association has estimated that there is a loss of $81,000 per day in Boston as a result of traffic delay. Trucking in Boston is extremely expensive. These losses ramify out to merchants, manufacturers, commuters, and many other interests.[22] Many proposals have been made to extend a through arterial across the Common, thus relieving the extreme congestion on Tremont and Beacon streets, the two arterials bordering the park.[23] Earlier suggestions, prior to the construction of the subway, called for street car tracks across the Common. But "the controlling sentiment of the citizens of Boston, and of large numbers throughout the State, is distinctly opposed to allowing any such use of the Common."[24] Boston has long suffered from land shortage and unusually high real estate values as a result both of the narrow confines of the peninsula comprising the city center and as a result of the exclusion from income-yielding uses of so large a tract as the Common.[25] A further difficulty has arisen from the rapid southwesterly extension of the business district in the past two decades. With the Common lying directly in the path of this extension the business district has had to stretch around it in an elongated fashion, with obvious inconvenience to shoppers and consequent loss to businesses.

The Common is not the only obstacle to the city's business expansion. No less than three colonial burying-grounds, two of them adjoined by ancient church buildings, occupy downtown Boston. The contrast that is presented by 9-story office buildings reared up beside quiet cemeteries affords visible evidence of the conflict between "sacred" and "profane" that operates in Boston's ecological pattern. The diseconomic consequences of commercially valuable land being thus devoted to non-utilitarian purposes go even further than the removal from business uses of a given amount of space. For it is a standard principle of real estate that business property derives added value if adjoining properties are occupied by other businesses.[26] Just as a single vacancy will depreciate the value of a whole block of business frontage, so a break in the continuity of stores by a cemetery damages the commercial value of surrounding properties. But, even more than the Common, the colonial burying-grounds of Boston have become invested with a moral significance which renders them almost inviolable. Not only is there the usual sanctity which attaches to all cemeteries, but in those of Boston there is an added sacredness growing out of the age of the grounds

and the fact that the forebears of many of New England's most distinguished families as well as a number of colonial and Revolutionary leaders lie buried in these cemeteries. There is thus a manifold symbolism to these old burying-grounds, pertaining to family lineage, early nationhood, civic origins, and the like, all of which have strong sentimental associations. What has been said of the old burying-grounds applies with equal force to a number of other venerable landmarks in central Boston. Such buildings as the Old South Meeting-House, the Park Street Church, King's Chapel, and the Old State House—all foci of historical associations—occupy commercially valuable land and interrupt the continuity of business frontage on their streets. Nearly all of these landmarks have been challenged at various times by real estate and commercial interests which sought to have them replaced by more profitable uses. In every case community sentiments have resisted such threats.

In all these examples we find a symbol-sentiment relationship which has exerted a significant influence upon land use. Nor should it be thought that such phenomena are mere ecological "sports." Many other older American cities present similar locational characteristics. Delancey street in Philadelphia represents a striking parallel to Beacon Hill, and certain in-town districts of Chicago, New York, and Detroit, recently revived as fashionable apartment areas, bear resemblances to the Beacon Hill revival. The role of traditionalism in rigidifying the ecological patterns of New Orleans has been demonstrated in a recent study.[27] Further studies of this sort should clarify even further the true scope of sentiment and symbolism in urban spatial structure and dynamics.

As a third line of evidence for our hypothesis we have chosen a rather different type of area from those so far considered. It is a well known fact that immigrant ghettoes, along with other slum districts, have become areas of declining population in most American cities. A point not so well established is that this decline tends to be selective in its incidence upon residents and that this selectivity may manifest varying degrees of identification with immigrant values. For residence within a ghetto is more than a matter of spatial placement; it generally signifies acceptance of immigrant values and participation in immigrant institutions. Some light on this process is afforded by data from the North End of Boston. This neighborhood, almost wholly Italian in population, has long been known as "Boston's classic land of poverty."[28] Eighteen percent of the dwellings are eighty or more years old, and sixty percent are forty or more years old.[29] Indicative of the dilapidated character of many buildings is the recent sale of a 20-room apartment building for only $500. It is not surprising then to learn that the area has declined in population from 21,111 in 1930 to 17,598 in 1940.[30] To look for spatially referable sentiments here would seem futile. And yet, examination of certain emigration differentials in the

North End reveals a congruence between Italian social structure and locational processes. To get at these differentials recourse was had to the estimation of emigration, by age groups and by nativity, through the use of life tables. The procedure consists of comparing the actual 1940 population with the residue of the 1930 population which probably survived to 1940 according to survival rates for Massachusetts. Whatever deficit the actual 1940 population may show from the estimated 1940 population is a measure of "effective emigration." It is not a measure of the actual volume of emigration, since no calculation is made of immigration *into* the district between 1930 and 1940.[31] Effective emigration simply indicates the extent of population decline which is attributable to emigration rather than to death. Computations thus made for emigration differentials by nativity show the following: (Table 2.)

Thus the second generation, comprising but 59.46 percent of the 1930 population, contributed 76.42 percent of the effective emigration from the North End, whereas the first generation accounted for much less than its "due" share of the emigration. Another calculation shows that where the effective emigration of second generation

TABLE 2. EFFECTIVE EMIGRATION FROM THE NORTH END, BOSTON, 1930 TO 1940, BY NATIVITY

Nativity	1930 Population	Per Cent of 1930 Pop. in Each Nativity Group	Effective Emigration 1930–1940	Per Cent of Emigration Accounted for by Each Nativity Group
American-born (second generation)	12553	59.46	3399	76.42
Italian-born (first generation)	8557	40.54	1049	23.58
Totals	21110	100.00	4448	100.00

Calculated from: census tract data and survival rates.

Italians represents 27.08 percent of their number in 1930, that of the first generation represents only 12.26 percent of their number in 1930.

Equally clear differentials appear in effective emigration by age groups. If we compare the difference between the percentage which each age group as of 1930 contributes to the effective emigration, and the percentage which each age group comprised of the 1930 population, we find that the age groups 15–24 account for much more than their share of effective emigration; the age groups 35–64 account for much less than their share.[32] In Table 3

TABLE 3. DIFFERENCE BETWEEN PERCENTAGE CONTRIBUTED BY EACH AGE GROUP TO EFFECTIVE EMIGRATION AND PERCENTAGE IT COMPRISED OF 1930 POPULATION

Age Groups as of 1930	Differences between Percentages	
	Male	Female
under 5	−1.70	−0.33
5–9	+0.38	+.004
10–14	+0.21	+2.66
15–19	+4.18	+3.01
20–24	+2.04	+2.35
25–34	−0.97	−0.07
35–44	−2.31	−1.09
45–54	−1.43	−1.17
55–64	−2.29	−1.19
65–74	−1.13	−0.59
75 and over	uncalculable	

Calculated from: census tract data and survival rates.

the figures preceded by a plus sign indicate "excess" emigration, those preceded by a minus sign indicate "deficit" emigration. In brief, the North End is losing its young people to a much greater extent than its older people.

These differentials are in no way startling; what is interesting, however, is their congruence with basic Italian values, which find their fullest institutionalized expression in the North End. Emigration from the district may be viewed as both a cause and a symbol of alienation from these values. At the core of the Italian value system are those sentiments which pertain to the family and the *paesani*. Both of these put a high premium upon maintenance of residence in the North End.

Paesani, or people from the same village of origin, show considerable tendency to live near one another, sometimes occupying much of a single street or court.[33] Such proximity, or at least common residence in the North End, greatly facilitates participation in the *paesani* functions which are so important to the first generation Italian. Moreover, it is in the North End that the *festas*, anniversaries, and other old world occasions are held, and such is their frequency that residence in the district is almost indispensable to regular participation. The social relationships comprised by these groupings, as well as the benefit orders, secret societies, and religious organizations, are thus strongly localistic in character. One second generation Italian, when asked if his immigrant parents ever contemplated leaving their North End tenement replied:

No, because all their friends are there, their relatives. They know everyone around there.

It is for this reason that the first generation Italian is so much less inclined to leave the North End than the American born Italian.

Equally significant is the localistic character of the Italian family. So great is its solidarity that it is not uncommon to find a tenement entirely occupied by a single extended family: grandparents, matured children with their mates, and grandchildren. There are instances where such a family has overflowed one tenement and has expanded into an adjoining one, breaking out the partitions for doorways. These are ecological expressions, in part, of the expected concern which an Italian mother has for the welfare of her newly married daughter. The ideal pattern is for the daughter to continue living in her mother's house, with she and her husband being assigned certain rooms which they are supposed to furnish themselves. Over the course of time the young couple is expected to accumulate savings and buy their own home, preferably not far away. Preferential renting, by which an Italian who owns a tenement will let apartments to his relatives at a lower rental, is another manifestation of the localizing effects of Italian kinship values.

Departure from the North End generally signifies some degree of repudiation of the community's values. One Italian writes of an emigrant from the North End:

I still remember with regret the vain smile of superiority that appeared on his face when I told him that I lived at the North End of Boston. "*Io non vado fra quella plebaglia.*" (I do not go among those plebeians.)[34]

As a rule the older Italian is unwilling to make this break, if indeed he could. It is the younger adults, American-born and educated, who are capable of making the transition to another value system with radically different values and goals.

Residence in the North End seems therefore to be a spatial corollary to integration with Italian values. Likewise emigration from the district signifies assimilation into American values, and is so construed by the people themselves. Thus, while the area is not the conscious object of sentimental attachment, as are Beacon Hill and the Common, it has nonetheless become a symbol for Italian ethnic solidarity. By virtue of this symbolic quality the area has a certain retentive power over those residents who most fully share the values which prevail there.

It is reasonable to suggest, then, that the slum is much more than "an area of minimum choice."[35] Beneath the surface phenomenon of declining population there may be differential rates of decline which require positive formulation in a systematic ecological theory. Such processes are apparently refractory to analysis in terms of competition for least impeditive location. A different order of concepts, corresponding to the valuative, meaningful aspect of spatial adaptation, must supplement the prevailing economic concepts of ecology.

NOTES

1. See Everett C. Hughes, "The Ecological Aspect of Institutions," *American Sociological Review.* 1 : 180–9, April, 1936.
2. This assumption of a correspondence between the maximum utility of a private association and that of the community may be questioned within the framework of marginal utility analysis. See particularly A. C. Pigou, *The Economics of Welfare.* Second Edition, London: 1924, Part II, ch. 8. For a clear presentation of the typical posi-

tion see Robert Murray Haig, "Towards an Understanding of the Metropolis—the Assignment of Activities to Areas in Urban Regions," *Quarterly Journal of Economics.* 40:402–34, May, 1926.
3. Georg Simmel, "Der Raum und die näumlichen Ordnungen der Gesellschaft," *Soziologie.* Munich: 1923, pp. 518–22; *cf.* Hughes, *op. cit.*
4. John R. Shultz, *Beacon Hill and the Carol Singers.* Boston: 1923, p. 11.

5. *Bulletin of the Society for the Preservation of New England Antiquities.* 4:3, August, 1913.
6. Josephine Samson, *Celebrities of Louisburg Square*, Greenfield, Mass.: 1924.
7. Abbie Farwell Brown, *The Lights of Beacon Hill.* Boston, 1922, p. 4.
8. *Cf.* W. Lloyd Warner and Paul S. Lunt, *The Social Life of a Modern Community.* New Haven, 1941, 107, on this pattern.
9. *The Boston Transcript.* April 12, 1930.
10. Harriet Sisson Gillespie, "Reclaiming Colonial Landmarks," *The House Beautiful.* 58:239–41, September, 1925.
11. *The Boston Transcript.* December 6, 1922.
12. *The Boston Transcript.* March 18, 1933.
13. *The Boston Transcript.* January 29, 1927.
14. *The Boston Transcript.* April 12, 1930.
15. *The Boston Transcript.* January 10, January 29, 1931.
16. Speech of William Everett, quoted in *The Boston Transcript.* March 7, 1903.
17. T. R. Sullivan, *Boston New and Old.* Boston: 1912, pp. 45–6.
18. Joshua H. Jones, Jr., "Happenings on Boston Common," *Our Boston.* 2:9–15, January, 1927.
19. *Cf.* Emile Durkheim, *The Elementary Forms of the Religious Life.* London: 1915, p. 345.
20. St. 1859, c. 210, paragraph 3; Pub sts. c 54, paragraph 13.
21. M. A. De Wolfe Howe, *Boston Common.* Cambridge: 1910, p. 79.
22. Elisabeth M. Herlihy, Ed., *Fifty Years of Boston.* Boston: 1932, pp. 53–4.
23. See, for example, letter to editor, *The Boston Herald.* November 16, 1930.
24. *First Annual Report of the Boston Transit Commission.* Boston: 1895, p. 9.
25. John C. Kiley, "Changes in Realty Values in the Nineteenth and Twentieth Centuries," *Bulletin of the Business Historical Society.* 15, June, 1941, p. 36; Frank Chouteau Brown, "Boston: More Growing Pains," *Our Boston.* 3, February, 1927, p. 8.
26. Richard M. Hurd, *Principles of City Land Values.* New York: 1903, pp. 93–4.
27. H. W. Gilmore, "The Old New Orleans and the New: A Case for Ecology," *American Sociological Review.* 9: 385–94, August, 1944.
28. Robert A. Woods, Ed., *Americans in Process.* Boston, 1903, p. 5.
29. Finance Commission of the City of Boston, *A Study of Certain of the Effects of Decentralization on Boston and Some Neighboring Cities and Towns.* Boston: 1941, p. 11.
30. Aggregate population of census tracts F1, F2, F4, F5: *Census Tract Data, 1930 Census*, unpublished material from 15th Census of the United States, 1930, compiled by Boston Health Department, table 1; *Population and Housing—Statistics for Census Tracts, Boston.* 16th Census of the United States, 1940, table 2.
31. By use of *Police Lists* for two different years a count was made of immigration into a sample precinct of the North End. The figure (61) reveals so small a volume of immigration that any use of it to compute actual emigration by age groups would have introduced statistical unreliability into the estimates. Survival rates for Massachusetts were computed from state life tables in: National Resources Committee, *Population Statistics, 2. State Data.* Washington: 1937, Part C, p. 38. The technique is outlined in C. Warren Thornthwaite, *Internal Migration in the United States.* Philadelphia: 1934, pp. 19–21.
32. Obviously most of the emigrants in the 15–24 age group in 1930 migrated while in the age group 20–29; likewise the emigrants in the 35–64 age group migrated while in the 40–69 age group.
33. William Foote Whyte, *Street Corner Society.* Chicago: 1943, p. xix.
34. Enrico C. Sartorio, *Social and Religious Life of Italians in America.* Boston: 1918, pp. 43–4.
35. R. D. McKenzie, "The Scope of Human Ecology," in Ernest W. Burgess, Ed., *The Urban Community.* Chicago: 1926, p. 180.

35. The Place of Social Structure in the Determination of Land Use — William H. Form

William Form makes use of several examples of land use, building, and zoning decisions in the region around Lansing, Michigan, to illustrate his argument that four organizational complexes influence the otherwise "free" forces of the real estate and housing market. These four are the real estate industry which owns, buys, or sells land and the buildings which occupy it; the large production and service industries and utilities which constitute the major consumers of land; the private individual home owners anxious to preserve the nearby amenities which lend value to their dwellings; and finally, the government. It is the local government which establishes standards for land use. The administrative units of these governments provide the forum through which the interests of the competing forces are resolved. The paper contains a plea that students of ecological processes devote more effort to empirical research dealing with the operation of the four organizational complexes and that models of spatial structure and urban growth incorporate these forces as explanatory variables.

William H. Form is Professor of Sociology at Michigan State University. Several of his published works are cited on page 333 of this volume.

Deriving a satisfactory theory of land use change is a pressing problem for both ecologists and urban sociologists.[1] Most of the current thinking on this subject revolves around the so-called ecological processes. A brief inspection of the literature reveals, however, a lamentable lack of agreement on the definition, number, and importance of the ecological processes.[2] It is apparent that the economic model of classical economists from which these processes are derived must be discarded in favor of models which consider social realities.

In studying land use change, this paper proposes that ecology abandon its subsocial non-organization orientations and use the frame of reference of general sociology. Even though the focus of attention of ecology may remain in the economic realm, a sociological analysis of economic behavior is called for. This means that most of the current ecological premises must be converted into research questions capable of sociological verification.

The first step is to analyze the social forces operating in the land market. Obviously the image of a free and unorganized market in which individuals compete impersonally for land must be abandoned. The reason for this is that the land market is highly organized and dominated by a number of interacting organizations. Most of the latter are formally organized, highly self-conscious, and purposeful in character. Although at times their values and interests are conflicting, they are often overlapping and harmonious. That is, their relationships tend to become structured over a period of time. From a study of this emerging structure one obtains a picture of the parameters of ecological behavior, the patterns of land use change, and the

From *Social Forces*, Vol. 32, No. 4 (May 1954), pp. 317–323. Reprinted by permission.

institutional pressures which maintain the ecological order.

Four Organizational Congeries in the Land Market

The interacting groups, associations, and relationships which comprise this emerging structure may be identified by asking such questions as: (a) Who are the largest consumers of land? (b) Which organizations specialize in dealing with land? and (c) Which associations mediate the conflicts of land use? Preliminary research suggests that, among the many associations and interests in American society, four types of social congeries or organizational complexes dominate the land market and determine indirectly the use to which land is put.

The first and perhaps most important of these congeries is the real estate and building business.[3] Since they know more about the land market of the city than comparable groups, it is suggested that the study of the real estate-building groups (along the lines of occupational-industrial sociology) would provide more insight into the dynamics of land use change then present studies which are based on the sub-social ecological processes. The analysis of real estate organizations is an especially good starting point to build a sociological ecology because these organizations interact with all of the other urban interests which are concerned with land use.[4]

The second social congeries which functions in the land market are the larger industries, businesses, and utilities. While they may not consume the greatest quantities of land, they do purchase the largest and most strategic parcels. Unknowingly their locational decisions tend to set the pattern of land use for other economic and non-economic organizations. Most of the land use decisions of these central industries and businesses are a response to peculiar historic circumstances in the community. Therefore it would seem fruitless to describe *a priori* the geometric shape of the city as a series of rings, sectors, or diamonds.

The third social constellation in the land market is composed of individual home owners and other small consumers of land. In a sense their position is tangential to the structure or important only under rather unusual circumstances. Most of their decisions on where to buy, when to buy, and what land to buy are fitted into an administered land market and are not, as many would assume, individual, discrete, free, and unrelated. The social characteristics of the consumers, their economic power, degree of organization, and relations to other segments of the community help explain the role they play in the market of land decisions.

The fourth organizational complex is comprised of the many local governmental agencies which deal with land, such as the zoning boards, planning commissions, school boards, traffic commissions, and other agencies. This organizational complex is loosely knit internally, for its segments often function at cross purposes. Their relations to other groups in the community vary with political currents. Unlike other organizations, these governmental agencies are both consumers of land and mediators of conflicting land use interests. Thus political agencies not only acquire land to placate private and public pressures, they are also called upon to resolve conflicts between different types of land consumers. Moreover, some of these governmental agencies try to fulfill a city plan which sets the expected pattern of the ecological development of the city.

These four organizational complexes[5]—real estate, big business, residents, and government—do not comprise all of the organizational entities which participate in land use decisions. However, they are the main ones. Once identified, the problem is to find the nature of the social relationships among these organizational complexes. Is a stable pattern discernable? How does the pattern manifest itself in physical space? In what direction is the pattern emerging as a response to inter-institutional trends in the broader society? To answer these questions, an analytical model is needed to appraise the social relations among the four organizational congeries identified above.

Elements in the Analytical Model

Sociologists have not yet derived completely satisfactory schema to analyze interorganizational relations, either in their structural or dynamic dimensions. However, ecologists are dependent on such general schema as have already been worked out. Some of the basic elements in the analytical scheme to appraise the relations among the four land consuming groups are described below.

1. The first element in the model is the amount and types of economic resources which each "grouping" has to buttress its land use decisions. Obviously the resources of the four "groupings" differ considerably. Thus, industry has property and capital which are somewhat greater and more mobile than those of the real estate industry. In addition to their tax resources, governmental agencies have the power to expropriate land in their own name or in the name of any interest which can control them. The individual home owner and the small businessman, on the other hand, not only have the smallest but the least organized economic resources. The economic resources of each group must be carefully gauged in each community where there is a contest to control particular parcels of land. However, economic resources comprise only one cell in the paradigm needed to analyze the structural setting of land use changes.

2. The second factors which merit consideration are the manifest and latent functions of each "grouping" in the land market. Thus, the functions of the real estate industry include, in addition to maximizing its earnings, bringing knowledge of available land to different segments of the community. Moreover it tries to organize the land market and control land values to assure itself stability and continuity of income.[6] In the process of so doing, the realtors come into contact with political, citizen, and business agencies.[7] The land interests of big business, on the other hand, are much more specific and spasmodic than those of the real estate business. The desire of businessmen to have large stretches of land under one title, to obtain land additions close to present plant operations, and to dominate the landscape of the community, often leads them to make diseconomic decisions which are in conflict with those of other groups.

Government agencies have quite different and sometimes conflicting functions to perform. Among these are: protecting present tax values, acquiring parcels of land for specific public or quasi-public uses, altering certain land use patterns to conform to the plan of the "city beautiful," acting as a clearing house and communication channel for those who need land use data. Most important, they mediate conflicts in land use and exercise their legitimate authority for groups which curry their favor.

Individual residents and small businessmen are mostly concerned with preventing changes in land use. They tend to be defensive-minded and sentimentally attached to their neighborhoods and to fight to prevent the encroachment of usages which would threaten present economic and social investments. In general, resident groupings do not play dynamic roles in changing urban land usages.

3. The internal organization of these four groupings differs considerably. Knowledge of this factor is important to assess the degree to which they may be mobilized to fight for control over desired lands. Often small, unified, and organized groups with meagre economic resources can dominate larger, richer, and more loosely knit groups in a land struggle. These four "groupings" differ in their internal structure and external relations. There is an urgent need for research to study the cleavages, cliques, alliances, and arrangements found within and among these groupings. However, certain trends may now be noted.

The real estate industry is slowly emerging from a haphazard aggregation of local agents to a tightly organized professional or fraternal society which seeks to establish control over the land market.[8] Big business and industry, on the other hand, have typically bureaucratic structures capable of marshalling tremendous resources in the community for or against other land-interested groups. Municipal agencies, though individually powerful, are often unaware of each other's activities. Therefore they tend to comprise a loosely knit of bureaus which often function at cross purposes. Since many governmental agencies are tied into the fabric of private associations, they are united to common action only under unusual external pressures. Individual residents and small businesses are the most loosely organized.[9] In fact, they tend to remain unorganized except under "crisis" conditions.

4. Each grouping has an accountability pattern differing in its consequences for action. Each has different kinds of pressures and influences to which it must respond. For example, the real estate organizations are primarily accountable to themselves and sometimes to their largest customers, the building industry and the utilities. On the other hand, the local managers of larger corporations tend to be accountable to other managers, stockholders, and board members who may not reside in the community. Thus, local managers may have to respond in their land decisions to pressures generated outside of the community. Municipal agencies are formally accountable to the local citizens who are, *according to the issues*, realtors, individual landlords, businessmen, educational, political, or any other organized interest.

Each of the four social congeries being considered is organized differently as a pressure group interested in land use policies. Each, in a sense, lives in a power situation which consists of its relation to the other three. Different kinds of alliances are made among them and among their segments, depending on the issues. The types of collective bargaining situations which arise among them must be studied in a larger context in order to understand the sociology of land use decisions. For example, businessmen who are sometimes appointed as members of city planning commissions may be constrained to play roles incongruous with their business roles. As members of residential and recreational organizations they may be forced to make decisions which may seem contradictory to their economic interests.

5. In land decisions involving the whole

city, the image which each grouping has of the city must be appraised. The realtors are usually the most enthusiastic boosters of the city. They envision an expanding city with an ever-growing land market, for this assures them income and security. Consequently, they exert pressure on the municipal agencies to join them in their plans for the "expansive city."

However, municipal officials do not conceive of the city primarily as a market. They see it as the downtown civic center, the city beautiful, and the planned community. Although desiring an expanding city, they are equally concerned with the politics and aesthetics of locating parks, avenues, schools, and other services. At times their aesthetic-political plans conflict with the boom ideology of the realtors and the industry-oriented plans of businessmen. Indeed this is almost inevitable in some situations, for politicians must secure votes to remain in office. Plans for different areas of the city must be weighed in terms of how they affect votes.[10]

The industrialists' conception of the community tends to be more partial than that of any other group. Since industries often have allegiances to non-community enterprises, they are not necessarily enamoured by the vision of the expansive city or the city beautiful. They are inclined to view the city primarily as their work plant and residence. They usually regard the existence of their enterprises as economic "contributions" to the city. Therefore they feel that any land decisions they desire as businessmen, golfers, or residents are "reasonable and proper" in view of their "contribution" to the locality. When their demands are not met, they can threaten to remove the industry to more favorable communities.

The citizen's view of the city is also segmental. He tends to envision it as his neighborhood, his work plant, and "downtown." These are the areas he wants to see protected, beautified, and serviced. Since residents do not comprise a homogeneous group, obviously their community images differ. The nature of the intersection of the segmentalized city images of these four social congeries provides one of the parameters for studying their interaction. Needless to say, other non-ecological images that these groups have of themselves and of each other have a bearing on their relations. However, since the problems of this paper are more structural than social psychological, this area will not be expanded.

6. Other factors in the analytical scheme may be derived which point to the different orientations and relationships existing among these groups. For example, their primary value orientations differ. For government, community "service" is ostensibly the chief value; for real estate, it is an assured land market; for business, it is profitable operations; for the resident, it is protection. Another distinction may be in terms of the amount and type of land interests of the groups. Whereas real estate is interested in all of the city's land, municipal agencies are more interested in communal lands, and industry is concerned with its private land use. The future task of sociologists will be to select the most important interactional areas of these groups to locate the forces responsible for land use patterns and changes.

Land Use Changes in a Zoning Context

Following the selection of some of the important dimensions in the paradigm, the task is to characterize briefly the pattern of the relationships among the four "groupings." In the broadest sense, the model to be followed is that used in analyzing the collective bargaining structure and process.[11] An excellent place to begin observing the "collective bargaining" relations among these groupings is in the zoning process of cities. Zoning is recommended because the methodological problems of studying it are minimal, and yet the kinds of intergroup relations found there are not unlike those in non-zoning relations.

Since almost every city of any consequence in the United States is zoned, any significant deviation in a pattern of land use necessarily involves a change in zoning. It would appear then that sociologists and ecologists should study the relations of land-interested agencies to municipal agencies.[12] Most zoning commissions tend to freeze an already existing pattern of land use. If they formulate plans for city growth, these plans tend to correspond to a sector image of expanding areas of ongoing land use. This results in a rather rigid ecological structure which inevitably generates pressures for changes. Since such changes involve obtaining the consent of municipal agencies, a political dimension insists itself in the study of ecological processes.

Traditional ecologists may object to this social structural and political approach to problems of land use change. They may suggest that the ecological concept of "dominance" provides the answer to the question of which group will determine land use or land use change. An examination of this concept in the ecological literature reveals a basic shortcoming. Ecological dominance refers to economic control in the symbiotic sense; it provides no analytical cues to appraise the relations among organizations which comprise the structure dealing with land use changes.[13]

Traditional ecologists may object that the proposal to study the relations of the four land "groupings" in a political context is merely a methodological innovation, in that the *results* of such a study would point to the same pattern of land use change available by recourse to the traditional ecological processes. They may reason that determination of land use after all is an economic struggle or process, in which the most powerful economic interests determine to what use land will be put. While it is true, they may agree, that this process is not as simple and as impersonal as hitherto believed, the end result is very much the same.[14]

The writer has recently been gathering cases of zoning changes that have occurred in Lansing, its fringe, and in the outlying areas. In addition, cases have been observed where attempts to institute zoning changes have failed. In both types of changes the questions were asked: (a) Did naked economic power dictate the decision to change or not to change the zoning? (b) Could the outcome of these cases be predicted by using a cultural ecology frame of reference? A brief analysis of the cases revealed that no simple economic or cultural analysis could account for success or failure of zoning changes. The actual outcome could be better analyzed on the basis of the paradigm suggested above. Four cases will be briefly summarized to suggest typical kinds of alliances found in attempts to change land use.

In Lansing, the zoning commission may recommend changes in zoning but the City Council must approve of them. This means that all changes in land use must occur in a political context. In 1951, a local metal fabricating plant asked the Council to rezone some of its property from a residential to a commercial classification so that an office building could be erected on it. The residents of the area, who are mostly Negroes, appeared before the

Council urging it to refuse the request on the ground that the company had not lived up to legal responsibilities to control obnoxious smoke, fly-ash, traffic, and so on. In addition, they contended that space for Negro housing was limited and re-zoning would deprive them of needed space. Moreover, they hinted that the company's request came indirectly from a large corporation which would eventually obtain the property. In short, they urged rejection of the request not on its own merits but on the basis that the company had not lived up to its community re-sponsibilities. Company spokesmen denied any deals, promised to control air pollution, and got labor union spokesmen to urge rezoning. The Council complied. Four months later all of the properties of the company, including the rezoned area, were sold to the large corporation in question.

Here is a clear case of economically powerful interests consciously manipu-lating land uses for their purposes. The question arises: why did not the large corporation itself ask for rezoning? Appar-ently, it realized that greater resistance would have been met. The local company is a medium-sized, old, home-owned enterprise which has had rather warm relations with its employees. The large corporation, on the other hand, is a large, impersonal, absentee-owned corporation that has at times alienated local people.[15] Therefore, its chances of getting this property without fanfare were increased by the use of an intermediary.

Yet business does not always win. In another case, a respectable undertaker established a funeral parlor in a low income residential area. The local residents ob-jected strenuously to the presence of the business. The legal aspects of the case remained obscure for a time because the undertaker insisted he did not embalm bodies in the establishment. In a pre-liminary hearing he appeared to have won a victory. The aroused residents called upon the Republican ward leader who promised to talk to the "authorities." Just before a rehearing of the case, the under-taker decided to leave the area for he was reliably informed that the decision would go against him.

Struggles between businessmen and government do not always work out in favor of the former. Currently, the or-ganized businessmen of East Lansing are fighting an order of the State Highway Commission which has passed a no parking ordinance to apply to the town's main thoroughfare. The retailers are fearful that they will lose business if the order holds. Since business will not be able to expand in the same direction if the order holds, pressure to rezone residential areas in the community for commercial and parking purposes will be forthcoming. In a com-munity where residents are a strong, vocal, upper middle status group majority, such pressure may be resisted strongly. Clearly a power struggle involving the State, local businessmen, local government, and the residents will determine the ecological pattern of the city.[16] A knowledge of their relationships is needed to predict the outcome of the struggle and the future ecological changes in the community.

S. T. Kimball has documented a case where the failure to inaugurate zoning involved the same kind of social structural analysis of group relations as suggested above. Kimball studied a suburban rural township where the upper middle status groups failed in a referendum to obtain zoning in the face of an industrial invasion of the area. An analysis of the case showed that the issue would be misunderstood if studied as a struggle of economic interests. In fact, the industrial interests were not an important variable in the case. The failure of the referendum was accounted for by analysis of five types of relationships: (a) those among the suburbanites, (b) those within the township board, (c) those between the supervisor and his constituents, (d) those between the farmers and suburbanites, and (e) those between the supervisor and the informal "leaders" in the community.[17]

Conclusions

This paper has proposed the need to consider social structure in addition to ecological and cultural factors in the study of changes in land use. The traditional ecological processes are no longer adequate tools to analyze changes in land use. These processes, like most ecological concepts, are based on models of eighteenth century free enterprise economics. Yet fundamental changes in the structure of the economy call for new economic models which in turn call for a recasting of general ecological theory. The new vital trend of cultural ecology does not do this adequately, for it considers the structural realities of urban society only indirectly.

This paper proposes that ecological change be studied by first isolating the important and powerful land-interested groupings in the city. Certain elements in an analytical scheme have been proposed to study the collective bargaining relationships among these groupings. The *forces* that operate in land use change may well be studied in the socio-political struggles that are presently occurring in the area of zoning. A brief survey of some changes in urban zoning points to the greater adequacy of the sociological over the traditional ecological analysis for understanding and predicting land use changes.

NOTES

1. For purposes of simplification this paper will limit itself to a consideration of land use change in middle-size, growing, industrial cities of the United States. Historical analysis of land use change is not within the province of this paper because of the methodological difficulties in reconstructing the ecological processes.

2. One reason for this confusion centers on the controversy whether human ecology should be related to or divorced from biological ecology. Amos H. Hawley claims that the difficulties of human ecology arise from its isolation from the mainstream of ecological thought in biology; see his "Ecology and Human Ecology," *Social Forces*, 22 (May 1944), pp. 399–405. Warner E. Gettys is of the opinion that human ecology should free itself from its primary dependence on organic ecology: see his "Human Ecology and Social Theory," *Social Forces*, 18 (May 1940), pp. 469–476.

3. It appears that an interpenetration of organization and interests of these two groups is increasing so rapidly in American cities that for many purposes they may be conceived as one interest group.

4. This is strongly suggested by strikingly parallel studies in two different types of cities. Cf. Everett C. Hughes, A Study of a Secular Institution: The Chicago Real Estate Board (unpublished Ph.D. dissertation, University of Chicago, 1928); Donald H. Bouma, An Analysis of the Social Power Position of the Real Estate Board in Grand Rapids, Michigan (unpublished Ph. D. dissertation, Michigan State College, 1952).

5. Each organizational complex is comprised of groups, associations, aggregations, social categories, and other types of social nucleations. To facilitate communication, the term "grouping" will be used to refer to this organizational complex. I am indebted to Professor Read Bain for pointing to the need for terminological clarification in matters dealing with interaction of different types of social nucleations.

6. See Everett C. Hughes, "Personality Types and the Division of Labor," in Ernest W. Burgess (ed.), *Personality and the Social Group* (Chicago: University of Chicago Press, 1929), especially pp. 91–94.

7. *Ibid.* Hughes indicates that the real estate industry is a loose federation of different types of businessmen. Each type plays a different role to correspond to its clientele and market.

8. *Ibid.*

9. Higher status areas of the city are usually more formally organized to protect land uses than are lower status areas. The formation of neighborhood "improvement and betterment" associations stabilizes land use and resists the invasion of other land uses.

10. For an illuminating case history of this, see

William Foote Whyte, *Street Corner Society* (Chicago: University of Chicago Press, 1947), pp. 245–252.

11. Herbert Blumer, "Sociological Theory in Industrial Relations," *American Sociological Review*, 12 (June 1947), pp. 271–278. See also the articles in Richard A. Lester and Joseph Shister (eds.), *Insights into Labor Issues* (New York: The Macmillan Company, 1948); William Foote Whyte, *Pattern for Industrial Peace* (New York: Harper and Brothers, 1951); H. D. Lasswell, *Politics* (New York: McGraw-Hill, 1936).

12. Richard Dewey, "The Neighborhood, Urban Ecology, and City Planners," *American Sociological Review*, 15 (August 1960), pp. 502–507.

13. See R. D. McKenzie, *The Metropolitan Community* (New York: McGraw-Hill, 1933), pp. 81–313; Don J. Bogue, *The Structure of the Metropolitan Community* (Horace J. Rackham School of Graduate Studies, University of Michigan, 1949), pp. 10–13.

14. In this respect the position of ecologists is not significantly different from the Marxist analysis of land use changes. This may explain the appeal of the ecological approach to some otherwise sophisticated sociologists. I am indebted to G. P. Stone for the elaboration of this idea.

15. For example, workers insist that during the depression the company recruited Southerners rather than local labor.

16. My colleague, G. P. Stone, suggests that it begins to appear that the State's position will force a very unusual ecological phenomenon: a business district turning its back to the main highway and reorienting itself to the "backyards," as it were.

17. Solon T. Kimball, "A Case Study of Township Zoning," *Michigan Agricultural Experiment Station Quarterly Bulletin*, 28 (May, 1946), p. 4.

Urban Locality Groups

PART V

The aggregation of people into dense settlements gives rise inevitably to a wide variety of organized and semiorganized groups. Some of these groups are organized around a single set of social functions, such as work or worship, represented by the social institutions of the economy and the church respectively. In the typical American urban community these institutions and groups draw their membership from a population which often is dispersed. Some of the problems of this situation have been discussed in earlier sections.

The readings in the present section are concerned with the other kinds of groups which arise in response to the fact that, even in urban society, people share a local area in common. These are the groups known as neighborhoods or local communities. No matter how often members of modern urban society may move about daily within a metropolitan region to work, to shop, or for recreation, they nevertheless reside in one specific part of the region. The sociologist is interested in understanding the role that the experience of living in these local areas still plays in the life of an American city dweller.

The first group of selections examines the question of whose needs are most effectively served by the neighborhoods and the local communities, and the interactions between these local areas and their functions within the metropolitan region and society as a whole. The awareness of the neighborhood as a significant social group and the attachment to it seem to vary depending upon the social class and the income level of the residents, their sex, the position of families in the life cycle, and the physical characteristics of the local area and its location within the metropolitan complex.

The readings in the second section consider the relevance of the local community to the political process. One of the distinguishing characteristics of urbanization in the United States is the degree to which many political decisions affecting schools, water supply, and land use continue to be the formal responsibility of small local governments. Considerable strain has developed, however, in the community's exercise of these functions because fiscal and administrative power to handle these problems is at the same time the province of the metropolis, the federal, and the state authorities. Some politicians and social scientists simply accept the confusing allocation of power and learn to play a political "game" to deal with it. Others are calling for a more "rational" reorganization of the lines of authority through the establishment of metropolitan government.

Urban Neighborhoods and Social Interaction

36. Rural-Urban Status Differences   Albert J. Reiss, Jr.
in Interpersonal Contacts

Reiss's paper is an example of a close and refined attempt through careful empirical research to investigate the relative impact of residential setting and occupation on social interaction. It is based on a study of the time budgets of 350 men in the urban, rural-nonfarm, and rural-farm settlements in the Nashville, Tennessee region. Reiss's major conclusion is that the distinction between agricultural and nonagricultural occupations is a more useful index of the type and frequency of interpersonal contacts within a community than the rural or industrial composition of the residential setting itself.

Albert J. Reiss, Jr., is Professor of Sociology and Director of the Center for Research in Social Organizations at the University of Michigan. Several of his published works are cited on page 27 of this volume.

Sociologists customarily describe the ideal type of personal contacts in cities as anonymous, segmental, and impersonal and contrast them with the intimate and personal type in rural areas.[1] A large number of studies offer general support for this description, but most give data for only a rural *or* an urban setting.[2] Comparisons between the two settings are therefore made by inferring the characteristics for one of them.

This paper reports the result of a pilot study to test several hypotheses about differences in types of interpersonal contacts among urban, rural—non-farm and rural-farm residents, the time-budget being used in gathering data. Sorokin and Zimmerman, who provide the most precise statement of supposed differences in the quality and quantity of social contact or interaction of rural and urban residents,[3] state a single hypothesis as to quantitative aspects: "the number of contacts per individual in a given unit of time is greater in urban than rural life." Qualitative differences are described in five hypotheses:

1. The area of the contact system of a member of a rural community, as well as that of the rural community as a whole, is spatially more narrow and limited than the area of a member of an urban community and of the urban community as a whole.
2. . . . Face to face relations occupy a less [sic] proportion of the whole interaction system of an urbanite than of a rural individual.
3. . . . The interaction system of an urbanite is woven, to a greater proportion than in the case of a rural individual, out of impersonal and to a less degree out of personal relations.
4. . . . In the totality of relations which compose the network of the interaction system of an urban individual, the part composed of casual, superficial and short-lived relations, in contrast to permanent, strong, and durable relations, occupies a much more conspicuous place than in the interaction system of a rural dweller.
5. . . . The relations are more flexible, less durable, and more impersonal; the whole network of this system of interaction is to be marked by greater complexity, greater plasticity, differentiation, manifoldness, and, at the same time by greater superficiality, "standardization," and mechanization than the network of the interaction system of a rural dweller.

The data from this pilot study permit only a partial test of the first four hypotheses. A sixth hypothesis, which follows from several of the postulates underlying these hypotheses, is also tested. Since agricultural work is less often organized on the basis of personal contacts than is non-agricultural and since in rural areas contacts are relatively fewer in frequency than in non-rural, the rural person is expected to spend a greater part of his time in isolation.

A growing body of evidence shows that the quantity and quality of social interaction is a function of socio-economic status, as well as of residential location. The major hypothesis advanced in sociological literature is that the amount of impersonal contact varies directly with socio-economic status. A corollary is that formal group participation varies more or less directly with socio-economic status, while informal varies inversely among the urban[4]. This paper also examines status, within each residential category, as a further test of the hypotheses.

Residents of high and low socio-economic status classified as rural-farm (RF), rural—non-farm (RNF), and urban residential, comprise the six populations.[5] They were not selected by uniform sampling criteria.

The urban population of the Nashville, Tennessee, Standard Metropolitan Area (SMA) was classified into white-collar and manual-worker census tracts and four white-collar and three manual-worker tracts were randomly selected. A 25 percent random sample of dwelling units was selected in each of these tracts and a respondent twenty years old and over was interviewed. The RNF and RF respondents were selected from a county south of the Nashville SMA. Two village communities located at maximum distance from the city center were selected, the rural area within a four-mile radius of them, and the major traffic artery from the central city to the areas. A respondent twenty years old or over in every fourth dwelling unit with a male head of household was then interviewed. The place of work of RNF respondents was not held constant. Some worked in the SMA, while others were employed in the villages or in rural locations, such as motel and dam sites, and so on. The population for which comparisons are made is white married males, age twenty to sixty-five, with a regular full-time job. These criteria were imposed to eliminate known sources of variation by sex, marital status, age, and employment status.

Time-Budgets The allocation of an individual's time during a single day was chosen as the measure of the amount and kind of personal contact. A budget of time was obtained for the nearest previous workday and the last full day off. This paper reports the data for only the workday.

The time-budget opened with the statement: "Now, we would like to know how you spent your time yesterday. We want to know just how much time you spent doing different things during the day and whom you spent it with. Suppose we begin with the time you got up yesterday: what time did you get up?" This was followed by, "What did you do when you first got up? Did you spend the time with anyone, or were you more or less alone? Whom were you with? and, how close are they to you?" Each new activity or block of time was similarly explored until the person said he went to sleep. Interviewers were specifically instructed to get the information so that it could be coded into one of the following mutually exclusive categories:

1. *Intimate kinship*, such as nuclear family members and extended kin members.
2. *Close intimate friends*, friends defined as "very close," "my best friend," etc.
3. *Close associate or client*, a close friend deriving from a work context, whether or not actually seen at work.
4. *Good friend*, a friend defined as "close," "just a good friend," etc.
5. *Distant associate or casual acquaintance*, either a fellow worker who is not defined as a friend or a person with whom one has a "speaking acquaintance."
6. *Cordial recognition*, defined as a person whom one recognizes in address, or "just someone to whom I say 'hello'".
7. *Pure client*, defined as a person whom one doesn't know personally, but one with whom contact is made, or with whom interaction takes place in a client relationship.

For analytical purposes, Nos. 1–4 are defined as "primary contacts"; Nos. 5–7 as "secondary contacts"; Nos. 6 and 7 as "impersonal contacts." As the total time awake was obtained, most persons also had some time with "no personal contact."

Part of the daily activity was also allocated to one of three contexts: time spent at work on a job; time spent in exposure to mass media; and time spent where secondary contacts are probable. Persons need not have experienced any personal contact to be coded active in that situation. Classification into these three situations is independent of the classification for interpersonal contacts. The same period of time, therefore, may be coded in both the contact and the situation class.

There are, of course, many problems of classification in allocating time to social situations and types of contact. Several types of contact may occur at a single time, for example, or the situation may include more than one type of activity. This problem was met by asking each respondent to allocate the time among the various types of persons with whom contemporaneous contact was made. It is clear from the time-budgets that urban dwellers spend more time in situations with more than one type of contact than do rural dwellers; the criterion adopted here masks this difference. Similarly, social contact among persons with whom the most intimate relationships are maintained may vary from mingling to copulation. In a strict sense, this study simply allocates daily contact time to persons with whom one has a particular *qualitative* relationship and to types of social situations, given certain *structural* characteristics. The quality and content of the interaction are not usually known.[6]

The time at which a time-budget is obtained affects the allocation of daily time. Seasonal and weekly differences in work influence both the amount of time spent at it, the situation, and the kind of daily contacts. The allocation of time also varies for individual households, owing to such circumstances as the temporary presence of guests or the temporary absence of a member. Such shifts in the daily round cannot be considered atypical and deserve analysis in themselves. They are not controlled in this study, except insofar as the interviewing of all urban respondents in April or May and of all RNF and RF respondents in May or in July allows gross seasonal variations.

Structural characteristics of the society likewise affect the social allocation of time. Age, sex, marital and occupational status are roughly controlled in this study either by selection of respondents or by statistical procedure. Others, such as the size of the family, the presence of preschool children, religious affiliation, the availability of mass media, and type of work are not controlled. A partial listing of some forty structural correlates of time-allocation was made for this study. Obviously, it would take simultaneous study of a very large population of respondents to control variation from all these sources.

Testing Procedures The time-budget was recorded in minutes for the waking hours of the day. Respondents erred sometimes in the allocation of minutes spent in a particular activity or relationship, since each was asked to recall the previous day. The error is readily apparent in their frequent "rounding" of numbers of minutes to figures ending in 0 and 5. The allocation of time is perhaps more reliable for activities represented in the "daily round" than for others. Pretests showed that the procedure of having respondents "follow the clock" with their report of daily activity provides a more reliable estimate of time than is obtained if the respondent is simply asked to "recall his day."

The mean and standard deviation were chosen as the measures of central tendency and dispersion for each group, and the null hypothesis of differences in means and variances was tested. The comparison of variances of rural and urban residential contexts is open to question on the grounds that one might logically expect greater variation within urban than rural contexts, since the urban is more heterogeneous in occupational composition. Ideally, occupational composition should be more satisfactorily controlled in comparisons than it is in this study, but our sample size does not permit a more detailed occupational classification. The difference between means was tested by the conventional T-test, which assumes that the populations do not differ significantly with respect to their variances. When the variances differed significantly, unless n_1 was equal to n_2, the standard error of the difference between means was calculated by using the estimates of the two population variances rather than a common estimate of the population variances. A two-tailed test of significance was used only when direction was not predicted.

There are 225 comparisons of types of interpersonal contact and contact situation for high- and low-status urban RNF and RF categories in Tables 2 and 4 involving tests of significance for proportions, for means, and for variances. For purposes of testing the hypotheses in this study, however, attention is directed to the *pattern* of significant differences among the comparisons by residence and status for a type of interpersonal contact or contact situation rather than on each significant comparison.

Tables 1–4 in this paper provide data and statistical tests for fifteen residential area-status group comparisons, but the tests of particular hypotheses do not refer to all comparisons. Zero-order comparisons of either status or residential categories with

respect to type of interpersonal contact or situation can be made by recombining information in the tables.

The present study relies solely on a cross-section comparison to test the hypotheses, and historical inferences, therefore, should be drawn only with extreme caution. Conclusions from a comparison of an urban community of today with an ideal typical description of a rural or urban community of a century ago may be highly misleading. Differences in personal contacts among urbanites of one hundred years ago and today could be greater, in fact, than the difference between residents of rural and urban areas at either time, for variation over time in some types of contact may be greater than that between categories at a particular time.

TABLE 1. PER CENT REPORTING SOME WORKDAY CONTACT OR SITUATIONS, BY RESIDENCE AND STATUS

Type of Interpersonal Contact or Contact Situation	Urban		RNF		RF	
	High	Low	High	Low	High	Low
No. of cases	176	75	27	24	28	21
Per cent reporting any contact with:						
1. Intimate kinship	97	99	90	100	100	100
2. Close intimate friend	33	39	80	42	36	24
3. Close associate or client	71	59	25	13	14	*
4. Good friend	32	37	30	38	18	10
5. Distant associate or client	43	44	65	38	46	33
6. Cordial recognition	10	12	*	4	4	*
7. Pure client	45	33	40	29	4	19
Per cent reporting workday time in:						
8. No interpersonal contact	86	81	90	92	82	71
9. Primary contact (1–4)	100	100	100	100	100	100
10. Secondary contact (5–7)	76	68	95	58	50	43
11. All impersonal contact (6–7)	51	41	40	33	7	19
12. All interpersonal contact (1–7)	100	100	100	100	100	100
13. Total waking time	100	100	100	100	100	100
Per cent of total waking time in:						
14. Job situations	100	100	100	100	100	100
15. Mass-media situations	87	88	55	45	61	53
16. Secondary situations	95	87	90	79	36	24

* No time reported for any respondent.

TABLE 2. SIGNIFICANT RESIDENCE AND STATUS GROUP DIFFERENCES IN PROPORTIONS OF RESPONDENTS REPORTING CONTACT FOR TYPES OF INTERPERSONAL CONTACTS AND SITUATIONS (*P* VALUES)*

Type of Interpersonal Contact or Contact Situations	Urban High Status versus					Urban Low Status versus				RNF High Status versus			RNF Low Status versus		RF High Status versus
	Urban Low	RNF High	RNF Low	RF High	RF Low	RNF High	RNF Low	RF High	RF Low	RNF Low	RF High	RF Low	RF High	RF Low	RF Low
1. Intimate kin	−	+	−	−	−	+	−	−	+	−	−	−	=	=	=
2. Close intimate friend	−	−†	−	−	+	−†	−	+	+	+†	+	+†	+	+	+
3. Close associate or client	+	+†	+†	+†	++	++	++	++	++	+	+	++	−	+‡	+‡
4. Good friend	−	+	−	++	+‡	++	−	++	+‡	−	+	+	+	+‡	+
5. Distant associate or client	−	−	+	−	+	−	+	−	+	+	+	+	−	+	+
6. Cordial recognition	−	+†	++	−	++	++	+	+	++	−	+	+†	+	++	++
7. Pure client	+	+	+	+†	+‡	+	+	++	+	+	+†	+	+‡	+	−
8. No interpersonal contact	+	−	−	+	+‡	−	−	−	+	=	+	+	+	+	+
9. Primary contact (1–4)	=	=	=	=	=	=	=	=	=	=	=†	=†	=	=	=

10. Secondary contact (5–7)	+	–‡	+	+‡	++	–†	+	++	++	++	++	+	+
11. All inpersonal contacts (6–7)	+	+	+	+‡	+†	+	+†	+‡	+‡	+	+	+	–
12. All interpersonal contacts (1–7)	=	=	=	=	=	=	=	=	=	=	=	=	=
13. Total time awake (1–8)	=	=	=	=	=	=	=	=	=	=	=	=	=
14. Total time in job situation	=	=	=	=	=	=	=	=	=	=	=	=	=
15. Total time in mass-media situations	–	++	++	++	++	++	+	++	+	+	+	–	+
16. Total time in secondary situations	+	+‡	++	+†	+†	+	+	++	+†	+†	+†	++	+

* The significance of the difference between proportions was determined from monographs (Joseph Lubin, "Nomographs for Determining the Significance of the Differences between the Frequencies of Events in Two Contrasted Series or Groups," *Journal of the American Statistical Association*, XXXIV (September, 1939), 540–41. The nomographs report *P* levels for only a critial ratio of 2 (0.0455) and of 3 (0.0027); levels are reported as 0.005 and 0.003, respectively, in the body of the table. The +, –, and = signs refer to the direction of the difference in each comparison.
† 0.003 level of significance.
‡ 0.05 level of significance.

Sorokin and Zimmerman's first hypothesis states that the urban individual and the urban area have a more extensive spatial contact system than do rural persons and rural areas. The distance between workplace and residence is one rough measure, assuming that the greater the distance between the two, the greater the territory over which contact obtains. Using this rough measure of spatial contact, the three residential settings are ranked thus: RNF, urban, and RF; and the hypothesis is not accepted. It seems likely that urban inhabitants may have a larger spatial area of contact if all modes of communication are mapped in territorial space. If this is true, then we might say that city people spread their daily symbolic contacts but not their direct physical contacts over a larger territory than do RNF inhabitants.

If we postulate that contacts with mass media are a measure of an extensive spatial contact system, we have a second test of the hypothesis. Every household in the study had either a radio or a television set and often a telephone and a daily newspaper. Every male, therefore, was potentially exposed to the mass media. The data show a higher proportion of urban than of RNF or RF males exposed to mass-media situations, irrespective of status. Mean exposure time was significantly greater for urban males than for RF males or RNF males of low status. But there are no significant differences by status either in the proportion of males who spend some time in daily contact with mass media or in mean amount of contact with media within the RNF and RF residence categories (see Tables 1–4). This result is consistent with the expectation that urban persons would have a greater range of contact than rural persons, except that RNF males of high status are more like urban than rural males in their exposure time to mass media.

Significantly more of the urban and RNF than RF males, regardless of status, had some exposure to secondary situations (line 16 in Tables 1 and 2). Urban and RNF males, likewise, have a higher mean exposure and variance in exposure to secondary situations than do RF males, but no significant differences of this kind are found between urban and RNF males (line 16, Tables 3 and 4). If we postulate that secondary contacts are generally spatially more diffuse than primary ones— a questionable postulate—it appears that non-agricultural workers have a more extensive spatial contact system than do those in agriculture.

These tests of our first hypothesis suggest that residential setting may be less important than occupational situs in determining the range of social contact. Men with nonagricultural employment, even when they reside in village or open country, more often are exposed to secondary contact situations than are males in agriculture. There are probably two main reasons for this: the nature of their job situations and their movement to and from places of work.

Primary social relations are said to be involved in a smaller proportion of the total interaction system of an urban than of a rural individual. There are a number of ways to test this second hypothesis, and much depends upon the definition of an "indirect interaction system" as part of the total system of social interaction. Sorokin and Zimmerman argue, by deduction, that the interaction system of an urbanite consists of a larger network of indirect contacts —persons whom one never sees—than does that of the typical rural person; hence the actual face-to-face, or primary, relations of an urbanite are a smaller proportion of the total interaction system. No data are available on the amount of indirect interaction

TABLE 3. MEAN AND STANDARD DEVIATION OF TIME SPENT IN SPECIFIED TYPES OF INTERPERSONAL CONTACT SITUATIONS BY RESIDENCE AND STATUS

Type of Interpersonal Contact or Contact Situation	Means (in Minutes)						Standard Deviations (in Minutes)					
	Urban		RNF		RF		Urban		RNF		RF	
	High	Low	High	Low	High	Low	High	Low	High	Low	High	Low
1. Intimate kinship	322	355	282	285	334	401	125	102	176	158	222	255
2. Close intimate friend	43	35	117	93	72	79	108	86	134	140	141	195
3. Close associate or client	223	191	54	21	33	*	215	224	125	66	109	*
4. Good friend	34	54	51	89	64	8	82	114	112	155	173	25
5. Distant associate or client	113	134	215	140	155	123	181	193	239	220	204	201
6. Cordial recognition	8	20	*	27	2	*	31	81	*	120	11	*
7. Pure client	111	48	87	53	1	7	190	117	135	89	4	16
8. No interpersonal contact	119	133	181	241	297	311	140	167	168	234	286	291
9. Primary contact (1–4)	622	634	498	485	507	488	256	251	226	266	281	271
10. Secondary contact (5–7)	233	202	308	222	158	130	225	219	205	222	207	202
11. All impersonal contact (6–7)	120	68	87	81	3	7	193	140	135	139	12	16
12. All interpersonal contact (1–7)	855	836	806	707	665	618	156	181	182	244	291	293
13. Total time awake	974	968	985	948	962	928	92	76	64	76	86	70
14. Total time in job situations	498	491	539	514	641	640	131	77	155	98	138	142
15. Total time in mass media situations	121	125	71	70	62	44	85	89	111	87	65	53
16. Total time in secondary situations	367	324	378	269	71	20	197	242	227	259	111	48

* No time reported for any respondent.

TABLE 4. SIGNIFICANT RESIDENCE AND STATUS GROUP DIFFERENCES IN INTERPERSONAL CONTACTS AND SITUATIONS (P VALUES)*

Type of Interpersonal Contact or Situation	Urban High Status versus					Urban Low Status versus				RNF High Status versus			RNF Low Status versus		RF High Status versus
	Urban Low	RNF High	RNF Low	RF High	RF Low	RNF High	RNF Low	RF High	RF Low	RNF Low	RF High	RF Low	RF High	RF Low	RF Low
1. Intimate kinship	−	+	+	(−)	(−)	(+)	(+)	(+)	(−)	−	−	−	−	−	−
2. Close intimate friend	(+)	−†	−	−	(−)	−†	(−)	(−)	(−)	(−)	+	+	+	+	−
3. Close associate or client	+	(+)‡	(+)‡	(+)‡	§	−†	−	−	−	+	+	+			
4. Good friend	(−)	(−)	(−)	§	(+)‡	(+)‡	(+)‡	(+)‡	§	+	+	*	−	§	§
5. Distant associate or client	(−)	(−)	+	−	(+)†	+	−	(−)	(+)†	−	−	(+)	+	(+)†	(+)
6. Cordial recognition	(−)	§	−	−	§	−	−	(+)	+	+	§	§	(+)	§	§
7. Pure client	(+)†	+	(+)†	(+)‡	(+)‡	§	−	(+)†	(+)†	+	(+)†	(+)†	(+)†	(+)†	−
8. No interpersonal contact	+	−	(−)†	(−)†	+	−	−†	(−)†	(−)†	−	+	(−)‡	−	−	−
9. All primary contact (1–4)	−	††	††	††	††	††	††	††	††	+	−	+	−	−	+

10. All secondary contact (5–7)	+	−	+	+	++	−	+	+	++	++	+	+	+	+
11. All impersonal contact (6–7)	(+)†	+	+	(+)‡	(+)†	−	−	+	(+)‡	(+)†	(+)†	(+)†	+	−
12. All interpersonal contact (1–7)	+	+	(+)	(+)†	(+)†	+	+	+	(+)†	(+)†	++	+	+	+
13. Total time awake (1–8)	+	−	+	+	+	−	+	++	+	+	++	+	+	+
14. Total time in job situation	(+)	−	−	++	+	(−)	+	+	−	−‡	−	−	−†	+
15. Total time in mass media situations	−	+	++	(+)‡	(+)‡	+	++	++	(+)	(+)	(+)	+	+	+
16. Total time in secondary situations	+	−	−	(+)‡	(+)‡	−	+	+	(+)‡	(+)‡	(+)‡	(+)‡	(+)	(+)

* The + and − signs refer to the direction of the difference in each comparison. Parentheses indicate that the variances differ significantly at the 0.02 level.
† Means differ significantly at the 0.05 level.
‡ Means differ significantly at the 0.001 level.
§ No time is reported for any respondent in at least one of the groups; the mean difference, therefore, is not calculated.

contacts, since no satisfactory operational definition of them was developed when the study was designed. It is difficult to say, for example, whether a rural dweller's indirect contact with a state or federal authority is greater or less than that of an urban resident, in view of agricultural subsidies, flood-control programs, and the like. The tests of the hypothesis, therefore, were limited to measures based on the actual amount of time spent in interaction.

All the respondents had some primary contact on the workday as shown by line 9 of Tables 1 and 2. This follows from the fact that all respondents were married males. While all men had some exposure to primary contacts during the day, the average urban male reported a significantly greater number of minutes of primary contact than did the average RNF or RF person, regardless of status (see Tables 3 and 4). There are no significant differences between RNF and RF males in total time spent in primary contacts. Table 4 also shows that there are no significant differences between any of the groups in variances in amount of daily primary contacts, despite differences in mean contact. Urban males, on the whole, exhibited no greater variability in this respect than did the RNF or RF. On the average, an urban employed, married male spends over 10 hours a day in primary interaction as compared with, roughly, 8 hours for the law-status RNF or RF male. Urban males, therefore, spend more actual time in primary contacts than do the RNF or RF. But urban males also spend more time on *all* personal contacts than do the low-status RNF and all RF. If one computes a ratio of the average time in primary contact to the average time in all personal contact (ratio of line 9 to line 12 in Table 3) for each residence-status group, the ratios for high- and low-status groups, respectively, are 0.73 and 0.76

for urban, 0.62 and 0.68 for RNF, and 0.76 and 0.79 for RF males. The differences are not particularly large. Certainly, the average urban male does not spend considerably less of his total time in interaction in primary contacts than does the average rural male. It appears that RNF males spend the least part of the total time in interaction in primary contacts, but this difference cannot be attributed to any single type of primary contact.

The third hypothesis—that the interaction system of the urban as compared with the rural individual is, to a greater degree, made up of impersonal relations—is a corollary of hypothesis 2. The types of impersonal relations defined for this study were those of cordial recognition and pure-client relations. The major finding is that urban and RNF males have a higher average amount of impersonal contact than do RF males (line 11, Tables 3 and 4). Only about one-tenth or fewer of the men in any residential setting or status group had contacts of cordial recognition on their workday, as Table 1 shows. It is not surprising, therefore, that there are no sizable significant differences in mean duration of contact in cordial relationships.

The pure-client relationship, however, is clearly not rural. The RF males have pure-client contacts much less often than do urban and RNF males, although the results are not statistically significant for all status categories (line 7 of Table 2). A separate tabulation also shows that no RF male had a pure-client relationship on the job, in contrast to at least two-fifths of the high-status and one-fifth of the low-status urban and RNF males. Urban and RNF males, regardless of status, have a significantly higher mean duration of pure-client contacts than do RF males (line 7 of Tables 3 and 4). The high-status urban male, as expected, has the greatest average contact in a client role, averaging almost 2 hours a day. This average, in fact, is significantly and appreciably above that of all categories except RNF persons of high status. There is also a significantly higher variance for pure-client contacts for urban and RNF than for RF males. High-status urban and RNF males, in fact, tend to have significantly greater variance in pure-client contacts than do the other residence-status groups, although the comparisons are not always statistically significant (line 7 of Tables 3 and 4). This apparently higher variance for high-status urban and RNF males is probably accounted for largely by differences in occupational role composition and job context. Some white-collar jobs—particularly professional and sales occupations—require almost exclusive contact with clients, while others require little, if any.

Sorokin and Zimmerman's fourth hypothesis also is closely related to the second and third hypotheses: that casual, superficial, and short-lived relationships comprise a greater proportion of the total of interaction relations than do the permanent, strong, and durable relationships. Lines 1–7 in all the tables provide comparisons for four types of primary and three types of secondary relationships which permit a partial test; they lend only parital support to it. RF males may have a somewhat greater proportion of their total contact in a primary interaction relationship than RNF males and perhaps urban males of high status, but the differences are small and certainly do not warrant a conclusion that the hypothesis is sustained. The findings on amount of time actually spent in primary and secondary situations tend to support the hypothesis. Urbanites increase their primary contact time over that of their rural counterparts by having

primary contacts at their work—an opportunity usually denied to rural males on small farms. Moreover, urban males make more personal contacts of the distinctly impersonal type—the pure-client relationship—than do the rural. These two types of relationships, then, are the major differentia. Yet, lest these differences be interpreted out of context, it must be remembered that the average urban person of high status—the extreme type—spends less than 2 hours a day in a pure-client relationship and only about 4 hours in all secondary contacts, while he spends over 10 hours in all types of primary interaction. His interaction time, therefore, is spent predominantly in primary relationships. These two types of relationships also appear clearly to reflect differences in opportunity for contact at work. Both the differences in primary contact with associates or clients and in the secondary pure-client type occur primarily at work. Non-agricultural work often provides opportunities for both types of contact—a primary friendship relation with a fellow or co-worker at the same or adjacent status levels and a secondary relationship with a member of the public or a client.

The final hypothesis is that the RF male spends a greater part of his waking time without any personal contact, given less opportunity for group contact in both work and non-work situations. There are no significant residence differences in the percentage of persons who spent some time in isolation (line 8 of Tables 1 and 2); however, RF males spend significantly more time in isolation and show greater variance than do urban (but not RNF) males, regardless of status (line 8, Tables 3 and 4).

The mean time spent in social isolation by the several residence-status groups can be expressed as a proportion of the mean time awake. These proportions, for high and low status, respectively, are 12.2 and 13.6 for urban, 18.4 and 25.4 for RNF, and 30.9 and 32.5 for RF males. It is readily seen that the average RF employed married male spends about a third of his day without any personal contact, as compared with only one-seventh of the waking time or urban employed married males, regardless of status; the RNF proportions are in between. It may be true that for single persons the urban environment is more conducive to living in almost complete isolation from social contact, but the typical urban married male in this study is less likely to spend part of his day isolated from social contact than is the typical RF married male. The average urban married male has more of primary contact and less of isolation than does the average married RNF or RF. The variance in amount of time spent without personal contact also is greater for RF than for urban married males. This at least suggests that the extremes of isolation (other than with intimate kin) are approached more closely by the RF than by the urban married male.

The modern period of Western society is often referred to as an age of potential leisure. This is attributed to the historical change in the amount of time spent at work by both agricultural and non-agricultural workers. The average time spent on the job was significantly longer for RF males than for RNF or urban males, regardless of status (line 14 of Tables 3 and 4). The average agricultural workers spent between 8 and 9 hours a day at work. The fact that the lowest variance for time spent on the job (line 14, Table 4) occurs for the non-agricultural workers of low status follows from the prevalence of a workday and week standardized by contract. The variance in length of workday for urban workers of

low status, in fact, is significantly below that of urban and RNF workers of high status and all RF workers.

The reduction in working hours provides considerable opportunity for persons to divide their waking hours among other activities (line 13 of Tables 3 and 4). There are a few significant differences between residence-status groups in the average duration of waking hours and no significant differences in variance. The mean waking interval is a little over 16 hours a day, with a standard deviation of 60–90 minutes, except for low-status RF persons. If one takes as a very crude measure of potential leisure the ratio of working hours to total hours awake, almost half the waking time of urban and RNF married males is spent outside the work context. These ratios for high- and low-status groups, respectively, are 51 and 51 for urban, 55 and 54 for RNF, and 67 and 69 for RF males. By contrast, roughly two-thirds of the waking time of RF persons is spent at work. Since, with the exception of RF persons of low status, there are no significant differences in total waking hours (and this is not enough to account for the observed differences), it is clear that the non-agricultural worker has a longer potential time for leisure than does the agricultural worker, at least on the workday.

Some attention was given to status differences in types of contact in referring to a combined residential area—status group difference. The status differentials in interpersonal contact are now examined within each of the three residential areas, though it is recognized that each test is not independent of the others in a sampling sense.

First of all, there are few status differences by residence in the proportion reporting some daily contact or in mean time spent in the several types of personal contact or contact situations (Tables 1–4). None of these status differences is significant in more than one of the three residential contexts. Urban groups of high and low status, in fact, show no significant differences in exposure to types of contact, and there are no significant differences in average time spent in personal contacts or contact situations between RNF or RF males of high and low status. Among urban inhabitants, males of high status have a greater mean contact in a pure-client relationship, and consequently in all impersonal contacts, than do urban males of low status. The same status differential is observed for RNF males, but it is not statistically significant. As noted, this probably is largely a consequence of differences in exposure to clients when at work.

There are somewhat more significant differences between high- and low-status groups in variances of time spent in personal contact and contact situations, even though there are few significant differences between them in average time spent in types of contact. None of the differences is observed in all residential settings, however.

Urban males of high status have a greater variance in contact with close intimate friends than do those of low status, but the latter have a greater variance in contact with good friends than do those of high status. The status difference in variance for all friendship contacts therefore disappears. High-status RF males, in contrast to high-status urban males, have a greater variance for contact with good friends than do those of low status; but the reverse, although not significant, is found for close intimate friends among RF males, so that the status difference in variance for all friendships also disappears for RF males. The apparent pattern then seems to be one where high-status urban and low-status

RF males show higher variance for contacts with good friends. This difference could well be a function of how high- and low-status males define "good" as compared with "close" friends—the distinction is difficult, in any case.

Urban males of high status have substantially greater variance in all impersonal contacts than do males of low status, but the difference is accounted for by the fact that high-status males have a greater variance in pure-client contacts, since low-status males have a substantially greater variance in contact in patterns of cordial recognition. Urban males of high status also show greater variance in the total time on their job than do those of low status. Both these patterns occur for RNF males, although they are not statistically significant. Hence white-collar workers are probably less homogeneous in their personal relations than are manual workers (in the non-agricultural situs).

The failure to reject the major null hypothesis about status differentials in interpersonal contact or in exposure to types of situation, independent of residence, is a surprising one, given both a general expectation of class differentials and the existing literature on them.

Only a few of the many possible reasons for this failure are mentioned here. The first is that differences in measurement account for the difference in conclusions. Most previous studies use some attribute of persons, such as their membership in certain groups, or a characteristic of their behavior, such as number of personal visits or meetings attended, as measures of personal contact and participation, and they also focus more on organizational structure. The present study measures times spent by the individual in a type of contact or situation. These are different dimensions of behavior. The time spent in many activities can be a negligible proportion of one's day: for example, the time spent in voluntary associations or in formal community organizations usually occupies only a very small proportion of a man's weekly, much less daily, time.

A second explanation is that our data are for very small samples, so that real, but small, differences may go undetected. Moreover, we examined only employed married males aged twenty to sixty-five; other age-sex-marital-status groups may show these expected differences. If this is the case, generalizations must be appropriately qualified. Fourth, the selection of our population in a southern locale may account for some differences, since it might be argued that the "more rural South" places high emphasis on primary relationships. This, conceivably, could affect the absolute allocation of time to a particular type of contact; but just how such an argument would apply to a failure to secure relative differences in residence-status comparisons is far from clear. Fifth, the limitation of our data to a single workday may limit our conclusion—the day-off could show a quite different pattern, although preliminary analysis suggests that this is not the case. Furthermore, a record of activity over an extended period might conceivably confirm the differences found in other studies in our population. Many previous studies measure contact for weekly, monthly, and even longer intervals. Generally, the longer the time, however, the less time "other-than-daily contact" will occupy of a person's total interaction time. A once-a-week contact with a friend, on the average, should account for less of the total weekly time than a daily contact, unless the time spent in the weekly contact is considerably longer. Finally, our measure of status is a simple dichotomy of white-collar and manual-worker status groups.

Such a gross distinction may mask true differences in status. On the other hand, the more status is refined in terms of specific operational indicators such as occupation, the more it may reflect non-status differences in the indicator.

The major findings with respect to status differences in types of interpersonal contact and exposure to contact situations are as follows:

1. There are no significant status differences in the proportion of respondents who had some contact or exposure, mean amount of contact or exposure, or variance in contact or exposure in types of interpersonal contact or time spent in contact, independent of residence.
2. When only the non-agricultural residential settings are considered (urban and RNF), there similarly are no clear-cut significant differences in the proportion with contact, mean amount, and variance in interpersonal contact or exposure to contact situations. High-status urban and RNF males both may have a greater mean contact and variance in a pure-client relationship and in total time in job situations than do low-status ones. These differences may be a function of only some white-collar jobs, however.

With respect to residence differences in exposure to different types of contact situations the major findings are as follows:

1. A higher proportion of urban employed married males than of RNF or RF males, regardless of social status, as exposed to mass media on their workday, and with greater mean exposure time.
2. Significantly more of the urban and RNF males (non-agricultural workers) than of RF males, regardless of social status, had some exposure to secondary situations, and they likewise had both higher mean exposure and variance in exposure to secondary situations.

3. There are no significant differences by residence in the proportion of persons who spent some time in isolation. But all RF males, regardless of status, spend significantly more time in isolation than do urban males, and they have a significantly greater variance in isolation as well.
4. The average time spent on the job was significantly greater for RF than for RNF or urban males, regardless of status.

Differences in types of interpersonal contacts for residential settings may be summarized as follows:

1. While almost all men had some exposure to primary contacts during the workday, the average urban employed male had a significantly greater average time in primary contact than did his RNF or RF counterpart, regardless of status. There was no such significant difference between RNF and RF males. Primary contact time *may* occupy a somewhat smaller proportion of the total inter-action time for urban and RNF males than it does for RF males.
2. Urban males do not show a greater amount of primary contact in all specific types of primary contacts, however. There is almost no significant variation in average daily contact with intimate kin and association with close intimate friends by residence. The major differentiating type is contact with a work associate or client. A significantly larger proportion of the urban than of the RNF or RF males, regardless of status, had contact with a close work associate or client on their workday, and they spend a greater average amount of their daily time in such contacts.
3. Urban and RNF males are more likely to have a greater mean amount of impersonal contact on their workday than are RF males. This impersonal contact consists largely of contact in the client-role relationship.

Sociologists who speculate about the findings of this paper may be tempted to use the findings to show that the differences between residential groups in the United States have almost disappeared, but, of course, the study was not designed to demonstrate this, since no comparative historical data are available. Others may use them to show that the ideal typical description of the decline of the kinship relationship in urban areas has been exaggerated, much as Axelrod has done in a recent paper.[7] This interpretation is similarly suspect, inasmuch as no bench-mark data are available for temporal comparison.

For those inclined to speculate about the theoretical implications of the findings, two conclusions appear of special relevance. The first is that the agricultural—non-agricultural situs distinction appears to discriminate better with respect to differences in personal contact than does the type of residential settlement. This observation is in keeping with that made by Sorokin and Zimmerman about thirty years ago:

> . . . Rural sociology is in the first place a sociology of an occupation group, namely the sociology of the agricultural *occupation*. Such is the first and fundamental criterion of differences between the rural and other, particularly urban, communities. From it follow a series of other differences between the rural and the urban communities, most of which are causally connected with the above difference in occupation.[8]

The second observation is that the theoretical constructs conventionally employed to type urban and rural interpersonal relations and contexts do not lend themselves too readily to research. And, when they are translated into operational terms, the findings apparently vary for subclasses of a general construct. Thus, for example, only the "pure-client" relationship appears to have much discriminatory power in the "secondary" or "impersonal" relations construct. It is not maintained here that these operational constructs are the most satisfactory for theory—they probably are not—but rather that more attention must be given to the analytical discrimination of constructs in theoretically based research investigations on differences in interpersonal contacts or relationships.

ACKNOWLEDGMENT

Financial support from the Institute of Research in the Social Sciences of Vanderbilt University and the assistance of A. Lewis Rhodes in gathering data and in statistical computations are gratefully acknowledged.

In this paper the now fashionable term *inter*personal is used interchangeably with the more acceptable *personal*, which seems to cover the ground quite adequately.

NOTES

1. The statement by Georg Simmel generally serves as a prototype; cf. his "The Metropolis and Mental Life," trans. in Kurt H. Wolff, *The Sociology of Georg Simmel* (Glencoe, Ill.: Free Press, 1950).
2. For a fairly complete summary of the early literature see P. A. Sorokin and C. C. Zimmerman, *Principles of Rural-urban Sociology* (New York: Henry Holt & Co., 1929), and P. A. Sorokin and Clarence Q. Berger, *Time-Budgets of Human Behavior* (Cambridge: Harvard University Press, 1938).
3. Sorokin and Zimmerman, *op. cit.*, pp. 48–58, 49, 51–54.
4. Among the most recent representative urban studies in this area, pertinent are Morris Axelrod, "Urban Structure and Urban Participation," *American Sociological Review*, XXI (February, 1956), 13–18, and Wendell Bell and Maryanne T. Force, "Urban Neighborhood Types and Participation in Formal Associations," *American Sociological Review*, XXI (February, 1956), 25–34. This relationship, commonly observed in urban areas, is not always verified in rural community studies; for example: "The white-collar groups had the highest scores for all three types of participation, although their superiority was less marked for informal than for formal and semi-formal participation" (Otis Dudley Duncan and Jay W. Artis, *Social Stratification in a Pennsylvania Rural Community* [Pennsylvania State College School of Agriculture, AES Bull. 543 (1951)], p. 38).
5. Among urban and RNF males, professional, technical, and kindred workers; proprietors, managers, and officials; sales workers; and clerical and kindred workers are the white-collar, non-agricultural occupations designated as "high status." All other occupations are "low status." Among RF males, all farm proprietors and managers are designated "high status"; all tenants, sharecroppers, and laborers "low status."
6. The conclusions of this study are limited by the selection of the particular population and by the criteria of allocating time among types of contact and types of situations. Alternative measures of contact or measures of interaction might easily result in different conclusions. Suppose, for example, that one knew the total number of persons seen (or met) during a day; urban persons probably have more such contacts in a day. Or suppose that the urban person works with a close friend more often than does a rural person: this does not preclude his also having a large number of indirect social contacts at work or contacts with persons he never even sees. While not all forms of social contact which are said to discriminate among persons in different environments are analyzed here, it should be clear that concepts like impersonal and personal contacts or indirect and direct contacts permit meaningful comparisons only if their operational referents are specified.
7. *Op cit.*, pp. 17–18.
8. *Op. cit.*, p. 16.

37. The Local Community: H. Laurence Ross
A Survey Approach

In discussions of the social organization of urban communities, there continues to be a good deal of debate about the significance of local areas to their residents. H. Laurence Ross chooses one of the best known upper-income and high prestige areas of any American city, Beacon Hill in central Boston, in which to investigate this issue. Making use of an interview schedule which gave respondents the opportunity to define the boundaries and characteristics of the area themselves, he finds that they regard it as an identifiable segment of urban space, and agree about its name and three of its four boundaries. The local community is also for them a convenient means through which to ascribe status and social position to the otherwise anonymous residents of the city. These functions of the local community persist despite the fact that residents of Beacon Hill carry on most of their activities, other than convenience shopping, in different parts of Boston. Ross does not examine additional features of the local community model, such as participation in organization and voluntary associations, but these are examined in other papers in this section.

H. Laurence Ross is Professor of Sociology and Law at the University of Denver. He is the editor of *Perspectives on the Social Order* (1968) and has written numerous articles on urban sociology and the sociology of law.

The model of the local community was proposed by Robert E. Park and Ernest W. Burgess as a framework for the description of social structure in American cities. The original model underlies several more recent investigations of urban life. Among the distinctive features of this model are the divisibility of the city into "natural" areas delimited by "natural" boundaries, the recognition of the areas as communities by their inhabitants, and the organization of social life within the areas around distinctive local facilities. This paper reports on a study using survey methods to investigate these aspects of the local community model. A further concern of the study was the status-ascriptive function suggested for named areas in the work of W. Lloyd Warner.

The research attempted, first, to determine whether named and bounded areas are recognized by a sample of urban residents who were asked to name and bound their own area of residence and to identify other named areas within the city. Second, the status-ascriptive functions were investigated through analysis of free responses to the stimuli of selected area names. Third, the residents were questioned concerning the location of various common activities that appeared to be relevant to the local community model. The results of this paper both amplify and qualify portions of the original model.

The Local Community Model

In the industrial metropolis, depicted by Simmel as a collection of overstimulated,

From *American Sociological Review*, Vol. XXXVII, No. 1 (February 1962), pp. 75–84. Reprinted by permission.

blasé, and reserved individualists, Robert E. Park and his colleagues noted many regions where social life was intense, informal, and intimate. Prototypical of such regions was the immigrant ghetto, integrated by the institutions of a quasi-folk society and isolated from other parts of the metropolis by language barriers and prejudice. The limits of the immigrant colonies were often marked by physical barriers to travel, such as elevated railway walls and watercourses. Impressed by the fact that the entire urban landscape was divided into small areas by the network of transportation and industry, these early ecologists put forward a model in which the interstices of this network, termed "natural areas," contained the units of urban social strcture, which they called "local communities." Starting with a map of Chicago containing the expected natural boundaries, they began a search for "the correspondence, if any, between this physical formation of the city . . . and the currents of the economic and social life of the city." The latter were determined by the following tests:

1. Well-recognized historical names and boundaries of local communities and the changes which these have undergone.
2. Dividing lines that are at present recognized by the residents, as when on one side of the street persons state that they live in one community and persons on the other side of the street state that they live in another community.
3. Boundaries of areas claimed by local organizations as businessmen's associations, by local newspapers, and by improvement associations, and in cases of dispute checking claims by plotting memberships of these groups.
4. Plotting membership or attendance or patronage of local community institutions or enterprises and noting the effect of barriers like parks and railroad lines.
5. Plotting the distributions and the movements of cultural groups like immigrant colonies and noting the effect of these barriers.[1]

According to Burgess, the model was appropriate to Chicago. On the other hand, simultaneously with this effort to demonstrate that the metropolis is made up of community areas segregated by natural boundaries, students following Park's research suggestions were noting certain limitations of the model, especially in some central city areas. Among these was Zorbaugh, who, after studying the New North Side "community" in Chicago, stated:

> . . . the older organization of the community, based on family ties and local associations, is being replaced by an organization based upon vocational interests and attitudes. This vocational organization cuts across local areas; defines itself spatially as city-wide; and takes much of a person's life out of the local community.[2]

In American cities of the fifties and sixties, many of the cultural differences that once distinguished among, and isolated, the local communities appear to have diminished. The large immigrant ghettoes of the early twentieth century have declined in size and have been reduced in variety and number, and the association "based on vocational interests and attitudes" appears increasingly prevalent. The question arises: can one identify today entities analogous to the local community as described by Park and his colleagues? Furthermore, if such entities are found, what functions do they serve in modern urban life?

Several recent urban studies imply the finding of local areas with properties similar to those given by the model cited above. Janowitz' concept of the community of limited liability represents a conditional confirmation of the model, in which he cites the proliferation of local communications media as evidence of residents' orientation to a local community, but stresses the partial and selective character of this orientation. This perspective is confirmed in Greer's studies of outlying urban areas. Greer stresses the local press, local organizations, and informal interaction as local community characteristics.[3] A somewhat similar approach appears in the "social areas" tradition of Shevky, Williams, Bell, and their students. This tradition is based on the demonstration of socially homogeneous areal units in several cities, and it offers a convincing typology for these units that has been found useful by other researchers.[4] On the other hand, some investigators, following the lead of Paul Hatt, have found a lack of homogeneity within small areal units, and a lack of congruence between reasonable alternative criteria of local organization, leading them to reject or to severely qualify the community model.[5] In the field of city planning, many writers take for granted the possibility of creating a community-like structure in the urban plan, but differ in their opinions as to whether a corresponding social organization can or should develop from such a plan.[6] In short, the local community model is still employed in much current urban theory and research, but with various degrees of confirmation arising from different empirical tests. The principal purpose of this paper is the submission of selected parts of the model to a new test through the use of survey techniques.

Recognition of Named Areas

With rare exceptions,[7] surveys concerned with the identification of a local community, in terms of respondents' naming and bounding an area in which their residences are located, have been unsuccessful. Typical are the findings of Riemer[8] in Milwaukee, Bloch *et al.*[9] in Chicago, Foley[10] in Rochester, McKenzie[11] in Columbus, and Smith, Form and Stone[12] in Lansing.

The present study was initiated on the assumption that these negative findings were in large part the result of methodological weaknesses, including the use of the ambiguous term "neighborhood" and the placement of questions concerning the name and boundary of the area at the end of questionnaires concerning "your block" or "the area within five blocks from home." Therefore, the first question asked of respondents in this study was, "What is the name of this part of [the city]?" There followed a request to state the boundaries of the area so named. The hypothesis to be tested was that residents agree on the name and boundaries of the area in which they live, and it was arbitrarily decided in advance that the criterion of "agreement" would be a simple majority.

A census tract in central Boston[13] was chosen for study. The choice was made in order to depart as much as possible from the ghetto prototype of the local community. The tract in question was an apartment house area. It contained population of mixed class and ethnic background. Because of a large proportion of young, unmarried people, the area had a very high mobility rate. Two hundred fifty respondents, representing 87 per cent of a random sample of households,[14] participated in the study.

Tables 1 and 2, presenting the distributions of names and boundaries given in answer to the above questions, show that there was a great deal more agreement in this study than in previously cited studies

TABLE 1. DISTRIBUTION OF NAMES ASCRIBED TO THE "PART OF TOWN" BY RESPONDENTS IN THE STUDY AREA

Name	Per Cent Using Name
Beacon Hill	68%
Modified form of Beacon Hill*	6
West End	23
Other name	2
D. K.	1
Total	100% (250)

* E.g., "the Back Side of Beacon Hill," "Bohemian Hill," etc.

that the respondents lived in a certain named and bounded area of the city. Majority agreement was found on a name for the area and on three of four boundaries. Moreover, the boundaries were those predicted in advance from natural area considerations. To the north, the boundary was a heavily traveled street, and to the south and west the boundaries were parks, major streets, and a river.

The presence of a second name for the area, on which a minority agreed, was not expected. It was noted that the boundaries given by respondents terming the area "the West End" tended to include territory lying farther north than the region defined by respondents using the name "Beacon Hill," and the hypothesis was advanced that the respondents might be living in a border region between two more clearly defined areas. In other to test this hypothesis, two small samples of people in tracts adjacent to the study area were asked the same questions. To the north, 24 respondents agreed unanimously that they lived in the West End. To the south, 22 of 23 agreed that they lived in Beacon Hill. Thus, the border region nature of the study area appears to explain the bimodal distribution of names among the original sample.

TABLE 2. DISTRIBUTION OF BOUNDARIES ASCRIBED TO THE "PART OF TOWN" BY RESPONDENTS IN THE STUDY AREA

Northern Boundary		Southern Boundary		Eastern Boundary		Western Boundary	
Street	Per Cent	Street	Per Cent	Street	Per Cent	Street	Per Cent
Cambridge	80%	Beacon* or Boston Common	81%	Joy	12%	Charles St., Charles River and Embankment††	87%
		Myrtle or Pinckney	5	State House and streets bordering	43		
				Scollay and Tremont†	21		
Other	9	Other	3	Other	9	Other	5
D.K., vague	11	D.K., vague	11	D.K., vague	15	D.K., vague	8
Total	100% (250)	Total	100% (250)	Total	100% (250)	Total	100% (250)

* Combined because Beacon Street forms the near border of the Boston Common.
† Combined because Tremont Street begins at and forms an extension of Scollay Square.
†† Combined because the Embankment is a park that follows the Charles River, and Charles Street parallels and borders the Embankment in the immediate vicinity of the census tract studied.

The question was raised whether areas of the metropolis other than the area of residence were commonly identifiable by name. A previous study by Kevin Lynch,[15] using a small and nonrandom sample of well-informed Bostonians, had located several named areas by asking the respondents to describe the city. Among these were three—the Back Bay, the North End, and the South End—that had also been recognized by Firey in his study of symbolism in ecology.[16] Professor Lynch sketched the boundaries obtained for these three areas from his respondents on a map prepared for the present study. The Beacon Hill-West End sample was asked if they knew the areas by name (no map was shown) and, if so, to name a street in each. The hypothesis that some[17] areas of the metropolis, in addition to the area of residence, are known as named areas, was tested according to the criterion that a majority of the respondents must be able to name a street within the boundaries sketched by Lynch. As many of the respondents were new to the city, and no measure of the accuracy of the Lynch boundaries (as against those determined by questioning a random sample of residents) was available, this could be expected to be a difficult test of the hypothesis. Yet the percentages of respondents correctly naming a street within the boundaries drawn by Lynch were 66 per cent for the North End, 80 per cent for the Back Bay, and 57 per cent for the South End. The hypothesis was therefore rather strongly confirmed.

In summary, it can be said that residents of the area studied regard themselves as living in a named area of the city, and agree on the boundaries of their area in all but one direction. The criterion of majority agreement was satisfied despite the fact that the study happened to be conducted in a border region formed by the inter-section of two clearly defined named areas. Furthermore, residents of this region can correctly identify several other named areas within the city. These results were achieved in spite of the fact that many residents were new to the city, and that the census tract studied was highly urbanized, being central to the city and heterogeneous in population.

Functions of the Named Area in Ascribing Status

Some sociologists, not primarily concerned with the study of local communities, have found the concept of named urban areas to be useful in other respects. One important use that has been made of area names is in ascertaining the social class of an individual. Warner's instructions for scoring the Index of Status Characteristics are illustrative:

> By previous knowledge or interview, establish the major social areas and their relative ranking . . . make a map of the areas and indicate the value of each area by putting its rating after its name on the map. Subareas of higher and lower ranking should be delineated and ranked. People living in the area know the differences.[18]

While these instructions, quoted in their entirety, are not very precise, Warner seems to be proposing the interview as a method for determining the named areas and finding out the degree of prestige associated with each area named. This technique would presumably be increasingly useful in large cities, where ratings that depend on intimate knowledge of individuals (for instance, Evaluated Participation) are less feasible.

Others have suggested that what is

useful to the sociologist is also useful to the average man. Shevky and Williams write:

> In urban-industrial society, the unfailing indicators of the social position of others readily accessible to everyone are houses and areas of residence. As every occupation is evaluated and generally accorded honor and esteem on a scale of prestige in society, so every residential section has a status value which is readily recognized by everyone in the city.[19]

Consideration of such names as Chinatown, Little Italy, Kilgubbin and Harlem suggests that ethnic connotations as well as status connotations are conveyed by the names of areas. A possible conclusion from these considerations is that area names play an important role in identifying the status and ethnicity of individuals, in a manner resembling that of occupational title for social class and family name for ethnicity. If area names are to perform this function in large cities, the names must be well-known, and the connotations they bear concerning class and ethnicity must be appropriate to the population of the

areas. The diffusion of knowledge of area names in different parts of the metropolis was suggested in the previous section of this paper. Evidence concerning the appropriateness or accuracy of the connotations evoked by names of urban areas will be presented in the following paragraphs.

In the study by Lynch cited above, certain parts of the named areas were designated core areas because of very high agreement on them by his respondents. The core areas were smaller than, and central to, the wider areas containing them. A census tract approximation of Lynch's core areas was used to determine selected demographic features for each of the named areas. Indices of social class and ethnic composition for the areas are presented in Table 3. Residents of the studied tract were asked to give a description of the three distant areas. Respondents denying knowledge of an area or citing a street not within the wider boundaries given by Lynch were not counted in the following tabulations. The descriptions, coded for mentions of class and ethnicity,

TABLE 3. INDICES FOR 1950 OF CLASS AND ETHNICITY FOR FIVE NAMED AREAS IN BOSTON

| | Named Area | | | | |
Index	North End*	Back Bay†	South End‡	Beacon Hill§	West End ‖
Percentage professionals, proprietors, managers, and officials in the labor force	8.0%	39.0%	9.7%	34.0%	13.8%
Percentage laborers and operatives in the labor force	46.2	3.7	27.5	6.4	31.3
Percentage of population foreign born	18.9	14.0	11.6	15.5	26.3
Percentage of population non-white	0.0	0.6	22.2	0.9	1.1

* Tracts F–2, F–4, and F–5.
† Tracts K–3 and K–5.
‡ Tracts I–1, I–2, I–3, I–4, L–1, L–4, and L–5.
§ Tracts K–1 and K–2.
‖ Tract H–1.
Source: *United States Census of Population: 1950. Vol. III, Census Tract Statistics.* Chapter 6.

TABLE 4. HOW RESPONDENTS CHARACTERIZE THREE NAMED AREAS IN TERMS OF STATUS

	Percentage of Those Demonstrating Knowledge of the Area Who Mention Class						
Community	White Collar	Blue Collar	Both	Total	No Mention	Grand Total	N
North End	1%	14%	1%	16%	84%	100%	166
Back Bay	33	4	3	40	60	100	199
South End	1	45	1	47	53	100	142

were compared with the demographic indices for each area. Among the three areas, it was expected that the Back Bay would be described as white-collar, in contrast to the other areas; that the South End would be seen as Negro; and that the North End would be seen as Italian, since 96 percent of its foreign-born were from Italy. Tables 4 and 5 support these expectations. Given the very open nature of the question,[20] the absolute number of class and ethnic symbols mentioned is evidence that these associations are among the first to be made to the stimulus of an area name.[21]

A similar pattern appears in Table 6, in which respondents thinking of themselves as living in Beacon Hill are compared with those thinking of themselves as living in the West End. In this tabulation, direct questions[22] were asked of the respondents about the class and national origin of the people in the area named, so the proportions mentioning class and ethnic composition cannot be taken as an index of the

salience of these characteristics. The respondents speaking of Beacon Hill thought of it as an upper- and middle-class area of North European Protestant stock. Those speaking of the West End thought of it as a working- and lower-class area of ethnic stock. These characterizations are supported, for the cores of these areas, by the census statistics presented in Table 3.

The preceding paragraphs have shown that accurate characterizations of class and ethnicity of the residents are among the salient connotations of area names. It follows that these names are available for use in social interaction between non-intimates in defining their respective statuses, as suggested by Shevky and Williams. This study is not able to supply proof that these names are actually used for this purpose, but one of the tabulations made suggests that people act as if this were so. The study took place in a border region between two named areas with different status connotations, and residents

TABLE 5. HOW RESPONDENTS CHARACTERIZE THREE NAMED AREAS IN TERMS OF ETHNICITY

	Percentage of Those Demonstrating Knowledge of the Area Who Mention Ethnicity						
Community	Negroes	Italians	Other Ethnic	Total	No Mention	Grand Total	N
North End	*	67%	1%	68%	32%	100%	166
Back Bay	*	*	4	4	96	100	199
South End	37%	*	7	44	56	100	142

* Not coded separately.

**TABLE 6. DIFFERENCES IN CHARACTER-
ISTICS ATTRIBUTED TO THE
AREA AMONG RESPONDENTS
IDENTIFYING WITH BEACON
HILL AND WEST END**

Class Designation of Area	Respondents Speaking of Beacon Hill	Respondents Speaking of West End
Upper or middle	70%	31%
Working or lower	27	66
Both, or D.K.	3	3
Total	100% (169)	100% (58)
Ethnic Designation of Area		
North European Protestant*	54%	7%
Ethnic†	24	81
Both, or D.K.	22	12
Total	100% (169)	100% (58)

* Old Yankee, English, Scottish, German, Dutch, Scandinavian origin.
† All other countries of origin.

of the region had a choice between the names of Beacon Hill and the West End. If people are socially typed by the name of their area of residence, those with a choice may be expected to choose the name with status connotations corresponding most closely to their own self-conceptions. Thus, in the present case, people conceiving of themselves as upper- and middle-class should tend to choose Beacon Hill as the name of their residence area, whereas people conceiving of themselves as work- ing- and lower-class should choose the West End, allowing a margin of error for working-class people who would like to "rise" to Beacon Hill and for middle-class people who do not accept the stereotype of the West End as working-class.

The results of the survey support the predictions. Among the respondents de- scribing themselves as upper- and middle- class, 81 percent "chose" Beacon Hill as their area of residence, compared with 58 percent of the respondents thinking of themselves as working- and lower-class. A similar situation exists with respect to national origin. Among the North Euro- pean Protestants, 76 percent "chose" Beacon Hill, as against 65 percent of the ethnics. Proximity to the cores of the respective areas was found to be associated with this decision, but cartographic analysis revealed that proximity operated inde- pendently, and that at any distance from the cores of the communities, working- and lower-class individuals were more likely to "choose" the working- and lower-class West End label for their area of residence.

The Named Area as a Community

The concept of community has several different meanings in sociology. According to a classical definition, "wherever any group, small or large, live together in such a way that they share, not this or that particular interest, but the basic conditions of a common life, we call that group a community."[23] Definitions of local com- munity implicit in empirical investigations focus on both interaction and institutions. The former focus, prominent in the work on suburban communities, is exemplified by such criteria as friendship, neighboring, par- ticipation in informal organizations, and orientation to communications media.[24] The latter focus, prominent in the Chicago tradition of concern with ethnic and central city communities, is ex- emplified by such criteria as membership in formal organizations and intensive use of distinctive local facilities.[25] Thus, the literature on local communities furnishes various criteria that could be framed as hypotheses concerning properties of named areas. This study investigated one of these criteria, the usage of local facilities.

Two studies of peripheral urban areas by Donald Foley served as a background and source of specific hypotheses for this work. While inspection of Foley's designs suggests that he never came to grips with what constituted "local" for his respondents, the parallel between his results and the findings in central Boston supports the general applicability of both.

Foley's first study[26] concerned a lower-middle-class area in northwestern St. Louis, containing elementary schools, churches, movie theaters, and "other facilities" as well as industries. Not available within the district were public high schools, large parks, and, aside from movies, professional entertainment facilities. A representative sample of families was polled to ascertain the location of various facilities used by all members of the family. Usage within the boundaries of the arbitrarily defined district was classified as local. Foley found that local food outlets and churches were used by the residents of this area, with 69 percent and 77 percent of the total uses, respectively, being local. On the other hand, only 5 percent of clothing, household equipment, and furniture shopping was local, and only 18 percent of employment was local, despite the presence of industry. A study of a peripheral area in Rochester[27] revealed a similar pattern,

where "local" was defined as "within five blocks from home."

The data from Boston are shown in Table 7. Because of the border nature of the census tract, both Beacon Hill and the West End were considered local, and the most liberal boundaries available (those sketched by Lynch) were used. All major categories of facilities were available within the area, although in variety and quality of stores the area was inferior to the adjacent central business district. Despite the differences between this area and those studied by Foley, and the different criteria of what is "local," the pattern is quite similar. Food shopping and church attendance are modally local, but all other facilities usages were found to be predominantly non-local. While the adjacent downtown area accounts for much non-local usage, it is noteworthy that non-local facilities usage *apart from the downtown area* far exceeds local facilities usage in all categories investigated except food shopping and church attendance. The non-local and non-downtown usage was fairly widespread throughout the metropolitan area. Respondents expressed preferences for suburban discount houses, for furniture and clothes from fashionable streets in the Back Bay, for roadhouse entertainment, and a host of items available in isolated

TABLE 7. DISTRIBUTION OF FACILITIES USED BY RESPONDENTS ACCORDING TO LOCATION OF FACILITY

Facility	Beason Hill and West End	Downtown	Other	Don't Use or D.K.	Total	
Food shopping	80%	*	18%	2%	100%	(250)
Clothing shopping	2	75	21	2	100	(250)
Furniture shopping	5	63	24	8	100	(250)
Work	22	28	34	16	100	(250)
Entertainment	22	37	34	7	100	(250)
Church	36	17	27	20	100	(250)

* Less than $\frac{1}{2}$ of 1%.

locations or in specialized business centers serving the entire metropolis.

In view of the support lent to the pattern found here by Foley's work, the proposal that the local community is organized around distinctive facilities must be strongly qualified. The nature of the qualification can be illustrated by considering the kinds of facilities that are locally used. While only food shopping and church attendance are modally local in these studies, the distribution of retail outlets in the city suggests that drugs, some kinds of banking, purchasing at variety stores, and other similar activities, are also typically local. This type of activity can be characterized as convenience shopping, involving goods which are used in small quantities and purchased fairly often, in which price differentials are not very important, and which are relatively highly standardized. It is, in other words, precisely in those lines in which goods are *not* strongly differentiated that local shopping is done. Goods and corresponding outlets that are distinctive appear to require a larger market than that supplied by a typical named area.

These data indicate that the local facilities usage of the modal urbanite, in the areas studied in this project and in Foley's previous work, tends to be confined to convenience goods. However, it should be kept in mind that local facilities usage in almost all categories appears greater than a chance model would predict, especially considering the absence of opportunities in the area.[28] Furthermore, a supplementary analysis revealed a slight tendency for some residents to use various local facilities more than other residents, supporting a model proposed by Merton in which the relevant community may be different for different people living in the same general locality.[29]

Summary and Conclusions

The research reported here supports the proposition, contained in the local community model of the metropolis, that the city is perceived by its residents as containing named areas, bounded by such barriers to travel as parks, rivers, and large streets. On the background of many studies yielding negative evidence, this study succeeded, using a new method that avoided the ambiguity of the term "neighborhood" and presented definitional questions at the beginning of the questionnaire.

The names of areas apart from the one of residence were found to be well-diffused in this study. Furthermore, these names were shown to have class and ethnic connotations that were in harmony with indices derived from the census. This evidence can be interpreted as support for the proposition that one function of named areas is the attribution of class and ethnic positions in the secondary social relations typical of the city.

An investigation of the proposition that residents of a named area use distinctive local facilities yielded generally negative results. Little use was made of local facilities except in items commonly termed convenience items, which are similar from area to area.

These results, based on a sample of households in one census tract in Boston, are statistically generalizable only to the census tract sampled. However, there is evidence to indicate that the results are not entirely due to peculiar local conditions in Boston and in the study area. In pre-tests of the questionnaire used in this study, residents of three Chicago "local communities" as defined by the Chicago Community Inventory—South Shore, Near North Side, and New City—were asked to name and bound their part of Chicago.

Agreement on name and boundaries in these areas compared favorably with that found in the Boston case, although residents of New City uniformly used the more pungent name of Back-of-the-Yards in referring to their area of residence. Similar results were found in a secondary analysis by the author of data gathered in outlying areas of Boston by Morton Rubin of Northeastern University. Consciousness of living in a named and bounded area thus does not appear to be confined to residents of high-status and historic areas of an old city. With respect to the other findings in this paper, Warner's use of the Index of Status Characteristics in various cities supports the characterization of named areas as a source of status ascription, and the previously noted similarity between areas in Boston and St. Louis and Rochester supports the generalizability of the results reported for use of facilities.

This study supports the local community conception of the city by demonstrating that named units with "natural" boundaries are recognized by residents of an urban area. It further suggests that named areas have a status-ascriptive function not stressed in the original model. The research qualifies an aspect of the model concerning the usage of local facilities. Other features of the local community model, such as the presence of participation in local organizations and a network of local friendships, were not specifically tested in this study, and await further research.

NOTES

1. Ernest W. Burgess, "Basic Social Data," in T. V. Smith and Leonard D. White, editors, *Chicago: An Experiment in Social Science Research*, Chicago: University of Chicago Press, 1929, pp. 47–66; see particularly p. 58.
2. Harvey Zorbaugh, *The Gold Coast and the Slum*, Chicago: University of Chicago Press, 1929, p. 241.
3. Morris Janowitz, *The Community Press in an Urban Setting*, Glencoe, Illinois: Free Press, 1952; Scott Greer, "Urbanism Reconsidered: A Comparative Study of Local Areas in a Metropolis," *American Sociological Review*, 21 (February, 1956), pp. 19–25; and Scott Greer, "Socio-Political Structure of Suburbia," *American Sociological Review*, 25 (August, 1960), pp. 514–526.
4. A general guide to work in the social areas tradition appears in Wendell Bell, "Social Areas: Typology of Urban Neighborhoods," in Marvin B. Sussman, editor, *Community Structure and Analysis*, New York: Thomas Y. Crowell, 1959, pp. 61–92.
5. Paul Hatt, "The Concept of Natural Area," *American Sociological Review*, 11 (August, 1946), pp. 423–427. See also William H. Form, Joel Smith, Gregory P. Stone, and James Cowhig, "The Compatibility of Alternative Approaches to the Delimitation of Urban Sub-Areas," *American Sociological Review*, 19 (August, 1954), pp. 434–440.
6. See, on the favorable side, Judith Tannenbaum, "The Neighborhood: A Socio-Psychological Analysis," *Land Economics*, 24 (November, 1948),

pp. 358–369. The chief critic is Reginald Isaacs. See "The Neighborhood Theory," *Journal of the American Institute of Planners*, 14 (Spring, 1948), pp. 15–23.
7. One exception is contained in Shirley Star, "An Approach to the Measurement of Interracial Tensions," unpublished Ph.D. dissertation, University of Chicago, 1950. She notes in passing that 81 per cent of the residents in one local community and 49 per cent of those in a second used the names attributed to the areas by the Chicago Community Inventory. The finding is vitiated by the fact that interviewers introduced the study as one of Grand Crossing or Auburn-Gresham, thus providing a set for questions on area name. Bell (*op. cit.*, p. 75) implies the use of names employed by residents in social area analysis. Scott Greer, in an unpublished research report, found that 98 per cent of residents of a part of Saint Louis County gave a distinctive name to their residential area. Names have been assigned to areas in countless studies in urban sociology, perhaps implying positive findings concerning agreement of residents to the name. An impressive example is in Calvin F. Schmid, "Urban Crime Areas: Part I," *American Sociological Review*, 25 (August, 1960), pp. 527–542, Figure 1. p. 528.
8. Svend Riemer, "Villagers in Metropolis," *British Journal of Sociology*, 2 (March, 1951) pp. 31–43.
9. Donald Bloch, *et al.*, "Identification and Participation in Urban Neighborhoods," unpublished M.A. thesis, University of Chicago, 1952.
10. Donald L. Foley, "Neighbors or Urbanites?"

mimeographed manuscript, Rochester: University of Rochester, 1952.

11. Roderick McKenzie, *The Neighborhood: A Study of Local Life in the City of Columbus, Ohio,* Chicago: University of Chicago Press, 1923.

12. Joel Smith, William H. Form, and Gregory P. Stone, "Local Intimacy in a Middle-Sized City," *American Journal of Sociology,* 60 (November, 1954), pp. 276–284.

13. Tract K-1, between Cambridge Street and Myrtle Street, Joy Street and the Charles River.

14. Twenty-nine refusals and nine non-contacted persons made up the rest of the sample. A check of age, sex, and occupational distributions of the respondents against census statistics for the tract showed no significant differences between the sample and the population on these variables.

15. Kevin Lynch, *The Image of the City,* Cambridge, Mass.: The Technology Press, 1960.

16. Walter Firey, *Land Use in Central Boston,* Cambridge, Mass.: Harvard University Press, 1947.

17. The sample of areas was not random, so no statistical generalization can be made.

18. W. Lloyd Warner *et al., Social Class in America,* Chicago: Science Research Associates, 1949, p. 238.

19. Eshref Shevky and Marilyn Williams, *The Social Areas of Los Angeles,* Berkeley Calif,: University of California Press, 1949, pp. 61–62.

20. "Tell me a little about the North End as you see it. What kind of a place is it? What makes it different from other neighborhoods in Boston?"

21. In contrast, the same comparison made on the variable of family status revealed little salience. In no case did as many as a quarter of the respondents mention age and/or marital status variables in their descriptions of the communities, although the Back Bay contains unusually large

numbers of young, single people and great stress could have been placed on this fact.

22. The question on class was based on that used by Richard Centers in *The Psychology of Social Classes,* Princeton, N. J.: Princeton University Press, 1951. It read: "When [the area] is mentioned, do you think first of the middle class, the lower class, the working class, or the upper class?" The question on national origin was, "When [the area] is mentioned, which of these groups do you think of first?" A card listing eleven broad national groups was presented with the question.

23. R. M. MacIver, *Society: A Textbook of Sociology,* New York: Farrar and Rinehart, 1937, pp. 8–9.

24. The works of Greer, Bloch *et al.,* and Janowitz, cited above, are examples of this focus.

25. This focus is illustrated by several of the studies in the Chicago Sociological Series, most notably Louis Wirth, *The Ghetto,* Chicago: University of Chicago Press, 1928, and Zorbaugh, *op. cit.* See also Foley, *op. cit.*

26. Donald L. Foley, "The Use of Local Facilities in a Metropolis," *American Journal of Sociology,* 56 (November, 1950), pp. 238–246.

27. Donald L. Foley, "Neighbors or Urbanites?", *loc. cit.*

28. The term "opportunities" is used as in Samuel A. Stouffer, "Intervening Opportunities: A Theory Relating Mobility and Distance," *American Sociological Review,* 5 (December, 1940), pp. 845–867.

29. For instance, about half the respondents with working- and lower-class self-descriptions, and half of those over 45 years of age, used local churches. See Robert K. Merton, "Patterns of Influence," in Paul Lazarsfeld and Frank Stanton, editors, *Communications Research 1948–1949,* New York: Harper, 1949.

38. The Neighborhood | Peter H. Mann

The term "neighborhood" is often used by sociologists and urban planners to express the relevance of group life at the level of local territories. It has become one of the most commonly used, and also abused, terms in the lexicon of urban sociological analysis. Peter Mann does yeoman service in cutting through the confusion. He emphasizes, first of all, the importance of distinguishing between neighborhoods as physical entities and as social or cultural units. Second, Mann explores the different aspects of social organization that can be considered in describing a neighborhood. Third, making use of an ideal-typical definition of what a neighborhood is, Mann examines the role of actual neighborhoods for the life of adults and children during different stages of the family life-cycles. He emphasizes that local areas are least important in the life of people who are employed and unmarried, but that they are critically necessary for the happiness of young mothers, little children, and old people. This way of looking at the neighborhood in terms of its place in the life of different subgroups of residents goes a long way toward clarifying the debate about the social function of neighborhood life.

Peter H. Mann is Senior Lecturer in Sociology at the University of Sheffield, in England. Several of his published works are cited on page 38 of this volume.

Everyone has neighbours, even the people in the Australian outback whose neighbours may be fifty miles away. For the word neighbourhood to have any meaning at all it is necessary to consider some particular criteria which can be applied to make the term useful in urban sociology. A person has neighbours and therefore the limits of his acquaintance may be said to limit his neighbourhood. But such a way of looking at things is obviously not in keeping with the general understanding of the word. A neighbourhood is usually thought of more in geographical terms as a distinct part of a town or city, which may be distinct by virtue of certain boundaries (e.g. made by roads, railways, rivers, parks, etc.) and marked out from other neighbourhoods by a certain homogeneity of housing within the area. As a corollary of the similarity of housing, there can be expected a certain homogeneity of social class within the given neighbourhood. The geographical, or physical, elements and the social ones do not always go together, and indeed the above definition would not always result in two observers delimiting neighbourhoods in any given town being in agreement.

Ruth Glass discusses this problem when she considers two alternative definitions of neighbourhood and the implications of them.[1] In the first definition—"a distinct territorial group, distinct by virtue of the specific physical characteristics of the

area and the specific social characteristics of its inhabitants"—she is giving an objective working definition which could be used for drawing boundaries according to reasonably clear physical features and objective social ones such as rateable values, occupational status of residents and so on. Indeed, the "J" index[2] is a practical way of working out neighbourhoods on such a pattern. Glass's second definition is less clearly objective when neighbourhood is described as "a territorial group, the members of which meet on common ground within their own area for primary social activities and for organized and spontaneous social contacts." The terms used in the second definition are much less simple than those of the first in so far as observation is concerned and Glass goes on to suggest indices which can be used to further define such terms as "primary social activities" and "organised and spontaneous social contacts." Maps showing catchment areas for schools, youth and adult clubs and shops of various types are given as examples of this method. If the catchment areas for the different institutions coincide to a large degree and the pattern of catchment areas corresponds to that of distinct territorial groups of people

From *An Approach to Urban Sociology* (London: Routledge & Kegan Paul; New York: Humanities Press, 1965), Chap. 6, pp. 150–170. Reprinted by permission.

then it can be said that social activities are concentrated within the areas of the territorial groups and the territorial groups therefore qualify as neighbourhoods. In fact, in Middlesborough, about which Ruth Glass wrote, social activities were dispersed rather than concentrated. By observational methods, therefore, the idea of neighbourhood is a difficult concept to elaborate. The general idea is obviously one of things in common—a common type of housing and amenities, some sort of common interests amongst inhabitants and some sort of common pattern of social life. But viewed as a distinct *area* within which these things are to be found the concept is difficult to apply. Most of us who live in towns will use the word "neighbourhood" at some time or other. The phrases such as "It wasn't a very nice neighbourhood that they lived in," or "They have a very nice house in a good neighbourhood" would not be meaningless to the hearer. On the other hand they would be far from precise sociological explanations. All that is being said here is that some vague area round where A or B lives is not very nice or is good. But the area is an undefined one, apart from the obvious vagueness of such words as "nice" and "good." Districts within a town or city may have names of their own, often derived from old villages swallowed up in the urban growth, but a residential suburb with the name of, say, "Uppercliffe," is not exactly the same as a neighbourhood. Carpenter[3] makes a distinction as follows. "The most distinctive characteristics of a neighbourhood are its relation with a local area sufficiently compact to permit frequent and intimate association and the emergence out of such association of sufficient homogeneity and unity to permit a primary or face-to-face social grouping endowed with a strong sense of self-consciousness and capable of

influencing the behaviour of its several constituents." Carpenter then, however, goes on to make qualificatory statements about the neighbourhood which are of considerable interest. He writes,

The neighbourhood is to be found in towns and cities, especially in residential areas which are not over-densely populated and which possess a population for the most part homogeneous and exhibiting a low rate of mobility. The characteristic processes of urbanism are, however, hostile to the preservation of neighbourhood life in that they promote a high degree of population density, a low rate of permanency of residence and considerable heterogeneity of population. The existence in the city of an intricate network of secondary group associations also tends to break down the group spirit, which is the fulcrum [*sic*] of neighbourhood life; as does also the ease with which the urban dweller may wrap himself in the cloak of anonymity and thus escape from the surveillance upon which primary group control depends. With the breakdown of the neighbourhood in cities there have grown up pseudo-neighbourhoods that may be broadly defined as residential areas. Such areas exhibit some similarity to true neighbourhoods in that they may show a considerable degree of homogeneity, especially when identified with particular racial or other ethnic groups, and also in that they operate in a large measure to condition the behaviour of their residents. On the other hand they are far too numerously populated to present anything remotely resembling the close limited primary group community life characteristics of the generic neighbourhood; such uniformities of conduct and attitudes as they display may more accurately be described as products of sectionalized culture patterns.

This particularly lengthy quotation is given here because there is so much in it that enables us to look closely at this difficult concept of neighbourhood.

The essence of Carpenter's initial definition, in the ideal type situation, is that the neighbourhood is a self-conscious primary grouping capable of influencing behaviour. Thus there is awareness of mutual rights and obligations between the group members if they are to be so influenced. This self-consciousness is backed up by homogeneity of the local people and stability of residence as shown by a low rate of mobility. The factor of being "not over-densely populated" is difficult to make much of since the yardstick by which a neighbourhood is decided to be not over-densely populated is not given. But if the urban development results in a high density, then this, with mobility and heterogeneity, go against the ideal pattern. Secondary group development is seen to detract from the importance of the neighbourhoods primary contacts, and social control becomes less effective as anonymity in the larger group becomes more easily obtainable. Thus, the "pseudo-neighbourhood" according to Carpenter may still demonstrate homogeneity and some conditioning or social control (nothing is said about mobility), but the high density of population militates against the true primary group control which is, rather, replaced by a general uniformity of behaviour of a less personal kind.

Carpenter's ideas on neighbourhood are of especial interest here because he places together so many important factors of the neighbourhood, the one to be dealt with first being the aspect of primary relationships and control. If the neighbourhood is in truth a grouping of people who have primary relationships with each other to such a level that a real social control is exercised over the relationships, then obviously the group must be a small one.

Whilst any numerical estimate would be pure guess-work, a figure of over a hundred families would probably be getting towards the limits of such control. Also there must be considered the reasons why primary relationships do ensue between the people; there must be some sort of forces making for interaction. If the neighbourhood group is an isolated one, cut off from other people and having no other contacts available, then it is fairly obvious that relationships within the group will be important, simply because there are no others to have. Also if the group is composed of people with special ties at bind the members together then it may be expected that interaction will be high. The obvious examples would be the ties of kinship, economic ties because of economic interdependence, or perhaps because of religious or ethnic similarities. Whilst Carpenter only actually instances social and ethnic similarities in the case of the pseudo-neighbourhoods, it may be supposed that the homogeneity in his usage applies to social class in its more general form. But one may certainly expect that the more people have in common with each other, even if it be only, say, a similarity of age, then the more things they will be conscious of sharing and the more this will be likely to make reciprocal understanding possible. And it is upon reciprocal understanding that the whole of society is based.

The neighbourhood then is really a small group of people, rather than an unspecified size of group denoted by the phrase "not over-densely populated," and it is a group which recognises its bonds and acknowledges the social controls operating over the members. The pseudo-neighbourhood, or residential area, may exhibit some of the characteristics of the ideal type neighbourhood of Carpenter's definition, but size of population (rather than density) is likely to restrict the detailed primary group controls, and all that will be found will be some such similarities of behaviour, perhaps derived more from general characteristics such as race or sub-cultural patterns.

The true neighbourhood would obviously be a very small group of people and it is obviously Carpenter's argument that it is unlikely to be found in modern urban society. What we must consider against Carpenter's ideas, is what we do actually find in modern cities.

The suggestions to be put forward for consideration are based upon the incontrovertible fact that people of different sexes, different ages and different social classes have different types of interests and different physical areas within which interests are pursued. Overall generalisations about how "people" act in the neighbourhoods of the modern city tend to be generalisations which must cover small children still in romper suits right through to old age pensioners in wheelchairs. For example, Roper says of urban life that

> Families live in close proximity with little in common . . . The great mobility in the large city tends to keep communities and neighbourhoods in continual flux . . . In the city one does not call upon one's neighbours simply because they live near, nor does one aid in sickness or distress except in emergency cases. The city aids its poor and distressed through impersonal channels. Newspapers take the place of country gossip and one may live for years without knowing one's neighbour.[4]

All these generalisations about city life might be true in some cases, and indeed in many cases, yet everyone knows of neighbours who call simply because they are neighbours and consider it a neighbourly duty to welcome newcomers to a district. Help in sickness and distress is often given in cases other than emergencies. Newspapers may be read, but local gossip does not disappear because of them. Some people may not know their neighbours of years' standing; others will know everything about the people who moved in two weeks ago.

But obviously every instance of the lack of personal relationships in the city can be offset by quoting cases of intense relationships. These contradictory examples do not get us much further. Attempts to define the boundaries of the physical neighbourhoods may be sterile in that they bear so little relation to social relationships. It is more useful to consider social relationships themselves rather than to worry about where neighbourhoods begin and end. To do this one can use a functional type of approach based on the life-cycle of the human being.

For example, if we take as a starting point the young child of pre-school age, the environment at birth, and before mobility develops, is the cot, pram or play-pen, and the neighbourhood is an irrelevant concept to the child itself (though not to the mother as we shall see later) because it (or rather he or she) is not a social creature at all.[5] But when the child becomes mobile and makes its own first social contacts, in playing with other children, then the first relationship with the neighbourhood is made. Here we find the small child playing in garden or on the pavement with other neighbouring children. The contacts made are likely to be restricted to a range of a few houses in either direction and contacts across a road which carries traffic are likely to be more restricted. The relationships made at this stage of development are obviously greatly determined by propinquity, and actual next-door children are likely to become playmates much more than children separated by as few as half a dozen houses, simply because access is so simple and mothers can know where they are. As the children grow a little older and means of transport are given to them (scooters, tricycles and small bicycles) the pavement becomes a means of communication and the network of relationships is extended to houses further along the road. But within the pre-school age range it is customary for pavement edges to form boundaries and the world on the other side of the road may well be a different social group. From random, but fairly routine, observations, I would suggest that the higher the social class the more the child is likely to be restricted in the area covered at this and immediately subsequent stages in the life-cycle. Of course, middle class people tend to live in houses with gardens at relatively low densities, while many lower class people live at high densities in terraces with only pavements and yards. For the latter, then, it follows that there are more chances of contact in a given area and play cannot be restricted to a safe enclosed garden under mother's eye if no garden exists. But in addition to this I would speculate that working class children tend to be given a freedom to roam at an earlier age than middle class ones, and some of the tiny children that one sees in working class areas roaming the streets alone lead one to wonder that so few are involved in traffic accidents. But when the pavement is the only playground then restrictions cannot be imposed even if they are desired.

When the child becomes of school age, at five in this country at the moment, its horizons are widened greatly by the daily journeys to and from the local school. Of course, the child has been shopping and visiting with his parents on innumerable occasions before going to school, but it is at school age that the journeying becomes his own journeying rather than someone else's. For the normal child in this country who attends the local education authority school (private schools raise separate questions) it is usual to attend the school nearest to the home. In some cases a certain amount of zoning of children is done by the education authority when officials visit homes to make censuses of the future school populations. Parents may then be told which school this child should attend when he is five and so a catchment area principle is used for allocating children to the primary schools. In this way the child becomes not only a part of a school group, but also a part of a geographical group. It may well be that the school catchment area is a fairly arbitrary one drawn around the school merely with a compass or a set square and its relation to any social factors is purely fortuitous. In most primary schools there is some mixing of social classes, since few natural neighbourhoods contain only houses with one class of people in them. But the mixing is likely to be less in areas of dense working class bye-law housing, or on council estates, where virtually the whole population is of working class type. In the middle class areas, or the transitional areas where the lower middle classes form a "buffer zone" between middle and working, there is likely to be more mixture, with some working class housing mixed in with the middle class. The point is that the primary school is the first real social institution in which the child meets his peers on a selection basis not governed by parental control. After a few years of careful choosing of suitable playmates for her offspring, the mother must now stand back and let her child make his own choice from amongst the forty-odd other specimens in his class. An interesting field of social-psychological research is open here as to the factors operating in the making of first friendships. From random observations I would suggest that like does tend to mate with like in most cases, and that social class does have an, albeit unconscious, effect on the friendships made. This is not to suggest that snobbishness is rife at the tender age of five, but perhaps more that children at this age already recognise children with their own type of manners, etiquette and interests. It is by no means irrelevant also to note that gentle parental pressures on their children may affect friendship patterns, and the careful pruning of invitations to tea or birthday parties can have a decided effect on the selections made.

The initial social contacts of the first classes of the primary school often lay the foundations for friendship which last all through the infant and junior schools. If the school is one which "streams" children at the age of seven, it may well be that a process of social class selection also takes place, since it is claimed by some psychologists and sociologists that even at this early age social class and measured intelligence show some correlation. But for more general social contact, the years in the junior school, between the ages of seven and eleven, are years when the range of interests of the children widen, both socially and physically. It is in this stage that children become very socially conscious and can take part in their first organised groups, such as cubs and brownies, church choirs and so on. In many cases this may mean after-school activities with already established school friends, but it is activity in a new milieu, and with a less authoritarian type of organisation. Also in the local voluntary groups, the children meet children from other schools, perhaps from private

schools, and they learn to interact with new types of adults. The essence of these voluntary groups such as cubs and brownies is that they are neighbourhood groups and in going to them the young children are widening their horizons of experience and taking in neighbourhood interests which extend further than just the end of their own road.

In many of the activities associated with the period at primary school the child is learning to stand on his or her own feet in social relationships with other children and adults. But at this stage parental control and guidance, and protection against undesirable or even dangerous social contacts is needed. At the age of eleven in this country a major break in the child's life occurs with its transference to the secondary school. It is not possible to make any complete generalisations since multilateral and comprehensive schemes obviously have very different social effects on the neighbourhoods. But whatever scheme is adopted it is extremely likely that the child at eleven will (*a*) go to a school with more children than his primary school, (*b*) go to a school which will bring him into contact with children over a wider geographical range.

It is interesting to note that in the case of the selective authorities, children are usually allowed to rank their preferences for grammar schools and so it may well be that a child gives first vote to a school on the other side of the town. In the case of children not selected for grammar schools there is rarely a choice given and they are expected to attend the nearest secondary modern school as directed by the education authority. This has the result that the grammar school child is likely to mix with a more geographically varied group than the secondary modern child, and thus has opportunities for wider contacts built into his educational system. In the case of comprehensive and quasi-comprehensive systems it is customary for a large comprehensive school to serve a particular catchment area. Often the comprehensive school is "fed" by a stipulated group of primary schools, so that the child at five years knows which school he will attend right the way through his educational career up to, or beyond, the age of fifteen. In this case there is a distinctive type of enlarged neighbourhood pattern created, and it is easy to delimit the catchment areas for primary and secondary schools.

In terms of social development the secondary school stage is a most interesting one for young people, since it is at this stage that their interests really cover a wider neighbourhood than before. The growing freedom of choice in their activities coupled with freedom of travel, on cycle or unescorted on public transport, means that they are now at a stage when choice can be made as to *where* any chosen activity shall be pursued. For example, if the boy wishes to be a boy scout he may be able to join a school group, a local church group, a local non-church group, or he may decide to join the group of which his best friend at school is a member right away on the other side of town. In informal sport he may decide that the best football or cricket pitches are in a park three miles from home, but with his bicycle to take him there the journey is worthwhile. If the local cinema still exists it may no longer be attractive when one is allowed to go to the big picture houses in the town centre. The essential point being made here is that to the young person the neighbourhood is still meaningful; the local churches, guides, scouts, cinemas, parks and so on still have a meaning. But now they are in competition with other attrac-

tions of a similar type, or even a different type, which may be located in other residential areas, or in the town centre, and the mobility of the young person is now becoming very much less limited. There is now competition for the young person's interests and in voluntary associations he need not be limited to his own neighbourhood. As the children grow older and become young teenagers their interests widen and so does their breadth of knowledge of the town or city as a whole. At the age when young people begin to go dancing, it is quite common to begin the first hesitant steps at the local church hall, scout huts or other similar neighbourhood institutions. But as skill develops the interest often turns from the local three-piece in the parish hall to the big bands, bright (or soft) lights of the town centre dance halls and all their more glamorous attractions, not to mention the possibilities of new faces. Thus as the children grow older the neighbourhood fulfils their needs less and less and the opportunities offered by the urban community as a whole have greater attractions. So it may be that in the middle teens, and especially if the young people leave school at fifteen or sixteen to go to work the daily travel to work may well complete the break with the neighbourhood. It is at this stage that the harassed parent typically laments of his son or daughter that he (or she) is never in, and the charge is made, "You treat this house like a hotel." The comparison with an hotel is, of course, too extreme to be real, but the meaning is significant, that the young person uses the home as a centre from which he, or she, will go out to a wide variety of interests, the home having the principal function of providing a place to sleep and eat.

At the stage of life where the young person is employed and unmarried the neighbourhood may well have its fewest functions. Having few ties and many opportunities, young people can make full use of all the facilities of leisure, sport, entertainment and culture that the city has to offer: This is the time of life when the individual can follow his own wishes, not having to worry about responsibilities to other people too much, and it is a time when the seeking of marriage partners takes place.

When young people do marry, and today they are marrying at a fairly early age, they have the immediate problem of where to live. In the working class marriages they are fortunate if they can at once find a house to rent that could be regarded as a possible permanent residence. Rarely are council dwellings available for newly-weds and the renting of private houses is a matter of chance or knowing the right people. House purchase is rarely possible for young people with few savings and below average wages. Some couples live for a time with in-laws, some find themselves rooms of a temporary kind, but few are lucky enough to find a place to "settle" immediately on marriage. In the middle classes house purchase is likely to be envisaged, but a flat is a more likely start to the marriage until sufficient capital for a mortgage deposit has been saved. Thus two things tend to work against the newly-weds having any strong neighbourhood feeling. The first is the likelihood of them living in an area where flats or rooms are common and where mobility is high. And secondly, today the wife is likely to continue working for some time after marriage. The first point results in young married couples living in areas where they may well have similarities of interest with other couples of their own recent marital status, but the transience of so much of the residential population

militates against any real group feeling. For these young couples mobility is still the great advantage which makes is possible for them to get about, to retain their links with relatives and friends, to keep up their activities in voluntary associations and clubs. When the wife works she may well use the neighbourhood shopping facilities very little, much of the household shopping being done near her work at lunch-time or on the way home. Thus the young couple in rooms in the house converted to flats may have little feeling of neighbourhood and only regard their local district as being convenient for the accommodation it offers, its proximity to work (if in the inner zone) and the transport facilities which it has for getting about the city. Young couples living with in-laws may well be in more permanent residential areas, but for them the temporary nature of the accommodation is unlikely to be forgotten and in the doubling-up within the household the younger couple have no real status of their own at all. They are merely lodgers in someone else's property and as such cannot be expected to have the same local feelings as the proper residents.

The next stage in the life-cycle comes when the wife has her first child, and for analysis purposes we will assume that at this stage the couple either rent or buy more permanent accommodation, even though it is well known how very many couples, especially in London, are not so fortunate as to be able to do this. If the young wife, on producing her first child, gives up work, even if only temporarily, the neighbourhood comes to have a very real meaning for her. From the stage of having no ties at all to hamper her mobility about the city, she suddenly finds herself tied so completely that the home, at times, can become a virtual prison. Mobility is limited by the needs of feeding times and the distance that can be covered when pushing a pram. Transporting the infant on buses becomes a major tactical operation requiring careful thought as to all possible hazards, and the wife whose husband will either lend her his car or provide her with one of her own lives in a different world from her non-car-owning sister. For the normal pram-pushing mother the local shopping expedition may well become the main outing of the day, or even week. What little research has been done on wives going out with their husbands in the evenings shows that this happens much more rarely once children arrive. Only the middle classes seem to accept the idea of paid baby sitters, and in the working classes a relative is almost always required if the baby is to be left. In a recent Birmingham survey in a working class area "89 mothers of children under 12 were asked if they were ever able to go out with their husbands in the evening and what arrangements they made about the care of the children on these occasions. As many as 47 said that they never went out with their husbands alone in the evening; either they took the children as well or their husbands stayed at home to let them go out; more than half said they never went out in the evening at all."[6] Only 4 respondents mentioned using paid baby-sitters. For the mother with a baby or babies, therefore, the neighbourhood has a very real meaning, yet for the husband who is out at work all day, and who may still be able to maintain some of his outside contacts at pub or club in spite of the young baby, the neighbourhood need not mean very much. He may have a garden to work in at times, but this does not necessarily produce many social contacts, although allotment gardening is a more obvious source of social interaction. But while the baby in the pram may make

acquaintances for the mother at the shops, and maybe result in a whole range of new friends being made, the husband is less likely to be brought within this orbit. Reimer suggests that "Community of interest exists among young married couples who are raising infants or young children of almost the same age," and Gist and Halbert say that "children are incurably addicted to 'neighbouring' and in areas where they are numerous intimate relationships arise between families faced with a common problem of rearing the young." To some extent this may be true, but studies of working class behaviour in this country tend to show that reliance on the older generation, reliance upon "mum," is extremely widespread, and in this there may be a different culture pattern between the U.S.A. and England. But even allowing that young people with young children share common problems, it is questionable as to whether *intimate* relationships arise from them. Such relationships as do arise are likely to be limited to the mothers, and the fathers may hardly be touched by them at all. Further, the relationships between the mothers may be limited to the common interests that surround children and child-rearing. For example, mothers of young children frequently have other children to tea with their own offspring, but the reciprocal tea parties are by no means repeated at adult level with reciprocal visits between husbands and wives; the relationships are limited to the children. Finally, it should not be assumed that the social relationships which arise from interaction between children are always amicable ones. Children can be excellent dividers as well as uniters and many an adult coolness can develop from the quarrels of young children, and the problems of the children of "decent" parents playing with "rough" neighbours have caused many a local tiff. Without the children the parents may never have had harsh words.

Nevertheless, at the stages when children are dependent creatures in need of adult care and attention, the housewife is likely to find the neighbourhood having a real meaning for her and instances of reciprocal help in baby minding whilst one person goes to the shops, taking neighbours' children to school with one's own and, even, baby-sitting in the evening are common examples of ways in which the mothers free themselves temporarily from the bonds of their children. In new housing areas, particularly when there are large numbers of young parents faced with problems of child-rearing, garden making, council-petitioning for better roads or the provision of a school, reciprocal help is a commonplace and a real feeling of community is readily observable. It is less clear in areas where young couples are in a minority and a young mother may find herself with the only pram in the road and empty houses around her all day where wives are out at work.

When the children are older, and are settled at school for most of the day, the housewife obviously is less restricted in her movements, and when baby-sitters are no longer needed (possibly when the eldest child is left in charge) both parents can have unlimited evenings out if they wish. But at this stage of the life-cycle the parents are getting a little older and are not likely to be wanting to dash back to the local Locarno ballroom where they met fifteen years ago. These couples may enjoy going out together more to the cinema, theatre, restaurant and public house, and in voluntary organisations such as churches, community centres, tennis clubs and musical societies the married couples whose children are "off their hands" are often the backbone of the organisation, being mature enough and free enough to undertake many duties. In this way the neighbourhood often does have more meaning for these slightly older married couples, and when their children are grown up and married they may well take greater interest in the local activities since their domestic interests have now decreased with their children's departure. But it should be borne in mind that these people are not tied to the neighbourhood, and with present trends they are quite likely to be car owners and so unlimited in their geographic range of interests and activities.

It is when old age begins to make its mark that the wider range of activities will be reduced, particularly when ill-health or a greater sensitivity to inclement weather develops. Old people who do not have their own transport become much more dependent upon local shops and delivered goods, and their needs may become the focus for neighbourly help. In urban life many services for old people, such as home-helps, district nurses and W.V.S. meals-on-wheels are organised on a city wide basis. But equally there are many local clubs for old people and innumerable neighbourly acts on the part of younger neighbours in helping with shopping, cleaning, gardening, snow-clearance, to mention only a few. When one partner of the marriage dies the dependency of the relict may become very great and neighbourly visits may at times be the only form of real social intercourse that remains. From the dependency of youth the wheel has turned full circle to the dependency of old age.

In this analysis of the life-cycle it has been made apparent that the needs of the individual in regard to the neighbourhood vary tremendously according to sex, age and family status. At times there are few needs which the neighbourhood is the appropriate body to fill; at other times the neighbourhood is a very meaningful concept indeed. But what is essential to the analysis is the continuous recognition that the neighbourhood is a *part* of the town or city; it is a sub-section of the city, not an entity in itself apart from the city. Recognition of this fact is essential for an appreciation of the position of the neighbourhood in the urban structure.

The emphasis upon the importance of primary relationships in the neighbourhood has led to consideration of the neighbourhood as a primary group in itself, and from this comparisons between villages and neighbourhoods have been made. In some cases these have been extremely valuable, at other times (as will be shown) they have been dangerously misleading.

Many years ago the American sociologist E. A. Ross gave an interesting contrast between village and city. He wrote of the village that "When communication is difficult and slow, you accept as intimates your blood kinsmen and neighbours, because you see them often, you know them best and they are right at hand in case you need them. Even if they are dour and touchy, even if their ways and ideas grate upon you, you fraternise with them for there is no one else to consort with. Even though with them you cannot be quite yourself or follow your bent, you adapt yourself to them from dread of becoming a social outcast." In the urban neighbourhood by contrast, "Modern methods of communication and transportation make possible a wide psycho-social and territorial range. The person's activities are not necessarily located in his home community, nor are the participants in these activities his neighbours. Home becomes significant as a place of retirement from the varied

stimuli of social activity, and neighbouring tends to be redefined as unwarranted intrusion."[7] This last phrase is echoed in a much more recent book by Reimer when he says, "To relax from his working day, the city dweller seeks a residential environment where he will be free from the constant alertness that is forced upon him by mingling with the motley crowd of a heterogeneous urban population. To relax in his private life, the city dweller wants to be with 'his own kind'."[8]

These comments on the neighbourhood may usefully be placed against Carpenter's definition so as to elucidate the principal functions of the neighbourhood. In his ideal type neighbourhood Carpenter describes a "primary group spirit which is the fulcrum of neighbourhood life," but this is recognised as being broken down by all the processes of urbanisation. Indeed, so much of an ideal type is Carpenter's neighbourhood that it seems almost contradictory to think of it as an urban concept at all. Logically it could be argued that if all the forces of urbanism are "hostile" to the preservation of neighbourhood life, then how can the neighbourhood be an urban phenomenon? One is led to the conclusion that Carpenter is speaking of a phenomenon that may have existed in the past when towns were small, communications were slow and when all the conditions of which Ross writes were present. But such conditions, which would be typical of the situations described by Flora Thompson in *Lark Rise to Candleford*,[9] are pertinent only to social structures now dead and gone. In a predominantly rural area they may still obtain, but the general picture of the neighbourhood is such that one would have to conclude that it cannot exist in present-day urban society. If this is so, then Carpenter's definition of neighbourhood is an abstraction, and only his definition of the "pseudo-neighbour-hood" or "residential area" is dealing with reality today. The similarity between the ideal-type neighbourhood and the old-time village is however very close and it may now be of value to make a brief comparison between the village and city so as to put the modern concept of neighbour-hood (or residential area of Carpenter) into perspective.

The generalised picture of the rural village before urbanisation had developed in the late nineteenth and early twentieth centuries is of a small community, prob-ably no more than a few hundred people in all, many of whom were interrelated through local marriages. Mobility was slight and the village was relatively isolated, even a few miles' journey being a major expedition. The occupational structure was closely linked to agriculture, its service industries and its by-products. Occupation tended towards a hereditary system and there were close relationships between home, work and leisure. The village had its social hierarchy with squire, parson, schoolteacher, shopkeepers and post office, but social mobility was slight, indeed almost a caste system. Nevertheless re-lationships were face to face and people knew each other as *whole* people and not just as segments of people in specialised roles. Social control was thus a strong factor and the individual had strong rea-sons to conform since social isolation or ostracism were very real sanctions. Being born and bred to this environment, though, the individual could adjust fairly readily to it, since no real alternatives were known. The few misfits might leave the village altogether or would become out-casts if they remained.

The contrast with the contemporary city is tremendous. Populations are huge and no individual can possibly know more than a fraction of the inhabitants. Relationship by kin and inter-marriage loses its import-ance in the community as a whole, though it may have vestiges remaining in some parts. Mobility is great, with both public and private transport, and moving from district to district is a new, important feature. Occupations are diverse, and few are hereditary. Production, distribution, commerce and administration have no such unifying bond as clear and striking as have agriculture and the land. Home has little relationship to workplace and with different occupations within the family, the working members split up all over the city. The social hierarchy of the city is complex and impersonal; classes replace individual statuses and one rarely knows many people as *whole* people. Opportu-nities for social mobility abound and a person is evaluated for what he is, or what he has, rather than by the ascribed status he derives from his father and family. Social control is less effective, since face-to-face relationships and intimate know-ledge of another's business cannot operate over a total community of tens of thou-sands of people. Anonymity is more easily obtained in the city centre and its institu-tions, but in the urban ethos it is "not done" to take too much interest in other people's lives anyway.

Obviously then the village of the past and the city of the present bear little similarity to each other. The differences are historical and concerned with size and complexity of structure. Comparison be-tween the village and the urban neighbour-hood is then a possible next step, since it may be felt that the neighbourhood, being a part of the town, may still demonstrate the characteristics of the village. But the above comparison between village and city must show how misleading such a comparison would be. The urban neighbourhood is not an entity in itself, as is the village, it is merely a part, and a part difficult to define at that, of the whole city, and as our previous life-cycle analysis showed, the neighbourhood is only a "some functions" unit as contrasted with the "all functions" of the village (even though the functions may be on a small scale).

Both Ross and Reimer suggest that the neighbourhood is a place of retreat from the *total* urban life; it is a place where the individual can relax, with as little strain as possible, with people of his own sort. This means that he expects to find rest in the neighbourhood from the varied social contacts of city life, and their attendant social adjustments, in a social area where he can expect the people around him to think and act as he himself does. He thus has expectations of a similar outlook on life amongst his neighbours, particularly in so far as life in the neighbourhood itself is concerned. So if people want to go out from the neighbourhood to work in other parts of the city, if they want to spend their leisure time in the city centre, these things do not particularly matter *unless* in some way they affect the neighbourhood. If Mr. Jones across the road goes off to work in his car each morning, wearing his dark suit, white shirt and bowler hat, his actual job does not really matter. But if he suddenly starts going out in greasy overalls, big boots and a cloth cap then it can matter because Mr. Jones is affecting the social status of the area in moving down the scale from an *apparent* non-manual occupation to a manual one. The interesting point is that if he went to his work as a factory hand in a car and business suit probably many people locally would be completely unaware of the dangerous situation that was at hand since so much of the assessment is done through

visual evidence. Similarly if the respectable Mr. and Mrs. Smith attended drunken orgies on the other side of town it would not affect the social life of their own neighbourhood at all so long as their behaviour never came to light. If the facts *did* come to light an interesting situation would probably arise. It might be hazarded that some neighbours would be greatly affronted and would cut the Smiths dead; others might well take the view that so long as they didn't hold the drunken orgies in the Smith's house then it was really no one's business locally. The point at issue is essentially whether the behaviour of a particular person is relevant to the neighbourhood itself. Obviously there are differences of opinion between individuals and between neighbourhoods themselves as to what constitutes correct neighbourhood behaviour, but the essential factor is a recognition that life is not confined to the neighbourhood in anything like the way it is in the hypothetical village.

There are three points to be considered about the urban neighbourhood. Firstly, since it is a fact that cities divide their residential areas according to social class criteria, one must have some knowledge of the social class of any given area. Secondly, one must try to discover what functions the neighbourhood actually provides for the residents. Thirdly, one must try to discover the active behaviour which constitutes neighbourliness.

In a study[10] carried out in an urban district adjacent to Nottingham I attempted some enquiries into these problems. The place was West Bridgford, an urban district of approximately 25,000 population, which lies on the south side of the River Trent. Whilst socially it is mainly a residential suburb of Nottingham it is a local government area separate from the city and it has strong local loyalties and activities of its own. Six different types of housing areas were selected for sample enquiries; older type terrace houses, medium-sized pre-1914 semi-detached houses, pre-1914 large semi and detached houses, modern council houses, modern medium-sized semi-detached houses and modern large detached houses. The occupants of the houses of the samples interviewed were asked about their use of amenities in the town and Nottingham city, their leisure activities, their associational memberships and their neighbourly behaviour. It was interesting to note that whilst the middle class people were much more active in organisations and clubs than were the working classes, the top people in the middle classes (i.e. the most well-to-do in the best residential districts) were less active *locally* and tended more to do shopping and to join activities in the city or the county area. In neighbourly activity the patterns differed between working class and middle class, with the former having more informal neighbouring in the way of "popping in" to the neighbours, the latter having more formal neighbouring in the way of giving coffee parties or evening entertaining in the home. Thus the neighbourhood means different things to different people and only a detailed typology of behaviour according to certain chosen criteria could do justice to the variety of patterns to be found in various types of neighbourhood.

It is therefore of considerable interest to enquire into the thoughts which lie behind the idea of the neighbourhood as a principle for town planning. Briefly put, the general theme that has been developed is that our modern cities are growing to such a size and such a complexity that some breakdown of them into smaller social units is needed if they are to retain their essentially "human" characteristics. An official statement made in 1944 put the case as follows,[11] "Something like half the population of England and Wales lives in towns which have a population of over 50,000. In these larger towns especially a sense of neighbourhood has been lost to great numbers of the inhabitants. The town is generally too large to be fully understood as a social unit, and the neighbourhood, the immediate environment of the many inhabitants, has lost or never had a full identity." The report notes then that large housing estates built between the wars were just as bad as, if not worse than, older parts of the towns in their inadequacy in stimulating neighbourly feeling. The report continues, "For the proper social well-being of the large town, then, it is necessary to work out some organisation of its physical form which will aid in every way the full development of community life and enable a proper measure of social amenities to be provided and arranged to advantage in each residential neighbourhood. The idea of the "neighbourhood unit" arises out of an acknowledgment of the necessity of doing this and offers the means of doing it."

NOTES

1. R. Glass, *The Social Background of a Plan*, London, 1948.
2. P. G. Gray, T. Corlett and P. Jones, "The Proportion of Jurors as an Index of a District," *Social Survey*, London, 1951.
3. N. Carpenter, *Encyclopaedia of the Social Sciences*, New York, 1933, p. 357.
4. Marion Wesley Roper, *The City and the Primary Group*, Chicago, 1935.
5. That is to say, not social outside the home environment.
6. *Responsibility in the Welfare State*, Birmingham Council of Christian Churches, 1961, p. 27.
7. E. A. Ross, *Principles of Sociology*, New York, 1938 edition.
8. S. Reimer, *The Modern City*, New York, 1952.
9. Flora Thompson, *Lark Rise to Candleford*, Worlds Classics, London, N.D.
10. Peter H. Mann, "Community and Neighbourhood with Reference to Social Status," Ph.D. Thesis, University of Nottingham, 1955.
11. Site Planning and Layout in Relation to Housing; Report of a Study Group of the Ministry of Town and Country Planning in *Design of Dwellings*, Ministry of Health, H.M.S.O., London, 1944.

39. Voluntary Associations and Neighborhood Cohesion
Eugene Litwak

A familiar concern of urban sociology is the tension between large functional organizations (such as industrial corporations) and the local community. It has been held by some that the local voluntary organization plays a mediating role between these two major organizational forces, a role which is made more plausible by the strikingly high rate of participation in voluntary organizations by contemporary, middle-class Americans. It is not clear, however, what the significance of this mediating role is. Does the voluntary association operate as a quasi-primary group supplementing the personal and social integration functions of the local neighborhood and the family? Or is the voluntary association really a tool through which the large corporation influences opinion at the local level to support industry's economic goals and political programs?

Eugene Litwak attempts to resolve this debate by making explicit the assumptions involved in each of the viewpoints. From this, he goes on to examine the available evidence provided by previous empirical studies. Litwak concludes that modern industrial bureaucracies do not necessarily succeed in dominating local communities, but that they do seek to dominate them. The capacity of local groups to resist domination requires an unusual ability to be flexible and to deal with unanticipated events, even when they lack the breadth and sophistication to cope with major technological and organizational problems at the national and regional level.

Eugene Litwak is Professor of Social Welfare Research at the University of Michigan. He is the author of numerous articles in the field of social organization.

The purpose of this paper is to investigate the relationship between voluntary associations and such local community primary groups[1] as the neighborhood. Two opposing hypotheses will be studied:

1. Mature industrial bureaucracies put pressures on their members to utilize voluntary associations and to *disaffiliate* from local community and neighborhood primary groups.[2]
2. Mature industrial bureaucracies put pressures on their members to utilize voluntary associations to *affiliate* with community and neighborhood primary groups.

It should be clear that both approaches stress the importance of voluntary associations. They disagree only regarding their functions, i.e., integrative or substitutive for local community and neighborhood primary groups.

In order to investigate these alternative points of view, the major assumptions of each will be made explicit and evaluated as to their capacity to explain key studies of the past. The literature reviewed in this connection will be highly selective; an effort will be made to choose one or two studies representing the pros and cons of each issue rather than to summarize the major studies in each field.[3]

The position taken in this paper is that the traditional assumptions supporting the first hypothesis can not be maintained in light of important bodies of data. Counter suggestions to these traditional views will be presented which do explain discrepancies in past studies and which support the hypothesis that voluntary associations integrate individuals into local neighborhood and community groups.

Following this analysis, specific predictions regarding the relationship between geographical mobility and club affiliations will be derived from the alternative hypothesis discussed above. New empirical material will be used to evaluate these differing predictions which in turn have a direct bearing on the larger issues in dispute.

Traditional Assumptions

1. Assumption That National Instruments of Control Are More Efficient Than Local Ones One of the major reasons that voluntary associations and industrialization are thought to be antithetical to local community and neighborhood primary group cohesion is that industrialization is most efficiently carried forth in large nationally centralized bureaucracies.[4] The major tools of interaction with and control of the rest of the society takes place through highly centralized national organs, e.g., Congress, national trade associations, the mass media.[5] The national base of industry permits management to see the advantages for social control of these highly centralized mass organs. This particular group of assumptions receives support from studies such as those done by Mills and Ulmer[6] and Schulze.[7] The former study shows a negative relation between towns dominated by large concerns and local welfare while the latter study argues that managements of national concerns have fewer commitments to the local community. The assumption that centralized efficiency leads to national identification would be most persuasive if a series of directly contradictory studies were not also available. Thus Fowler[8] provides evidence which

From *American Sociological Review,* Vol. XXVI, No. 2 (April 1961), pp. 258–271. Reprinted by permission.

goes counter to Mills and Ulmer while several studies dispute Schulze's conclusions.[9] It can be seen, therefore, that this traditional view does not completely meet the test of empirical verification, and must be modified if it is to explain American social behavior.

2. Assumption That Short Tenure Means Lack of Commitment Another assumption commonly underlying the view that industrialization and voluntary associations are negatively related to neighborhood primary group cohesion is that a national bureaucratic industrial organization in order to rationalize its labor must move its management around quite frequently. This means that the management of such concerns is unlikely to remain in a given community very long. Individuals with short tenure are less likely to identify with a primary group than others and therefore the management of national concerns is less likely than others to identify with a local community.[10] Such speculations have received some indirect empirical support from studies such as Angell's which argue that mobility is negatively related to local community welfare.[11] Again this would seem to be a very plausible position were there not available a series of counter studies. Thus Whyte,[12] Festinger,[13] and others[14] provide evidence indicating that individuals, living for a short while in a community, can develop strong community cohesion.

3. Assumption That Voluntary Organizations Are Formal and Therefore Antithetical to Primary Groups There is still a third assumption which, together with the other two, generally supports the view that voluntary associations are negatively related to neighborhood primary group cohesion. It is that voluntary associations are formal bureaucratic organizations and as such are antithetical to local community primary groups.[15] Again there is empirical evidence to the contrary. One group of studies indicates that there is a positive relation between friendship formation and affiliation in voluntary association.[16] Another series of studies suggests that affiliation with voluntary associations is related to local community identification.[17] In short, all three assumptions which underlie the view that industrialization and voluntary associations are negatively related to local community and neighborhood primary group cohesion cannot be maintained in the light of important bodies of empirical data. This raises the question whether alternative assumptions can be developed which in fact could meet such a test.[18]

An Elaboration of Previous Assumptions

1. Assumption of Change One way to reconcile these seemingly contradictory studies is to argue that we are in a period of change and that therefore a certain amount of contradictory evidence should be anticipated. For instance, the Mills and Ulmer study was done in 1940 while the contradictory Fowler study was done nearly ten years later. During this period there seems to have been a continued shift in the local community perspectives of large organizations. In 1940, for example, approximately 56 per cent of local community chest funds were gathered under business aegis while in 1950 this figure had risen to approximately 75 percent, and in 1958 it was approximately 85 percent.[19] The question arises whether this trend represents a superficial ideological façade or derives from basic organizational needs of large industrial concerns. To answer this question requires a re-analysis of the previous assumptions.

2. The Assumption That National and Local Commitment Maximize Social Control a. *Internal production needs and local commitment* Those who argue that the large size of a concern places management on a social peak from which it can view the national instruments of control forget that such a vantage point also permits surveillance of the local instruments of control. For instance, when a small businessman has an employee who is continually tardy, he might dismiss him and seek another without too much concern for the community basis for the worker's tardiness. However, the manager of a large plant employing 10,000 workers who finds a 20 percent tardiness or turnover rate cannot so easily dismiss the matter as one of personal idiosyncracy. He is in a much better position to see the relation to local community problems—poor transportation, poor recreation, poor crime prevention, poor schooling, etc. In short, it is maintained that there are immediate internal production demands which force the management of large national concerns to be highly committed to local community cohesion.[20]

b. *External production needs and local commitment* In addition to these internal production needs there are usually external ones which equally demand local community identification. Generally the larger the business becomes the more publicly exposed are its management's decisions and the more obvious it becomes to the general public that there is a relation between these "pure" business decisions and overall public welfare.[21] Thus, the very magnitude of the steel concerns makes it quite obvious to the public (via the press) that there is a direct relation between their prices and the problem of inflation. Granted that we live in a democracy, it quickly becomes apparent to the mangement of large concerns that business prerogatives exercised under public scrutiny become subject to public control. Management, in order to insure its point of view against hostile groups, e.g., the union, has consciously sought to control the public.[22] In addition it has discovered that issues frequently have little meaning unless they can be translated into immediate local terms.[23] This pragmatic experience of management in effect documents the theoretical argument that states that primary groups are frequently the most satisfactory social instruments for establishing reality.[24]

c. *The theory that the combination of large organizations and primary groups maximize control* To assert management's pragmatic justification of local community involvement would not be persuasive regarding future trends if this were not consistent with a strong theoretical position on social control.

The view that social control is best exercised through highly centralized national organizations such as the mass media rests on the same reasoning that Weber develops regarding the efficiency of bureaucracy in a mass society—its capacity to hire specialists who can make decisions based on knowledge, not favoritism, and its ability to reach the largest number of people with a given message.[25] However, to point out these efficiencies is not to overlook the deficiencies of such centralized organizations. In heeding the critics[26] of Weber's formulations it can be maintained that large organizations suffer from two defects: (1) they are relatively inflexible, able only to deal with standardized events, and (2) they have long complicated channels of communication which prevent quick reaction to unanticipated events. The latter defect partly accounts for the former.

By contrast, the primary group, because of its small size, may have a very quick flow of information and can exhibit great flexibility and speed in dealing with non-uniform events. However, it lacks the capacity of the large organization to reach great masses of people. Nor can it provide the expertise of specialization.

As a consequence, when it is important to reach a large audience with a standard message, the mass media are most useful. On the other hand, where one is faced with a highly differentiated audience or with a hostile audience necessitating great flexibility, primary groups are most advantageous for social control.

However, where maximal social control is desired, then both the mass media and the primary group should be used in conjunction. This combines the virtues of specialization and wide message dissemination with speed and flexibility. There is no reason why the two systems cannot be coordinated providing suitable social mechanisms are at hand.[27] The opinion leader is one case in point.[28] He acts to coordinate the message of the mass media with the needs of the primary group. Inkeles' discussion of the agitator in Russia is an even clearer example of how maximal social control is consciously sought by coordinating mass media with primary group behavior.[29] Lipset, and others, in their discussion of Nazi Germany point out that under this highly centralized political regime the drive for maximal social control led to a growing awareness of the needs for development and control

of local neighborhood block groups to supplement the formal mass organs.[30]

In short, it is argued that because of the internal and external demands of productivity as well as the strong theoretical reasons for a combination of primary group and large organization, management's current enthusiasm for local community identification represents an enduring facet of mature bureaucratic[31] society and is not a superficial ideological façade.

3. Assumption That Formal Organizations Can Speed Up Socialization and Minimize the Problem of Short Tenure If the process for integrating individuals into the group can be accelerated, then the problem of short tenure and local community identification can be solved. There is some evidence that the modern corporation seeks to accelerate integration through such mechanisms as (a) encouraging a "frontier attitude" among its employees so that native and stranger will take a positive view towards each other,[32] (b) encouraging the development of common values and roles which makes it easier for the stranger to learn the group norms,[33] (c) encouraging a "stepping stone reference group" orientation[34] so that individuals can integrate into their present group and still retain their mobility aspirations, (d) encouraging individuals to view their personality objectively as something which can be improved, thereby opening up new areas for public discussion and increased potential contact,[35] (e) encouraging a planning orientation in community development which will maximize friendship,[36] (f) providing economic aid for those who move and freeing their time for social contacts,[37] and (g) encouraging the localization of voluntary associations which integrate individuals speedily into the community.[38] In short, the answer to the argument that short tenure leads away from local primary group identification is that group structure can be so changed that socialization is accelerated. The modern corporation, because it is faced with the need to accelerate socialization within the confines of its organization, has developed these mechanisms for speedy integration which, granted the foregoing discussion on local community commitment, are easily transferred to the neighborhood.[39]

4. *Assumption That Voluntary Organizations Can Integrate Individuals into Primary Groups* To complete the discussion, it is necessary to know under what conditions formal organizations such as voluntary associations can accelerate the integration of individuals into primary groups.

a. *Public criteria of membership* One integrative advantage the voluntary association has over many forms of interaction is the fact that its availability can be publicly advertised. As a consequence, it is relatively easy for a stranger to locate and assess its merits without investing a great deal of effort.

b. *Initiative comes from either stranger or native* A second factor permitting the voluntary association to integrate strangers faster than most other forms of interaction is the fact that initiative for joining the organization can generally come from either the stranger or the native. By contrast, in many friendship relationships a stranger would be considered "pushy" if he initiated contact. As a consequence, there is greater probability that one will make contacts in voluntary associations than in other types of voluntary social relations.

c. *Membership consists of potential primary group members—neighbors* The two mechanisms mentioned thus far are generic for quick social integration, but by themselves do not imply a primary group integration. This will only occur if, in addition, the membership of the voluntary association consists of potential primary group members. Since primary group membership generally involves much face to face contact, this means that membership in voluntary associations must consist of groups such as local neighbors who have the potential for face to face contact outside the association.

d. *Membership does not conflict with existing primary groups—the family* Where membership in the voluntary association is restricted to one sex, it frequently sets up a conflict between family and voluntary association, i.e., participation in one group is at the expense of the other. Where both spouses are eligible for membership in the voluntary association, this potential conflict is minimized while the possibility of primary group contact is maximized—assuming that either spouse can act as an agent for the other in forming neighborhood friendship primary group.[40]

e. *Voluntary associations deal with issues in terms of local primary group interests* Where the voluntary organization deals with issues that are local and relevant to primary groups such as school issues, local recreation facilities, local religious or racial issues, local political issues, etc., it makes it much easier for the stranger to learn what the norms of the primary groups are prior to making his primary group contacts. All of the advantages of anticipatory socialization[41] occur.

f. *The voluntary association permits great membership participation* Formal voluntary associations can be organized in a variety of ways. Those which stress membership participation are most likely to lead to socialization into primary groups. This is a consequence of the fact that membership participation leads to more contacts between members rather than between professional staff and members.

In short, if the above conditions held, it would be argued that voluntary associations might well act to integrate individuals into neighborhood primary groups.

Re-examination of Conflicting Evidence

With the traditional assumptions and their modifications made explicit, attention may now be turned to a re-examination of conflicting evidence mentioned in the foregoing discussion to see in what sense the conflicts can be resolved. The evidence will be organized under general categories deduced from the modified traditional assumptions.

1. Where two studies made at different time periods provided conflicting evidence regarding large scale organizational orientation toward local community identification, the evidence was considered as supportive of the modified assumptions if the data from the later study showed that the executives of the large organizations took a more positive view toward local community than did those in the earlier investigations.[42]

2. Where two studies were made in the same time period it was necessary to differentiate between top management, middle management, and lower management. Pressures for change in this case start at the top, since they are a function of centralization. In this connection there can be little doubt that the official position of most top management of large organizations is to urge local community identity.[43] For example, Rossi's study, which reported little inclination of management to identify locally, must be further analyzed to see if the investigator did not group together the various managerial strata. In effect, he may have been reporting on the more numerous middle and lower management persons who are last to feel organizational pressures for local community participation.[44] If this were the case, his evidence should be re-analyzed to see if any trend emerges by level of managerial responsibility. Such a trend would be supportive of the modified assumptions here suggested.

3. Concerns engaged in public conflict or especially exposed are much more likely to be sensitive to the needs of local community identification than those having relatively peaceful relations or not publicly exposed. Thus utilities which are open to public scrutiny via government rate fixing agencies should be much more sensitive than other concerns to the need for local community identification. The Schulze[45] study, which argues small identification between management and local community, indicates that in fact the local community leaders do everything management could want. Where the local community acts as an instrument of company policy the company can afford the luxury of public indifference to the community. Quite the opposite would be true if the local community opposed company policy, e.g., on local tax policies, schooling, etc. This may well explain the difference between the Pellegrin and Coates study[46] and that by Schulze. The Pellegrin and Coates investigation was carried out in a large city where there is much greater likelihood of diverse needs and, therefore, organized opposition

to management (i.e., unions and local business groups). Furthermore, the very size of the community prevents the informal mind-reading act that governmental officials of small communities can practice.[47] Schulze's attempt to discount the factor of informal influence must be weighed against his report that management felt the local officials were doing everything management wanted.[48] This leaves the reader to assume that the overlap was fortuitous or that in fact the forms of influence were too subtle for Schulze to discern. In either case it is felt that these statements throw great doubt on the long term reliability of Schulze's assertions that management has little concern with local community affairs.[49]

4. Granted mobility, there is likely to be greater local identification in places populated by the executives of large organizations than in other types of communities. Such management dominated communities are likely to be more consistently in agreement with top management views because they have the fewest counter pressures from the traditional business groups. Thus the Whyte, Festinger, and Litwak studies dealt with new suburbs where there were large concentrations of management people. By contrast, the Angell study was made with a more diffused population.[50] It, therefore, would be necessary for studies such as Angell's to further differentiate in their analysis between management of bureaucratic concerns and traditional business concerns. It will be hypothesized that the former group will be less affected by short tenure than the latter.[51]

5. With regard to affiliation in voluntary associations, any evidence indicating that management people tend to affiliate in organizations that deal with local issues, consist of neighbors, permit joint husband and wife affiliation, permit great membership participation, and involve an active publicizing as well as recruiting of newcomers would be presumptive evidence that voluntary associations are being used to integrate individuals into primary groups.

The function of voluntary associations for integrating primary groups will be elaborated below. However, before doing so the limits of the foregoing rules for resolving conflicting data should be clearly understood. All of these rules assume that conflicts in data are reasonable as long as they can be ordered along the right time dimension or in terms of the theoretically expected groups.

The Use of Voluntary Associations for Local Neighborhood Integration

1. The Three Stages of Integration Up to this point this paper has concentrated on showing how conflicts in previous studies can be explained. Now attention will be turned to some specific hypotheses generated from the foregoing consideration and dealing with new data. If voluntary associations are indeed used by many to integrate into local neighborhood groups, then a three stage theory of neighborhood integration might be suggested. The first stage consists of a radical change, i.e., a person who has just moved from one city to another. The move is correlated with a whole host of major social changes, e.g., job changes, school changes for the children, disruption of extended family and old friendship ties. It is argued that at this first stage individuals are so heavily involved with their own immediate family and occupational problems that they have little time to consider neighborhood integration.

The second stage comprises families who have settled their immediate family problems and are ready to integrate into the neighborhood but who have not resided therein long enough to form local friendships. Such individuals may well turn to voluntary associations to help speed up their friendship formation. Finally, the third stage consists of individuals who have lived in the neighborhood for some time and have had an opportunity to make friends. Such individuals are not as likely as those in the second stage to use voluntary associations because the integrative functions of these associations are partly taken over by friendship relations. However, they will still use voluntary associations more than the first stage families because where there is much neighborhood turnover, such associations are necessary (even for the long term resident) to form new friendships. In short, what is hypothesized is an asymmetrical curvilinear relation between neighborhood integration and affiliation with voluntary associations.

By contrast, if voluntary associations are used to substitute for local neighborhood relations there should be little effect from a move. Once the initial crisis period is over there should be a modest monotonic relation between length of residence and associational affiliations. The assumption is that the longer the residence the more likely individuals are to find out about available associations and therefore the more likely they are to join.

To investigate these propositions, information from a survey of 920 white married women with at least one child under 19 who had moved into a new house or apartment within a three year period prior to the survey (June-October, 1952)[52] was used. The entire sample came from suburbs of Buffalo, New York. To operationalize affiliation with voluntary associations respondents were asked, "What organizations or social clubs do you belong to?"[53] To index type of move all respondents were classified as follows: (a) whether they had relatives living in town; and (b) whether they were newcomers or long term residents in their current neighborhood.[54] The three stages of integration were operationalized by cross-classifying respondents by length of residence in the neighborhood and place where their relatives reside. The first stage group (the "least settled") consists of all those who have no relatives in town and who have resided in the neighborhood nine months or less. The second stage families (the "moderately settled") consist of two groups: (1) those who have relatives in town, but have resided in the neighborhood nine months or less, and (2) those who have no relatives, but have resided in the neighborhood more than nine months. Finally, the third stage families (the "most settled") consist of those who have relatives in town and who have lived in their neighborhood more than nine months.

If these definitions are accepted, the data are consistent with the speculations that voluntary associations are used to integrate people into the local neighborhood. The "moderately settled" group has, on the average .85 (328 cases) affiliations, the "most settled" group has, on the average .70 (484 cases) affiliations, while the "least settled" group has .49 (108 cases).

2. Occupational Resources and the Three Stages
Most studies of voluntary associations report a positive association between occupational-economic resources of the respondent and the voluntary associations[55] to which he belongs. It is necessary therefore to take this factor into account before proceeding with the analysis of the three stages. For the above

TABLE 1. THE "MODERATELY SETTLED" GENERALLY HAVE MOST CLUB AFFILIATIONS AT EACH OCCUPATIONAL LEVEL

	Most Settled *	Moderately Settled †	Least Settled ‡
Stationary upper class§	1.18 (106)	1.26 (97)	.34 (44)
Upwardly mobile class	.91 (127)	.84 (123)	.53 (38)
Downwardly mobile class	.67 (77)	.77 (48)	.29 (17)
Stationary manual class	.34 (174)	.45 (60)	.00 (09)

* Individuals with relatives in town who have lived in their current neighborhood 9 months or more.
† Either individuals with relatives in town who have lived in their current neighborhood less than 9 months or individuals without relatives in town who have lived in their current neighborhood more than 9 months.
‡ Individuals with no relatives in town who have lived in their current neighborhood less than 9 months.
§ For definition of occupational class see footnote 56.

analysis may well be explained by a peculiar distribution of occupations among the three stages, i.e., with the middle stage group having more upper class people and the first stage group having mostly working class people.

Table 1 reveals that with the partial exception of the upward mobile the same pattern holds for each occupational level[56]— the center cell in each row has higher average club affiliations than either extreme. At the same time, it can be seen from Table 1 that occupational resources also play a role. In 8 out of 9 possible comparisons the top cell in each column (the stationary upper class group) has a greater average club affiliation than any other cell in the column.

3. Neighborhood Orientation and Stage of Move Relates to Neighborhood Integration The reader has already noted that the preceding analysis has been made with the implicit assumption that the respondents desire to integrate into the neighborhood. A somewhat different patterning of data would occur if the respondents had no desire to integrate into the neighborhood. For instance, where individuals are negatively oriented toward their neighbors, the longer their residence, the more likely they are to realize the differences and the

more likely they are to seek to dissociate from their neighbors. In this case they may use voluntary associations as a bridge out of the neighborhood.

The differences in patterns of affiliation can be specified as follows: (1) Those positively oriented to the neighborhood should have an asymmetrical curvilinear relation between club affiliation and neighborhood integration; (2) Those negatively oriented towards the neighborhood should have a positive monotonic relation between club affiliation and neighborhood integration. In order to investigate these hypotheses an attempt was made to operationalize orientation towards the neighborhood. Each of two types of neighborhood[57] (upper and manual-middle) was classified in terms of its family norms. Three family value positions were defined—extended, nuclear, and non-family oriented.[58] The upper class neighborhood was characterized by an extended family orientation while the manual neighborhood was non-family oriented.[59] The nuclear family orientation was equally prevalent in both groups. On this basis the population was divided into three groups: (1) those whose values conformed to their neighbors; (2) those whose values were deviant from their neighbors; and (3) those who could not be classified.

Under the assumption (partially confirmed)[60] that value homophily is the dominant trend in friendship formation, all individuals adhering to the value held by their neighbors were considered positively oriented. Value deviants were characterized as negatively oriented and all others were regarded as unclassified. Because of the marginal distribution on the value items only the extremes could be classified as positively and negatively oriented.

As Table 2 indicates, among those positively oriented towards their neighbors the moderately settled have the highest club affiliations in 7 out of 8 comparisons. By contrast, among those negatively oriented towards their neighbors the "most settled" have the highest club affiliations in 8 out of 8 comparisons. What is most interesting is that the largest group consisting of those whose neighborhood orientation could not be classified display the same pattern of affiliation as the positively oriented, i.e., asymmetrical curvilinear relation in 7 out of 8 instances.

The joint hypotheses for negatively and positively oriented can be partially tested by examining the first two columns where they make opposite predictions for their respective groups. It can be seen that in 7

TABLE 2. AMONG THOSE POSITIVELY ORIENTED TOWARD THEIR NEIGHBORS*
THE MODERATELY SETTLED INDIVIDUALS HAVE GREATEST CLUB
AFFILIATION WHILE AMONG THOSE NEGATIVELY ORIENTED THE MOST
SETTLED HAVE THE GREATEST CLUB AFFILIATION

	Most Settled	Moderately Settled	Least Settled
Positive Neighborhood Orientation			
Stationary upper class	.91 (35)	1.63 (27)	.17 (06)
Upwardly mobile class	.52 (29)	1.18 (33)	.87 (08)
Downwardly mobile class	.59 (27)	1.00 (14)	.00 (03)
Stationary manual class	.36 (56)	.36 (22)	.00 (03)
Total group	.58 (147)	1.09 (96)	.40 (20)
Negative Neighborhood Orientation			
Stationary upper class	1.87 (15)	1.05 (21)	1.00 (07)
Upwardly mobile class	1.30 (27)	.69 (26)	.57 (07)
Downwardly mobile class	.94 (16)	.40 (05)	.00 (02)
Stationary manual class	.52 (27)	.44 (09)	.00 (01)
Total group	1.08 (85)	.77 (61)	.65 (17)
Unclassified Neighborhood Orientation			
Stationary upper class	1.16 (56)	1.14 (49)	.23 (31)
Upwardly mobile class	.93 (71)	.72 (64)	.39 (23)
Downwardly mobile class	.62 (34)	.72 (29)	.42 (12)
Stationary manual class	.29 (91)	.52 (29)	.00 (05)
Total group	.71 (252)	.81 (171)	.21 (71)

* Positively oriented is defined as either those living in working class neighborhoods who have non-family orientation or those living in upper class neighborhoods who have extended family orientations. These are the norms of the respective neighborhoods. Negatively oriented are all people in those neighborhoods holding the opposite values. Unclassified are all individuals holding nuclear family values since these are approximately equally distributed in both groups.

out of 8 cases the differences go in the direction predicted.

The asymmetrical pattern of club affiliations for the positively oriented as opposed to the monotonic affiliations for the negatively oriented can most clearly be seen from Figure 1 dealing with the total populations of the respective groups. This particular patterning of findings is entirely consistent with the view that voluntary associations are being used to integrate individuals into local neighborhood primary groups, though it would take additional data of a kind not collected in this study to certify this point.

Yet this analysis might well serve a purpose in clarifying previous studies which related length of residence to affiliation in voluntary associations. A re-analysis of some of these studies suggests some support for the hypothesis here presented.

Basil G. Zimmer[61] points out that migrants tend to join more clubs the longer they live in a given place. However, when he sub-divides his data and confines himself to the migration which is most likely

to include management of bureaucratic organizations (between cities or among those with a college background) his data indicate an asymmetrical curvilinear relation. If Form's data[62] are organized in terms of the length of residence of his average respondent rather than age of houses, the pattern has some marked similarities to the overall pattern of Zimmer's study. There is a sharp cleavage between the recent mover and the remainder of the population. For this latter group, affiliation with clubs is not related to length of residence in a straightforward positive manner. Moreover, if the three studies of communities dominated by administrative people or potential administrative people are examined, it can be seen that there is an asymmetrical curvilinear relation between club affiliation and average length of residence. (The three studies were conducted in Westgate, composed of married students from the Massachusetts Institute of Technology, and Greenbelt, Maryland, investigated at two different time periods, and predominantly

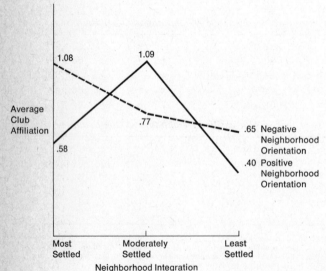

Figure 1. Neighborhood orientation by average club affiliation.

composed of government officials or white collar workers.) Freeman, and others,[63] point out that there is a correlation between length of residence and club affiliation, but report only the summary measures. A re-analysis of their data is necessary to see if an asymmetrical curvilinear hypothesis might account for their data much better. Wright and Hyman[64] suggest that there is no relation between length of residence and club affiliation. However, they do not differentiate the bureaucratic from other types of migrants nor do they separate the extreme newcomer from all others. Their "least settled" group is composed of those who have lived at their present address five years or less. Evidence from all other studies indicates that major differences in club affiliation occur during the first or at most, second year of residence. If their data could be reanalyzed along these lines the asymmetrical hypotheses could be partially tested.

In short, this somewhat limited review of the literature would suggest that where the data can be grouped in terms of the three stages of integration, and where bureaucratic groups can be analyzed separately, there is a definite tendency towards an asymmetrical curvilinear relationship between length of residence and club affiliation. This would of course be greatly magnified according to the hypotheses advanced here if the authors could further distinguish between positive and negative orientation towards the respondents' neighborhood.

Conclusion

The foregoing discussion has sought to present evidence supporting the view that modern industrial bureaucratic organizations encourage local as well as national community participation.

Our thesis is not that modern industrial bureaucracies will dominate local communities, but only that they will seek to dominate them. This qualification is inserted because the same pressures that make the modern industrial organization sensitive to the utility of local communities will operate with regard to any large centralized organization, i.e., unions, political parties, and church groups. The issue of who will eventually exercise power involves additional considerations and is beyond the scope of this paper.

To establish fully the conclusion of this paper further research on the quality of social relations in voluntary associations is necessary: (a) Do such organizations permit total family affiliations? (b) Does membership consist of neighbors or people who are accessible outside of the organization? (c) Is membership participation encouraged? (d) Are the issues dealt with in terms of their local primary group implications? For each of these aspects of voluntary association there must either be a trend analysis or some ahistorical method of testing the trend by using prototypical groups. Are executives most under the influence of mature bureaucratic organizations also most likely to exhibit these forms of behavior? Are communities most nearly dominated by such people more likely to exhibit these modes of behavior? Are executives in the top administrative positions most likely to encourage them? Are companies most publicly exposed (public utilities or large concerns in conflict with unions) most likely to urge this behavior?

If future studies tend to substantiate the position taken in this paper it is believed that a general principle of social control can be advanced as follows: Mature bureaucratic centralization leads to an explicit effort to coordinate and use formal organizations and local primary groups to maximize social control because the formal organization provides expertness and breadth of coverage but is inflexible and unable to deal with non-uniform events. The primary groups provide flexibility and ability to deal with the unanticipated, but has little expertness or breadth of coverage. Where these two groups can be coordinated then maximal control is achieved, i.e., expertness, breadth of coverage, and flexibility.

NOTES

1. The classical definition of primary group involved the simultaneous presence of the following elements: non-instrumental relations, diffuse relations, permanent relations, face to face relations, and positive affect. See Charles H. Cooley, "Primary Groups," in Paul Hare, E. F. Borgatta, and R. F. Bales, editors, *Small Groups*, (New York: Alfred A. Knopf, 1955), pp. 15, 17. The usage in the present paper is somewhat different and might more strictly be referred to as "modified" primary groups. It is argued here that the elements used by Cooley for defining primary groups are independent of each other and consequently there are groups that may have four out of the five factors. Such groups would not completely match the primary groups described by Cooley but would be closer to them than to the groups he designated as secondary and would differ in this regard from those we are designating as voluntary associations.

2. This point of view is implied in the works of Herbert Goldhamer, "Voluntary Associations in the United States," in Paul K. Hatt and Albert J. Reiss, Jr., editors, *Cities and Society: The Revised Reader in Urban Sociology*, (Glencoe: The Free Press, 1957), pp. 593–594; and Louis Wirth, "Urbanism as a Way of Life," *Cities and Society . . . op. cit.*, pp. 46–64 *passim*.

3. This limitation is imposed because the more exhaustive analysis is not necessary for presenting the issues. However, if the propositions here presented are to be thoroughly tested by future investigators the more complete review is necessary.

4. Max Weber, *From Max Weber: Essays in Sociology*, translated and edited by H. H. Gerth and C. Wright Mills (New York: Oxford University Press, 1946), pp. 196–244. For a detailed analysis of this argument see E. Litwak, "Primary Group Instruments for Social Control in Industrialized Society: The Extended Family and the Neighborhood" (Unpublished Ph.D. Dissertation, Columbia University, 1958), pp. 17–23.

5. C. Wright Mills, *The Power Elite* (New York: Oxford University Press, 1956), pp. 305, 307, best illustrates this kind of analysis.

6. C. Wright Mills and M. J. Ulmer, "Small Business and Civic Welfare, Report of the Smaller War Plants Corporation to the Special Committee to Study Problems of American Small Business," Senate Document No. 135, 2nd Session, Washington, 1946.

7. Robert O. Schulze, "The Role of Economic Dominants in Community Power Structure," *American Sociological Review*, 23 (February, 1959), pp. 3–9.

8. Irving A. Fowler, "Local Industrial Structures, Economic Power, and Community Welfare," *Social Problems*, 6 (Summer, 1958), pp. 41–51.

9. See R. J. Pellegrin and C. H. Coates, "Absentee-Owned Corporations and Community Power Structure," *American Journal of Sociology*, 61 (March, 1956), pp. 413–419; William H. Whyte, Jr., *The Organization Man* (New York: Simon and Schuster, 1956), pp. 295–296; and Floyd Hunter, *Community Power Structure* (Chapel Hill: The University of North Carolina Press, 1953), pp. 60–114, pp. 171–207.

10. This assumption would indirectly be supported by George C. Homans' theoretical discussion in *The Human Group* (New York: Harcourt, Brace and Company, 1950), p. 36, when he argues that continued contact is one of the four major requisites for group cohesion. It would be more directly supported by Simmel's view that relatively constant membership is necessary for group cohesion. See Walter Firey, *Land Use in Central Boston* (Cambridge: Harvard University Press, 1947), p. 177.

11. Robert Cooley Angell, "The Moral Integration of American Cities," *American Journal of Sociology* 57, Part 2 (July, 1951), pp. 119–120. Though Angell points out that short tenure is likely to lead to a lack of moral integration, he also argues that when voluntary associations such as churches and schools were oriented towards the local community they could reduce this lack of integration. In addition, he suggests that problems of short tenure may be licked in the future by rapid socialization. *Op. cit.*, p. 121.

12. Whyte, *op. cit.*, pp. 295–296 ff.

13. Leon Festinger, "Architecture and Group Membership," *Journal of Social Issues*, 7 (Nos. 1 and 2, 1951), pp. 158 ff.

14. E. Litwak, "Reference Group Theory, Bureaucratic Career, and Neighborhood Primary Group Cohesion," *Sociometry*, 23, (March, 1960), pp. 72–84.

15. Goldhamer *op. cit.*, pp. 593–594.

16. Wendell Bell and Marion D. Boat, "Urban Neighborhoods and Informal Social Relations," *American Journal of Sociology*, 62 (January, 1957), pp. 391–398; Morris Axelrod "Urban Structure and Social Participation," *American Sociological Review*, 21 (February, 1956), pp. 13–18.

17. Charles R. Wright and Herbert H. Hyman, "Voluntary Association Memberships of American Adults: Evidence from National Sample Surveys," *American Sociological Review*, 23 (June, 1958), pp. 292–293; Howard Freeman, Edwin Novak, and Leo Reeder, "Correlates of

Membership in Voluntary Associations," *American Sociological Review*, 22 (October, 1957), pp. 528–533.

18. An alternative approach would be to argue that the contradictory evidence is a function of inadequacies in some of the foregoing studies. This is not explored here.

19. This is a rough estimate pieced together from information in F. Emerson Andrews, *Corporation Giving* (New York: Russell Sage Foundation, 1952), pp. 156–158; and United Community Funds and Councils of America, *Trends in Giving, 1958*, Bulletin #199, pp. 1, 4.

20. Crawford H. Greenwalt, President of E. I. Du Pont de Nemours & Company has made explicit this dependence of the company on the local community:

   ". . . The roots of the modern corporation are far too deep to permit an irresponsible attitude towards its public duty. Even more so than the individual, the corporation is concerned with tenure, for its life extends over the life times of many individuals. The time was, I suppose, when the proprietor of a business, having offended public sensibilities, could pull up stakes and be out of town before morning, possibly only a step or two ahead of avenging justice. But the Du Pont Company along with modern industry is here to stay, and it is fully mindful . . . that its destinies are bound up with the general benefit. . . ." *Business Laws and Ethics*, March 29, 1954, pp. 8–9.

21. Some excerpts from a General Electric Company pamphlet, *Good Business Citizenship*, p. 3, highlights management's sensitivity to external social pressures and the need to identify business interest with the wider community:

   ". . . . The corporation is an artificial entity. It has no obligations or freedoms in its own right and separate from its role as the *composite agent* or servant of its customers, owners, employees, suppliers, and other involved segments of the public. Its whole mission is to integrate the individual contributions and resulting claims of all of these groups in their balanced best interests. . . . This brings us face to face with the questions of how far a corporate enterprise should go in its efforts to erase the misconceptions that now make it difficult, or even impossible, to carry out this mission; and what is the best way to assure its future welfare in light of the real and growing forces which are now bent on further worsening our business climate which is already not anything like what is required for corporate survival and growth. How we answer these questions—and how the above contributor-claimants look upon General Electric's *over-all operations and profits as being in the public interest*—will largely determine how effective we will be *permitted* to be in our daily operations. . . ."

   Sigmund Diamond has documented the historical swing of the businessman self-image from one narrowly defined by business success to one which blurs the lines between business and community welfare. See his *The Reputation of the American Businessman* (Cambridge: Harvard University Press, 1955).

22. This is represented in the advice General Electric gives to its employees to burrow from within:

   "YOU SHOULD JOIN UP. Active good personal citizenship in your local community means teaming up with a few other key individuals or joining local service groups, civic associations, political organizations, and the like, and becoming an active member in these groups. Sometimes this includes joining up in organizations where the opposition already has active members and is effectively controlling the activities and resolutions of these so-called 'public interest' groups. And when you do join up, you should exert the full weight of your personal influence to focus the organization's attention on the important specific locally determined objectives. . . ." *Op. cit.*, p. 19.

23. Again General Electric provides an ideal statement of this point, *op. cit.*, p. 11.

   "These serious threats which face the profitable operation and growth of our businesses . . . must be met at their source—in each of our plant areas. A better business climate can only be brought about by going to work on *specific locally determined objectives*. These locally determined objectives may apply to local problems which affect our business and our community, or the objectives may apply to national or state problems, or a combination at those different levels . . . the job is just too big to yield to an attack on a broad front. What is needed is *direct action at the local level* to identify and eliminate deterrents to profitable operation and growth at the community level. Only when we have sufficient activity at the grass roots level and *tailored to the needs at that level* can we expect to achieve a ground swell which will make itself felt state-wide and even nationally."

24. Elihu Katz and Paul F. Lazarsfeld, *Personal Influence* (Glencoe, Illinois: The Free Press, 1955), pp. 15–30. For a detailed review see E. Litwak, "Some Policy Implications in Communications Theory with Emphasis on Group Factors," *Education for Social Work, Proceedings of the Seventh Annual Program Meeting* (New York: Council on Social Work Education, 1959), p. 99 ff.

25. Max Weber, *op. cit.*, pp. 196–244.

26. Peter Blau points out that the larger the organization becomes, the more idiosyncratic and complex the events it must cover, the more complex the rules must be to govern these events, and the less efficient general rules become, necessitating internalization of organizational values and the localization of discretion. See *Bureaucracy in Modern Society* (New York: Random House,

1956), pp. 58, 62; Julian Franklin, "Bureaucracy and Freedom," in *Man in Contemporary Society*, Vol. I, prepared by the Contemporary Civilization Staff of Columbia University (New York: Columbia University Press, 1955), pp. 941–942. Franklin suggests that large organizations are unable to deal with complex issues because of their lack of flexibility. Merton's discussion of trained incapacity in bureaucracy reflects the same issue as does Selznick's point that it is difficult to operationalize organizational goals and make them completely consistent with the self interests of the administrators. See Robert K. Merton, "Bureaucratic Structure and Personality," in R. K. Merton, A. P. Gray, B. Hockey, and H. C. Selvin, editors, *Reader in Bureaucracy* (Glencoe: The Free Press, 1952), p. 364, and Philip Selznick, "A Theory of Organizational Commitments," *ibid.*, pp. 194–203.

27. For an elaboration of this point of view see Eugene Litwak, "The Need for Models of Bureaucracy Which Permit Maintenance of Conflicting Social Relations" (mimeographed).

28. Katz and Lazarsfeld, *op. cit.*, pp. 15–134, *passim*.

29. Alex Inkeles, *Public Opinion in Soviet Russia* (Cambridge: Harvard University Press, 1951), pp. 67–134, *passim*.

30. Seymour Martin Lipset, Martin A. Trow, and James S. Coleman, *Union Democracy* (Glencoe: The Free Press, 1956), pp. 73–83, *passim*. The authors argue that governments turn to local primary groups during periods of crisis when control must be maximal. The discussion in this paper supplements this line of reasoning by suggesting that centralization and clear lines of communication (i.e., bureaucratization) will also lead to the use of primary groups for social control.

31. During its formative years the industrial bureaucracy had to differentiate itself from the surrounding agricultural community which stressed occupational nepotism. In a mature industrial society there is far less economic pressure for nepotism, which means the bureaucracy can afford to be closer to the outer community. See E. Litwak, "The Use of Extended Family Groups in the Achievement of Social Goals," *Social Problems*, 7 (Winter, 1959–60), pp. 184–185.

32. For the general conditions under which positive orientation leads to friendship, see R. K. Merton and P. F. Lazarsfeld "Friendship as Social Process," in Morroe Berger, Theodore Abel, and Charles H. Page, editors, *Freedom and Control in Modern Society* (New York: Van Nostrand, 1954). The entire body of literature dealing with reference group orientation and anticipatory socialization would be relevant. See R. K. Merton and A. S-Kitt, "Contributions to the Theory of Reference Group Behavior," in R. K. Merton and P. F. Lazarsfeld, editors, *Continuities in Social Research: Studies in the Scope and Method of the "American Soldier"* (Glencoe: The Free Press, 1957), pp. 87–89. Discussions indicating the effects of social contacts on orientations are also relevant. For a summary of this literature see Gerhart Saenger, *The Social Psychology of Prejudice*, (New York: Harper and Brothers, 1953), pp. 213–229.

33. Many of the studies on friendship indicate that they tend to be based on value or role homophily. See "Friendship as Social Process," *op. cit.*

34. Litwak, "Reference Group Theory . . . ," *op. cit.*

35. For an illustration of this phenomenon see Whyte, *op. cit.*, pp. 351 ff.

36. There are many studies which indicate that local neighborhood friendship can be affected by the physical planning of housing. For one good illustration see Festinger, *op. cit.*, pp. 158 ff. The only question at issue is whether the large organization will encourage this kind of planning.

37. See Whyte, *op. cit.*, pp. 276–277.

38. Since this is the main burden of the present paper it will be discussed below in some detail.

39. Many studies of industrial bureaucracies have pointed out the positive function of informal primary group developments for production efficiency. Blau, *op. cit.*, pp. 58–62, has highlighted one major function performed by these groups. If primary groups are functional for production then the large corporation faces the problem of reconciling this primary group development with the need to move personnel on the basis of merit and rational labor allotment. In short, the corporation is faced internally with the same problems faced by the neighborhoods. It would be argued that the corporations (a) tend to develop the same mechanisms of integration which are necessary in the neighborhood and (b) tend readily to transfer these mechanisms to the neighborhood because of the relation of local neighborhood to their internal production demands. Whyte's discussion of the "Social Ethic" would readily be translatable into the mechanism of neighborhood cohesion. See Whyte, *op. cit.*, pp. 3–46.

40. Joint participation may take place by belonging to the same organization (i.e., church) or by belonging to an affiliate (i.e., women's auxiliaries) or by informal participation (i.e., holding meetings at house when spouse is present). This must be specified when the hypothesis is researched.

41. Merton and Kitt, *op. cit.*, pp. 87–89.

42. Mills and Ulmer, *op. cit.*, Fowler, *op. cit.*

43. Though this point has not been systematically documented, the present author wrote letters in 1958 to the following concerns regarding their local community programs: General Electric, Standard Oil of New Jersey, General Motors, Du Pont, Radio Corporation of America, Ford Motor Company, and U.S. Steel. From each of these companies he received literature, and from two of the companies unsolicited requests to come down to their headquarters to discuss the problem. In all cases it was made quite clear that management policy was to maximize local community collaboration. Interviews with some of the officials at the home offices of these concerns indicate that local management does not always understand or participate in the general policy stressed by the home office. But these interviews also suggested that this lack of understanding was to a large extent a function of the newness of policy and the fact that pressures for local community identification were initially most clearly felt by top management. To point out as Schultze does (*op. cit.*, pp. 8–9), that the home office of a given corporation is undecided on its policy of local community

identification is to obscure the significant historical trend. It is further necessary to know if this indecision represents a strategic turning point in company policy—from a lack of local community concern to a greater one.

The qualitative picture suggested above must be documented by more systematic evidence if the point of view suggested here is to be accepted.

44. Schulze, *op. cit.*, p. 8.
45. Schulze, *op. cit.*, pp. 8–9.
46. Pellegrin and Coates, *op. cit.*, pp. 413–419.
47. For a classic discussion of informal modes of influence in a small town see R. S. Lynd and H. M. Lynd *Middletown in Transition* (New York: Harcourt Brace, 1937), pp. 38–39.
48. Schulze, *loc. cit.*
49. In addition, it should be pointed out that the large organizations did participate in other areas of local community life—i.e., welfare. During the 1959 local chest drive the community studied by Schulze was still reeling from the impact of a recession. Yet this community reached its chest goals much more quickly than a nearby highly prosperous university community and this was directly a consequence of the large lump sum donations of the corporations to the local community. Furthermore, since Schulze's study there has developed among many large organizations (e.g., General Electric, Ford Motor Company, Michigan Bell Telephone) a program to encourage local *political* activities among its employees. Though this is far from systematic evidence against Schulze's conclusion it should be clear to the reader that managements' views on the issue of local political affiliations are still in flux.
50. Whyte, *op. cit.*, pp. 295–296 ff; Festinger, *op. cit.*, pp. 158 ff; Litwak, "Reference Group . . . ," *op. cit.*; Angell, *op. cit.*, pp. 119–120.
51. The hypothesis advanced thus far has been put in its strongest form. However, a weaker form (more easily defended) would still be very significant. It would be that while short tenure leads to a weakening of neighborhood identification, local neighborhood groups still retain their cohesiveness and viability because of the mechanisms for acceleration of socialization. This hypothesis in effect puts a lower limit on the amount of disintegration likely to occur in modern urban centers.
52. For a complete description of the sample, see Glenn H. Beyer, Thomas W. Mackesey, and James E. Montgomery, *Houses Are for People: A Study of Home Buyer Motivations* (Ithaca: Cornell University Housing Research Center, 1955), pp. 52–54. This study was made up of five discrete samples chosen on a semi-experimental basis to determine the effects of housing design. To define these five samples a varied set of criteria was used: (a) house design; (b) income level; (c) density (in some cases all members of the same block who met the criteria were chosen and in other cases people were selected on a random area sample); (d) only people with children under 19; (e) only people who had moved into or rented a house within a three-year period were selected; (f) the sample was stratified by renters and owners. With these diverse criteria and kinds of samples it is extremely difficult to determine what constitutes

a proper statistical test of significance. As a best estimate, sign tests were used where 9 or more signs were available while the Wilcoxon matched-pairs signed-ranks test was used where less than 9 signs were available. No attempt was made to test the hypothesis within each occupational group but only to show that since the same pattern (by inspection) held in each occupational group there is little statistical likelihood that occupational distribution can explain the findings.
53. Though the wives were asked this question, the context of the question was such that it was assumed that they would include their husbands' clubs as well. A content analysis of the clubs showed that many more women's clubs were mentioned then men's. This leads to the conclusion that men's clubs may have been underreported and much of what is said must be restricted to the women's clubs until this point is clarified.
54. The specific questions asked were as follows: "Do either you or your husband have close relatives living in the Buffalo area?"; "On about what date did the family move into this house?"
55. For a recent study see Wright and Hyman, *op. cit.*, pp. 288–289.
56. Since there is some question that occupational mobility as well as occupational differences may affect voluntary associations, an occupational mobility classification was used which would permit both kinds of comparisons. For a discussion of the mobility issue see Richard F. Curtis, "Occupational Mobility and Membership in Formal Voluntary Associations: A Note on Research," *American Sociological Review*, 24 (December, 1959), pp. 846–848. In order to classify all individuals into mobility categories, they, as well as the fathers of their husbands, were gathered into the U. S. Census occupational categories and these were in turn grouped as follows:

Upper Class: (a) professional, technical, and kindred workers; and (b) managers, officials and proprietors (except farmers);
Middle Class: (a) clerical and kindred workers; and (b) sales workers;
Manual Class: (a) craftsmen, foremen and kindred workers; (b) operatives and kindred workers; (c) service, household and others; and (d) laborers.

The husband and husband's father's occupations were then cross-classified against each other to provide four occupational categories as follows:

(1) Stationary upper class: Husband and husband's father are in the upper class.
(2) Upwardly mobile: Husband's father is in a lower occupational group than husband.
(3) Downwardly mobile: Husband's father is in a higher occupational group than husband.
(4) Stationary manual: Husband's father and husband are both in the manual group.

Eliminated from the analysis are all cases where the husband's father was a farmer and where both husband and father are from the middle class. The latter group was very small and rather than blur the analysis by categorizing them with either of the stationary groups they were eliminated.

57. The sampling procedure was such that in a good part of the sample everyone on the block having children was interviewed; in the rest of the sample, there was great geographical contiguity, with most of the respondents living in houses put up by five builders. As a consequence, all respondents could be classified in terms of common neighborhoods; these neighborhoods could in turn be classified into two types—upper class and manual-middle class. Upper class neighborhoods were characterized as such where 51 percent or more of the inhabitants of the geographical area were currently members of upper class occupations. For the details of the neighborhood classification, see E. Litwak, *Primary Group Instruments of Social Control*, (Unpublished Ph.D. dissertation, Columbia University, 1958), pp. 63–64, 169–171.

58. The "extended family oriented" were those individuals who very much agreed to either one of the following two items: "I want a location which would make it easy for relatives to get together;" "I want a house with enough room for our parents to feel free to move in." However, since only four per cent of the population very much agreed to the second term, it is the first item which basically defines extended family orientation. Nuclear family orientation was defined by individuals who very much agreed to the following two items but not the preceding ones: "Generally I like the whole family to spend evenings together;" "I want a house where family members can spend time together." A non-family oriented individual is one who did not answer "I very much agree" to any of the above items. The items formed a Guttman scale pattern which is described in Litwak, *Primary Group Instruments . . . , op. cit.*, pp. 43–47.

59. For an elaboration of this analysis, see *ibid.*, pp. 169–171, 317.

60. In general it was true (*ibid.*, pp. 171–173, 240), that value conformists had more friends in the neighborhood than those who were deviants.

61. Basil G. Zimmer, "Participation of Migrants in Urban Structures," in Hatt and Reiss, *op. cit.*, pp. 736–737.

62. William H. Form, "Stratification in Low and Middle Income Housing Areas," *Journal of Social Issues* 7 (Nos. 1 and 2, 1951), pp. 116–117.

63. Freeman, *op. cit.*, pp. 532–533.

64. Wright and Hyman, *op. cit.*, p. 292.

40. The Social Structure and Political Process of Suburbia   Scott Greer

Previous papers have been concerned mostly with the central city, but the concepts of neighborhood and local community are, of course, relevant to the suburbs as well. In the case of the suburbs, however, it appears that the involvement of residents in neighborhood life often leads to an interest in political affairs at the municipal level. Scott Greer's objective is to account for this process. He distinguishes four levels of local territoriality, each representing a wider area of concern, spatially and socially: the household, the neighborhood, the local area, and the municipality. Greer develops the notion that the constraints of each level set up a demand for social organizations to be developed at a higher level until finally, people's concern for the fate of their families leads them inexorably to turn to local politics as a means of controlling their own situation and fate. He recognizes that not all suburbanites react in this fashion, that many prefer to remain isolated, to interest themselves only in neighborhood affairs, and to save their political energies for dealing with issues at the national level.

Scott Greer is Professor of Sociology and Political Science and Director of the Center for Metropolitan Studies at Northwestern University. Several of his published works are cited on page 277 of this volume.

Three aspects of suburban society are emphasized in the recent literature: the demographic characteristics of the population, the associational structure, and the political structure. Suburban population tends to be more middle-class, ethnic, and family-centered than that of the central city; in the suburb the neighborhood and perhaps the local community are more important *loci* of association than in the city; and suburbia characteristically has smaller governmental units than the cities, and has more of them.

General theory is hazy, unarticulated, and incomplete with respect to the manner in which these three aspects of suburban society are related. Those committed to each approach neglect the others, or assume a non-existent integration. Duncan and Reiss, who emphasize differences in population composition, accept political boundaries as meaningful for their analyses.[1] Those who are more concerned with ecological processes derive demographic differences from ecological position and the economic dependence of suburbs upon the central city, paying little attention to the political structures which contain and define their data.[2] On the other hand, Robert Wood's recent treatment of suburban political structure emphasizes the political form of the municipality in the suburbs as a determinant for both recruitment to suburbia and the staying power of the suburban governmental enclaves.[3] Wood does not, however, explore the interrelations between political structure and the variables emphasized by the demographers and ecologists; again, a "loose fit" is assumed. Finally, recent work by Bell postulates a "quest for community" which implies that associational structure is a major selective factor in migration to suburbia and a stabilizing factor in the suburban trend, but one which

cannot be subsumed under the "housing market" or the "political climate" of suburbia.[4]

In this paper an effort is made to integrate and order these three aspects of suburbia and to develop a systematic theory of the relationships among population type, associational patterns, communication system, and political structure congruent with the present state of research findings and capable of further test and evaluation. The paper emphasizes the organizational level of analysis, and concentrates upon the explanation of the immediate organizational structure—that is, the spatially defined group as it exists in the suburbs.

This strategy differs from several current and traditional approaches. It does not move directly from the most general levels of societal structure to the observables (ordinarily the person-to-person relationship) or *vice versa*, as is common in the work of Durkheim, Parsons, Riesman, Weber, and other analysts of large-scale society.[5] Nor does this approach assume away the nature of interaction, as in much work by contemporary ecologists.[6] Both general theory and ecology and "macroscopic" approaches which emphasize the congruity and interdependence of social trends at a high level of abstraction. If, however, one takes seriously the intermediate-level constructs implied by these approaches—social class, bureaucracy, and occupational strata—one finds striking

An expanded and revised version of a paper read at the annual meeting of the American Sociological Association, September, 1959. I wish to thank, for their critical reading and creative suggestions, Aaron Cicourel and Harold Guetzkow of Northwestern University, and Wendell Bell of The University of California, Los Angeles.

From *American Sociological Review*, Vol. XXV, No. 4 (August 1960), pp. 514–526. Reprinted by permission.

anomalies when studying the local community. Thus suburbanites, disproportionately made up of white-collar bureaucrats (the "organization men" and the "other directed"), are precisely the people who cling most fiercely to the autonomy of the small municipalities when merger with the central city is in question. Their involvement in large-scale organizational systems does not determine their behavior in the community. In view of the viability or staying power of the suburban communities, one must ask: To what extent is this behavior appropriate to occupational scenes transferred, if at all, to the residential area? To raise this question is to require that the relevant area of social action, the residential community itself, be approached with a conceptual scheme appropriate to its own characteristics as a field for social action.

Thus, the strategy adopted here is to move from the macro-level, using census data for an aggregate description, but spelling out the steps by which one reaches the micro-level of household organization. This procedure provides a method of analyzing the social structure of the suburb—neighborhood, local residential community, and municipality. Such an approach then leads back to the macrolevel. Indexes based upon census data, however, now become measures of conditions under which spatially defined social groups become probable.[7]

Population Type and Life Style

The transformation of a predominantly agricultural and rural nation into an increasingly metropolitan nation may be summarized as an increase in societal scale. Many sequences of change are fundamental causes of this process and many secondary changes ensue.[8] For present purposes, changes in the kind of *differentia* which cut across the societal unit are emphasized. Occupation, for example, is a rather unimportant differentiator within small-scale society, and ethnic variations are usually absent. In modern cities, however, nothing is more impressive than the differences in culture, life chances, deference, and power associated with variations in occupation and ethnic identity.

A third dimension emphasized here is urbanism, or life style. By urbanism we refer to the life-ways of sub-segments which have become differentiated on a continuum ranging from a familistic to an extremely urban mode of life.[9] Such a continuum first emerged from the analysis of census tract populations, and the indexes developed to measure it apply to such aggregates.[10] Toward the urban end of the continuum are neighborhoods of apartment houses with single persons, childless couples, and one-child families predominating; toward the other end are single-family dwelling units inhabited by families with several children, in which the woman, not a member of the labor force, plays the role of wife and mother. This definition of urbanism, emphasizing household organization and its consequences, excludes much that is usually encompassed in the term, but this limited meaning appears in the term, but this limited meaning appears to be especially relevant to the present analysis of spatially defined groups in the metropolis.

The familistic type of neighborhood approximates, of course, the typical image of suburbia. Although suburbs have no monopoly of such populations, they tend to be more consistently inhabited by familistic households than any other part of the urban agglomeration. One important reason for such concentration lies in the demand and supply of sites for family living. Studies of suburban residents indicate the high evaluation they place on the physical and social facilities for child-rearing and home-making, including the prerequisite for this life, private space, indoors and out. The site demanded is one which allows for the play of children in safe and "pleasant" places, space for growing flowers, vegetables, and grass, for keeping pets, for patio exercise, and the like.[11] With the existing patterns of land allocation in urban regions, however, a large area per person is available at moderate price only on the outskirts of the built-up districts. To be sure, the relationship between demand and supply is far from perfect; as Schnore implies, many persons might settle for equivalent lodgings in the middle of the city.[12] But the point is moot—until new, single-family dwellings, rather than high-rise public housing developments, replace the tenements and rowhouses near the centers, we will not know how many "suburbanites" are fleeing the city and how many are forced to move outward because no other acceptable housing is available. Meanwhile, the family-oriented population continues to seek and find its sites on the growing edge of the city.

The local associational structure of a population can be derived from such sociological characteristics as family-orientation, for contiguity indicates the likelihood of contact, homogeneity indicates the likelihood of similar interests, and population type indicates the specific content which may plausibly be inferred for those interests.[13] Thus the use of indexes which aggregate persons by geographical sub-areas implies contiguity and the relative homogeneity of the residential neighborhood. Specifically, the urbanism index developed by Shevky and Bell as a

measure of average life-style yields social attributes of the geographically defined subpopulation, hypothesized here as crucial for spatially-based social interaction.[14] The less urban and more familistic the neighborhood, the more important is the dwelling unit as a site for everyday life, and for a particular kind of life.

The type and rate of interaction, however, is not specified in detail by this set of statements. All that is proposed, at this point in the argument, is that spatially defined interaction is related to the familistic character of the suburban population. In order to translate such interaction into social structure and political process, it is necessary to relate the gross variations in population type to a theory of spatially defined-organization.

The Organizational Structure of the Suburbs

The bifurcation of work and residence is sometimes taken as one of the defining characteristics of the suburban population.[15] But this bifurcation holds for most of the population in a metropolis; any local residential area is segmental in nature, Because a living area is the site for some, but not all, of the basic social activities of its residents,[5] Janowitz calls it the "community of limited liability."[16] Such a community, however, encompasses some very crucial structures and therefore has constraining force—which allows the social scientist some predictive and explanatory power.

The definition of social organization used in the present discussion emphasizes functional interdependence. As the unit of analysis, we shall emphasize the spatially defined group. The locality group, or community, is thus viewed as a special case of the social form elsewhere defined as "an aggregate in a state of functional interdependence, from which emerges a flow of communication and a consequent ordering of behavior."[17]

Geographical contiguity, however, has no self-evident sociological meaning. It may become the basis for interdependence only when it constitutes a field for social action. We consider below three such fields, concentric in scope: the neighborhood, the local residential community, and the municipality. Using the definition of the group stated above, we ask three questions about each of these levels of organization: What constitutes the functional independence of the members? What are the channels of communication and the contents of the communication flow? What kind of ordered behavior results?

The Neighborhood If the residents of a neighborhood consist of households with familistic ways of life (and consequently similar interests) existing in close proximity, there is a high probability of intersecting trajectories of action. Since surrounding households constitute important and inescapable parts of any given household's organizational environment, there emerge problems of social order, maintenance, and aid. Specifically, it is necessary to regulate the play of children, child-adult relations, and adult-adult relations to the degree that these represent possible blocks to the orderly performance of the household's way of life. To the extent that contiguous sites overlap visually, aurally, and (sometimes) physically, it is also necessary to regulate the use of the sites. The unsightly yard, the noises of the night, the dangerously barricaded sidewalk may constitute such blocks. Finally, similarity of life routines indicates a probable similarity of equipment and tasks: thus the interchangeability of parts is possible. This may range from the traditional borrowing of a cup of bourbon to the baby-sitting pool.

To be sure, similar problems arise in the apartment house districts characterized by a highly urban way of life, but the structure of the neighborhood and the nature of the population result in different kinds of order. The lower rate of communication, due to lack of common or overlapping space, and the separation of routines in time, result in a greater dependence upon formal norms (rules of the building, laws of residency) and upon formal authorities. Thus the apartment house manager, or even the police, may be useful for the maintainance of order and the site. (Their utility, from household to *concierge* to police, is evident in the reliance placed upon such organizations by the state in various European countries). In the suburbs, however, life-style and the relationships among the sites force inter-household communication.

Communication in the neighborhood may take place at many levels, but in viewing the suburban neighborhood as an organizational unit we shall emphasize casual interaction among those whose paths necessarily intersect. In the adjoining backyards, at bus stops, and local commercial facilities, considerable social interaction is well nigh unavoidable. This interaction may become elaborated into relatively permanent cliques—kaffeeklatsch groups, pools, and the like—and frequently results in a network of close friendships. These differ from "neighboring," or participation in the neighborhood organization, just as friendship within any organization differs from the ongoing structure of activity common to the aggregate.

The resulting patterns of behavior, the

structured action, probably vary a good deal according to the type of neighborhood; however, the ubiquity of the phrase "the good neighbor" seems to indicate some generalized role system and normative structure.[18] Orderliness, accessibility in time of need, and cleanliness are salient characteristics rooted in the functional interdependence discussed above. Individual members conform to such norms (whether or not they love their neighbors) because the norms facilitate their ongoing household enterprises.

But the neighborhood is a microcosm. Nor is it the only spatially based social structure mediating between the household and the metropolis. The neighborhood then is a precipitate of interacting households; participation in its does not necessarily indicate a role in the larger local area as community or as political unit. The neighborhood produces, at the least, some order among the small enclave of residents, and communication relevant to the nearby scene.

The Local Residential Area Neighbors in the suburbs tend to have similar interests, for their ways of life have similar prerequisites, while in the local residential area interdependence results when similar interests are transformed into common interests, based upon the common field in which they operate. Spatial aggregates are the distributing units for many goods and services—public schools, commerical services, and various governmental aids and are frequently available to the individual only through his residence in a geographically delimited aggregate. To the degree that this is true of vital resources, the population of a local residential area is functionally interdependent.[19] At the same time space, as the site of common activities (street, sidewalk, park, playground), is a base of interdependence, as in the neighborhood.

The local residential community as here defined includes a number of neighborhoods. It may or may not be coterminous with a political unit. What is its minimal organizational structure? Communication relevant to the area ordinarily takes place through two channels, the community press and voluntary organizations. While each is a communication channel, we shall stress the communications function of the press and the action function of the voluntary organization.

The local community press in the suburbs, widely distributed and widely read, is a medium available to almost all residents of most local areas.[20] Its utility stems directly from the interdependence of activities within the local area; supported by local merchants, it provides support in turn for the various formal organizations which constitute the "community." To be sure, all areas are not now serviced by a community press, but so useful is the medium (and consequently, so lucrative) that it is rapidly "covering" the suburban areas of contemporary cities. As the press develops where there is a market for its services, this should occur most consistently and widely among the familistic populations.

The suburban paper is quite similar to that described by Janowitz—parochial in its interests, reporting almost exclusively upon local happenings, translating metropolitan events into their effects on the local areas, seldom reporting national events.[21] Such local personages as merchants, bureaucrats, and organizational leaders constitute the actors on this stage. Insofar as the local area is a social fact, the latter is reflected in the press and at the same time reinforced in the process of reflection, for the press in perpetuating lines of communication stabilizes norms and roles. If it is chiefly a merchandising mechanism in its economic function, it is also a public platform for the area in its social and political functions.

But what of the local area without a separate government? In this case, what kind of structured action is indicated as the third term in the definition of the area as a social structure? Noting again that spatially defined organization in the residential area is loose, unstructured, and does not engage all of the residents, here we emphasize participation in the local formal organizations. Such organizations are segmental in their membership and purposes; they include those residents who are dependent upon them for basic necessities to their way of life. Community-oriented organizations, improvement associations, child-centered organizations, some fraternal and service clubs are examples. They are particular to the area, their membership is largely limited to those living there, and they are instruments of persuasion and control with respect to various community problems, projects, and festivals. Furthermore, if there is no political structure they are the *only* existing structures through which an interdependence specific to the area (issuing in local problems), communicated through the press (as "community issues"), become manifested in social action.

The Suburban Municipality The typical political structure of metropolitan suburbia viewed as a whole is a crazy-quilt of many small municipalities having various eccentric shapes and displaying little obvious order in their boundaries. It is likely, however, that many of these municipalities are roughly coterminous with one or more social communities of the kind discussed above. To the degree that this is the case, the seemingly arbitrary lines on the map may come to represent social communities. The congruence of municipal boundaries with a local residential community permits the translation of common interests into a polity. The common field of activity (and the various segmental interests sited in this field) is contained within a formal organizational structure having the power to control, within wide limits, some of the basic goods and services of the residents. Thus streets, parks, schools (and, to a degree, commerical and residential development) are not only sources of interdependence—their control is so structured as to allow effective action by the interdependent population. Furthermore, taxation, police power, and other governmental attributes are assigned to the local municipality.

Where such is the case, an additional level is added to the structured action which results from interdependence and the flow of communication within the residential community: political action within a political community.[22] Communication now incorporates well defined political norms and roles, the latter including the governmental official, political leader, voter, local taxpayer, and so on. But this type of organizational structure does not displace the kinds of voluntary community organizations indicated earlier. Certain modes of action tend to become allocated to the governmental organization; others remain the functions of private and semi-private groups (including the neighborhoods).

The organizational structure of suburbia may be summarized as follows: (1) The overlapping activities of households result in the neighborhoods, which exist as a kind of network spreading throughout the familistic population (for neighborhoods overlap as do households, and the neighborhood structure of a metropolis fre-

TABLE 1. SOCIAL-POLITICAL STRUCTURES OF SUBURBIA

	Source of Interdependence	Channels of Communication	Structured Action
Neighborhood:	Overlapping field Similar interests	Informal interaction Casual visiting	Regulated interaction Maintenance of the site Mutual aid
Local Area:	Common field Common interests	Community press Local organizations Informal interaction	Segmental interests protection Diffuse community action (outside political structure)

Municipality:	Common field
	Common interests
	Common organizational
	  structure coterminous
	  with both
		Local governmental
		  functions
		Local political orga-
		  nizations
		Local non-political
		  organizations
		Community press
		Informal interaction
			Law-abiding (local), tax-paying
			
			Voting, holding office
			Attending meetings
			Use of bureaucratic structure for
			  complaints and appeals
			Organization of electoral
			  campaigns

quently resembles St. Augustine's definition of God, an infinite circle whose center is everywhere and whose periphery is nowhere). (2) Larger residential areas with a degree of functional interdependence constitute "communities of limited liability." They exhibit communication through informal relations and the community press, and action through voluntary private and semi-private organizations. (3) In many cases, political units are roughly coterminous with, or include, one or more social communities. Neighborhoods are probably nearly omnipresent, though a network need not include all households; so are communities, but they vary widely in degree of organization; political communities may or may not exist. In the summary presented in Table 1, each analytical category is sketched in for each organizational level.

Relations between Organizational Levels in Suburbia

The four types of organization discussed above—household, neighborhood, local

residential area, municipality—are, generally, of ascending order as to size and descending order as to the probability of face-to-face or "primary" relations. They are also arranged in an order which indicates an increasing possibility of common "public" interest and action and, therefore, of policy relevance. Thus as formal policy becomes possible, representation rather than universal participation is a necessity.

The neighborhood, as the first level beyond the individual household, is very likely to generate interhousehold friendships and visiting patterns; neighboring then may be part of the informal communication flow of the area. The neighborhood, however, is not apt to form polity beyond the conventional "rules of the road," nor is it apt to be a representational unit for any larger collectivity. The social products of the neighborhood *per se* are small-scale order, mutual aid, and friendship. The lack of a formal structure oriented to the collective needs and problems of the inhabitants probably facilitates the performance of those minimal tasks discussed earlier: the informal and, indeed, often unspoken norms relevant to the group allow for considerable flexibility and effective control of deviation. But unformalized norms and unspecialized roles are suitable only for a given routine, and preferably one requiring little precision. The self-ordering of the neighborhood is an ordering of routine interaction, with wide limits of tolerance.

For these reasons, the neighborhood is not formally related to any other level of spatially based organization: it is too small to constitute an administrative sub-unit of a larger system and too informal to constitute a base for independent representation in a larger system. The interaction of households produces a luxuriant network of neighborhoods in the suburbs, but these have little direct significance for the polity.[23] Their chief contribution to other organizational systems is one of communication: they are a site for conversational ferment.

The household is related to the larger local area through formal organizations sited in the area. These include public and business structures and such "auxiliary" voluntary formal organizations as PTA and service club, as well as voluntary organizations built upon independent functional bases. In general, local organizations are concerned with common activities of specific segments of the residential population in the area.[24] The same household activities and interests which produce involvement in these area-wide segmental organizations also produce interest in the flow of local communication through informal relationships and the community press. Thus household members are differentially related to local formal organizations, while their reading of the press (and conversation with others) permits a familiarity with the organizations and actors of the local areas as a whole.

In the present approach, the agencies of local government, although they possess distinctive political functions, are also viewed as segmental structures. For, despite its conventional identity with a geographical space and its population, local government has only limited powers and duties and affects only a small part of the residents' activities.

The non-governmental organizational structure of the local area is related to the suburban municipality through the congruence of fields of action (and convergence or conflict of interests between voluntary organizations and governmental agencies. Possible interrelations of the two kinds of structures include, for example, the use of private organizations as representatives of community interests before the government, the overlapping leadership role within both government and private organizations, and the private organization as a political faction or party. Each of these would strengthen the argument that the local government is "truly representative of the community;" at the same time, each would have important consequences for the effectiveness of, and the constraints upon, local governmental agencies in dealing with problems and issues.

Thus, we should expect an overlapping membership between voluntary organizations and the municipal electorate. If the members of local organizations are exceptionally sensitive to community news as reported in the press, and if at the same time the community press reports governmental affairs extensively and frequently, the persons most active in local voluntary organizations should be highly informed about the *dramatis personae* of community polity. Insofar as they are committed members of common interest organizations, they would be particularly aware of governmental decisions, for these frequently affect voluntary organizations. And, even though they do not read the local paper, they should be unusually aware of information concerning the local residential community through their organizational activities, neighboring, and local friendships.

In short, neighborhood structures involve a large proportion of the suburban population, are loosely related to the local area communication system, but are not formally related to larger organizational networks. The local residential community and the municipality both involve a smaller proportion of the population (and one that is largely composed of the same individuals), but their scale and functions are such that they "stand for" the total population with respect to many basic activities.

Types of Relationship to Community Organization

If there are predictable and orderly relationships between households, neighborhoods, residential communities, and municipalities, we can spell out the possible logical combinations, and can examine the distribution of community roles and the consequences for forms of behavior other than those built into the typology. In constructing types we emphasize neighborhood, local area, and governmental structure.

From the previous discussion may be deduced three levels of relationship to local social structure: (1) involvement in the small-scale system of the neighborhood, (2) a role in segmental structures based upon certain interests common to some people in the local area, and (3) a place in the flow of communication representing the local area "as a whole."

Dichotomizing each attribute for simplicity yields eight logically possible combinations. Some of these, however, are inconsistent with the framework sketched out earlier. If we consider separately the possible relations between neighborhood interaction, community roles, and access to the communication flow, the theory, with its emphases upon the communication functions of neighboring and of the local press and the social consequences of roles in local organizations, leads to the conclusions that there are no necessary relationships between (1) neighboring and community roles and (2) neighboring and reading the local press, but that there *is* a necessary relationship between a community role and participation in the communication network, either through neighboring or the press or both. A person with a role in the local organizational network but who neither reads the paper nor visits with his neighbors behaves inconsistently with the general hypothesis.

Following the procedures and qualifications discussed above results in the "organizational types" presented in Table 2. The rubrics in the right-hand column of the table are something more than summaries and something less than fully explicated types. The local "isolate," on the one hand, and the "multi-level participator," on the other, are clearly extremes. "Neighborhood actors" have defined positions only within the neighborhood system (although they may read the paper for gossip and entertainment). "Voyeurs" read the papers only as spectators of the community; they do not hold positions in role-systems and are otherwise comparable to isolates. "Community actors" may avoid their neighbors but, through common commitments, may still participate in area-wide formal organizations.

TABLE 2. "ORGANIZATIONAL TYPES" IN SUBURBIA

	Neighborhood Interaction	Local Community Role	Access to Communication Flow	Type
I.	Yes	Yes	Yes	Multi-level participator
II.	Yes	Yes	No	Community actor (A)
III.	No	Yes	Yes	Community actor (B)
IV.	Yes	No	Yes	Neighborhood actor (A)
V.	Yes	No	No	Neighborhood actor (B)
VI.	No	No	Yes	Voyeur
VII.	No	No	No	Isolate
VIII.	No	Yes	No	Error

Population Type and Organizational Type
Certain associations are implied by the theory. Life style as the basis for similar interests at the neighborhood level and for common interests at the local area level should be a key variable in producing associational patterns. Thus, considering the urbanism dimension of the geographical subarea as a rough measure of life style among contiguous populations, we expect neighboring to increase consistently as urbanism declines. Within a sample from neighborhoods at a given level of urbanism, however, variation in neighboring should be a result of variation in the life style of individual households: neighboring should increase with homeownership, number of children in the family, presence of wife in the household during the day. (The opposite extreme is the single person or childless couple with a working wife, who live in a rented apartment.)

One may object that the latter attributes of individual households would be a simpler and more reliable index than the urbanism of the geographical sub-area, clearly a possibility. However, neighborhoods are aggregates of persons in given sub-areas, and such aggregates cannot be inferred from a sample that is random with respect to neighborhood. If individual household attributes are the only data,

we cannot allow for "the neighboring type of people" who live in areas where most women work, there are few children, and neighboring is difficult.[25] Contrariwise, considering only the average nature of the neighborhood, we lose the deviants within it. For these reasons, both aggregate and household attributes are significant.

The same logic should lead to similar relationships between the urbanism of the residential population and membership in local organizations. Commitment to the areas, as measured by commitment to home area, as measured by commitment to home, public schools, and other household investments, should increase as urbanism declines. Within the households residing in given types of area, however, those who are most concerned with the local residential area should be most apt to belong to formal organizations of a "community" nature.

The prediction of discrepancy between neighboring and activity in community organizations is based upon the hypothesis that in some familistic areas the neighborhood interaction system includes persons whose interests are deviant (for example, the post-parental couple, the non-family female), but that such interaction does not necessarily lead to a concern with broader community interest. And, *vice versa*, persons may be "good citizens" in the community at large although they are not involved with immediate neighbors. Thus urbanism should be related to both neighboring and community participation, but not necessarily through the identical group of actors.

Finally, the urbanism of the neighborhood should be associated with access to the local communication flow. The same variations in household commitment producing increased participation in neighborhood and local area organizational networks should increase the value of communication relevant to the residential community. As a consequence of these relationships, the constructed types of local "actors" (see Table 2) should vary with the urbanism of the neighborhood. Moving from urban districts towards familistic suburbs, we should find an increasing proportion of the adult population involved in the small-scale neighborhood and in the larger residential area as organizational systems—with isolates becoming a decreasing proportion.

A Note on Social Rank A relationship is often postulated between participation in formal community organizations and social rank (occupation, education, and income levels of the respondents or their neighborhoods or both). With social rank, however, as with age and sex, we are dealing with role variations which cut across the larger society, and these should have about the same effect *within* each type of neighborhood and, within the neighborhood, within each category of local actors. When social rank is controlled, therefore, community participational type should remain a major differentiator with respect to involvement and competence in the affairs of the local residential area.

Nevertheless, we would expect more community actors in upper-status neighborhoods, and among persons with more education, income, and with higher prestige occupations, for these persons may be expected to have more organizational memberships. At each level of social rank, however, the urbanism of the neighborhood should be salient, for it reflects the variations in life style relevant to spatially defined organization. Thus isolates should vary little by social rank, once the urbanism of the neighborhood is controlled. The chief effect of decreasing social rank would then be a decrease in community-level actors and an increase in neighborhood-level actors. Lower-status neighborhoods of low urbanism would be, not so much "massified and fragmented," as organized on the small-scale basis of the neighborhood. At each level of social rank, urbanism should make a major difference in the distribution of participational types.

This theory leads then to the proposition that urbanism *as such* has an independent predictive power for the identification of types of community actors because it indicates aspects of the population conducive to a greater or lesser generation of spatially defined groups. A corollary proposition is that type of community actor is a more powerful predictive instrument for many kinds of *local* organizational behavior than the social rank of the resident or his neighborhood and municipality.

Governmental Structure It was indicated above that governmental structure adds another organizational level, provides a "mold" for community activity, a focus for the policy-oriented, and a set of roles for the actors on the stage of the local community press. As an additional segmental organization, local government is a voluntary formal organization in that it provides further opportunities for involvement in the residential area's affairs. Therefore, if residential sub-areas are classified by organizational and governmental structure, we should expect the following rank order of competence and involvement in local affairs: areas with (1) autonomous organizational and governmental structures, (2) autonomous organizational but not governmental structures, (3) autonomous governmental but not organizational structures, and (4) areas with neither structure. Type (1) would include the suburban municipality which is a "social fact" as well as a governmental artifact; (2) would include the "local communities" in the unincorporated suburbs; (3) would probably be found in the areas now surrounded by the central city but still retaining political autonomy or in the areas immediately contiguous to the more urban neighborhoods of the city; (4) would be found, for the most part, in the central city.

Such a scheme points up the probability that incorporation will tend to increase public communication and action within a familistic area, for government summarizes many segmental common interests. If we consider the further possibility of applying the organizational types presented earlier to the probabilities of interaction within the political system, the analysis becomes more pertinent to the general problem of relating political and non-political social systems.

Political System and Residential Community

Three general types of actors summarize the seven types presented in Table 2: isolates, neighborhood actors, and community actors. These terms are used below as shorthand for the description of organizational conditions and memberships producing each type.

With respect to the political and proto-political processes in suburbia, we may ask: To what degree does the suburban population participate in a local political system? Participation here refers to *competence* (the possession of adequate and accurate information on the political process) and *involvement* (including voting in local elections).

Interaction within the community-wide system is a clue to probable involvement in the polity (and, consequently, voting, electioneering, standing for office, and other manifestations). We assume that the action role is pursued only within a group context, and that the membership groups available in the suburbs are the various community-wide organizations. Such membership is thus considered a prerequisite to involvement in community politics; similarly involvement emerges from a functional commitment to the local area at other levels. Involvement, however, does not necessarily imply competence. We consider competence as the probable result of participation in the flow of communication *relevant to the community-wide system*. This may result from informal interaction (friendship or neighboring) or the community press or both. The general types of community actors should behave quite differently within the role system of the local municipality.—These hypotheses are suggested by the following tabular presentation:

	Involve-ment	Com-petence
Isolates	Low	Low
Neighborhood actors	Higher	Higher
Community actors	Highest	Highest

The difference between political settings is crucial for testing the general hypothesis of organizational scale. If the three types of actors are further categorized by the political structure of their residential areas, isolates should differ little in their competence, whether they live in unincorporated or incorporated areas: they should be largely incompetent. Neighbors should be relatively incompetent in each area. But community actors in the incorporated areas should have more knowledge about community organization, for there is more to know. For example, they should know a larger number of leaders, for their governmental structure provides such parochial leaders. When political leaders are subtracted from their knowledge, however, they should have a general backlog of information on local leadership quite similar to those who live in unincorporated areas: organization type should be a predictor when political structure is controlled.

Two implications may be drawn from this discussion which are relevant to the current controversy about metropolitan governmental reform. First, the areas in which a viable, small-scale, local governmental process is likely are those of familistic populations, within which there are many community actors and few isolates—whether or not such areas are now incorporated. Second, the strength of the resistance to the "merger" of the central city and the suburbs should be found concentrated in those areas with a strong organizational network involving a large proportion of the adults in the residential community. In fact, the rank order of opposition should be correlated with the rank order, stated above, of competence and involvement in local affairs by areal attributes. At the low end of the resulting continuum would be those who live in the highly urban neighborhoods of the central city, for whom the local residential community has little meaning—and these persons are usually strong supporters of metropolitan "integration."

Some Derived Hypotheses

Further applications of the theoretical scheme are possible and tempting. It is desirable at this point, however, to apply the theory to some derived observational requirements. The following hypotheses, implicit or explicit in the above discussion, merely illustrate a much larger number of possibilities. They are now being tested against data from a large-scale survey of the suburban population of one of the major metropolitan areas. The hypotheses are stated briefly, but are consistent with the foregoing theoretical presentation.

Urbanism, Life-style, and Organizational Participation Thirty-four specific hypotheses under this category may be presented as the following six propositions:

(a) Despite the varying effects of social rank, ethnicity, and the characteristics of individual municipalities, urbanism is negatively related to neighboring, participation in formal organizations situated in the area, readership of the local press for local community news, and the incidence of community actors; urbanism is positively related to the incidence of isolates and voyeurs (hypotheses 1 through 6).

(b) When urbanism is controlled, social rank is positively related to the incidence of community actors, and negatively related to the incidence of neighborhood actors (hypotheses 7 and 8).

(c) Despite the varying effects of unit characteristics, the presence of children in the household is positively related to neighboring, participation in formal organizations situated in the area, and the incidence of community actors; it is negatively related to the incidence of isolates and voyeurs (hypotheses 8 through 11).

(d) When the presence of children in the household is controlled (and despite the varying effects of other unit characteristics), urbanism continues to have discriminating power with respect to the six participational variables indicated in (a) above (hypotheses 12 through 17).

(e) When the urbanism of the census tract of residence is controlled (and despite the varying effects of other unit characteristics), the presence of children in the household has discriminating power with respect to the participational variables indicated in (a) above (hypotheses 17 through 22).

(f) Despite the varying effects of other unit variables, urbanism and the presence of children in the household are conducive to the same types of organizational participation. Specifically, extremely high participation rates characterize those who live in low urban areas and have children, with respect to neighboring, belonging to local organizations, and reading the local press; the opposite holds for those without children in highly urban areas. With respect to the constructed types, the most community actors and the fewest isolates and voyeurs inhabit low urban neighborhoods with children in the households; the opposite holds for high urban neighborhoods among childless households (hypothesis 23 through 34).

Organizational Participation and Political Behavior Forty additional specific hypotheses are stated as the following seven more general formulations:

(a) Because it indicates involvement in the local area as an organizational system, participation in local organizations is positively related to voting, naming local leaders, and knowing the electoral rules. Because it indicates participation in the flow of communication in the area, readership of the press is related to naming leaders and knowing the rules. This also holds for neighboring with respect to naming leaders and knowing the rules. Neither neighboring nor readership of the press has a strong relationship with voting when organizational membership and the other unit of the pair is controlled (hypotheses 35 through 43).

(b) When the logically possible combinations are reduced to five, isolates (who neither read, neighbor, nor belong), voyeurs (who neither neighbor nor belong but who read the press), neighborhood actors (who neighbor but do not belong), deviants (who belong but neither neighbor nor read the press), and community actors (who belong and either neighbor, read, or do both), the following relative distributions result:

Type	Competence		Involvement
	Knows		
	Names	Rules	Votes
Isolates	—	—	—
Voyeurs	+	+	—
Neighbors only	+	+	+
Community actors	+ +	+ +	+ +
Deviants	—	—	+

(Hypotheses 44 through 58).

(c) When age, sex, and education (as an index of social rank) are controlled, each age, sex, and educational category will manifest the same variation by organization type (hypotheses 59 through 64).

(d) If competence and involvement are considered simultaneously, those competent and not active should be concentrated among the voyeurs, those active and not competent among the deviants, those active and competent among the community actors, those neither active nor competent, among the isolates (hypotheses 65 through 68).

(e) The rank order of the distribution of community actor types should be (1) local area coinciding with municipality, (2) local area without municipality, (3) municipality without local area, and (4) district with neither residential area organization nor political structure (hypothesis 69). This, in turn, should result in a similar rank order of ability to name leaders (hypothesis 70). The same rank order should hold for resist-ance to metropolitan integration movements (hypothesis 71).

(f) With incorporation controlled, the organizational types should have similar ability to name local leaders (hypothesis 72).

(g) If political office-holders and past office-holders are eliminated, organizational types in incorporated and unincorporated areas should have similar abilities to name local leaders, although a somewhat larger number should be able to do so in the incorporated areas. Therefore, naming of nonpolitical leaders should be related to the urbanism of the area (hypotheses 73 and 74).

NOTES

1. Otis Dudley Duncan and Albert J. Reiss, Jr., *Social Characteristics of Rural and Urban Communities:* 1950, New York: Wiley, 1956.
2. E.g., Walter T. Martin, "The Structuring of Social Relationships Engendered by Suburban Residence," *American Sociological Review*, 21 (August, 1956) pp. 446–453.
3. Robert C. Wood, *Suburbia, Its People and Their Politics,* Boston: Houghton Mifflin, 1959. See especially Chapter 4, "The Nature of Suburbia."
4. Wendell Bell, "Social Choice, Life Styles, and Suburban Residence," in W. A. Dobriner, editor, *The Suburban Community,* New York: Putnam's 1958, pp. 225–247.
5. Emile Durkheim, *Suicide,* translated by John A. Spaulding and George Simpson, edited with an Introduction by George Simpson, Glencoe, Ill.: Free Press, 1951; Talcott Parsons, *The Social System,* Glencoe, Ill.: Free Press, 1952; David Riesman, Reuel Denney, and Nathan Glazer, *The Lonely Crowd,* New Haven: Yale University Press, 1950; Max Weber, *The Theory of Social and Economic Organizations,* translated by A. M. Henderson and Talcott Parsons, edited with an Introduction by Talcott Parsons, New York: Oxford University Press, 1947. To bring matters up to date, see the work of the Detroit Area Study, which moves immediately from individual characteristics to such societal dimensions as the stratification system: *A Social Profile of Detroit, 1956, A Report of the Detroit Area Study of the University of Michigan,* Ann Arbor: Detroit Area Study, Department of Sociology and the Survey Research Center of the Institute for Social Research, 1957.
6. Amos H. Hawley, *Human Ecology: A Theory of Community Structure,* New York: Ronald, 1950;
   Otis Dudley Duncan and Beverly Duncan, "Residential Distribution and Occupational Stratification," *American Journal of Sociology,* 60 (March, 1955), pp. 493–503; Leo F. Schnore, "The Growth of Metropolitan Suburbs," *American Sociological Review,* 22 (April, 1957), pp. 165–173.
7. In the exposition of the theory that follows, the author has assumed the dogmatic but simplifying device of expressing many discrete hypotheses as valid propositions. These hypotheses, couched in testable form, conclude this paper.
8. See, e.g., Fred Cottrell, *Energy and Society,* New York: McGraw-Hill, 1955; Godfrey and Monica Wilson, *The Analysis of Social Change,* Cambridge: At the University Press, 1954; Eshref Shevky and Wendell Bell, *Social Area Analysis,* Stanford: Stanford University Press, 1955.
9. The term *urbanism* is used to refer to a concept Shevky has denoted as "urbanization" and Bell as "family status" or "familism." In general, urbanism implies that the higher the index reading, the nearer the approach to an ideal typical "urbanism as a way of life." Both the earlier terms are awkward, have disturbing connotations in the literature, and are sometimes downright misleading.
10. The index of urbanism is discussed in Shevky and Bell, *op. cit.*, pp. 17 and 55–56. For evidence of the independence and importance of this dimension, see the factor analysis studies: Wendell Bell, *A Comparative Study of the Methodology of Urban Analysis,* unpublished Ph.D. thesis, University of California, Los Angeles, 1952; Maurice D. Van Arsdol, Jr., Santo F. Camilleri, and Calvin Schmid "The Generality of Urban Social Area Indexes," *American Sociological Review,* 23 (June, 1958), pp. 277–284. For a test of the index, using sample

survey data, see Scott Greer and Ella Kube, "Urbanism and Social Structure," in Marvin Sussman, editor, *Community Structure and Analysis*, New York: Crowell, 1959, pp. 93–112.

11. See the findings reported by Bell (in Dobriner, *op. cit.*) and by Richard Dewey in "Peripheral Expansion in Milwaukee County," *American Journal of Sociology*, 53 (May, 1948), pp. 417–422. Seventy-two per cent of Bell's respondents who had moved from Chicago into two middle-rank suburbs listed physical characteristics as a reason for moving to the suburbs; 50 per cent of their responses reflected improvement in privacy and geographical space. Dewey's respondents gave as reasons for their move, in order, "better for children," "less congested," "cleaner," and "larger lot," as the four most popular ones.

12. Schnore, *op. cit.* A polemical statement of the possibility is found in William H. Whyte, Jr., "Are Cities Un-American?" in Editors of *Fortune*, *The Exploding Metropolis*, Garden City, N. Y.: Doubleday, 1958.

13. This argument is presented in another context by Wendell Bell in "A Probability Model for the Measurement of Ecological Segregation," *Social Forces*, 32 (May, 1954), pp. 357–364.

14. By relative homogeneity we mean no more than the probability that differences by a chosen criterion are greater between areas than is true within each area.

15. See, e.g., Martin, *op. cit.*

16. Morris Janowitz, *The Community Press in an Urban Setting*, Glencoe, Ill.: Free Press, 1952. See esp. Chapter 7, "The Social Dimensions of the Local Community."

17. Scott Greer, *Social Organization*, New York: Random House, 1955. The spatially defined group and the changing nature of the urban sub-community are discussed in Chapters 4 and 5.

18. The norms may vary of course by social rank and ethnicity; to simplify the argument the effects of these dimensions are considered irrelevant in the major hypotheses. Social rank is discussed in a later section.

19. The reader may question the existence of such "local areas" as social fact. However, scattered evidence indicates that the map of the city breaks down into sub-units for the residential population, whether or not these are congruent with ecologically defined "natural areas." The nature and consequences of economic decentralization are explored by Foley, of social and economic decentralization by Janowitz. See Donald L. Foley, "The Use of Local Facilities in a Metropolis," *American Journal of Sociology*, 56 (November, 1950), pp. 238–246, and *Neighbors or Urbanites? The Study of a Rochester Residential District*, Rochester, N. Y.: University of Rochester, 1952; and Janowitz, *op. cit.* A more recent study reports a strong definition of sub-areas among residents of Boston. See Laurence Ross, *The Local Community in the Metropolis*, unpublished Ph.D. thesis, Harvard University, 1959. Furthermore. 98 per cent of the residents of suburban St. Louis County accept the notion and give a distinctive name to their residential area (unpublished research report, Metropolitan St. Louis Survey)

20. Thus 84 per cent of Janowitz's respondents were readers of their local press (*op. cit.*). Similar findings are reported for a Los Angeles suburban sample of those who received the paper (85 per cent) over 92 per cent were regular readers; see Scott Greer and Ella Kube, *Urban Worlds: A Comparative Study of Four Los Angeles Areas*, Los Angeles: Laboratory in Urban Culture, 1955 (processed).

21. Janowitz, *op. cit.*

22. This does not imply an automatic evolution which presumes that through time interdependence must result in communication and order. The precise processes by which organizational structures evolve are not spelled out here; they would be desirable but are not essential to the purposes of the present paper.

23. The reader will recall the widely reported relationship between the voting of respondents and their neighbors; hoewever, the significant variables in the present discussion are quite different. Reference here is to *participation* (not direction of vote) in *local* elections, while neighbors are distinguished from friends (the latter is a subcategory). Near-dwelling friends may indeed influence voting in Presidential elections; this is not the proposition presented above.

24. They may be coded as: child-centered, community-political and fraternal-service, for those most intimately related to the affairs of the local residential area. The remaining voluntary organizations may be usefully coded as either work-related or church-related.

25. Greer and Kube, *op. cit.*, report a diminution in neighboring among non-working women, as the proportion of working women in a neighborhood increases. They explain this as a consequence of declining opportunities for neighboring.

Urban Community Power and Decision-Making

41. Power in Local Communities | William Spinrad

The paper by Greer, which concluded the previous section of this volume is indicative of the growing interest in the politics of suburban communities. William Spinrad deals mostly with the problems of politics and decision-making in cities. Using the extensive literature on community power developed over the last two decades by political scientists and sociologists, he discusses several key issues that are of paramount scholarly concern in this field. How should power and influence be defined in order to make them relevant to the functioning of cities? What research procedures can be employed for discovering the locus of power and the methods for arriving at decisions? Which groups attempt to wield power and what combination of motivations and situations lead them to seek influence over events? What is the power structure of the cities?

Spinrad answers the last question by coming out on the side of those who believe in the pluralistic nature of urban decision-making. In opposing the emphasis placed on business influence in many early studies, he argues that businessmen are generally reluctant to expose themselves to criticism from the local electorate. The important decision-makers are more likely to be top government officials and their professional advisers. Even when business groups enter the political arena—as they do, say to support downtown renewal—they share power and influence with these other local people.

William Spinrad is Professor of Sociology at Adelphi University and the author of many articles in the field of political sociology.

Since Floyd Hunter published his study of "Regional City" about a decade ago, many social scientists have devoted their attention to the study of community power.[1] Whatever comments we will make on some of the specific material, we would initially like to welcome this trend in the allocation of the professional resources of the social science fraternity. Particularly in the area of community research, this had been a relatively neglected subject, with the conspicuous exception of the Lynds' monumental study of Middletown.[2] The detailed cataloguing of the status structure was too often the dominant, in fact sometimes the only, theme. Longing for a simple stratification model in which everyone fits, more or less, into an obviously assignable place, the students of American communities tended to avoid the more complicated task of striving to learn "who got things done," why and how. It was, therefore, especially pleasing to read that in the old New England city of New Haven very few of the "social notables," the members of status-exclusive clubs, had any crucial role in the community decision-making process under review.[3]

The efforts at community power analysis have been many, the findings plentiful, the interpretations challenging. But, despite several suggestive attempts, thorough systematization is still wanting; the relation between the "power variable" and the entire community social structure is barely sketched. Let this preliminary appraisal not be misconstrued. The critique which follows is prefaced not only with praise for a worthwhile direction of social scientific inquiry but an appreciation of the valuable material that already exists. It is offered as a modest set of directives for future work in the area.

Several recently published volumes provide a springboard for an excursion into the field. An elaborate compendium of existing data on "public leadership" by Bell, Hill, and Wright offers little assistance to those who seek a comprehensive organization of ideas on the subject.[4] Marshalling a vast array of information, it initially classifies the methods by which leadership is located. The categories listed are: formal position, reputation, degree of social participation, opinion leadership, and role in specific decisions or events. The probability that each type will be drawn from particular demographic groups —sex, age, race, nationality, religion, social class, etc.—is assessed on the basis of reported investigations. Finally, the authors present the various findings on public attitudes towards leadership and motivations for leadership. As a catalogue of source material, the book can serve a useful purpose. But no attempt is made to organize or interpret the information. There are thus no summary statements, no attempts to develop models, no formulated clues to assist further discussions about community power. And these are precisely what are needed.

This brief consideration of the volume includes one additional caution. In its formulations, "public leadership" becomes a gross, diffuse concept. The "opinion leader," for instance, can hardly be equated with the other categories. Directed towards locating interpersonal communication networks, one general conclusion from opinion leadership research is that many, many people influence some others on some questions.[5] Such inquiries, valuable in their own sphere, scarcely provide any insight into community "power."

From *Social Problems*, Vol. 12 (Winter 1965), pp. 335–356. Reprinted by permission of the author, the journal, and The Society for the Study of Social Problems.

A meaningful organization of the field would be a posing of the major contending analyses. This, in essence, is the function of a symposium entitled *Power and Democracy in America.*[6] Despite its rather grandiose title and the variety of subjects considered by the major contributors and the editors, the core of the book is the debate between two students of community power, Delbert Miller and Robert Dahl. Utilizing their own researches and other relevant material, the two scholars generally represent and expound the two opposite sides of the methodological and analytical conflict that has characterized recent community power discussion. Miller favors the "reputational" form of investigation and finds a pyramidal, quasi-monolithic structure dominated by a "business elite" more or less typical. He is thus quite in accord with the findings of Hunter's original study. Dahl, utilizing "event analysis," searches for evidence of specific decision makers on particular issues, and concludes that a relatively pluralistic power structure is more prevalent. Of course, the divergencies are more complex and detailed, but these are the summary statements around which the discussion evolves.

The reputational technique, which has, with many variations, become fairly widespread in use, seeks to get knowledgeable informants to select, from a list of leading figures in community organizations and institutional areas, those whom they considered most powerful in "getting things done." Those chosen were then interviewed to learn about the personal and social relations among them, and which people they would themselves solicit if they wanted something adopted or achieved. Reviewing many studies with this research emphasis, including his own "Pacific City," Miller's conclusions are, essentially, the following:[7]

1. Businessmen are overrepresented among "key influentials" and dominate community policy-making in most communities.[8]
2. Local governments are weak power centers. The elected officials are mostly small businessmen, local lawyers, and professional politicians. Policy on important questions is formulated by organized interests groups under the influence of the economic dominants. City councils merely respond to their pressures.
3. Representatives of labor, education, religious, and "cultural" groups are rarely key influentials, are underrepresented in city councils.
4. In vivid contrast, Miller reports his investigations of "English City," like "Pacific City" a seaport community of about 500,000 population. Businessmen constitute only a minority of the "key influentials." Labor is significantly represented. There is also an appreciable number from educational, religious, welfare, and "status" leaderships. Furthermore, the city council is the major arena of community decision making, the party organizations the directing groups.

Noting differences between "Regional City" and "Pacific City," Miller does not insist that the power pattern is identical in all American communities. In fact, he develops a typology of possible structures which will be later considered. But the modal type is clearly sketched, particularly in contrast with the findings of his British study.

Dahl's counter propositions are based primarily on his study of New Haven, summarized in the symposium and more fully elaborated in his book *Who Governs?*[9] The power structure of New Haven is seen as relatively pluralistic or, to use his terminology, one of "dispersed inequalities," a metamorphosis from earlier days of oligarchal dominance by "aristocratic patricians" and "enterpreneurs" successively. This is initially indicated in the change in political leadership with the rise of the "ex plebeians" from various ethnic groups, often with proletarian backgrounds. The attention is, however, more to the examination of decision-leadership in three issue areas—political nominations, public education, and urban redevelopment, which Dahl insists are both representative and salient. The method in such "event analysis" is typically one of chronological narration of who did what, when, and what effect it had, in this instance supplemented by a more precise systematic tabulation of the kinds of people who held formal positions in the organizations concerned with the above issues and of those who initiated or vetoed significant decisions.

The refutation of the business dominance thesis is quite explicit. Some two hundred "economic notables" were located. Within the issue-areas studied, a significant number occupied formal positions only in connection with urban redevelopment (about fifty), of which seven were actually considered decision leaders. None were formally involved in public education, a handful in political parties.

Even within the area of urban redevelopment, the decision-making role of businessmen was considered minor. Their contributions came largely through their participation in the "Citizens Action Committee," organized by the Mayor with the objective of legitimizing decisions and providing an arena in which objections to the program could be anticipated and avoided. Neither the Committee, nor individual businessmen or business groups, were responsible for many crucial decisions. Dahl believes that they could, if vigorously

in opposition, have blocked proposals, but the political officials, led by the Mayor, prevented such contingencies by a "capacity for judging with considerable precision what the existing beliefs and the commitments of the men on the CAC would compel them to agree to if a proposal were presented in the proper way, time, and place."[10] In general, business groups possess many "resources," but they are also limited by many power "liabilities," so that they simply appeared as "one of the groups out of which individuals sporadically emerge to influence the policies and acts of city officials."[11] "Like other groups in the community, from the Negroes on Dixwell Avenue to teachers in the public school, sometimes the Notables have their way and sometimes they do not."[12]

In the decision areas studied, the "inequalities" are not so widely "dispersed." Only a few people make the key decisions in each issue area, but they achieve their hegemony by accepting the indirect influence of larger groups. Nominations are generally determined by a few party leaders, but with attention to the wishes of their followers within the party organizations, especially sub-leaders and representatives of ethnic groups. Most important redevelopment decisions were made by the Mayor and appropriate staff officials, with full sensitivity to the need for getting support from business and other groups. Major public education policy was directed by the Mayor and his appointees on the Board of Education; superintendents, principals, and teachers' organizations played some part, but mostly to mobilize support for public education. A few public and party officials thus constituted the directing leadership, each in his own province, with the office and personality of the dynamic Mayor, Richard Lee, supplying the unifying force. We have advisedly called the leading group a "directing" rather than a "dominating" oligarchy. It apparently got its way less from authority or influence, in the communication sense, than from the ability to please others, particularly potentially opposing groups. In fact, the political leaders favored the existence of organized groups as a means of legitimizing their decisions and mobilizing support, as well as providing an arena where various sentiments could be expressed and somewhat satisfied. The Citizens Action Committee in the urban redevelopment field was one such example. Similarly, school principals and the Board of Education utilized PTAs "to head off or settle conflicts between parents and the school system."[3]

Dahl does not maintain that the New Haven pattern he describes is the only one possible or existent. Like Miller, he offers a model of power types which will be later discussed. But the New Haven analysis provides the basic elements around which most of the varied forms are structured.

The dispute between the two major contending approaches to American community power is thus, more or less, joined. Partly methodological, it is, at least initially, a disagreement between a business-elite dominance thesis and an acceptance of a relative pluralism. It is also a disagreement about the role of local government and political leadership. Dahl believes that mayors and their staff have increasingly become the initiators and organizers of important community decisions. Miller insists that the political leaders are uncertain about themselves and wait for the cues of others, while businessmen have a clearly defined image "and thus act with more assertion."[14]

A third recent volume further helps locate the principal disputes on the subject.

Edward Banfield's *Political Influence*, utilizing even analysis, narrates, with a detailed chronology, how decisions involving six very specific community problems were arrived at or, in most cases, blocked or compromised.[15] In all cases, there was a divided opinion around significant forces and individuals. The actual list of issues should be of some interest: proposals for extending a particular hospital's facilities, reorganization of welfare administration, a state subsidy for the Chicago Transit Authority, a plan for a vast business center, the creation of a large Chicago branch of the University of Illinois, the building of an extensive Exhibition Hall. At the time of publication, only the last had been achieved. The welfare reorganization plans had produced a compromise; in all other cases, the contending elements had forced a general stalemate.

Banfield's accounts are in the nature of the best type of scholarly journalistic history. They contain extensive details, but little systematic treatment. However, his interpretations are organized around several summary ideas. Initially, he does not discount the possibility of business dominance. In essence, he believes that the resources of the leading Chicago businessmen, representing the top officials of leading national corporations and prominent regional commercial and banking institutions, offer an apparently unlimited power potential. Yet, he insists that, in his investigations, the "richest men in Chicago are conspicuous by their absence."[16] In fact, "big businessmen are criticized less for interfering in public affairs than for 'failing to assume their civic responsibilities.'"[17]

Businessmen do not dominate community decisions because of lack of unity, lack of interest, and because of the "costs" of intervening on any issue, including the encouragement of counter pressures. Their vital interests are not at stake and they are relatively satisfied with what is done. When their interests are more aroused, either because of some visible economic stake or because of personal predilections, particular business organizations may become heavily involved and be very influential. For instance, the disputed Exhibition Hall was built because it was a pet project of Colonel Robert McCormack and his successors on the Chicago *Tribune*. But, usually businessmen are only casually concerned or on all sides of most of the questions studied.

Typically, the most influential people in the community-decision making in Chicago are: "the managers of large organizations, the maintenance of which is at stake, a few 'civic leaders' whose judgment, negotiating skill, and disinterestedness are unusual and above all, the chief elected officials."[18] The organizations referred to are specified as those supported by "customers" rather than "members."[19] They may be profit-making businesses, public agencies which give free services, or public and semi-public agencies which sell services. In most cases, the involved organizations are public and the executives are civil servants, though Banfield describes them as "fighting politicians" rather than "bureaucrats."[20]

However, the most influential leaders in this megalopolis, as in the medium-sized city of New Haven, are the elected political officials, especially the Mayor. Banfield is thus on the side of Dahl against Miller. But, the leadership of Mayor Richard Daley, so frequently bracketed with Mayor Lee of New Haven as one of the "strong" mayors of our times, appears to be less forceful. Though both chief executive and official leader of the powerful Democratic

machine, he is faced with many limitations on the exercise of power, even within the political realm. He needs the cooperation of other elected officials, "irregulars" within his own party, elected officials of the other party (especially the Republican Governor in the period under study). He may be, and in this study actually was, blocked by the courts, Voters may veto proposals, as on a bond referendum, and, of course, the possibility of electoral opposition in the next election must always be considered. Above all the Mayor and his associates, like anyone who seeks to wield power in specific situations, has limited resources of "working capital." These cannot be "used up" for every challenge that arises.

Like the business dominants, Banfield seems to consider the political leaders as potentially omnipotent when they go "all out" on any question. But this would require depleting their limited working capital. They have to contend with other power groups besides those mentioned—national government in some cases, businessmen, other strong community elements that may be affected or aroused. They are, therefore, in practice, slow to take up issues and seek compromises. The initiative on most questions thus comes from the maintenance and enhancement needs of the type of formal organization listed. Other organizations may then support, oppose, or strive for modification. The following are some examples: A hospital tries to expand. Another hospital, for its own reasons, opposes. The *Tribune* wants an Exhibition Hall, the owners of another Hall oppose. The state, city, and county Welfare Departments have varying positions on reorganization plans. Attempts are made to line up different elements of the "public" on each side. The political leaders may then adjudicate or support one side or the other, but rarely with all their resources.

The varying positions of Miller, Dahl, and Banfield have been presented in some detail not so much to assess their ideas and their work at this juncture, but because their combined efforts do suggest the kinds of questions that have to be probed. These include the following:

1. Of what does community power consist and how does one locate it? This involves the general question of methodology.
2. Who attempts to wield power in which situation? Power motivation is generally ignored by Miller, is of great importance to Dahl and Banfield.
3. How are important community decisions made? Miller appears to see most community-relevant decisions as a simple reflection of the values and efforts of the business elite and its subordinates. Dahl and Banfield pay attention to the motivation, resources and tactics of specific groups and individuals.
4. What is the power position of particular groups? Emphasis has been on business and local government.
5. What is the prevailing power picture in the community? Corollary questions include the relation between power and other features of particular communities. Comparisons among communities is thus an inherent element of such analyses.

The remainder of this discussion is an attempt to elaborate and, to some extent, answer those questions, utilizing the material already reviewed as well as those of other students in the area. Our formulations are, of course, very tentative; we hope, in any case, that they can be guides for those looking for more complete answers, either in the research already undertaken or in the subsequent investigation which, we hope, is forthcoming.

Orientation and Methodology: What Is Community Power and How Is It Located?

What is community power? Initially, the term "community power" demands clarification. Appending the concept of "influence," which is, more or less, assumed to be synonymous, adds to the confusion. The traditional theoretical emphasis, summarized in Weber's formula—"the chance of a man or of a number of men to realize their own will in a communal action even against the resistance of others who are participating in the action"—is generally irrelevant to most discussions of American community power.[21] The orientation actually utilized is more in line with Bertrand Russell's description of power as "the production of intended effects."[22] Investigations have concentrated on the ability to and/or the practice of deciding what is to be done in, for, by the community. Power over people is thus an implicit, but rarely explicit, feature of the investigations. Furthermore, a "Machiavellian" model of power, which depicts individual power maintenance and enhancement as ends in themselves, must yield to approaches which seek to relate the exercise of power to other interests and values. Similarly, the long list of descriptions of types of power, bases of power, mechanisms of power, the distinctions among "power," "authority," "social control," et al., seem operationally outside the scope of the literature on American community power analysis.[23]

In essence, the focus is characteristically on community decisions, actual or potential, even if the methodology is "reputational." The basic question becomes who has more to say, or can have more to say, about things which are important to many people in the community. This is one of the reasons why such dissections of local power operations should be distinguished from those of the larger society, as exemplified by the nation.[24] There may be similarities between the city and the nation which can at times provide appropriate illustrations from one to develop some contentions about the other. Perhaps an ultimate comprehensive model would fit community power analysis into a more general framework of "power in society." But, at present, it is best to stay in one's own domain. An inventory of research on communities does not furnish a ready appraisal of "Power and Democracy in America."

The extrapolation of the findings from local community studies to the national picture, as in the attempt of some of the contributors to the above-named volume, represents a casual reductionism, a view of the operations of the great society and the smaller units as, a priori, identical—a common enough fallacy in American social science. As an example, the Hunter-Miller research has frequently been interpreted as lending support to C. Wright Mills' "power elite" thesis.[25] Whatever the validity of each and their superficial similarities, the respective formulations are quite different, partially because they deal with different orders of phenomena. Mills postulates a triumvirate of national elites—business, political, and military— with coordinated aims and interchangeable personnel. He does not depict business "dominance" over other groups with different power motivations, but a composite grouping with similar interests. When there is conflict, the elite thesis may not hold, but he believes that the realities of American society, in toto, relegate such conflicts to "middle-range" decisions. On the local level, there is no pressing need for such coordination; all decisions there tend, in his approach, to be middle-range.

In fact, those investigated in community studies appear quite minor, in terms of the future of society. If Mills' contentions were accurate, they would thus be quite compatible with any community power analysis yet offered.[26]

Methodology The variations in the findings are often, but not always, correlated with the method of inquiry— *reputation* vs. *event* analysis. A more obvious set of criteria, *formal position*, has been attempted and rejected. One study disclosed that the economic and political "office holders" were not typically community leaders by reputation.[27] Another revealed that the formal leaders were not directly involved in decision-making.[28] Research-wise, these conclusions may be pertinent, but they are subject to further probing as analytical interpretations, as later discussed.

Both of the major approaches have obvious virtues and defects, as apparent in their application. The "reputation" material is relatively codifiable and systematic, allows for ready replication and comparison. The criticisms are also obvious and often enough noted: the arbitrary choice of informants which can initially bias the findings, the "circularity" of the interviews (influentials talking about "influentials"), the acquired information suggesting "power potential" rather than "power utilization," the vagueness of the question wording, the possibility that the informant's observations may reflect folklore rather than knowledge, the possibility that "status" is automatically identified with power.[29] The tone is frequently a kind of groping inside-dopester exposé rather than a depiction of the institutional complexities of the contemporary American community.

The event analysis has more of the feel

of the precise socio-political processes. It dwells on what has been done, not about what could be done, though ad hoc discussions of resources available are significantly added, in many cases, as additional variables. Some of the institutional arrangements, conflicts and coalitions, problems and issues are available to the reader. At least, up to now, the defects and dangers are also glaring. Choice of issues involves neglecting others. Are those which are chosen representative? Are they salient to the functioning of the city, to the analysis of the power structure, or even to the specific purposes of the inquiry? Are the cases generalizable to the entire city decision-making process or only to particular types of decision-making?

One study did strive for an elaborate systematization of specific decisions.[30] Examining action on almost forty issues in the city of Syracuse, the researchers, through documentation and interviews, were able to locate the crucial decision-makers in each case. The quest was for a precise statistical summation of the more relevant social characteristics of these "influentials." Through factor analysis of these characteristics, a large proportion of the decisions could be grouped, i.e., the same types of people were involved in these types of decisions. The technique warrants continued applications and the results, referred to from time to time in this paper, were suggestive. But serious deficiencies remain. All the issues seem to have been given equal weight, and the problems of generalizability, pertinence, etc. still remain.

If the reputation approach sometimes resembles a quantification of a gossip column, some event descriptions appear like detailed journalistic case histories, good and comprehensive examples of the genre, but all with inherent dangers. The New Haven and Syracuse studies do offer more precise and ordered material, but they are not constructed so as to give us a clear-cut systematic picture of power in the community. The ideas are seminal, the evidence is there, but the data are still subject to the charge of selective choice.

In summary, the reputation approach appears to be comprehensive and methodologically neat; the question to be posed is: how relevant are the answers to meaningful hypotheses about community power. Event studies present the proper queries, search in the right directions, and provide tentative answers. But the answers remain partial and, usually, insufficiently systematized. Yet the author's predilection is towards the event approach, somehow systemized. It tends to be more concrete, to be accompanied by greater attention to the socio-political life of the community, to suggest more suitable insights into such elements as motivation for power utilization and power potential and, generally, to produce more fruitful results. However, our objective is not principally to appraise methodology. The discussion which follows utilizes material however obtained, though the method of acquiring the data is, necessarily, at least an implicit feature of our evaluation.

Location of power and the social structure
As a preliminary caution, it is necessary to point out that the full meaning of "power" in a community or society may not be directly available to any of the above techniques. Those who are powerful in specific crucial institutional areas of community life may neither possess the appropriate reputations nor participate in many significant community-relevant decisions. Their power comes from the functions of their institutions. The decisions they make within their apparently limited sphere may

be so consequential for the rest of the community or society that they are inherently "powerful," as long as the positions of their groups are maintained.

This is particularly true of "business" in a "business society." One may then speak of an ultimate "business power" on the national level, and to some extent locally, even if political leadership is not generally under their control. Dominating the economy (with appropriate veto power from other groups), they have power over the national livelihood, even if this power is less a matter of concrete decisions than of merely maintaining their institutional structures. Their power then may rest on the legitimacy of their institutions, not on how much they may control the direct decisions of government. Put another way, under the conditions of the existing economy, business must make money and businessmen must run their businesses accordingly. Secondly, no programs which involve economic activity can succeed without their participation or, at least, against their veto. Their specific roles in concrete decisions of political or other community relevance is another matter, related to specific situational factors. The varying interpretations of the power of business groups in communities are, in that sense, inadequate answers to the basic questions about the position of "business" in the social system. But this limitation may be irrelevant to the purposes of community investigations, which come back to the issue of who does or can make the important community-relevant decisions. Of course, the exercise of power within a specific institutional area, like business, may impel businessmen to strive to wield power on other community decisions.

Motivation for Decision-making

In the relatively pluralistic American community, power over decisions is not an automatic reflection of a prescribed hierarchal role description. A significant variable that emerges from the literature is the motivation to intervene in a particular decision-making process. Such motivation is simply a product of the extent to which that decision is salient to the group and/or the individual.

Group Saliency Factors Several types of group saliency factors are listed here, not with any logical organization, which does not seem obvious at this point, but as a list of the kinds of elements observed in the literature. They include: group power maintenance or enhancement in specific areas, furtherance of economic "interests" in the traditional sense, defense and extension of values. Contrariwise, non-intervention may imply that relative power, economic interests, and values are being achieved without such decision intervention.

Group power in community The general lines of this type of motivation are indicated in the methodological note and the review of Banfield's narratives. A community decision which may limit or enhance the relative power of groups will impel intervention by the leaders of such groups. This rather simplistic formula may be better understood by noting the converse, the non-intervention by potentially powerful groups when their power positions are not at stake. Returning again to our methodological note, this is one reason why business groups do not throw their resources into every question that arises. For instance, one of the discussants in the *Power and Democracy in America* volume, noting that businessmen collect philanthropic funds but leave the question of disbursement, the genuine decision-making aspects, to welfare professionals, remarks: "Perhaps the crucial issue is whether or not the allocation of funds is of relevance to the businessmen. If, in fact, they have no interest in, or are satisfied with, the allocation, their lack of concern may reflect not their weakness or fear of defeat but the realization that there is little power challenge involved."[31]

Similarly, the oft-noted ambivalence of officials of large absentee corporations toward participation in community activities, except when middle-management is prodded by the company for public relations reasons, is partly a reflection of the fact that their local and, of course, their national power positions, are rarely affected.[32] On the other hand, local government officials were among the few citizens actively concerned about metropolitan government reorganization plans, for the future of their "domains" might be at stake.[33]

One other power motivation may be noted, the search for power in some areas to compensate for powerlessness in other areas of the potentially powerful. The dominant role of businessmen in civic and philanthropic organizations may thus be seen as an outlet for power loss in local government.[34]

In summary, power groups will intervene in decisions when their bases of power are the issue. There seems to be little evidence of a drive towards generic power imperialism in American communities. Rather, the impulsion seems to be towards the maintenance and enhancement of the group's position in these particular "areas" of power within which it operates, which, to repeat, may involve an inherent power over many "areas."

Economic interests The literature likewise supports the almost truistic statement that intervention in decision-making will vary with the extent to which an issue has definite economic relevance to a group. In Banfield's discussion of proposed Chicago projects, those businessmen who would clearly gain business advantages were most vigorous in pushing for them, those who might lose a competitive position thereby were actively, if sometimes surreptitiously, in opposition.[35] Absentee corporations may have little concern about local problems which have little effect on the enterprises; however, in the communities where they have large home offices they may be actively involved in redevelopment decisions. In the Syracuse study, the local "aristocratic commercial leadership" were heavily represented in "Downtown Development" decisions, the "new management" elite of industrial corporations in those of "Industrial Interest."[36] In a study of the politics of a small town, merchants who would be adversely affected by a rerouting of traffic were decisive in defeating an attempt to change a highway through town.[37] Unions may be only tangentially concerned about community problems except when the economic interests of members are directly involved.[38]

Urban renewal offers a particular area in which economic interests may be at stake. Therefore, observers, with the possible exception of Dahl, find that many business groups are, quite appropriately, conspicuously engaged in decision-making about such questions.[39] An additional type of power exercise around economic interests is the ever present striving to lower governmental expenditures and to maintain lower taxes. Much of the intervention in small town or suburban community politics is concerned with little else.[40]

Values Such "interests" may or may not be closely identified with group values, particularly those which are manifestly politically relevant, and especially when some aspect of the group's legitimacy in the social structure is at issue. Public welfare expenditures can be considered an ideological challenge to a private business approach to solving community problems. Therefore, businessmen oppose such expenditures, actively work at private philanthropic alternatives, or get into official government positions where they can combat the "welfare state" philosophy.[41] People will spend as much on private activities as it would cost in taxes if the same effort were undertaken by government agencies.[42] Businessmen will push for a tax-supported subsidy to a private bus company rather than sanction a publicly-owned bus line.[43]

Perhaps the converse again reveals the nub of the question more clearly. Intervention by potential power wielders is less likely when neither the legitimacy nor the resources of the power base is threatened. Especially is this true of businessmen. Why bother with the effort, and costs, of trying to marshal resources on every decision, even of business relevance? As long as you can run your business, let the others have their particular decision-areas. This has been part of the traditional attitude of big business towards "corrupt" municipal political machines. Such a non-intervention orientation will, of course, be even more likely when there is a general satisfaction, or at least minimal antagonism towards what others are doing, especially if it may help your "interests." Why should New Haven businessmen spend their valuable time in the details of urban renewal planning, except when prodded by the Mayor? He and his staff seem to be doing a good enough job.

Somewhat surprisingly, the literature contains few other explicit examples of intervention in decisions because of group values beyond those of business groups. There are descriptions of those who get involved in decisions because of group "tastes" (art, mental health), professional orientation (health), life style (home owners striving to maintain a neighborhood).[44] Especially surprising is the comparative absence of accounts of group "ideological" motivation, secular and religious.

Conclusion The literature emphasizes decision intervention by business groups when the issues have some direct association with maintenance or enhancement of area of power, direct economic interests, or business "values." Such an accent is, to some extent, a reflection of the nature of prevailing arguments in the field, so often focused on "business power" hypotheses. But there is enough material to suggest, and one may add plausible further speculations, that motivations for attempts to exercise power on any community-relevant decision is similar for all groups. Certainly, the activities of civil rights groups on questions salient to them implies concern about power maintenance, interests, and values. Similar analysis can be applied to religious bodies, professional organizations, etc. which are insufficiently treated in the literature, as well as specific government bodies, who receive more attention. The research and analytical directive can almost be summed up as: find out why the leaders of a particular group should care about a particular controversy, find out why it does or does not mean enough to the group to warrant marshalling resources in the light of the possible contending forces.

Personal Factors *Role* The specific individual role requirements may be as consequential as the group aspects in determining the degree of intervention in decision-making. This has been the point of the many analysts who emphasize the central power position of the Mayor, his staff, and the responsible professionals in government agencies. In the context of the problems and structure and public expectations of the contemporary American cities, to do their jobs, especially to do them well, they have to become actively involved in many important decisions, have to utilize their power resources. In former times, when their role expectations were less demanding, they could more readily avoid power utilization and decision responsibility.

Career Attempts at power utilization may not be inherent in the role, but may enhance the possibility of success in that role and resultant career opportunities. It becomes an estimate of how to "do the job well," which may mean trying to foster or alter particular decisions. This could characterize some "go-getting officials," bureaucrats, professionals, perhaps some city managers. The mayor who wants to make a "name for himself," whatever the purpose, would be such an example, as in the case of Mayor Lee of New Haven. The pressure of corporations to get middle management to participate in civic organizations has been previously described. This is apparently the principal reason why many do participate, for it can become an appropriate mechanism for a favorable judgment in the corporation hierarchy or, in some cases, the opportunity to get known and thus shift to a position outside the corporation.

Personality Because of the nature of the inquiries, there has been little explicit attention to personality factors, which are frequently central in some general models of "power striving." It is appropriate to suggest, however, that motivations for exercise of power include this variable. It may be related to career strivings, to role performance, to group power maintenance, or to some combination thereof, as, for instance, the attempted use of power by anxious individuals who feel that their individual roles and careers are threatened by an assumed threat to their group's power. How this can be meaningfully studied is not readily answerable.

Conclusion Motivation for an effort at decision-making, or power wielding, in a situation where there is controversy, or possibility of controversy, is a product of, among other things, the extent to which the issue is deemed salient to the appropriate actors. Among the elements involved, as noted in the literature, are: the possible effects on the relative power position of a group; the economic interests of a group (or individual); the relevance to legitimacy, values, and life styles; the role demands and career aspirations of individuals.

Who Are the "Powerful," How, and Why?

As spelled out, those who have most to say about community relevant decisions are appropriately motivated to intervene in that decision. The measure of their "power," to what extent they will have their "way," requires some consideration of the following elements:

Formal Features *Formal position* The formal position of groups of individuals within the social structure involves being assigned the ultimate function of making the relevant decisions. With the popularity of "invisible government" approaches implicit in so much of the Hunter-Miller type of finding, it is important that this be initially emphasized. Even Vidich and Bensman, who frequently use the "invisible government" label in depicting the structure of a rural community, actually describe a "power elite" quartet which has important formal positions in the local government and party.[45]

The formal function of particular organizations is related to the kinds of decisions in which such organizations are involved. Thus, it should not be surprising that government officials play more of a role in decisions which have to be made by a government agency, have less to say when they are not officially assigned this responsibility. Private philanthropy projects are illustrative. Those with money collect from others with money. The money collectors, or rather the directors of money collections, are in the obvious position of deciding what is to be done with the money if they so wish. Similarly, since businessmen have to build private redevelopment and private civic projects, they will have much to say about those projects, whoever else may be involved.

If the formal position, or formal organization, require decisions on a subject, and if the issue is salient to the position or organization, the occupant is likely to be, in some manner, an important participant in the decision-making process. Thus, in the contemporary context, school superintendents are important in school decisions, expert officials in municipal departments are assigned decision responsibilities within their sphere and, above all, the "wishes" of the leaders of city governments today inherently carry great weight. In contrast, the officials of small towns and suburbs are not, by constitutional requirement or popular expectations, presumed to have much of an independent decision role, and few issues are very salient to them.[46] Therefore, their governments tend to be "weak."

However, as already indicated, some studies reveal that the formal leaders may not be either those who have power by reputation or those directly involved in important decisions. Their roles may be limited to that of "lending prestige or legitimizing the situations provided by others."[47] Those others, labeled as the "Effectors," are generally the underlings —particularly government personnel and the employees of the large private corporations.

Such interpretations tend to confuse "formal position" with "formal organizations." Comparatively lower range personnel of organizations may be involved in the actual decision process, but it is the position in the entire social structure of their organizations which gives them the ability and the motivation to make decisions. Furthermore, this decision-making potential and impetus would not exist without and cannot, in most instances, be counter to the more formal leadership of the organization. In essence, power-wielding hardly exists outside organization role. Whether the reputation or decision approach is used, the decision-makers are thus usually found rooted in some formally organized matrix.

There remains one formally assigned decision-making entity in a democracy with open contests—the electorate. Elections for office are rarely emphasized in the literature. In most of the communities studied, the incumbents or their likely successors seem fairly secure in tenure. But there are several indications of need to make a "good showing" in elections, as a popular legitimizing of their policies, a way of enhancing careers, a method of mobilizing followers, or simply because the role of a politician requires getting more votes. The "power" of the electorate, in this widespread situation of municipal government continuity, is that of a variety of publics toward whom politicians somehow try to appeal even if any comparative lack of appeal may not mean loss of political power. Referenda present a different picture. A formal requirement for popular approval limits the decision-making capabilities of any political leader or anyone else involved in such a decision. In the extreme case of suburban school officials, the decision-making option becomes very narrow.[48] The communication "appeals" then become of vital concern, the response to those appeals a direct expression of power by the electorate or sections thereof.

As a final consideration, the background of formal decision-makers, the element so frequently emphasized in traditional "elite" analysis, is rarely emphasized in community studies. Such features are occasionally stated, more frequently implied, but are rarely explicitly considered. In essence, such an approach states that because of common interests and values, the orientation of formal decision-makers is directed towards the reference group of those of similar origin, who, therefore, become powerful. It is not utilized because contemporary role, organization, etc. of those in formal positions seems to provide a more meaningful focus.

Access to formal decision-makers The notion of "access" to those who formally make decisions, particularly government officials, is evident in many studies of national and state politics. All discussions of "pressure groups" in local affairs dwell on, except when referenda are involved,

some means of "getting to" and thus affecting those who have the official decision-making responsibility. This is the assigned task of the "effectors" in corporations.[49] But, in most reputational studies and typical accompanying business dominance emphasis, as well as in various notions of "invisible government," much more is implied. The government is assumed to be a weak power center. Businessmen, as well as other groups "behind the scenes," possess formal and informal communication channels to government officials. Since the former represents "strength," the communications will be heeded.[50] To the extent that this process does occur, it should not be interpreted as a symptom of decision by intrigue. It is merely a reflection of the existing power relationship.

Formal structure The propensity and ability to make decisions may be related to the formal *structure* of the group and the formal relations with other groups. The power of local government, for instance, may be greater if staffed by full-time rather than part-time officials, and if elections are partisan rather than "nonpartisan."[51] The existence of a structure for making decisions and formal resources for implementing them may be other variables. Thus, Dahl describes how earlier attempts at urban redevelopment proved unsuccessful because there was no available political process for agreement, nor appropriate financial sources.[52] The Federal Housing Act of 1949 provided both. The "strong mayor" tendency is partly buttressed by the city charter provisions which give the chief executive authority and responsibility for so many decisions. Small towns and suburban governments frequently decide little because they are not constitutionally so assigned and would not have the formal means for executing such decisions if they were made.

Banfield describes two contrasting types of groups with varying formal decision-making potentials. "Civic organization" leaders do not have a mandate to take positions on certain controversial issues, it would be difficult to get the membership to make such decisions, and the organizations could not be readily mobilized to support them if adopted. Leaders of private corporations and the type of public bodies he describes can make such decisions and, to some degree, commit their organizations to them.[53]

The list of formal limitations to power exercise can be readily extended. Local governments have to receive state and Federal approval for many actions. As already described, electorate support is a definite limitation when referenda are required, a latent control in candidate elections. Courts may act as a check on many political decisions. Corporation employees operating in community affairs may require corporation approval for their actions.[54] In summary, in American communities today, effective exercise of power is partially dependent on the existence of appropriate formal mechanisms and the lack of formally restricting structures.

Values *Legitimate position of decision-maker* The legitimacy of the formal decision-maker or decision-making group in the specific area also obviously affects his likely success, i.e., his relative power. Businessmen, local government officials, school officials, professionals and experts *should*, with appropriate checks, make decisions in their respective spheres. The followers of traditional political machines grant their leaders the "right" to select nominees and officials. The decline of the machine is, among other things, a reflection of the loss of that "legitimate" function.

Extending the concept further, the "legitimate wisdom" of particular people in specific areas may influence decisions even if they are not necessarily the official decision-makers or share this function with others. This is especially evident when status is an ingredient of power, as in Hunter's "Regional City." Other examples from the literature include the University of Illinois officials in the conflict over expansion described by Banfield and the specialists in such areas as mental health and the arts in the Syracuse study.[55] A well-known individual case is that of Robert Moses in New York City and State, who has generally had so much power over many decisions because, among other reasons, officials and publics tend to accept his "record."[56]

Values of specific groups When the values of specific groups are more in accord with prevailing community values their opinions are more likely to produce the desired decisions, no matter what the formal decision mechanisms. This implies substantive value agreement, not merely acceptance of the legitimate role of particular people. Theses about business dominance are frequently accompanied by interpretations of a "broad dissemination of business values: what is good for business is good for the community."[57]

But value agreement may not be so inclusive. Differing values may prevail in different areas of disputes, and there may be value conflicts and contradictions. The business viewpoint may or may not prevail in the face of popular demands for "welfare," "justice," etc., as should be very obvious by now. These are, in effect, the values which provide a power potential for government officials in the contemporary city, further augmented by a widespread normative consensus in favor of "community redevelopment." Educators and education officials face two conflicting popular values in achieving their aims— a strong commitment to education as a social goal and a desire for "economy."

If the sought-for decision is to be achieved by more open propagandistic appeals to many publics, either as an effort at pressure politics or to achieve a particular popular vote, "values" may be consequential in more complex fashion. It is not merely that general values are inherently associated with particular groups, but specific situational values are utilized to get support. This seems little more than a restatement of a simple dictum of communication and opinion analysis, but it implies something more: that one of the means for achieving power in a specific decision area is the ability to mobilize organized groups and unorganized publics by appeals to salient values. To use an illustration by Dahl, "right to work" referenda, even though pushed by powerful business groups, pass when farmers were sufficiently aroused and fail when labor unions were properly mobilized.[58] In this instance, "power" is closely associated with "influence" in the communication sense. The strong motivations of the would-be decision-maker are effectively transferred to a receptive audience, which, by vote or pressure on the formal decision-makers, affects what is decided. Unfortunately, systematic analysis of such processes are rare in the community literature. Description of *prior* consideration of possible value pressures in formulating policy or maneuvering to secure consensus are more evident. Certainly, any inquiry into current civil rights controversies throughout the country,

almost completely absent in community studies to date, would have to accentuate communication and mobilization around values.

Concern with communication implies attention to communication channels. An assumed ingredient of a position of power is the ability to utilize such channels, whatever they may be. The local press is especially identified as an important decision-making mechanism. But, as with so many claims about opinion formation, such contentions have hardly been tested. In fact, the role of the local press has been seriously questioned.[59] Its "power" may rest more on the belief in its potential rather than any realization, as exemplified by the attention given to the opinions of the editors of the *Chicago Triubne*.[60]

Other Factors *Money and numbers as resources* The importance of money as a power variable in contemporary American communities requires little elaboration, except for the caution that it is not all powerful, will not always be utilized except when thoroughly motivated, will not be on the same side on many questions. Even if more fully utilized it can be countered by the opposing feature of numbers, as recognized as far back as Aristotle. As important in communities as mere quantity are the mobilization around dominant values and/or interests and, sometimes, the degree of access to official decision-makers.

Sanctions The use of "power over" to facilitate "power for," a common enough expectation, is rarely clearly indicated in the literature. Hunter does describe uses of deliberate pressures to silence or remove opposition from strategic positions.[61] Other possible examples are: removal of funds, closing down business, strikes, threats of resignation. When existent, these are typically implicit rather than stated.

Conclusion In summary, who makes the community relevant decisions or has more say about them? First of all, those who make them are those who are supposed to make them, because of their officially assigned positions or because this is their approved legitimate bailiwick. When the decision is not directly within their formally-designed domain, the appropriate formula should be along these lines: those who are properly motivated by the saliency of an issue, capable of committing and mobilizing their groups, having access to those who have the ability and the impulsion to make the appropriate formal decisions, possessing some form of legitimacy in the decision-area, capable of and utilizing appeals to the values and interests of many publics, able further to mobilize either large numbers or those in strategic positions (using whatever resources can be called upon), and somehow having an opposition with as few as possible of these advantages, will win out, i.e., will exercise their power over a particular area around a specific decision.

Power Position of Business and Local Government

Although many groups thus can and do exercise power in American communities, the major contentions are, quite appropriately about the two major institutional groups, business and local government. The foundations of their respective power positions are accordingly appraised in line with the previous formulations.

Business Banfield offers this conjecture about possible behavior of leading Chicago businessmen: "In some future case—one in which their vital interests are at stake—they may issue the orders necessary to set in motion the lower echelons of the alleged influence hierarchy."[62] Whatever the results of such an effort, this would imply a crucially divisive issue in the community, a quasi "revolutionary" conflict in which some aspect of legitimacy is debated. None of this appears in the literature. Business power within its own institutional area is hardly an issue in contemporary American communities. Beyond this, the following emerges from the literature.

The most important resources of businessmen are obviously the possession of money—their own and of others whose money can be utilized—and status. For many who postulate business elite dominance, these are the only factors involved, for there is the casual assumption that, in American society, wealth, status, and power are automatically correlated. Additionally, there is the generally accepted legitimacy of business values and the expertise of businessmen. Material interest in the city compels concern about many decisions. There is frequently close internal communication among businessmen.

But the inherent limitations to their exercise of power are also evident, as already suggested. The legitimacy of businessmen and their values is not accepted in all areas of community life and by all people.[63] Conflict of interest and opinion among businessmen is as evident as cohesion. Communication may not be as easy as assumed, especially through their far-flung organizations.[64] The process of formal decision-making on an issue is not always readily available, and potentially divisive decisions, within business organizations or in the community, are avoided. Public relations may be more important than power wielding for its own sake. There is little desire for political activity by corporation officials unless pushed by the companies' desire for a proper public image.

Businessmen expect public officials to handle the political problems and, unless seriously dissatisfied with what is done, will rarely intervene with any vigor. When economic interests are involved, they may participate, but often as supporters and legitimizers of the outspoken proponents. Their role in political affairs may be more extensive when local government is weak or when intervention does not brook serious opposition. In essence, they would then be responding to a "power vacuum," even though it is one of long standing. Their "citizen" activity may tend to be in civic, service, and philanthropic organizations, where objectives are clear, methods "clean," and controversy minimal, and the thorny arena of political conflict avoided. The exceptions, to repeat, are situations when *direct economic interests are involved*. Small local businessmen and professional people may be more involved in political affairs, particularly in smaller communities, because of more direct material interest, status strivings, or greater value concerns about the community.

Local government The basis for the power position of local government can be sketched more briefly. Despite the growing nationalization of government and politics and the checks that automatically follow, municipal government power has grown within the following context: the necessary functions of the government in solving complex contemporary problems and the accompanying role of professionals; a popularly supported plebeian-based political organization, typically with some ties to labor organizations and ethnic groups; a formal political structure which accents the power potential of the mayor and "partisan" organizations and elections. Traditional political machines are typical, though often diminished in power and appeal, but they are rarely involved in major policy decisions. Relative lack of power of political leaders and their staff professionals is correlated with the comparative absence of the above and the power of business groups, because of specific community configurations and historical antecedents, including the dominant position of local-based business and the slowness of change.

The Power Structure of American Communities

All that has been said tends to substantiate a pluralistic interpretation of American community power. People try to exercise power when a particular decision is salient and/or required. This obviously means that different groups in the community will be more involved in different kinds of decisions. Many groups possess appropriate resources, internal decision-making mechanisms, access to those who make the necessary formal decisions, widely accepted legitimacy and values, means for communicating to and mobilizing large publics. The investigation of power then becomes a study of discrete decision-making processes, with many sectors of the population revealing varying degrees of impact on different type decisions.[65]

But summary statements about American community power should go beyond such casual nominalism, as they must transcend facile monolithism. Some decisions are obviously more salient to the community than others. Power motivation, formal decision-making potential, resources, access, communication facilities may be widespread, but there are significant differences. To use the abused cliché, some are more equal than others. The two important dominant groups remain businessmen, of varying types, and local government officials. The pattern of American community power observed is mostly a matter of the respective positions of these two groups and their relation with the residual "all other groups."

Despite their disagreement about the prevailing power picture, Miller and Dahl offer models of possible power structure which are not too dissimilar.[66] Both allow for completely pluralistic patterns, with either particular spheres of influence for specific groups or open struggles by relatively equal groups on the same issues. To Miller, these are subordinate aspects in most American communities. To Dahl, they exist but are less likely possibilities than a system of comparative pluralism with *coordination by the political leadership* in different ways in different communities, a variant not specifically indicated by Miller. Finally both accept the possibility of domination by an economic elite, but Dahl generally relegates such situations to the past while Miller insists that this pattern, with all its variations, is most common in the United States today.

A more composite replica of these typologies is that of Rossi, with his simple division into "monoliths" and "polyliths."[67] The former is typically business elite dominant. In a polylith, local government is the province of the political leaders, backed by strong parties and working class associations.[68] The rest of his formulation is in accord with our previous discussion. Civic associations and community chests are in the hands of the leaders of business and staff professionals. A polylith is associated with strong political parties, based upon class political attitudes, frequently with ethnic concomitants. In response, economic leaders (and others), may advocate changes in government structure (non-partisan elections) to thwart some of the power of political parties. Absentee corporation officials will tend to set themselves off from purely local political concerns. In monoliths, conflicts tend to take on the character of minor revolts, like the revolutionary postures of the powerless in authoritarian countries.

All this can be restated in terms of what has already been spelled out. Business elite dominance appears most characteristic of communities when the dominant businessmen are most motivated to participate in community decisions (company towns, established commercial aristocracies, etc.) and/or when there are fewer rival power centers. The polylith is characterized by both the leadership of government officials and relative pluralism. Decision-making is widespread among many groups, depending upon motivation, resources, and the other listed ingredients. Businessmen are an important part of the power picture, but only as part of the above formula. In fact, a large section avoids the arena of political decisions, except when very pressing, because of the efforts demanded and risks inherent, and concentrates on the private areas of community decision-making, such as civic associations and philanthropic activities, where there is little opposition in power or ideology. The political leaders are the necessary co-ordinators in such a complex pattern and their power rests on the fairly strong power position of many groups—especially political parties, trade unions, ethnic groups, staff professionals, etc.—and the importance of governmental decisions today.

To complete our review, one additional presentation must be described. Political

Scientist Robert Salisbury states that what others would consider polylithic structures are, in most cases, evidence of a "new convergence."[69] A new power triumvirate has arisen to solve the vital problems of the contemporary city. Its elements have already been sufficiently identified: the business interests directly dependent on the condition of the city, particularly the downtown area; the professionals, technicians, experts engaged in city programs; the mayor, generally secure in his tenure. What Salisbury emphasizes is that this constitutes a coordinate power group; the mayor is the most influential, but he appears to be only the first among equals.

The leadership convergence directs most mayor decisions, particularly those that involve allocation of scarce resources; some of these, like redevelopment and traffic control, can determine the future of the city. The rest of the population—other organized groups, other politicians, and unorganized publics—are part of the process in three ways: they must be "sold" on certain issues, especially if referenda are in order; their interests and needs must be somewhat satisfied and/or anticipated; some demands must be responded to, such as race relations. Salisbury, however, believes that the importance of the last process can be exaggerated. Specifically, he insists that Banfield's selection of issues tends to magnify the initiative of the groups outside the "convergence." The more vital questions should, with few exceptions such as race relations, reveal the initiating, as well as decision-making position, of the triumvirate.

Salisbury's analysis can thus supply the basis for the concluding statements of this essay. Power over community decisions remains a matter of motivation, resources, mechanisms of decision-making, mobilization of resources, etc. On many, many decisions, various groups may initiate and win out, as in Banfield's account and in some of the descriptions of Dahl and others. Current disputes about race relations offer a fitting example where this more pluralistic interpretation, including both the ideas of spheres of influence and competing pressures around a common issue, may be readily applicable. But on the most salient community issues a directing leadership can be observed. In some communities, for the reasons outlined, the decision leaders have been, and may still be, particular business interests. In most of them, a new pattern has emerged, a polylithic structure in which business groups and local government each lead in their own domains. But the urgent problems of the past World War II era in most large cities have brought some business groups into the same decision area as the local government and the ever growing crop of experts. The extent to which the businessmen are involved may vary, as in the different accounts of the role of businessmen in urban renewal in different cities.

Does the rest of the population, organized and unorganized, become merely an audience called on occasionally to affirm and applaud these "big decisions?" Salisbury may have overstated his case. Many groups may initiate, veto, modify, pressure in all decision areas, in accord with the ingredients frequently listed. But those who are part of the new power convergence cannot be circumvented. In some manner, they have the responsibilities and will generally have to assume a decision-making role in all major decisions.

To return to the original debate, whatever evidence is available tends to support Dahl's emphasis against Miller's. Most American communities reveal a relatively pluralistic power structure. On some community-relevant questions, power may be widely dispersed. On the most salient questions, many groups may have an effect on what is decided, but the directing leadership comes from some combination of particular business groups, local government, and, in recent developments, professionals and experts. Communities differ

and communities change in the power relations among these elements. A suggestive hypothesis holds that the tendency has been towards their coordination into a uniquely composite decision-making collectivity.[70]

NOTES

1. Floyd Hunter, *Community Power Structure: A Study of Decision Makers*, Chapel Hill: The University of North Carolina Press, 1953.
2. Robert S. Lynd and Helen M. Lynd, *Middletown in Transition*, New York: Harcourt, Brace, 1957.
3. Robert Dahl, *Who Governs? Democracy and Power in an American City*. New Haven and London: Yale University Press, 1961, pp. 63–69.
4. Wendell Bell, Charles J. Hill, Charles R. Wright, *Public Leadership*, San Francisco: Chandler Publishing Co., 1961.
5. See Elihu Katz, "The Two-Step Flow of Communication: An Up-To-Date Report of an Hypothesis, *Public Opinion Quarterly* 21, (Spring, 1957), pp. 61–78.
6. *Power and Democracy in America*, edited by William V. D'Antonio and Howard J. Ehrlich, Notre Dame, Indiana: University of Notre Dame Press, 1961.
7. Actually, the major bulwarks for his thesis are his own and Hunter's research, plus a series of inquiries by Charles Loomis and his associates in Southwestern United States for which no published citations are given. The other references offered actually reveal much more complex patterns. See *Ibid.*, pp. 38–71.
8. *Ibid.*, p. 61.
9. Dahl, *op. cit.*
10. Dahl, *op. cit.*, p. 137.
11. *Ibid.*, p. 72.
12. *Ibid.*, p. 75.
13. *Ibid.*, p. 156.
14. D'Antonio and Ehrlich, *op. cit.*, p. 136.
15. Edward C. Banfield, *Political Influence*, New York: The Free Press of Glencoe, 1961.
16. *Ibid.*, p. 288.
17. *Ibid.*, p. 287.
18. *Political Influence*, p. 288.
19. *Ibid.*, p. 265.
20. *Ibid.*, p. 266.
21. *From Max Weber: Essays in Sociology*, translated, edited, and with an introduction by H. H. Gerth and C. Wright Mills, New York: Oxford University Press, Galaxy Book, 1958, p. 180.
22. Bertrand Russell, *Power: A New Social Analysis*, London: Unwin Books, 1962, p. 25.
23. Game models of decision-making, which pose analogies of combatants striving to win out over each other, are apparently as inapplicable as other orientations which emphasize "power over" rather than "power to." Dahl, for instance, has

offered such a theoretical model, which he does not seem to utilize in his own community power analysis. See Robert A. Dahl, "The Concept of Power," *Behavioral Science*, 3 (July, 1957), pp. 201–215.
24. A symposium of a few years ago on national power, which included such participants as Robert Lynd, C. Wright Mills, and Harold Lasswell, contained little overlap with most of the material on community power. See *Problems of Power in American Democracy*, edited by Arthur Kornhauser, Detroit: Wayne State University Press, 1959.
25. C. Wright Mills, *The Power Elite*, New York: Oxford University Press, Galaxy Books 1959, especially pp. 269–297.
26. One scholar has postulated a particular "convergence" of such power on the local level, as later discussed. See Robert Salisbury, "Urban Politics: The New Convergence of Power," paper delivered at meetings of American Political Science Association, New York, September, 1963.
27. Robert O. Schulze and Leonard U. Blumberg, "The Determination of Local Power Elites," *American Journal of Sociology*, 63 (November, 1957), pp. 290–296.
28. Linton C. Freeman, Thomas J. Fararo, Warner Bloomberg Jr., and Morris H. Sunshine, "Locating Leaders in Local Communities: A Comparison of Some Alternative Approaches," *American Sociological Review*, 28 (October, 1963), pp. 791–798.
29. For a thorough criticism see Raymond E. Wolfinger, "Reputation and Reality in the Study of Community Power," *American Sociological Review*, 25 (October, 1960), pp. 636–644.
30. Linton C. Freeman, Warner Bloomberg Jr., Stephen S. Koff, Morris S. Sunshine, Thomas J. Fararo, "Local Community Leadership," Publications Committee of University College, Syracuse University, 15, 1960; Linton C. Freeman, Thomas J. Fararo, Warner Bloomberg Jr., Morris H. Sunshine, "Metropolitan Decision Making," Publications Committee of University College, Syracuse University, 28, 1962.
31. D'Antonio and Ehrlich, *op. cit.*, p. 125.
32. Peter H. Rossi, "The Organizational Structure of an American Community," in *Complex Organizations*, edited by Amitai Etzioni, New York: Holt, Rinehart and Winston, Inc., 1962, pp. 301–312;

Ronald J. Pellegrin and Charles H. Coates, "Absentee-Owned Corporations and Community Power Structure," *American Journal of Sociology*, 61 (March, 1956) pp. 413–419; Robert O. Schulze, "The Role of Economic Dominants in Community Power Structure," *American Sociological Review*, 23 (February, 1958), pp. 3–9.

33. Scott Greer, *Metropolitics: A Study of Political Culture*, New York: John Wiley and Sons, Inc., 1963.

34. Peter H. Rossi, "Theory and Method in the Study of Power in the Local Community," paper presented at meetings of American Sociological Association, New York, August, 1960.

35. Banfield, *op. cit., passim.*

36. Freeman, *et al.*, "Local Community Leadership," *op. cit.*

37. Werner E. Mills Jr. and Harry R. Davis, *Small City Government: Seven Cases in Decision Making*, New York: Random House Studies in Political Science, 1962, pp. 31–43.

38. Dahl, *Who Governs? op. cit.*, pp. 253–255.

39. Peter H. Rossi and Robert A. Dentler, *The Politics of Urban Renewal: The Chicago Findings*, New York: The Free Press of Glencoe Inc., 1961; Robert C. Wood, *1400 Governments: The Political Economy of the New York Metropolitan Region*, Cambridge, Mass.: Harvard University Press, 1961, pp. 158–169; Salisbury, *op. cit.*

40. Robert C. Wood, *Suburbia: Its People and Their Politics*, Boston: Houghton Mifflin Co., 1959, pp. 161–197, *passim;* Arthur J. Vidich and Joseph Bensman, *Small Town in Mass Society*, Princeton, New Jersey; Princeton University Press, 1958, pp. 109–136.

41. Pellegrin and Coates, *op. cit.;* Hunter, *op. cit.*, pp. 207–227.

42. Vidich and Bensman, *op. cit.*, pp. 128–136.

43. Mills and Davis, *op. cit.*, pp. 55–72.

44. Freeman, *et al.*, "Local Community Leadership," *op. cit.*, Dahl, *op. cit.*, pp. 192–199; Banfield, *op. cit., passim.*

45. Vidich and Bensman, *op. cit.*, especially pp. 217–221.

46. Wood, *Suburbia, op. cit.*, pp. 153–255, *passim.*

47. Freeman, *et al.*, "Locating Leaders," *op. cit.*, pp. 797–798.

48. Wood, *op. cit.*, pp. 192–194.

49. Freeman, *et al.*, "Locating Leaders," *op. cit.*

50. Hunter, *op. cit.*, pp. 83–113, 171–205.

51. Rossi, "Theory and Method," *op. cit.*, pp. 26–29.

52. Dahl, *op. cit.*, p. 116.

53. Banfield, *op. cit.*, pp. 288–295.

54. Pellegrin and Coates, *op. cit.*

55. Banfield, *op. cit.*, pp. 165–166; Freeman, *et al.*, "Local Community Leadership," *op. cit.*

56. Wood, *1400 Governments, op. cit.*, pp. 163–166.

57. D'Antonio and Ehrlich, *op. cit.*, p. 126.

58. *Ibid.*, p. 106.

59. Greer, *op. cit.;* Alvin J. Remmenga, "Has the Press Lost Its Influence in Local Affairs," in *Urban Government*, edited by Edward C. Banfield, New York: The Free Press of Glencoe, Inc., 1961, pp. 379–389.

60. Banfield, *Political Influence, op. cit.*, pp. 212–217, 222–231.

61. Hunter, *op. cit.*, pp. 176–179.

62. Banfield, *Political Influence, op. cit.*, p. 288.

63. See Dahl in D'Antonio and Ehrlich, *op. cit.*, p. 109.

64. Banfield, *op. cit.*, pp. 295–296.

65. A political science text on the government of New York City thus concludes simply by listing six power groups in the city, who among others, appear to be important decision-makers in particular areas. See Wallace S. Sayre and Herbert Kaufman, *Governing New York City*, New York: Russell Sage Foundation, 1960.

66. D'Antonio and Ehrlich, *op. cit.*, pp. 62–70; Dahl, *op. cit.*, pp. 184–189.

67. Rossi, "Theory and Method," *op. cit.*, pp. 24–43.

68. A good example is provided in the description of Lorain, Ohio, by James B. McKee, "Status and Power in the Industrial Community," *American Journal of Sociology*, 58 (January, 1939), pp. 364–370.

69. Salisbury, *op. cit.*

70. One type of community does not seem to fit any model described—the ever growing residential suburb. Perhaps, the reason is that is does not constitute a genuine "community."

42. Urban Politics: The New Convergence of Power
Robert H. Salisbury

Robert Salisbury's paper puts the pluralistic conception of urban decision-making in an historical context. He points out that during the nineteenth century power in the larger American cities was principally in the hands, first, of a patrician class, and then of commercial and mercantile interests founded on manufacturing and industry. Their influence came by default. Following the great waves of European migration around the turn of the century, this power was challenged by political machines responding to working-class demands. The result was the division of influence between an economic elite, which exercised power behind the scenes, and a political elite, led by the party boss. The problems of the cities have recently proven too severe to withstand such diffusion of power. Elected officials possess formal authority but do not command the financial resources on which effective urban policy depends. The business interests are threatened by conditions of decay in central city areas and can no longer afford to turn their back on the gritty, day-to-day issues which confront the mayor's office. Both groups rely on the expert advice of professional planners and managers. This "new convergence" represents an advance over earlier power structures, but it still may be too weak to master the political problems of urban communities today.

Robert H. Salisbury is Professor of Political Science and Chairman of the Department at Washington University in St. Louis. He is coauthor of *State Politics and the Public Schools* (1964) and has contributed to several other volumes and scholarly journals. His work has dealt mainly with urban politics, comparative state politics, and public policy analysis.

Economically, culturally, and in many ways even politically, the United States has become a thoroughly urban nation.[1] One aspect of this urbanization is that scholars have increasingly paid attention to phenomena occurring in cities. Sociologists, political scientists, economists, geographers, and historians have all developed urban subfields of specialization; and in recent years the sub-fields have been infused with the great enthusiasm of virtual armies of researchers. When these efforts are combined with those of architects, planners, social workers, administrative managers, and all the other urbanists asking questions about life in the city, the resulting stack of data, reports, proposals, admonitions, and manifestos is truly staggering. Inevitably,

perhaps, concern for the substance of city life gets mixed with concern for the methods of inquiry. Both, of course, are legitimate and important areas of concern. Each helps illuminate and is illuminated by the other. Specifically, the study of power structure—a basic issue for all political inquiry—has come to focus very largely on the city. In the process, both the substantive and methodological issues surrounding this generic political question— the question, as Dahl puts it, of Who

An earlier version of this paper was presented to the 59th Annual Meeting of the American Political Science Association, New York, September 5, 1963.

From *The Journal of Politics*, Vol. 26, No. 4 (November 1964), pp. 775–797. Reprinted by permission.

Governs?—have been involved in virtually every discussion of urban affairs in recent years.[2]

Yet despite, or perhaps because of, this special ferment some important gaps on this question—who governs the city?—have remained. Many of these relate to the basic criticism to be made of almost all urban studies, the absence of comparative dimensions. Serious, theoretically sophisticated social and political analysis of urban data is relatively new on the scholarly scene, however. It is perhaps not so surprising therefore that so little genuine comparative work has been undertaken. One may be encouraged by the very recent emergence of a number of comparative studies.[3] Most of these, however, deal with relatively small communities. One who is interested in general patterns of big city politics must deal with a series of case studies, each study dealing with a single community. Each study then serves its author as the empirical foundation for a series of generalizations about politics (or society—the sociologists have been firmly in the tradition since the days of the Lynds). Some of these are brilliant. At best, however, they are sophisticated insights and theoretical conjectures built upon descriptions of a single case which, one hopes intuitively, may fit a larger number of cases.

The limitations of the data are compounded by variations in conceptual apparatus and/or data-gathering technique. One wishes that there were a clear basis for determining that Atlanta was or was not a pyramid-shaped monolith; that Springdale was "really" controlled by a caucus, and that New Haven actually conforms to Dahl's analysis.[4] None of these three was studied in a manner which permits accurate comparisons with the other two (or twenty more which might be named), and

hence no generalizations about either of two central points is possible. First, what is (are) the structure(s) of power in American cities? Second, what are the principal independent variables affecting the shape, scope and operation of these putative structures? It may turn out that each city is unique and no useful generalizations can be made using the city as the unit of analysis. Or the city may really be the most useful microcosm of the political system in which all essential processes, structures, and relationships can be found. The professional conclusion probably lies somewhere between. We will not know without systematic comparative study.

One major effort at synthesis of exciting materials about city, principally big city, politics is that of Edward C. Banfield and James Q. Wilson.[5] To a large extent they draw upon the same materials as this essay, and there are many areas of agreement. There are important differences, too, however, both in conclusions and approach. Thus Banfield and Wilson give only passing attention to the historical dimension of urban politics. I propose to examine the question of the structure of power and do so over time. By viewing the city historically a number of critical elements, particularly those which have changed, can be seen more clearly than if a more strictly contemporaneous study were made. My discussion focuses upon the big cities in the United States that experienced major growth prior to World War I. The pattern I shall describe may apply to other communities as well, but my model city in what follows is heterogeneous in ethnic and racial terms, contains considerable industry and a suburban ring, is experiencing core city decay, and is, in short, what those who write about urban problems generally have in mind when they refer to "the city."

Anyone who talks about urban structures of power must take a stand on two related questions: what is meant by power and how does one go about trying to establish its empirical dimensions. By "structure of power" I mean the set of relationships among community roles, durable over time, through which relationships scarce resources are allocated in a community. I am primarily concerned with those allocations which involve decisions by governmental agencies. We should recognize, however, the shifting importance over time of public allocations to the total of allocations made in the community, and remember, too, that public and private actions are always mixed together, nowhere more than in the city. I shall not give attention to the allocation of all those resources that might be deemed scarce, but only those that are of substantial volume or scope. I recognize the difficulty of drawing clear distinctions between "important" and "unimportant" decisions, but there *is* a difference, and it is recognized by decision-makers in a city. Thus the structure of power affecting a primary fight over the nomination for recorder of deeds may bear no relationship to the structure within which the city's urban renewal program is determined. In such a case it is only the latter that is of much interest; the decisions involve much more substantial resource allocations and the structure of power involved is therefore a more important one.

In short, we shall examine the most crucial structures of policy-relevant power in the large American city and attempt partly to identify and partly to postulate a pattern of development that seems warranted by the histories and present circumstances of several such cities. In doing so we must necessarily make comparisons among fragments of data drawn from sources that are widely diverse in concept and method. The result must obviously fall short of definitive status, but hopefully it may at least provide some stimulus to systematic comparative research in urban data.

II

Two systematic historical studies of urban power structure are those of New Haven by Dahl and Cibola by Schulze.[6] Both identify patterns of change that, despite considerable differences between the communities, are roughly similar. Much of the other published material on American urban history can be read as confirming this general pattern.[7]

Dahl finds that political office in New Haven was dominated first by the "patricians," then by the "entrepreneurs," and finally by the "ex-plebes." Patrician dominance rested upon oligarchic control of all of the major resources from which influence could be fashioned. "(S)ocial status, education, wealth, and political influence were united in the same hands."[8] The entrepreneur's prominence emerged as wealth and social standing were separated, and the new men of business displaced the patricians in controlling economic resources. The entrepreneurs, moreover, were popular as the crabbed patricians were not. But the increasing immigrant labor force led to changing standards of popularity, and by about 1900 "(P)opularity had been split off from both wealth and social standing. Popularity meant votes; votes meant office; office meant influence."[9] The resulting pattern Dahl refers to as one of "dispersed inequalities." Many actors possess politically relevant resources but none possesses enough to dominate a broad range of actions. Particular actors exercise influence over particular policy decisions depending on the resources relevant to that decision, and several types of coalitions may aggregate the influentials concerned with specific problems, but no continuous structure of influence is operative for the broad range of public decision.

Robert Schulze describes a similar historical pattern in. Cibola except that Cibola, a much younger community, had no patrician era. Instead it experienced two stages, local capitalism and nonlocal or absentee capitalism. In the former stage, until 1900, the economic dominants were also the political dominants. They held public office as well as controlling local economic resources and their preeminent social standing reinforced their hegemony. After 1900 Cibola increasingly became an economic satellite and local economic resources came increasingly under the control of national firms. Local officials of these firms did not involve themselves in the active influence structure of the community, much less hold office. Rather, there developed a separate category of influentials, the public leaders, whose influence rested primarily upon such factors as popularity and commitment to the locality. Schulze describes this as a bifurcation of power, but it may not be amiss to suggest that Schulze's data permit the inference that Cibola is more polylithic—influence is widely dispersed and discontinuous—than the bifurcation image implies.

Both Dahl and Schulze give support to the general view that roughly from the end of the Civil War until 1900 American cities were dominated by the merchantry. Where the community had long existed as a substantial population center, notably in the East, the entrepreneurs were likely, as Dahl describes, to have displaced the patricians. Where there hardly had been a

city in the ante-bellum years, there were no patricians to displace, and the commercial elite, relatively open to talents and money, but an elite nonetheless, dominated all the major institutions of the community. Political offices were typically held for short terms with each important merchant expected to contribute some time to the marginal activity of public office-holding.

Although the economic elite of the mercantile city dominated political institutions as well, it is unlikely that much additional influence accrued to them as a result. Public authority did relatively little in this stage or urban development. Only gradually were such elemental functions as water supply and sewage disposal, street construction and maintenance, police and fire protection undertaken.[10] In many cases, too, the initial phases of service were provided by a mixture of public and private effort that mirrored the mixture of public and private position held by influentials. Public improvements were undertaken not only to make life possible in the increasingly crowded and extended city, but also as "booster activities." "Let's put good old ——— on the map!" was an oft-repeated watchword of civic promotion. As McKelvey notes, chambers of commerce were formed to promote economic development in a number of post-Civil War cities,[11] and the promotion of canals, railroads, exhibition halls, and—the classic booster gimmick—the World's Fair, all were part of the merchantry's effort to sell their particular community to the nation. Boosterism, even for the one-shot, short-run promotion, almost invariably involved a complex intermixture of public and private efforts and rested, therefore, on an elite which dominated both public and private office.

. The gradual expansion of public services, however, had a significance for the structure of influence that booster gimmicks did not. Water and sewer systems, schools, streets, parks, police and fire were functions that required continuous operation by larger and larger corps of public employees. With the industrial growth of the city, the object for which boosterism strove, more and more people, requiring near-geometric increases in services, came to the city. Further, the new immigrants came to work in the new industries. Whereas the mercantile city had been as nearly classless as the frontier itself, the industrial city was the site of a differentiated class structure; differentiated by income and life chances, by ethnic origins, by religion, and by political potential.

At the same time, the industrial economic giant viewed the city very differently from the merchant. He was far less dependent on local sales or real estate values and thus less concerned with growth itself. His was a contingent investment in the community—gradually in the several communities housing his several branches—and his civil liability was therefore limited just as the corporate form limited his legal liability. His participation in the allocation of community resources, while potentially great, was infrequent and discontinuous. He was concerned only to protect his relatively narrowly defined corporate interests, not a generalized pattern of influence.

The merchantry had been deeply committed to the city in an economic and emotional way that was missing from the industrial manager. In the industrial city the modes by which civic obligations were discharged became more diverse and more specialized. Service on special boards or committees for libraries or schools, or parks, or slum dwellers was increasingly the way that the local notables—and their wives!—made their community

contributions. These were likely to be structurally separated from the main body of governmental institutions and something of a preserve for "the best people," insulated from "politics." In addition, the slowly growing concern for planning the City Beautiful and reforming inefficient or corrupt government provided larger and larger amounts of "program material" for the luncheon clubs and merchants' association.[12] That occasionally reform campaigns would actually elect a mayor or effect a change in governmental operation did not cancel the fact that economic and social influence had been separated from political influence, and that each now (ca. 1900) rested on a different social base.

An autonomous political elite was, of course, a function of expanded governmental activity and a growing working class population that altered the numerical balance of the city. As Dahl points out, not only were the political entrepreneurs now more popular than the economic entrepreneurs but the criteria of political popularity changed. Effective representation of the Booster spirit and promotion of industrial growth gave way to effective representation of the needs of the poor for elemental services and the promotion of the political organization itself. The boss and his machine we now recognize to have been functional for the newly industrial city; a growing army of public job-holders was recruited, a vast immigration was socialized and provided means of advancement in the urban society, welfare needs were at least minimally provided for, further extensions of public improvement programs were constructed, albeit expensively, and specific services were rendered to the economic elites as well. Railroad spurs, street car franchises, assessment adjustments, police protection of imported labor and a variety of other benefits could be conferred upon business by governmental agencies, even though the latter were no longer controlled by the businessmen themselves. Although businessmen were often appalled and sometimes intimidated by the "new men" of city politics, they rarely intervened or even protested against the system in any continuous way.

Surely a portion of the reason that the boss remained in power was that although government was far more formidable in this period than formerly, the major decisions allocating resources in the city were still made by private interests. Governmental functions were no doubt of crucial importance to the machine itself and to its followers, but, for the most part, they were of marginal importance to the private sector of the economy. It therefore made relatively little difference whether they were done well or not. This is the obverse of the point that economic notables tended to withdraw from civic involvement after about 1900. Not only did the changing city pretty well force them out of office; it was quite rational for them to tend their private gardens and only enter the political arena on behalf of specific policy questions with an immediate payoff to their specialized economic concerns.

What Schulze describes as the bifurcation of power between economic and political elites was thus a function of a changing industrial and social order in the city supported by the enlarged opportunities for political entrepreneurs in the growth of governmental activity. At the same time, the economic and social notables were fragmented by the split between absentee and local capital, the diffusion of energies in a myriad of specialized civic but largely nonpolitical enterprises, and finally by the exodus from the city's corporate limits of the middle class. The efforts of the Progressive WASPs to reform local government, to cleanse the stables of municipal corruption, were in the main doomed by the inexorable movements of people. The middle class moved to suburbia and put political popularity—the ability to get elected—permanently on a working class basis.

The final seal on the bifurcation was effected by the shift of the voting habits of the urban working class to overwhelming Democracy. From the beginning of the New Deal more and more of the large cities became safely Democratic. The metropolitan middle class maintained its Republican loyalties with respect to the national scene, but in local matters a modus vivendi on a business-like basis with the Democratic leadership—a matter of necessity for those with local interests at stake—was often achieved.

Yet the Democratic partisan hegemony provided a kind of cover by which middle class values could reappear in the public decisions of a working class city. By the end of the 1940's the machines were fading. The disciplined delivery of votes was rarely possible, at least on a city-wide basis, and the professionalization of the city bureaucracy was well along. Political office still went to those who mustered majorities from a predominantly working class city electorate but the circular pattern that characterized the era of "Politics for Profit"—votes gave power, power provided favors, favors provided votes—was increasingly broken. It is significant that a move toward "Good Government"—meaning rational policy making—came from within the political stratum itself in these years in Chicago, St. Louis, Pittsburgh, and New Orleans. This move coincided with a change in the agenda of urban resource allocation, and this change in turn has led to a change in the structure of influence.

III

I propose to designate the contemporary structure of urban power as the "new convergence." It is similar in many ways to what Dahl calls the executive-centered coalition. It is headed, and sometimes led, by the elected chief executive of the city, the mayor. Included in the coalition are two principal active groupings, locally-oriented economic interests and the professional workers in technical city-related programs. Both these groupings are sources of initiative for programs that involve major allocations of resources, both public and private. Associated with the coalition, also, are whatever groups constitute the popular vote-base of the mayor's electoral success. Their association is more distant and permissive, however. Their power to direct specific policy choices is severely limited. In the following pages I shall examine each element in the coalition as well as some of the groups in the city that largely lack power. In all cases I am concerned with power that is relevant to key resource allocation decisions.

In the period roughly centered on the turn of the century business leadership was transformed from local to absentee capital, from merchantry to corporate managers. Accompanying this shift in economic organization was a shift in community political commitment and orientations, and this shift, in the direction of reduced interest, coincided with and reinforced the burgeoning autonomous political organization. Now, however, I am saying that business plays an important role in the structure of city affairs. The apparent contradiction points to some complexities in the notion of "business."

First, some kinds of business never experienced the nationalizing effects of industrial reorganization. These often remained intimately associated with politics throughout the era of the bosses. Real estate dealers, building supply firms, insurance agents, and corner confectioneries were always likely to have an iron or two in the political fire. They still do, but these interests are not part of the coalition we are examining. Their interests are small with respect to resource allocations, and they deal in channels that are peripheral to the main body of decisions. Their politics is a kind of eternal process which goes on in many different kinds of worlds without affecting them. Petty business and petty politics are thus handmaidens but irrelevant to the larger issues of power.

The large international corporation continues to regard the local scene with the same investment calculus described earlier. In general, the branch plant will do only as much about the community as is required to develop and maintain an image of good corporate citizenship, and this is far less than is necessary for power or even concern about community resource allocation.[13] Occasionally, the needs of the firm may require it to intrude into the community political system, but such intrusions would be very much on an *ad hoc* basis. The same is likely to be true of large, nationally-oriented unions.[14] The exception occurs when the union or the firm has a large home office or plant in the city or has grown large from a base in a particular community. Then "good citizenship" may require more than charitable work and involve the company or union leadership in larger urban policy issues.

The most active business firms in the new convergence, however, are those with major investments in the community, which are dependent on the growth of a particular community, and which have come to recognize that all the major issues and decisions of the city affect their interests.[15] Furthermore, they all share a growing concern with that congeries of problems labeled "core city decay." They include the major banks, utilities, railroads, department stores, large real estate firms, and metropolitan newspapers. Functionally, the list is remarkably similar from city to city. Also similar is the fact that active concern with community affairs is relatively recent, largely post-World War II, and coincides with the perception of threat to tangible "downtown" economic values. Finally, the re-entry of these groups into the active quest for power coincides with the weakening of the party-political dominance of the governmental arena. This permitted the numerically inferior business groups to assert their claims on a more continuous basis than formerly had been the case. In Chicago, where the machine did not weaken so much, the loop businessmen continued to operate a largely *ad hoc* basis.[16] Elsewhere, however, the downtown business interests articulated their concerns more forcefully and organized their community-centered energies more efficiently than ever before. Instead of boosterism, business-centered groups helped to trigger a variety of problem-solving programs such as redevelopment and traffic revision and provided continuing support for efforts at solving other problems such as delinquency and crime. Much of the lay leadership of public campaigns for bonds, for example; much of the stimulus to action itself; and much of the private portion of new investment necessary to redevelopment came from this newly organized group. It is important to recognize, however, that, although the support and stimulus of downtown business was and is an essential element in the coalition that dominates decisions in the city, downtown business does not constitute a power elite. It does not run the city, or call the shots for its puppets.

The second element in the coalition—one would be tempted to call it the Civic Establishment except that the term may connote more tradition-based power than this coalition possesses—is composed of the technician, the professional, the expert. As Barry Karl has pointed out, the innovative function of the Progressive reform groups has largely been taken over by the professional.[17] The social worker has replaced Jane Addams. The social scientist in a Charles Merriam has replaced the amateur politician/reformer. Police administration, comprehensive budgeting and capital programming, systematic traffic control, land use planning, and renewal and rehabilitation have all become, in one degree or another, the domains of the expert. Technical criteria play a far greater role than before in determining choices, and the specification of alternatives is likewise largely a function of the technician who, often alone, knows what is possible.[18]

Perhaps the policy area most obviously dominated by the expert is that of public education. Teachers and school administrators not only set the agenda for action. They provide most of the arguments and evidence relevant to the choices that can be made and constitute the most active and powerful interests participating in the decision-making process. If non-professionals protest against certain policies—Negroes denouncing *de facto* segregation, for example—the professional educators cite technical educational criteria as a sufficient justification for their decisions and frequently carry the day.

The existence of professional skills

relevant to city problems is, of course, a relatively new feature on the urban scene. Even now we are a long way from a technocracy, for the skills fall far short of the problems. Nevertheless, the growth of what broadly may be called applied social science has added a significant number of new people in new roles to the urban system, and these people help articulate and specify the problems and alternative courses of action for the other interests in the coalition. In this way the technician exercises power over resource allocation that is every bit as real as that of the economic interests or authority-wielders.

Let us turn to the peak of the loose coalition of interests that dominate today's urban scene, the mayor. He presides over the "new convergence," and, if the coalition is to succeed, he must lead it. More than anyone else he determines the direction of urban development; yet his sanctions are few, his base of support insecure. The mayor is both the most visible person in the community and, on questions of public policy, probably the most influential. Yet his is a classic example of the separation of influence and power.[19] Few big-city mayors have significant patronage resources. Even fewer use their appointments to give themselves direct leverage over policy. Although the mayor in a partisan city is necessarily elected through processes that involve the ward organizations, no big-city mayor, not even Daley, can be regarded as the creature of the machine. Rather the mayor is an individual who has 1) sufficient mass appeal and/or organizational support to win election, 2) enough awareness of the complexity of urban problems to rely heavily on a professional staff for advice and counsel, and 3) the ability to negotiate successfully with the economic notables in the city to mobilize both public and private resources

in efforts to solve core city economic and social problems.

Successful electioneering in the city requires that the candidate be palatable to a lower income constituency, especially to Negroes. Where there remain vestiges of party organization with vote-delivering capabilities the successful candidate must have some appeal for them, too. An ethnic background or family association that evokes support from the delivery wards is often helpful. At the same time, however, the successful mayoral candidate is likely to appeal to that portion of the urban electorate which historically has been reformist or mugwumpish in orientation.[20] He personifies good government by his espousal of professionalism in local administration. Frequently his personal style, despite his name or political forbears, is thoroughly white-collar and middle class. He is relatively articulate on local television, and his campaigns are likely to stress his competence at communal problem-solving rather than the particular group benefits that may accrue following his election. Nor is this mere campaign talk. His administration concentrates on solving or alleviating particular problems rather than building memorials or dramatizing the city's commercial prospects. Again, this posture requires collaboration with those possessing the relevant resources, the experts and the businessmen.

Obviously, there are variations in the way the mayoral role is played. From city to city and mayor to mayor many differences may appear. The main lines of demarcation may be twofold, however. Some mayors, possessing the gifts of self-dramatization, may more fully personify the programs of the city than others. This has little effect on the content of the decisions but may have consequences in terms of support. Mayors may also differ in the degree to which they actively seek out problems and solutions. Banfield describes Daley waiting for things to come to a head; other mayors more actively seek either to forestall the problem entirely or to structure the whole process through which the issue develops. The latter distinction may be related to the structure of the city; the larger and more diverse the city, the less effectively can the mayor actively shape the problem-solving process.

Of what is mayoral influence composed? Much of it is contained in the office itself. Of all the roles in the community none is so well situated with respect to the flow of information concerning the city's problems. This alone gives the occupant of the office a great advantage over other influentials. He knows more about more things than anyone else. Although his patronage power may be relatively slight, his budgetary authority is typically substantial. Insofar as he, by himself or in a board or commission, presents the budget to the council, he is determining much of the agenda for the discussion of public affairs, and no one else in the city can compete with him. Third, his ability to co-opt persons into *ad hoc* committees is unmatched in the city. As the only official with formal authority to speak for the entire city, he can confer legitimacy on co-opted leaders as no one else can. Thus, if he chooses to, a shrewd mayor may have a good deal to say about who shall be regarded as leaders and who shall not. Negotiations on civil rights issues in a number of cities illustrate the point well. Finally, as noted earlier, the mayor is, or soon becomes, far better known in the community than anyone else, and is far better able to command and structure public attention.[21]

A considerable factor in the mayor's ability to structure public debate is his superior access to and influence over the press. City hall reporters not only cover his office closely but their view of city problems is very largely gained through their daily contacts with the official city fathers. The latter, in turn, are cordial and by being helpful can be reasonably assured that most of the news stories out of city hall will reflect mayoral interpretation. The newspapers as major businesses with their economic future tied to the local community and its elites are likely to favor editorially a mayor whose style embraces their interests. Thus even though the editors may differ with some specific recommendation of the mayor, they give him general support, while through them the mayor communicates his conceptions of city problems and program. One result, of course, is to make it difficult for others to challenge successfully the incumbent mayor for re-election.[22] Thus despite the unstable character of the coalition's base—predominantly low income voters and downtown businessmen—the mayor, once elected, may serve a good many terms. No outsider can find a sufficiently sharp wedge of controversy to drive between the disparate elements, or sufficient visibility to exploit whatever gaps develop.

Nevertheless, the mayor is influential only relative to other groups in the city. He is not powerful relative to the problems he tries to solve. The mayor cannot determine by fiat or, apparently, any other way that the economic resources of the city shall increase, that crime and poverty shall decline, that traffic shall move efficiently. He only has rather more directly to say about how the problems shall be approached than anyone else.

This discussion omits those cities which have adopted the council-manager form of government. In Kansas City or Cincinnati, for example, the aggregative and legitimating functions are less likely to be performed by the mayor who is seldom more than the ceremonial head of the city. The manager can rarely perform these functions either, since they are largely incompatible with his professional role. The result may be that the functions are not performed at all. On the other hand, the manager does possess some of the elements of leadership, especially information. As Banfield and Wilson note, the manager "sits at the center of things, where all communication lines converge. In the nature of the case, then, the councilman must depend on him for their information. Whether he likes it or not, this gives him a large measure of control over them."[23]

IV

The "new convergence" we have described actively seeks out solutions to certain problems it regards as critical to the city's growth. This activist posture may be viewed as somewhat at variance with the approaches to decision-making described by Dahl and by Banfield. Dahl suggests that in New Haven the coalition led by Mayor Lee has actively sought to resolve certain major issues with Lee serving as the principal negotiator among the contending forces. But, says Dahl, Lee selected issues with a view towards their effect upon his chances for re-election. Permanently conditioning the mayor's strategy was the fact that "the mayor and his political opponents were constantly engaged in a battle for votes at the next election, which was always just around the corner."[24] So far as most large cities are concerned, this may greatly overstate the impact of the necessity for re-election on the specific choices made by the mayor and his allies. We shall try to suggest both the role of the electorate and some of the more immediate restraints upon mayoral choice-making in a moment.

Banfield's analysis of Chicago leads to the conclusion that issues are raised primarily by large formal organizations, some of which are governmental and some of which are not.[25] As the maintenance or enhancement needs of the organization require governmental decisions they enter the political arena and usually seek the support of Mayor Daley. Daley himself, however, operates in primarily a reflexive fashion. Although he desires to "do big things," he must move slowly and cautiously, fearful of generating further controversies, and aware that the ponderous and intricate structure of power he heads can be disrupted and his influence capital used up if he moves too soon or too often. But Banfield selects issues that illustrate this argument. His cases fall far short of representing the range of major resource allocation decisions for Chicago. It may still be true, therefore, that Daley initiates or actively participates in the process involved in making other decisions. Certainly it seems that other big-city mayors do.[26]

I focused originally on the processes of allocating scarce resources. These processes may sometimes involve bitter conflict among rival interests. They may sometimes be resolved, however, in a highly consensual way. Particularly is this likely to be the case when the technical experts play a large role in shaping the decision. Much of the time such major areas of public policy as expressway planning, zoning, and budget-making are determined in ways that evoke little complaint or dispute. The fact that no one in the city effectively objects to the decision makes the decision no less important in terms of resource allocation.

A closely related aspect of urban decision-making is that a great many decisions are made in a fashion that may best be described as habitual. The pressures on the time and attention of decision-makers are such that many decisions must continue to be made (or avoided) as they have been in the past. No continuing calculation can be made of the costs and benefits for each area of possible choice. Much is done routinely. Much is left undone in the same way. Control of the routine is largely in the hands of the technicians with the mayor in the best position to alter it at the margins.

Some issues are forced "from the outside," of course. Things which city leaders would prefer not to have to deal with may be pressed in the fashion Banfield describes. Race relations issues generally come under this category. Almost every large city mayor has been compelled to take action, not because he or his coalition particularly wanted to, but because they were forced to by external pressure.

The recent demands of militant Negro groups have often been concentrated on city hall, however, even when the substance of the demands dealt with jobs in private employment. Negro leaders have correctly identified the mayor as the appropriate figure to convene local elites in order to negotiate agreements that will open job opportunities to Negroes. Militant Negroes have often greatly over-estimated the power of the mayor to effect a satisfactory solution, however. For while he is in a stronger position than any other person or group or functioning organization, his resources and those of his allies may fall far short of the requirements.

Pressure from the constituency would not be the usual way for policy to be initiated, however. The bulk of the city's working agenda is made up of proposals drawn up by the city's own technicians to meet problems identified by them or by their allies in the problem-oriented sectors of the community. The need for new revenue sources, for example, is perceived by the mayor and his staff long before public pressure is exerted, and it is the mayoral coalition which seeks a viable solution to the problem.

Not all mayors, not all corps of technicians, and not all downtown business groups are equal in ability to perceive problems, devise solutions, or negotiate settlements. One of the significant variables that distinguishes one city's political system from another is the energy and imagination of its newly convergent elites. In some cities solutions may be found that escape the leaders of another. It is probably true, however, that these differences have been narrowed somewhat by the collaboration among urban elites throughout the nation. The American Municipal Association and the U.S. Conference of Mayors provide organized communication networks that link the political executives. So does HHFA in its field. So do the various associations of urban technicians in their respective specialties. The metropolitan press facilitates a certain amount of interchange with respect to both problems and solutions in urban areas. Thus there has developed some degree of consensus as to what should be done and some uniformity in the structure of power by which action may be accomplished.

Cities vary with respect not only to energy and skill of leadership but in tangible resources, public and private that may be mobilized for reallocation. In Pittsburgh, for example, there was probably no available substitute for the Mellon cash. In St. Louis the scarcity or stodginess or both of local private capital has made the redevelopment task more difficult.

These are variables involved in the power structure of a community. That there are also variations in the range and severity of the problems cities face is obvious and complicates further the task of comparative analysis.

V

I have suggested that a large portion of the content of urban public policy is provided directly by one or more of the three main elements of the governing coalition; the mayor, the technical experts, and the downtown business community. They identify the problems, they articulate the alternative actions that might be taken, and they themselves take most of the relevant actions. This structure of decision-making provides no immediate role for the community-at-large, the voters; and, although Dahl may overstate the significance of their role in limiting New Haven's executive-centered coalition, they do play a role in resource allocations, and so do the organized groups that represent segments of the electorate that are outside the dominant coalition.

Dahl's attribution of "weight" to the electorate seems to be based on the relatively intense partisan competition in New Haven, and it may be reinforced by the need to run every two years. But in many cities the direct competition for office is neither so sharp nor so frequent. The tenure in office of prominent mayors such as Tucker, Daley, or Wagner suggests that survival in office may not always require the close attention to voter desires that Dahl suggests. Particularly is this likely in a city where elections are partisan, for the safety of the Democratic ticket is not often in question in many of these cities. The primary may occasionally present peril to the incumbent, and in both partisan and non-partisan cities incumbents sometimes lose. But there is little evidence to show that mayors, or other elected executives for that matter, have any reliable way of perceiving voter needs very accurately or consciously building support for himself among them. The new mayor may say, with Richard Daley, that "good government is good politics," in part because he doesn't have the option to engage in any other kind.

Nevertheless, generalized constituency sentiment remains a factor that affects policy-making, albeit in a secondary, boundary-setting way. It works primarily in three ways. First, the technician as social scientist often takes into account the interests and needs of the public he hopes to serve when making his plans and recommendations. If he proposes an enlarged staff of case workers for the Welfare Department, he does so partly because in some sense he expects the public to benefit. It is rarely, however, because any public demand for the larger staff is expressed. Rather, the technician believed the proposal would be "good" for the constituents. Secondly, the electorate must make certain broad choices directly. Bond issues and tax rates must often be voted upon; other types of referenda must be approved; key policy-making officials must be elected. Very often this involves "selling the public" on the desirability of the proposal. They have not demanded it. They often have no strong predispositions one way or another except perhaps for a class-related bias on public expenditures in general. But this approval is required, and in anticipation of the limits of tolerance the key decision-makers must tailor their proposals. This is influence, of course, but of a general and largely negative kind. Thirdly, there is the active demand stemming directly from the constituents to which policy-makers respond, but which response would not have been made in the absence of the public demand. Some of these demands go counter to the policies espoused by the coalition; spot zoning, for example, or construction unions' demands on the building code. In some instances the coalition may have the power to block the demands; in other cases, not. Some demands, however, are more difficult to deal with because, if they arise, they cannot be blocked by the exercise of power, but at the same time they are so controversial that almost any solution is likely to damage the overall position of the leaders. As we have noted, many of the issues of race relations are in this category. The city fathers have not agitated these issues, but once raised they must be met.

As we assign "the public" to a largely secondary role, we must also relegate those officials most closely associated with immediate constituency relationships to a similarly secondary position. Councilmen or aldermen, ward leaders, and other local party leaders are likely to play only supportive or obstructive roles in the community's decision-making process. The demands for action do not come from or through them, they are not privy to the councils either of the notables or the experts. They may well play out their traditional roles of precinct or ward politician, but, unlike the machine leader of yore, these roles are separated quite completely from those of policy-making. Even in Chicago, where the mayor's position in part depends on his vote-getting strength through the party organization, very little participation in policy-making filters down to the ward leaders. Similarly, William

Green's rise to power in the party organization in Philadelphia had little effect on the content of public policy. It is essential to see that the difference between the policy-making leadership and the "politicians" is more than rhetorical. It carries a substantial impact on the content of policy.[27]

Even though neither the party professionals nor the electorate generally are active participants in the process of resource allocation, is not the top political leadership, specifically the mayor, constrained by his desire for re-election? In part, of course, the answer is yes. In partisan cities the mayor must be nominated and elected on the party ticket, and, particularly in the primary, this may involve getting party organization support. In a non-partisan community too, the mayor must get enough votes to win. It does not follow, however, that there is much connection between what is needed to gain votes and the specific decisions made once in office. Dahl emphasizes the vote-getting popularity of Richard Lee's program in New Haven, especially of urban renewal. Yet that popularity was not really evident in advance of the decisions and was largely dissipated within a very few years. Doubtless Mayor Collins has increased his popularity in Boston by rationalizing and reducing the fiscal burden, but, if Levin is at all correct, his election was not a mandate for *any* particular decisions he has made.[28] The same, I think, could be argued for Dilworth, Tucker, and others of the "new mayors." Certainly the limits of public understanding and acceptance constitute restraints upon the decision-making system, but these are broad restraints, rarely specific in directing choices, and operating largely as almost subconscious limits to the kinds of choices that may be made.[29]

VI

It may not be amiss to conclude this discussion by juxtaposing three quite different strands of thought concerning the urban scene. On the one hand, Dahl and his associates have generally denied the existence of a single structure of power in the city. We have argued, not contradicting Dahl but changing the emphasis, that on a substantial set of key issues such a structure may be discerned. Hunter, *et al*, have stressed an essentially monolithic structure heavily weighted in behalf of the economic elites. We have stressed the central role of elected political leadership. Finally, such writers as Lewis Mumford and Jane Jacobs, less interested in the problems of power, have doubted the capacity of the urban community to serve man's essential needs at all. In a sense, we are suggesting that each may be partly correct, partly wrong. The coalition of interests headed by the mayor may indeed lack the resources, public and private, separately or combined, to solve the com-munal problems now dominating the civic agenda. This is the irony that lies behind the convergence of power elements in the modern city. Where once there seemed to be ample resources to keep what were regarded as the major problems of urban life within quite tolerable limits, now, with far more self-conscious collaboration of governmental and private economic power than ever before, and with those structures of power themselves larger and more extensive than ever, the capacity to cope with the recognized problems of the environment seems almost pathetically inadequate. Partly, this may be because the problems have changed in magnitude, and, partly, that we perceive their magnitude in more sophisticated fashion. In any case, it makes the notion of an elite with ample power to deal with the urban community if ever it chooses to, seem a romance, a utopian dream. Like other municipal utopias—Progressive-era reform or today's metropolitan reorganization—it may be yearned for but largely unrealized.

NOTES

1. For a most comprehensive and thoughtful history of urban growth in America see Blake McKelvey, *The Urbanization of America* (New Brunswick, New Jersey: Rutgers University Press, 1963).
2. Robert A. Dahl's study of New Haven was a classic of political science almost before it was published. See *Who Governs*? (New Haven: Yale University Press, 1961). Dahl chose not to integrate his findings with those available concerning other communities, and in a number of respects one may argue that his conclusions are limited to the New Haven context. One cannot deny, however, that the larger question of how to approach the study of power has been given theoretically sophisticated stimulus from the work of Dahl and his associates. See Nelson W. Polsby, *Community Power and Political Theory* (New Haven: University Press, 1963). For a convenient summary of many of the items in the large monographic literature on community power structure, see Charles Press, *Main Street Politics* (East Lansing: Michigan State University Institute for Community Development, 1962).
3. Recent attempts to engage in genuinely comparative analysis include Oliver P. Williams and Charles Adrian, *Four Cities* (Philadelphia: University of Pennsylvania Press, 1963); Amos H. Hawley, "Community Power and Urban Renewal Success," American Journal of Sociology, VIII (1963), pp. 422–31; Leo F. Schnore and Robert R. Alford, "Forms of Government and Socio-economic Characteristics of Suburbs," *Administrative Science Quarterly*, VIII (1963), pp. 1–17.
4. See the categorization suggested by Peter Rossi, "Power and Community Structure," *Midwest Journal of Political Science*, IV (1960), p. 398.
5. *City Politics* (Cambridge: Harvard University Press, 1963).
6. Robert Schulze, "The Bifurcation of Power in a Satellite City," in M. Janowitz, ed., *Community Political Systems* (Glencoe, Illinois: The Free Press of Glencoe, Illinois, 1961), pp. 19–81.

7. The volume of historical work dealing with American cities is immense in weight but often disappointing when it comes to the questions of greatest interest to political scientists. McKelvey's work is masterful both as a summary and as an introduction to the literature. *Op. cit.*, *passim*.

8. Dahl, *op. cit.*, p. 24.

9. *Ibid.*, p. 51.

10. See McKelvey, *op. cit.*, pp. 12–13.

11. *Ibid.*, p. 43.

12. The suggestion that civic reform issues provide "program material" and sometimes little else is developed in Edward Banfield, *Political Influence* (New York: The Free Press of Glencoe, 1961), pp. 298, ff.

13. See the provocative essay by Norton Long, "The Corporation and the Local Community," in Charles Press, ed., *The Polity* (Chicago: Rand McNally & Co., 1962), pp. 122–136.

14. See Banfield and Wilson, *op. cit.*, pp. 277–80.

15. See *Ibid.*, Ch. 18.

16. See Banfield, *Political Influence*, pp. 291, ff. Banfield himself emphasizes the tangible conflicts of interest which divide Chicago business interests. Even so, however, one may suspect that without the Daley machine Loop business interests would have developed more commonality of interests.

17. See *Executive Reorganization and Reform in the New Deal* (Cambridge: Harvard University Press, 1963), Ch. 1.

18. Banfield and Wilson note that the city manager often acquires power by virtue of "his virtual monopoly of technical and other detailed information." *op. cit.*, p. 175. They pay little attention to the possibility that other technicians in the city bureaucracy may acquire power over limited segments of policy in the same manner. Banfield and Wilson do note that in many cities it is the bureaucracy which can initiate and implement change but do not concede increasing significance to this group. See pp. 218–23.

19. Banfield and Wilson suggest that as the mayor's machine-based power has declined his formal authority has increased, by virtue of reformers' efforts to achieve greater centralization. They recognize, of course, that the increased authority does not compensate for the loss of power. Moreover, in the contemporary city the scope of the perceived problems and needs is often so broad that the strongest political machine could have done little about it from its own resources. Providing investment capital to rebuild downtown or opening employment opportunities for Negroes must be negotiated in the broader community. The mayor is likely to be the chief negotiator and neither formal authority nor political clout is as effective as bargaining skills. *Ibid.*, p. 336, ff.

20. Lorin Peterson greatly overstates the case for connecting contemporary urban influentials with the mugwump tradition, but there is something in his argument. See *The Day of the Mugwump* (New York: Random House 1961).

21. Scott Greer found that Mayor Tucker was the only person in the St. Louis community, city or suburbs, with any substantial visibility with respect to community-wide issues. *Metropolitics* (New York: John Wiley & Sons, 1963), pp. 106–7.

22. Banfield and Wilson note that the city hall reporter "is likely to be in a symbiotic relationship with the politicians and bureaucrats whose activities he reports. "*op. cit.*, p. 316. They do not conclude, however, that this relationship strengthens the elected leadership. Indeed, they imply the opposite. See, e.g., p. 325. This difference in judgement calls for more systematic empirical analysis that is presently available.

23. *Ibid.*, p. 175. Banfield and Wilson, however, do not make this point concerning the position of the mayor in non-manager cities.

24. *Political Influence*, p. 214.

25. *Ibid.*, p. 263, ff.

26. In addition to Dahl's discussion of Mayor Lee's active role, one may cite as particularly pertinent the discussions of Philadelphia, Detroit, Nashville and Seattle reported in the appropriate volumes of Edward Banfield, ed., *City Politics Reports* (Cambridge: Joint Center for Urban Studies, mimeo). My own research in St. Louis, the initial foundation for much of the argument in this essay, certainly leads to this conclusion.

27. For an illustration, see Robert H. Salisbury, "St. Louis: Relationships among Interests, Parties and Governmental Structure," *Western Political Quarterly*, XIII (1960), pp. 498–507.

28. See *The Alienated Voter* (New York: Holt, Rinehart and Winston, 1960).

29. Banfield and Wilson also discuss a shift in the contemporary city, at least in political style, from working class to middle class. They conclude that the new style politician, reflecting middle class values in a working-class city, will be compelled to offer broad inducements to the electorate in the form of major civic accomplishments if he wishes reelection. *Op. cit.*, p. 329 ff. This argument, like Dahl's, seems to me to assume that the urban electorate "shops" more actively than I think it does. It also assumes that political leaders in the urban community are more acutely conscious of their reelection problems than I think they are.

43. The Dynamics of Community Controversy

James S. Coleman

The outcome of decisions on local issues cannot be inferred from knowledge of the community's power structure alone. It is necessary also to take into account the natural tendency of community controversies to develop in particular directions, as well as the social structure that provides the context in which power is exerted. Both these conditions are the concern of James Coleman in the following selection taken from a short monograph reviewing research on community conflict.

Coleman points out that local controversies have their own dynamic whereby the response of groups within the community to potential issues of conflict produces reactions that intensify public debate. He describes several components of this dynamic, including the conversion of specific issues into general concerns, the emergence of totally new issues, and the polarization of interest groups among the citizenry. Coleman believes that four elements of the community's social structure can influence the course of the conflict. These are (1) the degree to which residents identify with the community, (2) the ratio of organizations and associations to population, (3) the distribution of organizational participation among residents, and (4) the extent to which memberships in associations are interlocking.

James S. Coleman is Professor of Social Relations at Johns Hopkins University. He is the author of *Equality of Educational Opportunity* (1966), *Adolescents and the Schools* (1965), and *Introduction to Mathematical Sociology* (1964).

The most striking fact about the development and growth of community controversies is the similarity they exhibit despite diverse underlying sources and different kinds of precipitating incidents. Once the controversies have begun, they resemble each other remarkably. Were it not for these similarities, Machiavelli could never have written his guide to warfare, and none of the other numerous works on conflict, dispute, and controversy would have been possible.[1] It is the peculiarity of social controversy that it sets in motion its own dynamics; these tend to carry it forward in a path which bears little relation to its beginnings. An examination of these dynamics will occupy the attention of this paper.

One caution is necessary: we do not mean to suggest that nothing can be done about community controversy once it begins. To the contrary, the dynamics of controversy *can* be interrupted and diverted —either by conscious action or by existing conditions in the community. As a result, although the same dynamic tendencies of controversy are found in every case, the actual development in particular cases may differ widely. In the discussion below, the unrestrained dynamic tendencies will be discussed.

Changes in Issues

The issues which provide the initial basis of response in a controversy undergo great transformations as the controversy develops. Three fundamental transformations appear to take place.

Specific to General   First, specific issues give way to *general* ones. In Scarsdale, the school's critics began by attacking books in the school library; soon they focused on the whole educational philosophy. In Mason City, Iowa, where a city-manager plan was abandoned, the campaign against the plan started with a letter to the newspaper from a local carpenter complaining that the creek overflowed into his home. This soon snowballed, gathering other specific complaints, and then gave way to the general charge that the council and manager were dominated by local business interests and had no concern for the workingman.

Most of the controversies examined show a similar pattern. (Even those that do not are helpful, for they suggest just why the pattern *does* exist in so many cases. Political controversies, for example, exhibit the pattern much less than do disputes based primarily on differing values or economic interests. The Athens, Tennessee, political fight began with the same basic issue it ended with—political control of the community (Key, 1950). Other political struggles in which there is little popular involvement show a similar restriction to the initial issue.)

It seems that movement from specific to general issues occurs whenever there are deep cleavages of values or interests in the community which require a spark to set them off—usually a specific incident representing only a small part of the underlying difference. In contrast, those disputes which appear not to be generated by deep cleavages running through the community as a whole, but are rather power struggles within the community, do not show the shift from specific to general. To be sure, they may come to involve the entire community, but no profound fundamental difference comes out.

This first shift in the nature of the issues, then, uncovers the fundamental differences which set the stage for a precipitating incident in the first place.

New and Different Issues   Another frequent change in the issues of the dispute is the emergence of quite *new and different* issues, unrelated to the original ones. In the Pasadena school controversy, the initial issue was an increased school budget and a consequent increased tax rate. This soon became only one issue of many; ideological issues concerning "progressive education," and other issues, specific as well as general, arose. In another case, a controversy which began as a personal power struggle between a school superintendent and a principal shifted to a conflict involving general educational principles when the community as a whole entered in (Warner et al., 1949, pp. 201–204). A study of the adoption of the city-manager plan in fifty cities (Stone, Price, and Stone, 1940, pp. 34–38) shows that in one group of cities, designated by the authors "machine-ridden," the controversy grew to include ethnic, religious, political, and ideological differences. Political campaigns generally, in fact, show this tendency: issues multiply rapidly as the campaign increases in intensity.

There are two different sources for this diversification of issues. One is in a sense "involuntary"; issues which could not have been raised before the controversy spring suddenly to the fore as relationships between groups and individuals change.

We see how this operates in an argument between two people, e.g., in the common phrases used to introduce new issues: "I hesitated to mention this before but now ..." or, "While I'm at it, I might as well say this too...." As long as functioning relations exist between individuals or groups, there are strong inhibitions upon introducing any issue which might impair the functioning. In a sense the stable relation suppresses topics which might upset it. But once the stability of the relation *is* upset, the suppressed topics can come to the surface uninhibitedly. We suggest that exactly the same mechanisms are at work in the community as a whole; networks of relations, however complex, act in the same fashion.

But in many other cases, illustrated best by political disputes, the diversification of issues is more a purposive move on the part of the antagonists, and serves quite a different function: to solidify opinion and bring in new participants by providing new bases of response. Again, this is evident in the two-person argument: each antagonist brings to bear all the *different* arguments he can to rationalize his position to himself and to convince his opponent. Just the same thing occurs in community conflict: each side attempts to increase solidarity and win new adherents from the still uncommitted neutrals by introducing as many diverse issues as will benefit its cause. Both these function—sincreasing solidarity among present members, and gaining new members—are vital; the first aids in the important task of "girding for action" by disposing of all doubts and hesitancies; the second gains allies, always an important aim in community conflict.

The issues introduced must be very special ones with little potential for disrupting the group that initiates them. They are almost always "one-sided" in the sense that they provide a basis for response only in one direction, and they gain their value by monopolizing the attention of community members. In controversies where a challenge is offered to an incumbent administration, the issue of "maladministration" is, typically, a one-sided issue; the administration can only offer defense and hope that attention soon shifts elsewhere. In school controversies, the issue of Communist subversion in the schools is one-sided; as long as it occupies the attention of the community, it is to the advantage of school critics. In contrast, the issue "progressive education *vs.* traditional education" offers no differential advantage to either side (unless, of course, progressive education can be identified by its opponents as "Communistic") until one group can prove to the majority of the community that one approach is better from all points of view. Analysis of the different functions of different kinds of issues can be found in Berelson, Lazarsfeld, and McPhee (1954), and in Coleman (1955, p. 253).

Disagreement to Antagonism A third change in the nature of issues as a controversy develops is the shift from *disagreement* to *antagonism*. A dispute which began dispassionately, in a disagreement over issues, is characterized suddenly by personal slander, by rumor, by the focusing of direct hostility. This is one of the most important aspects in the self-generation of conflict: Once set in motion, hostility can sustain conflict unaided by disagreement about particular issues. The original issues may be settled, yet the controversy continues unabated. The antagonistic relationship has become direct: it no longer draws sustenance from an outside element—an issue. As in an argument between friends, a discussion which begins with *disagreement* on a point in question often ends with each *disliking* the other.[2] The dynamics which account for the shift from disagreement to antagonism are two: "involuntary," and deliberate. Simmel explains the involuntary process by saying that it is "expedient" and "appropriate" to hate one's opponent just as it is "appropriate" to like someone who agrees with you (1955, p. 34). But perhaps there is a stronger explanation: we associate with every person we know certain beliefs, interests, traits, attributes, etc. So long as we disagree with only one or a few of his beliefs, we are "divided" in our feelings toward him. He is not wholly black or white in our eyes. But when we quarrel, the process of argument itself generates new issues; we disagree with more and more of our opponent's beliefs. Since these beliefs constitute *him* in our eyes, rather than isolated aspects of him, his image grows blacker. Our hostility is directed toward him personally. Thus the two processes—the first leading from a single issue to new and different ones, and the second leading from disagreement to direct antagonism— fit together perfectly and help carry the controversy along its course.[3] Once direct antagonism is felt toward an opponent, one is led to make public attacks on him.

Perhaps it would be fruitful to set down a little more precisely the "involuntary" processes which we suggest operate to shift issues from one disagreement to a multitude, ultimately to antagonism. In a diagram it might look something like this:

Men have a strong need for *consistency*. If I disagree violently with someone, then it becomes psychologically more comfortable to see him as totally black rather than gray.[4] This drive for consistency may provide the fuel for the generalization processes in Steps 3 and 4 of the diagram.

Apart from these "involuntary" or "natural" processes, the use of personal charges by the antagonists is a common device to bypass disagreement and go directly to antagonism. Sometimes consciously, often unconsciously, the opposing nuclei attempt to reach new people through this means, drawing more and more of the community to their side by creating personal hostility to the opponent.[5] In political disputes the degeneration to personal charges is particularly frequent. V. O. Key notes that in the South, state political campaigns are often marked by candidates' personal attacks on each other. He suggests that such attacks grow in the absence of "real" issues (1950, pp. 194–200). This seems reasonable since the use of personal attacks may be an attempt to incite antagonism in cases where there is not enough disagreement for the natural processes of conflict to operate. In other words, the attacks constitute an attempt to stimulate controversy artificially—a "short-cut" —by bypassing a stage in the process which might otherwise let the conflict falter. Such actions would seem to occur only when community leaders need to gain the support of an otherwise apathetic

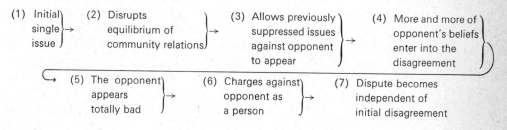

(1) Initial single issue → (2) Disrupts equilibrium of community relations → (3) Allows previously suppressed issues against opponent to appear → (4) More and more of opponent's beliefs enter into the disagreement → (5) The opponent appears totally bad → (6) Charges against opponent as a person → (7) Dispute becomes independent of initial disagreement

community which has no real issues dividing it.

In another group of controversies, focused around certain value differences, the shift to personal attacks is sometimes immediate, and seems to be a result of real disagreement and incipient antagonism. School controversies often begin with personal charges against teachers or principals of moral impropriety, or, more frequently in recent days, subversion. Why is it that personal attacks in these instances succeed in creating immediate hostility within the community, while other kinds of personal attacks are viewed with disfavor by the community, that is, until the late, intense stages of controversy when all inhibiting norms and constraints are forgotten? The reason may be this: When a personal accusation refers to behavior viewed as extremely illegitimate by community members it outweighs the norm against personal attacks. Presumably the community members put themselves in the place of the attacker and say, in effect, "If I knew these things to be true, would I feel right about speaking out publicly?" When the charges concern sexual immorality or political subversion, many persons can answer "yes" to such a question;[6] thus they feel unconcerned about making the kind of attacks that they would ordinarily never allow except in the heat of dispute.[7] These attacks, in turn, quickly create the heat that might be otherwise slow in coming.

Changes in content and character of issues constitutes only one kind of change going on in the development of a controversy; at the same time, the whole structure of organizations and associations in the community is undergoing change as well. The nature of these changes is examined below.

Changes in the Social Organization of the Community

Polarization of Social Relations As controversy develops associations flourish *within* each group, but wither *between* persons on opposing sides. People break off long-standing relationships, stop speaking to former friends who have been drawn to the opposition, but proliferate their associations with fellow-partisans. Again, this is part of the process of stripping for action: getting rid of all social encumbrances which impede the action necessary to win the conflict. Polarization is perhaps less pronounced in short-term conflicts, and in those in which the issues cut across existing organizational ties and informal relations. But in all conflicts, it tends to alter the social geography of the community to separate it into two clusters, breaking apart along the line of least attachment.

The Formation of Partisan Organizations In many types of community conflict, there are no existing organizations to form the nuclei of the two sides. But as the controversy develops, organizations form. In a recent controversy in Cincinnati over the left-wing political history of the city planning director (Hessler, 1953), supporters of the director and of the councilman who hired him formed a "Committee of 150 for Political Morality." This Committee used considerable sophistication in the selection of a name and in their whole campaign. Rather than remain on the defensive, and let the opposition blanket the community with charges of subversion, this Committee invoked an equally strong value—of morality in politics—and took the offensive against the use of personal attack by their opponents. This technique constitutes a way in which controversy can be held on a relatively high plane: by invoking community norms against smears, using these very norms as an issue of the controversy. If the norm is strong, it may keep the controversy "within bounds."

In general, as a dispute intensifies the partisans form *ad hoc* groups which have numerous functions while the controversy lasts: they serve as communication centers, as communication becomes more and more important within each side and attenuates between groups; they serve as centers for planning and organizing partisan meetings and other activities; and especially they can meet quickly—in a situation where speed is of utmost importance—any threat or challenge posed by the opposition.

The most common variation upon this theme is the union; in industrial disputes, the union is a defense organization *already* in existence; in a real controversy, it takes on all the aspects of the usual partisan organizations: secrecy, spirited meetings, pamphleteering, fund-raising.[8]

The Emergence of New Leaders As partisan organizations are formed and a real nucleus develops around each of the opposing centers, new leaders tend to take over the dispute; often they are men who have not been community leaders in the past, men who face none of the constraints of maintaining a previous community position, and feel none of the cross-pressures felt by members of community organizations. In addition, these leaders rarely have real identification with the community. In the literature they often emerge as marginal men who have never held a position of leadership before. A study of the fight against city-manager plans pictures the leaders of the opposition as men personally frustrated and maladjusted (Stene and Floro, 1953, pp. 21–39). The current desegregation fights have produced numerous such leaders, often young, one a former convict, usually from the outside. (*Life*, 1954; *Southern School News*, 1956.)

The new leaders, at any rate, are seldom moderates; the situation itself calls for extremists. And such men have not been conditioned, through experience in handling past community problems, to the prevailing norms concerning tactics of dispute.

One counter-tendency appears in the development of these organizations and the emergence of their leaders. In certain conflicts, e.g., in Cincinnati, one side will be composed primarily of community leaders, men of prestige and responsibility in the community. Though such groups carry on the functions of a partisan organization, they act not to lower the level of controversy, but to *maintain* or raise it. As did the Committee of 150 (and the ADA in Norwalk, Connecticut, and other groups in other controversies), they attempt to invoke the community's norms against personal attacks and unrestrained conflict. Sometimes (as in Cincinnati) they are successful, sometimes not.

In the face of all the pressures toward increasing intensity and freedom from normal constraint this last development is puzzling. The source of the reversal seems to be this: in certain controversies (particularly those having to do with the accusation of subversion), one side derives much of its strength from personal attacks and derogation, that is, from techniques which, were they not legitimated by patriotism or sex codes or similar strong values, would be outlawed by the community. Thus, to the degree that such methods are permitted, the attackers gain; and to the degree that community norms are upheld against these methods, the advantage is to the attacked. The more the attacked side can invoke the norms defining legitimate controversy, the more likely it is to win.

Invocation of community constraints is almost the sole force *generated by the conflict itself* which acts in a restraining direction. It is a very special force, and which appears to operate *only* under the conditions discussed above. Even so, it represents one means by which some controversies may be contained within bounds of normal community decision-making.

Community Organizations as the Controversy Develops As conflict develops, the community's organizations tend to be drawn in, just as individual members are. It may be the American Legion, the P.T.A., the church, the local businessmen's association; if its members are drawn into the controversy, or if it can lend useful support, the organization will be under pressure from one or both sides to enter the controversy. This varies, of course, with the nature of the organization and the nature of the dispute.

At the same time there are often strong pressures, both within the organization and without, to remain neutral. From within: if its members hold opposing sentiments, then their disharmony forces the organization itself to remain neutral. And from without: the organization must maintain a public position in the community which might be endangered by taking sides in a partisan battle threatening to split the community.

Examples of internal and external constraints on community organizations and leaders are not hard to find. In the Denver school controversy a few years ago, the county P.T.A. felt constrained to dissociate itself publicly from the criticisms of the school system made by their retiring president (Martin, 1951). In Hastings, New York, the positions were reversed: the school administration and teachers remained neutral while a battle raged over the P.T.A. election (McPhee, 1954). Similarly, in the strike in Gastonia, North Carolina, local ministers felt constrained not to take a public position (Pope, 1942, p. 283). If they had done so, the course of the strike might have been quite different as religious matters entered in explicitly. In some fights over the city-manager plan, businessmen's associations tried to keep out because the plan was already under attack for its alliance with business interests (Stene and Floro, 1953, p. 60); and in at least one fluoridation controversy, doctors and dentists were reluctant to actively support the fluoridation plan, singly or as a group, because of possible community disfavor affecting business (Mausner, 1955).[9] In another case, union leaders who had originally helped elect a school board could not bring their organizations to support a superintendent the board had appointed when he was accused of "progressivism" and favoritism to ethnic minorities. Their own members were too strongly split on the issue (McKee, 1953, p. 244). Ministers who were in favor of allowing Negro children to use the community house were influenced by the beliefs of influential members of their churches not to take a stand (The Inquiry, 1929, pp. 58–59). Even in Scarsdale, which was united behind its school board, the Town Club incurred disfavor with a minority of its members, who supported the school's critics, for taking as strong a stand as it did.

In sum, both community organizations and community leaders are faced with constraints when a dispute arises; the formation of a combat group to carry on the controversy and the emergence of a previous unknown as the combat leader are in part results of the immobility of responsible organizations and leaders. Both the new leader and the new organization are freed from some of the usual shackles of community norms and internal cross-pressures which make pre-existing organizations and leaders tend to soften the dispute.

The immobility of organizations resulting from a lack of internal (or sometimes external) consensus is one element which varies according to the kind of issue involved. This is best exemplified by different issues in national politics: when the issue is an economic one, e.g., Taft-Hartley legislation, groups mobilize on each side of the economic fence; labor unions and allied organizations *vs.* the National Association of Manufacturers, trade associations, and businesses themselves. When the issue has to do with tariffs, the composition of each side is different,[10] but there is still a mobilization of organizations on both sides. Sometimes the issue cuts directly across the organizations and institutions in society, thus immobilizing them, e.g., "McCarthyism," which blossomed such a short time ago. Labor unions never opposed McCarthy—their members were split. The Democratic party never opposed him—its constituency was split. Few of the powerful institutions in the country had enough internal consensus to oppose McCarthy. As it was, he drew his followers from all walks of life and from all levels of society. The cross-pressures resulting from lack of internal group consensus were reinforced by external pressures against opposing McCarthy, for all the values of patriotism were invoked by his forces. Almost the only organizations with neither internal nor external pressure against taking sides were the professionally patriotic groups like the

American Legion and the DAR. If the issue had not immobilized labor unions and the Democratic party then opposition to McCarthy would have been much more effective.[11]

The Increasing Use of Word-of-Mouth Communication As the controversy proceeds, the formal media of communication —radio, television, and newspapers—become less and less able to tell people *as much* as they want to know about the controversy, or the *kinds of things* they want to know. These media are simply not flexible enough to fill the insatiable need for news which develops as people become more and more involved. At the same time, the media are restricted by normative and legal constraints against carrying the kind of rumor which abounds as controversy proceeds. Word-of-mouth communication gradually fills the gaps, both in volume and in content, left by the mass media. Street-corner discussion amplifies, elaborates, and usually distorts the news that it picks up from the papers or the radio. This interpersonal communication offers no restraints against slander and personal charges; rather, it helps make the rhetoric of controversy consistent with the intensity.

Summary

Several characteristic events carry the controversy toward its climax. The most important changes in *issues* are: (a) from specific disagreements to more general ones, (b) elaboration into new and different disagreements, and (c) a final shift from disagreement to direct antagonism. The changes in the *social organization* of the community are as follows: the polarization of social relations as the controversy intensifies, as the participants cut off relations with those who are not on their side, and elaborate relations with those who are; the formation of partisan organizations and the emergence of new, often extremist partisan leaders to wage the war more efficiently; and the mobilization of existing community organizations on one side or the other. Finally, as the pace quickens and the issues become personal, word-of-mouth communication replaces the more formal media. It now remains to examine some of the reciprocal causations constituting the "vicious circles" or "runaway processes" so evident in conflict. These should give somewhat more insight into the mechanisms responsible for the growth of conflict.

Reciprocal Causation and the Developing Dispute

The inner dynamics of controversy derive from a number of mutually reinforcing relations; one element is enhanced by another, and, in turn, enhances the first, creating an endless spiral.[12] Some of the most important relations depend heavily upon this reciprocal reinforcement; if one or more of these cycles can be *broken*, then a disagreement already on the way to real conflict can be diverted into normal channels.

Mutual Reinforcement of Response Relations between people contain a built-in reciprocity. I smile at you; if you smile back, I speak to you; you respond, and a relationship has begun. At each step, my reaction is contingent upon yours, and yours, in turn, contingent upon mine.[13] *If* you fail to smile, but scowl instead, I may say a harsh word; you respond in kind, and another chain of mutual reinforcement builds up—this time toward

antagonism. It is such chains which constitute not only the fundamental character of interpersonal relations, but also the fundamental cycle of mutual effects in controversy. Breaking that cycle requires much effort. The admonition to "turn the other cheek" is not easily obeyed.

The direct reinforcement of response, however, is but one—the most obvious—of the mutually reinforcing relations which constitute the dynamics of controversy. Others, more tenuous, are more easily broken.

The Mutual Effects of Social and Psychological Polarization As participants in a dispute become psychologically "consistent," shedding doubts and hesitancies, they shun friends who are uncommitted, and elaborate their associations with those who feel the way they do. In effect, the psychological polarization leads to social polarization. The latter, in turn, leads to mutual reinforcement of opinions, that is, to further psychological polarization. One agrees more and more with his associates (and disagrees more and more with those he *doesn't* talk to), and comes to associate more and more with those who agree with him. Increasingly, his opponents' position seems preposterous—and, in fact, it *is* preposterous, as is his own; neither position feeds on anything but reinforcing opinions.

The outcome, of course, is the division of the community into two socially and attitudinally separate camps, each convinced it is absolutely right. The lengths to which this continually reinforcing cycle will go in any particular case depends on the characteristics of the people and the community involved. It is these characteristics which provide one "handle" for reducing the intensity of community conflict.

Polarization and Intensity: Within the Individual and Within Each Side As the participants become psychologically polarized, all their attitudes mutually reinforcing, the *intensity* of their feeling increases. One of the consequences is that inconsistencies within the individual are driven out; thus he becomes even more psychologically polarized, in turn developing a greater intensity.

This chain of mutual enforcement lies completely *within* the individual. But there is an analogous chain of reinforcement on the social level. As social polarization occurs (that is, the proliferation of associations among those who feel one way, and the attenuation of association between those who feel differently), one's statements meet more and more with a positive response; one is more and more free to express the full intensity of his feeling. The "atmosphere" of the group is open for the kind of intensity of feeling that previously had to remain unexpressed. This atmosphere of intensity, in turn, further refines the group; it becomes intolerable that anyone who believes differently maintain association within the group.

These are examples of reciprocal causation in community conflict, as they appear in the literature of these controversies. They constitute the chains which carry controversy from beginning to end as long as they remain unbroken, but which also provide the means of softening the conflict if methods can be found to break them. It is important to note that these reciprocal relations, once set in motion by outside forces, become independent of them and continue on their own. The one continuing force at work is the drive of each side to win, which sets in motion the processes described above; it carries the conflict forward "under its own steam,"

so to speak. But reciprocal relations also affect the initial drive, amplifying it, changing it; no longer is it simply a drive to win, but an urge to ruin the opponents, strip them of their power, in effect, annihilate them. This shift in goals, itself a part of a final chain of reciprocal causation, drives these processes onward with ever more intensity.

Gresham's Law of Conflict The processes may be said to create a "Gresham's Law of Conflict": the harmful and dangerous elements drive out those which would keep the conflict within bounds. Reckless, unrestrained leaders head the attack; combat organizations arise to replace the milder, more constrained pre-existing organizations; derogatory and scurrilous charges replace dispassionate issues; antagonism replaces disagreement, and a drive to ruin the opponent takes the place of the initial will to win. In other words, all the forces put into effect by the initiation of conflict act to drive out the conciliatory elements, replace them with those better equipped for combat.

In only one kind of case—exemplified best by the Cincinnati fight in which one side formed the "Committee of 150 for Political Morality"—"Gresham's Law of Conflict" did not hold. As we have said, it was to the *advantage* of that side—not altruism—to invoke against the opponents the community norms which ordinarily regulate a disagreement.

Yet a rather insistent question remains to be answered: if all these forces work in the direction of increasing intensity, how is it that community conflicts stop short of annihilation? After all, community conflicts *are* inhibited, yet the processes above give no indication how. Forces *do* exist which can counteract these processes and bring the dispute into orderly channels—

forces which are for the most part products of pre-existing community characteristics, and may be thought of here as constituting a third side in the struggle.[14] Primarily this "third force" preserves the community from division and acts as a "governor" to keep all controversies below a certain intensity.

In part the variations in these forces in the community are responsible for the wide variation in the intensity of community conflicts. Thus, a conflict which reaches extreme proportions in one community would be easily guided into quieter channels in another.

Certain attributes of the community's leadership, techniques which are used—or not used—at crucial points to guide the dispute into more reasonable channels, also affect the development of conflict. These methods, along with the pre-existing community attributes, constitute the means by which a disagreement which threatens to disrupt the community can be kept within bounds.

The Social Structure: Difference Among Communities

In the sections below are examined four variations in the social organization of the community which appear to be the most crucial for the course of controversy: (1) variation in *identification* with the community; (2) in the *density* of organizations and associations in the community; (3) in the *distribution* of participation among the citizens; and (4) in the *interlocking* of organizational memberships.

Identification with the Community Itself
The very existence of disagreement and controversy depend on involvement and identification. But when community members are highly involved with the community per se, identifying their own future with that of the community, that identification carries its own consequences as disagreement proceeds. Particularly, it appears to modify and constrain the disagreement. People who feel apart, and *unidentified*, are quickest to overstep the bounds of legitimate methods and carry the dispute into disruptive channels. When there are few or none who are identified, then there are essentially no norms to restrain the opposing sides. Conversely, if most people and organizations in the community are identified with community as a whole, then the potentially disruptive effects of the dispute are felt by all; there are conscious attempts at reconciliation. People are greatly concerned with what is happening to "their" community and will fight more quickly to see it go the way they want it to; at the same time, identification constrains them from letting a controversy get out of bounds and thus disrupt the community. In effect, communities whose members are highly involved will have more controversies, and feelings will be more intense about the issues, but these controversies are likely to be carried on within ordinary democratic processes without degenerating into a "fight to the finish."[15] Identification with the community, then, is one factor which works against the dynamic tendencies of conflict; apparently it does so in two ways: (a) By inhibiting the use of personal attacks which can initiate a controversy. The constraints exist because the value of the community as a whole overrides the importance of other values to the would-be attacker. (In this connection, it is interesting to note that when a member of a school board, or someone else highly involved with the community, makes a derogatory charge

against a teacher, he seldom makes it publicly, but forces the teacher to resign through board pressure. When some community member on the outside has such a charge, he often makes it publicly, creating a controversy in the community.) (b) By not allowing the dispute to degenerate from a disagreement over issues to direct antagonism. Identification inhibits participants from resorting to direct attacks upon their opponents. The community's norms against such tactics come into play; the more strongly the participants are identified with the community, the more effective are these norms.

Identification with the community thus interrupts the process of degeneration of conflict at the crucial point: where it turns from disagreement to direct antagonism. It is this antagonism, together with the personal attacks which go along with it, that leaves scars on a community, creating lasting cleavages and increasing the likelihood of future conflicts. Community identification helps preserve the *form* of controversy, restricting it to those procedures necessary to resolution of the problem, and inhibiting those which create lasting bitterness. This is not to say, of course, that identification with the community makes the *content* of the outcome optimum. Such identification with the community often means identification with the existing power structure. In communities and other kinds of organizations, the norm "unity above all" is employed often to dispel criticism of authority, quell uprisings, and defeat those who oppose the status quo. Identification with the community seems to act as a *conservative* influence on the content of the outcome. Whether this is "good" or "bad" in any particular case depends upon one's perspective. The effect on the *form* of the outcome, by contrast, is good by any

standards; the controversy is inhibited from deteriorating into an unrestrained fight.

Organizational Density Closely related to the phenomenon of identification with the community is the proliferation of organizations and associations within it— the "organizational density" of the town. Some communities have little, outside the churches, as a framework of social organization; other have lodges, women's clubs, veterans' groups, businessmen's clubs, art clubs, book review clubs, Parent-Teachers Associations and other school-related clubs, the Scouts, church missionary societies, Granges, and a long list of others.

The number of voluntary associations in most communities is enormous. In the thirties Warner found a New England town of 17,000 with 800 adult voluntary organizations (1953, p. 192), and an Illinois town of 6,000 had 133 in the forties (1949).

The organizational density of a town has distinct effects—direct and indirect— on dispute. (a) The direct consequences should be obvious. In a highly organized town, the pressure to take sides is very great; every association provides such a pressure. Consequently, any controversy which begins with a mere portion involved is likely to pull in quickly the whole community. In contrast, in a community in which the framework of social life is attenuated, a small part of the community can have its disputes without involving the majority—unless, of course, they are mobilized by a demagogue in the ways suggested earlier.

(b) The indirect effect of these organizations is the creation of a psychological identification with the community.[16] Depending on the nature of the organization, this effect may be great or small; some organizations, e.g., churches, P.T.A.'s, civic luncheon clubs, and women's clubs, are very much identified with the community. Others, however—veterans' groups, lodges, country clubs, and labor unions—are often less so. In any case, such community identification has the consequences discussed earlier. As a result, high organizational density in a community tends to draw the community into controversy, but it also acts to regulate the controversy and contain it.

Distribution of Participation In many towns, only the upper- and upper-middle class people are prolific joiners; lower-class people largely fail to participate. One author concludes that in the two towns he investigated, only 20 per cent of the community members were in any community-linked organizations.[17] The existence of religious, business, and labor groups (not included in the figure above) raises this level considerably, but some of these organizations customarily refrain from taking sides in a controversy.

The higher participation rates of higher social strata have been documented in study after study.[18] The consequences of this differential participation for the lower stratum are two: (a) lower-status people will less often be drawn into community controversy; (b) when they are drawn into controversy, they will be less constrained in their activities and quicker to reduce the controversy to personal derogation and attack. Note that these two consequences arise not from anything intrinsically "different" about lower-status people, but only from their differential participation in community activities. In recent school controversies, for instance, these consequences are similarly evident among high-status persons who were previously inactive in community organizations.

In highly stratified communities, therefore, a large proportion of the community is likely to remain effectively out of the conflict—but, when and if this group does enter, the level of controversy is likely to drop quickly. Probably the most stratified communities are relatively isolated towns with diverse industries; probably the least stratified are small suburban communities which have grown up since the end of World War II.

Interlocking of Memberships Organizational affiliations and informal relations provide the chain which links different members of the community together; if these affiliations are confined mostly within ethnic groups, or economic strata, or religious groups, and fail to tie these groups to one another, the lines of cleavage are already set. Many communities do lack these ties: old suburban communities with an influx of new residents, for example, in which the new residents are sharply differentiated from the old by occupation, age, and ethnicity, show very little association between the two groups.[19] Many New England towns are like this; the immigration waves deposited in these communities people who differed so much from the old Yankees that few ties sprung up between them.[20]

Another group of communities with similar lines of cleavage are the "service" towns; resort towns are the best example. It was in some part the division into "natives" and resort colonists which prompted the Peekskill riots (Rorty and Raushenbush, 1950). Only belatedly, after the riots, were attempts made to bring into community organizations some of the more stable resort people. True, these riots were in large part due to the existence of Communists and fellow-traveling groups among the summer colonists. It would hardly be possible—or to the Peekskill residents, desirable—to integrate these groups into the community, but many of the antagonisms which led to the riots might have been dispelled by closer association between some of the summer residents and the "natives."

This example illustrates one of the sources of recent community conflict in growing suburban towns where people's opinions receive continual reinforcement from fellow-workers—that is, from people outside the community. At home, divergent views are not forced to conform to those of others in the community; when some incident occurs, this divergence manifests itself in irreconcilable views. If suburbanites had to work day-by-day in the same small community, much of the reconciliation would have taken place over a long period of time, before the incident occurred. Port Washington, Long Island, is a good example; nationally active right-wingers live next door to dedicated advocates of the left-wing. They carry out their activities, of course, not in Port Washington, but in New York City.

This change in American life has given to social relations in small towns a *voluntary* quality that they never had before. People choose their associates, and more important, choose with whom not to associate. The consequences of this are not yet fully evident, but its effect on the structure of a community is clear. It allows small groups with similar interests and beliefs to become socially isolated from one another.[21] A lack of identification with others in the community becomes possible, as well as a much broader divergence of opinion than ever existed in communities where men are constrained to work with others. Two consequences for community conflict are the greater difficulty of reaching consensus from such an

extended spread of opinion, and the inability of opposing groups to "understand" each other. Thus there is a greater likelihood of imputing evil motives to the others, and directing antagonism against them.

Cross-Pressures Individuals have many associations in a community, many roles to play, and many attachments to groups and individuals. If these attachments are spread throughout the community as a whole, then the individual has in a sense internalized many different elements in the community. Similarly, each attitude or value the individual holds toward various aspects of life—whether derived from his background, his everyday experiences, or some other source—may be viewed as something outside himself, which he has internalized and made part of his psychological self.[22]

When a controversy arises in a community, any one of these objects and values can act as a basis of response; if it becomes involved in controversy, then it "takes with it" the individual who has attachments to it. The individual who has attachments to many elements in the community very often finds himself pulled in opposing directions as the controversy broadens. One group of people to whom he feels close is on one side; others to whom he feels equally close are on the other. His friends at work feel one way; his social friends feel another. His fellows at the American Legion post are more on one side; the people on his Community Chest Committee on the other. Unable to commit himself fully to one side or the other, he either withdraws from the dispute, or, taking sides, is still beset by doubts and fears, unable to go "all out" against the enemy.

These are the kinds of responses which

might be predicted for a man torn by cross-pressures; and these are the responses which such men have been found to make at least in political campaigns. Voting studies indicate that the person in a cross-pressured situation—say, a middle-class (i.e., pulled toward the Republicans) Catholic (i.e., pulled toward the Democrats)—is slow in deciding in favor of a candidate; he vacillates from one to the other, and often fails to show up at the polling booth.[23]

The consequences of this phenomenon are of extreme importance for community conflict primarily for one reason: some communities, with a high *density* of associations and organizations, and with great *interlocking* of these associations, create this potential for cross-pressure in their members; others, less tightly knit, do not. Among the first communities, part of the conflict is located within each person, part within each small group of friends, part within larger organizations, and only the remainder at the level of the community itself. In the community which does not create in its members the potential for cross-pressure, individuals are consistent; groups of friends are of one mind; and organizations are unified—all the conflict is shifted to the level of the community itself.[24]

The situation may be visualized by means of graphs which show the differing responses to an issue in the two kinds of community. On the horizontal axis in the graph below is located, from left to right, the individual, the small group, the larger organization or association, and the community. The vertical axis represents the amount of discord within each of these entities. The points which are on line A-A' represent the "normal" or "equilibrium" degree of discord within each of these entities when no particular controversy exists. Though such a line cannot be located exactly, it is obvious that the amount of normal discord increases as the size of the entity increases. The line B–B' is the line of maximum discord which the entity can tolerate. Again, there is no precise location intended; but again we know that an individual can tolerate a certain degree of internal conflict before he reaches neurosis, that a group can tolerate a greater degree of division before it breaks up, and, at the extreme, a community can stand a certain—and much greater—degree of division before it breaks apart permanently.

The question is, what happens when the two extreme types of communities are faced with an issue? Figure 2 shows what seems to occur when the community is

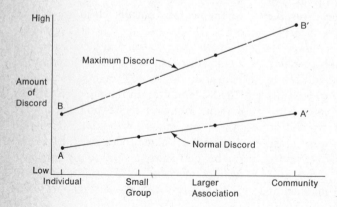

Figure 1

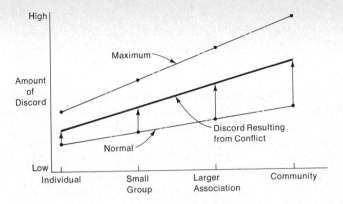

Figure 2

highly integrated, when part of the conflict is absorbed at each level.

It will be seen that the absorption of part of the controversy at each level means that each level moves toward the line of maximum discord, but that—in this idealized representation—none comes near the maximum. In contrast, in a community in which there were few lines tying together the major groups in town (say, two ethnic groups), conflict in its later stages would be as shown in Figure 3. Individuals, small groups of friends, and larger organizations (i.e., each ethnic group) will have mobilized their forces, becoming internally consistent through the processes discussed earlier, and shifting all the discord to the community level. This pushes up community discord to the danger point at which permanent cleavages are created. There are numerous intermediate cases, of course—most frequently, conflict within large associations or organizations. Individuals are internally consistent, small groups are unified, but large secondary associations are split, thus absorbing part of the conflict at this level.

These graphical representations should indicate the differential consequences for community conflict of social structures which are integrated to varying degrees. Although these consequences are not directly derived from empirical data on community conflict—for no data of precisely this sort have been systematically gathered—they are consistent with numerous descriptive accounts of the course of controversy in different communities. In

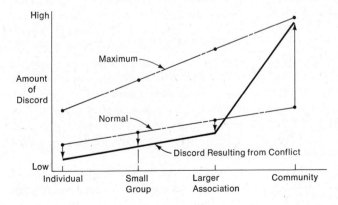

Figure 3

another sense, however, they are derived from a conceptual approach to community controversies which is implicit in much that has gone before.

Again, it must be emphasized that these mitigating effects of the social structure upon community conflict provide no rough-and-ready tool which can be brought in overnight to help contain a conflict already at hand. To bind together more closely the many persons, groups, and organizations which exist in a community is no simple task; it is not accomplished quickly, particularly when such factors as the economic structure of the community are working against integration. But to the degree that such social structure does exist, it provides a strong and sure safeguard against the kind of conflict which creates a permanent cleavage in the community.

The Economic Structure

The effects of the community's economic structure in inhibiting or promoting community conflict have been treated under other headings. At this point it is useful to summarize these effects on the three economic variations noted: "service" towns in which townspeople derive their income from outsiders; "self-contained" towns, in which men both live and work; and economic "appendages," in which most men commute to work outside town.

(a) In each of these, characteristic issues arise to provoke controversy. In economically self-contained towns, it is often issues of direct economic interest and of political control; in the others it is more often value differences deriving from differing backgrounds and experiences.

(b) In the stratified, self-contained communities, participation in the controversy will ordinarily be restricted to the upper and middle strata, while in the one-class commuting towns it will be more evenly spread throughout the community.

(c) When lower classes participate in controversy in stratified towns, the dispute is likely to get particularly acrimonious.

(d) The voluntary aspect of relations among residents who need only to live together and not to work together—in new suburbia—tends to segregate the community into discrete value-homogeneous groups, and to create diverse consequences for controversy.

The Mass Media of Communication

The local newspaper has often played an important role in community conflict. In Norwalk, Connecticut, for example, an account of the VFW's plan for reporting subversives by a sympathetic reporter in the Norwalk *Hour* set off the controversy. In this same conflict, the *Hour*, as well as nation-wide newspaper and television coverage, played an important part in the succeeding phases of the controversy.

In Scarsdale, an article in the New York *Herald-Tribune* brought into the open what had been private sniping at the school administration's book selection procedure. This article prompted a front-page statement in the local weekly paper signed by eighty-one prominent citizens. This statement set the tone for the remainder of the controversy.

In the Cicero riots, the Calumet *Index* acted both as a *transmitter* of opinion from members of the community (it published inflammatory letters), and as a *source* of opinion in its editorials and in its handling of the news.

In the Pasadena school controversy which led to Goslin's ouster, his administration incurred the antagonism of reporters from the outset; the subsequent reporting of school news was never sympathetic to the administration.

These examples could be multiplied endlessly; characteristically, the local newspaper carries out important functions in community conflict. Some conflicts have *started* with a crusading newspaper editor, or simply as a news scoop—making public a deal or maneuver which creates a real issue when it is brought into the open. When the newly-appointed city-manager in Madison, Wisconsin, took a long lease in the most expensive hotel in town, though his appointment was for less than half the period of the lease, the subsequent newspaper stories quickly aroused sentiment against him.

Whether the local newspaper creates an issue through editorial activity or sensationalist reporting, or whether it merely seeks out and reports events which create an issue, it is true that many controversies are born when community members unsuspectingly open their newspaper one morning. Similarly, in times of disaster or crisis, the mass media become of crucial importance. Any disturbance of the normal flow of life which seems to be the result of "external" agents sends people to the media for guidance. There is graphic evidence of the power of radio in the "Invasion from Mars" scare, created by the Orson Welles radio drama, and the subsequent use of radio to calm the misled listeners (Cantril, Gaudet, and Herzog, 1940).

Mass media, however, seem to play a smaller role in community controversy than they do in crises such as floods, bombing attacks, or explosions when people must know what to *do*: where to go for safety, how to organize to meet the disaster, how to get in touch with families, and other such pressing problems of action. The mass media can direct action most readily. In times of community dispute, however, the problem is what to *think*, how to make up one's mind. Because people depend on their friends and neighbors more often than mass media in matters of opinion, because mass media cannot legitimately transmit derogatory information and personal attacks as individuals can, and, finally, because the interpersonal networks are still intact (which is often not true in a disaster), the mass media play a less important role.

It has been suggested that another function of local newspapers and radios during controversy is direct *persuasion*, that is, convincing people to take one or the other side. The role of mass media in persuasion has been studied many times over, and the results have been much the same: little if any effect (Klapper, 1950). In one analysis of the partisan content of newspapers in presidential election campaigns from 1792 to 1940, no correlation was found between support by a majority of the newspapers and election results (Mott, 1944). Other studies have shown that information campaigns and community drives which depend on the mass media seem to have little impact on public opinion; quite to the contrary, they sometimes boomerang and have an effect opposite to that intended (Lazarsfeld and Kendall, 1945).

In contrast to field studies, however, *experimental* work in the effects of mass communication shows that the media are indeed effective in persuasion.[25] The major source of this discrepancy between field and experiment is not hard to locate. Experimental studies have asked the question: What is the effect of the mass media on individuals? Field studies, on the other hand, pose the question: What is the effect of mass media on a particular social unit (American society, a single town, etc.)? In a field situation, exposure to the persuasiveness of the mass media is neither complete, nor random. People expose themselves to what they *want* to hear or see; and this corresponds largely to their pre-existing opinions. (See, for example, Hyman and Sheatsley, 1952.) The mass media, used selectively in this way, have more a *reinforcing* effect than anything else. Their persuasiveness is expended on those who are already persuaded. In the experimental studies, however, *everyone* is exposed; selectivity cannot occur, and an effect is evident. But community controversies are not experimental situations, and the *direct persuasive effect* of the mass media seems negligible.

In some situations, of course, the mass media do show persuasive ability. In war bond drives, for example, radio was quite effective (Merton, 1946). When there is a monopoly of communication, the mass media show results (Lazarsfeld and Merton, 1952). But a community conflict situation constitutes anything but a monopoly on communication, because interpersonal discussion is of extreme importance.

Finally, it should be noted that the *indirect* effect of the mass media may be great: communication which starts with the newspaper or radio, and is mediated by group discussions, may ultimately have an important effect.[26]

The local mass media, then, particularly the newspaper, are of considerable importance, both in setting off a controversy and in communicating views and events to the community as a whole. In *persuasion*, however, the mass media appears to have little importance in comparison to the interpersonal networks.

A word should be added about national mass media. Television has played some role in at least three incidents concerning civil liberties: in Norwalk; in Indianapolis where the Civil Liberties Union was prevented from meeting; and during the desegregation controversy in Clinton, Tennessee. The first two incidents were quickly dissipated, perhaps more quickly than they would have been without the nationwide publicity; the effect of the third remains to be seen. Similarly, magazine publicity seems in some cases to have exposed the activities of right-wing groups and reduced their influence, e.g., the *McCall's* article which touched on the activities of Allan Zoll and Lucille Crain (Morse, 1951).

On the basis of meagre evidence, it appears that these responsible and respectable media have modified the intensity of disputes by viewing them in a new context, dispassionately, making them appear irrational and sometimes even ridiculous. In the glare of national attention, some disputes have cooled and dissipated more quickly than they might have otherwise. National media, presenting disputes in the context of a norm of orderly democratic processes, have apparently served as a valuable aid in keeping controversy within the bounds of reasonable debate.

Yet such publicity can have quite different effects. In some cases, unfavorable national publicity, together with strong community identification, has provided greater intensity of feeling among the adherents of one side. Representative John Rankin of Mississippi is said to have remarked that he was defeated in the 1948 primary only because Drew Pearson and Walter Winchell had for the first time stayed out of the fight against him. His constituents apparently viewed such opposition as Northern, big-city meddling, and reacted against it by voting him in.

One other national channel of communication has played an extremely important role at critical points in some disputes. National, right-wing organizations such as Allan Zoll's have on hand comprehensive biographical material on the past associations, affiliations, and activities of people with liberal or radical histories. At a moment's notice, these materials are sent to local followers, who then use them to discredit the person involved, ordinarily an opposition leader. Because of the personal basis of these attacks, they are often the incidents which set off a dispute or which transform a quiet disagreement into a bitter controversy. Unless these "facts" are met with immediate rebuttal, they are often extremely effective in molding opinion and dispersing the opposition.

Full, accurate measurement of the effect of the mass media in any community conflict has yet to be made. Such research is extremely difficult; each conflict is unique and one cannot serve as a control for another. It is not possible to say what a conflict would have been like if the local newspaper had handled its news, editorials, or letters-to-the-editor differently. Yet knowledge about the effects of the mass media is crucial, because it is certain that they play an important part in community controversy.

Conclusion

This, then, is a picture of the general aspects of community controversy drawn from the existing literature. There are elements peculiar to each different case, but as the discussion above indicates, there appear to be a number of general properties which these conflicts hold in common. Over and over again, as one case study after another was examined, the same patterns appeared: the same kinds of feelings were generated between the participants; the same kinds of partisan activity occurred.

Why have there been these remarkable similarities? Apparently, the autonomous nature of conflicts creates them. Once set off, controversies develop quite independently of the incident. Early stages generate later ones; conflicts which began quite differently end up alike: the community divided into opposing factions, angry and adamant, arguing about old quarrels which have nothing to do with the original issue.

Yet these controversies are not determinate things which grind their way unswervingly to the end. They may take a number of courses; the outcome may range from amicable resolution to bitter name-calling. Modifying factors which differ among communities may intensify controversy or reduce its tensions. Although the initiation of the controversy and the particular issue which sets it off are not extremely important in determining the course of the dispute, numerous characteristics of the community *are* important, and seemingly minor events during the growth of controversy can be important as well.

This state of affairs is a fortunate one from the point of view of the future prospects of knowledge about community controversy. It permits us ultimately to make general statements about the growth of community conflict, and about the factors in the community which affect this growth. Such generalizations make the study of community controversy per se a valuable implementation of our knowledge about community life. As community living takes on new vigor in our society, and as new patterns of suburban living emerge in America today, the study of these matters becomes of particular importance.

Little has been said in this report about the need for more research on certain aspects of community conflict. Yet it is surely evident in the very exposition that at many points our knowledge is limited. In order to develop a useful theory of community controversy, which can point the way to democratic decision-making in the community, much research must be done. In the present report, the attempt has been made to organize what knowledge is available—together with much speculation—so that it might be of maximum use both for the practical problems of controversy as they arise in the community and for designing further research which can someday provide a theory of community controversy.

NOTES

1. The one man who emphasized particularly the possibility of abstracting principles of conflict from particular situations of conflict is Georg Simmel, who wrote several essays on the subject. Unfortunately, Simmel never got around to writing a comprehensive theory of conflict, though he did set down a number of insights into particular aspects. See Simmel (1955). Lewis Coser has brought together the best of Simmel's insights and elaborated on them (Coser, 1956).

2. Conversely, a relationship which begins with two people *agreeing* in tastes and interests often ends with both *liking one another*. For a discussion of the process through which this occurs, see Merton and Lazarsfeld (1954).

   Georg Simmel notes the formal similarities between relations of positive and negative attachments, contrasting these with *absence* of relationship. He suggests that the psychological processes generating antagonism are just as fundamental as those generating liking. Simmel also notes the difference between a negative relationship based on disagreement over an outside object, and one which needs no such object, but is directly antagonistic. See Simmel (1955, p. 34, 36, passim), and Coser (1956).

3. It should be emphasized that these suggestions for processes are highly tentative; systematic research into the psychological dynamics involved in these changing relations would contribute greatly to our knowledge about the development of controversy.

4. One might speculate that this tendency would be stronger among those who tend to personalize easily; they move more quickly perhaps from specific disagreement to hostility toward the opponent as a whole. Feuds among hill people (who are highly "person-oriented"), for example, seem to bear this out. Thus the course of controversy may vary greatly in two communities, simply as a result of differences in "person-orientation."

5. Whether or not persons previously neutral can be brought into the controversy seems to depend greatly upon the time at which they are confronted with the alternative. If the antagonists are too involved too early they are viewed with puzzlement and distaste and detachment by neutrals. The situation is much the same as confronts a man arriving sober in the middle of a drunken party: he cannot join in because these people are "too far gone" for him to experience the events of the party as they do. The similarity between an orgy of community controversy and a drunken orgy is more than superficial in this and other respects. People collectively "forget themselves" in ways they may be ashamed of later. One of the major questions of community conflict concerns the processes through which this "forgetting" occurs.

6. It is a matter of the relative strengths of different values; some, like those against immorality and subversion, override the values against personal slander. If we knew the relative strength of certain social values among various segments of the population, we would be far better able to judge the course of controversy ranged around a certain issue. But we lack even methods for measurement.

7. In contrast to "putting oneself in the place of the attacker," those who hold civil liberties to be of great importance evidently put themselves in the place of the attacked, and ask themselves how it would feel to be unjustly charged in this fashion. It appears that the *variations in relative values* between these two groups cause them to identify with opposing parties in a case of such charges. Thus they are immediately brought in on one side or the other in such a dispute.

8. See Pope's (1942) graphic account of union operations in Gastonia, North Carolina, and Jones's (1941) discussion of union activity in Akron.

9. There is some evidence that men in certain occupations are more sensitive than others to public opinion and thus less willing to commit themselves to either side and less able to hold on to a position of principle. On the Pasadena school board, the two members most sensitive to the mass mood were a retail merchant and an undertaker (both, it should be noted, like doctors and dentists, have a retail product to sell) (Hurlburd, 1950, p. 31 ff.). This and other evidence leads to the hypothesis that persons who have a clientele or set of retail customers in town cannot generally

be trusted to stand up against a majority though they believe in the cause. Or even more generally, it seems that such men cannot *start* a controversy, since the initiator is always in a minority; neither can they continue against the initiator once he has gained the majority.

10. Sometimes labor unions and trade associations find themselves on the same side of the fence. The issue over an increase in watch tariffs saw the watchmakers' union and the manufacturers on the same side; both opposed a principle laid down by a tariff commission headed by the president of a steel company.

11. Interestingly, what is at one time an aid is at another time a hindrance; a movement with little organizational opposition also has little organizational support, and finds it difficult to become institutionalized without a coup.

12. The dynamics of controversy is a topic for the theoretician in sociology; it comes as close as any area of social life to constituting a closed system, in which all the effects are from variables within the system. When a theory of controversy does exist, the sets of mutually reinforcing relations like those examined in this section will constitute the heart of the theory.

13. Talcott Parsons (1951, p. 36) who studies this characteristic of interpersonal relations in detail, speaks of it as the "double-contingency of interpersonal relations." Parsons has a full discussion of this aspect of relations between persons.

14. This is not to say that some of these forces are not *within* the partisans themselves. Insofar as this is true, it leads to one of the important mechanisms by which conflict can be restrained.

15. Again, a comparison with controversy in different labor unions is apt. It became evident in a recent study of the printers' union that in comparison with many other unions, this union had (a) more identification of the members with their union and their trade; (b) more controversies, many times over issues which never created a stir in other unions; (c) less personal derogation and fewer factional upheavals, but instead a recognition of the other side's right to exist and right to differ. The mechanism seems quite the same in unions and in communities. See Lipset, Trow, and Coleman (1956), Chap. 4.

16. The disorganized New England town mentioned earlier (Homans, 1950), provides one more illustration of the fact that when men have not been involved in community affairs, they attribute little legitimacy to authority. In this case the community as a whole lost its regard for authority as social participation in community activities dropped.

17. John M. Foskett, "Participation and Non-Participation in the Policy Formation Process at the Community Level," (Abstract of paper delivered at the 48th Annual Meeting of the American Sociological Society, 1953).

18. One of the most recent of these, giving references to previous studies, is Foskett (1955). See also Floyd Hunter (1953), for a more sophisticated discussion of the particular statuses consistent with participation in Community organizations.

19. Yonkers, New York, is sharply divided into "old nesters" on the west side, and new "carpet-baggers" on the east side. The physical division of the town, as well as ethnic and style-of-life differences, accentuates the social division and discourages association. See a series of four articles by Harrison E. Salisbury (1955).

20. Circumstances faced by New England communities, however, need not mean a perpetuation of social divisions. One study reports the history of two towns in the Connecticut River Valley; both were faced with the assimilation of the Poles. In one town the Poles are full integrated, with many threads of association tying them to the community at large. In the other, there remains cleavage which has paralyzed the town. (The Inquiry, 1929, p. 124–26).

21. However, one author notes an opposing tendency. Granville Hicks (1953) points out that the one organization in his town which cuts across classes and differing backgrounds is the horse club. It is voluntary, leisure-activity organizations like this which proliferate in the new suburbia, and these organizations may bring closer together people with differing values and class backgrounds. Much work needs to be done in this area.

22. See G. H. Mead (1934, pp. 309, 315 ff.) for a discussion of the concept of self and the process of internalizing objects outside one's physical self into the psychological self.

23. See Berelson, Lazarsfeld, and McPhee (1954); see also Lipset, Lazarsfeld, Barton, and Linz (1954), Kriesberg (1949).

24. For a more general discussion of the levels at which conflict is resolved in various kinds of political system, see Coleman (1955).

25. The major work in this field is that of Carl Hovland and his associates, first in the army, and in his recent book (1953).

26. Little research in this area exists, but for a careful examination of related research and a discussion of the general problem, see Katz and Lazarsfeld (1956).

REFERENCES

Berelson, Bernard, Lazarsfeld, Paul F., and McPhee, William. *Voting*. Chicago: University of Chicago Press, 1954.

Cantril, Hadley, Gaudet, Hazel, and Herzog, Herta. *The Invasion from Mars*. Princeton: Princeton University Press, 1940.

Coleman, James. "Political Cleavage within the International Typographical Union." Unpublished Ph.D. dissertation, Columbia University, 1955.

Hessler, William H. "It Didn't Work in Cincinnati," *The Reporter*, IX (December 22, 1953), 13–17.

Hyman, Herbert H., and Sheatsley, Paul B. "Some Reasons Why Information Campaigns Fail," in *Readings in Social Psychology*, G. E. Swanson, T. M. Newcomb, and E. L. Hartley (eds.). New York: Holt, revised edition, 1952.

Key, V. O. Jr. *Southern Politics*. New York: Knopf, 1950.

Klapper, Joseph T. *The Effects of Mass Media*. New York: Columbia University, Bureau of Applied Social Research, 1950.

Lazarsfeld, Paul F., and Merton, Robert K. "Mass Communication, Popular Taste, and Organized Social Action," in *Readings in Social Psychology*, G. E. Swanson, T. M. Newcomb, and E. L. Hartley (eds.). New York: Holt, revised edition, 1952.

Lazarsfeld, Paul F., and Kendall, Patricia L. *Radio in Health Education*. New York: Columbia University Press, 1945.

"Outsider Stirs Up Small Town Trouble," *Life*, XXXVII (October 11, 1954), 45–46.

Martin, Lawrence. "Denver, Colorado," *Saturday Review* ("The Public School Crisis"), XXXIV, September 8, 1951, 6–20.

Mausner, Bernard and Judith. "A Study of the Anti-Scientific Attitude," *Scientific American*, CXCII (February, 1955), 35–39.

McKee, James B. "Organized Labor and Community Decision-making: A Study in the Sociology of Power." Unpublished Ph.D. dissertation, University of Wisconsin, 1953.

McPhee, William. "Community Controversies Affecting Personal Liberties and Institutional Freedoms in Education." Unpublished memorandum, Columbia University, Bureau of Applied Social Research, July, 1954.

Merton, Robert K. *Mass Persuasion: The Social Psychology of a War Bond Drive*. New York: Harper, 1946.

Morse, Arthur D. "Who's Trying to Ruin Our Schools?" *McCall's* (1951), reprinted in *Freedom and Public Education*, Ernest O. Melby and Morton Puner (eds.). New York: Praeger, 1953.

Mott, Frank Luther. "Newspapers in Presidential Campaigns," *Public Opinion Quarterly*, VIII (1944).

Pope, Liston. *Millhands and Preachers*. New Haven: Yale University Press, 1942.

Rorty, James, and Raushenbusch, Winifred. "The Lessons of the Peekskill Riots," *Commentary*, X (October, 1950), 309–23.

Simmel, Georg. *Conflict and the Webb of Intergroup Affiliations.* Glencoe: The Free Press, 1955.

Southern School News, III, (October, 1956), p. 15.

Stene, Edwin K., and Floro, George K. *Abandonment of the Manager Plan.* Lawrence, Kansas: University of Kansas, 1953.

Stone, Harold S., Price, Don K., and Stone, Kathryn H. *City Manager Government in the United States.* Chicago: Public Administration Service, 1940.

The Inquiry, *Community Conflict.* New York, 1929.

Warner, W. Lloyd and Associates. *Democracy in Jonesville.* New York: Harper, 1949.

Warner, W. Lloyd. *American Life: Dream and Reality.* Chicago: University of Chicago Press, 1953.

44. The Local Community as an Ecology of Games   Norton E. Long

Contemporary urban communities, particularly metropolitan regions, are notoriously weak as decision-making units. The territorial range of their problems does not correspond to the boundaries of municipal power. Challenges arise from conditions operating on the national scale and can often be handled only by federal programs, over which the city governments have little control. Many of the most knowledgeable and competent urban citizens do not care about local affairs. Norton Long analyzes why cities continue to survive in spite of these short-comings in political capacity. He explains their success in terms of the American cultural tradition of conducting social institutions as if they were games. Groups play at achieving their goals, and community needs are met because bankers, trade unionists, and professionals soon discover they are interdependent and must cooperate in order to survive. These games are tied together at the top by what Long calls the " social game," the exchange of prestige and status among the leading members of the important institutions of urban life.

Long's argument is facile and amusing, and it offers an accurate description of the way in which many influential members of the community look upon their roles. However, it is not clear whether he really believes that the urban game, as it now operates, compensates for the lack of effective government in cities.

Norton E. Long is Professor of Political Science at the University of Illinois. He is author of *The Polity* (1962) and coauthor of *Metropolitics: A Study of Political Culture* (1963).

The local community whether viewed as a polity, an economy, or a society presents itself as an order in which expectations are met and functions performed. In some cases, as in a new, company-planned mining town, the order is the willed product of centralized control, but for the most part the order is the product of a history rather than the imposed effect of any central nervous system of the community. For historic reasons we readily conceive the massive task of feeding New York to be achieved through the unplanned, historically developed cooperation of thousands of actors largely unconscious of their collaboration to this individually unsought end. The efficiency of this system is attested to by the extraordinary difficulties of the War Production Board and Service of Supply in accomplishing similar logistical objectives through an explicit system of orders and directives. Insofar as conscious rationality plays a role, it is a function of the parts rather than the whole. Particular structures working for their own ends within the whole may provide their members with goals, strategies, and roles that support rational action. The results of the interaction of the rational strivings after particular ends are in part collectively functional if unplanned. All this is the well-worn doctrine of Adam Smith, though one need accept no more of the doctrine of beneficence than that an unplanned economy can function.

While such a view is accepted for the economy, it is generally rejected for the polity. Without a sovereign, Leviathan is generally supposed to disintegrate and fall apart. Even if Locke's more hopeful view of the naturalness of the social order is taken, the polity seems more of a contrived artifact than the economy. Furthermore, there is both the hangover of Austinian sovereignty and the Greek view of ethical

primacy to make political institutions seem different in kind and ultimately inclusive in purpose and for this reason to give them an over-all social directive end. To see political institutions as the same kind of thing as other institutions in society rather than as different, superior, and inclusive (both in the sense of being sovereign and ethically more significant) is a form of relativistic pluralism that is difficult to entertain. At the local level, however, it is easier to look at the municipal government, its departments, and the agencies of state and national government as so many institutions, resembling banks, newspapers, trade unions, chambers of commerce, churches, etc., occuping a territorial field and interacting with one another. This interaction can be conceptualized as a system without reducing the interacting institutions and individuals to membership in any single comprehensive group. It is psychologically tempting to envision the local territorial system as a group with a governing "they." This is certainly an existential possibility and one to be investigated. However, frequently, it seems likely, systems are confused with groups, and our primitive need to explain thunder with a theology or a demonology results in the hypostatizing of an angelic or demonic hierarchy. The executive committee of the bourgeoisie and the power elite make the world more comfortable for modern social scientists as the Olym-

This paper is largely based on a year of field study in the Boston Metropolitan area made possible by grants from the Stern Family Foundation and the Social Science Research Council. The opinions and conclusion expressed are those of the author alone.

pians did for the ancients. At least the latter-day hypothesis, being terrestrial, is in principle researchable, though in practice its metaphysical statement may render it equally immune to mundane inquiry.

Observation of certain local communities makes it appear that inclusive over-all organization for many general purposes is weak or non-existent. Much of what occurs seems to just happen with accidental trends becoming cumulative over time and producing results intended by nobody. A great deal of the communities' activities consist of undirected co-operation of particular social structures, each seeking particular goals and, in doing so, meshing with others. While much of this might be explained in Adam Smith's terms, much of it could not be explained with a rational, atomistic model of calculating individuals. For certain purposes the individual is a useful way of looking at people; for many others the role-playing member of a particular group is more helpful. Here we deal with the essence of predictability in social affairs. If we know the game being played is baseball and that X is a third baseman, by knowing his position and the game being played we can tell more about X's activities on the field than we could if we examined X as a psychologist or a psychiatrist. If such were not the case, X would belong in the mental ward rather than in a ball park. The behavior of X is not some disembodied rationality but, rather, behavior within an organized group activity that has goals, norms, strategies, and roles that give the very field and ground for rationality. Baseball structures the situation.

It is the contention of this paper that the structured group activities that coexist in a particular territorial system can be looked at as games. These games provide the players with a set of goals that give them a sense of success or failure. They provide them determinate roles and calculable strategies and tactics. In addition, they provide the players with an elite and general public that is in varying degrees able to tell the score. There is a good deal of evidence to be found in common parlance that many participants in contemporary group structures regard their occupations as at least analogous to games. And, at least in the American culture, and not only since Eisenhower, the conception of being on a "team" has been fairly widespread.

Unfortunately, the effectiveness of the term "game" for the purposes of this paper is vitiated by, first, the general sense that games are trivial occupations and, second, by the pre-emption of the term for the application of a calculus of probability to choice or decision in a determinate game situation. Far from regarding games as trivial, the writer's position would be that man is both a game-playing and a game-creating animal, that his capacity to create and play games and take them deadly seriously is of the essence, and that it is through games or activities analogous to game-playing that he achieves a satisfactory sense of significance and a meaningful role.

While the calculability of the game situation is important, of equal or greater importance is the capacity of the game to provide a sense of purpose and a role. The organizations of society and polity produce satisfactions with both their products and their processes. The two are not unrelated, but, while the production of the product may in the larger sense enable players and onlookers to keep score, the satisfaction in the process is the satisfaction of playing the game and the sense in which any activity can be grasped as a game.

Looked at this way, in the territorial system there is a political game, a banking game, a contracting game, a newspaper game, a civic organization game, an ecclesiastical game, and many others. Within each game there is a well-established set of goals whose achievement indicates success or failure for the participants, a set of socialized roles making participant behavior highly predictable, a set of strategies and tactics handed down through experience and occasionally subject to improvement and change, an elite public whose approbation is appreciated, and, finally, a general public which has some appreciation for the standing of the players. Within the game the players can be rational in the varying degrees that the structure permits. At the very least, they know how to behave, and they know the score.

Individuals may play in a number of games, but, for the most part, their major preoccupation is with one, and their sense of major achievement is through success in one. Transfer from one game to another is, of course, possible, and the simultaneous playing of roles in two or more games is an important manner of linking separate games.

Sharing a common territorial field and collaborating for different and particular ends in the achievement of over-all social functions, the players in one game make use of the players in another and are, in turn, made use of by them. Thus the banker makes use of the newspaperman, the politician, the contractor, the ecclesiastic, the labor leader, the civic leader—all to further his success in the banking game— but, reciprocally, he is used to further the others' success in the newspaper, political, contracting, ecclesiastical, labor, and civic games. Each is a piece in the chess game of the other, sometimes a willing piece, but, to the extent that the games are different, with a different end in view.

Thus a particular highway grid may be the result of a bureaucratic department of public works game in which are combined, though separate, a professional highway engineer game with its purposes and critical elite onlookers; a departmental bureaucracy; a set of contending politicians seeking to use the highways for political capital, patronage, and the like; a banking game concerned with bonds, taxes, and the effect of the highways on real estate; newspapermen interested in headlines, scoops, and the effect of highways on the papers' circulation; contractors eager to make money by building roads; ecclesiastics concerned with the effect of highways on their parishes and on the fortunes of the contractors who support their churchly ambitions; labor leaders interested in union contracts and their status as community influentials with a right to be consulted; and civic leaders who must justify the contributions of their bureaus of municipal research or chambers of commerce to the social activity. Each game is in play in the complicated pulling and hauling of siting and constructing the highway grid. A wide variety of purposes is subserved by the activity, and no single overall directive authority controls it. However, the interrelation of the groups in constructing a highway has been developed over time, and there are general expectations as to the interaction. There are also generalized expectations as to how politicians, contractors, newspapermen, bankers, and the like will utilize the highway situation in playing their particular games. In fact, the knowledge that a banker will play like a banker and a newspaperman like a newspaperman is an important part of what makes the situation calculable and permits the players to estimate its possibilities for their own action in their particular game.

While it might seem that the engineers of the department of public works were the appropriate protagonists for the highway grid, as a general activity it presents opportunities and threats to a wide range of other players who see in the situation consequences and possibilities undreamed of by the engineers. Some general public expectation of the limits of the conduct of the players and of a desirable outcome does provide bounds to the scramble. This public expectation is, of course, made active through the interested solicitation of newspapers, politicians, civic leaders, and others who see in it material for accomplishing their particular purposes and whose structured roles in fact require the mobilization of broad publics. In a sense the group struggle that Arthur Bentley described in his *Process of Government* is a drama that local publics have been taught to view with a not uncritical taste. The instruction of this taste has been the vocation and business of some of the contending parties. The existence of some kind of over-all public puts general restraints on gamesmanship beyond the norms of the particular games. However, for the players these are to all intents as much a part of the "facts of life" of the game as the sun and the wind.

It is perhaps the existence of some kind of a general public, however rudimentary, that most clearly differentiates the local territorial system from a natural ecology. The five-acre woodlot in which the owls and the field mice, the oaks and the acorns, and other flora and fauna have evolved a balanced system has no public opinion, however rudimentary. The co-operation is an unconscious affair. For much of what goes on in the local territorial system co-operation is equally unconscious and perhaps, but for the occasional social scientist, unnoticed. This unconscious co-operation, however, like that of the five-acre woodlot, produces results. The ecology of games in the local territorial system accomplishes unplanned but largely functional results. The games and their players mesh in their particular pursuits to bring about over-all results; the territorial system is fed and ordered. Its inhabitants are rational within limited areas and, pursuing the ends of these areas, accomplish socially functional ends.

While the historical development of largely unconscious co-operation between the special games in the territorial system gets certain routine, over-all functions performed, the problem of novelty and breakdown must be dealt with. Here it would seem that, as in the natural ecology, random adjustment and piecemeal innovation are the normal methods of response. The need or cramp in the system presents itself to the players of the games as an opportunity for them to exploit or a menace to be overcome. Thus a transportation crisis in, say, the threatened abandonment of commuter trains by a railroad will bring forth the players of a wide range of games who will see in the situation opportunity for gain or loss in the outcome. While over-all considerations will appear in the discussion, the frame of reference and the interpretation of the event will be largely determined by the game the interested parties are principally involved in. Thus a telephone executive who is president of the local chamber of commerce will be playing a civic association, general business game with concern for the principal dues-payers of the chamber but with a constant awareness of how his handling of this crisis will advance him in his particular league. The politicians, who might be expected to be protagonists of the general interest, may indeed be so, but the sphere of their activity and the glasses through which they see the problem will be determined in great part by the way they see the issue affecting their political game. The generality of this game is to a great extent that of the politician's calculus of votes and interests important to his and his side's success. To be sure, some of what Walter Lippmann has called " the public philosophy" affects both politicians and other game-players. This indicates the existence of roles and norms of a larger, vaguer game with a relevant audience that has some sense of cricket. This potentially mobilizable audience is not utterly without importance, but it provides no sure or adequate basis for support in the particular game that the politician or anyone else is playing. Instead of a set of norms to structure enduring role-playing, this audience provides a cross-pressure for momentary aberrancy from gamesmanship or constitutes just another hazard to be calculated in one's play.

In many cases the territorial system is impressive in the degree of intensity of its particular games, its banks, its newspapers, its downtown stores, its manufacturing companies, its contractors, its churches, its politicians, and its other differentiated, structured, goal-oriented activities. Games go on within the territory, occasionally extending beyond it, though centered in it. But, while the particular games show clarity of goals and intensity, few, if any, treat the territory as their proper object. The protagonists of things in particular are well organized and know what they are about; the protagonists of things in general are few, vague, and weak. Immense staff work will go into the development of a Lincoln Square project, but the twenty-two counties of metropolitan New York have few spokesmen for their over-all common interest and not enough staff work to give these spokesmen more substance than that required for a "dogooding" newspaper editorial. The

Port of New York Authority exhibits a disciplined self-interest and a vigorous drive along the lines of its developed historic role. However, the attitude of the Port Authority toward the general problems of the metropolitan area is scarcely different than that of any private corporation. It confines its corporate good citizenship to the contribution of funds for surveys and studies and avoids acceptance of broader responsibility. In fact, spokesmen for the Port vigorously reject the need for any superior level of structured representation of metropolitan interests. The common interest, if such there be, is to be realized through institutional interactions rather than through the self-conscious rationality of a determinate group charged with its formulation and attainment. Apart from the newspaper editorial, the occasional politician, and a few civic leaders the general business of the metropolitan area is scarcely anybody's business, and, except for a few, those who concern themselves with the general problems are pursuing hobbies and causes rather than their own business.

The lack of over-all institutions in the territorial system and the weakness of those that exist insure that co-ordination is largely ecological rather than a matter of conscious rational contriving. In the metropolitan area in most cases there are no over-all economic or social institutions. People are playing particular games, and their playgrounds are less or more than the metropolitan area. But even in a city where the municipal corporation provides an apparent overall government, the appearance is deceptive. The politicians who hold the offices do not regard themselves as governors of the municipal territory but largely as mediators or players in a particular game that makes use of the other inhabitants. Their roles, as they conceive them, do not approach those of the directors of a TVA developing a territory. The ideology of local government is a highly limited affair in which the office-holders respond to demands and mediate conflicts. They play politics, and politics is vastly different from government if the latter is conceived as the rational, responsible ordering of the community. In part, this is due to the general belief that little government is necessary or that government is a congery of services only different from others because it is paid for by taxes and provided for by civil servants. In part, the separation of economics from politics eviscerates the formal theory of government of most of the substance of social action. Intervention in the really important economic order is by way of piecemeal exception and in deviation from the supposed norm of the separation of politics and economics. This ideal of separation has blocked the development of a theory of significant government action and reduced the politician to the role of registerer of pressure rather than responsible governor of a local political economy. The politics of the community becomes a different affair from its government, and its government is so structured as to provide the effective actors in it neither a sense of general responsibility nor the roles calling for such behavior.

The community vaguely senses that there ought to be a government. This is evidenced in the nomination by newspapers and others of particular individuals as members of a top leadership, a "they" who are periodically called upon to solve community problems and meet community crises. Significantly, the "they" usually are made up of people holding private, not public, office. The pluralism of the society has separated political, ecclesiastical, economic, and social hierarchies from one another so that the ancient union of lords spiritual and temporal is disrupted. In consequence, there is a marked distinction between the status of the holders of political office and the status of the "they" of the newspapers and the power elite of a C. Wright Mills or a Floyd Hunter. The politicians have the formal governmental office that might give them responsible governing roles. However, their lack of status makes it both absurd and presumptuous that they should take themselves so seriously. Who are they to act as lords of creation? Public expectation neither empowers nor demands that they should assume any such confident pose as top community leaders. The latter position is reserved for a rather varying group (in some communities well defined and clear-cut, in others vague and amorphous) of holders for the most part of positions of private power, economic, social, and ecclesiastical. This group, regarded as the top leadership of the community, and analogous to the top management of a corporation, provides both a sense that there are gods in the heavens whose will, if they exercise it, will take care of the community's problems and a set of demons whose misrule accounts for the evil in the world. The "they" fill an office left vacant by the dethronement of absolutism and aristocracy. Unlike the politicians in that "they" are only partially visible and of untested powers, the top leadership provides a convenient rationale for explaining what goes on or does not go on in the community. It is comforting to think that the executive committee of the bourgoisie is exploiting the community or that the beneficent social and economic leaders are wearying themselves and their digestions with civic luncheons in order to bring parking to a congested city.

Usually the question is raised as to

whether *de facto* there is a set of informal powerholders running things. A related question is whether community folklore holds that there is, that there should be, and what these informal power-holder should do. Certainly, most newspapermen and other professional "inside dopesters" hold that there is a "they." In fact, these people operate largely as court chroniclers of the doings of the "they." The "they," because they are "they," are newsworthy and fit into a ready-made theory of social causation that is vulgarized widely. However, the same newspaperman who could knowingly open his "bird book" and give you a run-down on the local "Who's Who" would probably with equal and blasphemous candor tell you that "they" were not doing a thing about the city and that "they" were greatly to be blamed for sitting around talking instead of getting things done. Thus, as with most primitive tribes, the idols are both worshiped and beaten, at least verbally. Public and reporters alike are relieved to believe both that there is a "they" to make civic life explicable and also to be held responsible for what occurs. This belief in part creates the role of top leadership and demands that it somehow be filled. It seems likely that there is a social-psychological table of organization of a community that must be filled in order to remove anxieties. Gordon Childe has remarked that man seems to need as much to adjust to an unseen, socially created spiritual environment as to the matter-of-fact world of the senses.

The community needs to believe that there are spiritual fathers, bad or good, who can deal with the dark: in the Middle Ages the peasants combated a plague of locusts by a high Mass and a procession of the clergy who damned the grasshoppers with bell, book, and candle. The Hopi Indians do a rain dance to overcome a drought. The harassed citizens of the American city mobilize their influentials at a civic luncheon to perform the equivalent and exorcise slums, smog, or unemployment. We smile at the medievals and the Hopi, but our own practices may be equally magical. It is interesting to ask under what circumstances one resorts to DDT and irrigation and why. To some extent it is clear that the ancient and modern practice of civic magic ritual is functional—functional in the same sense as the medicinal placebo. Much of human illness is benign; if the sufferer will bide his time, it will pass. Much of civic ills also cure themselves if only people can be kept from tearing each other apart in the stress of their anxieties. The locusts and the drought will pass. They almost always have.

While ritual activities are tranquilizing anxieties, the process of experimentation and adaptation in the social ecology goes on. The piecemeal responses of the players and the games to the challenges presented by crises provide the social counterpart to the process of evolution and natural selection. However, unlike the random mutation of the animal kingdom, much of the behavior of the players responding within the perspectives of their games is self-conscious and rational, given their ends in view. It is from the over-all perspective of the unintended contribution of their actions to the forming of a new or the restoration of the old ecological balance of the social system that their actions appear almost as random and lacking in purposive plan as the adaptive behavior of the natural ecology.

Within the general area of unplanned, unconscious social process technological areas emerge that are so structured as to promote rational, goal-oriented behavior and meaningful experience rather than mere happenstance. In these areas group activity may result in cumulative knowledge and selfcorrective behavior. Thus problem-solving in the field of public health and sanitation may be at a stage far removed from the older dependence on piecemeal adjustment and random functional innovation. In this sense there are areas in which society, as Julian Huxley suggests in his *The Meaning of Evolution*, has gone beyond evolution. However, these are as yet isolated areas in a world still swayed by magic and, for the most part, carried forward by the logic of unplanned, undirected historical process.

It is not surprising that the members of the "top leadership" of the territorial system should seem to be largely confined to ritual and ceremonial roles. "Top leadership" is usually conceived in terms of status position rather than specifiable roles in social action. The role of a top leader is ill defined and to a large degree unstructured. It is in most cases a secondary role derived from a primary role as corporation executive, wealthy man, powerful ecclesiastic, holder of high social position, and the like. The top-leadership role is derivative from the other and is in most cases a result rather than a cause of status. The primary job is bank president, or president of Standard Oil; as such, one is naturally picked, nominated, and recognized as a member of the top leadership. One seldom forgets that one's primary role, obligation, and source of rational conduct is in terms of one's business. In fact, while one is on the whole pleased at the recognition that membership in the top leadership implies—much as one's wife would be pleased to be included among the ten best-dressed women—he is somewhat concerned about just what the role requires in the expenditure of time and funds. Furthermore, one has a suspicion that he may not

know how to dance and could make a fool of himself before known elite and unknown, more general publics. All things considered, however, it is probably a good thing for the business, the contacts are important, and the recognition will be helpful back home, in both senses. In any event, if one's committee service or whatever concrete activity "top leadership" implies proves wearing or unsatisfactory, or if it interferes with business, one can always withdraw.

A fair gauge of the significance of top-leadership roles is the time put into them by the players and the institutionalized support represented by staff. Again and again the interviewer is told that the president of such-and-such an organization is doing a terrific job and literally knocking himself out for such-and-such a program. On investigation a "terrific job" turns out to be a few telephone calls and, possibly, three luncheons a month. The standard of "terrific job" obviously varies widely from what would be required in the business role.

In the matter of staffing, while the corporation, the church, and the government are often equipped in depth, the top-leadership job of port promotion may have little more than a secretary and an agile newspaperman equipped to ghost-write speeches for the boss. While there are cases where people in top-leadership positions make use of staff from their own businesses and from the legal mill with which they do business, this seems largely confined to those top-leadership undertakings that have a direct connection with their business. In general, top-leadership roles seem to involve minor investments of time, staff, and money by territorial elites. The absence of staff and the emphasis on publicity limit the capacity of top leadership for sustained rational action.

Where top leaderships have become well staffed, the process seems as much or more the result of external pressures than of its own volition. Of all the functions of top leadership, that of welfare is best staffed. Much of this is the result of the pressure of the professional social worker to organize a concentration of economic and social power sufficient to permit him to do a job. It is true, of course, that the price of organizing top leadership and making it manageable by the social workers facilitated a reverse control of themselves—a control of whose galling nature Hunter gives evidence. An amusing sidelight on the organization of the "executive committee of the bourgeoisie" is the case of the Cleveland Fifty Club. This club, supposedly, is made up of the fifty most important men in Cleveland. Most middling and even upper executives long for the prestige recognition that membership confers. Reputedly, the Fifty Club was organized by Brooks Emery, while he was director of the Cleveland Council on World Affairs, to facilitate the taxation of business to support that organization. The lead time required to get the august members of the Fifty Club together and their incohesiveness have severely limited its possibilities as a power elite. Members who have tried to turn it to such a purpose report fairly consistent failure.

The example of the Cleveland Fifty Club, while somewhat extreme, points to the need on the part of certain activities in the territorial system for a top leadership under whose auspices they can function. A wide variety of civic undertakings need to organize top prestige support both to finance and to legitimate their activities. The staff man of a bureau of municipal research or the Red Feather Agency cannot proceed on his own; he must have the legitimatizing sponsorship of top influentials. His task may be self-assigned, his perception of the problem and its solution may be his own, but he cannot gain acceptance without mobilizing the influentials. For the success of his game he must assist in creating the game of top leadership. The staff man in the civic field is the typical protagonist of things in general—a kind of entrepreneur of ideas. He fulfils the same role in his area as the stock promoter of the twenties or the Zeckendorfs of urban redevelopment. Lacking both status and a confining organizational basis, he has a socially valuable mobility between the specialized games and hierarchies in the territorial system. His success in the negotiation of a port authority not only provides a plus for his taxpayers federation or his world trade council but may provide a secure and lucrative job for himself.

Civic staff men, ranging from chamber of commerce personnel to college professors and newspapermen, are in varying degrees interchangeable and provide an important network of communication. The staff men in the civic agencies play similar roles to the Cohens and Corcorans in Washington. In each case a set of telephone numbers provides special information and an effective lower-echelon interaction. Consensus among interested professionals at the lower level can result in action programs from below that are bucked up to the prestige level of legitimitization. As the Cohens and Corcorans played perhaps the most general and inclusive game in the Washington bureaucracy, so their counterparts in the local territorial system are engaged in the most general action game in their area. Just as the Cohens and Corcorans had to mobilize an effective concentration of top brass to move a program into the action stage, so their counterparts have to mobilize concentrations of power sufficient for their purposes on the local scene.

In this connection it is interesting to note that foundation grants are being used to hire displaced New Deal bureaucrats and college professors in an attempt to organize the influentials of metropolitan areas into self-conscious governing groups. Professional chamber of commerce executives, immobilized by their orthodox ideology, are aghast to see their members study under the planners and heretics from the dogmas of free-enterprise fundamentalism. The attempt to transform the metropolitan appearance of disorder into a tidy territory is a built-in predisposition for the self-constituted staff of the embryonic top metropolitan management. The major disorder that has to be overcome before all others is the lack of order and organization among the " power elite." As in the case of the social workers, there is a thrust from below to organize a "power elite" as a necessary intrument to accomplish the purposes of civic staff men. This is in many ways nothing but a part of the general groping after a territorial government capable of dealing with a range of problems that the existing feudal disintegration of power cannot. The nomination of a top leadership by newspapers and public and the attempt to create such a leadership in fact by civic technicians are due to a recognition that there is a need for a leadership with the status, capacity, and role to attend to the general problems of the territory and give substance to a public philosophy. This involves major changes in the script of the top-leadership game and the self-image of its participants. In fact, the insecurity and the situational limitations of their positions in corporations or other institutions that provide the primary roles for top leaders make it difficult to give more substance to what

has been a secondary role. Many members of present top leaderships are genuinely reluctant, fearful, and even morally shocked at their positions' becoming that of a recognized territorial government. While there is a general supposition that power is almost instinctively craved, there seems considerable evidence that at least in many of our territorial cultures responsibility is not. Machiavellian *virtu* is an even scarcer commodity among the merchant princes of the present than among their Renaissance predecessors. In addition, the educational systems of school and business do not provide top leaders with the inspiration or the know-how to do more than raise funds and man committees. Politics is frequently regarded with the same disgust as military service by the ancient educated Chinese.

It is possible to translate a check pretty directly into effective power in a chamber of commerce or a welfare agency. However, to translate economic power into more general social or political power, there must be an organized purchasable structure. Where such structures exist, they may be controlled or, as in the case of *condottieri*, gangsters, and politicians, their hire may be uncertain, and the hired force retains its independence. Where businessmen are unwilling or unable to organize their own political machines, they must pay those who do. Sometimes the paymaster rules; at other times he bargains with equals or superiors.

A major protagonist of things in general in the territorial system is the newspaper. Along with the welfare worker, museum director, civic technician, etc., the newspaper has an interest in terms of its broad reading public in agitating general issues and projects. As the chronicler of the great, both in its general news columns and in its special features devoted to society and business, it provides an organizing medium for elites in the territory and provides them with most of their information about things in general and not a little of inside tidbits about how individual elite members are doing. In a sense, the newspaper is the prime mover in setting the territorial agenda. It has a great part in determining what most people will be talking about, what most people will think the facts are, and what most people will regard as the way problems are to be dealt with. While the conventions of how a newspaper is to be run, and the compelling force of some events limit the complete freedom of a paper to select what events and what people its public will attend to, it has great leeway. However, the newspaper is a business and a specialized game even when its reporters are idealists and its publisher rejoices in the title "Mr. Cleveland." The paper does not accept the responsibility of a governing role in its territory. It is a power but only a partially responsible one. The span of attention of its audience and the conventions of what constitute a story give it a crusading role at most for particular projects. Nonetheless, to a large extent it sets the civic agenda.

The story is told of the mayor of a large eastern metropolis who, having visited the three capital cities of his constituents—Rome, Dublin, and Tel Aviv—had proceeded home via Paris and Le Havre. Since his staff had neglected to meet the boat before the press, he was badgered by reporters to say what he had learned on his trip. The unfortunate mayor could not say that he had been on a junket for a good time. Luckily, he remembered that in Paris they had been having an antinoise campaign. Off the hook at last, he told the press that he thought this campaign was a good thing. This gave the newsmen some-

thing to write about. The mayor hoped this was the end of it. But a major paper felt in need of a crusade to sponsor and began to harass the mayor about the start of the local anti-noise campaign. Other newspapers took up the cry, and the mayor told his staff they were for it—there had to be an antinoise campaign. In short order, businessmen's committees, psychiatrists, and college professors were mobilized to press forward on a broad front the suppression of needless noise. In vindication of administrative rationality it appeared that an antinoise campaign was on a staff list of possibilities for the mayor's agenda but had been discarded by him as politically unfeasible.

The civic technicians and the newspapers have somewhat the same relationship as congressional committee staff and the press. Many members of congressional committee staffs complain bitterly that their professional consciences are seared by the insistent pressure to seek publicity. But they contend that their committee sponsors are only impressed with research that is newsworthy. Congressional committee members point out that committees that do not get publicity are likely to go out of business or funds. The civic agency head all too frequently communicates most effectively with his board through his success in getting newspaper publicity. Many a civic ghost-writer has found his top leader converted to the cause by reading the ghosted speech he delivered at the civic luncheon reported with photographs and editorials in the press. This is even the case where the story appears in the top leader's own paper. The need of the reporters for news and of the civic technicians for publicity brings the participants of these two games together. As in the case of the congressional committee, there is a tendency to equate accomplishment with publicity. For top influentials on civic boards the news clips are an important way of keeping score. This symbiotic relation of newsmen and civic staff helps explain the heavy emphasis on ritual luncheons, committees, and news releases. The nature of the newspapers' concern with a story about people and the working of marvels and miracles puts a heavy pressure for the kind of story that the press likes to carry. It is not surprising that civic staff men should begin to equate accomplishment with their score measured in newspaper victories or that they should succumb to the temptation to impress their sponsors with publicity, salting it to their taste by flattering newspaper tributes to the sponsors themselves. Despite the built-in incapacity of newspapers to exercise a serious governing responsibility in their territories, they are for the most part the only institutions with a long-term general territorial interest. In default of a territorial political party or other institution that accepts responsibility for the formulation of a general civic agenda the newspaper is the one game that by virtue of its public and its conventions partly fills the vacuum.

A final game that does in a significant way integrate all the games in the territorial system is the social game. Success in each of the games can in varying degrees be cashed in for social acceptance. The custodians of the symbols of top social standing provide goals that in a sense give all the individual games some common denominator of achievement. While the holders of top social prestige do not necessarily hold either top political or economic power, they do provide meaningful goals for the rest. One of the most serious criticisms of a Yankee aristocracy made by a Catholic bishop was that, in losing faith in their own social values, they were undermining the faith in the whole system of final clubs. It would be a cruel joke if, just as the hard-working upwardly mobile had worked their way to entrance, the progeny of the founders lost interest. The decay of the Union League Club in *By Love Possessed* is a tragedy for more than its members. A common game shared even by the excluded spectators gave a purpose that was functional in its time and must be replaced—hopefully, by a better one. A major motivation for seeking membership in and playing the top-leadership game is the value of the status it confers as a counter in the social game.

Neither the civic leadership game nor the social game makes the territorial ecology over into a structured government. They do, however, provide important ways of linking the individual games and make possible cooperative action on projects. Finally, the social game, in Ruth Benedict's sense, in a general way patterns the culture of the territorial ecology and gives all the players a set of vaguely shared aspirations and common goals.

45. Metropolitan Government, 1975: Robert C. Wood
An Extrapolation of Trends

No matter how competent and effective local governments become, whether at the level of the city or of the suburb, their success is limited because the problems that give rise to political issues extend beyond the boundaries of a single municipality. This is so especially in metropolitan areas. Consequently, there has been a good deal of interest in the possibility of establishing legal and administrative structures with authority over the affairs of an entire region and responsive to the demands of a metropolitan electorate.

Robert Wood subjects the proposals in favor of metropolitan government to reasoned criticism. He reviews the variety of economic and social forces that have stimulated these plans and discusses both their advantages and costs. Wood also notes the considerable evidence in support of the view that, for all their inefficiencies, metropolitan regions function with amazing resilience. He points to a number of trends that make this possible, including the extraordinary prosperity of urban regions, the emergence of federal grant-in-aid programs, the reduction of municipal corruption, the continued attractiveness of central city locations for business and residence, and the political involvement of suburbanites in local affairs. In the end, Wood seems to be so impressed with the potentialities in the current situation that he backs away from advocating a single metropolitan government. Instead, he proposes three alternative options for the future governing of the metropolis, each of which, in his view, offers numerous benefits to the residents of urban communities.

Robert C. Wood is Professor of Political Science at Massachusetts Institute of Technology and Director of the Joint Center for Urban Studies. He has served as Under Secretary, Department of Housing and Urban Development, Washington, D. C. He is the author of *Metropolis Against Itself* (1963) and *Suburbia, Its People and Their Politics* (1958) and coauthor of *1400 Governments: The Political Economy of the New York Metropolitan Region* (1964).

I

Growth and change in almost every aspect of American life form the backdrop of the studies of metropolitan regions and provide a concomitance of forces from which an analyst must choose. Innovations in transportation and communication, changes in housing construction and residential finance, mutations in the pattern of industrial development, almost instinctive aspirations for space and separate family accommodations, all play their part. So do the rising birth rate, the tradition of restlessness, nourished and intensified by the depression and the wars, the surging "upward mobility" within the middle class, prosperity and the family ethic.

From this concomitance, most of us who discuss the "metropolitan dilemma" and who call for radical reorganization of

A paper presented at the annual meetings of the American Political Science Association, New York City, September 1957.

From *The American Political Science Review*, Vol. LII (March 1958), pp. 108–122. Reprinted by permission.

metropolitan government have traditionally selected three forces as being of major importance. The first is the pattern of population growth and distribution within the typical SMA, in particular the disproportionate increase in suburban residential population traceable for at least thirty years.[1] The second is the slow diffusion of industry and large commercial activities throughout the area which has been taking place as new enterprises build their factories and shopping centers in fringe areas and old ones desert the central city to join them.[2] The third is also diffusive in character, although less tangible: the gradual spread of the cultural ethos of the metropolis to enfold formerly independent communities and to blanket the hinterlands with a common set of mores and values.[3] To most of us, each of these trends, taken alone, appears to have negative consequences for the fragmented pattern of government in metropolitan areas, and taken together, they seem to point positively in the direction of a common conclusion.

The now familiar negative aspects of suburban population growth are primarily three. The first concerns the costs of metropolitan governments. The journey to work, which the separation of residence and place of sustenance imposes, appears both to burden unfairly the central city and to impose crushing demands on the suburbs. The core is required to handle the cost of servicing a daytime population thirty to fifty percent in excess of its permanent number; the suburbs have unnecessarily large capital budgets since, in the welter of jurisdictions, economies of scale and size cannot be realized. Duplication and overlapping of facilities between suburbs and the core city and among suburbs result.

The population shift and the journey-to-work pattern which ensues appear to have a second negative effect. They seem to lead to a deterioration in the political process. The sturdy burgher class deserts the city, but the rigor of the commuting schedule makes its effective participation in suburban affairs unlikely. Big city politics is seen as becoming increasingly a struggle between the very rich and the very poor; suburban governments are held to be controlled by the old residents, merchants, and real-estate dealers, with only an occasional high-minded foray by the League of Women Voters. Most metropolitan inhabitants have their feet in at least two political jurisdictions; they are half-citizens, disfranchised either in law or in fact.

Third, what politics remains is likely to be bifurcated. As the suburban exodus goes on, we are told that the fringe and the central city are drifting farther and farther apart, the former increasingly Republican, the latter Democratic, so that the metropolitan areas are likely to be split into two warring camps. Prospects for mutual cooperation and understanding diminish, the metropolitan situation becomes cast in a rigid mold, and the opportunity for responsible consideration of regional problems diminishes.[4]

These implications of suburban growth *per se* seem dismal enough, but the second force of industrial diffusion adds a further difficulty. It appears to compound the metropolitan fiscal problem by making impossible an orderly matching of resources to requirements, by taking away revenues from the jurisdictions which need them most. Again, the plight of the central city is highlighted. Its tax base, already weakened by a large proportion of tax-exempt property devoted to educational and cultural purposes, is weakened further by the departure of business. Slums and blighted areas take the place of busy commercial districts, renewal efforts become more difficult, and welfare and public safety costs increase. Meanwhile in the outer ring some suburbs receive windfalls from new industry, but adjoining ones are saddled with the expenses of the workers living in cracker-box houses and putting four children per family through school. Because population and economic location patterns do not coincide, the traditional inequities and inadequacies of the American local tax structure are further intensified.[5]

As the metropolis extends its cultural influence, a third set of "negative" consequences ensues. Discrete local communities disappear; friendships become scattered randomly throughout the area; associations made in the course of work are different from those developed in residential neighborhoods. Only the ties of kinship and the stultifying communications of mass-media remain to bind men together.[6] This development is thought to have two untoward effects: first, as men wander aimlessly in the lonely crowd, the capacity of existing units of government to function vigorously and effectively is impaired for they no longer engender civic consciousness and a sense of belonging. Second, without regional institutions, no loyalty to a higher order is possible. All that remains is a weak notion of metropolitan patriotism, a New Yorker's superficial pride in being part of the Big Show. So regional problems find no vehicle for their solution and the capacity to look ahead, to plan rationally, to awake a regional consciousness is lost.

In a positive sense and in a broad way observers believe these trends are interrelated and that they lead to a common conclusion so far as political analysis is concerned. The separation of home and place of work, the rise of "nuclear centers of dominance" in the metropolitan economic system, the spread of metropolitan culture, taken together seem to signify that a metropolitan community has come —or is coming—into being. We have been imprecise about what the word "community" means. Rarely are political scientists as rigorous in their definitions as, for example, one of the panel members from a companion discipline has been.[7] But generally, we have assumed that if an aggregate of people in a given area achieve economic autarchy, if social intercourse extends over the area, and if common mores and customs exist, the basic foundations for a genuine community are present. The three factors we have studied seem to indicate that fairly self-sufficient metropolitan economic systems have developed, that social interaction now takes place across the entire area, and that a growing consensus about values is at hand. The prerequisites for the metropolitan community appear imbedded then in the trends we emphasize today.

Given this positive interpretation, the common conclusion is that for a single community, there should be a rationally constructed set of political institutions. The metropolitan dilemma is defined as the existence of many governments within a common economic and social framework. The metropolitan solution has been seen in variations on the theme "one community —one government" by any one of the half dozen ingenious political inventions. Running through all these recommendations is the premise that if somehow present units of government are brought together, if they can share resources and administrative responsibilities, the negative consequences of the forces now at work will be avoided and their impact guided into useful channels. If such reorganization is not forthcoming, we have generally believed these areas face governmental crises of substantial proportions. To drift with the tide is to court political, financial, and administrative disaster for urban government in the United States.

II

The facts on which the case for metropolitan government depends are quite real, and we have not misread the figures. Yet nothing demonstrates the complexity of analysis so well as the results of our reliance on three trends, and three trends alone. Despite our predictions, disaster has not struck: urban government has continued to function, not well perhaps, but at least well enough to forestall catastrophe. Traffic continues to circulate; streets and sewers are built; water is provided; schools keep their doors open; and law and order generally prevail. Nor does this tolerable state of affairs result from an eager citizenry's acceptance of our counsel: we know only too well that our proposals for genuine reform have been largely ignored.

It may be, of course, that the breaking point has simply not been reached. There is certainly little sign that the tide of suburban growth is ebbing, or that industrial diffusion is slowing down, or that the representatives of the new American character are remorseful now that their values have been so cruelly exposed. If we are to look forward to 1975, we have good reason for believing that these trends will continue until the "linear city" is in being on both our coasts and probably in regions in between. Yet conditions were already serious enough in the nineteen-twenties to prompt investigation and to set loose prophecies of doom. Developments have continued unabated, and it is a fair question, given the technological changes of recent years and the stubborn public reluctance to listen to our counsel, to ask if we have discovered the whole story.

If we dip back into the arrays of factors and forces at work in metropolitan regions, other trends appear, and the more they are studied, the more important they appear. In effect, when other trends, formerly left unexplored, are reviewed, they seem to operate as countervailing forces that modify the trends on which we have concentrated our attention. At times they abate the consequences our basic factors imply; at times, they change the relationships we have assumed existed. And, at least in one important respect, they present a completely different picture of the SMA than we have been accustomed to portraying.

For example, while it is true that the disproportionate growth in suburban population has accelerated since World War II, that growth has been accompanied by an extraordinary period of prosperity. As the dominant feature of our economy for the past 15 years, inflation has swollen the cost of government, but it also swelled, although belatedly, the revenue. Urban governments have managed spectacular increases in their tax returns in the past few years, and we are told by no less authority than the President's Commission on Intergovernmental Relations that the potential of the property tax is by no means realized.[8] Moreover, the rising level of incomes has an economic consequence quite apart from any particular tax structure: once basic necessities of life are satisfied, higher tax burdens, however imposed, are more tolerable, and borrowings become easier, so long as the market is not surfeited.[9] Thus communities may be forced to a general reassessment of property values, or they may skate on fiscal thin ice, but they need not undertake a general structural reorganization. Metropolitan governments may be forced to pay the excessive costs which the fragmented pattern requires, but they have been able to do so without encountering municipal bankruptcy.

Nor should other forces which bolster the capacity of metropolitan governments to sustain themselves be overlooked. While no major structural reform has been accomplished, state and federal grants-in-aid have helped support critical services and new municipal tax sources have been discovered and utilized. The plight of the central city has been to some extent relieved by grants and shared taxes, and by state assumption of important responsibilities. The commuter has either directly by earnings taxes or indirectly through his payments to state and federal governments contributed some of his share to the core municipality. The special district has been used more and more frequently to sidestep statutory debt limits, to tap new revenue sources, and to scale jurisdictional barriers in important functional fields. And some suburbs have been content to forego services, to get along with amateur governments, and to ignore the welfare state in order to remain autonomous.[10]

In less easily explicable ways, the deterioration of the urban political process seems to have been checked. Healthy signs of reinvigorated, capable political leadership have appeared in many of our large cities. Newcomers in suburbia have won important political battles, over schools and public improvements. Even the prophecy that the suburbs are irrevocably Republican and the central city irrevocably Democratic seems suspect in the light of the most recent election returns.[11] The party battleground is more complex than previously supposed.

While the apparently obvious consequences of disproportionate suburban growth have been modified, other developments have affected the revenue side of the picture. Metropolitan areas as a whole have continued to hold their own in relative economic importance, and industry has continued to move out to the fringe. Yet, by concentrating on the pattern of industrial diffusion alone, we have overlooked even more important economic changes which sharply modify the "mismatched supply and demand" thesis.[12]

The first of these is the shift in consumer demands. As output and income per worker have grown, and per capita consumption has risen, a relative decline has occurred in the consumption of agricultural products and a relative increase in the demand for "services." Employment has expanded dramatically in the fields of trade, amusement, research, education, medical care—the white collar category in general. Since these are the fields where real output per man has not increased very rapidly, the proportion of the labor force thus absorbed expands more rapidly than the absolute decrease in other categories would imply.

Second, the structure of manufacturing activities has changed. Not only have industry classifications included a larger number of truly white collar workers— management, advertising, special repair and maintenance staffs—but manufacturing processes and products have become increasingly specialized. An increasing number of specialists offer intermediate processes and products to a number of different industries, and their facilities provide the small manufacturer with "external economies" which allow him to compete effectively with larger firms. There are an increasing number of "unstandardized" final products, too, as firms depart from offering a few stable lines and present their customers with an array of choices.

Together with the decline in the pull of raw material sources as a locational factor, the relative increase in transportation costs, and the growing size of metropolitan markets, these changes in demand and in the structure of manufacturing help explain the continued growth of urban areas as entities. More important for our purposes, they move in the direction of counterbalancing the consequences of the industrial diffusion trend within metropolitan regions.

The rise in the importance of "services" in the urban economy means a broadening of the non-residential tax base exclusive of industrial plants. Offices, salesrooms, medical buildings, trade establishments of all sorts and sizes, while not as advantageous to municipalities in their cost-revenue ratios as manufacturing plants, still return more in taxes than they demand in public services.[13] As the white collar occupations grow in importance, the facilities in which they work become part of the resource base, and as they are scattered through the region in general they provide additional sources for revenue quite apart from those supplied by factories. If only industrial location trends are studied, this growing number of service establishments is overlooked and important increments to the resource base omitted.

The changes within the structure of manufacturing also make an exclusive reliance on the industrial location trends undependendable, particularly since, quite frequently, only larger firms are singled out for attention. The increasing specialization which characterizes more and more modern manufacturing means that the processes in any given industry from receipt of raw material to delivery of finished goods may

be dispersed throughout a region. Large plants and service facilities may drift toward the suburbs in search of cheaper space, but this does not necessarily mean that former locations in the central city or inner ring remain deserted.

On the contrary, many small firms frequently find a location within the central city attractive, for here are available all the specialists in the intermediate stages of production whose services can be contracted for to permit competition with the larger plants. Other "external economies" arise: fractional use of transportation facilities at less-than-carload or truckload lots, urban public services—police and fire protection, water and sewage facilities—which might not exist in the suburbs, rented space, a larger labor market, and so on. The appearance of unstandardized end products also enhances the central city's position, for purchases usually depend on visual inspections, and when styles and grades of material are important, inventories have to be kept within strict limits. These conditions make the core attractive as a "seed-bed" for industrial development, and take up the slack as larger firms depart.

Moreover, for all firms, large and small, the central city offers certain unstandardized inputs which are best provided in a central location. Advertising agencies, law firms, banks, home offices, some types of salesrooms, are activities which require proximity with their competitors, both because of the irregular schedule in which they may be used, and because "knowledge of the industry," gossip of the trade, face-to-face confrontation are prerequisites for doing business. Here again the central city offers advantages which few suburbs can yet supply.

When the changes in the manufacturing structure are considered, neither the central city nor the suburbs seems in such desperate straits as are often described. As industrial diffusion goes on, and available land is taken up, more suburbs will receive "windfalls." More will actively search them them out as well, for changes in plant architecture and the elimination of unfavorable site conditions, smoke, smells, water pollution, mean that many suburbs formerly hostile to development, will become enamoured of "light industry." Those who do not want, or will not find, industry will have their resources bolstered by service establishments following the market or by special facilities within an industry which can be separated from the parent plant.

Meanwhile, the central city is likely to find alternative economic activities, plants of small firms, business offices of large ones, and the cluster of professional and semi-professional services on which both depend. Moreover, the overriding necessity of these economic activities to maintain their central location makes their response to tax changes highly inelastic. Existing levies can be increased, or even new taxes on earnings and income imposed, and these special groups will still "stay put." Together with continued prosperity and a rise in real income, this inelasticity helps explain the recent successes in discovering new revenue sources. It further reduces the "certain" consequences of financial crises, which population and industrial trends have been thought to portend, to the status of mere possibilities, less likely than alternative courses of development.

Not only are our demographic and economic series suspect, but the less tangible hypothesis of "metropolitan dominance" comes in for critical scrutiny also. Without questioning the accuracy of the measures of newspaper circulation, postal delivery areas, telephone exchanges and journey-to-work patterns which imply the existence of a metropolitan "community," contradictory trends can be established. It is possible to submit that each region is an economic entity, that it has a circulatory and communication system of its own, and still argue that a scatteration of society has accompanied the scatteration of government; that metropolitan growth promotes a "huge mosaic of massed segregation of size, class, and ethnic groups" a "crazy quilt of discontinuities."[14]

Admittedly, as indicated earlier, when we speculate about community, we are talking about a nebulous term. The models used for the study of community are many; the essential elements of community life are still uncertain and their relative importance unweighed.[15] Yet it is significant that when authorities speak of the break-up of local communities in the metropolitan area, and the onrush of metropolitan dominance, their departure point is almost always the primary community, preliterate society, savage village or feudal holding where economic autarchy, social isolation and consensus of values were most complete.[16] Such a community, if it ever existed at all, never existed in the United States. Our archetype has been the New England town or the hamlet of the Old Northwest, both quite different in their organization of space and their feeling for community affairs, but both relatively sophisticated types, having substantial economic and social intercourse with the outside world, numbering speculators and entrepreneurs among their inhabitants, and displaying mature political systems. While their differences were many, the common elements of these communities were the qualities of propinquity, homogeneity, interdependence, and equality, which produced our ideal local government—grassroots democracy.[17]

If these qualities are taken as the essentials of smalltown life, then modern suburbs may be on the way to finding a substitute for economic self-sufficiency and social isolation to promote a sense of community consciousness. They may be using their political boundaries to differentiate the character of their residents from their neighbors and using governmental powers—zoning, residential covenants, taxation, selective industrial developments—to promote conscious segregation. From the variety of classes, occupations, income levels, races and creeds which the region contains, a municipality may isolate the particular variant it prefers and concentrate on one type of the metropolitan man. In a sense it may even produce a "purer" type of community than the American archetype, because it has a wider range of choice and it need not reproduce all the parts of a self-contained economic system. It can simply extract the particular functions it chooses to support, and achieve a social homogeneity never before possible.

Moreover, growth itself may aid and abet the process of strengthening community bonds in subareas of metropolitan regions. To the extent that a feeling of fellowship waxes strong in the early stages of community growth, that "political democracy evolves most quickly while the process of organization and the solving of basic problems are still critical," many suburbs may resemble earlier American towns in their political and social processes.[18] At any rate, provocative comparisons have been made between group and individual characteristics in modern housing developments—the acknowledgment of equality and the recognition of interdependence in Levittown and Park Forest—and frontier towns of old.[19]

A thesis that small communities are reappearing in the metropolitan areas, that the high-water mark of the process of communal disintegration has passed, is conjectural. But so is the rationale for the new metropolitan man, unattached and unrooted, and some interesting statistics support the first hypothesis. For one thing, the existence of fragmented governments do break up the area into manageable proportions—more suburbanites live in towns between 10,000 and 25,000 than in towns of any other size.[20] For another, modern suburbs have captured that portion of the middle class most oriented, in terms of education, occupation, income and family status, toward being responsible members of their locality. [21]Third, subareas in metropolitan regions are displaying a tremendous variety in their economic functions, social rank and ethnic and occupational order.[22] Most important of all, this variety does not seem to be random in nature, but the result of conscious coalescing according to a pattern of spatial homogeneity. In brief, each suburb may be gathering its chosen few to its bosom, and not just in the broad terms which Burgess and Hoyt have outlined.[23] More specifically, a clustering according to occupations seems to be taking place, in which different occupations, representing different status points in the social spectrum, put space between each other; and the wider the social differences, the further apart the members of disparate occupations live within the metropolitan area. Tracing this development in the Chicago metropolitan area, Otis and Beverly Duncan found a consistent pattern of residential segregation among occupations and a preference for neighbors with closely related occupations.[24]

If this process of natural neighborhoods goes on in an area in which each neighborhood is equipped with a local government, then instinctive feelings of community are enhanced by the fact of legal and political power. A cultural *sui generis* results, and the existence of separate political institutions, separate powers to be exercised, individual elections to be held, reinforces the bonds which make the neighborhood. Within the region as a whole, we may be witnessing a popular attempt to dissect the metropolitan giant into small pieces, and to cap each with legal authority and some degree of civic consciousness.

To the extent that this is true, the notion of one metropolitan community may be misleading, and the characterization of modern culture as new may be overdrawn. Economically the region may be one, but it may be powerless to bid for the loyalties of its residents against the claims of the smaller neighborhoods. Its inhabitants may be conformists, gregarious, adjusted, seeking approval from their peer groups, participating eagerly in every form of social endeavor; but these qualities may not signify a new dominant culture. Instead, they may mark a return to the smalltown life De Tocqueville found, an expression of protest against the stratified, pecuniary structure of the Victorian city, a desire to recreate again the "...opportunity for companionship and friendship, for easy access to local services, and for certain forms of security...," a new vision of open-country culture to stand against the metropolis.[25]

There are not enough reliable data over a long enough period of time to weigh the relative pulls of metropolitan dominance and grassroots renaissance. But there are enough data to allow us to be sceptical of the one community hypothesis, particularly when the history of public resistance to metropolitan reform is on our side. At least it seems clear that local loyalties are by no means abandoned,

and that, if by some political sleight-of-hand, a metropolitan government is created, it may not find the instinctive springs of support and popular understanding which is supposed to be anxiously waiting for the creation of regional institutions.

III

So far this analysis has undertaken only to expand the frame of reference in which metropolitan politics and government is usually considered, to bring other factors and forces under review, and to qualify conclusions derived from a limited review of empirical facts. The results of the inquiry certainly do not unveil the metropolitan future, nor do they indicate what steps should be taken. Our findings to date have been tentative and negative. Seriously adverse financial or political effects may not be arising from suburban growth. There may be no shortage of resources for the central city or the inner ring. There may not be one community to bring into maturity. In short, there may not be the metropolitan crisis which so many of us have expected for so long, either now or in the future.

This does not mean that there are no metropolitan problems, nor that there is no case for reform. Problems there are aplenty: ugly implications of the growing segregation of classes, races, and occupations in suburban ghettoes; marginal costs and wastes and inefficiencies in government finance and organization to be eliminated, the overriding issue as to whether we will realize the potential, in politics, in land use, in social intercourse, in the amenities of existence which metropolitan regions promise. We may not face catastrophe, but this is no reason for countenancing one-hour commuting schedules, for permitting blight, for condoning the repellent sprawl of cheap commercial developments, inadequate parks, congested schools, mediocre administration, traffic jams, smog, pollution, and the hundred and one irritations which surround us. Even if we can exist in the present metropolis, the fact of survival does not excuse a failure to plan the future with more care, to avoid the mistakes we have made in the past and to bestow a more worthwhile legacy.

Yet while these are real problems and genuine issues, they are not categorical necessities. They are fundamentally questions of value and of judgment, of what we should and should not do, and of how much. In short they are issues for political science to tackle in its traditional way, and no trend is clear enough to give us the easy answer "we have to do it one way." Alternatives are before us; choice remains, and the burden of responsibility is off the shoulders of the economist and the sociologist and back again on ours.

Within this normative framework, the alternatives are several and, in this analysis, only a brief summary of their implications can be undertaken. But those which seem most important are three—greenbelts, grassroots or gargantua—and they are genuine alternatives. Quite frequently, we have tended to think of metropolitan planning, federation and consolidation as related steps to the single goal of achieving political institutions suitable to the metropolitan community. In practice, we have frequently chosen between them on grounds of political expediency. Yet, these reforms do not move in the same direction; they lead us down quite different paths and, in a certain sense, a choice among them can be "extrapolated" too. In a reasoned way we can explore the implications which a certain set of values have for the future, judged by the benchmark of constitutional democracy. When this is done, though the task of metropolitan reform is complicated, its objectives are clarified. The discussion proceeds on the basis of a comparison of the values involved, in place of an excitable response to "inexorable" trends.

So far as the greenbelts alternative is concerned, the vision of order, balance, and beauty has timeless appeal for political philosophy as it has for the profession of planning. There are overtones of Plato and Aristotle, "an organic sense of structural differences," a corporate whole, in the concept, and there is the tough-minded insistence of Patrick Geddes, Ebenezer Howard, and Lewis Mumford that the vision is practical. When technology promises so much in terms of the capacity to shape nature to man's purposes, when the age of abundance is actuality, it seems reprehensible to permit the shapeless metropolitan sprawl. With such little effort, balanced communities could come into being, rational transportation systems provided, land set aside for recreational and cultural purposes, and the way cleared for Jefferson's common man to find "life" values in place of monetary values. The promise of individual dignity is combined with the aesthetics of a pastoral scene from which insects are banished and in which running water is supplied, and the metropolitan region becomes a true commingling of the best of rural and urban virtues.

There is of course a serpent in the garden of greenbelts as there was a crucial flaw in the Greek polis. Who defines the shape and substance of beauty, who determines the balance of each community, who arbitrates good taste, who decides the values of life? The advocates of greenbelts have always answered with injured innocence "the people," but they have been peculiarly reluctant to specify the means by which the people decide. They have, in modern times, reluctantly admitted that planning is properly a staff function; but when the chips are down, they have been scornful of the politician who curries votes, and indignant at his intrusion. The planners who have gained the most notoriety are those who have been the most ready to ignore the role of the elected official, to be contemptuous of the slow process of popular deliberations, and to hold themselves aloof from the electoral process. In short, while one implication of the greenbelt philosophy is harmony, another is in twentieth century socialism, American municipal style. Until the defenders of this alternative are much more specific as to the ways and means they can suggest to reconcile their values with the public's in a liberal tradition, we are rightly suspicious of their plans.

In contrast, the grassroots alternative clearly avoids the danger of professional controls imposed from above, and of an excessive commitment to communal order and balance. If we retain our belief in the efficacy of small communities and small governments which spring spontaneously into being, there is actually very little action called for at all. Given the accuracy of the economic and social statistics reviewed earlier, the likelihood of suburban governments disappearing or of crises forcing an expansion of public authority does not appear great. We can drift with the tide, fairly confident that the course of events will produce the best possible arrangement for the metropolitan complex.

This wedding of an ancient image in American political folklore to favorable modern trends makes the second approach both attractive and plausible. First the existence of all shapes and sizes of communities within the region offers an individual a freedom of choice as to where and how he wishes to live. Second, the continued segregation of occupations, classes, and races fits in well with modern doctrine on how to "manage" social conflict. Let each man find his own, abstain from social contact with antagonistic elements, abjure political disagreement and debate by joining a constituency which shares his values, and his tensions, anxieties, and uncertainties are relieved. The virtues of small-town life come to the fore, and the elemental qualities of neighborliness, friendship, and civic spirit are revived.

Yet even though the grassroots thesis has ample precedent in our history, underneath it lurk some assumptions which seem unpalatable. The individual who chooses his community in the metropolitan free-market in the same way in which he buys his car is essentially a laissez-faire man. He pursues his own self-interest to the maximum, and depends on a natural order of events to provide for the common good. Local governments become truly a bundle of services, to be purchased by those who can afford them without regard to more general social consequences. Those with resources insulate themselves from those without them, and issues of equity and humanitarianism become muted. The garden city planners may place too much reliance on the social nature of man, but grassroots advocates reach toward the opposite extreme of unfettered individualism.

Further, given the general American consensus on values, our basic commitment to democracy and capitalism, the management of social conflict is not likely to be our most pressing public problem. The pressures for conformity, the profoundly anti-individualistic element which punishes the deviate so swiftly in our society, the absence of variety, are more serious issues. Encouraging a scatteration of communities and governments in the metropolitan area does not solve this problem; it intensifies it. The individual may be free to choose his community, but once this selection is made, it is difficult for him to change his values if he wishes to stay in his own home town. The small community is friendly and comfortable and it promises fraternity, but it is also intolerant, inquisitive, barren of privacy. It is at least an open question whether this creation of political boundaries around disparate groups and classes is an appropriate development in a democracy, or whether it truly frees the individual in the manner its advocates intend. Perhaps variety, disagreement, discussion, and debate are to be encouraged rather than avoided.

To the extent this proposition is true, there is something to be said for the third alternative—of gargantua—the creation of a single metropolitan government or at least the establishment of a regional superstructure which points in that direction. If genuine metropolitan political institutions and processes are provided, the excessive marginal costs which overlapping and duplication bring about are reduced, a genuine arena exists for debate about meaningful issues which affect the area as a whole, and there is an opportunity to realize the metropolitan potential which is at our disposal.

In this scheme, decisions about the regional destiny are not the exclusive province of professional value-makers; they lie with the constituency as a whole. Freedom of choice remains for the individual, for the entire variety of spectacles and experiences which a metropolis offers is open to him. But, in a political sense, this freedom is accompanied by responsibility. A man cannot escape his neighbor by retreating to an exclusive suburb; he has to face him, to persuade or be persuaded. Political parties cannot rest secure in the knowledge that they have preponderant majorities in particular jurisdictions; they compete in a region with so many diverse temperaments and outlooks, as almost to guarantee a close two-party fight. Harmony does not appear automatically, it is painfully put together by compromise, by adjustments, by trial and error.

A plea for gargantua is not an attack against neighborhoods, against the importance of "moral integration" or against the need for fellowship and companionship. It is simply a plea against confusing these socially desirable qualities with the prerequisites of good government, against equipping neighborhoods with political prerogatives. We do not have, in the philosophical sense, a conservative tradition in the United States which emphasizes communal purpose and morality or gradations in social status. We have instead a liberal tradition, however confused in its definition of individualism and beset with contradictions; and the essence of that tradition is a distinction between society and government, a preference for legal contractual relationships in public affairs in place of personal ones. Solutions which either in the name of the public good or paradoxically in the name of rampant individualism emphasize communal bonds excessively, seek harmony instinctive or contrived, and discourage variety, are alien to the highest purpose of that tradition. Men have always found privacy, civility, and urbanity, the marks of civilization, in great cities even though they have often paid the price of anonymity and loneliness. They are most likely to find the same qualities there today.

In the end, the case for metropolitan reform, the drive for larger governments and for one community is as strong as ever. It is not a case built on necessity, on the threat of impending disaster, or on the consequences of modern technology. It is a case dependent on value judgments and philosophical disputation. But it is a strong case and perhaps a more appealing and persuasive one once its norms have been frankly admitted, and pretensions of scientific objectivity left behind. Metropolitan reform may not have been right so far as its analysis of empirical data is concerned, but it has always been righteous in the best sense of the word, and it remains righteous today.

NOTES

1. *Cf.* Victor Jones, *Metropolitan Government*, (Chicago, 1942); John C. Bollens, *The States and the Metropolitan Power* (Chicago, 1956); the National Conference on Metropolitan Problems, East Lansing, 1956, and individual metropolitan area surveys. Several of these rely on population trends almost exclusively to develop reform proposals. Amos H. Hawley, *The Changing Shape of Metropolitan America* (Glencoe, 1956), analyzes demographic developments. SMA means the Census Bureau's "standard metropolitan area."

2. *The Future of Cities and Urban Redevelopment*, Part II, Coleman Woodbury, editor (Chicago, 1953), and *Financing Metropolitan Government*, a symposium conducted by the Tax Institute (Princeton, 1955), place special emphasis on this trend.

3. For a general summary of this position, see S. A. Queens and D. B. Carpenter, *The American City* (New York, 1953), Chapter 7; R. D. McKenzie, *The Metropolitan Community* (New York, 1933), Chapter 9; and Don J. Bogue, *Structure of the Metropolitan Community* (Chicago, 1949).

4. Edward C. Banfield, "The Changing Political Environment of City Planning," a paper delivered at the 1956 meeting of the Association.

5. This conclusion is a major point in almost every description of metropolitan government. Charles Adrian, in *Governing Urban America* (New York, 1955), Chapters 2 and 11, gives an able summary of this and the other negative consequences discussed earlier.

6. An authoritative review of past and current literature dealing with the character of the metropolitan community is found in Scott Greer's "Individual Participation in Mass Society," a paper prepared for Conference Study of the Community, Northwestern University, 1956.

7. Conrad Arensberg, "American Communities," *The American Anthropologist*, vol. 57, pp. 1143–1162 (Dec. 1955). See also Albert J. Reiss, "Some Logical and Methodological Problems in Community Research," *Social Forces*, vol. 33, pp. 51–57 (October, 1954).

8. Allen P. Manvel, "Trends in Municipal Finance," *Municipal Yearbook*, 1957, showing the doubling of annual revenues for the 481 largest cities between 1942 and 1955 and the six-fold increase in non-property taxes.

9. Projecting the municipal bond market is a risky business and certainly a strong case can be made that cities have explored this avenue to the limit in the last few years. Over the long run, however, if continued prosperity is assumed, it seems clear that municipal offerings will continue to play an important part in the investment market.

10. Non-property tax revenue accounted for 27% of all local revenue in 1953. State and federal aid was about 8 billion dollars. It is also worth noting that an inverse relation usually exists between grants and non-property taxes by local units of government, so that units incapable of exploring a broader tax structure are bolstered disproportionately by aid formulae. For a fuller discussion, see The American Assembly, *The Forty-Eight States: Their Tasks as Policy Makers and Administrators* (New York, 1955).

11. Relatively little attention has been given to the subject of metropolitan voting behavior, and no general hypotheses seem firmly established. The Banfield analysis assumed a constant city Democratic majority of 60% and a Republican suburban majority of 60%. This assumption may be unrealistic after close analysis of the 1952 and 1956 national elections. For 14 metropolitan areas showing increasing Republican strength in 1952 over 1948, the gain in 8 central cities was greater than in their suburbs. In 1956, Republican central city gains continued, only San Francisco and Los Angeles managing a slight Democratic comeback. In spot Congressional elections in suburban St. Louis, sharp Democratic gains were registered between 1946 and 1954. A study of Boston metropolitan elections, state and national, between 1940 and 1954, showed 15 suburban towns growing increasingly Republican, 9 increasingly Democratic, and 13 changing from Republican to Democratic. While these analyses do not provide anything like a firm basis for positive speculation they do cast considerable doubt on the theory of suburban "conversion" to Republicanism, so prevalent in recent years.

12. In the following discussion of metropolitan economic developments, the analysis is based upon interim findings of the New York Metropolitan Region Study. I am indebted to Raymond Vernon, Director of the study, and the other economists on the staff for their patient revelations of the mysteries of regional economics. The study has not yet reached the point where the trends discussed can be stated in quantitative terms, and considerable modifications of the reasoning here summarized may take place before the project's conclusion in 1959. At the present time, however, these findings appear fairly well substantiated. The Study, and the economists therein are, of course, not responsible for the interpretations and inferences I have made so far as metropolitan government is concerned.

13. George A. Duggar, "The Tax System and a Responsible Housing Program," unpublished Ph.D. Dissertation, Harvard University, 1956, Ch. 6.

14. Arensberg, *op. cit.*

15. Reiss, *op. cit.*

16. Greer, *op. cit.*

17. Stanley Elkins and Eric McKitrick, "A Meaning for Turner's Frontier," *Political Science Quarterly*, Vol. 69, pp. 321–353, and pp. 565–602 (Sept. and Dec., 1954).

18. *Ibid.*, p. 325.

19. *Ibid.*

20. Otis Duncan and Albert J. Reiss, Jr., *Social Characteristics of Urban and Rural Communities, 1950* (New York, 1956). The citations here are both with respect to conclusions in the book, as well as an indication of source data from which independent statistical series have been developed.

21. *Ibid.*

22. *Ibid.*

23. Ernest W. Burgess, "Urban Areas" in *Chicago, An Experiment in Social Science Research*, ed. T. V. Smith and L. D. White (Chicago, 1929), pp. 113–138, and Homer Hoyt, *The Structure and Growth of Residential Neighborhoods in American Cities* (Washington, 1939).

24. Otis D. and Beverly Duncan, "Residential Distribution and Occupation Stratification," *The American Journal of Sociology*, Vol. 60, pp. 493–503 (March, 1955).

25. Woodbury, *op. cit.*, p. 367.

PART VI

Urban Environment and Social Behavior

Urban sociology has long been interested in the influence of the physical environment on behavior and social organization. In pursuing this interest, sociologists have tended to focus their research on the significance of density levels, the impact of dwelling unit design, the role of site planning or the spatial arrangements of dwellings, and the influence of the location of community facilities and work places. Studies of the effects of these environmental factors have proliferated recently, largely as a response to the development of government programs which aim to improve the quality of urban life through public housing, urban renewal and redevelopment, and suburban community planning.

Looked at in historical perspective, the rise of the city and the experience of living in conditions of high population density seem clearly to have contributed to the emergence of individuated personality types and the differentiated forms of social organization associated with modern society. The relationship of spatial factors to cultural and psychological phenomena is more ambiguous, however, when the conditions being studied are all variations in similar patterns of urban density. For example, moving poor people from relatively crowded and dilapidated slums to new, clean, and more spacious housing projects sometimes improves their physical health but is unlikely to reduce the incidence of social pathologies such as neurosis, divorce, or delinquency. Indeed, in some cases the destruction of old neighborhoods apparently diminishes the capacity of the migrant to function effectively even though a reduction in population concentration has occurred. The advantages of greater spaciousness are outweighed by the costs involved in having abandoned or lost the familiar social networks and cultural life-styles that were developed in slum areas. In the case of suburban settlements, which have been criticised for lacking the qualities of community integration that are found in some slums, considerable effort has been devoted to arranging houses, driveways, and backyards in a manner that would encourage intimacy and community spirit. However, the impact of these physical arrangements in bringing people together is of very short duration. What seems to count among neighbors in the long-run are the norms, values, and social characteristics they share in common rather than their physical proximity. The various studies indicate that the true significance of the physical environment is the way in which it encourages or enables desired patterns of behavior to develop when the culture, social organization, and attitudes of the users of these environments already dispose them toward adopting these patterns. Any thorough understanding of the relationship between the spatial environment and behavior depends upon a theory of urban form that recognizes the symbolic meanings that space can have for people and the complex interrelations between different scales of the environment and social and cultural factors.

46. Housing and Its Effects | Alvin L. Schorr

In the first part of this century, there was a widespread belief that if you took a person out of a slum and rehoused him in a more commodious environment, he would turn into a good middle-class citizen. After several decades of housing and renewal efforts, beginning with the New Deal period, this view has come to be rejected. It has become fashionable to say that "You can take the person out of the slum, but it is much harder to take the slum out of the person."

Alvin Schorr asserts that both the older and the now prevailing view represent oversimplifications of a complex causal relationship between the physical environment and social action. He suggests that the effects of housing can be understood only if one is careful to distinguish among the types of behavior and pathology, the characteristics of the population which is rehoused, the quality of their previous housing, and the elements of the housing environment which are transformed. In the following selection, Schorr examines the published research literature in terms of these distinctions and concludes that the impact of physical housing on human behavior is probably now being understated.

Alvin L. Schorr, Professor of Sociology at Brandeis University, has served as Deputy Assistant Secretary for Individual and Family Services, Department of Health, Education and Welfare, Washington, D. C. He is the author of *Explorations in Social Policy* (1968), *Poor Kids* (1966), *Social Security and Social Services in France* (1965), *Slums and Social Insecurity* (1964), and *Filial Responsibility in the Modern American Family* (1960). He is also Editor in Chief of *Social Work*.

Is There a Causal Relationship?

Whether housing affects people and how are old questions. They were examined in Glasgow about 1870, when the city took power to clear land and "reconstitute" neighborhoods. Examining the effects on people who were moved, J. B. Russell found himself perplexed in a way that seems painfully modern. Finding conclusions difficult, he wrote:

> A gutter-child from the Bridgegate is a very complicated production . . . . The evil which the Improvement Trust sets itself to remedy was worked in successive generations, and the good which it desires to effect cannot be exhausted in a period short of the life of one generation, if not of several.

That we have not come very far beyond this conclusion in a century may be a product of several factors. First, personal experiences testify so dramatically to the effect of housing that one is encouraged to approach research in somewhat patronizing fashion. Second, the motivation to conduct research has been chiefly to produce political action. The ideas that are useful for moving legislatures—crime, immorality, and ability to pay taxes—are too mixed and, over time, too inconsistent to prove very deeply into human behavior.

From Alvin L. Schorr, *Slums and Social Insecurity: An Appraisal of the Effectiveness of Housing Policies in Helping to Eliminate Poverty in the United States* (Washington, D. C.: U.S. Government Printing Office, 1963), Chapter I: "Housing and Its Effects," pp. 7–33, and Appendix A: "Evidence of the Effects of Housing," pp. 141–144. Reprinted by permission.

Third, approached for theoretical purposes, the question of the effect of housing presents difficult problems of definition and method. Does housing mean the house or the neighborhood, and are they separable? Is it at all possible to disentangle the physical facts of housing from the family's image of it, and what is the relative importance of each?

Weighing the net meaning of all the evidence that is available, one must conclude that the placement of houses and apartments in relation to one another and to the total city (downtown, suburban) clearly influences family and social relationships. Though there is no solid evidence, there is at least a hint of the effect of such factors as internal physical arrangement and space per person. In one direction the evidence is overwhelming: *extremely poor* housing conditions perceptibly influence behavior and attitudes.

Let us list the forms in which these effects of housing may be found. A division into three types of effects will be useful. First, some effects are caused by housing, in the sense that both house and neighborhood are included in the term. In this sense, we shall discuss the effect of housing when it is viewed as a symbolic extension of one's self, as a factor in increasing or minimizing stress, as a cause of good or ill health, and as a factor in feelings of satisfaction. A second type of effect may be attributed to physical housing alone—its space, its state of repair, its facilities, and its arrangement. Such physical conditions may influence privacy, child-rearing practices, and housekeeping or study habits. Finally, other effects may flow from the neighborhood or its relationship to the rest of the city. Effects really cannot be divided neatly into three like this; the division is a matter of convenience and emphasis only.

Effects of House and Neighborhood

Housing and Self-Perception El Fanguito, in San Juan, P.R., was known, before it was cleared, as the largest slum[2] in the world. But many residents neglected to mention it when researchers asked them to name a slum.[3] The first redevelopment proposal in the city of Milwaukee, announced in 1947, was defeated by residents. One woman's statement was reported by the *Milwaukee Journal*: "Slums, they call us. Why that's a terrible word—those are our homes, our shrines. We live there."[4] The inertia, not to say intransigence, of those slum residents who resist being moved in one city after another makes it plain that they do not view their surroundings with the same contempt as city planners and municipal officials. Slum neighborhoods may serve other functions that are useful to residents—we shall be discussing these at greater length—but one factor at work is that house and place are regarded as extensions of one's self. In the words of a study in the Chelsea area of New York:

> Housing ... has represented much more than physical structures. Housing is/has become a subject of highly charged emotional content: a matter of strong feeling. It is the symbol of status, of achievement, of social acceptance. It seems to control, in large measure, the way in which the individual, the family, perceives him/itself and is perceived by others.[5]

Thus, one evaluates his surroundings far from objectively, and himself in terms of his surroundings. How indeed call a house a slum if this is to tell the tenant he is a slum dweller!

To the middle-class reader, the social elements that are involved in identifying himself with his housing may be evident. These are the common coinage of deciding where to live: Who is accepted there? Are they my kind of people? Is it a step up or down? What will it do for me and my children? Whom shall I meet? The physical elements of self-evaluation may not be so evident. Indeed, it has been suggested that our culture tends to put out of mind the deep personal significance of what has been called the "nonhuman environment." It is interesting and perhaps also just that psychoanalysts are among the first to bring back to our minds a relationship that more primitive societies understand. Harold F. Searles writes:

> It seems to me that, in our culture, a conscious ignoring of the psychological importance of the nonhuman environment exists simultaneously with a (largely unconscious) *overdependence upon* that environment. I believe that the actual importance of that environment to the individual is so great that he *dare* not recognize it. Unconsciously it is felt, I believe, to be not only an intensely important conglomeration of things *outside* the self, but also a large and integral *part* of the self.[6]

If physical surroundings are a mirror to us all, they will reflect an especially disturbing image to the people who, lacking the simplest amenities, are made aware of the riches that others quite normally own and consume.

The reciprocal effects of housing and self-evaluation may flow in two directions. On one hand, people who feel they are worth more may avoid slums or low-status neighborhoods, if this is at all possible. Thus Moss Hart, assured of the success of his first play, moved his family within hours, leaving behind apartment, furniture, and clothing. He wrote:

> Each piece of furniture in the cramped dim room seemed mildewed with a thousand double-edged memories. The ghosts of a thousand leaden meals hovered over the dining room table. The dust of countless blackhearted days clung to every crevice of the squalid ugly furniture I had known since childhood.[7]

Who are the people who are eager to improve their housing? Studies show them to be the young, the families who are ambitious for their children, the people who wish to improve their status. (As this listing may suggest, it appears that acceptance of change is a family rather than an individual attribute.)[8,9,10] The physical move is a social move, an evidence of aspiration and a functional step in improving one's social or economic situation.

On the other hand, living in poor housing itself influences self-evaluation and motivation. This is the heart of the question we are dealing with, whether causality moves *from* housing *to* attitudes and behavior. A good deal has been written about the pessimism that is common to poor people, the readiness to seize the present satisfaction and let the future care for itself, and the feeling that one is controlled by rather than in control of events.[11] Indeed, so well do we understand these feelings that it has become necessary to be reminded that there is considerable variability, not to say aspiration, among even the very poor.[12,13] Studies of families living in deteriorated neighborhoods make the same point: pessimism and passivity present the most difficult barriers to rehabilitating neighborhoods or relocating families.

However, where vigorous effort has gone into upgrading neighborhoods—in Chicago, Baltimore, New Orleans, and Miami—observers have seen people "who dropped their old, fatalistic attitudes and embraced new feelings of pride and optimism. . . ."[14] This observation should not be exaggerated; only some people, more in Baltimore and fewer in Miami, responded. Scientifically controlled studies give more ambiguous evidence about the effect of changing housing on self-evaluation. The two or three that have been done do not appear to span an adequate period of time, nor do they have adequate instruments to measure motivation and self-evaluation. It seems clear that families who have improved their housing feel they have improved their situation and status.[15,16] A substantial, controlled sample of families who moved to improved housing showed higher "general morale" but no change in aspirations.[17]

Certain factors appear to operate selectively to determine who will respond to a change in housing. Apparently, improvement has to go beyond the simplest physical facilities before a change in attitude shows. That is, while sheer physical need continues to occupy the family's attention, attitude is not affected.[18,19] Even when their parents are not responding at all, children change their feelings about "the whole of life"—a change particularly noticeable in school.[20,21] There is evidence that children who are rehoused are "considerably more likely to be promoted at a normal pace. . . ."[22,23] Another factor is that opportunity needs to be genuinely present; otherwise indifference or escapist activities offer equally acceptable retreats.[24,25] There needs, finally, to be some basic educational and cultural attainment; in a sense, this is another way of saying that opportunity must be genuinely present.

Stress In attempting to describe the link between culture and personality, while both are changing, stress appears to be a useful concept. For example, it has been proposed that migration from a rural to an urban setting places "excessive adjustive burdens" on migrants. Insofar as these stresses cannot be absorbed by the individual or the group with which he surrounds himself, he will show some form of ill health.[26] How housing affects families and individuals is a special form of the same general question, and stress has been offered as a tie. That is, housing may affect behavior by contributing to or dissipating stress. The use of such an intervening concept has at least two advantages over attempts to relate housing inadequacies (noise, for example) directly to behavioral consequences (irritability). It accounts for differences in reaction between individuals of the same general background. In other words, it introduces the idea that some people have more effective adjustive mechanisms than others—patently a factor that influences reactions. Second, it accounts for the effect of certain factors which would not otherwise appear to be relevant (the relation of filth to migraine headaches, for example).

Almost any housing quality that affects individuals may be interpreted as stressful—crowding,[27] dilapidation and cockroaches,[28] or a high noise level.[29] Two further stressful factors are social isolation and inadequate space. There is some evidence that aged people who live alone are more likely to require psychiatric hospitalization than those living with families. Accumulating research suggests "that any environment which tends to isolate an individual from others offers a stress that will lead to distinguishable personality changes. . . ."[30,31] The adequacy of internal space will be considered at greater length later. For the moment, it is significant that the amount of space per person and the way space is arranged to promote or interfere with privacy have been related to stress.

Though the point is mentioned frequently in the literature, it has perhaps been put most cogently by James S. Plant. He refers to——

... the mental strain arising from constantly having to "get along" with other people. ... In the strain of having constantly to adapt to others there is a continuous challenge to the integrity of [the child's defenses] and the child gives to us beautifully the irritable, restless, insecure picture which proclaims this ever-present threat. Often adults feel the strain of having to adjust to others if they are persistently in a group for a period of time. We see children who have never known any other situation.[32]

We speak here of a reaction to extreme stimulation, without attempting to distinguish between attitudes of one socioeconomic class and another. In dealing specifically with internal space, we shall see that such a distinction is important.

Health Particularly in studies that correlate poor housing with poor health, substantial evidence links the two together. We may accept as causally related those illnesses for which correlations are demonstrated *and* the mechanisms that are operating are well understood. Daniel Wilner has offered a classification of these:

1. Acute respiratory infections (colds, bronchitis, grippe), related to multiple use of toilet and water facilities, inadequate heating or ventilation, inadequate and crowded sleeping arrangements.
2. Certain infectious diseases of childhood (measles, chickenpox, and whooping cough), related to similar causal factors.
3. Minor digestive diseases and enteritis (typhoid, dysentery, diarrhea), related to poor facilities for the cold storage of food and to inadequate washing and toilet facilities.

4. Injuries resulting from home accidents, related to crowded or inadequate kitchens, poor electrical connections, and poorly lighted and unstable stairs.
5. Infectious and noninfectious diseases of the skin, related to crowding and facilities for washing.[33]

Other diseases that, one may be confident, may be caused by poor housing include lead poisoning in children from eating scaling paint[34] and pneumonia and tuberculosis.[35] It is not surprising, therefore, to find that morbidity and mortality rates also correlate with adequacy of housing. With understandable exceptions —for example, an increase in infectious illness among young people newly exposed to one another[36]—controlled studies confirm that improved housing reduces the incidence of illness and death.[37]

Satisfaction Satisfaction is a somewhat different type of effect from those that have so far been discussed. Concepts such as health and optimism, though subjectively experienced, retain a degree of consistency from one group to another. Satisfaction is defined entirely by the current situation. Though the questions may vary from study to study, in each study "satisfaction" is defined as the answer to one or more specific questions. "Do you have complaints about this housing development?" "Do you like living here? Much? Little?" Consequently, satisfaction means only what each question means in the context in which it is asked. Used in association with other kinds of observations, measures of satisfaction provide additional leads and insights regarding experience with housing. They are therefore used with some frequency.

Satisfaction may be defined as the absence of complaint when opportunity for complaint is provided, or as an explicit statement that the person likes his housing. In these senses, satisfaction has at one time or another been shown to be positively related to the following housing characteristics: a set of beliefs about one's house, as distinguished from its physical properties[38]; the market value of the house[39]; ownership as opposed to rental[34]; one's neighbors or one's view of them[41]; close friendship or kinship ties in the neighborhood[42]; space per person[43,44]; the number of rooms per family[45]; the availability of space for separate uses[46,47]; the possession of a kitchen or bathroom of one's own[48]; and the absence of certain deficiencies (vermin, etc.).[49] Frequently such findings are based on correlations, but are confirmed, when confirmation is sought, by studies that follow families from poor to improved housing.

The relationship between such housing characteristics and satisfaction is plausible; unfortunately paradoxical findings also turn up. For example, the residents of a defense housing project, though their houses were more commodious, were less satisfied than residents of a project for student veterans.[50] Evidently, the circumstances under which families move into housing has an overriding influence on their attitude. Again, 6 percent of a small group of white-collar workers and 21 percent of a group of semiskilled and unskilled workers had been living with relatives. However, complaints about overcrowding flowed in the opposite direction. Twenty-nine percent of the white-collar group and 6 percent of the semiskilled and unskilled complained that they were overcrowded.[51] It has been argued that this represents a class difference in evaluation of privacy.[52] A final example: People living in crowded accommodations turned out, on the average, to be more satisfied than people who were less crowded. It is suggested that

those who were dissatisfied had managed to improve their accommodations and only the comparatively satisfied were still crowded.[53]

Thus, it appears that housing influences satisfaction, but within the limits of several general qualifications. First, satisfaction expresses a relationship between where a person has lived and his current housing. Thus, one man may be less satisfied with a mansion than another man with a small apartment, depending on where each lived earlier. Second, the housing that people want (and about whose lack they will complain) is related to what seems to them to be practical. Practicality, in turn, does not reach too far from what a family already has. "Needs," writes Svend Riemer, "appear, are satisfied, and fade out, only to make place for new needs."[54] Finally, there is not one housing satisfaction but several. General "residential satisfaction," "house satisfaction," and "neighbor satisfaction" have been identified as important.[55] Any specific factor under consideration may disappear in or be canceled out by the effect of another factor.

Effects of Physical Housing

We turn now to the effects that may be attributed to physical housing alone. Most research attention has been paid to the adequacy of internal space—or its inadequacy, which is crowding. A number of signs suggest that crowding is the key housing factor affecting low-income families. Measures of maladjustment to the home are "most strikingly" related to crowding.[56] The need for more space is the dominant reason that families, when they can afford it, change one house or apartment for another.[57] Crowding appears to be the major housing characteristic that influences health.[58] The effects of crowding have been more extensively investigated than other housing qualities, through perhaps only because crowding is more easily measured.

Crowding has been measured in a variety of ways. A count of persons per bed, used in Great Britain in the 19th century, does now seem to be out of date. Thus does the demise of standards in itself reflect progress. The American Public Health Association some years ago established space requirements by number of square feet —400 square feet for one person, 750 for two, 1,000 for three, and so on.[59] A standard of square feet may be suitable for builders and housing inspectors, for whom it is intended, but presents difficulties for enumeration or research. An easier standard to use counts the number of people per room in a housing unit. One person or less per room is considered adequate. Earlier standards counted 1.5 or 2 persons per room as adequate. A similar standard relates the number of people to the number of bedrooms—one bedroom for two people, two for three or four people, and so on. Number of people, number of bedrooms, and total space required may be combined into a more complicated formula. Thus, three people in two bedrooms required about 554 square feet.[60] There has been some interest, finally, in developing definitions more descriptive of family functioning. "Use crowding" describes the situation in which a room designated for one function (living room) is used also for a different function (bedroom).[61] Though such a definition has not been greatly elaborated, it holds the promise of taking into account both space and family needs at the same time. A numerical space measure, on the other hand, assumes that all families carry on more or less the same activities in the same ways.

Psychological Effects of Crowding It has already been noted that crowding, along with other physical and social factors, bears a relationship to stress and self-perception. Plant[62] identified four other psychological consequences of crowding. "The first is the challenge to the sense of individuality. . . ." Because he is so rarely alone, the child fails to learn to look to himself for the real satisfactions of life. "The second is the challenge to the child's illusions about other people. . . ." Brought into unavoidable contact with adult weakness and greed, children find it difficult to build up identifications with hero-parents or other ideals. "The third is the challenge to any illusions about sex." Crowding makes "the physical aspect of the sexual life primary instead of realizing it as largely the symbol of idiomatic personal relationships." Finally, he noted "the challenge to an objective study of the world or its problems. [Crowded children] are so much *in* life that they can rarely look *at* it." Plant writes out of his experience with children, but the analysis applies to adults as well.

These are clinical conclusions, undemonstrated and indeed untested. If they are accurate, what would one expect of the adult who is a product of crowded housing? He should tend to be gregarious, to look outside himself for stimulation, and to be comparatively uninterested in solitary pursuits. He is likely to be cynical about people, not to say organizations and governments. Sexual expression should be regarded as a physical matter, rather than an element of a relationship. He should feel unable to understand clearly the events that move him, let alone feel able to take hold of and move events. Such a description is consistent with the findings of studies of slum inhabitants, as well as with the broader descriptions of lower class culture. Obviously, we do not conclude that crowding is the single or the major element that produces a "culture of poverty." More likely, the personality of the slum dweller is "overdetermined." That is, crowding keys in with other deprivations, each reinforcing the other, to shape the slum dweller.

One insight that is somewhat similar to Plant's *has* been tested. It is suggested that if male children sleep with their mothers for a year or more, drastic measures must be provided at adolescence to break the mother-son bond. Analysis of 56 societies confirms that such a sleeping arrangement tends to be followed by rituals that enforce separation. Our own society does not enforce separation except, perhaps, in requiring military service—and that rather late. It is suggested that the consequences, where a strong relationship with the mother has not been interrupted, are delinquency or open rebellion against paternal authority.[63] The relevance of this analysis lies in the likelihood that where there is crowding, such a sleeping arrangement will persist.

Something more may be said about the effects of crowding on sexual behavior. Bingham Dai writes:

As a slum child I had frequent clandestine sex experiences. No attempt was made to hide the facts from me. People laughed at small children's acts toward sex expression.[64]

A number of accounts, usually at second-hand, tend to link seeing and doing rather simply together. For example, youths in the "pilot area" of Baltimore, though they responded to community rehabilitation efforts, showed least change in their sexual behavior. Probation officers and recreation leaders felt that the poor example set by adults was responsible.[65]

However, the material that is available suggests a different sequence.

Having reviewed the literature of lower class sexual behavior, Lee Rainwater writes:

The sexual stimulation that comes in all of these cultures [Mexico, Puerto Rico, England, the United States] from the close living together of children and adults is apparently systematically repressed as the child grows older. The sexual interests stimulated by these and other experiences are deflected for the boys onto objects defined as legitimate marks (loose women, careless girls, prostitutes, etc.) and for the girls simply pushed out of awareness with a kind of hysterical defense (hysterical because of the fact that later women seem to protest their ignorance too much).[66]

How is it, then, that many poor youngsters do have sex relations and that they show high rates of venereal disease and illegitimacy? Why, in particular, would girls, in having relations, permit themselves to be defined as loose? Conceivably, in the hope of getting a husband where husbands are comparatively unavailable. Conceivably, for favors and payment. And conceivably, for an appearance of regard which comes particuarly hard to the girl whose does not value herself very highly. Moreover, it has been noted from time to time that where genuine opportunity is not or does not seem to be available, energy is "diverted to sex, recreation, and gambling."[67,68,69] In effect, then, we see crowding as providing a high degree of sexual stimulation which may lead, for some girls, to expression after a tortuous course through repression, boredom, and discouragement. It is not so appealing a picture as the simpler one. As for youngsters who do not react in this way, some will reject sexuality categorically, defending themselves from one problem with another.

In the sense in which we have been discussing crowding, it is almost purely a lower class phenomenon. Yet there is a serious issue whether it is middle-class city planners or lower-class slum dwellers who feel strongly about crowding. The issue is raised particularly at the level of public policies concerning forced relocation. On one hand, there has been a series of the effect of crowding that demonstrate its undesirable consequences. (Some of these studies, at least, leave the impression that the researcher himself placed a sufficiently high value on solitude to influence his conclusions.)[70,71] On the other hand, there are studies that suggest that other, conflicting values are more important to lower-class families than the privacy that adequate space permits. For example, in a new Chilean housing project residents moved furniture from their living rooms into the hall so they could be together, as was their custom. Again, though some people may wish to have privacy, others may feel frightened when they cannot see and hear their neighbors.[72]

It does not appear impossible to reconcile the two points of view. For one thing, privacy is not the opposite of crowding, though it is sometimes treated as if it were. It is hard to be private while crowded but the Chileans, for example, were convivial even though they had more than adequate space. Further, there does not appear to be a genuine difference of opinion whether poor people wish to live "seven deep."[73] The differences are rather these: If space of minimimum adequacy is provided, will working-class and middle-class people have similar desire for *additional* space?[74] This question is susceptible of research and has hardly been resolved. Poor families express much more modest desires about space, as about everything else. We have already indicated, however,

that such expressions are colored by what a family has and what seems practical.

The second real difference is this: Are there poor people who wish to yield, for the adequate space they would presumably like, the familiar secure neighborhood that may be crucially important?[75] This question seems less likely to be resolved by research. The problem is, in a sense, in motion. If crowding leads to a preference for being with people, as Plant suggests, then the provision of adequate space will be followed by the need for it. There is an interesting example of this transition in an English study of families rehoused from 19th-century dwellings to a housing estate.[76] They had lived long in densely populated housing, with the closeness and warmth that are characteristic of some slums. Upon moving, the families reported a decrease in tension, particularly between fathers and daughters, as privacy became more readily available. No one would any longer sleep in the living room. On the other hand, some unnecessary sharing of bedrooms persisted during the year of the study; homework and other tasks were done in company, by choice. One perceives, all intermixed, the families' interest in changing, the strain in changing, and the limiting conditions that old and new structures place upon their living patterns.

It is not only attitudes about space that are in transition; the whole value system of a poor family may be in motion. While some families would cast their lot with familiarity, others—depending on age, family situation, and so forth—would plump for improved housing. (We should tag them "upwardly mobile" and feel that we understand them.) Thus, a categorical choice between space and familiarity may elude us. Yet it becomes clear that one cannot assume that all families wish or should wish to move: This is in fact the policy issue at which the argument is usually aimed: Renewal and relocation policies need to take account of the families who do not wish to move.

Other Effects of Crowding and Layout We have noted the effect of housing on health. It is appropriate to add, in speaking of direct physical effects of housing, that fatigue and too little sleep may be consequences of seriously inadequate housing. The point is frequently made that crowding leads to irritations and interruptions. Reviewing cases, Dr. Lemkau concludes that these in turn "lead to unproductive expenditure of energy which in turn ends in overfatigue. . . ."[77] A study of working-class Negroes in Chicago in 1945 revealed that most of them slept less than 5 hours a night. The study ascribes this finding simply to lack of space for beds.[78] It is hardly necessary to point out the relationship of rest to health.

We have dealt so far almost exclusively with the effects of crowding on personal feelings and behavior. We need also to take account of family activities, particularly the function of child rearing. The effect of crowding on intra-family friction is observed in various connections. For example, one reason that suburban families gain in morale is that, with more space, family members no longer get in each other's way.[79] A small kitchen gives difficulty to the housewife trying to prepare food and cope with children or other adults at the same time.[80]

One result of seriously inadequate space appears very often to be that family members spend their time out of doors.[81,82] An illustration was observed in families moving to small apartments in Vienna, who began to seek outside recreation they had not used before. When recreation was not available, families showed aggravation of any predisposition to neurotic behavior.[83] The tendency to spend time outside the home may be a particularly serious matter in relation to children. It has been observed that they do not study;[84] more than that, they are not within reach of parental control. Study of low-income families in the District of Columbia suggests strikingly early "cutoff points" in parental will and ability to control children. Children do, indeed, seem to seize control —some as early as at the age of six.[85,86] One can hardly overlook the relevance of such a pattern to the fact that children cannot reasonably be kept in the house. Inside the house, and at an earlier point in the child's life, another kind of problem exists. If there is an arrangement for him to keep a certain number of things, to set up projects, and so forth, the more or less natural course is to protect the child from adults, and vice versa. If space does not permit such an arrangement, a wholly different problem arises. One study concluded that the problem arises for most families with two children in two-bedroom apartments. The inevitable consequence is a certain amount of tension, more for the "permissive" than the "traditional" families.[87]

In discussing the influence of crowding upon family relationships, it is well to bear in mind that those who are crowded together may not be only the husband and wife and their children. The group frequently includes other relatives or nonrelatives. There was a good deal of concern about doubled-up families following World War II, as it was felt that the scarcity of housing forced an undesirable situation upon them.[88] With housing now more plentiful, it may be supposed that larger family groups live together out of choice. We shall see, in discussing the strategies that the poor use to secure housing, that doubling up is not only a matter of choice.

It should be clear that the arrangement of space, as well as the amount of space, may be influencing behavior. Where space is grossly inadequate, it is difficult to see the effects of another variable. Where the basic amount of space is adequate, however, such questions arise as the effect of devoting increased proportions of the cost of a house to appliances rather than space and the effect of one-story compared with two-story houses. (These particular questions were listed by Catherine Bauer in 1952,[89] and remain quite untouched a decade later.)

Such study as has been done of the effects of internal design has chiefly sought to find the preferences of families. (Preferences, like satisfaction, may be difficult to interpret.) Thus, one of the earliest studies[90] established that, if the dining room has to be eliminated for reasons of economy, low-income families prefer the kitchen to the living room for eating. An English study has found it useful to observe family preferences, as well as to ask questions about them. It finds the kitchen to be especially important to family life; half the housewives had someone with them while preparing meals. Whether families eat in a kitchen or living room, this study finds, is strongly dependent on personal preference.[91] The choice of illustrations about eating and the kitchen is not accidental; these are the functions that have interested researchers. (Working-class women also view the kitchen as the most important room in the house.)[92]

In any case, preferences are hardly a satisfactory indication that housing has an effect upon attitudes and behavior. "There is little evidence," Rosow[93] writes, "that satisfaction with new housing is directly related to liveability resulting *from design*

per se, except when there is a significant improvement in housing, especially where people come from substandard housing, or occupants are particularly conscious of housing in highly literate, sophisticated terms." On the other hand, students such as Svend Riemer[94,95] have supposed that internal design has an important effect upon patterns of family living.[96,97,98] In fact, there is little evidence either way. It is unfortunate that these factors have received so little research attention. Architects and builders are left to rely almost entirely upon tradition and intuition.

Neighborhood Effects

Social and Family Relationships Having complained about the lack of research into the human effects of internal arrangement of space, fair play compels a balancing acknowledgement. The effects of place and neighborhood upon social and family relationships have occupied one of the main streams of social science research. Occasionally it is rewarding to wonder what moves research in one direction more than another. Surely, we live in a time when relationships occupy the center of our stage. The building of entire communities at once, a comparatively recent development, focuses attention on a natural laboratory for observing interaction. By contrast, the natural laboratory that is *inside* the house or apartment escapes attention. Further, the data that have become available represent a convergence of several rather different developments: small group research; research into class, particularly working class, patterns; the simultaneous flowering of interest and disenchantment (if disenchantment can flower) in the suburban rearrangement; and concern (irritation? anger? guilt?) at the slum dwellers who conduct a characteristically unconcerted stay-in strike against urban renewal. One suspects, too, that some sociologists may be charmed by a quasi-physical scientific relationship between human elements and the compounds they form.

Observation of planned or large-scale housing development appears to have established that "those people who reside closest to each other in terms of distance, physical orientation, or accessibility tend to become friends or form closely knit social units."[99,100,101] An analogy to physics leads us to Boyle's law of social interaction: The physical space that neighbors occupy in inversely proportional to the likelihood of interaction. In the planned, fairly homogeneous communities that have been studied, social interaction tends to be high. Because these studies have been done in young communities, it is uncertain whether the influence of physical proximity remains significant over a period of time. Longer range observations hint that, as the community ages, friendships tend to form more around formal organization and occupation and less in response to simple proximity. Two phases of reaction of a new population have been distinguished: Phase I—eager interaction and mutual help, and Phase II—selective, restrictive interaction and withdrawal.[102] A second qualification of the law of social interaction is touched on in appendix A: Families may move to suburban communities because they want to socialize. That they do socialize, then, can hardly be attributed to the physical nature of the suburbs. Gans[103] has offered a third qualification. He points to the substantial social and economic homogeneity of the communities that have been studied. Since the families' behavior patterns, values, and interests are alike, they naturally tend to form friendships

with one another. Homogeneity, he argues, is more significant in creating a large number of friendships than is proximity. Even within homogeneous groups, however, physical placement influences friendships.

Whether one evaluates physical proximity as crucial or secondary, it seems clear that it has an influence on social relationships. One detects that this conclusion leaves officials and builders with an unwelcome sense of importance. They are called upon to exercise judgment, but what sort of judgment? How much social interaction is desirable? It has been pointed out that if people are close together, enmities may be increased as well as friendships.[104] They may join community organizations out of displeasure with their neighbors as well as pleasure.[105] Moreover, neighborhood friendships may carry a family along in a pattern not their own and not quite satisfying. Describing the cost of "happiness," Whyte writes:

> Suburban families ". . . sense that by their immersion in the group they are frustrating other urges, yet they feel that responding to the group is a moral duty and so they continue, hesitant and unsure, imprisoned in brotherhood."[106]

In response to this dilemma, there has been increasing emphasis on planning blocks and neighborhoods so that families are left free to choose whether or not they wish to socialize, and how. We shall be returning to this concept in the next chapter.

The evidence we have been discussing cuts across socioeconomic class, and it treats families at or near the point of their arrival in the community. There have been a number of observations of working-class families after the fact, so to speak. That is, the families are observed in the neighborhoods in which they have lived for some time, neighborhoods they have formed and of which they are a product. This material suggests that it is not only social interaction that is influenced by a family's location but the nature of family relationships as well. Moreover, social and family relationships flow together; change in one changes the other. It is important to bear in mind that these studies generally describe moderately deteriorated neighborhoods with fair proportions of stable families. The social networks of the more deteriorated, disorganized neighborhoods in the United States have not been described as carefully.

In the neighborhoods that have been described, families tend to be centered around the mother—one sees references to the "matriarchy of the slums."[107] The father is engaged at work and socially with other men. Family membership is concentrated in the locality; the most active ties are with other members of the family. It appears that it is the closest relatives of the parents, rather than more distant ones, who are significant. Proximity makes for frequent contacts with relatives and other neighbors, casually in passing and less casually on the sidewalk or in the corner tavern. Neighbors tend perforce to be deeply involved in one another's family life. There is considerable closeness to a group of people, but comparatively little singling out of intimate friends in the middle-class manner. There is considerable attachment to the place in itself. Relationships are identified with locality and it is difficult to conceive them separately. Two characteristics of working-class areas appear to be unique:

> . . . the interweaving and overlap of many different types of interpersonal contacts and role relationships, and . . . the organiza-

tion and concrete manifestations of these relationships within a common, relatively bounded spatial region.[108]

Researchers report, occasionally with some warmth of their own, that the mood of these neighborhoods is one of warmth, of security, and of identity.[109,110,111,112, 113,114,115,116,117]

It is evident that, if they were moved, many of these families would find it difficult to maintain their patterns of relationship. The impact of one change must somehow be reflected: As locality and the extended family are no longer coterminous, it is no longer possible to be neighborhood centered and extended family centered at once. A complex series of adjustments that depends on the precise circumstances gets under way. For example, a group of relocated old people faced the problem of finding meaningful activity and keeping in touch with their children. The children undertook to come to the old people, shifting to weekend visits from the more casual daily contact that had been typical. For weekday activity, the old men and women turned to other old people in their immediate neighborhood.[118,119] Study in France suggests that old people living in a crowded, deteriorated neighborhood develop with those who happen to be neighbors ties that "rapidly become effective and full substitutes for kinship relationships."[120] The development of this pattern, though it was not customary for them, suggests a highly flexible patterning of family and neighborly relationships dependent upon the neighborhood.

Younger family groups who move may develop a family-centered society in the place of the neighborhood-centered society they have known. The change is not only expressed in the degree of the contact with one person or another but, as one might expect, in the kind of contact. There is a shift from spending time with collateral relatives to husband and wife or children. Marital disagreement diminishes, and sharing of household chores increases. Less contact with distant relatives is accompanied by more contact with neighbors.[121] There may be a relatively easy or eager shift in pattern, and gains may be perceived. "There is a tendency for the conjugal type of family to discover itself and for the obligations of kinship to be relaxed."[122] Contacts with relatives, though less frequent, may be more satisfactory because there is more to talk about and less interruption.[123]

On the other hand, it has been pointed out that it is not only distance from relatives and friends that is a new factor to families that move, but "the lack of both an ideology and of a physical framework in which suitable fresh relationships could develop"[124]. There may be unfamiliarity with telephones, and other substitutes for face-to-face contact. The concepts of friendly but limited intercourse with neighbors and of formal organizations may come slowly, and with strain, to families who have not known them. It somewhat simplifies the problem to view it as one of reestablishing in a new community the relationship that were possible in the former one, if that were possible. For some of the families, the meaning of the move includes a wish or readiness to exchange old patterns for new ones. Other families, as we have noted, cannot navigate the change or resent it.[125,126]

Even for young families, the shift from neighborhood-centered to family-centered activity is only one possible sequence. A move to fairly dense, centrally located new housing, may not produce as much alteration. For example, a Baltimore study of rehoused families finds them more proud of and involved in their new neighbor-hoods than the families who remained in poor housing.[127,128] We must also note explicitly that some part of the effect of a neighborhood on families is an effect of demographic selectivity. A suburban neighborhood, currently at least, draws a high percentage of families with young children. They will be interested in the PTA and school taxes. High rates of membership in certain kinds of organizations and interest in local political affairs may seem to be a response to neighborhood. It is also, of course, a response to the stage of the family cycle. So, too, it has been noted that slum neighborhoods are hospitable to those who seek anonymity because others with the same aim are already there.

Evidence of the Effects of Housing

There are, in general, three types of evidence of the effects of housing on attitudes and behavior. Most prevalent, undoubtedly, is the personal or case observation. There is testimony by slum dwellers and by those who know them at firsthand. Teachers speak of children being unable to study for lack of space and quiet, of being unable to bring friends home, of being unable even to stay at home.[129] Social workers speak of poor sanitation, of doors without locks so that drunks and vagrants wander in, of single rooms that serve as family dwellings.[130] A doctor describes a woman who visited him weekly for advice on relieving her headaches and on dealing with defective plumbing and with ratholes. When she could move, her migraine vanished with her maintenance problems.[131] These are convincing observations though homely, or perhaps because homely. They focus on the effect of extreme housing conditions, making it plain that such conditions interfere with the myriad daily activities necessary to normal personal care and family life.

Apart from case observation, the largest body of material on the relationship of housing and human behavior has been developed in attempting to correlate the two. Poor housing correlates to a high degree with rates of illness and death, with the rate of mental illness, with juvenile and adult delinquency, and with other social problems such as chronic drinking and illegitimacy. These studies are subject to the criticism that a correlation is not necessarily a causal relationship. Nevertheless, the sheer volume of them has been persuasive to social scientists and to legislators. ". . . Any common sense evaluation," wrote Gunnar Myrdal in 1944, "will tell us that the causation, in part, goes *from* poor housing *to* bad moral, mental and physical health."[132] A long line of researchers have made more or less similar statements.

Nevertheless, it is well worth distinguishing between the evidence that bears on illness and death rates and the evidence about social pathology. The connecting links between poor housing and poor health are well understood. For example, crowding and inadequate heating or ventilation speed the spread of acute respiratory infections and other infectious diseases.[133] Establishing a correlation confirms a conclusion already based on an understanding of the disease process. But we are very far from being able to furnish such explanations in regard to juvenile delinquency, mental illness, and illegitimacy. In the absence of such connecting links, the limitations of correlations ought not to be lightly waved aside.

The risks of correlations may be illustrated in relation to juvenile delinquency. A review of studies in 1936 concluded that delinquency was associated with substandard housing. "With respect to the juveniles at least," it said, "the conclusion can scarcely be escaped that the housing, if not the chief factor, was at least a very significant factor accounting for the delinquent behavior."[134] In the intervening years, distinguished studies have confirmed the correlation. However, the possibility that poor housing and delinquency could both be attributed to a third factor was pointed out by Bernard Lander. Using Baltimore census material, he demonstrated simple correlations between juvenile delinquency, on one hand, and overcrowding and substandard housing, on the other. He then manipulated his data to rule out the effect of such factors as percentage of nonwhites in an area and median educational level, with the result that the "correlations between overcrowding, substandard housing and delinqency are reduced to zero. . . ."[135] Thus, physical housing appeared to be somehow related to delinquency but not a causal factor. After correcting for other factors, Lander found that only two of the traits being tested continued to correlate with juvenile delinquency: the racial heterogeneity of an area and the percentage of homes rented instead of owned. He presents the hypothesis that these traits are symptomatic of anomie which, in turn, leads to high rates of juvenile delinquency.[136] Presumably, other hypotheses may be advanced. The point illustrated is that the effect of housing is not established by correlations, as it would be if the connecting mechanism were well defined. A correlation without a solid base in theory is like a wedding ring in a man's vest pocket—interesting to speculate upon, perhaps, but it can be fitted to more than one finger.

The third type of evidence compares the behavior and attitudes of people in different types of housing. Because of the public issues involved, the comparison is usually between substandard or crowded housing and adequate housing. Other types of comparison are also made: established versus new neighborhoods[137,138] planned versus unplanned neighborhoods[139,140], and racially homogeneous versus racially mixed housing.[141,142,143] The comparison is most frequently made by study of the same families before and after a move; a few studies use control groups at the same point in time. Comparison studies focus on the effects of housing on juvenile delinquency rate,[144] on morale and social status,[145] on aspirations and attitude,[146] on physical and mental health,[147,148] and on social behavior and family relationships.[149,150] Evidence from controlled comparisons of families in poor and adequate housing tends to be substantial, though subject to various difficulties that must be taken into account.

One difficulty—that the change from one type of housing to another may be linked with any number of other changes, known and unknown—is strikingly illustrated by an English study of the early 1930s'. Over a 5-year period (1928–32) the health officer of the town of Stockton compared the death rates of families who had moved to modern dwellings and of families who had remained behind in slums. The death rate for those who moved increased substantially over the rate for those who remained behind; it may be imagined that the difference caused some stir. In the end, it was noted that families in new housing were paying twice as much rent just when the depression struck. Because their income was marginal, higher rent led to poorer nutrition—thus, better housing to a higher death rate.[151] In this case the hidden factor produced unanticipated results and caused a search. More troublesome are hidden factors that produce anticipated results: that rehousing may select the younger families who are able to move, the better educated families whose values make them ready to move, or the comparatively acceptable families who can filter through whatever requirements are placed upon admission to new housing.

Somewhat similar to the problem of hidden factors is that of distinguishing between cause and effect. For example, Herbert Gans argues that, though a move to a suburban community may be followed by higher family morale and more socializing, the suburb per se does not cause the new behavior. On the contrary, it is the wish of families to socialize that causes them to move to the suburbs. Suburban living may reinforce their predispositions, but this effect is minor.[152]

Conclusion

Though the evidence is scattered, taken as a whole it is substantial. The type of housing occupied influences health, behavior and attitude, particularly if the housing is desperately inadequate. In the terms that we use today, "desperately inadequate" means that housing is dilapidated or lacks a major facility such as running water. In these terms, 13 million homes in the United States were inadequate in 1956. In addition, about 6 million were crowded.

Housing, even when it is minimally adequate, appears to influence family and social relationships. Other influences of adequate housing are uncertain. Lack of evidence is not the same as negative evidence. One would hope that eventually research could move on from the iron law of housing research—that research into effects is bound to the lowest housing standards in existence. Research that focuses on the effects of *optimum* housing or on the internal arrangement of adequate housing also has its place.

Those influences on behavior and attitudes that have been established bear a relationship to whether people can move out of or stay out of poverty. The following effects may spring from poor housing: a perception of one's self that leads to pessimism and passivity, stress to which the individual cannot adapt, poor health, and a state of dissatisfaction; pleasure in company but not in solitude, cynicism about people and organizations; a high degree of sexual stimulation without legitimate outlet, and difficulty in household management and child rearing; and relationships that tend to spread out in the neighborhood rather than deeply into the family. Most of these effects, in turn, place obstacles in the path of improving one's financial circumstances. Obstacles such as those presented by poor health or inability to train children are obvious. Those presented by having ties centered in one's neighborhood rather than in one's wife and children are less direct, but significant. Such a family, for example, is less likely to move if a better job requires it.

Reviewing a large number of discussions of the evidence, one may conclude that the impact of physical housing on human behavior is generally understated. Why should this be so? First, because we are only now emerging from a period of absorption in psychological man. Psycho-

logical man, being infinitely adaptable, would not be greatly influenced by his physical surroundings. Our growing interest in a sociological understanding of man holds the seed of a comparable misunderstanding. Psychological man, if he was Buddhist in his introspectiveness, was at least dynamic. Seen sociologically, one gets a broader, more eclectic view of man, but may tend to see him so intricately involved in his current relationships as to be unable to change. This is not a sound sociological view, but it is reflected in the conclusions of some studies.

Second, the heavy reliance on technology and material gain that has characterized our progress may require a degree of blindness to its effect on people. In failing to discern the impact of housing on people, we leave ourselves free to think, we are meeting their needs through technology. At the same time, we are left free to overlook the possible human costs of material progress.

A final reason that the impact of physical housing may tend currently to be understated has to do with the stage of sophistication of research into housing. The research that is available, and is cited here, is partial and requires to be pieced together. A conception has yet to be developed that sees man in relation to his physical environment. Until such a scheme is developed, and research adapted to it, we shall not fully perceive the relationship of man to shelter. Meanwhile, we shall build houses.

NOTES

1. Ferguson, Thomas, and Pettigrew, Mary G., "A Study of 718 Slum Families Rehoused for Upwards of Ten Years," *Glasgow Medical Journal*, vol. 35, 1954, pp. 183–201.

2. The term "slum" has been used to describe houses, neighborhoods, and people—and conditions that are physical, moral, and social. Here, slum means a house that is dilapidated, lacking in facilities, or overcrowded to a point that seriously interferes with health, safety, or the reasonable conduct of family life. Housing in an area where slums predominate is considered slum housing, even if otherwise satisfactory.

3. Back, Kurt W., *Slums, Projects and People: Social Psychological Problems of Relocation in Puerto Rico*, Duke University Press, Durham, N.C., 1962.

4. Woodbury, Coleman, ed., *The Future of Cities and Urban Redevelopment*, University of Chicago Press, Ill., 1953, p. 379.

5. Hudson Guild Neighborhood House and New York University Center for Human Relations and Community Studies, *Human Relations in Chelsea*, 1960. Report of the Chelsea Housing and Human Relations Cooperative Project, p. 60.

6. Searles, Harold F., *The Nonhuman Environment in Normal Development and in Schizophrenia*, Internal Universities Press, Inc., New York, 1960, p. 395.

7. Hart, Moss, *Act One*, Random House, New York, 1959, p. 437.

8. Back, Kurt W., *op. cit.*

9. Rossi, Peter H., *Why Families Move*, a Study in the Social Psychology of Urban Residential Mobility, The Free Press, Glencoe, Ill., 1955.

10. Rubin, Morton; Orzack, Louis H.; and Tomlinson, Ralph, "Resident Responses to Planned Neighborhood Redevelopment," *Community Structure and Analysis*, ed. by Marvin Sussman, Thomas Y. Crowell Co., New York, 1959, pp. 208–234.

11. Kluckhohn, Florence, and Spiegel, John P., "Integration and Conflict in Family Behavior," Report No. 27, Group for the Advancement of Psychiatry, Topeka, Kans., August 1954.

12. Lewis, Hylan, "Child Rearing Among Low Income Families in the District of Columbia." Address to the Washington Center for Metropolitan Studies, June 8, 1961, processed.

13. Rohrer, John H., Edmonson, Munro S., with Lief, Harold; Thompson, Daniel; and Thompson, William, *The Eighth Generation*, Harper & Bros., 1960.

14. Millspaugh, Martin, and Beckenfeld, Gurney, *The Human Side of Urban Renewal*, ed. by Miles Colean, Fight-Blight Inc., Baltimore, Md., 1958, p. 61.

15. Chapin, F. Stuart, *Experimental Designs in Sociological Research*, Harper & Bros., New York, 1955, revised edition.

16. Wilner, Daniel M., et al., *The Housing Environment and Family Life*, ch. XVII, "Summary and Conclusions," July 1960, processed. See note 128.

17. *Ibid.*

18. Bateman, Richard W., and Stern, Herbert J., *op. cit.*

19. Back, Kurt W., *op. cit.*

20. Bateman, Richard W., and Stern, Herbert J., *op. cit.*

21. Jackson, William, "Housing and Pupil Growth and Development," *The Journal of Educational Sociology*, vol, 28, No. 9, pp. 370–380, May 1955. Reports an unpublished Ph.D. thesis, "Housing as a Factor in Public Growth and Development," New York University, 1954.

22. Wilner, Daniel M., and Walkley, Rosabelle Price, "The Effects of Housing on Health, Social Adjustment and School Performance," Mar. 23, 1962. Presented at the 39th Annual Meeting of the American Orthopsychiatric Association, Los Angeles, Calif. See note 128.

23. Wilner, D. M.; Walkley, R.P., Pinkerton, T.; and Tayback, M., *The Housing Environment and Family Life: A Longitudinal Study of the Effects of Housing on Morbidity and Mental Health*, The Johns Hopkins Press, Baltimore, Md., 1962, pp. 11.

24. Davis, Allison, "Motivation of the Underprivileged Worker," *Industry and Society*, ed. by William Foote Whyte, McGraw-Hill, New York, 1946, pp. 84–106.

25. Sarchet, Bettie, cited in Millspaugh, Martin, and Breckenfeld, Gurney, *The Human Side of Urban Renewal, op. cit.*, p. 11.

26. Cassel, John; Patrick, Ralph; and Jenkins, David, "Epidemiological Analysis of the Implications of Culture Change: A Conceptual Model," *Annals of the New York Academy of Sciences*, vol. 84, Dec. 8, 1960, pp. 938–949.

27. Davis, Allison, *op. cit.*

28. Berle, Beatrice Bishop, *80 Puerto Rican Families in New York City*, Columbia University Press, New York, 1958.

29. Mumford, Lewis, *The City in History*, Harcourt, Brace, New York, 1961, p. 473.

30. Lemkau, Paul V., *Mental Hygiene in Public Health*, second edition, McGraw-Hill, New York 1955, p. 381.

31. Faris, Robert L., cited in F. Stuart Chapin, "Some Housing Factors Related to Mental Hygiene," *American Journal of Public Health*, vol. 41, No. 7, July 1951, p. 841.

32. Plant, James S., "Some Psychiatric Aspects of Crowded Living Conditions," *American Journal of Psychiatry*, vol. IX, No. 5, March 1930, pp. 849–860. Or see Plant, James S., "Family Living Space and Personality Development," in *A Modern Introduction to the Family*, ed. by Norman W. Bell and Ezra F. Vogel, The Free Press of Glencoe, Ill., 1960, pp. 510–520.

33. Wilner, Daniel M.; Walkley, Rosebelle Price;

and Tayback, Matthew, "How Does the Quality of Housing Affect Health and Family Adjustment," *American Journal of Public Health*, vol. 46, No. 6, June 1956, pp. 736–744.

34. New York Academy of Medicine, "Report of the Subcommittee of Housing of the Committee on Public Health Relations," *Bulletin of the New York Academy of Medicine*, June 1954.

35. Pond, M. Allen, "The Influence of Housing on Health," *Marriage and Family Living*, vol. XIX, No. 2, May 1957, pp. 154–159.

36. Wilner, Daniel M., et al., *op. cit.*

37. Wilner, Daniel, and Walkley, Rosabelle Price, *op. cit.*

38. Mogey, John, and Morris, Raymond, "An Analysis of Satisfaction," 1960, typescript.

39. Riemer, Svend, "Maladjustment to the Family Home," *American Sociological Review*, vol, 10, No. 5, October 1945, pp. 642–648.

40. Back, Kurt W., *op. cit.*

41. Ross, Peter H., *op. cit.*

42. Fried, Marc, and Linderman, Erich, "Sociocultural Factors in Mental Health and Illness," *American Journal of Orthopsychiatry*, vol. XXXI, No. 1, January 1961, pp. 87–101.

43. Reimer, Svend, *op. cit.*

44. Cottam, H. R., cited in Chapin, F. Stuart, "Some Housing Factors Related to Mental Hygiene," *American Journal of Public Health*, vol. 41, No. 7, July 1951, p. 841.

45. Mogey, John, and Morris, Raymond, *op. cit.*

46. Chapin, F. Stuart, "Some Housing Factors Related to Mental Hygiene," *American Journal of Public Health*, vol. 41, No. 7, July 1951, pp. 839 845.

47. Chapin, F. Stuart, "The Effects of Slum Clearance and Rehousing on Family and Community Relationships in Minneapolis," *American Journal of Sociology*, vol. 43, No. 5, March 1938, pp. 744–763.

48. Mogey, John, and Morris, Raymond, *op. cit.*

49. Wilner, Daniel M; Walkley, Rosabelle Price; and Cook, Stuart W., *Human Relations in Interracial Housing*, University of Minnesota Press, Minneapolis, 1955.

50. Kennedy, Robert Woods, "Sociopsychological Problems of Housing Design," *Social Pressures in Informal Groups*, ed. by Leon Festinger, Stanley Schachter, and Kurt Back, Harper & Bros., New York, 1950, pp. 202–220.

51. Dean, John P., "The Ghosts's of Home Ownership," *Journal of Social Issues*, vol. VII, Nos. 1 and 2, 1951, pp. 59–68.

52. Rosow, Irving, "The Social Effects of the Physical Environment," *Journal of the American Institute of Planners*, vol. XXXII, No. 2, May 1961, pp. 127–133. (Originally published as "Specialists' Perspectives and Spurious Validation in Housing," *Marriage and Family Living*, vol. XIX, No. 3, August 1957, pp. 270–278.)

53. Back, Kurt W., *op. cit.*

54. Reimer, Svend, "Architecture for Family Living," *Journal of Social Issues*, vol. VII, Nos. 1 and 2, 1951, pp. 140–151.

55. Mogey, John, and Morris, Raymond, *op. cit.*

56. Reimer, Svend, "Maladjustment to the Family Home," *op. cit.*

57. Rosow, Irving, *op. cit.*

58. Pond, M. Allen, *op. cit.*

59. American Public Health Association, Committee on the Hygiene of Housing, *Planning the Home for Occupancy*, Public Administration Service, Chicago, Ill., 1950.

60. International Union of Family Organization, *Minimum Habitable Surfaces*, Family Housing Commission, Cologne, 1957.

61. Chapin, F. Stuart, "The Relationship of Housing to Mental Health," working paper for the Expert Committee on the Public Health Aspects of Housing of the World Health Organization, June 1961, mimeographed.

62. Plant, James S., *op. cit.*, pp. 850–854.

63. Whiting, John W. M.; Kluckhohn, Richard; and Anthony, Albert, "The Function of Male Initiation Ceremonies at Puberty," in *Readings in Social Psychology*, ed. by Eleanor E. Maccoby, Theodore M. Newcomb, and Eugene L. Hartley, Henry Holt & Co., New York, 1958, pp. 359–370.

64. Dai, Bingham, "Some Problems of Personality Development Among Negro Children," Chapter 32 of *Personality in Nature, Society, and Culture*, ed. by Clyde Kluckhohn and Henry A. Murray, New York, Alfred A. Knopf, 1949, pp. 437–458. Dai's article abridged from an article in *Sociological Foundations of the Psychiatric Disorders of Childhood*, Woods Schools, May 1946, pp. 67–100, p. 446.

65. Millspaugh, Martin, and Breckenfeld, Gurney, *op. cit.*

66. Rainwater, Lee, "Marital Sexuality and the Culture of Poverty." An expanded version of a paper read at the Plenary Session on Sex and Culture of the 60th Annual Meeting of the American Anthropological Association, Philadelphia, 1961, mimeographed, p. 5.

67. A not dissimilar nomination: television, flashy cars, and taverns.

68. Millspaugh, Martin, and Breckenfeld, Gurney, *op. cit.*

69. Davis, Allison, *op. cit.*

70. Chapin, F. Stuart, *op. cit.*

71. Chapin, F. Stuart, *ibid.*

72. Fried, Marc, "Some Implications of Housing Variables for Mental Health, a Reply to Professor F. Stuart Chapin," *Memorandum A4 of the West End Research Project* of the Center for Community Studies, Department of Psychiatry, Massachusetts General Hospital and the Harvard Medical School, Jan. 5, 1961.

73. One sentence troubled a Miami Junior Leaguer all night, and she subsequently organized a Slum Clearance Committee for Coconut Grove in Miami. The sentence occurred in a talk by the Reverend Theodore R. Gibson: "My people are living seven deep."

74. Rosow, Irving, *op. cit.*

75. Gans, Herbert, J., "The Human Implications of Current Redevelopment and Relocation Planning," *Journal of the American Institute of Planners*, vol. XXV, No. 1, February 1959, pp. 15–25.

76. Hole, Vere, "Social Effects of Planned Rehousing," *The Town Planning Review*, vol. XXX, No. 2, July 1959, pp. 161–173.

77. American Public Health Association, Committee on the Hygiene of Housing, *op. cit.*, p. 1.

78. Davis, Allison, *op. cit.*

79. Gans, Herbert J., "The Effect of a Community Upon Its Residents: Some Considerations for Sociological Theory and Planning Policies." Presented to the American Sociological Association, St. Louis, Mo., Sept. 1, 1961.

80. Hall, Edward T., "The Language of Space,"

81. *Journal of the American Institute of Architects*, vol. XXXV, No. 2, February 1961, pp. 71–74. There is this alternative: "One of the things I hate about this place," Mrs. Daniels says, "is, a man comes home from work and takes off his pants and there is no place to hang them. No closets, no place even to throw them down. All you can do, you must eat and go to bed, and maybe look at television."

82. Ashmore, Harry S., *Other Side of Jordan*, W. W. Norton, New York, 1960, p. 56.

83. H. Strotzka cited in F. Stuart Chapin, "The Relationship of Housing to Mental Health," p. 7. Working paper 3A for the Expert Committee on the Public Health Aspects of Housing of the World Health Organization. Meeting in Geneva, June 19–26, 1961.

84. Jackson, William S., "Housing and Pupil Growth and Development," *The Journal of Educational Sociology*, vol. 28, No. 9, pp. 370–380, May 1955. Reports an unpublished Ph.D. thesis, "Housing as a Factor in Public Growth and Development," New York University, 1954.

85. Lewis, Hylan, "Child Rearing Practices Among Low Income Families in the District of Columbia. Presented at the National Conference on Social Welfare, Minneapolis, Minn., May 16, 1961, mimeographed.

86. Riemer, Svend, "Sociological Theory of Home Adjustment," *American Sociological Review*, vol. 8, No. 3, June 1943, pp. 272–278.

87. Blood, Robert O., Jr., *Developmental and Traditional Child-Rearing Philosophies and Their Family Situational Consequences*, Doctoral thesis, University of North Carolina, Chapel Hill, 1952.

88. American Public Health Association, Committee on the Hygiene of Housing, *op. cit.*

89. Gottmann, Jean, *Megalopolis*, The Twentieth Century Fund, New York, 1961.

90. National Housing Agency, *The Liveability Problems of 1,000 Families*, Washington, D. C., October 1945.

91. Allen, Mrs. P. G., "Meals and the Kitchen," *Housing Centre Review*, vol. 5, 1955, pp. 14–17.

92. Rainwater, Lee, and Handel, Gerald, *Status of Working Class in Changing American Society*, Social Research, Inc., Chicago, February 1961.

93. Rosow, Irving, *op. cit.*

94. Riemer, Svend, "Sociological Theory of Home Adjustment," *op. cit.*

95. Riemer, Svend, "Sociological Perspective in Home Planning," *American Sociological Review*, vol. 12, No. 2, April 1947, vol. XXVI, No. 10, October 1959.

96. There have been some quite distinguished supposers: Winston Churchill said that "We shape our buildings and afterwards our buildings shape us." Said Queen Juliana, "There is absolutely no point in letting the world be run by nervous wrecks. Everybody should try to find a spot to be alone to concentrate and think of everything an adult and responsible person should think about. The result might be astonishing."

97. Merton, Robert K., "The Social Psychology of Housing," *Current Trends in Social Psychology*, Wayne Dennis, et al., 1948, University of Pittsburgh Press, Pennsylvania, pp. 163–217.

98. Pond, M. Allen, *op. cit.*

99. Form, William H., "Stratification in Low and Middle Income Housing Areas," *Journal of Social Issues*, vol. VII, Nos. 1 and 2, 1951, pp. 109–131.

100. Festinger, Leon; Schachter, Stanley; and Back, Kurt, *Social Pressures in Informal Groups*, Harper & Bros., New York, 1950.

101. Fisher, Ernest M., "A Study of Housing Programs and Policies." Prepared for the U. S. Housing Administrator, January 1960. Included as a working paper in *Interim Report on Housing the Economically and Socially Disadvantaged Groups in the Population*. Conference sponsored by the Metropolitan Housing and Planning Council of Chicago, Feb. 26–27, 1960, in cooperation with Action, Inc., of New York.

102. Mogey, John M., *Family and Neighborhood*, Oxford University Press, New York, 1956.

103. Gans, Herbert J., "Planning and Social Life: Friendship and Neighbor Relations in Suburban Communities," *Journal of the American Institute of Planners*, vol. XXVII, No. 2, May 1961, pp. 134–140.

104. Wallace, Anthony F. C., "Planned Privacy: What's Its Importance for the Neighborhood?" *Journal of Housing*, vol. 13, No. 1, January 1956, pp. 13–14.

105. International Research Associates, Inc., *The April 1958 Benchmark Survey: Some Implications for Policy*. Prepared for Chelsea Closed Circuit Television Project, Feb. 25, 1959, New York City.

106. Whyte, William H., Jr., *The Organization Man*, Simon & Schuster, New York, 1956, pp. 365.

107. Mogey, John M., "Changes in Family Life Experienced by English Workers Moving From Slums to Housing Estates," *Marriage and Family Living*, vol. XVII, No. 2, May 1955, pp. 123–128.

108. Fried, Marc, and Gleicher, Peggy, "Some Sources of Residential Satisfaction in an Urban Slum," *Journal of the American Institute of Planners*, vol. XXVII, No. 4, November 1961, pp. 305–315.

109. Mogey, John M., *op. cit.*

110. Mogey, John M., *ibid.*

111. Fried, Marc, and Gleicher, Peggy, *op. cit.*

112. Fried, Marc, and Lindermann, Erich, "Sociocultural Factors in Mental Health and Illness," American Journal of Orthopsychiatry, vol. XXXI, No. 1, January 1961, pp. 87–101.

113. Hole, Vere, *op. cit.*

114. Gans, Herbert J., *op. cit.*

115. Campleman, Gordon, "Some Sociological Aspects of Mixed-Class Neighborhood Planning," *The Sociological Review*, vol. XLIII, sec. 10, 1951. Reprinted by the Le Play House Press, Ledbury, Herefordshire, England.

116. Michel, Andrée V., "Kinship Relations and Relationships of Proximity in French Working-Class Households," in *A Modern Introduction to the Family*, ed. by Norman W. Bell and Ezra F. Vogel, The Free Press of Glencoe, Ill., 1960, pp. 287–294.

117. Woodbury, Coleman, ed., *The Future of Cities and Urban Redevelopment*, University of Chicago Press, Ill., 1953.

118. The study reports that public housing for the aged proved highly appropriate to their new social pattern.

119. Frieden, Elaine, "Social Differences and Their Consequences for Housing the Aged," *Journal of the American Institute of Planners*, vol. XXVI, No. 2, May 1960, pp. 119–124.

120. Michel, Andrée V., *op. cit.*

121. Mogey, John M., *op. cit.*

122. *Ibid.*

123. Hole, Vere, *op. cit.*

124. *Ibid.*, p. 171.

125. 84–year old Ezekiah Cunningham, the neighborhood grocer in the path of a renewal project, said this more concisely: "Well, it seems like they're handin' out a passel o' joy and a passel o' sorrow."

126. Howes, Rev. Robert G., *Crisis Downtown, a Church-Eye View of Urban Renewal*, National Conference of Catholic Charities, Washington, D. C., December 1959, p. 10.

127. Wilner, Daniel M., and Walkley, Rosabelle Price, "The Effects of Housing on Health, Social Adjustment and School Performance," Mar. 23, 1962. Presented at the 39th Annual Meeting of the American Orthopsychiatric Association, Los Angeles, Calif.

128. Wilner, D. M.; Walkley, R. P., Pinkerton, T.; and Tayback, M., *The Housing Environment and Family Life: A Longitudinal Study of the Effects of Housing on Morbidity and Mental Health*, The Johns Hopkins Press, Baltimore, Md., 1962.

129. Jackson, William S., *op. cit.*

130. Dumpson, James R., "The Human Side of Urban Renewal," *The Welfarer*, vol. XIII, No. 10, October 1960, pp. 1–6.

131. Berle, Beatrice Bishop, *op. cit.*

132. Myrdal, Gunnar, *An American Dilemma*, Harper & Bros., New York, vol. 1, 1944, p. 1290.

133. Wilner, Daniel M.; Walkley, Rosabelle Price; and Tayback, Matthew, *op. cit.*

134. Federal Emergency Administration of Public Works, Housing Division, *The Relationship Between Housing and Delinquency*, Research Bulletin No. 1, Washington, 1936.

135. Lander, Bernard, *Towards an Understanding of Juvenile Delinquency*, Columbia University Press, New York, 1954.

136. *ibid.*, p. 79.

137. Mogey, John M., *op. cit.*

138. Frieden, Elaine, *op. cit.*

139. Festinger, Leon, Schachter, Stanley, and Back, Kurt, *op. cit.*

140. Whyte, William H., Jr., *op. cit.*

141. Deutsch, Morton, and Collins, Mary Evans, *Interracial Housing*, University of Minnesota, Minneapolis, 1951.

142. Merton, Robert K., "The Social Psychology of Housing," *Current Trends in Social Psychology*, Wayne Dennis, et al., 1948, University of Pittsburgh Press, Pennsylvania, pp. 163–217.

143. Wilner, Daniel M.; Walkley, Rosabelle Price; and Cook, Stuart W., *op. cit.*

144. Barer, Naomi, *op. cit.*

145. Chapin F. Stuart, *op. cit.*

146. Back, Kurt W., *op. cit.*

147. Wilner, Daniel M.; Walkley, Rosabelle Price; Schram, John M.; Pinkerton, Thomas C.; and Tayback, Marrhew, "Housing as an Environmental Factor in Mental Health: The Johns Hopkins Longitudinal Study," *American Journal of Public Health*, vol. 50, No. 1, January 1960, pp. 55–63.

148. Wilner, Daniel M.; Walkley, Rosabelle Price; Williams, Huntington; and Tayback, Matthew, "The Baltimore Study on the Effects of Housing on Health," *Baltimore Health News*, vol. XXXVII, No. 6, June 1960, pp. 45–52.

149. Hole, Vere, *op. cit.*

150. Mogey, John M., *op. cit.*

151. Ferguson, Thomas, and Pettigrew, Mary G., "A Study of 718 Slum Families Rehoused for Upwards of Ten Years," *Glasgow Medical Journal*, vol. 35, 1954, pp. 183–201.

152. Gans, Herbert J., "The Effect of a Community Upon Its Residents: Some Considerations for Sociological Theory and Planning Policies." Presented to the American Sociological Association, St. Louis, Mo., Sept. 1, 1961.

47. Some Sources of Residential Satisfaction in an Urban Slum

Marc Fried
and
Peggy Gleicher

In a paper included in Part III of this volume, Seeley said that slum areas are useful environments for many groups in the urban population. Fried and Gleicher consider some of the reasons why this should be so, focusing on the processes through which a working-class, largely Italian community, develops a positive association with a particular segment of the city's space. They point out that the devotion of Boston's West Enders to their houses and streets was the result of three factors: (1) it was a stable neighborhood; families had lived there for most of their lives and it was, therefore, an environment in which they were at ease; (2) their friendship and kin relations were located in the area; and (3) the West Enders had learned behavior patterns for using the public and private space of the area that was denied to them in the middle-class neighborhoods of Boston. The authors frame their discussion of these attitudes toward space in terms of their implications for urban renewal and public housing policy.

Marc Fried is Research Professor and former Director of the Institute of Human Sciences, Boston College. He has written extensively in the fields of social and clinical psychology and social problems. Currently, he is working on a study of the effects of rural-to-urban migration on Negro status and achievement.

Peggy Gleicher is Research Associate at the Institute for Human Sciences, Boston College.

The gradual deterioration of older urban dwellings and the belief that such areas provide a locus for considerable social pathology have stimulated concern with altering the physical habitat of the slum. Yet the technical difficulties, the practical inadequacies, and the moral problems of such planned revisions of the human environment are also forcing themselves upon our attention most strikingly.[1] While a full evaluation of the advantages and disadvantages of urban renewal must await studies which derive from various disciplines, there is little likelihood that the vast sums currently available will be withheld until there is a more systematic basis for rational decisions. Thus it is of the utmost importance that we discuss all aspects of the issue as thoroughly as possible and make available even the more fragmentary findings which begin to clarify the many unsolved problems.

Since the most common foci of urban renewal are areas which have been designated as slums, it is particularly important to obtain a clearer picture of so-called slum areas and their populations. Slum areas undoubtedly show much variation, both variation from one slum to another and heterogeneity within urban slum areas. However, certain consistencies from one slum area to another have begun to show up in the growing body of literature. It is quite notable that the available systematic studies of slum areas indicate a very broad working-class composition in slums, ranging from highly skilled workers to the non-working and sporadically working members of the "working" class. Moreover, even in our worst residential slums it is likely

Reprinted by permission of the *Journal of the American Institute of Planners* (Volume XXVII, No. 4, November 1961).

that only a fairly large and visible minority) are afflicted with one or another form of social pathology. Certainly the idea that social pathology in any form is decreased by slum clearance finds little support in the available data. The belief that poverty, delinquency, prostitution, and alcoholism magically inhere in the buildings of slums and will die with the demolition of the slum has a curious persistence but can hardly provide adequate justification for the vast enterprise of renewal planning.

In a larger social sense, beyond the political and economic issues involved, planning for urban renewal has important human objectives. Through such planning we wish to make available to a larger proportion of the population some of the advantages of modern urban facilities, ranging from better plumbing and decreased fire hazards, to improved utilization of local space and better neighborhood resources. These values are all on the side of the greater good for the greatest number. Yet it is all too apparent that we know little enough about the meaning and consequences of differences in physical environment either generally or for specific groups. Urban renewal may lead, directly and indirectly, to improved housing for slum residents. But we cannot evaluate the larger effects of relocation or its appropriateness without a more basic understanding than we now have of the meaning of the slum's physical and social environment. This report is an initial essay toward understanding the issue. We shall consider some of the factors that give meaning to the residential environment of the slum dweller. Although the meaning of the environment to the resident of a slum touches only one part of the larger problem, it is critical that we understand this if we are to achieve a more effectively planned and designed urban environment.[2]

The Significance of the Slum Environment

People do not like to be dispossessed from their dwellings, and every renewal project that involves relocation can anticipate considerable resistance, despite the best efforts to insure community support.[3] It is never quite clear whether most people object mainly to being forced to do something they have not voluntarily elected to do; or whether they simply object to relocation, voluntary or involuntary. There is, of course, considerable evidence for the commitment of slum residents to their habitat. Why this should be so is less clear and quite incomprehensible in the face of all middle-class residential values. In order to evaluate the issue more closely we shall consider the problem of the meaning and functional significance of residence in a slum area. Although we are primarily concerned with a few broadly applicable generalizations, a complete analysis will take better account of the diversities in the composition of slum populations.

The fact that more than half the respondents in our sample[4] have a long-standing experience of familiarity with the area in which they lived before relocation suggests a very basic residential stability. Fifty-five per cent of the sample first moved to or were born in the West End approximately 20 years ago or more. Almost one-fourth of the entire sample was born in the West End. Not only is there marked residential stability within the larger area of the West End, but the total rate of movement from one dwelling unit to another has been exceedingly low. Table 1 gives the distribution of movement from one dwelling unit to another within the ten years prior to the interview. It is readily evident that the largest proportion of the sample has made very few moves

TABLE 1. NUMBER OF MOVES IN PREVIOUS TEN YEARS

Moves	Number	Per cent
Totals	473	100
None	162	34
One	146	31
Two	73	15
Three or more	86	19
No answer	6	1

indeed. In fact, a disproportionate share of the frequent moves is made by a small group of relatively high-status people, largely professional and semiprofessional people who were living in the West End only temporarily. Regardless of which criterion we use, these data indicate that we cannot readily accept those impressions of a slum which suggest a highly transient population. An extremely large proportion shows unusual residential stability, and this is quite evenly distributed among the several levels of working-class occupational groups.

The Slum Environment as Home What are the sources of this residential stability? Undoubtedly they are many and variable, and we could not hope to extricate the precise contribution of each factor. Rents were certainly low. If we add individually expended heating costs to the rental figures reported we find that 25 per cent were paying $34 a month or less, and 85 per cent paying $54 a month or less. But though this undoubtedly played a role as a background factor, it can hardly account for the larger findings. Low rental costs are rarely mentioned in discussing aspects of the West End or of the apartment that were sources of satisfaction. And references to the low West End rents are infrequent in discussing the sources of difficulty which people expected in the

course of moving. In giving reasons for having moved to the last apartment they occupied before relocation, only 12 per cent gave any type of economic reason (including decreased transportation costs as well as low rents). Thus, regardless of the practical importance that low rents must have had for a relatively low income population, they were not among the most salient aspects of the perceived issues in living in the West End.

On the other hand, there is considerable evidence to indicate that living in the West End had particular meaning for a vast majority of West End residents. Table 2

TABLE 2. FEELINGS ABOUT THE WEST END

Feelings	Number	Per cent	
Totals	473	100	
Like very well	174	37	75
Like	183	38	
Mixed like-dislike	47	10	14
Indifferent	18	4	
Dislike	25	5	10
Dislike very much	23	5	
No answer	3	1	

shows the distribution in response to the question, "How do you feel about living in the West End?", clearly indicating how the West End was a focus for very positive sentiments.

That the majority of West Enders do not remain in or come back to the West End simply because it is practical (inexpensive, close to facilities) is further documented by the responses of the question, "Which neighborhood, this one or any other place, do you think of as your real home, that is where you feel you really belong?" It is quite striking that fully 71 per cent of the people named the West End as their real home, only slightly less than the proportion who specify liking the West End or liking it very much. Although there is a strong relationship between liking the West End and viewing it as home, 14 per cent of those who view the West End as home have moderately or markedly negative feelings about the area. On the other hand, 50 per cent of those who do not regard the West End as home have moderately or markedly positive feelings about the area. Thus, liking the West End is not contingent on experiencing the area as that place in which one most belongs. However, the responses to this item give us an even more basic and global sense of the meaning the West End had for a very large proportion of its inhabitants.

These responses merely summarize a group of sentiments that pervade the interviews, and they form the essential context for understanding more discrete meanings and functions of the area. There are clearly differences in the details, but the common core lies in a widespread feeling of belonging someplace, of being "at home" in a region that extends out from but well beyond the dwelling unit. Nor is this only because of familiarity, since a very large proportion of the more recent residents (64 per cent of those who moved into the West End during 1950 or after) also showed clearly positive feelings about the area. And 39 per cent of those who moved in during 1950 or after regard the West End as their real home.[5]

Types of Residential "Belonging" Finer distinctions in the quality and substance of positive feelings about the West End reveal a number of variations. In categorizing the qualitative aspects of responses to two questions which were analyzed together ("How do you feel about living in the West End?" and "What will you miss most about the West End?"), we distinguished three broad differences of emphasis among the positive replies. The three large categories are: (1) *integral belonging:* sense of *exclusive* commitment, taking West End for granted as home, thorough familiarity and security; (2) *global commitment:* sense of profound gratification (rather than familiarity), pleasure in West End and enjoyment; and (3) *discrete satisfaction:* specific satisfying or pleasurable opportunities or atmosphere involving no special commitment to *this* place.

Only a small proportion (13 per cent) express their positive feelings in terms of logically irreplaceable ties to people and places. They do so in often stark and fundamental ways: this is my home; it's all I know; everyone I know is here; I won't leave. A larger group (38 per cent) are less embedded and take the West End less for granted but, nonetheless, express an all-encompassing involvement with the area which few areas are likely to provide them again. Their replies point up a less global but poignant sense of loss: it's one big happy family; I'll be sad; we were happy here; it's so friendly, it's handy to everything and everyone is congenial and friendly. The largest group (40 per cent) are yet further removed from a total commitment but in spite of the focused and discrete nature of their satisfaction with the interpersonal atmosphere or the convenience of the area, remain largely positive in feeling.

Differences in Foci of Positive Feelings Thus, there is considerable variability in the depth and type of feeling implied by liking the West End; and the West End as home had different connotations for different people. For a large group, the West End as home seems to have implied a comfortable and satisfying base for moving out into the world and back. Among this group, in fact, the largest proportion were more concerned with accessibility to other places than with the locality itself. But for more than half the people, their West End homes formed a far more central feature of their total life space.

There is a difference within this larger group between a small number for whom the West End seems to have been the place *to* which they belonged and a larger number for whom it seems rather to have been the place *in* which they belonged. But for the larger group as a whole the West End occupied a unique status, beyond any of the specific attributes one could list and point to concretely. This sense of uniqueness, of home, was not simply a function of social relationships, for the place in itself was the object of strong positive feelings. Most people (42 per cent) specify both people and places or offer a global, encompassing reason for their positive feelings. But almost an equally small proportion (13 per cent and 10 per cent, respectively) select out people or places as the primary objects of positive experience.

With respect to the discrete foci for positive feelings, similar conclusions can be drawn from another question: "Which places do you mostly expect to miss when you leave the West End?" In spite of the place-orientation of the question, 16 per cent specify some aspect of interpersonal loss as the most prominent issue. But 40 per cent expect to miss one of the places which is completely identified with the area or, minimally, carries a specific local identity. The sense of the West End as a local region, as an area with a spatial identity going beyond (although it may include) the social relationships involved, is a common perception. In response to the question: "Do you think of your home in the West End as part of a local neighborhood?"[6] 81 per cent replied affirmatively. It is this sense of localism as a basic feature of lower-class life and the functional significance of local interpersonal relationships and of local places which have been stressed by a number of studies of the working class[7] and are documented by many aspects of our data.

In summary, then, we observe that a number of factors contribute to the special importance that the West End seemed to bear for the large majority of its inhabitants.

1. Residence in the West End was highly stable, with relatively little movement from one dwelling unit to another and with minimal transience into and out of the area. Although residential stability is a fact of importance in itself, it does not wholly account for commitment to the area.

2. For the great majority of the people, the local area was a focus for strongly positive sentiments and was perceived, probably in its multiple meanings, as home. The critical significance of belonging in or to an area has been one of the most consistent findings in working-class communities both in the United States and in England.

3. The importance of localism in the West End, as well as in other working-class areas, can hardly be emphasized enough. This sense of a local spatial identity includes both local social relationships and local places. Although oriented around a common conception of the area as "home," there are a number of specific factors dominating the concrete meaning of the area for different people.

We now turn to a closer consideration of two of these sets of factors: first, the interpersonal networks within which people functioned and, in the subsequent section, the general spatial organization of behavior.

Social Relationships in Physical Space
Social relationships and interpersonal ties are not as frequently isolated for special attention in discussing the meaning of the West End as we might have expected. Despite this relative lack of exclusive salience, there is abundant evidence that patterns of social interaction were of great importance in the West End. Certainly for a great number of people, local space, whatever its independent significance, served as a locus for social relationships in much the same way as in other working-class slum areas.[8] In this respect, the urban slum community also has much in common with the communities so frequently observed in folk cultures. Quite consistently, we find a strong association between positive feelings about the West End and either extensive social relationships or positive feelings about other people in the West End.[9] The availability of such interpersonal ties seems to have considerable influence on feelings about the area, but the absence of these ties does not preclude a strongly positive feeling about the West End. That is, despite the prominence of this pattern, there seem to be alternative sources of satisfaction with the area for a minority of the people.

The Place of Kinship Ties Following some of the earlier studies of membership in formal organizations, which indicated that such organizational ties were infrequent in the working class, increasing attention has been given to the importance of kinship ties in lower-class groups.[10] Despite the paucity of comparative studies, most of the investigations of working-class life have stressed the great importance of the extended-kinship group. But the extended-kinship group, consisting of relationships beyond the immediate family, does not seem to be a primary source of the closest interpersonal ties. Rather, the core of the most active kinship ties seems to be composed of nuclear relatives (parents, siblings, and children) of both spouses.[11] Our data show that the more extensive these available kinship ties are within the local area, the greater the proportion who show strong positive feeling toward the West End. These data are given in Table 3 and show a quite overwhelming and consistent trend in this direction. Other relationships point to the same observation: the more frequent the contact with siblings or the more frequent the contact with parents or the greater the desire to move near relatives, the greater the proportion who like the West End very well.

The Importance of the Neighbor Relationship Important as concrete kinship ties were, however, it is easy to overestimate their significance and the relevance of kinship contacts for positive feelings about

TABLE 3. EXTENSIVENESS OF KIN IN WEST END BY FEELINGS ABOUT WEST END

Extensiveness of kin in West End	Number of respondents		*Feelings about West End (per cent)*		
		Totals	Strongly positive	Positive	Mixed negative
None	193	100	29	46	25
Few	150	100	37	38	25
Some	67	100	45	31	24
Many	52	100	58	27	15

the residential area. Studies of the lower class have often neglected the importance of other interpersonal patterns in their concentration on kinship. Not only are other social relationships of considerable significance, but they also seem to influence feelings about the area. The similar effects of both sets of relationships is evident in Table 4, which presents the association between feelings about the West End and the personal importance of relatives versus friends.[12] A greater proportion (50 per cent) have a strong preference for relatives, but a large group (31 per cent) indicates a strong preferential orientation to friends. More relevant to our immediate purpose there is little difference among the three preference groups in the proportions who have strong positive feelings about the West End.

In view of the consistency in the relations between a wide variety of interpersonal variables and feelings about the West End, it seems likely that there are alternaitve paths to close interpersonal ties of

which kinship is only one specific form.[13] In fact, the single most powerful relation between feelings about the West End and an interpersonal variable is provided by feelings about West End neighbors (Table 5). Although the neighbor relationship may subsume kinship ties (i.e., when the neighbors are kin), the association between feelings about neighbors and feelings about the West End is stronger than the association between feelings about the West End and any of the kinship variables. Beyond this fact, the frequent references to neighbors and the stress on *local* friendships lead us to suggest that the neighbor relationship was one of the most important ties in the West End. And, whether based on prior kinship affiliation or not, it formed one of the critical links between the individual (or family) and the larger area and community.

Localism in Close Interpersonal Ties Since the quality of feeling about the West End is associated with so wide a diversity of

TABLE 4. PREFERENCE FOR RELATIVES OR FRIENDS BY FEELINGS ABOUT WEST END

Preference for relatives or friends	Number of respondents	Feelings about West End (per cent)			
		Totals	Strongly positive	Positive	Mixed negative
Relatives preferred	232	100	39	39	22
Mixed preferences	81	100	35	32	33
Friends preferred	148	100	36	42	22

TABLE 5. CLOSENESS TO NEIGHBORS BY FEELINGS ABOUT WEST END

Closeness to neighbors	Number of respondents	Feelings about West End (per cent)			
		Totals	Strongly positive	Positive	Mixed negative
Very positive	78	100	63	28	9
Positive	265	100	37	42	21
Negative	117	100	20	39	41

interpersonal relationships, it is not surprising that the majority of people maintained their closest ties with West Enders. The distribution of relationships which were based in the West End or outside the West End are given in Table 6. The

TABLE 6. WEST END DWELLING OF FIVE CLOSEST PERSONS

Five closest persons	Number	Per cent	
Totals	473	*100*	
All West End	201	*42*	*60*
Mostly West End	85	*18*	
Equally West End and outside	13	*3*	
Mostly outside West End	70	*15*	*25*
All outside West End	46	*10*	
Unspecified	58	*12*	

striking proportion whose closest ties are all or mostly from the West End is clearly evident. As we would expect on the basis of the previous results, the more exclusively a person's closest relationships are based in the West End, the greater the likelihood that he will have strong positive feelings about the West End.

A few significant factors stand out clearly from this analysis.

1. Although the kinship relationship was of considerable importance in the West End, as in other working-class communities, there were a number of alternative sources of locally based interpersonal ties. Among these, we suggest that the neighbor relationship is of particular importance, both in its own right and in its effect on more general feelings about the area.

2. There is considerable generality to the observation that the greater one's interpersonal commitments in the area, in the form of close contact or strongly positive feelings, the greater the likelihood of highly positive feelings about

the area as a whole. This observation holds for all the forms of interpersonal relationship studied.

What is perhaps most striking about the social patterns of the West End is the extent to which all the various forms of interpersonal ties were localized within the residential area. Local physical space seems to have provided a framework within which some of the most important social relationships were embedded. As in many a folk community[14] there was considerable overlap in the kinds of ties which obtained: kin were often neighbors; there were many interrelated friendship networks; mutual help in household activities was both possible and frequent; many of these relationships had a long and continuous history; and the various ties often became further intertwined through many activities within a common community.

The street itself, favorite recreation areas, local bars, and the settlement houses in the area all served as points of contact for overlapping social networks. Thus the most unique features of this working-class area (although common to many other working-class areas) were: (a) the interweaving and overlap of many different types of interpersonal contacts and role relationships, and (b) the organization and concrete manifestation of these relationships within a common, relatively bounded spatial region. It is these characteristics which seem to have given a special character and meaning both to the quality of interpersonal relationships and to the area within which these relationships were experienced.

We have repeatedly stressed the observation that, granting the importance of local social relationships, the meaning of "localism" in the West End included places as well as people. It is difficult to document the independent significance of either of these factors, but the importance of the physical space of the West End and the special use of the area are evident in many ways. Previously we indicated the importance of physical areas and places as sources of satisfaction in the West End. We now wish to consider more systematically the way in which the physical space of the area is subjectively organized by a large proportion of the population. In understanding the importance of such subjective spatial organization in addition to the significance of local social relationships, we can more adequately appreciate the enormous and multiply derived meaning that a residential area may have for people.

Subjective Spatial Organization

There is only a fragmentary literature on the psychological, social, or cultural implications of spatial behavior and spatial imagery. The orientation of the behavioral sciences to the history, structure, and dynamics of social relationships has tended to obscure the potential significance of the nonhuman environment generally and, more specifically, that aspect of the nonhuman environment which we may designate as significant space. Although there have been a number of important contributions to this problem, we are far from any systematic understanding of the phenomena.[15] We do not propose to discuss the problems or concepts, but only to start with a few very primitive considerations and to observe the working-class relationship to space in several respects. We are primarily concerned with the way in which space is organized or structured in defining the usable environment and in providing restrictions to or

freedom for mobility in space.[16] In this way we may hope to see more broadly the constellation of forces which serve to invest the residential environment of the working class with such intense personal meaning.

Spatial Usage Patterns in the Middle Class There are undoubtedly many differences among people in the way space is organized, according to personality type, physiological disposition, environmental actualities, social roles, and cultural experience. We wish to focus only on some of those differences which, at the extremes distinguish the working class quite sharply from higher-status groups. Although we do not have comparative data, we suggest that in the urban middle class (most notably among relatively high-status professional and business groups) space is characteristically used in a highly *selective* way. The boundary between the dwelling unit and the immediate environs is quite sharp and minimally permeable. It is, of course, possible to go into and out of the dwelling unit through channels which are specifically designated for this purpose. But walls are clear-cut barriers between the inside of the dwelling unit and the outer world. And even windows are seldom used for any interchange between the inner world of the dwelling unit and the outside environment (except for sunlight and air). Most of us take this so much for granted that we never question it, let alone take account of it for analytic purposes. It is the value of the "privacy of the home." The dwelling unit may extend into a zone of lawn or garden which we tend and for which we pay taxes. But, apart from this the space outside the dwelling unit is barely "ours."

As soon as we are in the apartment hallway or on the street, we are on a wholly *public* way, a path to or from some-place rather than on a bounded space defined by a subjective sense of belong-ing.[17] Beyond this is a highly individualized world, with many common properties but great variability in usage and subjective meaning. Distances are very readily trans-gressed; friends are dispersed in many directions; preferred places are frequently quite idiosyncratic. Thus there are few physical areas which have regular (cer-tainly not daily) widespread common usage and meaning. And contiguity between the dwelling unit and other significant spaces is relatively unimportant. It is primarily the channels and pathways between individualized significant spaces which are important, familiar, and com-mon to many people. This orientation to the use of space is the very antithesis of that localism so widely found in the work-ing class.

The Territorial Sense in the Working Class Localism captures only a gross orientation toward the social use of an area of physical space and does not sufficiently emphasize its detailed organiza-tion. Certainly, most middle-class observers are overwhelmed at the degree to which the residents of any working-class district and, most particularly, the residents of slums are "at home" in the street. But it is not only the frequency of using the street and treating the street outside the

house as a place, and not simply as a path, which points up the high degree of per-meability of the boundary between the dwelling unit and the immediate environ-ing area. It is also the use of all channels between dwelling unit and environment as a bridge between inside and outside: open windows, closed windows, hallways, even walls and floors serve this purpose. Frequently, even the sense of adjacent human beings carried by noises and smells provides a sense of comfort. As Edward Ryan points out:[18]

> Social life has an almost uninterrupted flow between apartment and street: children are sent into the street to play, women lean out the windows to watch and take part in street activity, women go "out on the street" to talk with friends, men and boys meet on the corners at night, and families sit on the steps and talk with their neighbors at night when the weather is warm.

It is not surprising, therefore, that there is considerable agreement between the way people feel about their apartments and the way they feel about the West End in general (Table 7). Without attempt-ing to assign priority to feelings about the apartment or to feelings about the West End, it seems likely that physical barriers which are experienced as easily permeable allow for a ready generalization of positive or negative feelings in either direction.

We would like to call this way of struc-turing the physical space around the actual

TABLE 7. FEELINGS ABOUT THE APARTMENT BY FEELINGS ABOUT WEST END

Feelings about apartment	Number of respondents	Feelings about West End (per cent)			
		Totals	Like very well	Like	Mixed-dislike
Like	367	100	43	40	17
Mixed-indifferent	41	100	20	42	39
Dislike	60	100	12	30	58

residential unit a *territorial* space, in contrast to the selective space of the middle class. It is territorial in the sense that physical space is largely defined in terms of relatively bounded regions to which one has freedom or restriction of access, and it does not emphasize the path function of physical space in allowing or encouraging movements to or from other places.[19] There is also evidence, some of which has been presented in an earlier section, that it is territorial in a more profound sense: that individuals feel different spatial regions belong to or do not belong to them and, correspondingly, feel that they belong to (or in) specific spatial regions or do not belong.[20]

Spatial Boundaries in the Local Area In all the previous discussion, the West End has been treated as a whole. People in the area did, in fact, frequently speak of the area as a whole, as if it were an entity. However, it is clear that the area was differently bounded for different people. Considering only the gross distinction between circumscribing the neighborhood as a very small, localized space in contrast to an expansive conception of the neighborhood to include most of the area, we find that the sample is about equally split (Table 8). It is apparent, therefore, that the territorial zone may include a very small or a very large part of the entire West End, and for quite a large proportion it is the former. For these people, at least, the boundary between dwelling unit and street may be highly permeable; but this freedom of subjective access does not seem to extend very far beyond the area immediately adjacent to the dwelling unit. It is also surprising how little this subjective sense of neighborhood size is affected by the extensiveness of West End kin or of West End friends. This fact tends to

support the view that there is some degree of independence between social relationships and spatial orientations in the area.[21]

TABLE 8. AREA OF WEST END "NEIGHBORHOOD"

Neighborhood	Number	Per cent
Totals	473	*100*
Much of West End: all of area, West End specified, most of area, large area specified	191	*40*
Part of West End: one or two streets or less, a small area, a store	207	*44*
People, not area: the people around	17	*4*
Not codeable	58	*12*

Thus, we may say that for almost half the people, there is a subjective barrier surrounding the immediately local area. For this large group, the barrier seems to define the zone of greatest personal significance or comfort from the larger area of the West End. However, it is clearly not an impermeable barrier. Not only does a large proportion of the sample fail to designate this boundary, but even for those who do perceive this distinction, there is frequently a sense of familiarity with the area beyond.[22] Thus, when we use a less severe criterion of boundedness than the local "neighborhood" and ask people how much of the West End they know well, we find that a very large proportion indeed indicate their familiarity with a large part or most of the area (Table 9).[23] Although almost half the people consider "home ground" to include only a relatively small local region, the vast majority is easily familiar with a greater part of the West End. The local boundaries within the West End were, thus, boundaries of a

TABLE 9. AREA OF WEST END KNOWN WELL

Area	Number	Per cent	
Totals	473	100	
Just own block	27	6 }	20
A few blocks	65	14	
Large part	66	14 }	64
Most of it	237	50	
Uncodeable	78	16	

semi-permeable nature although differently experienced by different people.

The Inner-Outer Boundary These distinctions in the permeability of the boundaries between dwelling unit and street and across various spaces within the larger local region are brought even more sharply into focus when we consider the boundary surrounding the West End as a whole. The large majority may have been easily familiar with most or all of the West End. But it is impressive how frequently such familiarity seems to stop at the boundaries of the West End. In comparison with the previous data, Table 10 demonstrates

TABLE 10. FAMILIAR AREAS OF BOSTON

Area	Number	Per cent
Totals	473	101
West End only: no other area, none	141	30
Adjacent area: North End, esplanade	216	46
Contiguous areas: East Boston, Cambridge	98	21
Nearby areas: Revere, Malden, Brookline	12	3
Metropolitan Boston, beyond "nearby" areas	1	0
Outside Boston area	3	1
No answer	2	0

the very sharp delineation of the inner space of the West End from the outer space surrounding the West End. The former is generally well explored and essentially familiar, even though it may not be considered the area of commitment. The latter is either relatively unknown by many people or, if known, it is categorized in a completely different way. A relatively large proportion are familiar with the immediately adjacent areas which are directly or almost directly contiguous with the West End (and are often viewed as extensions of the West End), but only slightly more than a quarter (26 per cent) report familiarity with any other parts of the Boston area. Thus there seems to be a widely experienced subjective boundary surrounding the larger local area and some of its immediate extensions which is virtually impermeable. It is difficult to believe that people literally do not move out of this zone for various activities. Yet, if they do, it apparently does not serve to diminish the psychological (and undoubtedly social) importance of the boundary.[24]

These data provide considerable evidence to support, if they do not thoroughly validate, the view that the working class commonly organizes physical space in terms of a series of boundaries. Although we do not mean to imply any sense of a series of concentric boundaries or to suggest that distance alone is the critical dimension, there seems to be a general tendency for the permeability of these boundaries to decrease with increasing distance from the dwelling unit. Significant space is thus subjectively defined as a series of contiguous regions with the dwelling unit and its immediately surrounding local area as the central region. We have referred to this way of organizing physical space as *territorial* to distinguish it from the more highly *selective* and individualized use of space which seems to characterize the middle class. And we suggest that it is the territorial conception and manner of using physical space which provides one of the bases for the kind of localism which is so widely found in working-class areas.

In conjunction with the emphasis upon local social relationships, this conception and use of local physical space gives particular force to the feeling of commitment to, and the sense of belonging in, the residential area. It is clearly not just the dwelling unit that is significant but a larger local region that partakes of these powerful feelings of involvement and identity. It is not surprising, therefore, that "home" is not merely an apartment or a house but a local area in which some of the most meaningful aspects of life are experienced.

Conclusions

The aims of urban renewal and the sources of pressure for renewal are manifold: among the objectives we may include more rational and efficient use of land, the elimination of dilapidated buildings, increase in the municipal tax base, and the improvement of living conditions for slum dwellers. Although the social benefit to the slum dweller has received maximum public attention, it is always unclear how the life situation (or even the housing situation) of the working-class resident of a slum is supposed to be improved by slum clearance or even slum improvement. Public housing has not proved to be an adequate answer to this problem for many reasons. Yet public housing is the only feature of renewal programs that has even attempted to deal seriously with this issue.

In recent years, a number of reports have suggested that concern about slum conditions has been used to maneuver public opinion in order to justify use of eminent domain powers and demolition, largely for the benefit of middle- and upper-status groups. Although we cannot evaluate this political and economic issue, we do hope to understand the ways in which dislocation from a slum and relocation to new residential areas has, in fact, benefited or damaged the working-class residents involved. It is all too apparent, however, that the currently available data are inadequate for clarifying some of the most critical issues concerning the effects of residential relocation upon the subject populations.

We know very little about slums and the personal and social consequences of living in a slum. We know even less about the effects of forced dislocation from residential areas on people in general and on working-class people specifically. But rational urban planning which, under these circumstances, becomes urban *social* planning, requires considerable knowledge and understanding of people and places affected by the plans. It is incumbent upon us to know both what is wrong with the slum and with slum life and what is right about slums and living in slums.[25] It is essentially this question, formulated as the meaning and consequences of living in a slum, that has motivated our inquiry into the sources of residential satisfaction in an urban slum. In turn, this study provides one of the bases for understanding the ways in which dislocation and relocation affect the patterns of personal and social adaptation of former residents of a slum.

In studying the reasons for satisfaction that the majority of slum residents experience, two major components have emerged. On the one hand, the residential area is the region in which a vast and interlocking set of social networks is localized. And, on the other, the physical area has considerable meaning as an extension of home, in which various parts are delineated and structured on the basis of a sense of belonging. These two components provide the context in which the residential area may so easily be invested with considerable, multiply determined meaning. Certainly, there are variations both in the importance of various factors for different people and in the total sense which people have of the local area. But the greatest proportion of this working-class group (like other working-class slum residents who have been described) shows a fairly common experience and usage of the residential area. This common experience and usage is dominated by a conception of the local area beyond the dwelling unit as an integral part of home. This view of an area as home and the significance of local people and local places are so profoundly at variance with typical middle-class orientations that it is difficult to appreciate the intensity of meaning, the basic sense of identity involved in living in the particular area. Yet it seems to form the core of the extensive social integration that characterizes this (and other) working-class slum populations.

These observations lead us to question the extent to which, through urban renewal, we relieve a situation of stress or create further damage. If the local spatial area and an orientation toward localism provide the core of social organization and integration for a large proportion of the working class, and if, as current behavioral theories would suggest, social organization and integration are primary factors in providing a base for effective social functioning, what are the consequences of dislocating people from their local areas? Or, assuming that the potentialities of people for adaptation to crisis are great, what deeper damage occurs in the process? And, if there are deleterious effects,

are these widespread or do they selectively affect certain predictable parts of the population? We emphasize the negative possibilities because these are closest to the expectations of the population involved and because, so frequently in the past, vague positive effects on slum populations have been arbitrarily assumed. But it is clear that, in lieu of or along with negative consequences, there may be considerable social benefit.

The potential social benefits also require careful, systematic evaluation, since they may manifest themselves in various and sometimes subtle ways. Through a variety of direct and intervening factors, the forced residential shift may lead to changes in orientations toward work, leading to increased satisfaction in the occupational sphere; or, changes may occur in the marital and total familial relationship to compensate for decreased kinship and friendship contacts and, in turn, lead to an alternative (and culturally more syntonic) form of interpersonal satisfaction; or, there may be either widespread or selective decreases in problems such as delinquency, mental illness, and physical malfunctioning.

A realistic understanding of the effects, beneficial and/or deleterious, of dislocation and relocation from an urban slum clearly requires further study and analysis. Our consideration of some of the factors involved in working-class residential satisfaction in the slum provides one basis for evaluating the significance of the changes that take place with a transition to a new geographic and social environment. Only the careful comparison of pre-relocation and post-relocation data can begin to answer these more fundamental questions and, in this way, provide a sound basis for planning urban social change.

ACKNOWLEDGMENTS

This report is part of a study entitled *Relocation and Mental Health: Adaptation Under Stress*, conducted by the Center for Community Studies in the Department of Psychiatry of the Massachusetts General Hospital and the Harvard Medical School. The research is supported by the National Institute of Mental Health, Grant No. 3M 9137-C3. We are grateful to Erich Linde- mann, the Principal Investigator, and to Leonard Duhl of the Professional Services Branch, NIMH, for their continued help and encouragement. Edward Ryan has contributed in many ways to the final formulations of this paper, and Chester Hartmann and Joan Levin have given help- ful criticism and advice.

NOTES

1. Herbert Gans, "The Human Implications of Current Redevelopment and Relocation Plan- ning," *Journal of the American Institute of Planners*, Vol. 25, No. 1 (February 1959), pp. 15–25.
2. This is one of a series of reports on the meaning and significance of various aspects of working-class life. This group of studies will provide a basis for a subsequent analysis of the impact of relocation through a comparison of the pre-relocation and the post-relocation situation. The population of the original area was predominantly white, of mixed ethnic composition (mainly Italian, Polish, and Jewish). The many ethnic composition differences do not vitiate the larger generaliza- tions of this study.
3. This does not seem limited to contemporary relocation situations. Firey reports a similar phenomenon in Boston during the nineteenth century. Walter Firey, *Land Use in Central Boston* (Cambridge: Harvard University Press, 1947).
4. These data are based on a probability sample of residents from the West End of Boston inter- viewed during 1958–1959. The sampling criteria included only households in which there was a female household member between the ages of 20 and 65. The present analysis is based on the pre- relocation data from the female respondents. Less systematic pre-relocation data on the husbands are also available, as well as systematic post- relocation data for both wives and husbands and women without husbands.
5. It is possible, of course, that we have obtained an exaggerated report of positive feelings about the area because of the threat of relocation. Not only does the consistency of the replies and their internal relationships lead us to believe that this has not caused a major shift in response, but, bearing in mind the relative lack of verbal facility of many of the respondents and their frequent tendencies to give brief replies, we suspect that the interview data often lead to underestimating the strength of sentiment.
6. This question is from the interview designed by Leo Srole and his associates for the Yorkville study in New York.
7. The importance of localism in working-class areas has been most cogently described by Richard Hoggart, *The Uses of Literacy* (London: Chatto and Windus, 1857), and by Michael Young and Peter Wilmot, *Family and Kinship in East London* (Glencoe: The Free Press, 1957). In our own data, the perception of the area as a local neigh- borhood is largely independent of the individual's own commitment to the area.
8. Many of the studies of working-class areas make this point quite clear. Cf. Hoggart, *op. cit.*; Young and Wilmott, *op. cit.*; Herbert Gans, *The Urban Villagers* (Glencoe: The Free Press, forthcoming); J. M. Mogey, *Family and Neighbour- hood* (London: Oxford University Press, 1956); Madeline Kerr, *People of Ship Street* (London: Routledge and Kegan Paul, 1958).
9. These associations between feelings about the West End and interpersonal variables include interpersonal relationships outside the West End as well. Thus there is the possibility that an inter- related personality variable may be involved. We shall pursue this in subsequent studies.
10. The importance of kinship ties for working-class people was particularly brought to the fore by Floyd Dotson, "Patterns of Voluntary Associa- tion Among Urban Working Class Families," *American Sociological Review*, 1951, Vol. 25, pp. 687–693.
11. This point is made by Young and Wilmott, *op. cit.* In this regard as in many others, the similarity of the East End of London and the West End of Boston is quite remarkable.
12. The "Preference for Relatives or Friends" item is based on four separate questions presenting a specific situation and asking if the respondent would prefer to be associated with a relative or friend in each situation.
13. We do not mean to imply that this exhausts the special importance of kinship in the larger social structure. There is also evidence to suggest that some of the basic patterns of the kinship relation-

ship have influenced the form of interpersonal ties more generally in the urban working class. This issue is discussed in Marc Fried and Erich Lindemann, "Sociocultural Factors in Mental Health and Illness," *American Journal of Orthopsychiatry*, 1961, Vol. 31, pp. 87–101, and will be considered further in subsequent reports.

14. Ward Goodenough gives an excellent description of a similar pattern on Truk. Cf. Ward Goodenough, *Property, Kin, and Community on Truk* (New Haven: Yale University Publications in Anthropology, No. 46, 1951).

15. There are a number of rich and provocative discussions of selected aspects of space-oriented behavior. Cf. Paul Schilder, *The Image and Appearance of the Human Body* (London: Kegan Paul, Trench, Trubner, and Co., 1935); and *Mind: Perception and Thought in Their Constructive Aspects* (New York: Columbia University Press, 1942); Erik Homburger Erikson, "Configurations in Play—Clinical Notes," *Psychoanalytic Quarterly*, 1937, Vol. 6, pp. 139–214; H. A. Witkin, *Personality Through Perception* (New York; Harper, 1954); Edward T. Hall, "The Language of Space," *Landscape*, Fall 1960. The studies of the animal ecologists and the experimental studies of spatial orientation have considerable bearing on these issues. A recent contribution to the literature of urban planning, Kevin Lynch's *The Image of the City* (Cambridge: The Technology Press, 1960) bears directly on the larger problems of spatial orientation and spatial behavior in the urban environment, and its analytic framework has proved useful in the present formulations.

16. We shall not touch on a related problem of considerable interest, the basic modes of conceiving or experiencing space in general. We assume a close relation between general conceptions of space and ways of using spatial aspects of specific parts of the environment, but an analysis of this problem is beyond the scope of the present discussion.

17. The comment of one reader to an early draft of this paper is worth quoting, since it leads into a fascinating series of related problems. With respect to this passage, Chester Hartman notes: "We tend to think of this other space as anonymous and public (in the sense of belonging to everyone, i.e., no one) when it does not specifically belong to us. The lower-class person is not nearly so alienated from what he does not own." To what extent is there a relationship between a traditional expectation (even if occasionally belied by reality) that only *other* people own real property, that one is essentially part of a "propertyless class" and a willingness to treat any property as common? And does this provide a framework for the close relationship between knowing and belonging in the working class in contrast to the middle-class relationship between owning and belonging? Does the middle-class acceptance of legal property rights provide a context in which one can *only* belong if one owns. From a larger psychological view, these questions are relevant not merely to physical space and physical objects but to social relationships as well.

18. This comment is a fragment from a report on ethnographic observations made in the area.

19. These formulations, as previously indicated, refer to modal patterns and do not apply to the total population. Twenty-six per cent do select out the "accessibility" of the area, namely, a path function. The class difference, however, is quite striking since 67 per cent of the highest-status group give this response, but only 19 per cent of the lowest-status group and between 28 per cent and 31 per cent of the middle- (but still low-status) groups select out various types of "accessibility."

20. Without attempting, in this report, a "depth" psychological analysis of typical patterns of working-class behaviors, we should note the focal importance of being accepted or rejected, of belonging or being an "outsider." Preliminary evidence from the post-relocation interviews reveals this in the frequent references to being unable to obtain an apartment because "they didn't want us" or that the landlord "treated us like dirt." It also emerges in the frequently very acute sensitivity to gross social-class differences, and a sharp sense of not belonging or not fitting in with people of higher status. Clarification of this and related problems seems essential for understanding the psychological and social consequences of social-class distinctions and has considerable implication for urban residential planning generally and urban renewal specifically.

21. The social-class patterning is also of interest. Using the occupation of the head of household as the class criterion, there is almost no difference among the three working-class status levels in the area included as a neighborhood (the percentages who say "much or all of the area" for these three groups are, respectively, 51 per cent, 46 per cent, and 48 per cent). But only 38 per cent of the high-status group include much or all of the West End in their subjective neighborhood.

22. Of those who include only part of the West End in their designation of their neighborhood, 68 per cent indicate they know a large part or most of the West End well. Naturally, an even higher percentage (87 per cent) of those who include much or all of the West End in their neighborhood are similarly familiar with a large part or all of the area.

23. We used the term "neighborhood" for want of a better term to designate the immediate local area of greatest significance. On the basis of his ethnographic work, however, Edward Ryan points out that this term is rarely used spontaneously by West Enders.

24. Unfortunately, we do not have data on the actual frequency of use of the various areas outside the West End. Thus we cannot deal with the problem of the sense of familiarity in relation to actual usage patterns. However, in subsequent reports, we hope to pursue problems related to the bases for defining or experiencing physical-spatial boundaries and the various dimensions which affect the sense of commitment to and belonging in physical areas.

25. There is, of course, the evident danger of considering a social pattern on the basis of "right" and "wrong" which, inevitably, merely reproduce our own transitory values. A careful and thorough analysis, however, provides its own correctives to our all-too-human biases.

48. Planning and Social Life | Herbert J. Gans

A major interest of research on suburban communities has been the effect of the low density and other spatial features of suburban settlement on friendship formation and neighbor relations. Planners and social critics have held, for example, that social behavior could be greatly influenced merely by making certain changes in the location of houses or the design of streets—a kind of environmental determinism. Gans takes the view that the commonality of values and attitudes among residents—what he calls "homogeneity"—is more important in determining whether neighbors will become friends than are spatial patterns. The desire of most suburbanites for a homogeneous population runs counter to the traditional conviction of planners who believe in the importance of balanced neighborhoods where people of different age groups, social classes, ethnic backgrounds, and races live side by side. Gans doubts the capacity of planners to redirect the preferences of suburban residents, but he does believe that they should be offered the maximum opportunity to choose among communities with different spatial patterns and mixes of population types and classes.

Herbert J. Gans is Professor of City Planning at Massachusetts Institute of Technology. Several of his published works are cited on page 70 of this volume.

Studies of wartime housing projects and postwar suburban subdivisions have shown that the residents of these developments do a considerable amount of visiting with the nearest neighbors, and may select their friends from among them. Social relationships appear to be influenced and explained by *propinquity*.[1] As a result, they are affected by the site plan and the architectural design, which determine how near people will live to each other. In fact, the authors of one study of social life have suggested that:

"The architect who builds a house or designs a site plan, who decides where the roads will and will not go, and who decides which directions the houses will face and how close together they will be, also is, to a large extent, deciding the pattern of social life among the people who will live in those houses."[2]

Conversely, other studies of social life have shown that people tend to choose friends on the basis of similarities in backgrounds, such as age and socio-economic level; values, such as those with respect to privacy or child rearing; and interests, such as leisure activity preferences.[3] These findings suggest that social relationships are influenced and explained by people's *homogeneity* with respect to a variety of *characteristics*, although it is not yet known exactly what combination of characteristics must be shared for different social relationships. This explanation would imply that the planner affects social life not through the site plan but through decisions about lot size or facility standards that help to determine, directly or indirectly, whether the population of an area will be homogeneous or heterogeneous with respect to the characteristics that determine social relationships.[4]

Reprinted by permission of the *Journal of the American Institute of Planners* (Volume XXVII, No. 2, May 1961).

The two explanations raise a number of issues for planning:

1. Whether or not the planner has the power to influence patterns of social life.
2. Whether or not he should exert this power.
3. Whether some patterns of social life are more desirable than others, and should, therefore, be sought as planning goals. For example, should people be encouraged to find their friends among neighbors, or throughout, or outside their residential area? Should they be politely distant or friendly with neighbors?

If propinquity is most important in determining friendship formation and neighbor relations, the ideal patterns—if such exist—would have to be implemented through the site plan. If homogeneity of characteristics is most important, the planner must decide whether to advocate homogeneous residential areas, if he wishes to encourage friendliness and friendship among neighbors; and heterogeneous ones, if he wishes to encourage more distant neighbor relations and spatially dispersed friendship.

Although the available research does not yet permit a final explanation of the patterns of social life, a preliminary conclusion can be suggested. This permits us to discuss the implications for planning theory and practice.

Propinquity, Homogeneity, and Friendship

The existing studies suggest that the two explanations are related, but that homogeneity of characteristics is more important than propinquity.[5] *Although propinquity initiates many social relationships and maintains less intensive ones, such as "being neighborly," it is not sufficient by itself to* create intensive relationships. *Friendship requires homogeneity.*

Propinquity leads to visual contact between neighbors and is likely to produce face-to-face social contact. This is true only if the distance between neighbors is small enough to encourage one or the other to transform the visual contact into a social one.[6] Thus, physical distance between neighbors is important. So is the relationship of the dwellings—especially their front and rear doors—and the circulation system.[7] For example, if doors of adjacent houses face each other or if residents must share driveways, visual contact is inevitable.

The opportunity for visual and social contact is greater at high densities than at low ones, but only if neighbors are adjacent horizontally. In apartment buildings, residents who share a common hallway will meet, but those who live on different floors are less likely to do so, because there is little occasion for visual contact.[8] Consequently, propinquity operates most efficiently in single-family and row-house areas, especially if these are laid out as courts, narrow loops, or culs-de-sac.

Initial social contacts can develop into relationships of varying intensity, from polite chats about the weather to close friendship. (Negative relationships, varying from avoidance to open enmity are also possible.) Propinquity not only initiates relationships, but it also plays an important role in maintaining the less intensive ones, for the mere fact of living together encourages neighbors to make sure that the relationship between them remains positive. Propinquity cannot determine the intensity of the relationship, however; this is a function of the characteristics of the people involved. If neighbors are homogeneous and feel themselves to be compatible, there is some likelihood that the relationship will be more intensive than an exchange of greetings. If neighbors are heterogeneous, the relationship is not likely to be intensive, regardless of the degree of propinquity. *Propinquity may thus be the initial cause of an intensive positive relationship, but it cannot be the final or sufficient cause.*

This is best illustrated in a newly settled subdivision. When people first move in, they do not know each other, or anything about each other, except that they have all chosen to live in this community—and can probably afford to do so.[9] As a result, they will begin to make social contacts based purely on propinquity, and because they share the characteristics of being strangers and pioneers, they will do so with almost every neighbor within physical and functional distance. As these social contacts continue, participants begin to discover each other's backgrounds, values, and interests, so that similarities and differences become apparent. Homogeneous neighbors may become friends, whereas heterogeneous ones soon reduce the amount of visiting, and eventually limit themselves to being neighborly. (This process is usually completed after about three months of social contact, especially if people have occupied their homes in spring or summer, when climate and garden chores lead to early visual contact.) The resulting pattern of social relationships cannot be explained by propinquity alone. An analysis of the characteristics of the people will show that homogeneity and heterogeneity explain the existence *and the absence* of social relationships more adequately than does the site plan or the architectural design. Needless to say, the initial social pattern is not immutable; it is changed by population turnover and by a gradual tendency to find other friends outside the immediate area.[10]

If neighbors are compatible, however, they may not look elsewhere for companionship, so that propinquity—as well as the migration patterns and housing market conditions which bring homogeneous people together—plays an important role. Most of the communities studied so far have been settled by homogeneous populations. For example, Festinger, Schachter, and Back studied two student housing projects whose residents were of similar age, marital status, and economic level. Moreover, they were all sharing a common educational experience and had little time for entertaining. Under these conditions, the importance of propinquity in explaining visiting patterns and friendship is not surprising. The fact that they were impermanent residents is also relevant, although if a considerable degree of homogeneity exists among more permanent residents, similar patterns develop.

Propinquity, Homogeneity, and Neighbor Relations

Although propinquity brings neighbors into social contact, a certain degree of homogeneity is required to maintain this contact on a positive basis. If neighbors are too diverse, differences of behavior or attitude may develop which can lead to coolness or even conflict. For example, when children who are being reared by different methods come into conflict, disciplinary measures by their parents will reveal differences in ways of rewarding and punishing. If one child is punished for a digression and his playmate is not, misunderstandings and arguments can develop between the parents. Differences about house and yard maintenance, or about political issues can have similar consequences.

The need for homogeneity is probably greatest among neighbors with children of equal age and among immediately adjacent neighbors. Children, especially young ones, choose playmates on a purely propinquitous basis. Thus, positive relations among neighbors with children of similar age are best maintained if the neighbors are comparatively homogeneous with respect to child-rearing methods. Immediately adjacent neighbors are likely to have frequent visual contact, and if there is to be social contact, they must be relatively compatible. Some people minimize social contact with immediately adjacent neighbors on principle, in order to prevent possible differences from creating diagreement. Since such neighbors live in involuntary propinquity, conflict might result in permanently impaired relationships which might force one or the other to move out.

Generally speaking, conflicts between neighbors seem to be rare. In the new suburbs, current building and marketing practices combine to bring together people of relatively similar age and income, thus creating sufficient homogeneity to enable strangers to live together peaceably. In the communities which I have studied, many people say that they have never had such friendly neighbors. Where chance assembles a group of heterogeneous neighbors, unwritten and often unrecognized pacts are developed which bring standards of house and yard maintenance into alignment and which eliminate from the conversation topics that might result in conflict.

The Meaning of Homogeneity

I have been stressing the importance of resident characteristics without defining the terms homogeneity and heterogeneity.

This omission has been intentional for little is known about what characteristics must be shared before people feel themselves to be compatible with others. We do not know for certain if they must have common backgrounds, or similar interests, or shared values—or combinations of these. Nor do we know precisely which background characteristics, behavior patterns, and interests are most and least important, or about what issues values must be shared. Also, we do not know what similarities are needed for relationships of different intensities or, for any given characteristics, how large a difference can exist before incompatibility sets in. For example, it is known that income differences can create incompatibility between neighbors, but it is not known how large these differences must become before incompatibility is felt.

Demographers may conclude that one community is more homogeneous than another with respect to such characteristics as age or income, but this information is too general and superficial to predict the pattern of social life. Social relationships are not based on census data, but on subjectively experienced definitions of homogeneity and heterogeneity which terminate in judgments of compatibility or incompatibility. These definitions and judgments have received little study.

Sociologists generally agree that behavior patterns, values, and interests—what people think and do—are more important criteria for homogeneity than background factors.[11] My observations suggest that in the new suburbs, values with respect to child rearing, leisure-time interests, taste level, general cultural preferences, and temperament seem to be most important in judging compatibility or incompatibility.

Such interests and values *do* reflect

differences in background characteristics, since a person's beliefs and actions are shaped in part by his age, income, occupation, and the like. These characteristics can, therefore, be used as clues to understanding the pattern of social relationships. *Life-cycle stage* (which summarizes such characteristics as age of adults, marital status, and age of children) and *class* (especially income and education) are probably the two most significant characteristics. Education is especially important, because it affects occupational choice, child-rearing patterns, leisure-time preferences, and taste level. *Race* is also an important criterion, primarily because it is a highly visible—although not necessarily accurate—symbol of class position.[12]

Background characteristics provide crude measures that explain only in part the actual evaluations and choices made by neighbors on a block. Until these evaluations themselves are studied—and then related to background data—it is impossible to define homogeneity or heterogeneity operationally. Since considerable criticism has been leveled at the new suburbs for being overly homogeneous—at least by demographic criteria—such research is of considerable importance for the planner's evaluation of these communities and for the planning of future residential areas.

Variations in Homogeneity

The degree of population homogeneity varies from suburb to suburb. Moreover, since residents usually become neighbors by a fairly random process—for example, by signing deeds at the same time—many combinations of homogeneity and heterogeneity can be found among the blocks of a single subdivision.[13] In some blocks, neighbors are so compatible that they spend a significant amount of their free time with each other and even set up informal clubs to cement the pattern. In other blocks, circumstances bring together very diverse people, and relationships between them may be only polite, or even cool.

Whyte's studies in Park Forest led him to attribute these variations to site planning features. He found that the small "courts" were friendly and happy; the larger ones, less friendly and sometimes unhappy. He also found that the residents of the smaller courts were so busy exchanging visits that, unlike those of the larger ones, they did not become active in the wider community.[14] My observations in Park Forest and in Levittown, New Jersey, suggest, however, that homogeneity and heterogeneity explain these phenomena more effectively.[15] When neighbors are especially homogeneous, blocks can become friendly, regardless of their size, although the larger blocks usually divide themselves into several social groupings. Block size is significant only insofar as a small block may *feel* itself to be more cohesive because all sociability takes places within one group. In the larger blocks, the fact that there are several groups prevents such a feeling, even though each of the groups may be as friendly as the one in the smaller block.

Community participation patterns can be explained in a similar fashion. If the block population is heterogeneous, and residents must look elsewhere for friends, they inevitably turn to community-wide clubs, church organizations, and even civic groups in order to meet compatible people. If participation in these organizations is based solely on the need to find friends, however, it is likely to be minimal, and may even cease, once friendships are established. This type of membership differs considerably from civic or organizational participation proper. The distinction between the two types is important. Whyte recommends that site planners encourage participation by making blocks large enough to discourage excessive on-the-block social life. While this might increase the first type of participation, it cannot affect the second type. People who are inclined to be really active in community-wide organizations are a self-selected minority who will desert the social life of the block, regardless of the block's layout or of the neighbors' compatibility. They are usually attracted to community participation by pressing community problems and by interest, ambition, or the hope of personal gain. Site planning techniques cannot bring about their participation.

The Role of Propinquity

Given the importance of homogeneity in social relationships, what role remains for propinquity? Since propinquity results in visual contact, whether voluntary, or involuntary, it produces social contact among neighbors, although homogeneity will determine how intensive the relationships will be and whether they will be positive or not. Propinquity also supports relationships based on homogeneity by making frequent contact convenient. Finally, among people who are comparatively homogeneous and move into an area as strangers, propinquity may determine friendship formation among neighbors.

In addition, some types of people gravitate to propinquitous relationships more than others. Age is an important factor. As already noted, children choose their playmates strictly on a propinquitous basis, though decreasingly so as they get older. This is why parents who want their young children to associate with playmates of similar status and cultural background must move to areas where such playmates are close at hand.

Among adults, the importance of propinquity seems to vary with sex and class. Women generally find their female friends nearby, especially if they are mothers and are restricted in their movements. In fact, young mothers must usually be able to find compatible people—and therefore, homogeneous neighbors—within a relatively small radius. Should they fail to do so, they may become the unhappy isolated suburban housewives about whom so much has been written. My observations suggest that most women are able to find the female companionship they seek, however. In addition, the increase in two-car families and women's greater willingness to drive are gradually reducing the traditional immobility of the housewife.

The relationship between propinquity and class has received little study. Generally speaking, the "higher" the class, the greater the physical mobility for visiting and entertaining. Thus, working-class people seem to be least mobile and most likely to pick their friends on a propinquitous basis. However, since they visit primarily with relatives, they may travel considerable distances if relatives are not available nearby.[16] Upper-middle-class people seem to go farther afield for their social life than do lower-middle-class ones, in part because they may have specialized interests which are hard to satisfy on the block.

Propinquity is also more important for some types of social activities than others. In America, and probably everywhere in the Western world, adolescents and adults socialize either in peer groups—people of similar age and sex—or in sets of couples. Peer groups are more likely to form on the basis of propinquity. For example, the members of that well-known suburban peer group, the women's "coffee klatsch," are usually recruited in the immediate vicinity. Since the participants indulge primarily in shop talk—children, husbands, and home—the fact that they are all wives and mothers provides sufficient homogeneity to allow propinquity to function.[17] For couples, homogeneity is a more urgent requirement than propinquity, since the two people in a couple must accept both members of all other couples. The amount of compatibility that is required probably cannot be satisfied so easily among the supply of neighbors within propinquitous distance.

The role of propinquity also varies with the size of the group, and with the activities pursued. The larger the group, the less intensive are the relationships between participants, and the less homogeneity is required. If the group meets for a specific activity, such as to celebrate a major holiday or to play cards, the behavior that takes place is sufficiently specialized and habitual that the participants' other characteristics are less relevant. If the group meets for conversation, more homogeneity of values and interests is required.[18]

Limitations of These Observations

The foregoing comments are based largely on observations and studies in new suburban communities. Little is known about the role of propinquity and homogeneity in established communities, although there is no reason to expect any major differences.[19] Whatever differences exist are probably due to the reduction of much of the initial homogeneity in established communities through population turnover. The same process is likely to take place in new communities. Move-outs create a gap in established social groupings. Newcomers may be able to fill this gap—provided they are not too different from those they have replaced. Even so, it is hard for a newcomer to break into an established coffee klatsch or card party, and only people with a little extra social aggressiveness are likely to do so. In addition, there is the previously noted tendency of the original residents to find new friends outside the immediate area and to spend less time with neighbors. As a result of these processes, patterns of social life in new communities will eventually resemble those in established areas.

Most of my observations are at present only hypotheses that need to be tested by more systematic research. Two types of studies are especially important. The first should investigate the influence of resident characteristics by analyzing the existence of propinquitous relationships among a variety of blocks, all similar in site plan and architectural design but differing in the degree of homogeneity among neighbors. The second study should analyze the impact of site plans and housing design on propinquity, by studying subdivisions which differ in physical layout but are occupied by similar kinds of residents.

Conclusions

At the beginning of this paper, I raised three questions: whether the planner had the power to influence patterns of social life; whether he ought to use this power; and if so, whether ideal patterns existed which should be advocated as planning goals. These questions can now be answered in a preliminary fashion.

The planner has only limited influence

over social relationships. Although the site planner can create propinquity, he can only determine which houses are to be adjacent. He can thus affect visual contact and initial social contacts among their occupants, but he cannot determine the intensity or quality of the relationships. This depends on the characteristics of the people involved.

The characteristics of the residents can be affected to some small degree by subdivision regulations, lot-size provisions, facility standards, or by any other planning tools which determine the uniformity of the housing to be built and the facilities to be provided—and can therefore affect the degree of homogeneity or heterogeneity among the eventual occupants. The planner has considerably less influence, however, than the private and public agencies which combine to finance, build, and market houses. These in turn respond to housing demand—and to the fact that most buyers are willing to accept similarity in house type and want a fair degree of homogeneity in their neighbors.

Consequently, within the context of present planning powers and practices, the planner's influence on social relationships is not very great. Whether or not it should be greater can only be decided on the basis of value judgments about patterns of social life.

Needless to say, a wide variety of value judgments can be formulated. My own judgment is that no one ideal pattern of social life can be—or should be—prescribed, but that opportunity for choice should be available both with respect to neighbor relations and friendship formation.

Neighbor relations should be positive; no benefits, but many social and emotional costs, result from life in an atmosphere of mutual dislike or coolness. Beyond this point, however, the intensity of relationships should not be a subject for planning values. Whether neighbors become friends, whether they remain friendly, or whether they are only polite to each other should be left up to the people who come to live together. Each type of relationship has its pros and cons, but none is so much more desirable than another that it should be advocated by the planner.

Friendship formation is a highly personal process, and it would be wrong for anyone to presume to plan another person's friendships. Moreover, one pattern of friendship does not seem to me to be preferable to any other. Finding one's friends on the block is convenient, although propinquity may encourage so much social contact that no time is left for friends who live farther away. Also, propinquity may make life on the block difficult if the friendship should cease to be friendly. Dispersal of friendship over a larger residential area may help people to know their community a little better, but unless they are already interested in gathering and using such knowledge, this is not likely to make much difference to them, or to the community.

Prescribing the opportunity for choice requires also that no one should be forced into any social relationship not of his own choosing. For example, no site plan should so isolate blocks from one another that residents must find it too difficult to maintain social contacts outside the block. Likewise, no residential area should be so heterogeneous in its population make-up that it prevents anyone from finding friends within the area; nor should it be so homogeneous that residents socialize only on their own block.

Implications for Planning Practice

Detailed implications cannot be spelled out until considerably more data are available on the relative roles of propinquity and homogeneity. Some guides can be suggested, however.

The site planner should not deliberately try to create a specific social pattern, but he should aim to provide maximum choice. If possible, the site plan should contain a variety of house-to-house relationships, so that residents who desire a large number of visual and social contacts and those who prefer relative isolation can both be satisfied. If density requirements permit, however, the site planner should not locate dwelling units within such close physical and functional distance to each other that the occupants are constantly thrown together and forced into social contact. In areas of single-family houses, the planner should avoid narrow courts. In rowhouse developments, soundproof party walls are necessary. In addition, some type of separation between houses should be provided to shield front and rear doors from those of adjacent houses. Since Americans seem to dislike complete and permanent separation from neighbors, however, something less irrevocable than a solid wall is desirable.

Blocks and courts should be so laid out that they do not become prisons. At the same time, however, they should not be spread out in such a fashion that all visual and social contact between neighbors is prevented. This is a problem in areas of very low density, where lots are so large that neighbors have difficulty in meeting each other.[20]

If and when sufficient research has been done to establish the relationship between site planning and social life on a sounder empirical basis, the concept of voluntary resident placement should be explored. Thus if the studies indicate that some locations in a site plan will inevitably result in greater social contact than others, potential occupants should be informed so that they can take this fact into account in choosing their houses.[21]

Since homogeneity is an important determinant of social relationships, some degree of homogeneity on the block would seem to be desirable. This would encourage positive relationships among neighbors and would allow those who want to find friends in the immediate vicinity to do so without impairing the ability of others to seek friends on the outside. If blocks are too homogeneous, however, those people who differ from the majority are likely to be considered deviants, and may be exposed to social pressure to conform or sentenced to virtual isolation. Conversely, heterogenous blocks would produce cool and possibly negative relations among neighbors and would eliminate the chance to make friends on the block.

The proper solution is a moderate degree of homogeneity, although at this point no one knows how to define this degree operationally or how to develop planning guides for it. Moreover, the planner lacks the power to implement such guides. *My observations suggest that, by and large, the present crop of suburban communities provides the degree of homogeneity described here. Consequently, the planner need not worry about his inability to intervene.*

My proposals in behalf of residential homogeneity are based on the value judgments defended here and apply only to one phase of residential life. Planners have long debated whether residential areas should be homogeneous or heterogeneous. Some planners, who give higher priority to other planning values, and are more concerned with other phases of residential life, have advocated balanced communities, with heterogeneous populations.

ACKNOWLEDGMENTS

I am indebted to Paul Davidoff, John W. Dyckman, Lewis Mumford, Janet and Tom Reiner, Melvin M. Webber, and William L. C. Wheaton for helpful critiques of earlier versions of this paper.

NOTES

1. The principal postwar studies are: R. Merton, "The Social Psychology of Housing," in Wayne Dennis (ed.), *Current Trends in Social Psychology* (Pittsburgh: University of Pittsburgh Press, 1947), pp. 163–217; T. Caplow and R. Foreman, "Neighborhood Interaction in a Homogeneous Community," *American Sociological Review*, Vol. 15 (1950), pp. 357–366; L. Festinger, S. Schachter, and K. Back, *Social Pressures in Informal Groups* (New York: Harper & Bros., 1950); L. Festinger, "Architecture and Group Membership," *Journal of Social Issues*, Vol. 7 (1951), pp. 152–163; L. Kuper, "Blueprint for Living Together," in L. Kuper (ed.), *Living in Towns* (London: Cresset Press, 1953), pp. 1–202; W. H. Whyte, Jr., "How the New Suburbia Socializes," *Fortune*, August 1953, pp. 120–122, 186–190, and *ibid.*, *The Organization Man* (New York: Simon and Schuster, 1957), Chapter 25. See also the earlier researches and some negative findings cited by I. Rosow, "The Social Effects of the Physical Environment," *Journal of the American Institute of Planners*, Vol. 27 (1961), pp. 127–133. The discussion that follows draws on these studies and on my own research and observations in two suburban communities, Park Forest, Illinois and Levittown, New Jersey.

2. Festinger, Schachter, and Back, *op. cit.*, p. 160. See also Merton, *op. cit.*, p. 208.

3. See, e.g., P. Lazarsfeld and R. Merton, "Friendship as a Social Process: A Substantive and Methological Analysis" (Part I: Substantive Analysis, by R. Merton), in M. Berger, T. Abel, and C. Page (eds.), *Freedom and Control in Modern Society* (New York: Van Nostrand, 1954), pp. 21–37.

4. Hereafter, when I describe a population as homogeneous or heterogeneous, I always mean with respect to the characteristics that are relevant to the particular aspect of social life under discussion, although for stylistic reasons, the qualifying phrase is usually left out.

5. The relationship between propinquity and homogeneity is considered in most of the studies cited in footnote 1. See, e.g., the discussion by Kuper, *op. cit.* pp. 154–164, and by Rosow, *op. cit.* p. 131.

6. If the physical distance is negligible, as between next door neighbors, social contact is likely to take place quickly. When neighbors are not immediately adjacent, however, one or the other must take the initiative, and this requires either some visible sign of a shared background characteristic, or interest, or the willingness to be socially aggressive. This is not as prevalent as sometimes imagined. Although the new suburbs are often thought to exhibit an inordinate amount of intra-block visiting, I found that on the block on which I lived in Levittown, New Jersey, some of the men who lived three to five houses away from each other did not meet for over a year after initial occupancy. The wives met more quickly, of course.

7. Festinger, Schachter, and Back call this "functional distance." *Op. cit.*, pp. 34–35.

8. Festinger, *op. cit.*, p. 157. See also A. Wallace, *Housing and Social Structure* (Philadelphia: Philadelphia Housing Authority, 1952). In urban tenement areas, where neighbors are often related or from the same ethnic background, there may be considerable visiting between floors. A high degree of homogeneity can thus overcome physical obstacles.

9. Home buyers do not, however, move into a new area without some assurance that neighbors are likely to be compatible. They derive this assurance from the house price (which bears some correlation to purchasers' income level), from the kinds of people whom they see inspecting the model homes, and from the previous class and ethnic image of the area within which the subdivision is located.

10. See W. Form, "Stratification in Low and Middle Income Housing Areas," *Journal of Social Issues*, Vol. 7 (1951), pp. 116–117.

11. For one study which deals with this problem, see Lazarsfeld and Merton, *op. cit.* They concluded that the sharing of values is more important than the sharing of backgrounds.

12. Studies such as M. Deutsch and M. Collins, *Interracial Housing* (Minneapolis-University of Minnesota Press, 1951) and E. and G. Greer, *Privately Developed Interracial Housing* (Berkeley: University of California Press, 1960), suggest that

...vely homogeneous in class ...es are no obstacle to social ...e is no longer a criterion of ...s especially true in middle- ...as occupied by professional ...rger subdivisions. Smaller ones are ... ...t settled randomly, but are occupied by ... ...ps, for example related households or members of an ethnic group moving *en masse* from another area.

14. Whyte, *The Organization Man*, pp. 333–334.
15. These comments are based on observations, however, rather than on systematic studies. Macris studied visiting patterns in Park Forest in 1957 and found considerably less intrablock visiting than did Whyte. He also found that there was almost no visiting at all between tenants and homeowners, even though they were living in physical propinquity in the area he studied. This suggests the importance of neighbor homogeneity. D. Macris, "Social Relationships Among Residents of Various House Types in a Planned Community," unpublished master's thesis, University of Illinois, 1958.

16. M. Young and P. Willmott, *Family and Kinship in East London* (London: Routledge and Kegan Paul, 1957).
17. There must, however, be general agreement about methods of housekeeping, getting along with husbands, and child rearing. Since these methods vary with education and socio-economic level, some homogeneity of class is necessary even for the coffee klatsch.
18. The kinds of gatherings which Whyte studied so ingeniously in Park Forest were mainly those of peer groups indulging in single-purpose activities. This may explain why he found propinquity to be so important.
19. See Rosow, *op. cit.*, p. 131.
20. Erich Lindemann (in a personal conversation) has reported that this resulted in an upper-income community which he and his associates have studied. The large lots which satisfy the status needs of their owners also create loneliness for women who have no social contacts in the larger community.
21. See the discussion of this proposal by Whyte, *The Organization Man*, p. 346.

49. A Theory of Urban Form   Kevin Lynch
and
Lloyd Rodwin

Two difficulties arise in trying to understand the way in which the physical environment of the city influences human behavior. One is to develop an analytical framework for describing and classifying the characteristics of the environment that conceivably can influence social action. The second is to describe the purposes and goals of the city in a manner that will allow an urban design proposal to be examined and evaluated in the light of how it may produce a more effective and humane urban community.

The paper by Lynch and Rodwin is one of the few efforts made by students of urban life to grapple with these difficulties. They put forth a sixfold classification of urban design systems, in terms of spaces and buildings, the number of these elements, their density, their grain or degree of differentiation in the urban landscape, the focal organization of plans, and the generalized pattern of spatial distribution. Although the authors do not list specific goals to be developed for a particular city, they do recommend a procedure and a set of criteria for arriving at goals and establishing priorities among them. Lynch and Rodwin conclude the paper with an application of their proposal to a hypothetical urban design problem.

Kevin Lynch is Professor of City Planning at Massachusetts Institute of Technology. He is the author of *Site Planning* (1962) and *The Image of the City* (1960) and coauthor of *The View From the Road* (1964).

Lloyd Rodwin is a Professor in the Department of City and Regional Planning at Massachusetts Institute of Technology, chairman of the faculty committee of the Harvard-MIT Joint Center for Urban Studies, and Director of the Special Program for Urban and Regional Studies of Developing Countries. He is the author of *Housing and Economic Progress* (1961) and *British New Towns Policy* (1956) and editor of *The Future Metropolis* and *Planning Urban Growth and Regional Development* (1968).

The principal concern of the physical planner is to understand the physical environment and to help shape it to serve the community's purposes. An outsider from some other discipline would ordinarily assume that such a profession had developed some ideas concerning the diverse effects of different forms of the physical environment (not to mention the reverse effects of nonphysical forces on the environment itself). And he might be equally justified in expecting that intellectual leaders in the profession had been assidously gathering evidence to check and reformulate these ideas so that they might better serve the practitioners in the field. A systematic consideration of the interrelations between urban forms and human objectives would seem to lie at the theoretical heart of city planning work.

But the exception would bring a wry smile to the face of anyone familiar with the actual state of the theory of the physical environment. Where has there been any systematic evaluation of the possible range of urban forms in relation to the objectives men might have? Although most attempts at shaping or reshaping cities have been accompanied by protestations of the ends towards which the shapers are striving, yet in fact there is usually only the most nebulous connection between act and protestation. Not only are goals put in a confused or even conflicting form, but also the physical forms decided upon have very little to do with these goals. Choice of

form is most often based on custom, or intuition, or on the superficial attraction of simplicity. Once constructed, forms are rarely later analyzed for their effectiveness in achieving the objectives originally set.

What does exist is some palliative knowledge and rules of thumb for designing street intersections, neighborhoods, and industrial areas, for separating different land uses, distinguishing different traffic functions, or controlling urban growth. Analysis of urban design is largely at the level of city parts, not of the whole. The prevailing views are static and fragmentary. When ideal models are considered, they take the form of utopias. These serve to free the imagination, but are not substitutes for adequate analysis.

There are some reasons for this unsatisfactory situation. The profession is still quite young, and most of its energies are concentrated in professional practice. The men in the field are far too preoccupied with practical problems to fashion new concepts. The profession itself developed from fields like architecture and civil engineering which have not been research minded. The professionals in the universities have taught practical courses and spent much of their time in outside practice. Research and theory under these circumstances were expendable. In the rough and

Reprinted by permission of the *Journal of the American Institute of Planners* (Volume XXIV, No. 4, Fall, 1958).

tumble of daily operations, preliminary notions such as economic base studies, land use master plans, neighborhood design, or zoning and subdivision controls serve a reasonably useful function.

But the planner's situation is changing rapidly. Most of our population now lives in metropolitan regions, and the metropolitan trend is still continuing. There is not only increasing dissatisfaction with our cities, but also an awareness that it is possible to make them more delightful and more efficient places in which to live and work. Tremendous public support has been generated by organizations like The American Council to Improve Our Neighborhoods. Housing, road building, and urban renewal programs are also providing powerful instruments for the transformation of our metropolitan environment. These changing circumstances and values are interesting symptoms of the age of leisure.

The planner's tools and concepts are being subjected to a severe test by this growing demand for action. Something better than rule of thumb and shrewd improvisation is required if his services are to warrant public appreciation. In short, we need better ideas, better theory. Formulated operationally, such theory can be tested, revised, and ultimately verified. Even if initially inadequate, theories can help to develop and extend our ideas, to make them more precise, embracing, and effective. Unless planners can devise more powerful ideas for understanding and controlling the physical environment, they are not likely, and perhaps do not deserve, to be treated as more than lackeys for the performance of routine chores.

Possible Analytical Approaches

It is not easy to create theories "full blown." Effective theories, as a rule, are products of many men's efforts constantly reworked into a more general and more systematic form. It is also hard to locate the best starting place. In tackling the problems of the physical environment one can employ a number of approaches ranging from the descriptive to the genetic, from problem-solving to process and function analyses. All have certain advantages and disadvantages.

Description is the most obvious approach, and perhaps the weakest, standing alone. To describe the physical environment more accurately is an important aim; but since these descriptive possibilities are endless, it is difficult to be sure what is and what is not crucial or relevant. Description works best when there is enough familiarity with significance to permit vividness and terse accuracy. Too little is known about the form of the physical environment, or even about the appropriate analytical categories for analyzing these forms, to handle effective description. Description alone, moreover, yields little insight as to the underlying mechanism of operation.

Studying how the physical environment is transformed might be another approach. The nature of the changes can be recorded, the difficulties and directions in transition, the conditions associated with the changes and the various social, economic, and political processes by which the alteration takes place. Often the historical, comparative, and genetic approaches are the best ways of following the dynamics of the physical environment. But there are limitations too; and these lie in the difficulty of disentangling the strategic variables which should be examined and of understanding the mechanism of change.

Another approach, now most current, is pragmatic. Each case can be considered more or less unique. The emphasis is on problem solving, or on shaping or re-shaping the physical environment to eliminate specific difficulties or to achieve specific effects. Limited generalizations or rules can be formulated; but the tendency is to emphasize the uniqueness of each problem and the inapplicability of "strato-spheric generalizations." The advantage here is the "realism"; the weakness is the handicap implicit in the assumption that general ideas and theories are of almost no value as guides for dealing with specific cases or classes of cases.

A more abstract variant of problem solving might be a study of the goal-form relationship. This approach is concerned with how alternative physical arrangements facilitate or inhibit various individual and social objectives. It is an approach directly keyed to action; it would, if perfected, suggest optimum forms or a range of them, once aspirations had been clarified and decided upon. Its weakness is its static nature; and its strength lies in the emphasis on the clear formulation of goals and on the probable effects of various forms of physical organization. The more that is learned about these effects, the more light will be shed on the process and perhaps even on the mechanism of change. Simi-larly, descriptive techniques and genetic and historical approaches might prove more effective if the emphasis were on objectives and if the evidence sought were related to the effectiveness of the environ-ment in serving these ends. Problem solving, too, might be more systematic, less haphazard and subject to rules of thumb, if it were grounded on more solid knowledge of goal-form relationships.

This paper proposes to set forth an approach to such a theory. It will therefore necessarily deal first with the problem of analyzing urban form, secondly with the formulation of goals, and thirdly with the techniques of studying the interrelations between such forms and goals.

Criteria for Analytical Categories of Urban Form

Since the work on urban form has been negligible, the first task is to decide what it is and to find ways of classifying and describing it that will turn out to be useful both for the analysis of the impact on objectives and for the practical mani-pulation of form. Without a clear analytical system for examining the physical form of a city, it is hardly possible to assess the effect of form or even to change it in any rational way. The seemingly elementary step of formulating an analytical system is the most crucial. Upon it hangs all the rest; and while other questions, such as the statement of objectives or the analysis of effects, may be partly the task of other disciplines, the question of city form cannot be passed off.

There are a number of criteria which a workable system must meet. First, it must apply to cities and metropolitan areas and be significant at that scale. This is simply an arbitrary definition of our particular sphere of interest, but it conceals an important distinction. There are many environmental effects which operate at larger scales (such as the influence of climate or the distribution of settlement on a national level), and even more which are effective at a smaller scale (such as the decoration of a room or the siting of a group of houses). Cities are too often regarded simply as collections of smaller environments. Most traditional design ideas (shopping centers, neighborhoods, traffic intersections, play spaces, etc.) reflect this tendency. It is usually assumed that well-designed neighborhoods, with good roads and sufficient shopping and industry, automatically produce an optimum settlement. As another example, many planners are likely to think that a beautiful city is simply the sum of a large series of small areas which are beautiful in themselves.

But this may be no more true than that a great building is a random collection of handsome rooms. Every physical whole is affected not only by the quality of its parts, but also by their total organization and arrangement. Therefore, the first criterion for form analysis is that it identify form qualities which are significant at the city or metropolitan scale, that is, which can be controlled at that scale and which also have different effects when arranged in different patterns that are describable at that scale. This criterion excludes, without in any way denying their importance, such features as intercity spacing (describable only beyond the city level) or the relation of the front door of a house to the street (which is hard to describe on the city scale unless uniform, difficult to control at that level, and whose city-wide pattern of distribution would seem to be of no importance).

The second criterion is that categories must deal solely with the physical form of the city or with the distribution of activities within it; and that these two aspects must be clearly and sharply separated. City and regional planners operate primarily upon the physical environment, although mindful of its complex social, economic, or psychological effects. They are not experts in all the planning for the future that a society engages in,

but only in planning for the future development of the physical and spatial city: streets, buildings, utilities, activity distributions, spaces, and their interrelations. Although cries of dismay may greet such a reactionary and "narrow" view, the currently fashionable broader definitions lead in our judgment only to integrated, comprehensive incompetence.

A planner in this sense is aware that the final motive of his work is its human effect, and he should be well grounded, for example, in the interelation between density and the development of children in our society. He must be quite clear that the physical or locational effects may often be the least important ones, or operate only in conjunction with other circumstances. Above all, he has to understand that the very process of achieving his proposed form, the way in which the group decides and organizes itself to carry it out, may turn out to be the most decisive effect of all. Nevertheless, he takes the spatial environment as the focus of his work, and does not pretend to be a sociologist, an economist, an administrator, or some megalomaniacal supercombination of these.

Physical form and the spatial distribution of activities in the city are partly contained in the traditional "land use" categories of the planning field. Unfortunately, these categories are analytically treacherous.

It is true that their very ambiguity is often useful in field operation, where they can be made to mean what the user wants them to mean. But for theoretical study these categories thoroughly confound two distinct spatial distributions: that of human activity, or "use" proper, and that of physical shape. The traditional concept of "single-family residential use," for example, unites a certain kind of activity:

family residence (and its concomitant features of eating, sleeping, child-rearing, etc.) with a type of isolated physical structure, called a "house," which is traditionally allied with this activity. This works tolerably well in a homogeneous society, as long as people behave with docility and continue to reside in families in these houses. But if they should choose to sleep in buildings we call factories, then the whole system would be in danger. Even under present circumstances "mixed uses," or structures used now for storage, now for selling, now for religious meetings, cause trouble.

The pattern of activities and the physical pattern are often surprisingly independent of each other, and they must be separated analytically if we are to understand the effect of either. In practice, planners operate primarily upon the physical pattern, while often aiming to change the activity pattern via the physical change. Only in the negative prohibitions of some parts of the zoning ordinance do planners operate directly upon the activity pattern itself. By sharp distinction of the two, it is possible to explore how activity pattern and physical pattern interact, and which (if either) has significant effects in achieving any given objective.

This paper, however, will develop primarily the notion of the urban physical pattern, leaving the question of the activity pattern for another effort. This is done not to prejudge the relative importance of the two, but for clarity of analysis and because at present most planners operate primarily upon the physical rather than the activity patterns. The time may come, of course, when city planners may manipulate the distribution of activities in an equally direct manner. Even should this time not come and should our influence on activities continue to be indirect, it

would be important to know the consequences of activity distribution.

Such nonspatial factors as the range of family income, political organization, or the social type of a city are excluded by this second criterion. This paper will also exclude factors such as the distribution of work place versus sleeping place or the quantity of flow on city streets. These latter are activity categories, properly considered under their own heading.

A third criterion of our analytical system, which adds to the problems of constructing it, is that it must be applicable to all types of urban settlement, used by any human culture. An American city, a Sumerian settlement, or a future Martian metropolis must all be capable of being subsumed under it. The categories must reach a level of generality that might be unnecessary in simply considering present-day cities in the United States. Not only is this necessary for complete analysis, but also by making our categories truly general we may uncover new form possibilities not now suspected. For example, dwelling-units-per-acre cannot be used as a basic descriptive measure, since some settlements may not have sleeping areas organized into dwelling units. (The fact of having such an organization, of course, may be part of a physical description.)

A fourth criterion is that the categories must eventually be such that they can be discovered or measured in the field, recorded, communicated, and tested. Lastly, the crucial test: all the factors chosen for analysis must have significant effect on whatever goals are important to the group using the facilities and must encompass all physical features significant for such goals.

Our aim is to uncover the important factors that influence the achievement of certain human objectives. Therefore the categories allowable here will depend upon the objectives chosen and on the threshold effect considered significant. The categories used might shift with each new study. It is necessary, however, to set up one system of form categories so that comparisons may be made from one study to another. Therefore one must begin by considering the familiar human purposes and by guessing what physical features might be significant for those purposes. Subsequent analysis and testing will undoubtedly modify the categories based on this criterion.

In summary, the criteria for an analytic system of city form are that the categories of analysis must:

1. Have significance at the city-wide scale, that is, be controllable and describable at that level
2. Involve either the physical shape or the activity distribution and not confuse the two
3. Apply to all urban settlements
4. Be capable of being recorded, communicated, and tested
5. Have significance for their effect on the achievement of human objectives and include all physical features that are significant

Proposed Analytical System

While several types of analytical systems might be considered, we have attempted to develop a set of abstract descriptions of the quality, quantity, or spatial distribution of various features, of types that are present in some form in all settlements. The abstractness of this system makes it difficult to conceptualize. It also divides up the total form of city, although not spatially, and it therefore raises the problem of keeping in mind the interrela-

tions among categories. But for generality, clarity, and conciseness—and perhaps even for fresh insights—it seems to be the preferable method and will be followed in the rest of this paper.

A system for activity pattern would probably require a description of two basic aspects: flows of men and goods, on the one hand, and, on the other, the spatial pattern of more localized activities such as exchange, recreation, sleeping, or production. Although this side of the analysis will be omitted in order to concentrate on physical pattern, a similar breakdown is feasible in the physical form description: (a) the flow *system*, excluding the flow itself and (b) the distribution of adapted space, primarily sheltered space.

These are quite similar to the familiar duet of land use and circulation, with the content of activity removed. It may be remarked that an overtone of activity still remains, since the physical facilities are divided between those primarily used for flow, and those accommodating more fixed activities. This is a very convenient division, however, and seems to be a regular feature of all settlements.

There are many cases, of course, in which a given physical space is used both for flow and for other activities. Usually the other activities are alongside the flow, or sometimes intermixed with it, and here the space must be subdivided, or simply counted in both categories. Occasionally there may be a cyclical shift in use, as when a road is shut off for a street dance. Then, if this is important, a temporal shift of the facility from one category to another must be made. It is even conceivable that a city could contain mobile facilities in which both circulation and other activites are performed simultaneously, on the analogy of the ocean liner. But perhaps that can be faced when it happens on a scale that would be significant in a city.

Except for these difficulties, then, the division into flow system and adapted space is a convenient one. The former is usually easy to identify, and includes all the roads, paths, tubes, wires, canals, and rail lines, which are designed to facilitate the flow of people, goods, wastes, or information. The latter category, that of adapted spaces, although it seems tremendously broad, has sufficient basic similarity to be treated as an entity. It consists of all spaces that have been adapted in some way to be useful for some one or several significant noncirculatory activities.

In this country's climate, the key spaces of this nature are those enclosed and with a modified climate, that is, the city's "floor space." Eslewhere enclosure may be less important. Almost everywhere, however, the adaptation includes some modification of the ground plane, even to the cultivation of a field; and the key activities are often likely to take place in at least sheltered, if not enclosed, spaces. But in any case, the fundamental thing done to our physical environment, besides providing means for communication, is to provide spaces for various activities, to adapt the quality of those spaces, and to distribute in an over-all pattern.

Since many of the primary adaptations of a space, such as enclosure or the provision of a smooth, level, hard, dry ground plane, are useful for many different activities, spaces are often used interchangeably. A "store-front" may be used as a store, an office, a church, a warehouse, or even a family residence. This interchangeability argues for the usefulness and necessity of generalizing adapted space into one category. Within it, one may dissect as much as necessary, dividing

enclosed floor space from open space, picking out tall structures from the floor space category, or hard-surfaced lots from total open space. Occasionally, purely for convenience, it may be necessary to use activity-oriented names, such as "office structure," or "parking lot." But, whenever this is done, reference is being made solely to a physical type and not to its use.

Each one of these two general categories, flow system and adapted space, could also be broken down in a parallel way for more exact analysis.

1. *Element types* The basic types of spaces and of flow facilities can be described qualitatively in their most significant aspects, including the extent to which the different types are differentiated in character, or to which they grade into each other.

2. *Quantity* The quantities of houses or streets, in length or capacity or size, can then be enumerated, to give total capacity and scale.

3. *Density* Next the intensity with which spaces or channels are packed into a given unit area can be stated; as a single quantity, if uniform, but more likely as

ranges of intensity and as average and typical intensities. This is a familiar idea when applied to adapted space, particularly enclosed space, as is exemplified in the concept of the floor-area ratio. The same idea could be applied to the circulation system, calculating intensity as the flow capacity which passes in any direction through a small unit area and mapping the variation of this ratio (as in potential vehicles per hour-acre).

5. *Focal organizations* The spatial arrangement and interrelation of the key points in the total environment can be examined. These might be the density peaks, the concentrations of certain dominant buildings types, the key open spaces, or the termini or basic intersections of the circulation systems. Consideration of the arrangement of such key points is often a shorthand method of expressing total pattern.

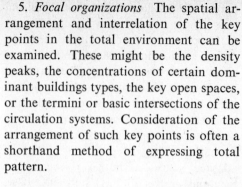

4. *Grain* The extent to which these typical elements and densities are differentiated and separated in space can be defined as coarse or fine in terms of the quantity of a given type that is separated out in one cluster, and sharp or blurred in terms of the manner of separation at the boundary. Thus, house and factory building types might typically be separated in one city into large pure clusters, sharply differentiated at the edges; while in another town the grain might be very fine and the transitions generally blurred. Again, the outdoor spaces migh be blurred and undifferentiated or, in the circulation system, footpaths and vehicular pavements might be sharply and coarsely separated. Essentially, this quality refers to the typical local interrelations between similar or dissilimar elements, but without reference as yet to total pattern.

6. *Generalized spatial distribution* This could be taken as a catchall which included the entire analysis. What is meant here is the gross pattern in two- (or three-) dimensional space, as might be expressed on a greatly simplified map or model. It would include such items as outline (or the shape of the city with reference to the noncity) and the broad pattern of zones occupied by the basic element and density types. One city might have a single central density peak; another a circle cut by pie-shaped zones of "factory" buildings; another a flow system on a rectangular grid; still another might have a uniform pattern of small interconnecting enclosed outdoor spaces surrounded by a deep belt of free-flowing space punctuated by tall masses. Such a description would be needed whenever the notation of type,

quantity, density, grain, and pattern of key points was insufficient to describe the significant total pattern.

Finally, of course, it would be necessary to interrelate the two basic categories, to show where the flow termini came with reference to the density peaks, for example, or to relate the pattern of the flow system to the general open space pattern.

The method given above is proposed as a basic system of analyzing a city's form in accordance with the original criteria. It does not try to cover all the physical features of a city, which are endless, but concentrates on those considered significant at that scale. Only systematic testing in real cities will indicate whether all the important features are included.

An Example of the Analytical System

Since this system may be difficult to follow in the abstract, it will perhaps clarify the proposal to use it in describing an imaginary settlement named Pone. Like any town, Pone is best described by the use of both words and precise drawings, but here words and a simple sketch must suffice.

a. Pone is made up of six types of adapted space: dirt-floored rooms, 20 by 20 feet, roofed with thatch and enclosed by adobe, each structure being free standing; concrete-floored shed spaces, 75 feet by up to 300 feet, in corrugated iron, sometimes single and sometimes in series horizontally; multistory concrete structures containing from fifty to two hundred 10 by 10 foot rooms; walled-in cultivated spaces of rectangular shape, varying from ½ to 3 acres; walled, stone-paved spaces pierced by paths; irregular bare dust-covered spaces which take up the remainder of the area. Pone has four types of flow

channels: four-foot dirt paths, unenclosed; thirty-foot cobbled roads, enclosed in semicircular tubes of corrugated iron; an interconnecting waterproof system of four-inch pipes; and some telegraph wires.

b. There are ten thousand adobe rooms, totaling 4,000,000 square feet; fifty shed spaces, totaling 1,000,000 square feet; and four multistory structures, with 40,000 square feet of floor space. There are five thousand cultivated spaces occupying 5,000 acres, two walled and paved open spaces of 10 acres each; and the leftover dust covers 1,200 acres. There are three miles of cobbled road, each with a capacity of 400 mulecarts per hour in both directions; and 60 miles of dirt path, each able to carry 2000 persons per hour in either direction. There are 20 miles of pipe and 2 miles of wire.

c. Density of adobe rooms varies continuously from a floor-area ratio of 0.003 to 0.3; that of the sheds from 0.3 to 0.9 (with a tendency to group at the two extremes), while the tall structures are uniformly at 5.0. Road-capacity density varies from a peak of 1,600 carts per hour-acre to a low of 20; path-capacity density varies from 4,000 persons per hour-acre to 50.

d. The three types of enclosed space are sharply differentiated and separated in plan. Cultivated spaces are mixed coarsely with the adobe rooms, while the irregular dusty areas are finely distributed throughout. Roads and paths are sharply separated and do not interconnect except at the shed spaces. Any intersections are at separated grades. They are also coarsely separated, since the roads are associated with the shed spaces.

Wires and pipes follow along paths. Pipes are dispersed, but wires serve only sheds and the multistory structures.

· *e.* Focal points in this organization are

the two rectangular paved open spaces. The first is central to the area of adobe rooms, and is the focus of converging paths. It corresponds to the peak of room density and to one of the peaks of path density. The other focal point is flanked by the multistory structures, occurs at another convergence and density peak of the path system, and is touched upon by the road system. Here occurs the major terminus and interchange point of that road system. The wire lines all pass through a central switchboard in one of the multistoried structures. The pipe lines have a single source just beyond the town boundary.

f. The settlement is round and compact, with no holes. The multistoried structures and second focus occur at the center, with the sheds occupying a narrow pie-shaped sector outwards from this. The focus of room density is slightly off center. The road system is a rectangular grid of irregular spacing, tying to the sheds, to the second focal point, and, by a single line, to the outside. The path system is irregular and capillary, but converges and intensifies at the two focal points, as noted above.

In theory (and particularly if we could use more drawings) we now know enough of the physical form to judge its value for various basic purposes at the city level of significance. One is tempted to object: Isn't this meaningless, if one knows nothing of the life that is going on within that form? Lifeless, yes, and saying little or nothing about the society of Pone (though one may make some guesses); but yet adequate, if you want to test its cost, or productive efficiency (given some productive system), or comfort (given some standards). Certainly it is the first step in trying to disentangle the effects of physical form per se, and the first step even if one wants to study the results of physical form in relation to activity pattern, or social organization, or politics. (To describe New York City in this way would, of course, take a few more pages.)

Problems of Goal Formulation

What will be the goals against which we will test this city? Unfortunately for a neat and workmanlike job, they might be almost

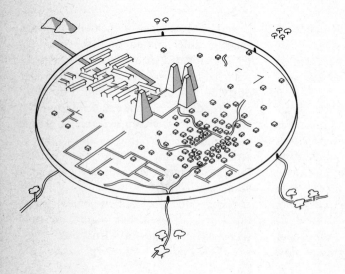

anything. One group inhabiting Pone might find it highly satisfactory, another might find it useless or even dangerous, all depending on their several purposes and the variations in their cultures. Is there any method by which relevant goals might be set out and related to these environmental shapes? Unhappily for the reader, we now find that we must digress to consider the problems of setting up a goal system. Only after this is done will it be possible to return to the implications of the forms themselves.

The possible goals must first be considered. This may cause some confusion, since such a collection is not likely to be consistent or unified. It must be distinguished from a goal *system*, i.e., a set of selected objectives which are coherent, unified, and capable of guiding action. Construction of ,such a system is the desirable result of considering goal possibilities, but it can only be brought to completion by a particular group in a particular situation. Thus the possible range of goals might include both the preservation of individual life at all costs and also the maximization of human sacrifice. A particular system would have to choose, or, more probably, settle upon some intermediate stand; and this stand should be related to its other objectives.

Probably the most confusing aspect of this question is not the infinite number of goal possibilities, but rather their range of generality. Some objectives, such as "goodness," may seem to regulate almost every action, but to do so in such a vague and generalized way as to be of little help in choice. Others, such as the goal of having all children say "please" when asking for things at the table, are very clear in their implications for action, but quite limited in their application and their consequences. These two goals are interconnected only

by a long chain of explanations, situations, and interactions. It is difficult to be sure that one follows from the other and hard to weight their relative importance in relation to other goals.

To avoid such confusions, it is important that any one goal system should contain only objectives which are at approximately the same level of generality. We may smile when someone admonishes a child to "be good, and keep your fingernails clean!" But we are also exhorted to build city additions that will be good places to live in and will keep valuations high. In many cases, of course, there may be no real confusion, as when the second point is the true objective and the first is only a verbal blind.

Similarly, it is meaningless to consider beauty and fresh paint as alternative objectives: they do not operate at the same level. Each objective may in its turn looked upon as a means of attaining some objective higher up the scale of generality. Shouting at recruits may be considered a means of overawing them, with the goal of developing obedience, which is itself directed to the building of a disciplined military force, having as its objective the winning of wars, which may be thought of as a way to gain security. When constructing a rational system for guidance in any particular situation, what must be built up is a connected hierarchy of goals, considering possible alternatives only at the same level of generality and checking lower levels for their relevance to upper levels of the system.

The more general objectives have the advantage of relative stability: they are applicable to more situations for larger groups over long spans of time. They have the corresponding disadvantages of lack of precision and difficulty of application in any specific problem. Very often, in goal systems of real life, such general objectives may have very little connection with objectives farther down the list, being, rather, top-level show pieces, or covers for hidden motives. The operating goals are then the intermediate ones, those which actually regulate action. To develop a rational set of goals, however, the connection must be sought out, or the motives that are the true generalized goals must be revealed. The aim is to produce a system that is as coherent as possible, although this again is rare in reality.

Since reference back to very general goals is a painful one intellectually, most actions must be guided by intermediate, more concrete, objectives, which can be referred to more quickly. Only the most serious steps warrant reference to fundamentals, while everyday decisions depend on customs and precepts that are actually low-level goals. City building is important enough to be referred back to more than simple precepts; but even here decisions cannot always be brought up to the highest level of generality, since the analysis is so complex. Therefore reliance must be placed upon goals of an intermediate level. But these intermediate goals should be periodically checked for their relevance to more general objectives and to the changing situation, as well as for consistency among themselves.

It is a besetting sin to "freeze" upon rather specific goals and thus risk action irrelevant to a new situation. If it is observed, for example, that growing cities have been prosperous ones, attention may focus upon increase of population size as an objective. Actions will be directed toward stimulating growth, regardless of any consequences of dislocation, instability, or cost. Industries may be brought in which will depress the wage level and the general prosperity, because no one has

stopped to examine the objectives that lie behind the growth objective, i.e., to ask the simple question: "Why do we want to grow?" Because of this continuous tendency to fix upon goals at too specific a level, it is a wise habit to challenge current goals by always pushing them back at least one step up the ladder of generality.

Criteria for the Choice of Goals

What will be the criteria for the choice of goals in our case? If they are rational, they should be internally consistent. There should, moreover, be some possibility of moving toward their realization, now or in the future. Otherwise they are simply frustrating. To have operational meaning, they must be capable of being contradicted, thus permitting a real choice. And finally, the goals must be relevant to city form, since there are many human objectives which are little affected by environmental shape. Therefore, given one's basic values and the values of the culture in which one is operating, it is necessary to develop a set of useful intermediate objectives which are consistent, possible, operational, and relevant to the task in hand.

Devising such objectives is difficult; and it is not made easier by the fact that a planner is an individual responsible for actions or recommendations in an environment used by large numbers of people. He is not concerned simply with his own values, nor even with their interaction with the values of another individual with whom he can communicate, which is the situation of the architect with a single client. The planner's client is a large group, a difficult client to talk to, often incoherent, and usually in some conflict with itself.

To some extent the planner can rely on democratic processes to establish group objectives; to some extent he must use sociological techniques to uncover them. Often he is forced, or thinks he is forced, to rely upon his own intuition as to group objectives—a most hazardous method, since the planner is himself likely to be a member of a rather small class of that society. In any event, he must make every effort to understand his own values, as well as to uncover and clarify the goals of the society he is working for.

His troubles do not stop here. Even if he had perfect knowledge of group goals, and they proved to form a completely consistent system, he is still faced with the issue of relating them to his own personal values. He cannot be solely the handmaiden of the group, but has some responsibility (should he differ) to urge upon them a modification of their goal system or to acquaint them with new alternatives. He has a complicated role of leader and follower combined and must resolve this for himself. This is true of many other professional groups.

And should the public goals, as is most likely, prove to be internally inconsistent or in transition, then the planner must mediate these conflicts and changes. He must find the means of striking a balance and the way of preparing for the new value to come without destroying the old value still present.

But to all these everyday woes we can at the moment simply shrug our theoretical shoulders. Give us a consistent and operational system of objectives, a system possible and relevant and organized properly by levels, and we will show you the environmental forms to achieve these objectives. If your goals are superficial or shortsighted, so much the worse. That is your concern, not ours.

In western culture, general and accepted goals would probably cluster around the worth of the individual human being, around the idea of man as the measure, with an emphasis on future results and yet on the importance of process as well as final achievement. Basic values for the individual might include such things as:

a. Health, equilibrium, survival, continuity, adaptability
b. Coherence, meaning, response
c. Development, growth, stimulus, choice, freedom
d. Participation, active use of powers, efficiency, skill, control
e. Pleasure, comfort

Upon the basis of such generalities, one can make for himself (or for his group) a set of broad goals. One way of conveniently organizing such goals may be the following:

a. Regarding the relation of men and objects: Those goals
   1. having to do with direct functioning: biological or technical goals, such as the achievement of an environment which sustains and prolongs life;
   2. having to do with sensuous interactions: psychological or esthetic goals, such as the creation of an environment which is meaningful to the inhabitant.
b. Regarding the relation of men and men: Those goals
   1. having to do with interpersonal relations: sociological and psychological goals, ' such as constructing surroundings which maximize interpersonal communications;
   2. or having to do with group functioning; social goals such as survival and continuity of the group.

It is important to see that a mere listing of objectives is insufficient even at this generalized level, if a policy of relative emphasis is not also included. Any real action may work for one goal and against the other, or be more or less helpful in relation to another action. Yet the choice must be made. Therefore a statement of objectives must be accompanied by a statement of relative importance: that, for example, group survival is valued above individual survival, although both are valued. More precisely, it will have to be said that, in such-and-such a circumstance, group survival is more valued.

Since attainment of human objectives almost always entails the use of scarce resources, the next level of objectives are the economic. In their most general form, they can be described as the attainment of ends with the maximum economy of means, while keeping or making the resource level as high as possible. In all these general objectives, moreover, there is an intertwining of means and ends, of process and final achievement. Particularly where "final" achievement may be as long delayed or even as illusory as it is in city development, the attainment of objectives may be affected more by the process itself than by final form that is being sought.

But the goal system at this level, however consistent and relevant, is still too general for effective application to city-form decisions. Moving down to lower levels for specific guidance, how can one define a "meaningful environment," for example, or the limits within which interpersonal communication is to be maximized?

It would be possible to move down the ladder step by step, ending with some such rule as "all buildings should by their exterior form reveal to any adult inhabitant of average education and intelligence their principal internal use," or even ". . . to accomplish this, the following building types shall have the following shapes. . . ." The latter is undoubtedly an example of

"misplaced concreteness"; but even the former poses problems in relating it back to the general descriptive categories of city form that were developed above. How does the "meaningfulness" of structure relate to density, or grain, or focal organization? In coming down the ladder of specificity we may find we have slipped away from relevance to form at the city scale, or have developed precepts which have multiple and complex effects on the various categories of city form.

Since the formulation of specific objectives is unavoidable, it would be preferable that they be reorganized by being grouped in terms of their relevance to the descriptive categories. Such organization is simply a tactical move, but a crucial one. It involves running through the list of descriptive categories of city form, and choosing (by intuition or prior experience) those general objectives that seem most relevant to that aspect of form.

For example, the following general goals are probably affected in some important way by the "grain" of adapted spaces in an urban settlement:

a. Optimum interpersonal communication
b. Maximum choice of environment for the individual
c. Maximum individual freedom in construction
d. Optimum esthetic stimulus
e. Maximum productive efficiency
f. Maximum productive flexibility
g. Minimum first cost
h. Minimum operating cost

By thus selecting and grouping our general goals, a hypothesis is being asserted, that, for example, "the grain of city facilities has significant (if unknown) effect on the first cost of constructing them." Such hypotheses may prove untrue, in which case the group of goals must be revised or, equally likely, it may indicate that some other objective not originally listed is also significantly affected and must be added to the list.

One objective may be significantly affected by more than one form quality and will thus appear in more than one group. Another objective may be little influenced by any one quality alone, but rather by the nature of the combination of two or more, such as the total effect of grain and density together. This is a separate point, to which we will later return.

The critical nature of the form categories previously selected now becomes apparent, since they impose their pattern upon the entire investigation. If they are not in themselves highly significant, or if they are inconsistent or poorly organized, the work must be redone. Nevertheless, by bringing in the relation to form thus early in our consideration of objectives, a much more economical and systematic attack is possible. The objectives not only contain hypotheses of relevancy, but are really turning into action questions, for example: "What grain of spaces gives a minimum first cost?"

It must be made clear that, if physical forms are considered in insolation, such action questions are not answerable. No relation between grain and first cost can be established until a construction process is postulated. Or, for another example, the impact of the grain of spaces on interpersonal communication depends also on the activity occupying those spaces. Nevertheless, once given a construction process or an activity distribution which is held constant during the test, then the differential impact of various grain alternatives can be analyzed. Thus, in a given activity context, the results of various physical patterns might be studied. Often, a principal result of a given physical pattern may

occur via the manner in which it changes an activity distribution, given an assumption as to a fixed association between certain forms and certain activities.

The same limitations apply to the study of activity patterns in isolation, which are meaningless without reference to the facilities available for communication, insulation, and so on. Eventually, there would be a more complex level of analysis, in which both activity distribution and form might be allowed to vary simultaneously. Even here, however, a general cultural context is still required.

Once the general goals are arranged in terms of the type, quantity, density, grain, focal organization, and pattern of the adapted spaces and the flow system (and in the process just those objectives have been selected out which may be most critically affected by these qualities), and once a general context of culture and activity has been chosen, a more concrete level of analysis is possible. The level should be specific enough to say that "city A is closer to this objective than city B." The meaning of terms must be put in an operational, and often quantitative, way. For example, "what density of spaces allows a reasonable journey from home to work" might become: "what density (or densities) allows 75 percent of the population to be within 30 minutes' time distance of their place of work, providing no more than 10 percent are less than 5 minutes away from their work place?" Different city models could now be tested by this criterion.

Not all goals could be put in this quantitative form, of course. But they would at least have a testable wording, such as: "what is the density at which there is maximum opportunity for interpersonal communication within the local group, without destroying the ability of the individual to achieve privacy when desired?" Such formulations are likely to contain the words maximum, or minimum, or optimum.

The caution must be repeated that, while satisfyingly specific, such goals require continuous rechecking for relevance to the general goals and the changing situation. The home-to-work objective, for example, is simply a definition of the original word "reasonable." Next year, or in India, it might be different.

Goal Form Interaction

Having established an analytical system of urban form and groups of objectives cast in relevant operational terms, the next problem we have is the interaction of form with goal. One might begin either by considering the grain of adapted space and the objectives significantly related to it, or, alternatively, a fundamental objective and the form aspects related to it. If one of the goals is minimum first cost, for example, are the shed spaces of Pone cheaper to build when concentrated as they are in a coarse grain than if they were dispersed throughout the adobe spaces in a fine grain? Or, perhaps, does the grain of dispersion make no difference whatever? Undoubtedly, the effect of grain on cost may differ for different types of space. For example, while the grain of shed spaces was critical because they were built by mass site fabrication methods, the grain of adobe spaces might be indifferent, since they were put up singly by hand in any case. Or it might be found that disperson of the multistory spaces among the shed spaces did not affect their cost, but dispersion among the adobe spaces did. Only in certain cases could generalizations as to grain, per se, be made.

More often, the grain of a certain type of adapted space would have to be the subject of a conclusion.

The grain of the shed spaces may also affect productive efficiency. To test this, one may assume a type of activity, a given productive system, similar to the assumption of construction methods to test the cost implications. To do so does not mean that activity distribution slips in by the back door; we are still testing the impact of one or another physical quality upon the functioning of an activity which is held constant during the test. That is, given a factory system of production, which operates more easily in the wide-span shed spaces of Pone than anywhere else in the city, is that productive system more efficient if all the sheds are close together or if they are dispersed?

In this manner, the goal implications of grain could be analyzed, testing each for relevance and effect, and ending by a search to see if significant goals have been left out. If this system is successful, one should be able to say that, given such-and-such a culture, this particular grain gives best results if your goal system has these particular elements and emphases, and another grain would be better for another system. Alternatively, the objective of minimum first cost could be explored throughout all its ramifications, resulting in a statement that, given a certain culture, this particular total urban form can be constructed at a minimum first cost.

These are final stage results, difficult to attain. Partial, and still useful, conclusions are more likely, such as: if this is the contemporary American society and, if the *only* goal is productive efficiency, then here is the grain to use for this type of adapted space (or: there are several equally good distributions or, perhaps, the grain is of no consequence). Of course, the answer is likely to be still more qualified. One may have to add that this grain is best in a city of small size, another in the larger city; or that optimum grain cannot be separated from density or pattern.

One further note must be made. The *process* of achieving goals or of reshaping form is, in cities, as important as the long-range goal or form. Building a new city of a specific shape may have vital side-effects on the administrative acts and organization required; sequence of development has as much to do with cost as final density. Moreover, one may have important goals which have to do mainly with the process itself, for example, that development decisions be arrived at democratically, or that people be allowed to participate in planning their dwellings, regardless of the final result.

The goal-form method, then, consists in ordering form analysis and definition of objectives so that their interrelation can be considered in a systematic and rational manner. It helps to pose the problem. There it blesses the investigator, and drops him in the mud. It has no further bearing on the analysis of any given interrelation. Each such analysis is likely to be unique and to demand its own method of solution. One might be amenable to mathematical methods; another, to sociological tools; a third, solvable only by subjective analysis; a fourth, by full-scale field tests. There is no guarantee, of course, that the fifth may be solvable at all. What is proposed is merely a way of attacking the central problems of cities in a methodical way.

This "merely," however, may in time open up new possibilities, simply because the problems are more precisely put. If the important physical properties of cities can be clearly defined, and if an operational standard can be set, such as one regarding commuting times, we may be able to study the implications of complex forms by means of new mathematical methods or with such aids as the high-speed computers.

Complex Form and Goal Relationships

If form qualities and goals could be analyzed and disposed of one by one, then in time a complete structure could be built with relative ease. Unfortunately (and this is perhaps the most vulnerable point of the system) physical patterns and goals have a habit of complex interaction. There is not one goal, but many; and the presence of other goals influences the force of the original one. The city forms, which we have herded into arbitrary categories to make our analysis possible, in truth make one pattern. It is not always easy to discuss the impact of grain without specifying density or size. The consequences of the distribution of adapted spaces rests partly on the flow system allied with it.

Thus there are frequently situations where a given goal may not only be influenced by more than one form aspect, but also may at times be affected by such an intimate interaction of aspects that there is no separable cause. A convenient system of notation for such a situation might be as follows, imagining that we are concerned with five goals, A, B, C, D, and E, which have the relationships with form (shown in the accompanying diagram).

Achievement of goal is influenced by:

A–(1) space type; (2) flow system size
B–(1) space, density, and grain combined; (2) focal organization of space and flow system combined
C–(1) space, size, and flow system pattern combined

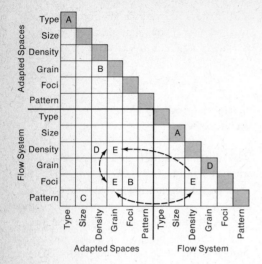

Adapted Spaces   Flow System

D–(1) grain of flow system; (2) density of space and flow system combined

E–(1) grain of space, and density and focal organization of flow system all combined

Here the appearance of a goal in the top diagonal (shaded squares) indicates that it relates to a single form quality at a time. Elsewhere its appearance shows that it is influenced by a pair of form qualities that must be considered together. One goal is shown (E) which is effected by an inseparable combination of three, and must therefore be shown as a connected triangle. If a three-dimensional notation system were used, it could occupy a single solid cube. Higher interactions would require more complicated notations.

This figure would change, of course, as the system of descriptive categories was modified. It is simply a convenient way of reminding ourselves what must be taken into account in studying goal-form interaction. It indicates, incidentally, that in this particular case two aspects of form (space pattern and flow system type) happen to be the ones that have no bearing on any

goal. All the rest are involved in one way or another.

Probably these analytical methods could handle situations where pairs of qualities were involved. Triads of qualities become much more difficult, and many more are likely to make analysis impossible. Some questions may therefore be answerable, and others may resist our best efforts.

To complete the example, consider the city of Pone again. The people of Pone are simple-minded; they have few wants. They have only three goals relevant to city form:

1. Maximum individual privacy, when not producing
2. Maximum defensibility in war
3. Maximum productive efficiency

In case of conflict, goal 2 takes precedence, then goal 3. The Ponians are a simple and a rather grim people.

These goals are set in the following situation: the town produces various kinds of simple consumer goods, which it exports to the surrounding countryside in return for raw materials. This production is most easily carried out in the shed spaces, directed by control functions in the multistory spaces. But the town also produces a large part of its food supply in the cultivated spaces within its limits. Other life functions, beyond production and distribution, are traditionally carried out in the adobe rooms or in the paved open spaces. Wars are fought by ground action, with simple shortrange weapons, and may occur suddenly.

The following matrix indicates the probable relevancy of various form aspects to the three goals:

That is, objective 1 is affected by the type, density, and grain of adapted spaces, all acting singly. Objective 2 is influenced by the pattern of spaces and by the density, grain and focal organization of the flow system, acting singly. It is also the prey of the combined action of the size and density of the adapted spaces. This is true because, although the larger the city the greater the defensive army that could be raised for war and the higher the density the more compact the defensive perimeter, yet in combination they may work in another way. A large, very dense city might quickly succumb to food shortages, owing to the lack of adequate internal cultivated spaces. Therefore the optimum solution is likely to be a function of size in relation to density. Finally, objective 3 is related to the type and grain of spaces and the type and density of the flow system, acting singly, plus the combined effect of the spatial and flow-system focal organizations. The matrix indicates that the size and pattern of the flow system are meaningless to the Ponians.

The analysis on all these separate points could then be carried through and the total balance struck, comparing the actual form of Pone with any other forms within the reach of this people. One might come out with some such conclusion as: given these goals, the actual form is probably the optimum available, with the following modifications:

a. For the privacy objective, a new type of space should be substituted for the single-room adobe space.

b. For the defense objective, a better balance of size and density could be struck, particularly if the unused dust spaces were eliminated. Furthermore, if the capacity density of the flow system were stepped up and the system dispersed at finer grain throughout the settlement, then defense would be simplified.

c. For the production objective, an increase in flow capacity density would also facilitate efficiency.

As was stated at the beginning, the high planners of Pone would also have gone on to a study of the consequences of the activity distribution in the city, and they would have ended with a higher level study of the interrelation of activity and form. But probably the reader has had enough.

Evaluation

Application of this method to a modern metropolis would obviously be far more complicated and, necessarily, more fragmentary. But the basic technique should still be applicable, though it would call for descriptions at a larger scale and goals less precisely formulated. Since the whole technique is analytical, a study of isolated parts, it will tend to give first approximations, rather coarse conclusions bristling with "ifs." It would nevertheless be the elementary knowledge upon which much more refined, and in particular much more fluid and integrated methods could be constructed.

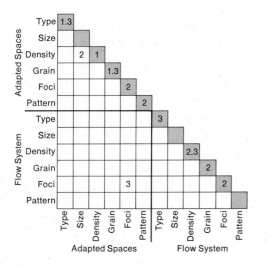

To the student of the physical environment, perhaps the most attractive features of goal-form studies are the new possibilities for research and theory. Regardless of the inadequacy of our present formulations there is a need to test and explore both the range and appropriateness of form categories. Hardly anything is known of how they interact and what the possibilities are for substitution. And instead of fragmentary notions, such as the differentiation of traffic networks, the separation or mixing of land uses, and the organization of neighborhood units, there is the prospect of a general theory of urban form for the city as a whole. If some measure of success is achieved in developing such a general theory, it should not prove too difficult to fit these miscellaneous doctrines into this broader framework, especially since these doctrines purport to modify city form in line with some more or less definite objectives.

Goal-form studies also suggest a new lead for examining city planning history. Instead of the traditional historical survey of civic design accomplishments, the adequacy of urban forms might be examined in the light of some of the major goals of different cultures. The same approach might be applied with profit to current history. Significant contemporary plans for communities might be studied to see how adequately the goals are formulated and how explicitly they are related to the physical forms proposed.

The essence of progress for most disciplines lies in finding ways of systematizing as well as extending present knowledge. Goal-form studies offer a springboard for city and regional planning to achieve this extension and synthesis.

But aside from the elegance or logic of the theoretical framework, such an analytical system may find its ultimate usefulness in providing the raw material for planning decisions. Eventually it should tell the planner: "If your only aim is productive efficiency, and if other elements are like this, and if your society does not change, then this form is the best one yet found to do the job." This is the underpinning for what in part must remain a complex art, an art yet beyond the determinability of scientific knowledge in three ways. First, in that the more complex interactions are most likely to elude rigorous theory and depend on personal judgment. Second, because the method is indifferent to the choice of values, and the choice or clarification of objectives is a fundamental part of the art of planning. And thirdly, because the method can do no more than test form alternatives previously proposed. The creative task of imagining new form possibilities, as in all other realms of art and science, lies beyond it, although the analytical system may be suggestive in this work.

50. The Metropolis and Mental Life | Georg Simmel

For all the discussion of the influence of urban life on mental health, there still is no better description and analysis of the urban personality than this classic paper by Georg Simmel. The particular qualities of the urban mentality include an emphasis on cognitive modes of apprehending, responses based on rational calculation, precision and punctuality in the scheduling of events and commitments, a blasé attitude toward the world, reserve in personal encounters, and extreme individuation. Simmel looks upon the city not only as the propagator of this consciousness over the last several centuries, but also as the arena in which new forms of social organization, designed to support this type of personality, have been evolving.

It should be realized that in attributing the modes of personal adaptation described to the urban condition, Simmel, to some degree, is speaking metaphorically. The personality Simmel depicts is as much the heritage of modern, industrial, mass society as it is of the growth of cities and the increasing urbanization of populations.

Georg Simmel (1858–1918) was Professor of Sociology at the University of Strasbourg. His most well-known works are *Sociology of Religion* (English translation, 1959), *Conflict* (English translation, 1955), and *The Web of Group Affiliations* (English translation, 1955).

The deepest problems of modern life derive from the claim of the individual to preserve the autonomy and individuality of his existence in the face of overwhelming social forces, of historical heritage, of external culture, and of the technique of life. The fight with nature which primitive man has to wage for his *bodily* existence attains in this modern form its latest transformation. The eighteenth century called upon man to free himself of all the historical bonds in the state and in religion, in morals and in economics. Man's nature, originally good and common to all, should develop unhampered. In addition to more liberty, the nineteenth century demanded the functional specialization of man and his work; this specialization makes one individual incomparable to another, and each of them indispensable to the highest possible extent. However, this specialization makes each man the more directly dependent upon the supplementary activities of all others. Nietzsche sees the full development of the individual conditioned by the most ruthless struggle of individuals; socialism believes in the suppression of all competition for the same reason. Be that as it may, in all these positions the same basic motive is at work: the person resists to being leveled down and worn out by a social-technological mechanism. An inquiry into the inner meaning of specifically modern life and its products, into the soul of the cultural body, so to speak, must seek to solve the equation which structures like the metropolis set up between the individual and the super-individual contents of life. Such an inquiry must answer the question of how the personality accommodates itself in the adjustments to external forces. This will be my task today.

The psychological basis of the metropolitan type of individuality consists in the *intensification of nervous stimulation* which results from the swift and uninterrupted change of outer and inner stimuli. Man is a differentiating creature. His mind is stimulated by the difference between a momentary impression and the one which preceded it. Lasting impressions, impressions which differ only slightly from one another, impressions which take a regular and habitual course and show regular and habitual contrasts—all these use up, so to speak, less consciousness than does the rapid crowding of changing images, the sharp discontinuity in the grasp of a single glance, and the unexpectedness of on-rushing impressions. These are the psychological conditions which the metropolis creates. With each crossing of the street, with the tempo and multiplicity of economic, occupational and social life, the city sets up a deep contrast with small town and rural life with reference to the sensory foundations of psychic life. The metropolis exacts from man as a discriminating creature a different amount of consciousness than does rural life. Here the rhythm of life and sensory mental imagery flows more slowly, more habitually, and more evenly. Precisely in this connection the sophisticated character of metropolitan psychic life becomes understandable—as over against small town life which rests more upon deeply felt and emotional relationships. These latter are rooted in the more unconcious layers of the psyche and grow most readily in the steady rhythm of uninterrupted habituations. The intellect, however, has its locus in the transparent, conscious, higher layers of the psyche; it is the most adaptable of our inner forces. In order to accommodate to change and to the contrast of phenomena, the intellect does not require any shocks and inner upheavals; it is only through such upheavals that the more conservative mind could accommodate to the metropolitan rhythm of events. Thus the metropolitan type of man—which, of course, exists in a thousand individual variants—develops an organ protecting him against the threatening currents and discrepancies of his external environment which would uproot him. He reacts with his head instead of his heart. In this an increased awareness assumes the psychic prerogative. Metropolitan life, thus, underlies a heightened awareness and a predominance of intelligence in metropolitan man. The reaction to metropolitan phenomena is shifted to that organ which is least sensitive and quite remote from the depth of the personality. Intellectuality is thus seen to preserve subjective life against the overwhelming power of metropolitan life, and intellectuality branches out in many directions and is integrated with numerous discrete phenomena.

The metropolis has always been the seat of the money economy. Here the multiplicity and concentration of economic exchange gives an importance to the means of exchange which the scantiness of rural commerce would not have allowed. Money economy and the dominance of the intellect are intrinsically connected. They share a matter-of-fact attitude in dealing with men and with things; and, in this attitude, a formal justice is often coupled with an inconsiderate hardness. The intellectually sophisticated person is indifferent to all genuine individuality, because relationships and reactions result from it which cannot be exhausted with logical operations. In the same manner, the individuality of phenomena is not commensurate with the pecuniary principle. Money is concerned only with what is common to all: it asks for the exchange value, it reduces all quality and individuality to the question: How much? All intimate emotional relations between persons are founded in their individuality, whereas in rational relations man is reckoned with like a number, like an element which is in itself indifferent. Only the objective measurable achievement is of interest. Thus metropolitan man reckons with his merchants and customers, his domestic servants and often even with persons with whom he is obliged to have social intercourse. These features of intellectuality contrast with the nature of the small circle in which the inevitable knowledge of individuality as inevitably produces a warmer tone of behavior, a behavior which is beyond a mere objective balancing of service and return. In the sphere of the economic psychology of the small group it is of importance that under primitive conditions production serves the customer who orders the good, so that the producer and the consumer are acquainted. The modern metropolis, however, is supplied almost entirely by production for the market, that is, for entirely unknown purchasers who never personally enter the producer's actual field of vision. Through this anonymity the interests of each party acquire an unmerciful matter-of-factness; and the intellectually calculating economic egoisms of both parties need not fear any deflection because of the imponderables of personal relationships. The money economy dominates the metropolis; it has displaced the last survivals of domestic production and the direct barter of goods; it minimizes, from day to day, the amount of work ordered by customers. The matter-of-fact attitude is obviously so intimately interrelated with the money economy, which is dominant in the metropolis, that nobody

can say whether the intellectualistic mentality first promoted the money economy or whether the latter determined the former. The metropolitan way of life is certainly the most fertile soil for this reciprocity, a point which I shall document merely by citing the dictum of the most eminent English constitutional historian: throughout the whole course of English history, London has never acted as England's heart but often as England's intellect and always as her moneybag!

In certain seemingly insignificant traits, which lie upon the surface of life, the same psychic currents characteristically unite. Modern mind has become more and more calculating. The calculative exactness of practical life which the money economy has brought about corresponds to the ideal of natural science: to transform the world into an arithmetic problem, to fix every part of the world by mathematical formulas. Only money economy has filled the days of so many people with weighing, calculating, with numerical determinations, with a reduction of qualitative values to quantitative ones. Through the calculative nature of money a new precision, a certainty in the definition of identities and differences, an unambiguousness in agreements and arrangements has been brought about in the relations of life-elements— just as externally this precision has been effected by the universal diffusion of pocket watches. However, the conditions of metropolitan life are at once cause and effect of this trait. The relationships and affairs of the typical metropolitan usually are so varied and complex that without the strictest punctuality in promises and services the whole structure would break down into an inextricable chaos. Above all, this necessity is brought about by the aggregation of so many people with such differentiated interests, who must integrate their relations and activities into a highly complex organism. If all clocks and watches in Berlin would suddenly go wrong in different ways, even if only by one hour, all economic life and communication of the city would be disrupted for a long time. In addition an apparently mere external factor, long distances, would make all waiting and broken appointments result in an ill-afforded waste of time. Thus, the technique of metropolitan life is unimaginable without the most punctual integration of all activities and mutual relations into a stable and impersonal time schedule. Here again the general conclusions of this entire task of reflection become obvious, namely, that from each point on the surface of existence—however closely attached to the surface alone—one may drop a sounding into the depth of the psyche so that all the most banal externalities of life finally are connected with the ultimate decisions concerning the meaning and style of life. Punctuality, calculability, exactness are forced upon life by the complexity and extension of metropolitan existence and are not only most intimately connected with its money economy and intellectualistic character. These traits must also color the contents of life and favor the exclusion of those irrational, instinctive, sovereign traits and impulses which aim at determining the mode of life from within, instead of receiving the general and precisely schematized form of life from without. Even though sovereign types of personality, characterized by irrational impulses, are by no means impossible in the city, they are, nevertheless, opposed to typical city life. The passionate hatred of men like Ruskin and Nietzsche for the metropolis is understandable in these terms. Their natures discovered the value of life alone in the unschematized existence which cannot be defined with precision for all alike. From the same source of this hatred of the metropolis surged their hatred of money economy and of the intellectualism of modern existence.

The same factors which have thus coalesced into the exactness and minute precision of the form of life have coalesced into a structure of the highest impersonality; on the other hand, they have promoted a highly personal subjectivity. There is perhaps no psychic phenomenon which has been so unconditionally reserved to the metropolis as has the blasé attitude. The blasé attitude results first from the rapidly changing and closely compressed contrasting stimulations of the nerves. From this, the enhancement of metropolitan intellectuality, also, seems originally to stem. Therefore, stupid people who are not intellectually alive in the first place usually are not exactly blasé. A life in boundless pursuit of pleasure makes one blasé because it agitates the nerves to their strongest reactivity for such a long time that they finally cease to react at all. In the same way, through the rapidity and contradictoriness of their changes, more harmless impressions force such violent responses, tearing the nerves so brutally hither and thither that their last reserves of strength are spent; and if one remains in the same milieu they have no time to gather new strength. An incapacity thus emerges to react to new sensations with the appropriate energy. This constitutes that blasé attitude which, in fact, every metropolitan child shows when compared with children of quieter and less changeable milieus.

This physiological source of the metropolitan blasé attitude is joined by another source which flows from the money economy. The essence of the blasé attitude consists in the blunting of discrimination. This does not mean that the objects are not perceived, as in the case with the half-wit, but rather that the meaning and differing values of things, and thereby the things themselves, are experienced as insubstantial. They appear to the blasé person in an evenly flat and gray tone; no one object deserves preference over any other. This mood is the faithful subjective reflection of the completely internalized money economy. By being the equivalent to all the manifold things in one and the same way, money becomes the most frightful leveler. For money expresses all qualitative differences of things in terms of "how much?" Money, with all its colorlessness and indifference, becomes the common denominator of all values; irreparably it hollows out the core of things, their individuality, their specific value, and their incomparability. All things float with equal specific gravity in the constantly moving stream of money. All things lie on the same level and differ from one another only in the size of the area which they cover. In the individual case this coloration, or rather discoloration, of things through their money equivalence may be unnoticeably minute. However, through the relations of the rich to the objects to be had for money, perhaps even through the total character which the mentality of the contemporary public everywhere imparts to these objects, the exclusively pecuniary evaluation of objects has become quite considerable. The large cities, the main seats of the money exchange, bring the purchasability of things to the fore much more impressively than do smaller localities. That is why cities are also the genuine locale of the blasé attitude. In the blasé attitude the concentration of men and things stimulates the nervous system of the individual to its highest achievement so that it attains its peak. Through the mere quantitative intensification of the

same conditioning factors this achievement is transformed into its opposite and appears in the peculiar adjustment of the blasé attitude. In this phenomenon the nerves find in the refusal to react to their stimulation the last possibility of accommodating to the contents and forms of metropolitan life. The self-preservation of certain personalities is bought at the price of devaluating the whole objective world, a devaluation which in the end unavoidably drags one's own personality down into a feeling of the same worthlessness.

Whereas the subject of this form of existence has to come to terms with it entirely for himself, his self-preservation in the face of the large city demands from him a no less negative behavior of a social nature. This mental attitude of metropolitans toward one another we may designate, from a formal point of view, as reserve. If so many inner reactions were responses to the continuous external contacts with innumerable people as are those in the small town, where one knows almost everybody one meets and where one has a positive relation to almost everyone, one would be completely atomized internally and come to an unimaginable psychic state. Partly this psychological fact, partly the right to distrust which men have in the face of the touch-and-go elements of metropolitan life, necessitates our reserve. As a result of this reserve we frequently do not even know by sight those who have been our neighbors for years. And it is this reserve which in the eyes of the small-town people makes us appear to be cold and heartless. Indeed, if I do not deceive myself, the inner aspect of this outer reserve is not only indifference but, more often than we are aware, it is a slight aversion, a mutual strangeness and repulsion, which will break into hatred and fight at the moment of a closer contact, however caused. The whole inner organization of such an extensive communicative life rests upon an extremely varied hierarchy of sympathies, indifferences, and aversions of the briefest as well as of the most permanent nature. The sphere of indifference in this hierarchy is not as large as might appear on the surface. Our psychic activity still responds to almost every impression of somebody else with a somewhat distinct feeling. The unconscious, fluid and changing character of this impression seems to result in a state of indifference. Actually this indifference would be just as unnatural as the diffusion of indiscriminate mutual suggestion would be unbearable. From these typical dangers of the metropolis, indifference and indiscriminate suggestibility, antipathy protects us. A latent antipathy and the preparatory stage of practical antagonism effect the distances and aversions without which this mode of life could not at all be led. The extent and the mixture of this style of life, the rhythm of its emergence and disappearance, the forms in which it is satisfied —all these, with the unifying motives in the narrower sense, form the inseparable whole of the metropolitan style of life. What appears in the metropolitan style of life directly as dissociation is in reality only one of its elemental forms of socialization.

This reserve with its overtone of hidden aversion appears in turn as the form or the cloak of a more general mental phenomenon of the metropolis: it grants to the individual a kind and an amount of personal freedom which has no analogy whatsoever under other conditions. The metropolis goes back to one of the large developmental tendencies of social life as such, to one of the few tendencies for which an approximately universal formula can be discovered. The earliest phase of social formations found in historical as well as in contemporary social structures is this: a relatively small circle firmly closed against neighboring, strange, or in some way antagonistic circles. However, this circle is closely coherent and allows its individual members only a narrow field for the development of unique qualities and free, self-responsible movements. Political and kinship groups, parties and religious associations begin in this way. The self-preservation of very young associations requires the establishment of strict boundaries and a centripetal unity. Therefore they cannot allow the individual freedom and unique inner and outer development. From this stage social development proceeds at once in two different, yet corresponding, directions. To the extent to which the group grows—numerically, spatially, in significance and in content of life—to the same degree the group's direct, inner unity loosens, and the rigidity of the original demarcation against others is softened through mutual relations and connections. At the same time, the individual gains freedom of movement, far beyond the first jealous delimitation. The individual also gains a specific individuality to which the division of labor in the enlarged group gives both occasion and necessity. The state and Christianity, guilds and political parties, and innumerable other groups have developed according to this formula, however much, of course, the special conditions and forces of the respective groups have modified the general scheme. This scheme seems to me distinctly recognizable also in the evolution of individuality within urban life. The small-town life in Antiquity and in the Middle Ages set barriers against movement and relations of the individual toward the outside, and it set up barriers against individual independence and differentiation within the individual self.

These barriers were such that under them modern man could not have breathed. Even today a metropolitan man who is placed in a small town feels a restriction similar, at least, in kind. The smaller the circle which forms our milieu is, and the more restricted those relations to others are which dissolve the boundaries of the individual, the more anxiously the circle guards the achievements, the conduct of life, and the outlook of the individual, and the more readily a quantitative and qualitative specialization would break up the framework of the whole little circle.

The ancient *polis* in this respect seems to have had the very character of a small town. The constant threat to its existence at the hands of enemies from near and afar effected strict coherence in political and military respects, a supervision of the citizen by the citizen, a jealousy of the whole against the individual whose particular life was suppressed to such a degree that he could compensate only by acting as a despot in his own household. The tremendous agitation and excitement, the unique colorfulness of Athenian life, can perhaps be understood in terms of the fact that a people of incomparably individualized personalities struggled against the constant inner and outer pressure of a de-individualizing small town. This produced a tense atmosphere in which the weaker individuals were suppressed and those of stronger natures were incited to prove themselves in the most passionate manner. This is precisely why it was that there blossomed in Athens what must be called, without defining it exactly, "the general human character" in the intellectual development of our species. For we maintain factual as well as historical validity for the following connection: the most extensive and the most general contents and forms of life are most inti-

mately connected with the most individual ones. They have a preparatory stage in common, that is, they find their enemy in narrow formations and groupings the maintenance of which places both of them into a state of defense against expanse and generality lying without and the freely moving individuality within. Just as in the feudal age, the "free" man was the one who stood under the law of the land, that is, under the law of the largest social orbit, and the unfree man was the one who derived his right merely from the narrow circle of a feudal association and was excluded from the larger social orbit—so today metropolitan man is "free" in a spiritualized and refined sense, in contrast to the pettiness and prejudices which hem in the small-town man. For the reciprocal reserve and indifference and the intellectual life conditions of large circles are never felt more strongly by the individual in their impact upon his independence than in the thickest crowd of the big city. This is because the bodily proximity and narrowness of space make the mental distance only the more visible. It is obviously only the obverse of this freedom if, under certain circumstances, one nowhere feels as lonely and lost as in the metropolitan crowd. For here as elsewhere it is by no means necessary that the freedom of man be reflected in his emotional life as comfort.

It is not only the immediate size of the area and the number of persons which, because of the universal historical correlation between the enlargement of the circle and the personal inner and out freedom, has made the metropolis the locale of freedom. It is rather in transcending this visible expanse that any given city becomes the seat of cosmopolitanism. The horizon of the city expands in a manner comparable to the way in which wealth develops; a certain amount of property increases in a quasi-automatical way in ever more rapid progression. As soon as a certain limit has been passed, the economic, personal, and intellectual relations of the citizenry, the sphere of intellectual predominance of the city over its hinterland, grow as in geometrical progression. Every gain in dynamic extension becomes a step, not for an equal, but for a new and larger extension. From every thread spinning out of the city, ever new threads grow as if by themselves, just as within the city the unearned increment of ground rent, through the mere increase in communication, brings the owner automatically increasing profits. At this point, the quantitative aspect of life is transformed directly into qualitative traits of character. The sphere of life of the small town is, in the main, self-contained and autarchic. For it is the decisive nature of the metropolis that its inner life overflows by waves into a far-flung national or international area. Weimar is not an example to the contrary, since its significance was hinged upon individual personalities and died with them; whereas the metropolis is indeed characterized by its essential independence even from the most eminent individual personalities. This is the counterpart to the independence, and it is the price the individual pays for the independence, which he enjoys in the metropolis. [The most significant characteristic of the metropolis is this functional extension beyond its physical boundaries.] And this efficacy reacts in turn and gives weight, importance, and responsibility to metropolitan life. Man does not end with the limits of his body or the area comprising his immediate activity. Rather is the range of the person constituted by the sum of effects emanating from him temporally and spatially. In the same way, a city consists of its total effects which extend beyond its immediate confines. Only this

range is the city's actual extent in which its existence is expressed. This fact makes it obvious that individual freedom, the logical and historical complement of such extension, is not to be understood only in the negative sense of mere freedom of mobility and elimination of prejudices and petty philistinism. The essential point is that the particularity and incomparability, which ultimately every human being possesses, be somehow expressed in the working-out of a way of life. That we follow the laws of our own nature—and this after all is freedom—becomes obvious and convincing to ourselves and to others only if the expressions of this nature differ from the expressions of others. Only our unmistakability proves that our way of life has not been superimposed by others.

Cities are, first of all, seats of the highest economic division of labor. They produce thereby such extreme phenomena as in Paris the remunerative occupation of the *quatorzième*. They are persons who identify themselves by signs on their residences and who are ready at the dinner hour in correct attire, so that they can be quickly called upon if a dinner party should consist of thirteen persons. In the measure of its expansion, the city offers more and more the decisive conditions of the division of labor. It offers a circle which through its size can absorb a highly diverse variety of services. At the same time, the concentration of individuals and their struggle for customers compel the individual to specialize in a function from which he cannot be readily displaced by another. It is decisive that city life has transformed the struggle with nature for livelihood into an inter-human struggle for gain, which here is not granted by nature but by other men. For specialization does not flow only from the competition for gain but also from the underlying fact that the seller must always seek to call forth new and differentiated needs of the lured customer. In order to find a source of income which is not yet exhausted, and to find a function which cannot readily be displaced, it is necessary to specialize in one's services. This process promotes differentiation, refinement, and the enrichment of the public's needs, which obviously must lead to growing personal differences within this public.

All this forms the transition to the individualization of mental and psychic traits which the city occasions in proportion to its size. There is a whole series of obvious causes underlying this process. First, one must meet the difficulty of asserting his own personality within the dimensions of metropolitan life. Where the quantative increase in importance and the expense of energy reach their limits, one seizes upon qualitative differentiation in order somehow to attract the attention of the social circle by playing upon its sensitivity for differences. Finally, man is tempted to adopt the most tendentious peculiarities, that is, the specifically metropolitan extravagances of mannerism, caprice, and preciousness. Now, the meaning of these extravagances does not at all lie in the contents of such behavior, but rather in its form of "being different," of standing out in a striking manner and thereby attracting attention. For many character types, ultimately the only means of saving for themselves some modicum of self-esteem and the sense of filling a position is indirect, through the awareness of others. In the same sense a seemingly insignificant factor is operating, the cumulative effects of which are, however, still noticeable. I refer to the brevity and scarcity of the inter-human contacts granted to the metropolitan man, as compared with social intercourse in the small town. The temptation to appear "to the point,"

to appear concentrated and strikingly characteristic, lies much closer to the individual in brief metropolitan contacts than in an atmosphere in which frequent and prolonged association assures the personality of an unambiguous image of himself in the eyes of the other.

The most profound reason, however, why the metropolis conduces to the urge for the most individual personal existence —no matter whether justified and successful—appears to me to be the following: the development of modern culture is characterized by the preponderance of what one may call the "objective spirit" over the "subjective spirit." This is to say, in language as well as in law, in the technique of production as well as in art, in science as well as in the objects of the domestic environment, there is embodied a sum of spirit. The individual in his intellectual development follows the growth of this spirit very imperfectly and at an ever increasing distance. If, for instance, we view the immense culture which for the last hundred years has been embodied in things and in knowledge, in institutions and in comforts, and if we compare all this with the cultural progress of the individual during the same period—at least in high status groups—a frightful disproportion in growth between the two becomes evident. Indeed, at some points we notice a retrogression in the culture of the individual with reference to spirituality, delicacy, and idealism. This discrepancy results essentially from the growing division of labor. For the division of labor demands from the individual an ever more one-sided accomplishment, and the greatest advance in a one-sided pursuit only too frequently means dearth to the personality of the individual. In any case, he can cope less and less with the overgrowth of objective culture. The individual is reduced to a negligible quantity, perhaps less in his consciousness than in his practice and in the totality of his obscure emotional states that are derived from this practice. The individual has become a mere cog in an enormous organization of things and powers which tear from his hands all progress, spirituality, and value in order to transform them from their subjective form into the form of a purely objective life. It needs merely to be pointed out that the metropolis is the genuine arena of this culture which outgrows all personal life. Here in buildings and educational institutions, in the wonders and comforts of space-conquering technology, in the formations of community life, and in the visible institutions of the state, is offered such an overwhelming fullness of crystallized and impersonalized spirit that the personality, so to speak, cannot maintain itself under its impact. On the one hand, life is made infinitely easy for the personality in that stimulations, interests, uses of time and consciousness are offered to it from all sides. They carry the person as if in a stream, and one needs hardly to swim for oneself. On the other hand, however, life is composed more and more of these impersonal contents and offerings which tend to displace the genuine personal colorations and incomparabilities. This results in the individual's summoning the utmost in uniqueness and particularization, in order to preserve his most personal core. He has to exaggerate this personal element in order to remain audible even to himself. The atrophy of individual culture through the hypertrophy of objective culture is one reason for the bitter hatred which the preachers of the most extreme individualism, above all Nietzsche, harbor against the metropolis. But it is, indeed, also a reason why these preachers are so passionately loved in the metropolis

and why they appear to the metropolitan man as the prophets and saviors of his most unsatisfied yearnings.

If one asks for the historical position of these two forms of individualism which are nourished by the quantitative relation of the metropolis, namely, individual independence and the elaboration of individuality itself, then the metropolis assumes an entirely new rank order in the world history of the spirit. The eighteenth century found the individual in oppressive bonds which had become meaningless—bonds of a political, agrarian, guild, and religious character. They were restraints which, so to speak, forced upon man an unnatural form and outmoded, unjust inequalities. In this situation the cry for liberty and equality arose, the belief in the individual's full freedom of movement in all social and intellectual relationships. Freedom would at once permit the noble substance common to all to come to the fore, a substance which nature had deposited in every man and which society and history had only deformed. Besides this eighteenth-century ideal of liberalism, in the nineteenth century, through Goethe and Romanticism, on the one hand, and through the economic division of labor, on the other hand, another ideal arose: individuals liberated from historical bonds now wished to distinguish themselves from one another. The carrier of man's values is no longer the "general human being" in every individual, but rather man's qualitative uniqueness and irreplaceability. The external and internal history of our time takes its course within the struggle and in the changing entanglements of these two ways of defining the individual's role in the whole of society. It is the function of the metropolis to provide the arena for this struggle and its reconciliation. For the metropolis presents the peculiar conditions which are revealed to us as the opportunities and the stimuli for the development of both these ways of allocating roles to men. Therewith these conditions gain a unique place, pregnant with inestimable meanings for the development of psychic existence. The metropolis reveals itself as one of those great historical formations in which opposing streams which enclose life unfold, as well as join one another with equal right.

However, in this process the currents of life, whether their individual phenomena touch us sympathetically or antipathetically, entirely transcend the sphere for which the judge's attitude is appropriate. Since such forces of life have grown into the roots and into the crown of the whole of the historical life in which we, in our fleeting existence, as a cell, belong only as a part, it is not our task either to accuse or to pardon, but only to understand.[1]

NOTE

1. The content of this lecture by its very nature does not derive from a citable literature. Argument and elaboration of its major cultural-historical ideas are contained in my *Philosophie des Geldes* [The Philosophy of Money; München und Leipzig: Duncker und Humbolt, 1900].

PART VII

Urban
Policy and Planning

Most urban sociologists are not content only to describe and analyze existing conditions in urban communities. They also wish to project the future course of events, given observable trends in the present; to speculate about alternative and possibly more desirable future conditions for cities; and to discuss methods for planning social change. These concerns are reflected in this section. The selections are intended to indicate the relevance of the theoretical and research materials of previous sections to the major issues of urban policy and thus emphasize the bridge between scientific sociology and the normative and applied dimensions of the discipline.

The first section includes articles that report current ideas about the likely course of urban development in the United States. Most of the articles also imply a criticism of the values that urbanism in this country now seems to be following. The papers reflect virtually the full range of proposals now being set forth for reorganizing the urban social order, the cities, and the metropolitan regions. The proposals include the view that the era of the city is now past and its demise should be encouraged; that the growth of the spread city is the natural and salutary result of modern advances in technology; and that the great challenge for the future is to restore the viability of neighborhoods and local communities. The articles examine both the city as a physical entity and urbanization as a social and cultural phenomenon.

The readings in the second section deal with methods and processes for planning urban change. Whichever type of proposal for the future described in the first part is chosen, there will be questions about the chances for achieving it and how these chances can be maximized. Insofar as most organized human activity involves some degree of forethought and effort to attain goals, social change in some measure is always planned change. "Planned change" in the context of the planning professions, however, implies a particular strategy. Goals must be articulated and discussed. Procedures for evaluating the goals must be developed, hopefully in response to the wishes and needs of the public. Alternative means for attaining selected goals must be weighed. The implementation of this general process raises questions about the capacity of American society to adopt it, its compatibility with traditions of democracy and the rules of urban politics, and the readiness of the planning professions and disciplines like sociology to make an effective contribution.

Projected Trends and Policy Alternatives

51. Order in Diversity: Community Without Propinquity

Melvin M. Webber

Melvin Webber's paper discusses a major urban social trend of our time—the dissociation of the occupational and social groups with which people identify and which offer them emotional satisfaction from the locales and territories in which they reside. Webber details the various forces responsible for this split, including the rise of efficient mass communication systems, developments in transportation technology, and the increase in the size of urban and metropolitan populations. He takes a sanguine view of these forces and their impact, arguing that groups based on "place" are anachronistic, no longer of great social-psychological relevance to individuals, and that needs once served by them are now met by "interest communities." According to Webber, the development of the interest community explains the viability of spread city physical patterns, such as we find in Los Angeles and throughout the Southwestern states. It also has contributed to the emergence of wholly new and diverse subcultures, different from the ethnic subcultures based on European immigration. In Webber's view these original forms of social life provide a new foundation for sustaining American traditions of freedom, individuality, and social mobility.

Melvin M. Webber is Professor of City Planning at the University of California, Berkeley, and coauthor of *Explorations into Urban Structure* (1964). He is a former editor of the *Journal of the American Institute of Planners*.

The spatial patterns of American urban settlements are going to be considerably more dispersed, varied, and space-consuming than they ever were in the past—whatever metropolitan planners or anyone else may try to do about it. It is quite likely that most of the professional commentators will look upon this development with considerable disfavor, since these patterns will differ so markedly from our ideological precepts. But disparate spatial dispersion seems to be a built-in feature of the future—the complement of the increasing diversity that is coming to mark the processes of the nation's economy, its politics, and its social life. In addition, it seems to be the counterpart of a chain of technological developments that permit spatial separation of closely related people.

At this stage in the development of our thinking, students of the city are still unable to agree even on the nature of the phenomena they are dealing with. But it should surprise no one. For the plain fact of the matter is that, now, when the last rural threads of American society are being woven into the national urban fabric, the idea of city is becoming indistinguishable from the idea of society. If we lack consensus on an organizing conceptual structure of the city, it is mainly because we lack such a structure for society as a whole. The burden, then, rests upon all the arts, the humanities, and the sciences; and the task grows increasingly difficult as the complexity of contemporary society itself increases and as rapidly accumulating knowledge deprives us of what we had thought to be stable pillars of understanding.

In previous eras, when the goals, the beliefs, the behavior, and the roles of city folk were clearly distinguishable from those of their rural brethren, and when urban settlements were spatially discrete and physically bounded, schoolboy common sense was sufficient to identify the marks of "urbanness." Now all Americans are coming to share very similar cultural traits; the physical boundaries of settlements are disappearing; and the networks of interdependence among various groups are becoming functionally intricate and spatially widespread. With it all, the old symbols of order are giving way to the signs of newly emerging systems of organization that, in turn, are sapping the usefulness of our established concepts of order.

Especially during the last fifteen years, the rapid expansion of the large metropolitan settlements has been paralleled by a rising flood of commentary, reporting and evaluating this remarkable event; and we have developed a new language for dealing with it. Although the scholarly contributions to this new literature tend to be appropriately restrained and the journalistic and polemic contributions characteristically vituperative, the emerging patterns of settlement are typically greeted by both with disapproval if not frantic dismay. By now almost everyone knows that the low-density developments on the growing edge of the metropolis are a form of "cancerous growth," scornfully dubbed with the most denunciatory of our new lexicon's titles, "urban sprawl," "scatteration," "subtopia," and now "slurbs"—a pattern of development that "threatens our national heritage of open space" while "decaying blight rots out the city's heart" and a "demonic addiction to automobiles" threatens to "choke the life of our cities." Clearly, "our most cherished values" are imperiled by what is synoptically termed

From *Cities and Space: The Future Use of Urban Land*, Lowdon Wingo, Jr., ed. Published by The Johns Hopkins Press for Resources for the Future, Inc. Reprinted by permission.

"urban chaos." However, such analysis by cliché is likely to be helpful only as incitement to action; and action guided by obsolescent truths is likely to be effective only as reaffirmation of ideology.

We have often erred, I believe, in taking the visual symbols of urbanization to be marks of the important qualities of urban society; we have compared these symbols with our ideological precepts of order and found that they do not conform; and so we have mistaken for "urban chaos" what is more likely to be a newly emerging order whose signal qualities are complexity and diversity.

These changes now taking place in American society may well be compatible with—and perhaps call forth—metropolitan forms that are neither concentrated nor concentric nor contained. Sympathetic acceptance of this proposition might then lead us to new ways of seeing the metropolis, ways that are more sensitive to the environmental qualities that really matter. We might find new criteria for evaluating the changes in metropolitan spatial structure, suggesting that these changes are not as bad as we had thought. In turn, our approach to metropolitan spatial planning would be likely to shift from an ideological campaign to reconstruct the preconceived city forms that matched the social structures of past eras. Instead, we might see the emergence of a pragmatic, problem-solving approach in which the spatial aspects of the metropolis are viewed as continuous with and defined by the processes of urban society—in which space is distinguished from place, in which human interaction rather than land is seen as the fruitful focus of attention, and in which plans limited to the physical form of the urban settlement are no longer put forth as synoptic statements of our goals.

Metropolitan planning, then, would become the task of mutually accommodating changes in the spatial environment and changes in the social environment. And, because so much of the future is both unknowable and uncontrollable, the orientation of our efforts would shift from the inherently frustrating attempt to build the past in the future to the more realistic strategy of guiding change in desired directions—from a seeking after predesigned end-states to a continuing and much more complex struggle with processes of becoming.

So radical a revision of our thoughtways is not likely to come easily, for we are firmly devoted to the a priori values that we associate with land (especially with open land), with urban centers (especially with the more concentrated and culturally rich centers), and with certain visual attributes of the urban settlement (especially those features that result from the clean boundary line and the physical separation of different types of objects). And, above all, we are devoted to a unitary conception of order that finds expression in the separation of land uses, the classifiable hierarchy of centers, and the visual scene that conforms to classical canons.

So, let us briefly reconsider the idea of city and review some of the current and impending changes to see what their consequences are likely to be for future urbanization in the United States. We can then re-examine the idea of urban space to see how we might allocate it with some greater degree of rationality.

The Qualities of "Cityness"

In the literature and in the popular mind, the idea of city is imprecise: the terms "city," "urban," "metropolitan," and the various other synonyms are applied to a wide variety of phenomena. Sometimes we speak of the city as though it were simply an artifact—an agglomeration of buildings, roads, and interstitial spaces that marks the settlements of large numbers of people. On other occasions we refer not to physical buildings but to concentrations of physical bodies of humans, as they accumulate in nodal concentrations at higher densities than in "nonurban" places. At other times we refer to the spatial concentration of the places at which human activities are conducted. At still other times we mean a particular set of institutions that mark urban systems of human organization, where we mean to identify the organizational arrangements through which human activities are related to each other—the formal and the informal role allocating systems and the authority systems controlling human behavior. In turn, we sometimes refer to patterns of behavior, and sometimes we mean to distinguish the social value systems of those people and groups that are "urban" from those that are "nonurban."

The values, the ways of life, the institutional arrangements, and the kinds of activities that characterize people living in high-density clusters amidst large concentrations of buildings have been traditionally quite different from those of people living on farms or in small settlements. The large American city has been distinguished by a particular set of these characteristics, and yet, depending upon the specific purposes of our examination, not all these characteristics are necessary conditions of urbanness.

Large numbers of the people concentrated at the centers of New York, Chicago, and most other large metropolitan areas are recent migrants from "rural" areas. Their values, their life styles, their occupational skills, and their social institutions are certainly undergoing rapid change, but, nonetheless, these people are still rural villagers and are likely to retain many of their ways through at least another generation. After an intensive study of the residents of Boston's West End, Herbert Gans could best typify these second- and third-generation descendants of Italian immigrants as "urban villagers," whose way of life in the geographic center of a large metropolitan settlement has retained strong similarities to the patterns inherited from the villages of Italy.[1] The cultural diversity typified by the West Enders living adjacent to Beacon Hill residents—rather than any particular social pattern—is one of the distinctive marks of the city.

The city also is frequently equated with the greatest variety of economic activities; modern urbanization is often conceived as the counterpart of industrialization. Industrialization carries with it an increasingly fine division of labor and, hence, an increasing interdependence among men having specialized skills, who exchange many types of goods and services with one another. As the industrial development process evolves, increasing varieties of goods and services are produced; purchasing power and hence consumer demands rise; and the economy moves ever further from the self-sufficiency of nonurban primitive societies.

Relatively few products and occupations are exclusively associated with urbanization. At an early date in history we might have been able to distinguish nonurban production from urban production by separating the extractive industries (agriculture, forestry, fishing, and mining) and their related occupations from all others. But this is no longer clear. When the skills of farmers and miners are so closely approximating those of men who work in factories and executive suites, the distinction is hard to retain. And when fishermen live on San Francisco's Telegraph Hill, when oilworkers are an industrial elite, and when farmers and foresters hold university degrees and maintain laboratories and research plots, it becomes very difficult indeed to avoid the conclusion that these men are more firmly integrated into the urban society than are Boston's West Enders.

To say this is not to extend the proposition that the amalgamation of the once-rural and once-urban societies is accompanying a movement to an "other-directed" "mass society." The opportunities for a diversity of choices are clearly much greater in the United States today than they were 150 years ago when industrialization and the opportunities for social mobility were just beginning to stir new ideas and new ways into a poorly educated and unskilled population. Despite some gloomy predictions of the impending impacts of the mass communications media and of the pressures for conformity, the American population is realizing expanding opportunities for learning new ways, participating in more diverse types of activities, cultivating a wider variety of interests and tastes, developing greater capacities for understanding, and savoring richer experiences.

In the next fifty years it is likely that the rate at which the opportunities for learning and for social mobility expand will be even greater than in the last sixty years, when millions of uneducated immigrants from all over the world were integrated into every stratum of American society. Urban life, the communications media, and the public education systems are not likely to reduce all to a lowest common mediocrity. They are more likely to open doors to new ideas, to increased opportuni-

ties for being different from one's parents and others in the subculture in which one was reared—as those who have enjoyed these benefits already know and as the American Negroes are coming to know. Rather than a "mass culture" in a "mass society" the long-term prospect is for a maze of subcultures within an amazingly diverse society organized upon a broadly shared cultural base. This is the important meaning that the American brand of urbanization holds for human welfare.

During the past half-century the benefits of urbanization have been extended to an ever-growing proportion of the population: differentials in income distribution have narrowed; formal and informal educational opportunities have spread; Americans have flooded into the middle class. Access to information and ideas has thereby been extended to larger and larger percentages of the population, and this has been greatly abetted by the increasing ease of communication and transportation, *across* space, bringing books, periodicals, lectures, music, and personal observation to more and more people. As the individual's interests develop, he is better able to find others who share these interests and with whom he can associate. The communities with which he associates and to which he "belongs" are no longer only the communities of place to which his ancestors were restricted; Americans are becoming more closely tied to various interest communities than to place communities, whether the interest be based on occupational activities, leisure pastimes, social relationships, or intellectual pursuits. Members of interest communities within a freely communicating society need not be spatially concentrated (except, perhaps, during the formative stages of the interest community's development), for they are increasingly able to interact with each other wherever they may be located. This striking feature of contemporary urbanization is making it increasingly possible for men of all occupations to participate in the national urban life, and, thereby, it is destroying the once-valid dichotomies that distinguished the rural from the urban, the small town from the metropolis, the city from the suburb.

The Spatial City

Nothing that I have just said depends upon any specific assumption about the spatial patterns in which urbanites distribute themselves. I am contending that the essential qualities of urbanness are cultural in character, not territorial, that these qualities are not necessarily tied to the conceptions that see the city as a spatial phenomenon. But throughout all of human history these nonspatial qualities have indeed been typically associated with populations concentrated in high-density urban settlements.

Although, as some have suggested, there may be certain psychological propensities that induce people to occupy the same place, there seems to be almost universal agreement among urban theorists that population agglomeration is a direct reflection of the specialization of occupations and interests that is at the crux of urbanism and that makes individuals so dependent upon others. Dependency gets expressed as human interaction—whether through direct tactile or visual contact, face-to-face conversation, the transmission of information and ideas via written or electrical means, the exchange of money, or through the exchange of goods or services. In the nature of things, all types of interaction must occur through space, the scale of which depends upon locations of the parties to the transaction. It is also in the nature of things that there are energy and time costs in moving messages or physical objects through space; and people who interact frequently with certain others seek to reduce the costs of overcoming space by reducing the spatial distances separating them. Population clusterings are the direct expression of this drive to reduce the costs of interaction among people who depend upon, and therefore communicate with, each other.

As the large metropolitan areas in the United States have grown ever larger, they have simultaneously become the places at which the widest varieties of specialists offer the widest varieties of specialized services, thus further increasing their attractiveness to other specialists in self-propelling waves. Here a person is best able to afford the costs of maintaining the web of communications that he relies upon and that, in turn, lies at the heart of complex social systems. Here the individual has an opportunity to engage in diverse kinds of activities, to enjoy the affluence that comes with diversity of specialized offerings; here cultural richness is not withheld simply because it is too costly to get to the place where it can be had.

The spatial city, with its high-density concentrations of people and buildings and its clustering of activity places, appears, then, as the derivative of the communications patterns of the individuals and groups that inhabit it. They have come here to gain accessibility to others that inhabit it. They have come here to gain accessibility to others and at a cost that they are willing and can afford to pay. The larger the number of people who are accessible to each other, the larger is the likely number of contacts among pairs, and the greater is the opportunity for the individual to accumulate the economic and cultural wealth that he seeks.

Having come to the urban settlement in an effort to lower its costs of communication, the household or the business establishment must then find that location within the settlement which is suitable to it. The competition for space within the settlement results in high land rents near the center, where communication costs are low, and low land rents near the edge of the settlement, where communication costs are high. The individual locator must therefore allocate some portion of his location budget to communication costs and some portion to rents. By choosing an outlying location with its typically larger space he substitutes communication costs (expended in out-of-pocket transportation payments, time, inconvenience, and lost opportunities for communication with others) for rents. And, since rent levels decline slowly as one leaves the built-up portions of the urban settlement and enters the agricultural areas, while communication costs continue to rise as an almost direct function of distance, very few have been wont to move very far out from the center of the urban settlement. The effect has traditionally been a compact settlement pattern, having very high population and employment densities at the center where rents are also highest, and having a fairly sharp boundary at the settlement's margin.

It is this distinctive form of urban settlement throughout history that has led us to equate urbanness with agglomerations of population. Some architects, some city planners, and some geographers would carry it still further, insisting that the essential qualities of the city are population agglomerations and the accompanying building agglomerations themselves; and they argue that the configurations and qualities of spatial forms are themselves objects of value. The city, as artifact or as locational pattern of activity places, has thus become the city planners' specific object of professional attention throughout the world; and certain canons have evolved that are held as guides for designers of spatial cities.

Sensitive to the cultural and economic productivity of populations residing in large and highly centralized urban settlements, some city planners have deduced that the productivity is caused by the spatial form; and plans for future growth of the settlement have therefore been geared to perpetuating or accentuating large, high-density concentrations. Other city planners, alert to a different body of evidence, have viewed the large, high-density city as the locus of filth, depravity, and the range of social pathologies that many of its residents are heir to. With a similar hypothesis of spatial environmental determinism and looking back with envy upon an idealization of the small-town life that predominated in the eighteenth and early nineteenth centuries, this group of planners has proposed that the large settlements be dismantled, that their populations and industries be redistributed to new small towns, and that all future settlements be prevented from growing beyond some predetermined, limited size.

Others have offered still other ideal forms. The metropolitan plan for the San Francisco Bay Area and Washington's Year 2000 plan propose star-like configurations surrounding a dominant center, with major subcenters along each of the radials.[2] The Greater London Plan calls for a somewhat similar pattern of subcenters surrounding central London, but these are to be spatially free-standing towns at the outer edge of a permanent greenbelt.

Alert to the external economies that accompany large agglomerations, while sensitive to the problems that accompany high density and large size. Catherine Bauer Wurster has eschewed both the British New Towns doctrine and the American metropolitan growth patterns. She urges instead that major new settlements be separated from one another and limited to some half-million inhabitants each.[3] Others have proposed slightly different modifications to the Bay Area–Washington, the Greater London, and the Wurster schemes in the official plans prepared for Detroit, Atlanta, and Denver.

Despite some important differences among these proposals, however, they all conform to two underlying conceptions from which they stem:

1. The settlement is conceived as a spatial *unit*, almost as though it were an independent artifact—an independent object separable from others of its kind. The unit is spatially delineated by a surrounding band of land which, in contrast to the unit, has foliage but few people or buildings. In some of the schemes subunits are similarly delineated by green-belts; in others they are defined as subcenters, as subsidiary density peaks of resident and/or employed populations; but the unitary conception holds for all.

2. Whether the desired population size within the unit is to be large or small, whether subunits are to be fostered either as subsettlements within greenbelts or as subcenters within continuously built-up areas, the territorial extent of the "urbanized area" is to be deliberately contained, and a surrounding permanent greenbelt is to be maintained. The doctrine calls for distinct separation of land that is "urbanized" and land that is not. The editors of *Architectural Review* stated the contention with effective force, in "Outrage" and "Counter Attack," when they pleaded, for sharply bounded separation of city, suburb, and country:

> The crime of subtopia is that it blurs the distinction between places. It does so by smoothing down the differences between types of environment—town and country, country and suburb, suburb and wild—rather than directly between one town and another. It doesn't deliberately set out to make Glen Shiel look like Helvellyn; it does so in fact by introducing the same overpowering alien elements—in this case blanket afforestation and the wire that surrounds it—into both. The job of this issue [of the magazine] is to get straight the basic divisions between types of environment, and to suggest a framework for keeping each true to itself and distinct from its neighbors.[4]

Behind both ideas are the more fundamental beliefs that urban and rural comprise a dualism that should be clearly expressed in the physical and spatial form of the city, that orderliness depends upon boundedness, and that boundaries are in some way barriers. I have already indicated that the social and economic distinctions between urban and rural are weakening, and it is now appropriate that we examine the spatial counterparts of this blurring nonspatial boundary. I believe that the unitary conceptions of urban places are also fast becoming anachronistic, for the physical boundaries are rapidly collapsing; and, even where they are imposed by legal restraints, social intercourse, which has never respected physical boundaries anyway, is increasingly able to ignore them.

Emerging Settlement Patterns

It is a striking feature of current, physical urbanization patterns that rapid growth is still occurring at the sites of the largest settlements and that these large settlements are to be found at widely scattered places on the continent. The westward population movement from the Atlantic Seaboard has not been a spatially homogeneous spread, but has leapfrogged over vast spaces to coagulate at such separated spots as the sites of Denver, Houston, Omaha, Los Angeles, San Francisco, and Seattle.

This is a very remarkable event. Los Angeles, San Francisco, San Diego, and Seattle, as examples, have been able to grow to their present proportions very largely as the result of a rapid expansion of industries that are located far from both their raw materials and their customers. The most obvious of these, of course, are the producers of aircraft, missiles, and electronic equipment which use materials manufactured in the East, in Canada, and throughout the world, and then sell most of their product to firms and governments that are also spatially dispersed. They seem to have been attracted to the West by its climate, its natural amenities, and by a regional style of life that their employees seem to find attractive. Once there, they are highly dependent upon good long-distance transportation. And, since successful management of these industries depends upon good access to information about technical processes, about markets, and about finance, they are equally dependent upon good long-distance communication.

It seems clear that the scale of growth there would not have been possible without first the railroad, ocean freighters, and the telegraph and then the telephone, the highways, and the airlines. All of these changes, we must remember, are very recent occurrences in the history of urban man. (The centennial of the Pony Express

was celebrated in 1961, and the Panama Canal is scarcely two generations old.) These technological changes have made it possible for individual establishments to operate efficiently thousands of miles away from the national business center at New York, the government center at Washington, and the industrial belt between Boston and Chicago, to which they are very intimately linked. At least at this territorial scale, it is apparent that economic and social propinquity is not dependent upon spatial propinquity.

These distant metropolitan areas continue to attract a wide variety of specialized firms and individuals, and most of them still prefer to locate *inside* these metropolitan settlements. It is impressive that the television industry, which requires such intricate co-ordination and split-second timing, has chosen to operate primarily out of two metropolitan areas at opposite ends of a continent, yet its establishments are located within the midst of each. Similarly, the financial institutions and administrative offices of corporations which also rely upon quick access to accurate information are attracted to locations within the midst of these settlements. The reasons are apparent.

Just as certain businesses must maintain rapid communications with linked establishments in other metropolitan areas throughout the nation and throughout the world, so too must they maintain easy communication with the vast numbers of local establishments that serve them and that in turn are served by them. The web of communication lines among interdependent establishments within the large urban settlements is extremely strong. Today it is possible to break off large chunks of urban America and place them at considerable distances from the national urban center in the East, but it does not yet seem possible for these chunks to be broken into smaller pieces and distributed over the countryside.

Nevertheless, the events that have marked the growth of widely separated metropolitan settlements force us to ask whether the same kinds of processes that induced their spatial dispersion might not also come to influence the spatial patterns of individual metropolitan settlements as well. A business firm can now move from Philadelphia to Los Angeles and retain close contact with the business world in the East while enjoying the natural amenities of the West; yet it has little choice but to locate within the Los Angeles Basin where it would be readily accessible to a large labor force, to suppliers, and to service establishments. It is attracted to the metropolitan settlement rather than the more pleasant Sierra Nevada foothills because here the costs of overcoming distance to linked establishments are lower. *The unique commodity that the metropolitan settlement has to offer is lower communication costs.* This is the paramount attraction for establishments and, hence, the dominant reason for high-density agglomeration.

The validity of this proposition would be apparent if we were to imagine a mythical world in which people or goods or messages could almost instantaneously be transported between any two establishments—say, in one minute of time and without other costs of any sort. One could then place his home on whichever mountaintop or lakeside he preferred and get to work, school, or shops anywhere in the world. Goods could be distributed to factories or homes without concern for their distances from the point of shipment. Decision-makers in industry and government could have immediate access to any available information and could come into almost immediate face-to-face contact with each other irrespective of where their offices were located, just as friends and relatives could visit in each other's livingrooms, wherever each might live. With transport costs between establishments reduced to nearly zero, few would be willing to suffer the costs of high density and high rent that are associated with high accessibility to the center of the metropolitan settlements. And yet, accessibility to all other establishments would be almost maximized, subject only to the one-minute travel time and to restraints of social distance. Under these assumptions, urban agglomerations would nearly disappear. Were it not that the immobility of certain landscape and climatic features would induce many household and business establishments to seek locations at places of high natural amenity, that some people may have attitudinal preferences for spatial propinquity to others, and that some industrial processes cannot tolerate even one-minute travel times between industrial establishments, we would expect a virtually homogeneous dispersion across the face of the globe.

Of course, zero communication costs are an impossibility, but the history of civilization has been marked by a continuous decline in the effective costs of communication. Time costs and the costs of inconvenience between any given pair of geographic points have declined consistently; and the financial capacity to bear high dollar-costs has tended to counterbalance the high expenses attached to high speed and high comfort. The concomitant effect of very high speeds between distant points and slower speeds between nearby points has been nearly to equate the travel times between pairs of points on the surface of the earth. Certain improvements in transportation equipment that are now becoming possible could gradually reduce differential time costs of travel to nearly zero. The effects of this potential change on the spatial patterns of settlements would be dramatic.

Some Potential Changes in Transportation and Communication Technology

We are all aware of the fact that, within metropolitan areas in the United States, the widespread use of the automobile has freed the family's residence from the fixed transit lines that had induced the familiar star-like form of settlement. The pattern of residential scatteration at the growing edges of most metropolitan areas would clearly not have happened without the private car; indeed, this pattern was not apparent until the auto induced the suburban developments of the twenties. The telephone, the motor truck, and transportable water, fuels, and electricity have further abetted this lacy settlement boundary. And, of course, all these trends have been further nurtured by a rising level of average family income and by credit arrangements that have made it possible for the average family to choose—and get—one or more autos, telephones, and houses. Similarly the new communication devices, higher corporate incomes, and federal financial encouragement have made it possible for some foot-loose manufacturers and certain types of commercial establishments to locate in relatively outlying portions of metropolitan settlements.

To date, however, very few of these families and business establishments have chosen to locate very far from the metropolitan center, because the costs of maintaining the web of communications that are essential to their cultural and their economic well-being would simply be too high. Even though they might like to locate in a mountain setting, the benefits that would accrue from so pleasant a habitat seem to be far outweighed by the difficulties of maintaining contact with the various specialists they rely upon.

But today a great many of them are much farther away from the metropolitan center, in mileage distance, than they were even fifteen years ago, not to mention the differences that have occurred since the beginning of the century. Even so, a great many have chosen outlying locations without increasing their time distances to the center. Increased mileage distance carries a necessary increase in dollar costs, but the more sensitive component of communications costs in the locator's calculus seems to be the time costs, as the recent traffic studies and the phenomenal rise in long-distance telephone usage indicate.

Increases in travel speeds within most of the metropolitan settlements have been relatively modest as compared to the changing speeds of intermetropolitan travel that the airlines have brought. In part because the potentials of the new freeway systems have been so severely restrained by the countereffects of congestion and in part because the improvements in transit systems have been rare indeed, peak-hour travel speeds have not increased appreciably. But off-peak increases have been great in some places, and some changes are imminent that are likely to cause an emphatic change.

Where the urban freeway systems are uncongested, they have induced at least a doubling in speed and in some places a quadrupling—and the freeways do run freely in off-peak hours. As the urban freeway systems that are now under construction are extended farther out and connected to one another, an unprecedented degree of freedom and flexibility will be open to the traveler for moving among widely separated establishments in conducting his affairs. A network of freeways, such as that planned for the Los Angeles area, will make many points highly accessible, in direct contrast to the single high-access point that resulted from the traditional radial transit net. Even if new or improved high-speed fixed-route transit systems were to be superimposed on freeway networks, the freeway's leveling effect on accessibility would still be felt. And the positive advantages of automobiles over transit systems—affording, at their best, door-to-door, no-wait, no-transfer, private, and flexible-route service—make it inconceivable that they will be abandoned for a great part of intrametropolitan travel or that the expansion of the freeway systems on which they depend will taper off. We would do well, then, to accept the private vehicle as an indispensable medium of metropolitan interaction—more, as an important instrument of personal freedom.

There has been a great deal of speculation about characteristics of the evolutionary successor to the automobile, but it is probably too early to predict the exact form it will take. I would hazard some confident guesses, though, that it will not be a free-flight personal vehicle because the air-traffic control problems appear to be insoluble, that it will be automatically guided when on freeways and hence capable of traveling safely at much higher speeds, but that it will continue to be adaptable to use on local streets. If bumper-to-bumper movement at speeds of 150 miles per hour or more were to be attained, as current research-and-development work suggests is possible, greater per lane capacities and greater speeds would be realized than any rapid transit

proposals now foresee for traditional train systems. When these on-route operating characteristics are coupled with the door-to-door, no-wait, no-transfer, privacy and flexible route-end service of the personal vehicle, such a system would appear to be more than competitive with any type of rapid transit service now planned—with two important qualifications. The costs would have to be reasonable, and the land use patterns would have to be compatible with the operating characteristics of the transportation system.

A system that would be capable of moving large numbers of cars into a small area within a short period of time would face the parking dilemma in compounded form. Although unpublished reports of the engineers at The RAND Corporation suggest that it would be mechanically possible and perhaps even economically feasible to build sufficient underground parking facilities on Manhattan to store private cars for all employees and shoppers who arrive there daily, the problem of moving large numbers of cars into and out of the garages during brief periods would call for so elaborate and costly a maze of access ramps as to discourage any serious effort to satisfy a parking demand of such magnitude. Before such an all-out effort is made to accommodate the traditional central business district to the private motor car, the summary effect of thousands of locational decisions by individual entrepreneurs would probably have been to evolve a land use pattern that more readily conforms to the auto's operating characteristics. With further increases in mass auto usage—especially if it could attain bumper-to-bumper, 150 mph movement— we are bound to experience a dispersion of many traditionally central activities to outlying but highly accessible locations. The dispersed developments accompanying the current freeways suggest the type of pattern that seems probable. Here, again, Los Angeles offers the best prototype available.

In What Sense Is Urban Space a Resource?

I have been suggesting that the quintessence of urbanization is not population density or agglomeration but specialization, the concomitant interdependence, and the human interactions by which interdependencies are satisfied. Viewed from this orientation, the urban settlement is the spatial adaptation to demands of dependent activities and specialists for low communication costs. It is helpful, therefore, to view the spatial city as a communications system, as a vastly complex switchboard through which messages and goods of various sorts are routed.

Information, ideas, and goods are the very stuff of civilization. The degree to which they are distributed to all individuals within a population stands as an important indicator of human welfare levels—as a measure of cultural and economic income. Of course, the distribution of this income is determined predominantly by institutional rather than spatial factors— only the rare Utopian has even suggested · that the way to "the good society" is through the redesign of the spatial city. And yet, space intervenes as a friction against all types of communication. Surely,· salvation does not lie in the remodeled spatial city; but, just as surely, levels of cul-· tural and economic wealth could be increased if the spatial frictions that now limit the freedom to interact were reduced. This is the important justification for city planning's traditional concern with space.

In the very nature of Euclidean geometry, the space immediately surrounding an urban settlement is limited. Given a transportation communication technology and its accompanying cost structure, close-in space has greater value than distant space, since nearby inhabitants have greater opportunities to interact with others in the settlement.

But as the transportation-communication technologies change to permit interaction over greater distances at constant or even at falling costs, more and more outlying space is thereby brought into the market, and the relative value of space adjacent to large settlements falls. Urban space, as it has been associated with the economies of localization and agglomeration, is thus a peculiar resource, characterized by increasing supply and by ever-declining value.

These cost-reducing and space-expanding effects of transportation-communication changes are being reinforced by most of the technological and social changes we have recently seen. The patterns of social stratification and of occupations, the organizational structures of businesses and of governments, the goods and the ideas that are being produced, and the average individual's ranges of interests and opportunities are steadily becoming more varied and less tradition-bound. In a similar way, the repercussions of these social changes and the direct impacts of some major technological changes have made for increasing diversity in the spatial structures of urban settlements.

· Projections of future change, and especially changes in the technologies of transportation and communication, suggest that much greater variation will be possible in the next few decades. It is becoming difficult to avoid the parallel prediction that totally new spatial forms are in the offing.

· To date, very few observers have gone

so far as to predict that the nodally concentric form, that has marked every spatial city throughout history, could give way to homogeneous dispersion of the nation's population across the continent; but the hesitancy may stem mainly from the fact that a non-nodal city of this sort would represent such a huge break with the past. Yet, never before in human history has it been so easy to communicate across long distances. Never before have men been able to maintain intimate and continuing contact with others across thousands of miles; never has intimacy been so independent of spatial propinquity. Never before has it seemed possible to build an array of specialized transportation equipment that would permit speed of travel to increase directly with mileage length of trip, thus having the capability of uniting all places within a continent with almost-equal time distance. And never before has it seemed economically feasible for the nodally cohesive spatial form that marks the contemporary large settlement to be replaced by drastically different forms, while the pattern of internal centering itself changes or, perhaps, dissolves.

A number of informed students have read the same evidence and have drawn different conclusions. Observing that the consequences of ongoing technological changes are spatially neutral, they suggest that increased ease of intercourse makes it all the more possible for households and business establishments to locate in the midst of high-density settlements. This was essentially the conclusion that Haig drew when he wrote, ". . . Instead of explaining why so large a portion of the population is found in urban areas, one must give reasons why that portion is not even greater. The question is changed from 'Why live in the city?' to 'Why not live in the city?'"[5]

I am quick to agree that many of the recent and the imminent developments are ambiguous with respect to space. They could push urban spatial structure toward greater concentricity, toward greater dispersion, or, what I believe to be most likely, toward a very heterogeneous pattern. Since administrative and executive activities are so sensitive to the availability and immediacy of accurate information—and hence of good communications—they may be the bellwether of future spatial adjustments of other activities as well, and they therefore warrant our special attention.

The new electronic data-processing equipment and the accompanying procedures permit much more intensive use of downtown space than was ever possible with nonautomated office processes; but they can operate quite as effectively from an outlying location, far removed from the executive offices they serve. The sites adjacent to the central telephone exchange may offer competitive advantages over all others, and establishments relying upon computers, that in turn are tied to the long-distance telephone lines, seem to be clustering about the hub of those radial lines in much the manner that they once clustered about the hub of the radial trolley lines. At the same time we can already observe that outlying computer centers are attracting establishments that use their services.

The recent history of office construction in midtown New York, northwest Washington, and in the centers of most large metropolitan areas is frequently cited as clear evidence of the role that face-to-face contacts play in decision-making and of the importance of spatial propinquity in facilitating face-to-face contact. And yet, simultaneously, large numbers of executive offices have followed their production units to suburban locations, and some have established themselves in outlying spots, spatially separated from their production units and from all other establishments. The predominant movement in the New York area has been to the business center, but the fact that many have been able to move outside the built-up area suggests that a new degree of locational freedom is being added.

The patterns in Washington, Detroit, and Los Angeles clearly suggest that the walking-precinct type of central business district (CBD), with its restricted radius, compactness, and fixed-route transit service, is not the only effective spatial pattern for face-to-face communication. Washington's governmental and private offices are dispersed over so wide an area that few are within easy walking distance of each other. Meetings typically call for a short auto trip, either by taxi or private car. In Detroit and especially in Los Angeles, establishment types that have traditionally been CBD-oriented are much more dispersed throughout the settled area. Relying heavily upon the automobile, Los Angelenos seem to be able to conduct their business face-to-face, perhaps as frequently as do New Yorkers. Highly specialized firms employing highly specialized personnel are located in all parts of the Los Angeles Basin—in some places within fairly compact subcenters, in other places in quite scattered patterns. But the significant feature is this: few linked establishments are within walking distances of each other, and an auto trip is thus an adjunct to a face-to-face meeting.

Even with a moderate speed of automotive travel, considerable mileage can be covered within a short time. At door-to-door average speeds of only 15 mph, it takes about four minutes to get to another's office a mile away; and, especially for long-distance trips, average travel speeds are considerably higher, probably exceeding 50 mph door-to-door off-peak in Los Angeles. Although I know of no measurements of this sort having been made, I would guess that (after adjusting for the total number of establishments within the metropolitan area) an establishment on Wilshire Boulevard in Los Angeles has as many linked establishments within a given time-distance as does a similar establishment at Rockefeller Center.

Comparable studies of traffic patterns in New York and Los Angeles will be completed within a few years, and it will then be possible to compare travel-time costs to commuters and shoppers, as well as to men who need to transact business face-to-face. I think it is safe, to predict, however, that large differences will not be found, that Los Angelenos are just about as accessible to their work places and to the various urban service establishments as are New Yorkers, and perhaps even more accessible. Moreover, I would expect to find that Los Angeles residents maintain as diverse a range of contacts, that they interact with others as frequently and as intensively, that they are participants in as broad and as rich a range of communications as the resident of any other metropolitan area. I believe the popular notion among outsiders that Los Angeles is a cultural desert, is a myth whose basis lies in the ideology of metropolitan form. We have equated cultural wealth and urbanity with high-density cities; since Los Angeles is not spatially structured in the image of the culturally rich cities we have known, some have therefore inferred that life there must be empty and deprived of opportunity. It is strikingly apparent, however, that nearly seven million people and their employers seem to find this an amiable habitat and that Easterners continue to arrive at a rapid rate. It is also apparent that a considerable part of its attractiveness has been the natural setting and the opportunities to engage in activities outside the urban settlement itself.

If most of the social and technological changes I have mentioned were in fact neutral in their spatial impacts, this itself would represent a powerful new factor at work on the spatial organization of cities. Prior dominant modes of transportation and communication, traditional forms of organization of business and government, the older and more rigid patterns of economic and social stratification, and prior educational and occupational levels and opportunities all exerted positive pressures to population agglomeration around dominant high-density business-industrial-residential centers. If these pressures for concentration and concentricity are ebbing, the effects of counter processes will be increasingly manifest.

The Ascent of Amenity as Locational Determinant

Throughout our history, the locations and the internal arrangements of our cities have been predominantly shaped by the efforts of individual establishments to lower the costs of transporting goods, information, and people. If our speculations concerning the secular declines in these costs should prove to be valid, we can expect that the nontransportable on-site amenities will come to predominate as locational determinants.

Population growth in California, Arizona, Florida, and other naturally favored places can be largely attributed to the favorable climate and landscape. At smaller scale, in turn, new residential accommodations and new industrial es-

tablishments are being developed at those sites whose natural conditions are most favored by groups of various types. This is a very remarkable development; the luxury of locational choice is now being extended to ever-increasing numbers within an increasingly diverse population.

During the past sixty years the work week of American manufacturing workers has fallen from about 59 hours to something under 40, while wages have risen from an average of about $450 per year to about $4,700 (in constant 1947–49 dollars from about $1,250 to about $4,000 per year). The prospects are for a continuing reduction in working hours and for a continuing rise in disposable income, perhaps accompanied by a narrowing of the extremes in income distribution. When compounded by the availability of credit, higher levels of education, lowering ages of retirement, and a further dispersion of middle-class ways to larger proportions of the population, the range of choice open to most people—including the range of locational choice—is certain to increase greatly.

Although it is undoubtedly true that the success of recent suburban developments to some extent reflects rather limited choices available within the contemporary metropolitan housing markets, it is also apparent that for most of their inhabitants these developments represent marked improvements in living standards. Most suburbanites in the upper-income brackets have made free locational choices, since they could afford more central sites. Even a recent disenchantment with suburban life has not refuted the compatibility of low-density housing developments with middle-class preferences for spaciousness, with middle-class attitudes about distance, with current status criteria, and with child-oriented family life.

Among certain professional groups that have recently been in high demand (most notably those specialists associated with research and development in the electronics, missiles, and petrochemical industries) the preferences for suburban-type residential environments within pleasant natural settings seem to have been so strong as to have affected the locations of these industries in California, Long Island, and the suburbs of Boston. To attract these skilled persons, whole industries have moved. Very few have chosen locations very far removed from the universities and the business complexes to which they are closely linked, but it is significant that they have tended to select outlying spots. With increasing leisure time, increasing mobility via automobiles, and increased spending power, we can expect the average family to take much greater advantage of outdoor recreational activities available in the countryside accessible to its home. As transportation facilities are improved and week-ends lengthen, families will be able to travel longer distances than before. Some will prefer to locate their homes near recreational facilities, and the recreation place might even replace the work place as the major determinant of residential locations.

The range of locational choice is broadening at the same time that changing characteristics of the national population are breeding increasing diversity in people's locational preferences. Simultaneously, all segments of the national population are being woven into an increasingly complex social, political, and economic web, such that no person and no group is entirely independent of all other persons and all other groups. The growing pluralism in American society is more than a growing multiplicity of types of people and institutions. Each person, each group bound by a community of interests, is integrally related to each other person and group, such that each is defined by its relations to all others and that a change in one induces a change in all others.

The kinds of information that can be read from maps showing urbanized areas or land use patterns are therefore likely to be misleading. Suggesting that settlements of one size or another are in some way independent units, in some way separated from each other and from the spatial field in which they lie, maps of this sort miss the essential meaning of urbanization. Whether the maps represent existing patterns or plans for future patterns, they present static snapshots of locational patterns of people or buildings or activity places and say nothing (except as the reader may interpolate) about the human interaction patterns that are at the heart of complex social processes. When people can interact with others across great distances and when they can readily move themselves into face-to-face positions as the need to do so arises, it scarcely matters whether a greenbelt intervenes or whether the space between them and their associates is used for houses and factories. Surely Los Angeles is an integral part of the national urban system, despite the 2,500-mile-wide greenbelt that separates it from New York. Surely Bakersfield is as integral a part of the southern California urban system as is Pasadena, despite the intervention of the Tehachapi Mountains and some 90 miles. Surely the researchers in Los Alamos are as much a part of the world-wide community of atomic physicists, as if they happened to be at Brookhaven or Berkeley or Argonne.

Spatial separation or propinquity is no longer an accurate indicator of functional relations; and, hence, mere locational pattern is no longer an adequate symbol of order. The task of the spatial planner is therefore considerably more difficult than we have traditionally thought. The normative guides that we have used have been oriented primarily to the form aspects that can be represented on maps and have applied static and simplistic concepts of order that are not consonant with the processes of growing and complex urban systems.

It is a fairly simple matter to prepare a land use plan for a territory, if its spatial organization is to follow any one of the simple universal models that city planners have promulgated. Sites for "self-contained and balanced" new towns are readily found, and site plans are readily made. It is quite another matter to get the townspeople to behave as though they comprised a "self-contained and balanced community"—nor would many of us really want them to be deprived of the enriched lives that come with free communication with the "outside world." Plans for increased centrality and higher density can also be portrayed readily within the traditional idiom of land use planning; but, again, it is hard to believe that the advocates would be willing to deprive the residents of the opportunities to choose outlying locations. Nevertheless, whether small town or large concentration, the rules are clear and simple; the variables to be accounted are limited in number and in complexity; and the solution is determined before the problem is attacked.

It is considerably more difficult, however, to plan for diversity in settlement and land use patterns, for here the formal rules of urban form are not very helpful. No single scheme can be taken as a rule to be applied to all establishments and to all places. Rather, the locational requirements of the many diverse groups of establishments must establish the rules,

and the optimum pattern would then resemble none of the doctrinal models.

The optimum land use pattern of the future metropolis is likely to be highly diversified. Since transportation costs will never fall to zero, the external economies associated with clusterings of similar and dissimilar establishments will continue to induce certain types of establishments to seek centers and subcenters of many types. Some of these will be of the familiar employment and shopping-center types, whether in the CBD or in the unitary "regional center" molds. Other establishments, mutually linked to a third type of establishment, will undoubtedly continue to cluster about it wherever it may be, whether it be a stock exchange, a major university, an airport, or a large manufacturer or retailer. Other establishments will form subcenters, largely as a result of their mutual desire to occupy a particularly pleasant site, although such growth inducements are self-limiting, of course. Those establishments that depend upon good access to information will undoubtedly continue to seek locations that best facilitate easy communication. For some, formal meeting places that accommodate scheduled encounters will suffice, and for many of these the airports and the convention halls are already serving a large part of their requirements. Others, such as the ladies' garment industry and the securities exchanges, may be so sensitive to changes in styles and/or market conditions as to induce even more intensive business concentrations of the sort that Manhattan typifies.

Simultaneously, the optimum patterns would include scattered developments for a great variety of establishments in a great variety of land use mixes and density patterns. For those manufacturers who prefer to locate factories and workers' housing near mountain skiing and hiking areas, for those lone wolves who prefer solitude and possibly a part-time farm, and for all those for whom a high-speed auto drive is no commuting deterrent, we can expect (and should encourage) scattered developments of the type now becoming common east of Boston and north of New York.

The future land use pattern will certainly not be one of homogeneous dispersion. Transportation and communication costs will never permit that, and the very uneven distribution of favored climates and landscapes would strongly discourage it. But a much greater degree of dispersion is both likely and desirable, while centers and subcenters of various compositions and densities persist and grow in a range of sizes spanning the whole spectrum from "center" to "sprawl."

If we are willing to accept the idea that the optimum urban settlement and land use patterns are likely to be as pluralistic as society itself, then the conceptions of spatial order will follow from our conceptions of social order. Our spatial plans, then, will be plans for diversity, designed to accommodate the disparate demands upon land and space made by disparate individuals and groups that are bound up in the organized complexity of urban society.

Planned Allocation of Urban Space

One of the planner's major tasks is to delineate the probable range of real future choice—the envelope within which goal-directed actions are likely to pay off. I read the evidence concerning the qualities and magnitudes of some uncontrollable aspects of future change to say that many of the spatial forms to which we have aspired are no longer within that envelope.

Moreover, I contend that we have been searching for the wrong grail, that the values associated with the desired urban structure do not reside in the spatial structure per se. One pattern of settlement and its internal land use form is superior to another only as it better serves to accommodate ongoing social processes and to further the nonspatial ends of the political community. I am flatly rejecting the contention that there is an overriding universal spatial or physical aesthetic of urban form.

Throughout this essay I have laid heavy emphasis upon the communication patterns that bring people into contact with others and that have created our traditional settlement patterns. I have done so because communication is a very powerful influence that has scarcely been studied. But it is not my view that this is the only important factor affecting urban spatial structure, or that the criteria for planning the spatial structure for complex urban communities stem from this relationship alone. No simple cause-and-effect relationships are likely to be uncovered in this field, for the maze of relationships within such complex open systems as urban societies are such that a change in one part of the web will reverberate to induce changes throughout all parts of the web. The problem of planning for the optimum utilization of urban space is far more complex than our present understanding permits us to even realize.

No attempt will be made here to catalogue the kinds of criteria that a rigorously conducted planning effort would need to weigh. I leave this omission not from modesty—only ignorance. But a few considerations can be mentioned, if only to suggest that my ignorance may not be complete.

I have chosen to deal with space, not with land, because, for the paramount purposes of men who engage in non-extractive industries, the surface of the earth has meaning as representation of communication distance rather than as inherent characteristics of the soil. I have contended that all space is urban space, since interaction among urbanites takes place through, or is inhibited by, all space. Space has significance for the urban planner primarily because of the implications that locational patterns have for fruitful interaction, hence for social welfare.

For some purposes, however, the surface of the earth does have meaning as soil or as minerals or as water storage; and in this context planners are indeed concerned with allocating *land* judiciously. With the prospect of increasing space utilization by urban activities, a growing conflict is inevitable between land users and space users. Fortunately the rate of increase in agricultural productivity continues to outpace the rate of population increase in the United States; and, in the face of embarrassing agricultural surpluses, the conflict is likely to thrive only in ideological disputes rather than in market competition.

Largely, I suspect, as vestige of our agrarian ancestry, many city planners and others hold to a rather fundamentalist belief in land. Land is seen as a scarce and sacred resource to be saved against those who would "encroach" upon and "desecrate" its natural features. To use good soils for housing is frequently decried as wasteful of a valuable natural resource, all the more objectionable because these changes are effectively irreversible. But the answer is surely not that simple. There may indeed be areas that would most profitably be retained in crops rather than in houses and factories, but in the places where the question arises the balance is probably more often in favor of the houses and factories. The values inherent in accessibility, that make those places attractive to the house buyer, are quite likely to weigh more heavily than the values to be derived from crops. But no answers can be found a priori. Each site must be evaluated for the relative costs and benefits implicit in the alternative purposes for which it might be used.

Similarly, lands that might provide the recreational opportunities that are increasingly in demand might also be used for other purposes. But, again, no doctrinaire answers are likely to be found supportable. Again, each site must be subjected to an analysis of the welfare implications implicit in the substitutable uses. The benefits from recreational use are quite as real as those deriving from farms and houses. Within the total spatial field, places for recreational activity need to be developed. But no ready solutions are in hand; certainly the greenbelt doctrine in itself is insufficient basis for the investments that are required.

Within any given territory at any given time, space is finite. Present and future demands for it are highly diverse in their requirements, but we can surely learn enough about the characteristics of each type of user to equip ourselves to make more rational allocations than would occur under unguided market conditions. The task is not to "protect our natural heritage of open space" just because it is natural, or a heritage, or open, or because we see ourselves as Galahads defending the good form against the evils of urban sprawl. This is a mission of evangelists, not planners.

Rather, and as the barest minimum, the task is to seek that spatial distribution of urban populations and urban activities

that will permit greater freedom for human·
interaction while, simultaneously, providing freer access to natural amenities
and effective management of the landscape
and of mineral resources.

This is no mean task. And probably the

meanest part of the task will be to dis-
abuse ourselves of some deep-seated
doctrine that seeks order in simple map-
pable patterns, when it is really hiding in
extremely complex social organization,
instead.

NOTES

1. Herbert J. Gans, *The Urban Villagers* (New York:
   The Free Press of Glencoe, Inc., 1962).
2. Parsons, Brinckerhoff, Hall, and Macdonald,
   *Regional Rapid Transit: Report to the San Fran-
   cisco Bay Area Rapid Transit Commission* (San
   Francisco and New York: Parsons, Brinckerhoff,
   Hall, and Macdonald, 1956). National Capital
   Planning Commission and the National Capital
   Regional Planning Council, *Policies Plan for the
   Year 2000* (Washington: U.S. Government Print-
   ing Office. 1961).

3. Catherine Bauer Wurster, "Framework for an
   Urban Society," in *Goals for Americans: The Report of the President's Commission on National
   Goals* (New York: Prentice-Hall, 1960).
4. "Counter Attack," *Architectural Review*, 1955,
   pp. 355–56.
5. Robert M. Haig, "Toward an Understanding of
   the Metropolis," *New York Regional Survey, Regional Survey of New York and Its Environs*, Vol. 1
   (New York: Regional Plan Association, Inc.
   1927).

52. Moral Values and Community | Robert A. Nisbet

*Democratic theory has long held that the small territorial community is the cornerstone of
freedom and creativity in American society. As Webber pointed out in the previous selection,
these kinds of communities are now disappearing and are being replaced by communities based
on the common occupational interests of their members, regardless of whether or not they live
in close proximity to one another. Can these new forms of community really serve the functions
performed by the neighborhood and other residential groups, and do they provide a sufficient
basis for the survival of democracy, individualism, and an integrated social order?*

*In general, Robert Nisbet answers these questions affirmatively, but with some reservations.
Citing a variety of sociological materials, including the theoretical writings of Durkheim and
recent studies of British working-class settlements, he discusses the reasons why large-scale
bureaucracies and modern institutions lack the capability to develop the sense of loyalty,
responsibility, and autonomy that democratic politics require. He is scornful of those who
advocate the establishment of community centers as a means for developing community spirit
at the local level, on the grounds that these centers and the activities they symbolize are
functionally irrelevant to the demands of American society today.*

Robert A. Nisbet is Professor of Sociology and former Vice-Chancellor and Dean of the College of
Letters and Science at the University of California, Riverside. He is the author of *Tradition and Revolt*
(1968), *The Sociological Tradition* (1966), and *Community and Power* (1962).

The relationship between man, the community, and environment is one of the lasting themes to which every generation makes its contribution based upon knowledge and historical circumstances. To a large extent this relationship is dependent upon the system of authority and function which exists in society at large. During the Middle Ages, when centralized authority did not exist, local units tended to be strong and to enlist the loyalties of their members. The downfall of medieval communities came about in very large part as the result of centralization both of political authority and economy during the Renaissance and the Reformation. The basic problem of the community in the Western world is therefore to be seen in terms of what happened historically to the structure of power and function in the larger society. It is very difficult to maintain the eminence of the small, local units when the loyalties and actions of individuals are consolidated increasingly in the great power units represented by the nation states in the modern world.

But the problem of community is also a problem in values. Because of the widespread emphasis upon technique, mechanism, rationalization of authority, monopoly of economic activity, there has been a general disinclination in the social sciences and in modern planning to remain closely concerned with the problem of human values. Quite apart, however, from the ultimate origin of human values, we know that their nurture and transmission from generation to generation depends upon groups small enough to provide the medium of learning but possessed of sufficient significance to give them a meaningful role so far as the cultivation of values is concerned. Such values as love, honor, and loyalty do not, cannot, thrive in a sociological vacuum.

It is well known in the study of language that the meanings of words and sentences depend upon understandings which exist prior to the utterance of the words themselves. It is equally true that all formal statements of value contain and depend upon certain prejudgments which give formal judgments their roots of meaning and even possibility of communication. Without some kind of agreement upon the unspoken but powerful prejudgments, all efforts to derive meaning from and to reach agreement about the explicit judgments are fruitless. Most of the world's conflicts of faith and action take their departure from lack of agreement about prejudgments rather than from dissention about formal judgments; and these are never within the reach of the language analyst. Finally, it is but an extension of the foregoing to emphasize that the communities of assent on which the spoken word depends, and the silent prejudgments which give meaning and efficacy to formal judgments of value, are themselves reinforced and contained by the more tangible communities of interest and behavior that compose a social organization. No one of these three sets of elements is causative or crucial. They exist as inseparable aspects of the one unified phenomenon. Apart from residual values themselves, human associations can have no more meaning than those which exist in the animal world. But apart from communities of men, the values themselves will not long remain important and meaningful to their human beings.

A wise philosopher, Susanne Langer has written:

From *International Review of Community Development*, No. 5 (1960), pp. 574–582. Reprinted by permission.

The mind, like all other organs, can draw its sustenance only from the surrounding world; our metaphysical symbols must spring from reality. Such adaptation always requires time, habit, tradition, and intimate knowledge of a way of life. If, now, the field of our unconscious symbolic orientation is suddenly plowed up by tremendous changes in the external world and in the social order, we lose our hold, our convictions, and therewith our effectual purposes. . . . All old symbols are gone, and thousands of average lives offer no new materials to a creative imagination. This, rather than physical want, is the starvation that threatens the modern worker, the tyranny of the machine. The withdrawal of all natural means for expressing the unity of personal life is the major cause of the distraction, irreligion, and unrest that mark the proletariat of all countries.[1]

It is not strange that in our century we should see so many evidences—in practical behavior and also in philosophy and literature—of the kind of dislocation of moral value to which Dr. Langer refers. The vast changes in government, economy, and technology have had a striking impact upon men's social relationships. In the 18th century the central problem taken by philosophers was the problem of authority, and out of it came the theory and jurisprudence of the modern nation state. In the 19th century the central problem seemed to be economic, and in the works of the great economists of the 19th century, we see the outlines created of the industrial world to which all of us, increasingly, belong. In the 20th century it is the moral-social problem that has become uppermost. And it has become uppermost because of the profound changes which have taken place in state and economy.

What are the dislocations and deprivations which have driven so many, in this age of economic abundance and political welfare, to a quest for security and a general concern for community? They lie, I think, in the realm of the small primary personal relationships of society—the relationships that mediate directly between man and his larger world of economic, moral, and political and religious values. Our problem is concerned with all of these values and their greater or less acceptability to the individual. It is this that makes our problem also social. It is social in the exact sense that it pertains to the small areas of membership and association in which human values are made meaningful and compelling to human beings.

Behind the spreading sense of insecurity and alienation in western society, behind all of the popular as well as academic preoccupation with the problem of community, there is growing realization that the traditional primary relationships of men have become, in certain areas, functionally irrelevant to the larger institutions of society, and sometimes meaningless to the moral aspirations of individuals.

A great deal of the character of contemporary social action has come from the efforts of men to find in large scale organizations, especially political ones, those values of status and intellectual security which were formally acquired in church, family, and neighborhood. How else can we explain the success of such movements in the modern world as Communism, Nazism except as mass movements designed to confer upon the individual some sense of that community which has been lost under the impact of modern social changes. The horror and tragedy are that such political movements have been based upon, and dedicated to, force and terror.

Too often the problem of modern community is blurred under the phrase, "social disorganization." Such a term is made to cover too great a diversity of conditions. In any society as complex as ours it is unlikely however that all aspects are undergoing a similar change. Thus it can scarcely be said that the state, as a distinguishable relationship among human beings, is today undergoing disorganization, for in most countries, including western Europe and the United States the political relationship is being enhanced above all other forms. The contemporary state, with all its apparatus of bureaucracy, has become more powerful, more cohesive, and is endowed with more functions than at any time in its history.

Nor would it be sensible to speak of disorganization of the great impersonal relationships which we find in our society in the form of the large private and semi-public organizations of an educational, economic, and charitable nature. Large-scale labor organizations, political parties, welfare organizations, and business corporations show a continued and even increasing prosperity, at least when measured in terms of institutional significance. It may be true that these organizations do not offer the degree of individual identification that makes for a sense of social belonging but it would hardly be accurate to apply the word disorganization to these immense and influential organizations.

The problem of disorganization, if we are to use the term, must be located more precisely with respect to those types of relationship which have actually undergone dislocation. These, as I have indicated above, are the relationships of the smaller, inter-personal sort. It is worth remembering that when Durkheim first addressed himself to the problem of community in his *Division of Labor*, he did so in the optimistic belief that modern industrialism was creating a new and more viable form of solidarity than had ever been known in the history of the human race. This new form of solidarity, Durkheim said, was organic; organic in the sense it would be based upon division of labor, with each element of the system thereby made the more dependent upon all other elements. Durkheim distinguished this form of solidarity from the old and traditional form which he called mechanical. Mechanical solidarity, Durkheim defined, as that which exists when all human beings are pursuing identical functions.

It was Durkheim's bold argument that such difficulties and maladjustments as we now find in the society around us stem from the fact that organic solidarity has only incompletely and imperfectly come into existence. When the last evidences of mechanical solidarity are erased and when the new system based upon division of labor is functioning perfectly, all such maladjustments will disappear. Men will be drawn to one another not on the basis of ancient traditional interest but on the basis of felt, mutually perceived, functional interdependence.

Such was Durkheim's contention, but, as he himself came to realize after he finished the *Division of Labor* the argument could not really be sustained. Therefore we find Durkheim in his next great work, *Suicide*, proclaiming the need for the re-establishment of forms of association akin to those which existed successfully in the ages characterized by mechanical solidarity. Only these, he was forced to conclude, can rescue modern man from the loneliness and functional inadequacy that he finds in the industrial system around him. Thus, although Durkheim failed in the prime effort of his first great book, he set a problem that he came to answer brilliantly—but very differently, from what he had originally intended—that is, through human communities within industry and the state which would restore once again the sense of solidarity and inspire men with a deep devotion to moral purpose.

The great inadequacy of Durkheim was in failing, however, to search for those natural and autonomous communities of individuals which have developed somehow even within the great impersonal spaces of the modern state. Durkheim accepted the perspective of modern society as being almost unrelievedly impersonal, atomistic, and mechanical. It was for this reason that Durkheim argued the necessity of contriving and establishing from the ground up new forms of community life which would give the individual a sense of identification. This view corresponded, of course, with the view taken by many of the early sociologists in the United States and elsewhere, a view which saw the small primary groups becoming historically archaic and replaced by large "secondary" associations. The argument was that such primary groups as family, neighborhood, and local community are undergoing a process of disappearance, to be replaced by the greater associations of a secondary character based upon economic or educational or religious interest alone. But more careful study in recent decades reveals that even in the largest cities, primary groups of an autonomous and self perpetuating character are to be found.

I should like to refer in this connection to the fine study of the family in London done by Michael Young and Peter Willmott.[2] In this study it was discovered that, contrary to popular sociological belief, the extended family still has great relevance in the lives of many of the people in the lower class areas of London. Furthermore, when thousands of these individuals, under a program of planning, were removed from their slum areas and placed in model housing some distance away from the slums, considerable unhappiness was the consequence. Such unhappiness was the result of small families being separated from relatives on whom they had traditionally depended for a great deal of their human association. In short, well-intended but insufficiently prepared planning had taken modern sociology at its face value and assumed that only the small conjugal family was of any significance in the lives of individuals and that such families could safely thereby be removed.

I think this study of the family could undoubtedly be supplemented and reinforced by other studies of the kinds of small communities which exist, and which are all too frequently neglected by planning which takes the view that cities are merely collections of atomistic individuals.

Much thought is being given these days to the need for community centers, especially in the suburbs and in many of the "model" towns which are coming into existence in so many parts of the world. Such centers are considered as essential to the development of a community spirit. But I do not think there is very much hope for any one of these centers in the instilling of a sense of community purpose so long as they are regarded as mere adornments to the functions and loyalties which actually exist and are related to day to day lives. A community center will be important to individuals only insofar as it adapts itself to the activities and concerns which exist naturally among a people but which need only leadership and guidance to evoke their full manifestation. Such centers can hardly operate successfully in a social desert: that is an area inhabited simply by individuals impersonally united by economic or religious interests but not through the affiliations which actually give life and meaning to one's existence.

The old communities—tribe, clan, joint

family, and guild—were held together to a very large extent by sacred, even religious, bonds. The towns of the Middle Ages, which are sometimes, perhaps uncritically, praised as ideal communities, sheltered the lives of their citizens by religious, civic, and economic associations, each of which aspired to be a kind of enlarged family, and was small enough to arouse deep personal loyalty. The reason why religion has figured so prominently in social history is that in any community a feeling of meaning, of shared purpose, is essential to the prosperity of the community. Religion, traditionally, has been the vessel in which most of the shared meanings and purposes of a deeper sort have been carried. But, it must be emphasized, religion is not indispensable so long as there is some other pattern of meanings and purposes which will do the same thing.

It may well be asked: why should we seek communities at all? Is it not sufficient, in an age of the welfare state that we should live simply and solely in terms of the great regulations, laws, and associations which this state provides? It is often said that today, for the first time in human history, the state has become a benevolent and protective association which is able to meet both the social and the physical demands of people formerly met by a plurality of smaller communities. To this we must say firmly, however, that the state which possesses the power to do things *for* people has also the power to do things to them. Freedom cannot be maintained in a monolithic society. Pluralism and diversity of experience are the essence of true freedom. Therefore even if the state were able to meet the basic problems of stability and security through its own efforts, we should have to reject it as the solution simply because of our concern for the problem of freedom.

However it is to be noted that the state does not even serve the security need. No large-scale association can really meet the psychic demand of individuals because, by its very nature, it is too large, too complex, too bureaucratized, and altogether too aloof from the residual meanings which human beings live by. The state can enlist popular enthusiasm, can conduct crusades, can mobilize on behalf of great "causes," such as wars, but as a regular and normal means of meeting human needs for recognition, fellowship, security, and membership, it is inadequate. The tragedy is that where the state is most successful in meeting the needs for recognition and security, it is most tyrannical and despotic, as the histories of Communist Russia and Nazi Germany have made clear. The only proper alternative to large-scale, mechanical political society are communities small in scale but solid in structure. They and they alone can be the beginning of social reconstruction because they respond, at the grass roots, to fundamental human desires: living together, working together, experiencing together, being together. Such communities can grow naturally and organically from the most elementary aspirations, they remain continuously flexible, and, by their very nature, they do not insist upon imposing and rigid organizations.

Not only for purposes of viable social planning, as contrasted with the mechanical type of planning, but also for purposes of motivation and general creativity, the contexts of informal association must be understood. These, we have learned full well, are indispensable to the nurture of vigorous and creative personality. They are also crucial to the preservation of political freedom.

When the basic principles of modern liberalism were being formulated by such men as Locke, Adam Smith, and Jefferson, the image of man that existed then in the philosophical mind was one constructed out of such abstract traits as reason, stability, security, and indestructible motivations toward freedom and order. Man alone was deemed to be inherently self-sufficing, equipped by nature with both the instinct and reason that could make him autonomous.

What we can now see with the advantage of hindsight was that the founders of liberalism were unconsciously abstracting certain moral and psychological attributes from a social organization and considering these as the timeless natural qualities of the individual, who was regarded as independent of the influences of any historically developed social organization. Those qualities were qualities actually inhering to a large extent in a set of institutions and groups, all of which were aspects of historical tradition. But, with the model of Newtonian mechanics before them, the moral philosophers insisted on reducing everything to human atoms in motion, to natural individuals driven by impulses and reason deemed to be innate in man.

Given this image of man as inherently self-sufficing, given the view of communities and groups as merely secondary, as shadows of the solid reality of man, it was inevitable that the strategy of freedom should have been based upon objectives of release and the emancipation of man from his fettering institutions.

A creative society would be one in which individuals were "emancipated" from all types of social relationship. A free society would be, similarly, one in which human beings were morally and socially, as well as politically, free from any kind of authorities and institutional functions. The ideal, insensibly, became one of a vast mass of individuals separated from one another in social terms, participating only through the impersonal mechanisms of the market and of the legal state.

Thus, in Bentham's terms the fundamental cement of society would be provided not through groups and close personal relationships, but through certain "natural" identifications of interest rising in almost equal part from man's instinctual nature and from his reason. "It is not strange," George E. Adams has written, "that the self discovery and self-consciousness of the individual should have steadily mounted higher as the environment of individuals more and more takes on the form of an impersonal, causal, and mechanical structure. For the mobility and freedom of the individual can be won only as he becomes detached from his world; his world becomes separated from him only when organized and defined in objective and impersonal terms."[3]

In strictly sociological terms, what this means is that the individual's community was becoming an ever more remote thing to him in the 19th century. Because of profound shifts in the structure of authority and functions of society, more and more men were being made small parts in a social machine ever larger, ever more impersonal, ever more regimented. With authority becoming more and more objectified and externalized, the consequences were deleterious to those primary forms of authority with which man had traditionally and subjectively identified himself for ages. These ceased to be important. Their moral virtues were transferred as it were to him, even as their historic authorities were being transferred to the state.

But what we have learned under the guidance of studies in modern social psychology is that the rationalist image of man is theoretically inadequate and practically intolerable. We have learned that man is not self-sufficing in social isolation, that his nature cannot be deduced simply from elements innate in the germ plasm, and that between man and such social groups as the family, local group, and interest associations there is an indispensable connection. No conception of individuality is adequate that does not take into consideration the many ties which normally bind the individual to others from birth to death.

Individuality cannot be understood except as the product of normatively oriented interaction with other persons. Whatever may lie neurologically in the human being, we know that a knowledge of man's actual behavior in society must take into consideration the whole stock of norms and cultural incentives which are the product of social history. The normative order in society is fundamental to all understanding of human nature. We do not see, think, react, or become stimulated except in terms of the socially inherited norms of human culture.

But the normative order is itself inseparable from the associative order. Culture does not exist autonomously; it is always set in the context of social relationships. Only thus do the ends and patterns of culture make themselves vivid and evocative to human beings. And we have learned that with the dislocation of the social relationships which immediately surround the human being there occurs also a disruption of his cultural or moral order. The intensity of personal incentive, whether in the context of therapy or day to day life of the normal human being tends to fluctuate with the intensity of meaningful social relationships. This is what we have learned from studies of motivation in learning, from studies of character formation, and from observation of personal morale in all kinds of stress situations.

The philosophy of individualism, John Dewey wrote a generation ago,

> ignores the fact that the mental and moral structure of individuals, the pattern of their desires and purposes, change with every great change in social constitution. Individuals who are not bound together in associations, whether domestic, economic, religious, political, artistic, or educational, are monstrosities. It is absurd to suppose that the ties which hold them together are merely external and do not react into mentality and character, producing the framework of personal disposition.[4]

So too with creativeness. Admittedly, it is the freedom of persons that is crucial. Great works of art or literature or science are not created by anonymous organizations. They are the concrete results of personal performance. But from the obvious centrality of the person in intellectual or cultural achievement it does (not) follow that such achievement is the sole consequence of innate individual forces nor that it is the result simply of processes of separation. To be sure there is in the achievement of any great work, whether it be a painting or a treatise in metaphysics, a relatively high degree of detachment in the minds of the creator. But we are still compelled to regard the important interdependences between the creator and his community.

Creation is individual, or at most the work of a small group, but much creative work would never have been done apart from such communities as the guilds, colleges, philosophical societies, monasteries, and institutes. In such organizations as these the informal, the spontaneous, and the autonomous types of relationship assume great importance. In them the creative process can move freely, tensions can be relaxed and inhibitions overcome. Sparks are thrown off by difference rubbing on difference in small compass. Imaginations are fired. Admittedly, small groups can be as deadly as large ones, but the important point is that, unlike more formal types of asssociations, small and informal groups are not likely to last for long when their purpose is dead and their fellowship flagging. They are not saved by

by-laws or dues investe̸... resources run out.

In conclusion, the search̸... of community must be a c... All the resources of knowl... be brought to bear on the prob̸ ... . Neither moral values, nor fellowship, nor freedom can easily flourish apart from the existence of diverse communities each capable of enlisting the loyalties of its members.

NOTES

1. *Philosophy in a New Key*. London and New York, 1948, p. 235.
2. *Family and Kinship in East London*. London, 1957.
3. *Idealism and the Modern Age*. New Haven, 1919, p. 35.
4. *Individualism Old and New*. New York, 1930, pp. 81–2.

53. The Uses of City Neighborhoods | Jane Jacobs

Belief in the dominance of the spread city pattern and in the need for communities based on conditions other than residential propinquity leaves unexamined the question how older cities, such as those which dominate the Eastern, Central, and Southern portions of the nation, should be reorganized in order to make them effective and attractive urban environments. Jane Jacobs addresses herself to this issue. She claims that established cities can begin to function well only if they form a hierarchy of spatial units, in which each unit is given the power to control its local social order. Mrs. Jacobs believes that there are three such units—the neighborhood, the district, and the city—and in this selection she discusses the first two. She argues that neighborhoods should be the locus of informal social control and the units through which children are acquainted with the rules of urban life. The neighborhood is defined by the street and much of her article is given over to a discussion of how to make streets lively and safe. The district is intermediate in size between the city and neighborhood. It is the unit through which the policy and plans of the municipality can be translated and tested against the will and needs of its residents, and in turn, can serve as the channel through which the interests of the public are communicated to the mayor and other officials at the top. Mrs. Jacobs is in favor of giving districts formal status in the administrative and political structure of urban government—a proposal which is gaining wider acceptance in many large cities today.

Jane Jacobs is a social critic and author of *The Death and Life of Great American Cities* (1961) and *The Economy of Cities* (1969).

...ighborhood is a word that has come to sound like a Valentine. As a sentimental concept, "neighborhood" is harmful to city planning. It leads to attempts at warping city life into imitations of town or suburban life. Sentimentality plays with sweet intentions in place of good sense.

A successful city neighborhood is a place that keeps sufficiently abreast of its problems so it is not destroyed by them. An unsuccessful neighborhood is a place that is overwhelmed by its defects and problems and is progressively more helpless before them. Our cities contain all degrees of success and failure. But on the whole we Americans are poor at handling city neighborhoods, as can be seen by the long accumulations of failures in our great gray belts on the one hand, and by the Turfs of rebuilt city on the other hand.

It is fashionable to suppose that certain touchstones of the good life will create good neighborhoods—schools, parks, clean housing and the like. How easy life would be if this were so! How charming to control a complicated and ornery society by bestowing upon it rather simple physical goodies. In real life, cause and effect are not so simple. Thus a Pittsburgh study, undertaken to show the supposed clear correlation between better housing and improved social conditions, compared delinquency records in still uncleared slums to delinquency records in new housing projects, and came to the embarrassing discovery that the delinquency was higher in the improved housing. Does this mean improved shelter increases delinquency? Not at all. It means other things may be more important than housing, however, and it means also that there is no direct, simple relationship between good housing and good behavior, a fact which the whole tale of the Western world's history, the whole collection of our literature, and the whole fund of observation open to any of us should long since have made evident. Good shelter is a useful good in itself, as shelter. When we try to justify good shelter instead on the pretentious grounds that it will work social or family miracles we fool ourselves. Reinhold Niebuhr has called this particular self-deception, "The doctrine of salvation by bricks."

It is even the same with schools. Important as good schools are, they prove totally undependable at rescuing bad neighborhoods and at creating good neighborhoods. Nor does a good school building guarantee a good education. Schools, like parks, are apt to be volatile creatures of their neighborhoods (as well as being creatures of larger policy). In bad neighborhoods, schools are brought to ruination, physically and socially; while successful neighborhoods improve their schools by fighting for them.[1]

Nor can we conclude, either, that middle-class families or upper-class families build good neighborhoods, and poor families fail to. For example, within the poverty of the North End in Boston, within the poverty of the West Greenwich Village waterfront neighborhoods, within the poverty of the slaughterhouse district in Chicago (three areas, incidentally, that were all written off as hopeless by their cities' planners), good neighborhoods were created: neighborhoods whose internal problems have grown less with time instead of greater. Meantime, within the once upper-class grace and serenity of Baltimore's beautiful Eutaw Place, within the one-time upper-class solidity of Boston's South End, within the culturally privileged purlieus of New York's

Morningside Heights, within miles upon miles of dull, respectable middle-class gray area, bad neighborhoods were created, neighborhoods whose apathy and internal failure grew greater with time instead of less.

To hunt for city neighborhood touch-stones of success in high standards of physical facilities, or in supposedly competent and nonproblem populations, or in nostalgic memories of town life, is a waste of time. It evades the meat of the question, which is the problem of what city neighborhoods do, if anything, that may be socially and economically useful in cities themselves, and how they do it.

We shall have something solid to chew on if we think of city neighborhoods as mundane organs of self-government. Our failures with city neighborhoods are, ultimately, failures in localized self-government. And our successes are successes at localized self-government. I am using self-government in its broadest sense, meaning both the informal and formal self-management of society.

Both the demands on self-government and the techniques for it differ in big cities from the demands and techniques in smaller places. For instance, there is the problem of all those strangers. To think of city neighborhoods as organs of city self-government or self-management, we must first jettison some orthodox but irrelevant notions about neighborhoods which may apply to communities in smaller settlements but not in cities. We must first of all drop any ideal of neighborhoods as self-contained or intro-verted units.

Unfortunately orthodox planning theory is deeply committed to the ideal of sup-posedly cozy, inward-turned city neigh-borhoods. In its pure form, the ideal is a neighborhood composed of about 7,000 persons, a unit supposedly of sufficient size to populate an elementary school and to support convenience shopping and a community center. This unit is then further rationalized into smaller groupings of a size scaled to the play and supposed man-agement of children and the chitchat of housewives. Although the "ideal" is seldom literally reproduced, it is the point of departure for nearly all neighborhood renewal plans, for all project building, for much modern zoning, and also for the practice work done by today's architec-tural-planning students, who will be in-flicting their adaptations of it on cities tomorrow. In New York City alone, by 1959, more than half a million people were already living in adaptations of this vision of planned neighborhoods. This "ideal" of the city neighborhood as an island, turned inward on itself, is an important factor in our lives nowadays.

To see why it is a silly and even harmful "ideal" for cities, we must recognize a basic difference between these concoctions grafted into cities, and town life. In a town of 5,000 or 10,000 population, if you go to Main Street (analogous to the con-solidated commercial facilities or com-munity center for a planned neighborhood), you run into people you also know at work, or went to school with, or see at church, or people who are your children's teachers, or who have sold or given you professional or artisan's services, or whom you know to be friends of your casual acquaintances, or whom you know by reputation. Within the limits of a town or village, the connections among its people keep crossing and recrossing and this can make workable and essentially cohesive communities out of even larger towns than those of 7,000 population, and to some extent out of little cities.

But a population of 5,000 or 10,000

residents in a big city has no such innate degree of natural cross-connections within itself, except under the most extraordinary circumstances. Nor can city neighborhood planning, no matter how cozy in intent, change this fact. If it could, the price would be destruction of a city by converting it into a parcel of towns. As it is, the price of trying, and not even succeeding at a misguided aim is conversion of a city into a parcel of mutually suspicious and hostile Turfs. There are many other flaws in this "ideal" of the planned neighborhood and its various adaptations.[2]

Lately a few planners, notably Reginald Isaacs of Harvard, have daringly begun to question whether the conception of neighborhood in big cities has any meaning at all. Isaacs points out that city people are mobile. They can and do pick and choose from the entire city (and beyond) for everything from a job, a dentist, recreation, or friends, to shops, entertainment, or even in some cases their children's schools. City people, says Isaacs, are not stuck with the provincialism of a neighborhood, and why should they be? Isn't wide choice and rich opportunity the point of cities?

This is indeed the point of cities. Furthermore, this very fluidity of use and choice among city people is precisely the foundation underlying most city cultural activities and special enterprises of all kinds. Because these can draw skills, materials, customers or clienteles from a great pool, they can exist in extraordinary variety, and not only downtown but in other city districts that develop specialties and characters of their own. And in drawing upon the great pool of the city in this way, city enterprises increase, in turn, the choices available to city people for jobs, goods, entertainment, ideas, contacts, services.

Whatever city neighborhoods may be, or may not be, and whatever usefulness they may have, or may be coaxed into having, their qualities cannot work at cross-purposes to thoroughgoing city mobility and fluidity of *use*, without economically weakening the city of which they are a part. The lack of either economic or social self-containment is natural and necessary to city neighborhoods—simply because they are parts of cities. Isaacs is right when he implies that the conception of neighborhood in cities is meaningless—so long as we think of neighborhoods as being self-contained units to any significant degree, modeled upon town neighborhoods.

But for all the innate extroversion of city neighborhoods, it fails to follow that city people can therefore get along magically without neighborhoods. Even the most urbane citizen does care about the atmosphere of the street and district where he lives, no matter how much choice he has of pursuits outside it; and the common run of city people do depend greatly on their neighborhoods for the kind of everyday lives they lead.

Let us assume (as is often the case) that city neighbors have nothing more fundamental in common with each other than that they share a fragment of geography. Even so, if they fail at managing that fragment decently, the fragment will fail. There exists no inconceivably energetic and all-wise "They" to take over and substitute for localized self-management. Neighborhoods in cities need not supply for their people an artificial town or village life, and to aim at this is both silly and destructive. But neighborhoods in cities do need to supply some means for civilized self-government. This is the problem.

Looking at city neighborhoods as organs of self-government, I can see evidence that only three kinds of neighborhoods are useful: (1) the city as a whole; (2) street neighborhoods; (and 3) districts of large, subcity size, composed of 100,000 people or more in the case of the largest cities.

Each of these kinds of neighborhoods has different functions, but the three supplement each other in complex fashion. It is impossible to say that one is more important than the others. For success with staying power at any spot, all three are necessary. But I think that other neighborhoods than these three kinds just get in the way, and make successful self-government difficult or impossible.

The most obvious of the three, although it is seldom called a neighborhood, is the city as a whole. We must never forget or minimize this parent community while thinking of a city's smaller parts. This is the source from which most public money flows, even when it comes ultimately from the federal or state coffers. This is where most administrative and policy decisions are made, for good or ill. This is where general welfare often comes into direct conflict, open or hidden, with illegal or other destructive interests.

Moreover, up on this plane we find vital special-interest communities and pressure groups. The neighborhood of the entire city is where people especially interested in the theater or in music or in other arts find one another and get together, no matter where they may live. This is where people immersed in specific professions or businesses or concerned about particular problems exhange ideas and sometimes start action. Professor P. Sargant Florence, a British specialist on urban economies, has written, "My own experience is that, apart from the special habitat of intel-lectuals like Oxford or Cambridge, a city of a million is required to give me, say, the twenty or thirty congenial friends I require!" This sounds rather snooty, to be sure, but Professor Florence has an important truth here. Presumably he likes his friends to know what he is talking about. When William Kirk of Union Settlement and Helen Hall of Henry Street Settlement, miles apart in New York City, get together with *Consumers' Union*, a magazine located still other miles away, and with researchers from Columbia University, and with the trustees of a foundation, to consider the personal and community ruin wrought by loan shark-installment peddlers in low-income projects, they know what each is talking about and, what is more, can put their peculiar kinds of knowledge together with a special kind of money to learn more about the trouble and find ways to fight it. When my sister, Betty, a housewife, helps devise a scheme in the Manhattan public school which one of her children attends, whereby parents who know English give homework help to the children of parents who do not, and the scheme works, this knowledge filters into a special-interest neighborhood of the city as a whole; as a result, one evening Betty finds herself away over in the Bedford-Stuyvesant section of Brooklyn, telling a district group of ten PTA presidents there how the scheme works, and learning some new things herself.

A city's very wholeness in bringing together people with communities of interest is one of its greatest assets, possibly the greatest. And, in turn, one of the assets a city district needs is people with access to the political, the administrative, and the special-interest communities of the city as a whole.

In most big cities, we Americans do reasonably well at creating useful neighborhoods belonging to the whole city. People with similar and supplementing interests do find each other fairly well. Indeed, they typically do so most efficiently in the largest cities (except for Los Angeles which does miserably at this, and Boston which is pretty pathetic). Moreover, big-city governments, as Seymour Freedgood of *Fortune* magazine so well documented in *The Exploding Metropolis*, are able and energetic at the top in many instances, more so than one would surmise from looking at social and economic affairs in the endless failed neighborhoods of the same cities. Whatever our disastrous weakness may be, it is hardly sheer incapability for forming neighborhoods at the top, out of cities as a whole.

At the other end of the scale are a city's streets, and the minuscule neighborhoods they form, like our neighborhood of Hudson Street for example.

In the first several chapters of this book I have dwelt heavily upon the self-government functions of city streets: to weave webs of public surveillance and thus to protect strangers as well as themselves; to grow networks of small-scale, everyday public life and thus of trust and social control; and to help assimilate children into reasonably responsible and tolerant city life.

The street neighborhoods of a city have still another function in self-government, however, and a vital one: they must draw effectively on help when trouble comes along that is too big for the street to handle. This help must sometimes come from the city as a whole, at the other end of the scale. This is a loose end I shall leave hanging, but ask you to remember.

The self-government functions of streets are all humble, but they are indispensable. In spite of much experiment, planned and unplanned, there exists no substitute for lively streets.

How large is a city street neighborhood that functions capably? If we look at successful street-neighborhood networks in real life, we find this is a meaningless question, because wherever they work best, street neighborhoods have no beginnings and end setting them apart as distinct units. The size even differs for different people from the same spot, because some people range farther, or hang around more or extend their street acquaintance farther than others. Indeed, a great part of the success of these neighborhoods of the streets depends on their overlapping and interweaving, turning the corners. This is one means by which they become capable of economic and visual variation for their users. Residential Park Avenue in New York appears to be an extreme example of neighborhood monotony, and so it would be if it were an isolated strip of street neighborhood. But the street neighborhood of a Park Avenue resident only begins on Park, quickly turns a corner off it, and then another corner. It is part of a set of interweaving neighborhoods containing great diversity, not a strip.

Isolated street neighborhoods that do have definite boundaries can be found in plenty, to be sure. They are typically associated with long blocks (and hence with infrequent streets), because long blocks tend almost always to be physically self-isolating. Distinctly separate street neighborhoods are nothing to aim for; they are generally characteristic of failure. Describing the troubles of an area of long, monotonous, self-isolating blocks on Manhattan's West Side, Dr. Dan W. Dodson of New York University's Center for Human Relations Studies notes: "Each [street] appears to be a separate world of its own with a separate culture. Many of those interviewed had no conception of the neighborhood other than the street on which they resided."

Summing up the incompetence of the area, Dr. Dodson comments, "The present state of the neighborhood indicates that the people there have lost the capacity for collective action, or else they would long since have pressured the city government and the social agencies into correcting some of the problems of community living." These two observations by Dr. Dodson on street isolation and incompetence are closely related.

Successful street neighborhoods, in short, are not discrete units. They are physical, social and economic continuities—small scale to be sure, but small scale in the sense that the lengths of fibers making up a rope are small scale.

Where our city streets do have sufficient frequency of commerce, general liveliness, use and interest, to cultivate continuities of public street life, we Americans do prove fairly capable at street self-government. This capability is most often noticed and commented on in districts of poor, or one-time poor people. But casual street neighborhoods, good at their functions, are also characteristic of high-income areas that maintain a persistent popularity—rather than ephemeral fashion —such as Manhattan's East Side from the Fifties to the Eighties, or the Rittenhouse Square district in Philadelphia, for example.

To be sure, our cities lack sufficient streets equipped for city life. We have too much area afflicted with the Great Blight of Dullness instead. But many, many city streets perform their humble jobs well and command loyalty too, unless and until they are destroyed by the impingement

of city problems too big for them, or by neglect for too long a time of facilities that can be supplied only from the city as a whole, or by deliberate planning policies that the people of the neighborhood are too weak to defeat.

And here we come to the third kind of city neighborhood that is useful to self-government: the district. This, I think, is where we are typically most weak and fail most disastrously. We have plenty of city districncts in name. We have few that function.

The chief function of a successful district is to mediate between the indispensable but inherently politically powerless, street neighborhoods, and the inherently powerful city as a whole.

Among those responsible for cities, at the top, there is much ignorance. This is inescapable, because big cities are just too big and too complex to be comprehended in detail from any vantage point—even if this vantage point is at the top—or to be comprehended by any human; yet detail is of the essence. A district citizens' group from East Harlem, in anticipation of a meeting it had arranged with the Mayor and his commissioners, prepared a document recounting the devastation wrought in the distict by remote decisions (most of them well meant, of course), and they added this comment: "We must state how often we find that those of us who live or work in East Harlem, coming into daily contact with it, see it quite differently from . . . the people who only ride through on their way to work, or read about it in their daily papers or, too often, we believe, made decisions about it from desks downtown." I have heard almost these same words in Boston, in Chicago, in Cincinnati, in St. Louis. It is a complaint that echoes and re-echoes in all our big cities.

Districts have to help bring the resources of a city down to where they are needed by street neighborhoods, and they have to help translate the experiences of real life, in street neighborhoods, into policies and purposes of their city as a whole. And they have to help maintain an area that is usable, in a civilized way, not only for its own residents but for other users—workers, customers, visitors—from the city as a whole.

To accomplish these functions, an effective district has to be large enough to count as a force in the life of the city as a whole. The "ideal" neighborhood of planning theory is useless for such a role. A district has to be big and powerful enough to fight city hall. Nothing less is to any purpose. To be sure, fighting city hall is not a district's only function, or necessarily the most important. Nevertheless, this is a good definition of size, in functional terms, because sometimes a district has to do exactly this, and also because a district lacking the power and will to fight city hall—and to win—when its people feel deeply threatened, is unlikely to possess the power and will to contend with other serious problems.

Let us go back to the street neighborhoods for a moment, and pick up a loose end I left dangling: the job, incumbent upon good street neighborhoods, to get help when too big a problem comes along.

Nothing is more helpless than a city street alone, when its problems exceed its powers. Consider, as an illustration, what happened with respect to a case of narcotics pushing on a street in uptown West Side Manhattan in 1955. The street on which this case occurred had residents who worked all over the city and had friends and acquaintances outside the street as well as on it. On the street itself they had a reasonably flourishing public

life centered around the stoops, but they had no neighborhood stores and no regular public characters. They also had no connection with a district neighborhood; indeed, their area has no such thing, except in name.

When heroin began to be sold from one of the apartments, a stream of drug addicts filtered into the street—not to live, but to make their connections. They needed money to buy the drugs. An epidemic of holdups and robberies on the street was one answer. People became afraid to come home with their pay on Fridays. Sometimes at night terrible screaming terrorized the residents. They were ashamed to have friends visit them. Some of the adolescents on the street were addicts, and more were becoming so.

The residents, most of whom were conscientious and respectable, did what they could. They called the police many times. Some individuals took the initative of finding that the responsible outfit to talk with was the Narcotics Squad. They told the detectives of the squad where the heroin was being sold, and by whom, and when, and what days supplies seemed to come.

Nothing happened—except that things continued to get worse.

Nothing much ever happens when one helpless little street fights alone some of the most serious problems of a great city.

Had the police been bribed? How is anybody to know?

Lacking a district neighborhood, lacking knowledge of any other persons who cared about this problem in this place and could bring weight to bear on it, the residents had gone as far as they knew how to go. Why didn't they at least call their local assemblyman, or get in touch with the political club? Nobody on the street knew those people (an assemblyman has about 115,000 constituents) or knew anybody who did know them. In short, this street simply had no connections of any kind with a district neighborhood, let alone effective connections with an effective district neighborhood. Those on street who could possibly manage it moved away when they saw that the street's situation was evidently hopeless. The street plunged into thorough chaos and barbarism.

New York had an able and energetic police commissioner during these events, but he could not be reached by everyone. Without effective intelligence from the streets and pressure from districts, he too must become to a degree helpless. Because of this gap, so much good intent at the top comes to so little purpose at the bottom, and vice-versa.

Sometimes the city is not the potential helper, but the antagonist of a street, and again, unless the street contains extraordinarily influential citizens, it is usually helpless alone. On Hudson Street we recently had this problem. The Manhattan Borough engineers decided to cut ten feet off our sidewalks. This was part of a mindless, routinized city program of vehicular road widening.

We people on the street did what we could. The job printer stopped his press, took off of it work on which he had an urgent deadline, and printed emergency petitions on a Saturday morning so the children, out of school, could help get them around. People from overlapping street neighborhoods took petitions and spread them father. The two parochial schools, Episcopal and Catholic, sent petitions home with their children. We gathered about a thousand signatures from the street and the tributaries off it; these signatures must have represented most of the adults directly affected. Many businessmen and residents wrote letters, and a representative group formed a delegation to visit the Borough President, the elected official responsible.

But by ourselves, we would still hardly have had a chance. We were up against a sanctified general policy on street treatment, and were opposing a construction job that would mean a lot of money for somebody, on which arrangements were already far advanced. We had learned of the plan in advance of the demolition purely by luck. No public hearing was required, for technically this was merely an adjustment in the curb line.

We were told at first that the plans would not be changed; the sidewalk must go. We needed power to back up our pipsqueak protest. This power came from our district —Greenwich Village. Indeed, a main purpose of our petitions, although not an ostensible purpose, was to dramatize to the district at large that an issue had erupted. The swift resolutions passed by district-wide organizations counted more for us than the street-neighborhood expressions of opinion. The man who got our delegation its appointment, Anthony Dapolito, the president of the citizens' Greenwich Village Association, and the people on our delegation who swung the most weight were from other streets than ours entirely; some from the other side of the district. They swung weight precisely because they represented opinion, and opinion makers, at district scale. With their help, we won.

Without the possibility of such support, most city streets hardly try to fight back— whether their troubles emanate from city hall or from other drawbacks of the human condition. Nobody likes to practice futility.

The help we got puts some individuals on our street under obligation, of course, to help other streets or aid more general district causes when help is wanted. If we neglect this, we may not get help next time we need it.

Districts effective at carrying the intelligence from the streets upward sometimes help translate it into city policy. There is no end to such examples, but this will do for illustration: As this is written, New York City is supposedly somewhat reforming its treatment for drug addicts, and simultaneously city hall is pressuring the federal government to expand and reform its treatment work, and to increase its efforts at blocking narcotics smuggling from abroad. The study and agitation that have helped push these moves did not originate with some mysterious " They." The first public agitation for reform and expansion of treatment was stirred not by officials at all, but by district pressure groups from districts like East Harlem and Greenwich Village. The disgraceful way in which arrest rolls are padded with victims while sellers operate openly and untouched is exposed and publicized by just these pressure groups, not by officials and least of all by the police. These pressure groups studied the problem and have pressed for changes and will continue to, precisely because they are in direct touch with experiences in street neighborhoods. The experience of an orphaned street like that on the Upper West Side, on the other hand, never teaches anybody anything—except to get the hell out.

It is tempting to suppose that districts can be formed federally out of distinct separate neighborhoods. The Lower East Side of New York is attempting to form an effective district today, on this pattern, and has received large philanthropic grants for the purpose. The formalized federation system seems to work fairly well for purposes on which virtually everyone is agreed, such as applying pressure for a new

hospital. But many vital questions in local city life turn out to be controversial. In the Lower East Side, for example, the federated district organizational structure includes, as this is written, people trying to defend their homes and neighborhoods from obliteration by the bulldozers; and it also contains the developers of cooperative projects and various other business interests who wish the governmental powers of condemnation to be used to wipe out these residents. These are genuine conflicts of interest—in this case, the ancient conflict between predator and prey. The people trying to save themselves spend much of their effort, futilely, trying to get resolutions adopted and letters approved by boards of directors that contain their chief enemies!

Both sides in hot fights on important local questions need to bring their full, consolidated, district-scale strength (nothing less is effective) to bear on the city policy they want to shape or the decisions they want to influence. They have to fight it out with each other, and with officials, on the plane where the effective decisions are made, because this is what counts in winning. Anything that diverts such contenders into fragmenting their power and watering their efforts by going through "decision-making' motions with hierarchies and boards at ineffectual levels where no responsible government powers of decision reside, vitiates political life, citizen effectiveness and self-government. This becomes play at self-government, not the real thing.

When Greenwich Village fought to prevent its park, Washington Square, from being bisected by a highway, for example, majority opinion was overwhelmingly against the highway. But not unanimous opinion; among those for the highway were, numerous people of prominence, with leadership positions in smaller sections of the district. Naturally they tried to keep the battle on a level of sectional organization, and so did the city government. Majority opinion would have frittered itself away in these tactics, instead of winning. Indeed, it was frittering itself away until this truth was pointed out by Raymond Rubinow, a man who happened to work in the district, but did not live there. Rubinow helped form a *Joint* Emergency Committee, a true district organization cutting through other organizational lines. Effective districts operate as Things in their own right, and most particularly must their citizens who are in agreement with each other on controversial questions act together at district scale, or they get nowhere. Districts are not groups of petty principalities, working in federation. If they work, they work as integral units of power and opinion, large enough to count.

Our cities possess many islandlike neighborhoods too small to work as districts, and these include not only the project neighborhoods inflicted by planning, but also many unplanned neighborhoods. These unplanned, too small units have grown up historically, and often are enclaves of distinctive ethnic groups. They frequently perform well and strongly the neighborhood functions of streets and thus keep marvelously in hand the kinds of neighborhood social problems and rot that develop from within. But also, just such too small neighborhoods are helpless, in the same way streets are helpless, against the problems and rot that develop from without. They are shortchanged on public improvements and services because they lack power to get them. They are helpless to reverse the slow-death warrants of area credit-blacklisting by mortgage lenders, a problem terribly difficult to fight even with impressive district power. If they develop

conflicts with people in adjoining neighborhoods, both they and the adjoining people are apt to be helpless at improving relationships. Indeed, insularity makes these relationships deteriorate further.

Sometimes, to be sure, a neighborhood too small to function as a district gets the benefit of power through possessing an exceptionally influential citizen or an important institution. But the citizens of such a neighborhood pay for their "free" gift of power when the day comes that their interests run counter to those of Papa Bigwheel or Papa Institution. They are helpless to defeat Papa in the government offices, up where the decisions are made, *and therefore they are helpless also to teach him or influence him.* Citizens of neighborhoods that include a university, for example, are often in this helpless fix.

Whether a district of sufficient potential power does become effective and useful as an organ of democratic self-government depends much on whether the insularity of too small neighborhoods within it is overcome. This is principally a social and political problem for a district and the contenders within it, but it is also a physical problem. To plan deliberately, and physically, on the premise that separated city neighborhoods of less than district size are a worthy ideal, is to subvert self-government; that the motives are sentimental or paternalistic is no help. When the physical isolation of too small neighborhoods is abetted by blatant social distinctions, as in projects whose populations are price-tagged, the policy is savagely destructive to effective self-government and self-management in cities.

The value of city districts that swing real power (but in which street neighborhoods are not lost as infinitesimal units) is no discovery of mine. Their value is rediscovered and demonstrated empirically over and over. Nearly every large city has at least one such effective district. Many more areas struggle sporadically to function like districts in time of crisis.

Not surprisingly, a reasonably effective district usually accrues to itself, with time, considerable political power. It eventually generates, too, whole series of individuals able to operate simultaneously at street scale and district scale, and on district scale and in neighborhoods of the city as a whole.

To correct our general disastrous failure to develop functional districts is in great part a problem of city administrative change, which we need not go into at this point. But we also need, among other things, to abandon conventional planning ideas about city neighborhoods. The "ideal" neighborhood of planning and zoning theory, too large in scale to possess any competence or meaning as a street neighborhood, is at the same time too small in scale to operate as a district. It is unfit for anything. It will not serve as even a point of departure. Like the belief in medical bloodletting, it was a wrong turn in the search for understanding.

If the only kinds of city neighborhoods that demonstrate useful functions in real-life self-government are the city as a whole, streets, and districts, then effective neighborhood physical planning for cities should aim at these purposes:

First, to foster lively and interesting streets.

Second, to make the fabric of these streets as continuous a network as possible *throughout* a district of potential subcity size and power.

Third, to use parks and squares and public buildings as part of this street fabric; use them to intensify and knit together the fabric's complexity and multiple use. They should not be used to island off different uses from each other, or to island off subdistrict neighborhoods.

Fourth, to emphasize the functional identity of areas large enough to work as districts.

If the first three aims are well pursued, the fourth will follow. Here is why: Few people, unless they live in a world of paper maps, can identify with an abstraction called a district, or care much about it. Most of us identify with a place in the city because we use it, and get to know it reasonably intimately. We take our two feet and move around in it and come to count on it. The only reason anyone does this much is that useful or interesting or convenient differences fairly near by exert an attraction.

Almost nobody travels willingly from sameness to sameness and repetition to repetition, even if the physical effort required is trivial.[3]

Differences, *not duplications*, make for cross-use and hence for a person's identification with an area greater than his immediate street network. Monotony is the enemy of cross-use and hence of functional unity. As for Turf, planned or unplanned, nobody outside the Turf can possibly feel a natural identity of interest with it or with what it contains.

Centers of use grow up in lively, diverse districts, just as centers of use occur on a smaller scale in parks, and such centers count especially in district identification if they contain also a landmark that comes to stand for the place symbolically and, in a way, for the district. But centers cannot carry the load of district identification by themselves; differing commercial and cultural facilities, and different-looking scenes, must crop up all through. Within this fabric, physical barriers; such as huge traffic arteries, too large parks, big institutional groupings, are functionally destructive because they block cross-use.

How big, in absolute terms, must an effective district be? I have given a functional definition of size: big enough to fight city hall, but not so big that street neighborhoods are unable to draw district attention and to count.

In absolute terms, this means different sizes in different cities, depending partly on the size of the city as a whole. In Boston, when the North End had a population upward of 30,000 people, it was strong in district power. Now its population is about half that, partly from the salutary process of uncrowding its dwellings as its people have unslummed, and partly from the unsalutary process of being ruthlessly amputated by a new highway. Cohesive though the North End is, it has lost an important sum of district power. In a city like Boston, Pittsburgh or possibly even Philadelphia, as few as 30,000 people may be sufficient to form a district. In New York or Chicago, however, a district as small as 30,000 amounts to nothing. Chicago's most effective district, the Back-of-the-Yards, embraces about 100,000 people, according to the director of the district Council, and is building up its population further. In New York, Greenwich Village is on the small side for an effective district, but is viable because it manages to make up for this with other advantages. It contains approximately 80,000 residents, along with a working population (perhaps a sixth of them the same people) of approximately 125,000. East Harlem and the Lower East Side of New York, both struggling to create effective districts, each contain about 200,000 residents, and need them.

Of course other qualities than sheer population size count in effectiveness—especially good communication and good morale. But population size is vital because it represents, if most of the time only by implication, votes. There are only two ultimate public powers in shaping and running American cities: votes and control of the money. To sound nicer, we may call these "public opinion" and "disbursement of funds," but they are still votes and money. An effective district—and through its mediation, the street neighborhoods—possesses one of these powers: the power of votes. Through this, and this alone, can it effectively influence the power brought to bear on it, for good or for ill, by public money.

Robert Moses, whose genius at getting things done largely consists in understanding this, has made an art of using control of public money to get his way with those whom the voters elect and depend on to represent their frequently opposing interests. This is, of course, in other guises, an old, sad story of democratic government. The art of negating the power of votes with the power of money can be practiced just as effectively by honest public administrators as by dishonest representatives of purely private interests. Either way, seduction or subversion of the elected is easiest when the electorate is fragmented into ineffectual units of power.

On the maximum side, I know of no district larger than 200,000 which operates like a district. Geographical size imposes empirical population limits in any case. In real life, the maximum size of naturally evolved, effective districts seems to be roughly about a mile and a half square.[4] Probably this is because anything larger gets too inconvenient for sufficient local cross-use and for the functional identity that underlies district political identity. In a very big city, populations must therefore be dense to achieve successful districts; otherwise, sufficient political power is never reconciled with viable geographical identity.

This point on geographical size does not mean a city can be mapped out in segments of about a square mile, the segments defined with boundaries, and districts thereby brought to life. It is not boundaries that make a district, but the cross-use and life. The point is considering the physical size and limits of a district is this: the kinds of objects, natural or man-made, that form physical barriers to easy cross-use must be somewhere. It is better that they be at the edges of areas large enough to work as districts than that they cut into the continuity of otherwise feasible districts. The fact of a district lies in what it *is* internally, and in the internal continuity and overlapping with which it is used, not in the way it ends or in how it looks in an air view. Indeed, in many cases very popular city districts spontaneously extend their edges, unless prevented from doing so by physical barriers. A district too thoroughly buffered off also runs the danger of losing economically stimulating visitors from other parts of the city.

Neighborhood planning units that are significantly defined only by their fabric and the life and intricate cross-use they generate, rather than by formalistic boundaries, are of course at odds with orthodox planning conceptions. The difference is the difference between dealing with living, complex organisms, capable of shaping their own destinies, and dealing with fixed and inert settlements, capable merely of custodial care (if that) of what has been bestowed upon them.

In dwelling on the necessity for districts, I do not want to give the impression that an effective city district is self-contained either economically, politically or socially. Of course it is not and cannot be, any more

than a street can be. Nor can districts be duplicates of one another; they differ immensely, and should. A city is not a collection of repetitious towns. An interesting district has a character of its own and specialites of its own. It draws users from outside (it has truly urban economic variety unless it does), and its own people go forth.

Nor is there necessity for district self-containment. In Chicago's Back-of-the-Yards, most of the breadwinners used to work, until the 1940's, at the slaughterhouses within the district. This did have a bearing on district formation in this case, because district organization here was a sequel to labor union organization. But as these residents and their children have graduated from the slaughterhouse job, they have moved into the working life and public life of the greater city. Most, other than teen-agers with after-school jobs, now work outside the district. This movement has not weakened the district; coincident with it, the district has grown stronger.

The constructive factor that has been operating here meanwhile is time. Time, in cities, is the substitute for self-containment. Time, in cities, is indispensable.

The cross-links that enable a district to function as a Thing are neither vague nor mysterious. They consist of working relationships among specific people, many of them without much else in common than that they share a fragment of geography.

The first relationships to form in city areas, given any neighborhood stability, are those in street neighborhoods and those among people who do have something else in common and belong to organizations with one another—churches, P-TA's, businessmen's associations, political clubs, local civic leagues, fund-raising committees for health campaigns or other public causes, sons of such-and-such a village (common clubs among Puerto Ricans today, as they have been with Italians), property owners' associations, block improvement associations, protesters against injustices, and so on, ad infinitum.

To look into almost any relatively established area of a big city turns up so many organizations, mostly little, as to make one's head swim. Mrs. Goldie Hoffman, one of the commissioners of Philadelphia's redevelopment agency, decided to try the experiment of casing the organizations, if any, and the institutions in a drear little Philadelphia section of about ten thousand people, which was up for renewal. To her astonishment and everyone else's, she found nineteen. Small organizations and special-interest organizations grow in our cities like leaves on the trees, and in their own way are just as awesome a manifestation of the persistence and doggedness of life.

The crucial stage in the formation of an effective district goes much beyond this, however. An interweaving, but different, set of relationships must grow up; these are working relationships among people, usually leaders, who enlarge their local public life beyond the neighborhoods of streets and specific organizations or institutions and form relationships with people whose roots and backgrounds are in entirely different constituencies, so to speak. These hop-and-skip relationships are more fortuitous in cities than are the analogous, almost enforced, hop-and-skip links among people from different small groupings within self-contained settlements. Perhaps because we are typically more advanced at forming whole-city neighborhoods of interest than at forming districts, hop-skip district relationships sometimes originate fortuitously among

people from a district who meet in a special-interest neighborhood of the whole city, and then carry over this relationship into their district. Many district networks in New York, for instance, start in this fashion.

It takes surprisingly few hop-skip people, relative to a whole population, to weld a district into a real Thing. A hundred or so people do it in a population a thousand times their size. But these people must have time to find each other, time to try expedient cooperation—as well as time to have rooted themselves, too, in various smaller neighborhoods of place or special interest.

When my sister and I first came to New York from a small city, we used to amuse ourselves with a game we called Messages. I suppose we were trying, in a dim way, to get a grip on the great, bewildering world into which we had come from our cocoon. The idea was to pick two wildly dissimilar individuals—say a headhunter in the Solomon Islands and a cobbler in Rock Island, Illinois—and assume that one had to get a message to the other by word of mouth; then we would each silently figure out a plausible, or at least possible, chain of persons through whom the message could go. The one who could make the shortest plausible chain of messengers won. The headhunter would speak to the headman of his village, who would speak to the trader who came to buy copra, who would speak to the Australian patrol officer when he came through, who would tell the man who was next slated to go to Melbourne on leave, etc. Down at the other end, the cobbler would hear from his priest, who got it from the mayor, who got it from a state senator, who got it from the governor, etc. We soon had these close-to-home messengers down to a routine for almost everybody we could conjure up, but we would get tangled in long chains at the middle until we began employing Mrs. Roosevelt. Mrs. Roosevelt made it suddenly possible to skip whole chains of intermediate connections. She knew the most unlikely people. The world shrank remarkably. It shrank us right out of our game, which became too cut and dried.

A city district requires a small quota of its own Mrs. Roosevelts—people who know unlikely people, and therefore eliminate the necessity for long chains of communication (which in real life would not occur at all).

Settlement-house directors are often the ones who begin such systems of district hop-skip links, but they can only begin them and work at opportune ways to expand them; they cannot carry the load. These links require the growth of trust, the growth of cooperation that is, at least at first, apt to be happenstance and tentative; and they require people who have considerable self-confidence, or sufficient concern about local public problems to stand them in the stead of self-confidence. In East Harlem, where, after terrible disruption and population turnover, an effective district is slowly re-forming against great odds, fifty-two organizations participated in a 1960 pressure meeting to tell the Mayor and fourteen of his commissioners what the district wants. The organizations included P-TA's, churches, settlements, and welfare groups, civic clubs, tenant associations, businessmen's associations, political clubs, and the local congressman, assemblyman and councilman. Fifty-eight individuals had specific responsibilities in getting up the meeting and setting its policy; they included people of all sorts of talents and occupations, and a great ethnic range—Negroes, Italians, Puerto Ricans, and undefinables. This represents a lot of hop-skip district links. It has taken years and skill on the part of half a dozen people to achieve this amount of network, and the process is only starting to reach the stage of being effective.

Once a good, strong network of these hop-skip links does get going in a city district, the net can enlarge relatively swiftly and weave all kinds of resilient new patterns. One sign that it is doing so, sometimes, is the growth of a new kind of organization, more or less district-wide, but impermanent, formed specifically for *ad hoc* purposes.[5] But to get going, a district network needs these three requisites: a start of some kind; a physical area with which sufficient people can identify as users; and Time.

The people who form hop-skip links, like the people who form the smaller links in streets and special-interest organizations, are not at all the statistics that are presumed to represent people in planning and housing schemes. Statistical people are a fiction for many reasons, one of which is that they are treated as if infinitely interchangeable. Real people are unique, they invest years of their lives in significant relationships with other unique people, and are not interchangeable in the least. Severed from their relationships, they are destroyed as effective social beings—sometimes for a little while, sometimes forever.[6]

In city neighborhoods, whether streets or districts, if too many slowly grown public relationships are disrupted at once, all kinds of havoc can occur—so much havoc, instability and helplessness, that it sometimes seems time will never again get in its licks.

Harrison Salisbury, in a series of *New York Times* articles, "The Shook-Up Generation," put well this vital point about city relationships and their disruption.

"Even a ghetto [he quoted a pastor as saying], after it has remained a ghetto for a period of time builds up its social structure and this makes for more stability, more leadership, more agencies for helping the solution of public problems."

But when slum clearance enters an area [Salisbury went on], it does not merely rip out slatternly houses. It uproots the people. It tears out the churches. It destroys the local business man. It sends the neighborhood lawyer to new offices downtown and it mangles the tight skein of community friendships and group relationships beyond repair.

It drives the old-timers from their broken-down flats or modest homes and forces them to find new and alien quarters. And it pours into a neighborhood hundreds and thousands of new faces . . .

Renewal planning, which is largely aimed at saving buildings, and incidentally some of the population, but at strewing the rest of a locality's population, has much the same result. So does too heavily concentrated private building, capitalizing in a rush on the high values created by a stable city neighborhood. From Yorkville, in New York, an estimated 15,000 families have been driven out between 1951 and 1960 by this means; virtually all of them left unwillingly. In Greenwich Village, the same thing is happening. Indeed, it is a miracle that our cities have any functioning districts, not that they have so few. In the first place, there is relatively little city territory at present which is, by luck, well suited physically to forming districts with good cross-use and identity. And within this, incipient or slightly too weak districts are forever being amputated, bisected and generally shaken up by misguided planning policies. The districts that are effective enough to defend themselves from planned disruption are eventually trampled in an unplanned gold rush

by those who aim to get a cut of these rare social treasures.

To be sure, a good city neighborhood can absorb newcomers into itself, both newcomers by choice and immigrants settling by expediency, and it can protect a reasonable amount of transient population too. But these increments or displacements have to be gradual. If self-government in the place is to work, underlying any float of population must be a continuity of people who have forged neighborhood networks. These networks are a city's irreplaceable social capital. Whenever the capital is lost, from whatever cause, the income from it disappears, never to return until and unless new capital is slowly and chancily accumulated.

Some observers of city life, noting that strong city neighborhoods are so frequently ethnic communities—especially communities of Italians, Poles, Jews or Irish—have speculated that a cohesive ethnic base is required for a city neighborhood that works as a social unit. In effect, this is to say that only hyphenated-Americans are capable of local self-government in big cities. I think this is absurd.

In the first place, these ethnically cohesive communities are not always as naturally cohesive as they may look to outsiders. Again citing the Back-of-the Yards as an example, its backbone population is mainly Central European, but all kinds of Central European. It has, for example, literally dozens of national churches. The traditional enmities and rivalries among these groups were a most severe handicap. Greenwich Village's three main parts derive from an Italian community, an Irish community and a Henry Jamesian patrician community. Ethnic cohesiveness may have played a part in the formation of these sections, but it has been no help in welding district cross-links—a job that was begun many years ago by a remarkable settlement-house director, Mary K. Simkhovich. Today many streets in these old ethnic communities have assimilated into their neighborhoods a fantastic ethnic variety from almost the whole world. They have also assimilated a great sprinkling of middle-class professionals and their families, who prove to do very well at city street and district life, in spite of the planning myth that such people need protective islands of pseudosuburban "togetherness." Some of the streets that functioned best in the Lower East Side (before they were wiped out) were loosely called "Jewish," bit contained, as people actually involved in the street neighborhoods, individuals of more than forty differing ethnic origins. One of New York's most effective neighborhoods, with an internal communication that is a marvel, is the midtown East Side of predominately high-income people, utterly undefinable except as Americans.

In the second place, wherever ethnically cohesive neighborhoods develop and are stable, they possess another quality besides ethnic identity. They contain many individuals who stay put. This, I think, more than sheer ethnic identity, is the significant factor. It typically takes many years after such groups have settled in for time to work and for the inhabitants to attain stable, effective neighborhoods.

Here is a seeming paradox: To maintain in a neighborhood sufficient people who stay put, a city must have the very fluidity and mobility of use that Reginald Isaacs noted, as mentioned early in this chapter, when he speculated whether neighbor-

hoods can therefore mean anything very significant to cities.

Over intervals of time, many people change their jobs and the locations of their jobs, shift or enlarge their outside friendships and interests, change their family sizes, change their income up or down, even change many of their tastes. In short they live, rather than just exist. If they live in diversified, rather than monotonous, districts—in districts, particularly, where many details of physical change can constantly be accommodated—and if they like the place, they can stay put despite changes in the locales or natures of their other pursuits or interests. Unlike the people who must move from a lower-middle to a middle-middle to an upper-middle suburb as their incomes and leisure activities change (or be very outré indeed), or the people of a little town who must move to another town or to a city to find different opportunities, city people need not pull up stakes for such reasons.

A city's collection of opportunities of all kinds, and the fluidity with which these opportunities and choices can be used, is an asset—not a detriment—for encouraging city-neighborhood stability.

However, this asset has to be capitalized upon. It is thrown away where districts are handicapped by sameness and are suitable, therefore, to only a narrow range of incomes, tastes and family circumstances. Neighborhood accommodations for fixed, bodiless, statistical people are accommodations for instability. The people in them, as statistics, may stay the same. But the people in them, as people, do not. Such places are forever way stations.

NOTES

1. In the Upper West Side of Manhattan, a badly failed area where social disintegration has been compounded by ruthless bulldozing, project building and shoving people around, annual pupil turnover in schools was more than 50 percent in 1950–60. In 16 schools, it reached an average of 92 percent. It is ludicrous to think that with any amount of effort, official or unofficial, even a tolerable school is possible in a neighborhood of such extreme instability. Good schools are impossible in any unstable neighborhoods with high pupil turnover rates, and this includes unstable neighborhoods which *also* have good housing.

2. Even the old reason for settling on an ideal population of about 7,000—sufficient to populate an elementary school—is silly the moment it is applied to big cities, as we discover if we merely ask the question: Which school? In many American cities, parochial-school enrollment rivals or surpasses public-school enrollment. Does this mean there should be two schools as presumed neighborhood glue, and the population should be twice as large? Or is the population right, and should the schools be half as large? And why the elementary school? If school is to be the touchstone of scale, why not the junior high school, an institution typically far more troublesome in our cities than the elementary school? The question "Which school?" is never asked because this vision is based on no more realism about schools than about anything else. The school is a plausible, and usually abstract, excuse for defining *some* size for a unit that comes out of dreams about imaginary cities. It is necessary as a formal framework, to preserve designers from intellectual chaos, and it has no other reason for being. Ebenezer Howard's model towns are the ancestors of the idea, to be sure, but its durability comes from the need to fill an intellectual vacuum.

3. Thus it was discovered in Jefferson Houses, in East Harlem, that many people who had lived in the project four years had never laid eyes on the community center. It is at the dead end of the project (dead end, in the sense that no city life, only more park, lies beyond). People from other portions of the project had no normal reason for travelling to it from their portions and every normal reason not to. It looked, over there, like more of the same. A settlement-house director in the Lower East Side, Dora Tannenbaum of Grand Street Settlement, says of people in different building groupings of an adjacent project: "These people cannot seem to get the idea they have anything in common with one another. They act as if the other parts of the project were on a different planet." Visually these projects are units. Functionally they are no such thing. The appearance tells a lie.

4. The Back-of-the-Yards in Chicago is the only significant exception to this rule that I know of.

5. In Greenwich Village, these frequently run to long, explicit names: e.g., the Joint Emergency Committee to Close Washington Square Park to All but Emergency Traffic; the Cellar Dwellers' Tenant Emergency Committee; the Committee of Neighbors to Get the Clock on Jefferson Market Courthouse Started, the Joint Village Committee to Defeat the West Village Proposal and Get a Proper One.

6. There are people who seemingly can behave like interchangeable statistics and take up in a different place exactly where they left off, but they must belong to one of our fairly homogeneous and ingrown nomad societies, like Beatniks, or Regular Army officers and their families, or the peripatetic junior executive families of suburbia, described by William H. Whyte, Jr., in *The Organization Man*.

54. Living Space for the New Millions | Erwin A. Gutkind

The long-run historical trend toward large-scale and relatively dense urban settlement is an inescapable accompaniment of the population explosion, not only in the United States but throughout the world. Despite this trend, the form of urban settlement in the future is highly ambiguous. One of the major issues is the eventual role of the central city in a metropolitan or regional complex. Underlying Jane Jacobs' defense of the neighborhood and district in the previous selection is the belief that downtown cores have certain unique qualities and functions and, therefore, that the central city should continue to dominate surrounding suburban settlements.

E. A. Gutkind is one of the leading spokesmen for an alternative viewpoint. His fundamental argument is that a broad historical perspective reveals the declining significance of the traditional city as a progressive force in the advance of civilization. He claims that most planners, including urban sociologists, have tended to overlook this fact. Gutkind says we must acknowledge the twilight of cities and plan accordingly. He advocates that we adopt as guiding principles the ideas of decentralization and dispersal and that we employ the instruments of city, regional, and national planning to hasten the day when an organic and integrated urban region becomes a reality.

Erwin A. Gutkind (1896–1968) was Research Professor of City Planning in the Institute for Environmental Studies at the University of Pennsylvania. He was the author of the *Urban Development* series (1964–   ) and of numerous other books, including *International History of City Development* (1964), *The Twilight of Cities* (1962), and *Community and Environment* (1954).

Our environment is expanding, but the interplay of space, scale, and sprawl continues to spread disorder over ever-larger regions and growing spheres of urban and rural existence. No determined attempts have been made to cope with this situation on a large scale through a systematic physical and cultural decentralization and dispersal of the congested conurbations. The outburst into the wide unexplored spaces of the world, which in the Renaissance heralded the beginning of a new age, is repeated today with far greater intensity in scope and character.

To conquer space, to explore the universe, are realizable ambitions of mankind. New energies are released. A new vision of life is born, and with it a keen awareness of unlimited possibilities takes hold of the mind of an ever-growing number of people. Just as in the Renaissance the discovery of new lands and new inventions transformed the attitude to life and left its mark on all works of man, on the urban and rural environment, so today the impact of the emerging possibilities will revolutionize our environment more fundamentally than at any other period of history, with the exception of the agricultural and urban revolutions.

It is a great demand that is made upon

us. Many cherished ideas will have to be discarded. New ideals have to be evolved and absorbed: and although it is not too likely that the Malthusian problem will be solved by interstellar migrations, the imagination, the power, and the enthusiasm that are the agents of this outward drive into the universe cannot fail to reshape the scale and the character of our terrestial actions.

But apart from these considerations, there are very cogent and practical reasons that should make us pause for reflection. The most obvious reason is the population explosion. Where will the new millions live and how will they be accommodated? In cities, even if the urban environment is improved?

The scriptural injunction, "Increase and multiply," is no longer a sensible proposition. The world population is now exceeding 2.7 billion and doubling about every fifty years. The present rate of increase, of 1 per cent per year, is rising, and according to the demographic estimates of the United Nations will have reached 3 per cent by the year 2000.

About 10,000 years ago the total population of the world engaged in hunting and food gathering may have been something over five million. After the agricultural revolution and in the early stages of the urban revolution the total had exceeded eighty-six million. At the time of Christ it had risen to perhaps 250 million. The first doubling to 500 million took 1,600 years; the next doubling to one billion only 250 years, in 1850; the third doubling to two billion only eighty years, in 1930. If the present trends continue, the total population will have reached four billion in the late 1970's—a doubling in about forty years—and over six billion by 2000.

Population growth is most rapid in the underdeveloped countries, in Asia, Latin America, and most of Africa, where about two-thirds of the world's population live in conditions that are near or below the subsistence minimum. If this development persists unchecked, it will divide the world even more sharply than political rivalries into two antagonistic groups: the "have" and the "have-not" blocs. This is the over-all picture.

In this country, the United States, there will be more than 300 million by 2000, but this prospect does not seem to provoke serious thought on the environmental problems which this increase will create. David Riesman remarks on this attitude of the younger American generation in *Problems of United States Economic Development*, The Committee for Economic Development:

> Serious discussion of the future is just what is missing in the United States. . . . We live now, think later. . . . I think we fear opacity of the future, and try not to pierce it with concrete plans. . . . What we fear to face is more than total destruction; it is total meaninglessness.

This attitude will not solve the problems of the urban and suburban chaos nor will it help to revitalize the rural areas. The population of the U.S.S.R. was, at the beginning of 1959, according to the All-Union census, somewhat over 208 million, and the natural increase exceeded $3\frac{1}{2}$ million per year. The urban population had risen from 60.4 million before the war to almost 100 million in 1959, and the number of cities and urban-type settlements from 2,759 in 1939 to 4,616 in 1959.

This increase continued up to the initiation of the Virgin Lands Program in 1954; then it began to decline and the population in the eastern areas increased by 16 million, a trend that is likely to continue. Although the rate of growth of the urban population is very considerable, it seems that great efforts are being made to settle large numbers of the population in rural areas—an effort that, if successful, would reduce the pressure on the cities.

China is in a different position. Of its almost 650 million people, a majority live in rural areas. By 1955 about 100 million lived in cities, a number that has risen during the last years. China has twenty-five cities with a population of more than 500,000 but, the bulk of the urban population lives in small market towns. Nearly 75 percent of the total population are concentrated in 15 percent of the national territory, in the eastern lowlands and hills, and in Szechwan, the most populous province.

These three countries represent three different types of population problems, but have in common the pressure of a growing population upon the urban areas and on the available space in general. India and Pakistan are in positions not too dissimilar to that of China. It would go far beyond the scope of this work to go into a detailed investigation of their national differences. The most threatening problem is everywhere the same: the population explosion forces a new assessment of how the new millions—in some cases also the old millions—can be settled and housed in a dignified manner that will disperse the vast urban conglomerations and create a balanced structure of settlement over the whole national territory.

Decentralization and Dispersal

The goal of a new structure of settlement is not to change the urbanite into a suburbanite. Nor is it anything like the production of numerous blueprints for new communities, green belts, parkways, and rural areas—possibilities only discussed among those who fail to understand that life cannot be pressed into the strait jacket of preconceived schemes or narrow ideas. The large-scale and long-term plans that are needed cannot be anything else but a flexible framework for future action. But what should be absolutely clear is the direction in which we intend to move ahead, and the delineation of those areas which are to be thinned out and those which are to be developed. Furthermore, if we want to create a dynamic equilibrium of settlement, we should think and act in processes, not according to notions of static entities. How can we proceed?

In broad terms our task is threefold: the replacement of the built-up areas which are "lost" through the thinning-out and through the reduction of population and building density in the cities, the conversion of hitherto undeveloped or not fully developed areas into living space for the new millions, and an organic integration of the old and the new areas over large regions. The guiding principles to achieve these goals are decentralization and dispersal. The instruments are city, regional, and national planning.

Decentralization and dispersal are interdependent. They affect urban and rural areas alike. Decentralization should be understood not in the narrower sense of a decentralization of industry but in its broader meaning of decentralization of settlement, that is, the loosening up of urban districts. Dispersal, on the other hand, spreads beyond the confines of the area from which the overflow of population is to be drained. Thus, decentralization proceeds within a narrower space than dispersal, and dispersal begins where decentralization ends.

Decentralization remains focused on a

center. It is a procedure that does not diminish the importance of the center as such, but changes the spatial structure and interdependence and the functions radiating from it within its sphere of influence. Dispersal affects more or less widely separated places and areas and creates new mental and material relationships to a new environment. A clear distinction between both these principles is essential, if the different types of planning are not to be confused and are to serve as really efficient instruments. Both, decentralization and dispersal, have a dual effect: they influence the places, districts, and regions from which people migrate and those to which they move.

Decentralization is a term much used—and misused—today. Its equivalent on the Continent is the German term *Entballung der Staedte*, the decongestion of cities. The problem is the same everywhere, and, unfortunately, the resulting misunderstandings are also identical. Decentralization, as it is mostly understood, is the development of suburbs on the fringes of the central city, which is preserved as substantially the same compact entity that it has been before: the all-absorbing and domineering influence on the life of the decentralized units.

This "decentralization," however, has nothing to do with an organic decentralization that affects the core city and its surroundings at the same time and with the same intensity. It does not lead to a systematic loosening up of the overcrowded urban areas, nor does it lead to a balanced physical, social and economic integration of the metropolitan area.

The instruments of planning are, as mentioned above, city, regional, and national planning. These are interdependent, like decentralization and dispersal, and should be used simultaneously or the

results will be a patchwork of unrelated reforms that, after a short time, will be more difficult to improve than the present situation.

In order to forestall wrong expectations and to clarify the exact objectives of this investigation, it may be pertinent to repeat that in this connection it is neither possible nor desirable to produce a manual of city planning, a sort of "do-it-yourself" pamphlet on how to proceed. Here we are exclusively concerned with the methods in general, how they should be applied, and what the results should be. And further: the aim is the transformation of the urban and rural environment on a large scale through the redistribution of the fundamental needs of homes, work, distribution and circulation, leisure and recreation, social intercourse, and cultural stimulation.

And finally, I want to confute one argument that is, as I know from experience, most likely to be put forward, namely, that the following suggestions are basically not different from the usual plans for the decentralization of urban areas. To the best of my knowledge, there is not one single proposition that tries to eliminate the traditional role of the city as an all-absorbing center. All proposals, even if they envisage a fairly far-reaching decentralization, leave the central city intact and maintain its spirit and its core. Frank Lloyd Wright's *The Disappearing City* comes, perhaps, nearer to the ideas propounded in this work, although they have not been thought out and worked out in intelligible form.

I do not pretend for a moment that my own ideas offer a final solution or that they cannot be criticized on any reasonable ground. On the contrary, I hope that they will stimulate discussion and reassessment. But I do maintain that they deviate fundamentally from all the patterns which have been suggested as possible city development, be they stars or fingers, wedges or rings, galaxies or a combination of several of these pattern-book models.

For me, and many like-minded people, the twilight of cities is a fact, and I cannot convince myself that it is possible or useful to revive something that is dead, namely, the city. I have to rely on the indulgence of the reader, "your humble patience, pray," if I venture once more to ask for his objective and unbiased reflection on my insistence that the starting point of the following proposal is not city renewal but city dispersal. It may be that my ideas fall short of the expectations I have raised and that the last remarks are regarded as an expression of apologetic diffidence. The first may be true; the second is definitely not.

City or Local Planning   This procedure generates centrifugal tendencies and furthers existing trends working in the same direction. The process is reversed: in the past centripetal forces formed and sustained the urban structure even where cities expanded or grew amorphous at the periphery.

This new type of city planning aims at a radical thinning-out of the total urban area through population movement, and transfer of activities and buildings and equipment to other places, which regional or national schemes, or both, have assigned as suitable locations for similar functions in the new structure of settlement. This is the program. The *methods* to realize it are:

1. No slums are to be rebuilt; the areas gained by slum clearance are to be retained as open spaces.
2. The core of the urban area is to be loosened up by the evacuation of commercial enterprises, entertainment and cultural institutions, and small industries located in the central area, gradually increasing in scope and intensity till the densely built-up area is converted into a central open space.
3. The open spaces thus gained are to be interrelated as a continuous park system connecting the former slums, the central open space, and the thinned-out residential quarters and industrial districts. Gradually this will turn what has been a congested urban area into a park landscape merging into the open country.

Slum clearance   Slums cannot be demolished before new accommodation is available and industries and white-collar jobs are redistributed through regional allocation. Consequently, slum clearance and dispersal of the core areas are a combined operation. The areas reclaimed in this process may be small and widely dispersed, sometimes consisting of only a few isolated plots. Nevertheless, they form the original nuclei of the comprehensive scheme of dispersal. In the beginning they may serve as neighborhood playgrounds or recreation areas that can easily be prepared for this purpose. As provisional amenities they do not involve a major expenditure.

The urban core   It has been mentioned above that the scarcity of space is felt first in the cities. It may, therefore, seem to be absurd to suggest a further reduction of space exactly in the area where congestion is greatest. To define this procedure in these terms is, of course, self-contradictory because the causes that have produced the congestion—buildings and streets—are removed and the area previously confined by them is converted into an open space. In other words, the space needed for these buildings, streets, and squares is shifted to other places within the regional scheme.

In general, urban centers are to be redeveloped as central open spaces and not to be rebuilt. After all, as has been explained on the foregoing pages, there is no need to preserve these overgrown tumors in the centers of cities. They are a disturbing legacy of the past, dating back to the Middle Ages.

There is no justification for retaining the concentration of offices and shops in the heart of the urban communities—especially not now, when the cities are spilling over into the countryside and when these concentrations are the main reason why all our cities suffer from an accelerated arteriosclerosis and stagnation. Shopping centers, with a great variety of shops and even with opportunities for specialized shopping, are moving out to the suburbs. Economic activities are redistributed from the older central districts to the fringe areas; retail trades, household services, warehousing, and other industrial services follow the same trend.

In a study, *Guiding Metropolitan Growth*, made by the Committee for Economic Development in 1960, this outward movement has been investigated in detail, although the recommendations advocated in this statement on national policy maintain the essential principles of metropolitan growth.

Of thirteen million dwelling units erected in nonfarm areas from 1946 through 1958, approximately eleven million, or 85 percent, have been located outside central cities. Both sales and jobs in retail lines have dropped steadily in the core as a proportion of the New York region over a 25-year period with the outer rings registering the corresponding gains. . . . A gradual but unremitting relative decline in manufacturing jobs located in central cities is also discernible. [On the other hand] certain types of activities show little inclination to deconcentrate. Business and governmental services requiring face-to-face relationships

or dependence upon a large pool of female labour continue to exercise a strong preference for office space in the core of large metropolitan areas.

This latter conclusion may be correct for the time being, that is, within the present structure of settlement, but there is no reason to assume that this will not or cannot change in different conditions. Face-to-face relationships are more and more replaced by telephone or other media of communication, and grow increasingly impersonal the more the trend toward the organized irresponsibility of committees or of large trusts becomes the order of the day.

Then there are the "gray areas" between the business core and the suburbs, where in the first quarter of this century the majority of families lived. Since 1945 the exodus from these areas has gathered momentum, and lower income groups, including racial minorities, have moved into these potential slums.

Industries, especially those producing standardized goods, are shifting to horizontal-line processing in one-story plants and are thus forced out of the crowded districts to larger sites outside the urban areas where industrial districts or trading estates can be developed.

Taking all these movements together, there is a definite "natural" trend away from the core of cities. A determined prompting and persuasion is, therefore, not out of place and would ultimately produce results which are already in the making.

However, old ideas and habits die hard. It is not surprising to observe that city centers are treated in development plans almost as a Holy of Holies. They seem to be sacrosanct, and not only their existence but also their expansion are taken for granted. The possibility of reducing the central conglomerations never enters the minds of planning officials. They rationalize *ex post facto* what they believe to be the only "reasonable" solution, without even faintly realizing that there may be other ideas that should at least be investigated. Their attitude is reminiscent of Christian Morgenstern's Palmström, when after a street accident, in which he was knocked down by a car, he concludes "*dass nicht sein kann, was nicht sein darf.*" (In a free translation this means: "that nothing can be that ought not to be.")

In this mood they lay down the law that a "vital" center will continue to exist and to develop as the decision making area of a metropolis. But why is it "vital"? Is decision-making an activity that must be concentrated in the center? True, it may affect a majority of citizens, but only a relatively small number are needed to make decisions. Moreover, in this affluent society an ever growing number of urbanites are contracting out of active participation in politics, because they know from experience that their vote has no purpose other than to enable the various parties to play musical chairs, and that the new team forgets only too easily the promises made during the election campaign. This may be regrettable, but it can certainly not be altered by concentrating decision-making in the central city.

Why do city planning officials assume as an undeniable fact that the trend towards greater need for office space will continue? Of course, it will continue, if no other opportunities are offered elsewhere. I believe that it is almost impossible to argue with planners who are overwhelmed by the pressure of daily routine work and are not free to propose more radical changes or to convince the city fathers that this preservation of the *status quo*, even with some modifications, is unrealistic.

Traffic congestion will increase if retail trades and cultural activities continue to be packed together in the core area. This approach will not solve the problem. It is a retrogressive "solution" that will make matters worse. It retains basically the concentric development of the urban area, and prefers a static pattern to an organic and linear decentralization.

The central open space would eliminate the most disturbing features of urban congestion and of a deceptive urban attraction. It would revitalize the communal structure and create a focal area that is the real property of all inhabitants, their genuine community center, which the park system spreads to all parts of the region.

Only a small number of the activities previously concentrated in the core city are to be grouped together within a small area. This would include certain branches of the administration and possibly some headquarters of large commercial enterprises. A careful investigation would have to precede the selection of the institutions that would qualify for a location in a relatively narrow compass. They would form the *Desk City*, empty at night and used only in daytime. This City can be located at the fringes of the central park, loosely laid out with ample open spaces, underground access roads, and garages.

Parks and parkways The grid of parks and parkways is the first prerequisite for a rational tidying up of the whole amorphous urban mass. A green belt, or green islands interspersed between the built-up areas, green wedges penetrating to the center from the periphery are insufficient means to achieve this end. Nature should be omnipresent, not merely as a Sunday amenity but as an indispensable part of everyday life, on the daily walks to the schools, to the shopping centers, to the stations, and to other parts of the community.

The atmosphere, the mental and sentimental influence of our environment, can create conditions that are essential to our well-being, even more essential than the satisfaction of our material needs. Verdure not only within easy reach but within direct view of every inhabitant resembles the keynote of a polyphonic composition. Every settlement of the future should be a park community. Even the industrial districts, with the possible exception of those for heavy industry, can be made partners in this revolution of environment, situated in green surroundings near playing fields and in direct connection with the open landscape.

The realization of this goal would be the final fulfillment of the hopeful beginning inaugurated over two hundred years ago by John Wood's plan for Bath. His plan marked the end of an era which excluded Nature from the built-up urban areas. In Bath this principle was abandoned. The architects opened their town to the open country. They built the new quarters on the hilly slopes of the surrounding land and made Nature an essential element of the whole. With this decision modern city planning was born. It is left to us to draw the ultimate conclusions from this sublime example—not only in theory but in practice. The far-reaching integration of Nature with architecture has a profound effect on the structure and atmosphere of the community. [See accompanying table.]

EFFECTS OF INTEGRATION OF NATURE WITH ARCHITECTURE

It creates:	It rejects:
A unifying element.	Piecemeal incoherence.
A stimulus to the dramatization of social life and the revivification of individual life.	Self-centered insensibility.

It generates:	It ends:
A spill-over of the population into the region.	Overcrowding and high density.
A direct interaction between the region and the urban area.	Disfiguration and misuse of the countryside by urban sprawl.
Intimate awareness by the townspeople of the cycle of Nature.	Antagonism between city and country.

It produces:	It abolishes:
A loosening up of the block system.	Rigidity.
A splitting up of the block front.	Uniformity.
A disintegration of the speculative lot system.	Cut-to-pattern buildings.

It provides:	It prevents:
A steady flow of fresh air.	Stagnation and pollution of the air.
Free access to sun and light.	Sunless and drab rooms.
An easy opportunity for recreation.	Indoor rustiness.

It enforces:	It avoids:
Diversity of layout and buildings.	Repetition.
Regeneration of architecture and space relations.	Traditional humbug.
Reorganization of traffic.	Stop-gap modifications.

The character of the streets will gradually change. Instead of dull and uniform canyons, the streets will be open ribbons, rhythmically articulated by groups of buildings with free views of other parts of the community. The uninterrupted walls of houses, the continuous block fronts, will disappear. Traffic arteries will be so laid out that they only skirt the communities, never passing through any urban or rural settlement. Consequently, they will no longer converge on a center, the less so as central areas have ceased to exist as attracting focal points. Secondary access roads will lead to the residential and industrial districts, providing a grid of communications over the whole area.

The separation of fast traffic from residential, recreational, and working district, and the organic direction of local traffic with a minimum of interference in all those areas where the pedestrian is king, not the automobile, restore to life one of the most essential elements which lift it above the level of a narrow parochialism: mobility, a possibility that everyone wants to exploit and to enjoy, that has been lost in the chaos of our congested cities and highways. We shall deal with this problem later in detail.

Some general observations may clarify the consequences of the ideas put forward on the foregoing pages. Physical dispersal without a simultaneous cultural dispersal leads nowhere. It would make all efforts illusory, and maintain the old-fashioned unity by centralization instead of creating integration by organic dispersal over a wide area. The new mobility enables us to reexamine the need for a concentration of cultural institutions in the most populous communities.

What cultural opportunities can be offered as public services? I am not refer-ring to the inevitable seond- and third-rate cinemas and other commercialized entertainments that cater to the lower level of uncritical enjoyment. The cultural media that provide for enrichment and creative development of the mind belong to another category. In this connection I am thinking exclusively of those institutions which can give a distinctive character to a community and whose formative and attracting power is strong enough to radiate over a wide area.

To this group belong all educational services, such as universities and colleges, libraries, opportunities for adult enlightenment, and, of course, schools, which are in any case dispersed all over the country. Furthermore, there are museums, exhibitions, theaters, concert halls, and other similar opportunities. All the cultural goods these institutions can provide are mobile. There is no need whatsoever to regard them as "fixed industries" that must be located in only a few big cities.

In the new structure of settlement there may be university towns similar to those which already exist, as, for instance, Princeton, Oxford, and Cambridge, but of a purer character, not spoilt by the encroachment of industries. There may be places where theater and opera performances imprint their mark on the life of the community. There may be museum towns from which traveling exhibitions are regularly sent out. There may be festival towns where special entertainments are organized. The rudiments of this dispersal do exist, and it is necessary only to evolve them further and to get rid of the notion that most of these opportunities should be concentrated in one or several big cities.

None of these institutions, let us repeat, is fixed to one place, but each can be made the focal point of the communal life of a small community. Their accessibility will be improved because our mobility is increased. To drive to a place, say, 20 or 30 miles away, over first-rate roads will take less time than to squeeze through traffic jams, to stop at innumerable red lights, and to face the almost insuperable problem of parking.

Would it not be an exciting adventure to lift the visit to a museum or a theater out of the routine of everyday life by surrounding it with the atmosphere of a festive occasion, and to attend a performance or look at works of art in a setting of natural beauty, instead of in an environment that makes relaxation impossible, whose noise and smell impair concentration and enjoyment? Is the popularity of open-air performances not perhaps an indication of this desire for a more stimulating environment?

In any case, the dispersal of cultural amenities to small communities is justified for two reasons: their removal from the hustle and bustle of the big cities and the need to make them revitalizing factors of the life of small communities. Their creative effectiveness will increase because they are more easily accessible and, above all, because the atmosphere surrounding them radiates the special attraction of something unusual.

It is astonishing to observe how strongly city planners are influenced by stereotyped patterns of urban development. The past and theoretical rigidity make them insensitive to the potentialities inherent in our situation. Virtually all metropolitan development schemes are based on the preservation of a city center, even if a far-reaching decentralization is suggested. The patterns for this decentralization are more or less the time-honored stars or rings or similar figures. A particularly ingenious city planner has even promoted the idea of a shifting center that would wander with the extension of the city.

This *idée fixe* has taken such a hold over their minds that they fail to see the great possibilities a flexible and unbiased approach to the reshaping of our environment offers. They cannot shed the notion of metropolitan growth, as though a metropolis or a big city is something permanent, something unique that is not subject to fundamental change. Change is permanent, however, not cities, and this change can be sometimes violent and most destructive, if it is not voluntarily and in time brought under control.

The advocates of urban supremacy are apparently convinced that metropolitan existence will be the normal way of life in the future. This may or may not be so. Looking at the world today, we can see ourselves heading for an antstate, and a decaying urban civilization spreading over our planet in spite of, or just because of, its inner contradictions.

If this is what the exponents of an unmitigated urbanization expect, would it not be more reasonable to try to remedy the causes, instead of treating the symptoms with small doses of homeopathic drugs, such as drawing-board patterns of layout or lovely clover-leaves and similar patent medicines? Why does this school of thought assume that a systematic and large-scale dispersion would make easy accessibility to rural land unnecessary and would impair spontaneous communication and choice of residence? Why would small communities have a high density at the center and why would the flow of activities and traffic converge at the center of each community? On what grounds can small communities that have come into existence in an organic regional development be equated with satellite towns in the usual sense, or, by implication, can only a metropolis be "imaginable" and not dispersed small communities? And why is the encouragement of continued metropolitan agglomerations accepted as the gospel of city planning? Why are all these assumptions put forward as guiding principles of city planning?

The answer is simple: it is contained in the tacit postulate of continued metropolitan agglomeration. I do not want to repeat the arguments against this policy, but I do believe that this approach to the grave problems of an unchecked urbanization is not only sterile but dangerous, and that the danger, which inevitably will grow in intensity, can be avoided by a determined turning away from outworn doctrines and a serious search for solutions more attuned to the future.

Regional Planning Looked at from the vantage point of our present situation, in this case from the existing cities, regional planning exerts a pull away from the urban areas, while within the region it tends towards concentration and interdependence of hitherto more or less isolated settlement units. Although this is perhaps too doctrinaire and theoretical an explanation, it may help to clarify the difference between city and regional planning.

Before we proceed to define the meaning and purpose of regional planning, a few words on metropolitan planning may be pertinent. I have often been asked what is the difference between city and metropolitan planning. My answer has always been: none—metropolitan planning merely covers a larger area but works on the same erroneous principles and uses the same methods. Metropolitan planning, as understood in this country, is mostly concerned with some administrative or organizational adjustments or, at best, with the preservation of open spaces. It does not, or if at

all, only very timidly, try to interfere with the mushroom growth of suburbs or similar outlying excrescences of the metropolis.

Moreover, the term metropolitan planning is often mixed up with "regional" planning, thus confusing the issues even more. What is meant by this terminology is merely the metropolitan region, which is in any case a rather elusive something. Metropolitan planning should disappear from the vocabulary and the program of work of city planners and be made part and parcel of genuine regional planning. It could have been useful if it had at least begun to introduce some order into the chaotic mess of urban sprawl and to develop a system of functional spacing as the first step toward an organic redistribution of settlement and industry. This opportunity has passed. The metropolitan tentacles are grabbing more and more land.

An alleviation of this unrestricted absorption of the countryside into the metropolitan whirlpool can be expected only from regional planning, from a mutual adaptation of city and region, and from a coordinated transformation of the urban and rural areas in which the level of organic redevelopment would simultaneously rise as in communicating pipes. This does not mean a ruralization of urban areas or an urbanization of rural areas, but a leveling-up of both to a higher standard of cultural and material evolution and a reinstatement of human values as the supreme arbiters of all our efforts to revitalize the environment.

In every age and in most countries of the world Ideal Cities have been designed, and in some cases, built. They enshrined the purest and highest aspirations and a vision of the future. Today, Ideal Cities can no longer fulfill this mission. While only a few generations ago the village and the small town were almost self-sufficient units, today the world is our unit of thinking and acting.

But it is not only the world that is shrinking. Every country is undergoing the same transformation. In other words, the scale of our actions is widening. Translated into the language of city planning, this means that we have to design plans for the Ideal Region and for a country as a whole. All our cities have developed on ground plans conceived for small towns. They belong to an era that was far removed from our age with its violent social and economic, scientific and technological changes. Hitherto our efforts to reshape the urban and rural environment have not been attuned to this disturbing outlook. Intense mental exertions and clear vision are needed to adapt our ideas to these new conditions.

The *Ideal Region* is the result of a far-reaching redistribution of settlement, industry, and population, and of a reshaping of the environment in such a manner that it can absorb the new millions and offer them a dignified and productive existence. This demands the preparation of large-scale and long-term plans for vast regions within which a new structure of settlement can systematically grow up, and every community can serve distinctive functions as an organic part of the whole. This is the program for the Ideal Region. Let us not forget that the Ideal Cities of the past were social fanfares expressing the conscience and the longing of their age. The Ideal Region should do the same for our time.

What is a region and what is the meaning of regional integration? As long as the relations between town and country were relatively simple, it was not too difficult to find a workable size for a region. So it was in medieval Europe and in China where the towns were centers of a hinterland one days' journey in distance to and from the town. It was similar too in the Colonial period of the United States, when Philadelphia was the largest city because its hinterland was then the largest with the most fertile farmland. Today these simple relations, and with them the easy fixation of a well-defined region, have ceased to exist. Modern means of transport make boundaries illusory and bind together regions that are actually separated.

Regionalism is the result of functional spacing within a certain area. It is a process of gradual growth from inside this area; but it stretches out beyond the regional sphere towards other regions, establishing manifold contacts with them. Regionalism is a unifying force coordinating all activities that make up the life of a region.

The following quotation from *American Regionalism* by Odum and Moore gives an excellent summary of the problems involved:

Of great significance in the culture economy of regionalism [is] the decentralisation of people, of culture, and of pathology [which] may be attained in the new frontiers of American life. . . . Yet again such decentralisation does not apply only to the metropolitan regions or the planned towns and communities round the great cities. It takes into account the whole phenomenon of the new mobility of people, the migrations to and from cities, it comprehends movements to and from farms, providing technical ways for the reintegration of agrarian culture.. . . It points to the development of new frontiers of . . . culture which may provide new centres of health and recreation, of opportunity or urban decentralisation where surplus wealth may be expended or normal culture develop. . . . In the second place the region differs from the mere locality or pure geographic area in that it is characterised not so much by boundary lines and actual limits, by extension from a centre, and by fringe or border margins which separate one area from another. A key attribute of the region is, therefore, that it must be a *constituent unit in an aggregate whole or totality*. Inherent in the *region* as opposed to the mere locality or the isolated section is the essence of unity of which it can exist as a part. . . . In this more vital sense urbanism or metropolitanism is not regionalism in so far as urban centres seek their own ends regardless of relationships to other great centres or in opposition to national or rural ends.

Regionalism, as the connecting link between national and local planning, has to play a decisive role in the process of decentralization and dispersal. Its factual expression is, as already mentioned, the regional structure of settlement as produced by functional spacing. Functional spacing leads to two different, though closely interdependent, results; it assigns certain functions to each individual community, thus giving it a special character, and it balances this distribution of functions among the individual settlements of the region,

Neither the size of a settlement nor the number of its inhabitants nor its distance from the next place can determine the functions it can exert. On the contrary, the functions determine the size, distance, and number. The idea is that settlements with the same functions, especially with the same central services, can be equally spaced from each other. A hierarchy of communities where each rank controls those below it would be the opposite of everything national and regional planning stands for. It would perpetuate the existing structure and prevent coordination of the

individual communities and collaboration between them as equal partners in regional integration.

We must look at the region as a whole and lift as many services as possible onto a regional basis. This point of view would mean an equal distribution of some basic services among all settlements of the region. It would also alter the relationship of some other functions, and it would provide a flexible framework for the complicated interblending of the numerous expressions and needs of modern life.

Regional integration embraces the *whole* life of a region. Social forces are the prime movers of the process. Economic factors are the buttresses giving them stability and guaranteeing their smooth working. Social and economic activities must be conceived and pursued on a regional basis, balancing local interests and rivalries.

In the social sphere an elastic framework of social services reaching every community and every citizen on an equal level must be developed, so that home life, recreation, social intercourse, and cultural activities find ever-widening opportunities and increasing stimulation. In the economic sphere a similar framework must be devised for the provision of work and the distribution of goods and all material amenities over a network of public utility services, bringing scientific and technological innovations within easy reach of every inhabitant of the region. This is, of course, only a rough classification of the manifold factors involved, but it will show the need for integration on a regional level.

Regional integration means the equal distribution of cultural and material goods over the whole region. It produces a regional association of all communities within a given area, rivaling each other in quality but not in quantity. It is, as it were, a neighborhood unit on a regional scale, which focuses the interests of its inhabitants on a common task and on a common purpose without reducing them to the narrow dullness of parochialism.

Regional integration demands:

1. Planning from the top and the bottom at the same time
2. Organic growth from within
3. Unity of rural and urban districts in the cultural, social, and economic sphere
4. Interregional balance of internally homogeneous regions

Planning from top to bottom What is meant by planning from the top and the bottom at the same time? If we attempted to plan a region from the top, delimiting its size, redistributing its population and industry, developing a green grid, assessing its main activities, and allocating them among the different districts and localities within it, without taking into account the approach from the bottom, the local conditions and characteristics, we would create something like an empty shell.

At best the result would be a rigid framework within which the individual communities would lack functional interdependence and a balanced socio-economic structure. In other words, we must apply both the deductive and the inductive method, the former starting from the configuration as a whole and the latter leading from the particular to the general.

The approach from the top means that we must envisage a region as one functional unit and that every community within this unit may become a regional center for a particular purpose. In terms of physical and social planning, this approach implies physical and cultural decentralization and dispersal, resulting in a functional interrelationship between the community units.

There should, however, be no mistake; the physical environment this adaptation to new conditions creates is merely a means not an end in itself. It is the physical framework within which every human activity can be carried on and every individual and social need can be fulfilled with the highest degree of efficiency. The regional plan should assign size, status, and function to the individual communities, replacing their subordination to the absorbing influence of the big cities and their sometimes overspecialized structure with a vigorous coordination and diversity.

Planning from the top consists, therefore, of a twofold approach. First, it is a diagnosis of the special character of the region as a whole and of the forces that make up the functional network of the region. Secondly, it is a modification of the existing pattern and a bringing-out of the inherent potentialities in the interaction all over the region. Consequently, planning a region from the top is not a mere redistribution of what exists, but an eminently formative task, initiating a greater productivity and a rational adaptation of the natural resources of man's needs.

A simple example may be helpful. If we move to a new house, the first thing we do is adapt it in general to our personal taste and convenience. We brood over the best use of the different rooms; each should fulfill its purpose efficiently, and all together should form an integrated dwelling unit. The use of a number of rooms has been fixed from the very beginning; they correspond, as it were, to the natural resources of the region, such as coal, water, and fertile agricultural areas. Here we will build up our "fixed industries," cooking, washing, storing, and so on. The main issue with which we are confronted is how we intend to arrange our life.

These and similar considerations will be foremost in our mind before we settle down to furnish the individual rooms—the different "communities" of the house. To follow up the simile of the "region," both approaches—the approach from the top, the adaptation of the house to our needs and aspirations in general, and the approach from the bottom, the practical and attractive furnishing of the rooms—are interlocked, and we must think of both at the same time. And in each respect we are concerned first of all with bringing out the best qualities and developing the potentialities latent in the house and in each room.

The approach from the bottom—the furnishing of the rooms—is, in the main, an allocation of functions to the individual communities and districts of the region. We must know what every place and every district can offer under the existing conditions and what potential development promises the highest cultural and material returns. We must avoid a lopsided or a self-contained structure of communities and districts. However, it is not sufficient that every community and every district—urban and rural—produces what is best suited to it. It is essential that every activity can be carried on with the highest efficiency and that it is conceived as part and parcel of the regional scheme.

Organic growth Organic growth from within means the development of the constituent parts of the body, in this case the region, to their fullest capacity, by the provision of the right vitamins as a natural source of energy in the form most rapidly absorbed and used by the body. Vitamins are, in this connection, the right quality and the right quantity of social

and economic services, which widen the opportunity of every community and district and of every citizen for a continuous expansion in the production and the use of goods and result in a rising standard of living for the *whole* population.

No body can grow without exercise, and no mind can develop without intellectual adventure. Both need, therefore, the appropriate tasks. These tasks can be provided in the form of work, recreation, and social intercourse. But favorable results can be expected only if every part of the "body" region is balanced to all the others and not impeded in its working. To achieve this goal, it is necessary to eliminate waste of resources, of time and space, and—to follow up the comparison —to eliminate all substances that have produced regional and local arteriosclerosis and to increase the efficiency of services and the scope of consumption and life in general.

Unity of urban and rural districts As for the unity of rural and urban districts in the cultural, social, and economic sphere, we can restrict our comments to four principles.

Regional integration is the result of unity by diversity but not of uniformity by repetition. Unity by diversity means that the inhabitants of the region have a diverse opportunity in the choice of their occupation, their living places, and their recreational possibilities. Industrial and agricultural activities must be soundly balanced within the region as a whole, and within every district and every community there should be a sufficient number of different industries to make a lopsided development of the labor market impossible. In general, unity by diversity will put the interdependence of all communities on a new basis if all cultural, social, and economic services and opportunities are accessible on the same level of quality and quantity to the whole population.

A regional scheme must embrace the whole region without any discrimination between rural and urban districts. It is an indivisible plan in a spatial sense just as much as in a structural sense. Let me quote in this connection a passage from Mumford's *The Culture of Cities*. It gives the essence of the problem we have to solve.

> Plans must result in a more complicated pattern and a more comprehensive life for the region, for this geographic area can only now, for the first time, be treated as an instantaneous whole for all functions of social existence. Instead of trusting to the mere massing of population to produce the necessary social concentration and social drama, we must now seek these results through deliberate community planning and closer regional linkages. One might call this new method of designing city and region in working partnership the principle of unity by apportioned distribution rather than unity by centralisation. The latter means physical spreading and control from a dominant centre, whereas the first means functional spotting. Any one part of such a complex may become, for a special purpose, the centre of the region.

Interregional balance Regional integration does not stop at the boundaries of the individual regions. It makes provision for interregional cooperation. Consequently, a regional scheme must take into account not only the forces working within the region but also those of other regions. The former have the tendency to move outward, while the latter exert their influence inward upon the region.

It is comparable to a railway station: its layout in general and its technical installations in detail handle the outgoing and incoming trains. The internal structure depends not only on the number of passengers and the quantity of goods arriving in this particular place but also on the impact of the traffic along the whole length of all the lines converging on it. The station building itself is a clearly delimited entity, but around it spreads the web of the railway tracks and the marshaling yards, interspersed with numerous sheds and other constructions, forming a marginal area.

The same holds good for a region except that for administrative reasons its exact delimitation defies precision. Its actual boundaries are marginal areas, but not dotted lines like those on maps. These areas are traversed by long filaments thrust out from any population center within the region to other centers far away in other parts of the country.

The main conclusion that should be drawn from the foregoing definition of regional planning is that it does not stop outside the boundaries of urban areas. The Ideal Region comprises both rural and urban areas, including what was previously the metropolis or the big regional city. The ideal and functional preponderance of urban agglomerations has disappeared. Their activities and social and cultural attractions have been distributed among the new regional community units.

The new environmental structure will need several generations to materialize, but the groundwork should be laid and the direction in which our efforts are to move should be charted now. This is the minimum we can do if we expect posterity to look back at our time not with a feeling of despair and contempt but with pride and gratitude for the insight and vision of our own generation.

In the course of this work I have repeatedly warned of the realism of the so-called realists and of the planners for chaos. I have to repeat this warning, for in the short period since the first hesitant steps toward regional planning experience has already taught us that these groups of pseudo-planners will do all in their power to oppose and to thwart this development. They are the same people who believe that they are "modern" and "progressive," when they fill their homes with labor and money-saving gadgets. They are the same zealots who hope to imprison the spirit of the future in the mold of outworn social ideals. Their self-deceptions make them blind to the profound changes that are going on in the mind of humanity as a whole. They fail to see that even words are changing their meaning—that ideas take on a totally different sense and that their implications are far removed from what they have been in the past.

This revolution of the mind that is spreading all over the world is tantamount to a crisis of consciousness. This crisis is the most potent force demanding a transformation of our environment, on a scale and with an intensity that has not occurred in previous eras. What distinguishes it even from the agricultural and urban revolutions is that we are more conscious—or that we are at least more able to be conscious—of the changes we initiate ourselves and that we can make these changes deliberately and, if we want, systematically.

I admit that the picture is not too bright, if we look at the world stage, especially at the political scene, where the human drama is enacted. The Cold War is perhaps the most telling example. It is fought with slogans, with prestige values, and with the obsolete weapons of power politics, not with ideas, human values, or the clarity

and integrity of purpose that alone can release the creative faculties of groups and individuals. Like many other spheres of life, city planning has been a victim of this unfortunate attitude.

And yet we should try to rid ourselves of the comforting but dangerous escape into a world of double standards: one for Sundays, brimming over with shallow and pious intentions and a consummate conciliation of personal interests and vague public ideals, and one for weekdays, full of socalled realistic and pragmatic tinkering with details. There is but one standard that should dominate all our thoughts and actions. The standard of the highest morality and of the highest human values should be our only yardstick. We are still far removed from this goal, but we should exert all our efforts to follow the road that leads in this direction.

The creation of a physical environment for the masses and for the individuals who compose the masses is a step in this direction. The dynamic equilibrium between the whole and the parts has been submerged in our subconscious. It has to be restored, to be brought to the surface—but without surface values. There is now much talk going on about functional design, but where is the harmony of functional and social forces in the reformation of our environment? It does not exist—not yet.

Some people, the image-chasers, hope to resuscitate the image of the city by making it "legible." Why do they not try to create the image of a region? Are they too timid to adapt their ideas to the expanding scale, expanding in scope and diversity? Whence this mental timidity? We need a greater flexibility of mind and a new vision and, above all, to use Mirabeau's famous exhortation: *De l'audace! Encore de l'audace! Toujours de l'audace!*

Regional planning, if rightly understood,

demands this ever-present audacity. It will encounter great obstruction and difficulties. But so does the conquest of space. Why should we not be genuine realists? Why not employ the same energy, the same inventiveness, and all our means to this terrestrial adventure and adapt our environment, before we land a man on the moon, to the challenge of the new world that is emerging, in which generations to come must live?

National Planning Just like local and regional planning, regional and national planning overlap. National planning is primarily concerned with the working out of principles, not with detailed investigations or with the working out of comprehensive plans. Regional and national planning have gained recognition in Europe and parts of Asia as indispensable instruments for improving the environment. In this country there still exists a widespread distrust of everything concerned with planning. The climate is not too propitious, and it may be doubtful whether anything beyond local planning will ever be fully utilized. What are the essential problems that are the proper domain of national and interregional planning? Are these problems really so antagonistic to the present trend, and are they so new that the distrust is justified?

Regional planning, and for that matter "national" planning, have existed in antiquity, in the Greek city-states and in Roman times, as urban-rural integration of large areas. In the Middle Ages the urban region included towns and their surrounding countryside. This dynamic interaction began to dissolve when industrial development disintegrated the physical and social structure of settlement and finally broke down the clearly defined boundaries of the urban sphere of influence.

Today the problems are greater, but the task has remained the same: to restore a sound balance between city and country and between regions. Living space for the new millions has to be provided. Nobody will deny that it is impossible to accommodate the population increase in the existing urban conglomerations, even if they are improved by city renewal, which in any case would not appreciably increase the dwelling space but rather reduce it, if renewal means a loosening-up of the urban area. Consequently, one of the main tasks of national planning is sorting out regions as reception or evacuation areas for the growing population. This should be done only by a very general apportionment, but the main trends of a redistribution of population and industry should be defined.

Other tasks that have already been undertaken and solved with considerable success in the United States are the preservation of national parks, the mobilization of water and other resources, and the building of a grid of interstate highways. All this involves not only physical but also economic planning and far-reaching sociological investigations and a national land-use policy.

In general, national planning should provide a guidance system that is flexible enough to serve as the basis for future plans and decisions going beyond local and purely regional interests and to balance conflicting pressures which inevitably emanate from too parochial an attitude among competing communities and regions. The mere concentration of population in a given area will never contribute anything to social awareness and collective creativity, the essential prerequisites of a community spirit and a fertile dramatization of social life.

After all that has been explained on the

foregoing pages there is no need to enter into a detailed description of what national planning should be. I have done this in my *Creative Demobilization*. But we may summarize the main lines of action which are instrumental in the planning of new settlements and in the reshaping of those already existing. They are:

1. The articulation of large regions, through a system of *linear arteries* forming the primary grid of parks, parkways, and highways, to serve the functional needs of recreation and circulation.
2. The differentiation of the apportioned living space, through a system of *spatial zoning* organizing the available land into residential and nonresidential areas, to serve the functional needs of housing and working.
3. The subdivision of these areas through a system of *functional spotting*, providing the secondary grid of open spaces and roads, to serve the functional needs of the local units, their internal structure, layout, and interconnected groupings.

All these three methods should be combined and applied simultaneously and systematically over vast regions. They are the fundamentals of local, regional, and national planning and, if wisely used, can inaugurate an era of a creative revolution of environment.

Whatever the defenders of a "flexible *status quo*" may say, the twilight of cities is a fact, and the imperative need to provide sufficient and stimulating living space for the new millions is also a fact. We have the means to harmonize these two truths and to make them the cornerstones of the transformation of our urban and rural environment on a large scale. We can do it—but only if we will it, and attune our vision to the future.

55. The Pattern of the Metropolis | Kevin Lynch

Kevin Lynch's paper reviews most of the important plans for the spatial organization of urban regions that have been proposed by planners and social scientists. He begins by describing three elements that are critical for distinguishing among alternative proposals: the structural condition and density of buildings, the system for moving persons and goods through urban space, and the location of fixed activities such as stores, schools, and cultural facilities. Using this classification system, Lynch proceeds to point out the behavioral and organizational implications of five different plans: the dispersed sheet, the galaxy of settlements, the core city, the star, and the ring. These names are his labels for well-established design forms in the city planning and urban studies traditions. Lynch finds each of the plans wanting in several respects, and he therefore offers another proposal of his own, which he calls "the multicentered net." In this proposal, settlements would be dispersed, to take advantage of the amenity provided by low density, while at the same time, major activities would be concentrated in several large centers. This would assure a sufficient population base to support specialized activities, including cultural endeavors, luxury shopping, and central government functions. The paper ends with a consideration of the policies and strategies that our society would have to follow to bring this proposal to fruition.

It should be noted that the approach Lynch adopts in this paper is an outgrowth of the conceptual framework he and Lloyd Rodwin presented in their paper included in Part VI of this book.

Kevin Lynch is Professor of City Planning at Massachusetts Institute of Technology. Several of his published works are cited on page 757 of this volume.

The pattern of urban development critically affects a surprising number of problems, by reason of the spacing of buildings, the location of activities, the disposition of the lines of circulation. Some of these problems might be eliminated if only we would begin to coordinate metropolitan development so as to balance services and growth, prevent premature abandonment or inefficient use, and see that decisions do not negate one another. In such cases, the form of the urban area, whether concentrated or dispersed, becomes of relatively minor importance.

There are other problems, however, that are subtler and go deeper. Their degree of seriousness seems to be related to the particular pattern of development which has arisen. To understand these problems we must begin by evaluating the possible alternatives of metropolitan form. Therefore, consider the form of the metropolis as if it existed in a world free of pressures or special interests and on the assumption that massive forces can be harnessed for reshaping the metropolis for the common good—provided this good can be discovered. How should such power be applied?

We begin by deciding which aspects of the metropolitan pattern are crucial. We can then review the commonly recognized alternative patterns, as well as the criteria that might persuade us to choose one over

another. Finally, we may hope to see the question as a whole. Then we will be ready to suggest new alternatives, and we will have a technique for choosing the best one for any particular purpose.

The Critical Aspects of Metropolitan Form

There are at least three vital factors in assessing the adequacy of the form of the metropolis, once its total size is known. The first of all is the magnitude and pattern of both the structural density (the ratio of floor space in buildings to the area of the site) and the structural condition (the state of obsolescence or repair). These aspects can be illustrated on a map by plotting the locations of the various classes of density ranging from high concentration to wide dispersion, and the various classes of structural condition ranging from poor to excellent. Density and condition provide a fundamental index of the physical resources an urban region possesses.

A second factor is the capacity, type, and pattern of the facilities for the circulation of persons: roads, railways, airlines, transit systems, and pathways of all sorts. Circulation and intercommunication perhaps constitute the most essential function of a city, and the free movement of persons happens to be the most difficult kind of circulation to achieve, the service most susceptible to malfunction in large urban areas.

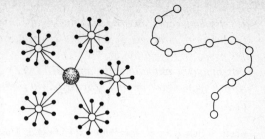

Figure 2. Focal organization.

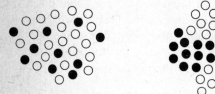

Figure 1. Grain.

The third factor that makes up the spatial pattern of a city is the location of fixed activities that draw on or serve large portions of the population, such as large department stores, factories, office and government buildings, warehouses, colleges, hospitals, theatres, parks, and museums. The spatial pattern of a city is made up of the location of fixed activities as well as the patterns of circulation and physical structure. However, the distribution of locally based activities, such as residence, local shopping, neighborhood services, elementary and high schools, is for our purpose sufficiently indicated by mapping the density of people or of buildings. Hence, if we have already specified structural density and the circulation system, the remaining critical fact at the metropolitan scale is the location of the city-wide activities which interact with large portions of the whole.

When we come to analyze any one of these three elements of spatial pattern, we find that the most significant features of such patterns are the grain (the degree of

intimacy with which different elements, such as stores and houses, are intermixed), the focal organization (the interrelation of the nodes of concentration and interchange as contrasted with the general background), and the accessibility (the general proximity in terms of time of all points in the region to a given kind of activity or facility). In this sense, one might judge that from every point the accessibility to drugstores was low, uneven, or uniformly high, or that it varied in some regular way, for example, high at the center and low at the periphery of the region. All three aspects of pattern (focal organization, grain, and accessibility) can be mapped, and the latter two can be treated quantitatively if desired.

It is often said that the metropolis today is deficient as a living environment. It has suffered from uncontrolled development, from too rapid growth and change, from obsolescence and instability. Circulation is congested, requiring substantial time and a major effort. Accessibility is uneven, particularly to open rural land. The use of facilities is unbalanced, and they become increasingly obsolete. Residential segregation according to social groups seems to

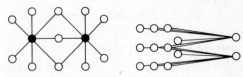

Figure 3. Accessibility.

be growing, while the choice of residence for the individual remains restricted and unsatisfactory. The pattern of activities is unstable, and running costs are high. Visually, the city is characterless and confused, as well as noisy and uncomfortable.

Yet the metropolis has tremendous economic and social advantages that override its problems and induce millions to bear with the discomforts. Rather than dwindle or collapse, it is more likely to become the normal human habitat. If so, the question then is, what particular patterns can best realize the potential of metropolitan life?

The Dispersed Sheet

One alternative is to allow the present growth at the periphery to proceed to its logical conclusion but at a more rapid pace. Let new growth occur at the lowest densities practicable, with substantial interstices of open land kept in reserve. Let

older sections be rebuilt at much lower densities, so that the metropolitan region would rapidly spread over a vast continuous tract, perhaps coextensive with adjacent metropolitan regions. At the low densities of the outer suburbs, a metropolis of twenty million might require a circle of land one hundred miles in diameter.

The old center and most subcenters could be dissolved, allowing city-wide activities to disperse throughout the region, with a fine grain. Factories, offices, museums, universities, hospitals would appear everywhere in the suburban landscape. The low density and the dispersion of activities would depend on and allow circulation in individual vehicles, as well as a substantial use of distant symbolic communication such as telephone, television, mail, coded messages. Accessibility to rural land would become unnecessary since outdoor recreational facilities would be plentiful and close at hand. The permanent low-density residence would displace the summer cottage.

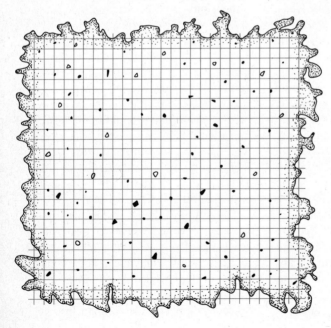

Figure 4. The dispersed sheet.

The system of flow, concerned solely with individual land (and perhaps air) vehicles, should be highly dispersed in a continuous grid designed for an even movement in all directions. There would be no outstanding nodal points, no major terminals. Since different densities or activities would therefore be associated in a very fine grain, the physical pattern similarly might encourage a balanced cross-section of the population at any given point. Work place and residence might be adjacent or miles apart. Automatic factories and intensive food production might be dispersed throughout the region.

Frank Lloyd Wright dreamed of such a world in his Broadacre City.[1] It is this pattern toward which cities like Los Angeles appear to be moving, although they are hampered and corrupted by the vestiges of older city forms. Such a pattern might not only raise flexibility, local participation, personal comfort, and independence to a maximum, but also go far toward solving traffic congestion through the total dispersion and balancing of loads. Its cost would be high, however, and distances remain long. Accessibility would be good, given high speeds of travel and low terminal times (convenient parking, rapid starting); at the very least it would be evenly distributed. Thus communication in the sense of purposeful trips ("I am going out to buy a fur coat") might not be hindered, but spontaneous or accidental communication ("Oh, look at that fur coat in the window!"), which is one of the advantages of present city life, might be impaired by the lack of concentration.

Although such a pattern would require massive movements of the population and the extensive abandonment of equipment at the beginning, in the end it might promote population stability and the conservation of resources, since all areas would be favored alike. It gives no promise, however, of heightening the sense of political identity in the metropolitan community nor of producing a visually vivid and well-knit image of environment. Moreover, the choice of the type of residence would be restricted, although the choice of facility to be patronized (churches, stores, etc.) might be sufficiently wide.

The Galaxy of Settlements

We might follow a slightly different tack while at the same time encouraging dispersion. Instead of guiding growth into an even distribution, let development be bunched into relatively small units, each with an internal peak of density and each separated from the next by a zone or zero structural density. Depending on the transport system, this separation might be as great as several miles. The ground occupied by the whole metropolis would increase proportionately; even if the inter-spaces were of minimum size, the linear dimensions of the metropolis would increase from thirty to fifty per cent.

City-wide activities could also be concentrated at the density peak within each urban cluster, thus forming an over-all system of centers, each of which would be relatively equal in importance to any of the others. Such a metropolitan pattern may be called an "urban galaxy." The centers might be balanced in composition or they might vary by specializing in a type of activity, so that one might be a cultural center, another a financial center.

The system of flow would also be dispersed but would converge locally at the center of each cluster. It might be organized in a triangular grid, which provides such a series of foci while maintaining an easy flow in all directions over the total area. Since median densities remain low, while

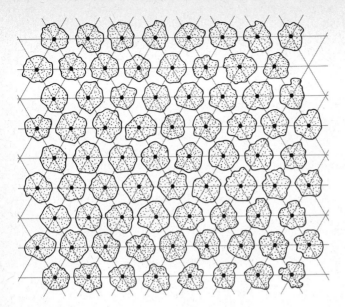

Figure 5. The galaxy.

the centers of activity are divided into relatively small units, the individual vehicle must be the major mode of transportation, but some supplementary public transportation such as buses or aircraft running from center to center would now be feasible.

While it retains many of the advantages of the dispersed sheet, such as comfort, independence, and stability, this scheme probably enhances general communication, and certainly spontaneous communication, through creating centers of activity. It would presumably encourage participation in local affairs by favoring the organization of small communities, though this might equally work against participation and coordination on the metropolitan scale. In the same sense, the visual image at the local level would be sharpened, though the metropolitan image might be only slightly improved. Flexibility might be lost, since local clusters would of necessity have relatively fixed boundaries, if interstitial spaces were preserved, and the city-wide activities would be confined to one. kind of location.

The factor of time-distance might remain rather high, unless people could be persuaded to work and shop within their own cluster, which would then become relatively independent with regard to commutation. Such independent communities, of course, would largely negate many metropolitan advantages: choice of work for the employee, choice of social contacts, of services, and so on. If the transportation system were very good, then "independence" would be difficult to enforce.

This pattern, however, can be considered without assuming such local independence. It is essentially the proposal advocated by the proponents of satellite towns, pushed to a more radical conclusion, as in Clarence Stein's diagram.[2] Some of its features would appear to have been incorporated into the contemporary development of Stockholm.

The pattern of an urban galaxy provides a wider range of choice than does pure dispersion, and a greater accessibility to open country, of the kind that can be maintained between clusters. This pattern has a somewhat parochial complexion and lacks the opportunities for intensive, spontaneous communication and for the very specialized activities that might exist in larger centers. Local centers, too, might develop a monotonous similarity, unless they were given some specific individuality. That might not be easy, however, since central activities tend to support and depend on one another (wholesaling and entertainment, government and business services, headquarters offices and shopping). A compromise would be the satellite proposal proper: a swarm of such unit clusters around an older metropolitan mass.

The Core City

Those who are enamored with the advantages of concentration favor a completely opposite policy, one that would set median structural densities fairly high, perhaps at 1.0 instead of 0.1. (In other words, let there be as much interior floor space in buildings as there is total ground area in the city, instead to only one-tenth as much.) If we consider the open land that must be set aside for streets, parks, and other such uses, this means in practice the construction of elevator apartments instead of one-family houses. The metropolis would then be packed into one continuous body, with a very intensive peak of density and activity at its center. A metropolis of twenty million could be put within a circle ten miles in radius, under the building practice normal today.

Parts of the city might even become "solid," with a continuous occupation of space in three dimensions and a cubical grid of transportation lines. (The full application of this plan could cram a metropolis within a surprisingly small compass: twenty million people, with generous spacing, could be accommodated within a cube less than three miles on a side.) Most probably there would be a fine grain of specialized activities, all at high intensity, so that apartments would occur over factories, or there might also be stores on upper levels. The system of flow would necessarily be highly specialized, sorting each kind of traffic into its own channel. Such a city would depend almost entirely on public transport, rather than individual vehicles, or on devices that facilitated pedestrian movement, such as moving sidewalks or flying belts. Accessibility would be very high, both to special activities and to the open country at the edges of the city. Each family might have a second house for weekends; these would be widely dispersed throughout the countryside and used regularly three or four days during the week, or even longer, by mothers and their young children. The city itself, then, would evolve into a place for periodic gathering. Some of the great European cities, such as Paris or Moscow, which are currently building large numbers of high-density housing as compact extensions to their peripheries, are approximating this pattern without its more radical features.

Such a pattern would have an effect on living quite different from that of the previous solutions. Spontaneous communication would be high, so high that it might become necessary to impede it so as

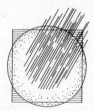

Figure 6. The core.

to preserve privacy. Accessibility would be excellent and time-distance low, although the channels might be crowded. The high density might increase discomfort because of noise or poor climate, although these problems could perhaps be met by the invention of new technical devices. As with the previous patterns, the choice of habitat would be restricted to a single general type within the city proper, although the population could enjoy a strong contrast on weekends or holidays. The nearness of open country and the many kinds of special services should on the whole extend individual choice. Once established, the pattern should be stable, since each point would be a highly favored location. However, a very great dislocation of people and equipment, in this country at least, would be required to achieve this pattern.

Such a metropolis would indeed produce a vivid image and would contribute to a strong sense of the community as a whole. Individual participation, on the other hand, might be very difficult. It is not clear how running costs would be affected; perhaps they would be lower because of the more efficient use of services and transportation, but initial costs would undoubtedly be very high. The segregation of social groups, as far as physical disposition can influence it, might be discouraged, although there is a level of density above which intercommunication among people begins to decline again. Certainly this solution is a highly rigid and unadaptable one in which change of function could be brought about only by a costly rearrangement.

The Urban Star

A fourth proposal would retain the dominant core without so drastic a rever-

sion to the compact city. Present densities would be kept, or perhaps revised upward a little, while low-density development at the outer fringe would no longer be allowed. Tongues of open land would be incorporated into the metropolitan area to produce a density pattern that is star-shaped in the central region and linear at the fringes. These lines of dense development along the radials might in time extend to other metropolitan centers, thus becoming linear cities between the main centers. The dominant core, however, would remain, surrounded by a series of secondary centers distributed along the main radials. At moderate densities (less than the core pattern, and more than the sheet), the radial arms of a metropolis of comparable size might extend for fifty miles from its own center.

The metropolitan center of the star pattern would again contain the most intensive types of city-wide activity. Elsewhere, either in the subcenters or in linear formations along the main radials—whichever proved the more suitable—these activities would be carried on at a less intense level. The system of flow would logically be organized on the same radial

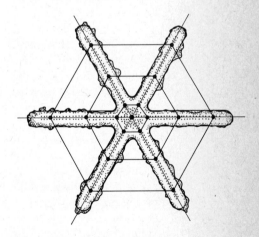

Figure 7.   The star.

pattern, with supplementary concentric rings. An efficient public transportation system of high capacity could operate along the main radials, whereas the ring roads could accommodate public transit of lower intensity. To some degree, travel by individual vehicles, although discouraged for centrally bound flows, would be practicable in other directions.

This pattern is a rationalization of the manner in which metropolitan areas were developing till the individual vehicle became the usual means of travel. It is the form the city of Copenhagen has adopted as its pattern for future growth;[3] Blumenfeld has discussed it at length.[4] This form retains the central core with its advantages of rapid communication and specialized services yet permits the location of other kinds of major acitvities. Lower residential densities are also possible. Individual choice should be fairly wide, both in regard to living habitat, access to services, and access to open land—this land lies directly behind each tongue of development, even at the core, and leads continuously outward to true rural land.

Movement along a sector would be fairly fast and efficient, although terminals at the core might continue to be congested and, with continued growth, the main radials might become overloaded. Movement between sectors, however, would be less favored, especially in the outer regions; there distances are great, transit hard to maintain, and channels costly, since they would span long distances over land they do not directly serve. Accessibility to services would be unequal as between inner and outer locations.

The visual image is potentially a strong one and should be conducive to a sense of the metropolis as a whole, or at least to the sense of one unified sector leading up to a common center. Growth could occur

radially outward, and future change could be accomplished with less difficulty than in the compact pattern, since densities would be lower and open land would back up each strip of development. The principal problems with this form are probably those of circumferential movement, of potential congestion at the core and along the main radials, and of the wide dispersion of the pattern as it recedes from the original center.

The Ring

In the foregoing, the most discussed alternatives for metropolitan growth have been given in a highly simplified form. Other possibilities certainly exist—e.g., the compact high-density core pattern might be turned inside out, producing a doughnut-like form. In this case the center would be kept open, or at very low density, while high densities and special activities surround it, like the rim of a wheel. The principal channels of the flow system would then be a series of annular rings serving the high-intensity rim, supplemented by a set of feeder radials that would converge at the empty center. In fact, this is essentially a linear system, but one that circles back on itself and is bypassed by the "spokes" crossing the "hub." This system is well-adapted to public transportation, both on the ring roads and the cross radials, while individual vehicles might be used for circulation outside the rim.

Densities along the rim would have to be rather high, while those beyond the rim could be low. A system of weekend houses might also be effectively employed here. The central area could either be kept quite open or devoted to special uses at low densities. City-wide activities could be spotted round the rim in a series of intense centers, supplemented by linear patterns along the annular roadways. There would be no single dominant center but rather a limited number of strong centers (an aristocracy rather than a monarchy). These centers might also be specialized in regard to activity—finance, government, culture, etc.

This pseudo-linear form, like the radial tongues of the star plan, has the linear advantages: a high accessibility, both to services and to open land; a wide choice of habitat and location of activities; and a good foundation for efficient public transit. Congestion at any single center is avoided, yet there is a high concentration. In contrast to the galaxy or satellite form, the variety and strong character inherent in the specialized centers would have some hope of survival because of the relatively close proximity of these centers.

The visual image would be strong (though perhaps a little confusing because of its circularity), producing a clear impression of the centers around the rim in contrast to the central openness, and of the way they connected with each other in sequence. The whole metropolis would seem more nearly like one community. One of the most difficult problems would be that of growth, since much development beyond the rim would soon blur the contour and require a new transportation system. A second concentric ring might be developed beyond the first, but it would negate some of the advantages of the first ring and would demand massive initiative by the central government to undertake its development. Another difficulty would be that of control. How can the belts of open land or the accessible center be kept free of building? Even if this problem were solved satisfactorily, a dilemma is also likely to arise in regard to the size of the ring: should it be small enough for the

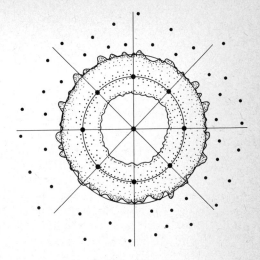

Figure 8. The ring.

major centers to be in close proximity to one another or big enough to allow all the residences and other local activities to be related to it?

One classic example of this form exists, although on a very large scale—the ring of specialized Dutch cities that surround a central area of agricultural land: Haarlem, Amsterdam, Utrecht, Rotterdam, The Hague, and Leiden. This general pattern is now being rationalized and preserved as a matter of national policy in the Netherlands. In our own country, the San Francisco Bay region appears to be developing in this same direction.

The ring tends to be rather rigid and unadaptable as a form. It would require an extreme reshaping of the present metropolis, particularly with regard to transportation and the central business district; but it might dovetail with an observable trend toward emptying and abandoning the central areas. The plan could be modified by retaining a single major center, separated by a wide belt of open space from all other city-wide activities to be disposed along the rim.

It may be noted that this use of open land in concentric belts ("green belts") is exactly opposite to its use as radial tongues in the star form.

The Objectives of Metropolitan Arrangement

Many other metropolitan forms are hypothetically possible, but the five patterns described (the sheet, the galaxy, the core, the star, and the ring) indicate the variation possible. One of the interesting results of the discussion is to see the appearance of a particular set of values as criteria for evaluating these forms. It begins to be clear that some human objectives are intimately connected with the physical pattern of a city, while others are very little affected by it. For example, there has been little discussion of the healthfulness of the environment or of its safety. Although these factors are influenced by the detailed design of the environment, such as the spacing of buildings or the provision for utilities, it is not obvious that the specific metropolitan pattern has any significant effect on them so long as we keep well ahead of the problems of pollution and supply. Psychological well-being, on the other hand, may be affected by the shape of the urban environment. But again, we are too ignorant of this aspect at present to discuss it further.

We have not referred to the efficiency of the environment in regard to production and distribution. This represents another basic criterion that probably is substantially affected by metropolitan pattern, but unfortunately no one seems to know what the effect is. "Pleasure" and "beauty" have not been mentioned, but these terms are nebulous and hard to apply accurately. A number of criteria have appeared, however, and it may well be worth while to summarize them. They might be considered the goals of metropolitan form, its fundamental objectives, either facilitated or frustrated in some significant way by the physical pattern of the metropolis.

The criterion of choice heads the list. As far as possible, the individual should have the greatest variety of goods, services, and facilities readily accessible to him. He should be able to choose the kind of habitat he prefers; he should be able to enter many kinds of environment at will, including the open country; he should have the maximum of personal control over his world. These advantages appear in an environment of great variety and of fine grain, one in which transportation and communication are as quick and effortless as possible. There may very likely be some eventual limit to the desirable increase of choice, since people can be overloaded by too many alternatives, but we do not as yet operate near that limit for most people. In practice, of course, to maximize one choice may entail minimizing another, and compromises will have to be made.

The ideal of personal interaction ranks as high as choice, although it is not quite so clear how the optimum should be defined. We often say that we want the greatest number of social contacts, so as to promote neighborliness and community organization, minimize segregation and social isolation, increase the velocity and decrease the effort of social exchange. And yet, while the evils of isolation are known, we are nevertheless beginning to see problems at the other end of the scale as well. Too much personal communication may cause breakdown, just as surely as too little. Even in moderate quantities, constant "neighborliness" can interfere with other valuable activities such as reflection, independent thought, or creative work. A high level of local community organization may mean civic indifference or intergovernmental rivalry when the large community is involved.

In this dilemma, a compromise could be found in saying that potential interaction between people should be as high as possible, as long as the individual can control it and shield himself whenever desired. His front door, figuratively speaking, should open on a bustling square, and his back door on a secluded park. Thus this ideal is seen as related to the ideal of choice.

Put differently, individuals require a rhythmical alternation of stimulus and rest—periods when personal interchange is high and to some degree is forced upon them, to be followed by other periods when stimulus is low and individually controlled. A potentially high level of interaction, individually controlled, is not the whole story; we also need some degree of spontaneous or unpremeditated exchange, of the kind that is so often useful in making new associations.

The goal of interaction, therefore, is forwarded by many of the same physical features as the goal of choice: variety, fine grain, efficient communication; but it puts special emphasis on the oscillation between stimulus and repose (centers of high activity versus quiet parks), and requires that communication be controllable. In addition, it calls for situations conducive to spontaneous exchange. Storehouses of communication, such as libraries or museums, should be highly accessible and inviting, their exterior forms clearly articulated and expressive of their function.

These two objectives of choice and interaction may be the most important goals of metropolitan form, but there are others of major importance, such as minimum first cost and minimum operating cost. These seem to depend particularly on continuous occupation along the major transportation channels, on a balanced use of the flow system, both in regard to time and direction of flow, a moderately high structural density, and a maximum reliance on collective transport.

Objectives of comfort, on the other hand, related principally to a good climate, the absence of distracting noise, and adequate indoor and outdoor space, may point either toward generally lower densities or toward expensive ameliorative works, such as sound barriers, air conditioning, and roof-top play areas. The important goal of individual participation may also indicate lower densities and an environment that promotes an active relation between an individual and his social and physical milieu, thus giving him a world that to some extent he can manage and modify by his own initiative.

We must also consider that the urban pattern will necessarily shift and expand, and therefore it is important to ask whether the adjustment to new functions will be relatively easy, and whether growth, as well as the initial state, is achievable with a minimum of control and central initiative and intervention. Adaptability to change seems to be greater at lower densities, since scattered small structures are readily demolished or converted. Both an efficient transport system and some form of separation of one kind of activity from another are also conducive to flexibility. Discontinuous forms like the galaxy or the ring require special efforts to control growth, for these patterns raise problems such as the appearance of squatters and the preservation and use of intervening open land.

Stability is a somewhat contradictory goal; it takes into account the critical social and economic costs of obsolescence, movement of population, and change of function. It is very possible that stability in the modern world will be impossible to maintain, and it runs counter to many of the values cited above. The criterion of stability may then be restated: if change is inevitable, it should be moderated and controlled so as to prevent violent dislocations and preserve a maximum of continuity with the past. This criterion would have important implications as to how the metropolis should grow and change.

Finally, there are many esthetic goals the metropolis can satisfy. The most clear-cut is that the metropolis should be "imageable," that is, it should be visually vivid and well structured; its component parts should be easily recognized and easily interrelated. This objective would encourage the use of intensive centers, variety, sharp grain (clear outlines between parts), and a differentiated but well-patterned flow system.

The Relation of Forms to Goals

We have now treated a number of objectives that are crucial, that are on the whole rather generally accepted, and that seem to be significantly affected by the pattern of the metropolis: the goals of choice, interaction, cost, comfort, participation, growth and adaptability, continuity, and imageability. Other goals may develop as we increase our knowledge of city form. What even these few imply for city form is not yet obvious; moreover, they often conflict, as when interaction and cost appear to call for higher densities, while comfort, participation, and adaptability achieve optimal realization at lower levels. Nevertheless, we have immediate decisions

to make regarding the growth of urban areas, and if we marshall our goals and our alternatives as best we can, we can the better make these decisions.

The clarifying of alternatives and objectives has an obvious value, for this will permit public debate and the speculative analysis of the probable results of policy as related to any given form. Yet this kind of approach will soon reach a limit of usefulness unless it is supported by experimental data. Such experimentation is peculiarly difficult in regard to so large and complex an organism as a metropolis. To some degree we can form judgments drawn from such different urban regions as Los Angeles, Stockholm, and Paris, but these judgments are necessarily distorted by various cultural and environmental disparities. Possibly we can study certain partial aspects of city form, such as the effects of varying density or the varying composition of centers, but the key questions pertain to the metropolitan pattern as an operating whole. Since we cannot build a metropolis purely for experimental purposes, we can only build and test models, with some simplified code to designate pattern. By simulating basic urban functions in these models, tests might be run for such criteria as cost, accessibility, imageability, or adaptability. Such tests will be hard to relate to the real situation, and it is difficult to see how certain objectives (such as interaction or participation) can be tested, yet this technique is our best current hope for experimental data on the implications of the total metropolitan pattern.

Dynamic and Complex Forms

Until we have such experimental data, what can we conclude from our imaginary juxtaposition of metropolitan form and human goals? Each of the alternatives proposed has its drawbacks, its failures in meeting some basic objectives. A radical, consistent dispersion of the metropolis appears to restrict choice, impair spontaneous interaction, entail high cost, and inhibit a vivid metropolitan image. A galaxy of small communities promises better, but would still be substandard as regards choice, interaction, and cost, besides being harder to realize. A recentralization of the metropolis in an intensive core appears to entail almost fatal disadvantages in cost, comfort, individual participation, and adaptability. The rationalization of the old metropolis in a star would work better if central congestion could be avoided and free accessibility maintained, but this form is less and less usable as size increases. The ring has many special advantages but raises great difficulties in cost, adaptability, and continuity with present form.

Of course, these are all "pure" types that make no concessions to the complications of reality and they have been described as though they were states of perfection to be maintained forever. In actuality, a plan for a metropolis is more likely to be a complex and mixed one, to be realized as an episode in some continuous process, whose form involves rate and direction of change as well as a momentary pattern.

For example, let us consider, on the basis of the little we know, a form that might better satisfy our aspirations, if we accept the fact of metropolitan agglomeration: this form is in essence a variant of the dispersed urban sheet. Imagine a metropolis in which the flow system becomes more specialized and complex, assuming a triangular grid pattern that grows at the edges and becomes more

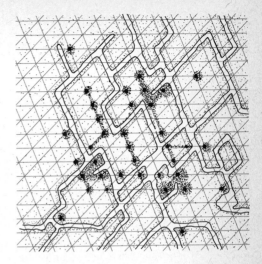

Figure 9. The multicentered net.

specialized in the interior. Many types of flow would be provided for. Densities would have a wide range and a fine grain, with intensive peaks at junctions in the circulation system and with linear concentrations along major channels, but with extensive regions of low density inside the grid. Through the interstices of this network belts and tongues of open land would form another kind of grid. Thus the general pattern would resemble a fisherman's net, with a system of dispersed centers and intervening spaces.

City-wide activities would concentrate in these knots of density, which would be graded in size. In the smaller centers the activities would not be specialized, but the larger centers would be increasingly dominated by some special activity. Therefore the major centers would be highly specialized—although never completely "pure"—and would be arranged in a loose central cluster, each highly accessible.

A metropolis of twenty million might have, not one such cluster, but two or three whose spheres of influence would overlap. These clusters might be so dense as to be served by transportation grids organized in three dimensions, like a skeletal framework in space. Elsewhere, the network would thin out and adapt itself to local configurations of topography. This general pattern would continue to specialize and to grow, perhaps in a rhythmically pulsating fashion. With growth and decay, parts of the whole would undergo periodic renewal. Such a form might satisfy many of the general criteria, but each particular metropolis is likely to encounter special problems. Even so, the description illustrates the complexity, the indeterminacy, and the dynamic nature of city form that are inherent in any such generalization.

Perhaps we can make such a proposal more concrete by stating it as a set of actions rather than as a static pattern. If this were the form desired, then the agencies of control would adopt certain definite policies. First, they would encourage continued metropolitan agglomeration. Second, they would begin to construct a generalized triangular grid of channels for transportation, adapting its interspacing and alignment to circumstances, but aiming at raising accessibility throughout the area as a whole. This grid would provide for many different kinds of flow and would have a hierarchy of its own—that is, the lines of circulation would be differentiated with respect to the intensity and speed of their traffic. Third, peaks of activity and density would be encouraged, but in sharply defined areas, not in rings whose density gradually declines from the center. The present metropolitan center would be encouraged to specialize and thus loosen into a cluster, while one or two major rival centers might develop elsewhere in the network, rather than allowing a general dispersal of city-wide activities.

Such major specialized centers might be given even greater local intensity, with multi-level circulation, perhaps as a three-dimensional system of public rights-of-way.

Fourth, every effort would be made to retain, acquire, or clear a system of linked open spaces of generous size that pervaded the network. Fifth, a wide variety of activities, of accommodation, and of structural character, dispersed in a fine-grained pattern, would be encouraged. Once the concentration of special activities and the arrangement of higher densities in centers and along major channels had been provided for, then zoning and other controls would be employed only to maintain the minimum grain needed to preserve the character and efficiency of the various types of use and density, and large single-purpose areas would be avoided. Sixth, the form of centers, transportation channels, and major open spaces would be controlled so as to give as vivid a visual image as possible. Seventh, the agency would be committed to continuous rebuilding and reorganization of successive parts of the pattern.

Such a set of policies would mean a radical redirection of metropolitan growth. Whether this plan is feasible or worth the cost would require serious consideration. Even if this pattern were chosen, there would still be many crucial questions of relative emphasis and timing to be weighed. If life in the future metropolis is to be worthy of the massive effort necessary to build it, the physical pattern must satisfy human values. The coordination of metropolitan development, however obligatory, will not of itself ensure this happy result. Coordination must be directed toward some desired general pattern, and, to define this, we must clarify our alternatives and the goals they are meant to serve.

NOTES

1. Frank Lloyd Wright, "Broadacre City," in *Taliesin*, October 1940, vol. 1, no. 1.
2. Clarence Stein, "City Patterns, Past and Future," *Pencil Points*, June 1942.
3. *Skitseforslag tol egnsplan for Storkobenhaven:* Copenhagen regional plan. Summary of the preliminary proposal, 1948–1949, with list of contents and notes explaining all illustrations of the preliminary proposal, translated into English.
4. Hans Blumenfeld, "A Theory of City Form," *Society of Architectural Historians Journal*, July 1949.

The Planning of Urban Change

56. Foundations of Urban Planning | F. Stuart Chapin, Jr.

Cities and other urban communities have not escaped the general tendency in modern society to assign the responsibility for controlling social processes and administrative structures to specially trained personnel. The profession that has been given much of this burden is the city planning profession, which now has over 6,000 members in the United States alone. In the view of F. Stuart Chapin, Jr., the problems the profession is expected to cope with are primarily social in character. However, the work of the profession transcends the focus of the social science disciplines because it is intrinsically interdisciplinary in its concerns. It involves innovation as well as investigation, and the application of planning knowledge is an art as much as a science. The role of the planner is to formulate and guide an orderly process of urban development. Chapin describes the steps in this process, which include decision-making, goal specification, program evaluation, and program reorientation. In the final portion of the paper he describes various interpretations of the urban social and political structure that are the basis for the way the city planning practitioners now handle the planning process. Many of these approaches will be familiar to students of urban sociology.

F. Stuart Chapin, Jr., is Professor of Planning and Research Professor in the Institute for Research in Social Science, University of North Carolina. He is the author of many books and research monographs, including *Household Activity Systems* (1966) and *Urban Land Use Planning* (second edition, 1965). He is coeditor of *Urban Growth Dynamics in a Regional Cluster of Cities* (1962).

As long as the human species has been in possession of a faculty for reasoning, man has sought to influence the course of events. Early he learned that foresight in the exercise of this power provided a means for achieving certain predetermined objectives. When man utilizes such a means-end mechanism, he is engaging in "planning." By this definition, planning, then, has something of the quality of universality about it. As a professional group, planners acknowledge that they are dealing with the elements of a concept that many fields utilize. They make no exclusive claim to the concept, but since the whole of their effort both in theory and practice is with the study and application of planning in the pursuit of specific needs and problems of human existence, they have come to have a very direct and consuming interest in many facets of planning.

While we might take various paths, for example, we might study planning in the framework of "resource planning" or "regional planning," in this discussion we are concerned with "urban planning," the application of foresight to achieve certain preestablished goals in the growth and development of urban areas. In making urban planning our subject, we are immediately specifying a locus for the study and practice of planning. We are identifying a specific kind of locale, with a particular economic life, political context, and social organization. We are making this entire microcosm a subject for study, but focusing attention on particular choices in the kind of living environment and the means for achieving each that assures the best possible accommodation of the residents' goals of urban life. It should not be surprising then, to find that the theory and practice of urban planning as it is evolving in this country has a means-ends flavor. Thus, we see American effort in

planning theory and research tending to focus on (1) "the planning process" and (2) "urban structure and form," and at the practicing level, attention centering around (1) planning administration and (2) the "comprehensive plan." This discussion will have an emphasis on the first pair of fundamentals and will make only passing reference to the pair cast in the practicing framework. Throughout, our concern is with contemporary emphases of planning. The development of planning thought extending back to the literature on social action and utopias is a large and significant part of the field which is omitted from this paper.

"Foundations of urban planning," accordingly, is pursued in the following three parts. First, we begin with some distinguishing characteristics of the field as a background to understanding its orientations as they have evolved to date. Second, we focus on the *process* orientations, and thirdly, we examine the *structure-form* orientations of the field.

The Nature of Planning

Urban planners work in a three-dimensional world and, along with a concern for the city as an economic entity and a social system, possess a direct and absorbing interest in the physical make-up of the city and its visual form—not only how the city functions but also how the city affects man's senses and thereby slips into his consciousness, and how, in turn, this affects his living experiences or, more basically, his values and his behavior. We will come to the urban planners' concern with the functional aspects of the city and the perceptional aspects in the last part of this paper.

To understand more fully the nature of planning, we may look at planning first as a field that is a supradiscipline in the sense that it takes a transdisciplinary view of urban phenomena. Next, we may view planning as a field having a central concern for innovation. Finally, we may view planning as a focus for the conjunction of the sciences and the arts. These ways of viewing urban planning suggest the basis for the differentiation of this field from all others that may be concerned in one way or another with urban phenomena.

Transdisciplinary Character of Planning

The supradisciplinary aspect of urban planning springs from a basic preoccupation the field has with the relatedness of many phenomena in the urban scene. This is in contrast to other fields. Among other things, the economist is concerned, for example, with the market process as an element of the urban economy, the political scientist, with the process of public policy formulation, and the sociologist, with the social control processes. Each discipline essentially has a prior claim on the indicated subject area in the sense that it has developed through the years special knowledge and skills to deal with it. Each discipline to an extent may seek out and draw from another discipline where knowledge and skills join or overlap. But as the market process, the public policy formulating process, social control processes, or other processes associated with other fields interact in multisystem frameworks, there develops a science for the study of the relatedness of these processes which no one of the component fields is fully equipped or disposed to undertake. So, to deal with related aspects

of processes that cross into several discipline areas, new fields of specialization emerge. Planning, operations research, and regional science are examples. Planning was the first strong specialization of this kind to develop and assume the characteristics of a distinct field, and urban planning is the most firmly established option today in this field.

Urban planning deals with another kind of relatedness. We have been using a "means" orientation to illustrate the role that planning plays in studying interrelationships among the different "process" systems functioning in the urban milieu. We might also use a "place" concept as the counterpart of an "ends" orientation to examine relatedness of urban phenomena in space. In the same way that each discipline may use the notion of "process," each for its own special reasons may examine the spatial dispositions of phenomena under study and seek to understand their distribution in space. When the interrelationships of these spatial configurations are examined in the framework of over-all urban structure and form, they become of special interest to the field of urban planning. In both the process and structure-form orientations, "relatedness" is of special interest to planning researchers. In the practice of planning, its counterpart is "coordination," which is a way of insuring relatedness in efforts at modifying structure-form elements in the city's make-up.

Innovational Aspect of Planning

Now, if we add to this view of planning a second view, the innovational aspect, we have another basis for differentiating planning from many of its related fields. Social scientists normally apply their knowledge to a means-ends framework in a kind of clinical manner, that is, they may propose different means and ends in a hypothetical framework to test theories or models or they might take a "what would happen if" approach and reason out the consequences of their means-ends schema in the real world. The planning researcher is no less experimental in his research and study, but the ultimate application of his knowledge involves an innovational aspect, that is, it involves the use of the planning process as a means and certain forms of spatial organization in the urban environment as ends in fulfillment of certain defined community goals.

Planning seeks knowledge not for knowledge's own sake but for its applications to the needs of man. In this sense, it is constantly modifying the very phenomena it seeks to study. Thus, the innovational feature of planning gives it a "science plus" aspect, with the end being sought not simply a dispassionate study of "what is," but also "what could be" and "what should be." To put it another way, planning is a combination of the descriptive, projective, and prescriptive. Pure science seeks to understand the nature of phenomena, how it functions and what laws govern its make-up and its transformations. Science will also seek to project the observed behavior of the subject under study to discover "what could be" under specific assumptions governing the projections. But when value judgments enter the picture, as in prescriptive approaches, the "plus" or innovational feature comes into prominence. This, of course, is not unique to planning but is generally characteristic of the professions that apply science to achieve particular ends.

Conjunction of the Social Sciences and the Arts We see urban planning in its broadest usage when we look at it as a field in which the social sciences and the arts coalesce. What may be loosely referred to as "basic planning," on the one hand, and what increasingly is referred to as "urban design," on the other, have long been recognized as related components of urban planning. However, in American planning practice, urban design has been in eclipse for some time, and planning programs have not often accorded urban design studies more than token consideration in the plan preparation stage. Thus, in the normal course of events, urban planning practitioners have commissioned or undertaken economic studies, demographic analyses, housing investigations, thoroughfare studies, etc., and they have applied these findings to the organization and use of space in preparing a general plan for growth and development of the urban area. But, until very recently, few planning programs have undertaken basic design analyses as an essential part of the preparation of a land development plan. The city plans developed in the recent past have been criticized as being a somewhat sterile and mechanistic conception of the future city, often insensitive to the visual and "the human scale." Perhaps because of this imbalance in urban planning, the complementing aspect of planning as a science and planning as an art has been slow to become recognized. One explanation for the imbalance persisting as long as it has may be found in the widely held notion that design is entirely an intuitive field and not researchable. In the last ten years, however, there has been a general swing away from this position, and there has been a steadily increasing interest in urban design research, and even in the application of social science research techniques to the study of urban design.

While the method of approach to research employed by the design researcher can never be fully likened to that of the social science researcher, both follow a system of reasoning backed by well-established principles and tenets. However, the social scientist seeks a product that meets different tests than those the designer uses as his tests. For example, frequently the social scientist will strive for a result that can be replicated, one that can be replicated with number-perfect precision. The designer seeks another kind of universal. He seeks a universal that in some situations will achieve uniqueness in the result rather than exact duplication. While the practicing designer who applies these universals always must rely on a mixture of intuition, artistic creativity, and experience-tempered judgments, which preclude any likelihood of replication, the design researcher is now seeking to bring to him approaches that combine social science and design knowledge.

Post–World War II developments in the planning field have brought these two ancestral trails of planning into a closer relationship. Current thought seeks a conjunction of these two paths through research and, at the practicing level, through improved procedures and defined information flows in the course of a planning study. Conceptual developments in planning thought reflect the growing area of relationship. Of particular interest in this respect is the shift from a "unitary approach" in planning (emphasis on the single, detailed, and invincible scheme) to an "adaptive approach" (emphasis on an evolutionary scheme which is based on a firm set of development policies embodied in a general plan but which is progressively adapted to recognize unpredictable elements of change and technology).[1] Under the adaptive approach, urban design can be continuously brought into play in translating the basic plan concepts of urban structure into urban forms that have visual meaning on the site. In this sense, in the same way that basic planning analyses must be continuously investigating new considerations brought to light by science and technology, urban design must be continuously prescribing changes in urban form in adaptation to changes uncovered in basic planning analyses. These information flows may proceed in steady progression or occur in feedback sequences. Thus, in the long pull, urban analyses may lead to an urban design expression which feeds back a behavioral impact that modifies the analytical requirements and calls for a somewhat modified emphasis in a new design expression. The affinity of these two traditionally separated areas of learning is especially clear in the field of urban planning. We will return to urban design again in the last part of this paper.

As must be evident from the foregoing discussion, planning has parallels with other fields, but it also has distinctive features. Three of these features that differentiate planning from other fields are: (1) its multidisciplinary ties, (2) its innovational bias, and (3) its joint identification with the sciences and the arts. We may now go on to examine two rather fundamental orientations to urban planning. In some respects these orientations constitute areas of specialization in the field. To the extent that researchers must have a focus, these offer two focal areas in which to achieve some depth in their investigations. To the extent that practitioners utilize both orientations as integral parts of one profession, the separation implied in the term "orientations" is artificial.

Process Orientations

Process is an old chestnut of the social sciences, but because of its dynamic quality is continues to offer a useful approach to the study of certain phenomena. Every field has introduced refinements into the literature on the nature of process in applying dynamic features of the concept to its own needs. So, it is not surprising to find *planning process* a source of frequent searching commentary in the urban planning field.

The concept of process has both a technical and a behavioral usage in the field. The technical usage generally relates to stages of planning in some defined work program of the planning agency. Thus, we see reference to the establishment of a work program which proceeds from a specification of what is needed to how a study is to be done and in what order the work is to be executed. The planning agency might, therefore, establish a work program for the preparation of a land development plan and specify the elements as an economic study, a population study, and a land use study. It might then proceed to the scheduling of specific analyses to be undertaken—say, an input-output analysis as a means of testing economic growth assumptions; a population forecast as a means of studying the implications of the economic growth assumptions; and a holding capacity analysis of open land adaptable for various uses as a means of estimating the implications of the economic and population assumptions for land development patterns. Once the work program is specified, the technical process of planning then proceeds to data collection, analysis, and the preparation of plans, cost analyses, and recommendations. This kind of technical application of the concept constitutes one specific meaning of process within the planning field.

The behavioral usage of process in planning literature is in a tradition not unlike that found in the social sciences generally. In current planning thought, this usage of the *planning process* has to do with a *sequence of action* which begins with establishing certain goals, involves certain decisions as to alternative ways of achieving these goals and eventually takes the form of steps for carrying out decisions, followed by evaluation and perhaps a new sequence of action. It is this usage which will be followed in the discussion below. The sequence falls into these stages:

Goal specification stage
Decision-making stage
Plan execution, evaluation, and
reorientation stage

In discussing these stages, we will take the view that these three stages occur in cycles which proceed in a circular rather than a straight-line sequence, with one sequence of action moving into a second, and a second into a third, and so on. Throughout, our concern will be with *process*, reserving *content* or substance of goals, decisions, and follow-through for consideration in the final section of the discussion.

Before examining these stages of the planning process, we need some kind of differentiation between the various actors and the roles they portray throughout the three stages of the sequence. In other words, goals, decisions, execution, and evaluation each involve the questions, "by whom" and "for whom." Who specifies the goals? Who decides among the specified goals? Who follows through on decisions? And who evaluates the consequences? Moreover, for whom are goals, decisions, follow-through, and evaluation made—for what group? The residents? The leaders? Or the officialdom of the city?

Clearly, these actors can be cast in a number of different role combinations, multiplying the complexities of the ways in which the planning process can be studied many times. For purposes of this discussion, we shall give officialdom the center of the stage and cast other actors as "walk-ons" who interact with city officials as the planning process progresses through the three-act sequence we have noted above. To simplify things still further, the spotlight will most frequently focus on the urban planner to observe how he takes part in the planning process in relation to other city officials, civic leaders and the general public. Along the lines of the following Daland-Parker nomenclature, we will need to be aware that at each stage the role or combination of roles the planner assumes under any particular set of circumstances may vary according to whether he is functioning in an *institutional role* as an administrative official in local government, in a *professional role* as a practitioner of the precepts of the planning profession, in a *political innovation role* as he relates his actions to political channels and the political "influentials" in the community, or in an *educational role* as he relates his actions to the grass roots citizenry of the community at large.[2]

Goal Specification With these differentiations as to actors and roles, let us now direct our attention to the dynamic aspects of the planning process, the sequence of action through the three stages of the process. Goal specification is a logical point of entry into the circular sequence we have identified with the planning process. At the outset, it might be observed that while goals of planning have been in

the forefront of planning thought since the early literature on utopias, only in relatively recent times has the identification of goals been made an integral part of the technical work of planning. This spotlighting of goals bids well to be a characteristic of the sixties, not alone in planning, but pervading many fields. (Witness the work of the President's Commission on National Goals in 1960.)

Until relatively recently, goals specified in the course of the planning process were identified on the basis of the planner's perception of community goals. His sources for these goal statements were, in part, a combination of observation and experience in his contacts with the public, with civic groups and with pressure groups of all kinds and, in part, his own intuitive view of what the goal content should be. The intuitive approach to the definition of goals is a holdover from the design origins of the field. While the design aspect of the field must always draw on the intuitive creativity of the artist, particularly when proposals for achieving goals are translated into design expressions, the identification of community goals need no longer be an intuitive matter.

What constitutes a valid basis for the identification of the goals of a populace? The nebulousness of identifying goals that have one and the same meaning to both the average urbanite and the decision maker is difficult enough, but how are goals to be arrayed and given meaning in combinations that have never been articulated or viewed before by the general public or even the decision maker in any goal form of physical development? Though the problems are difficult, research is beginning to shed some light on these questions, and effort is being directed toward the identification and measurement of group goals, that is, widely held goals, and the intensity with which goal concepts are held by groups of city residents.

Contemporary thinking on the identification of planning goals is increasingly turning to the use of survey research methods in the study of attitudes. Except for Branch's early experiment in a public opinion poll, the application of these methods to goal identification for planning has been very recent.[3] Wilson's work offers an illustration of the directions in which research is currently moving.[4] One of several planning research studies at the University of North Carolina concerned with the identification of goal perceptions with respect to the living qualities of cities, this study experiments with a series of devices for getting at attitudes. It uses direct questions to probe for responsiveness on physical features of goal forms that are associated with "livability" in the city, and in a complementary line of questioning it seeks to get at past behavior that might also shed light on goals. Thus, questions are asked on reasons for past choices in the selection of the hometown. Similarly, residents are queried on reasons for choosing the neighborhood in which they settled in the one or more communities that had been picked as hometowns, and questions are asked that indicate the intensity of satisfaction with respect to these past choices. As an indirect approach, game techniques are used to induce respondents to simulate their choices and thus divulge what their current satisfactions are likely to be with respect to goals. At the Massachusetts Institute of Technology, Lynch has experimented with other approaches.[5] In some home interview experiments, he has respondents take imaginary trips through their city and comment on features in the community that they consider to be noteworthy. On other occasions he actually makes trips through parts of the city with respondents using tape-recorded interviews to obtain on-the-spot responses of residents as they pass through their community.

One important distinction between public opinion polls and attitude surveys might be borne in mind here. Without getting into the specifics of definitions, we might remember that polls seek direct measures of satisfaction and dissatisfaction with widely recognized problems or issues. Attitude studies frequently focus on less obvious and sometimes hidden problems which are not fully understood or perhaps may not even be recognized by the general public. In this connection, it is interesting to speculate on the political overtones of any attempt to use poll findings or even the results of attitude surveys as a basis for public forum and a "popular vote" on goals. If the public views a survey as a "vote," conflict may be intensified, or created, where none existed before. Thus, the solicitation of opinion on goals may lead to conflicting expectations among a populace which are politically irreconcilable and potentially a source of widespread dissatisfaction. On the other hand, attitude studies devoid of hoop-la and taken simply as one of an array of aids to decision making, may be politically innocuous.

Even though the older value-laden approaches to goal identification are being superseded, the act of selecting the goal combinations to be introduced into the planning process is still a subjective matter. The establishment of standards to be used in determining how widely held a goal must be before it is given prominence in a goal combination requires a value judgment. To devise goal combinations meaningful to decision makers and at the same time bracket the many divergent planning goals that are held by residents, also unquestionably involves an exercise of judgment. More importantly, when the planner identifies a series of "goal forms," (say, a "nucleated form," a "diffused form," and a "compact form" of urban development) as alternative approaches to satisfying goal preferences of the general public, he is imputing to these goal forms certain living qualities that match up with public goal preferences. Here again value judgments are involved.

Ex post facto, correspondence between goals and goal forms can be demonstrated, but when correspondence is sought ahead of time, it is necessary for the planner to make a judgment. In other words, whereas survey research methods may assist in goal identification, they are not likely to be very helpful in eliciting any meaningful response on design forms with which respondents have had no direct experience. Some kinds of preferences can be inferred or forecast from choices made in areas of questioning where there has been direct experience, but as yet techniques have not been devised which can predict with any great reliability what respondent reactions will be to new and unfamiliar design forms. Thus, it is still necessary for the planner to use value judgments in making up the goal combinations and in devising alternative goal forms from which decision makers can make a choice. Moreover, the designer must still depend upon his design ingenuity and the sales appeal of a new idea in securing acceptance of new and unique design expressions.

The specification of goal combinations in the form of alternatives often involves a variety of other goals. Thus, for example, to implement a general goal of revitalizing the central business district, established as an objective in the local planning effort, the planning agency may put before city council another set of goal alternatives—a choice between maintaining the central business district as a single strong center or promoting the development of a series of decentralized satellite centers.

In addition to ramifications of one goal leading to others, the specification of goal forms in terms of alternatives means greater complexity in the entire sequence of action in the planning process.[6] That is to say, any particular goal combination obviously involves several successive investigative cycles of action before a choice is made. Such systems of linked investigative actions bear a resemblance to what will be recognized from decision-making theory as "decision chains."

Another order of complexity may be introduced by varying the actors and by varying the roles taken in the specification of goals. If we put the spotlight on the urban planner alone and vary the roles he may be disposed to play, there can be considerable variation in the way goals are presented. For example, in a political innovation role the urban planner may be sensitive to the tipping point at which decision makers will tend to act or not act. He may, therefore, specify goal forms entirely with reference to the tipping point. If he functions solely as a professional, he may present choices without consideration of the political feasibility of his goal forms. On the other hand, where the goal has no policy ramifications and where no issue is involved, role may be relatively less important, and goal specification can be quite perfunctory, direct, and uncomplicated. So, we may conclude that goal specification is very complexly interwoven into the action sequence, sometimes varying according to the policy implications behind the goal, sometimes varying with the actors dominating a particular issue at a particular time, and sometimes varying with the political climate prevailing at the time.

At this juncture we begin to note that "goal specification" is a somewhat elusive term, and when too much emphasis is given to it as a "stage," it has a slightly static ring. Clearly, from the above discussion, goal specification consists of many linked frames in the film of action we are inspecting, and to get at the dynamic aspect of the action sequence, for all practical purposes, we cannot attach too great importance to stages as such. Indeed, stages as used here are really only convenient labels for breakpoints in the action sequence which we have introduced in order to observe some of the variables of the planning process.

Decision Making   Let us now inspect a breakpoint in the action sequence which will give us some insight into the dynamics of the decision-making stage of the action sequence. This is the stage in which alternative courses of action for the fulfillment of goals are considered and evaluated, and a selection is made. For purposes of this discussion, while keeping the urban planner near the front of the stage, we will focus the spotlight on the city council as the decision-making unit and consider the role of the urban planner only in relation to the city council in this setting.

Using Simon's three-part sequence of steps to decision making, and the Meyerson-Banfield adaptation of it, we may think of this stage in the planning process as involving: (1) consideration of all action alternatives within the framework of conditions that prevail and goals sought; (2) evaluation of the consequences following from the pursuit of each action alternative, including the change of conditions predicted and the extent of goal achievement anticipated; and (3) selection of the

alternative that in the light of consequences and in consideration of goals is the most preferable course of action.[7]

Now, let us assume that a decision must be made on how to maintain the central business district as a single strong center. Our first step is to examine the action alternatives. Although additional alternatives or other combinations of alternatives might be proposed, the following are adequate for purposes of illustration:

First action alternative: Hold-the-line approach   A program emphasizing more efficient use of the existing street system through strategic traffic engineering solutions (one-way streets, removal of on-street parking, etc.) and the provision of off-street parking under self-liquidating projects, coupled with a concerted effort to get downtown property owners to undertake a face-lifting and general refurbishing of their properties.

Second action alternative: Rehabilitation approach   A program providing for limited strategic revisions in street layout (street closings, new connecting links, etc.) and the provision of public off-street parking, coupled with the introduction of a mall, open squares, or shopping courts worked into a unifying design for the organization of space and circulation in the central area.

Third action alternative: Redevelopment approach   A program providing for some reallocation of uses between central and outlying centers, the reorganization of uses and circulation systems within the central business district and a general renewal of the central area by a public redevelopment program and private action of downtown property owners according to a unifying and balanced design.

Of course, a fourth alternative would be no action, that is, do nothing. In this connection, it may be noted that inaction as well as action may produce additional actions in the decision chain.

While very general in their meaning, these action alternatives obviously are arrayed in an ascending order of the involvement of local government and in the extent of capital outlay commitment. They also constitute a gradation in the decisiveness with which they go at the problem. If backed up with supporting data, action alternatives can be compared as to costs and benefits; they can be compared in terms of the nonmonetary aspect of the choice, that is, the extent of satisfaction each alternative offers or how close each solution comes to achieving the goal. The city council theoretically can proceed to make a rational decision.

Prevailing policies and even the absence of policy may have an important bearing on the outcome of a decision. We may note also that the outcome can be governed by policy considerations of both a higher and lower order. If we view policies as tending to fall into a hierarchical array that range from the topmost strategic kind of consideration on down to those that constitute more detailed and specific kinds of considerations that follow from previous higher order policies, we must recognize that in making a choice between two or more action alternatives at any intermediate point in the hierarchy, decision makers, consciously or unconsciously, are making higher order commitments as well as involving themselves in additional decisions that must subsequently be made down the line.[8] Thus, implicit in a decision on any one of the above choices is a prior, higher order policy decision that a single strong center is to be actively promoted in the future growth

and development of the metropolitan area. Whether or not this policy was deliberated on, a decision on any one of the action alternatives listed above constitutes a commitment in the allocation of resources for many years to come to a kind of transportation system that must be able to accommodate very large numbers of people, bringing them into the central area with a minimum of delay and a maximum of comfort. Whether consciously or not, a commitment to a single strong center is a rejection of a different kind of transportation system, one which seeks to bring relatively smaller numbers of people to several centers. Down the hierarchy, implied are decisions on particular implementing schemes of vastly different scope and differing amounts of capital outlay. Thus, every decision has reference points to a broad array of policies of higher or lesser order.

Of course, what has been said about decision making in the action sequence is greatly simplified. First, it might be noted that the alternatives submitted to the city council are not fixed alternatives and often are modified in form and content in the course of the decision-making sequence. It is a prerogative of decision makers, often a consciously exercised prerogative, to restrict, extend, or otherwise modify the scope of their decision area. This can happen when the staff, which is involved in specifying the alternatives and the implications of each, is not in possession of all of the relevant political information. Secondly, and related to this consideration, are the underlying behavioral variables to decision making. There is a whole body of literature on political behavior dealing with leadership and role playing in decision making and how, in turn, the impact of these vary with the issue being decided upon and the alignment of pressure groups. No less important, there are the background variables deeply embedded in the attitudes and value systems of each actor. Finally, it should be noted that we have used illustrations assuming a situation where no other units of local government are involved and where no special authorities exist. The dynamics of intergovernmental decision making and the interjurisdictional aspects of decision making in a "fractionalized" metropolitan governmental situation of course add tremendously to the complexities of this and other stages of the action sequence.

Plan Execution, Evaluation, and Reorientation Continuing with our stage framework and breaking into the action sequence at another point, we come to the post-decision making stages consisting of what we have termed the execution, evaluation, and reorientation stage of planning. The steps in this stage coalesce to a considerable degree from the time one is initiated until the last is completed, and since the follow-through on one decision is the take-off for the next, we shall treat all of them together.

Plan execution may be any one or a combination of several of the following measures. It may be a public improvement —a new water plant, a school expansion program, or an extension to the expressway system. It may be clearance of a slum and carrying out a redevelopment plan. It may be accomplished through regulatory measures—the adoption of a minimum housing standards ordinance or a revision of the zoning ordinance. However, from the moment a decision is made evaluation begins, and eventually a new or modified view of the intended action may emerge. The evaluation of the effects of a decision may result in reorientation and may subsequently involve take-off on a new action sequence. Evaluation by the city council reflects consideration of the unanticipated side effects as well as repercussions from the anticipated effects of their earlier decision. Perhaps no new action sequence ensues directly related to the previous one and the planning process substantially achieves the goal for which action was initiated in the original instance. On the other hand, the dynamics of the situation may produce a new sequence, with a change of goals, a change of action alternatives, and a change of decisions. The featured actors and the walk-on actors and their roles may vary, and the new sequence of action may involve additional actors and modified roles from those that were involved in preceding action sequences.

In summary, it may be observed that the process orientations of urban planning have a distinct behaviorial emphasis and involve the applications of knowledge of human behavior to the study of man's actions in adapting his environment to his living needs. The planning process is the means mechanism used in achieving adaptation. Although greatly simplified in order to give an overview of the process orientation in planning, the urban planning process consists of a sequence of stages which tend to proceed from goal specification to decision making to execution, evaluation, and reorientation. It is now appropriate to turn to the substance with which this process is concerned namely, the urban environment, particularly its spatial structure and form.

NOTES

1. I am indebted to Donald L. Foley for this nomenclature which he developed in a session at the Urban Studies Seminar, Chapel Hill, August 14, 1961.
2. Robert T. Daland and John A. Parker, "Roles of the Planner in Urban Development," in F. Stuart Chapin, Jr., and Shirley F. Weiss, eds., *Urban Growth Dynamics* (New York: John Wiley & Sons, Inc., 1962).
3. Melville C. Branch, Jr., *Urban Planning and Public Opinion: National Survey Research Investigation* (Princeton: Bureau of Urban Research, September 1942). See also *Urban Planning and Public Opinion: A Pilot Study* (Princeton: Bureau of Urban Research, February 1942).
4. Robert L. Wilson, "Livability of the City: Attitudes and Urban Development," in Chapin and Weiss, eds., *Urban Growth Dynamics.*

5. Kevin Lynch, *The Image of the City* (Cambridge: The Technology Press and Harvard University Press, 1960).
6. Some planning agencies identify only one goal form, i.e., one scheme for the physical development of the urban area, and subsequently follow up in the decision-making stage with recommendations based on the one goal choice. However, increasingly planning agencies are considering goal forms in terms of alternatives before a decision is reached on a single goal form.
7. Herbert A. Simon, *Administrative Behavior* (New York: The Macmillan Company, 1957), p. 67. Martin Meyerson and Edward C. Banfield, *Politics, Planning and the Public Interest* (New York: The Free Press of Glencoe, 1955), p. 314.
8. For a fuller discussion, see F. Stuart Chapin, Jr., *Urban Land Use Planning* (New York: Harper & Row, Publishers, 1957), pp. 267–273.

57. The Goals of Comprehensive Planning   Alan Altshuler

The planning profession aspires to deal with the problems of urban communities according to a rational process that takes into account a wide range of values, norms, and social and economic conditions. However, when this ideal is applied in practice it often runs aground on the realities of urban and suburban politics. Alan Altshuler reports several instances in which exactly this situation occured in two cities he studied. It leads him to raise the question whether the planner's claim to represent the general public interest really can be sustained. Altshuler points out that statements about goals and values which planners make are usually too abstract to serve as a basis for deciding among concrete urban design and administrative alternatives. The profession itself admits that the test of its ability to state the public interest is whether these statements are accepted in community debates. In the cities Altshuler studied it proved difficult to elicit public discussion of planning proposals; there also was some confusion about which groups within the communities were the relevant constituencies. These and other experiences lead Altshuler to question the entire philosophical and logical foundation of comprehensive planning theory. He advocates that planners lower their sights and begin to base the ideology of the professional role on middle-range planning.

Alan Altshuler is Associate Professor of Political Science at Massachusetts Institute of Technology and the author of *The City Planning Process: A Political Analysis* (1965).

Those who consider themselves comprehensive planners typically claim that their most important functions are: one, to create a master plan which can guide the deliberations of specialist planners, two, to evaluate the proposals of specialist planners in the light of the master plan, and three, to coordinate the planning of specialist agencies so as to ensure that their proposals reinforce each other to further the public interest. Each of these functions requires for ideal performance that the comprehensive planners understand the overall public interest, at least in connection with the subject matter (which may be partial) of their plans; and that they possess causal knowledge which enables them to gauge the approximate net effect of proposed actions on the public interest.

Comprehensiveness and the Public Interest

This paper is concerned with some ways in which city planners have approached the first of these two requirements; that is, that they understand the public interest. Contrary to most students of planning, I consider it the more interesting one. If comprehensive planners deal with a great many more areas of public policy than specialists, their factual and causal knowledge in each area is bound to appear shallow by comparison with the specialists in it. Their claims to comprehensiveness, therefore, if they are to be persuasive, must refer primarily to a special knowledge of the public interest.

Every government planner, no matter how specialized, must be guided by *some* conception of the public interest. Since, plans are proposals of concerted action to achieve goals, each must express his conception as a goal or series of goals for

his community. He will probably conceive these goals as constantly shifting rather than highly stable, as always intermediate rather than final, and as more in the nature of criteria than of concrete destinations. Community goal conceptions are likely to have these characteristics because of the limitations on collective human foresight and imagination. Nonetheless, it is impossible to plan without some sense of community goals, call them what you will. Moreover, for the planning process in any community to be democratic, and I assume in these pages that it should be, the goals must win approval from a democratic political process.

The *comprehensive* planner must assume that his community's various collective goals can somehow be measured at least roughly as to importance and welded into a single hierarchy of community objectives. In addition, he must argue that technicians like himself can prescribe courses of action to achieve these objectives without great distortion or harmful side effects of a magnitude sufficient to outweigh the gains achieved through planning. We may conceive a continuum of faith in the feasibility and desirability of comprehensive planning. The "ideal type" defender of comprehensive planning would contend that a serious effort should be made to plan the future evolution of all important economic and social patterns in detail. Other defenders would limit their support to the planning in general outline of change in particular strategic variables.

Certainly few sophisticated American defenders of planning believe that planners can achieve a total comprehensiveness of perspective on any issue. Many do believe,

Reprinted by permission of the *Journal of the American Institute of Planners* (Volume XXXI, No. 3, August, 1965).

however, that professional planners can come closer to achieving it on numerous vital issues than other participants in the urban decision process. The primary purpose of this paper is to explore some of the foundations of this belief.

It should be noted that the explicit claims of practicing planners often suggest that a fair approximation of genuine comprehensiveness is currently attainable. By way of illustration, some cases studies I wrote several years ago[1] provide evidence. They were conducted in two midwestern cities whose programs had especially good reputations among planners consulted. Let us label these cities A and B. Both had nonpartisan forms of government, weak political party organizations, and strong civil service merit systems. City A had a commission form of government; City B had a strong council-weak mayor system. City A had a population of roughly 300,000; City B, 500,000.

One case study involved the evolution of a land use plan for City A. The planning director's conception of the plan's function is described in his published introduction to it:

> The total city planning process, of which land use planning is but one part, involves a continuing program of deriving, organizing, and presenting a comprehensive plan for the development and renewal of [the city] . . . The plans must be economically feasible, and must promote the common good, and at the same time [must] preserve the rights and interests of the individual.

Long discussions with every planner involved in the plan's preparation persuaded me that these words were meant literally. City planning was comprehensive and for the common good, not for any lesser objectives. Several members of the planning staff had vigorously criticized the previous planning director for offering advice freely to operating agencies without first developing, or even trying to develop, a comprehensive plan. The predecessor himself, however, had justified his recommendations in terms of their overall "effect on community life." For example, he had written in a publication on the city's proposed freeway system that, while others had considered the cost of the freeways and their effect on traffic, the City Planning Board had "special responsibilities posed by virtue of its function and status as an advisory representative citizens' group concerned with the development of all facets of the community's life."

A second case study concerned the location of a new city-county hospital in City A. In the course of a prolonged controversy, politicians turned finally to city planners to interpret the overall public interest. The City Planning Board shied from this challenge out of political prudence, but the planning staff of the city's Housing and Redevelopment Authority accepted it eagerly. Both groups of planners stated confidently in interviews that they were better equipped to recommend a wise decision than the city's consultant hospital architect, whose primary concern was how best to build a hospital. They believed that because their perspective was broader, their recommendation was very likely to be more rational.[2]

A third case study described the evolution of a central area plan for City B. The plan's primary author, with the full support of his planning director, cast its arguments in the broadest possible terms. Its operational goal was clearly a limited one: economic growth. The planner felt, however, that he had to justify the goal itself. He stressed the functions of downtown as bearer of culture, disseminator of news and ideas, haven for unique activities, supplier of taxes to support all public services, and so on. When interviewed, he emphasized that his concern was to enrich the lives of all citizens, not to line the pockets of downtown businessmen. It was merely fortuitous, he believed, that in this case the interests of property owners and those of society coincided. He admitted freely, as did all the planners in both cities, that no plan or evaluation could be entirely comprehensive. His (and their) disclaimer was perfunctory, however, as if only a minor detail were at stake. He wrote, for example, that the central area plan could not truly be termed comprehensive because: "there are and always will be elements—new aspects—yet to be studied and yet to be decided upon." He thus rejected a conception of comprehensiveness that I have termed useless; that is, that the comprehensive plan should deal with everything. In short, he admitted that the object of any decision is necessarily limited, at very least in time, but he preserved the implication that the planner's approach—that is, his goal orientation—to the object may be comprehensive.

Planners generally agree that the method of discovery of community goals can in the final analysis only be public discussion. Planners may propose alternative articulations, but goal statements can have no claim to represent community thought unless the community or its "legitimate" representatives ratifies them after serious discussion and deliberation. The primary problem in theory, then, should be to guide the vigorous discussion and to decide when it has gone on long enough. The primary problem in practice, it developed in the two cities studied, was to get any sort of discussion going at all, and then to keep it going.

The planners of City A hoped, for

example, that vigorous discussion would follow publication of their land use plan. No one showed any interest in discussing it, however. The reason seemed to be that the plan's stated goals were too general. No one knew how their application would affect him in practice. Those who were not completely uninterested in the plan had learned long ago to be suspicious of "utopian" generalities. As a result, non-planners decided with uncoordinated unanimity to ignore the plan until someone proposed specific applications of it. Only at this point, they felt, would there be anything comprehensible—whether or not comprehensive—to argue about.

The planners of City B argued that the City A planners' premises were wrong, and would have been wrong even if discussion of their plan had developed. For a discussion truly to influence the planning process, they said, it had to begin before detailed planning got under way. In their view, no one could effectively interpolate changes into a plan after it was complete without upsetting its internal harmony. If one of the goals of a plan were changed, then in theory every specific recommendation should be altered to some extent. No one had the time or intellectual energy, however, to do this when a plan had already taken definite shape. The crucial phase in the evolution of any plan, then, was the development of its first draft. Goals should be determined before this phase moved far along. They themselves tried to obtain approval for planning goals before developing their central area plan. They decided at the start that they needed a goal statement which would be both "operational" and acceptable to all "reasonable" citizens of the city. By "operational," they meant that progress toward the goal could be objectively measured, and that the broad costs, both tangible and spiritual, of striving toward it could be forseen. Comprehensive goals, they judged, could not be operational. Therefore, reasonable men could not pass on them intelligently. It followed that goals could win intelligent public approval only if they were partial. The question was: *how* partial? Perhaps it was possible to articulate, and plan to achieve, highly general goals even if not truly comprehensive ones.

They endeavored to bring about a public discussion of essential goal options before preparing the detailed plan. Planners had applied themselves to downtown economic problems in recent years, and had developed a fairly integrated theory explaining characteristic downtown problems. Consequently, City B's planners were able to present their preferred goals with tightly reasoned arguments behind them. The parts were related and mutually reinforcing. The man of affairs with a limited amount of time could quickly grasp the objectives and the main lines of reasoning on which the recommendations were based. The most general operational goal that the planners proposed was "the economic growth of downtown." They recognized that this goal was itself deceptive, however, in that it sounded noncontroversial but the measures necessary to its accomplishment could not be. In their publications on downtown planning goals, therefore, they choose to emphasize what they termed "design goals." These were in fact *types* of projects that had been tried in other cities. The planners explained the relationship between these types of proposals and the economic problems facing urban downtowns in the current period. It was possible to discuss the types of dislocation that might be expected, and so on, without bringing in specific project proposals. The discussion was a model of compre-

hensible argument in favor of middle range (that is, operational but still general) planning goals. It is doubtful that existing theory was (or is) sufficiently developed to support comparable justifications of goal recommendations at any other range of city planning activity.[3]

Even in this area, however, the specific financial costs and unintended side effects that would arise on application in City B were difficult to foresee. Any intelligent discussion of planning goals had to take these (or their unpredictability) into account. For the discussion to be fully useful, the planners judged, its participants had to be willing to inform themselves about planning detail at some significant expenditure of time and effort. The discussion had to continue throughout the planning process, which itself would have peaks of activity but no final termination. Since the overall goal was partial, the discussants had to be urged to consider the full complexity of its side effects. This they could not do if they confined themselves to examination of the central economic reasoning behind the "design goals."

The first problem was how to find appropriate discussants. The comprehensive planner's search is more complicated than that of any specialist. He cannot be satisfied to consult a narrow constituency. Presumably he should understand every important goal of each of society's members. If he must deal in practice with groups rather than individuals, he should not limit himself to constellations of interest that maintain permanent formal organizations. But the planners knew of no way to approach the city's "potential" groups. These would not become actual groups unless some immediate threats activated their potential members; some potential groupings of interest that the observer might identify would not become actual even then. Even those theoretically capable of being activated, however, currently had no leaders to speak for them. The abstract discussion of goals could seldom seem sufficiently immediate to spur them to organize and choose representatives. It seemed that in no other public endeavor than general goal determination was the disproportion greater between the number of groups that might reasonably become involved and the number that would.

The planners soon found that they could carry on a continuing discussion only with men whose jobs required them to spend time on the study and discussion of civic affairs. Only a few organizations in the city had such men on their payrolls. All of these fit into a few categories. Most were large downtown business firms or organizations of businessmen. A few good government groups (supported mainly by the contributions of businesses or businessmen) had representatives who took an interest in city planning, but for the most part they were in the same position as planners; they could talk abstractly about the public interest but they could not claim any special ability to represent particular interests. The other permanent organizations in the city did not have representatives spending the bulk of their time observing civic affairs. Each had a few continuing interests (racial issues, taxes, city hiring policy, and so forth) and became politically active only when immediate threats to these arose.

Making the best of this situation, the planners tried to carry on a discussion of goals with the professional "civic affairs" representatives of downtown business. These professional discussants, however, lacked the power to commit their firms to anything. Consequently, as the discussion became more specific they became more and more noncommittal. The businessmen who had the power to commit their firms to specific courses of action had neither the time nor interest to engage in long discussions with the city planners. In a short while, even the professional discussants found that they had no time to study each tentative planning formulation with care. Thus, a major difficulty was revealed (as it probably would have been in most cities). Even had the planners been able to handle all the complexity of life, they would not have found laymen willing or able to evaluate their work.

If it is so difficult to spur well-informed discussion even of such limited goals as those of the central area plan, the following question necessarily demands attention: what should be considered an adequate discussion of planning goals? Was the discussion in this case adequate even though the only participants were businessmen who took only mild interest in the discussion and were concerned only with direct economic costs and consequences? One might say that it was, because other groups could have entered the discussion to raise additional points had they wished. I was not able to find any elected officials in City B, however, who accepted this reasoning. Most were rather inarticulate about their objectives, but some were able to state their views quite precisely. Their central line of reasoning may be summarized briefly. Downtown businesses are "organizations in being." They are accustomed to watching the civic scene and searching for issues likely to affect their interests. They enter the discussion of any proposal at a very early stage and understand its potential impact on their interests relatively early. Other members of the public, however, tend to reach awareness that something is in issue and conceptualize their interests much more slowly. After the perception begins to clarify most take quite some time to organize. There is an enormous range in the amount of time, and in the degree of immediacy of a threat or opportunity, that it takes to move different groups of people with potential interest in a proposal to the threshold of organizational expression. Government never moves slowly enough or poses issues clearly enough to give everyone his say. It is fair to say that only when government moves at a snail's pace and deals with issues of rather direct and immediate impact can a significant proportion of the great multitude of interests express themselves. Therefore, democratic planning of a highly general nature is virtually impossible. No legislature or committee of interest group leaders can rationally evaluate a statement of general goals. Its members cannot, in the absence of specific project proposals and citizen reactions to them, predict how the countless measures needed to accomplish the goals will affect the overall quality of community life or the interests of their own constituents and organizations. Consequently, they are likely to prefer operating on levels where comprehension and prediction are more feasible, even if this means fragmenting policy choices rather than integrating them. In practice, this means that they will rarely commit themselves to let general and long-range goal statements guide their consideration of lower-level alternatives.

There are, no doubt, many American local politicians who would not find the preceding argument a compelling one. In localities lacking a coherent "power elite" firmly committed to a plan, however, it has a high degree of plausibility as a prescription for political survival. Its specific dictates are bound to be, at a minimum, a "project" rather than a "general planning" orientation and a disinclination to deal with controversial issues.

Basis for Authority

The point was made in the previous section that truly comprehensive goals tend not to provide any basis for evaluating concrete alternatives. It is thus difficult to stir political interest in them and impossible to plan rationally in their service. Recognizing this, many contemporary planners claim to practice middle-range planning—planning for the achievement of goals that are general, but still operational.

The middle-range planning ideal clearly has much to recommend it. It permits the promise of meaningful political discussion and approval of planning goals, even if (as we have seen) the achievement may be highly elusive. From the viewpoint of the general planner, however, it has one crucial flaw. It provides no basis for the planner to claim to understand the overall public interest. Men who plan to achieve operational—even though relatively general—goals are specialists, not comprehensive planners. Consequently, they have no *obvious* theoretical basis for claiming to know better than other specialists how far each specialist goal should be pursued, and with what priority.

The case for efforts at genuinely comprehensive planning has generally rested heavily on the thought that planners can resolve conflicts among goals in expert fashion. If they cannot, if they can only articulate specialist goals, then elected officials would seem required to act as the comprehensive arbiters of conflict. If it is assumed that arbiters operate most successfully when all important considerations are presented vigorously to them, one may argue reasonably that each important cluster of operational goals should be defended by a separate agency. Philip Selznick, for instance, has contended that leaders who wish to maximize their influence should structure their organizations so that the lines of jurisdiction-dividing sub-units are those along which important issues are likely to arise. His reasoning is that if issues arise within sub-units, they are likely to be decided by the sub-unit head, without the chief executive becoming aware of them. It is when sub-units themselves come into conflict that arbiters at the next higher levels are most likely to learn of issues.[4] Delegation of overall authority to arbitrate, in this view, even within the framework of highly general goal statements, is bound to transfer the substance of power from the delegator to the delegatee. If the delegator retains appellate jurisdiction he may dilute this effect. The more that he is committed to uphold the comprehensive policy vision of the delegatee, however, the less will he feel free to do so. In trying to persuade politicians to commit themselves to the policy visions of planners, defenders of comprehensive planning must contend that the politicians will benefit their constituents by doing so. To the extent that the planners themselves lack comprehensive perspectives, however, this contention becomes less and less plausible.

Beyond this, even in pursuit of their own specialist goals, planners operate in a world of whole objects, not analytical aspects. They cannot conceive means that will further the operational goals of primary interest to them without also affecting innumerable others in uncontrolled fashion. Many planners recognize this, and try not to serve their stated operational goals exclusively. The operational goal of City B's central area plan, for example, was downtown economic growth. Its authors realized, however, that they could not reasonably ignore other goals. They wrote and spoke as though the cultural, political, spiritual, recreational, and other functions of downtown could never conflict with each other or with the economic function. In practice, they were saved by their common sense; they did not press their pursuit of economic goals sufficiently far to spur public awareness of potentially serious conflicts. Conceivably, they might have listed all the significant operational goals they hoped to serve, but they would still have been left with the problem of balancing them. In short, every concrete object of planner attention is a miniature of the whole. The important analytical problems that arise in planning for an entire urban area arise also in planning any section of it.[5] Perhaps the only solution is frankly to adopt a specialist orientation, even while remaining willing to adjust specific proposals as highly distasteful side effects become apparent. It may still be plausible to maintain, however, that planners are custodians of values that somehow deserve to take precedence over the values propounded by other specialists. Let us consider the most persuasive lines of reasoning frequently advanced in support of this view.

One of the most straightforward was stated by Allison Dunham in a well-known article several years ago.[6] He claimed to have found after a survey of the planning literature that planners almost invariably believed that, at the very least, they were the officials best qualified to evaluate site proposals for every kind of facility. They based their position on the premise that planners were experts in the impact of land uses on each other. The argument, in other words, was not that planners were "wiser" than operating agency officials, but that on certain types of issues their specialty deserved first place in the hierarchy of specialties.

On this point two queries come to mind. First, are the impacts of uses on each other regularly more important in site decisions than the intended purposes of each use? Second, can locational problems be separated meaningfully from all other problems? Let me illustrate by referring to the controversy (mentioned previously) about where in City A to locate the new city-county hospital. One powerful group was anxious to locate the hospital between the city's two largest private hospitals (which in turn were one block apart) in the downtown area. They argued that the three hospitals combined could support a great deal of expensive equipment, could attract outstanding internes and residents more easily than any one alone, and might provide the base within a few years for development of a medical school in the city. The city's planners favored a site just outside the downtown area, emphasizing the traffic congestion that would result from locating the new hospital in the immediate vicinity of the two old ones. Each side advanced other arguments as well, but these were the main ones, and for my purpose it is not necessary to judge the overall merit of either position. It is only necessary to consider the general issues which were posed: first, how much cost in traffic congestion should be accepted to obtain how much benefit to health? and second, is traffic congestion more a locational problem than building a medical center? The proponents of the three-hospital medical center argued that its benefits could be obtained only by building on the site they proposed. No others in the immediate vicinity were available. They considered the site favored by the city

planners to be wholly unacceptable. The only way to argue that planners should normally be given the benefit of the doubt in disputes of this kind is to say, as Dunham did, that specialists think of the needs of their constituents, while planners think of the impact of specialist proposals on others. In this case, the constituents were sick people and hospital staff personnel, while the "others" included many of the same people, but in their other capacities: as drivers and investors, for instance. The key question is whether the "others" should have had any more presumptive right to prevail than the recognized constituents.

Another objection to this definition of planner competence is that it provides only the haziest indication of the legitimate jurisdiction of planners and of government. Just what is a locational decision? It is hardly enough to say, as planners generally have, that locational decisions are those that have an impact on surrounding property or people. Almost anything I do to my property affects my neighbor in some way. For instance, if I rent out rooms in my single-family home, I have changed the use of my land and therefore made a locational decision, by a common planning definition. Should government therefore control everything, as it already controls my right to rent out rooms? Planners deny that it should, but they have rarely asked where the cutoff point should be. They have generally been satisfied to say that government should intervene only in cases of "substantial" harm, and that common sense will prevail in interpreting the word "substantial." They may be right, but this formulation gives the citizen no theoretical guidance as to whose common sense should prevail in cases of disagreement between other decision-makers and planners.

A second persuasive line of reasoning to support the view that planners should generally prevail in such disputes is that they alone among city officials analyze city problems from an overall point of view. Operating agency officials cannot rise above their day-to-day administrative chores, and in any event their perspectives are conditioned by the narrow responsibilities of their departments. Even politicians typically devote most of their time to maintaining contacts with, and to performing errand boy services for, their constituents. In dealing with legislative proposals, they generally focus on details of immediate interest to vocal groups rather than on the overall picture. In most cities, moreover, councilmen are elected from wards; in many they work only part time at their jobs; and in some each councilman heads a city department. Only planners can devote all their time to thought about city problems at the most general level.

The most obvious criticism of this position is that freedom from operating responsibility may not be the best condition in which to make high-level decisions. Some prominent decision-makers have argued that it is a poor one. Winston Churchill, for example, has written that Stafford Cripps became restive and hypercritical of his colleagues while serving as parliamentary whip during World War II. What he needed, according to Churchill's diagnosis, was responsibility which would absorb his energies and give him a sense of the concrete issues. Those who are free from operating responsibility, concluded Churchill, tend to develop an unhelpful watchdog mentality. It is unhelpful because they usually think too abstractly to be cogent critics of complex choices among policies.[7] Similarly, Chester Barnard has written that study and reflectiveness without operating responsibility tend to lead to the treatment of things by aspects rather than wholes, to a disregard of factors which cannot be expressed precisely, and to an underestimation of the need for artistry in making concrete decisions. Because so many crucial factors cannot find expression in words, Barnard concluded, the interdependencies of social life can only be grasped intuitively. Only men of long and responsible experience are likely to acquire very much of this intuitive grasp, and therefore only such men—who will also grasp the supreme difficulty of planning in this "world of unknowns"—are qualified to plan.[8] This is unquestionably a rather mystical position, but it is no less for that a respectable and forceful one.

Barnard and Churchill agree, then, that freedom from responsibility for operating decisions is anything but fit training for planning.[9] Those who accept their view are likely to believe that any one of a number of city officials may qualify better than the planning director to serve as the wise chief advisor of politicians on broad policy issues. In cities A and B, the city councils consistently acted on this belief. To the extent that they desired coordination of public works, they normally relied on their city engineers to achieve it. When the City Council of B decided to separate capital budgeting from ordinary budgeting, it set up a committee composed of politicians and civic leaders. The committee was given a small staff headed by a former city councilman. Planners were shut out of the capital budgeting process entirely. When the City Council of A decided that it needed a special advisor on the interstate freeway program, it appointed the incumbent city engineer, who had been about to retire. When the city engineer of B left the city government for private employ, his successor proved inadequate (in the City Council's view) for the unofficial task of coordinating city public works. Within a year, the Council lured him back into government, giving him the title of Development Coordinator. The city's planners believed that they should have been given the job, but they could offer no strong arguments to support their view that the engineer was less able to take the overview than they. The politician most responsible for bringing him back told me that the planners thought too abstractly and with insufficient regard to cost; whereas the engineer, though less articulate, understood the infinite, inexpressable complexity of governmental choice. In fairness to the planners, it should be added that the engineer had made his entire career in City B, looking to the City Council for his raises, perquisites, and promotions. He had risen primarily because of his technical competence, to be sure, but also because the councilmen felt confident that he would not embarrass them politically and that his overriding loyalty was to themselves. The Planning Director, by contrast, had been chosen after a national search by a citizens' committee (advised by a nationally known planning consultant), had been on the local scene for two years, and had his primary base of political support outside the city government entirely. It should be mentioned that the last factor was not due to simple ineptitude on the Planning Director's part. He had chosen his strategy consciously and deliberately, judging that the city government would support effective general planning only if—and, even then, only perhaps—pressured by outside groups to do so.

A third defense that planners frequently make of their aspiration to be more than "mere" specialists is that governmental efficiency is served by having one agency keep track of everything that every city agency does, calling attention to conflicts and to means of coordinating effort for the benefit of all. The distinction between coordination and planning, however, is of practical importance only so long as planners have no power. Without power, they can as coordinators simply try to persuade groups of specialists that their respective interests will be served by improved coordination. As soon as planners begin to impose solutions or advise politicians to impose them, however, they have entered the substantive planning field. That is, they have set their perception of the public interest on substantive matters against those of the specialists who have rejected their advice. Similarly, when planners request authority to prepare a city's capital budget, they cannot justify the request on grounds of "simple efficiency," which would have to be established by the criteria of all the specialists' own goals. They must assert, at least implicitly, that they have some means of choosing among the values entrusted to each operating agency. In other words, they must claim to have goals. And the coordination of action in pursuit of substantive goals is, if it is anything, substantive planning.

One might say that the planner needs coordinative power only because some specialists stupidly or obstinately refuse to cooperate with others in the interests of "simple efficiency," even though no significant values are threatened. The specialists' answer is that no one can determine that this is the case in any particular controversy without examining it in detail. Philip Selznick has illustrated this point clearly in his analysis of the history of the Communist party.[10] The party refused to cooperate with other leftist parties in the decade before the Popular

Front, despite the obvious threat of fascism. Yet this period of isolation, Selznick contends, made the party a much more valuable tool to its masters during and after the Popular Front period. During the isolation period, the "character" of the party developed and became incorruptible. This extreme example illustrates a simple point: that cooperation and isolation in themselves have important effects on organizations. If an agency head claims that a measure advanced in the name of efficiency actually threatens important values—and any agency head who refuses the advice of the planning director will say this—no outsider can refute him until he examines the bases of his arguments in detail. If we assume that most agency heads are men of good conscience, we can likewise assume that they will have some reasons that seem genuinely sufficient to them, and that will seem so as well to at least some reasonable out-siders. In the end, no act of coordination is without its effect on other values than efficiency.

Closing

The purpose here is not to disparage the ideal of comprehensive planning, but rather to challenge the planning profession to reinforce its most fundamental theoretical arsenal.[11] Some of the issues raised may seem overly theoretical, and in the immediate sense perhaps they are—though to me they appeared quite close to the surface in the two cities I studied. In the long run, however, comprehensive planning and evaluation will have little effect on American cities unless their goal premises can be established in sufficiently compelling fashion (both politically and intellectually) to make politicians take notice.

NOTES

1. These case studies appear as chapters 2–5 of my book, *The City Planning Process* (Ithaca: Cornell University Press, 1965). Versions of three of them have already been published separately by the Inter-University Program as "The Ancker Hospital Site Controversy," "A Land-Use Plan for St. Paul," and "Locating the Intercity Freeway."
2. The words "rational" and "wise" are often used interchangeably in evaluating public choices. This is in accord with the usage of natural law philosophers, but not with that of contemporary economic and social theorists. For the latter, the term "rational" refers to the efficiency of means where ends are known. "Wisdom" refers to deep understanding and the ability to make what are considered "good" judgments on complex human issues, when goals and efficient means are not generally known.

   Consequently, the planners' use of the word "rational" in the classic sense to defend their distinctly modern "expert" recommendations makes for confusion of thought. This confusion has a political function, however. It conveys the impression that expert logic or technique can produce "good" decisions on complex human issues.
3. A major reason for this, of course, is that in no urban sections but downtown do simple economic goals seem entirely adequate. Outside the United States, planners often consider them inadequate even for downtown. See, for example, the British Town and Country Planning Association's analysis of central London problems: "The Paper Economy" (London: Town and Country Planning Association, 1962).
4. Philip Selznick, *Leadership in Administration* (Evanston: Row, Peterson, and Company, 1957).
5. The more limited objects (e.g., neighborhoods instead of whole cities) do present somewhat different, if not lesser, problems to the comprehensive planner. Cause and effect are easier to trace on the small scene, and important differences of interest are likely to be fewer. On the other hand, if planners emphasize the common interest of each homogeneous unit, they may well accentuate the differences between units.
6. Allison Dunham, "A Legal and Economic Basis for City Planning," *Columbia Law Review*, LVIII (May, 1958), pp. 650–71.
7. Winston Churchill, *The Second World War*, Vol. IV: *The Hinge of Fate* (Boston: Houghton-Mifflin Co., 1950), p. 560.

   Churchill was not arguing against the making of large decisions by generalists, of course. He himself was Prime Minister. Nor was he criticizing the British practice of concentrating authority within the civil service in the hands of generalists. Several points may be noted. The generalists in a British ministry exercise all formal power of decision not exercised by the minister himself. They bear responsibility as well for deciding which issues, and which specialist analyses of them, are important enough for the minister to consider. The elite corps of the generalists, the Administrative Class, are expected on entry only to think, write, and speak clearly, and to have done well in their subject of undergraduate concentration. Any subject will do, although subjects fit for "gentlemen" (i.e., men devoted to culture rather than making a living), notably the classics, have traditionally predominated. British adminstrators have no formal technical training for their work at all. They are platonic rather than functional leaders, but matured on responsibility rather than study. Those at the higher levels are notably unsympathetic to the ideal of general planning. They take well-known pride in deciding "each case on its merits."

Parenthetically, where city planners are employed in British ministries, they are considered technicians, capable of contributing useful advice on specialized aspects of issues, but not of being entrusted with the power to make decisions.

8. Chester Barnard, *Organization and Management* (Cambridge: Harvard University Press, 1948), ch. 4.
9. It should be clear that when I speak of "planning" in this article, I mean the work of determining overall policy guidelines for public activity, and means of implementing them. No single individual or agency makes such determinations alone in an American community. The recommendations of some, however, are bound to carry more weight than those of others. The crucial questions at issue in this section are (1) whether the views of planning agencies on controversial policy issues should normally be granted presumptive validity in the absence of strong evidence discrediting them; and (2) whether the training and career patterns of professional city planners equip them well for planning at the higher levels.
10. Philip Selznick, *The Organizational Weapon* (Glencoe: The Free Press, 1960).
11. I have made a beginning effort at reinforcement in my article, "Reason and Influence in the Public Service," which is scheduled to appear in a forthcoming issue of the *Public Administration Review* and as chapter 7 of my book, *The City Planning Process*.

58. Social Planning, Social Planners, and Planned Societies John W. Dyckman

City planning is by no means the only "urban" planning tradition in this country. Other professions, too, specify the goals of American communities and plan their activities in terms of rational programs for achieving them. Social workers, for example, try to base welfare activities on a systematic consideration of the needs of the total society. Similarly, architects, economic planners, public administrators, and city managers propose to widen the scope of their professional influence into something analogous to comprehensive planning. In recent years all branches of planning have tended to merge their efforts in response to the accelerating rate of urban growth, the decay of the central cities, and the greater awareness of "hard-core" urban poverty. As a result, several programs sponsored by municipal, state, and federal levels of government now carry the label of "social planning."

John Dyckman reviews the several meanings of the term "social planning." He distinguishes between societal planning, or the generation of goals and programs aimed to deal with the group and individual needs of American society as a whole; programming for selected social goals, such as the War on Poverty; and the emerging tendency in several professions based on "hard" sciences, including engineering and economic planning, to incorporate a

concern for social values. Dyckman says that the fundamental values and basic social insti-
tutions of the United States obstruct the application and implementation of social planning
methods. Much of his paper is devoted to a description and evaluation of the strategies that
must be developed for circumventing and overcoming these obstacles.

John W. Dyckman is Professor of City and Regional Planning and Chairman of the Department of City and Regional Planning of the University of California, Berkeley. For information on his other published work see page 439.

Social planning is a belated and tentative response of American planners to functional lag. Physical planning, particularly of cities, has been accepted as a legitimate activity at the governmental level for more than half a century. Economic planning, though partial and inconstant, has been an established part of the governmental scene since the 1930's. Social planning, on the other hand, has been openly recognized only more recently, and then it has proceeded under a cover of confusion which has prevented public debate on its scope and its intentions.

For the most part, social planning in the USA is defensive, and arises from the crises which are spun off as by-products of action programs of government. Public intervention in urban development and renewal, for example, has cast up problems of relocation which are so intertwined in the fabric of social life of the affected communities that "social" planners are called upon for relief.

At the same time, the residual issues of the affluent society are so clearly social issues that earlier concerns of physical and economic planning have in some cases given way to priorities for direct planning of social outcomes. The Poverty Program, for example, recognizes that the problem of poverty is not merely a problem of economics, but is also a problem of the culture of poverty which can be addressed only by direct social action. Juvenile

delinquency, mental health, and a range of other social ills are, in the view of the behavioral scientists who examine them, more than economic problems. Indeed, there are many who argue that a planned economy cannot eliminate these problems. The presence of social pathology alongside planning then becomes an argument against an excessively "materialistic" view of society. Paradoxically, opponents of the excessive economic determinism often attributed to Marxism are cast in the role of advocates of increasing planning in the social sphere.

Other types of social planning have been made necessary by rejection of the "planned society" of socialist economists. The whole complex of welfare services which have grown up in the United States were traditionally, and still remain, devices to compensate for the wastage and breakage in a competitive, individual-serving, industrial society. They have existed to cushion the blow of this competitive struggle for those so disadvantaged as to be unable to compete effectively. The traditional social services, both privately and publicly provided, are ad hoc solutions for specific problems. They have not, until recently, drawn upon a common context or comprehensive planning outlook.

Reprinted by permission of the *Journal of the American Institute of Planners* (Volume XXXII, No. 2, March, 1966).

The notion of coordinated social services, of planned cooperation between agencies, is relatively recent in the field of social welfare and social work. But even where such coordinating councils exist in cities or metropolitan areas, their planning is roughly advisory (except for determinations which enter into the division of the Community Chest) and lacks measures of progress which would guide the allocative decisions. Even more important, the social goals which planning would presumably help to advance are vague and are often stated so as to obscure rather than to adjudicate differences between the goals of the independent agencies.

As a result, there is a great deal of remedial social action, and some social planning in the United States, but this goes on in the absence of even a schematic societal plan which will guide the individual plans of the operating agencies. Societal planning in the United States is principally hortatory, as in the National Goals Reports issued during the Eisenhower Administration.

Some of the most thoughtful work on the meaning of social planning in the American context was instituted several years ago under the direction of Everett Reimer for the Puerto Rican Planning Board. Reimer, assisted by Janet Reiner, commissioned thoughtful papers by Herbert Gans, Abraham Kaplan, and other consultants, and produced many useful internal memoranda. In one of these papers Gans clearly distinguished "societal planning" from "social programs." The former is much more difficult to treat, since it entails some specification of the goals of the society, while the latter are farther along in the "means" end of the means-end continuum. Gans developed a paradigm for locating programs and actions in this framework which is an excellent statement

for orientation to the problem of social planning in the context of the remedial actions of social agencies traditional in the United States.[1]

Let us extend this line of reasoning, and take *social planning* to mean the effort to plan for the fate of a whole society. This view emphasizes the interdependence of activities and the shared consequences of program actions. It recognizes that there may be unplanned consequences of planned actions, and that these may deserve attention equal to that given the programs themselves. Much of the concern with social planning among city planners in the United States stems from the unplanned social dislocations and stresses that follow upon public programs such as redevelopment. In a comparable vein, the interest in social planning in developing economies arises from similar stresses that follow upon planned economic development. Indeed, the former draws heavily on the literature developed in the latter, and both have made liberal use of studies developed in crisis situations such as bombings, floods, and deportations. The problems of disrupted working class urban neighborhoods described by Gans and others are in one perspective a pale copy of the disruptions and strains on social goals of political realization, social justice, and cultural self-expression which have accompanied pursuit of the goal of economic development in preindustrial societies.

When societal goals are advanced by unilateral programs of service agencies, unexpected or perverse results may emerge. Thus the goals of economic justice may dictate an emphasis on low-cost meritorious consumer goods such as housing, and the goals of social justice may indicate that the housing should be placed in neighborhoods as favored as those claimed by higher income groups, but the actual programs for achieving these goals may make for outcomes that disturb the harmonious relations between groups, aggravate class tension, and encourage some forms of antisocial actions. Programs of economic development have almost inevitably favored certain classes whose cooperation was vital to the program, to the relative disadvantage of others. More specifically, these programs have been concerned with incentives necessary to realization of the goals, such as high rewards to entrepreneurs, which may have been paid for by relatively disadvantaged groups. One can proliferate examples of this kind, both in economic development and in urban renewal. These examples dramatize the need for a true social planning framework in which to evaluate the social consequences of individual programs.

To clarify these relations, we might distinguish three operational meanings of *social planning*, and three levels of action.

1. At the societal planning level, social planning means the selection of the social goals of the nation or state, and the setting of targets for their achievement. It requires a ranking of these goals, and assessment of the cost (in terms of other objectives) of achieving them, and judgments of the feasibility of such programs.

2. Social planning, in a closely related meaning, involves the application of social values and action criteria to the assessment of programs undertaken in the pursuit of economic or political goals. Thus, it can mean the testing of the consequences—in terms of intergroup or interpersonal relations—of everything from broad economic development programs to specific redevelopment projects.

3. Social planning can mean specifically "social" programming arising from the broad social goals of the community. The traditional welfare activities of public and private agencies have been the principal focus of such planning in the United States. The coordination of programming for and by the multitude of caretaker agencies that have grown up in our free enterprise economy is a popular task for this type of social planning.

Much of the discussion of social planning, and the identification of activities under this label, belongs in the third category. It is my contention that this category has developed in a variety of directions without an adequately specified set of objectives at the first and second levels. This view is independent of considerations of the planned society, though subsequent discussion will make clear that the latter are not irrelevant to it.

Social planning has long been treacherous ground for the city planner because of the ever present danger that the expert determination of need might degenerate into the imposition of class or professional prejudices upon a resistant clientele. Social planning, in the sense of determination of the social needs of a community or a group within the community is torn between the desire to require certain levels of consumption of merit goods on the one hand, and the recognition of the legitimacy of individual choice on the other. Many social planners assert that their interest is in the maximization of opportunity, or freedom of choice. But as a practical matter, no society has found a feasible way of maximizing choice for all groups or individuals at all times. For the exercise of one man's choice is a limitation on the freedom of choice of another.

It is not surprising that social planning has often turned away from goals, in the direction of means. For one thing, it is firmly in the tradition of modern clinical

psychology, and the positivism of sociology, to accept individually determined
ends as legitimate, and to emphasize means
of realizing these ends. But it is a matter of
some subtlety, worthy to challenge the
professional social actionist, or clinical
caretaker, to emphasize the manipulation
of behavior, rather than the alteration of
goals of behavior. Let us consider some
of the problems encountered in these tasks.

**Finding Appropriate Remedies:
Diagnosis of the Client**

Remedial social planning is necessary
in our society because the major forces
shaping our lives are unplanned. Social
planning has come to the fore because we
have been unable to predict, control, or
shape the repercussions of technological
change or of our planned programs.
Because we do not plan our technology,
but allow it to follow opportunistic lines,
we do not control the repercussions of its
development. These repercussions cast up
many of the persistent social problems of
our times, such as the sharp segregation
of the poor, the aged, and the minorities
in the cities; the left-behind regions of
economic depression; the unemployable
cadres of displaced workers; and the
great gaps in educational attainment. In
many respects, the advanced technological
societies need therapeutic social planning
as badly as the countries experiencing the
stresses of early technological change. For
example, urban renewal, which was embraced avidly by liberals and city planners
in 1949 at passage of the Housing Act,
has proven a specific source of embarrassment and friction to liberal politicians for
fifteen years. It is the realization of this
fact that has created the call for a Domestic
Peace Corps in the United States.

These problems have traditionally been
easier to identify in the newly developing
economies. One might swiftly recognize
the particular problems raised for Puerto
Rican planning by a host of world and
hemispheric developments: the emergence
of a new stage in world industrialization;
the extension of the urban life style and
the obliteration of differences between city
and country in the most industrially
developed nations; the sharpening of
differences between the "educated" and
"uneducated"; the development of new
technological advances in transportation
and communication. Until a Michael
Harrington, or some other prophet, calls
attention to the lags in our perception,
we are likely to miss the similar phenomena which take place in societies starting
from a more favored base. It is the merit
of urban renewal that it called attention
to problems of the city, to implications of
public intervention in the city, and to
undeveloped perspectives in city planning.

Further, the issue of relocation in urban
redevelopment emphasizes the interdependence of the social fabric of communities. It has underlined the reality that one
cannot intervene in any important portion
of this web without disrupting the structure and entangling himself in the consequences.

But the urban renewal issue is complicated by the complexity of modern government and its ingrown bureaucracy in
response to technological pressures operating through the inexorable drive of
organizational efficiency. In the course of
this transformation of government, many
of the more purely "social" concerns,
which were adequately handled in the
days when political community and social
community were identical, have disappeared in the larger governmental
apparatus. As a result, the need for social

planning is one symptomatic side effect of the organizational conquest of government. This bureaucratization is present at all levels—the distance between the local communities and city government is evident at a public hearing in a major city on the subject of a freeway location or a redevelopment proposal—though it is most intense at the federal level, where the bureaucracies are relatively rationalized and professionalized. Because we have not been conscious of the organizational and technological revolutions in our modern life, we approach the discovery of disparities between local community feeling and bureaucratic objectives with indignation. Truly effective social planning, even in a limited therapeutic sense, would need to deal more self-consciously with the relation between local social objectives and larger organizational requirements.

It is largely this sense of bureaucratic distance, which exists between city planners and citizens, almost equally with practitioners of welfare services and their clients, that has led to the social planning emphasis on *client analysis*. Presumably, by detailed sociological analysis of the client population, akin to the market analysis conducted by firms seeking outlets for their products, social planning can be equipped to overcome this bureaucratic disability. Client analysis has drawn upon, and has developed, substantial insights into the aspirations and motives of the target populations. Presumably, client analysis will also help uncover and recognize the interest of groups who are disenfranchised of power, and whose real aspirations would rarely be reflected in public programs. This more dynamic, or even revolutionary, aspect of client analysis has been widely stressed by social planners operating in minority group areas. It may be likened to a caretaker variant of the civil rights position that the society must do some things to help disadvantaged groups which have not yet been discovered by the disadvantaged groups themselves. In the advertising analogy, client analysis thus leads to taste-making, as well as taste-serving.

In this latter formulation, the client analysis position strikes a responsive note in the ideology of city planners, who have commonly felt that the citizens of the megapolitan world must be saved from themselves. In the social planning context, the inarticulate disadvantaged are saved from a temporary ignorance of their own best interests in order that they can more effectively express those interests over time.

The client analysis position, however, has one great advantage over that of traditional city planning. It explicitly identifies these interests, and neither subsumes them in vague categories of public interest, nor freely ascribes the prejudices of the bureaucracy to the long run best interest of the poor. Client analysis, moreover, begins from the presupposition that many of the bureaucratic standards will be ill-suited to serve the real client population. Nevertheless, one cannot escape the reality that social planning with client analysis merely substitutes market research for the operations of the market. That is, client analysis notwithstanding, social planning is the antithesis of laissez-faire.

Social planning, in fact, cannot escape the ire of the conservatives by adopting some of the instruments of the market. Indeed, the violence of objections to the rent supplements included in last year's Housing Bill is evidence that indirectness and subtlety in social programs, which place a greater premium on planning than on direct action, may be more deeply resented by opponents of the programs' purposes. One is reminded that the late Senator Bricker belaboured his compatriot Senator from Ohio, Robert Taft, for introducing the "Trojan Horse" of private redevelopment into the publicly subsidized 1949 Housing Act. There is no particular ground for believing that social planning and market mechanisms make public spending any more palatable to enemies of the programs. The very informational requirements of social planning may make the priests of that planning more suspect of hoarding secrets.

Caretakers and Long-run Client Interests

Most social planners have at least a modified "caretaker" orientation. In his statement on "Meeting Human Needs" in *Goals for Americans*, the report of the President's Commission in 1960, James P. Dixon, Jr. wrote, "[society] can develop ways by which people can meet their own needs more readily and fruitfully, and it can develop ways by which society as a whole can meet needs that would otherwise be unmet. There are individuals who will not meet their own needs, and others who cannot."[2] The caretaker responsibility presumably extends to those who will not as well as those who cannot. Few societies take a wholly permissive view towards freedom of choice. In addition to the collective goods which we make available for the use of all citizens, from national defense to national parks, there are public programs encouraging the consumption of certain goods and services, and discouraging others. Economists recognize that societies encourage the consumption of the "merit" goods and discourage the consumption of demerit goods. Thus we exempt certain foods from sales taxes and

place punitive taxes on alcohol, tobacco, and other products, and severely restrict the use of narcotics.

Americans have been understandably wary of social planning, since these responsibilities place the planners in the role of caretakers of "safety," "health," and "morals." The technological competence of highly organized government is today so great that there is widespread suspicion and apprehension about government power. We are afraid of the information handling capabilities which modern technology has placed at the disposal of government, for the "disutopians" have warned us of the threat to liberty which may lurk in such power. We all tend to be slightly apprehensive about the governmental capacity for storing information about the individual and recalling it by means of the social security number, zip code, or other identification. These fears may be legitimate even when it is recognized that the information technology is itself morally indifferent, and can be used with equal effect for widely approved and undesirable social purposes. The issue of what is "desirable" is an openly divisive one. Humanists have never been reluctant to prescribe remedies for fellow humans, but a central problem of democratic planning, as Davidoff and Reiner have emphasized, is that of preserving an adequate area of individual choice in the face of expert judgments of the "good."[3]

This issue is a persistent stumbling block in all social planning programs aimed at overcoming some of the undesirable consequences of our great technical efficiency. The Poverty Program is split, from the very start, on disagreement over the meaning of poverty. The traditional libertarian nineteenth century economists argue that the problem of poverty is one of inadequate income, and the provision of that income will eliminate the poverty. Some of the contemporary liberals argue the contrary, maintaining that there is a culture of poverty independent of income which cannot be redressed by simple money payments. The choice of a measurement of poverty engages this issue. A "market basket" approach as contrasted with an income level approach commits one to a definition of poverty in terms of merit goods, and required consumption, rather than income payment. In short, it takes some of the choice away from the poor, and refers the determination to an objective standard.

In social planning, the caretaker issue directly confronts choice. The case of planning for mental health, for example, is fraught with instances of value conflict. Even at the margin, where relatively clear-cut issues of community interest can be adduced, there are few clear-cut policy directions. Take the control of dischargees from mental hygiene programs. It serves the cause of effective treatment to continue the contact with the patient over a period of time. To maintain this contact normally requires a legal hold on the patient. But it is a matter of great administrative delicacy to decide when the imposition of that hold, usually by court order, is genuinely "protective," and when it is a violation of the patient's civil liberties.

In such cases, the welfare economics rule, crudely paraphrased, would be to restrain the patient only when the marginal social benefit from the continuing contact exceeds the marginal social cost of diminishing individual liberty. In practice, the probability of relapse once removed from contact is the decisive "factual" input. When the social cost of relapse, weighted by the probability of relapse once the patient is removed from contact, exceeds the social cost of deprivation of liberty multiplied by the probability of such deprivation in enforced contact, the restraint is justified. Clearly, administrators may be divided on their relative valuation of the social damage of the behavior of the mentally ill and of freedom to come and go at will. But it is sometimes overlooked that the social sciences, on which such calculus is dependent for its "factual" inputs, are often equally at variance over the behavioral probabilities. As Hans Morgenthau once observed, social sciences are not only uncertain about the nature of causes, given effects, but are also uncertain about the evaluation of the effects, given the causes.

The problem of choice is therefore shifted uncomfortably to the social planner. He finds that he must have a theory of long-run client interests. If he is to engage in this perilous activity, he cannot afford the luxury of positivist detachment. He will not be handed a ready-made packet of goals in the form of a set of well-ordered preference functions, and the task of discerning "latent" goals will take great patience and much free interpretation. The enterprise of social planning has always been facilitated by strong ideology. At the least, it requires determined leadership.

Social Planning and Social Leadership

If the democratic ideals of decentralized decision and individual choice are to be pursued concurrently with the officially defined community goals of health and welfare, including increased consumption of meritorious goods and services, extraordinary efforts must be made to bulwark the choosing processes of the disadvantaged with vast amounts of technical information, political leverage, and economic means. In particular, it may be necessary for the poor and disadvantaged to have their own planners. This realization is quickly forced upon those who hold uncompromisingly democratic goals, and who become engaged in the action processes. For example, Paul Davidoff has on various occasions urged that planners take up the role of advocates for the disadvantaged.[4]

The problem is closely analogous to that of foreign aid. In making grants or loans to underdeveloped nations, the donors are always faced with the difficult task of insuring efficient use of the funds, without imposing imperialistic controls. The difficulties in such action may account for the predilection in Soviet aid programs for concrete development projects, rather than outright grants. If the projects chosen are popular, some of this difficulty can be avoided. Presumably, if federal programs followed indigenous market choice rather than bureaucratic determination of merit, they would provide freedom schools, key club memberships, and cut-rate Cadillacs rather than public housing, Job Corps camps, and school lunches. It would then be up to local planners, working in the community as advocates, to both extend the impact of the actual choices of the community, and to reshape the choice, by dramatizing the relations between means and ends.

Taken seriously programs like the rent subsidy provisions of the present Housing Act, which are aimed at encouraging the consumption of merit goods, entail a basic reeducation of consumers. Indeed, real incomes measured by consumer satisfaction, may not go up in the short run under such programs even if the objective level of consumption is raised. (In the case of relocation of slum dwellers in housing estates in England, Ireland, and elsewhere, there is even some evidence that the objective level of living has at times declined slightly with the increased consumption of a particular merit good, housing.)

The closer one gets to the community level, and the closer to the client, the more acute are these problems of individual liberty and choice. The main problem of social planning at the national level is to establish social goals which are attainable, or at least approachable, which can be given some hierarchical ordering, and which can be programmed. National planners should use program guides, standards, and other bureaucratic controls sparingly, lest they make demands on localities which are unreasonable in this sense.

At the local level, where these goals are to be implemented, the democratic ideal would hold out the opportunity for citizens to participate in defining the operational form of their goals. In practice, however, there is a tendency toward organizational efficiency which requires each local agency action to be measured against the operating rules of output which are established by the national bureaucracies. While planning as an activity is independent of the issue of centralization, the same organizational forces that make for planning push for the efficiencies realizable by central control. What is more, the planners are often impatient with the delays, losses, and frictional costs imposed by decentralized administration. The conduct of the Antipoverty Program is an example of such costs, and the uneasiness which these arouse in the planners.

Social Planning and Administrative Efficiency

The Great Society is determined to be The Efficient Society, not content to provide butter with its guns, but bent on having the most Bang for the Buck and the smoothest spreading, high-score product in Dairyland. The success of economic thinking in the Defense Department's planning and the great growth of efficiency analysis techniques supported by government contract effort have encouraged governmental planners to apply performance tests to social welfare programs as well as to military procurement. The city planning profession, which has long vacillated between social utopianism and managerial efficiency aims, now must increasingly accommodate to the imposition of the latter by the administering federal bureaucracies. Local social planning has barely begun to digest the implications of this trend.

The drive for evaluation of the effectiveness of social service programs is eminently reasonable. In the absence of well articulated national social goals, individual program progress is difficult to measure; in a society only recently concerned with defining more subtle measures of social progress than income and employment some confusion of direction is to be expected. The presence of established bureaucracies poised to soak up the new program funds does not reassure the operations analyst. After all, what percentage of applicants to the U.S. Employment Service are placed in jobs by that service? What percentage of referrals to Mental Health clinics are successfully treated? Existing welfare agencies tend to be audited in terms of operations performed, not results achieved. Senator Ribicoff's recent observation that federal agencies may lack the competence to administer the new social programs enacted by Congress is only half the picture; Congress has failed to give clearly the direction of results expected from these programs. Administrative audits may be premature until these purposes are clarified. There is even a danger that too-hasty efficiency measures will impede the development of these goals, for the latter must be defined by the interactions between the clients and the supply agencies.

Since a prime goal of administration is efficiency, and since individuals may be legitimately indifferent to the efficiency of the system or organization, individual behavior is a friction to be overcome in administration. Resistance to the imposition of preference rankings from above is a fundamental democratic tenet, but it is almost inevitably in conflict with programs planned by experts, whether social planners or physical planners. Efficiency-minded physical planners become impatient at the economic and engineering inefficiencies produced by obdurate human behavior, and the social planners, since the origins of the settlement house movement, have marvelled at the capacities of the poor for resisting "self-betterment."

Robert Moses, one of the more impatient of planners, recently gave vent to this common annoyance, commenting on an engineering feasibility report for a proposed Long Island Sound crossing which he favors. Since the feasibility depends, to some extent, on the ability of the planners to persuade people to use the crossing at times other than summer months and week-ends, Mr. Moses complained that "the usual short season, dependent on the opening and closing of schools, and occasional mid-summer peak loads due to silly, gregarious travel hours, are the despair and curse of those who operate our seashore." The stickiness of this behavior puzzled Mr. Moses, for he continued, "as to hourly schedules, why should motorized lemmings instinctively crawl in huge armies to cast themselves into the sea just at high noon, instead of staggering their arrivals? Why can't they listen to radio and other mechanical instruction? Why must a driver behave like an ant, and if he must, why isn't he an obedient ant?"[5]

The administrative, or management, sciences differ in their approach to planning, depending on the scope and degree of control exercised by the management. More centralized management leans to a "hard" style, with decentralized or democratic management styles featuring a "soft" approach. The mnemonic public administration acronym POSDOORB (plan, organize, staff, direct, coordinate, report, budget) is appropriate to the hard style, while its counterpart DECOCOMO (decide, communicate, coordinate, motivate) is more representative of the soft. The soft style in administrative planning does not ask why man is not an obedient ant, it assumes that strict obedience is not feasible, and that manipulation of the actor's motives will be necessary to achieve the desired performance. But both POSDOORB and DECOCOMO are "top-down" procedures, as the words "direct" and "decide" reveal. The ends, in either case, are given.

The Community Action Committees set up by the Office of Economic Opportunity in its "Poverty Program" wish to have a hand in setting these ends. They wish to exploit the "maximum feasible participation" phrase in the enabling legislation to take a major part in the direction of the program. The Bureau of the Budget, guardian of administrative efficiency and witting or unwitting ally of the established big-city political machinery, has moved to curb the power of the clients in policy-making. Administrative efficiency and mass democracy have often been in conflict; Veblen's Engineers could not leave the conduct of the economy to so anarchic a mechanism as the Price System. Elites and the electorate are constantly in tension, both about the proper ends of the society and the appropriate forms of participation in decision-making.

Social Planning and Radical Reform

Proponents of social planning in the United States are impeded from developing a coherent plan of action by the ideological strictures of the society in which they operate. Our pragmatic, conservative, democratic ideology holds that *one*, the structure of power cannot be changed from below, and *two*, behavior and taste cannot be changed from above. Under the first, not only are revolutionary *means* excluded, but radical ends are ruled out as well. By the canons of presupposition *two*, democracies must resist the imposition of preferences upon the weak by the strong. Despite welfare economists' demonstration that aggregation of individual values into a community value function is greatly facilitated by acceptance of the preference of authority as the preference of the group (the dictatorship case) this convenience is denied social planners.

Given these limitations, social planning is split, with its left wing rejecting presupposition *one* and accepting *two*; an administrative right accepting *one* but altering *two*; and a political right accepting both *one* and *two* and insisting on confining operations within the alternatives of the status quo. Only the last mentioned has no crisis of legitimation. Radical social planners bent on changing the distribution of power and available actions to maximize individual choice and administrative social planners accepting the power distribution and attempting to secure behavior of the wards to conform to the tastes of their guardians are both pushing for social change. The left wishes substantial redistribution so that its clients will be allowed to transform themselves (along lines of their choosing) while the administrative right wants the clients to transform themselves so that the whole game will work more smoothly, even if the chief beneficiaries of smoother functioning prove to be the more powerful. Examples of these ideal types are not hard to find in city planning.

The task of the radical social planners is difficult. Society is less tolerant of those who would tamper with the goals than of those who would alter the means, and its organized apparatus is especially uneasy at efforts to incorporate machinery for regularly changing the goals, through radical indulgence of free choice, even when the rhetoric of the social planners uses venerated slogans. The experience of Mobilization For Youth in New York is evidence that revolutionary programs guided by social planners are not likely to be treated by the custodians of civil order with the degree of indulgence sometimes accorded illegal sit-ins. Mobilization For Youth, moreover, was challenging the local governmental administration more directly than it was threatening some vague "power structure." This was true even when it supported tenant movements, for the slum landlords "power" is vested in their relations with local political figures rather than in connections with financial and economic powers.

In comments at the workshop on "Centrally Planned Change" two years ago, John R. Seeley expressed the fear that the federal involvement in traditional local social planning would create a more formidable bureaucratic administrative barrier to the "grass roots" choice school of social planning. Observing that "a number of the executive departments of the federal government have moved into a species of planning and plan-forcing on a scale so massive as to constitute almost a new force in American life, and, incidentally, to render peripheral and probably powerless the previous incumbents of "the social planning activity," he went on to cite Karl Mannheim as labelling "correctly the major danger on which would turn the fate of planning as between the dictatorial and democratic varieties. The former fate would be sealed if planning fell into the hands of the bureaucracies."[6] But the dilemma for social planning leadership is clearly not "bureaucracy or grass roots," but "what bureaucracy?" In a society in which the "establishment" has vast bureaucratic, rationalizing, technically competent apparatus at its disposal, can a more tolerant, permissive, choice-maximizing movement succeed in redistributing power? And if the radical social planners are allowed to keep presupposition *two* on condition that they give up their opposition to *one*, that is, that they retain democratic choice at the price of foregoing revolutionary redistribution, will they not become the leaders of the lost, the counselors of despair?

This tension in the leadership condition of the radical social planners in the American ghetto slums has been bared by the anarchic outbreaks of Harlem last summer and Los Angeles this year. The democratic social planner resists being made a recruitment officer for the Establishment. He wants the client to be taken on his own terms, to be taken seriously as an arbiter of his own values. He may even attempt to protect indigenous forms and life styles when they are illegal. But he has no revolutionary role or power. In a direct confrontation of authority and the frustrated aspirations of his clients, he has no function, for he cannot relinquish or curb his doctrine of self-determination—that would mean rejection of position *two*—and he cannot speedup the transfer of power.

Social Planning, Social Science, and Societal Goals

At best, our contemporary social planning can achieve some coordination of welfare agency efforts, some limited participation by community groups in welfare planning, and a readiness to be measured against such goals as the discerning savants of our society can muster. Positive social science, which is steadfastly descriptive, and determined to be value-free, can play an important diagnostic role, but without the informing graces of ideology it is remarkably mute on prescription. Social scientists tell us of the plight of the bottom fifth of our society, of the obstacles to social mobility, of the frustrating flight of meaningful work, of intergenerational transmission of dependency, and even of the private grasp of public decision, but they leave program to the reformers and ideologues. Ideologically sustained societal planning, as the socialist experiments show, virtually dispenses with social science.[7]

The ideological socialists are steadfast in their commitment to equity principles, though in practice efficiency considerations of economic development may be allowed to supersede these as "temporary" expedients. The utilitarian postulates of the economic-efficiency administrative analysts are regarded by social critics as convenient oversimplifications. As a nation we have slipped into a program of broad social reform which involves the organization of our economy, of the space organization of our cities, and even of interpersonal relations, without benefit of societal planning. At the same time our social scientists have compiled some of the best social statistics in the world, and have supported these with unexcelled social analysis and a great deal of partial social theory. At the local community level we are on the verge of comprehensive social accounts.[8]

We are now in an increasingly good position to measure the impact of public programs on their various clients, to establish the benefits and costs of programs, and to measure, in limited terms, the efficiency of public actions, thanks to a host of social studies, social measurements, and social accounts. Our social intelligence system is potentially powerful. Some, like Seeley, fear that this power will be manipulated by the planner-bureaucrats. Others feel, somewhat wryly, that the bureaucrats will keep this knowledge from being mobilized for social action. The "broad citizen involvement and participation" sought in community social planning is frustrated by the lack of basic social democracy. Without this involvement, the political legitimacy of social planning is open to challenge, for we have no consensus on a national social program to guide the community effort.

In any event, the social democracy which is a precondition to collective social planning in a political democracy depends on social gains which will be engineered, for the most part, from Washington. The achievement of economic democracy, the securing of equality in civil rights, the abolition of gross regional differences in education, and other major social gains will be forged by federal power, or not at all. But the societal plan which will set the targets against which all the ad hoc programs will be measured does not exist.

If such national social planning were to be instituted in the USA, substantial reorganization and improvement of our social data might be required. It is obvious, for example, that the relation of economic planning to social planning requires a national manpower policy, and that the latter, in turn, requires a national manpower budget with great regional and local detail. The material for such a budget is abundantly available, but the policy— which would require the setting of targets on full employment, local and regional labor force mobility, and similar matters —is not available to organize the data.

Social science can inform policy directly, as well as contribute to social accounting. The findings of social scientists have influenced the highest councils in the land, as the wholesale citation of Myrdal's *American Dilemma* by the Supreme Court in its civil rights decisions showed, and the revival of brain-trusting style in the executive branch is now graced by richer social science material than was available to the New Deal. At times it seems we have fallen back on "objective" social science findings because our political ideology offers so few positive guides to social reconstruction. Thus a program which

might be openly embraced in other countries out of commitment to an ideology might be introduced in the USA under the seemingly nonarbitrary cloak of social "science." There is a danger in this process, for it could lead to the tyrannical "scientism" predicted by intellectual opponents of planning.

More likely, however, it would lead to much ad hoc social planning. For the social scientists cannot supplant the goal-making role of ideology, or relieve the political decision makers of their responsibility for setting the public preference scale and the targets to be embodied in a societal plan. The protection of the citizen against administrative abuses, the biases of planners, the condescension of caretakers, and all arbitrariness in social planning depends upon the open articulation of coherent national social goals, and the public acceptance of social planning targets. The Poverty Program, Appalachia Bill, aid to education, and other "Great Society" Acts need a national social accounting against which to be measured. Even more, they need a national social plan which articulates policy, and target dates, for achieving minimum levels of income and consumption, direction and amount of redistribution of population, reduction of intergenerational dependency, equalization of education, and a host of other social goals.

ACKNOWLEDGMENT

Parts of this article are based on "Memorandum on Social Issues in Planning in Puerto Rico," which I prepared while on a consulting team under the leadership of Professor Robert B. Mitchell in San Juan in July of 1963.

NOTES

1. Herbert Gans, "Memorandum," an unpublished paper of the Puerto Rican Planning Board.
2. James P. Dixon, Jr., "Meeting Human Needs," *Goals for Americans*, The Report of the President's Commission on National Goals (Prentice-Hall, 1960), p. 249.
3. P. Davidoff and T. Reiner, "A Choice Theory of Planning," *Journal of the American Institute of Planners*, XXVIII (May, 1962), 103–115.
4. Good statements of the Davidoff position may be found in: Paul Davidoff, "The Role of the City Planner in Social Planning," *Proceedings of the American Institute of Planners, 1964 Annual Conference*, pp. 125–131, and, "Advocacy and Pluralism in Planning," *Journal of the American Institute of Planners*, XXX (November, 1964), 331–338.
5. Remarks by Robert Moses on the proposed Long Island Sound Crossing, Triborough Bridge Authority, 1965.
6. John R. Seeley, "Central Planning: Prologue to a Critique," *Centrally Planned Change: Prospects and Concepts*, ed. Robert Morris (New York: National Association of Social Workers, 1964), p. 58.
7. A well-documented case for this conclusion appears in a yet-unpublished paper on Soviet Social Science prepared by Peter R. Senn for the Annual Meeting of the American Association for the Advancement of Science at Berkeley, December, 1965.
8. See Harvey Perloff, "New Directions in Social Planning," *Journal of the American Institute of Planners* XXXI (November, 1965), 297–303.

59. The Community Development Process

Loureide J. Biddle
and
William W. Biddle

America has always had a distaste for large-scale, centralized planning by experts. When this country has supported planned efforts, they usually have been limited programs developed through the voluntary efforts of small communities, or in the terminology of the Biddles, "the microprocesses of the nucleus." While this ideology has become less central to the thinking of the planning professions as a consequence of urbanization and the growth of the societal scale, its spirit has remained alive and even has had something of a revival in the community action programs of the War on Poverty and the Model Cities program.

William and Loureide Biddle are leading theorists as well as ardent practitioners of the community development movement. The following selection, taken from their major book, looks at modern planning ideas from the perspective of the average citizen who is the object of the city planner's proposals. The Biddles aim to show community residents how they should cope with these proposals, to make programs more responsive to local needs. At the same time, the selection discusses reasons why planners ought to stimulate participation and gives instructions on how to encourage it. The objective the Biddles strive for is "creative tension," a vital interrelationship between the constraints of the larger society and the interests of the citizens who are closest to urban problems.

Loureide J. and William W. Biddle are community development consultants. They are coauthors of *Encouraging Community Development* (1968), *The Community Development Process* (1965), and *Growth Toward Freedom* (1957). William W. Biddle is author of *The Cultivation of Community Leaders* (1953).

A basic nucleus represents a microprocess in the midst of a society that admires gigantism. A larger nucleus provides a means by which several of these micro-processes may be able to relate themselves to huge, attention-getting events and large-scale planning. The comprehensive solution to problems, well-financed, affecting the lives of great numbers of people, and administered from the top, represents a macroprogram. One of the bars to the progress of community development is the widespread belief that only in macro-programs is there hope. According to this viewpoint, microprocesses are foredoomed to frustration.

Macroprograms are characteristically inaugurated by government; the bigger (and therefore more significant?) are federal—for only big government can command the huge sums necessary. But big foundations, big businesses, big churches, big labor unions, these and other great concentrations of decision-making power can also be expected to originate and finance such programs.

A few of the problems that assail modern man are solvable on the simpler local scene. But the bulk of the difficulties, especially the more worrisome ones, must find more comprehensive solutions. Does this mean, as many believe, that reliance must be placed upon the macro-solution in which there is little or no place for the microprocesses of local initiative?

Can the small-scale and local processes of development we have been describing have influence upon the monumental forces of our time? Can they have any appreciable effect upon the thinking of the great decision makers, upon the policy-determining events, the large-scale planning, and the much publicized social movements of a mass-communicated age? There are no easy answers to such ques-

tions of democratic vitality. There never have been.

By studying the past it is possible to discover that important movements and headline-claiming events often have had humble beginnings. More important for the future, however, is this: No one can know what the possibilities may be for ordinary citizen contribution to the flow of history until there is more research into the encouragement of human self-development, much of which must begin in local experience.

A development of people to accompany the development of economic systems and facilities is being called for by the more democratic policy makers and sensitive planners. They are questioning whether their programs can succeed without corresponding changes in the human beings who are affected. The more humane these decision makers are, the more they ask for favorable development in persons through participation in the processes of self-chosen change. But most of them do not know how to expedite human growth in the midst of the grand-scale planning. Community development processes provide one approach for experimentation—a local participative democracy by which people may learn to become contributors to the great decisions of our time.

An Era of Large-scale Decision Making

Perhaps the ordinary citizen has always lived with the sense of being overwhelmed by the decisions of the great and powerful.

If so, the problem has become more acute in the modern era, when policies are determined, plans are made, and administration is centered in distant capitals of government and of financial control. The freedom left even to members of local power structures, let alone to ordinary citizens, is steadily reduced.

More and more, the great decisions from distant offices of central power call upon individuals to acquiesce. More and more, the instruments of mass persuasion increase the tendency to make a virtue of conformity. More and more, the necessities of interdependence on expanding scale make mockery of claims to individual and local independence. Nationally determined behaviors and standards tend to replace those determined at the community level. And these distantly determined pressures call for some change in people's loyalties and habits. Even the advocates of conservatism call for a change, even if the change is only a return to some (presumed) earlier way of life.

Many of the pressures toward community and individual conformity are governmental, but there are other pressures as powerful and as insistent. Acquiescence in centralized decisions is demanded by huge employers (corporations with nationwide operations or with the ability to control the policies of local businesses) and employee associations (labor unions with national or international authority). Various national churches tend to exercise centralized controls, partly because they are in a position to allocate funds. National welfare programs insist (as they should) upon minimum standards. Health organizations seek conformity to better sanitation, diet, and immunization practices. Educational extension enterprises seek the spread of better agricultural practices, better traffic control, cleaner cities. And the list of recommended conformities is endless.

Those who would cultivate citizen initiative cannot avoid urging the people to accept conformity. The problem becomes especially acute when the controllers ask the people to acquiesce in some belief or behavior that is manifestly good—according to the controller. It is easy to urge independence of decision making when obviously bad habits are to be resisted. But what of the changes that distant decision makers "know" to be beneficial? All digit telephone dialing and ZIP codes for mail delivery are "convenient" and "efficient." All such centrally determined changes are forced upon the citizens, who are asked to acquiesce. The only opportunity for independence is found in resistance. And this is often condemned as stubbornness.

Perhaps the benefit in efficiency is demonstrable from these and other changes distantly decided, in an age of centralized mechanization. But how do ordinary persons who benefit from acquiescence also develop as a result of responsible decision making of their own? And can their own initiative be fitted into these and other changes planned from above?

One aspect of life in a mass-persuaded age offers some prospect of hope of a modicum of individual autonomy. This is the existence of multiple persuasions in a free society. Competing advertising is the most obvious, though very limited, example. Rival political and religious propagandas represent another invitation to freedom of choice. Multiplicity of persuasions, however, grant only the opportunity to choose. It does not provide the experience of intelligent responsibility, upon which autonomy must rest.

Too often, traditional discussions of freedom have been limited to choosing by isolated individuals, as though a single person could hope to resist the organized pressures of a massive social system. Is the only admired free man then the unusual individual resister who can stand out against social pressure and even of historical trends? If so, then freedom is denied to ordinary persons, and responsible freedom (that grows out of participation in change) is denied even to the resister.

Dealing with Distant and Impersonal Authority

A community development nucleus, especially a larger one, provides a means by which an increasing number of ordinary citizens may develop a local voice to influence the great decisions of our time. This is a possibility even though the active members will constitute a small minority of a population at any one time. This is true as long as the door is held constantly open for all to participate if and when they see fit. Experience indicates that when this invitation to participation is kept open, even those who remain inactive develop a proprietary conviction that their point of view has been represented. A community nucleus gives a voice to those who will, to contribute to the large-scale, centralized deciding of our time.

As centralized controls increase, ordinary citizens can hope for independence mainly in a reactivation of localism. But that local initiative can no longer be effective if it relates itself only to processes locally controlled. It must address itself also to the great problems, the macroprograms, the distant decision makers. Community nuclei can provide this renewal of localism, but only as their members acquire the skill needed to deal constructively with bureaucrats, experts, and programs that seek to regiment individuals and "educate" the public.

Dignity to Cope with the Powerful Self-confidence to converse with the powerful on a man-to-man basis is notably lacking in the contemporary ordinary citizen. It is not easy to restore, or create anew, such dignity or confidence in one's self. The assurance that "I" have opinions important enough to gain the attention of influential people is not acquired by mere reassurance. Such conviction grows out of discussion of important matters that helps the discusser to discriminate between important and unimportant opinions.

Nucleus experience provides help in achieving this discrimination. And self-confidence grows when citizens have studied and discussed enough to know that they know what they are talking about. Additional skill in discrimination may be acquired by using the nucleus as a place for examining, criticizing, and verbally resisting the multitudinous persuasions that push everyone toward conformity. This resistance is strongest and most effective when it is not a blanket negativism. but recognizes that all of us must conform at many points, but by our own intelligent choosing. And we learn to resist in the same way.

A task which most nuclei undertake, if they last long enough, is the learning of how to live with omnipresent persuasions, persuaders and wielders of power. Membership in the nucleus provides a sense of group support for conclusions reached or negotiations undertaken. No longer is the single person a lone resister. He is a spokesman for a thoughtful and emotionally supportive group. As such, he can afford to be discriminative, accepting some ideas but opposing others, supporting his conclusions with the reasons for decision.

One of the most interesting and gratifying experiences occurs when a nucleus invites in an awesome person for consultation, or when it sends a delegation to a distant office or to an organization not easily approached. The quizzing, conversation, or petitioning tends to be dignified, with assurance on the part of the member that he is within his rights and can deal with powerful persons as an equal in human dignity. Or he concludes that seemingly impersonal institutions are made up of, or conducted by, human beings who have weaknesses and strengths similar to his own.

Living with Experts The representatives of the massive controlling institutions that dominate the lives of ordinary people often appear as experts. These persons, all wise in a limited field, are on the increase as life becomes more complex, as all of us become more dependent upon specialized knowledge, which an ordinary person cannot possess. More and more, the people of specialized wisdom are employed by the institutions (churches, universities, governments, local and federal, and so on) or are licensed by authorities (medical doctors, radio and TV repairmen, qualified auto mechanics, and many others).

Learning to live with these indispensable experts, while at the same time retaining or strengthening a sense of autonomy is, for the ordinary citizen, a problem. It will continue to be a problem, and of increasing difficulty. When a citizen nucleus is used as a local instrument for seeking solutions, it becomes apparent that many different relationships to experts must be tried out, evaluated and modified, adapted and readapted over the changing years. Living with experts in such a manner as to build autonomy and local dignity will prove difficult, but it is necessary.

When the experts respond to invitations from the nuclei or give time to delegations from them, the members become aware of the old cliché definition: An expert is a man who knows all the answers, but does not understand the questions. They discover that he is likely to examine their problem, not within the context of its reality, but within the categories of his field of specialization. He is inclined to offer help as an illustrative case for his isolated wisdom. His approach is likely to be learnedly doctrinaire, not helpfully addressed to the worries and frustrations of people.

In learning to live with experts, therefore, the task of the larger nucleus is to help these specialists learn how to apply their wisdom to problems as these arise, to people as they are. Much patience is required of the members as they confer time and again with the specially-trained. Such patience has its reward, for the interaction of the nucleus with the experts may cause changes in the specialists themselves for which they become grateful —after they have learned how much more useful their skills can be, in the perspective of practical living. But the patience that enables the experts to learn this is an outgrowth of the dignity that the citizen has attained, a dignity that is not threatened by the unrelated self-assurance so often characteristic of the specialist.

The specialists' resistance to the learning of practicality is likely to arise when they discover that their own cherished field of competence needs to be coordinated with the specialities of other experts. They are frequently reluctant to admit that their expertness does not provide all the answers or that real-life problems are seldom classifiable within the prescribed boundaries of any one specialty. Helping the experts to cooperate in order to be more useful may prove even more difficult than achieving a belief in one's own dignity.

Bureaucrats Are Human Most of the contacts of nucleus members with big decisions, and the institutions that make them, are with the lesser figures, the employed staff who are frequently described as bureaucrats (and who often prove more inflexible than the top-level decision makers). A bureaucrat does not necessarily pose as an expert. He is rather the enforcer and defender of the decisions that his superiors have made. Nucleus members can best deal with such functionaries when they realize that bureaucrats are also human. When these lesser lights are most impersonal and inflexible, they are but responding to a difficult assignment that leaves them little room for making decisions of their own.

A first step toward effective relations with the bureaucracy is taken when the citizens bring themselves to understand the position of the bureaucrat, rather than to blame him for the policy others have adopted. A second step is taken when the citizens come to accept the policy, for the present, even though they realize that it is inadequate. For though the enforcer of the rule may sometimes be persuaded to admit the inadequacy of the policy—if he is not pressed to allow a special exception —changes in the rule are to be sought at a higher level. Nucleus members can often influence this higher policy-making level.

Acceptance of the conclusion that bureaucrats are unfeeling marionettes, indifferent to "our" needs, leads easily to that sweeping condemnation by category to which all of us are liable. The discovery that they are human, even as you and I, opens the way for enlisting a few in the interests and enterprises of a nucleus that serves the common good. A basic principle

is involved: When a massive bureaucracy becomes too inflexible to meet human problems, a few individual bureaucrats may be won over, if they are appealed to on a dignified human level. A few may be persuaded to suggest to higher-level decision makers ways to attain greater flexibility. These recommendations can supplement the appeals from the citizens.

Local Implementation of Large-scale Decision Many national policies and programs depend for their success upon cooperation from local initiative. This is true of federal legislation, of supreme court decisions, and of the programs that derive from both; it is also true of planning agencies, national, state, and regional. The administrators of these programs, frequently finding themselves at a loss because the arousing of local participative responsibility is so difficult, react by developing an attitude of discouraged helplessness, which might be referred to as the "Frustration of the Bureaucrat." There are myriad examples of large-scale programs that have failed or have had only a qualified success, because they have lacked vigorous local participation.

Most federal programs that spend money upon the local scene require the participation of committees representative of community interests in the proposing and approving of activities. In setting up such programs, the Congress intentionally decentralizes responsibility. The good intention has been difficult to implement, however; in thousands of committees that have been served by the federal programs, no vigorous nucleus of concerned citizens has existed, nor has it been possible to create such a nucleus to meet the requirements of specific legislation. Committees, it is true, have been set up, but they are often nominal associations poorly representative of citizen interest, if not wholly inactive. And the frustration of the bureaucrat has increased.

When the Supreme Court laid down the dictum that public schools must integrate the races with "all due deliberate speed," the actual pattern and pace of integration was left to the decision of local authorities. The implementation of the Court's order and the working out of a response to a growing national consensus that the justice of the Negroes' suit could not be denied, both of these had to be consummated by locally decided changes. A nucleus group that speaks with the conscience of good will then becomes an instrument for influencing school board, merchants' associations, churches, or any other influential decision-making body. After the tumult and the shouting (of the demonstrations for civil rights) have died, there remains the task of experimentally working out the programs that will recognize and satisfy the demands and aspirations of Negro citizens. This task is an opportunity for the local nucleus of good will. The actual patterns of integration must be discovered at the local level, where the members of the two races meet in daily living.

The controversies that receive national attention, but must find some solution on the local scene, will increase in the years to come. The admission of Negroes to first-class citizenship, is but a beginning. Federal legislation, court decisions, changes in the national conscience, all will bring new pressures for local initiative to work out community aspects of national change. The problem is not so much how to relate the small-scale deciders on the community scene to the large-scale problem and program, as how to persuade local citizens to form the association for local initiative— a larger nucleus of good will—that can

take its part in the totality of consciously chosen development.

The Democratization of Planning

Even as the controversies over change must be expected to increase, so must the amount of planning increase. Change will need guidance. But is planning an activity limited to a particular breed of experts? Or is it one in which the ordinary citizen of initiative and good will may participate?

Two tacit assumptions underlie much planning: first, that it is a single-shot beginning for improvement, resulting in a "master plan" evolved by experts and subject to only minor modification in the implementing; second, that democratic participation has been achieved when the citizens (vaguely referred to as "the public"), or their spokesmen, have acquiesced in the "master plan" at "public hearings."

Two contrary assumptions need to be made explicit for democratic realism: first, that planning is a never-ending obligation, to be carried on continuously in an age of change; second, that some means for giving voice to the inarticulate needs to be worked out in order to achieve bona fide citizen participation.[1]

> . . . It is encouraging to note that experts in this field are beginning to speak of dynamic planning; that is, planning that is flexible in design and responsive to change. As [Maxwell] Fry put it at a meeting of architects, "We would be better employed in searching for the rules that govern nature and nature's creature, man; for if this city is to be built it will be built not by one man but many, and not by architects only." . . . The idea is growing that planning can succeed only if it becomes increasingly a shared activity; the different organized

groups in the community must have a part in it. This is an idea that was emphasized in a widely read book by [Barbara] Wootten who argued that such control is safest in the hands of the man and woman on the street. . . . Progress would be slow, but the results would be more lasting. . . .

The processes of community development provide a promising means for the democratization of planning. But two points of sensitivity, at least, need to be kept in mind by the encouragers and the citizen participants: First, it is exceedingly difficult to get ordinary people to voice authentic feelings and opinions, for many average citizens do not know how to express their positive desires; indeed, until they have acquired the dignity conferred by self-confidence, they often do not know that they have positive desires. Second, the contribution from ordinary citizens, once achieved, must be continued indefinitely, so that planners may learn to accept and to live with authentic spokesmen for the citizen interest—so that ordinary citizens may increase their effectiveness as a result of their participation in the making of important decisions.

The processes that offer promise move from basic nuclei to a larger nucleus. The latter becomes effective as it relates itself to many agencies, government offices, institutions, powerful individuals, and the planners, through whom these decision makers operate.[2]

A responsible larger nucleus can be helpful to planners at many points. It can endorse the idea of and necessity for planning and use its influence to assure financial support. It can bring problems to the planners' attention. It can help in the collecting of data. It can join in the discussion of the objectives for a community and of the priorities for progress. The actual technical details of blueprints and specifications remain the responsibility of the trained experts. The administering of the plans and of the supporting laws remains the responsibility of trained experts. The enactment of supporting legislation remains the responsibility of government. But when nucleus members have contributed their thinking to the process by which the plans were evolved and supported, their interest can help planners keep the emerging common good in mind.

When the members of the large nucleus become involved in planning processes, they frequently discover new necessities for self-discipline. They curb their tendencies to become partisan for particular segments of the population. They also become aware of some of the human tragedy involved in any program of improvement. When the way is cleared for new highways or bridges or housing developments, some people must be ousted from their homes or their land. When zoning ordinances are passed and enforced, when sanitation regulations are adopted, even when children are compelled to go to school, the individual's freedom of choice is curtailed. It is seldom that any important improvement can be brought about without hurting someone. The members of the larger nucleus, aware of the possibilities for tragedy, can urge the adoption of measures that will minimize the hurt. And they can often help to assuage the injury, by insisting that decent homes be found for those who have been ousted and by explaining to the people the necessity for sanitation and education and other self-disciplines in the complexities of modern life.

By preserving a concern for the common good, independent of government or of other authority, a larger nucleus can help to make planning humane. And the planners and administrators can be helped to develop confidence in the good sense that ordinary people can learn to exhibit.

From Alienation to Dignity

The fact that ordinary persons resist planning, or stay away from public hearings, or attend only to attack and criticize, is a sign of their alienation from life and from one another, a malaise that is characteristic of our time. There are numerous other signs: a sense of hopelessness, a widespread conviction that "we" can do nothing to improve bad situations, an apathetic refusal to stir out of the accepted routines of life, a fear of making choices, even when it is evident that the traditional ways of life can no longer serve.

Experienced encouragers of community development are aware of local climates of alienation that can infect an entire population. Indeed, they are wise to assume that the citizens' first response to any proposals for action (and even the later responses) may indicate apathy and reflect a hopeless disbelief in "our" ability to do anything positive. The community development process becomes one means for moving from a prevailing alienation to a dignity of belief in "ourselves"—for individuals—for all the people in an area of growing initiative.

Nucleus members who have had the experience of standing up to persons in authority develop a belief in their own significance. They discover that the reputedly powerful often are also hemmed in by circumstance, that they also may be frustrated and impatient, that some who appear to be unapproachable actually welcome contacts. The ability to dominate another person is not necessary to the overcoming of alienation. The opportunity

to be heard, to be taken seriously, to make a contribution to important decisions, these are necessary. Necessary also is the growing sense of an effective "we-ness." This awareness of collective influence comes to replace, in part, some loss of the significance of "I," overwhelmed by authoritarian decision and by the sweep of uncontrolled events. Many "I's" begin to gain significance out of association with and effective "we."

It should be noted that the community development process is only one of many that may help persons to mature in dignity. Other processes may be more effectively used in some cases, as for those maladjusted persons who can afford individual professional attention.[3] But for the great number of ordinary people, many adequately conceived and administered community development processes seem to promise the most practical means for stimulating growth in citizen dignity.

A basic nucleus can bring to a few the dignity that comes with participation in an important decision. A larger nucleus can increase the number and can create a social atmosphere conducive to personal dignity for many in a local area. But the totality of people benefited is microscopic as compared with the massed need in our metropolitan-dominated society. Can the microprocesses be multiplied in sufficient quantity to lift a considerable proportion of the population?

This question poses a challenge to the great institutions that make the large-scale decisions which set up macroprograms. Might some or several of these institutions establish a well-financed and properly staffed program directed toward stimulating thousands of nuclei that become effective through larger nuclei? And if they did, would they be wise enough to diminish their long-standing desire to seek citizen conformity? Could they come to admire a large-scale effort that seeks an increase of local and personal variety in initiative? Tentatively, we give a "yes" answer to this query, taking into consideration the frailties exhibited by every human being and posing against this the genuine democratic aspiration to be found in many institutions that operate within an atmosphere of freedom.

But a more fundamental question is: Can these institutions expect to succeed in their macroprograms if there is not built into them some corresponding effort directed toward stimulating the growth of local citizens? Our tentative answer is "no." To make available to people a program of growth in democratic competence is as necessary as are the macroefforts of improvement. Persons achieve competence most surely when they learn to contribute to and help guide the macroprograms set up to improve their conditions.

A Creative Tension

The tension between large-scale programs and small-scale community processes will always exist. The first grows out out of legislative and administrative decisions that apply to a whole region or nation. The second grows out of citizen decisions, locally made in face-to-face experience. When the voice of local initiative is strengthened through larger nuclei, the tension can be made creative.

No panacea for the multiplying problems of accelerating change is to be found in community development. Nor are sure solutions to be found in grandiose planning. Both ordinary people and planners, legislators and administrators, must be prepared to seek solutions by experimentation. Community development processes may be used to supplement the thinking of the great deciders by making available to them the creative ideas of citizens who are closest to the problems. The best progress will be made, not by a macroprogram alone, or by a microprocess alone, but by a greater process that establishes a vital interrelationship between the two.

In the processes of community development, the citizens tend to mature; they are no longer content merely to complain. And because they are contributing to the planning process, they become less dependent upon winning and less upset by losing.

The members of larger nuclei can remain close to the people and to the human suffering that is caused by unsolved problems. They are in a position both to expedite and to be creatively critical of experimental tryout of programs. They can give support to programs while criticizing them.

NOTES

1. Nels Anderson, *The Urban Community: A World Perspective* (New York: Holt, Rinehart and Winston, 1959), p. 476.
2. For an example of how this process may operate, see Julia Abrahamson, *A Neighborhood Finds Itself* (New York: Harper and Row, 1959), and Herbert A. Thelen and Bettie Belk Sarchet, *Neigh-* *bors in Action* (Chicago: University of Chicago Press, 1954).
3. For individual psychotherapy, see Carl R. Rogers, *Client-centered Therapy* (Boston: Houghton Mifflin, 1951). For small groups, see the works of the National Training Laboratories and others working in the field of Group Dynamics . . .

60. Social Planning: A New Role for Sociology   Herbert J. Gans

The professions concerned with planning the development of urban communities have made great strides toward increasing their own skill and competence, in improving the quality of urban life, and in helping to make the administration of urban affairs more rational and efficient. However, the planning and caretaking professions have encountered numerous problems for which their present intellectual resources are inadequate, especially in the areas of poverty, race, and housing. Gans suggests that these failures pose a challenge to sociology, one that discipline can meet by orienting itself more in the direction of policy concerns, particularly policies focused on guided mobility planning for poor whites and blacks. Gans specifies four functions of urban sociology in relation to the work of the planning and caretaking professions: (1) the development of theoretical schemes to guide planning; (2) improved methods for determining social goals; (3) the formulation of programs for achieving goals; and (4) the conduct of research which evaluates action programs. Gans believes that if sociologists carry out these functions a branch of sociology will develop that will be equal in resources, productivity, and intellectual standing to theoretical-empirical sociology.

Herbert J. Gans, both a sociologist and a city planner, is Professor of City Planning at Massachusetts Institute of Technology. Several of his published works are cited on page 70 of this volume.

Around the turn of the century, a number of the pioneers of American sociology were deeply involved in the social-action issues of their day, especially those concerning the welfare of the city and its less fortunate residents.[1] They participated in such reform movements as city planning, public recreation, "good government," sanitation and public health, and they helped to establish settlement houses, philanthropic agencies, and a variety of other social-welfare programs and services. Sometimes they functioned purely as researchers, but in many cases they also played advisory or participant roles in policy formation and program development. Insofar as they were helping to shape community goals and to choose the methods to be used for achieving these goals, they were participating in what is today being called "social planning."

As these reform movements took hold, they became institutionalized as public agencies and municipal activities. Concurrently, lay leaders and volunteer workers, including the sociologists among them, were replaced by paid professionals. The departure of the sociologists can be explained by three factors. First, with the rapid growth of sociology as an academic discipline, sociologists began to spend most of their time as teachers. Second, the subsequent boom in sociological research

Part one of Chapter 16 from *The Uses of Sociology* edited by Paul F. Lazarsfeld, William H. Sewell, and Harold L. Wilensky, © 1967 by Basic Books, Inc., Publishers, New York. Permission granted also by George Weidenfeld and Nicolson, Ltd. This is an expanded and revised version of a paper prepared for the 1962 meetings of the American Sociological Association, Washington, D. C.

and the attempt to create a scientific sociological method discouraged sociologists from participating in action programs and even from doing research on controversial issues. Third, the professionals who took over the new bureaucracies developed techniques of service and of caretaking, to use Erich Lindemann's apt phrase, which left little room for the sociologist. Thus, city planning was carried out by engineers and architecturally trained practitioners who believed that the goals of their calling—the good community and the good life—could be attained by architectural and site-planning methods and that the alteration of the physical environment was the main priority. Recreation officials sought to achieve the same goals by supplying supervised facilities, such as the playground, park, and community center, in the belief that these would attract users to interact with professionally trained leaders who would teach them "constructive" and "wholesome" forms of leisure behavior. Public-health officials turned to clinics, and social workers to settlement houses, as well as to case-work techniques. Only in some caretaking agencies, notably those dealing with delinquents and older lawbreakers, did sociologists continue to find a function. In the others, they participated only as, occasional consultants or as sporadic, and usually uninvited, critics.[2]

In the last two decades, the barrier between the planning and caretaking professions and the sociologists has begun to break down. This has come about for two reasons. First, the more thoughtful members of these professions have been realizing that the traditional techniques were not working so well as was being claimed. For example, the caretakers' success among European immigrants and their children was not being duplicated with the Negro and Puerto Rican newcomers to the city, and some professionals went so far as to suspect that all along their techniques had been effective largely because of the existence of highly mobile and self-selected clients among the European immigrants. In short, these professions began to realize that they were not reaching their intended clients, and as Richard Cloward has put it, what they had mistaken for service was only the illusion of service. In the call for new approaches, they began to turn to the social sciences for help. Their decision to do so was also affected by the new prestige of the social sciences and by the availability of research and other funds for sociological help. Indeed, today it is fashionable for professional agencies of all kinds to hire sociologists.

Second, social scientists themselves have begun to take an interest in the work of these professions. Thanks to the activities of the federal government and private foundations, behavioral scientists from a number of disciplines are doing research and developing ways of applying social-science knowledge to their programs. This, too, has cut down the barriers between them.

Planning for Guided Mobility: The Proposal Stage, 1962

Of all the welfare-oriented professions, perhaps none has grown faster in the postwar era than city planning. Although the modern city-planning movement emerged in the middle of the nineteenth century, much of its growth has come in the last fifteen to twenty years, stimulated by the federally supported programs of urban redevelopment (now called urban renewal), which began with the passage of the 1949 Housing Act. The planners and the "housers" were concerned mainly with eliminating slums and conserving the less blighted structures and neighborhoods, but in addition to these "physical" goals they also sought social ones. Thus, they hoped not only that slum clearance would provide the slum dwellers with better housing but that these people would adopt middle-class ways of life. After a decade of experience, however, it has become clear that tearing down the slums and moving their occupants elsewhere may have improved their housing conditions—although it did not even do this very often—but it did not reduce their poverty or radically change their ways of life.[3] Crime, delinquency, alcoholism, school failure, unemployment, mental illness, and other disabilities of the low-income population have not been reduced by alterations in the physical environment.[4]

As a reaction to the shortcomings of urban renewal, a new approach is being developed which has been given many names, including human renewal, community development, gray-area programs, and social planning.[5] Broadly speaking, the purpose of this approach is to find nonphysical ways of helping the low-income population and reducing deviant behavior. This goal is hardly novel, and in essence the new approach is only the most recent version of the never-ending attempt to help the deprived elements of society improve their living standards. What is new is the involvement of city planners in this effort and the fiscal scale of the programs that are being developed.

The term *social planning* has been used most often to describe these programs, if only to distinguish them from the physical planning methods used in urban renewal.[6] The term itself was borrowed from the social-welfare profession, which has long used it to refer to the co-ordination of the activities of the many individual agencies that provide social service in the city by councils of social agencies, community chests, or United Fund organizations.[7] The programs now being developed by city planners and others are not exactly plans in the usual sense of the word, and they are no more nor less social than any other form of human activity. From a sociological perspective, such programs might best be described as schemes for *guided mobility*, or, more correctly, for guided lower-class mobility, since they propose to induce mobility among people whom sociologists describe as lower-class (or in the Warnerian terminology, lower-lower-class).

It should be noted, however, that none of the agencies conceived or conceptualized their efforts in this way, and they did not see themselves as encouraging mobility, guided or unguided, for they did not think systematically about what changes they sought to encourage in their clients. Moreover, since the programs are aimed at helping those individuals who are attracted to them, rather than entire population groups, their actual mobility potential is low. Indeed, it seems likely that they will principally help people who are already upwardly mobile. Needless to say, there is no intent to change the class structure of American society, but only to help the people who are at the bottom of the hierarchy.

Guided-mobility plans have been springing up with considerable rapidity. As of 1962 they existed or were being readied in such cities as New York, Chicago, Los Angeles, Philadelphia, Boston, Pittsburgh, Washington, Oakland, and New Haven, to name only a few. Many of them are specifically geared to the prevention of juvenile delinquency and thus are primarily focused on services for young people; for example, the Mobilization for Youth project in New York City.[8] Others, especially those emanating from city-planning agencies, seek to deal with all age groups of the population.[9]

Although most of these projects have not proceeded beyond the drafting of prospectuses, the soliciting of financial support, and the recruitment of staff, some over-all similarities in their goals and programs are already apparent. It should be noted that any generalizations that can be made are highly preliminary, for the programs are likely to change as they move from the exhortatory language of the fund-raising brochure to actual implementation in the field.

By and large, the guided-mobility plans emphasize four major programmatic goals: to extend the amount and quality of present social services to the hard-to-reach lower-class population; to offer new methods of education, especially in the area of job training; to reduce unemployment by retraining and the creation of new jobs; and to encourage self-help both on an individual and group basis, notably through community participation and neighborhood organization. In addition, programs in recreation, public health, delinquency prevention, and housing are often included in the plan.

Generally speaking, the programs being proposed reflect the fact that guided-mobility plans are developing out of an alliance between city planners, the suppliers of social services, and experts in community organization. For one thing they are organized to deal not with social structures and peoples, but with neighborhoods and their residents. Often the neighborhoods are chosen because of the physical renewal projects taking place in them. Conversely,

some plans also include areas which are not occupied by lower-class people. Moreover, the proposals stress the use, not of whatever functional services are needed to solve problems, but of public—and physical—*facilities*, such as the school, the recreation center, or the clinic. These emphases are contributed by city planners and reflect traditional programmatic concepts of the planning profession.

Furthermore, the programs propose that the services offered by these facilities and by social-service agencies generally be increased beyond present levels and that they be co-ordinated. Instead of separate agencies each working individually with the same clients, the proposal is to have these agencies work in concert, or at least to know what the others are doing. This technique reflects a long-term goal of the suppliers of social services, and is a part of their concept of social planning. And, finally, the schemes call for new efforts to reach the previously unreached by using professional community organizers and other caretakers working in the neighborhood, much like the detached street or gang worker in delinquency prevention, and by finding nonprofessional "natural leaders" who will carry the message and the services of guided mobility to people who shy away from contact with public facilities and professional staffs. This is the contribution of community organization.

Some of the plans stress the increased use of present techniques, while others call for the development of new ones. Some proposals are highly sophisticated, but by and large it is fair to say that most of them are from a sociologist's perspective quite unsophisticated and even naïve. This naïveté takes several forms.

First, many of the plans are based on the traditional goal of persuading the lower class to become middle class, both in behavior and values, and they hope to attain this goal by the traditional means of confronting this population with middle-class services and staffs. Although there are proposals to call on "natural" or "indigeneous" leaders who are not middle class, their function will be to bring the low-income population in touch with the middle-class staff and services. Moreover, the proposals are quite optimistic that the lower-class clients will assent to this confrontation and that rapport with them can be achieved. Beyond that, it is believed that once rapport is obtained, they are willing and able to resort to self-help and to formal organization to achieve the goals set for them.

Also, the programs proposed in these plans are determined less by the needs and present conditions among the intended clients than by the skills and services of the programmers. Indeed, variations in programs among the individual cities can be related to the characteristics of the sponsoring agencies in each. As a result, the plans frequently give as much attention to such essentially low-priority programs as improvements in leisure behavior, training in citizenship, and the stimulation of neighborhood consciousness as to such much higher priority needs as job opportunities, higher incomes, and solutions to basic social and psychological problems prevalent in the lower-class population.

Similarly, not only does the city planners' concern with neighborhood divert the programs to goals of neighborhood cohesion or stability, and so use guided mobility as a means to physical-renewal aims, but, more important, it overestimates the importance of the role that the neighborhood plays in the life of the lower-class population. Thus, the proposals run the

danger that in prescribing for the neighborhood they may sidestep the real problems.

In some cases, the naïvéte I have described stems from traditional program emphases among the sponsors. In other cases, it follows from the fact that the agencies running the guided-mobility programs cannot do much to change basic structural deficiencies of the society. They can do little to create more jobs for low-income people and to remove the practices of racial discrimination that prevent access to the available jobs and other opportunities. Even so, more often the naïveté is based on the absence of a conceptual and theoretical framework about the nature of lower-class life and accompanying processes of social deprivation and disorganization. For example, most of the proposals do not seem to be aware of the concepts of class, social stratification, or social mobility. A theoretical framework is required to allow the formulators of action programs to move from an understanding of present conditions and their causes to the setting of goals and to the development of programs that will achieve these goals. In a word, what the plans need, but now lack, is the sophistication and rationality that can be supplied by social-science theory and data. These alone will not produce miracles, but they may prevent some politically and financially costly failures.

Criticism is always easy, and my comments have failed to call attention to the pioneering thought and effort that have gone into these plans. Even so, I think that social scientists could do much to help improve them, and I believe that they should take part in them. In fact, the remainder of this chapter is primarily an appeal asking sociologists to do just that. In elaborating the appeal, I shall also indicate my conception of the direction that guided-mobility theory and planning programs ought to take.

The Role of Sociology in Planning Against Poverty

What can sociologists do? It goes without saying that they can do research *about* guided-mobility planning, studying the issues involved and the programs themselves in order to add to our theoretical knowledge in the fields of class, urban life, social disorganization, and deviant behavior. They can also conduct research *for* these programs, and they will undoubtedly be asked to do so in the coming years, either on a staff or consultant basis. But I believe that the sociologist ought to be more than a detached researcher and that he should participate more directly in social-action programs. The guided-mobility planners can use the sociologist in at least four ways: for the *development of a theoretical scheme to guide the planning*, for *goal determination*, for *means or program development*, and for *the evaluation of action programs*.

Although research about the nature and dynamics of lower-class life is still in its infancy, the main outlines of a theoretical scheme can be set out in brief.[10] The low-income population can be divided into the *working class* and the *lower class* (upper-lower and lower-lower in the Warnerian scheme). The former is distinguished by relatively stable semiskilled or skilled blue-collar employment and by a way of life that centers on the family circle, or extended family. The lower class is characterized by temporary, unstable employment in unskilled—and the most menial—blue-collar jobs and by a way of life equally marked by instability. S. M.

Miller has aptly described it as crisis-life.[11] Largely as a result of the man's occupational instability, the lower-class family is often matrifocal or female-based. This is most marked among the Negro population, in which the woman has been the dominant figure since the days of slavery, but it can also be found in other groups suffering from male occupational instability. Although this type of family organization has some stable and positive features, especially for its female members, the hypothesis has been suggested that it raises boys who lack the self-image, the aspirations, and the motivational structure that would help them to develop the skills necessary to function in the modern job market.[12] Also it may prevent boys from participating in a "normal" family relationship in adulthood, thus perpetuating the pattern for another generation. These conditions are, of course, exacerbated by racial and class discrimination, low income, slum and overcrowded housing conditions, as well as illness and other deprivations which bring about frequent crises. Under these conditions, lower-class people are not motivated to develop mobility aspirations, but instead defend themselves against frustration by rejecting the rest of the world and by searching for what gratifications are available, including such forms of retreat as alcohol and narcotics.

The result is a vicious cycle of lack of opportunity and of aspiration. To begin with, the lower class suffers from lack of occupational opportunities and access to education and social institutions. These deprivations create social-structural and cultural patterns which inhibit many people from developing the values and skills needed to take advantage of the opportunities if they were available. If and when they do become available, these inhibitions thus prevent mobility from taking place. Without aspirations, available opportunities cannot be used; but without opportunities, few people in their right mind are motivated to develop aspirations that may be frustrated.

This vicious cycle can, however, be broken. Opportunities must precede aspirations, not only because many lower-class people do develop the requisite motivation to take advantage of opportunities, only holding it in abeyance until opportunities appear, but also because the remainder will not develop the needed aspirations without evidence that opportunities will be open to them. For example, a number of studies show that educational aspirations are quite strong in the Negro community, but that a variety of factors and forces erode them as children become older and are socialized into the ever present lower-class culture.[13] If the proper educational opportunities were available, the aspirations would not need to erode so often.

This sketchy theoretical scheme has implications for action programs. To begin with, it suggests that the working-class population needs guided-mobility plans much less urgently than the lower class, especially given the scarcity of public funds and political "capital" for social change. Not only the working class has achieved a reasonable amount of economic stability, if not affluence, but its members also have skills to maneuver in the modern labor market. The lower class, on the other hand, suffers from much more intense deprivation and is capable of filling only jobs which are rapidly disappearing from the economy. Its need for help is infinitely greater.

The theoretical scheme also suggests two types of action programs for this population. First, it is necessary to increase opportunities for jobs as well as for educational skills—and equally important, credentials—that permit the holding of skilled blue- and white-collar jobs and to reduce discrimination based on ascribed aspects of race and class. Second, methods must be found to develop the aspirations, motivations, and skills needed for these opportunities. Insofar as their development may be hindered by the dynamics of the female-based family and other elements of lower-class life, changes in the social structure and culture of the lower class may be required before the psychological prerequisites can develop.

Although this theoretical scheme is preliminary and as yet unsupported by sufficient empirical verification, it is sufficient to allow me to consider the other three functions the sociologist can play in guided-mobility planning and to raise some of the questions which must be answered before such planning can be successful.

Perhaps the most important function is the determination of goals. The planners must begin by asking what problems are to be solved and what goals are to guide the problem-solving process. Is it the amelioration of antisocial and self-destructive behavior or, beyond that, the elimination of all lower-class behavior which is visible and displeasing to the dominant middle-class culture? Or is the aim the traditional one of making middle-class citizens out of the lower class?

These questions are framed from the point of view of the sponsors and suppliers of guided-mobility plans. The sociologist should, however, shift the focus of questions to the clients of these plans. Thus he must ask: What do lower-class people find desirable and undesirable in their way of life; also, which aspects of this life are pathological for them, regardless of their own attitudes, and which are likely to lead to pathological consequences for others in the society? Needless to say, the determination that a behavior pattern is pathological must be based on empirically valid and reliable evidence to prevent the facile labeling of deviant or only culturally different behavior as pathological. The sociologist must also ask: What is the goal of the lower-class individual? Is he content with social instability, wanting only economic stability for himself and his children? Or does he want middle-class ways for him and them? Or is his goal, at least in the foreseeable future, to become working class, to achieve the stability of employment, family life, and group membership that distinguishes it from his own ways? And if this is so, as seems quite likely, what are the dominant aspects of working-class life that he wants and how do they differ from both his present ways and the middle-class ones of the programmers of guided mobility?

These questions are only a sample of the ones that need to be asked. Once they are answered—even if only in the preliminary forms necessary to get action programs started—the sociologist can help to develop the means necessary to achieve the goals; that is, by participating in the development of programs of action. It is here that he can perhaps make his most useful contribution. As already noted, caretakers and city planners are often wedded to techniques that give the illusion of service rather than service, proposing inadequate or irrelevant means for the right goals. Moreover, the sociologist is trained to look for basic processes, functions, and causes, so that he can see fairly clearly what means do and do not achieve the goals for which they are intended. For example, he can demonstrate with little effort that improved playgrounds or

new school buildings will not by themselves contribute much to cure the pathologies of lower-class life.

Means necessarily depend on the goals selected for action. If the primary goal is to help lower-class people achieve working-class status and culture, the methods to be chosen will seek to overcome the two types of obstacles that now stand in the way: lack of opportunities and absence of the proper aspirations, motivations, and skills. In order to deal with this question here, I limit the discussion to that portion of the lower-class population which can most easily respond to opportunities; that is, the people who can work and learn, who might be called the *adaptable poor*. It thus excludes the minority of lower-class people who are either too old or physically and otherwise disabled—the people whom Hylan Lewis has aptly called the *clinical poor*.[14] Among the adaptable group, it is useful to distinguish between those who are potentially middle or working class—who have the requisite emotional, intellectual, and other cultural attributes for responding to opportunities—from those who do not and are in that sense culturally more lower class.

As already indicated, both types need programs that increase job and other opportunities, higher incomes, the reduction of discrimination, and access to schools and a variety of social services. This is more easily said than done. The establishment of better schools and social services is comparatively simple to program if funds and staff are available. Of course, the services must be designed to attract the intended clients. Moreover, incentives may be necessary to induce people to use these services, especially on a long-term basis. For example, money payments to students may persuade lower-class parents who are skeptical about education to send them to school. Similarly, grants in lieu of wages might allow men with families, who dropped out of school in adolescence, to return in their twenties when they have realized the importance of education.

The provision of more jobs and the elimination of discrimination are much more difficult to accomplish. In a society in which the number of jobs cannot keep up with population growth, no one has yet come up with ways of determining, much less instituting, the needed structural changes that will create more jobs, or for that matter, of channeling them to a population that is least able to compete for them. These are challenges for economic and political planners, for people who can devise "social inventions" to overcome the opposition of vested interests, and for politicans willing to carry out the difficult process of creating change.

The potentially middle- or working-class segment will be able to respond to these opportunities with a relatively small amount of help, but the remainder of the lower-class population—and the proportion is unknown—must be aided by methods that will help individuals, families, and other groups to develop the emotional, intellectual, and social responses necessary to allow them to take hold of such opportunities.

This requires a catalogue of generalizations about the characteristics of the attitudes and skills that are lacking and the social and psychological causes of their absence. This, in turn, takes the inquiry into the nature of lower-class problems. Is it aspirations for mobility that are lacking, or the motivations to pursue these aspirations, or the emotional, intellectual, and social skills that are necessary to implement both? And what causes these to be absent? Is the female-based family at fault; and if so, in what ways does it inhibit people from responding to opportunity? Is it the matriarchal dominance which is said to emasculate boys and send them on the way to familial and other forms of marginality? Or is it the lack of male models in the child-rearing process? If so, could surrogate models be provided by guided-mobility programs? Or are there deeper, dynamic factors which require the presence of a stable father figure? He is not so easily supplied. Or does the problem lie less with the family structure than with parental lack of education, the thought processes taught by lower-class parents, and the skills required to succeed in lower-class surroundings which are learned from siblings and peers and differ sharply from the skills needed to do well in school? Is it the inability to concentrate, to use words as concepts rather than as tools in interpersonal struggles, or is it simply the absence of books and privacy for study at home, or perhaps the unskilled and culturally myopic teacher that causes the problems? Or is the source of the difficulties to be found in the high rate of mental illness among the lower-class population and the fact that the youngster is from his earliest days surrounded by many people who are mentally ill, including even his parents?

Once these questions are answered and basic causal processes are isolated from psychological symptoms, program planning must determine whether the needed attitudes and skills can be encouraged or whether adults and even adolescents who have grown up in a lower-class milieu have so hardened their defenses against deprivation that they can no longer change. In that case, perhaps only young children can be helped effectively, and much of the effort might best be spent on rescuing them from the negative elements in the lower-class milieu. After that it, must be determined to what extent these attitudes and skills can be taught either by formal or informal methods and to what extent they can come about only as a result of structural changes in lower-class life. If the latter is true, then preschool forms of education may be less effective than attempts to remove children from the lower-class milieu through day-care centers, summer camps, foster parents, and even boarding schools and "children's societies" modeled on those in the Israeli collectives.

Finally, there is the important and equally difficult problem of developing rapport with a population which has traditionally rejected contact with caretakers and is so despairing of being helped that it has often turned aside all aid in order to save what little dignity it is able to maintain.

I am not suggesting that the sociologist can answer these questions or that action programs can be developed to achieve the desired goals. Many of the questions have no answers at present, and action programs will have to be experimental until the right ones are found. All the sociologist can do is to work with other behavioral scientists to help programmers achieve the best methods, provided, of course, that he is invited to do so. Since guided mobility is a form of social mobility, the extensive sociological literature on this topic may provide useful leads for action programs.

The fourth function of the sociologist is that of evaluation: analyzing the action programs in terms of their consequences and finding out whether or not they have achieved the intended goals and without undesirable side effects. Because many of the programs will be experimental, the sociologist can help set them up so that they can be studied and evaluated most effectively. Evaluation research is already

an accepted field of inquiry in sociology, and although its method and techniques are still primitive, and much more research must be done before it can become a mature branch of sociology, its relevance needs no more discussion here.

The Need for Policy-Oriented Sociology

The four functions I have proposed for the sociologist in guided mobility require considerable theoretical exploration and much more detailed theory building, but they do not require any radical theoretical innovation, for they are based on a theory of planning which has its roots in the social sciences and can be "plugged into" a number of sociological theories, including symbolic interactionism, action theory, and the structural-functional approach. They do, however, require some changes in the use of research, in the conceptualization of theory, and in professional self-definition.

Most of the questions which must be answered before planning can take place on a rational basis have not yet been sufficiently studied; yet the planners cannot wait for further research. Sociologists who participate in guided-mobility programs must be able to come to conclusions on the basis of past research, a modicum of impressionistic observation, and a large amount of freewheeling hypothesizing— that is, guessing. They must gamble further by being willing to build the products of this highly unscientific approach into experimental programs. There is no doubt that this type of sociological endeavor will lay the practitioner open to criticism from colleagues in the discipline as being unscientific or controversial, but it will be countered by appreciation—and the surrender of an ancient stereotype about the unwillingness of sociologists to come to conclusions—on the part of the planners.

Moreover, the sociologist must revamp the concepts that he uses so that they can answer the questions posed by the plan and in such a way that they will lead to ideas and techniques for action programs. Concepts framed for theory and for action differ considerably, and while not every sociologist has the skill and imagination for social invention, his concepts must be able to help those who do and who make up action programs. While it is important for these programs to have a theoretical understanding of lower-class behavior patterns and attitudes, it is much more important for them to know how lower-class people may be helped. For example, the guided-mobility planners who want to provide aid to lower-class Negro women must know what kinds of help these women need most urgently and how the always limited resources can be allocated with this priority in mind. Is their first need for a direct income grant, or for help in finding a job, or for job training, or for better housing, or for assistance in taking care of the children? Also, if the first priority were an income grant, what kind of grant would be least humiliating, least likely to create further dependency, and least likely to reduce even more the function of the father? If the first priority were for assistance in child care, what kind of assistance would be accepted by women without making them feel that they are inferior mothers or that they might be losing their children to strangers practicing a different culture? And perhaps most important, if jobs for Negro men are not yet available, what kinds of aid will maintain the positive functions of the female-based family but will also reduce the dysfunctions for its male members?

Answers to questions like these will also force the sociologist to make unaccustomed value judgments. A question about what aspects of lower-class life are undesirable differs sharply from the usual question of what lower-class life is like. For example, the sociologist must frame value judgments on the issue of Negro family structure. Coming from a culture in which the two-parent nuclear family is the norm, he must decide whether or not to suggest programs that would maintain the Negro female-based family. Part of the problem is, of course, empirical; he must have data to determine whether such a family is functional for the present social and economic position of its various members and how these members feel about the kind of family in which they are living. But even if such a family is a functional and wanted solution, the sociologist in an action program still has to decide for himself whether he can propose programs that will maintain this family type for yet another generation.

Many similar questions must be answered about other behavior patterns and attitudes that differ from the middle-class ones with which most sociologists identify. And whether he functions as a researcher or joins those who design action programs, the sociologist must make value judgements about behavior patterns, institutions, and attitudes which he has not made before. This is not so difficult as it might appear, for the basic value judgment—that society can and ought to be improved—already lurks in the hearts and minds of most contemporary sociologists. Even so, large ideological steps must be taken to get from the prevalent liberalism of the social-problems approach to the kind of radical social innovation that is needed to make guided-mobility programs successful, especially when these involve the redistribution of power, income, opportunities, and prerogatives.

Moreover, what is needed is a pragmatic radicalism, oriented less to classical concepts of revolution than to techniques for changing social, economic, and political institutions which resist change.

What I have been describing here is applied or, more correctly, *policy-oriented* sociology. This type of analysis is not new; it was practiced among the early sociologists, if only in a primitive way, and it has become popular in our time among sociologists working in market research, medical sociology, and wherever else their efforts are used in policy formulation and decision making. Planning for guided mobility is just another, although much broader, topic for policy-oriented sociology. If sociologists become involved in it, their work may speed the development of a branch of sociology which is explicitly concerned with policy formation and should be equal, in resources, productivity, and intellectual standing to traditional theoretical-empirical sociology. Given similar developments in other disciplines, the social sciences may one day be more help in solving the pressing questions of our society than has heretofore been the case. Needless to say, I believe this to be a desirable goal.

ACKNOWLEDGMENTS

I am grateful to Robert Dentler, Elmer Luchterhand, Peter Marris, and Frances Piven for comments on earlier drafts of this chapter.

NOTES

1. This is not to slight European sociologists, although their participation was more at the national than the local community level.
2. See, for example, the highly relevant—but rejected—critique of the settlement house by William F. Whyte, Jr., *Street Corner Society*, 2nd ed. (Chicago: University of Chicago Press, 1955), pp. 98–108, 275–276, 354–356. See also Herbert J. Gans, "Redefining the Settlement's Function for the War on Poverty," *Social Work*, IX (October, 1964), 3–12.
3. Marc Fried, "Grieving for a Lost Home," in Leonard J. Duhl, ed., *The Urban Condition* (New York: Basic Books, 1963), pp. 151–171; Chester Hartman, "The Housing of Relocated Families," *Journal of the American Institute of Planners*, XXX (November, 1964), 266–286; and Herbert J. Gans, "The Failure of Urban Renewal: A Critique and Some Proposals," *Commentary*, XXXIX (April, 1965), 29–37.
4. See, for example, Irving Roscow, "The Social Effects of the Physical Environment," *Journal of the American Institute of Planners*, XXVII (1961), 127–133; and D. Wilner, R. Walkley, T. Pinkerton, and M. Tayback, *Housing Environment and Family Life* (Baltimore: John Hopkins Press, 1962).
5. More specifically, the approach developed first as an attempt to counteract the failure of relocation programs to help the slum dwellers. In some cities, it grew out of urban-renewal planning for skid-row districts and the fear that if the derelict population of such areas were simply relocated in the normal manner, skid row would spread to other residential areas. For this and other reasons, attempts are under way to "rehabilitate" this population as part of the relocation process. In yet other cities, and especially in projects financed by the Ford Foundation, the aim was to prevent the deterioration of so-called "gray areas" into slums.

   The term *gray area* was initially coined by researchers in the New York Metropolitan Region study to describe deteriorating working-class areas beyond the present slums which would decline further with the increasing suburbanization of residents and industry in the coming generation and would thus be gray in mood. The term may have originated from map-coloring habits, in which the slums are often colored black and the less deteriorating areas gray. There might also be a racial connotation, since the areas are now often occupied by whites, but are likely to become nonwhite in the future.
6. The term *social planning* has also been applied to plans which attempt to outline social goals for the entire society, an approach that might better be called *societal planning*. For example, the Central Planning Board of Puerto Rico has been working on a social plan for the island. This project

developed as a reaction by the then incumbent governor, Muñoz Marín, to the emphasis on economic planning and grew out of his appeals for an "Operation Serenity" to slow down the urbanizing and industrializing influences of the "Operation Bootstrap" program which brought industry to Puerto Rico.

7. Davis McEntire, "Social Planning and Urban Renewal," in George S. Duggar, ed., *The New Renewal* (Berkeley: Bureau of Public Administration, University of California, 1961), pp. 117–126.

8. Mobilization for Youth, Inc., *A Proposal for the Prevention and Control of Delinquency by Expanding Opportunities* (New York: Mobilization for Youth, mimeographed, December, 1961).

9. Illustrative of such plans are: City of Oakland, *Proposal . . . for a Program of Community Development* (Oakland, California, City of Oakland, mimeographed, June, 1961, revised December, 1961); *Action Housing Inc., . . . Urban Extension . . . in the Pittsburgh Area* (Pittsburgh: Action Housing, mimeographed, September, 1961); Action for Boston Community Development, *A Proposal for a Community Development Program in Boston* (Boston: A.B.C.D., mimeographed, December, 1961); and Community Progress Inc., *Opening Opportunities: New Haven's Comprehensive Program for Community Progress* (New Haven: Community Progress, mimeographed, April, 1962). My comments about the plans below are based on these and on other published and unpublished documents which I have examined, as well as on discussions about existing and proposed plans in which I have participated in several cities. My description of these plans is an ideal type and does not fit exactly any one of the proposals now in existence.

10. A more detailed formulation is presented in Herbert J. Gans, *The Urban Villagers: Group and Class in the Life of Italian-Americans* (New York: Free Press of Glencoe, 1962), Chapters 11, 12. For a somewhat similar scheme, see Mobilization for Youth, *op. cit.*, Chapter 2. An excellent brief statement of the nature of lower-class life is contained in Walter B. Miller, "Lower Class Culture as a Generating Milieu of Gang Delinquency," *Journal of Social Issues*, XIV (1958), 5–19.

11. S. M. Miller, "Definition of Lower Class: Some Notes for Discussion," unpublished Memorandum, p. 4. See also S. M. Miller and Frank Riessmann, "The Working Class Subculture: A New View," *Social Problems*, IX (1961), 86–97.

12. See, for example, W. B. Miller, *op. cit.*

13. Harlem Youth Opportunities, Inc., *Youth in the Ghetto* (New York: H.A.R.Y.O.U., 1964); Richard A. Cloward and J. A. Jones, "Social Class: Educational Attitudes and Participation," in A. H. Passow, ed., *Education in Depressed Areas* (New York: Bureau of Publications, Teachers College, Columbia University, 1963), pp. 190–264; and Hylan Lewis, "Culture, Class and the Behavior of Low Income Families," paper presented at the Conference on Low Income Culture, New York, June, 1963, mimeographed.

14. *Ibid.*

Name Index

Subject Index

937

About the Editors

Robert Gutman is Professor of Sociology at Rutgers College and at the Urban Studies Center, Rutgers University, and Visiting Professor of Architecture and Urban Planning at Princeton University. He has taught at the Institute for Architecture and Urban Studies in New York City and at the University of London, Stanford University, Dartmouth College, and Columbia University. In addition to numerous contributions to books and professional journals, his published work includes *The Mark of Oppression: A Psycho-Social Study of the American Negro* (with Abram Kardiner and Lionel Ovesey) and *Birth and Death Registration in Massachusetts, 1639–1900*. He has served as Associate Editor of the *American Sociological Review* and as Advisory Editor of the *American Journal of Sociology*.

David Popenoe is Associate Professor of Sociology at Douglass College, Rutgers University, and was formerly Director of Academic Affairs of the Rutgers Urban Studies Center. He has taught at the University of Pennsylvania and at New York University. He is editor of *The Urban-Industrial Frontier;* coeditor with Robert Gutman of a special issue of *The American Behavioral Scientist*, "Urban Studies: Present Trends and Future Prospects in an Emerging Academic Field"; and author of a forthcoming introductory textbook in sociology. He has been an advisory editor and is now Associate Review Editor of *Journal of the American Institute of Planners*.